The Handbook of Adult Clinical Psychology

The Handbook of Adult Clinical Psychology

An evidence-based practice approach

Edited by Alan Carr and Muireann McNulty

LONDON AND NEW YORK

First published 2006 by Routledge
27 Church Road, Hove, East Sussex BN3 2FA

Simultaneously published in the USA and Canada
by Routledge
270 Madison Avenue, New York NY 10016

Reprinted 2007

Routledge is an imprint of the Taylor & Francis Group, an informa business

Typeset in Times by
RefineCatch Limited, Bungay, Suffolk
Printed and bound in Great Britain by
TJ International Ltd, Padstow, Cornwall
Paperback cover design by Sandra Heath

This publication has been produced with paper manufactured to strict environmental standards and with pulp derived from sustainable forests.

British Library Cataloguing in Publication Data
A catalogue record for this book is available from the British Library

Library of Congress Cataloging-in-Publication Data
The Handbook of adult clinical psychology : an evidence based practice approach / edited by Alan Carr & Muireann McNulty.
p. cm.
Includes biographical references and index.
ISBN 1–58391–853–1 – ISBN 1–58391–854–X (pb.)
1. Clinical psychology – Handbooks, manuals etc. I. Carr, Alan. II. McNulty, Muireann.
RC467.2.H34 2006 616.89 – dc22

ISBN13: 978–1–58391–853–1 (hbk)
ISBN13: 978–1–58391–854–8 (pbk)

ISBN10: 1–58391–853–1 (hbk)
ISBN10: 1–58391–854–X (pbk)

Dedication

This book is dedicated to the late Joan Carr who died in December 2005. Her life was an example to us all of how to face adversity with courage and optimism.

Contents

List of tables

List of figures

Editors

Professor Alan Carr is Director of the clinical psychology training programme at the National University of Ireland, Dublin. Having trained in Ireland and Canada, he worked in the NHS in the UK before returning to Ireland to work at University College Dublin. He has written and edited over twenty volumes, including the second edition of the *Handbook of child and adolescent clinical psychology* and the *Handbook of intellectual disability and clinical psychology practice* (edited with Gary O'Reilly, Patricia Noonan Walsh and John McEvoy), both of which were published by Routledge in 2006 along with the current volume.

Dr Muireann McNulty is the Clinical Co-ordinator of the clinical psychology training programme at the National University of Ireland, Dublin and Senior Psychologist at the St John of Gods Hospital, Dublin. Dr McNulty trained in Ireland and the USA. She then worked in the NHS in the UK before returning to Ireland to work at UCD and the St John of God Adult Mental Health Services in Dublin. Dr McNulty developed the adult clinical psychology curriculum for the clinical psychology training programme at University College Dublin and has co-ordinated teaching in this area for a number of years.

Contributors

Gordon J. G. Asmundson, PhD, Professor of Health Studies and Psychology, Kinesiology and Health Studies, 3737 Wascana Parkway, University of Regina, Regina, SK, Canada, S4S 0A2.

Tony Bates, PhD, Director of the MSc in CBT, Department of Psychiatry, Trinity College Dublin and Principal Psychologist at the Department of Psychology, Jonathon Swift Clinic St James' Hospital, Dublin, Ireland.

Paul Bebbington, FRCPsych, Professor of Social and Community Psychiatry, Head of Department of Mental Health Sciences Royal Free and University College London Medical School 48 Riding House Street, London W1N 8AA.

Alberto Blanco-Campal, D Psych Sc, Clinical Psychologist, North Eastern Area of the Health Service Executive, Drogheda, and School of Psychology, University College Dublin, Belfield, Dublin 4, Ireland.

Tasha M. Burwinkle, PhD, Department of Anaesthesiology, Box 356540, University of Washington, Seattle, WA 98195, USA.

Alan Carr, PhD, Director of the Doctoral Programme in Clinical Psychology, University College Dublin, Belfield, Dublin 4, Ireland and Consultant Clinical Psychologist and Marital and Family Therapist, Clanwilliam Institute, Dublin, Ireland.

Karin Carter, D Phil, Psychology Services, Bolton Salford and Trafford Mental Health NHS Trust, Bury New Road, Prestwich, Manchester M25 3BL, UK.

Jessica Carty, BA, Australian Centre for Post Traumatic Mental Health, University of Melbourne, 330 Waterdale Road, Heidelberg Heights Victoria 3081, Australia.

Mark Creamer, PhD, Director, Australian Centre for Post Traumatic Mental Health, University of Melbourne, 330 Waterdale Road, Heidelberg Heights Victoria 3081, Australia.

Padmal de Silva, PhD, Senior Lecturer, Department of Psychology, Kings College, University of London, and Institute of Psychiatry, De Crespigny Park, London SE5 8AF, UK.

Patricia Furer, PhD, St Boniface General Hospital M 5–409 Tache Ave, Winnipeg, MB, Canada, R2H 2A6.

David Hemsley, PhD, Professor of Psychology and Director of the Doctoral Programme in Clinical Psychology, Department of Psychology, Institute of Psychiatry, De Crespigny Park, London SE5 8AF, UK.

Steve Jones, PhD, Senior Lecturer in Clinical Psychology, University of Manchester, Academic Division of Clinical Psychology, 2nd Floor Research and Teaching Centre, Wythenshawe Hospital, Manchester M23 9LT, UK.

Kathryn E. Korslund, PhD, Associate Director, Behavioral Research and Therapy Clinics, University of Washington, Department of Psychology, Box 351525, Seattle, WA 98195–1525, USA.

Elizabeth Kuipers, PhD, Professor of Psychology, Department of Psychology, Institute of Psychiatry, De Crespigny Park, London SE5 8AF.

Janice R. Kuo, MS, University of Washington, Department of Psychology, Box 351525, Seattle, WA 98195–1525, USA.

Dominic Lam, PhD, Clinical Tutor, Doctoral Programme in Clinical Psychology, Department of Psychology, Institute of Psychiatry, De Crespigny Park, London SE5 8AF, UK.

Carolien Lamers, PhD, Lecturer in the School of Psychology, University of Wales Bangor, Brigantia Building, College Road, Bangor LL57 2DG, Wales, UK.

Marsha M. Linehan, PhD, Professor of Psychology, University of Washington, Department of Psychology, Box 351525, Seattle, WA 98195–1525, USA.

Barbara S. McCrady, PhD, Professor and Clinical Director, Centre of Alcohol Studies, Rutgers University, 607 Allison Road, Piscataway, NJ 08854–8001, USA.

Muireann McNulty, PhD, Clinical Co-ordinator of the Doctoral Programme in Clinical Psychology, University College Dublin, Belfield, Dublin 4, and Senior Clinical Psychologist, Cluain Mhuire Family Centre, Hospitaller Order of St. John of God, Newtownpark Avenue, Blackrock, Co. Dublin, Ireland.

Stephen McWilliams, MD, Registrar in Psychiatry, Cluain Mhuire Family Centre, Hospitaller Order of St. John of God, Newtownpark Avenue, Blackrock, Co. Dublin, Ireland.

Raymond W. Novaco, PhD, Professor of Psychology, University of California, Irvine, CA 92697–7085, USA.

Eadbhard O'Callaghan, MD, Professor of Psychiatry, Department of Psychiatry, University College Dublin, Belfield, Dublin 4 and Consultant Psychiatrist Cluain Mhuire Family Centre, Hospitaller Order of St. John of God, Newtownpark Avenue, Blackrock, Co. Dublin, Ireland.

Emmanuelle Peters, PhD, Lecturer in Clinical Psychology, Box PO77, Institute of Psychiatry, King's College London, De Crespigny Park, Denmark Hill, London SE5 8AF and Honorary Consultant Clinical Psychologist, South London & Maudsley NHS Trust.

John L. Taylor, PhD, Head of Psychological Therapies & Research, Northgate & Prudhoe NHS Trust, Psychology Department, Northgate Hospital, Morpeth, Northumberland, NE61 3BP, UK and Lecturer in Psychology at the University of Newcastle, Newcastle upon Tyne, Tyne and Wear, UK.

Steven Taylor, PhD, Professor, Department of Psychiatry, University of British Columbia, Vancouver, British Columbia, Canada, V6T 2A1.

Dennis C. Turk, PhD, John and Emma Bonica Professor of Anesthesiology & Pain Research, Department of Anaesthesiology, Box 356540, University of Washington, Seattle, WA 98195, USA.

John R. Walker, PhD, St Boniface General Hospital M 5–409 Tache Ave, Winnipeg, MB, Canada, R2H 2A6.

Adrian Wells, PhD, Reader in Psychology, Academic Division of Clinical Psychology, University of Manchester, Rawnsley Building, Manchester Royal Infirmary, Oxford Road, Manchester, M13 9WL, UK.

Craig A. White, ClinPsyD, PhD, Deputy Director of Psychological Services/ Macmillan Consultant in Psychosocial Oncology, Honorary Professor of Clinical Psychology, University of Paisley, Consulting and Clinical Psychology Services, Pavillion 7, Ayrshire Central Hospital, Killwinning Rd, Irvine, Ayrshire, KA12 8SS, Scotland, UK.

Bob Woods, PhD, Professor of Psychology, The Institute of Medical and Social Care Research, Wheldon Building, University of Wales, Bangor, LL57 2UW, Wales, UK.

Foreword

This *Handbook of adult clinical psychology: An evidence based practice approach* provides clinical psychologists in training with a comprehensive practice handbook to help build the skills necessary to complete a clinical placement in the field of adult mental health. While practical in orientation, the book is based solidly on empirical evidence. This book is one of a set of three that cover the lion's share of the curriculum for clinical psychologists in training in the UK and Ireland. The other two volumes are the *Handbook of child and adolescent clinical psychology* (Second Edition) (by Alan Carr) and the *Handbook of intellectual disability and clinical psychology practice* (edited by Gary O'Reilly, Patricia Noonan Walsh, Alan Carr & John McEvoy).

This book is divided into five sections. Section 1 covers general frameworks for practice (classification and epidemiology; CBT, psychodynamic, systemic and biomedical models; and general assessment procedures). Section 2 deals with mood problems (depression, bipolar disorder and managing suicide risk). Section 3 focuses on anxiety problems (generalized anxiety disorder, panic disorder, obsessive-compulsive disorder, post-traumatic stress disorder and social phobia). Section 4 deals with psychological problems linked to physical health (somatoform disorders, chronic pain, adjustment to cancer, eating disorders and substance abuse). Section 5 focuses on schizophrenia, borderline personality disorder, psychological problems in older adults, anger management and depersonalization disorder.

The chapters on clinical problems explain how to assess and treat the condition in an evidence-based way with reference to case material. Interventions from cognitive-behavioural, psychodynamic, interpersonal/systemic and biomedical approaches are described where there is evidence that they are effective for the problem in question. Skills-building exercises and further reading for psychologists and clients are included at the end of each chapter.

Preface

There is growing awareness of the applicability of the methods and findings of clinical psychology to an ever widening range of problems. This has resulted in a considerable expansion of training both within the UK and Ireland, but no course can be expected to provide exposure to all possible approaches with every clinical group. This volume provides a comprehensive coverage of clinical psychology, which will certainly be of great value both to trainees and those involved in organizing programmes. The opening chapters are particularly useful to those entering the profession, dealing as they do with the variety of conceptual frameworks within which clinical psychologists operate, from developmental to biomedical.

A valuable feature of this book is the way in which a historical perspective to our understanding of disorder is combined with detailed case studies illustrating particular forms of intervention. In addition to traditional references, the chapters highlight further reading for both practitioners and their clients. There are also guides to appropriate assessment instruments; it might have been useful to highlight these not subject to copyright and hence available without extortionate cost to clinicians!

Clinical services are increasingly influenced by the demand for a clear evidence base for psychological interventions and this volume illustrates the ways in which clinical psychology has responded to this challenge. Indeed, the impressive array of contributors includes many who have been in the forefront of developments in treatment techniques. This is by far the most complete volume of its type currently available. Although its target audience will be clinical psychologists, it will also be found useful by undergraduates hoping to enter the profession and by psychiatrists.

David Hemsley
Professor of Abnormal Psychology
Director of Clinical Psychology Training
Institute of Psychiatry, London
August 2005

Acknowledgements

We are grateful to the American Psychiatric Association for permission to reprint diagnostic criteria from: *Diagnostic and statistical manual of the mental disorders* (Fourth Edition-Text Revision, DSM-IV-TR, Published in 2000 by the APA in Washington, DC) for the following disorders: major depressive episode (p. 356); manic episode (p. 362); generalized anxiety disorder (p. 476); panic attack (p. 432); obsessive-compulsive disorder (pp. 462–463); post-traumatic stress disorder (pp. 467–468); social phobia (p. 456); somatization (p. 490); hypochondriasis (p. 507); pain disorder (p. 503); anorexia nervosa (p. 589); bulimia nervosa (p. 594); substance abuse (p. 199); substance dependence (pp. 197–198); schizophrenia (pp. 312–313); borderline personality disorder (p. 710) and depersonalization disorder (p. 532).

Thanks to the World Health Organization for permission to reprint diagnostic descriptions from: *The ICD-10 classification of mental and behavioural disorders, clinical descriptions and diagnostic guidelines* (Published in 1992 by the WHO in Geneva) for the following disorders: depressive episode (pp. 119–120); mania (pp. 112–115); generalized anxiety disorder (pp. 140–141); panic attack (pp. 139–140); obsessive-compulsive disorder (pp. 142–144); post-traumatic stress disorder (pp. 147–148); social phobia (pp. 136–137); somatization (pp. 162–163); hypochondriasis (pp. 164–165); persistent somatoform pain disorder (pp. 168–169); anorexia nervosa (pp. 176–177); bulimia nervosa (pp. 178–179); harmful psychoactive substance use (pp. 74–75); psychoactive substance dependence syndrome (pp. 75–76); schizophrenia (pp. 86–88); emotionally unstable personality disorder, borderline type (pp. 204–205) and depersonalization-derealization syndrome (pp. 171–172).

Thanks to John Wiley publishers and Dr Wells for permission to reproduce a diagram of the Metacognitive Model of generalized anxiety disorder from: Wells, A. (1997). *Cognitive therapy of anxiety disorders: A practice manual and conceptual guide.* Chichester, UK: Wiley.

Thanks to Guilford Press, Dr Clark and Dr Wells for permission to reproduce a diagram of the cognitive model of the processes that occur when a socially phobic individual enters a feared social from: Clark, D. M. & Wells,

A. (1995). A cognitive model of social phobia. In R. Heimberg, M. Leibowitz, D.A. Hope & F.R. Schneier (Eds.), *Social phobia: Diagnosis, assessment and treatment* (pp. 69–93). New York: Guilford Press.

Thanks to Oxford University Press and Dr Fairburn for permission to reproduce a diagram of the cognitive-behavioural model model of bulimia from: Fairburn, C. (1997). Eating disorders. In D. Clark & C. Fairburn (Eds.), *The science and practice of cognitive behaviour therapy* (p. 212). Oxford: Oxford University Press.

Thanks to Oxford University Press, Dr McCrady and Dr Epstein for permission to reproduce a table of the medical consequences of heavy use of alcohol or other drugs from: McCrady, B. S. & Epstein, E. E. (1999). *Addictions: A comprehensive guidebook.* New York: Oxford University Press.

Thanks to the National Academy Press and the Institute of Medicine for permission to reproduce a terminological map from: Institute of Medicine (1990). *Broadening the base of treatment for alcohol problems.* Washington, DC: National Academy Press.

Thanks to Dr Prochaska, Dr DiClemente, Dr Norcross and the American Psychological Association for permission to reproduce a spiral model of the stages of change from: Prochaska, J. O., DiClemente, C. C. & Norcross, J. C. (1992). In search of how people change. Applications to addictive behaviours. *American Psychologist,* 47, 1102–1114.

Thanks to Dr Hunter and colleagues and Elsevier Press for permission to reproduce a diagram of a cognitive-behavioural model of depersonalization disorder from Hunter, E.C., Phillips, M.L., Chalder, T., Sierra, M. & David, A.S. (2003). Depersonalisation disorder: A cognitive-behavioural conceptualisation. *Behaviour Research and Therapy*, 41, 1451–1467.

Thanks to Dr Sierra, Dr Berrios and Elsevier Press for permission to reproduce a diagram of a neurobiological model of depersonalization from: Sierra, M. & Berrios, G.E. (1998). Depersonalisation: Neurobiological perspectives. *Biological Psychiatry*, 44, 898–908.

Section 1

Conceptual frameworks

Chapter 1

Normal psychological development in adulthood

Alan Carr and Muireann McNulty

When adults develop psychological problems, such as depression, anxiety or the other difficulties described later in this book, these problems do not occur in a vacuum; they occur within the context of the family lifecycle. Challenges within the lifecycle can contribute to the development of psychological problems and such difficulties might also compromise the capacity to complete important developmental tasks. It is for this reason that the approach to the practice of adult clinical psychology outlined in this volume begins with a consideration of the normal family lifecycle.

FAMILY LIFECYCLE

Most models of the family lifecycle are based on the norm of the traditional nuclear family, with other family forms being conceptualized as deviations from this norm (McGoldrick & Carter, 2003). One such model is presented in Table 1.1. This model delineates the main tasks to be completed by the family at each stage of development. After considering this model in some detail, other lifecycle models will also be considered.

Leaving home

In the first two stages of family development, the principal concerns are with differentiating from the family of origin by completing school, developing relationships outside the family, completing one's education and beginning a career. The capacity to make and maintain stable, supportive and satisfying friendships is determined by many historical, personal, and environmental factors. Adult attachment style is particularly important, and this has its roots in childhood attachment experiences. Compared to people with anxious attachment styles, those with a secure attachment style tend to develop better-quality peer relationships that hold up under stress (Allen & Land, 1999). A fuller discussion of attachment style will be given below. With respect to personality traits, extraversion, agreeableness and stability (as opposed to

Table 1.1 Stages of the family lifecycle

Stage	*Tasks*
1. Family-of-origin experiences	• Maintaining relationships with parents, siblings and peers • Completing school
2. Leaving home	• Differentiation of self from family of origin and developing adult to adult relationship with parents • Developing intimate peer relationships • Beginning a career
3. Premarriage stage	• Selecting partners • Developing a relationship • Deciding to marry
4. Childless couple stage	• Developing a way to live together based on reality rather than mutual projection • Realigning relationships with families of origin and peers to include spouses
5. Family with young children	• Adjusting marital system to make space for children • Adopting parenting roles • Realigning relationships with families of origin to include parenting and grandparenting roles • Children developing peer relationships
6. Family with adolescents	• Adjusting parent–child relationships to allow adolescents more autonomy • Adjusting marital relationships to focus on mid-life marital and career issues • Taking on responsibility of caring for families of origin
7. Launching children	• Resolving mid-life issues • Negotiating adult to adult relationships with children • Adjusting to living as a couple again • Adjusting to including in-laws and grandchildren within the family circle • Dealing with disabilities and death in the family of origin
8. Later life	• Coping with physiological decline • Adjusting to the children taking a more central role in family maintenance • Making room for the wisdom and experience of the elderly • Dealing with loss of spouse and peers • Preparation for death, life review and integration

Based on Carter, B. & McGoldrick, M. (1999). *The expanded family lifecycle. Individual, family and social perspectives* (Third Edition). Boston: Allyn & Bacon.

neuroticism) facilitate the development of friendships (John & Srivastava, 1999). At an environmental level, opportunities in school, leisure activities, the family and the community to meet with peers, at least some of whom have similar attributes, skills and values, are important for the development of friendships. Lack of such opportunities, an anxious attachment style and a personality profile characterized by extreme neuroticism all render people vulnerable to developing psychological problems at this stage of the lifecycle.

Forming a couple

From Table 1.1 it can be seen that in the third stage of the family lifecycle model, the principal tasks are those associated with selecting a partner and deciding to marry or cohabit. In the following discussion, the term 'marriage' is used to cover both traditional marriage and the more modern arrangement of long-term cohabitation. Adams (1986) views mate selection as a complex process that involves four stages. In the first phase partners are selected from among those available for interaction. At this stage, empirical studies show that people select mates who are physically attractive and similar to themselves in interests, intelligence, personality and other valued behaviours, and attributes. The popular idea that opposites attract is a myth unsupported by empirical evidence. In the second phase there is a comparison of values following revelation of identities through self-disclosing conversations. If this leads to a deepening of the original attraction then the relationship will persist. In the third phase, there is an exploration of role compatibility and the degree to which mutual empathy is possible. Once interlocking roles and mutual empathy have developed, the costs of separation begin to outweigh the difficulties and tensions associated with staying together. If the attraction has deepened sufficiently and the barriers to separation are strong enough, consolidation of the relationship occurs. In the fourth and final phase a decision is made about long-term compatibility and commitment. If a positive decision is reached about both of these issues, then marriage or long-term cohabitation may occur. When partners come together they are effectively bringing two family traditions together, and setting the stage for the integration of these traditions with their norms and values, rules, roles and routines into a new tradition. Couple formation and marriage entail the development of a series of important relationships: the marital relationship, kinship relationships and later parent–child relationships, all of which have the potential to contribute to happiness and well-being (Carr, 2004). Marriage and psychological adjustment are intimately linked (Carr, 2000); single people are more likely to develop psychological problems. Psychological disorders can both cause marital conflict and such conflict can contribute to the aetiology and maintenance of psychological difficulties.

Marriage

In the fourth stage of the family lifecycle model, the childless couple must develop routines for living together that are based on a realistic appraisal of the other's strengths, weaknesses and idiosyncrasies rather than on the idealized views that formed the basis of their relationship during the initial period of infatuation.

Marital satisfaction

The following demographic factors are associated with marital satisfaction (Newman & Newman, 2002):

- high level of education
- high socio-economic status
- similarity of spouse's interests, intelligence and personality
- early or late stage of family lifecycle
- sexual compatibility
- for women, later marriage.

The precise mechanisms linking these factors to marital satisfaction are not fully understood. However, the following speculations seem plausible. Higher educational level and higher socio-economic status probably lead to greater marital satisfaction because, where these factors are present, people probably have better problem-solving skills and fewer chronic life stresses such as crowding. Although there is a cultural belief that opposites attract, the research results show that similarity is associated with marital satisfaction, probably because of the greater ease with which similar people can empathize with each other and pursue shared interests. Marital satisfaction drops during the child-rearing years and satisfaction is highest before children are born and when they leave home. During these periods, it may be that greater satisfaction occurs because partners can devote more time and energy to joint pursuits and there are fewer opportunities for conflict involving child management. Most surveys find wide variability in the frequency with which couples engage in sexual activity but confirm that it is sexual compatibility rather than frequency of sexual activity that is associated with marital satisfaction.

Marital interaction

Studies of belief systems and interaction patterns of well-adjusted couples show that they have distinctive features (Carr, 2000; Gottman, 1993; Jacobson & Gurman, 1995). These include:

- respect
- acceptance
- dispositional attributions for positive behaviour
- more positive than negative interactions
- focusing conflicts on specific issues

- rapidly repairing relationship ruptures
- managing differing male and female conversational styles
- addressing needs for intimacy and power.

Well-adjusted couples attribute their partners' positive behaviours to dispositional rather than situational factors. For example, 'She helped me because she is such a kind person', not 'She helped me because it was convenient at the time'. The ratio of positive to negative exchanges has been found to be about five to one in happy couples (Gottman, 1993). So even though well-adjusted couples have disagreements, this is balanced out by five times as many positive interactions. When well-adjusted couples disagree, they focus their disagreement on a specific issue, rather than globally criticizing or insulting their partner. This type of behaviour is a reflection of a general attitude of respect that characterizes happy couples. Well-adjusted couples tend to rapidly repair their relationship ruptures arising from conflict and they do not allow long episodes of non-communication, sulking or stonewalling to occur. Sometimes, well-adjusted couples resolve conflicts by agreeing to differ. The specific process of agreeing to differ reflects a general attitude of acceptance. Distressed couples, in contrast, have difficulties in many of the areas listed above and this relationship distress is often associated with a psychological disorder in one or both partners.

There is good evidence that men and women have different conversational styles. Men use conversation predominantly to convey task-focused information and to resolve task-related problems. Women use conversation predominantly to make and maintain relationships (Tannen, 1990). In their communication with each other, well-adjusted couples find ways to manage these differing conversational styles so that psychological intimacy can be fostered rather than compromised. So males in such relationships make efforts to use conversation to make and maintain their relationship with their partner and females are tolerant of the challenge that this poses. Difficulties and disagreements about communication and intimacy on the one hand, and the power balance or role structure of the relationship on the other, are central themes for distressed couples and are often key concerns for couples in which one member has a psychological problem (Jacobson & Gurman, 1995). With respect to intimacy, males usually demand greater psychological distance and females insist on greater psychological intimacy. With respect to power, males commonly wish to retain the power and benefits of traditional gender roles whereas females wish to evolve more egalitarian relationships. In well-adjusted couples, partners' needs for intimacy and power within the relationship are adequately met, and partners have the capacity to negotiate with each other about modifying the relationship if they feel that these needs are being thwarted.

Types of marriage

Fitzpatrick (1988) and Gottman (1993) have both identified three types of stable, satisfactory marriage in questionnaire and observational studies. I have termed these 'traditional', 'androgynous' and 'avoidant' couples. Characteristics of these types of marriage are summarized in the first part of Table 1.2. Traditional couples adopt traditional sex roles and lifestyles and take a low-key approach to conflict management. Androgynous couples strive to create egalitarian roles and take a fiery approach to conflict resolution. Avoidant couples adopt traditional sex roles but live parallel lives and avoid conflict. Two types of unstable couple were identified in Gottman's (1993) study. In Table 1.2, I have labelled these 'conflictual' and 'disengaged' couples. The former engage in conflict but without resolution and the latter avoid conflict much of the time. Gottman found that in all three stable types of couple the ratio of positive to negative verbal exchanges during conflict resolution was 5:1. For both unstable types of couples the ratio of positive to negative exchanges was approximately 1:1. Gottman and Fitzpatrick's work highlights the fact that there are a number of possible models for a stable marital relationship. Their work also underlines the importance of couples engaging in conflict with a view to resolving it rather than avoiding conflict. Negativity is only destructive if it is not balanced out by five times as much positivity. Indeed, negativity may have a prosocial role in balancing the needs for intimacy and autonomy and in keeping attraction alive over long periods.

Families with children

In the fifth stage of the family lifecycle model given in Table 1.1, the main tasks are for couples to adjust their roles as marital partners to make space for young children, for couples' parents to develop grandparental roles and for children as they move into middle childhood to develop peer relationships. The development of positive parenting roles involves couples establishing routines for meeting children's needs for:

- safety
- care
- control
- intellectual stimulation.

Developing these routines is a complex process. Routines for meeting children's needs for safety include protecting children from accidents by, for example, not leaving young children unsupervised and also developing skills for managing frustration and anger that the demands of parenting young children often elicit. Routines for providing children with food and shelter, attachment, empathy, understanding and emotional support need to be

Table 1.2 Five types of couples

Stability	*Type*	*Characteristics*
Stable	Traditional couples	• They adopt traditional sex roles • They privilege family goals over individual goals • They have regular daily schedules • They share the living space in the family home • They express moderate levels of both positive and negative emotions • They tend to avoid conflict about all but major issues • They engage in conflict and try to resolve it • At the outset of an episode of conflict resolution, each partner listens to the other and empathizes with their position • In the later part there is considerable persuasion
	Androgynous couples	• They adopt androgynous egalitarian roles • They privilege individual goals over family goals • They have chaotic daily schedules • They have separate living spaces in their homes • They express high levels of positive and negative emotions • They tend to engage in continual negotiation about many issues • Partners disagree and try to persuade one another from the very beginning of episodes of conflict resolution • A high level of both positive and negative emotions
	Avoidant couples	• They adopt traditional sex roles • They have separate living space in their homes • They avoid all conflict • They have few conflict resolution skills • Partners state their case when a conflict occurs but there is no attempt at persuasion or compromise • They accept differences about specific conflicts as unimportant compared with their shared common ground and values • Conflict related discussions are unemotional
Unstable	Conflictual couples	• They engage in conflict without any constructive attempt to resolve it • Continual blaming, mind-reading, and defensiveness characterize their interactions • High levels of negative emotion and little positive emotion are expressed • Attack–withdraw interaction pattern

Continued overleaf

Table 1.2 continued

Stability	*Type*	*Characteristics*
	Disengaged couples	• They avoid conflict and have few conflict resolution skills • Brief episodes of blaming, mind-reading, and defensiveness characterize their interactions • Low levels of negative emotion and almost no positive emotion is expressed • Withdraw–withdraw interaction pattern

Based on Gottman, J. (1993). The roles of conflict engagement, escalation and avoidance in marital Interaction: A longitudinal view of five types of couples. *Journal of Consulting and Clinical Psychology, 61*, 6–15, and Fitzpatrick, M. (1988). *Between husbands and wives: Communication in marriage*. Newbury Park, CA: Sage.

developed to meet children's needs for care in these various areas. Routines for setting clear rules and limits; for providing supervision to ensure that children conform to these expectations; and for offering appropriate rewards and sanctions for rule following and rule violations meet children's need for control. Parent–child play and communication routines for meeting children's needs for age-appropriate intellectual stimulation also need to be developed if the child is to show optimal emotional and intellectual development. The parenting process and parental mental health are closely linked. The demands of meeting children's needs, particularly if parents have high level of stress and low levels of social support, can contribute to the development of psychological disorders such as depression (Brown, 2000). Also, where parents have a psychological disorder they can have difficulty meeting their children's needs and this might adversely affect their children's development (Luthar, 2003).

Attachment styles

Children develop secure emotional attachments to their parents if their parents are attuned to their needs for safety, security and being physically cared for and if their parents are responsive to children's signals that they require their needs to be met (Bowlby, 1988; Cassidy & Shaver, 1999). Where caregivers are attuned to infants' needs and meet them reliably, infants develop an internal working model of their caregiver as a secure base from which to explore the world and so show considerable confidence in doing so. Where caregivers fail to meet their infants' needs in a reliable way, infants develop internal working models of their caregivers as unreliable and a view of themselves as insecure. Four child–parent attachments that show continuity over the lifecycle and affect the way adult romantic attachments are formed are given in Figure 1.1 (Cassidy & Shaver, 1999). Securely attached children and

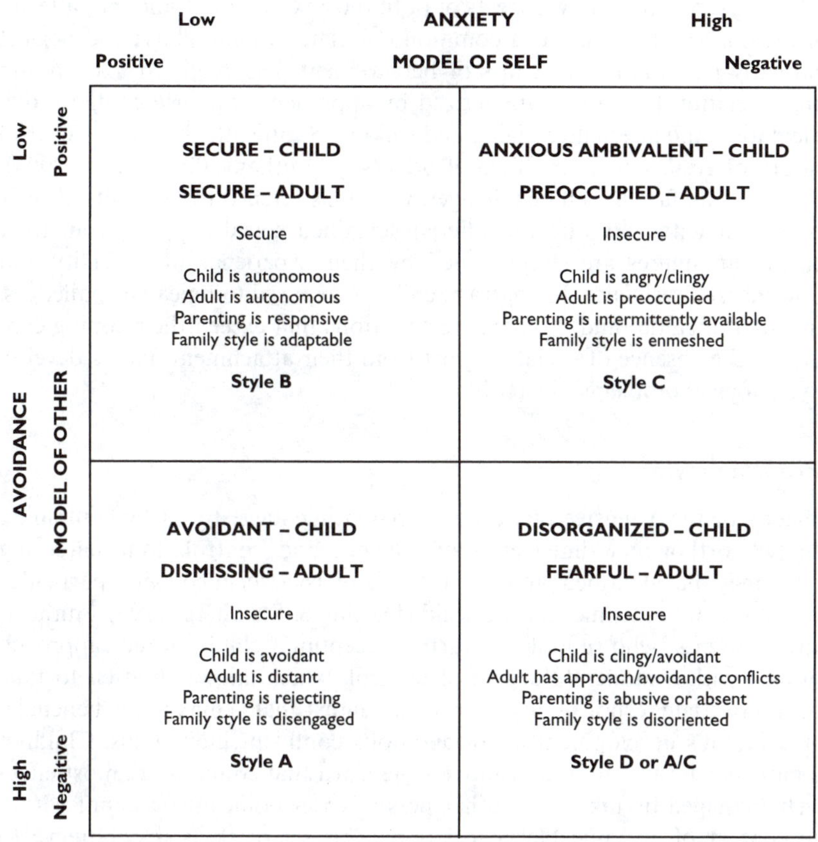

Figure 1.1 Characteristics of four attachment styles in children and adults.

Based on Cassidy, J. & Shaver, P. (1999). *Handbook of attachment*. New York: Guilford, and Carr, A. (2000b). *Family therapy: Concepts, process and practice*. Chichester: Wiley, p. 167.

marital partners react to their parents or partners as if they were a secure base from which to explore the world. Parents and partners in such relationships are attuned and responsive to the children or partner's needs. While a secure attachment style is associated with autonomy, the other three attachment styles are associated with a sense of insecurity. Anxiously attached children seek contact with their parents following separation but are unable to derive comfort from it. They cling and cry or have tantrums. Marital partners with this attachment style tend to be overly close but dissatisfied. Avoidantly attached children avoid contact with their parents after separation; they sulk. Marital partners with this attachment style tend to be distant and dissatisfied. Children with a disorganized attachment style following separation show aspects of both the anxious and avoidant patterns. Disorganized attachment is a common correlate of child abuse and neglect and early parental absence, loss or bereavement. Disorganized marital and family relationships are characterized by approach-avoidance conflicts, disorientation and alternate clinging and sulking. Secure attachment is a central feature of resilience in the face of adversity (Luthar, 2003; Walsh, 2003). Children who face difficult challenges, who are stretched to the limits of their coping capacity and who are offered sustained social support from their attachment figures are strengthened by their experience of adversity and show marked resilience. In contrast, children exposed to repeated challenges, stresses, difficulties and problematic situations that exceed their coping capacity in the absence of social support from their attachment figures develop psychological problems in later life.

Parenting styles

Reviews of the extensive literature on parenting suggest that by combining the two orthogonal dimensions of warmth and control, four parenting styles may be identified and each of these is associated with particular developmental outcomes for the child (Darling & Steinberg, 1993). Authoritative parents who adopt a warm, accepting, child-centred approach coupled with a moderate degree of control, which allows children to take age-appropriate responsibility, provide a context that is maximally beneficial for children's development as autonomous confident individuals. Children of parents who use an authoritative style learn that conflicts are most effectively managed by taking the other person's viewpoint into account within the context of an amicable negotiation. This set of skills is conducive to efficient joint problem solving and the development of good peer relationships and consequently the development of a good social support network. This parenting style is also conducive to good moral development (Kagan & Lamb, 1987). Children of authoritarian parents who are warm, accepting but controlling tend to develop into shy adults who are reluctant to take initiative. The parents' disciplinary style teaches them that unquestioning obedience is the best way to manage interpersonal differences and to solve problems. Children of permissive parents who are warm and accepting but lax in discipline lack the competence in later life to follow through on plans and show poor impulse control. Children who have experienced little warmth or acceptance from their parents and who have been either harshly disciplined or had little or inconsistent supervision may develop psychological problems as adults.

Supportive grandparental roles

In addition to developing parental roles and routines for meeting children's needs, a further task of this stage is the development of positive grandparental roles and the realignment of family relationships that this entails. Neugarten and Weinstein (1964) identified a number of different types of grandparental roles. First, there were those that adopted a formal role and were not involved in child care but loving and emotionally involved with the grandchildren. The second role was essentially fun-seeking and these grandparents acted as playmates for the grandchildren. The third type of grandparental role was that of a distant figure who had little contact with grandchildren. The fourth role type was that of parental surrogate and these grandparents assume the role of parent to the grandchildren so that the mother could work outside the home. The final grandparental role was that of a reservoir of family wisdom who occupied a powerful patriarchal or matriarchal position within the extended family. Where grandparents adopt roles that are supportive of parents and grandchildren, they contribute to family resilience. Where they adopt roles that greatly increase the demands on parents and grandchildren, without offering support, then they can contribute to parental psychological problems.

Families with adolescents

In the sixth stage of the family lifecycle model presented in Table 1.1, which is marked by children's entry into adolescence, parent–child relationships require realignment to allow adolescents to develop more autonomy. Concurrently, demands of caring for ageing grandparents may occur. This is an extremely complex and demanding stage of the family lifecycle, particularly for parents, and the demands of this period can lead to or exacerbate parental psychological disorders.

Problems in adolescence

Good parent–child communication and joint problem-solving skills facilitate the renegotiation of parent–child relationships and the growth of adolescent autonomy. Results of empirical studies of adolescent relationships with parents, peers and partners contradict many commonly held misconceptions (Hill, 1993; Papalia, 2000). Psychoanalytic writers, on the basis of clinical observations of distressed adolescents, argued that parent–child conflict is the norm in adolescence. Epidemiological studies of adolescents show that this is not the case. Although one in five families experience some parent–child conflict, only one in twenty experience extreme conflict. In most families, parent–adolescent quarrels are about mundane topics like untidiness, music, clothing and curfew time. They are rarely about values or ethics.

A traditional view of adolescence posits a gradual erosion of the quality of parent–adolescent relationships with a complementary increase in the quality of the adolescent–peer relationships; studies of attachment suggest that this is not the case. Secure attachments to parents are correlated with secure attachments to peers. Promiscuity in adolescence is not the norm. Most surveys show that a majority of older teenagers view premarital sex between committed partners as acceptable; premarital sex with multiple partners is viewed as unacceptable. Teenage pregnancy is a risk factor for adult social and psychological problems primarily because it can interfere with education and compromise the career prospects of the teenager. Adolescent marriages resulting from unplanned pregnancies run a high risk of dissolution, and these young families often develop multiple life problems and require particularly intensive multi-systemic intervention (Brunk et al., 1987).

Resilience in adolescence

Adolescence is a risky period (Hill, 1993). Opportunities for developing a wide variety of psychological problems that can continue into adulthood abound. Factors that have been found in longitudinal studies to characterize individuals who are resilient in the face of adversity are summarized in Table 1.3 (Luthar, 2003; Rolf et al., 1990; Rutter, 1999). Individuals are more likely to show good adjustment if they have an easy temperament and a high level of intellectual ability. A high level of self-esteem, an optimistic attributional style, a general belief in control over one's life and a specific belief that factors related to specific stresses may be controlled (high self-efficacy) are all associated with good adjustment. These traits (high IQ and easy temperament) and positive belief systems probably render individuals less vulnerable to becoming overly physiologically aroused and aggressive, or demoralized and depressed when faced with life stresses. Individuals are less adversely affected by life stresses if they have good planning skills, a sense of humour and the capacity to empathize with others. All of these coping skills can help individuals detach from deviant or incapacitated attachment figures (such as criminal or incapacitated parents) and deviant peers and seek out more resourceful and prosocial attachment figures and peers. Selecting or creating a positive social network (through marriage, positive school experiences, good friendships, or talented performance in sports or arts) can halt negative chain reactions or start positive chain reactions that facilitate personal development. Better adjustment to life stress occurs when individuals come from higher socio-economic groups, have good social support networks comprising family members and peers and attend schools that provide a supportive yet challenging educational environment. Secure attachment relationships to primary caregivers who adopt an authoritative parenting style and the involvement of both the mother and father in parenting are the major positive family factors associated with adolescents' adjustment to life stress.

Table 1.3 Factors associated with resilience in adolescence

Domain	*Factors*
Family factors	• Absence of early separation or losses • Secure attachment • Authoritative parenting • Father involvement
Community factors	• Positive educational experience • Good social support network (including good peer relationships, and involvement in organized religious activity) • High socio-economic status
Psychological traits	• High ability level • Easy temperament
Self-evaluative beliefs	• High self-esteem • Internal locus of control • Task related self-efficacy • Optimistic attributional style
Coping skills	• Planning skills • Sense of humour • Empathy skills • Skill in detaching from deviant attachment figures and peer groups • Skill in finding or creating a social supportive network • Skill in using unique talents (e.g. sport or music) to create social supportive network and avoid deviant network

Based on Rolf, J., Masten, A., Cicchetti, D., et al. (1990). *Risk and protective factors in the development of psychopathology*. New York: Cambridge University Press, and Rutter, M. (1999). Resilience concepts and findings: Implications for family therapy. *Journal of Family Therapy, 21*, 119–144.

The absence of childhood separations, losses, bereavements, parental mental health problems, criminality and marital discord also characterize the families of individuals who are resilient in the face of stress.

Caring for grandparents

Increasingly, with the lengthening of the average lifespan, the responsibility of caring for ageing parents is becoming a routine responsibility for men and women in mid-life. The stress associated with this role and the impending death of the ageing parent tends to be most acutely felt by daughters of ageing parents. Social support from family and friends and periodic relief or custodial care are important coping resources for such daughters to employ in managing the stresses of caring for ageing parents. In the absence of such supports, the risk of psychological disorder increases.

Launching

The seventh stage of the family lifecycle model in Table 1.1 is concerned with the transition of young adult children out of the parental home. Ideally, this transition entails the development of a less hierarchical relationship between parents and children. During this stage, parents are faced with the task of adjusting to living as a couple again, dealing with disabilities and death in their families of origin and adjusting to the expansion of the family if their children marry and procreate.

Mid-life review

As young adults grow up and begin to leave home, parents must contend not only with changes in their relationships with their maturing offspring but also with a mid-life re-evaluation of their marital relationship and career aspirations. This process, which may have begun in the previous lifecycle stage, takes on considerable momentum as the family home empties. Just as the notion of the universality of adolescent rebellion has not been supported by the results of carefully conducted community-based surveys, so also the popular concept of the mid-life crisis has been found to be a relatively rare phenomenon (Papalia, 2000; Santrock, 2002). Longitudinal studies show that many men and women in their forties become more introspective and re-evaluate their roles within the family and the world of work. For men, there may be a shift in values with an increased valuing of family life over work life. For women, there may be an increased emphasis on work over family. However, these changes in values rarely lead to changes that assume crisis proportions.

Gould (1981) has shown in an extensive study of clinical and non-clinical populations that the assumptions and belief systems learned within the family of origin are challenged in a gradual way over the course of adulthood and this process reaches a resolution in mid-life. Gould's findings are summarized in Table 1.4. The assumptions of childhood give a sense of safety and security. They include a belief in omnipotent thought, a belief in omnipotent protective parents, a belief in the absoluteness of the parents' world view and defences against a rage reaction to separation. Adult consciousness, however, is governed by an acceptance that we create our own lives according to beliefs and values that are different from those internalized in childhood.

In the late teens, if the adolescent is to be liberated from the family, the parents' world view must be appraised. Their parents' roles as protectors must be evaluated and their command over the youth's sexuality and body must be challenged. The conflict is between retaining a childhood role and trying out new roles.

In the twenties, within the work arena, the idea that life is fair and if you stick to the rules you will win, is challenged. With relationships, the idea that our partners can make up for our deficiencies and we can make up for theirs is also challenged. The idea that love can cure personal deficiencies must be given up during the twenties. For example, a talkative partner cannot make up for a quiet partner's style, nor can a nurturing partner fulfil all his or her partner's dependency needs. When these assumptions have been challenged, the person is in a position to differentiate sufficiently to establish a family separate from the family of origin.

The assumptions that are challenged up to the twenties relate to the outer world. In the thirties, assumptions about our inner selves or our relationships with ourselves are challenged. The person realizes that one can know something intellectually such as 'this row with my partner can be resolved through patient negotiation' and yet lack the emotional knowledge to work through the process of negotiation. In their thirties, people realize that they have many characteristics of their parents that they dislike. For example, they

Table 1.4 False assumptions challenged in adulthood

Period	*False assumption*	*Belief systems*
Late teens	I will always belong to my parents and believe in their world	• If I get any more independent it will be a disaster • I can only see the world through my parents' assumptions • Only they can guarantee my safety • They must be my only family • I don't own my body
Twenties	Doing it their way will bring results and they will guide me through difficulties	• If I follow the rules, I will be rewarded • There is only one right way to do things • Rationality, commitment and effort will always prevail over other forces • My partner will do those things for me that I cannot do for myself (i.e. give me a love-cure)
Thirties	Life is simple and controllable. There are no significant co-existing contradictory forces within me	• What I know intellectually, I know emotionally • I am not like my parents in ways that I don't want to be • I can see the reality of those close to me clearly • I can realistically identify and deal with threats to my security
Forties	There is no evil in me or death in the world. The sinister has been expelled	• My work or my relationships grant me immunity from death and danger • There is no life beyond this family • I am innocent

Based on Gould, R. (1981), *Transformations: Growth and change in adult life*. New York: Simon Schuster.

might treat their children unfairly. This has to be recognized if patterns are not to be repeated across generations. There must be an acceptance of a partner's evolution and growth and the fact that we cannot assume that we see that person's point of view today just because we saw it a year ago. There are many threats to security in mid-life both within marriage and the work place. Perceived threats within marriage are often projections, rather than realistic threats.

People in their thirties assume that the feelings of being mistreated or taken for granted are real threats from their partners rather than projections onto their partners of ways in which they were treated as children by their parents or significant others. The belief that we can always identify and deal with threats accurately must be challenged in mid-life.

In the forties, illusions of safety are challenged. For men, the most common illusion is 'If I am successful I will never be frightened again'. For women, the most widespread illusion is 'I cannot be safe without a man to protect me'. When these illusions are challenged, both men and women are freed from slavish adherence to career or marital roles to make the best use of their remaining years with an awareness of their mortality in mind. Within marriage, both husbands and wives must challenge the belief that there is no life outside the marriage. This might lead to them choosing to separate or choosing consciously to live together. The choice to remain married enriches the marriage. In mid-life there must be a reappraisal of the idea that we are innocent, as this is usually a defence against the childhood tendency to label certain emotional states as bad or unacceptable. There is an examination of how we label these emotional experiences rather than a continued attempt to try to deny them. For example:

- anger need not be labelled destructiveness
- pleasure need not be labelled as irresponsibility
- sensuality need not be labelled as sinfulness
- wicked thoughts need not entail wicked actions
- dissatisfaction need not be labelled as greed
- love need not be labelled as weakness
- self-concern need not be labelled as selfishness.

When these aspects of the self are relabelled, rather than denied, and integrated into the conscious self, a process of liberation and increased psychological vitality occurs. For Gould (1981), at the end of the mid-life period the adult experiences a consciousness where the guiding belief is 'I own myself', rather than 'I am theirs'. The sense of self-ownership gives life meaning. Where individuals have difficulty letting go of childhood assumptions and moving towards adult consciousness, psychological problems may develop.

Later life

In the final stage of the family lifecycle model in Table 1.1, the central issue is coping with loss associated with ageing, illness and the inevitability of death. The experience of loss may involve the following grief processes:

- shock
- denial or disbelief
- yearning and searching
- sadness
- anger
- anxiety
- guilt and bargaining
- acceptance.

There is not a clear-cut progression through these processes from one to the next (Stroebe, Hansson, Stroebe & Schut, 2001; Walsh & McGoldrick, 1991). Rather, at different points in time, one or other process predominates. There may also be movement back and forth between processes. All of the processes can give rise to problems significant enough to lead to a referral for psychological treatment.

Shock and denial

Shock is the most common initial reaction, it can take the form of physical pain, numbness, apathy or withdrawal. The person may appear to be stunned and unable to think clearly. This may be accompanied by denial, disbelief or avoidance of the reality of the bereavement, a process can last minutes, days, even months. During denial people may behave as if the dead family member is still living, albeit elsewhere. Thus, the bereaved may speak about future plans that involve the deceased. Terminally ill people may talk about themselves and their future as if they were going to live indefinitely.

Yearning and searching

A yearning to be with the deceased, coupled with disbelief about his or her death, may lead to frantic quests for the person who has died. During this process, those who have lost family members may report seeing them or being visited by them. Mistaking other people for the deceased is also a common experience during the denial process. With terminal illness, the yearning for health may lead to a search for a miracle cure and to involvement in alternative medicine.

Sadness

When denial gives way to a realization of the reality of death, profound sadness, despair, hopelessness and depression may occur. The experience of sadness may be accompanied by low energy, sleep disruption, a disturbance of appetite, tearfulness, an inability to concentrate and a retreat from social interaction. With terminal illness, despair, hopelessness and depression find expression in an unwillingness to fight the illness.

Anger

Complementing the despair process is an anger process, which is associated with the sense of having been abandoned. Aggression, conflict, and drug and alcohol abuse are some of the common ways that grief-related anger finds expression. With terminal illness, the anger may be projected onto family members or members of the medical team. Destructive conflicts within these relationships may occur, such as refusal to adhere to medical regimes, to take medication or to participate in physiotherapy. Someone with a terminal illness may feel angry about the physical or emotional suffering they are enduring or expect to endure as the illness progresses. They may also feel angry about the time, opportunities and experiences they expected to have but will not now have. Anger may be directed towards a God or at fate for allowing this to happen, at family members, friends or medical personnel who cannot share, remove or fully understand their illness, or at the self for things done or not done in the past.

Anxiety

The expression of anger may be followed by remorse or fear of retribution. Where a person has been lost through illness or accident, those grieving may worry that they too will die from similar causes. This can lead to a belief that one is seriously ill and to a variety of somatic complains, such as stomach aches and head aches. It may also lead to a refusal to leave home lest a fatal accident occur.

Guilt and bargaining

The guilt process is marked by self-blame for causing or not preventing the death of the deceased. Some individuals hold the belief that if they died this might magically bring back the deceased. Thus, the guilt process may underpin suicidal ideation or self-injury, which invariably leads to referral for mental health assessment. With terminal illness, the illness may be experienced as a punishment for having done something wrong. This sense of guilt underpins the bargaining process in which people facing death engage. The bargaining process may be carried out as imagined conversations with a deity, where the dying person makes promises to live a better life if they are permitted to live longer.

Acceptance

The final grief process is acceptance. With bereavement, the survivors reconstruct their view of the world so that the deceased person is construed as no longer living in this world, but a benign and accessible representation of them is constructed, which is consistent with their belief system. For example, a Christian may imagine that the deceased is in heaven. Atheists may experience the deceased as living on in their memory or in projects or photographs left behind. In terminal illness, acceptance involves a modification of the world view so that the future is foreshortened and therefore the time remaining is highly valued and is spent living life to the full rather than searching in vain for a miracle cure. For bereaved people new lifestyle routines are evolved as part of the process of accepting the death of a family member and families become re-organized to take account of the absence of the deceased person. With terminal illness, once the inevitability of imminent death has been accepted, routines that enhance the quality of life of the dying person may be evolved. A summary of the grief processes is presented in Table 1.5.

Positive reactions to loss

Reviews of empirical studies of bereavement confirm that there is considerable variation in grief processes and that for some people, in certain circumstances, bereavement and grieving lead to personal growth (Shackleton, 1983; Stroebe, 1993; Stroebe et al., 2001; Wortman & Silver, 1989). Depression following bereavement is not universal. Only about a third of people suffer depression following bereavement. Failure to show emotional distress initially does not necessarily mean that later adjustment problems are inevitable. Also, contrary to the popular myth that grief counselling is the panacea for loss, not everyone needs to work through their sense of loss by immediate intensive conversation about it. Different people use different strategies to cope with loss. Some use distraction or avoidance, while others use confrontation of the grief experience and working through. Those that effectively use the former coping strategy may not show emotional distress. The quality of family relationships and friendships may improve in response to bereavement or terminal illness, with supportive relationships being strengthened.

Negative reactions to loss

Results of empirical studies confirm that for some people bereavement is a particularly destructive experience that does not lead to personal growth and

Table 1.5 Behavioural expressions of themes underlying grief processes following bereavement or facing terminal illness

	Bereavement		*Terminal Illness*	
Grief process	*Underlying theme*	*Adjustment problems arising from grief processes that may lead to referral*	*Underlying theme*	*Adjustment problems arising from grief processes that may lead to referral*
Shock	• I am stunned by the loss of this person	• Complete lack of affect and difficulty engaging emotionally with others • Poor concentration	• I am stunned by my prognosis and loss of health	• Complete lack of affect and difficulty engaging emotionally with others • Poor concentration
Denial	• The person is not dead	• Reporting seeing or hearing the deceased • Carrying on conversations with the deceased	• I am not terminally ill	• Non-compliance with medical regime
Yearning and searching	• I must find the deceased	• Wandering or running away • Phoning relatives	• I will find a miracle cure	• Experimentation with alternative medicine
Sadness	• I am sad, hopeless and lonely because I have lost someone on whom I depended	• Persistent low mood, tearfulness, low energy and lack of activity • Appetite and sleep disruption • Poor concentration and poor school work	• I am sad and hopeless because I know I will die	• Giving up the fight against illness • Persistent low mood, tearfulness, low energy and lack of activity • Appetite and sleep disruption • Poor concentration and poor school work
Anger	• I am angry because the person I needed has abandoned me	• Aggression • Conflict with family members and others	• I am angry because it's not fair. I should be allowed to live	• Non-compliance with medical regime • Aggression

		• Drug or alcohol abuse • Poor concentration		• Conflict with medical staff, family members and peers • Drug or alcohol abuse • Poor concentration
Anxiety	• I am frightened that the deceased will punish me for causing their death or being angry at them. I am afraid that I too may die of an illness or fatal accident	• Separation anxiety, agoraphobia and panic • Somatic complaints, and hypochondriasis • Poor concentration	• I am frightened that death will be painful or terrifying	• Separation anxiety and regressed behaviour • Agoraphobia and panic
Guilt and bargaining	• It is my fault that the person died so I should die	• Suicidal behaviour	• I will be good if I am allowed to live	• Over-compliance with medical regime
Acceptance	• I loved and lost the person who died and now I must carry on without them while cherishing their memory	• Return to normal behavioural routines	• I know that I have only a short time left to live	• Attempts to live life to the full for the remaining time

Adapted from Carr, A. (1999). *Handbook of child and adolescent clinical psychology*. London: Routledge.

development (Shackleton, 1983; Stroebe, 1993; Stroebe et al., 2001; Wortman & Silver, 1989). A return to normal functioning following bereavement does not always occur rapidly. While the majority of people approximate normal functioning within two years, a substantial minority of bereaved people continue to show adjustment difficulties even seven years after bereavement. Extreme distress following bereavement commonly occurs in those who show protracted grief reactions. Resolution and acceptance of death does not always occur. For example, parents who lose children and those who lose a loved one in an untimely fatal accident can show protracted patterns of grief. Grief may have a marked effect on physical functioning. Infections and other illnesses are more common among bereaved people and this is probably due to the effect of loss-related stress on the functioning of the immune system. However, with the passage of time, immune-system functioning returns to normal. Just as bereavement may strengthen supportive family relationships, it may also weaken already discordant relationships and lead to family breakdown. While children's grief reactions tend to be briefer that those of adults, loss of a parent leaves young children vulnerable to depression in adult life. Adults bereaved as children have double the risk of developing depression when faced with a loss experience in adult life compared with their non-bereaved counterparts. Bereaved children most at risk for depression in adulthood are girls who were young when their parents died a violent or sudden death and who subsequently received inadequate care associated with the surviving parent experiencing a prolonged grief reaction.

Having considered a family lifecycle model that assumes lifelong monogamy, lifecycle models that address other types of family arrangements deserve attention, particularly those that evolve when separation, divorce and remarriage occurs.

LIFECYCLE STAGES ASSOCIATED WITH SEPARATION AND DIVORCE

Divorce is no longer an aberration in the normal family lifecycle but a normative transition for a substantial minority of families (Anderson, 2003; Greene et al., 2003; Hetherington & Kelly, 2002; Visher et al., 2003). Table 1.6 shows that family transformation through separation, divorce and re-marriage can be conceptualized as a process involving a series of stages (Carter & McGoldrick, 1999). This model outlines tasks that must be completed during various stages of the transformation process. Failure to complete tasks at one stage may lead to problems at later stages. The stress associated with family transformation through divorce may contribute to the development of psychological disorders and lead to a referral for psychological treatment.

Table 1.6 Extra stages in the family lifecycle entailed by separation or divorce and re-marriage

Stage	*Task*
1. Decision to divorce	• Accepting one's own part in marital failure
2. Planning separation	• Co-operatively developing a plan for custody of the children, visitation and finances • Dealing with the response of the families of origin to the plan to separate
3. Separation	• Mourning the loss of the intact family • Adjusting to the change in parent–child and parent–parent relationships • Avoiding letting marital arguments interfere with parent-to-parent co-operation • Staying connected to the extended family • Managing doubts about separation and becoming committed to divorce
4. Post-divorce period	• Maintaining flexible arrangements about custody, access and finances without detouring conflict through the children • Ensuring both parents retain strong relationships with the children • Re-establishing peer relationships and a social network
5. Entering a new relationship	• Completing emotional divorce from the previous relationship • Developing commitment to a new marriage
6. Planning a new marriage	• Planning for co-operative co-parental relationships with ex-spouses • Planning to deal with children's loyalty conflicts involving natural and step-parents • Adjust to widening of extended family
7. Establishing a new family	• Realigning relationships within the family to allow space for new members • Sharing memories and histories to allow for integration of all new members

Based on Carter, B. & McGoldrick, M. (1999). *The expanded family lifecycle. Individual, family and social perspectives* (Third Edition). Boston: Allyn & Bacon.

Decision to divorce

In the first stage, the decision to divorce occurs and accepting one's own part in marital failure is the central task. However, it is useful to keep in mind that many contextual factors contribute to divorce, including socio-economic status, urban/rural geographical location, age at marriage, premarital pregnancy, psychological adjustment and parental divorce (Faust & McKibben, 1999; Raschke, 1987). Divorce is more common among those from lower socio-economic groups with psychological problems who live in urban areas and who have married before the age of 20. It is also common where premarital pregnancy has occurred and where parental divorce has occurred. Divorce is less common among those from higher socio-economic groupings without psychological problems who live in rural areas and who have married after the age of 30. Where premarital pregnancy has not occurred and where the couples' parents are still in their first marriage divorce is also less common. The economic resources associated with high socio-economic status, the community integration associated with rural living, the psychological resources associated with maturity and the model of marital stability offered by non-divorced parents are the more common explanations given for the associations among these factors associated with divorce. The relationship between these various factors and divorce, while consistent, are moderate to weak. That is, there are significant subgroups of people who show some or all of these risk factors but do not divorce.

Separation

In the second stage of the lifecycle model of divorce, plans for separation are made. A co-operative plan for custody of the children, visitation, finances and dealing with families of origin's response to the plan to separate must be made if positive adjustment is to occur.

The third stage of the model is separation. Mourning the loss of the intact family, adjusting to the change in parent–child and parent–parent relationships; preventing marital arguments from interfering with interparental co-operation, staying connected to the extended family and managing doubts about separation are the principal tasks at this stage.

Divorce leads to multiple life changes that affect parental well-being and the impact of these changes on parental well-being is mediated by a range of personal and contextual factors (Anderson, 2003; Faust & McKibben, 1999; Greene et al., 2003; Hetherington & Kelly, 2002). Divorce leads custodial parents to experience major changes in their lives, including a change in residential arrangements, economic disadvantage, loneliness associated with social network changes, and role strain associated with the task overload that results from having to care for children and work outside the home. Non-custodial parents experience all of these changes with the exception of role strain but with the additional strain of missing daily contact with their children. Changes in divorced couples' residential arrangements, economic status, social networks and role demands lead to a deterioration in physical and mental health for the majority of individuals immediately following separation. Mood swings, depression, identity problems, vulnerability to common infections and exacerbation of previous health problems are all common sequelae for adults who have separated or divorced. However, for most people these health problems abate within two years of the separation.

Post-divorce period

The fourth stage of the lifecycle model of divorce is the post-divorce period. Here couples must maintain flexible arrangements about custody, access and finances without detouring conflict through the children; they must also retain strong relationships with the children and re-establish peer relationships. The stresses and strains of residential changes, economic hardship, role changes and consequent physical and psychological difficulties associated with the immediate aftermath of separation may compromise parents' capacity to co-operate in meeting their children's needs for safety, care, control, education and relationships with each parent (Amato, 2000; Faust & McKibben, 1999; Greene et al., 2003). Three distinct co-parenting styles have been identified in studies of divorced families (Hetherington & Kelly, 2002). When conflictual parenting occurs, all parental messages are passed through the child and this go-between role forced on the child is highly stressful and may lead to sustained adjustment problems. With co-operative parenting, a unified and integrated set of rules and routines about managing the children in both the custodial and non-custodial households is developed. This is the optimal arrangement but occurs in only about one in five cases. With parallel parenting each parent has his or her own set of rules for the children and no attempt is made to integrate these. Most children show few adjustment problems when parallel parenting occurs and this is the most common pattern. About a fifth of individuals from families where divorce has occurred develop significant long-term psychological problems (Hetherington & Kelly, 2002).

New relationships

Establishing a new relationship occurs in the fifth stage of the divorce lifecycle model. For this to occur, emotional divorce from the previous relationship must be completed and a commitment to a new marriage must be developed. The sixth stage of the model is planning a new marriage. This involves planning for co-operative co-parental relationships with ex-spouses and planning to deal with children's loyalty conflicts involving biological and step-parents. It is also important to adjust to the widening of the extended family.

In the final stage of the model, establishing a new family is the central theme. Re-aligning relationships within the family to allow space for new members and sharing memories and histories to allow for integration of all new members are the principal tasks of this stage.

Step-families have unique characteristics compared with families of first marriages (Hetherington & Kelly, 2002; Visher et al., 2003). On the positive side, parents in second marriages are more open in communication, more willing to deal with conflict, more pragmatic, less romantic and more egalitarian with respect to childcare and housekeeping tasks. On the negative side, compared with intact first marriages, step-families are less cohesive and more stressful. Step-parent–child relationships on average tend to be more conflictual than parent–child relationships from intact families. This is particularly true of step-father–step-daughter relationships and may be due to the daughter's perception of the step-father encroaching on a close mother–daughter relationship. Divorced adults with children in middle childhood and early adolescence who wish to re-marry should try to wait until after the children have reached about 16–18 years if they want their new relationship to have a fair chance of survival, because during the early teenage years (10–15) children's resistance to parental remarriage is at a maximum (Hetherington & Kelly, 2002).

LIFECYCLE STAGES ASSOCIATED WITH SINGLEHOOD

In recent years, in industrialized countries, there has been a decline in the numbers of traditional families. People are delaying marriage and childbearing, evidenced in the rise in the age of marriage and motherhood; in Ireland, 38% of women in married or cohabiting couples in the 25–34 age group had no children in 2002, compared to 28% in 1996 (Central Statistics Office, Republic of Ireland, CSO-RoI, 2003a). In the UK, the rate of marriage has fallen (Haskey, 1995), while the rates of divorce and serial cohabitation are rising (Ermisch, 2000). Almost three-quarters of adult women in the UK were married in the late 1970s, while in 1998 this figure had dropped to a little over a half. About three-quarters of first partnerships are cohabitations, rather than marriages, contributing to the rise in the marrying age (Ermisch, 2000). Further, the duration of cohabitation is about two years, with less than 5% lasting more than ten years (Ermisch & Francesconi, 2000). Of these, 53% of the couples married and the remainder parted (Ermisch & Francesconi, 2000). There are thus more households of single people, single parents, step-families, and cohabiting couples, For example, between 1996 and 2002 in Ireland, the number of single people grew by 15.5% while the number of married people grew by 7.2% (CSO-RoI, 2003a). Single-person households make up about a third of all homes (CSO-RoI, 2003b; Office for National Statistics UK, 2003). There is growing recognition that 'single' people include people in a steady relationship with someone with whom they do not live. About one-third of never married, childless women aged under 35 who fall into the demographic group of 'single' are in non-resident relationships or 'living apart together' (LAT); about two-fifths of these relationships endured for two years or more. The proportion of young people now who will never marry is about 20% (Ermisch, 2000).

Psychological theories of adult development traditionally include a stage of marriage; recent revisions concede that cohabiting may be an alternative to marriage. Against this normative model, someone who never formed a marriage or cohabiting relationship is seen as having failed to achieve a life goal; some personal deficit is often assumed during psychological assessment: poor social skills prevent forming or maintaining intimacy; autistic spectrum disorders; a debilitating neurotic condition that deters potential partners; a combination of low self-confidence, low self-esteem and intrusive symptoms such as anxiety or depression; deficits in character or personality; or a person's inability to identify or accept a homosexual sexual orientation.

While psychological difficulties may make it harder to form relationships, not least because of prejudice against those with mental health problems, surely not every person who does not marry or cohabit has a psychological problem? Other explanations apart from the pathological and alternative models of what is normal are needed.

Theories of 'normal' development are embedded in a Western cultural ideology that typically over-emphasizes the role of the individual and under-emphasizes the role of the environment in making causal attributions (the fundamental attribution error; Jones & Nisbett, 1972). Thus, theories construe staying single as reflecting stable, internal, traits and fail to recognize the influence of situational factors in the society or culture that may reduce the likelihood of finding a compatible partner, or being able to cohabit with that partner. As socio-economic status declines, life choices and options shrink, including occupational and geographical mobility, disposable income and free time. For example, it may be extremely difficult to find a partner when working people are also juggling the demands of caring for elderly parents, children, or ill family members with little community support. Similarly, people working more than one job to make ends meet may have little energy left for dating. People may not be able to afford to give up work to move across the country to live with a partner, or to afford the costs of marrying or setting up home with a partner. Some individuals are not given the chance to achieve intimacy because of prejudices operating in society, for example, prejudices against people from certain races or cultures, or against people with certain physical or intellectual disabilities.

More challenging still for a typically conservative profession is the idea that choosing not to be in an intimate relationship or choosing to 'live apart together' could be a valid and healthy life choice. The literature would be enhanced by some study of single people across the lifecycle, who are in or not in intimate sexual relationships, and who demonstrate high functioning and contribution to society. Rather than seeing an intimate sexual cohabiting relationship as a signifier of adult development or health, and its absence as a signifier of stagnation or poor health, it would be useful to look at the elements, and the quality, of intimacy in people in all marital and cohabiting situations. It may be that such abilities as the ability to form and maintain relationships over time, to repair inevitable ruptures in relationships, to communicate effectively and solve interpersonal problems, to demonstrate compassion and loyalty, to confide in others and guard the confidences of others, and to move flexibly between dependence and independence in response to life challenges, are better signifiers of healthy adult development.

GAY AND LESBIAN LIFECYCLES

A significant minority of individuals have gay or lesbian sexual orientations. When such individuals engage in therapy, it is important that frameworks unique to their sexual identity are used to conceptualize their problems, rather than frameworks developed for heterosexual people.

Gay and lesbian identity formation

Lifecycle models of the development of gay and lesbian identities highlight two significant transitional processes: self-definition and 'coming out' (Laird & Green, 1996; McWhirter & Mattison, 1984; Slater, 1995). The first process – self-definition as a gay or lesbian person – occurs initially in response to experiences of being different or estranged from same-sex heterosexual peers and later in response to attraction to and/or intimacy with peers of the same gender. The adolescent typically faces a dilemma of whether to accept or deny the homoerotic feelings he or she experiences. The way in which this dilemma is resolved is in part influenced by the perceived risks and benefits of denial and acceptance. Where adolescents feel that homophobic attitudes within their families, peer groups and society will have severe negative consequences for them, they may be reluctant to accept their gay or lesbian identity. Attempts to deny homoerotic experiences and adopt a heterosexual identity may lead to a wide variety of psychological difficulties, including depression, substance abuse, running away and suicide attempts, all of which may become a focus for therapy. In contrast, where the family and society are supportive and tolerant of diverse sexual orientations, and where there is an easily accessible supportive gay or lesbian community, then the benefits of accepting a gay or lesbian identity may outweigh the risks, and the adolescent may begin to form a gay or lesbian self-definition.

Once the process of self-definition as gay or lesbian occurs, the possibility of 'coming out' to others is opened up. This process of coming out involves coming out to other lesbian and gay people, to heterosexual peers and to members of the family. The more supportive the responses of members of these three systems, the better the adjustment of the individual.

In response to the process of 'coming out', families undergo a process of destabilization. They progress from subliminal awareness of the young person's sexual orientation to absorbing the impact of this realization and adjusting to it. Resolution and integration of the reality of the youngster's sexual identity into the family belief system depends on the flexibility of the family system, the degree of family cohesion and the capacity of core themes within the family belief system to be reconciled with the youngster's sexual identity (Laird & Green, 1996). Therapy conducted within this frame of reference aims to facilitate the processes of owning homoerotic experiences, establishing a gay or lesbian identity and mobilizing support within the family, heterosexual peer group, and gay or lesbian peer group for the individual.

Lifecycle stages

Slater (1995) has offered a five-stage lifecycle model for lesbian couples. In the first stage of couple formation the couple is mobilized by the excitement of forming a relationship but may be wary of exposing vulnerabilities. The management of similarities and differences in personal style so as to permit a stable relationship occurs in the second stage. In the third stage, the central theme is the development of commitment, which brings the benefits of increased trust and security and the risks of closing down other relationship options. Generativity through working on joint projects or parenting is the main focus of the fourth stage. In the fifth and final stage the couple learns to jointly cope with the constraints and opportunities of later life, including retirement, illness and bereavement on the one hand and grandparenting and acknowledging life achievements on the other.

McWhirter and Mattison (1984) developed a six-stage model for describing the themes central to the development of enduring relationships between gay men. The first four stages, which parallel those in Slater's model, are blending, nesting, maintaining and building. McWhirter and Mattison argue that the fifth stage in the gay couple lifecycle, which they term releasing, is characterized by each individual within the couple pursuing his own agenda and taking the relationship for granted. This gives way to a final stage of renewal, in which the relationship is once again privileged over individual pursuits.

Difficulties in managing progression through the lifecycle stages described here may lead gay and lesbian couples to seek therapy.

PERSONALITY DEVELOPMENT ACROSS THE LIFESPAN

While the family lifecycle models considered above offer a framework for considering interpersonal challenges across the lifespan, Erikson's model of personality development offers a useful framework for considering the major intrapsychic issues that individuals face at various points in the lifecycle. Within the model, the lifespan is divided into a series of stages, each of which involves facing a challenge or crisis that requires resolution (Erikson, 1959; Erikson, Erikson & Kivnick, 1986; McAdams & de St Aubin, 1998). If resolution occurs, a particular personal strength or virtue evolves; if it does not, a personal difficulty or vulnerability is engendered. The ease with which successive dilemmas are managed is determined partly by the success with which preceding dilemmas were resolved. Individuals who fail to satisfactorily resolve many dilemmas are particularly vulnerable to psychological problems, which may become a focus for treatment. Erikson's model is presented in Table 1.7. What follows is a summary of the main hypotheses entailed by this theory.

Table 1.7 Erikson's model of personality development

Stage	*Dilemma and main process*	*Virtue and positive self-description*	*Vulnerability and negative self-description*
Infancy 0–18 m	Trust versus mistrust Mutuality with caregiver	Hope I can attain my wishes	Detachment I will not trust others
Toddler years 18 m–3 y	Autonomy versus shame and doubt Imitation	Will I can control events	Compulsion I will repeat this act to undo the mess that I have made and I doubt that I can control events and I am ashamed of this
Pre-school years 3 y–6 y	Initiative versus guilt Identification	Purpose I can plan and achieve goals	Inhibition I can't plan or achieve goals so I don't act
Middle childhood 7 y–11 y	Industry versus inferiority Education	Competence I can use skills to achieve goals	Inertia I have no skills so I won't try
Adolescence 12 y–20 y	Identity versus role confusion Role experimentation	Fidelity I can be true to my values	Confusion I don't know what my role is or what my values are
Young adulthood 21 y–34 y	Intimacy versus isolation Mutuality with peers	Love I can be intimate with another	Exclusivity I have no time for others so I will shut them out
Middle age 34 y–60 y	Productivity versus stagnation Person–environment fit and creativity	Care I am committed to making the world a better place	Rejectivity I do not care about the future of others, only my own future
Old age 60 y+	Integrity versus despair Introspection	Wisdom I am committed to life, I accept myself, my parents, my life but I know I will die soon	Despair I am disgusted at my frailty and my failures

Based on Erikson, E (1959). *Identity and the life cycle*. New York: International University Press.

Trust versus mistrust

The main psychosocial dilemma to be resolved during the first eighteen months of life is trust versus mistrust. If parents respond to infants' needs in a predictable and sensitive way, the infant develops a sense of trust. In the long-term, this underpins a capacity to have hope in the face of adversity and to trust, as adults, that difficult challenges can be resolved. If the child does not experience the parent as a secure base from which to explore the world, the child learns to mistrust others and this underpins a view of the world as threatening. This may lead the child to adopt a detached position during later years and difficulties with making and maintaining peer relationships may occur.

Autonomy versus shame and doubt

The main psychosocial dilemma in the pre-school years (eighteen months to three years) is autonomy versus shame and doubt. During this period children become aware of their separateness and strive to establish a sense of personal agency and impose their will on the world. Of course, sometimes this is possible, but other times their parents will prohibit them from doing certain things. There is a gradual moving from the battles of the terrible twos to the ritual orderliness that many children show as they approach school-going age. If parents patiently provide the framework for children to master tasks and routines, autonomy develops. As adults, such children are patient with themselves and have confidence in their abilities to master the challenges of life. If parents are unable to be patient with the child's evolving wilfulness and need for mastery, and criticize or humiliate failed attempts at mastery, the child will develop a sense of self-doubt and shame. The lack of patience and parental criticism will become internalized and children will evolve into adults who criticize themselves excessively and who lack confidence in their abilities. In some instances, this may lead to the compulsive need to repeat their efforts at problem solving so that they can undo the mess they have made and so cope with the shame of not succeeding.

Initiative versus guilt

In the early school years (three to six years), the main psychosocial dilemma is initiative versus guilt. When children have developed a sense of autonomy in the pre-school years, they turn their attention outwards to the physical and social world and use their initiative to investigate and explore its regularities with a view to establishing a cognitive map of it. The child finds out what is allowed and what is not allowed at home and at school. Many questions about how the world works are asked. Children conduct various experiments and investigations, for example by lighting matches, taking toys apart, or playing doctors and nurses. The initiative versus guilt dilemma is resolved when the child learns how to channel the need for investigation into socially appropriate courses of action. This occurs when parents empathize with the child's curiosity but establish the limits of experimentation clearly and with warmth. Children who resolve the dilemma of initiative versus guilt act with a sense of purpose and vision as adults. Where parents have difficulty empathizing with the child's need for curiosity and curtail experimentation unduly, children may develop a reluctance to explore untried options as adults because such curiosity arouses a sense of guilt.

Industry versus inferiority

In middle childhood (six to twelve years), the main psychosocial dilemma is industry versus inferiority. Having established a sense of trust, autonomy and initiative, the child's need to develop skills and engage in meaningful work emerges. The motivation for industry may stem from the fact that learning new skills is intrinsically rewarding and many tasks and jobs open to the child may be rewarded. Children who have the aptitude to master skills that are rewarded by parents, teachers and peers emerge from this stage of development with new skills and a sense of competence and self-efficacy about these. Youngsters who fail and are ridiculed or humiliated develop a sense of inferiority and in adulthood lack the motivation to achieve.

Identity versus role confusion

The establishment of a clear sense of identity – that is, a sense of who I am – is the major concern in adolescence. When adolescents experience a moratorium, in which many roles are explored, they go to develop a strong commitment to vocational, social, political and religious values, a virtue Erikson refers to as fidelity, and usually have good psychosocial adjustment in adulthood. When the adolescent does not experience a moratorium and explore new roles, identity remains diffuse.

Intimacy versus isolation

The major psychosocial dilemma for people who have left adolescence is whether to develop an intimate relationship with another or move to an isolated position. People who do not achieve intimacy experience isolation. Difficulties with establishing intimate relationships typically emerge from experiences of mistrust, shame, doubt, guilt, inferiority, and role confusion associated with failure to resolve earlier developmental dilemmas in a positive manner.

Productivity versus stagnation

The mid-life dilemma is that of productivity versus stagnation. People who select and shape a home and work environment that fits with their needs and talents are more likely to resolve this dilemma by becoming productive. Productivity may involve procreation, work-based productivity or artistic creativity. Those who become productive focus their energy into making the world a better place for further generations. Those who fail to select and shape their environment to meet their needs and talents may become overwhelmed with stress and become burned out, depressed or cynical on the one hand or greedy and narcissistic on the other.

Integrity versus despair

In later adulthood, the dilemma faced is integrity versus despair. A sense of personal integrity is achieved by those who accept the events that make up their lives – the good and the bad – and integrate these into a meaningful personal narrative in a way that allows them to face death without fear. Those who avoid this introspective process, or who engage in it and find that they cannot accept the events of their lives or integrate them into a meaningful personal narrative that allows them to face death without fear, develop a sense of despair. This despair entails a sense of self-rejection for one's past failures and current frailties. The process of integrating failures, disappointments, conflicts, growing incompetencies and frailty into a coherent life story is very challenging. The positive resolution of this dilemma in favour of integrity rather than despair leads to wisdom. Research on lifespan development shows that people do face the psychosocial dilemmas entailed by Erikson's theory and develop the virtues or vulnerabilities associated with the successful or unsuccessful resolution of them. However, the passage through the stages is more variable than the theory suggests and people can return to past stages in later life (Valliant, 1977).

DIVERSITY

The lifecycle models and related research findings presented in this chapter have all been informed by a predominantly Western, white, middle-class, Judeo-Christian, socio-cultural tradition. However, in Westernized countries, we now live in a multi-cultural, multi-class context. An increasingly significant proportion of clinical psychologists' patients are from ethnic minority groups. Also, many are not from the affluent middle classes but survive in poverty and live within a subculture that does not conform to the norms and values of the white, middle-class community. When such individuals engage in therapy, a sensitivity to these issues of race and class is essential (Patel, 2000; Hays, 2001).

This type of sensitivity involves an acceptance that different patterns of organization, belief systems, and ways of being in the broader socio-cultural context may legitimately typify individuals and families from different cultures. People from different ethnic groups and subcultures may have differing norms and styles governing communication, problem-solving, rules, roles and routines. They may have different belief systems involving different ideas about how progression through the lifecycle should occur, how relationships should be managed, how marriages should work, how parent–child relationships should be conducted, how the extended family should be connected, and how relationships between families and therapists should be conducted. For example, traditional theories of human development prioritized separation from parents as a key task of adolescence and early adult life over the capacity to develop mature adult relationships. This reflected the well-documented Western bias of valuing individuation and independence in adult development (Loevinger, 1976). Thus, clinicians usually looked at events such as moving out of the parental home to set up an independent home unit as signifiers of moving towards adult maturity. More recently, theories of human development have sought to redress this relative neglect of life goals of connectedness and relationship with the introduction of the concept of interdependence and theories about how abilities to relate develop over the lifespan (Josselson, 1992). Being able to be mature and maintain relationships with the family of origin and community might be a better model of mature functioning, particularly for clients from non-Western cultures; for example, an adult client's decision to live with parents until marriage, as is expected in a culture, could reflect psychological health and may not represent pathology. Most importantly, clinical psychologists must be sensitive to the relatively economically privileged position that most occupy with respect to patients from ethnic minorities and lower socio-economic groups. We must also be sensitive to the fact that we share a responsibility for the oppression of minority groups. Without this type of sensitivity we run the risk of illegitimately imposing one set of norms and values on clients and furthering this oppression.

SUMMARY

Psychological problems occur within the context of the lifecycle. The family lifecycle can be conceptualized as a series of stages, each characterized by a set of tasks that must be completed to progress to the next stage. Failure to complete tasks may lead to adjustment problems. In the first two stages of family development, the principal concerns are with differentiating from the family of origin by completing school, developing relationships outside the family, completing one's education and beginning a career. In the third stage, the principal tasks are those associated with selecting a partner and deciding to marry. In the fourth stage, the childless couple must develop routines for living together that are based on a realistic appraisal of the other's strengths, weaknesses and idiosyncrasies. In the fifth stage, the main task is for couples to adjust their roles as marital partners to make space for young children. In the sixth stage, which is marked by children's entry into adolescence, parent–child relationships require re-alignment to allow adolescents to develop more autonomy. The demands of grandparental dependency and mid-life re-evaluation may compromise parents' abilities to meet their adolescents' needs for the negotiation of increasing autonomy. The seventh stage is concerned with the transition of young adult children out of the parental home. During this stage, the parents are faced with the task of adjusting to living as a couple again, to dealing with disabilities and death in their families of origin and of adjusting to the expansion of the family if their children marry and procreate. In the final stage of this lifecycle mode the central task is coping with loss.

Family transformation through separation, divorce and re-marriage can also be viewed as a staged process. In the first stage, the decision to divorce occurs and accepting one's own part in marital failure is the central task. In the second stage, plans for separation are made. A co-operative plan for custody of the children, visitation, finances and dealing with families of origin's response to the plan to separate must be made if positive adjustment is to occur. The third stage of the model is separation. Mourning the loss of the intact family, adjusting to the change in parent–child and parent–parent relationships, preventing marital arguments from interfering with interparental co-operation, staying connected to the extended family and managing doubts about separation are the principal tasks at this stage. The fourth stage is the post-divorce period. Here couples must maintain flexible arrangements about custody, access and finances without detouring conflict through the children; they also need to retain strong relationships with the children and to re-establish peer relationships. Establishing a new relationship occurs, in the fifth stage. For this to occur, emotional divorce from the previous relationship must be completed and a commitment to a new marriage must be developed. The sixth stage of the model is planning a new marriage. This entails planning for co-operative co-parental relationships with ex-spouses and planning to deal with children's loyalty conflicts involving natural and step-parents. It is also important to adjust to the widening of the extended family. In the final stage of the model, establishing a new family is the central theme. Re-aligning relationships within the family to allow space for new members and sharing memories and histories to allow for integration of all new members are the principal tasks of this stage.

Lifecycle models of the development of gay and lesbian identities highlight two significant transitional processes: the process of self-definition as a gay or lesbian person and the process of coming out to other lesbian and gay people, to heterosexual peers and to members of the family. The more supportive the responses of other lesbian and gay people, heterosexual peers and members of the family, the better adjustment will be. Stage models for the development of lesbian and gay couple relationships have been developed that take account of their unique life circumstances.

The development of individual identity within a family context may also be conceptualized as a series of stages. At each stage, the individual must face a personal dilemma. The ease with which successive dilemmas are managed is determined partly by the success with which preceding dilemmas were resolved and partly by the quality of relationships within the individual's family and social context. The dilemmas are: trust versus mistrust, autonomy versus shame and doubt, initiative versus guilt, industry versus inferiority, group identity versus alienation, identity versus role confusion, intimacy versus isolation, productivity versus stagnation, integrity versus despair and immortality versus extinction.

When working with individuals from ethnic minorities and lower socio-economic groups, a sensitivity to issues of race and class is essential if the illegitimate imposition of norms and values from the dominant culture is to be avoided.

EXERCISE 1.1

Working in pairs, adopt the roles of interviewer and interviewee; reverse roles when the interview is over. The interviewer should invite the interviewee to describe: (1) how his or her family managed the task as the various stages of the lifecycle; (2) how he or she personally managed Erikson's psychosocial dilemmas; and (3) what strengths these developmental experiences have given him or her.

FURTHER READING FOR PRACTITIONERS

Carter, B. & McGoldrick, M. (1999). *The expanded family lifecycle. Individual, family and social perspectives* (Third Edition). Boston: Allyn & Bacon.

FURTHER READING FOR CLIENTS

Levinson, D. (1986). *Seasons of a man's life*. New York: Ballentine.

Sheehy, G. (1976). *Passages: Predictable crises of adult life*. New York: Dutton.

REFERENCES

Adams, B. (1986). *The family: A sociological interpretation* (Fourth Edition). San Diego: Harcourt Brace & Janovich.

Allen, J. & Land, D. (1999). Attachment in adolescence. In: J. Cassidy & P. Shaver (Eds), *Handbook of attachment* (pp. 319–335). New York: Guilford.

Amato, P. (2000). The consequences of divorce for adults and children. *Journal of Marriage and the Family*, 62, 1269–1287.

Anderson, C. (2003). The diversity, strengths and challenges of single-parent households. In: F. Walsh (Ed), *Normal family processes* (Third Edition, pp. 121–151). New York: Guilford.

Bowlby, J. (1988). *A secure base: Clinical implications of attachment theory*. London: Routledge.

Brown, G. (2000). Medical sociology and issues of aetiology. In: M. Gelder, J. Lopez-Ibor & N. Andreasen (Eds), *New Oxford textbook of psychiatry* (Volume 1, pp. 293–300). Oxford: Oxford University Press.

Brunk, M., Henggeler, S., & Whelan, J. (1987). Comparison of multisystemic therapy and parent training in the brief treatment of child abuse and neglect. *Journal of Consulting and Clinical Psychology*, 55, 171–178.

Carr, A. (1999). *Handbook of child and adolescent clinical psychology*. London: Routledge.

Carr, A. (2000). *Family therapy: Concepts, process and practice*. Chichester: Wiley.

Carr, A. (2004). *Positive psychology: The science of happiness and human strengths*. London: Brunner-Routledge.

Carter, B. & McGoldrick, M. (1999). *The expanded family lifecycle. Individual, family and social perspectives* (Third Edition). Boston: Allyn & Bacon.

Cassidy, J. & Shaver, P. (1999). *Handbook of attachment*. New York: Guilford.

Central Statistics Office (CSO), Republic of Ireland (2003a). *2002 Census of population – Volume 2 – ages and marital status*. Cork: CSO.

Central Statistics Office (CSO), Republic of Ireland (2003b). *2002 Census of Population – Volume 3 – household composition and family units*. Cork: CSO.

Darling, N. & Steinberg, L. (1993). Parenting styles as context: An integrative model. *Psychological Bulletin*, 113, 487–496.

Erikson, E. (1959). *Identity and the life cycle*. New York: International University Press.

Erikson, E., Erikson, J., & Kivnick, H. (1986). *Vital involvement in old age*. New York: Norton.

Ermisch, J. (2000). *Personal relationships and marriage expectations: Evidence from the 1998 British Household Panel Study*. Working Paper from the Institute for Social and Economic Research, University of Essex.

Ermisch, J. & Francesconi, M. (2000). The increasing complexity of family relationships: Lifetime experience of lone motherhood and stepfamilies in Great Britain. *European Journal of Population*, 16(3), 235–259.

Faust, K. & McKibben, J. (1999). Marital dissolution: Divorce, separation, annulment, and widowhood. In: M. Sussman, S. Steinmetz & G. Peterson (Eds), *Handbook of marriage and the family* (Second Edition, pp. 475–500). New York: Kluwer-Plenum.

Fitzpatrick, M. (1988). *Between husbands and wives: Communication in marriage*. Newbury Park, CA: Sage.

Gottman, J. (1993). The roles of conflict engagement, escalation and avoidance in marital interaction: A longitudinal view of five types of couples. *Journal of Consulting and Clinical Psychology*, 61, 6–15.

Gould, R. (1981). *Transformations: Growth and change in adult life*. New York: Simon Schuster.

Greene, S., Anderson, E., Hetherington, E., Forgatch, M., & DeGarmo (2003). Risk and resilience after divorce. In: F. Walsh (Ed), *Normal family processes* (Third Edition, pp. 96–120). New York: Guilford.

Haskey, J. (1995). Trends in marriage and cohabitation: The decline in marriage and the changing pattern of living in partnerships. *Population Trends*, 80, 5–15.

Hays, P. (2001). *Addressing cultural complexities in practice. A framework for clinicians and counsellors*. Washington, DC: American Psychological Association.

Hetherington, E. & Kelly, J. (2002). *For better or for worse: Divorce reconsidered*. New York: Norton.

Hill, P. (1993). Recent advances in selected aspects of adolescent development. *Journal of Child Psychology and Psychiatry*, 34, 69–99.

Jacobson, N. & Gurman, A. (1995). *Clinical handbook of couple therapy*. New York: Guilford.

John, O. & Srivastava, S. (1999). The big five trait taxonomy: History, measurement and theoretical perspectives. In: L. Pervin & O. John (Eds), *Handbook of personality* (Second Edition, pp. 102–138). New York: Guilford.

Jones, E. E. & Nisbett, R. E. (1972). The actor and the observer: Divergent perceptions of the causes of behaviour. In: E. E. Jones, D. E. Kanouse, H. H. Kelley, R. E. Nisbett, S. Valins, & B. Weiner (Eds), *Attribution: Perceiving the causes of behavior* (pp. 79–94). Morristown, NJ: General Learning Press.

Josselson, R. L. (1992). *The space between us: Exploring the dimensions of human relationships*. San Francisco: Jossey-Bass.

Kagan, J. & Lamb, S. (1987). *The emergence of moral concepts in young children*. Chicago: University of Chicago Press.

Laird, J. & Green, R. (1996). *Lesbians and gays in couples and families: A handbook for therapists*. San Francisco: Jossey-Bass.

Loevinger, J. (1976). *Ego development: Conceptions and theories*. San Francisco: Jossey-Bass.

Luthar, S. (2003). *Resilience and vulnerability: Adaptation in the context of childhood adversities*. Cambridge: Cambridge University Press.

McAdams, D. & de St Aubin, E. (1998). *Generativity and adult development*. Washington, DC: American Psychological Association.

McGoldrick, M. & Carter, B. (2003). The family lifecycle. In: F. Walsh (Ed), *Normal family processes* (Third Edition, pp. 375–398). New York: Guilford.

McWhirter, D. & Mattison, D. (1984). *The male couple: How relationships develop*. Englewood Cliffs, NJ: Prentice Hall.

Neugarten, B. & Weinstein, R. (1964). The changing American grandparent. *Journal of Marriage and the Family*, 26, 199–204.

Newman, B. & Newman, P. (2002). *Development through life* (Eighth Edition). Pacific Grove, CA: Wadsworth Publishing.

Office of National Statistics, UK (2003). *Census 2001: Households*. Online, available: http://www.statistics.gov.uk/cci/nugget.asp?id=350

Papalia, D. (2000). *Human development*. (Eighth Edition). New York: McGraw Hill.

Patel, N. (2000). *Clinical psychology race and culture. A training manual*. Oxford. BPS-Blackwell.

Raschke, H. (1987). Divorce. In: M. Sussman & S. Steinmetz (Eds), *Handbook of marriage and the family* (pp. 348–399). New York: Plenum.

Rolf, J., Masten, A., Cicchetti, D., et al. (1990). *Risk and protective factors in the development of psychopathology*. New York: Cambridge University Press.

Rutter, M. (1999). Resilience concepts and findings: Implications for family therapy. *Journal of Family Therapy*, 21, 119–144.

Santrock, J. (2002). *Lifespan development* (Ninth Edition). New York: McGraw-Hill.

Shackleton, C. (1983). The psychology of grief: A review. *Behaviour Research and Therapy*, 6, 153–205.

Slater, S. (1995). *The lesbian lifecycle*. London: Free Press.

Stroebe, M. (1993). Coping with bereavement: A review of the grief work hypothesis. *Omega Journal of Death and Dying*, 26, 19–42.

Stroebe, M., Hansson, R., Stroebe, W., & Schut, H. (2001). *Handbook of bereavement research: Consequences, coping and care*. Washington, DC: American Psychological Association.

Tannen, D. (1990). *You just don't understand: Women and men in conversation*. New York: Ballentine.

Vaillant, G. (1977). *Adaptation to life: How the best and brightest came of age*. Boston: Little Brown.

Visher, E., Visher, J., & Pasley, C. (2003). Remarriage families and step parenting. In: F. Walsh (Ed), *Normal family processes* (Third Edition, pp. 121–151). New York: Guilford.

Walsh, F. (2003). Family resilience: Strengths forged through adversity. In: F. Walsh (Ed.), *Normal family processes* (Third Edition, pp. 399–423). New York: Guilford.

Wortman, C. & Silver, R. (1989). The myths of coping with loss. *Journal of Consulting and Clinical Psychology*, 57, 349–357.

Chapter 2

Classification and epidemiology

Alan Carr and Muireann McNulty

This chapter offers an overview of the way psychological problems are classified in current versions of the World Health Organization's *International classification of diseases*, tenth edition (ICD-10; WHO, 1992a), the American Psychiatric Association's *Diagnostic and statistical manual*, fourth edition (DSM-IV; APA, 1994) and the American Psychiatric Association's *Diagnostic and statistical manual*, fourth edition text revisions (DSM-IV-TR; APA, 2000) along with a summary of the epidemiology of major categories of problems. The reliability and validity of the two classification systems are evaluated; strengths and weaknesses of categorical approaches to conceptualizing psychological problems are considered. The use of standardized diagnostic interviews, explicit diagnostic criteria and multiple diagnostic axes are all addressed. Differential diagnosis and comorbidity are also discussed.

FUNCTIONS OF CLASSIFICATION

In clinical psychology classification has three main functions. First, it permits information about particular types of problem to be ordered in ways that facilitate the growth of a body of expert knowledge. This information typically includes the accurate clinical description of a problem and the identification of factors associated with the aetiology, maintenance, course and possible management plans effective in solving the problem. Such expert information constitutes the basis for sound clinical practice. Second, classification systems allow for the development of epidemiological information about the incidence and prevalence of various problems. This sort of information is particularly useful in planning services and deciding how to prioritize the allocation of sparse resources. Third, classification systems provide a language through which clinicians and researchers communicate with each other.

Currently, the two major classification systems in widespread use are the ICD-10 WHO, 1992a) and the DSM-IV-TR (APA, 2000). The DSM-IV-TR is the textual revision of the fourth edition of the *Diagnostic and statistical manual of the mental disorders* of the American Psychiatric Association (APA, 1994). The ICD-10 is the tenth edition of the *International classification of diseases*. Psychological problems are classified in Chapter five of this system (WHO, 1992, 1993, 1996, 1997b). Four versions of this are available: the Clinical Descriptions and Diagnostic Guidelines (WHO, 1992a); the Diagnostic Criteria for Research (WHO, 1993); the Diagnostic and Management Guidelines for Mental Disorders in Primary Care: ICD-10, Chapter V, Primary Care version (WHO, 1996) and the Multiaxial Presentation of the ICD-10 for use in Adult Psychiatry (WHO, 1997b). The Clinical Descriptions and Diagnostic Guidelines versions give prototype descriptions of each disorder and general principles to follow in making a diagnosis. The Diagnostic Criteria for Research version gives explicit inclusion and exclusion criteria for making diagnoses on cases for inclusion in research studies. The Primary Care version gives guidance on differential diagnosis on the basis of primary complaints, making a definitive diagnosis and treatment planning. The Multiaxial version offers a way to concurrently code information about diagnosis, disability and contextual factors. It should be emphasized that while, in clinical practice, the DSM-IV-TR is viewed as the US alternative to the European ICD-10, in fact, the ICD-10 is not exclusively European; it is the instrument through which the World Health Organization (WHO), a United Nations (UN) Agency, collects data and compiles statistics on all diseases in all UN countries on all diseases. Although the DSM system is available only in English, the ICD has been translated into many widely spoken languages.

Both DSM and ICD are premised on a medical model of psychological difficulties. For this reason, they may be ideologically unacceptable to clinical psychologists who adopt cognitive-behavioural, psychodynamic, systemic, or other such frameworks as a basis for practice. However, the administration and funding of clinical services and research programmes is predominantly framed in terms of the ICD and DSM systems and so it is important for clinical psychologists to be familiar with them. What follows is a cursory summary of the main advantages and problems of both systems.

ADVANTAGES OF ICD-10 AND DSM-IV

Both systems contain fairly comprehensive groups of categories covering most psychological difficulties seen in clinical practice. Lists of the major categories from ICD-10 and DSM-IV-TR are given in Table 2.1. In both systems, for any case, the main diagnosis is given in categorical rather than dimensional terms. There has been an emphasis, within both systems, on hierarchical organization of main diagnostic categories, with a few broadband categories subsuming many narrowband categories. In both systems, each main diagnostic category is defined in atheoretical terms. For the most

Table 2.1 Main categories in DSM-IV-TR and ICD-10 classification systems

DSM-IV-TR	*ICD-10*
Disorders usually first diagnosed in infancy childhood or adolescence	Organic mental disorders
Delirium, dementia, amnestic and other cognitive disorders	Mental and behavioural disorders due to psychoactive substance use
Mental disorders due to a general medical condition	Schizophrenia, schizotypal and delusional disorders
Substance-related disorders	Mood disorders
Schizophrenia and other psychotic disorders	Neurotic, stress-related and somatoform disorders
Mood disorders	Behavioural syndromes associated with physiological disturbances and physical factors
Anxiety disorders	Disorders of adult personality and behaviour
Somatoform disorders	Mental retardation
Factitious disorders	Disorders of psychological development
Dissociative disorders	Behavioural and emotional disorders with onset usually occurring in childhood and adolescence
Sexual and gender identity disorders	
Eating disorders	
Sleep disorders	
Impulse control disorders	
Adjustment disorders	
Personality disorders	
Other conditions	

part, diagnostic categories are based on observable clusters of symptoms. This strategy was adopted to avoid the unreliability of diagnoses based on inferred intrapsychic variables that characterized earlier versions of both systems. However, in some instances organic or psychosocial aetiological factors are used to define disorders. For example, substance-related disorders are defined by the substances abused and exposure to a major stressor is one of the criteria for post-traumatic stress disorder. In both systems, a person may receive more than one major diagnosis and this provides a way of dealing with the problem of comorbidity.

The DSM-IV-TR is a multi-axial classification system. A multi-axial version of ICD-10 for use in adult mental health has been developed (WHO, 1997b). Multi-axial systems allow complex information about important facets of a case to be coded simply and briefly. In the DSM multi-axial system, the main diagnosis is given on axis I; personality disorders are categorically coded on axis II; medical conditions are categorically coded on axis III; psychosocial and environmental problems are listed on axis IV.

Global functioning is rated on a 100-point scale on axis V. In the tri-axial ICD-10 system for use in adult mental health settings, clinical diagnoses are coded on axis I; disabilities on axis II; and contextual factors on axis III.

Both the DSM and ICD systems are open to revision in the light of new information. In an appendix of DSM-IV, diagnostic criteria and axes for further study are included. Among these, a defensive functioning axis and a global assessment of relational functioning axis are outlined. The defensive functioning axis is based on psychodynamic therapy, theory and research (Valliant, 2000). The global assessment of relational functioning axis is based on family systems therapy, theory and research (Dausch, Milkowitz & Richards, 1996).

Although the diagnostic criteria of the current DSM and ICD systems are very similar, they are not identical. Studies comparing concordance rates show while that both systems yield similar rates for many disorders, there are notable exceptions. ICD-10 criteria yield higher prevalence rates of social phobia, post-traumatic stress disorder and harmful alcohol use disorders (Andrews, Henderson & Hall, 2001) but lower rates for personality disorders (Samuels et al., 2002). Many researches in the field want to work towards making the next revisions of the ICD and DSM system identical (First & Pincus, 1999).

ETHICAL AND PRACTICAL PROBLEMS WITH ICD-10 AND DSM-IV

Both of the current ICD and DSM classification systems have serious shortcomings. Their technical problems may be distinguished from ethical and pragmatic concerns, which will be addressed first. At an ethical level, ICD and DSM diagnoses pathologize vulnerable individuals who are relatively powerless to resist this process. That is, diagnoses focus on weaknesses rather than strengths and are couched in a pathologizing, pejorative discourse. The process of traditional diagnosis may lead individuals, their families and the community to view diagnosed patients as defective. If labelling leads to stigmatization, then it is only justifiable to the extent that the diagnoses given lead to treatment that ameliorates the problems described by the label. A counter-argument to this overall objection to labelling is that it is not the label that leads to stigmatization but the behavioural difficulties that the individual exhibits. Another argument is that the problems and the label combine to lead to stigmatization and that the benefits of some form of labelling probably outweigh the costs. However, labelling should be as benign as possible. The massive over-emphasis on pathology with little regard for personal strengths and resources shown by the DSM and ICD systems is unjustifiable. It would be very empowering to be able to say something like:

> Our assessment shows that you have many personal strengths and skills and are well supported by your partner and family. Because of this, you present with less severe sleep and mood problems than would otherwise occur following a trauma. The official ICD-11 and DSM-V diagnosis is *robust personal and family coping syndrome*.

Instead, our current classification systems inform pathologizing feedback, such as:

> Our assessment shows that following exposure to a trauma you are suffering from intrusive memories, attempts to avoid or suppress these, and episodes of anxiety. The official ICD-10 and DSM-IV diagnosis is *post-traumatic stress disorder.*

At the pragmatic level, surveys show that clinicians find the DSM system unhelpful in routine clinical practice (Jampala, Sierles & Taylor, 1986). A diagnostic label, or even a full multi-axial list of labels, offers very limited guidance on how to proceed clinically. In practice, many clinicians give an ICD or DSM diagnosis as an administrative chore. In the US, insurance companies often link payment to the presence of a DSM diagnosis. In parts of Europe, particularly in the public health services, funding may be linked to the completion of administrative forms on each patient seen, and these forms include a requirement to give an ICD diagnosis. Psychological interventions are rarely exclusively based on diagnosis, but on complex multi-factorial formulations, an issue that will be considered in greater detail below.

TECHNICAL PROBLEMS WITH DSM-IV AND ICD-10

The main technical problems with the DSM and ICD classification systems are low reliability, poor coverage, high comorbidity and low validity.

Reliability

In the past, a major problem with the ICD and DSM systems has been their poor inter-rater reliability. Clinicians who interviewed the same cases frequently reached different conclusions about the most appropriate diagnosis. It was hoped that the use of diagnostic criteria based on atheoretical observable symptoms would improve the unacceptably low reliability co-efficients obtained for many of the DSM-II categories. No such improvement was observed in carefully controlled studies comparing the DSM-II (in which no diagnostic criteria were given) and DSM-III (in which diagnostic criteria were first introduced) (e.g. Kirk & Kutchins, 1992; Mattison, et al., 1979).

However, in later studies that coupled the use of diagnostic criteria with standardized approaches to interviewing using instruments such as Structured Clinical Interview for DSM-IV-TR axis I disorders (SCID-I; First et al., 1997) or the Composite International Diagnostic Interview (CIDI; WHO, 1997a) the reliability of diagnoses could be improved from a kappa of about .6 to a kappa of about .7 or .8 (Meyer, 2002). Kappa reliability co-efficients must be above .7 to be classified as satisfactory. However, the highest reliabilities (kappas of .7–.9) occur when diagnoses are made on the basis of a synthesis of information drawn from multiple sources, including diagnostic interviews, interviews with other informants and behavioural observations of nursing or research staff (Meyer, 2002). Currently, for both DSM-IV-TR and ICD-10, establishing procedures for routinely obtaining satisfactory reliability for diagnoses remains a central challenge.

Coverage

Along with the use of diagnostic criteria, there has been a gradual narrowing of definitions of disorders to reduce within-category heterogeneity and improve reliability. This effort to improve within-category homogeneity has led to a problem of poor coverage. That is, many cases typically referred for consultation cannot be classified into clearly defined categories using either the ICD or DSM systems. Many referred cases do not quite meet all the diagnostic criteria and are 'subthreshold' conditions. Other cases present with significant and complex difficulties involved in coping with major life transitions and stresses, but these challenges that would benefit from psychological consultation do not constitute a diagnosable disorder. Still other cases present with a very wide range of difficulties and symptoms associated with a variety of diagnostic categories. Within the ICD and DSM classification systems, three strategies have been adopted to deal with these diagnostic dilemmas. The first is to include an undefined subcategory for many disorders to accommodate individuals who show constellations of subthreshold, atypical, or mixed patterns of symptoms. In the DSM, such categories are labelled *not otherwise specified* (NOS) and in the ICD the term *unspecified* is used, for example, *F29 unspecified non-organic psychosis*. The second solution to the coverage problem has been to include a list of problems, concerns and factors that may lead to referral but which fall outside the overall diagnostic framework. In the ICD system these are termed Z codes; in the DSM, they are referred to as V codes. For example, in the ICD-10, code Z64.0 is used when a person has *problems related to unwanted pregnancy*. In DSM-IV, code V61.20 is used if there is a *parent–child relational problem*. The third strategy to deal with the problem of presentations that do not fit one of the narrowly defined categories has been to allow for the coding of multiple diagnoses and consider these to be comorbid conditions.

Comorbidity

Comorbidity refers to situations where a person presents with a sufficiently wide range of symptoms for more than one diagnosis to be given. That is, the person simultaneously meets the diagnostic criteria for more than one diagnosis. Classification systems that permit the coding of comorbid diagnoses are valid and useful in circumstances where comorbid conditions are underpinned by differing biopsychosocial aetiological factors and where these multiple conditions require concurrent but distinctly different approaches to treatment. For example, a person with a long-standing diagnosis of bipolar disorder in later adulthood may come to meet the diagnostic criteria for dementia. Or a person with a diagnosis of Asperger's syndrome may develop a mood disorder in early adulthood in response to difficulties in making and maintaining friendships and romantic attachments. However, in other circumstances classification systems that permit coding comorbid conditions may be less useful. These include circumstances where the two comorbid conditions both arise from the same set of biopsychosocial aetiological factors and where a single approach to treatment is appropriate. For example, patients who show a complex set of clinical features that meet the criteria for both a mood disorder and an anxiety disorder are not uncommon. Neither is a presentation characterized by chronically low mood with episodes of extremely low mood that meets the diagnostic criteria for both dysthymia and major depression; this is often referred to as double depression. The usefulness of comorbid codings in these circumstances is questionable.

Comorbid presentations are more common in clinical than community populations. Within clinical populations, comorbid cases, for the most part, are less responsive to treatment. This is well documented for the personality disorders, which in DSM-IV-TR are coded on axis II. A strong association has been found between the presence of comorbid axis II diagnoses and poor response to treatment for a range of disorders, notably anxiety and mood disorders (Crits-Cristoph & Barber, 2003).

Validity

The validation of diagnostic categories within the DSM and ICD systems involves demonstrating that cases that meet the diagnostic criteria for a particular category share common critical characteristics. These include predisposing risk factors, precipitating factors that trigger the onset of the disorder, maintaining factors that lead to persistence or exacerbation of the disorder and protective factors that modify the impact of aetiological factors. Factors in each of these categories may be biological, psychological or social. The course of the disorder over time, and the response of cases to specific treatments, should also be shared to a fairly marked degree by cases falling within the same valid diagnostic category. Despite extensive research on many disorders, it is difficult to point to any one condition where validity on all of these criteria has been established. There is not a high level of specificity in the links between aetiological factors and many psychological problems. Furthermore, the course of any disorder and its response to treatment is highly variable and is strongly influenced for most disorders by comorbidity and the number of risk factors present.

The reason both the ICD and DSM systems have reliability, coverage and comorbidity difficulties that compromise their validity is because most psychological difficulties are not distributed within the population as disease-like categorical entities. Rather, they occur as dimensional psychological characteristics that are typically the outcome of the impact of a complex array of biopsychosocial predisposing, precipitating, maintaining and protective factors. It is therefore expedient for clinical psychologists to make use of dimensional frameworks and complex formulation frameworks in assessing many categorically defined problems. It is to these that we now turn.

DIMENSIONAL MODELS

Within DSM-IV and ICD-10, psychological problems are conceptualized in categorical terms. That is, it is assumed that within a population some people have psychological disorders and some do not, and that there are qualitative differences between those that do and do not meet the diagnostic criteria for specific disorders. Trait theories, in contrast, argue that a limited number of dimensions may be used to characterize important aspects of behaviour and experience. Traits are normally distributed within the population. So for any given trait (for example introversion–extraversion) most people show a moderate level of the trait, but a few people show extremely low or extremely high levels of the trait. Within a population, people who fall at the extreme ends of these dimensions may have the sorts of difficulties attributed in DSM-IV and ICD-10. However, these people differ from others only in the degree to which they show particular traits. For example, extreme introversion may lead to difficulties with making and maintaining social relationships and to a diagnosis of social anxiety disorder or avoidant personality disorder. Extreme neuroticism may lead to difficulties with mood and self-regulation and to the diagnosis of anxiety or mood disorders. Extreme conscientiousness may lead to obsessional ideas and compulsive behaviour and to a diagnosis of obsessive-compulsive disorder or obsessive-compulsive personality disorder.

In recent years, normal personality trait theory has come to be dominated by the Five Factor Model of Personality (Costa & Widiger, 2001). This model includes the following dimensions: neuroticism, extraversion, openness to experience, agreeableness and conscientiousness. The five factors have been derived from the semantic clustering of an exhaustive list of adjectives describing personality traits abstracted from dictionaries in a number of languages and extensive factor-analytic studies of self-report and observer-rated items based on these lists. Within the broad tradition of trait theory, historically there has been considerable controversy over the precise number of traits that may appropriately be used to describe personality functioning. For example, Eysenck (1990) argued that three traits (neuroticism, extraversion and psychoticism) could account for most aspects of personality functioning. In contrast, Cattell (1990) argued that sixteen traits were required. Differences in the number of traits in these models are due to differences in the factor-analytic methods used and the range of items analysed. The Five Factor Model of Personality builds on the insights of Eysenck, Cattell and others. The first two dimensions are the same as those proposed by Eysenck. Furthermore, the traits agreeableness and conscientiousness are two aspects of Eysenck's psychoticism factor. Disagreeable people are interpersonally cold and people low on conscientiousness disregard social conventions. Openness to experience refers to a dimension that extends from imaginative creativeness to constriction. Furthermore, secondary factor analyses of Cattell's sixteen factors yield broadband factors similar to some of those within the five-factor model.

The weight of evidence shows that 50% of the variance in major personality traits such as extraversion, neuroticism, openness to experience and conscientiousness may be accounted for by genetic factors (Paris, 1996). The mechanisms by which genetic factors influence personality traits are complex. Probably, multiple genes determine temperamental characteristics, and these interact with environmental influences in the development of personality traits. There is considerable evidence from longitudinal studies of the link between temperament and personality traits. Children with high activity levels and positive affect become extraverted. Children who are highly irritable and fearful show high levels of neuroticism in later life. Children who show attentional persistence later develop high levels of conscientiousness (Rothbart & Ahadi, 1994). Children with extreme temperamental characteristics may be more vulnerable to environmental stressors or they may elicit reactions from parent and others that exacerbate their extreme temperamental characteristics.

In contrast to the evidence for the role of genetic factors in the development of personality traits, there is little evidence for a major role of genetic factors in the development of personality disorders. Thus, it is probable that people with extreme levels of particular personality traits (which are 50% heritable) when exposed to particular types of family environments develop certain personality disorders. In prospective and retrospective studies, a wide variety of family-based risk factors have been found to predispose people to the development of personality disorder. These include separation from or loss of a parent, parental psychopathology and related impaired parenting, problematic parent–child relationships, extremely low or high levels of family cohesion, physical and sexual abuse, neglect and the absence of social support (Paris, 1996).

Trait theories of personality, particularly the Five Factor Model of Personality, have been applied largely to the study of personality disorders with some degree of success (Costa & Widiger, 2001). In DSM-IV, personality disorders fall into three clusters: cluster A, eccentric personality disorders (schizoid, schizotypal, paranoid); cluster B, erratic-dramatic personality disorders (border-line, anti-social, narcissistic, histrionic); and cluster C, anxious personality disorders (avoidant, dependent and obsessive-compulsive). Distinctive personality trait profiles have been empirically identified for each personality disorder and treatment strategies have been developed for problems associated with extreme levels of each of the five major personality traits. For example, extreme introversion is a central trait for most disorders in cluster A; extreme extraversion and low agreeableness or conscientiousness typify most disorders in cluster B; and high neuroticism characterizes all cluster C personality disorders.

Dimensional approaches have been used not only to address individual differences in personality but also to measure variation within highly specific domains such as mood, anxiety and psychotic experiences (Westen, Heim, Morrison, Patterson & Campbell, 2002). Multi-variate studies of self-report and symptom rating scales show that anxiety and depression both share a common negative affect factor, but that depression is uniquely associated with exceptionally low positive affect scores, while anxiety is characterized by exceptionally high scores on an autonomic arousal dimension. Multi-variate studies of psychotic symptoms has led to the inclusion in an appendix of DSM-IV of a dimensional approach to coding different symptom patterns in people with a diagnosis of schizophrenia as an alternative to subtyping. Four-point dimensional scales are used to rate the extent to which patients show positive symptoms (such as delusions and hallucinations), negative symptoms (such as flattened affect and avolition) and disorganization (including disorganized speech and behaviour). This may prove to be a more reliable and valid way of dealing with heterogeneity than suptyping people with schizophrenia as paranoid, disorganized and catatonic.

Dimensional approaches to diagnosing and conceptualizing psychological problems have the advantage of fitting better with the way many psychological characteristics are normally distributed within the population. However, there is little doubt that some psychological difficulties, such as bipolar disorder, are discretely distributed and so may be better accounted for within a categorical system (Craighead et al., 2002). Severe and profound intellectual disability is also distributed within the population as a categorical disease like entity, while mild and moderate intellectual disability appear to be distributed as the tail of a normal distribution of cognitive ability conceptualized in dimensional terms (Volkmar & Dykens, 2002).

Dimensional conceptualizations of psychological problems offer a useful framework for assessment in many instances. The use of reliable and valid self-report inventories and observer rating scales can readily be incorporated into routine clinical practice to provide assessments of the status of people on such dimensions. Furthermore, cut-off scores can be used, when administratively necessary, to translate dimensional scores into diagnoses. Finally, improvement or deterioration may be assessed in terms of changes in scores along dimensions. Manuals for most inventories, rating scales, and tests give rules for interpreting change scores which take into account the psychometric properties of the instrument.

COMPLEX FORMULATIONS

It is both a strength and a weakness of the DSM and ICD classification systems that, for the most part, diagnostic categories are defined in atheoretical terms. An atheoretical approach prevents the unreliability of diagnoses based on inferred biological, intrapsychic or interpersonal variables, which characterized earlier versions of both systems. However, an atheoretical classification system leaves clinicians without a way to conceptualize the complex array of biopsychosocial predisposing, precipitating, maintaining and protective factors relevant to specific disorders and their treatment. What follows is an encapsulation of some of the more important factors that may be considered in developing complex and relatively comprehensive formulations for psychological problems in adulthood.

Predisposing factors

Biological, psychological and social factors associated with early life may predispose people to developing psychological problems in adulthood (Rutter & Taylor, 2002). Genetic vulnerabilities, the consequences of prenatal and perinatal complications, and the sequelae of early insults, injuries and illnesses may predispose people to developing problems in later life. In addition to these biological predisposing factors, a number of psychological characteristics, traits and relatively enduring belief systems may also predispose people to developing psychological difficulties. Low intelligence, difficult temperament, extreme levels of major personality traits (introversion, neuroticism, conscientiousness and disagreeableness), low self-esteem and an external locus of control are some of the more important variables in this category. Important social predisposing factors for psychological problems include separation from or loss of a parent, parental psychopathology and related impaired parenting, insecure attachment to parents in early life, family disorganization and sustained exposure to marital discord, physical and sexual abuse, neglect and the absence of an adequate social support network in childhood.

Precipitating factors

Some psychological problems, such as autism, are present at birth. For others, the onset is quite gradual. For example, anti-social personality disorder may begin early in childhood as oppositional defiant disorder developing later into conduct disorder before evolving into a personality disorder at the end of adolescence. In other instances, the onset of psychological problems is very sudden and in response to a clear stressor, as in the case of post-traumatic stress disorder, or a build-up of life stresses, as in some cases of depression. Despite these variations, it is conceptually useful to distinguish precipitating factors from predisposing and maintaining factors, while recognizing that precipitating factors may not be identifiable in all instances. Psychological problems may be precipitated by acute life stresses such as loss experiences, humiliation, illness, injury, victimization, redundancy, financial difficulties or imprisonment (Brown, 2000). They may also be precipitated by lifecycle transitions such as leaving home, changing jobs, marriage or making a commitment to a long-standing relationship, having children, family conflict, children leaving home, parental decline, separation or divorce, or forming a new family (Carr, 2000).

Maintaining factors

Once psychological problems have developed, they may be maintained by psychological, social and biological factors. Beliefs about self-regulation and self-regulatory skills are important psychological maintaining factors. In particular, psychological problems may be maintained by poor self-efficacy beliefs, dysfunctional attributions, cognitive distortions, and dysfunctional coping strategies. Modifying these maintaining factors is a central aim of cognitive-behaviour therapy (described in Chapter 3). Other psychological maintaining factors include problematic attachment styles and immature defence mechanisms. These factors are a central focus in psychodynamic therapy, which will be considered in Chapter 4. Within the social domain psychological problems may be maintained by patterns of interaction within the marriage, the family, the wider social network and by the way in which the individual engages with treatment agencies. These include interaction patterns characterized by communication and joint problem-solving deficits, high stress and low support, inadvertent reinforcement of problem behaviour, conflict and violence, emotional enmeshment or disengagement and overly chaotic or rigid organization of the social system. These maintaining factors are addressed by systemic approaches to therapy, which will be considered in Chapter 5. Biological factors, notably the dysregulation of certain neurotransmitter systems, may maintain some psychological disorders. Psychopharmacological treatments target these systems; Chapter 6 addresses these biomedical interventions.

Protective factors

A variety of protective factors within the biological, psychological and social domains have been identified (Carr, 2003; Rapp, 1998). Within the biological domain, a personal history of good health and a family history indicative of little or no genetic vulnerability to psychological problems are protective factors. For people with a recurrent episodic disorder, a positive response to pharmacological treatment in a previous episode may be considered a protective biological factor, because it suggests that such a response may occur again. Within the psychological domain, a number of traits, relatively enduring belief systems and other personal attributes are notable protective factors. These include good premorbid adjustment and a history of having coped well with a similar problem in the past. Psychological mindedness, a capacity to understand psychological formulations of personal difficulties, and an acceptance that these difficulties may be addressed by engaging in psychological treatment are protective psychological factors also. Other protective psychological factors include average or above-average intelligence, a history of having an easy temperament, moderate to high levels of major personality traits (notably extraversion, emotional stability, conscientiousness, and agreeableness), high self-esteem, an internal locus of control, strong self-efficacy beliefs, an optimistic attributional style, functional coping strategies, a secure attachment style and mature defence mechanisms. Within the social domain a crucially important protective factor is the capacity to make and maintain a co-operative therapeutic alliance with professionals within the relevant treatment agency. Other protective factors within the social domain include current and past membership of a family and social system with good communication and joint problem-solving coupled with low stress and high emotional support.

From this encapsulation of some of the more important factors to consider in developing comprehensive formulations for psychological problems in adulthood, it is clear that multiple aetiological factors need to be considered, including positive factors. Positive protective factors are particularly important because highlighting these can motivate clients to engage in treatment, and building on these strengths may also serve as a focus for therapy.

WORLD PSYCHIATRIC ASSOCIATION'S INTERNATIONAL GUIDELINES FOR DIAGNOSTIC ASSESSMENT

One example of an attempt to meet the shortcomings of the ICD-10 and the DSM-IV is the World Psychiatric Association's International Guidelines for Diagnostic Assessment (IGDA; Mezzich et al., 2003). The IGDA attempts to offer an assessment and diagnostic framework that unifies the many systems used throughout the world, including the ICD-10, the DSM-IV, the Chinese

Classification of Mental Disorders (Chinese Medical Association, 1995), the Cuban Glossary of Psychiatry (Otero, 2000) and the Latin American guide for Psychiatric Diagnosis (Berganza et al., 2001). A central feature of this set of guidelines is its recognition of the need for cultural sensitivity in evaluating people with psychological difficulties. The guidelines also insist that diagnostic formulation should be based on multiple data sources, including clinical interviews with the patient, interviews with members of the patient's social network, past health and social care records and special investigations such as laboratory tests and psychometric assessments. The IGDA recommends the use of a four-category multi-axial system, with clinical disorders on axis I, disabilities on axis II, contextual factors on axis III, and quality of life on axis IV. The first three axes of this system are the same as those used in the ICD-10 multi-axial system for adults (WHO, 1997b). The IGDA recognizes that in addition to making a multi-axial diagnosis and standardized formulation, there is a requirement in each case to make a personalized ideographic formulation that explains the unique set of biopsychosocial factors contributing to each patient's specific difficulties, the patient's unique profile of personal and contextual strengths and a prognostic statement of expected outcome for the case. Treatment planning should be based on both the standardized and personalized formulations. Thus, clinicians should draw on available evidence from controlled trials in selecting the components of their overall treatment plan, but this should be tailored to the needs of the individual patient through reference to their idiographic formulation.

EPIDEMIOLOGY

While the classification of psychological disorders addresses the question: 'How many different sort of problems are there?', the central question for epidemiology is: 'How many people in the population have these problems?' Epidemiology is also concerned with the identification of factors associated with the distribution of diagnoses within populations. Data on the overall prevalence of psychological problems in major national surveys is given in Table 2.2. The table shows that between 12 and 29% of populations in Northern Ireland, the UK, the USA and Australia have psychological disorders at any one time. Depressive disorders, anxiety disorders and drug and alcohol dependence are particularly prevalent difficulties. Less than 1% of the population suffers from schizophrenia. Psychological disorders have clear demographic correlates (Henderson, 2000; Jenkins et al., 1997; Kessler et al., 1994; McConnell et al., 2002). Women have higher rates of depressive and anxiety disorders and men have higher rates of drug and alcohol dependence. Younger people have higher rates of disorder, especially drug and alcohol dependence. Married people, employed people and people with more education have lower rates of all disorders. In community surveys, about 40–50%

Table 2.2 Prevalence rates (in percentages) of common psychological disorders

Country		*UK*	*USA*	*Australia*	*Northern Ireland*
Prevalence period		1 Week	12 Month	12 Month	12 Month
Interview instrument		CIS-R	CIDI	CIDI-A	SCAN
Author		Jenkins et al.,	Kessler et al.,	Henderson	McConnell et al.,
Year		1997	1994	2000	2002
Number in study		*n* = 10,108	*n* = 8098	*n* = 10,641	*n* = 1242
Response rate		80%	82%	78%	74%
Any disorder*		27%	29%	22%	12%
Depression	Male	1.7	8.5	4.2	2.7
	Female	2.5	14.1	7.4	8.5
Anxiety	Male	2.8	11.8	7.1	2.4
	Female	3.4	22.6	12.1	4.7
Alcohol and drug abuse	Male	7.5	14.1	9.4	3.4
	Female	2.1	5.3	3.7	0.5
Schizophrenia	Male	0.4	0.5	0.4	0.4
	Female	0.4	0.6	0.4	0.4

CIS-R, Clinical Interview Schedule-Revised (Lewis et al., 1992); CIDI, Composite International Diagnostic Interview (World Health Organization, 1997a); SCAN, Schedules for Clinical Assessment in Neuropsychiatry (WHO, 1992b).
* Based on estimates reported in Andrews et al. (2001).

of the people who meet the diagnostic criteria for one disorder also meet the criteria for another disorder and about a fifth of people in community surveys meet the criteria for three or more disorders (Kessler, 1995). People with multiple comorbid disorders have greater disability, are more intensive service users and are poorer responders to treatment (Andrews, Slade & Issakidis, 2002). In community surveys, about 9–13% of cases have DSM-IV personality disorders and 5–6% have ICD-10 personality disorders (which have higher diagnostic thresholds) (Samuels et al., 2002). Personality disorders are more prevalent among males than females, younger than older people and those who are unmarried rather than married.

SUMMARY

Currently, the DSM and ICD classification systems are used in the US and Europe, respectively, to facilitate clinical practice, communication and research. These systems have the advantages of being multi-axial, including diagnostic criteria and allowing for the coding of psychosocial stresses and adaptive functioning. However, both the DSM-IV and ICD-10 have poor coverage, yield high levels of comorbidity and, in most instances, many diagnostic categories have only fair levels of reliability and validity. The problems may be due to the dimensional distribution of most psychological problems within the population and the fact that most psychological difficulties are associated with a complex constellation of predisposing, precipitating, maintaining and protective factors. Community studies yield prevalence rates of 12–29% for axis I disorders and 4–13% for personality disorders. Prevalence rates vary with demographic factors, including gender, age, educational level, employment status and marital status.

EXERCISE 2.1

Working in pairs, adopt the roles of interviewer and interviewee; reverse roles when the interview is over. The interviewer should invite the interviewee to describe a minor difficulty he or she had in the past five years. Then, using the section in the chapter on complex formulations, try to identify the predisposing, precipitating, maintaining and protective factors that were associated with this minor difficulty.

FURTHER READING FOR PRACTITIONERS

American Psychiatric Association (APA) (2000). *Diagnostic and statistical manual of the mental disorders (Fourth Edition-Text Revision) DSM-IV-TR*. Washington, DC: APA.

Beutler, L. & Malik, M. (2002). *Rethinking the DSM: A psychological perspective*. Washington, DC: American Psychological Association.

World Health Organization (WHO) (1992). *The ICD-10 classification of mental and behavioural disorders*. Geneva: WHO.

ASSESSMENT INSTRUMENTS

First, M., Spitzer, R., Gibbon, R., & Williams, J. (1997). *Structured Clinical Interview for DSM-IV-TR Axis I Disorders (SCID-I), Clinician Version*. Washington, DC: American Psychiatric Press. Online, available: http://www.appi.org

First, M., Spitzer, R., Gibbon, R., Williams, J., & Benjamin, L. (1997). *Structured Clinical Interview for DSM-IV-TR Axis II Personality Disorders (SCID-II)*. Washington, DC: American Psychiatric Press. Online, available: http://www.appi.org

Lewis, G., Pelosi, A. J., Araya, R. C., & Dunn, G. (1992). Measuring psychiatric disorder in the community: The development of a standardised assessment for use by lay interviewers. *Psychological Medicine*, 22, 465–486. Revised Clinical Interview Schedule is available: http://www.bris.ac.uk/Depts/Psychiatry/resh/cis.htm

Loranger, A. (1999). *International Personality Disorder Examination (IPDE)*. Odessa, FL: PAR. Online, available: http://www.parinc.com/product.cfm?ProductID=164.

World Health Organization (WHO) (1992). *Schedules for clinical assessment in neuropsychiatry*. Geneva: WHO.

World Health Organization (1997). *Composite International Diagnostic Interview. Version 2*. (CIDI). Geneva: WHO. Online, available: http://www.who.int/msa/cidi/

REFERENCES

American Psychiatric Association (APA) (1994). *Diagnostic and statistical manual of the mental disorders (Fourth Edition; DSM-IV)*. Washington, DC: APA.

American Psychiatric Association (APA) (2000). *Diagnostic and statistical manual of the mental disorders (Fourth Edition-text revision; DSM-IV-TR)*. Washington, DC: APA.

Andrews, G., Henderson, S., & Hall, W. (2001). Prevalence, comorbidity, disability and service utilization: Overview of the Australian National Mental Health Survey. *British Journal of Psychiatry*, 178, 145–135.

Andrews, G., Slade, T., & Issakidis, C. (2002). Deconstructing current comorbidity: Data from the Australian national survey of mental health and well-being. *British Journal of Psychiatry*, 181, 306–314.

Berganza, C., Mezzich, J., Oteero-Ojeda, A. et al. (2001). Latin American guide for psychiatric diagnosis: A cultural overview. In: J. Mezzich & H. Fabrega (Eds), *Psychiatric clinics of North America* (pp. 433–446). Philadelphia, PA: Saunders.

Brown, G. (2000). Medical sociology and issues of aetiology. In: M. Gelder, J. Lopez-Ibor & N. Andreasen (Eds), *New Oxford textbook of psychiatry* (Volume 1, pp. 293–300). Oxford: Oxford University Press.

Carr, A. (2000). *Family therapy: Concepts, process and practice*. Chichester: Wiley.

Carr, A. (2003). *Positive psychology*. London: Psychology Press.

Cattell, R. (1990). Advances in Cattellian personality theory. In: L. Pervin (Ed), *Handbook of personality: Theory and research* (pp. 101–110). New York: Guilford.

Chinese Medical Association (1995). *Chinese classification of mental disorders* (Second Edition, revised). Nanjing: Dong Nan University Press.

Costa, P. & Widiger, T. (2001). *Personality disorders and the five-factor model of personality* (Second Edition). Washington, DC: American Psychological Association.

Craighead, E., Miklowitz, D., Frank, E., & Vajk, F. (2002). Psychosocial treatments for bipolar disorder. In: P. Nathan & J. Gorman (Eds), *A guide to treatments that work* (Second Edition, pp. 263–276). New York: Oxford University Press.

Crits-Cristoph, P. & Barber, J. (2002). Psychological treatments for personality disorders. In: P. Nathan & J. Gorman (Eds), *A guide to treatments that work* (Second edition, pp. 611–624). New York: Oxford University Press.

Dausch, B., Miklowitz, D., & Richards, J. (1996). Global Assessment of Relational Functioning Scale (GARF): 11. Reliability and validity in a sample of families of bipolar patients. *Family Process*, 35, 175–189.

Eysenck, H. (1990). Biological dimensions of personality. In: L. Pervin (Ed), *Handbook of personality: Theory and research* (pp. 244–276). New York: Guilford.

First, M. & Pincus, H. (1999). ICD-10 v. DSM -IV. A response. *British Journal of Psychiatry*, 175, 205–209.

Henderson, S. (2000). The contribution of epidemiology to psychiatric aetiology. In: M. Gelder, J. Lopez-Ibor & N. Andreasen (Eds), *New Oxford textbook of psychiatry* (Volume 1, pp. 308–319). Oxford: Oxford University Press.

Jampala, V., Sierles, F., & Taylor, M. (1986). Consumer's views of DSM III. Attitudes and practices of US psychiatrists and 1984 graduate residents. *American Journal of Psychiatry*, 143, 148–153.

Jenkins, R., Bebbington, P., Farrell, M. et al. (1997). The national psychiatric morbidity surveys of Great Britain – initial findings from the household survey. *Psychological Medicine*, 27, 775–789.

Kessler, R. (1995). Epidemiology of psychiatric comorbidity. In: M. Tsuang, M. Tohen, & G. Zahner (Eds), *Textbook in psychiatric epidemiology* (pp.179–198). New York: Wiley.

Kessler, R., McGonagle, K., Zhao, S. Nelson, C., Hughes, M., Eshleman, S., Wittchen, H., & Kendler, K. (1994). Lifetime and 12-month prevalence of DSM-III-R psychiatric disorders in the United States. *Archives of General Psychiatry*, 51, 8–19.

Kirk, S. & Kutchins, H. (1992). *The selling of DSM: The rhetoric of science in psychiatry*. New York: Aldine de Gruyter.

Mattison, R., Cantwell, D., Russell, D., & Will, L. (1979). A comparison on DSM–11 and DSM–111 in the diagnosis of childhood psychiatric disorders-11. Interrater agreement. *Archives of General Psychiatry*, 36, 1217–1222.

McConnell, P., Bebbington, P., McClelland, R., Gillespie, K., & Houghton, S. (2002). Prevalence of psychiatric disorder and the need for psychiatric care in Northern Ireland. *British Journal of Psychiatry*, 181, 214–219.

Meyer, G. (2002). Implications of information gathering methods for a refined taxonomy of psychopathology. In: L. Beutler & M. Malik (Eds), *Rethinking the DSM: A psychological perspective* (pp. 69–105). Washington, DC: American Psychological Association.

Mezzich, J., Berganza, M., Von Cranach, M., Jorge, M., Kastrup, M., Murphy, R., Okasha, A., Pull, C., Sartorius, N., Skodol, A., & Zaudig, M. (2003). Essentials of the World Psychiatric Association's international guidelines for diagnostic assessment (IGDA). *British Journal of Psychiatry*, 182 (Suppl 45).

Otero, A. (2000). *Tercer Closario Cubano de Psiquiatria*. (*Third Cuban glossary of psychiatry*). Havana: Psychiatric Hospital.

Paris, J. (1996). *Social factors in the personality disorders. A biopsychosocial approach to aetiology and treatment*. Cambridge: Cambridge University Press.

Rapp, C. (1998). *The strengths model: Case management with people suffering from severe and persistent mental illness*. New York: Oxford University Press.

Rothbart, M. & Ahadi, A. (1994). Temperament and the development of personality. *Journal of Abnormal Psychology*, 103, 55–66.

Rutter, M. & Taylor, E. (Eds) (2002). *Child and adolescent psychiatry* (Fourth Edition). Oxford: Blackwell.

Samuels, J., Earton, W., Bienvenu, J., Brown, C., Costa, P., & Nestadt, G. (2002). Prevalence and correlates of personality disorders in a community sample. *British Journal of Psychiatry*, 180, 536–542.

Valliant, G. (2000). Adaptive mental mechanisms. Their role in positive psychology. *American Psychologist*, 55, 89–98.

Volkmar, F. & Dykens, E. (2002). Mental retardation. In: M. Rutter & E. Taylor (Eds), *Child and adolescent psychiatry* (Fourth Edition, pp. 697–710). Oxford: Blackwell.

Westen, D., Heim, A., Morrison, K., Patterson, M., & Campbell, L. (2002). Simplifying diagnosis using a proptype matching approach: Implications for the next edition of the DSM. In: L. Beutler & M. Malik (Eds), *Rethinking the DSM: A psychological perspective* (pp. 221–250). Washington, DC: American Psychological Association.

World Health Organization (WHO) (1992). *The ICD-10 classification of mental and behavioural disorders. Clinical descriptions and diagnostic guidelines*. Geneva: WHO. Online, available: http://www.informatik.fh-luebeck.de/icd/welcome.html

World Health Organization (WHO) (1993). *The ICD-10 classification of mental and behavioural disorders. Diagnostic criteria for research*. Geneva: WHO.

World Health Organization (WHO) (1996). *Diagnostic and management guidelines for mental disorders in primary care. The ICD-10, Chapter V, Primary care version*. Gottingen: WHO/Hogrefe and Huber.

World Health Organization (WHO) (1997a). *Composite International Diagnostic Interview – Version 2.1 (CIDI)*. Geneva: WHO. Online, available: http://www.who.int/msa/cidi/

World Health Organization (WHO) (1997b). *Multiaxial presentation of ICD-10 for use in adult psychiatry*. Cambridge: Cambridge University Press.

Chapter 3

Cognitive behaviour therapy

Alan Carr and Muireann McNulty

The cognitive behaviour therapy (CBT) tradition incorporates a range of psychotherapeutic theories and practices, including behaviour therapy, behaviour modification, cognitive therapy and cognitive behaviour therapy, all of which have their roots in learning theories (Rachman, 1997). Within CBT it is assumed that problematic thoughts, feelings and behaviour patterns are learned through the same processes as normal thoughts, feelings and behaviour. These learning processes include operant and classical conditioning, and various cognitive processes such as modelling and identification. Therapy involves coaching clients to replace problematic habits with more adaptive ways of thinking, feeling, behaving and interacting with others. This coaching process is based on the principles of learning theory. The small constituent habits that make up psychological disorders are identified through careful interviewing and observation. The personal and situational antecedents, the co-occurring psychological states and the personal and situational consequences associated with problematic habits are identified. Specific CBT treatment programmes are designed for specific problems and the efficacy and effectiveness of these empirically evaluated. CBT programmes typically include interventions that alter antecedents that signal the onset of problematic thoughts, feelings and behaviour; interventions that challenge non-adaptive beliefs and styles of information processing that accompany problematic behaviour; and interventions that change the consequences of problematic thoughts, feelings and behaviour so that more adaptive alternatives to problematic patterns are developed and re-inforced. Evidence from treatment outcome studies reviewed in Nathan and Gorman (2002) provide support for the efficacy and effectiveness of CBT for depression and anxiety disorders. CBT is also an effective component of multi-modal treatment programmes for bipolar disorder, positive psychotic symptoms, pain management, management of some illnesses, and problems associated with some personality disorders, particularly border-line personality disorder.

LEARNING PROCESSES AND PROBLEM DEVELOPMENT

Within the CBT tradition it is assumed that psychological problems are acquired and may be altered through a series of learning processes. These include:

- operant conditioning
- classical conditioning
- learning involving various cognitive processes.

Operant conditioning

The application of Skinner's (1957) principles of operant conditioning to understanding the aetiology and modification of problem behaviour began in the USA with pioneering work by a number of people including Ayllon and Azrin (1968) and Ullman and Krasner (1965). Within this framework, problematic behaviour is viewed as being maintained by the occurrence of specific antecedent conditions and/or by specific consequences that follow problematic behaviour.

Antecedents of behavioural problems, referred to as setting events, discriminative stimuli or cues, are specific situations or stimuli that regularly elicit problem behaviours. For example, in obsessive-compulsive disorder, situations involving dirt or perceived threat of contamination commonly elicit anxiety. Clients attempt to reduce anxiety by engaging in compulsive washing rituals that bring only temporary relief. An effective treatment for obsessive-compulsive disorder is exposure and response prevention. Here, the client is exposed to cues that elicit anxiety, but prevented from engaging in anxiety-reducing compulsive rituals. Initially, anxiety increases but eventually it subsides.

Problematic behaviour may be maintained by two specific classes of consequence: positive reinforcement and negative reinforcement. Positive reinforcement refers to situations where problematic behaviour is followed by a desired outcome or reward and this increases the probability that the behaviour will recur. For example, clients with border-line personality disorder who experience emotional relief after they cut their arms with a razor are more likely to do this again, because the sense of relief reinforces their arm-cutting behaviour. Responses that are negatively reinforced, by leading to avoidance or escape from distressing situations, are also more likely to recur. For example, chronic pain clients may find that sitting still allows them to avoid increasing the intensity of their pain, and so they are likely to do so repeatedly. Responses that are not positively or negatively reinforced are less likely to recur and so are extinguished. Responses that are punished may be temporarily suppressed.

In the field of adult mental health, token economies are a good example of a therapeutic intervention based on the principles of operant conditioning (Ayllon & Azrin, 1968). Token economies have been used in residential settings for clients who have serious skills deficits, for example people with chronic schizophrenia. Clients earn reinforcers (tokens) by engaging in certain target adaptive behaviours and tokens may be exchanged for items from a reinforcement menu of valued privileges. Pain behaviour programmes are another example of the application of operant learning principles to health problems (Fordyce, 1976). In these programmes, chronic pain clients with constricted lifestyles are socially reinforced for engaging in adaptive behaviour, but not reinforced for engaging in pain behaviour.

When people are learning complex new skills, they are most likely to learn these rapidly and accurately if complex skills are broken down into smaller simpler subskills. When learning individual subskills, these are acquired more efficiently if successive approximations to the subskill are reinforced through the process of shaping. Intermittent reinforcement is more effective than continuous reinforcement in helping people learn new responses and skills. In CBT, when coaching clients in problem solving and communication, the subskills that constitute these complex skills are taught one at a time and their application to easy and non-emotive topics occurs before tackling complex emotionally charged problems. Also, successive approximations to these skills are reinforced to gradually shape skill development.

Within the psychotherapeutic relationship, operant learning principles may be usefully applied. Therapists may extinguish problematic, destructive conversation by acknowledging it, but not selectively responding to it with intense interest. In contrast, therapists may reinforce adaptive, flexible, solution-oriented conversation by selectively attending and responding to it with positive remarks and inquiries. Large, complex problems may be broken down into smaller, more manageable tasks and successive approximations to plans for implementing adaptive solutions to these may be positively reinforced by selectively responding to them in an encouraging way.

Classical conditioning

The application of Pavlov's principles of classical conditioning to understanding the aetiology and modification of problem behaviour, notably anxiety, began with the work of Watson (1924) and Mowrer (1960) in the USA, Eysenck (1960) in the UK, and Wolpe (1958) in South Africa. In classical conditioning theory, it is proposed that if a neutral conditioned stimulus (CS) is paired with a strongly feared unconditioned stimulus (UCS), which elicits anxiety as an unconditioned response (UCR), then after one intense pairing or multiple less intense pairings of the CS and UCS, subsequent exposure to the previously neutral CS elicits anxiety, which is a conditioned response (CR). For example, a customer who was in his bank (CS) when a frightening robbery (UCS) occurred now experiences intense anxiety (CR) any time he enters a bank. Thus, banks have become cues for anxiety. Classical conditioning theory also proposes that generalization may occur where the class of situations that are cues for anxiety broadens. So, the client just mentioned not only became frightened of going into banks, but also of entering post offices and shops with high cash turnovers. Extinction, according to classical conditioning theory, occurs when the person is exposed to the cue (CS) repeatedly in the absence of the UCS. However, one of the problems with anxiety is that people tend to avoid situations that are cues for anxiety and so their anxiety does not extinguish (Mowrer, 1960).

Systematic desensitization, which is based on classical conditioning, involves coaching clients in relaxation skills, creating a hierarchy of feared imaginal and/or actual (*in vivo*) situations and pairing exposure to these feared situations with relaxation, starting with the least anxiety-provoking situation (Wolpe, 1958). Progress from one stage in the hierarchy to the next occurs when the feared situation no longer elicits anxiety or avoidance, that is when the conditioned anxiety response becomes extinct.

A problem with this very simple classical conditioning explanation of the development of phobias is that in some instances brief exposure to a weak unconditioned stimulus can eventually lead to the emergence of a phobia. Eysenck's (1979) incubation theory attempts to overcome the shortcomings of a simple classical conditioning explanation. He argued that anxiety initially develops through one-trial classical conditioning when a neutral object for which a person is biologically prepared to develop an extinction-resistant fear (CS) is paired with a strongly feared object (UCS) and this object elicits anxiety (UCR). Subsequent exposure to the previously neutral object (CS) elicits mild anxiety (CR). Repeated brief exposure to this previously neutral object (CS) leads to an increase in fear through a process of incubation. Brief exposure leads to anxiety (CR), which is effectively paired with the feared object and on the next brief exposure even more fear is elicited. Incubation is a positive feedback process where fear itself reinforces fear of the phobic object. This whole process occurs outside of cognitive control. Eysenck also argued that people who are constitutionally more neurotic and introverted are more likely to develop phobic anxiety through this incubation process. He also acknowledged that phobias develop only to a limited group of stimuli and that humans have preparedness, as a result of evolutionary processes, to develop phobias to these through a process of classical conditioning (De Sylva et al., 1977). According to this theory, treatment for phobias involves either gradual exposure (systematic desensitization), where clients confront their feared situations gradually from least to most fearsome, or complete exposure (flooding), where clients confront their most feared situation for an extended time period until anxiety subsides. Gradual exposure may be to the feared situation itself (*in vivo*) or to an image of the feared situation (imaginal). Thus, three procedures may be used to treat phobias: *in vivo* desensitization, imaginal desensitization and flooding. The theory predicts that the two *in vivo* methods – *in vivo* desensitization or flooding – should be more effective than imaginal desensitization. The use of relaxation skills or other coping strategies are only important insofar as they help the person tolerate remaining in the presence of the feared object. There is still controversy over details of the incubation theory as an explanation for the aetiology of phobias. However, a large body of research shows that exposure techniques such as desensitization and flooding, particularly *in vivo*, are very effective methods for treating phobias (Barlow et al., 2003).

Learning involving cognitive processes

While operant and classical conditioning theories of learning place greatest emphasis on the role of proximal external antecedents and consequences in acquiring psychological problems, cognitive learning theories and theories of cognitive therapy focus on the role of distal developmental factors and intra-psychic factors in the acquisition and modification of problematic behaviour patterns, beliefs and emotions.

Cognitive theories of psychopathology, such as that Aaron T. Beck (1976), propose that maladaptive schemas are built up through difficult experience, including exposure to early stressful life events, frustration of important needs, and modelling of and identification with early family relationships. A schema is a cluster of interconnected core beliefs about the self and others in significant relationships, the nature of the world, or the probable course of future events. From the core beliefs in a schema, a variety of problematic assumptions and rules develop. An assumption usually is conditional and takes the form of an 'if A, then B' statement, for example, 'If I am not liked by everybody, then I am worthless'. A rule usually takes the form, 'I must be perfect, otherwise I am worthless'. A core belief, in contrast, can usually be articulated as an absolute statement, for example, 'I'm worthless', 'Other people are untrustworthy', or 'The world is dangerous'. Schemas with assumptions and beliefs about loss render people vulnerable to depression. Those with assumptions and beliefs about pervasive, imminent danger render people vulnerable to anxiety disorders. With anger-management difficulties, schemas involve assumptions and core beliefs about entitlement and fairness.

Assumptions and core beliefs from schemas associated with common axis I disorders and personality disorders are given in Table 3.1. People have both adaptive and maladaptive schemas and at any particular time some schemas are active and some are inactive or latent. For episodes of axis I disorders, such as depression or anxiety, to occur, latent maladaptive schemas are activated in adulthood by schema-related major stressful life events. For example, experiences involving loss may activate depressive schemas. Once such latent schemas are activated, minor day-to-day stresses may trigger negative automatic thoughts. Negative automatic thoughts in turn typically

Table 3.1 Maladaptive schemas

Schema domain	*Schema*	*Core expectations, predisposing parenting experiences and sample beliefs*
Disconnection and rejection		Expectation that attachment needs will not be met arising from neglectful or abusive early parenting
	1 Abandonment/ instability	You will abandon me because you are unreliable, or angry, or favour someone else, or are about to die
	2 Mistrust/abuse	I cannot trust you because you will hurt me
	3 Emotional deprivation	You will not give me nurturance, or empathy or protection
	4 Defectiveness shame	I am inferior because of my appearance, or because of my sexual or aggressive urges and so you will reject me
	5 Social isolation	I am different from others and do not belong
Impaired autonomy		Expectation that one will not function independently arising from overprotective early parenting
	6 Dependence and incompetence	I am unable to handle everyday responsibilities without your help
	7 Vulnerability to harm or illness	I am in imminent danger from becoming ill, going crazy, having a serious accident or being a crime victim
	8 Enmeshment	I cannot separate from my parents because they need me, but I feel smothered and directionless
	9 Failure	I have failed to achieve my potential at school or work and I am stupid
Impaired limits		Deficient in following through on personal goals and commitments to others due to permissive early parenting
	10 Entitlement and grandiosity	I am entitled to whatever I want because I am special and I want power to control others
	11 Lack of self-control	I can't control my behaviour or complete plans because my appetites and impulses prevent me
Other directedness		Expectation that if meeting the need of others is prioritized, regardless of frustration of personal needs for autonomy, spontaneity and intimacy, then minimal personal needs for attachment and safety will be met
	12 Subjugation	If I suppress my wishes (which are probably not important to you) and my anger at you for making me suppress my wishes, then you will not abandon or hurt me, but I feel trapped because you coerce me into subjugation

	13 Self-sacrifice	If I suppress my wishes, and voluntarily meet your needs, then you will not abandon me or feel pain and I will not feel guilty or selfish, but I may end up feeling resentful
	14 Approval seeking	If I do all I can to meet your approval or get your attention and recognition or attain wealth and status, then you will not abandon me
Over-vigilance and inhibition		Expectation that if high standards of performance and ethical behaviour are prioritized, regardless of frustration of needs for autonomy, spontaneity and intimacy, then minimal personal needs for attachment and safety will be met
	15 Pessimism	Most important things in my life will probably go wrong, so I focus on the negative aspects of life and fear mistakes that will lead to personal and financial ruin without optimism
	16 Emotional inhibition	If I suppress my positive emotions and desires (joy, sex, etc.), hide my emotional vulnerabilities, and focus on rationality then you will not abandon or criticize me
	17 Hyper-criticalness	If I am not efficient and perfect and do not meet high ethical and achievement standards, then you will abandon or criticize me
	18 Punitiveness	If I or others make a mistake we deserve to be harshly punished and not forgiven

Based on Young, J., Klosko, J. & Weishaar, M. (2003). *Schema therapy: A practitioner's guide* (pp. 14–17). New York: Guilford.

lead to problematic mood states, problematic physiological changes associated with negative emotions, and problematic behaviour and interaction patterns. Collectively, these negative moods, physiological states, behaviour and interaction patterns confirm the non-adaptive world view entailed by the schema and so maintain the person's axis I disorder. For example, a male client with a depressive schema held the assumption, 'If everyone does not like me, then I am unlovable'. He passed a female friend in the street who did not say hello and had the automatic thought, 'She really hates me'. His mood dropped. He kept his head down, avoiding eye contact and hurried home, rather than greeting her warmly and humorously joking about her not saying hello. On his next trips out, he continued to avoid eye contact with others on the street, met fewer people every day, and gradually became more isolated and depressed about being disliked and unloved. His negative view of himself was thus confirmed. A diagram of the cognitive model is presented in Figure 3.1.

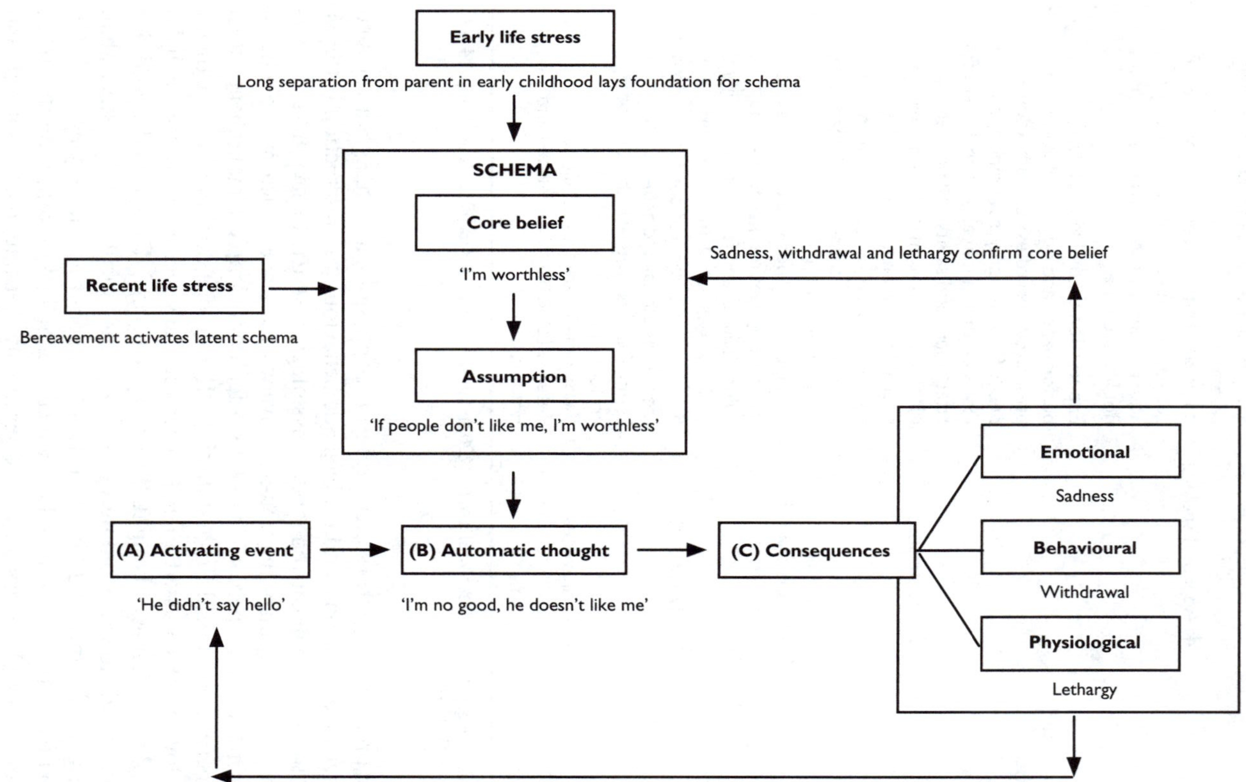

Figure 3.1 Cognitive therapy model.

Cognitive therapy also proposes that once schemas are activated, people become prone to interpreting ambiguous situations in problematic ways. The various logical errors that they make are referred to as cognitive distortions, some of which are listed in Table 3.2. CBT aims to train clients to monitor situations where negative automatic thoughts and cognitive distortions occur

Table 3.2 Cognitive distortions

Distortion	*Description*
All or nothing thinking (or dichotomous thinking)	Thinking in extreme categorical terms. For example, 'Either I'm a success or a failure'
Mental filter (or selective abstraction)	Filtering our positive aspects of the situation, selectively focusing on the negative aspects of a situation, and drawing conclusions from these. For example, 'I made a mistake earlier today so every thing I did today was wrong'
Over-generalization	Generalizing from one instance to all possible instances. For example, 'I failed that stats exam so I'll never be any good at stats'
Magnification or minimization	Exaggerating or under-emphasizing the significance of an event. For example, 'He said she didn't like me so that must mean she hates me', or, 'He said he likes me, but he probably doesn't mean it'
Personalization	Attributing negative feeling of others to the self. For example, 'He looked really angry when he walked into the room, so I must have done something wrong'
Emotional reasoning	Taking feelings as facts. For example, 'I feel like the future is black so the future is hopeless'
Discounting the positives	Believing that positive personal characteristics or achievements do not count in overall self-evaluation. For example, 'I passed that exam, but that was just good luck, I'm really no good at stats'
Mind reading	Assuming that others are reacting negatively to you without having evidence for this. For example, 'Her silence means that she doesn't like me'
Fortune telling	Predicating that things will turn out badly without having evidence to support this. For example, 'I will probably not enjoy the party'
Catastrophizing	Erroneously predicting extreme distress on the basis of limited evidence. For example, 'My heart is racing. I must be going to have a heart attack'
Labelling	Identifying completely with situational shortcomings. For example, 'I didn't just make a mistake, I proved that I'm a complete fool'
Should and must statements	Making absolute statements about how the self or others ought to be. For example, 'I should always be perfect and he should be loving'

Based on Beck, A. (1976). *Cognitive therapy and the emotional disorders*. New York: International Universities Press, and Burns, D. (1980). *Feeling good. The new mood therapy*. New York: Avon.

and to identify underlying assumptions and core beliefs, to evaluate the validity of these and to engage in activities both within therapy sessions and between sessions that provide evidence to refute them. These include collecting evidence that is inconsistent with negative beliefs and assumptions, achieving increasingly challenging goals so as to disprove negative beliefs and assumptions, and learning new coping strategies to help master these challenges.

Evidence from experimental studies reviewed in Clark and Fairburn (1997) and Williams et al. (1997) provide support for some of the mechanisms of problem development and resolution contained in CBT theory.

Clinicians who use cognitive therapy distinguish between 'hot' cognitions, which are strongly emotionally charged, and 'cold' cognitions that are associated with less intense emotions. It is accepted clinical lore that more therapeutic progress occurs when clients work with 'hot' cognitions in CBT (Greenberger & Padesky, 1995). Within cognitive science, this clinical insight has been addressed by Teasdale (1997), who distinguishes between specific propositional meanings and generic or schematic implicational meanings. For example, the specific propositional meaning of the sentence 'I feel worthless', is 'At present I am not worth anything'. In contrast, the generic or schematic implicational meaning is difficult to covey in words but it might be something like this: 'Lost and alone in a grey, grey land, on the edge of this arctic desert, my lover stands and then moves away without seeing me or caring, and I know that tomorrow and tomorrow and tomorrow will unfold like a dark, windswept, wasteland without hope or light or love'. Sensory features such as tone, poetic features of language, facial expressions and bodily movements all convey implicational meaning in addition to the propositional meaning of a statement. According to Teasdale, only generic or schematic implicational meanings are directly linked to emotions. Specific propositional meanings are less strongly and directly linked to emotions. Thus, cognitive therapy interventions that entail helping clients to marshal evidence for their worth by intellectually reviewing events that involved making a positive contribution in work or family life may be useful in changing propositional meanings. However, such interventions probably have limited impact on implicational meanings and long-term management of negative emotional states. In contrast, interventions that facilitate clients actively and wholeheartedly engaging in tasks, the outcome of which provides evidence for their worth, are more likely to change implicational meanings and to have a lasting effect on long-term mood management.

ASSESSMENT AND FORMULATION

The following description of CBT assessment, formulation and treatment is brief and over-simplified, but is based on more detailed and comprehensive discussions of CBT practice to which readers are referred for a fuller account (Barlow, 2001; Beck, 1976; Beck, 1995; Burns, 1999; Clark & Fairburn, 1997; Greenberger & Padesky, 1995; Hawton et al., 1989; Padesky & Greenberger, 1995; Young et al., 2003). CBT begins with engaging the client in an assessment process that leads to an individualized case formulation. The development of a strong therapeutic relationship is central to this engagement process. Within cognitive therapy the therapeutic relationship is one of collaborative empiricism. Therapist and client work together to gather evidence to develop and test-out a CBT formulation of the client's main difficulties. This formulation is a set of hypotheses about the development and maintenance of the client's list of problems. A CBT formulation details the way antecedent factors (A), intervening beliefs (B) and emotional, physiological, behavioural and cognitive consequences (C) maintain the client's main difficulties. This is often referred to as the ABC aspect or situational aspect of the formulation.

The formulation also specifies the underlying schemas that render the client vulnerable to his or her problems, other biopsychosocial vulnerabilities such as personality traits or genetic predispositions and the stressful life events that triggered the onset of the current episode of psychological disorder or syndrome. This is often referred to as the syndromal aspect of the formulation.

In complex cases, particularly where clients have comorbid personality disorders, a full case formulation involves a set of formulations, with one for each disorder specifying the ABCs for the main problems along with vulnerability factors and precipitating stresses for each disorder.

In developing the formulation, the therapist helps the client through a socialization process, into thinking about his or her psychological problems in CBT terms. That is, the client is invited to accept that it is useful to recognize that a build-up of specific life stresses triggered the current problems because of certain specific personal vulnerabilities, and that the client's day-to-day difficulties are maintained by the ABC connections. Clients learn that these maintaining factors are under their control and so can be changed through CBT. It follows from this that individualized CBT formulations are used as a basis for treatment planning. Most CBT treatment plans are composed of the limited number of procedures described later in this chapter. These procedures focus largely on monitoring and modifying ABC aspects of problem formulations. Also, for most common problems, such as mood and anxiety disorders, empirically supported treatment protocols that include effective problem-specific combinations of treatment procedures have been developed. Some of these protocols are described later in this book.

As with all intake interviews, it is good practice in CBT to form a contract for assessment specifying one or more sessions; the location, duration and timing of these; the importance of completing homework assignments, such as keeping a daily thought record or carrying out a schedule of agreed, between-session activities and bringing the results of homework to sessions for review. CBT is not a cure-all for psychological problems; available research evidence shows that certain CBT treatment protocols are useful for certain types of people with certain specific problems. Thus it is good practice to inform the client at the initial appointment that the assessment will be looking at, among other things, their suitability for CBT.

Problem list

The first part of a formulation is the problem list. To establish the list, invite clients to explain their situation and difficulties in such a way that they feel free to give a narrative account of many or all of the difficulties they face with limited interruption. Here is one way to offer such an invitation:

> Your GP, Dr Berkley, wrote and asked me to offer you an appointment. He said that your mood had been low and that you were having a lot of difficulties in your life. We have about an hour today to talk about these difficulties and for us to decide if this service might be useful to you. One way to start would be for you to tell me what your main difficulties are now and the story of how these have developed during your life. Can you tell me the story now please?

Some clients have difficulty giving a coherent self-directed narrative and require more detailed questioning. Here are some questions that may be asked to develop a problem list:

- What is the main problem that concerns you right now?
- What was the main difficulty you were facing that led you to contact our service?
- If I were to ask other people in your family/work place what they thought the main problem was, what do you think they would say?
- Can you tell me more about that?
- When did the problem start?
- Has anything (including past treatment) made it worse or better?

To build an alliance with the client, periodically empathize with the client, using phrases like:

- That sounds very difficult.
- I can see that you have been through a very challenging time with these problems.

To track fluctuations in problems over time, it is useful to use quantitative scaling questions:

- On a scale of 1 to 10, how bad is the problem now?
- On a scale of 1 to 10, how bad was the problem yesterday morning (yesterday evening, last week, last month, last year, when you were in such and such a situation)?
- How often does the problem occur each day (week, month, year)?
- Once the problem starts, how long does it go on for, how many minutes (hours, days, weeks, months)?

All of these types of enquiry can be followed up with probes like:

- Can you say more about that?
- Is there more that you would like to say about that?

Sometimes, it is useful to ask the client to recount a specific episode or incident to illustrate:

- Can you give me a specific example of that?

Periodically, summarize what the client has said and check the accuracy of this, to indicate that you are following and making sense of the story and that you want to get an accurate picture of the situation. For example:

> From what you've said so far, it seems to me that after you lost your job about a year ago, you became very sad, because it was not just a job; it was one of the most important things in your life. And at home, no-one understood this, so you found yourself withdrawing from your husband and children and spending more and more time on your own. Then, there were two episodes in the past six months, where you felt as if you were going to have a heart attack: one at the post office and one on a bus on the motorway. Since these, you have been frightened to go out without your husband. Have I got that part right?

Standardized self-report instruments and rating scales such as the Beck Depression Inventory (BDI-II; Beck et al., 1996) and Beck Anxiety Inventory (BAI; Beck & Steer, 1990) can also be used to identify difficulties for inclusion on the problem list. Common difficulties for problem lists include suicidal ideation, drug abuse, depressive symptoms as indicated by a high BDI score, anxiety symptoms as indicated by a high BAI score, difficulty leaving the house, medical difficulties such as diabetes, family problems such as marital discord or violence, occupational problems such as unemployment, and accommodation problems such as inadequate housing.

In some contexts it may be appropriate to write to clients and ask them to write out the list of problems with which they want help and to complete some screening inventories, such as the BDI and BAI, and post these into the clinic before the first appointment.

Diagnoses and prioritizing problems

As the problem list unfolds in an intake interview, it is worth thinking about whether clusters of problems might be inter-related and reflect a single disorder or syndrome. This process of clustering or grouping problems is challenging. Clinicians in training may wish to defer this process until the end of the first interview; with experience this process becomes easier. Thus, it may be more useful initially to move from constructing a problem list to ABC problem analysis, and then to go back to problem grouping and diagnosis after the first interview.

The multiple problems on a problem list should be grouped and ordered in a clinically meaningful way and, where appropriate, diagnoses given according to criteria in the locally used system, e.g. ICD-10 (WHO, 1992) or DSM-IV (APA, 2000). For example, suicidal ideation, depressive symptoms and sleep problems might all be grouped together as evidence for an episode of major depression. Anxiety symptoms, panic attacks and difficult leaving the house might be grouped together as evidence of panic disorder with agoraphobia. Chronic history of difficulties with independence and related difficulties might be coded dependent personality disorder. If ICD-10 is used, disabilities may be coded on axis II and contextual stresses on axis III. If DSM-IV-TR is used, health problems such as diabetes are listed on axis III, social stresses on axis IV and global assessment of functioning on axis V.

In prioritizing problems or syndromes to be addressed, those that place that client at risk of harming themselves or others should always be given first priority. Problems that may prevent the client from engaging in therapy, for example not taking essential medication such as lithium for bipolar disorder, should be the next priority. Problems that are priorities of the client should immediately follow problems in these first two categories.

ABC problem analysis

Some problems, such as difficulties arranging transport to therapy, require management rather than formulation and therapy. However, most psychological difficulties are amenable to ABC analysis. That is, for any instance of the problem, it is usually possible to identify antecedent situational cues, intervening automatic thoughts and psychological consequences. Situational antecedents include the environmental cues or interpersonal context within which problems occur. Automatic thoughts are the transient negative self-statements that are made in response to the situational antecedents. The consequences of situational antecedents and related negative automatic thoughts include changes in mood, such as increased depression, anxiety or anger. Typically, these mood changes involve physiological changes such as increases or decreases in arousal. They may also involve behavioural changes such as social withdrawal, avoidance or violence. Changes in the environment or the social context may also occur. For example, others may offer increased attention or withdraw. These environmental and contextual changes may in turn reinforce the problem behaviour, beliefs and mood states. An ABC problem analysis can be conducted by observing a client go through a micro-episode of problem behaviour within the consulting room. For example, a person with obsessive-compulsive disorder could be exposed to cues, such as dirt, that trigger obsessional thoughts and compulsive washing behaviour within an intake interview session. A second option is to invite clients to complete self-monitoring homework tasks, described below. A third option is to conduct a detailed ABC problem analysis interview using a line of questioning like this for each problem:

- Can you describe the last time the problem happened?
- What did you notice first?
- What happened next?
- What went through your mind in that situation?
- What story did you tell yourself about the situation?
- How did that make you feel?
- On a 10-point scale how much did your mood (anxiety, anger) go up or down?
- How did other people in the situation react?
- What brought the situation to a close?
- What did you lose or gain as a result of the situation?
- What was it about the way the situation ended that makes it more likely to happen again?

After an ABC problem analysis, summarize the analysis and inquire about its accuracy:

> Let me check if I have understood what happened on Wednesday correctly. You wanted to post the parcel, so you left your husband in the supermarket and went across to the post office. While you were in the queue, you felt your heart racing and noticed you were short of breath. You thought, 'I'm going to have heart attack'. Just to check that you really were having serious heart trouble, you focused all your attention on your racing heart, your shortness of breath, and the tingling feelings in your fingers. Then you noticed your heart rate accelerate. You couldn't catch your breath. The room looked unreal and you felt dizzy, so your ran out of the post office and bumped into your husband who was just opening the car door outside. You felt huge relief as he hugged you and helped you into the car and took you home. Gradually, your heart rate

> dropped and you could breathe OK. During this episode your anxiety level went from zero in the supermarket, to six when you first noticed your heart racing, to ten when you left the post office and back to three when you were driving home. And you now believe that in future you will not queue up in the post office in case you get another panic attack like that one. This is good because you now know how to avoid panic attacks and have prevented any more from happening. But it's also a problem because you have been finding that you hardly go out at all now and you have almost made yourself a prisoner in your own house. Is that what has happened?

In this section, ABC problem analysis has been presented as a relatively simple process. However, it can be quite complex. For example, in situations where clients with social phobia are required to interact with others (A), many believe that they will be negatively evaluated (B), and so adopt safety behaviours (avoiding eye contact, speaking quickly or evaluating what they have said) that impair their performance and in doing so may elicit negative feedback from others (C). They also focus their attention on interoceptive cues (such as increase heart and respiration rates) (A) and use these as a basis for forming an impression of how others view them (B), which in turn increases arousal, impairs their performance and elicits negative feedback from others (C), which confirms their beliefs that others will evaluate them negatively. For people with generalized anxiety disorder, a wide range of situations such as receiving a bank statement, an unexpected phone call or having a cold leads them to worry (A). They then find themselves worrying about the fact that they are worrying and believe that their worrying is out of control (B). This may lead them to try to distract themselves or suppress their tendency to worry (C), which in turn leads to an increase in worrying. Such complex ABC analyses associated with specific disorders are discussed later in this book.

Thought catching

One of the biggest challenges in learning to do an ABC analysis is teaching clients 'thought catching', that is, helping them to access and articulate negative automatic thoughts.

If clients have difficulty with thought catching, set up a challenging situation or a role-play in the consulting room, or invite them to imagine with their eyes closed that they are in a difficult or challenging situation. Watch for behavioural or physiological signs of a shift in their mood, such as a change in their facial expression or bodily position, eyes filling with tears, or changes in respiration, and then ask them one or more of the following questions:

- What was going through your mind just then?
- What did you just tell yourself?

- What do you guess you were thinking about just now?
- Were you thinking . . . (suggest a possible automatic thought) . . .?
- Were you thinking . . . (suggest a thought that is definitely not their automatic thought, for example 'Ice cream is cold but nice')?

Sometimes automatic thoughts have a strong visual component and a weaker verbal component. In these situations invite clients to describe the image they see and what message it conveys to them.

Only some automatic thoughts have a critical impact on emotional state. These are referred to as 'hot' thoughts. For example, in the automatic thought 'This is hard, very tricky, I can't do it, I'm so stupid' the client said 'I'm so stupid' was the 'hot' part of this automatic thought. A central part of teaching clients thought catching is helping them learn to isolate and record their 'hot' thoughts.

Precipitating, predisposing and protective factors

The ABC aspect of a CBT formulation explains how micro-episodes of the problem occur in day-to-day situations, and how these micro-episodes maintain the problem. However, the syndromal aspect of a CBT formulation explains why the overall episode of the disorder or syndrome occurred at this time for this client. To develop a syndromal formulation, precipitating stresses, predisposing vulnerability factors, and protective factors need to be identified.

Precipitating factors

Stresses that precipitate episodes of a disorder may be broadly classified as:

- 'Exit' events, involving loss (e.g. bereavement or unemployment).
- 'Entrance' events involving the formation of new relationships and assumption of new responsibilities (e.g. births, marriages, new friendships or work situations).
- Illnesses and injuries.
- Other lifecycle transitions and changes (e.g. moving house or financial difficulties).

Stressful events that have precipitated the onset of the current and previous episodes of the disorder can be identified by inviting clients to draw their lifelines, noting the periods when they had previous and current episodes of their disorder and indicating the stressful life events that preceded each episode. Lifelines are described in detail in Chapter 7.

Predisposing factors

Maladaptive schemas are the principal predisposing vulnerabilities of particular relevance to CBT syndromal formulations. These contain problematic core beliefs (such as 'I am inept') that inform automatic thoughts, of the type noted in ABC problem analysis (such as 'I can't do this'). These beliefs commonly concern the self, others, the world or the future. Schemas typically have their origins in early childhood and arise from exposure to early stressful life events, frustration of important needs and through modelling and identification in early family relationships. A list of common schemas is given in Table 3.2 (p. 69). Schemas may be assessed with the Young Schema Questionnaire (Young & Brown, 2001). They can also be assessed using the downward or vertical arrow technique (Burns, 1999). With this technique, write an automatic thought identified in a common and recurring but specific situation (using ABC problem analysis) at the top of a page and beneath it draw a downward arrow. Then write down the client's answer to this question beneath the downward arrow. Next, ask the client:

> Assuming this thought is true, tell me why this thought is upsetting to you? What does it mean about you (or others, or the world, or the future)?

Then draw a downward arrow beneath the answer and repeat the process a number of times until you arrive at the client's core belief. An example of a downward arrow exercise is given in Figure 3.2.

Other vulnerability factors requiring assessment for a comprehensive CBT formulation include personality traits such as neuroticism, and genetic predispositions. Personality traits may be assessed with the Revised NEO Personality Inventory (Costa & McCrae, 1992). Genetic predispositions can be assessed by taking a family history of psychological problems or drawing a genogram and noting blood relatives with psychological problems (as described in Chapter 7).

Protective factors and suitability for treatment

The probability that a treatment programme will be effective is influenced by a variety of protective factors. It is important that these are assessed and included in the later formulation because it is protective factors that usually serve as the foundation for therapeutic change. For CBT, particularly important protective factors are the capacity to form a good therapeutic relationship, accepting a CBT formulation of the problem (rather than an exclusively biological formulation) and a willingness to follow through on homework assignments. Indeed, these three protective factors may be considered the central criteria for assessing clients' suitability for treatment. Other more general protective factors (elaborated in Chapter 7) include a history of

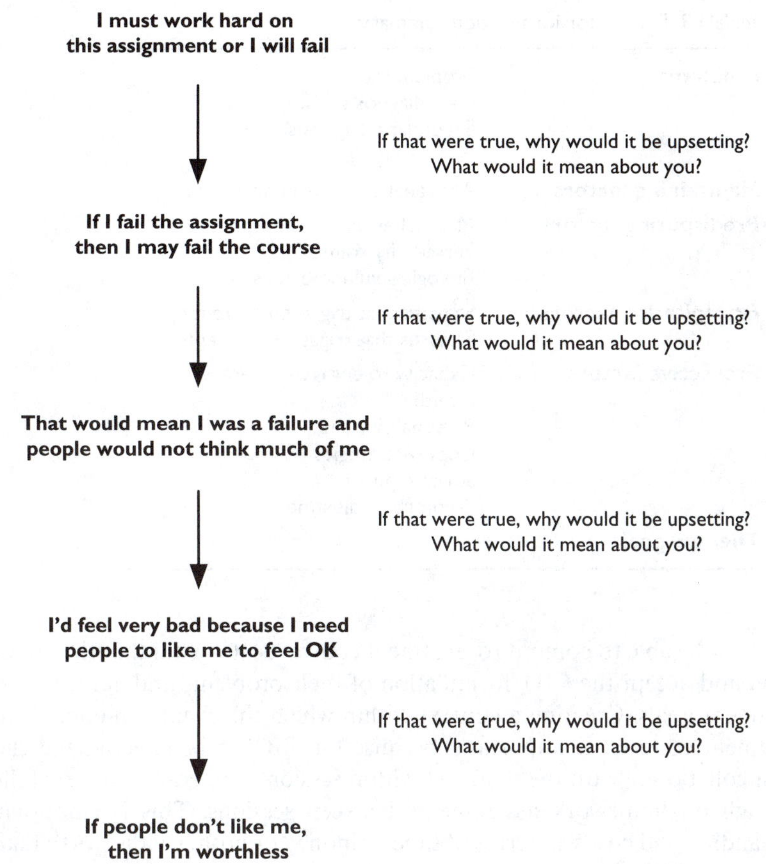

Figure 3.2 Downward arrow technique.

having coped well and recovered from previous episodes of the disorder, physical health and fitness, high self-esteem, an internal locus of control, high self-efficacy, an optimistic attributional style, functional coping strategies, good problem-solving skills, a good social support network, the capacity to make and maintain stable relationships, and a low level of life stress.

An example of a CBT formulation is given below in the section 'Contracting for treatment'. An outline of the main headings in a formulation is given in Table 3.3.

TREATMENT

Once intake assessment has been completed and a preliminary formulation has been constructed, the next step is to agree a contract for treatment. For

Table 3.3 Format for formulation summary

Problems	Problem list Main diagnosis Secondary diagnosis Personality disorder
Maintaining factors	ABC analysis of main problems
Predisposing factors	Main schemas Personality traits Biological vulnerabilities
Precipitating factors	Stresses that triggered current episode Stresses that triggered past episodes
Protective factors	Capacity to engage in therapy Health Personality traits Coping strategies Social support Premorbid adjustment
Therapy goals	

clients to be able to commit to treatment contracts, it is vital that they understand and accept the CBT formulation of their problems and agree with the treatment goals. Creating a context within which the client can commit to a treatment contract is important, because for CBT to be effective the client must collaborate with the therapist within sessions and co-operatively follow through on homework assignments between sessions. This is emotionally demanding and costly in terms of time or money or both, so it is worth taking time to establish a solid treatment contract.

Contracting for treatment

In forming the contract, the first step is to summarize the list of problems that led the client to seek treatment, order and prioritize these in a coherent way and check them for accuracy. The second step is to offer the ABC aspect of the formulation of the main presenting problem, and once again to check this for accuracy. The third step is to offer the syndromal aspect of the formulation, pointing out the schemas and related developmental experiences and genetic predispositions that rendered the client vulnerable to developing the current episode of the problem following recent life stresses. An accuracy check should also be made at this point. The fourth step is to highlight strengths and protective factors that suggest the client may benefit from CBT, and to suggest certain areas in which specific goals might be set. Before progressing to detailed goal setting, it is often useful to give the client an opportunity to discuss any reservations about committing to a treatment contract and to make it clear that you know that there are obstacles that may make it very difficult for the client to fully co-operate with treatment and to follow through on homework assignments:

> We are getting towards the end of this meeting, so it would be useful to check a few things with you at this point. The main difficulties that you have been struggling with have been controlling your low mood, managing your sleep and keeping your energy up. These problems are all related. They are all aspects of depression. The mood problem is your main concern. Can I check that that is the case? . . . We looked at a few situations where your mood is particularly low. These are situations where you try to handle demanding things at work or conflict at home. These activating events (the As of the situation), spark off certain negative beliefs for you, like, 'I can't do it' or 'they don't care about me any more' (the Bs of the situation). These beliefs, these stories that automatically go through your mind, have clear consequences for your mood (the Cs of the situation). Your mood drops. You feel you have no energy. You withdraw. And this convinces you that you were right to believe that you could not handle the situation. Can I check again, that this ABC sequence is what happens to you? . . . Now an important question is why you find yourself repeating this sort of pattern over and over again. From what you told me, my best guess is that when you were promoted at work and your wife became ill and was hospitalized, these two stresses, activated an old set of beliefs (a schema) that you learned as a child, when your mother went to hospital and you started school. Back then, you felt very sad, lost and alone. You made sense of the situation by believing that you somehow were responsible for your mother going away and that if you did well at school and were very popular with everyone, then your mother would return from hospital and care for you again. Does that fit for you? . . . Another part of the puzzle is that you may also be vulnerable to developing mood problems because you have inherited a nervous system that runs down under pressure. From what you told me, your father, uncle and grandfather also had mood problems, and you may have inherited a disposition to mood problems from them. Does that bit fit for you too? If you can accept this way of understanding your difficulties, then there are a number of things that you can do to get control over your mood, improve your sleep and get your energy back. You can learn to change your thinking style, so it's less pessimistic. You can increase your energy by gradually changing your daily activity routines. And you can learn some exercises to help you sleep better. You can also consider anti-depressant medication to help that part of your nervous system involved in mood regulation speed up again. However, this sort of therapy is not a guaranteed cure. It only works for two out of three people. You have a number of strengths that make me hopeful that you might be

> one of the lucky ones who can benefit from treatment. You're healthy and fit, motivated to come to an intake interview, you think about your difficulties in a psychological way and you have handled similar sorts of difficulties quite well in the past. However, this type of programme is a lot of hard work, ten sessions over twenty weeks. That's a big commitment of time (and money). There will be homework assignments to do. That may be inconvenient. And so I could understand that you might not want to go ahead with this right now. I need to check with you what your reservations are, and if you are ready to commit to all this hard work or not?

Where clients disagree with minor aspects of the formulation, it is valuable to take time to clarify inaccuracies and reach a shared and consensual position. Where clients cannot accept the formulation and insist that their difficulties are a reflection of an exclusively biological illness that can only be cured by medication, and think that CBT formulations and intervention will be of little value, arguing about the relative validity of biomedical versus biopsychosocial models of disorders is of little value. It is helpful in these instances to say that CBT can help people cope with the symptoms of a variety of biological illnesses, such as bipolar disorder, to relapse less frequently. The contract for treatment in such instances involves helping the person learning coping strategies to cope with a medical condition.

Goal setting and monitoring

With goal setting, the aim is to define clear, unambiguous, visualizable, measurable, positively stated goals for problem resolution. These goals allow the client and clinician to know in a concrete way when the presenting problems have been solved. Clients often state goals in vague terms, so it is important to ask questions that require specific details when goal setting. Useful questions for goal setting are:

- If your problems were solved, what specifically would be different about the way you spend your day?
- If you no longer had these difficulties, and we were watching a videotape of an average day in your life, what would we see you doing that you can't do now, but really want to be able to do?

Goals may also be framed as achieving a score below the clinical cut-off point on standardized scales such as the BDI or the BAI. Goals may involve being able to carry out a typical activity of daily living without interference from a problem behaviour, for example, being able to travel on public transport without having a panic attack. With problem drinking, it may be appropriate to set a maximum number of alcohol units per week as a goal, and with anorexia the goal may be achieving a target weight. In CBT, progress towards goals should be monitored regularly, for example weekly or monthly, using an agreed outcome measure. This is usually distinct from daily self-monitoring and diary keeping, which will be described next.

Where disagreement occurs about goals, the client's priorities should be followed unless these entail significant risks or interfere with therapy effectiveness. For example, managing imminent suicide risk or imminent risk of harm to others should always be a priority. Where clients have major substance use problems or severe anorexia, these should be prioritized over other difficulties, since intoxication and starvation interfere with the effectiveness of CBT.

Structuring sessions

Structure CBT sessions in the following way:

- orientation to the structure of the session
- check-in
- set agenda
- work through agenda, including reviewing homework
- agree homework
- summarize and request feedback.

Orientation

At the beginning of each session let the client know the structure you intend to follow. Here is one way to do this:

> Our meeting will last for an hour today and this is the way I suggest we use the time. We'll start by checking how you are now and how you have been since we last met. Then, we'll agree on an agenda. One thing I want to put on the agenda is how you managed the homework we discussed last week. You will probably have things you want to put on the agenda too. We'll try to cover most things on the agenda. And then towards the end of the session we will agree your next homework assignment. We'll finish up with a recap of the ground we have covered and I'll ask you for feedback on the session. Is that structure OK with you?

Check-in

The second task is to check how the client is now and how things have been since the last session. If self-report measures of symptoms, rating scales, or other indices of goal attainment have been completed, these should be checked too and improvement or deterioration noted. A common problem is for clients to move without agreement from the check-in process to discussing a recent crisis in detail. If this begins to happen, indicate that a discussion of the recent crisis may be an important item to put on the agenda.

Set agenda

The third task is to set an agreed agenda that can realistically be completed within the time available. A typical agenda might include homework review, discussion of coping with a recent crisis, planning for a challenge coming up in the near future and agreeing on homework. Checking homework is usually the first item on the agenda and agreeing a further homework assignment is often the last item on the agenda. Between these two items, clients may be invited to include a couple of additional items or clinicians may suggest items that may be included on the agenda. In early sessions, therapists may actively suggest additional agenda items. In later sessions, clients may be invited to take more responsibility for agenda setting. Usually, agenda items are related to therapy goals and to significant aspects of client's current life situation that facilitate or impede goal attainment. The agenda should be set and items on it prioritized collaboratively. Risky behaviour, including self-harm and violence, and behaviour that interferes with the effectiveness of therapy, such as difficulties with completing homework assignments, should always be prioritized. When setting an agenda, the challenge is to keep the agenda short, realistically manageable within the available time, and relevant to goal attainment.

Work through the agenda

The fourth task is to work through the agenda. In reviewing homework (often the first item on the agenda) intermittent praise should be given for successive approximations to well-completed homework assignments. Where assignments are incorrectly completed and the problem is a skills deficit, corrective instruction should be given. Where assignments are partially completed or not completed at all, obstacles to homework completion should be explored. Sometimes these obstacles are practical difficulties, such as being unable to manage the competing demands of work, family life and do homework assignments. However, resistance to doing homework is often related to schemas about self and others, such as those listed in Table 3.1 (pp. 66–67). Schemas associated with personality disorders that include assumptions such as 'I am stupid' or 'I cannot trust you because you will hurt me' often make it difficult for clients to complete homework assignments. In such cases, recognizing these schemas, inviting clients to collect evidence to challenging these assumptions, and learning to work around them is critical if CBT is to be effectively used to deal with axis I disorders such as depression or anxiety (Young et al., 2003).

In working through items on the agenda, such as managing a recent crisis or planning how to handle an upcoming challenge, the clinician's role is to manage time effectively and to facilitate problem solving using the CBT techniques described below. There are many obstacles in working through an agenda. Sometimes clients want to ventilate their feelings of sadness, anger, despondency and demoralization for long periods of time before moving into problem solving. It can be helpful to point out in an empathic way that this is occurring and asking if the client wishes to use the therapy time to do this or focus on problem solving.

On other occasions, clients will stray from the agenda and talk about items unrelated to the agreed agenda. It can be helpful to point out in an empathic way that this is occurring and invite the client to try to focus on the agenda items and possibly put the other items on the agenda for the next session.

Agree homework

The fifth task in a structured session is to agree homework assignments. The following guidelines make it more probable that clients will follow-through on invitations to complete homework:

- Collaboratively design simple homework tasks to fulfil specific functions and begin the homework in the session.
- Give a rationale for the homework linked to the work done in the session and overall treatment goals.
- Offer invitations to carry out homework clearly in simple language, inviting the client to do specific things.
- Describe homework briefly and break complex tasks into parts.
- Check that the client has understood the homework.
- Emphasize the importance of homework.
- Write down complex homework assignments.
- Mention any potentially negative side-effects of homework tasks and anticipate obstacles.
- State that homework will be discussed at the next session and convey an expectation of co-operation and success.
- Always review homework.

Summarize and request feedback

Throughout each session, you should periodically summarize what has occurred. However, it is particularly important at the end of the session to summarize the ground that has been covered and to ask the client for feedback on helpful and unhelpful aspects of the session. Here is an example of such a summary:

> Today we reviewed your homework, and it's clear that you are mastering the relaxation exercises, but having difficulty remembering to do them every day. We talked about you setting a fixed time of 9.30 each evening, after the news, to do them for the next fortnight. We spent most of the session exploring the way you interpreted a number of situations as very threatening to you last week when you visited your sister. We then agreed that for homework over the next week you would use this form to keep track of situations in which you experience anxiety, and the sorts of automatic thoughts that lead you to feel anxious. Is that a fair summary? . . . Can I just check with you, if there was anything that you found particularly useful about today's session, and if there was anything that jarred a bit and was unhelpful?

Treatment strategies

Within CBT, a group of cognitive strategies may be identified, the primary aim of which is to modify negative automatic thoughts and cognitive distortions and in doing so to alter negative mood states such as depression, anxiety and anger. Cognitive strategies also aim to reduce vulnerability to relapse by modifying core beliefs and assumptions about self, others, the world and the future contained in the underlying maladaptive schemas. Behavioural strategies, in contrast, aim to equip clients with skills to alter or cope better with activating events or to engage in activities that have a direct and positive impact on emotional states and are intrinsically reinforcing. They include scheduling activities, relaxation, pleasant events and physical exercise. Some of the more widely applicable CBT strategies are briefly described below. These constitute a menu that clinicians draw from in tailoring individualized CBT programmes for particular clients. The types of strategy chosen and the way in which they are sequenced should be determined by each client's formulation and treatment goals on the one hand, and the results of treatment outcome studies on the other. CBT treatment protocols for specific clinical syndromes are given in other chapters in this book.

Socratic questioning and guided discovery

Within CBT, for most therapeutic strategies, with the possible exception of skills training, the preferred interactional style is to use questions to elicit adaptive responses from clients. Through questioning in a planned way, therapists guide clients to discover how their problems are maintained and how problem-maintaining patterns may be modified. For example, when gathering evidence for and against a negative automatic thought, it is better to ask the client about such evidence than telling him or her what you think the evidence is, because this provides the client with the experience of discovering it for themselves and becoming committed to altering the problem beliefs. This approach is referred to as Socratic questioning, after the Greek philosopher Socrates, who believed that all people have the wisdom to solve their own problems; the role of the teacher is to ask questions that will elicit this wisdom and so guide students towards the good life.

Cognitive strategies

For cognitive strategies, the routine is as follows. First, give the rationale for using cognitive strategies:

> In our first meeting we both noticed that in many situations you have a tendency to look on the down side of things, to see the glass as half empty rather than as half full. It also seemed to both of us that this way of thinking lowered your mood. One way to take control of your mood and improve it is to start to question your tendency to look on the down side. We could begin by looking at that difficult situation you mentioned a few minutes ago. Would you be prepared to do that?

Begin with an ABC analysis of a specific situation. Invite the client to state or write down a negative automatic thought or assumption (B) that came to mind in response to a specific activating event (A), and ask him or her to rate the degree to which this is believed in on a scale from one to ten. The client can then be invited to state or write down the consequent emotion (C) felt and to rate its intensity on a scale from one to ten. Once this has been done, the client is invited to use a specific cognitive strategy, such as questioning the evidence for the belief or doing an experiment to test the validity of the belief. When the strategy has been used, the client is invited to state or write down an alternative balanced belief to replace the negative automatic thought or assumption. This alternative belief will have arisen from the cognitive treatment strategy. The alternative belief should fit with the new evidence given by using the strategy. Once the new belief has been stated or written down, the client rates the degree to which he or she believes it on a scale from one to ten; the client also states or writes down the emotion this new belief causes him or her to feel and rates its intensity on a scale from one to ten. Finally, the client is invited to note if there has been an improvement in his or her emotional state. This final step offers proof for the effectiveness of the cognitive strategy in improving the client's well-being.

Questioning the evidence

With this strategy, invite the client to list evidence for and against a negative automatic thought or assumption. Questioning the evidence involves inviting clients to distance themselves from the automatic thought or assumption and to accept that a problematic interpretation of an activating event is only one possible take on the situation, not true facts. Distancing sets the stage for stating the evidence for or against the negative automatic thought or assumption. The following questions can aid this process:

- In this situation you had the following thought . . . This is just one take on, or view of, the situation. What evidence can you give me that this interpretation of the situation is accurate?
- Can you think of anything that might not fit with that take on the situation?
- Is there another possible interpretation of the situation that is more helpful to you?
- Can you think of any evidence that supports this more helpful take on the situation?
- If your negative take on the situation is supported by the evidence, are things as bad as you have made them out to be – a real catastrophe – or just a temporary nuisance?
- If you cannot decide whether there is more evidence for an optimistic or pessimistic interpretation of the situation, which interpretation is most useful to you in terms of being happy and achieving your goals?
- Having questioned the evidence for your negative belief and found that it was not fully supported, what is your new and more balanced belief?
- On a scale of one to ten, how strongly do you believe this?
- What emotion do you feel right now, and how would you rate this emotion on a scale from one to ten?
- Is this rating higher or lower than the rating you gave before you questioned the evidence for your first take on this situation?
- Has questioning the evidence led to an improvement in how you feel right now?

A thought record that is specially designed for this technique is contained in Table 3.4. In the first three columns, the antecedents, beliefs and consequences associated with specific events that led to significant changes in the client's emotional state are listed. In the next two columns, evidence for and against the problematic automatic thought is given. In the sixth column, an alternative more balanced interpretation of the situation is recorded. Finally, the last column is used to record information about emotional and cognitive changes arising from questioning the evidence for the negative belief. This thought record can be used within therapy sessions to provide focus for questioning the evidence, and also as the basis for a homework assignment. Initially, clients are invited to use the first three columns to learn how to identify activating events, consequent mood changes, and to 'catch' automatic thoughts and beliefs. Later, when skill at pinpointing mood changing events and 'thought catching' has been refined, clients can be invited to fill in the last three columns. That is, to use questioning the evidence in their day-to-day lives as a coping strategy.

Table 3.4 Thought record for learning how to challenge automatic thoughts

Activating situation *When?* *Where?* *Who was there?* *What happened?*	**Beliefs** *What negative automatic thoughts went through your mind?* *How much did you believe them 1–10?* *What cognitive distortions did you make?* *Circle the hot thought*	**Consequences** *What emotions did you feel?* *How strong were they 1–10?* *How did you behave?* *How did your body react?* *What were the reactions of others?*	***What evidence was there for your beliefs?***	***What evidence was there against your beliefs?***	***What is your new balanced belief?*** *Rate how strongly you believe this 1–10*	***What was the outcome?*** *What emotions did you feel?* *How strong were they 1–10?* *How did you behave?* *How did your body react?* *What was the reaction of others?*

There are a number of common difficulties with this therapeutic strategy. Some clients have difficulty distinguishing thoughts from feelings. One way around this is to list a series of hypothetical situations and ask them to say what they would think and feel in each. Then, give feedback on whether they are correctly labelling thoughts and feelings for each of their responses. For clients who have difficulty identifying automatic thoughts, use the guidelines for 'thought catching' presented on pp. 76–77.

Behavioural experiments

Invite clients to set up an experiment that tests the validity of a negative automatic thought, assumption or core belief. For example, to test the belief 'I can't do anything right', clients could be invited to successfully complete one or more simple tasks inside or outside the therapy sessions. These might include reading a passage from a book, writing a three-item shopping list, or telling the story of how their best friend once did something good for them. By completing these tasks, clients have proved that they can do at least one or two things right. In setting up experiments there are a number of critical preparatory tasks. First, grade the size of the challenge in the experiments, start small and gradually work up towards more challenging experiments. Second, set specific times and places for experiments. Third, help the client design the experiment to test out whether a particular belief is true or false and write down the possible outcomes or predictions. Fourth, invite the client to anticipate possible problems to doing the experiment and collaborate on developing a list of strategies to overcome possible problems or setbacks. Fifth, ask the client to write down the outcome of the experiment and whether it supported his or her negative or positive predictions.

Safety behaviour experiments

Safety behaviour experiments are particularly appropriate as part of the treatment of certain anxiety disorders. Where anxious clients use anxiety-maintaining safety behaviours to cope, first invite them to identify the safety behaviours used in threatening situations. For social phobia, safety behaviours include avoiding eye contact to avoid seeing negative feedback from others, gripping objects tightly to reduce nervous shaking, and taking deep breaths to stay calm. For panic attacks, safety behaviours include reducing physical activity to prevent a feared heart attack, leaning on objects to prevent falling over, and suppressing worry to avoid losing control of one's mind. For hypochondriasis, frequent medical consultations and personal health checks to get health information are common safety behaviours. Once safety behaviours have been identified, invite clients to do an experiment in which they give up using safety behaviours and notice the impact of this on their anxiety levels. Giving up safety behaviours usually provides evidence that the feared consequence clients were avoiding with the safety behaviour does not occur. This weakens their anxious beliefs.

Belief surveys

Invite clients to ask a number of friends about the degree to which they believe in one of the clients' negative automatic thoughts, assumptions or beliefs. Their responses should be written down verbatim and these 'survey results' are brought into therapy to explore their impact on the degree to which clients still believe their negative automatic thoughts, assumptions or beliefs; the degree to which they believe more balanced alternatives; and the consequent impact of these cognitive changes on their emotional well-being.

Challenging distortions

Invite clients to identify the cognitive distortion within one of their negative automatic thoughts, assumptions or beliefs, with reference to the list in Table 3.1 (p. 66). Then invite them to list evidence to show the distortion is not always true. This provides a basis for rephrasing the belief without the distortion, a process that usually leads to a more balanced type of belief.

Thinking in shades of grey

Invite clients to rephrase one of their negative automatic thoughts or assumptions using language that reflects thinking in shades of grey, rather than black and white. Then, invite clients to list evidence to show that the statement involving shades of grey is probably more consistent with the evidence than the black and white statement.

Re-attribution

Invite clients to rephrase a negative automatic thought that attributes a failure experience to internal, global, stable personal characteristics as a statement that attributes failure to external, specific and transient factors. The other side of this strategy is inviting clients to rephrase one of their negative automatic thoughts in which they attribute a success experience to external, specific, and transient factors to internal, global, stable personal characteristics.

Cost–benefit analysis

Invite clients to list the costs of holding a negative automatic thought, assumption, or belief and the benefits of giving it up.

Focusing on the positive

Invite clients to replace negative automatic thoughts and assumptions that focus exclusively on problematic aspects of a situation with alternatives that focus on positive features of the situation. List evidence to support the positive alternative.

Showing self-compassion

Invite clients to rephrase negative automatic thoughts and assumptions that involve 'should', 'must', 'always' and 'never' statements in the compassionate language they would use if talking to a close friend who was in difficulty. These new statements will include words such as 'may sometimes' or 'might occasionally' rather than 'should never' and 'must always'. Then, invite clients to list reasons why they deserve the compassion of these kinder and more reasonable statements.

Using less extreme language

Invite clients to rephrase negative automatic thoughts, assumptions and beliefs in less extreme language and list the evidence to support these more reasonable statements.

Pie-chart analysis

Where clients hold beliefs that they are completely to blame or one hundred per cent responsible for some negative event, with high associated feelings of guilt or shame, invite them to indicate on a pie chart the percentage of responsibility that each of the other people involved in the situation had. Clients typically apportion less of the responsibility to themselves after this exercise, with associated lessening of guilt and shame. For example, a victim of an accident at work who believed he was completely responsible for the damage to himself and another worker was invited to show in the pie chart how responsible his co-worker, supervisor and employer were for the accident, This use of the pie-chart strategy changed his belief from being one hundred to forty per cent responsible.

Core belief test

For this cognitive schema-change strategy, begin by using the downward arrow technique mentioned earlier, an example of which is given in Figure 3.2, to identify a core belief about the self, others, the world or the future. Then invite clients within the session and later as homework to write down a list of pieces of evidence that show that the core belief is not one hundred per cent true all the time in all situations.

Positive daily log

For this cognitive schema-change strategy, the therapist does not begin and end the strategy in the way outlined at the beginning of the section, since the focus of this strategy is positive, not negative beliefs. Fortunately, everyone has both positive adaptive schemas as well as negative maladaptive schemas. Adaptive schemas include core beliefs such as 'I'm good', 'I'm competent' or 'I'm likeable'. With the positive daily log, the existence of adaptive schemas of positive beliefs about the self, others, the world and the future is first established through Socratic questioning. Positive automatic thoughts that occur following success or receiving support from others provide evidence for the existence of these positive schemas. After this discovery, clients are invited to rate the degree to which they believe a specific positive belief on a scale from one to ten; they are also invited to state or write down the emotion this new belief makes them feel and to rate its intensity on a scale from one to ten. As homework, clients are invited to keep a record of all positive events that happen each day that provide evidence for the truth of the positive belief in their adaptive schemas. In other words, they are invited to catch themselves being good, successful, likeable or competent as often as possible and immediately to write down these events in their logbook. The positive daily log is then reviewed in therapy and clients are invited once again to rate the degree to which they believe their positive belief on a scale from one to ten. They are also invited to state or write down the emotion this new belief makes them feel and to rate its intensity on a scale from one to ten. Finally, they are invited to note if there has been an improvement in their emotional state. This final step offers proof for the effectiveness of the cognitive strategy in improving their emotional well-being.

Behavioural strategies

For behavioural strategies, use the following routine. First, give a rationale for the behavioural method:

> In our first meeting we both noticed that in certain trigger situations you end up feeling anxious, sad or angry. One way to take control of your mood and improve it is to try to set situations up that are less distressing. Another way is to learn to tolerate being in difficult situations by using certain coping strategies. We could begin by looking at that difficult situation you mentioned a few minutes ago. Would you be prepared to do that?

Invite clients to state or write down a specific activating event, the consequent emotion that followed it, and to rate the intensity of this distressing emotion on a scale of one to ten. Once this has been done, clients are invited to use a specific cognitive strategy, such as using relaxation skills or distraction. When the strategy has been used, clients are invited to state or write down the emotion they feel and to rate its intensity on a scale of one to ten. Finally, invite clients to note if there has been an improvement in their emotional state. This final step offers proof for the effectiveness of the behavioural strategy in improving their well-being.

Distraction and thought stopping

Invite clients to identify the activating event that is leading to negative automatic thoughts and distressing moods, and then ask them to temporarily focus on some other aspect of the situation, engage in a distracting activity, or stop their negative automatic thoughts. Specific techniques include concentrating attention on another task, such as singing a song; focusing on an external physical object, such as a tree waving in the wind; actively postponing rumination until later that day; saying 'stop' loudly and banging a hand on a table or other surface; snapping an elastic band worn on the wrist or looking at a flash card with STOP written on it in large letters.

Time-out

Invite clients to identify the activating event that is leading to negative automatic thoughts and distressing moods, and then to temporarily withdraw from the situation. During this period of time-out, relaxation, physical exercise or cognitive strategies may be used to reduce emotional distress. Clients should re-enter the situation when they have calmed their distressing emotions. This is a particularly suitable technique for anger management.

Relaxation

Invite clients to identify the activating events that lead to negative automatic thoughts and distressing moods. Clients are encouraged to practise relaxation skills and use them in these situations to reduce anxiety. A set of relaxation exercises is given in Table 3.5. Customized relaxation tapes are a useful adjunct to direct instruction but relaxation tapes without instruction are of little clinical value. When coaching clients in relaxation, use a slow, calming tone of voice and repetition of instructions as required. For a minority of clients, relaxation exercises lead to increased tension. This may occur because the client is made aware of previously unnoticed body tension through completing the exercises. Alternatively, it may occur because focusing attention on somatic processes during the exercises induces anxiety. In such instances, work on only one or two muscle groups at a time and keep the training periods very short. Also request regular anxiety ratings and, when increases in anxiety occur, distract clients by asking them to engage in the visualization

Table 3.5 Relaxation exercises

RELAXATION EXERCISES

After a couple of weeks daily practice, you will have developed enough skill to use these exercises to get rid of unwanted body tension.

- Set aside 20 minutes a day to do these relaxation exercises
- Do them at the same time and in the same place every day
- Before you begin, remove all distractions (by turning off bright lights, the radio, etc.) and loosen any tight clothes (like belts, ties or shoes)
- Lie on a bed or recline in a comfortable chair with the eyes lightly closed
- Before and after each exercise breath in deeply and exhale slowly three times while saying the word 'relax'
- Repeat each exercise twice

Area	*Exercise*
Hands	Close your hands into fists. Then allow them to open slowly Notice the change from tension to relaxation in your hands and allow this change to continue further and further still so the muscles of your hands become more and more relaxed
Arms	Bend your arms at the elbow and touch your shoulders with your hands Then allow them to return to the resting position. Notice the change from tension to relaxation in your arms and allow this change to continue further and further still so the muscles of your arms become more and more relaxed
Shoulders	Hunch your shoulders up to your ears. Then allow them to return to the resting position Notice the change from tension to relaxation in your shoulders and allow this change to continue further and further still so the muscles of your shoulders become more and more relaxed
Legs	Point your toes downwards. Then allow them to return to the resting position Notice the change from tension to relaxation in the fronts of your legs and allow this change to continue further and further still so the muscles in the fronts of your legs become more and more relaxed Point your toes upwards. Then allow them to return to the resting position Notice the change from tension to relaxation in the backs of your legs and allow this change to continue further and further still so the muscles in the backs of your legs become more and more relaxed
Stomach	Take a deep breath and hold it for three seconds, tensing the muscles in your stomach as you do so. Then breath out slowly Notice the change from tension to relaxation in your stomach muscles and allow this change to continue further and further still so your stomach muscles become more and more relaxed
Face	Clench your teeth tightly together. Then relax. Notice the change from tension to relaxation in your jaw and allow this change to continue further and further still so the muscles in your jaw become more and more relaxed

Continued overleaf

Table 3.5 continued

Area	*Exercise*
	Wrinkle your nose up. Then relax. Notice the change from tension to relaxation in the muscles around the front of your face and allow this change to continue further and further still so the muscles of your face become more and more relaxed Shut your eyes tightly. Then relax. Notice the change from tension to relaxation in the muscles around your eyes and allow this change to continue further and further still so the muscles around your eyes become more and more relaxed
All over	Now that you've done all your muscle exercises, check that all areas of your body are as relaxed as can be. Think of your hands and allow them to relax a little more Think of your arms and allow them to relax a little more Think of your shoulders and allow them to relax a little more Think of your legs and allow them to relax a little more Think of your stomach and allow it to relax a little more Think of your face and allow it to relax a little more
Breathing	Breath in . . . one . . . two . . . three . . . and out slowly . . . one . . . two . . . three . . . four . . . five . . . six . . . and again Breath in . . . one . . . two . . . three . . . and out slowly . . . one . . . two . . . three . . . four . . . five . . . six . . . and again Breath in . . . one . . . two . . . three . . . and out slowly . . . one . . . two . . . three . . . four . . . five . . . six
Visualizing	Imagine you are lying on a beautiful sandy beach and you feel the sun warm your body Make a picture in your mind of the golden sand and the warm sun As the sun warms your body you feel more and more relaxed As the sun warms your body you feel more and more relaxed As the sun warms your body you feel more and more relaxed The sky is a clear, clear blue. Above you, you can see a small white cloud drifting away into the distance As it drifts away you feel more and more relaxed It is drifting away and you feel more and more relaxed It is drifting away and you feel more and more relaxed As the sun warms your body you feel more and more relaxed As the cloud drifts away you feel more and more relaxed (Wait for 30 seconds) When you are ready open your eyes ready to fact the rest of the day relaxed and calm

exercise described in Table 3.5. When relaxation skills have become well developed, clients may be coached in reducing the time required to relax by focusing on the muscle groups one at a time, allowing them to relax without movement, in time to their breathing and the mental self-instruction to relax as they exhale. After two weeks of homework practice, clients can progress to applied relaxation, where a rapid body scan of all muscle groups, paired with breathing exercises, and a mental self-instruction to relax is used as a relaxation coping strategy in day-to-day challenging situations.

Imagery

Imagery-based interventions can modify negative mood states. In imaginal systematic desensitization, clients are invited to master increasingly anxiety-provoking images of fearful situations through the use of relaxation and other coping strategies. For clients with post-traumatic stress disorder, situational cues may elicit vivid images that are more prominent than automatic thoughts. Also, some clients with a wide range of other psychological problems find that negative visual imagery rather than negative automatic thoughts are the main factor determining their negative emotional states. Where imagery is the primary determinant of mood, clients may be invited to relax using the skills described in the previous section. Then invite clients to bring to mind an agreed distressing image. Next, ask the client to imagine the 'movie' of the image progressing and having a positive rather than a negative outcome. The process is repeated with each negative image until cues that once called the negative image to mind now call the modified image to mind. This positive outcome is thus 'invented' collaboratively by the therapist and client.

Physical activity

Clients may be invited to use regularly scheduled periods of between thirty and ninety minutes of daily physical activity to activate them if lethargic and depressed, or to calm them down if anxious or angry. Physical activity may also be used as a coping strategy in specific situations. Invite clients to identify activating events that lead to negative automatic thoughts and distressing moods, and then to engage in physical activity following these activating events to enhance their emotional state.

Pleasant event scheduling

Clients may be invited to use regularly scheduled pleasant events to activate them if lethargic and depressed or to calm them down if anxious or angry. First, construct a grid with the hours of the day from rising (e.g. 7.00 a.m.) until retiring (e.g. 12.00 a.m.) down the left side of the page, and the days of the week across the top. Second, fill all routine obligations into this grid. Third, invite the client to list pleasant events on a separate sheet and then fill these into the vacant slots in the grid. Pleasant events can include things like breathing clean air, walking in the park, playing football with one's children or reading the paper. Make sure that there are at least seven pleasant events in each day (or one for every two waking hours).

Worry practice

Where clients are concerned that their worrying is out of control, invite them to engage in daily planned periods of worrying to gain control over the worry process.

Graded challenges

Invite clients to construct hierarchies of graded challenges. For anxiety disorders, these hierarchies will include increasingly feared situations. For anger control problems, increasingly provocative situations should be included in these hierarchies. For depression, tasks requiring increasing effort may be used. Arrange opportunities in therapy and as homework for clients to master challenges within their hierarchies, one at a time starting with the least challenging, while using various coping strategies to deal with distress or challenge of each step of the hierarchy.

Self-reward

Invite clients to use self-praise and tangible rewards (personal treats) for using coping strategies to deal effectively with activating events and negative automatic thoughts.

Communication skills

Activating events can be modified through clear communication. Communication skills include listening and speaking. Through modelling, rehearsal and shaping successive approximations to good performance, coach clients to listen without judging. Invite them to put their own opinions and emotions on hold, to summarize what they have heard the other person say and to check that their summary was accurate before replying. When coaching clients in speaking skills, ask them to decide on the points they want to make first. Then, through modelling, rehearsal and shaping, coach them to organize their points logically, say them clearly using 'I statements', and check that they have been understood. Coach clients to make their points without attacking, blaming, sulking or mind reading.

Support seeking

Support seeking is a specific communication skill. Through modelling, rehearsal and shaping successive approximations to good performance, coach clients to ask friends or family members for support to enhance their emotional state following challenging situations that have led to negative automatic thoughts and negative mood states.

Assertiveness

Assertiveness is a particular communication skill. Through modelling, rehearsal and shaping successive approximations to good performance, coach clients to ask people whose behaviour is distressing to them to change their behaviour using a statement format such as:

> 'When you do X, I feel Y; so I would prefer if you did Z. Thank you.'

Clients should be coached to state their requests without attacking, blaming or sulking and, if provoked, to mentally stand back, breath deeply, relax and start again: 'When you do X . . .'

Problem solving

Problem solving can be used to modify activating events. Through modelling, rehearsal and shaping successive approximations to good performance, invite clients to first break big vague problems into many smaller specific problems to be tackled one at a time. Second, define each of these in solvable terms. Third, focus on solving the specific problem at hand, not attacking the person or people involved in the problem. Fourth, generate many possible solutions to the problem in hand. Fifth, when all solutions are generated, examine the pros and cons of each, and select the best. Sixth, implement this solution, review progress, and modify the solution if it's not working. Finally, repeat this sequence as often as is necessary to solve the problem and celebrate success.

Decision making

Sometimes the principal activating event leading to negative automatic thoughts and a distressed mood state is a dilemma involving two possible course of action. Where clients face a dilemma about two courses of action and this is causing significant emotional distress, invite them to write down the pros and cons of each course of action and base their decision on the balance of pros and cons.

Coping strategies

Most of the therapeutic strategies listed in the previous two sections can by used by clients in their day-to-day lives as coping strategies. Lists of these coping strategies are given in Tables 3.6 and 3.7. A self-monitoring form on which clients can do an ABC analysis of problem situations and then indicate which coping strategies they used and the impact of using these on their cognitive and emotional state is given in Table 3.8. For recurring challenging

Table 3.6 CBT cognitive coping strategies

For all cognitive strategies follow this routine.

Before using the strategy
State or write down a negative automatic thought or assumption and rate the degree to which you believe in it on a scale from 1 to 10
State or write down what emotion this belief makes you feel and rate its intensity on a scale of 1 to 10

Then use the specific strategy

After using the strategy
State or write down an alternative balanced belief arising from using the strategy and that fits with the new evidence given by using the strategy and rate the degree to which you believe it on a scale of 1–10
State or write down what emotion this new belief makes you feel and rate its intensity on a scale of 1–10
Note if there has been an improvement in you emotional state

Question the evidence for a negative belief. List the evidence for and against a negative automatic thought or assumption

Do an experiment. Do an experiment to test the validity of a negative automatic thought or assumption

Do the experiment of giving up a safety behaviour. Identify the safety behaviour used in threatening situations. Then give it up and notice the impact of this on how strongly you hold your anxious beliefs

Conduct a survey. Ask a number of friends the degree to which they believe in one of your negative automatic thoughts or assumptions

Identify distortions. Identify the cognitive distortion that one of your negative automatic thoughts or assumptions entails with reference to the list in Table 3.1. List the evidence that shows that the distortion is not always true and restate the assumption without the distortion

Think in shades of grey. Rephrase one of your negative automatic thoughts or assumptions using language that reflects 'shades of grey' thinking rather than black and white thinking, and list the evidence to show the shades of grey statement is probably true

Make a re-attribution. Rephrase one of your negative automatic thoughts in which you attribute a failure experience to internal, global, stable personal characteristics to external, specific and transient factors. Rephrase one of your negative automatic thoughts in which you attribute a success experience to external, specific, transient personal characteristics to internal, global and stable factors

Do a cost–benefit analysis. List the costs of holding a negative automatic thought or assumption and the benefits of giving it up

Focus on the positive. Replace negative automatic thoughts and assumptions that focus exclusively on the negative with alternatives that focus on positive aspects of the situation and list evidence to support these alternatives

Show self-compassion. Rephrase negative automatic thoughts and assumptions that involve 'should' and 'must', 'always' and 'never' statements in the compassionate language you would use if talking to a close friend who was in difficulty. These new statements will include words such as 'may sometimes'. List reasons why you deserve the compassion entailed by these kinder and more reasonable statements

Use less extreme language. Rephrase negative automatic thoughts and assumptions in less extreme language and list the evidence that supports these more reasonable statements

Table 3.7 CBT behavioural coping strategies

Behavioural strategies

For all behavioural strategies follow this routine

Before using the strategy
State or write down the activating event and what emotion you feel and rate its intensity on a scale of 1 to 10

Then use the specific strategy

After using the strategy
State or write down what emotion you feel and rate its intensity on a scale of 1 to 10
Note if there has been an improvement in you emotional state

Use temporary distraction or thought stopping. Identify the activating event that is leading to negative automatic thoughts and distressing moods, and then temporarily focus on some other aspect of the situation, use thought stopping, or engage in a distracting activity

Take time-out. Identify the activating event that is leading to negative automatic thoughts and distressing moods. Then take a little time-out to relax, breathe, question the evidence for your distressing beliefs and calm down. Do not re-enter the situation until you have calmed your distressing emotion

Use relaxation skills. Identify the activating event that is leading to negative automatic thoughts and distressing moods, and then practice relaxation skills to reduce anxiety

Do physical activity. Identify the activating event that is leading to negative automatic thoughts and distressing moods, and then engage in physical activity to enhance your mood

Schedule a pleasant event. Identify the activating event that is leading to negative automatic thoughts and distressing moods, and then engage in a pleasant event to enhance your mood

Ask for support. Identify the activating event that is leading to negative automatic thoughts and distressing moods, and then ask a close friend or family member for support to enhance your mood

Behave assertively. Identify the activating event that is leading to negative automatic thoughts and distressing moods, and then rehearse and follow through on assertively asking the person whose behaviour is distressing to you to change their behaviour using a statement format like this 'When you do X, I feel Y so I would prefer if you did Z. Thank you.'

Practice worrying. Identify the worry pattern leading to negative automatic thoughts and distressing moods, and then engage in planned periods of worry to gain control over the worry process

Solve problems systematically. Identify the activating problem that is leading to negative automatic thoughts and distressing moods and break this big vague problem into many smaller specific problems. Define each of these in solvable terms. Generate many possible solutions. Examine the pros and cons of each, and select the best. Implement this solution, review progress, and modify the solution if it is not working. Repeat this sequence as often as is necessary and celebrate success

Make decisions systematically. Identify the activating dilemma that is leading to negative automatic thoughts and distressing mood. Write down the pros and cons of each course of action in this dilemma and base your decision on the balance of pros and cons

Face graded challenges. Organize situations that give rise to distressing emotions such as anxiety or anger into a hierarchy and arrange to master these one at a time starting with the least challenging, while using various coping strategies to deal with distress

Reward yourself for coping. Use intermittent self-praise and tangible rewards for using coping strategies to deal effectively with activating events and negative automatic thoughts

Table 3.8 Thought record for tracking the use of cognitive and behavioural coping strategies

Activating situation *When?* *Where?* *Who was there?* *What happened?*	***Beliefs*** *What negative automatic thoughts went through your mind?* *How much did you believe them 1–10?* *What cognitive distortions did you make?* *Circle the hot thought*	***Consequences*** *What emotions did you feel?* *How strong were they 1–10?* *How did you behave?* *How did your body react?* *What were the reactions of others?*	***What cognitive coping strategy did you use?*** *Questioned evidence for negative belief* *Did an experiment* *Gave up safety behaviour* *Did a survey* *Challenged distortion* *Thought in shades of grey* *Did re-attribution* *Did a cost–benefit analysis* *Focused on positive* *Was kind to myself* *Used less extreme language*	***What behavioural coping strategy did you use?*** *Used distraction* *Used time-out* *Used relaxation skills* *Did physical activity* *Had a pleasant event* *Asked for support* *Behaved assertively* *Practised worrying* *Used systematic problem solving* *Used systematic decision making* *Faced graded challenges* *Rewarded self for coping*	***What was the outcome?*** *What emotions did you feel?* *How strong were they 1–10?* *How did you behave?* *How did your body react?* *What were the reactions of others?*

situations, clients may be invited to write their own coping cards. On one side, the activating situation and/or negative automatic thought is written and on the other a preferred effective coping strategy for dealing with the challenging situation or negative automatic thought is written down. When facing these situations, cards are read and the coping strategies on them used.

DISENGAGEMENT

In the later sessions of a course of CBT, the main tasks are to fade out the frequency of sessions, to help clients understand the change process and to facilitate the development of relapse management plans. The interval between sessions is increased as the end of therapy is reached since this offers clients greater time periods within which to independently manage their own symptoms. This is an approximation to complete independent symptom management, which will follow when disengagement is complete.

The degree to which goals are being met is reviewed regularly in CBT, but towards the end of the session contract (for example six to ten sessions) conduct a thorough goal attainment review using interview and psychometric assessment procedures. Then, review the CBT formulation of the problem constructed in the early sessions and collaboratively explore how specific cognitive and behavioural strategies used during therapy led to positive changes in the client's thinking style, behavioural routines, and emotional state. Where limited progress was made, factors contributing to this may be explored.

In relapse management planning, clients are helped to forecast the types of stressful situations in which relapses may occur, their probable negative reactions to relapses and the ways in which they can use the lessons learned in therapy to cope with these relapses in a productive way. Relapses are often triggered by similar factors to those that precipitated the original problem or by a build-up of stressful life events. Once events that might precipitate a relapse have been identified, the negative automatic thoughts and consequent problematic emotional and behavioural reactions through which these events will be translated into a full-blown relapse are considered. A relapse management plan is then collaboratively developed. This will typically include constructing a CBT formulation and then using similar CBT strategies as were used in therapy to manage the potential relapse. One part of this relapse prevention process may involve holding weekly self-therapy sessions in which the client sets aside time to 'meet with themselves' and use the CBT session structure to check how they are, set an agenda, review homework, work through the agenda and set themselves homework for the next week. Where feasible, therapists can offer periodic follow-up relapse prevention or management sessions.

SUMMARY

CBT assumes that problematic thoughts, feelings and behaviour patterns are learned through the same processes as normal thoughts, feelings and behaviour. These learning processes include operant and classical conditioning, and various cognitive processes such as modelling and identification. Therapy involves coaching clients to replace problematic habits with more adaptive ways of thinking, feeling, behaving and interacting with others. CBT is an effective treatment for depression and anxiety disorders and is an effective component of multi-modal treatment programmes for bipolar disorder, positive psychotic symptoms, pain management, management of some illnesses, and problems associated with some personality disorders. CBT is a collaborative process involving the therapist and client. In the assessment and formulation stage of CBT, a contract for assessment is established, a problem list is drawn up and a formulation is constructed. The ABC situational aspect of a CBT formulation details the way antecedent factors (A), intervening beliefs (B) and psychological consequences (C) maintain the client's main difficulties. The syndromal aspect of a CBT formulation specifies the underlying schemas that render the client vulnerable to his or her problems and the stressful life events that triggered the onset of the current episode of psychological disorder. A treatment contract is formed on the basis of a CBT formulation and this specifies the goals and duration of therapy. CBT sessions follow a set format, which includes orientation to the structure of the session, check-in, agenda setting, homework review, working through the agenda, homework setting, summarizing and feedback. Through Socratic questioning and guided discovery, therapists help clients to see how their problems are maintained and how problem-maintaining patterns may be modified. CBT treatment programmes include cognitive and behavioural therapeutic strategies. Cognitive strategies aim to modify problem-maintaining automatic thoughts, assumptions and core beliefs (e.g. questioning the evidence for negative beliefs). Behavioural strategies aim to equip clients with skills to alter or cope better with activating events or to engage in activities that have a direct and positive impact on emotional states and which are intrinsically reinforcing (e.g. activity scheduling or relaxation skills training). In the final sessions of a CBT programme, the main tasks are to fade out the frequency of sessions, help clients understand the change process and facilitate the development of relapse management plans.

EXERCISE 3.1

Work in pairs. Adopt the roles of interviewer and interviewee and reverse roles when the interview is over. The interviewer should invite the interviewee to describe a minor mood problem that he or she had in the past week or two. Then, using the thought record in Table 3.4, do an ABC problem analysis and question the evidence for the automatic thought.

FURTHER READING FOR PRACTITIONERS

Barlow, D. (2001). *Clinical handbook of psychological disorders. A step-by-step treatment manual* (Third Edition). New York: Wiley.
Beck, J. (1995). *Cognitive therapy: Basics and beyond.* New York: Guilford.
Clark, D. & Fairburn, C. (1997). *The science and practice of cognitive behaviour therapy*. Oxford: Oxford University Press.
Hawton, K., Salkovskis, P., Kirk, J., & Clark, D. (1989). *Cognitive behaviour therapy for psychiatric problems: A practical guide*. Oxford: Oxford University Press.
Young, J., Klosko, J., & Weishaar, M. (2003). *Schema therapy: A practitioner's guide*. New York: Guilford.

ASSESSMENT TECHNIQUES

Mobilio, A., Hersen, M., & Bellack, A. (2002). *Dictionary of behavioural assessment techniques*. New York: Percheron Press.

FURTHER READING FOR CLIENTS

Benson, H. & Stuart, E. (1992). *The wellness book: A comprehensive guide to maintaining health and treating stress related illness*. New York: Scribner.
Burns, D. (1999). *The feeling good handbook – revised.* New York: Plume.
Butler, G. & Hope, T. (1995). *Manage your mind.* New York: Oxford University Press.
Davis, M., Eshelman, E., & McKay, M. (1995). *The relaxation and stress workbook* (Fourth Edition). Oakland, CA: New Harbinger.
Greenberger, D. & Padesky, C. (1995). *Mind over mood: Changing how you feel by changing the way you think*. New York: Guilford.
Madders, J. (1997). *The stress and relaxation handbook: A practical guide to self-help techniques*. London: Vermillion.
Prochaska, J., Norcross, J., & Di Clemente, C. (1995). *Changing for good.* New York: Avon.

REFERENCES

American Psychiatric Association (APA) (2000). *Diagnostic and statistical manual of the mental disorders (Fourth Edition-Text Revision) DSM-IV-TR*. Washington, DC: APA.
Ayllon, T. & Azrin, N. (1968). *The token economy*. New York: Wiley.

Barlow, D. (2001). *Clinical handbook of psychological disorders. A step-by-step treatment manual* (Third Edition). New York: Wiley.

Barlow, D., Raffa, S., & Cohen, E. (2003). Psychosocial treatment for panic disorders, phobias and generalised anxiety disorder. In P. Nathan & J. Gorman (Eds), *A guide to treatments that work* (Second Edition, pp. 301–336). New York: Oxford University Press.

Beck, A. (1976). *Cognitive therapy and the emotional disorders*. New York: International Universities Press.

Beck, A. & Steer, R. (1990). *Beck Anxiety Inventory*. San Antonio, TX: Psychological Corporation.

Beck, A., Steer, R. & Brown, G. (1996). *Beck Depression Inventory* (Second Edition; BDI-II). San Antonio, TX: Psychological Corporation.

Beck, J. (1995). *Cognitive therapy: Basics and beyond*. New York: Guilford.

Burns, D. (1980). *Feeling good: The new mood therapy*. New York: Avon.

Burns, D. (1999). *The feeling good handbook – revised*. New York: Plume.

Clark, D. & Fairburn, C. (1997). *The science and practice of cognitive behaviour therapy*. Oxford: Oxford University Press.

Costa, P. & McCrae, R. (1992). *Revised NEO Personality Inventory (NEO-PI-R) and NEO Five-Factor Inventory (NEO-FFI) professional manual*. Odessa, FL: Psychological Assessment Resources.

De Silva, P., Rachman, S., & Seligman, M. (1977). Prepared phobias and obsessions: Therapeutic outcome. *Behaviour Research and Therapy*, 15, 65–77.

Eysenck, H. (1960). *Behaviour therapy and the neuroses*. Oxford: Pergamon.

Eysenck, H. (1979). The conditioning model of neurosis. *The Behavioural and Brain Sciences, 2*, 155–199.

Fordyce, W. (1976). *Behavioural methods for chronic pain and illness*. St Louis: Mosby.

Greenberger, D. & Padesky, C. (1995). *Mind over mood: Changing how you feel by changing the way you think*. New York: Guilford.

Hawton, K., Salkovskis, P., Kirk, J., & Clark, D. (1989). *Cognitive behaviour therapy for psychiatric problems: A practical guide*. Oxford: Oxford University Press.

Mowrer, O. (1960). *Learning theory and behaviour*. New York: Wiley.

Nathan, P. & Gorman, J. (2002). *A guide to treatments that work* (Second Edition). New York: Oxford University Press.

Padesky, C. & Greenberger, D. (1995). *Clinician's guide to mind over mood*. New York: Guilford.

Rachman, S. (1997). The evolution of cognitive behaviour therapy. In: D. Clark & C. Fairburn (Eds), *The science and practice of cognitive behaviour therapy* (pp. 1–26). Oxford: Oxford University Press.

Skinner, B. (1957). *Verbal behaviour*. New York: Appleton Century & Crofts.

Teasdale, J. (1997). The relationship between cognition and emotion. The mind-in-place in mood disorders. In: D. Clark & C. Fairburn (Eds), *The science and practice of cognitive behaviour therapy* (pp. 67–94). Oxford: Oxford University Press.

Ullman, L. & Krasner, L. (1965). *Case studies in behaviour modification*. New York: Holt, Rinehart and Winston.

Watson, J. (1924). *Behaviourism*. Chicago: The People's Institute.

Williams, J., Watts, F., McLeod, C., & Matthews, A. (1997). *Cognitive psychology and emotional disorders* (Second Edition). Chichester: Wiley.

Wolpe, J. (1958). *Psychotherapy by reciprocal inhibition*. Stanford, CA: Stanford University Press.

World Health Organization (WHO) (1992). *The ICD-10 classification of mental and behavioural disorders. Clinical descriptions and diagnostic guidelines*. Geneva: WHO.

Young, J. & Brown, G. (2001). *Young's Schema Questionnaire: Special edition.* New York: Schema Therapy Institute.

Young, J., Klosko, J., & Weishaar, M. (2003). *Schema therapy: A practitioner's guide*. New York: Guilford.

Chapter 4

Psychodynamic therapy

Alan Carr and Muireann McNulty

Brief psychodynamic therapy (BPT) is an evidenced-based approach to clinical practice that falls within the psychoanalytic tradition (Crits-Cristoph, 1992; Crits-Cristoph & Barber, 1991; Gustafson, 1986; Lambert & Ogles, 2004; Ursano et al., 1998; Ursano & Ursano, 2000). BPT originated with the work of Sigmund Freud, who reported a number of cases of brief therapy based on dynamic principles. In the UK, Balint (Balint et al., 1972) and Malan (1995) have been central figures in this tradition. In the USA, important contributors to BPT include Sifneos (1987), Davenloo (1980), Mann (1973), Strupp (Strupp & Binder, 1984), Luborsky (1984) and Horowitz (Horowitz et al., 1984). The focus in this chapter is on the approach to BPT originated by David Malan (1995) at the Tavistock in the UK and developed by Leigh McCullough at Harvard in the USA (McCullough et al., 2003; McCullough-Vaillant, 1997).

CASE VIGNETTE

Michael, a forty-year-old man, came to therapy because of anxiety, depression and chest pains for which no physical basis could be found. Because of his work as a teacher in a local school, and voluntary work as a coach and committee member at a local football club, he was well respected in his local community. Happily married with three children, Michael had many friends and was an excellent footballer and coach. His family and developmental history were within normal limits, with no family history of psychological problems, no major early life stresses, no major family lifecycle problems, and no educational or occupational difficulties. Throughout his school and college career, Michael's academic, social and sporting performances were consistently excellent. He was team captain on many of his school teams and went on to play football for his county. When he was 22, he competed in regional football finals, about which his father was particularly proud. He came from a well-respected and stable family. His retired grandfather was formerly a chief fire officer for the county, and his father had worked, until his retirement five years previously, as a school principal at the school where Michael was first a pupil, then a teacher and more recently (within the last six months) a vice principal. Both his father and grandfather were highly regarded in the community. Great sportsmen, both played on their county football teams and had been coaches and referees. Both were devoted to their families. It was puzzling that a man with such a normal background should present for assessment of psychological problems.

In the two assessment sessions, Michael described three episodes of chest pain. The first occurred in his home-office at 6.30 p.m. on a Friday. It had been a busy day during which he finished a major proposal for changes at the school. The ideas for change were drafted by the new school principal but would probably meet some resistance from school staff. Michael had been working for a month on a presentation of the ideas to the school staff. In an informal meeting with the principal, he outlined the presentation. The principal praised him highly and asked him to redraft the presentation in preparation for a school staff meeting on Monday at 9 a.m., a very demanding task. Michael said he was more than willing to undertake this. Michael saw his GP that evening and on his advice rested for the weekend and Monday, and rescheduled the presentation for the following Thursday. The second episode of chest pain occurred about a month later in his car with his wife and children on a Sunday afternoon at about 5.00 p.m. on the way home from a visit to his wife's parents. It had been a pleasant visit, during which his wife's parents invited them to Christmas dinner, and despite their polite protests, would not take no for an answer. Michael and his wife had made plans to spend Christmas Day in their new house that year, rather than with either of their parents. Michael was disappointed about this change in plan but, so as not to offend his in-laws, said he would be delighted to have Christmas dinner with them. When he got the chest pain, his wife drove him home and he spent the evening and the next day resting. He mentioned to his wife that he hoped this did not occur when he was driving home from her parents' house on Christmas Day. The third episode of chest pain occurred six weeks later on a Wednesday evening at about 10.00 p.m. in the bar of his football club after a committee meeting. One issue that concerned him during the committee meeting had been the request by the chairman that some of the more longstanding members of the committee should step down to leave room for new people to join. Michael said in the meeting that he supported the chairman, because in principle he thought it was his duty to support the chair. However, Michael had been on the committee for years, enjoyed the role and hoped one day to be chairman himself. When he got the chest pains later that evening, his close friends from the committee tended to him and drove him home, rather than ordering him a taxi. He took that as an indication of their support for him and a token of the depth of their friendship.

After each of these three episodes, Michael visited his GP, who could identify no physiological cause for the 'attacks' and so after the third episode, referred Michael to a cardiologist. The cardiologist too could find no physical basis for the complaints and advised a psychological consultation, suggesting that the episodes were stress-related. Over the three months from the first episode to the consultation with the cardiologist, Michael had noticed his mood becoming more depressed and irritable. This led to conflict with other school staff, about which he felt uncomfortable, particularly in light of his recent promotion to vice principal. It also led to conflict with his children at home. Michael worried a great deal more than he used to about his health, his mortality, his popularity at the football club, making renovations to his new house and the amount of time he spent at work. A preliminary BPT formulation following the model set out in Figure 4.1 (described below) was made after two assessment sessions and Michael was judged to be suitable for BPT using the criteria set out in Table 4.3. Subsequently he completed 10 sessions of BPT, during which the chest pains no longer recurred. However, his anxiety and depression initially intensified and then later abated during the course of treatment. The BPT focused predominantly on restructuring defences and then restructuring affect, but not self–other restructuring, strategies summarized in Table 4.4. Details of the therapy are given below.

TRIANGLES OF CONFLICT AND PERSON

The model of psychodynamic practice described in this chapter and outlined in Figure 4.1 can be useful for work with clients referred for psychological

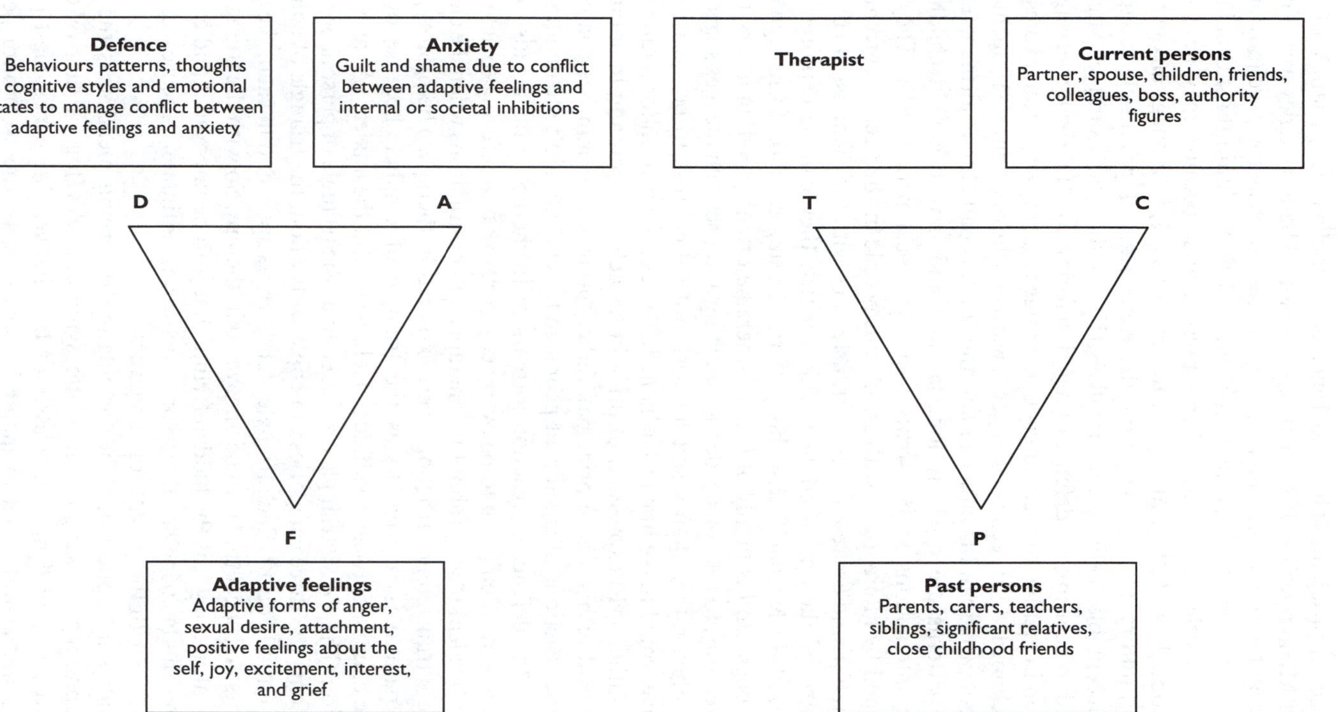

Defences (D) are used to manage conflict between anxieties (A) about expression of adaptive feelings and impulses (F). These D-A-F patterns began with past persons (P), are maintained by interactions with current persons (C), and are re-enacted as transference with the therapist (T).

Figure 4.1 Triangles of conflict and person.
Based on Ezriel, H. (1952). Notes on psychoanalytic group therapy: II. Interpretation. *Research Psychiatry*, 15, 119. Menninger, K. (1958). *Theory of psychoanalytic technique*. London: Imago. Malan, D. (1995). *Individual psychotherapy and the science of psychodynamics*. London: Arnold. McCullough-Vaillant, L. (1997). *Changing character: Short-term anxiety regulating psychotherapy for restructuring defences, affects and attachments*. New York: Basic Books.

therapy for difficulties with anxiety, depression, somatic complaints and interpersonal problems. The model includes Ezriel's (1952) triangle of conflict and Menninger's (1958) triangle of person. These triangles were linked by Malan (1995) and presented as the theoretical basis for psychodynamic treatment planning by McCullough-Vaillant (1997). Within this formulation model, difficulties with which clients present arise because they have used dysfunctional psychological defence mechanisms (D) to manage anxiety and other inhibitory affects (A) about the expression of potentially adaptive but unacceptable feelings and impulses (F). In the case example, Michael appeared to be using the defence of reaction formation (D) (being very agreeable when in fact he was very angry), to manage anxiety (A) about expressing his unacknowledged feeling of anger towards authority figures (F) including his school principal, his father-in law and the football club chairman. These D-A-F patterns are typically longstanding and have begun in childhood through interactions with parents and other past persons (P). They are maintained by interactions with significant people in the client's current life situation (C), and are re-enacted as transference with the therapist (T) during the course of therapy, a context within which they can be explored and understood. In Michael's case, his pattern of using reaction formation as a defence began in his family of origin, where he often agreed, in a very good humoured way, to take on academic, sporting and social challenges suggested by his father, rather than assert his wish not to, because to be assertive or aggressive would make him feel ashamed. The use of reaction formation won him his father's (P) expression of pride in his achievement, and in adult life the approval of his school principal, father-in-law and committee chairman (C). These reactions of significant people in his current adult life maintained his use of the defence of reaction formation. In therapy, Michael also used this defence by attempting to be overly co-operative and refusing to acknowledge ambivalent feelings about the therapist (T) in situations where he clearly did. These transference reactions were explored in therapy. The prototypical D-A-F pattern is referred to as the triangle of conflict, because of the dynamic conflict between the hidden feeling (F) and the anxiety (A) about its expression. The T-C-P triangle is referred to as the triangle of person, because it represents the three categories of people with whom the triangle of conflict may potentially occur. Each triangle stands on its apex, and in each, the apex represents an aspect that is to be uncovered in therapy. So with the triangle of conflict, ultimately it is the hidden feeling that is to be uncovered and experienced. With the triangle of person, uncovering ultimately focuses on the relationship with the parents or caregivers.

A final point concerning the formulation deserving mention is the role of precipitating stresses. Often, acute symptoms develop in the wake of increased personal demands, stresses or life changes. Michael's chest pains occurred in the wake of two major life changes. In the six-month period before the pains, he had been promoted to vice principal of the school and had moved into a house that was somewhat beyond his means. These two (self-created) demands created many opportunities for Michael to use his habitual defence mechanisms in ways that involved high personal costs, particularly denying his own need for fairness.

Core conflictual relationship theme method

There are a variety of other BPT formulation models other than that presented in Figure 4.1. Of these, the Core Conflictual Relationship Theme (CCRT) method deserves mention because of its significant impact on research in the field of BPT (Book, 1998). With the CCRT method, the therapist extracts three key elements from the client's account of a series of problematic relationship episodes in which the presenting problem occurred: (1) the client's wish (W), (2) the client's anticipated response of the other person (imagined response from the other, or RO), and (3) the client's response in the situation (actual response of self, or RS). So, in the case of Michael, in the vignette that opened this chapter, in the three episodes his wish (W) was to speak out in anger for being so unfairly treated. His imagined response of the other (RO) was violent or embarrassing retaliation against him. His actual response (RS) was to act in an overly co-operative way. When this formulation model is compared with the triangle of conflict of the formulation model in Figure 4.1, there are many similarities. The wish (W) and adaptive feeling (F) are both referring to the same phenomenon. The anticipated or imagined response of others (RO) is very similar to anxiety (A) in the triangle of conflict. The actual response of the client (RS) and the defence (D) in the triangle of conflict seem to refer to the same thing. In this chapter, the focus will be exclusively on the formulation model presented in Figure 4.1, but it is important to note that this is not the only model informing evidence-based practice of BPT.

AIMS OF BPT

The goal of BPT is to help clients resolve their presenting problems by targeting specific elements in their problem formulations:

- defence restructuring
- affect restructuring
- self–other restructuring.

The first aim of BPT, defence restructuring, has two parts: defence recognition and defence relinquishing. Defence restructuring aims to help clients recognize how they use defences to manage anxiety about having and expressing forbidden feelings about people in the T, C, P triangle. This is challenging because clients are often not fully conscious of their maladaptive patterns of using defences in response to anxiety about having strong, unacceptable feelings and the replication of such maladaptive patterns across T, C and P contexts. They also resist becoming conscious of the patterns and their replication across contexts because this involves acknowledging that they do in fact have strong forbidden feelings and impulses such as aggression, sexual desire, attachment, sadness and so forth. Defence relinquishing aims to increase clients' motivation to give up the use of defences. Giving up or reducing the use of defences in response to anxiety is difficult, as clients must tolerate the inhibitory anxiety about having and expressing hidden feelings. Clients habitually resisted accepting these affective experiences because they learned in childhood that to have these feelings is to risk rejection or punishment from their parents and those that provide them with safety and security. Michael had learned the lesson, 'If I am angry, I'm bad and will be abandoned'. Other common childhood lessons that lead to the inhibition of activating emotions are, 'Sex is dirty, so don't be rude or you will be punished', 'Don't be a show-off or no-one will like you', 'Big boys are not clingy, so stand on your own two feet', 'Don't be a cry-baby or you'll be rejected', 'Always be very, very careful or you will die' and so forth. These messages are often not only unconscious but sometimes preverbally encoded, making the development of insight into defences even more challenging.

The second goal of psychodynamic psychotherapy, affect restructuring, also has two parts: affect experiencing and affect expression. Affect experiencing aims to help clients fully experience and accept their forbidden adaptive feelings without anxiety. Affect expression aims to find socially acceptable ways to express feelings. For Michael, the implicit therapeutic goal was for him to permit himself to experience his anger towards authority figures and express it assertively. McCullough conceptualizes this process of accepting forbidden feelings without anxiety and without avoiding anxiety through using defence mechanisms as becoming desensitized to an affect phobia, a topic to which we will return in the next section. Accepting forbidden feelings is particularly challenging because it involves letting go of the belief that having strong forbidden feelings and expressing these will compromise safety and security.

The third goal of psychodynamic psychotherapy, self–other restructuring, is to help clients develop a more tolerant attitude towards themselves, a more accurate and compassionate view of others, and a more secure style of engaging in self–other attachments. This involves modifying the internalized models of self, others and relationships learned during childhood.

Dynamic conflict, affect phobia and desensitization

McCullough et al. (2003) have reframed dynamic conflict as affect phobias. In dynamic conflict people repeatedly develop anxiety (pole A of the triangle of conflict in Figure 4.1) when they experience the possible occurrence of a forbidden feeling such as anger or sexual desire (pole F of the triangle of conflict in Figure 4.1) and so use a defence mechanism (pole D of the triangle of conflict in Figure 4.1) to manage the anxiety and repress the hidden feeling. This is analogous to experiencing phobic anxiety (A) in response to a feared stimulus (F) and responding with escape or avoidance (D). In Michael's case this involved experiencing anxiety (A) in response to the forbidden feeling of anger towards authority (F) and responding with reaction formation (D), for example supporting the chairman who wanted him to leave the football club committee that he loved. Each time this process occurs, the hidden feeling (F) and anxiety (A) become more strongly associated through classical conditioning. Because the use of the defence mechanism (D) leads to a reduction in anxiety, the defence is negatively reinforced, and is more likely to be used again.

Through this reframing of dynamic conflict, McCullough argues that, in BPT, the role of the therapist is to desensitize the client to the anxiety-provoking (A) forbidden feelings (F). In Michael's case he needed to be desensitized to his fear of assertively expressing his anger to authority figures. Desensitization is achieved by exposing clients gradually to increasingly stronger 'doses' of forbidden feelings (F) and helping them to tolerate the anxiety (A) associated with this process until it subsides, while at the same time preventing them from using their habitual defence mechanisms (D) to escape from the anxiety-provoking situation. Thus, desensitization in BPT involves gradual exposure and response prevention. It is critical that the steps in this exposure process are finely graded and that clients master their anxiety to each graded dose of the forbidden feeling. If clients escape from experiencing a particular dose of the forbidden feeling before they have reduced the anxiety associated with it, they become more sensitized to it.

In BPT, desensitization involves helping clients bring forbidden feeling into consciousness, helping them tolerate and gradually reduce the anxiety this provokes, and then repeating the process with an even more anxiety-provoking dose of exposure to the forbidden feeling. During this cycle, the therapist helps the client keep anxiety within manageable limits, a process often referred to as 'containing' in psychodynamic practice. This is typically done by asking, 'What is the most painful/most frightening/hardest thing about these feelings?' and then exploring these anxieties.

For example, Michael was invited to focus on how he felt at the meeting in the football club just before he supported the chairman's proposal for long-standing members to step down from the committee. As he did so he became aware of increasing distress tinged with anger. When asked, 'What is the hardest thing about these feelings?' he gradually identified his anger at the chairman for suggesting he step down from the committee, a committee he some day wanted to chair. He also identified anxiety about expressing this anger because he believed that, to be a good man, he should support, rather than oppose, a leader, in this case the chairman. It took some time for his anxiety about this to subside because, for Michael, being angry at authority equated with being bad and being judged harshly or rejected by others,

Later in therapy, Michael showed strong physiological signs of emotional arousal when the therapist informed him that he needed to reschedule the appointment due to the emergence of an unforeseen event. Michael said that he completely understood, that the rescheduling was not a problem and that he would be happy to go along with it. When this transference reaction was explored and the parallels between Michael's reactions to the therapist (T) and the way Michael had reacted to his school principal, father-in-law, football club chairman in his current life (C), and his father during his childhood (P), he showed a large increase in distress and anxiety. When asked what was the hardest thing about these feelings, he identified his anger at the therapist for changing the arrangements and his anxiety about expressing this anger because it would lead to the therapist either humiliating or abandoning him.

These two events are examples of steps in a desensitization hierarchy for an affect phobia, with the discussion of a recent event (the football club situation) being less anxiety provoking than the here-and-now transference interpretation.

From the forgoing discussion, it is clear that, clinically, it is important to know what type of emotions are involved in typical BPT formulations and what types of defence mechanism are commonly used. These issues will be addressed in the next two sections.

Emotions

A list of some of the main emotions of concern in BPT is given in Table 4.1 (McCullough et al., 2003), divided into activating and inhibiting categories. Activating emotions motivate us to engage in approach behaviour and inhibiting emotions motivate avoidance. On the triangle of conflict in Figure 4.1, activating emotions occupy the lowest corner labelled F (for adaptive feelings) and inhibiting emotions occupy the top right-hand corner labelled A (for anxiety). Activating emotions include anger, sexual desire, attachment and positive feelings towards the self, joy, excitement and grief. Inhibitory emotions include anxiety, guilt and shame. Historically, within the psychodynamic tradition, because of Freud's hypotheses about their importance, there has been a strong focus on the activating emotions of sexual desire and anger. However, in McCullough-Vaillant's (1997) practice, the most common activating emotions underpinning core conflicts are anger, grief, attachment and positive feelings towards the self.

All of these emotions have important functions, which are listed in Table 4.1. They give us information about changes in our environment and motivate us to adapt to these changes. For example, anger lets us know that we are under threat and motivates us to assert our needs and protect ourselves against

Table 4.1 The functions of activating and inhibiting emotions, their adaptive and destructive expression, and anxieties that inhibit activating emotions

	Function	*Adaptive expression*	*Destructive expression*	*Anxieties that inhibit activating emotions*
Activating emotions (F)				
Anger	To assert needs, set limits, protect against boundary violations	Assertion	Aggression	I will destroy relationships
Sexual desire	To mate and reproduce	Mutual consenting sex	Predatory or promiscu- ous sex	I will become perverted and dirty
Attachment	To nurture others	Closeness, tenderness, care and trust	Relationship addiction	I will be engulfed
Positive feelings towards self	To nurture the self	Self-regard	Grandiosity	I will become selfish
Joy	To sooth the self	Self-soothing	Self-indulgence	I will be punished for feeling good
Excitement and interest	To explore the environment	Vigorous exploration	Reckless risk-taking	I will die from risk-taking
Grief	To accept loss, relieve pain and elicit attachment from others	Resolving loss	Succumbing to despair	I will never be happy again
Inhibiting emotions (A)				
Anxiety	Inhibit behaviour that could threaten safety or security	Careful avoidance of danger	Paralysis or extreme avoidance of danger	
Guilt	Inhibits behaviour that is unacceptable to others in society	Remorse	Self-attack	
Shame	Inhibits behaviour that is unacceptable to the self	Atonement	Self-hate	

Activating affects occupy the F corner of the triangle of conflict. Inhibiting affects occupy the A corner on the triangle of conflict. Based on McCullough, L., Kuhn, N., Andrews, S., Kaplan, A., Wolf, J., & Hurley, C. (2003). *Treating affect phobia: A manual for short-term dynamic psychotherapy.* New York: Guilford Press.

further boundary violations. Anxiety lets us know that we are in danger and may need to withdraw, rather then defend, our boundaries.

Sometimes emotions lead to adaptive behaviour. For example, anger expressed as assertion is adaptive. On other occasions, emotions lead to destructive behaviour. For example, anger expressed by violently attacking another physically or verbally. Similarly, inhibitory feelings may be adaptive, when for example anxiety leads us to withdraw from dangerous situations, or maladaptive, when anxiety leads us to withdraw from all spontaneous or adventurous activity.

During the course of development, in relationships with primary caregivers, we learn that emotions such as anxiety and shame signal the importance of inhibiting the destructive expression of activating emotions such as aggression. Anxiety and shame occur when children perceive that any expression of activating emotions is disapproved of by the caregiver, or fantasizes that their safety or security will be threatened if they express activating emotions such as aggression, sexual desire or joy. Defence mechanisms are used to manage the anxiety associated with the fears about expressing activating emotions, as well as allowing symbolic expression of the feeling.

Unfortunately, many defence mechanisms are fairly unsophisticated and lead not only to the exclusion of anxiety from consciousness, but to all vestiges of the activating emotion being excluded from consciousness as well. In such situations, not only is the destructive expression of the activating emotion inhibited, but also the adaptive expression of the activating emotion. This is problematic. When the adaptive expression of emotions such as anger, grief, attachment and positive feelings about the self are excluded from consciousness, people are left with 'missing capabilities' (Gustafson, 1986). Their capacities to assert themselves, let go of losses, form close relationships, explore the environment and nurture themselves are diminished.

Defence mechanisms

Defence mechanisms are ways of obtaining some degree of gratification by striking a compromise between, on the one hand, the experience and expression of forbidden feelings or activating emotions, such as anger or sexual desire, and, on the other hand, inhibiting the experience and expression of these emotions. Defence mechanisms are used when the client fears losing safety and security if feelings are experienced and expressed. The more primitive the defence mechanisms, the more likely it is that all aspects of the experience of this type of conflict will be unconscious.

A list of the main defence mechanisms is given in Table 4.2. The list is based on the defensive functioning scale in Appendix B of DSM-IV-TR (APA, 2000), which organizes defence mechanisms into seven levels depending on their degree of sophistication or maturity. At the highest or most adaptive level, defences regulate anxiety by allowing a balance to be achieved

Table 4.2 Defence mechanisms at different levels of maturity

Level	*Features of defences*	*Defence*	*The individual regulates anxiety (A) associated with conflicting wishes or prohibitive injunctions and adaptive feelings, impulses or perceived stresses (F) by . . .*
High adaptive level	Promote an optimal balance among unacceptable impulses and prosocial wishes to maximize gratification and permit conscious awareness of conflicting impulses and wishes	**Anticipation**	Considering emotional reactions and consequences of these before the conflict or stress occurs and exploring the pros and cons of various solutions to these problematic emotional states
		Affiliation	Seeking social support from others, sharing problems with them without making them responsible for them or for relieving the distress they entail
		Altruism	Dedication to meeting the needs of others and receiving gratification from this (without excessive self-sacrificing)
		Humour	Reframing the situation which gives rise to conflict or stress in an ironic or amusing way
		Self-assertion	Expressing conflict-related thoughts or feelings in a direct yet non-coercive way
		Self-observation	Monitoring how situations lead to conflict or stress and using this new understanding to modify negative affect

Continued overleaf

Table 4.2 Continued

Level	*Features of defences*	*Defence*	*The individual regulates anxiety (A) associated with conflicting wishes or prohibitive injunctions and adaptive feelings, impulses or perceived stresses (F) by . . .*
		Sublimation	Channelling negative emotions arising from conflict or stress into socially acceptable activities such as work or sports
		Suppression	Intentionally avoiding thinking about conflict or stress
Mental inhibitions	Keep unacceptable impulses, out of awareness	**Displacement**	Transferring negative feelings about one person onto another less threatening person
Compromise formation level		**Dissociation**	Experiencing a breakdown in the integrated functions of consciousness, memory, perception, or motor behaviour
		Intellectualization	The excessive use of abstract thinking or generalizations to minimize disturbing feelings arising from conflict
		Isolation of affect	Losing touch with the feelings associated with descriptive details of the conflict, trauma or stress
		Reaction formation	Substituting acceptable behaviours, thoughts or feelings which are the opposite of unacceptable or unwanted behaviours, thoughts or feelings that arise from a conflict
		Repression	Expelling unwanted thoughts, emotions or wishes from awareness

		Undoing	Using ritualistic or magical words or behaviour to symbolically negate or make amends for unacceptable impulses
Minor image distorting level	Distort image of self and others to regulate self-esteem	**Devaluation**	Attributing exaggerated negative characteristic to the self or others
		Idealization	Attributing exaggerated positive characteristics, to others
		Omnipotence	Attributing exaggerated positive characteristics or special abilities and powers to the self which make oneself superior to others
Disavowal level	Keep unacceptable impulses and ideas out of consciousness with or without misattribution of these to external causes	**Denial**	Refusing to acknowledge the painful features of the situation or experiences which are apparent to others
		Projection	Attributing to others one's own unacceptable thoughts, feelings and wishes
		Rationalization	Providing an elaborate self-serving or self-justifying explanation to conceal unacceptable thoughts, actions or impulses
Major image distorting level	Gross distortion or misattribution of aspects of the self or others	**Autistic fantasy**	Engaging in excessive daydreaming or wishful thinking as a substitute for using problem solving or social support to deal with emotional distress

Continued overleaf

Table 4.2 Continued

Level	*Features of defences*	*Defence*	*The individual regulates anxiety (A) associated with conflicting wishes or prohibitive injunctions and adaptive feelings, impulses or perceived stresses (F) by . . .*
		Projective identification	Attributing to others one's own unacceptable aggressive impulses. Then inducing others to feel these by reacting aggressively to them. Then using the other person's aggressive reactions as justification for acting out unacceptable aggressive impulses
		Splitting of self-image or image of others	Failing to integrate the positive and negative qualities of self and others and viewing self and others as either all good or all bad
Action level	Action or withdrawal from action	**Acting out**	Acting unacceptably to give expression to the experience of emotional distress associated with conflict or stress
		Apathetic withdrawal	Not engaging with others
		Help-rejecting complaining	Making repeated requests for help and then rejecting help when offered as a way of expressing unacceptable aggressive impulses
		Passive aggression	Unassertively expressing unacceptable aggression towards others in authority by overtly complying with their wishes while covertly resisting these

Level of defensive dysregulation	Failure of defences to regulate conflict related feelings leading to a breakdown in reality testing	**Delusional projection**	Attributing to others one's own unacceptable thoughts, feelings and wishes to an extreme degree
		Psychotic denial	Refusing to acknowledge the painful features of the situation or experiences which are apparent to others to an extreme degree
		Psychotic distortion	Viewing reality in an extremely distorted way

Based on American Psychiatric Association (2000). *Diagnostic and Statistical Manual of the Mental Disorders* (Fourth Edition-Text Revision, DSM-IV-TR, Defensive Functioning Scale, pp. 807–813), Washington, DC: APA.

between forbidden feelings or impulses and prosocial aspirations. This balance maximizes the possibilities of gratification. Also, while the balance is being achieved, the conflicting impulses and wishes are held in consciousness. Anticipation, affiliation, altruism, humour, self-assertion, self-observation, sublimation and suppression are adaptive defences. At the second level, the level of mental inhibitions or compromise formation, defences regulate anxiety by keeping forbidden feelings or impulses out of consciousness. Of these, repression is the prototypical defence. Other defences at this level include displacement, dissociation, intellectualization, isolation of affect, reaction formation, and undoing. Minor image distortion of the self or others, through devaluation, idealization or omnipotence occurs at the next level. Defences at this level regulate anxiety and self-esteem by enhancing or exaggerating positive aspects of the image of the self and one's allies and exaggerating negative attributes of others. This self-inflation, promotion of allies and demotion of foes is typical of the narcissistic personality and thus these defences are referred to as narcissistic defences. At the next level, anxiety associated with conflict between forbidden feelings or impulses and prosocial standards is regulated by disavowal through denial, projection or rationalization. Major image distortion to regulate anxiety associated with conflict occurs at the next level with consequent occasional cognitive slippage or loss of touch with reality. Splitting is the prototypical defence at this level. Here anxiety is regulated by demonizing some people, seeing them as 'all bad' and directing all unacceptable aggressive impulses towards them. Concurrently a subset of people is idealized, seen as 'all good' and all positive feeling projected onto them. This more extreme self-aggrandisement, idealization of allies and demonization of foes is typical of the border-line personality and thus these defences are referred to as border-line defences. At the action level, conflict-related anxiety is regulated by expressing it through behaviour, for example, aggressive or promiscuous sexual behaviour, or social withdrawal. Where there is a failure to regulate anxiety associated with conflict, the person may struggle to do so by breaking contact with reality and engaging in psychotic denial, distortion or delusional projection.

When learning BPT, it is important to keep in mind that defence mechanisms often involve the expression of strong emotions, in addition to masking activation emotions. For example, where one partner in a marriage experiences anxiety about having their attachment needs met and anxiety about expressing these needs, the anxiety may be regulated using the defence of denial, which can take the form of extreme rage at one's partner. In terms of the triangle of conflict in Figure 4.1, in these situations, the need for attachment is the forbidden feeling (F). The main anxiety is that expressing these needs will lead to rejection (A). The defence expressed as raging anger is denial (D) of the person's attachment to his or her partner. In emotion-focused couples therapy, the primary intervention is helping couples recognize and express their attachment needs. Rather than using rage as a defence to regulate anxiety about being rejected if attachment needs are expressed, the couple is encouraged to give up the defence, bear the fear of rejection, and express their need for attachment (Greenberg, 2002). Emotion-focused couples therapy is an evidenced-based therapeutic approach that shares some commonalities with BPT.

All defences entail primary and secondary gains. Primary gains are avoidance of the forbidden feeling including anger, grief, sexual desire and so forth. Secondary gains are positive spin-offs from using the defence and/or developing symptoms associated with using the defence. Common secondary gains are freedom from the responsibilities of asserting rights, replacing losses, facing personal challenges, managing interpersonal conflict and so forth. The more primitive a defence mechanism, the more likely it is that the defence and the hidden feeling will be unconscious and relatively inaccessible to conscious introspection. Also, the more primitive a defence the more likely it is that the repressed emotion will find expression elsewhere in the person's life. Malan (1995) refers to this as 'the return of the repressed'. That is, the forbidden feeling 'leaks' back into the person's life and often brings significant secondary gain. In the case of Michael, the primary gain from his use of reaction formation was avoidance of conflict with authority figures. The secondary gain from the symptoms was that it gave him a legitimate indirect way to express his opposition to the plans others had for him without having to assert himself directly or confront others. Thus, his chest pains were a nuisance for his school principal who had to reschedule the meeting. They reduced the chances of him leaving the football club committee because his close supporters would not want him to feel left out at a time when he was clearly vulnerable. They offered the possibility of avoiding Christmas dinner at his in-laws, since they might recur during his drive home on Christmas Day.

Over the lifespan, defences follow a developmental trajectory from the less sophisticated to the more sophisticated (Cramer, 1991). In a fifty-year longitudinal study of three large cohorts, Vaillant (2000) found that the use of adaptive or mature defences in early adulthood was predictive of midlife psychosocial functioning, social support, subjective well-being, marital satisfaction and income. The use of adaptive defences was also associated with less disability in middle life and greater resilience against developing depression in the face of multiple life stresses. The Defence Mechanism Rating Scales (Perry & Kardos, 1995) is the best available method for objectively rating defences from tapes or transcripts and the DSM-IV-TR defensive functioning scale in Table 4.2. is based on these. Strictly speaking, defences cannot be measured by self-report instruments because defences operate out of awareness. However, attempts have been made to measure conscious derivatives of unconscious defence mechanisms using self-report inventories such as the Defence Style Questionnaire (Bond & Wesley, 1996).

ASSESSMENT AND FORMULATION

The aim of assessment and formulation in BPT is to determine how the client's problems can be mapped out in terms of the triangle of defence and the triangle of person set out in Figure 4.1 and if the client is suitable for BPT.

Assessment interview

Prior to the assessment interview it is helpful to use a questionnaire, such as McCullough's (2003) Psychotherapy Assessment Checklist, to collect factual information on the client's presenting problems, current symptoms, current levels of stress and support, current level of functioning and past history. Using a pre-interview questionnaire reduces the need to use the interview for extensive fact-finding and detailed history taking. Thus the interview can be used for an in-depth exploration of episodes of the presenting problems, the identification of a core conflict as a focus for therapy and the formulation of the core conflict in terms of the triangles of conflict and person set out in Figure 4.1.

At the opening of the intake interview, it is essential to establish a contract for assessment. Assessment for BPT can take between one and three hours and may involve one long session or one to three shorter sessions. Explain to clients that the aim of the assessment process is to develop a shared understanding of their difficulties, determine if they have the sorts of difficulties that can benefit from BPT, and if so agree on a schedule of treatment sessions.

In the intake interview it is useful initially to ask the client to identify their main problems, to rate these on scales of 1 to 10 in terms of importance and then to give some very specific examples of the main problems. If clients give very general answers, it is important to request specific examples, because valid formulations can only be based on detailed accounts of specific incidents of significant problems. Here are some useful questions to elicit specific accounts of significant problems:

- 'What are the main difficulties or problems in your life at present?'
- 'Right now, on a scale of 1 to 10, how big a problem is each of these for you?'
- 'If you were to rank order your top three problems, which would be the one you most want help with now?'
- 'Can you tell me about the last time that problem happened?'
- 'How did it start and what exactly happened?'
- 'How were you feeling and how do you think the other person was feeling during this incident?'
- 'What was the hardest thing for you about this incident?'
- 'After the incident in what ways were you worse off and in what ways were you better off?'
- 'Can you tell me about another specific example of that sort of problem?'

When listening to the answers to these questions, do so with the triangle of conflict in mind, asking yourself questions about the forbidden feeling (F), the inhibitory anxiety (A) and the defence (D) being used.

First ask yourself, 'If the client were to express an adaptive activating emotion in this situation that showed compassion for both self and others or helped them deal with a loss or a boundary violation, what would the activating emotion be? Which of the emotions in Table 4.1 would it be?' The most common are anger, grief, attachment and positive feelings towards the self. Other possibilities are sexual desire, joy, excitement and interest.

A second question to ask yourself is, 'Assuming that the client is feeling anxiety, shame or guilt (inhibitory emotions) because of the danger of expressing an activating emotion, what must he or she be saying to him- or herself?' The answer to this question will take the form of a statement like this: 'I'm scared, ashamed or guilty of expressing X, because if I do, then Y will happen and that will mean something bad about myself or others or my relationships'. Common anxieties about expressing forbidden feelings are given in the right-hand column of Table 4.1.

The third question to ask yourself is, 'What is the client thinking, doing or feeling to manage his or her anxiety about expressing these forbidden feelings or to keep these forbidden feelings out of consciousness? Is the client using a defence listed in Table 4.2?'

The outcome of these three reflexive questions is a preliminary formulation in terms of the triangle of conflict, which takes the form: 'In this type of situation the client uses this defence (D), because they experience this anxiety (A), about this forbidden feeling (F)'.

With that preliminary D-A-F formulation in mind, proceed to ask the client about a few more specific similar episodes in different areas of their lives such as family, work and leisure contexts. Also ask about situations involving different symptoms or problems. Use the client's responses to these questions to gradually refine the D-A-F formulation based on the triangle of conflict. For Michael, three specific situations were identified in which chest pains occurred: one involving his school principal at work, one involving his father-in-law within a family context and one involving the chairman of the football club committee. He also recounted incidents in which he felt particularly anxious and depressed, which he identified as his other two main problems. These problems seemed to occur not in further episodes of interaction with others, but when he was reflecting on the three situations in which he experienced the chest pain. In Michael's case the D-A-F triangle of conflict formulation was that he used reaction formation as a defence (D) to regulate anxiety (A) about expressing the forbidden feeling of anger (F).

By asking for a series of situations in which the client's problems occurred and formulating these in terms of the triangle of conflict, the D-A-F formulation is refined. Hypotheses emerge about significant people in the client's life who occupy the C and P poles in the triangle of person. With Michael, it became clear that his school principal, his father-in-law and club chairman all occupied the C pole of the triangle of person. It seemed that Michael perceived all three as authority figures.

Once people who occupy the C pole of the triangle of person have been identified, the next step is to make a hypothesis, based on what they hold in common, about the types of people in the client's childhood who might have engaged in similar types of episodes with the client and enquire about these. For example, Michael was asked to describe situations from his childhood in which parents and teachers or coaches whom he saw as having authority over him expressed wishes about how he should manage challenging situations, and how he reacted in these situations. He described many situations in which he perceived their expressed wishes to be commands with which he felt compelled to co-operatively comply, despite the personal costs of this.

With examples of how the triangle of conflict has been played out at the C and P poles of the triangle of person, it is then possible to make hypotheses about how this core conflict will find expression within the therapeutic relationship at the T pole of the triangle of person. For Michael, the hypothesis was that if he engaged in therapy, it was probable that his transference reactions would involve reaction formation. That is, it was expected that when anger at the therapist was provoked by challenge or disappointment, he would behave in a very co-operative way rather than assertively expressing his anger towards the therapist. In fact this hypothesis was supported by Michael's reaction to the therapist's statement about rescheduling appointments mentioned earlier in the section on desensitization to affect phobias.

Once the core conflict has been formulated in terms of the triangles of conflict and person outlined in Figure 4.1, specific hypotheses may be made about the specific affect phobias to which the client needs to be desensitized. In Michael's case the hypothesis was that he was fearfully avoidant of expressing anger in an assertive way to authority figures. He needed to be exposed to increasingly stronger feelings of anger associated with such situations, while being prevented from using reaction formation to escape from the anxiety associated with experiencing these forbidden feelings.

At the end of the assessment phase the formulation is presented in terms of the triangles of conflict and person to the client. In offering the formulation, the elements should be presented from the least anxiety provoking to the most anxiety provoking. Tentative rather than definite language should be used throughout the process to minimize threat to the client and to allow scope for refinement based on feedback. In presenting the formulation, the specific examples, situations or episodes on which the general formulation is based are specified first. The sense of anxiety (A) or being ill at ease is presented second and the defence (D) used to manage this anxiety is interpreted third. The fourth and most anxiety-provoking aspect of the interpretation, the forbidden feeling (F) or impulse, is offered next in tentative language. Finally, links may be made within the triangle of person to the way this D-A-F pattern in the present (C) is replicating similar patterns learned in childhood through interacting with parents and caregivers (P). Here is how a formulation was presented to Michael, whose case vignette opened this chapter: For clarity, this interpretation is given here as a single paragraph, but it was spread over the second half-hour of the second assessment session and Michael responded to each aspect of the interpretation in detail.

'It seems that there is a recurring theme in the three episodes you have described. In all of them you noticed that the chest pain occurred after you had had a conversation in which you felt a bit ill at ease: the conversations with your school principal about the presentation, with your father-in-law about Christmas dinner and with the chairman of the committee about possibly stepping down (C). None of these was easy (A). Does that fit for you? . . . In all three of these conversations, you spoke in a very agreeable and co-operative way (D) with each of these people, and to some degree that made you feel a little less ill-at-ease? Is that accurate? . . . Now, this is speculation on my part, but another common thread in all of these situations is that you felt as if you were being asked to do something that for one reason or another was a bit difficult, put you out a bit or was not what you wanted to do. With your school principal, he wanted you to work through the weekend and produce a presentation for Monday morning. With your father-in-law, he wanted you to change your plans for Christmas Day. And the chairman at the football club wanted you to step down from a committee you enjoy contributing to. Does that fit with your view of the situation? . . . There is a possibility that in each instance you may have felt some irritation or anger with these three men for asking you to do things that may feel to you a bit unfair (F). I need to check that possibility with you . . . There is one further thing, I need to check with you. It may be that you felt unable to express your views about the unfairness of their requests or wishes because you have learned in the course of your life as you were growing up at home with your parents (P) that good men support those older or wiser or with greater authority than themselves? . . . So if we put these parts together . . . I'm wondering if you sense there may be links here between the chest pain, the agreeable way you spoke (D) to the three people (C) in the situations you described, your possible irritation or anger towards them (F) for their unfair requests and, your beliefs about not questioning the wishes of these sorts of people (A) that you learned as a youngster (P)?'

Overall, Michael accepted the formulation, but did, understandably, show resistance to accepting the degree of anger he felt towards authority figures, an issue that later became central to the therapy. The fact that he responded to the interpretation so well suggested that he was a suitable candidate for BPT.

Developing a psychodynamic formulation and offering it to clients in such a way that it is at least partially accepted is fraught with pitfalls. One problem is offering an inaccurate formulation that does not fit with the client's experience. To overcome this, always present interpretations very tentatively and check the degree to which the client can accept it. A second difficulty is interpreting the forbidden feeling (F) before interpreting the anxiety (A) and the defence (D), causing the client to intensify his or her defences. This is the most common mistake in the general category of 'interpreting too much to soon' and not pacing the process to match the client's readiness for insight. If this happens, shift the focus to an exploration of the client's experience of anxiety and the defences used to regulate it and then interpret the anxiety and the defence within the therapeutic relationship (T). That is, work towards making a transference interpretation. Here is an example:

'I noticed just now that when I suggested that your willingness to co-operate with people in authority (D) even when you perceived them making unfair demands on you might be your way of managing your fear (A) of expressing anger (F) towards them, this idea led you to give me a detailed account of a book you had read on the psychology of teamwork. You then said that this book said co-operation, not competition, was the key to good teamwork. I'm wondering if you could describe to me what the hardest thing was about listening to me suggesting the link between your co-operation with your school principal, and possible anger . . . Could there be a link between me asking you to consider a very difficult interpretation to accept and you responding with a helpful account of a book on teamwork? . . . It seems to be the same pattern as happened with your school principal. We both asked you to do something quite demanding and your response in each instance was a very high level of co-operation (D). Can we explore what the concerns (A) and feelings (F) might be that lead you to this level of co-operation?'

Assessing suitability for BPT

Clients particularly well suited to psychodynamic psychotherapy have some or all of the characteristics listed in Table 4.3 (Aveline, 1995; McCullough et al., 2003; Piper, et al., 2002). First, they experience sufficient psychological distress to be motivated to seek therapy and to commit to a therapeutic contract. Usually, people who have been 'sent' to therapy by a third party and have not actively sought out therapy themselves are insufficiently motivated to engage in and benefit from BPT. On this criterion, Michael was suited to therapy, having made an appointment himself at an outpatient clinic.

Second, those suited for BPT have the capacity to form a therapeutic alliance. This is typically evidenced by a history of having made and maintained at least one meaningful longstanding relationship in their lives. Piper et al. (2002) have developed a five-point quality of object relations scale for rating the capacity to make and maintain relationships based on clients' accounts of their relationships in childhood, adolescence and adulthood. (In the psychoanalytic tradition, 'object' is the term that has been used to refer to significant other people with whom we have relationships, notable caregivers or parents or key people in our adult networks.) Piper distinguishes between mature, triangular, controlling, searching, and primitive levels of object relations. At the mature level, the person engages in equitable relationships characterized by love, kindness and concern for others. At the

Table 4.3 Suitability criteria for brief psychodynamic therapy

Sufficient distress to be motivated
Capacity to form a therapeutic alliance – history of at least one good relationship
Psychologically minded – responds to trial interpretation
Capacity to tolerate strong affect without acting impulsively
Courage to explore more adaptive ways of managing conflict
Stable life situation and some social support
Clear focus for therapy stated as triangles of defence and person
GAF score above 50
To determine GAF score inquire about these areas in the past six months
Symptoms (depression, anxiety, anger control, somatic complaints etc.)
Social functioning (family, intimate relationships, peer relationships in leisure activities)
Educational or occupational functioning (at college or work)

100	**No symptoms** and superior social and occupational/educational functioning
90	**Minimal symptoms** (e.g. exam anxiety or occasional family conflict) and good social and occupational/educational functioning
80	**Transient symptoms** (e.g. concentration difficulties after a family argument) leading to slight impairment in social or occupational/educational functioning (e.g. temporary underfunctioning at work or school)
70	**Mild symptoms** (e.g. low mood and insomnia) **or mild impairment** in social or occupational/educational functioning (e.g. truancy, minor thefts) but can make and maintain relationships
60	**Moderate symptoms** (e.g. panic attacks, flat affect and circumstantial speech) **or moderate impairment** in social and occupational/educational functioning (e.g. few friends, conflict with people at work or school)
50	**Serious symptoms** (e.g. suicidal ideation, severe obsessional rituals, frequent shoplifting) or **serious impairment** in social or occupational/educational functioning (e.g. no friends, unable to keep a job)
40	**Some impairment in reality testing** or communication (e.g. speech at times illogical, obscure or irrelevant) or **major impairment in several areas**, such as work, school, family, judgement, thinking, mood (e.g. depressed man who avoids friends, neglects family and is unable to work)
30	Behaviour is considerably influenced by delusions or hallucinations or shows serious impairment in communication or judgement or inability to function in almost all areas
20	Some danger of hurting self or others or occasionally fails to maintain minimal personal hygiene or gross impairment in communication
10	Persistent danger of severely hurting self or others or persistent inability to maintain minimal personal hygiene or serious suicidal act with clear expectation of death

Based on McCullough, L., Kuhn, N., Andrews, S., Kaplan, A., Wolf, J., & Hurley, C. (2003). *Treating affect phobia: A manual for short-term dynamic psychotherapy*. New York: Guilford. Aveline, M. (1995). How I assess for focal therapy. In C. Mace (Ed), *The art and science of assessment in psychotherapy* (pp. 137–154). London: Routledge. Piper, W., Joyce, A., McCallum, M., Azim, H. & Ogrodniczuk, J. (2002). *Interpretive and supportive psychotherapies. Matching therapy and personality*. Washington, DC: American Psychological Association. American Psychiatric Association (2000). *Diagnostic and Statistical Manual of the Mental Disorders* (Fourth Edition-Text Revision, DSM-IV-TR, Global Assessment of Functioning Scale, p. 34), Washington, DC: APA.

triangular level, the person engages in real or fantasized triangular relationships marked by competition to win the affection of one person by gaining victory over another person. Michael was functioning at the mature level in his relationship with his wife but at the triangular level in his relationship with his father, the school principal and with the chairman of the club. At the controlling level, relationships are marked by well-meaning attempts to control or possess others. At the searching level, the person is constantly driven by an attempt to find a substitute for a lost caregiver, but the relief provided by substitutes inevitably give way to disillusionment and the re-experience of loss. At the primitive level the person becomes highly dependent on others and reacts with intense anxiety and anger to actual or potential disapproval, separation, or loss. The five levels of the quality of object relations partially correspond to attachment styles (Cassidy & Shaver, 1999). The mature level corresponds to a secure attachment style where there are positive internal working models of the self and others. The primitive level corresponds to a preoccupied attachment style where working models of the self and other are both negative. Piper et al. (2002) have shown in a series of studies that higher scores on this scale are associated with a better response to therapy.

The third characteristic of clients suitable for psychodynamic therapy is that they are psychologically minded. Piper et al. (2002) have shown a clear relationship between psychological-mindedness and outcome in psychodynamic therapy. Psychologically minded clients are willing to explore how personal difficulties may arise when particular defence mechanisms are used to deal with conflict between their impulses to act in certain ways and their aspirations to conform to societal norms. Psychologically minded people are also willing to explore how their characteristic ways of making and maintaining relationships have evolved over their life and how these relationship styles subserve their personal distress. One way to assess this psychological-mindedness is by offering a trial interpretation using the formulation involving the triangles of conflict and person set out in Figure 4.1. In the previous section, an example was given of how a trial interpretation was offered to Michael. His response to this trial interpretation was positive: he thought about if for a while, identified with some aspects of it and was willing to discuss it further. This underlined his suitability for therapy. Had he insisted that his chest pains were evidence of an undetected cardiac problem, and refused to consider a psychodynamic formulation, he would have been judged unsuitable for BPT.

The fourth characteristic of clients suitable for psychodynamic therapy is that they have the capacity to tolerate strong affect associated with interpersonal conflict without acting impulsively, and to explore this when it is enacted within the therapeutic relationship. A willingness to experience some degree of sadness, anger, anxiety or joy, often as part of recounting an intense emotional event, is good evidence for having met this criterion. Where emotional conflict has led to violence, self-harm or serious drug or alcohol abuse, this suggests the client has limited ability to tolerate strong conflict-related affect.

A fifth suitability criterion is having the courage to explore more adaptive ways of managing intrapsychic conflicts and interpersonal challenges. Where clients make it clear that they are ready to start changing the way they manage their feelings, their relationships, or their lives, this criterion is met.

A sixth criterion is the presence of a relatively stable life situation and some degree of social support. Socially isolated individuals with multiple life stresses and no stable job or home situation would not meet this criterion.

Finally, for time-limited therapy clients must be able to collaborate in establishing a clear focus for therapy. This is shown by a willingness to work collaboratively to develop a preliminary formulation based on the conceptual framework in Figure 4.1.

The DSM-IV-TR (APA, 2000) Global Assessment of Functioning (GAF) scale is useful in determining suitability for treatment. Clients with GAF scores above 50 are usually suitable for short-term psychodynamic psychotherapy (McCullough et al., 2003).

Clients with schizophrenia or other psychoses; severe drug dependence; suicidal intent; severe anger management problems; border-line, anti-social or narcissistic personality disorders; and moderate or severe intellectual disability are unsuitable for BPT. Clients with mood and anxiety disorders, somatoform disorders, and avoidant and dependant personality disorders have been shown in controlled trials to benefit from this approach to treatment (Crits-Cristoph, 1992; Piper et al., 2002; Ursano & Ursano, 2000).

TREATMENT

In BPT, the therapeutic contract has four key elements. First, a specified limited number of regular, frequent therapy sessions of fixed duration are scheduled. For example, these may be of fifty minutes duration and held once or twice a week at the same time in the same location and the session limit may vary from twelve to thirty sessions (three to six months). Second, clients agree that for the duration of therapy they will not make major life changes (such as moving countries or getting married), attempt suicide or contact the therapist outside agreed scheduled sessions. Third, the client is invited to report without censorship what comes into consciousness and not to 'edit out' apparently irrational or socially unacceptable thoughts, feelings, images, memories, dreams and fantasies that occur during the therapy sessions. Fourth, therapists adopt a style in which they convey to the client that they will listen attentively, offer interpretations and other interventions, but will not gratify the client's needs for personal information about the therapist or physical contact with the therapist.

The main BPT treatment strategies and techniques are listed in Table 4.4. They fall into three categories, in line with the main goals of BPT: to restructure defences, affects and self–other representations. As an overall guideline, therapy typically progresses from restructuring defences to affects. With very high-functioning clients, who obtain GAF scores between 70 and 80, it may be more efficient to begin with restructuring affect, since often the assessment process itself is sufficient to allow the client to want to relinquish defences. With low-functioning clients who obtain GAF scores close to 50, begin with self–other restructuring. Where people have border-line or narcissistic personality disorders, defence restructuring should be slowly paced

Table 4.4 Therapeutic goals, strategies and techniques in brief psychodynamic psychotherapy

Goals	*Strategies*	*Techniques*
Defence restructuring	**Defence recognition**	Pointing out defences against forbidden adaptive feelings
		Validating defences
		Pointing out existing exceptions to using defences
		Repeating pointing out defences until they are routinely recognized
	Defence relinquishing	Identifying costs and benefits and secondary gains of defences
		Tracing origins of defences and how they are now maintained
		Grieving losses due to defences
		Repeating relinquishing interventions to increase motivation to give up defences
Affect restructuring	**Affect experiencing**	Facilitating gradual exposure to the feared adaptive feelings and impulses
		Preventing use of old defences
		Repeating exposure and defence prevention until fear of forbidden feelings is desensitized
	Affect expression	Exploring new ways to express feared adaptive feelings *in vivo*
		Exploring ways to tolerate interpersonal conflict *in vivo*
		Repeating affect expression until new ways of expressing feared affect flow naturally
Self–other restructuring	**Self-restructuring**	Desensitization to positive feelings towards the self

	Facilitating viewing the self from the perspective of others
	Integrating positive and negative feelings towards the self
	Facilitating self-parenting
	Repeating self-restructuring interventions until positive self-feelings are no longer avoided and self-esteem improves
Other restructuring	Desensitization to nurturant feelings from others
	Empathy skills training to facilitate accurate and compassionate perception of others
	Integrating positive and negative views of others
	Identifying and restructuring 'addictive' attachments
	Repeating other-restructuring interventions until adaptive feelings within relationships are no longer avoided

Based on McCullough-Vaillant, L. (1997). *Changing character: Short-term anxiety regulating psychotherapy for restructuring defences, affects and attachments*. New York: Basic Books. McCullough, L., Kuhn, N., Andrews, S., Kaplan, A., Wolf, J., & Hurley, C. (2003). *Treating affect phobia: A manual for short-term dynamic psychotherapy*. New York: Guilford Press.

after self–other restructuring has occurred. However, these guidelines are not rigid and throughout the course of therapy interventions in all three categories are made.

Defence restructuring

The two main strategies for defence restructuring are defence recognition and relinquishment. The first aims to give the client insight into his or her defence. The second facilitates letting go of defences so that forbidden feelings may be experienced.

Defence recognition

With defence recognition, listen carefully to the client's uncensored account with the dynamic formulation developed during the assessment sessions in the back of your mind. Also hold in mind your hypothesis about the main forbidden feeling to which the client needs to be desensitized. When opportunities arise, tentatively point out where defences are used to manage anxiety associated with forbidden feelings. Explore with the client, or tentatively speculate out loud, what forbidden feeling (F) is being excluded from consciousness and why (A). In doing this, adopt an empathic collaborative position. Let the client know that you could understand why there might be a need to use the defence to keep certain feelings and ideas out of consciousness. Communicate that you are aware that the client may be experiencing guilt, shame or anxiety about forbidden feelings. In validating the client's defences, the aim is to help the client replace shame with self-compassion. It is essential to avoid pointing out defences in a way that clients will interpret as criticism, since this will compound the client's sense of shame, guilt and anxiety. Repeatedly point out defences until the client routinely recognizes when defences are used and reaches a position where defences are accepted as the best available way to cope with forbidden feelings at the time they were initially learned. But it is now time to find a better way. Here are some examples of defence recognition interventions:

- 'I noticed that when you talk about that painful time in your life, you speak without showing much feeling.'
- 'When you spoke of your mother's death, it looked like you were about to cry but you stopped yourself and quickly made a joke.'
- 'Just now you changed the subject before finishing your account of the argument with your husband. I'm wondering about that.'
- 'When you cry like this, it seems to make you feel worse rather than to bring relief. Is that the way it feels to you?'
- 'In that story, you portray yourself as a real villain and your sister as a paragon of virtue. Can you make sense of that?'
- 'It seems you criticized your brother but wanted to criticize someone else. Who might that have been?'

During defence identification, when opportunities arise, point out existing exceptions to using defences, and label these as strengths. For example:

- 'You say you have trouble with closeness, but Barry has been your friend since primary school.'
- 'You are down on yourself for so many things, so it's good today for you to tell me about your achievements.'

When clients resist acknowledging defences, invite them to do experiments that involve temporarily relinquishing their defences. For example, a client who does not accept that he uses avoidance of eye contact as a defence when talking about grief, may be invited as an experiment to describe what he feels when he sustains eye contact while talking about grief.

To summarize, the aim is to help clients recognize the defences they use, to wonder with the client about what is defended against and why, and to provide empathic support and validation to the client in this. An example of this with Michael follows:

Therapist: I notice that as you were telling me all the reasons why going to your in-laws for Christmas will be good for everyone in your family, your spoke very rapidly and seemed quite tense (D).

Michael: Yes, I suppose I do feel quite jumpy when I think about going.

Therapist: What's the hardest part about thinking of it?

Michael: I, just, well, being trapped there for the whole day [D]. (smiles wryly) Maybe I'm not so thrilled about going [F] . . . It's a bit of a nuisance, it's irritating.

Therapist: It seems like it is difficult for you to feel irritated [F] about having to go to your in-laws. I wonder if feeling irritated makes you feel very guilty [A]?

Michael: Well, it does a bit, I suppose. Yes, a lot really. I feel like I'm disappointing my wife's parents [C]. They love our kids and would love to see more of them, and Christmas is such a time for children that they really want to be part of it, on the day itself. They're really looking forward to it and I hate to be the one that stops it [A] happening just because I don't want to go [F]. It wouldn't be fair to them; they're old, they may not have many Christmases left with the kids, it would bring them a lot of happiness.

Therapist: It sounds to me very similar to other examples you've told me, where you expected yourself to put the needs of your 'elders', particularly your father and grandfather [P], above your own [D], something that was important in your family growing up.

Michael: Well, I suppose so. For instance, we always went to my mother's parents at Christmas time and my father didn't seem to mind. Although, now that I think of it, he never seemed to enjoy it much, he was a bit quiet and usually fell asleep for most of it. But yes, he still went, probably to show respect to his father-in-law, which I admire. I think I should be able to do that too. We were always encouraged as children to follow that example.

Therapist: You feel 'good' when you are pleasing your 'elders' [C and P] but it also sounds like you feel irritated and even angry [F] that you are so often sacrificing what you want. I wonder if feeling angry [F] makes you feel guilty and uncomfortable [A] so that it is easier to try to just please everyone [D]? Does that fit at all with how you feel about this Christmas issue?

Michael: Yes, a bit. I wouldn't say I feel angry, but irritated, yes. Yes, irritated [F]. It would be nice to spend Christmas in our own home, for once, cook what we want to eat, watch a film I want for

> a change. I'd probably be in better form too, for the kids. But it's really hard to ask for that without feeling selfish and mean.

Defence relinquishing

When clients are capable of routinely identifying their use of defences to regulate anxiety about experiencing or expressing forbidden feelings, the next step is to help them become motivated to let go of these defences, use them less frequently or use more adaptive defences. Begin by helping clients to identify the benefits and costs of defences. The primary gains for using any defences is avoidance of the forbidden feeling, for example grief or anger. The secondary gains are those positive outcomes associated with the defence and related symptoms, for example avoiding responsibilities and being cared for by others, avoiding unfamiliar life changes, avoiding closeness and achieving the safety of isolation. The main cost of using defences is that the adaptive function or capability associated with the forbidden affect is lost or compromised. So defences can prevent clients from asserting their rights when anger is inhibited, engaging in fulfilling sex when sexual desire is inhibited, maintaining supportive relationships when attachment is inhibited, nurturing the self when positive feelings towards the self are inhibited, facing personal challenges when excitement and joy are inhibited, and resolving and replacing losses when grief is inhibited.

Along with helping clients weigh up the costs and benefits of retaining and relinquishing defences, help them trace the origins of their defences in childhood and how they are now maintained in adulthood. Invite clients to describe situations involving their parents, siblings and carers in which they might have felt their safety and security would be threatened if they expressed their forbidden feelings, and help them to articulate how they began to use defences to inhibit the expression of these affects and impulses. Then invite them to explore how they continued to use these defences in adulthood with people other than their parents, siblings and carers.

After building self-compassion by tracing the origins of defences in childhood through to their maintenance in adulthood, and exploring costs and benefits of defences, some clients eventually arrive at a situation where they realize that their defences have cost them dearly. They recognize that there have been many missed opportunities in their lives where they could have acted assertively, or fulfilled their sexual needs or their needs for attachment, or felt positively about themselves or experienced joy or excitement or resolved their losses. Invite clients to grieve for these losses in therapy. All of these defence-relinquishing interventions need to be repeated to increase motivation to give up defences. However, letting go of defences is very anxiety provoking, so help clients to regulate this anxiety. For example, you may say, 'This way of handling, sadness/anger/closeness has had its downside but it has also stood you in good stead. You are thinking of handling these feelings in a different way now. So, I'm wondering what the most difficult thing about making this change is going to be?'

To summarize, the aim is to help clients increase their motivation to give up defences by helping them identify the pros and cons of defences, including primary and secondary gain; identify the origins and maintenance of defences; identify the maladaptive effects of using defences; grieve the losses associated with defence use; and identify and work towards using alternative adaptive behaviours or more mature defences. An example of this with Michael follows:

Therapist: When you think about trying to give up this pattern of saying nothing about what you want, what is the most difficult or overwhelming part of it for you?

Michael: Well, I don't know really, maybe, maybe asking and being told 'No', 'You shouldn't need that', or 'Who do you think you are? Why are you so special?' [A-rejection]

Therapist: It seems quite sad that you have learned to hide what you want so regularly from others. You've put others first for so long, it sounds like you don't often think about what you want or don't expect others to be interested in pleasing you or responding to what you need.

Michael: Yes, when you put it that way, it is sad. Lots of lost opportunities.

Therapist: Yes, maybe many times when you just suffered in silence you could have gotten so much more from situations.

Michael: Yes, I suppose so. I hadn't really thought about it, but yes, I think my wife would probably like to do things for me. She cares, but I don't often ask her for much. Hardly ever, really. And I can see how I've let people take advantage of me quite a bit, been the martyr a bit at work, not delegating enough, taking too much on and being a bit of a 'superman'. I think I do resent that more than I realized and it's wearing me out. But I'm not sure what else I can do . . .

Later in the session:

Therapist: And I wonder too about the panic attacks you've had recently. We've noticed that they happened when you wanted something but felt too guilty to ask and just went along. Can we talk about what was good and bad about those attacks?

Michael: Well, the downside was I felt awful, really unwell and scared, and a bit foolish too, in front of everyone.

Therapist: Yes, it sounded really unpleasant. I wonder if there was an upside too?

Michael: Well, I suppose in a sort of way, yes, in that people were very kind. I realized they cared quite a bit and they, well, they took some of the pressures off, stopped making so many demands on me.

Therapist: So while it was really unpleasant at the time and you felt foolish, it also helped you feel cared for and people backed off a little without you having to ask them to. Is that right?

Michael: Yes, I think so. Yes. There was a bit of an upside because I really don't like having to ask for things or having to say no to people.

Later in the session:

Therapist: I can see how guilty you feel about being irritated with your school principal when he asked you to co-ordinate the rosters for yard duty as well as meeting with those difficult parents after school. You seem really ashamed of feeling irritated. What is the most shameful piece about feeling irritated?

Michael: Well, I just feel so selfish, and small, and just, well, petty. They are small things to do for others, that I shouldn't feel annoyed. I shouldn't mind. I should just be able to do these things 'with a good grace' as my dad used to say. That was always the way it was in our house, you were never allowed to say no. If you could do a favour, well then you should do it and do it willingly.

Therapist: That's a tough standard to live up to, and a powerful message to get from your parents. No wonder it is so important to you now. But I wonder if it is a rule that you want to continue to live by, as an adult, or something you want to be more flexible with?

Michael: When you put it that way, well, I've never thought about it that way before. I just thought that was how everyone lives, although, no, they don't really, because most people aren't nearly as considerate or helpful as I try to be, which again, I think I resent. Probably other people aren't so bothered by feeling resentful and put upon too, they probably don't feel as irritated as often because they're not constantly trying to keep everyone happy. It would be nice not to always have to please everyone.

Affect restructuring

The two main strategies for affect restructuring are affect experiencing and expression. The first aims to desensitize the client to his or her forbidden feeling and the second facilitates the development of adaptive ways to express these feelings.

Affect experiencing

With affect experiencing, the aim is to help clients move in graded steps towards fully experiencing their forbidden feelings (F), without experiencing the punishing emotions of shame, guilt and anxiety (A), and without using their defences (D). Affect experiencing is a process of imaginal systematic desensitization. First, brief clients about the rationale and procedures for affect experiencing. Explain that to be able to use their feelings fully to help them live happier lives, they have to fully experience the feelings they habitually try to avoid. To do this, they will be invited to select a few situations in which they might have such feelings. Then in a relaxed state with their eyes closed, they will be asked to imagine themselves in these situations experiencing their forbidden feelings and tolerating the distress associated with this until it passes, and that this process will be repeated until the forbidden feelings no longer make them feel distressed. Agree on a series of interaction scenarios that they will use for the desensitization procedure. Then invite the client to relax, bring to mind in vivid detail an image of an agreed interaction with parents, siblings or carers from their past (P) or an interaction with significant people from their current life situation (C). The interaction must evoke the forbidden feeling. Ask the client to describe the interaction in detail and their experience of the forbidden feeling (F). Specifically ask them first to name the feeling. Clients often confuse feelings such as boredom and sadness, or anger and excitement. Then ask them to describe how the feeling is experienced physiologically in their body. Do they feel aroused, relaxed, ready for action or quiet and still? Then ask about the images that accompany the feeling. Encourage clients to describe in vivid detail what the feeling would make them want to do if they allowed it to guide their actions. For example, do they have images of standing up for their rights, or moving closer to someone, or crying to feel relief? As the anxiety, shame and guilt (A) concurrently arise, invite the client not to use their usual defences and to try to tolerate the anxiety by describing in detail the fear, shame or sense of guilt associated with experiencing the forbidden feeling. Help the client regulate anxiety by asking, 'What is the most difficult/frightening/humiliating thing about experiencing this feeling of rage/sexual desire/closeness/grief/joy/self-caring/excitement?' Some of the common anxieties that clients feel when they allow themselves to experience forbidden feelings are listed in the right-hand column of Table 4.1. Contain the clients' discomfort by letting them know that if they can stay with the forbidden feeling long enough, the anxiety, shame and guilt will pass. Empathize with their distress. This aspect of the process is very demanding, because it requires you to be able to tolerate high levels of intense negative affect, something that is easier to do if you have been through uncovering therapy yourself. Once clients have reduced their anxiety to the imagined scenario, invite them immediately to either imagine it again and allow them to experience the feelings more intensely or move on to another scenario which has the potential to more strongly evoke the forbidden feeling.

To intensify exposure to feelings, reflect back clients' statements about their feelings, and statements about the bodily sensations associated with these. For example, if a client says, 'When I see her like this I feel so sad, I feel the tears welling up inside me', this may be reflected back as, 'You feel so sad and the tears are welling up inside you'. Further intensify feelings by inviting clients to elaborate details of images associated with the forbidden feelings by asking questions such as, 'Can you describe exactly what you can see right now? Can you smell the smoke from your mother's cigarette? Notice the colour of the carpet and wallpaper?' Encourage clients to imagine the most extreme acts that their forbidden feelings might lead them to. Balint (1968) referred to the process of having these extreme fantasies based on forbidden feelings as regression in the service of the ego. They might include sadistic anger, promiscuous sex or infantile dependency. Tolerating experiencing these extreme forbidden feelings reduces the need to act out, and in this sense the regressive fantasies are in the service of the ego. It is important to reassure clients that it is acceptable to experience these imaginary outcomes of their adaptive emotions, which are distinct from actual courses of action they might take in real life. Invite clients describing scenarios from the past to say things that they would have said if they had been allowed to express their forbidden feelings. For example, 'If you had allowed yourself to feel these feelings back then, what would you have liked to say to your mother? . . . Can you tell her that now in your fantasy and see how it feels? . . . Now tell her again and notice the feeling.' Some clients find it helpful to imagine the person from their past sitting in an empty chair opposite them and then to conduct a dialogue with them. This practice, widely used by Gestalt therapists, is known as the empty-chair or two-chair technique.

The process of affect experiencing does not always run smoothly. A common error is to mistake an emotion used as a defence for a forbidden feeling. For example, tearful self-hating, victimized sadness used as a defence (D) to regulate anxiety (A) about expressing aggression (F) may be mistaken for the adaptive emotion of grief. Where clients are helped to intensify their experiencing of these defensive emotions, it inadvertently strengthens their defences and cuts them off even more from their forbidden feelings! However, this mistake can be spotted. If clients experience their emotions in their body and in their images as closing down the possibility of the adaptive actions listed in the third column of Table 4.1, then it is best to assume that the emotion is a defence (D) rather than a forbidden feeling (F). Another difficulty is that clients may misinterpret the invitation to experience and tolerate strong forbidden feelings as a licence to get their feelings out by shouting or crying or acting-out their feelings by hurting themselves or other people or damaging property. In these situations, help the client to calm down. Then explain that the aim of therapy is to be able to manage the forbidden feelings by tolerating experiencing and then deciding how to use this experience to do something adaptive rather than destructive. The process of desensitization takes time. Affect experiencing has to be repeated frequently for each of the client's main forbidden feelings. For example, Michael would be invited and encouraged to recognize and tolerate his own feelings of anger towards his school principal, the committee chairperson, therapist and father, without defending by being overly co-operative, and with assistance from the therapist in managing his fears about the negative effects of experiencing anger.

To summarize, the aim is to help clients be exposed in imagination to the forbidden feelings (F), without responding with a defence (D), and to support clients in managing the associated anxiety (A) until it subsides. An example of this with Michael follows:

Therapist: We talked about looking at some feelings in more depth. Let's stay with that example you brought up of how you felt tense after the principal made those three demands on you. Even as you talked about it, you seemed tense. Can you describe how you felt about him giving you all those tasks when he knew you were so busy?

Michael: Well, I think he' s busy too, we all are, but even still, I felt a bit annoyed because he'd just dumped a lot of other things on me recently. The more I do, the more I get to do, so I suppose, yes, I feel annoyed.

Therapist: Where do you experience that annoyance in your body?

Michael: Hmm, I'll have to think about that. Kind of agitated, like I want to let out energy, go for a run. So probably in my legs, the urge to do something physical.

Therapist: All that annoyance that you're holding in, if you were to experience it, what do you imagine doing or saying?

Michael: I don't know. Maybe shout at him to make him see what he's putting on me! Or shake him.

Therapist: So you want to shout at him or shake him.

Michael: Yes, make him stop taking me for granted, pushing me around! Not that I would, really.

Therapist: It's really common to want to shake or shout at someone. We're talking about feelings, not behaviours, and imagining something is not the same as doing it. You look a bit uncertain and tense right now . . .

Michael: Well, I just felt that what I said was just so, angry. I didn't realize I felt so angry about this. It just felt a bit, well, much. It really sounds like I'm over-reacting completely. I should just get on with the job.

Therapist: Yet that is what you normally try to do, to dismiss the anger and so you get a bit stuck. The process of sitting with this anger for a while may actually help you move on from it and give you back the energy you normally spend trying not to be angry.

Michael: Well, yes, it is exhausting trying to be so nice all the time. So you think we should keep at this?

Therapist: If you're ready, let's look at that annoyed feeling a bit more.

Affect expression

With affect expression, the aim is to facilitate clients' exploring adaptive ways to express forbidden feelings and to explore ways to tolerate interpersonal conflict in real-life (*in vivo*) situations rather than in imagination. Affect expression aims to help clients express anger as assertion, express sexual desire within mutually satisfying sexual relationships, express the need for attachment by engaging in close, trusting relationships, express positive emotions towards self and joy without shame or guilt, pursue interests enthusiastically, and express grief in a way that resolves losses. For clients to be able to express their emotions and needs in these ways, they require skills. In addition to expressive skills they also need receptive skills so that they can respond appropriately to the emotional expression of others. First, assess the clients' skills for expressing emotions and responding to the emotions of others in those areas where they have had an affect phobia. Ask the clients what they would do in situations where they wished to express forbidden feelings (F) in an adaptive way and role-play such situations. If clients have limited skills for expressing emotions and understanding and responding to specific emotional responses of others, coach them in communication, problem-solving and assertion skills (described in Chapter 3 on CBT). Help clients anticipate situations in which they may experience interpersonal conflict and invite them to be prepared to tolerate emotional discomfort, such as fears about the consequences of expressing emotions in these situations. Then invite clients, for homework, to enter situations *in vivo* that elicit their forbidden feelings, to tolerate these and adaptively express them, and tolerate the interpersonal conflict that may arise from them. For example, Michael would be invited to imagine and later role-play with the therapist a situation where he would say to his father-in-law that he and his family would be having Christmas dinner in their own house and would come love to come to dinner on New Year's Day instead. He might be given a homework task of broaching this with his wife first and later his father-in-law.

Repeat affect expression interventions until new ways of expressing forbidden feelings flow naturally.

One of the pitfalls with affect restructuring is to move from affect experiencing to affect expression too rapidly, before the affect phobia has been sufficiently desensitized. In these circumstances clients go through the motions of expressing forbidden feelings in new and adaptive ways without actually letting themselves experience the emotions. If this occurs, invite the client to go back to further affect experiencing work and then desensitize the client to their affect phobia.

To summarize, the aim is to help clients practise in 'real life' situations expressing feelings without defending so that anxiety subsides. The therapist helps the client to express emotion and tolerate expressions of emotions by others, to deal with interpersonal conflict that may arise and to integrate affects for better emotional expression. The therapist trains the client in skills, such as assertiveness, as needed. An example of this with Michael follows:

Therapist: This Christmas Day invite to your in-laws that you don't want to accept, perhaps that could be a way for you to practice expressing your wishes assertively. Could we look at that here today?

Michael: Okay, although I can just imagine how hurt they will look if I said we weren't coming.

Therapist: So at first they'd be very upset.

Michael: Oh yes, very. Disappointed. I feel guilty just imagining saying it.

Therapist: Let's try to work on that situation right now so that it is not so hard to do in reality. Remember in the last few weeks we've looked at assertiveness skills? Let's look at a few ways you might be able to broach this with them and a few ways you might respond if they express disappointment. Do you remember we talked about blending positive and negative statements in a situation where there was conflict?

Michael: Yes, I tried that this week with my wife and it worked quite well. I still felt a bit nervous and a bit guilty, but she responded really well.

Therapist: Great. Let's see if you could come up with one now for broaching things with your in-laws.

Michael: Well, let's see, 'We really appreciate you asking us for Christmas Day and we enjoy spending time with you over the holiday period. We also enjoy being in our own place, especially when we are not working and the kids are off school. Christmas Day in particular, the kids like to be home so they can use all their new gifts, they're so excited with what they get. We'd love to come and spend time with you later in the week. Could we come over on New Year's Day, and maybe you'd like to come to us the day after Christmas?'

Therapist: So how are you feeling after that?

Michael: Not so bad.

Therapist: What was the hardest part of saying that?

Michael: I felt a bit tense, bit apprehensive about what reaction I'd get, but generally okay.

Therapist: Okay, so shall we have a go at a role-play next and work on how you respond to how they react?

Michael: Okay, I'll give it a go. But to make it real, you'll have to look really disappointed when I tell you I'm not coming, so that it's real practice for what it's going to be like for me!

Self–other restructuring

With self–other restructuring the aim is to help clients develop a more accurate perception of the self and others and to treat the self and others with greater compassion. High-functioning clients with GAF scores above 60 require little self–other restructuring. But lower-functioning clients, particularly those with personality disorders, GAF scores at 50 or below, low self-esteem, poor impulse control, and difficulties making and maintaining relationships, require self–other restructuring before defence or affect restructuring can be attempted. These clients hold inaccurate views of themselves and others that are distorted by an inability to tolerate positive feelings about themselves or positive feelings from others. This avoidance of positive feelings about the self and positive emotions from others must be overcome before engaging in the type of therapy described so far in this chapter.

Self-restructuring

The aim of self-restructuring is to help clients be receptive to their own positive feelings about themselves, to view the self from the perspective of others, to integrate positive and negative feelings towards the self, and to engage in self-parenting. Desensitizing clients to phobias about positive feelings towards the self is central to achieving these aims. In terms of the triangle of conflict, the defence (D) for these types of affect phobias is usually self-devaluation and finds expression in self-neglect, self-hate, self-attack and, in extreme cases, self-harm. These defences are used to regulate anxiety, shame, guilt, contempt, and disgust (A) concerning experiencing or expressing positive feelings about the self (F) including self-compassion, self-esteem, self-respect, self-confidence and self-interest.

To elicit positive feelings about the self, invite clients to recount how they have been abused, neglected and hurt during their life. After each of these stories ask them, 'How do you think I feel after hearing that story about how you were hurt/let down/betrayed?' To this, clients may indicate that they believe you feel sad, concerned, sympathetic, and so forth. Confirm this and invite the client to explore their own feelings of compassion for themselves. For example, 'Yes, I feel really concerned that when you were a little girl you were hurt so badly. I'm wondering, if you can allow yourself to experience the same sort of feelings for this little girl?'

Typically, clients find these feelings inhibited by their self-devaluing defences and anxiety, shame and disgust. To help clients regulate these emotions, ask them questions such as, 'What is the hardest thing about feeling compassion for this hurt little girl?' A common response is for clients to say that they believe it is selfish to care for themselves. In response, point out that it is possible to care about a number of people (including the self) at the same time and that the care we show to others is enhanced if we are able also to care for ourselves. A second common response is for clients to say that they could not stand the pain it would bring to care for themselves. The implication is that if clients allow themselves to feel compassion for themselves, or joy now, they open themselves up to experiencing the grief associated with a lifetime of lost opportunities where they have not cared for themselves. In response, assure clients that the grief will be strong, and will hurt, but it will pass and create the possibility of experiencing self-compassion and joy in the future. By repeating this procedure of inviting clients to experience positive feelings about the self through asking them to imagine the compassion you feel for them, and then preventing them from using self-devaluating defences (D) and regulating their anxiety, shame and contempt (A), they gradually become desensitized to adaptive positive feelings about the self.

However, clients need to replace their self-devaluing defences with positive supports. Invite them to find role models who they admire and can emulate. Invite them to articulate how they would like to be if they could manage their lives in a better way. Help them to develop problem-solving, communication, assertiveness and self-care skills using the procedures outlined in Chapter 3 on cognitive behaviour therapy, so that they can solve problems in a balanced way rather than through excessive self-sacrifice or self-harm.

Another strategy for self-restructuring is facilitating viewing the self from the perspective of others. Regularly invite clients after they have recounted significant episodes from their current or past life to imagine how you perceive them, or how others in their social network might view them. Enquire how they would react if a stranger recounted similar incidents to them. A variation on this is to role-play recounting the incident, with the therapist taking on the role of the stranger and recounting an incident similar to that just recounted by the client. Invite clients to describe how hearing the incident makes them feel towards the stranger the therapist is role-playing.

A particularly important set of skills to be learned is recognizing and responding to personal needs in a compassionate way, so clients become their own 'good parents'. Here is a rationale for this intervention. 'We know your parents, at least some of the time, did their best to bring you up, but their best was not enough. Often they were not tuned in to what you needed and so often you were left needing. Now, as an adult you can change that. You can tune in to your needs and make careful plans for them to be met like a good parent'. Coach clients to become attuned to internal signals such as hunger, thirst, fatigue, danger, sexual arousal, loneliness, recognition, joy and the need for meaning in life. Help them to develop routines for meeting some of these needs (e.g. hunger and thirst) and to develop longer-term plans to meet others (the need for friendship) in the way that good parents would be attuned to their children's needs and attempt to meet them in a responsive way. This intervention is particularly important where clients disregard their own needs excessively or rely almost exclusively on others for having their needs met. Often, this latter adaptation appears as a 'relationship addiction', where clients cannot affirm themselves but rely exclusively on others to affirm their identities. Self-parenting helps such clients to move towards autonomy, and those who disregard their own needs to move towards interdependence.

Where clients have a fragile sense of self, repeat self-restructuring interventions until positive self-feelings are no longer avoided, self-esteem improves and clients have learned to act as their own 'good parents'.

Other restructuring

The aim of other restructuring is to help clients become receptive to the positive feelings of others towards them, to develop more accurate and compassionate perceptions of others, and to integrate positive and negative views of others. This involves desensitization to phobias about nurturant feelings from others in the client's current life (C), in the therapeutic relationship (T) and in the past (P). Where there is a phobia about nurturant attachment feelings from others (F), in terms of the triangle of conflict, the defence may be denial, devaluation or repression (D). With denial, clients do not believe others care about them. With devaluation, clients see the other person in a disparaging light, and so minimize the validity of their expressions of care. For example, 'When he says he loves me, I think he must be a real fool to fall for a loser like me'. With repression, the client keeps memories of positive past attachments unconscious. All of these defences are used to regulate anxiety and other inhibitory feelings, such as self-disgust (A) that arise at the thought of others caring about them.

To desensitize clients to positive feelings from the therapist (T) begin by giving them the rationale for doing so: 'Often, if we have been badly treated in the past, we mistakenly assume that others in our current lives, including friends, partners or therapists will also treat us badly. So we respond to others as if they care little for us, even when the other person cares a great deal. This habit makes it difficult to form lasting relationships. One way around it is to learn to recognize and respond positively to caring feelings from other people'. Then invite clients to say how they perceive you, the therapist. This usually elicits transference distortions in which clients typically attribute uncaring attitudes to the therapist. For example, 'You must think I'm such a loser, and you're only listening to me because it is your job'. In response to this, ask the client to look at your face and see if your expression is an uncaring one and to think back over the time you have spent together and see if there is any evidence that you might actually care for the client. As clients struggle with this, invite them to let you know what the most painful thing is about admitting that you might care for them. Repeat the process until clients become receptive to positive feelings from the therapist (T).

To desensitize clients to positive feelings from others in their current life (C), using guided imagery, invite them to imagine in detail increasingly more intense situations in which others express care for them. In each of these imagined scenarios, ask clients to indicate what the most painful thing is about hearing others' expressions of attachment to them, without using defences such as denial or devaluation. Repeat the process until clients become receptive to positive feelings from others in their current life.

To desensitize clients to positive feelings from significant carers in their past (P) begin by giving them the rationale for doing so. 'Often if we have been badly hurt or let down by others in the past who were supposed to care for us, we put all memories of positive attachments to these or other carers out of our mind. We actively try to forget them, because to remember them would hurt us too much. However, if we can be brave enough to search and find these memories of positive attachments from our childhoods, they can help us. We can use the memories of the good feelings we had in these childhood relationships as a reminder of the kinds of feelings we would like to have now in our relationships with friends and partners. These memories are like a map that let us know the kinds of emotions we want to feel when we make good friends'. Then invite them to think about people in their early life who made them feel special, who they looked up to, and who made them feel safe and secure when they were hurt or lonely. Ask clients to recount in explicit detail episodes in which their carer made them feel protected, safe or secure. Invite them to visualize these situations vividly. If they experience anxiety about admitting these feelings to consciousness, ask what the most painful thing is about allowing them to re-experience care and kindness from others. Repeat the process until clients become receptive to positive feelings from carers in their life (P).

To facilitate more accurate and compassionate perceptions of others in their current life, offer empathy skills training. Invite clients to role-play situations in which they misperceived others, but to take the role of the other person and the therapist take the role of the client. After these role-plays ask clients to summarize how the other person might have felt in the situation. Repeat the process using many different scenarios until clients learn how to accurately and compassionately judge others' feelings and intentions.

Some clients, particularly those with border-line personality disorders who have been abused in childhood, have 'addictive' attachments to others, especially romantic partners, who treat them badly. They repeatedly are attracted to, select and depend on these partners who are initially charming but ultimately abusive or unfaithful. Such clients find these relationships initially exciting because of these partners' charms, and attractive because they are familiar and recapitulate similar relationships with abusive carers. But ultimately these relationships are painful because they end in betrayal. By contrast, such clients find relationships with decent, caring partners boring and sometimes disgusting. To be able to let go of addictive relationships with uncaring partners, clients must be first desensitized to caring feelings of others, and their own positive feelings about the self. They must also be given the opportunity to grieve the lost opportunities for caring relationships in the past. The most useful rationale to give clients for this intervention is that lasting and satisfying relationships are based on generous love of others and not the addictive need for the approval of others. To be open to relationships based on generous love, rather than trapped into relationships based on the addictive need for approval, we have to be able to have positive feelings about ourselves and recognize and accept positive feelings from others, hence the need for desensitization to positive feelings from self and others.

Repeat all of these other-restructuring interventions until adaptive feelings within relationships are no longer avoided. This can be a slow process with people who have personality disorders.

As self and other restructuring progresses, clients become receptive to positive feelings to and from self and others. They gradually move towards seeing themselves and others more accurately and compassionately. A gradual realization comes that we all have mixed feelings about ourselves and others. We all have strengths and weaknesses. We have all achieved some good things in life and we have all made some unfortunate mistakes. Creating opportunities for clients to articulate this helps them to let go of the defence mechanism of splitting, so common in border-line personality disorder, and to integrate their positive and negative feelings about themselves and others.

Therapeutic relationship, resistance, transference and countertransference

A distinction is made within the psychodynamic tradition between the transference relationship and the real relationship between the client and therapist (McCullough-Vaillant, 1997). In the transference relationship, the client responds to the therapist (T) in the way that they responded to past caregivers (P), following engrained D-A-F patterns. In the real relationship, the therapist and client collaborate in a relationship based on mutual trust and respect. Both types of relationship occur during BPT and at any one time, one is more prominent than the other. In long-term psychoanalysis, the therapist creates a context where the transference relationship is given greater expression. In the approach to BPT described here, the real relationship is given primacy, although transference inevitably occurs and transference interpretations are made when therapists point out the occurrence of D-A-F patterns within the therapeutic relationship.

Resistance is commonplace in therapy. Resistance involves using various defences (D) to regulate anxiety (A) associated with the threat of uncovering forbidden feelings (F). In psychodynamic psychotherapy, clients typically become involved in resistance for good reasons. Resistance is the client's attempt to use defences that were effective in earlier life in ensuring safety, security and survival and avoiding threats to physical and psychological well-being. Clients may resist practical aspects of the therapeutic contract by making major life changes, attempting suicide, trying to contact the therapist outside office hours, missing sessions or coming late to sessions. They may resist procedural aspects of the contract by censoring the material they talk about in therapy, forgetting to tell the therapist about important material such as significant dreams, consistently rejecting the therapist's interpretations or demanding that the therapist gratify their curiosity about the therapist's private life or their desire for erotic contact with the therapist..

Within BPT, the therapist responds to resistance by offering interpretations of the resistance in a supportive, rather than punitive, way. It is crucial that such interpretations are not offered in a punitive way because typically, in the past, clients will have met with punitive reactions to their commonly used defences within the context of intimate or helping relationships.

The therapist's own immediate psychological reactions to the client's resistance is an important source of information about the impact of the client's defence mechanisms and relational styles on others such as their partners, friends, children, or close colleagues. Immediate, intense psychological reactions to clients are usually referred to as countertransference. In the case example at the beginning of the chapter, at one point in the treatment the client showed resistance by being overly co-operative. This elicited a countertransference reaction in the therapist of extreme irritation. This let the therapist know that in certain types of situation this client typically reacted by making people feel irritated. This information allowed the therapist to make the following interpretation in a supportive way: 'It seems that sometimes the way you go along with the wishes of others without fighting your corner may irritate them and make them place more demands on you, which in turn makes you go along with them even more. Do you want to explore that possibility?'

Distinctions are made between concordant and complementary countertransference reactions. With concordant countertransference reactions, the therapist experiences a deep empathy with the client's experience. For example, with a client who has experienced a major loss, the therapist may experience profound sadness and despair. With complementary countertranference reactions, the therapist experiences the interpersonal response invited by the client's reaction. For example, in response to the client blaming the therapist for not alleviating his or her suffering, the therapist might experience guilt and anger.

When therapists experience countertransference reactions, they are sometimes predominantly reflections of the impact of the client's typical defences and relational style. However, in other instances they may be predominantly reflections of the therapist's own unresolved sensitivities to particular issues.

For example, a therapist who has experienced child abuse, neglect or early bereavement might respond particularly intensely to the maladaptive defences and relational styles of a client who has experienced similar trauma. These predominantly personal countertransference reactions can compromise the therapist's capacity to offer supportive interpretations and maintain good therapeutic alliance. Therapists may find themselves alternating between attempts to gratify the client's need to be rescued and attempts to persecute the client for showing resistance. Because countertransference reactions that arise from therapists' personal life histories can compromise the capacity to respond therapeutically, it is particularly important for clinicians who practise psychodynamic therapy to receive regular supervision and to have undergone their own psychodynamic therapy. Such personal therapy also enhances therapists' capacity to empathize with clients' experiences of the challenges entailed by participating as a client in this type of therapy.

Termination

Because BPT is time limited, therapy is usually terminated when the session limit has been reached. At this point, for the half to two-thirds of cases that can benefit from this type of therapy, the presenting problems will have been partially, but not fully, resolved (Svartberg, et al., 2004; Winston et al., 1994). However, clients who responded to BPT will know how to recognize and relinquish defences and will have become partially desensitized to their main forbidden feelings, so they will have the skills required to independently continue the process that began in BPT. As the session limit is approached, if significant gains have been made, the interval between sessions can be increased. The changes in the presenting problems that have occurred may be reviewed and the reasons for these changes in terms of the model given in Figure 4.1 explored. Successes in reducing symptoms and solving presenting problems may be celebrated. Later sessions can be used to help clients develop the mature defence of anticipation. Possible situations in which they might be tempted to use old defences could be identified and more adaptive ways of managing these explored. Part of the process of preparing for future challenges is network building. Therapists may invite clients to begin to develop networks of relationships that will provide them with support when they face future challenges.

Termination is a loss experience. Clients could be invited to express how they feel about this loss, to grieve it, to articulate their positive and negative feelings about the therapist and the therapy process, and to anticipate how they will carry an internalization of the therapist with them in future. When they meet complex life challenges they can imagine what the therapist might say to them in those situations.

SUMMARY

Brief psychodynamic therapy (BPT) is an evidenced-based approach to clinical practice that falls within the psychoanalytic tradition and was exemplified here with reference to a model of practice originated by David Malan in the UK and further developed by Leigh McCullough in the USA. Within this BPT model it is assumed that psychological problems arise because dysfunctional psychological defence mechanisms (D) have been used to manage anxiety and inhibitory affects (A) about the expression of potentially adaptive, but forbidden feelings and impulses (F). These D-A-F patterns are typically longstanding and have begun in childhood through interactions with parents and other past persons (P). They are maintained by interactions with significant people in the client's current life situation (C), and are re-enacted as transference with the therapist (T) during the course of therapy, a context within which they can be explored and understood. BPT aims to help clients recognize and relinquish their dysfunctional defences and replace them with more mature defences. A second aim of BPT is to desensitize clients to the experience of forbidden feelings and impulses and help them develop adaptive ways to express these. A third aim of BPT, of particular relevance to clients with personality disorders, is to help them develop a more positive self-image and a capacity to engage in more positive relationships with others. Within BPT, specific therapeutic strategies are used to restructure defences, to restructure forbidden feelings and affects, and to restructure psychological representations of self and others. BPT begins with an assessment interview in which suitability for BPT is determined and a formulation is developed. Clients with GAF scores below 50 are unsuitable for all but the self–other restructuring stages of BPT. Treatment is premised on a time-limited contract and usually progresses from defence to affect restructuring. However, with low-functioning clients, it begins with self–other restructuring. Within the therapeutic relationship, transference, countertransference and resistance are managed in a planned way. In the termination phase, the way in which presenting problems were resolved is reviewed and grief associated with the ending of the therapeutic relationship is addressed.

EXERCISE 4.1

Using the case of Michael from the chapter case study, draw triangles of conflict and person, including his defences, anxieties and feelings in relation to the therapist, current and past people in his life.

Working in pairs, adopt the roles of interviewer and interviewee; reverse roles when the interview is over. Role-play the following therapist interactions with Michael:

1 Recognize his defences (D): help him discover what is defended against (F) and why (A), being mindful to provide empathy and validate his feelings.
2 Restructure his defences (D) and increase his motivation to give up defences: help him to:

   a identify pros and cons of defences
   b identify primary and secondary gain
   c identify the origins and maintenance of defences
   d identify the maladaptive effects of using defences
   e grieve the losses associated with defence use
   f identify and work towards using alternative adaptive behaviours or more mature defences.

3 Experience affect: help him to be exposed in imagination to the forbidden feelings (F), without responding with a defence (D), and support him in managing the associated anxiety (A) until it subsides.
4 Express affect in 'real-life' situations: Help him to:

   a express emotion and tolerate expressions of emotions by others
   b deal with interpersonal conflict that may arise
   c integrate affects for better emotional expression
   d learn and practice assertiveness skills.

FURTHER READING FOR PRACTITIONERS

Crits-Cristoph, P. & Barber, J. (1991). *Handbook of short-term dynamic psychotherapy*. New York: Spectrum.

Malan, D. (1995). *Individual psychotherapy and the science of psychodynamics* (Second Edition). London: Butterworth-Heinemann.

McCullough, L., Kuhn, N., Andrews, S., Kaplan, A., Wolf, J., & Hurley, C. (2003). *Treating affect phobia: A manual for short term dynamic psychotherapy*. New York: Guilford.

McCullough-Vaillant, L. (1997). *Changing character: Short-term anxiety regulating psychotherapy for restructuring defences, affects and attachments*. New York: Basic Books.

Ursano, R., Sonnenberg, S., & Lazar, S. (1998). *Concise guide to psychodynamic psychotherapy in the era of managed care: Principles and techniques*. Washington, DC: APA.

ASSESSMENT INSTRUMENTS

Bond, M. & Wesley, S. (1996). *Manual for the Defence Style Questionnaire*. Montreal, Quebec: McGill University. Write to Dr Michael Bond, Department of Psychiatry, Sir Mortimer B Davis – Jewish General Hospital, 4333 Chemin de la Cote Ste-Catherine, Montreal, Quebec, Canada H3T 1E4. Tel.: 514–3408210.

McCullough, L. (2003). *Psychotherapy assessment checklist*. Online, available: http://www.affectphobia.org/research.html

McCullough, L. (2003). *Achievement of therapeutic objectives scale*. Online, available: http://www.affectphobia.org/research.html

Perry, C. & Kardos, M. (1995). A review of defence mechanism rating scales. In: H. Conte & R. Plutchik (Eds), *Ego defences: Theory and measurement* (pp. 283–299). New York: Wiley. Contains a description of the Defence Mechanism Rating Scale, which is available from Sir Mortimer B Davis – Jewish General Hospital, 4333 Chemin de la Cote Ste-Catherine, Montreal, Quebec, Canada H3T 1E4.

Society for Psychotherapy Research is a good source of information on assessment instruments and research in the field. Web address: http://www.psychotherapyresearch.org

REFERENCES

American Psychiatric Association (APA) (2000). *Diagnostic and statistical manual of the mental disorders* (Fourth Edition-Text Revision; DSM-IV-TR). Washington, DC: APA.

Aveline, M. (1995). How I assess for focal therapy. In: C. Mace (Ed), *The art and science of assessment in psychotherapy* (pp. 137–154). London: Routledge.

Balint, M. (1968). *The basic fault. Therapeutic aspects of regression*. London: Tavistock.

Balint, M., Ornstein, O., & Balint, E. (1972). *Focal psychotherapy*. Philadelphia, PA: Lippincott.

Bond, M. & Wesley, S. (1996). *Manual for the Defence Style Questionnaire*. Montreal, Quebec: McGill University. Write to Dr Michael Bond, Department of Psychiatry, Sir Mortimer B Davis – Jewish General Hospital, 4333 Chemin de la Cote Ste-Catherine, Montreal, Quebec, Canada H3T 1E4. Tel.: 514–3408210.

Book, H. (1998). *Brief psychodynamic psychotherapy*. Washington, DC: American Psychiatric Press.

Cassidy, J. & Shaver, P. (1999). *Handbook of Attachment*. New York: Guilford.

Cramer, P. (1991). *The development of defence mechanisms: Theory, research, and assessment*. New York: Springer-Verlag.

Crits-Cristoph, P. (1992). The efficacy of brief psychodynamic psychotherapy: A meta-analysis. *American Journal of Psychiatry*, 149, 151–158.

Crits-Cristoph, P. & Barber, J. (1991). *Handbook of short-term dynamic psychotherapy*. New York: Spectrum.

Davanloo, H. (1980). *Short-term dynamic psychotherapy*. New York: Jason Aronson.

Ezriel, H. (1952). Notes on psychoanalytic group therapy: II. Interpretation. *Research Psychiatry*, 15, 119.

Gustafson, J. (1986). *The complex secret of brief psychotherapy*. New York: Norton.

Horowitz, M., Marmar, C., Krupnick, J., Wilner, K., Kaltreider, N., & Wallerstein, R. (1984). *Personality styles in brief psychotherapy*. New York: Basic Books.

Lambert, M. J. & Ogles, B. M. (2004). The efficacy and effectiveness of psychotherapy. In: M. J. Lambert (Ed), *Bergin & Garfield's handbook of psychotherapy and behavior change* (Fifth Edition, pp. 139–193). New York: Wiley.

Luborsky, L. (1984). *Principles of psychoanalytic psychotherapy: A manual for supportive/expressive treatment*. New York: Basic.

Malan, D. (1995). *Individual psychotherapy and the science of psychodynamics* (Second Edition). London: Butterworth-Heinemann.

Mann, J. (1973). *Time-limited psychotherapy*. Cambridge, MA: Harvard University Press.

McCullough, L. (2003). *Psychotherapy assessment checklist*. Online available: http://www.affectphobia.org/research.html

McCullough, L., Kuhn, N., Andrews, S., Kaplan, A., Wolf, J., & Hurley, C. (2003). *Treating affect phobia: A manual for short-term dynamic psychotherapy.* New York: Guilford.

McCullough-Vaillant, L. (1997). *Changing character: Short-term anxiety regulating psychotherapy for restructuring defences, affects and attachments*. New York: Basic Books.

Menninger, K. (1958). *Theory of psychoanalytic technique*. London: Imago.

Perry, C. & Kardos, M. (1995). A review of defence mechanism rating scales. In: H. Conte & R. Plutchik (Eds), *Ego defences: Theory and measurement* (pp. 283–299). New York: Wiley.

Piper, W., Joyce, A., McCallum, M., Azim, H., & Ogrodniczuk, J. (2002). *Interpretive and supportive psychotherapies. Matching therapy and personality*. Washington, DC: American Psychological Association.

Sifneos, P. (1987). *Short-term dynamic psychotherapy: Evaluation and technique* (Second Edition). New York: Plenum.

Strupp, H. & Binder, J. (1984). *Psychotherapy in a new key: Time-limited dynamic psychotherapy*. New York: Basic Books.

Svartberg, M., Stiles, M., & Seltzer, M. (2004). Randomized controlled trial of the effectiveness of short-term dynamic psychotherapy and cognitive therapy for cluster C personality disorders. *American Journal of Psychiatry*, 161, 810–817.

Ursano, R. & Ursano, A. (2000). Brief individual psychodynamic psychotherapy. In: M. Gelder, J. Lopez-Ibor & N. Andreason (Eds), *New Oxford textbook of psychiatry* Volume 2 (pp. 1421–1432). Oxford: Oxford University Press.

Ursano, R., Sonnenberg, S., & Lazar, S. (1998). *Concise guide to psychodynamic psychotherapy in the era of managed care: Principles and techniques*. Washington, DC: American Psychiatric Press.

Vaillant, G. (2000). Adaptive mental mechanisms. Their role in positive psychology. *American Psychologist*, 55, 89–98.

Winston, A., Laikin, M., Pollack, J., Samstag, L., McCullough, L., & Muran, C. (1994). Short-term psychotherapy of personality disorders: 2 year follow-up. *American Journal of Psychiatry*, 151, 190–194.

Chapter 5

Systemic couples therapy

Alan Carr and Muireann McNulty

CASE VIGNETTE

James and Sarah, a couple in their mid-twenties, were referred for therapy at a psychology clinic attached to a general hospital by a social worker. In the referral letter the social worker said that the couple had multiple problems. James had an explosive temper, which was frightening for Sarah and her two children. Sarah, who had a history of panic attacks, had developed a constricted lifestyle because of fears of having panic attacks when away from home. The couple argued constantly. The case was referred to social services by a health visitor who became concerned for the welfare of the couple's children, Kelly (4 years) and Luke (1 year), when conducting a routine developmental assessment visit with Luke around the time of his first birthday. The social worker visited the couple at their home and met with a frosty reception. The couple initially insisted that everything was OK and that no family evaluation or support were required. The social worker explained that she had a statutory obligation to evaluate the capacity of the parents to provide a safe and secure home environment for the children. One recommendation arising from the social worker's assessment was that the couple complete a programme of marital therapy to address the conflict between them, since this was interfering with their capacity to co-operatively meet their children's needs.

Because of the couple's ambivalence about attending therapy, invitations to an initial contracting meeting were sent to the referring social worker and the couple, with a request that the social worker arrange transportation for the couple to attend the psychology clinic. In the meeting the couple expressed their ambivalence about attending therapy, but the social worker pointed out that if the couple decided not to attend therapy, their children's names would be placed on an at-risk register held at her department. In light of this information, the couple agreed to attend two sessions during which an assessment would be conducted. If that indicated that they were suitable for therapy a further contract for ten sessions of therapy would be offered.

In the assessment sessions, it became clear that during episodes of conflict between James and Sarah, Sarah would not do something that James aggressively demanded, such as soothing the children or being attentive to his needs. In response James would criticize her, and she would initially fight back but eventually go quiet or have a panic attack. James would then back off. The couple would then not be on speaking terms for a few days. Gradually they would have increasingly more contact until the next episode. Sarah's beliefs, which underpinned her behaviour in these episodes, were that the demands of life, her children and her partner were too great for her to manage and she would usually fail. She also believed that arguments between couples were competitive exchanges that were won or lost. She believed that she could never beat James in an argument and so gave up each time, a process that reinforced her beliefs in her own lack of power to influence James. Also when she became frustrated she believed that her increased arousal was a sign that she was about to have a heart attack, a belief that often preceded her panic attacks. Sarah had learned this pessimistic way of viewing the world from her mother, who had long-standing depression, and from observing her parents' very unhappy marriage. James behaved as he did during problematic episodes because he believed that Sarah was being purposefully un-co-operative to punish him and that it was unfair that she didn't cherish him, because he devoted himself to her. He had a general disposition to believe that others were trying to take advantage of him, a hostile attributional bias that he had learned from his father. James had a conflictual relationship with his father, who treated his mother as James treated Sarah. A detailed diagram of this three-column formulation is given in Figure 5.1.

On the positive side, there were exceptional episodes where James helped rather than criticized Sarah when she was having difficulty soothing the children or cooking dinner, doing the washing or some other household job. In response she smiled at him and good feelings between them followed. James had learned from his mother that 'a little kindness goes a long way' and it was this belief that underpinned his

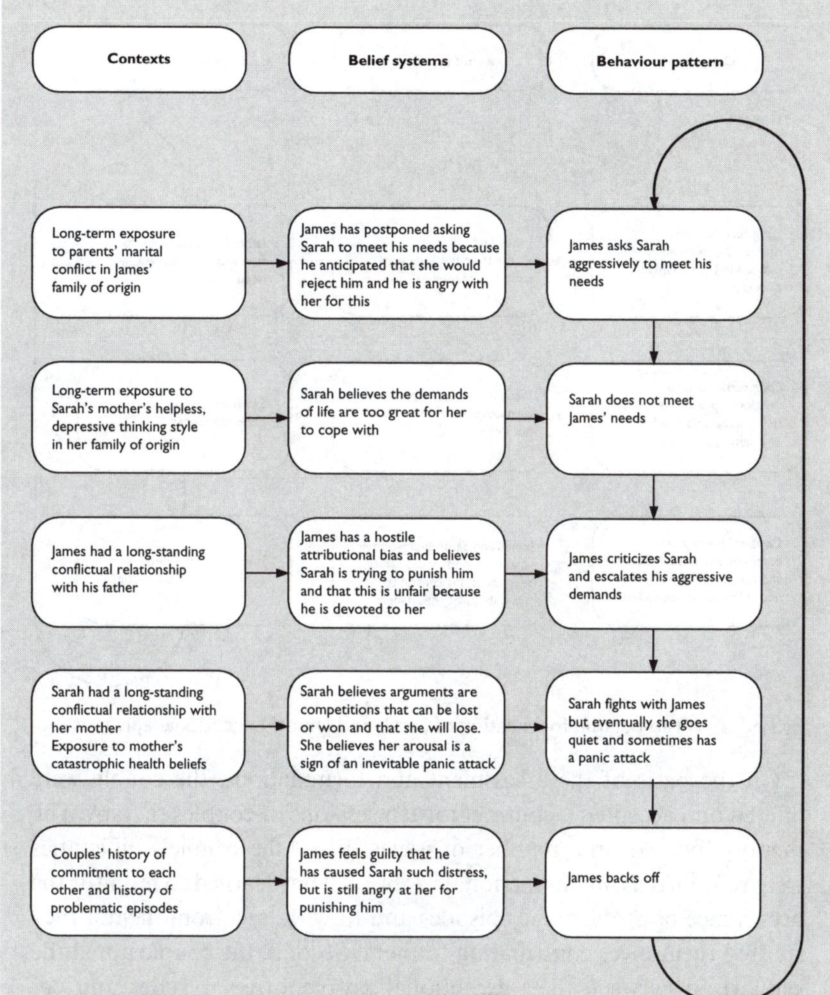

Figure 5.1 Three-column formulation of Sarah and James' problematic episodes.

generous behaviour. Sarah had learned that 'one good turn deserves another' from her dad, with whom she had a good relationship and this underpinned her good feelings when James was kind to her. A three-column formulation of exceptional episodes in which the problem would be expected to occur but did not is given in Figure 5.2. A genogram of the couple is given in Figure 5.3, which threw light on some of the contextual factors included in the third column of the two formulations.

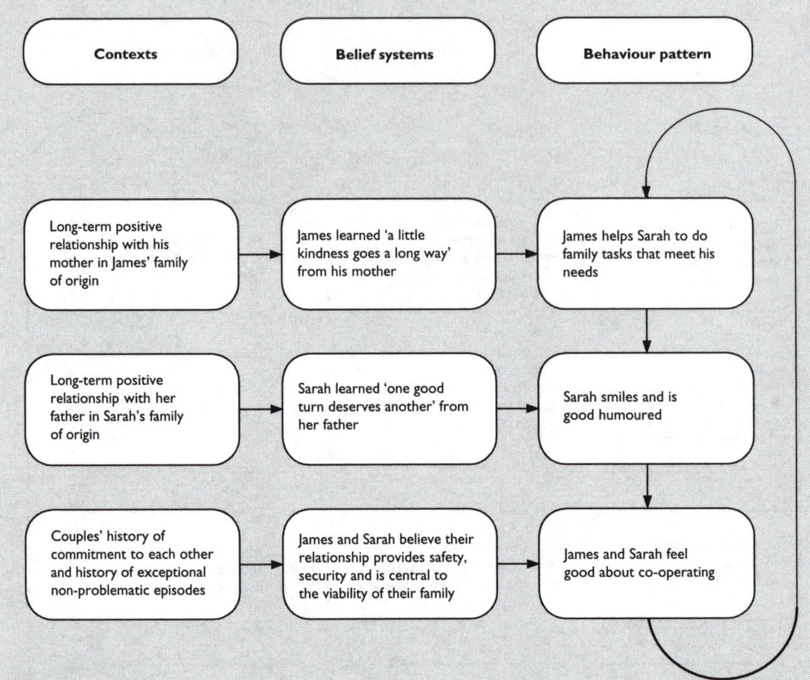

Figure 5.2 Three-column formulation of Sarah and James' exceptional episodes.

On the basis of the assessment and formulations, the couple were offered and accepted a contract for ten sessions of couples therapy. The therapy focused on a number of issues. First, the couple's difficulties were reframed as an interactional problem. They learned to monitor the occurrence of problematic episodes and to withdraw from them if they spotted themselves contributing to them. Second, the couple noted the similarities between their exceptional problem-free episodes and co-operative communication and problem-solving skills. They developed these skills further so they could apply them to potentially conflictual situations. Third, James learned to identify and express his attachment needs in a direct way, and to use this skill regularly to prevent a build-up of need-frustration and aggression. Fourth, Sarah was helped to control her panic attacks using a cognitive behavioural programme involving exposure to interoceptive cues and relaxation and copings skills training. Fifth, James helped Sarah overcome her agoraphobia through partner-assisted graded exposure to feared situations involving travelling away from the house for gradually increasing distances.

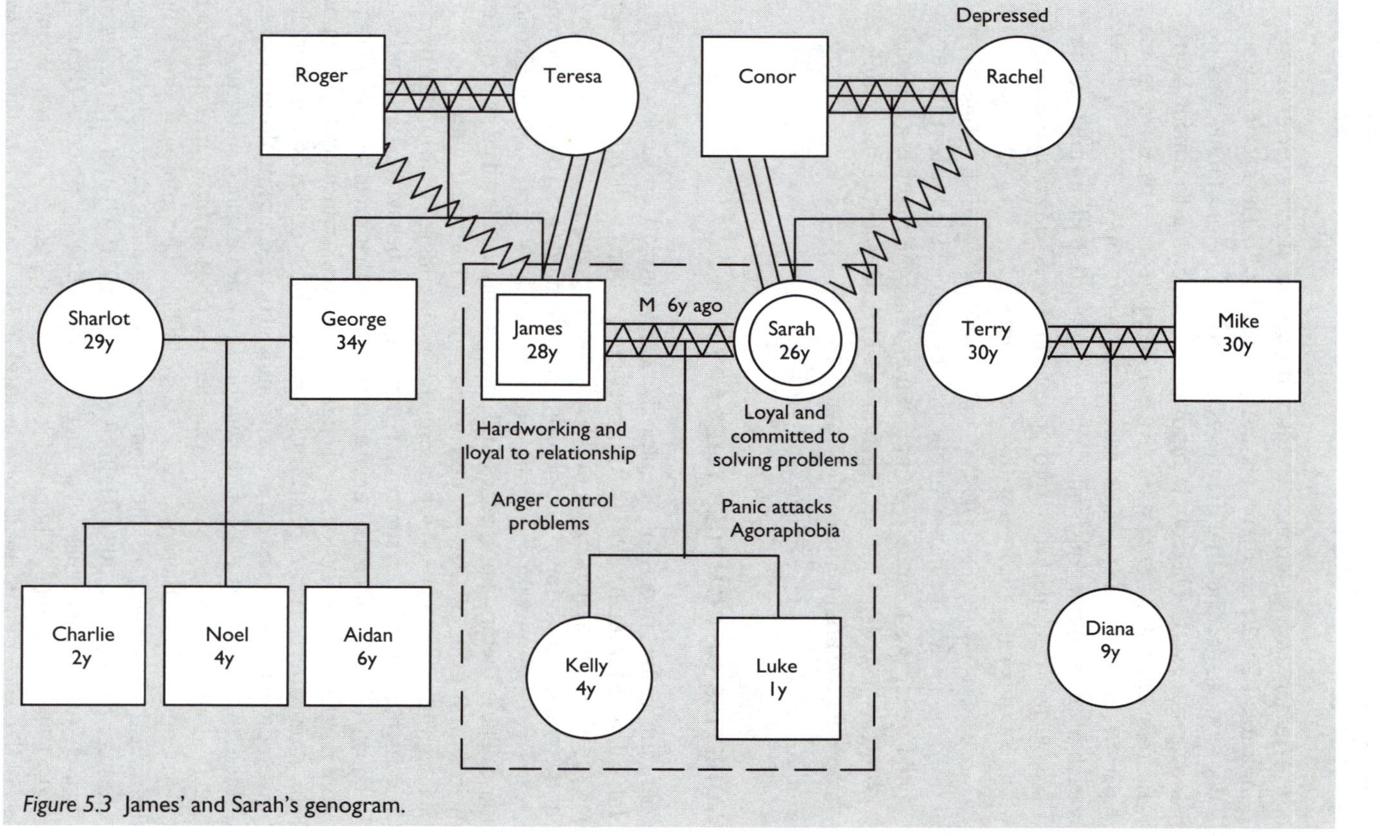

Figure 5.3 James' and Sarah's genogram.

After ten sessions a review conducted with the referring social worker indicated that the children were doing much better. The social services department decided that frequent monitoring of the family was no longer necessary. The couple reported the following treatment gains: the frequency of their unproductive arguments reduced from five to one per week, their marital satisfaction improved, supportive links with each of their families of origin were strengthened, both members of the couple reported marked improvements in James' anger management and Sarah's panic disorder with agoraphobia.

A relapse occurred a couple of years later at a time when Sarah began working outside the home for the first time since the birth of the first child. After two sessions focusing on managing the conflicts associated with the new demands on the family, the frequency of the couple's unproductive arguments reduced again.

VARIETIES OF COUPLES THERAPY

There are many models of couples therapy (Gurman & Jacobson, 2002; Halford & Markman, 1997). Approaches to couples therapy have been developed within systemic, cognitive-behavioural, and psychodynamic psychotherapeutic traditions. In addition, specific models of couples therapy have been developed for particular problems such as depression or alcohol abuse. These therapy approaches and models may be classified in terms of their central focus of therapeutic concern and in particular with respect to their emphasis on: (1) repetitive problem-maintaining behaviour patterns; (2) constraining belief systems that support these behaviour patterns; and (3) constitutional, contextual or historical factors that predispose couples to adopt particular belief systems and engage in particular problem-maintaining behaviour patterns (Carr, 2000). In the same vein, hypotheses and formulations about couple's problems and strengths may be conceptualized in terms of these three domains. Also, interventions may be classified in terms of the specific domains they target. This chapter describes an integrative approach to systemic couples therapy (ISCT; Carr, 2000). The approach draws on theoretical and clinical insights from a variety of models of couples therapy (Gurman & Jacobson, 2002; Halford & Markman, 1997) and the results of research on the effectiveness of particular couples therapy practices (Baucom et al., 1998; Carr, 2000, Chapter 17; Liddle et al., 2002; Pinsof & Wynne, 1995). Three-column formulation is central to ISCT and it is to this that we now turn.

BEHAVIOUR PATTERNS, BELIEF SYSTEMS AND BROADER CONTEXTS

In ISCT, for any problem, an initial hypothesis and later formulation may be constructed in which the behaviour pattern that maintains the problem is specified, the constraining belief systems that underpin the partners' roles in this pattern are outlined and the broader contextual factors that predispose couples to these belief systems and behaviour patterns are given. For example, in the vignette that opened this chapter, our initial hypothesis was that the couple got involved in regular conflictual patterns of interaction in which James' anger control problems and possibly Sarah's panic attacks might have played a part. Our second hypothesis was that the belief systems that underpinned their roles in these interaction patterns involved James having views about being entitled to certain things from Sarah, and Sarah believing that she was either in danger or powerless. Our third hypothesis was that these beliefs and behaviour patterns had their roots in adverse family-of-origin experiences. These hypotheses were checked-out during the assessment interviews and led to the development of the three-column problem formulation in Figure 5.1.

In ISCT, a couple's strengths may be conceptualized as involving exceptional interaction patterns within which the problem does not occur, empowering belief systems that inform partners' roles within these interaction patterns and broader contextual factors that underpin these competency-oriented belief systems and provide a foundation for resilience. For example, in the vignette that opened this chapter, our first strengths-oriented hypothesis was that occasionally the couple became involved in co-operative patterns of interaction. Our second hypothesis was that the belief systems that underpinned their roles in these interaction patterns involved James' and Sarah's commitment to their marriage and to raising their children together. Our third hypothesis was that these beliefs and behaviour patterns had their roots in positive family-of-origin experiences and positive experiences within their own relationship. These hypotheses were checked out during the assessment interviews and led to the development of the three-column exception formulation in Figure 5.2.

In light of formulations of a couple's problems and strengths, a range of interventions that address interaction patterns, belief systems and broader contextual factors can be considered. Those which fit best for the couple, make best use of their strengths, and for which there is best evidence of effectiveness may be selected. Some interventions aim primarily to disrupt problem-maintaining interaction patterns, for example, communication and problem-solving skills training. Others aim to help couples evolve more liberating and flexible belief systems, for example reframing difficulties viewed by couples as individual deficits, as shared interactional behaviour patterns. Still other interventions aim to modify the negative impact of broader contextual factors, for example, helping couples strengthen their social support networks.

THE THREE-COLUMN PROBLEM FORMULATION MODEL

To aid the processes of hypothesizing and formulating about couples' problems, ideas from many schools of couples therapy have been integrated into a three-column problem formulation model, presented in Table 5.1 (Carr, 2000).

Problem-maintaining behaviour patterns

Formulations and hypotheses in this style of practice must always include a detailed description of the problem and the pattern of behaviour in which it is embedded. This is placed in the right-hand column of a three-column formulation. The problem-maintaining behaviour pattern includes a description of what happens before, during and after the problem in a typical episode. Commonly, the pattern will also include positive and negative feelings. These offer clues as to why the pattern is rigid and repeats recursively. For example, James, in the vignette that opened the chapter, when describing a typical problematic behaviour pattern, said he shouted because he knew that in the end Sarah would give in, and this would make him feel like he had won. And Sarah said that she went quiet after the shouting got too loud because it brought relief. So feelings associated with winning and relief were critical to maintaining the behaviour pattern in which the problem was embedded.

Problems may be maintained by behaviour patterns involving ineffective attempted solutions (Shoham & Rohrbaugh, 2002). A minor problem, such as disagreeing about what TV station to watch, may become a major problem, such as a series of major near-violent rows, because of the way a couple try to repeatedly solve this difficulty using ineffective solutions, such as coercion. Confused communication may also maintain problem behaviour, often because it leads to a lack of clarity about partners' positions, wishes, feeling and expectations.

Behaviour patterns that involve high rates of negative, critical or punitive exchanges and low rates of positive, supportive exchanges between partners can maintain problems (Gottman, 1993). It was noted in Chapter 1 that a ratio of 5:1 positive to negative exchanges characterizes well-adjusted couples. Interaction patterns characterized by a lack of intimacy or a significant imbalance of power may also maintain relationship dissatisfaction and other problems (Jacobson & Christensen, 1996).

Symmetrical interactions in which, for example, aggression from one partner is responded to with aggression from another partner; or complementary behaviour patterns where, for example, increasing dependence or illness in

Table 5.1 Three-column problem formulation model for systemic couples therapy

Contexts	*Belief systems*	*Behaviour patterns*
Constitutional • Genetic vulnerabilities • Debilitating somatic states • Early illness or injury • Learning difficulty • Difficult temperament **Contextual** • Constraining cultural norms and values • Current lifecycle transitions • Home–work role strain • Lack of social support • Recent loss experiences • Recent illness or injury • Unemployment • Moving house • Poverty • Secret romantic affairs **Historical** • Major family-of-origin stresses: 1. Bereavements 2. Separations 3. Child abuse 4. Social disadvantage 5. Institutional upbringing • Family-of-origin parent–child problems: 1. Insecure attachment 2. Authoritarian parenting 3. Permissive parenting 4. Neglectful parenting 5. Inconsistent parental discipline 6. Lack of stimulation 7. Scapegoating 8. Triangulation • Family-of-origin parental problems: 1. Parental psychological problems 2. Parental drug or alcohol abuse 3. Parental criminality 4. Marital discord or violence 5. Family disorganization	• Denial of the problem • Rejection of a systemic framing of the problem in favour of an individualistic framing • Constraining beliefs about personal competence to solve the problem • Constraining beliefs about problems and solutions relevant to the presenting problem • Constraining beliefs about the negative consequences of change and the negative events that may be avoided by maintaining the status quo • Constraining beliefs about relationships with partners and other network members (e.g. differences are battles which can be won or lost) • Constraining attributional style (internal, global, stable, intentional attributions for problem behaviours) • Constraining cognitive distortions 1. Maximizing negatives 2. Minimizing positives • Constraining defence mechanisms 1. Denial 2. Passive aggression 3. Rationalization 4. Reaction formation 5. Displacement 6. Splitting 7. Projection	• The couple's or symptomatic partner's problem behaviour • The sequence of events that typically precede and follow an episode of the symptoms or problem behaviour • The feelings and emotions that accompany these behaviours, particularly positive feelings or payoffs • Patterns involving ineffective attempted solutions • Patterns involving confused communication • Patterns involving high rates of negative exchanges and low rates of positive exchanges • Patterns involving expression of negative emotions due to fears of attachment needs being unmet • Patterns involving lack of marital intimacy • Patterns involving a significant marital power imbalance • Symmetrical and complementary behaviour patterns • Enmeshed and disengaged behaviour patterns • Rigid and chaotic behaviour patterns • Coercive interaction patterns • Patterns involving inadvertent reinforcement • Triangulation of children • Patterns including lack of co-ordination among involved professionals and family members

Based on Carr, A. (2000). *Family therapy: Concepts, process and practice*. Chichester: Wiley.

one partner is met with increasing care-taking in another partner may also characterize problem-maintaining behaviour patterns (Haley, 1963).

Problems may be maintained by enmeshed, over-involved relationships and also by distant, disengaged relationships. Rigid repetitive interactions or chaotic unpredictable interactions may also maintain problems (Minuchin, 1974).

Coercive interaction patterns, where partners repeatedly engage in escalating aggressive exchanges that conclude with withdrawal and a sense of relief for all involved, may lead to escalations in relational aggression (Patterson, 1982). Problems may also be maintained when partners inadvertently reinforce each other's problem behaviour.

Problems may be maintained by triangulation, when partners involve children in their conflict (Minuchin, 1974). In a detouring-attacking triad, partners express their anger at each other through the child, who often has conduct problems. In a detouring-protecting triad, partners express their disappointment with each other through their joint concern about the child, who often has a psychosomatic complaint.

A lack of co-ordination among involved professionals including health, social service and other professionals can maintain problematic behaviour.

Problem-maintaining belief systems

Problem-maintaining behaviour patterns may be supported by a wide variety of constraining belief systems (Carr, 2000). Problem-maintaining behaviour patterns may persist because one or both partners deny the existence of the problem. For example, alcohol or drug problems may persist because the partner with the problem does not accept that there is a difficulty. Problem-maintaining behaviour patterns may persist because partners reject a systemic framing of the problem and so deny their role in either maintaining the problem or contributing to its resolution. For example, couples in which one partner is depressed may reject the idea that their difficulty in increasing supportive interaction within the couple may maintain the mood disorder. Problem-maintaining behaviour patterns may persist because couples believe that they are not competent to solve the problem. In the case vignette that opened the chapter, Sarah believed she was helpless to influence her problematic interactions with James. Problem-maintaining behaviour patterns may persist because partners have theories about the cause of the problem and the appropriate way to solve it that are not particularly useful. For example, where partners believe that anxiety, depression or other biopsychosocial difficulties are wholly biologically determined and require pharmacological treatment, this belief may underpin problem-maintaining behaviour, such as passivity.

Beliefs about the negative consequences of change and the negative events that can be avoided by maintaining the status quo may also underpin problem-maintaining behaviour. For example, a husband in a discordant marriage may persist in limiting his partner's freedom because he may believe that to treat her as an equal would involve him accepting a lower status and ultimately this would lead his wife to leave him.

There are many beliefs about couples' relationships that can maintain problem behaviour and these beliefs often take the form: 'A good husband or wife always does X in this type of situation' or 'If X does Y in a marriage then A should do B because it's right, fair, or feels like the right thing to do'.

An attributional style where internal, global, stable attributions are made for problem behaviour and external, specific, unstable situational attributions are made for good behaviour may lead partners to persist in problem-maintaining behaviour and to elicit problem-maintaining behaviour in each other (Finchman & Bradbury, 1992). Such attributions include defining the self or one's partner as 'bad, sad, sick or mad', although often more sophisticated labels than these are used. For example, couples may accuse each other of being intentionally hurtful or vindictive (i.e. 'bad') and this can support coercive interaction patterns characterized by low intimacy and power imbalance, which in turn maintains the couple's discord. Or couples may define one partner as neurotic (i.e. 'sick'). This can support extreme complementary interaction patterns characterized by extreme care-giving and care-receiving roles. Such roles compromise the intimacy and power balance within the relationship and maintain the couple's discord.

A belief system characterized by cognitive distortions such as maximizing negatives and minimizing positives may also support problem-maintaining interaction patterns. For example, a depressed husband who sees every glass as half empty rather than half full and every silver lining as part of a dark rain cloud, may find that this style of thinking leads him to behave in ways that prevent him from receiving the support he needs from his partner to break out of his depression. Cognitive distortions are listed in Table 3.2 and discussed in Chapter 3.

Certain problematic defence mechanisms may be central to belief systems that maintain problematic behaviour patterns. Defence mechanisms are used to regulate anxiety that accompanies conflict due to a desire to pursue one course of action while fearing the consequences of doing so. Problematic defence mechanisms include denial (as has already been mentioned) and also passive aggression, rationalization, reaction formation, displacement, splitting and projection. With passive aggression, rather than talking openly about a conflict of interests within the couple, one partner passively avoids co-operating with others. With rationalization, couples construct rational arguments to justify destructive behaviour. With reaction formation and displacement, rather than talking openly about a conflict of interests, one partner treats the other as if he or she were strongly admired and liked, but anger towards the true target of aggression may be displaced onto another family member or the partner at a later time. For example, a wife who feels her husband does not meet her intimacy needs may sing his praises and displace anger towards him onto her son, whom she criticizes for being inconsiderate and selfish. From this example, it may be seen that with displacement, strong negative feelings about one partner are directed towards another person. With splitting and projection, one partner views the other in black and white terms: as completely good and others as wholly bad, or as completely bad and others as wholly good. Whether they are seen as good or bad may vary from time to time. Where couples are married with children, some family members may be defined as wholly good and others as completely bad. Good qualities and intentions are projected onto the former, while bad qualities and negative intentions are projected onto the latter. Family members defined as good are cherished and those defined as bad are scapegoated. A comprehensive list of defence mechanisms is given in Table 4.2 and they are discussed in detail in Chapter 4.

Problem-maintaining contextual factors

Problem-maintaining behaviour patterns and the belief systems that support these may arise from predisposing factors rooted in constitutional vulnerabilities, stressful features of couple's current wider social context, and adverse family-of-origin experiences (Carr, 2000).

Partners may be predisposed to engage in problem-maintaining behaviour patterns and the belief systems that support these as a result of certain constitutional vulnerabilities (Schmaling & Scher, 2000). Common examples are vulnerability to schizophrenia, bipolar disorder, depression and the presence of debilitating somatic states, including cancer and chronic pain. A history of illness or injury, learning disabilities or a difficult temperament may also predispose to problematic beliefs and behaviour patterns.

Stressful or problematic features of couple's current wider social context can predispose them to problem-maintaining beliefs and behaviour patterns (Walsh, 2003). Cultural norms and values, such as extreme patriarchy or a commitment to the use of domestic violence to solve couple's problems, may underlie belief systems that support problem-maintaining behaviour patterns. Belief systems that support problem-maintaining behaviour patterns may be activated by lifecycle transitions, home–work role strain and lack of social support. Problem-maintaining belief systems may also be activated by recent loss experiences, such as bereavement or separation, illness, injury, unemployment, moving house or poverty. In couples where one partner is having an ongoing secret romantic affair, the confusion caused by this may also activate belief systems that support problem-maintaining behaviour patterns.

Major family-of-origin stresses that may predispose partners to hold problematic belief systems and fall into problem-maintaining behaviour patterns include bereavement, particularly death of a parent; separations from parents in childhood through illness or parental divorce; physical, emotional or sexual child abuse or neglect; social disadvantage and poverty and being brought up in an institution or in multiple foster-care placements. Individuals who have experienced these stresses early in life may develop belief systems that privilege the use of aggression, excessive interpersonal distancing, excessive interpersonal closeness or a chaotic unpredictable relational style in solving relationship problems (Walsh, 2003).

Family-of-origin parent–child socialization experiences that may predispose individuals to hold problematic belief systems and engage in problem-maintaining behaviour patterns include insecure attachment and authoritarian, permissive, neglectful or inconsistent parenting. Included here also are parenting styles that involve little parent–child interaction and intellectual situation and scapegoating (Newman & Newman, 2002). Family-of-origin parental problems that may predispose individuals to hold problematic belief systems and engage in problem-maintaining behaviour patterns include parental psychological problems, such as depression, parental drug or alcohol abuse, parental criminality, couple's discord or violence and general family disorganization (Newman & Newman, 2002). All of these non-optimal socialization experiences may give rise to the development of belief systems that in later life lead individuals to repeat these type of problematic relationships with their partners.

THE THREE-COLUMN EXCEPTION FORMULATION MODEL

To aid the processes of hypothesizing about exceptions and formulating these, ideas from many schools of therapy and findings from studies of resilience have been integrated into a three-column exception formulation model, presented in Table 5.2 (Carr, 2004; Luthar, 2003).

Exceptional behaviour patterns

Hypotheses and formulations about exceptional behaviour patterns include elements suggested by the literature on strengths and resilience (Carr, 2004; Luthar, 2003).

They include a description of what happened before, during and after the problem was expected to occur but did not. Commonly, the exceptional pattern will also include positive feelings. These offer clues as to how the exceptional pattern may be strengthened. For example, in the exception formulation given in Figure 5.2 the good feelings that followed co-operation offered a reason for James and Sarah to co-operate more in future. Exceptional behaviour patterns are often characterized by effective problem solving and clear communication. They usually involve a higher rate of positive, supportive rather than negative, critical exchanges between partners. A clear expression of needs, particularly attachment needs, a degree of

Table 5.2 Three-column exception formulation model for systemic couples therapy

Contexts	*Belief systems*	*Behaviour patterns*
Constitutional • Physical health • High IQ • Easy temperament **Contextual** • Good social support network • Low family stress • Balanced home and work roles • Moderate or high socio-economic status • Empowering cultural norms and values **Historical** • Positive family-of-origin experiences • Positive family-of-origin parent–child relationships • Secure attachment • Authoritative parenting • Clear communication • Flexible family organization • Good parental adjustment • Parents had good marital relationship • Successful experiences of coping with problems	• Acceptance of the problem • Acceptance of a systemic framing of the problem • Commitment to resolving the problem • Empowering beliefs about personal competence to solve the problem • Empowering beliefs about problems and solutions relevant to the presenting problem • Beliefs about the advantages of problem resolution outweigh beliefs about the negative consequences of change and the negative events that may be avoided by maintaining the status quo • Empowering beliefs about marital, and other family relationships particularly loyalty beliefs • Benign beliefs about the characteristics or intentions of partners and other network members • Optimistic attributional style (internal, global, stable, intentional attributions for productive behaviour and situational attributions for problem behaviour) • Healthy defence mechanisms: 1. Self-observation 2. Humour 3. Self-assertion 4. Sublimation	• The sequence of events that occur in those exceptional circumstances where the problem or symptom was expected to occur but does not occur • The feelings and emotions that accompany these behaviours, particularly positive feelings or payoffs • Patterns involving effective solutions and good problem-solving skills • Patterns involving clear communication • Patterns involving high rates of positive exchanges and low rates of negative exchanges • Patterns involving clear expression of attachment needs • Patterns supporting marital intimacy • Patterns supporting marital power sharing • Emotionally supportive (rather than enmeshed or disengaged) behaviour patterns • Flexible behaviour (not rigid or chaotic) patterns • Patterns including good co-ordination among involved professionals and family members

Based on Carr, A. (2000). *Family therapy: Concepts, process and practice*. Chichester: Wiley.

psychological intimacy and greater balance in the distribution of power (within the cultural constraints of the family's ethnic reference group) are common features of exceptional behaviour patterns. Exceptional behaviour patterns often involve emotional support and flexibility about rules, roles and routines. Within professional networks, exceptions tend to occur more commonly when there is good interprofessional co-ordination and co-operation between families and professionals.

Exceptional belief systems

Exceptional non-problematic behaviour patterns may be supported by a wide variety of positive belief systems (Carr, 2004). These belief systems always involve acceptance rather than denial of the problem and a willingness to accept responsibility for contributing to problem resolution. Commitment to resolving the problem and conviction that one is competent to so do are common features of these belief systems. When partners hold useful and empowering beliefs about the nature of the problem and its resolution, exceptions may also occur. The occurrence of exceptional behaviour patterns may be associated with the development of the belief that the advantages of resolving the problem outweigh the costs of change. Clients may construct narratives in which once-feared consequences associated with their presenting problems come to be seen as not so dreadful after all. Exceptions may occur when partners endorse positive and empowering beliefs about their relationship and about their role in the family. This may include a realization of how much partners care for each other and how important it is to be loyal to one's marriage or relationship.

Exceptions may also occur when partners develop benign beliefs about the intentions and characteristics of each other and come to view them as good people who are doing their best in a tough situation rather than vindictive people who are out to persecute them. An optimistic attributional style may also underpin exceptional, non-problematic behaviour patterns.

When exceptional behaviour patterns occur, sometimes they are associated with the use of healthy defence mechanisms to manage anxiety arising from conflicting desires to follow a course of action but also to avoid rejection or attack from others. Healthy defence mechanisms include self-observation, looking at the humorous side of the situation, being assertive about having one's needs met, and sublimation of unacceptable desires into socially acceptable channels such as work, art or sport. A full list of healthy defence mechanisms is given in Table 4.2 and they are discussed in detail in Chapter 4.

Contextual factors associated with resilience

Exceptional behaviour patterns and the productive belief systems that support these arise from protective factors that foster resilience (Carr, 2004; Luthar,

2003). These protective factors may be rooted in partners' constitutional characteristics, the couple's broader social context or their historical family-of-origin experiences. Important personal characteristics that contribute to resilience are physical health, high intelligence and easy temperament.

A good social support network, including friends and members of the extended family, and low extra-familial stress enhance a couple's chances of resolving the problems they bring to therapy. Well-balanced home and work roles, moderate or high socio-economic status and empowering cultural norms and values also contribute to resilience in the face of adversity.

Good parent–child relationships characterized by secure attachment, authoritative parenting and clear communication in the family-of-origin foster later resilience and strength. Successful experiences of coping with problems in the family-of-origin and the current relationship, flexible organization in the family-of-origin, good parental adjustment and a positive relationship between parents in the family-of-origin may also engender later resilience.

STAGES OF ISCT

In ISCT to help couples cope with symptoms and resolve problems, the overall strategy is to work co-operatively with them to formulate their difficulties and exceptional episodes (where their difficulties were expected to occur but did not using the three-column models outlined above). Once this has been achieved, treatment goals are set and a therapy plan developed that aims to increase the occurrence of exceptions, disrupt problematic behaviour patterns, transform problematic belief systems and address problem-maintaining contextual factors.

However, couples therapy is not that straightforward. Sometimes, couples have difficulty engaging in therapy. In the example that opened this chapter, Sarah and James probably would not have attended therapy at all without careful planning about who to invite to the initial sessions and what the focus of these meetings should be. Furthermore, many couples show marked improvement following assessment only. That is, once they develop a shared understanding of their difficulties and exceptional situations where their problems were expected to occur but did not, they spontaneously avoid problematic interactions and engage in exceptional non-problematic interactions instead. Finally, some couples come to therapy with one problem, such as depression or anxiety and, when this is resolved, request therapy for other difficulties such as sexual problems. To address these various challenges, within ISCT the process of therapy is conceptualized as a developmental stage-wise process.

The framework set out in Figure 5.4 outlines the stages of ISCT from the initial reception of a referral letter to the point where the case is closed

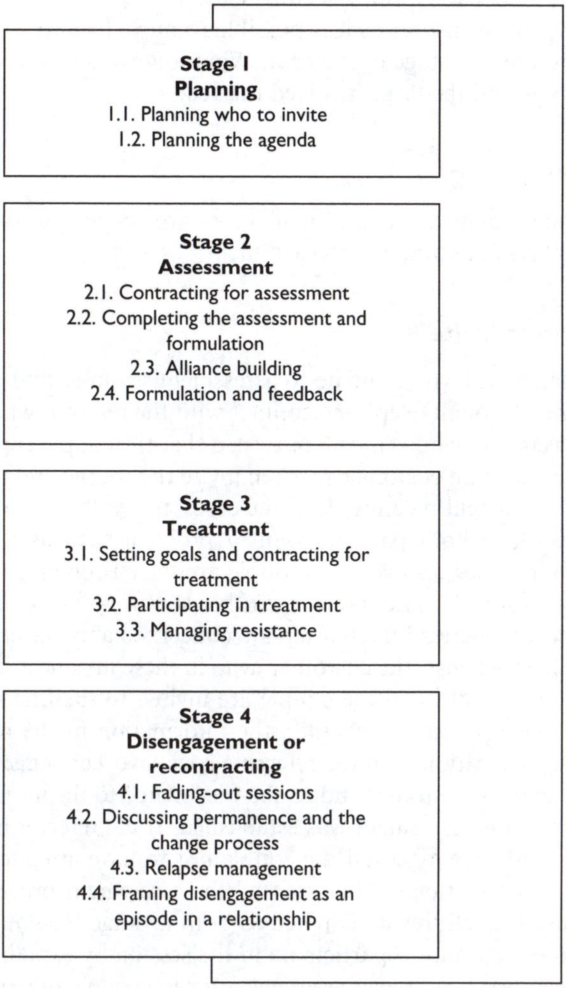

Figure 5.4 Stages of systemic couples therapy.
Based on Carr, A. (2000). *Family therapy: Concepts, process and practice*. Chichester: Wiley.

(Carr, 2000). The first stage is concerned with planning, the second with engagement and assessment, the third with treatment and the fourth with disengagement or recontracting for further intervention. At each stage, key tasks must be completed before progression to the next stage occurs. Failure to complete the tasks of a given stage in sequence or skipping a stage may jeopardize the consultation process. For example, attempting to conduct an assessment without first contracting for assessment may lead to co-operation difficulties if the couple find the assessment procedures arduous or threatening. Failure to complete assessment before treatment compromises decision making about goal setting and selecting specific therapy strategies. Therapy is a recursive process insofar as it is possible to move from the final stage of one episode to the first stage of the next. What follows is a description of the stages of therapy and the tasks involved in each.

Stage 1: Planning

In the first stage of therapy, the main tasks are to plan who to invite to the assessment sessions and what to ask them.

Planning who to invite

To make a plan about who to invite to assessment sessions, find out from the referral letter or through telephone contact with the referrer, who is involved with the problem and who is most concerned that the couple engage in treatment, i.e. who the main customer is. Then invite the couple and the customer to an intake assessment meeting. In some cases, this will be straightforward. For example, where both partners want a problem such as depression or relationship difficulties resolved, the couple are the customer. In other cases, where probation social services or some other statutory agency is concerned about the case, or where adult children are concerned about a parental problem such as alcohol abuse, the customer, who in these instances is usually not a member of the couple, and the couple are invited to the first interview. In the example that opened this chapter, the information in the referral letter and a phone conversation with the referring social worker suggested that the referrer was the main customer and so she was invited to the initial meeting at which a contract for assessment was established. If the referrer had not been invited, we would have expected the couple not to have attended the intake interview, or to have attended but resisted the assessment process. To avoid these problems, the referrer was invited to both arrange the couple's attendance at the interview and to participate in the session by explaining why she had made the referral and the consequences for the couple of participating in therapy or not doing so.

Planning what to ask: Agenda setting

If the referrer's concerns are vague and there is any degree of ambiguity about who the main customer for therapy is, the following questions may be asked, both in a preliminary telephone contact with the referrer and at the outset of the intake interview: 'What is the main problem that led to the referral? Who is most concerned that the problem be addressed now?' The next set of questions to ask are those that allow hypotheses based on preliminary three-column formulations of problems and exceptions to be checked. These questions should cover behaviour patterns, belief systems and specific contextual factors. The third set of questions should cover the couple's personal and family background, so that unanticipated contextual factors of relevance to a more accurate formulation of the problem may be identified. Prepare a list of lines of questioning to follow and refer to these throughout the assessment sessions.

Stage 2: Assessment

In the second stage there the three main tasks are: (1) establishing a contract for assessment; (2) completing the assessment and formulation; and (3) building a therapeutic alliance.

Contracting for assessment

Contracting for assessment involves the therapist and clients clarifying expectations and reaching an agreement to work together. Begin by explaining the referral route, for example:

'I thought to start I would explain my understanding of how you were referred here and check if that fits with your understanding. Dr Randell wrote to me and said that you were all concerned about Michael's depression. She took the view that you were both affected by this and so both of you might be able to help with solving the problem. So she referred you here. Is that your understanding of how the referral came about?'

The next priority is to outline what assessment involves and offer each partner a chance to accept or reject the opportunity to complete the assessment. Explain the way in which the interviews will be conducted, their duration, and the roles of the team (if a team or a supervisor behind a one-way screen is involved). For example:

'What we had in mind for today was to invite each of you to give your views on the problem. How you see it. What you think makes it worse or better. Who is most affected by it. How you think it might be solved. When each of you has given your view, we will take a break. During the break, I will take some time to think about all that you have said (or to talk with the team about their views of the situation) and then we can finish up by discussing what to do next. That is, I will be in a position to tell you if you have the type of problem we can help you with and if so how we think it would be best to proceed. These meetings usually take an hour or an hour and a half altogether. Can I check with each of you if you wish to have this meeting right now and if you wish to give your views on the problems that led to you coming here today?'

If a team is involved in the assessment process, clarify their roles. Also if a one-way screen is being used, mention its function. For example:

'In our clinic we have found that it's useful in helping couples solve problems if more than one therapist is involved. But it can be distracting if more than one of us is here in the interviewing room. So our practice is to work in teams, and for the rest of the team to watch the interview silently from the other side of that screen. It looks like a mirror, but the team can see us from the other room. Their job is to keep track of each person's different view of the situation and think about how best to solve the problem. Some members of the team are very experienced and some (like me) are in training. I will introduce you to them after the break (or now) if that's OK with you?'

If videotaping is used, a written consent form should be signed by both partners. It may also be useful to give a verbal explanation. For example:

'In our clinic we have found that we can get a clearer understanding of each person's different view of the situation if we video each session and then review it later. To get this service, you must sign a consent form. The form simply says that you want the video-review service and understand that the video is confidential and will not be shown to anyone except the clinical team.'

If, after a course of therapy, a therapist wants to use a tape for training purposes, then it is necessary to request written consent specifically for this. The audience to which the tape will be shown must be specified on the consent form with reference to local, national or international training events.

In the contracting meeting, highlight the voluntary nature of the assessment and clarify the limits of confidentiality. Normally, the contents of sessions are confidential unless there is evidence that a client is a serious threat to themselves or to others. For example, where there is evidence of suicidal intent or domestic violence, confidentiality may be breached.

Where one or both partners are confused about why they both have been invited for the intake interview when (in their opinion) only one of them has a problem, such as anxiety or depression, the following rationale may be given:

> 'Our guess is that both of you are affected by this problem, both of you have views on things that make the problem better or worse, and both of you may have views on how best to cope with it or resolve it in future. So we thought we might get a better understanding of the situation by talking to both of you.'

Enquiring about the presenting problem

Once a contract for assessment has been established, each partner may be invited to give his or her view of the presenting problem, the pattern of interaction around it and related belief systems. Ask about the nature, frequency and intensity of the problems; previous successful and unsuccessful solutions to these problems; and partners' views on the causes of these problems and possible solutions that they suspect may be fruitful to explore in future. Also ask questions to test specific hypotheses about the presenting problem based on your preliminary three-column problem formulation.

Questions about problem-maintaining behaviour patterns

Here are some questions that may be useful when enquiring about the presenting problem and the pattern of interaction in which it is embedded:

- Everybody has their own view of the problem. What we are interested in finding out is each person's view. These may all be quite different. That's OK. We are not looking for the right answer or the absolute truth, just each person's view of the problem.
- So, can you tell us how you see it?
- How did it start?
- How is it now?
- Can you tell me about the last time the problem occurred?
- If I were watching a video of the problem happening, what would I see in the lead up to it, during it, and after it?

- What were you each feeling during these episodes?
- What has made it better or worse?
- How have you tried to solve this problem?
- What solutions have worked in the past and which have not?
- Which solution do you keep trying again and again?
- In your previous attempts to solve this problem, when A said B did you understand what he or she meant?
- In your previous attempts to solve this problem, when X happened did you feel close to or distant from your partner?
- In your previous attempts to solve this problem, when X happened did you feel like you had more power or less power than your partner?
- In your previous attempts to solve this problem, when X happened, did you know what was going to happen next?
- In your previous attempts to solve this problem, when X happened, was the outcome a good thing or a bad thing for you or your partner?
- In your previous attempts to solve this problem, when X happened, did you believe that your partner was on your side or not?
- In your previous attempts to solve this problem, was it clear to you what the plan was for yourself, your partner, the social worker, the doctor and the probation officer?
- How have you tried to get a joint plan working?

Questions about problem-maintaining belief systems

What follows are some useful formats for questions to ask when interviewing about belief systems that support problem-maintaining behaviour patterns:

- Is there agreement between you about what the main problem is?
- Who holds the view most strongly that there is a problem?
- What explanation do you give for this problem?
- Is the problem more to do with the person or the situation?
- Has the problem got worse or better since you made your appointment to come here?
- What explanation do you offer for this improvement, deterioration or stability?
- In the past, has the problem been constant or fluctuating?
- How do you explain this stability or fluctuation?
- In the future, will you expect the problem to improve, deteriorate or remain stable?
- What explanation do you or others give for this expected change or stability?
- How does your explanation of the problem differ from that of your partner?
- If this problem were improving, what would you both be doing differently?

- If this problem were getting worse, what would you both be doing differently?
- If your mother/father/grandmother/grandfather/priest/rabbi, etc. were here with us, what advice would they give us about managing this problem?
- What roles should husbands/wives/doctors/social workers, etc. take in dealing with problems like these according to your mother/father/grandparents/religion/ethnic group?
- There is a downside to everything. What would be the downside to solving this problem?
- What would you lose?
- We often do one thing to avoid another problem. Just say you or your partner were dealing with this problem as you have been doing to avoid some other worse situation, what is it you are avoiding?
- To what extent do you believe that you can control this problem and to what extent do you believe it is out of your control?
- To what extent do you believe that your partner can control this problem and to what extent do you believe it is out of his/her control?
- How do you think the problem will be in a year if you keep going as you have been?
- Just say the problem got solved in the next few months, and I met you in a year's time and asked you what exactly had happened, what story would you tell me?

Questions about predisposing contextual factors

What follows are some useful formats for questions to ask when interviewing about contextual and historical predisposing factors:

- Over the past year, what have been the main changes that have occurred for you and your partner?
- Over the past year, what have been the main pressures on you at home and work?
- Over the past year, who has been most supportive of you and how have they shown this?
- How have you juggled the demands of work and home life over the past year?
- How has your health and that of your partner been over the past year?
- How would this type of situation have been handled in your family-of-origin?
- Can you describe how a comparable situation was handled in your amily-of-origin?
- Do you believe that any of the challenges or difficulties you faced as a youngster have affected your capacity to cope with the present problem?

- How would you describe your mother's/father's/carer's relationship with you during your childhood and adolescence?
- How would you describe your mother's and father's relationship with each other during your childhood and adolescence?
- How would you describe your mother's/ father's way of managing their lives during your childhood and adolescence?
- How would you describe family life (rules, role and routines) during your childhood and adolescence?

Enquiring about exceptions

Questions about exceptions include those about exceptional circumstances within which the problem does not occur, empowering belief systems and narratives that underpin these exceptions, and constitutional, contextual and historical factors that are the foundation of family resilience (deShazer, 1988; White, 1995).

Questions about exceptional behaviour patterns

The following are useful formats for questions to ask when interviewing about exceptional behaviour patterns:

- Tell me about an exceptional situation in which the problem was expected to occur but didn't.
- If I was watching a video of this exception what would I see in the lead up to it, during it and after it?
- What were you each feeling during this episode?
- Was there a turning point during this successful exception when you knew that you were going to manage the problem well?
- During this successful episode when you managed the problem well, when A said B did you understand what he or she meant?
- During this successful episode when you managed the problem well, when X happened did you feel close to or distant from your partner?
- During this successful episode when you managed the problem well, when X happened did you feel like you had more power or less power than your partner?
- During this successful episode when you managed the problem well, when X happened, did you know what was going to happen next?
- During this successful episode when you managed the problem well, was the outcome a good thing or a bad thing for you or your partner?
- During this successful episode when you managed the problem well, when X happened, did it feel like your partner was on your side?
- During this successful episode when you managed the problem well, was it clear to you what the plan was for yourself, your partner, the social

worker, the doctor and probation officer? How did you all get a joint plan working?

Questions about empowering belief systems

What follows are some useful formats for questions to ask when interviewing about empowering narratives and belief systems:

- What is your explanation for this successful exception in which you managed the problem well?
- Was your success more to do with your efforts, the efforts of your partner or the situation?
- To what extent do you believe that you can make these exceptions happen again and to what extent do you believe this is out of your control?
- To what extent do you believe that your partner can control these exceptions and to what extent do you believe that they are out of their control?
- Can you give other examples from the past to show that you or your partner were the main factor in managing this problem?
- In the future if you wanted to create another exceptional event in which yourself and your partner managed the problem well, what would you have to do?

Questions about predisposing protective factors and resilience

What follows are some useful formats for questions to ask when interviewing about protective predisposing factors:

- Can you describe a comparable situation in your family-of-origin, a situation where a problem was unresolved for a long time and then was managed successfully on one occasion?
- If your mother/father/grandmother/grandfather/priest/rabbi, etc. were here with us, what advice would they give us about making these exceptions occur again?
- What roles should mothers/fathers/husbands/wives/doctors/social workers, etc. take in making these exceptions happen again according to your mother/father/grandparents/religion/ethnic group?
- What challenges or difficulties did you face as a youngster that empowered you so that you could manage the present problem so well in this exceptional situation?
- If I were watching a video of your earlier life, what do you think I would see that would explain how you managed to handle the problem so well in this exceptional situation?

Developmental history and genogram construction

The process of taking a developmental history and genogram construction may be routinely incorporated into initial couples assessment sessions (McGoldrick, Gerson, & Shellenberger, 1999). In taking a couple's developmental history, it can create a positive climate in the session to begin by enquiring what attracted them to each other and how they met. From there, ask about the early years of the relationship and the good times they shared before their current problems began. Then ask about how the couple handled the various lifecycle stages listed in Table 1.1 (p. 4), such as having children, managing the process of child rearing and making space for the couple's relationship and so forth. Enquire about the way in which each partner noticed the problems developing and any theories they might hold about precipitating factors. Then, for each partner, enquire about their development within their family-of-origin, and how each managed the various lifecycle challenges of growing up, leaving home, developing a career and developing relationships prior to their current relationship.

While taking the couple's developmental history, concurrently begin constructing a genogram. A genogram is a family tree that contains clinically relevant information about family members and their pattern of organization. Genogram symbols are given in Figure 5.5 and a checklist of areas to cover in genogram construction is given in Table 5.3. It is useful to construct a genogram in a way that allows partners to see it as it is drawn. A flip chart or whiteboard may be used to facilitate this. Most of the genogram construction rules are contained in Figure 5.5. Once the genogram contains all important family members, invite partners to include other important details following the checklist in Table 5.3.

Genogram construction is a good opportunity to pinpoint and label partners' strengths. When asking about strengths, invite partners to identify and label their own and each other's positive attributes. This often has the impact of raising morale and diminishing hopelessness. Here are some examples of how to enquire about and label strengths:

- Can you describe the last time you noticed your partner doing X effectively? Would you agree that doing X well is one of his/her strengths?
- Does you partner work hard on some occasions? If so, would you say that being hardworking is one of their strengths?
- Does your partner help at home from time to time? If so, would you say that being kind and helpful are two of his/her strengths?
- Has your partner got a friend that s/he sees from time to time. If so, would you say that s/he is a loyal friend?
- How long have you been in a relationship? How many times have you separated or felt like leaving but not done so? Does this mean that you are loyal to your partner, that loyalty is one of your strengths?

Table 5.3 Information to include in genograms

People	**Demographics**	• Name • Age • Occupation
	Transitions	• Births • Deaths • Marriages, cohabiting relationships • Changing households • Leaving home • Foster care • Anniversaries of transitions
	Strengths	• Examples of having coped well with problems in the past • Work and school performance • Making and maintaining friendships • Sports and leisure • Special personal achievements
	Vulnerabilities	• Illnesses and hospitalizations • Psychological adjustment problems • Substance abuse • Anger control, violence and abuse • Criminality
Patterns	**Dyadic**	• Supportive alliances and coalitions • Stressful conflicts
	Triadic	• Triangulation where a child is required to take sides with one of two other family members (usually the parents) • Pathological triangles with denied cross-generational coalitions • Detouring-attacking triads where the parents express joint anger at the child, associated with conduct problems • Detouring-protecting triads where parents express joint concern about the child who presents with a psychosomatic or emotional complaint
	Complex	• Multi-generational dyadic patterns (e.g. mothers and daughters are close in three generations) • Multi-generational triadic patterns (e.g. triangulation occurs in two generations)

Based on Carr, A. (2000). *Family therapy: Concepts, process and practice*. Chichester: Wiley.

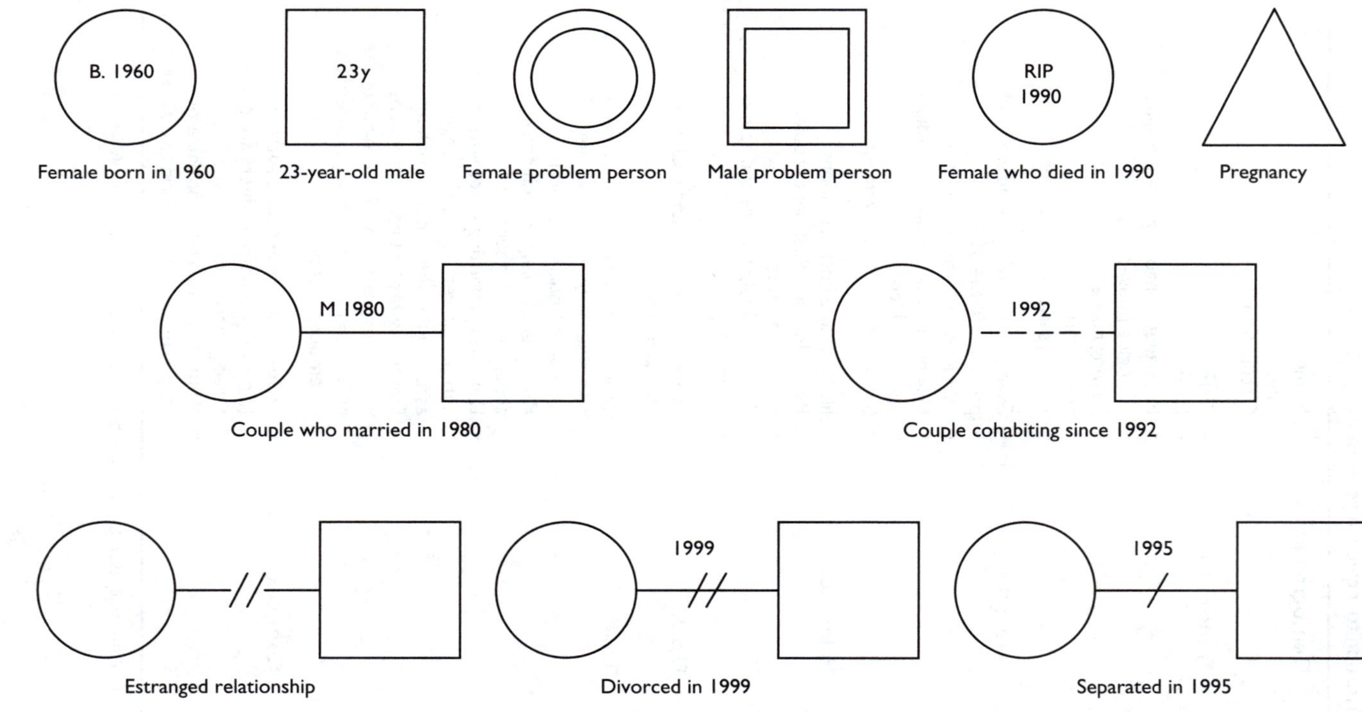
B. 1960
Female born in 1960
23y
23-year-old male
Female problem person
Male problem person
RIP
1990
Female who died in 1990
Pregnancy
M 1980
Couple who married in 1980
1992
Couple cohabiting since 1992
Estranged relationship
1999
Divorced in 1999
1995
Separated in 1995

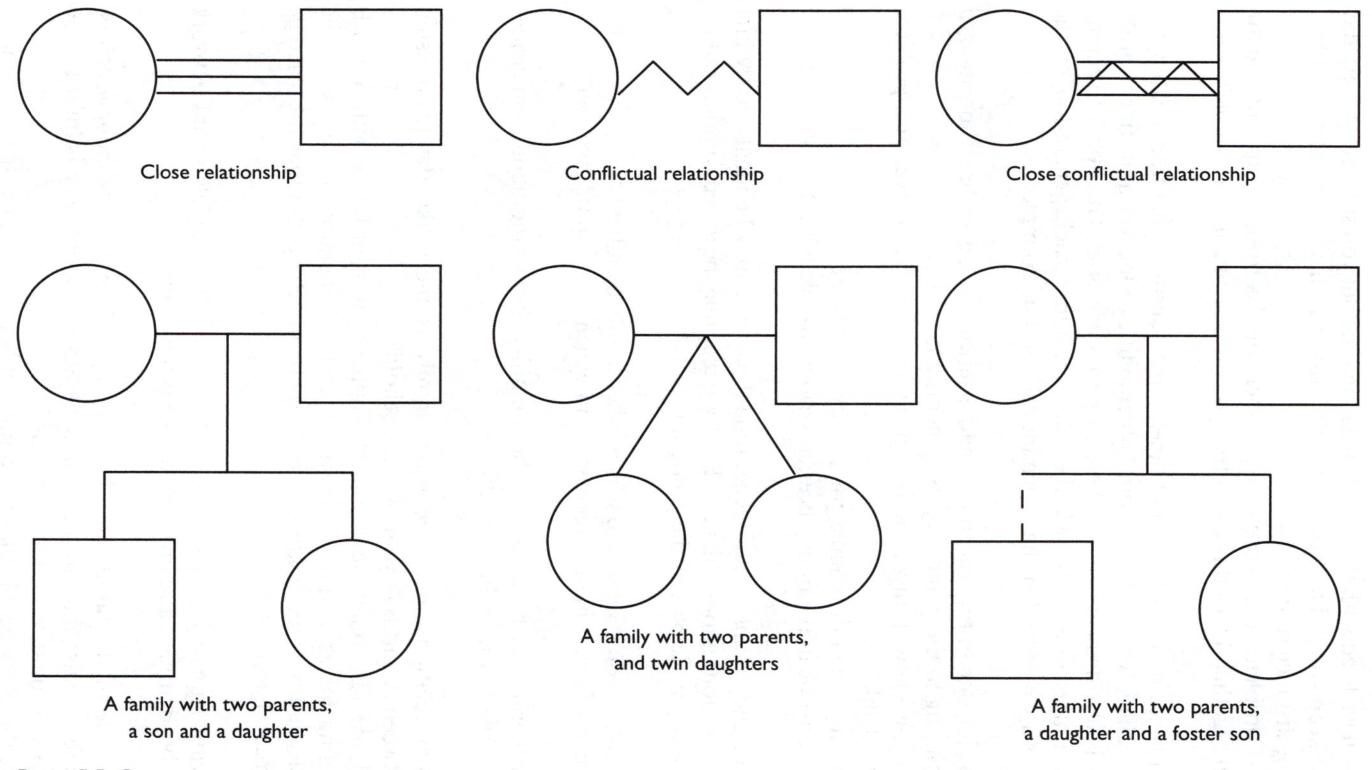

Figure 5.5 Genogram symbols.

- You have lived with this problem a long time but you still get up every day and keep going. Does this mean that that you have great stamina, like a long-distance runner?
- This problem could have caused other couples to break up, but you are still together. Does this mean that you are a strong united couple?

While it is useful to spend a lot of time asking questions that lead to strengths being labelled, when asking about vulnerabilities, illnesses, adjustment problems, it is less demoralizing if these enquiries are brief. One way of keeping such enquiries brief is to ask the question about each generation or the couple as a whole, rather than each individual. For example:

- Has anyone in this generation had a serious illness or been hospitalized [pointing to the grandparents' generation]?
- Do you know if anyone in this generation had bad nerves or a problem with drink?
- Has anyone in the couple got a really short fuse?
- Has anyone in the family been in serious trouble with the police?

Triangles and complex multi-generational patterns may be identified by first asking questions about alliances. Each partner may be asked to point out on the nuclear couple part of the genogram:

- Which of you is closest to which other family member?
- Which of you is in disagreement with which other family member?

Multi-generational patterns may be identified by asking about similarities between relationships. For example:

- What relationship in the wider family is most like the relationship between A and B in your own household?
- It looks like sometimes a triangle happened in your house with A and B joining forces against C. If we go back a generation or across to the households of aunts and uncles, is there anywhere else that this triangle pattern happens?

Significant supportive or stressful members of the couple's social network should be identified and included on the genogram:

- Outside of the family, are there any close friends (neighbours/doctors/professionals) that are important because they are very helpful to you and so should be on the genogram?
- Are there any people that are important because they cause your family a lot of hassle and so should be on the genogram?

To explore the amount of support or stress associated with extrafamilial relationships, some questions are useful in keeping this process brief:

- Which people in the family or wider network do you see on a daily basis and which do you see infrequently, like just at Christmas and Easter?
- Are these contacts a hassle or are they something you look forward to?

If partners looks forward to these contacts more than others, each partner may be asked of these contacts:

- Who looks forward to them the most?
- Who looks forward to them the least?

The management of developmental issues may be enquired about with reference to the frameworks outlined in Chapter 1. Questions may focus on how well partners managed particular lifecycle stages and transitions from one stage to the next. This offers further opportunities to pinpoint and label strengths. An example of a genogram for James and Sarah is presented in Figure 5.3 and the way salient aspects of the genogram were incorporated into the three-column problem and exception formulations has been outlined in the case vignette at the beginning of this chapter.

Questionnaires and rating scales

The *Golombok Rust inventory of marital state* (GRIMS; Rust, Bennun, Crowe, & Golombok, 1988) and the *Marital satisfaction inventory-revised.* (MSI-R; Snyder, 1997) are useful self-report instruments for routinely surveying couple's strengths and weaknesses. The Global Assessment of Relational Functioning Rating Scale, from the DSM-IV-TR, given in Table 5.4 is a useful non-intrusive way of rating couple functioning based on an intake interview.

Alliance building

In addition to providing information, the process of assessment also serves as a way for the couple and therapist to build a working alliance. Building a strong working alliance is essential for valid assessment and effective therapy. All other features of the consultation process should be subordinate to the working alliance, since without it, clients drop out of assessment and therapy or fail to make progress (Hubble, Duncan, & Miller, 1999; Norcross, 2002). The only exception to this rule is where the safety of a partner or family member is at risk; in such cases protection takes priority over alliance building.

Research on common factors that contribute to a positive therapeutic outcome and ethical principles of good practice point to a number of guidelines

Table 5.4 Global Assessment of Relational Functioning Scale

Score	*Description*
81–100	**Overall functioning**. The couple is functioning satisfactorily from partners' self-reports and from the perspective of observers
	Problem solving and communication. Agreed routines exist that help meet the needs of the couple. There is flexibility for change in response to unusual demands or events. Occasional conflicts and stressful transitions are resolved through effective problem solving and communication
	Organization. There is a shared understanding and agreement about roles and tasks. Decision making is established for each functional area. There is recognition of the unique characteristics and merits of each partner
	Emotional climate. There is a situationally appropriate optimistic atmosphere. A wide range of feelings is freely expressed and managed. There is a general atmosphere of warmth, caring and sharing values. Sexual relations are satisfactory
61–80	**Overall functioning**. The functioning of the couple is somewhat unsatisfactory. Over a period of time many, but not all difficulties are resolved without complaints
	Problem solving and communication. Daily routines that help meet the needs of the couple are present. There is some difficulty in responding to unusual demands or events. Some conflicts remain unresolved but do not disrupt the functioning of the couple
	Organization. Decision making is usually competent but efforts to control one another quite often are greater than necessary or are ineffective. There is not always recognition of the unique characteristics and merits of each partner and sometimes blaming or scapegoating occurs
	Emotional climate. A range of feelings is expressed but instances of emotional blocking and tension are evident. Warmth and caring are present but are marred by partners' irritability and frustrations. Sexual relations are reduced or problematic
41–60	**Overall functioning**. The couple have occasional times of satisfying and competent functioning together, but clearly dysfunctional, unsatisfying relationships tend to predominate
	Problem solving and communication. Communication is frequently inhibited by unresolved conflicts that often interfere with daily routines. There is significant difficulty in adapting to family stresses and transitional change
	Organization. Decision making is only intermittently competent and effective. Either excessive rigidity or significant lack of structure is evident at these times. Individual needs are often submerged by one partner's demands
	Emotional climate. Pain or ineffective anger or emotional deadness interferes with family enjoyment. Although there is some warmth and support between partners, it is usually unequally distributed. Troublesome sexual difficulties are often present

21–40	**Overall functioning.** The couple is obviously and seriously dysfunctional. Forms and time periods of satisfactory relating are rare **Problem solving and communication.** Couple's routines do not meet partners' needs. They are grimly adhered to or blithely ignored. Lifecycle changes generate painful conflict and obviously frustrating failures in problem solving **Organization.** Decision making is tyrannical or quite ineffective. Partners' unique characteristics are unappreciated or ignored **Emotional climate.** There are infrequent periods of enjoyment of life together. Frequent distancing or open hostility reflects significant conflicts that remain unresolved and quite painful. Sexual dysfunction is commonplace
1–20	**Overall functioning.** The couple has become too dysfunctional to retain continuity of contact and attachment **Problem solving and communication.** Couple routines for eating, sleeping, entering and leaving the home, etc. are negligible. Partners do not know each other's schedules. There is little effective communication between partners **Organization.** Couples are not organized to respect personal boundaries or accept personal responsibilities within the relationship. Partners may be physically endangered, injured or sexually assaulted **Emotional climate.** Despair and cynicism are pervasive. There is little attention to the emotional needs of others. There is almost no sense of attachment, commitment or concern for each other's welfare

Based on American Psychiatric Association (2000). *Diagnostic and Statistical Manual of the Mental Disorders* (Fourth Edition-Text Revision, DSM-IV-TR, pp. 814–816). Washington, DC: APA.

that therapists should employ in developing a working alliance (Hubble et al., 1999; Norcross, 2002). Warmth, empathy and genuineness should characterize the therapist's communication style. The therapist should form a collaborative partnership in which clients are experts on the specific features of their own relationships and therapists are experts on general scientific and clinical information relevant to the broad class of problems of which the presenting problem is a specific instance.

Neutrality and acceptance are central to the positioning of the therapist. Each partner in the couple must feel at the end of each session that the therapist understood, accepted and sympathized with his or her point of view. They must not feel judged or blamed, but rather experience the therapist as understanding that they were doing their best to manage a frustrating or intolerable situation. This is a challenging position to adopt since, in most couples sessions, both partners blame each other and invite the therapist to take sides with one or other partner.

Assessment should be conducted from a position of respectful curiosity in which the therapist continually strives to uncover new information about the problem and potential solutions and invites clients to consider the implications of viewing their difficulties as determined by multiple factors and from multiple different perspectives. This positioning counters the couple's attempt to find the 'one cause', the 'person who is to blame', or the 'single right answer'.

An invitational approach should be adopted in which clients are invited (not directed) to participate in assessment and treatment. Thus, if partners cannot follow through on homework assignments or activities in sessions, they do not feel guilty or blamed for not doing as directed.

There should be a balanced focus on strengths and resilience on the one hand and on problems and constraints on the other. This positioning fosters optimism without colluding with denial.

There should be an attempt to match the way therapy is conducted to the clients' readiness to change, since to do otherwise may jeopardize the therapeutic alliance. For example, if a therapist focuses on offering technical assistance with problem solving to clients who are still only contemplating change and needing help exploring the pros and cons of change, conflict will arise because the clients will feel coerced into action by the therapist and will probably not follow through on therapeutic tasks; the therapist may feel disappointed that the clients are showing resistance.

There should be an acknowledgement that clients and therapists inadvertently bring to the working alliance attitudes, expectations, emotional responses and interactional routines from early significant care-giving and care-receiving relationships. These transference and countertransference reactions, if unrecognized, may compromise therapeutic progress and so should be addressed when resistance to therapeutic change occurs. Methods for managing resistance will be discussed below.

Formulation and feedback

Once a formulation has been constructed, feedback is given to the couple about the formulation and treatment options are considered. During feedback, use all opportunities to label the couple's strengths, to build hope. Match the level of detail in giving feedback to the cognitive abilities and the emotional readiness of each member of the couple. It is also important to empathize with each partner's position when outlining the way in which the problem appears to have evolved. Usually, partners are well intentioned but under stress, and without adequate information they inadvertently contribute to problem development or maintenance. In the process of feeding back some or all of the formulation to couples, in order to maintain a good working alliance, regularly check that they have understood and accepted the formulation so far. Once the couple has understood and accepted the formulation, move on to goal setting. Here is an example of how feedback was given to James and Sarah, the couple mentioned in the opening vignette:

'Over the last two sessions we have worked together to try to understand the difficulties that brought you here. These problems are complex and challenging. I have been impressed with the way you have faced up to them. A lot of other couples would have thrown in the towel by now. I've been impressed that you have stuck together through this process. Even though things are sometimes very rough in your lives, you are loyal to each other and to your children and seem to want to work things out. At this stage I can let you know my view, my assessment of the situation. Then you have a chance to think about this and make a decision about whether to move on to treatment or not. Should I tell you my assessment of the situation now?

'It's clear to me that your difficulties follow a definite pattern that involves both of you, and it's hard to know where it begins or ends. But for the sake of simplicity, let's say the pattern begins with a disagreement, in which, James, you ask Sarah to do something for you because you feel stressed out, like calm the children down or treat you in a romantic way. But maybe you ask a bit aggressively because you think she's going to say no. And then you, Sarah, find it hard to co-operate with James because you feel like you have enough on your plate already. You're overloaded. Then, James, you criticize Sarah because it feels to you like she's punishing you, and that's not fair because you're doing your best. Then you, Sarah, fight back. But this gets you riled up. Sometimes you notice this, and hear your heart beating too fast and think you might have a heart attack. On those occasions you have a panic attack; a fairly scary experience. James, when you see this, you sometimes feel like it's your fault Sarah is having the attack and you then usually back off. Then there often is a gap of a few days where you are not on speaking terms. And then gradually the ice thaws between you. But the misunderstanding is not cleared up. So, the next time the pressure is on both of you and James, you ask Sarah to do something for you, the pattern repeats. I just want to check that pattern out with you.

'The other thing we have talked about over the last two sessions are exceptions, times when the pattern that makes you both feel so bad should have happened but didn't. There are times, James, when you help Sarah. Like when she is having difficulty with the children, or the car, or cooking dinner, or doing some other jobs. When you help her, she smiles at you or says something kind, and you both feel good. These exceptions give me hope that you may be able to sort out your difficulties.

Can I check that you both recognize these exceptional patterns I'm talking about?

'Now, from the stuff you've told me about your families, I suspect that for each of you, your part in the problem patterns and the exceptions comes in part from things you learned in the families you grew up in. But we can talk about that at another time . . . Right now, if you agree that these patterns are a useful way of looking at your problem and exceptions to it, the question is would you like to meet for a few more sessions to work on changing the problem pattern and bringing more of the exception patterns into your lives? You can let me know later what your answer is to that question.'

Stage 3: Treatment

In some cases, the process of assessment and formulation releases a couple's natural problem-solving skills and they resolve the problem themselves. In other cases, assessment leads on to contracting for an episode of treatment.

Setting goals and contracting for treatment

The contracting process involves establishing goals and outlining a plan to work towards these in light of the formulation. Clearly defined, realistic goals that are accepted by both partners and that are perceived to be moderately challenging are crucial for effective therapy. Ask questions like this to set long-term goals:

- Imagine, it's a year from now and the problem is solved. It's a Monday morning at your house. What is happening? Give me a blow-by-blow description of what everyone is doing.

Ask the following types of question to set short-term goals:

- What is the smallest thing that would have to change for you to know you were moving in the right direction to solve this difficult problem?
- Just say this problem was half-way better. What would be different about the way you talked to each other?

Ideally, progress towards goals should be assessed in an observable or quantitative way. For many problems, progress may be assessed using frequency counts, for example, the number of arguments or the number of compliments.

Ratings of internal states, moods and beliefs are useful ways of quantifying progress towards less observable goals. Here are some examples of scaling questions:

- You say that on a scale of one to ten your mood is now about three. How many points would it have to go up the scale for you to know you were beginning to recover?
- Last week on a scale of one to ten, you said your belief in X was four. How strongly do you believe X now?

When couples have set some treatment goals, a contract for further therapy may be set:

'There are pros and cons to continuing with this work to try and achieve the sorts of goals you have been talking about. You may want to go it alone from here on. Or you may want to attend some more meetings here with us. To benefit from therapy, you would need to attend about ten more sessions. That involves a lot of time and effort. Also, there is only a two out of three chance that you will benefit from therapy. So it's not a guaranteed solution and it's hard to say right now if you will be one of the lucky ones who can benefit. On the other hand, you are both good at this sort of work. You have a knack of making sense of your problems in a very thoughtful way and seem to be able to use these meetings well, so these two things suggest to me that you might benefit from further meetings. Should we discuss how you want to proceed now?'

Participating in treatment

Treatment may involve interventions that aim to alter problem-maintaining behaviour patterns, interventions that focus on the development of new belief systems that open up possibilities for problem resolution and interventions that focus on predisposing factors. Some interventions in each of these categories are listed in Table 5.5. As a broad principle of practice, it is probably most efficient to begin with interventions that aim to alter problem-maintaining behaviour patterns and the belief systems that underpin these, unless there is good reason to believe that such interventions will be ineffective because of the influence of constitutional vulnerabilities, broader contextual factors or historical family-of-origin issues. Only if interventions that focus on problem-maintaining behaviour patterns and belief systems are ineffective

Table 5.5 Interventions in systemic couples therapy to address factors within three-column formulations

Contexts	*Belief systems*	*Behaviour patterns*
Addressing constitutional factors • Psychoeducation about condition • Facilitating adherence to medication regime **Addressing contextual issues** • Network meetings • Changing roles • Building support • Rituals for mourning losses • Exploring secrets **Addressing family-of-origin issues** • Facilitate exploration of transgenerational patterns, scripts myths and relationship habits • Facilitate re-experiencing, expressing and integrating emotions from family-of-origin experiences, which underpin destructive relationship habits • Coach clients to reconnect with cut-off parental figures	**Reframing problems** • Frame problems in interactional terms • Frame problems in solvable terms • Frame intentions in positive terms **Pinpointing strengths** • Find unnamed obvious strengths • Attribute them to clients as defining characteristics **Relabelling** • Find negatively labelled behaviours • Relabel them in positive non-blaming terms **Presenting multiple perspectives** • Split messages • Reflecting team practice **Externalizing problems and building on exceptions** • Separate the problem from the person • Identify and amplify exceptions including pre-therapy improvements • Involve network members • Link the current life exceptions to the past and future • Build a new positive narrative based on the series of exceptions	**Creating a therapeutic context** • Contract • Lay ground rules • Facilitate turn taking • Manage time and space **Facilitating expression of unmet attachment needs** • Distinguish primary (vulnerable/adaptive) emotions from secondary (hard/ maladaptive) emotions • Facilitate intense expression and reception of primary emotions and attachment needs **Changing rates of positive and negative behaviour** • Behaviour exchange • Acceptance building **Problem-solving and communication skills training** • Communication skills training • Problem-solving skills training **Tasks to change behaviour patterns between sessions** • Symptom monitoring • Restraint • Managing graded challenges • Practising symptoms • Self-regulation

Based on Carr, A. (2000). *Family therapy: Concepts, process and practice*. Chichester: Wiley.

or clearly inappropriate is it efficient to move towards interventions that target predisposing factors. Select interventions that fit with a couple's goals, the three-column formulation of the problem and the exception formulation. Select interventions that are compatible with the couple's readiness for change. Where clients are ambivalent or uncommitted, these issues rather than action planning should be the focus of treatment. Interventions that are compatible with the couple's rules, roles, routines, belief systems and culture are probably preferable to those that are incompatible. Interventions that make best use of the couple's strengths are probably better than those that do not fully exploit the couple's own problem-solving and self-healing resources to the full. It is also preferable to select interventions that make best use of the therapist's or team's skills.

Behaviour-focused interventions

Interventions that aim to directly disrupt or replace problem-maintaining behaviour patterns include the following:

- creating a therapeutic context
- facilitating emotive expression of attachment needs
- changing rates of positive and negative behaviour
- problem-solving and communication skills training
- using tasks between sessions to change behaviour patterns.

Creating a therapeutic context

In every session, the process of creating a context for therapeutic work is an intervention that disrupts problem-maintaining behaviour patterns. In every session the contract for therapeutic work is re-established either implicitly or explicitly. Turn taking in speaking and listening is practised and the therapist, in collaboration with the couple and the agency, arrange for the session to take place for a period of uninterrupted time in an appropriate space to achieve agreed goals. However, in the first session these issues are addressed very explicitly (as described earlier in the section on contracting for assessment). In later sessions, pay regular attention to creating a therapeutic context by structuring the sessions in a way that promotes collaborative problem solving and that maintains a sense of fairness. A useful structure is to open each session by inviting participants to give a brief account of progress from their perspective. Note specific issues to be discussed in the heart of the session. Sometimes it is helpful to take a break before concluding the session to plan how the session might most usefully be concluded. Sessions may be concluded by simply inviting participants to continue the in-session conversation in the next session. In other instances, the strengths and commitment clients have shown during the session may be highlighted. Sometimes it is useful to conclude sessions by reframing clients' problems or highlighting multiple different perspectives. In still other instances, sessions may conclude by inviting clients to complete specific tasks for specific reasons before the next session.

Facilitating emotive expression of attachment needs

Where clients had insecure attachment styles in their families of origin, this may be replicated in their adult relationships. They may fear that their partners will not meet their attachment needs for companionship, support, satisfaction, security and safety. They may anticipate that if they let their partners know that they feel sad, frightened or in need of companionship, they will be rejected. This anticipation of rejection and the pain it would involve prevents them from letting their partners know that they feel vulnerable and needy. Instead, they assume rejection would occur and express anger at their partners because of this, often erroneous, expectation. However, their hostile attitude often elicits rejection from their partners and so their fears become a self-fulfilling prophecy. In such circumstances, an intervention central to emotionally focused couples therapy is appropriate (Johnson, 1996). Couples are helped to distinguish between secondary and primary emotional responses. Primary emotional responses include fear, sadness disappointment, emotional hurt and vulnerability. Anger and resentment are secondary emotional responses that occur when there is an expectation that attachment needs may not be met. The couple's problem may be reframed as one involving the miscommunication of primary attachment needs and related disappointments. Partners may be invited to express their attachment needs and related primary emotional responses in full and forceful ways, but not to give vent to their secondary emotional responses through blaming or guilt induction. When primary emotions such as sadness and disappointment are expressed, the partner listening to the emotional expression of attachment needs commonly experiences empathy and is moved to go some way towards meeting the other's attachment needs. If in a number of sessions the therapist can facilitate an intensification and repetition of such primary expressions of attachment needs, these may come to replace secondary emotional responses, such as anger and resentment.

Changing rates of positive and negative behaviour

Behavioural exchange techniques may be used to help flexible couples increase positive things that they do for each other. Facilitating emotional acceptance can increase positive exchanges and decrease negative exchanges in rigid couples by helping partners react to non-preferred behaviours with acceptance rather than negative responses (Jacobson & Christensen, 1996).

BEHAVIOURAL EXCHANGE

Where couples are strongly motivated to change, behavioural exchange interventions that directly aim to increase rates of positive exchanges between couples are appropriate. The rationale given is that happy couples spontaneously engage in five times more positive than negative exchanges, so planning an increase in positive exchanges will enhance relationship satisfaction. Behavioural exchange interventions involve generating lists of events that are valued by partners and arranging for them to do these things for each other in a way that is optimally reinforcing for both parties. This means in practice that 'givers' must be perceived to be giving freely and giving something that is valued by 'receivers', and 'receivers' must communicate that 'gifts' received were valued and that they are grateful. One option is to ask each partner to generate his or her own list of valued events, exchange the lists and then carry out one or more events each day as a 'gift' for their partner and notice the impact of this on relationship satisfaction. A more subtle option (Jacobson & Christensen, 1996) is for partners to generate what they believe their spouse's wish list to be. With this option, the therapist works with each partner while the other partner is an observer and helps to brainstorm all the things that they could do to make their partner happy. This creates a context within which 'receivers' hear 'givers' in conversation with the therapist focusing exclusively on the 'receiver's' needs and how these might be met through acts of generosity and caring. Then partners are invited, between sessions, to choose one or more items from their list that are not too taxing for them, and freely 'give' to their partners without mentioning that they are doing so, with a view to increasing the receiver's relationship satisfaction. A discussion of the impact of the task on couple's satisfaction is reserved until the next therapy session, where the 'givers' get feedback that can help them refine future attempts. If couples have difficulty generating pleasing things they can do for their partners, the Spouse Observation Checklist may be used (Wills, Weiss, & Patterson, 1974). This 409-item inventory covers a wide variety of activities in areas such as companionship, affection, sex, consideration, communication, activities with others, children and finances. Guidelines for giving homework assignments in ways that maximize the chances of adherence are given in Chapter 3 on CBT.

ACCEPTANCE BUILDING

With acceptance building, couples are helped to pinpoint within their problem-maintaining behaviour patterns instances where one partner responds negatively to another because he or she wants the partner to change, and to note how this leads to a symmetrical escalation of negative behaviour. They are then invited to disrupt this pattern by building acceptance. Four strategies are used for acceptance building: empathic joining around the problem, detachment from the problem, tolerance building and developing self-care skills. With the first two of these strategies, couples are helped to join forces against a perplexing dilemma such as whether to have more or less closeness in a relationship when partners have very different preferred levels of closeness. In the second two strategies clients are desensitized to their partner's difficult behaviour or helped to develop self-care skills to cope with it.

With empathic joining around the problem, invite each partner to say how the problem hurts them or makes life difficult for them and how this experience of being hurt makes them try to change their partner's behaviour in a coercive or destructive way. Then empathize with each partner's position in a compassionate way and show how their difficulty accepting each other maintains their problem-behaviour pattern. By modelling empathy and compassion you may promote acceptance. For example:

'You seem to be involved in a situation where anything you do to try to make things better, makes them worse. Mary, when you need to feel supported by John but suspect he wants to keep his distance, you ask him for support in a way that conveys that you are disappointed that he has let you down in the past. I guess you do this because you expect he will let you down again and you never ask for his support unless you really need it. John, you really need your space and to feel appreciated. Each time Mary asks you for support, in that way, you feel like she is criticizing and not understanding you and all you do for the family, so even before she's finished saying what's on her mind, you launch a counterattack or withdraw. The outcome of this usually is, Mary, you get little support and John, you feel even more criticized. It's clear you both care about each other a lot and fall into this trap because you are both trying to change the other person to be more supportive or less critical. So there is an opportunity here to make things different. But it's a hard road. It involves accepting that you face a common problem here. You care about each other. You want to support each other. You each want to be supported. But it's very hard for you to find a way to do this that does not end up in this trap.'

When building emotional acceptance through detachment, the key is to invite the couple to describe the problem as separate from either partner. So, for example, couples may be invited in all future conversations to consider the problem (such as depression, bipolar disorder, anxiety, episodes of conflict) as a detached entity that both of them have to cope with or solve. Invite couples to externalize the problem in all conversations about how to cope with or resolve it. It may be helpful for them to set up a chair or object in the therapy room or at home to represent the problem. Whenever the couple return to viewing each other as adversaries and blaming each other, remind them that they are a team who are dealing with a detached or externalized problem.

When building emotional acceptance through strengthening tolerance, couples may be invited to enact a problematic behaviour pattern, and tolerate the pain it causes them so that they will have practised this skill for managing relapses. This tolerance strengthening process is like desensitizing couples to each other's negative behaviour by exposing them to it in a controlled way, just as people with phobias are gradually exposed to feared situations. When this is done within sessions, invite couples to 'rehearse' how they will tolerate each other's negativity by having a typical conflict within therapy. When giving this as a homework assignment, invite couples to 'pretend' to have a typical conflict without informing their partners, and notice how they tolerate the negative emotions it elicits in them.

When building emotional acceptance through self-care, invite partners to explore ways of coping with their spouse's negative behaviours and getting their needs met in ways that do not involve their partners. Self-care skills include being able to pinpoint problem-maintaining patterns as soon as they begin, developing humour and assertiveness skills as ways of communicating that they have noticed the 'same old pattern' happening again, and consciously withdrawing from these problem-maintaining behaviour patterns as soon as they begin, in a non-punitive way. Self-care also involves developing self-soothing skills such as relaxation or meditation to manage arousal and social skills to manage the need for social support from others.

Communication and problem-solving skills training

Communication and problem-solving skills training equips couples with the skills necessary to talk in a clear way about new problems as they arise and then to develop plans for solving these problems co-operatively (Jacobson & Christensen, 1996). Give this rationale to couples before inviting them to participate in this type of skills training.

COMMUNICATION

Communication skills training involves coaching clients through modelling, role-play and feedback in fair turn taking; communicating messages clearly, directly and congruently to their partners; checking that one has been understood; listening in an empathic manner; paraphrasing partners' messages; and checking the accuracy of such paraphrases. With communication skills training, typical mistakes include interrupting before the other person has finished, failing to summarize what the other person said accurately, attributing negative malicious intentions to the other person, failing to check that the message was accurately sent, failing to check that the message has been accurately received, blaming and sulking.

PROBLEM SOLVING

Problem-solving skills training involves coaching couples through modelling, role-play and feedback in defining large daunting problems as a series of small solvable problems and, for each problem, brainstorming solutions; evaluating the pros and cons of these; selecting one; jointly implementing it; reviewing progress and modifying the selected solution if it is ineffective or celebrating success if the problem is resolved. When couples are observed trying to solve emotionally laden problems, often the first pitfall they slide into is that of problem definition. Many clients need to be coached in how to translate a big vague problem into a few small, specific problems. A second pitfall involves trying to solve more than one problem at a time. A third area of difficulty is helping couples to hold off on evaluating the pros and cons of any one solution until as many solutions as possible have been listed. This is important, since premature evaluating can stifle the production of creative solutions.

COACHING

Train couples in using one skill at a time. In each instance offer couples an intellectual understanding of the skills. Model the skills using an emotionally neutral example. Then invite clients to try using the skills to discuss a neutral topic in the session. Let the episode run for five or ten minutes, and take notes of various difficulties that occur. Often, couples need to be coached out of bad habits such as negative mind reading, blaming and sulking. The challenge in effective skills training is to help the clients avoid their habitual mistakes by praising them for gradual approximations to good communication. Criticizing clients for making mistakes tends to threaten the integrity of the therapeutic alliance and has little impact on skill refinement. Through giving feedback on each trial, couples move gradually to skill mastery. Once couples can use skills to address emotionally neutral topics, invite them to use them to discuss an emotionally 'hot' topic. When mastery has been achieved with 'hot' topics in therapy, offer skills practice with emotionally neutral topics as homework. Only when couples have mastered addressing neutral topics successfully at home should they be invited to address emotionally 'hot' topics as homework. A time and place free of distractions should be agreed and a time limit of no more than twenty minutes set for initial communication assignments and forty minutes when skills are better developed. Where couples with chronic problems successfully resolve a difficulty either in therapy or as homework, a vital part of the coaching process is to help them celebrate this victory. Here is one way to offer the invitation to do a communications training homework task:

'Schedule a specific time and place for the conversation. This should be a time when there is no pressure to be elsewhere and a place in which there are no distractions. Discuss one topic at a time, begin with an emotionally neutral topic. Later, you can move on to using these skills to talk about "hot" issues. Take turns fairly. Make the speaking turns brief.

'When speaking, your main goal is to help your partner understand your point of view. Decide the exact points you want to say. Organize them logically. Say them clearly and then check that you have been understood. When you are certain your partner has understood you accurately, allow space for a reply. When you are speaking, state your points without attacking, blaming or sulking. Frame your points as congruent *I-statements*. For example "I feel angry about what happened between us earlier today". This *I-statement* is better than a *You-statement* like "You started attacking me again today like you always do just to get at me".

'When you are listening, your main goal is to find out exactly what your partner thinks. Listen without interruption and, when your partner has finished speaking, summarize their key points. Check that you have understood what they have said accurately before you reply. When you are listening, avoid composing your reply, defending yourself, or attacking your partner. Try to listen without judging what is being said and avoid negative mind-reading where you attribute bad intentions to your partner.

You have shown that you can do all this here in therapy, so the invitation is to try to do this at home. We will review how you got on next week.'

Tasks between sessions

Couples may be invited to complete tasks between sessions that aim to disrupt or replace problem-maintaining behaviour patterns (Carr, 2000). Among the more widely used tasks are symptom monitoring, restraint, managing graded challenges, practising symptoms and self-regulation.

SYMPTOM MONITORING

For many difficulties, inviting couples to regularly record information decreases problem behaviour and symptoms and increases problem-solving behaviour. Where appropriate, invite clients to routinely record information about the main presenting problems, the circumstances surrounding their occurrence, completion of homework tasks and adherence to biomedical treatment regimes. Intensity ratings, frequency counts, durations and other features of problems or symptoms may be recorded where appropriate. Intrapsychic and interpersonal events that happen before, during and after problems may also be noted. When inviting clients to use a monitoring system, the chances of them co-operating is better if a simple and structured system is given, such as those described in Chapter 3 on CBT. Review monitoring charts regularly and invite couples to speculate on the reasons for changes in problems and related events.

RESTRAINT

When couples commonly make their problems worse by trying to solve them in their habitual ways, they can be advised to move slowly and restrain themselves from trying to change their situation too quickly, since this may have unexpected negative consequences (Shoham & Rohrbaugh, 2002).

MANAGING GRADED CHALLENGES

In cases where clients' fear and anxiety lead them to avoid particular situations, it may be appropriate to invite them to work towards facing the situation they fear most by gradually facing increasingly threatening situations. This type of intervention is appropriate where the fear is related to going out of the house or having arguments. For example, in couples where a member has agoraphobia and panic attacks, it may be appropriate to invite the non-symptomatic partner to escort the person with agoraphobia on increasingly longer outings to learn how to cope with such challenges in a supportive context. Where couples avoid conflict or avoid talking about couples issues and instead discuss the children, they may be invited to schedule increasingly longer conversations about couples issues each day. For example, over a three-week period they may be invited to lengthen their scheduled conversations from 5 to 15 minutes.

PRACTISING SYMPTOMS

With some problems, couples may be invited to practise the symptoms so as to gain control over them. For example, couples who argue regularly may be invited to set aside a designated time each day (e.g. 9.00–9.15 each evening) and confine their arguments to this period exclusively. They may be invited to do this so that they can learn to control the timing of the fights. If their arguments escalate rapidly, they may be invited to take one long turn each of about seven minutes in which they fully express all that they wish to say or listen to their partner doing so. This allows couples to gain control over the pacing of their fights. If they argue about a topic like jealousy, with one partner feeling particularly jealous, they may be invited during scheduled arguments over jealousy to reverse roles so that they can learn to understand each other's positions.

SELF-REGULATION TASKS

Within any relationship, partners have more control over their own behaviour than that of their spouse. Couples may be helped to use this insight to alter the problematic behaviour patterns in which they have become embroiled with their partners (Halford, 1998). A number of self-regulatory strategies may be used. First, they may learn to identify and state their needs more clearly as requests for specific positive actions on the part of their partners. Second, they can plan to selectively attend to their partner's positive exchanges within the relationship and use these as opportunities to respond to their partner in positive ways. Third, they can plan to avoid introducing negativity into the relationship by avoiding complaining and expressing aggression or other negative emotions within the relationship. This may involve identifying risky situations where such expressions are likely and avoiding or changing these. Fourth, they may plan to respond to negativity from their partner in ways that minimize their negative impact. For example, they may say they are taking time out, to avoid an escalating battle. Fifth, they may arrange to have needs that are unmet within the relationship fulfilled in other relationships or situations. For example, needs for companionship may be met by arranging activities with friends. Needs for self-esteem may be based on reflecting on one's own behaviour and values rather than relying on one's partner's evaluations. Sixth, they may be invited to explore their expectations of the relationship and consider altering these, so that they more closely fit with what their partner can provide. Finally, they may be invited to keep the option of leaving the relationship open as a possible way of reducing relationship distress.

Interventions that focus on belief systems

The following interventions focus largely on transforming belief systems:

- reframing problems
- pinpointing strengths
- relabelling

- presenting multiple perspectives
- externalizing problems and building on exceptions.

It is usually unnecessary to give a rationale for using these types of interventions, since they are broadly speaking an expression of a position that is fundamentally non-blaming, compassionate, optimistic and respectful of a couple's resourcefulness (Carr, 2000).

Reframing

With reframing, couples are offered a new framework within which to conceptualize a sequence of events, and this new way of conceptualizing the sequence of events makes it more likely that the problem will be resolved rather than maintained. The three-column formulation model offers a template for major reframes such as that given in Figure 5.1, but minor reframes of specific events may be offered throughout therapy. Reframe problems in non-blaming-interactional rather than blaming-individual terms, in solvable rather than uncontrollable or fixed terms and reframe partners' reasons for engaging in problem-maintaining behaviour as arising from positive rather than negative intentions.

Here are a couple of examples of minor reframes. Both partners in a distressed couple insisted that the main problem was that the other person was to blame because the other partner was 'a vindictive, mean, selfish bastard'. The following reframing was offered:

> 'When you disagree with each other strongly, you both end up blaming each other and calling each other names. From what you have each said to me, the main reason you do this is because each of you feels disappointment and a deep sense of loss that your wish for your partner to meet your needs has not been met. I wonder if you would be willing to explore ways that you might be able to meet each other's needs, so as to reduce the constant disappointment that you both battle?'

In couples therapy, reframing is often required when one partner in a couple overtly or covertly invites the therapist to side with him or her against the other partner. In conflictual couples, the request is usually for the therapist to act as judge and jury and agree that one partner is right and the other wrong. Reframe statements about one partner being right and the other wrong in relational terms such as:

> 'It seems that in this relationship you have developed equally valid yet distinctive viewpoints. Discussions about which is the correct viewpoint keep you connected in frequent passionate conversations. However, at some point you may wish to explore other ways of being connected besides arguing about whose viewpoint is right and whose is wrong.'

In non-conflictual couples involved in complementary relationships where one partner is defined as ill or weak and the other as competent and strong, the request is usually for the therapist to take on the job of supporting the supposedly weaker partner to take this burden off the supposedly stronger partner. Reframe statements about one partner being weak and the other strong in relational terms such as:

> 'It seems there is an acceptance that X is weaker than Y and so requires regular help and support from Y to keep going. It also seems that there is an invitation for me to assist with supporting X. I find this invitation difficult to accept because, from my vantage point, I am struck by the strength and competence that X shows in providing Y with the role of apparently being the strong and competent person in this relationship. It may be useful to explore other ways this strength could be used.'

Pinpointing strengths

Most distressed couples have lost sight of their many strengths. Help couples rediscover these by drawing their attention to them when things that the couple do in therapy provide evidence for their presence. Then attribute these strengths to the couple's defining characteristics. Such strengths include loyalty, sticking together through thick and thin, tolerance for distress, commitment to the idea that the relationship can improve, a shared history of a relationship that once worked well, thoughtfulness in trying to make sense of the relationship difficulties, the capacity to listen carefully to each other's viewpoints despite distress, self-control in avoiding violence, maturity in not involving the children in every battle and passion for, rather than apathy about, the relationship.

Relabelling

On a moment-to-moment basis during all stages of therapy, make use of the opportunities to highlight partners' strengths. This reduces demoralization and helps couples develop beliefs about each other's positive attributes and their ability to solve their own problems. With relabelling, offer positive or optimistic labels for ambiguous behaviour as a substitute for negative or pessimistic labels or attributions. For example, when a client says, 'He was standing there looking stupid, so I told him to get on with it', this may be relabelled by saying 'When he was thinking through what to do next, and you encouraged him to go ahead, what happened?' When a client says 'She needs to be at home when she is this ill' the sentiment may be reframed as, 'While she is recovering, how do you believe she should spend her time?'

Presenting multiple perspectives

Where couples have become polarized, they may be offered a message containing multiple perspectives that articulates and empathizes with the validity of each position, while also opening up the possibility of an alternative systemic framing of their difficulties (Papp,1982). For example:

> 'I was struck by the way each of you have distinctive styles for managing situations and have discussed this with two colleagues since we last met, to obtain their expert opinions on how best to proceed. One of my colleagues was taken by Mary's style. Mary, you have shown that your own personal style is to talk straight and say what is on your mind. So if you want John to know that you think a job needs to be done in the house, you tell him straight and don't beat about the bush. If he doesn't take notice, you tell him again. That is "the straight-talking approach". My other colleague was impressed by your style, John. You take a "thoughtful approach". You think things over a great deal before saying anything. This is a personal style and one that reflects your careful approach to this relationship. I suppose the question that is raised for me is, how can the best of both styles be brought to bear on the difficulties and distress you are both experiencing? Perhaps you have views on this you would like to air today?'

Externalizing problems and building on exceptions

To develop a positive belief system or narrative about their relationship, invite couples to externalize their difficulties as separate from the relationship. Then help them remember the exception formulation they constructed during assessment. Next ask them to recount in detail multiple instances of exceptional non-problematic episodes. Then, help them to explore ways to recreate exceptions like these in the future. As this positive narrative about their relationship evolves, invite them to speculate about what this way of defining themselves says about them as a couple. Invite them to recreate exceptions as a homework assignment and to involve other people from their social network in recognizing their positive definition of themselves as a resourceful and connected couple (White, 1995). Here is a line of questioning that may be used in this type of work:

- In our first meeting you told me that there were often exceptional times when the problem should have occurred but didn't. How have you both arranged from time to time to prevent these bad relationship habits from infecting your relationship?
- If I was watching a video of these exceptional episodes, what details would I see that were different from those episodes where bad relationship habits infect your relationship?
- Can you tell me about three or four of these episodes right now? . . .
- How could you use this information to arrange situations where your relationship is uninfected by these bad habits? . . . Is that something you would be willing to do?
- It seems that all of these positive and exceptional events are connected and reflect the degree to which you really care about each other. How do you imagine this central part of your relationship will find expression in the future? What will it look like?
- What do all of these exceptional events from the past and the ones that will happen in the future say about you as a couple?
- Do they say you are a couple that is kind? . . . committed? . . . caring? . . . passionate? etc. . . .?
- Who from your family would you most like to witness this aspect of your relationship?
- How could you let them know that you are a kind, committed, caring, passionate couple? . . . Is that something you would be willing to do?

Interventions that focus on broader constitutional factors

Interventions that aim to modify the impact of historical, contextual and constitutional predisposing factors or mobilize protective factors within these areas include the following:

- addressing constitutional factors
- addressing contextual issues
- addressing family-of-origin issues.

Addressing constitutional factors

Constitutional vulnerabilities may be genetic or they may involve debilitating somatic states, sequelae of early illness or injury, learning difficulties, or difficult temperament. Couples in which one partner has a constitutional vulnerability may require psychoeducation about the condition or vulnerability, help with ensuring the vulnerable partner adheres to a medication regime where this is appropriate, referral for medical consultation where appropriate and support in securing an appropriate placement if necessary.

PSYCHOEDUCATION

In psychoeducation, give both general information about the problem and a specific three-column formulation of the vulnerable family member's unique difficulties (McFarlane, 1991). Simplicity and realistic optimism are central to good psychoeducation. It is important not to overwhelm couples with information, so a good rule of thumb is to think about a case in complex terms but explain it to clients in as simple terms as possible. Put succinctly: 'Think complex – Talk simple'. Good clinical practice involves matching the amount of information given about the formulation and case management plan to the client's readiness to understand and accept it. A second important rule of thumb is to engender a realistic level of hope in psychoeducation by focusing on strengths and protective factors, as well as aetiological factors later. Put succinctly: 'Create hope – Name strengths'. Group psychoeducation offers a forum where couples can meet others in the same position and this has the benefit of providing additional support.

In psychoeducation, information on clinical features, predisposing, precipitating, maintaining and protective factors may be given along with the probable impact of the problem in the short and long term on cognition, emotions, behaviour, family adjustment, school adjustment and health. Details of the multi-modal treatment programme should be given both orally and in written form, if appropriate, in a way that is comprehensible to couples. It is important to highlight strengths that increase the probability that the vulnerable partner will respond positively to treatment and that the other partner will learn appropriate ways to respond to the vulnerable partner's symptoms. This should be balanced with a statement of the sacrifices that the couple will have to make to participate in the treatment programme. Common sacrifices include attending a series of consultation sessions, discussing difficult issues openly, completing homework assignments, being prepared for progress to be hampered by setbacks, learning to live with ongoing residual difficulties, accepting that episodes of therapy are time-limited and accepting that, at best, the chances are only two out of three that therapy will be helpful.

ADHERENCE TO MEDICAL REGIMES

Initially, in cases where non-adherence is a problem, it is important that couples are involved in understanding the regime and that the non-symptomatic partner is helped to support the vulnerable partner in complying with the regime. As adherence improves, more autonomous management of adherence should be encouraged. Adherence to medical regimes is maximized if the following guidelines are followed (Ley, 1988):

- Give a rationale for the regime.
- Set out the medication and medical care regime in simple language, inviting clients to do specific things.
- Describe the medication regime and medical care tasks briefly and break complex tasks into parts.
- Check that the clients have understood the regime.
- Emphasize the importance of adherence to the regime and the positive and negative effects and side-effects of both adherence and non-adherence.
- Write down complex tasks.
- State that adherence will be reviewed in every session and convey an expectation of co-operation.
- Always review adherence and respond favourably to adherence.
- Manage non-adherence in the way outlined for managing resistance described below.
- With adherent clients, encourage autonomous management of adherence.

Addressing contextual issues

Where factors in the wider social context hinder progress, the following interventions may be considered:

- network meetings
- changing roles
- building support
- mourning losses
- exploring secrets.

NETWORK MEETINGS

Where couples have multiple problems and are involved with multiple agencies and professionals, convene network meetings, especially if the problem solving within the network is poorly co-ordinated (Carr, 2000). Without good co-ordination, opportunities for using available resources effectively and synergistically may be lost. Instead, members of the network may inadvertently drift into problem-maintaining behaviour patterns.

Convene a network meeting to clarify or refine the three-column formulation and to agree on roles and responsibilities. Open review meetings with introductions, set the agenda and state that each person will have an opportunity to make a contribution. Make sure that everyone gets a fair hearing by helping the reticent to elaborate their positions and the talkative to condense their contributions. Summarize periodically to help members maintain focus. Above all, retain neutrality by siding with no one, and curiously enquiring about each person's position. Use time-out, if necessary, to integrate contributions, refine the formulation and elaborate options for action. Once the meeting accepts the refined formulation, request a commitment to develop or refine the action plan. Then work towards that by examining options and agreeing on which team members are responsible for particular parts of the programme. Minute all agreements and agree on further review dates.

When contributing to a network meeting, prepare points on your involvement in the case, your hypotheses and plans. Use slack time at the beginning of the meeting or during the tea break to build good working alliances with network members. Always introduce yourself before making your first contribution, if you are new to the network. Outline your involvement first and hypotheses and plans later. Make your points briefly and summarize your points at the end of each major contribution. When you disagree, focus on clarifying the issue not on attacking the person with whom you disagree. Keep notes on who attended the meeting, on the formulation and the plan agreed. If you have unresolved ambivalent feelings after the meeting, discuss these in supervision.

CHANGING ROLES

Stresses associated with lifecycle transitions described in Chapter 1 or home–work role strain can underpin problem-maintaining beliefs and behaviour patterns. Facilitating changes in partner's roles to address the way they jointly tackle these demands may be appropriate. Invite couples to identify the new demands at home and work and help them negotiate an equitable division of labour that is compatible with their strengths and cultural expectations.

BUILDING SUPPORT

Where lack of social support underpins problem-maintaining beliefs and behaviour patterns, this deficit can be addressed by providing a therapeutic forum where couples may confide their views and feelings. For chronic problems, refer couples to self-help support groups where they can meet with others who have similar problems to address long-term social support deficits. Where couples in nuclear families have become disconnected from their extended families, suggest that couples invite members of their extended families to sessions to develop supportive relationships with them.

MOURNING LOSSES

Where unresolved grief underpins problem-maintaining beliefs and behaviour patterns, couples may be helped to engage in rituals to mourn their losses (Walsh & McGoldrick, 1991). Bereavement, separation, illness, injury, unemployment and moving house are common loss experiences for couples. In Chapter 1 it was noted that adjustment to loss involves processes such as shock; denial; futile searching for the lost person, attribute or situation; despair and sadness; anger at the lost person or those seen as responsible for the loss; anxiety about other inevitable losses, including one's own death; and acceptance. These processes occur as couples change their belief systems so as to accommodate the loss. Couples become stuck in the mourning process for various reasons. In some cases couples have tried to short-circuit the grieving process and act as if they have grieved, but find that from time to time they become inexplicably and inappropriately angry or sad. In other cases, the expression of sadness or anger persists over years and so compromises the couple's development. Prescribing mourning rituals where lost members, attributes or situations are remembered in detail and couples then bid them farewell may be liberating for couples paralysed by unresolved grief.

EXPLORING SECRETS

Where the reason for the absence of therapeutic progress is obscure, it is worth considering that one or other partner is harbouring a family secret or having a secret affair. In these instances, ask the couple to consider the possible implications of such a hypothetical secret. Here are some useful questions to ask in such instances:

- It seems to me that there may be some unknown factor contributing to your distress, otherwise you would be making more progress than has occurred. I don't know what this unknown factor is. My guess is that if one of you knows what it is, you think that it would be least hurtful if you kept it a secret. So please, hold on to your secret if you have one. For now, let us assume that something secret is happening. If that were the case, how would each of you handle it. Is this something you are prepared to discuss?
- How would you react if you found out about this secret?
- If I was watching a video of the showdown when you found out about the secret, and say it was an affair, what would I see?
- What would it mean for your relationship if your partner was having an affair?

- If you found out your partner was having an affair and you decided to end this relationship, how would that pan out? What would each of you do?
- How would you forgive your partner?
- How would you expect your partner to make up for his/her infidelity?

Information from this line of hypothetical questioning may throw light on the reasons for lack of therapeutic progress. Addressing infidelity is covered in Chapter 24.

Addressing family-of-origin issues

Where there is the possibility that unresolved family-of-origin issues are compromising therapeutic progress, it is worth exploring transgenerational patterns, scripts and myths to help couples understand how relationship habits from their family-of-origin are influencing their current life situation. In some instances, it may be helpful to facilitate accessing, expressing and integrating emotions associated with adverse family-of-origin experiences that underpin destructive relationship habits. In others, it may be valuable to coach clients to reconnect with parents from whom they have become cut-off, so they can become free of triangulation in their families of origin and so stop replicating this in their families of procreation.

EXPLORING

Invite clients to explore transgenerational patterns, scripts and myths relevant to their difficulties in making therapeutic progress using their genograms as the focus for the following lines of questioning (Boszormenyi-Nagy et al., 1991; Friedman, 1991):

- I have noticed that no matter how hard you try to make sense of this problem and tackle it in a sensible way, you end up in difficulty. You have a way that you would like your relationships to be but you just can't seem to get it to work like that. Something is blocking you. One possibility is that you are carrying relationship habits from your family-of-origin in the back of your mind, and any time you are under stress you fall into these old habits. Would you like to explore this possibility?
- Look at your genogram and think about what have been the most important relationships in your life.
- What relationship habits did you learn from these relationships?
- In these relationships, how did you learn to live with giving and receiving care and support?
- Tell me how your parents and siblings received and gave support to each other?

- In these relationships, what did you learn about the way people should communicate with each other in families. How should husbands and wives or mothers and fathers talk to each other?
- Tell me how your parents and siblings talked to each other about important issues?
- In these relationships, how did you learn to deal with leading and following, the whole issue of managing power?
- Tell me about who was in charge in you family-of-origin and how others fitted in around this.
- In your family-of-origin, how did you learn to deal with conflict?
- What happened when your parents or siblings didn't agree about an important issue?
- What about triangles? Did people get stuck in triangles in your family-of-origin?
- Was anyone 'piggy-in-the-middle' between your parents or two other people?
- Are you still involved in a triangle in your family-of-origin?
- Who have you stayed close to?
- Who have you cut off?
- Have you ever tried to reconnect from your cut-off parent?
- What are you avoiding by being cut off? What is the disaster you guess would happen if you spoke intimately with the person from whom you are cut off?
- What does this exploration tell you about the possible relationship habits you have learned from your parents, siblings and other family members?
- When you try to do the sensible thing in solving the problem you have with your partner that brought you into therapy, how do these relationship habits interfere with this?
- Do you think that there are situations in which you can control the urge to follow through on these relationship habits you have received from your parents, siblings and other family members?
- What is it about these situations that allows you, to break these chains, these destructive relationship habits?
- Would you like to explore ways of weakening their influence on you?
- Before making this decision, I am inviting you to look at the downside of changing your relationship habits. One big problem is this: if you change the relationship habits you learned from your parents, you may feel like you are being disloyal to them. What are the consequences of that for you and for your relationship with them?

Lines of questioning such as this conducted over a number of sessions may lead in some instances to a realization that family-of-origin issues are interfering with effective problem solving with clients' current relationship with their partners. They may also lead clients to want to change these. Awareness of destructive relationship habits learned in the family-of-origin is rarely enough to liberate clients from slavishly following these habits when under stress.

RE-EXPERIENCING

One way to help clients weaken these relationship habits is to create a context within which they can remember and re-experience the highly emotional situations in which they learned them, and integrate these forgotten and destructive experiences into their conscious narrative about themselves (Greenberg, 2002). Invite clients within therapy sessions to close their eyes and visualize their memories of specific situations in which they learned specific relationship habits and tolerate experiencing the intense negative affect that accompanies such visualization experiences. Invite clients to verbalize the self-protective emotionally charged responses that they would have liked to have made in these situations to their parents or caregivers, within therapy sessions. Such responses may be made to a visualized image of their caregiver or to an empty chair, symbolizing their caregiver or parent. In addition, invite clients to write (but not send) detailed letters to their parents or caregivers expressing in graphic emotional terms how difficult they found their challenging early life experiences in which they learned their destructive relationship habits. These processes of re-experiencing and responding differently to early formative experiences help clients to gain control over their destructive relationship habits. Also when partners witness each other exploring and then re-experiencing stressful family-of-origin memories in this way, it helps them develop compassion for each other.

RECONNECTING

A further technique that helps clients to break free from inadvertently slipping into destructive relationship habits is to coach them to reconnect with parents from whom they have become cut off (Friedman, 1991). Invite clients to plan a series of visits with the parent from whom they are cut off and talk with them in an adult-to-adult mode, and avoid slipping into their old relationship pattern of distancing and cutting-off from the parent. Initially in these visits conversation may focus on neutral topics. However, greatest therapeutic gains tend to be made where clients can tell the parent in an adult manner how the parent's behaviour hurt, saddened or angered the client as a child and how this led to a long period of distancing and cut-off which the client would like to end and eventually replace with a less destructive relationship. Sometimes, clients find making such statements easier if they write them out with coaching from their therapists and rehearse them in therapy sessions prior to meeting with their parents.

Managing resistance

Resistance may take the form of clients not co-operating during therapy sessions, not completing tasks between sessions not attending sessions or refusing to terminate the therapy process (Carr, 2000). Resistance is common and often occurs because clients are ambivalent about the process of change. That is, they begin to doubt that the benefits of achieving therapeutic goals outweigh the costs of change, because change inevitably involves personal costs. When this occurs, the central task is to suspend all attempts at empowering clients to achieve their stated therapeutic goals and focus all therapeutic effort on addressing this ambivalence, no matter how long this takes. Only when clients have addressed their personal dilemmas about the costs of maintaining the status quo and the costs of changing their situation will they be in a position to return to the process of therapeutic problem solving. The main therapeutic task is to help the couple clearly and explicitly articulate their beliefs about the costs of change and to empathize with this ambivalence. These beliefs may involve feared catastrophes associated with change or a conviction about their powerlessness to change important aspects of their situation and the inevitable disappointment that will arise from trying and failing again. It is vital to avoid any hint of criticism when enquiring about ambivalence, since most clients when they experience ambivalence are already engaging in covert self-criticism. Here is the sort of question that may be asked to help clients address ambivalence about change:

> 'I sense that you believe you are between a rock and a hard place today, that you believe the costs of following through on the plans you have been making are too high. Let's take some time to talk about that today. What do you believe the downside will be for you in sorting this problem out?'

Stage 4: Disengaging or recontracting

In the final stage of therapy, the main tasks are to fade out the frequency of sessions, help the couple understand the change process, facilitate the development of relapse management plans and frame the process of disengagement as the conclusion of an episode in an ongoing relationship rather than the end of the relationship. In relapse management planning, help couples to forecast the types of stressful situation in which relapses may occur, their probable negative reactions to relapses and the ways in which they can use the lessons learned in therapy to cope with these relapses in a productive way. Most relapses are associated with a build-up of stressful life events and in some instances these then interact with constitutional vulnerabilities.

For example, clients with seasonal affective disorder are particularly prone to relapse in early winter, particularly if exposed to a high level of stress. Once couples have considered events that might precipitate a relapse, explore the ways in which their problem-maintaining interaction patterns and belief systems will translate a slip into a full-blown relapse. Enquire about their plans for handling this in light of the lessons learned in therapy. Disengagement is usefully constructed as an episodic event rather than as the end of a relationship. This is particularly important when working with couples who have chronic problems. Offer them a distant follow-up appointment or telephone back-up to help manage relapses. In some instances, the end of one therapeutic contract will lead immediately to the beginning of a further contract, for example where couples have addressed adult or couple's problems and want to progress to a discussion of parent–child issues.

SUMMARY

ISCT can be conceptualized as a developmental and recursive process involving the stages of planning, assessment, treatment and disengagement or recontracting. Specific tasks must be completed at each stage before progressing to the next. In ISCT, for any problem, an initial hypothesis and later formulation may be constructed in which: (1) the behaviour pattern that maintains the problem is specified; (2) the constraining belief systems that underpin the partners' roles in this pattern are outlined; and (3) the broader contextual factors that predispose couples to these belief systems and behaviour patterns are given. In addition, a similar three-column formulation may be constructed to explain exceptional episodes in which problems were expected to occur but did not happen. These three-column formulation models provide a template for guiding the assessment of the couple's problems and for planning therapy. Therapeutic interventions may be classified in terms of the specific domains they target within three-column problem and exception formulations, with some interventions targeting behaviour change, some targeting belief systems, and others focusing on contextual predisposing factors.

FURTHER READING FOR CLIENTS

Christensen, A. & Jacobson, N. (2002). *Reconcilable differences*. New York: Guilford.

Gottman, J. & Silver, N. (1999). *The seven principles for making marriage work*. London: Weidenfeld & Nicolson. This guide is based on years of research by Gottman.

Markman, H., Stanley, S., & Blumberg (1994). *Fighting for your marriage*. San Francisco, CA: Jossey Bass. This guide is based on a scientifically evaluated premarital programme.

FURTHER READING

Carr, A. (2000). *Family therapy: Concepts process and practice*. Chichester: Wiley.

Gurman, A. & Jacobson, N. (2002). *Clinical handbook of couple therapy* (Third Edition). New York: Guilford.

Halford, W. & Markman, H. (1997). *Clinical handbook of marriage and couples interventions*. New York: Wiley.

ASSESSMENT INSTRUMENTS

Rust, L., Bennun, L., Crowe, M., & Golombok, S. (1988). *GRIMS. The Golombok Rust Inventory of Marital State*. Windsor, UK: NFER-Nelson.

Snyder, D. (1997). Marital Satisfaction Inventory-Revised. Los Angeles, CA: Western Psychological Services.

Wills, T., Weiss, R., & Patterson, G. (1974). A behavioural analysis of the determinants of marital satisfaction. *Journal of Consulting and Clinical Psychology*, 42, 802–811. Describes the spouse observation checklist that can be ordered from Dr Robert L. Weiss, Oregon Marital Assessment Service, 3003 Willamette Street, Suite F, Eugene, OR 97405, USA. http://www.perry-psych.com/order02.htm

REFERENCES

American Psychiatric Association (APA) (2000). *Diagnostic and statistical manual of the mental disorders* (Fourth Edition-Text Revision, DSM-IV-TR). Washington, DC: APA.

Baucom, D., Shoham, V., Mueser, K., Daiuto, A., & Stickle, T. (1998). Empirically supported couple and family interventions for marital distress and adult mental health problems. *Journal of Consulting and Clinical Psychology*, 66, 53–88.

Boszormenyi-Nagy, I., Grunebum, J., & Ulrish D. (1991). Contextual therapy. In: A. Gurman & D. Kniskern (Eds), *Handbook of family therapy*. Volume 11 (pp. 200–238). New York: Brunner Mazel.

Carr, A. (2000). *Family therapy: Concepts process and practice*. Chichester: Wiley.

Carr, A. (2004). *Positive psychology*. London: Brunner-Routledge.

deShazer, S. (1988). *Clues: Investigating solutions in brief therapy*. New York: Norton.

Finchman, F. & Bradbury, T. (1992). Assessing attributions in marriage: The relationship attribution measure. *Journal of Personality and Social Psychology*, 62, 457–468.

Friedman, E. (1991). Bowen theory and therapy. In: A. Gurman & D. Kniskern (Eds), *Handbook of family therapy. Volume 11* (pp. 134–170). New York: Brunner Mazel.

Gottman, J. (1993). The roles of conflict engagement, escalation and avoidance in marital interaction: A longitudinal view of five types of couples. *Journal of Consulting and Clinical Psychology*, 61, 6–15.

Greenberg, L. (2002). *Emotion focused therapy*. Washington, DC: American Psychological Association.

Gurman, A. & Jacobson, N. (2002). *Clinical handbook of couple therapy* (Third Edition). New York: Guilford.

Haley, J. (1963). *Strategies of psychotherapy*. New York: Grune & Stratton.

Halford, W. (1998). The ongoing evolution of behavioural couples therapy: Retrospect and prospect. *Clinical Psychology Review*, 18, 613–634.

Halford, W. & Markman, H. (1997). *Clinical handbook of marriage and couples interventions*. New York: Wiley.

Hubble, M., Duncan, B., & Miller, S. (1999). *The heart and soul of change*. Washington, DC: APA.

Jacobson, N. & Christensen, A. (1996). *Integrative couple therapy: Promoting acceptance and change*. New York: W. W. Norton.

Johnson, S. (1996). *The practice of emotionally focused marital therapy: Creating connection*. New York: Brunner-Routledge.

Ley, P. (1988). *Communicating with patients: Improving communication satisfaction and compliance*. London: Croom Helm.

Liddle, H., Santisteban, D., Levant, R., & Bray, J. (2002). *Family psychology: Science-based interventions*. Washington, DC: APA.

Luthar, S. (2003). *Resilience and vulnerability: Adaptation in the context of childhood adversities*. Cambridge: Cambridge University Press.

McFarlane, W. (1991). Family psychoeducational treatment. In: A. Gurman & D. Kniskern (Eds), *Handbook of family therapy. Volume 11* (pp. 363–395). New York: Brunner Mazel.

McGoldrick, M., Gerson, R., & Shellenberger, S. (1999). *Genograms: Assessment and intervention* (Second Edition). New York: Norton.

Minuchin, S. (1974). *Families and family therapy*. Cambridge, MA: Harvard University Press.

Newman, B. & Newman, P. (2002). *Development through life* (Eighth Edition). Pacific Grove, CA: Wadsworth Publishing.

Norcross, J. (2002). *Psychotherapy relationships that work. Therapist contributions and responsiveness to patients*. New York: Oxford University Press.

Papp, P. (1982). The Greek chorus and other techniques of paradoxical therapy. *Family Process*, 19, 45–57.

Patterson, G. (1982). *Coercive family process*. Eugene, OR: Castalia.

Pinsof, W. & Wynne, L. (1995). Family therapy effectiveness: Current research and theory. Special Edition of the *Journal of Marital and Family Therapy*, 21 (4). Washington, DC: American Association of Marital and Family Therapy.

Rust, L., Bennun, L., Crowe, M., & Golombok, S. (1988). *GRIMS. The Golombok Rust Inventory of Marital State*. Windsor, UK: NFER-Nelson.

Schmaling, K. & Scher, T. (2000). *The psychology of couples and illness: Theory, research and practice*. Washington, DC: APA.

Shoham, V. & Rohrbaugh, M.J. (2002). Brief strategic couple therapy. In: A.S. Gurman & N.S. Jacobson (Eds), *Clinical handbook of couple therapy* (Third Edition, pp. 5–25). New York: Guilford.

Snyder, D. (1997). *Marital Satisfaction Inventory-Revised*. Los Angeles, CA: Western Psychological Services.

Walsh, F. (2003). *Normal family processes* (Third Edition). New York: Guilford.

Walsh, F. & McGoldrick, M. (1991). *Living beyond loss. Death in the family*. New York: Norton.

White, M. (1995). *Re-authoring lives*. Adelaide: Dulwich Centre Publications.

Wills, T., Weiss, R., & Patterson, G. (1974). A behavioural analysis of the determinants of marital satisfaction. *Journal of Consulting and Clinical Psychology*, 42, 802–811.

Chapter 6

Biomedical approaches and use of drugs to treat adult mental health problems

Stephen McWilliams and Eadbhard O'Callaghan

> Men will always be mad and those who think they can cure them are the maddest of all.
>
> (Voltaire)

INTRODUCTION

For millennia, choosing the most appropriate treatment for major psychological morbidity has been a controversial issue. Indeed, although Voltaire's assertion may seem a little pessimistic given our current level of knowledge, we are still admittedly engaged in a steep learning curve, driven largely by our hitherto lack of success. Since the days of the eighteenth-century French philosopher's remark, different eras have brought about various 'revolutionary' models of treatment, often complimented by the vehement vituperation of the remainder. So why have prognoses only recently begun to improve?

One reason may be that, until recently, an 'either/or' distinction was commonly applied to the treatment of major psychological morbidity in that, depending on the variety of therapist involved, a patient was typically treated with *either* a 'biological' approach involving pharmacotherapy *or* a 'psychological' approach utilizing psychotherapy. Recently, however, advances have demonstrated that psychological interventions can be highly effective in those disorders traditionally labelled as 'biologically based', whereas the converse might also be true. Indeed, appropriate treatment is usually a question of emphasis within a comprehensive treatment regime. For example, in psychotic illnesses and bipolar affective disorder, it is usually appropriate to place an emphasis on pharmacotherapy in the initial acute episode. Not only does this facilitate stabilization of the individual's mental state, but it also enables the person to benefit more from psychological and social therapies. Conversely, in the vast majority of anxiety-related illness, the emphasis is better placed on psychotherapy, with pharmacotherapy used as either a temporary adjunct or for situations where psychological therapies have failed. Meanwhile, most other conditions lie on a spectrum between the two.

As other chapters in this book deal with the psychological approaches used in treatment, we have taken the opportunity here to summarize some of the commonly used pharmacological therapies with a general reference to the ICD-10 (WHO, 1992) and DSM Classifications of Mental and Behavioural Disorders Fourth Edition-Text Revisions (APA, 2000). Words emphasized in italic are defined in the Glossary at the end of the chapter (p. 249).

PHARMACOKINETICS AND PHARMACODYNAMICS

Absorption and metabolism of drugs

Drugs can be taken orally, sublingually, rectally, intravenously, intramuscularly, *topically*, by inhalation or by slow-release intramuscular *depot*. Once inside the body, drugs must undergo the sequential processes of absorption, metabolism, distribution and elimination if they are to work optimally on the synaptic receptors of nerves.

Absorption of oral and rectal drugs occurs across the epithelium of the gastrointestinal tract. Such drugs are more likely to be absorbed quickly if they are highly lipid soluble, minimally alkaline or acidic, and small in terms of particle size; their absorption is also aided by moderate gastrointestinal motility and a good splanchnic flow of blood to the gut.

Orally and rectally absorbed drugs undergo first-pass metabolism in the wall of the gastrointestinal tract and in the liver by way of enzymes such as cytochrome P450. Some psychotropic drugs such as chlorpromazine and morphine undergo substantial first-pass metabolism, which means the oral dose needs to be much higher than the intravenous dose. Moreover, there are considerable variations between the doses needed by different individuals due to varying first-pass metabolism. Meanwhile, there are two phases of metabolism in the liver: phase one involving oxidation, reduction or hydrolysis of drugs and phase two involving conjugation and inactivation.

After metabolism, drugs are distributed through the body's various compartments, which include the intracellular fluid (approximately 40% of body weight), fat (20%) and extracellular fluid – composed of plasma (5%) and interstitial water (18%). Several factors determine where a drug will be distributed to; for example, drugs with a larger molecular size and drugs that bind strongly to plasma protein both tend to be confined to plasma. Meanwhile, highly lipid-soluble drugs tend to distribute themselves through the total body water, whereas lipid-insoluble drugs are unable to pass through cell membranes and are therefore confined to the extracellular compartment. Of note, highly lipid-soluble drugs that bind strongly to body fat tend to be difficult to remove by haemodialysis in cases of overdose.

The *blood–brain barrier*, consisting of a continuous layer of tightly joined *epithelial cells*, is particularly important in drug distribution, as psychotropic drugs must cross this barrier if they are to have any effect on the brain. The blood–brain barrier is more permeable to lipid-soluble drugs, during extreme stress and when inflammation occurs, such as in meningitis.

Finally, excretion of drugs takes place in the kidneys through three processes. *Glomerular filtration* occurs to most drugs except those tightly bound to plasma proteins, while drugs such as morphine and pethidine undergo active excretion and re-absorption in the renal tubules. Third, *passive diffusion* across the renal tubules may occur in the case of some drugs, for example those with high lipid solubility.

Receptor activation

Central to understanding how a drug works in the body is the concept of the synapse and the fact that the nervous system is not purely electrical but also chemical. Synapses are essentially 'gaps' in the nerves that travel both within the brain and from the brain to various parts of the body. These synapses contain chemical neurotransmitters that bind to receptors on cell membranes and cause receptor activation, resulting in cell function. Examples of neurotransmitters include dopamine, acetylcholine, noradrenaline, serotonin and histamine.

There are two important ways in which activation of receptors leads to cell function. First, activation may result in the opening and closing of ion channels. Examples include nicotinic acetylcholine (nACh) receptors, which are linked to a sodium channel; gamma amino butyric acid (GABAa) receptors, which are linked to a chloride channel; and others such as serotonin (5-HT$_3$) and glutamate receptors. In the case of the nACh receptors, five subunits (two alphas, a beta, a gamma and a delta) are clustered around a central transmembrane pore. When acetylcholine binds to the extracellular parts of the two alpha subunits, changes occur in the shape of their alpha helices, resulting in opening of the pore, which thus allows sodium ions to pass through and leads ultimately to an electrical impulse in the nerve.

The second method involves mobilization of G-protein, a chemical messenger that activates ion channels or other chemicals such as cyclic adenosine monophosphate (cAMP) and inositol phosphate. Receptors involved in this mechanism include muscarinic acetylcholine (mACh), adrenoceptors, neuropeptide and most serotonin receptors. G-protein consists of two subunits. The alpha subunit binds to the receptor and the beta subunit binds to the target.

These two mechanisms of receptor activation are important in understanding the current hypotheses linking neurotransmitter dysregulation, psychological morbidity and pharmacotherapy.

PSYCHOLOGICAL PROBLEMS AND PSYCHOPHARMACOLOGICAL TREATMENTS

Dementia (ICD-10: F00–03. DSM-IV: 290/294)

Dementia is a chronic, progressive and global decline in functioning that affects primarily memory, intellect and personality. It is usually irreversible, and its prevalence increases with age, from 5% of over–65s to 20% of over-80s. Aetiology includes degenerative causes such as Alzheimer's disease and Lewy body dementia; vascular causes such as multi-infarct dementia, and other causes such as tumours and AIDS.

With all types of dementia, the treatment emphasis is placed on social support, general care and good carer education, with pharmacotherapy largely confined to Alzheimer's disease in patients with a score on the Mini-Mental State Inventory of more than 12. Medication is comprised mainly of inhibitors of the enzyme acetylcholinesterase and includes donepezil, rivastigmine and galantamine.

Alcohol and substance abuse (ICD-10: F10–19. DSM-IV: 291/292/303–5)

This category in the ICD-10 refers to not just alcohol, but also opiates, cannabinoids, sedatives, cocaine, other stimulants (such as caffeine), hallucinogens, tobacco, volatile solvents and other psychoactive substances. Moreover, the classification includes criteria for acute intoxication, harmful use, dependence, withdrawal and psychosis, with common adverse effects including disinhibition, argumentativeness, aggression, labile mood, poor attention, impaired judgement and various physical complaints.

Alcohol abuse

Up to 30% of men and 10% of women consume alcohol in excess of the recommended maximum weekly amounts (21 units for men and 14 units for women). Meanwhile, up to 25% of men will be problem drinkers at some stage during their lives; the heaviest drinking occurs in the teens and early twenties, a time at which the 'binge drinking' phenomenon is most prevalent.

Detoxification from alcohol

In an abusive situation, the brain becomes accustomed to a certain level of alcohol within the body. In such cases, a sudden discontinuation of alcohol, leading to a drop in blood levels, places the individual at risk of withdrawal symptoms, which may occur within hours of the last drink and tend to peak at approximately 24–48 hours. Early withdrawal symptoms include tremor, restlessness, anxiety, sweating, insomnia, anorexia, nausea and vomiting, raised blood pressure, racing pulse and, occasionally, seizures; later symptoms may also include agitation, confusion, disorientation, continued changes in blood pressure and pulse, fever, paranoia and visual or auditory hallucinations. Symptoms, however, are usually mild to moderate and typically abate within 5–7 days of the last drink. In approximately 5%, severe withdrawal in the form of delirium tremens may develop.

Inappropriately managed alcohol withdrawal is associated with significant morbidity and mortality and thus it is important to adopt the correct general supportive and pharmacological measures. Benzodiazepines (e.g. alprazolam or chlordiazepoxide) represent the current treatment of choice for acute withdrawal. Although such drugs have intrinsic anticonvulsant properties, an additional anticonvulsant (e.g. carbamazepine) may be required for patients at high risk of seizures. Vitamin replacement, meanwhile, is often advisable as chronic alcohol abuse can lead to significant vitamin deficiencies, which may, in turn, lead to conditions such as Wernicke's encephalopathy and Korsakoff's psychosis.

Detoxification in the community is a safe option for most patients, although admission is often necessary where there is a history of delirium tremens, withdrawal seizures, poor adherence to medication, cognitive impairment, inadequate social support or previous failed community detoxification. Mild dependence can sometimes be treated supportively without medication, while moderate dependence requires a regime typically consisting of 10–20 mg of chlordiazepoxide four times daily, reduced gradually over 5 days.

Severe dependence requires larger doses of benzodiazepines in an inpatient setting, with close monitoring of blood pressure, pulse and symptoms of withdrawal using a recognized scale such as the Clinical Institute Withdrawal Assessment for Alcohol – Revised Version (CIWA-Ar). Benzodiazepines are best avoided until the patient is fully sober, at which point the drugs are ideally given flexibly for 24–48 hours, followed by a 5-day regime of gradually reduced dosage. Seizure prophylaxis is often advisable as detailed above, while oral or *parenteral* B-complex vitamins help to prevent deficiency syndromes such as Wernicke's encephalopathy.

Alcoholic hallucinosis characteristically involves third-person auditory hallucinations in clear consciousness. Voices are often derogatory or commanding in nature, while conversations and music may also be experienced. The onset of alcoholic hallucinosis, while often associated with withdrawal, is nevertheless a distinct entity from delirium tremens. The condition is very distressing for the patient and may require treatment with antipsychotic medication in addition to the withdrawal regime outlined above.

Maintaining abstinence

Drugs used to help maintain abstinence from alcohol include disulfiram (Antabuse), acamprosate, naltrexone and nalmefene. Disulfiram works by blocking the liver enzyme acetaldehyde dehydrogenase, which metabolizes alcohol. Patients who consume alcohol while taking disulfiram risk an unpleasant reaction involving nausea, headache and other symptoms due to an accumulation of partially metabolized alcohol (acetaldehyde). Of note, significant liver disease is a contraindication to disulfiram.

Acamprosate is a taurine derivative that enhances the functioning of the neurotransmitter GABA. In conjunction with important psychological measures, acamprosate has been shown to reduce craving and enhance abstinence. However, as with disulfiram, it must be used with caution in patients with liver disease.

Naltrexone is an opiate *antagonist* that reduces craving in patients abstinent from alcohol. Once again, liver function should be adequate before commencement.

Cocaine abuse

Cocaine is a stimulant that acts by inhibiting the reuptake of dopamine. It has a *half-life* of 50 minutes and is most commonly taken intranasally – either alone or with heroin – but can also be smoked. Although unpleasant and characterized by mood, sleep and appetite changes, withdrawal is rarely life-threatening and can be treated with short-term benzodiazepines. Some reports suggest that there may be a role for selective serotonin reuptake inhibitors (SSRIs) in preventing relapse.

Heroin abuse

It is hard to judge the prevalence of heroin abuse in view of its illicit nature; however, estimates suggest that it affects less than 1% of the population, with most new addicts being males in their twenties. Self-reporting of opiate dependence can be confirmed by testing urine and observing for signs of withdrawal. Pharmacotherapy for withdrawal can then be considered, alongside measures to address lifestyle, help with psychosocial issues, stabilize drug intake and reduce drug-related harm.

Pharmacotherapy primarily includes methadone, an opiate *agonist* used for detoxification and substitution therapy. Methadone is a controlled drug with a low lethal dose and a high potential for dependency and, as such, the indications and arrangements for its use are closely monitored. It is used only in patients who are dependent on opiate drugs, and its consumption is heavily supervised, especially in the initial few months. It is best prescribed in oral liquid formulation, as crushing and inappropriate injection of tablets has been reported in heroin abusers.

The starting dose of methadone depends on the patient's tolerance level and drug-taking history, taking into account the long half-life of methadone. As inappropriate dosing can be fatal, doctors are often cautious at first and commence treatment with dosages as low as 10–30 mg. This is increased gradually, usually by no more than 10 mg per week, although heavily dependent users may require larger dosage increases. As regular medical assessments are essential, patients usually attend daily for the first few days, allowing regular reviews and dosage titrations to take place and thus helping to reduce withdrawal symptoms. Outpatient stabilization can take 6 weeks or more, although inpatient treatment and dose reduction can occur more rapidly, with a linear reduction regime over as little as 10 days.

Acute intoxication is a contraindication to methadone treatment, the risk of fatal overdose being greater, while extreme caution is also practised in patients with severe hepatic or renal failure. If methadone overdose occurs, it is treated with naloxone. Once a patient is stable on methadone for a period of time, a contract may be negotiated to gradually and flexibly reduce the dosage by 5–10 mg weekly or fortnightly.

Other drugs used in the management of opiate withdrawal include lofexidine. This is a non-opiate drug that is less likely to be misused than methadone and is therefore useful in patients with less severe or lengthy drug histories. Side effects include sedation and occasional hypotension (low blood pressure). Alternative opiate-based drugs include LAAM (levo-alpha-acetyl-methadyl), a 'mu' receptor agonist with a long half-life, and buprenorphine, a partial 'mu' receptor agonist and a 'kappa' receptor antagonist. The latter is safer but may not be as effective.

Schizophrenia (ICD-10: F20–29. DSM-IV: 295)

The term 'schizophrenia' was first coined by the Swiss psychiatrist Eugen Bleuler in the early part of the twentieth century. Since then, the concept has become more refined and is regarded by the ICD-10 as a severe continuous or episodic psychotic illness that lasts at least 1 month and is experienced in clear consciousness. Schizophrenia is not, by definition, attributable to organic causes or drug abuse. Positive symptoms include delusions, auditory hallucinations, disorders of thought and bizarre behaviour; negative symptoms include flattened affect, poverty of speech, lack of motivation and social withdrawal.

Schizophrenia is classified into the paranoid type, with mainly hallucinations and delusions; the hebephrenic type, with preponderantly thought disorder and affective symptoms; the *catatonic* type, comprising bizarre psychomotor eccentricities; and finally the undifferentiated type. The onset of schizophrenia is usually in early adulthood; its secondary disabilities span personal, domestic, occupational and social spheres.

Neurotransmitter hypothesis of schizophrenia

Before we examine the pharmacotherapy used to treat schizophrenia it is important to discuss the dopamine hypothesis, on which such drug treatment is based. It is known that certain drugs, such as amphetamines, cause the release of dopamine, and also appear to cause clinical signs and symptoms similar to those of schizophrenia. Similarly, dopamine antagonists have been successfully used to treat psychotic signs and symptoms, their efficacy appearing to correlate specifically with their affinity for dopamine D_2 receptors. Further studies have shown an increased number of dopamine receptors in the limbic system of schizophrenic patients.

The dopamine hypothesis of schizophrenia is not flawless – we have not yet explained why the antipsychotic effects take weeks to occur following an immediate dopamine receptor blockade, or where other neurotransmitters such as serotonin, histamine, noradrenaline and glutamate come into the picture – but it provides us with a solid theoretical model on which many effective therapies are based.

Antipsychotic medication

Antipsychotic medication can be broadly divided into two categories: classical and atypical. Classical antipsychotics, such as chlorpromazine, first became available in the 1950s and, until recently, represented the first-line option in the treatment of schizophrenia. They are effective preponderantly against positive symptoms, their main drawbacks being their side-effects profile and their failure to have any significant effect on negative symptoms.

The quest for a side-effect-free antipsychotic, effective against both positive and negative symptoms, led to the development of atypical antipsychotics. The first of these to appear was clozapine, which became available in the 1970s. Despite its association with fatal *agranulocytosis* in 0.3% of patients, a vigilant monitoring service has facilitated its continued use in treatment-resistant schizophrenia. Moreover, its role has expanded recently, with studies suggesting some efficacy against suicide.

The 1990s witnessed the emergence of newer atypical antipsychotics, such as risperidone, olanzapine, quetiapine and ziprasadone, which can ameliorate both positive and negative symptoms with fewer extrapyramidal side effects than the classical antipsychotic. These medications now represent the first-line treatments for psychosis, particularly as parenteral and depot formulations become increasingly available.

As evidence suggests that a longer duration of untreated psychosis is linked to a more turbulent recovery and an increased likelihood of relapse, it is important to initiate treatment as soon as the diagnosis of schizophrenia is suspected. Treatment begins with an atypical antipsychotic at its lowest effective dosage, preferably in a single-dose regime, with 3–6 weeks allowed for a given dosage to work before adjusting upwards. If symptoms persist or if the drug is not tolerated, a second atypical antipsychotic represents the next-line treatment, followed by a classical antipsychotic or clozapine.

When it is necessary to exceed the pharmacologically recommended dosage (generally > 1 g equivalent of chlorpromazine; see Table 6.1), patients should be monitored closely, as recommended by the Royal College of Psychiatrists. It is noteworthy, however, that patients who respond to antipsychotic medication generally do so at around 600 mg of chlorpromazine equivalence for acute treatment and 400 mg of chlorpromazine equivalence for maintenance. Overall, approximately 60% of positive symptoms and 30–50% of negative symptoms respond to antipsychotics, with persistent non-response sometimes explained by inadequate dosage, misdiagnosis, comorbidity or non-adherence. Depot preparations may ameliorate the latter, while useful adjuncts to treatment include benzodiazepines, lithium and electroconvulsive therapy (ECT).

The importance of good maintenance and adherence cannot be overemphasized, as the risk of relapse never really disappears. Although psychological interventions such as CBT have been shown to improve symptomatology, adherence and social functioning, psychosocial measures remain a vital component of any comprehensive management strategy. Education of patients and carers, the involvement of voluntary organizations and supportive family psychotherapeutic measures are all extremely useful, especially in the context of an increased likelihood of relapse in home environments with high levels of expressed emotion.

The first step in management, however, is the trial of a suitable antipsychotic medication. Maximum dosages of the commonly used antipsychotic medications are given in Table 6.1.

Table 6.1 Maximum doses for common antipsychotic medications

Drug	*Dose equivalent to 1000 mg chlorpromazine*
Haloperidol	120 mg
Sulpiride	2400 mg
Zuclopenthixol	150 mg
Clozapine	900 mg
Amisulpiride	1200 mg
Olanzapine	20 mg
Ziprasidone	160 mg
Risperidone	16 mg
Haloperidol depot	300 mg every 4 weeks
Flupenthixol depot	400 mg per week
Zuclopenthixol depot	600 mg per week

Classical antipsychotics (daily dosage ranges given in brackets)

PHENOTHIAZINES

Group I phenothiazines have side-chains containing aliphatic-rings and include chlorpromazine (25–1000 mg) and promazine (400–800 mg). Group II phenothiazines comprise the piperazines, which include trifluoperazine (10–50 mg) and fluphenazine (1–20 mg). Group III phenothiazines comprise the piperidines, which include thoridazine (150–800 mg). Although the last group is rarely used nowadays because of its adverse effects on the heart, the other phenothiazines are still in use, not just for psychosis but also for agitation in the elderly, anxiety, nausea and autism.

The adverse effects of phenothiazines are common to many of the classical antipsychotics. The extrapyramidal symptoms, which include tardive dyskinesia, dystonia, parkinsonism and akathisia, are all described below; other important adverse effects include sedation, hypotension, hypothermia (low body temperature), hormonal disorders, convulsions, jaundice, abnormalities of heart rhythm and anticholinergic symptoms such as dry mouth, blurred vision, urinary retention and constipation. Moreover, phenothiazines interact with other medications such as lithium, anticholinergics, anticonvulsants, antidepressants and dopamine agonists. Blood monitoring is not required.

THIOXANTHENES

Flupenthixol (6–18 mg) and zuclopenthixol (20–150 mg) are available in an oral format and a depot injection; zuclopenthixol is also available as Clopixol Acuphase, an injection used in acute psychosis and manic states. Side effects are similar to those of phenothiazines and contraindications include comatose states, pregnancy and lactation. Blood monitoring is not required.

BUTYROPHENONES

Haloperidol (1–20 mg) and droperidol (20–120 mg four times daily) are available in oral and intramuscular preparations and are used to treat psychosis, agitation, mania, extreme anxiety and *Gilles de la Tourette* syndrome. Their adverse effects are similar to those of phenothiazines, while haloperidol interacts with chlorpromazine, fluoxetine, carbamazepine and terfenadine and is not normally used in lactating mothers. Blood monitoring is not required.

DIPHENYLBUTYLPIPERIDINES

Pimozide (2–20 mg) is used in both mania and psychosis and has side effects similar to those of phenothiazines. Serious cardiac arrhythmias may also occur, however, making it necessary to measure plasma potassium levels regularly. Pimozide may interact with diuretics and cardio-active drugs such as tricyclic antidepressants, while it is generally avoided in patients who have pre-existing heart conditions and in women who are pregnant or lactating.

SUBSTITUTED BENZAMIDES

Sulpiride (400–2400 mg twice daily) and amisulpiride (50–1200 mg twice daily) act primarily on dopamine D_2 and D_3 receptors and thus appear to cause less sedation and hypotension than many other antipsychotics. The side effects and interactions of sulpiride are otherwise similar to those of phenothiazines; high levels of the hormone prolactin can be a particular problem with amisulpiride. The latter is therefore contraindicated in lactating mothers and patients with prolactin-dependent tumours; both drugs are contraindicated in patients with *phaeochromocytoma*. Blood monitoring is not required.

Atypical antipsychotics

DIBENZODIAZEPINES

Arguably the biggest breakthrough in efficacious pharmacotherapy for schizophrenia has been clozapine, a most useful drug that frequently succeeds where others have failed. Like many 'wonder drugs', however, clozapine is not without its problems. Potential adverse effects include sedation, hypersalivation, weight gain, hypothermia, hormonal disorders, extrapyramidal and anticholinergic symptoms, hypotension and cardiac problems, convulsions, delirium, jaundice and blood disorders such as *neutropaenia* and potentially fatal *agranulocytosis*.

Despite this rather daunting list of adverse effects, a specialized Clozapine Monitoring Service helps to ensure the safety of the medication, facilitating blood tests and providing useful advice for doctors and patients. A strict and gradual dosing regime is recommended, particularly in the early phases of treatment, as many of the adverse effects are dose dependent. The usual starting dose is 12.5 mg once daily, with increases of 12.5–25 mg per day up to a therapeutic daily divided dosage of approximately 450 mg, or a plasma level of 350 mcg/l. This can usually be achieved in 3–4 weeks but can take longer if side effects prove problematic. With clozapine, adherence is particularly important because patients who miss more than 2 days of tablets require their dosages to be titrated upwards, once again, from the beginning.

Clozapine can interact with any drug that depresses the manufacture of while blood cells, for example carbamazepine, phenothiazines, SSRIs and risperidone, all of which may also increase clozapine levels. Smoking and phenytoin can decrease clozapine levels. Clozapine should be avoided in pregnant or lactating women.

THIENOBENZODIAZEPINES

Olanzapine (5–20 mg daily) is often used as a first-line treatment and is generally well tolerated, although its adverse effects include sedation, weight gain, hypotension, anticholinergic symptoms and raised liver function tests. Smoking and carbamazepine can reduce olanzapine levels to a small extent and the drug is contraindicated in patients with narrow angle *glaucoma* and in lactating mothers. Patients should ideally not drive or operate machinery while on olanzapine.

BENZIXASOLES

Risperidone (2–16 mg daily) is also used as a first-line treatment. Its side effects include agitation, hypotension, abdominal pain, anxiety and raised prolactin levels. Extrapyramidal symptoms are uncommon with risperidone at daily dosages of less than 8 mg, and interactions are similar to those of phenothiazines. Recently, risperidone consta – a slow-release preparation – was developed to replace tablets with a 3-weekly injection, thus giving the adherence advantages associated with a depot.

DIBENZOTHIAZEPINES

Quetiapine (150–400 mg twice daily) may be used as a first-line treatment. Adverse effects include hypotension, sedation, dry mouth, constipation, weight gain, dizziness and changes in liver and thyroid function. Quetiapine is used cautiously with any drug that inhibits the liver enzyme cytochrome P450 and is best avoided in pregnant or lactating women.

BENZISOTHIASOLES

Ziprasadone (40–160 mg daily) was recently licensed in Ireland and is available in oral and intramuscular preparations. Its adverse reactions include somnolence, nausea, postural hypotension, cardiac arrhythmias and, occasionally, dystonias (see below). It interacts with carbamazepine and some antiarrhythmics. Use should be avoided in pregnant or lactating women.

Extrapyramidal side effects and their management

Acute dystonia

Acute dystonia occurs in 2–10% of patients within hours to days of commencing therapy – usually with a classical antipsychotic – and is most common in young males. Spasm occurs to groups of muscles, leading to fixed postures such as involuntary protrusion of the tongue, clenched jaw muscles, *torticollis* (where a group of neck muscles becomes rigid) or oculogyric crisis (in which the head points involuntarily upwards with the mouth open wide and the eyes staring). Acute dystonia is extremely distressing and can result in poor adherence to therapy.

Treatment involves the immediate administration of intramuscular or intravenous anticholinergic medication such as procyclidine, followed by oral procyclidine or orphenadrine. The classical antipsychotic should be reduced in dosage or preferably changed to an atypical antipsychotic, which is less likely to cause dystonia at therapeutic doses.

Akathisia

Akathisia occurs in 20–25% of patients and involves a distressing subjective feeling of motor restlessness, usually involving the lower limbs. As it may lead to increased psychiatric disturbance, poor adherence and even suicide, medication dosage should be reduced, where possible, and supplemented with oral propranolol or a benzodiazepine. Anticholinergic medication is not indicated.

Parkinsonism

Parkinsonism occurs weeks to months after commencing treatment and is due primarily to a blockade of D_2 receptors in the basal ganglia. Symptoms include a mask-like facial expression, tremor, rigid muscles, a *festinant gait* and akathisia. The classical antipsychotic should ideally be reduced in dosage or switched to an atypical variety. Anticholinergic medication, such as procyclidine or orphenadrine, may also be useful.

Tardive dyskinesia

Tardive dyskinesia occurs months to years after commencing antipsychotics in up to 60% of patients, with the risk increasing further by 5% per year. It involves abnormal head and neck movements, progressing from tongue-rotating, lip-smacking and orofacial dyskinesia to choreoathetiod movements of the head, neck and trunk. Elderly patients, females and patients with organic brain damage or affective disorders are most at risk. There is little effective treatment and, indeed, reducing the antipsychotic dosage or adding an anticholinergic can actually aggravate symptoms, albeit temporarily. Switching to clozapine leads to some improvement in up to 70% but, overall, the best measure is prevention by favouring atypical antipsychotics and discontinuing any medication that may exacerbate movement disorders.

It is worth noting that tardive dyskinesia can occur in patients with schizophrenia who have never taken medication. This naturally leads to some confusion regarding the aetiology, with some experts hypothesizing that there may be an 'unmasking' process involved. Either way, tardive dyskinesia adds significantly to the stigmatization felt by patients with schizophrenia.

Neuroleptic malignant syndrome

This is a rare and idiosyncratic reaction presenting with fever, clouding of consciousness, muscle rigidity, unstable blood pressure, racing pulse and changes in levels of the enzyme creatinine phosphokinase. It represents a medical emergency and the mortality for untreated cases is as high as 18%. Treatment, in addition to general supportive measures and rehydration, involves immediate withdrawal of the offending antipsychotic and urgent transfer to a medical ward where oral bromocriptine or dantroline can be given. ECT can be effective in treating this condition. Recovery takes approximately 10 days, shortly after which time most patients can be prescribed another antipsychotic, such as clozapine.

Depot injections

Deep intramuscular depot preparations, in which the drug is dissolved in fractionated oil, are normally administered at intervals of 1–4 weeks, allowing the drug to diffuse slowly and evenly into the body's water compartments. Advantages include the avoidance of first-pass metabolism and improvement of adherence. As it is not possible to discontinue depots quickly in the event of adverse effects occurring, a small test dose is essential when commencing any depot for the first time. Such medications should ideally be given at the lowest therapeutic dose at intervals as lengthy as the licence will allow.

Treatment-resistant schizophrenia

For treatment-resistant patients who fail to respond to 6–12 months of clozapine therapy, adjuvant medications include sulpiride, lamotrigine, risperidone, omega-3-triglycerides, amisulpiride, haloperidol and nefazadone. Alternatively, olanzapine can be prescribed at high doses of up to 60 mg daily.

It is worth noting that, for patients who recover, the risk of relapse never really disappears. Shepherd et al. (1989) report that the overall prognosis of schizophrenia was poor, with only 22% of patients escaping with a single acute episode and no residual impairment of functioning. The remainder were found to experience recurrent episodes, with 35% having little or no residual impairment; 8% experiencing significant, non-progressive impairment; and 35% enduring significant, progressive impairment.

Treatment of schizoaffective disorder and psychotic depression

These disorders are treated with concomitant use of an antipsychotic and an antidepressant or mood stabilizer to address both affective and psychotic symptoms.

A note on cost

Atypical antipsychotics are usually more expensive than their classical counterparts but this does not necessarily make the latter more cost effective in clinical practice. For example, patients are known to adhere better to atypical antipsychotics, thus reducing their likelihood of relapse. Add this to the fewer associated intolerable side effects and any patient will tell you which type of medication is better value!

Hypomania, mania and bipolar affective disorder (ICD-10: F30–31. DSM-IV: 296/301)

The ICD-10 characterizes hypomania as a degree of elevated or irritable mood that lasts at least 4 days and is abnormal for the individual concerned. In addition, the diagnosis requires the presence of at least three symptoms from a long list that includes increased activity or restlessness, overtalkativeness, poor concentration, sleeplessness, overfamiliarity and reckless behaviour such as overspending.

Mania requires a more significant level of elevated or irritable mood lasting at least a week, with at least three signs from a list similar to that above but also including pressure of speech, racing thoughts, grandiosity and significant disinhibition.

For a diagnosis to stand, mania and hypomania must not be attributable to substance misuse or any organic cause. Up to 20% of manic patients have been found to have first-rank psychotic symptoms.

An ICD-10 diagnosis of bipolar affective disorder requires a current episode of mania or hypomania in addition to another previous instance of disturbed mood which, in itself, has met the criteria for a mixed affective, depressive, hypomanic or manic episode with or without psychotic symptoms. Of note, rapid-cycling bipolar affective disorder is characterized in the DSM-IV by four or more episodes of mood disturbances in a single year. Bipolar affective disorder affects men and women equally, the peak age of onset being 20–30 years. So, how might we treat mania, hypomania and bipolar affective disorder?

Initial sedation of hypomanic patients

For patients presenting with mania or hypomania, the first priority is to optimize their mood stabilizer dosage to reach a plasma level within its therapeutic range (see below). Antidepressant medications are ideally withdrawn immediately and a benzodiazepine (e.g. lorazepam) is prescribed, evaluated over a 2- to 3-day period and withdrawn after resolution of symptoms. If this fails, an antipsychotic (e.g. haloperidol, chlorpromazine or olanzapine) represents the next line in treatment, with evaluation over 1–2 weeks, at which point it can either be withdrawn or used as prophylaxis against future manic episodes. Further options involve antimanic agents such as lamotrigine and gabapentin.

Mood stabilizers

Lithium

As the most common mood stabilizer, lithium is used as prophylaxis against both bipolar and unipolar affective disorders, as well as in the treatment of acute mania. Moreover, it is used to augment the action of antidepressants in patients with treatment-resistant depression. Blood tests are essential when using lithium and include plasma levels, which should be monitored every 5 days until a safe and effective dosage is reached. Plasma levels should lie between 0.6 and 1.2 mmol/l and are taken routinely during maintenance – along with renal function – every 2–3 months. It is important to note that blood samples for lithium should be taken 12 hours after a given dose. As hypothyroidism occurs in 3–4% of patients on lithium, thyroid function should be monitored every 6 months.

The early side effects of lithium include thirst, nausea, loose bowel motions, fine tremor and *polyurea*. Other side effects, occuring in up to 30%, include weight gain, oedema, cardiac changes, nasal congestion and tardive dyskinesia. When plasma levels exceed 1.5 mmol/l, toxic effects can occur and include anorexia, vomiting, diarrhoea, coarse tremor, unsteady gait, slurred speech, confusion, drowsiness, eye changes, muscle twitching and convulsions. Very high levels of lithium can be fatal. Pregnancy is a relative contraindication to lithium therapy, especially in the first trimester when there is a risk of congenital defects such as *Ebstein's anomaly*. Other contraindications include thyroid disorders and compromised renal function, both of which are more likely in the elderly. Lithium interacts with haloperidol, thiazide diuretics, alcohol and a variety of cardioactive medications.

Bipolar patients who become depressed may need augmentation of their lithium with an antidepressant, and others suffering from rapid-cycling disorder may require augmentation with another mood stabilizer. Finally, care should be taken when discontinuing lithium as a 'rebound' relapse can sometimes occur.

Carbamazepine

Carbamazepine works by slowing down the recovery time of sodium channels in the nervous system. It has been shown to be as effective as lithium in preventing relapses of bipolar affective disorder and is also useful in treating rapid-cycling disorder. It is, however, thought to be less effective in the treatment of acute mania.

The side effects of carbamazepine include drowsiness, double vision, unsteady gait, rashes, headache, hypothyroidism and blood abnormalities such as *agranulocytosis* and *leucopaenia.* Regular blood tests are therefore needed, including thyroid function tests and a full blood count, in addition to drug plasma levels. The latter are recommended every 2 weeks for the first 2 months and, although there is no universally accepted therapeutic window for the drug, 8–12 mg/l is a reasonable guideline. Pregnancy is a contraindication to carbamazepine because neural tube defects may occur, and important interactions occur with antipsychotics, monoamine oxidase inhibitors (MAOIs), lithium and clozapine.

Sodium valproate

Sodium valproate, which works by inhibiting the enzyme GABA-transaminase, is used to treat mania, refractory bipolar affective disorder and rapid-cycling disorder. Moreover, it represents the first-line anticonvulsant for clozapine-induced seizures and may be used prophylactically when clozapine doses exceed 500–600 mg per day.

The adverse effects of sodium valproate include nausea, vomiting, diarrhoea, sedation, tremor, weight gain, unsteady gait and slurred speech; rare side effects such as a low platelet count and toxicity to the liver and pancreas may also occur. Sodium valproate can interact with lithium, antipsychotics, warfarin and aspirin and is contraindicated in pregnant or lactating women.

The response rates to mood-stabilizing medication vary depending on the context in which the manic event or bipolar illness occur. Overall, the rates are estimated at approximately 50% but may be as low as 30% in patients with a rapid-cycling disorder and as high as 70% in patients experiencing acute mania.

Depression (ICD-10: F32–33. DSM-IV: 296/300–1)

Depression is a common psychiatric illness, the prevalence of which appears to be on the increase. The overall lifetime risk for affective disorders probably exceeds 20%; it is more common in women than in men. For an ICD-10 diagnosis of depression, the episode must last at least 2 weeks, with a history of manic or hypomanic episodes absent, and substance abuse and organic illness ruled out as aetiological factors. Illness severity and the presence or absence of somatic symptoms vary within the disorder.

Neurotransmitter hypothesis of depression

Before we examine the pharmacotherapy used to treat depression, it is important to note the hypothesis on which the treatment of depression is based. The *monoamine* hypothesis of affective disorders states that depression is due to a functional deficit of monoamine neurotransmitters, such as serotonin and noradrenaline, whereas mania is due to their functional excess.

Evidence to support this theory includes the observation that mood improves in patients treated with tricyclic antidepressants (TCAs), which are known to block monoamine reuptake in the synapse. Similarly, mood improves in patients taking monoamine oxidase inhibitors (MAOIs), which prevent the breakdown of monoamines in the synapse; and in patients receiving electroconvulsive therapy (ECT), which is believed to work by increasing central responses to monoamines. Moreover, the antihypertensive drugs reserpine, which reduces monoamine storage, and methyldopa, which inhibits noradrenaline synthesis, are both noted to cause depression.

The monoamine hypothesis is not fully understood, however. We still have not worked out, for example, why cocaine and amphetamines inhibit noradrenaline uptake and yet fail to have any effect on depression, or why antidepressants have delayed clinical efficacy despite their immediate effects on monoamine transmission. Nonetheless, the monoamine hypothesis provides us with a solid theoretical model upon which many effective therapies are based.

With this in mind – and once the decision has been made to use an antidepressant – a starting dose is prescribed and assessed over 4–6 weeks. Should this prove ineffective, a second antidepressant of a different class may be tried before moving to the suggested treatments for refractory depression described below. An effective antidepressant should be continued for at least 4–6 months after resolution of symptoms and withdrawn gradually over 2–4 weeks to avoid re-emergence of symptoms. A synopsis of antidepressants is given below.

Tricyclic antidepressants

Tricyclic antidepressants (TCAs) include most of the older varieties of antidepressant, which work by inhibiting the reuptake of noradrenaline and serotonin in the synapse. These were, for many years, considered the 'gold standard' treatment for depression but they have become less popular recently due to their numerous associated adverse effects. Such effects mean that poor adherence can be a serious issue with TCAs, and particular varieties such as amitriptyline and dothiepin can be exceptionally dangerous in overdose. Table 6.2 presents treatment indications, daily dosages and half-lives of commonly used TCAs.

The adverse effects of TCAs are related to the blockade of specific neurotransmitter receptors. For example, anticholinergic effects – dry mouth, blurred vision, urinary retention and constipation – are associated with muscarinic M1 receptors and are worst with desipramine and nortriptyline. Some patients develop a tolerance for anticholinergic effects within a week or two, and the effects can be minimized further by titrating the dosage gradually or by using less-anticholinergic TCAs such as amitriptyline or imipramine.

Meanwhile, side effects associated with alpha-1-adrenergic receptors include postural hypotension, dizziness and cardiac arrhythmias, while histamine H1 receptors are linked to weight gain and sedation. The latter occurs more with amitriptyline and dothiepin than with nortriptyline or imipramine. TCAs are associated with various ECG changes, such as *heart block*, and are contraindicated in patients with a significant cardiac history. Other contraindications include enlarged prostate and narrow-angle *glaucoma*, while care should be taken in patients with epilepsy or diseases of the liver and kidney.

TCAs interact with several other important drugs, increasing the effects of alcohol, hypnotics, anxiolytics, antipsychotics, noradrenaline and adrenaline; TCAs can reduce the action of some antihypertensives. In particular, they can interact with MAOIs to produce central nervous excitation, hyperpyrexia and coma; trimipramine is the least likely TCA to do this. Finally, TCAs should be discontinued gradually to avoid the risk of a cholinergic rebound syndrome.

Table 6.2 Commonly used TCAs, treatment indicators, daily dosages and half-lives

Name	*Indications (depression and . . .)*	*Daily dosage*	*Half-life*	*Notes*
Amitriptyline	Childhood enuresis; migraine	10–150 mg	8–24 h	Metabolized to nortriptyline
Nortriptyline	As above	20–150 mg	18–96 h	Useful in the elderly
Imipramine	As above	75–300 mg	4–18 h	Metabolized to desipramine
Desipramine	Nil	75–200 mg	12–24 h	
Dothiepin	Nil	75–225 mg	11–40 h	
Lofepramine	Nil	70–210 mg up to TDS	1.5–6 h	Used in elderly: less cardiotoxic
Clomipramine	Obsessive-compulsive disorder; phobic states; cataplexy associated with narcolepsy	10–250 mg	17–28 h	

Selective serotonin reuptake inhibitors

Selective serotonin reuptake inhibitors (SSRIs), which are among the newest of the antidepressants, selectively inhibit the reuptake of serotonin in the synapse. They have several advantages over TCAs, largely related to their more acceptable side effect profile at effective dosages, leading, in turn, to greater adherence. In addition, fewer cardiotoxic side effects make SSRIs the drug of choice in depressed cardiac patients; they are also considerably safer in overdose and useful in a variety of additional disorders, apart from depression. Unfortunately, they may be less effective in severe depression, and one SSRI is reported – but not proven – to be associated with suicidal preoccupation. A synopsis of the commonly used SSRIs is given in Table 6.3.

Adverse effects are reported less frequently with SSRIs than with other antidepressants. Nausea and diarrhoea are the most common, occurring in 27% of patients; dry mouth occurs in up to 18%, sexual dysfunction reportedly in 15% and blurred vision in 5%. Meanwhile, insomnia occurs with all SSRIs except citalopram, and anorexia is associated with all except paroxetine. Sedation, however, is problematic in up to 21% of patients on paroxetine and fluoxetine, and anxiety symptoms occur in 15%. In addition, fluoxetine may be associated with low sodium and glucose levels in the blood.

The serotonergic syndrome is a more serious adverse effect, thought to be due to enhanced serotonergic transmission in the brainstem. It can occur with SSRIs, lithium and MAOIs and presents with fever, restlessness, agitation, diarrhoea, stomach cramps, tremor, exaggerated reflexes and impaired consciousness. Indeed, it is not unlike the neuroleptic malignant syndrome mentioned earlier and, moreover, can be fatal if left untreated.

Withdrawal symptoms have been reported occasionally with SSRIs, including paroxetine. Gradual withdrawal is therefore advised to avoid such symptoms, which include headache, dizziness, nausea, *paraesthesia*, sweating, tremor and occasional dystonias.

Table 6.3 Commonly used SSRIs, treatment indicators, daily dosages and half-lives

Name	*Indications (depression and . . .)*	*Daily dosage*	*Half-life*	*Notes*
Fluvoxamine	OCD	100–300 mg	15–22 h	Nausea more likely
Fluoxetine	Bulimia nervosa; OCD	20–60 mg	24–140 h	Not very sedating
Sertraline	OCD	50–200 mg	24–26 h	Can raise LFTs
Paroxetine	OCD; social phobia; panic disorder +/– agoraphobia	20–60 mg	24 h	Withdrawal effects
Citalopram	Panic disorder +/– agoraphobia	20–60 mg	33 h	Fewer interactions

LFTs, liver function tests; OCD, obsessive-compulsive disorder.

There are no absolute contraindications to SSRIs, although caution is advised for patients with epilepsy. It is important to note that SSRIs can interact badly with MAOIs, leading to excitation of the central nervous system, *hyperpyrexia* and even coma. Some SSRIs, moreover, may interact with other drugs such as propranolol, oral anticoagulants, phenytoin, carbamazepine and haloperidol.

Serotonin and noradrenaline reuptake inhibitors

Venlafaxine is a phenethylamine bicyclic derivative with pharmacological effects similar to the TCAs. Although its half-life is only 5 hours, while that of its active metabolite is 10 hours, a longer acting XL preparation is also available. The latter is used in depression at dosages of 75–300 mg; higher dosages have more influence over noradrenergic transmission and are used in generalized anxiety disorder.

The adverse effects of venlafaxine are relatively few in number due to its low affinity for cholinergic, histaminergic and alpha-1-adrenergic receptors. Nausea, hypertension and sexual dysfunction may occur and caution should be exercised in patients with hepatic or renal impairment. Moreover, it is avoided in patients taking MAOIs due to the risk of the serotonergic syndrome.

Monoamine oxidase inhibitors

The enzyme monoamine oxidase, which metabolizes a variety of neurotransmitters in the synapse, has two types of pharmacological inhibitor: irreversible and reversible. Irreversible MAOIs inhibit monoamine oxidase A (MAO-A) in the gastrointestinal tract and monoamine oxidase B (MAO-B) in the brain. As MAO-A preferentially breaks down serotonin and noradrenaline, its inhibitors are ideal for treating depression.

The irreversible MAOIs include drugs such as phenelzine, tranylcypromine and isocarboxazid and are generally reserved for patients with treatment-resistant depression. Phenelzine has traditionally had a role in treating phobias, panic disorder and atypical, non-biological types of depression, especially those associated with anxiety and hypochondriacal symptoms. The use of MAOIs, however, needs to be monitored closely. Possible adverse effects include *orthostatic hypotension*, oedema, insomnia, sexual dysfunction, weight gain, liver damage and psychosis. *Phaeochromocytoma* is an absolute contraindication; relative contraindications include cardiovascular disease, liver disease, diabetes, epilepsy and hyperthyroidism.

The importance of special dietary restrictions in patients taking MAOIs cannot be overemphasized. Foods rich in tyramine and drugs containing amines must be avoided at all costs because gastrointestinal MAO-A is also responsible for breaking down tyramine in the diet. If the latter is not metabolized, it builds up rapidly in the body and causes the release of noradrenaline, which, in turn, leads to a sudden pounding headache and potentially fatal rise in blood pressure otherwise known as the 'cheese reaction'.

Cheese is not the only food rich in tyramine, however. Other foods to be avoided include sources of degraded protein, such as liver, hung game, pickled herring, smoked fish and pate. Fava and broad bean pods are also off the menu, as are beer, Chianti wine, avocados and yeast or protein extracts such as Marmite, Bovril and Oxo. Drugs to be avoided include pethidine, morphine, cocaine, SSRIs, anaesthetics containing adrenaline and many commonly used cold and flu remedies. Furthermore, such restrictions remain in place for at least 2 weeks after the MAOI is discontinued.

Reversible inhibitors of monoamine oxidase A

Reversible inhibitors of monoamine oxidase A (RIMAs), such as moclobemide, are far less likely to cause the cheese reaction although the risk is by no means completely absent. Moderate quantities of mature cheese, for example, may still cause difficulty but, nonetheless, stringent dietary restrictions are usually not required. Meanwhile, the efficacy of RIMAs is similar to that of SSRIs and TCAs, while their side effects include insomnia, nausea, agitation and confusion. Of note, interactions can occur with cimetedine, pethidine and SSRIs, and caution should be exercised in patients using TCAs.

Electroconvulsive therapy

In 1938, Cerletti and Bini first used electricity to induce a seizure in a mute catatonic patient. Their work was based on the earlier research by physicians such as Phillipus Paracelcus and Ladislas Von Meduna. General anaesthetics were first used for electroconvulsive therapy (ECT) in 1951 and, since then, ECT has been further researched and refined to increase its efficacy and reduce its side effects.

ECT is currently the most effective treatment available for severe depression, especially where antidepressants have failed, where medicinal adverse effects have not been tolerated or where patients have previously responded well to ECT. Other indications include postnatal or psychotic depression and low mood associated with psychomotor retardation, where ECT may indeed be lifesaving, for example in the context of a suicidal patient who cannot wait 2 weeks for antidepressants to work.

Up to 80% of patients with acute mania respond to ECT, including many whose illnesses were resistant to the combined use of lithium and antipsychotics. The relapse rate, however, is higher for manic patients than for their depressive counterparts. ECT can also be used in catatonic stupor, various neurological conditions such as Parkinson's disease, and affective disorders associated with multiple sclerosis.

Despite a widespread confidence in the efficacy of ECT, many respected clinicians over the years have voiced dissatisfaction with the available evidence. For example, a recent article in *The Psychologist* (Johnstone, 2003) highlights a number of ongoing concerns regarding efficacy, ethics, the potential physical and psychological harm, and how little we know about the mechanism of action. Johnstone cites Greenblatt et al. (1964) and discusses their claim that ECT is effective in eight out of ten cases; he then reminds us that Buchan et al. (1992), conversely, found the procedure to be little better than placebo. Different studies have come to different conclusions; meanwhile Johnstone's article makes a valid point: that ECT research – like much of psychiatry – is still very much in its infancy.

Although we are still unsure of the mechanism by which ECT works so successfully, several plausible theories exist. One hypothesis draws a correlation between the manner in which ECT raises the seizure threshold and improves mood, and compares this to the mood-stabilizing properties of anticonvulsant medications such as sodium valproate and carbamazepine. Another theory suggests that changes in blood–brain barrier permeability associated with ECT may lead to improved mood, and yet another hypothesis notes EEG and neurochemical changes seen after the procedure. The theories are endless, yet a definitive mechanism is yet to be found.

ECT is normally given three times per week with, on average, six to twelve procedures performed in total. Informed, written consent is required and routine blood tests, an ECG, a chest X-ray and an anaesthetic review are normally necessary prior to the first session. As with any procedure requiring anaesthetic, the patient must fast for 12 hours before each session.

During the procedure, blood pressure, heart rate and blood oxygen saturation are all monitored along with an EEG reading. An intravenous anaesthetic is administered along with a muscle relaxant, before a few seconds of 100% oxygen is given via a mask. The electrodes are then placed in position near the temples before a small current is passed, lasting less than a second and producing a seizure that usually lasts 15–45 seconds.

Minutes later, the patient wakes up and may experience a brief period of confusion, headache or muscle stiffness which rarely lasts more than an hour. Short-term memory loss – perhaps the most famous side effect of ECT – may span a few days but rarely persists beyond 1 month. Overall, the mortality rate for ECT is 2 in 100,000, no more than that associated with the general anaesthetic.

Indeed, the procedure is a safe and effective means of treating severe depression, especially if a maintenance course of antidepressants is prescribed afterwards to help avoid relapse.

Treatment of refractory depression

There are a number of options open to patients who do not respond to antidepressants and psychotherapy alone. First, augmentation with sufficient lithium to achieve a plasma level of 0.4–0.6 mmol/l has been shown to ameliorate symptoms in approximately 50% of patients, although this naturally carries the risk of side effects associated with lithium and hence requires plasma monitoring. ECT can be used as outlined above and, should this also fail, venlafaxine in dosages above 225 mg daily is normally well tolerated and practicable in the primary-care setting provided blood pressure is monitored regularly. Tri-iodothyronine at dosages of 20–50 mcg daily can also prove expedient and is usually well tolerated, although it normally requires specialist supervision and regular monitoring of thyroid function. Meanwhile, other options include augmentation with tryptophan, pindolol, dexamethasone, lamotrigine, high-dose TCAs, a combined MAOI and TCA, bupropion and benzodiazepines.

So, what is the overall outcome of treatment? In a 1994 meta-analysis, Piccinelli and Wilkinson reported that 50% of patients recovered within 6 months and that the health of a further 25% was restored within a year. Whereas 10% were found to experience persistent treatment-resistant depression, 75% of recovered patients relapsed within a 10-year period.

Anxiety disorders (ICD-10: F40–42. DSM-IV: 300/308–9)

The ICD-10 categorizes neurotic and stress-related disorders into phobic disorders, including agoraphobia, social phobias and specific phobias; other anxiety disorders, such as panic disorder and generalized anxiety disorder; obsessive-compulsive disorder; and reactions to severe stress, incorporating adjustment disorders. Although each category has different diagnostic requirements, symptoms are broadly grouped into those involving autonomic arousal, the chest and abdomen, the mental state and general symptoms.

Anxiety disorders are relatively common. Estimates suggest that lifetime prevalence varies between 1–2% for panic disorder and 10–15% for social phobia, and the overall lifetime risk for anxiety disorders is 15–20%. Meanwhile, reported rates are higher in women for all types of anxiety disorder except social phobia, where rates are equal between genders. So, with this in mind, how do we treat anxiety disorders?

Cognitive behavioural therapy (CBT) almost always represents the first-line option, depending on the clinical aspects in question, the patient's suitability and the availability of an appropriately trained therapist. Good education of patients and carers is obviously a necessity and medications such as SSRIs and MAOIs may also be called on where there is comorbid depression, severely debilitating symptoms or failure of CBT alone. Meanwhile, in situations where the combination of CBT and medication proves unsuccessful, a review of the diagnosis may be necessary, to include examination of lifestyle issues such as caffeine consumption and drug abuse, and investigation for possible organic aetiology.

Benzodiazepines

Benzodiazepines, which work by increasing GABA function in the synapse, are used in the short-term management of severe and disabling anxiety. They were first introduced in the 1960s as a 'safe' alternative to barbiturates and became so successful that, before long, they were viewed as a panacea for every anxiety-related problem from broken marriages to redundancy. Indeed, at the height of their popularity, 31 million NHS prescriptions for benzodiazepines were being given out per year – enough to sedate three out of every four adults in the UK! Unsurprisingly, withdrawal and tolerance effects soon became apparent, the latter developing in as few as 14 days. The result is that there are now strict prescribing guidelines, issued by the Royal College of Psychiatrists, which state, for example, that benzodiazepines should not be prescribed for more than four consecutive weeks.

The symptoms of benzodiazepine withdrawal can include rebound anxiety, sweating, agitation, irritability, insomnia, muscle tension, nausea, lethargy, unsteady gait and blurred vision; seizures and paranoid delusions may also rarely occur. To avoid such symptoms, addicted patients should be weaned off their benzodiazepines by substituting with an equivalent dose of diazepam and then reducing the latter very gradually. Diazepam is used here because of its long half-life; the half-lives of other commonly-used benzodiazepines are shown in Table 6.4.

The adverse effects of benzodiazepines include drowsiness, unsteady gait and paradoxical aggression. Co-ordination may become impoverished and thus extreme care should be taken while driving or operating machinery. Meanwhile, the use of benzodiazepines during pregnancy can result in fetal anomalies, such as a cleft lip and palate. The effects of benzodiazepines are

Table 6.4 Benzodiazepines and their associated half-lives

Benzodiazepine	*Half-life*
Clonazepam	20–40 h
Chlordiazepoxide	5–30 h
Nitrazepam	24–40 h
Lorazepam	8–20 h
Temazepam	6–15 h
Oxazepam	6–20 h

exaggerated by alcohol, barbiturates, TCAs and antihistamines; their levels are increased by fluoxetine.

Buspirone

Buspirone, a type of azapirone, is a serotonin agonist that, unlike benzodiazepines, does not act directly on GABA, although it may have an indirect effect via dopamine. Used for the short-term management of generalized anxiety disorder at dosages of up to 60 mg, buspirone does not cause significant sedation or cognitive impairment and carries a low risk of dependence and withdrawal symptoms. Its anxiolytic effect, however, occurs gradually over 1–3 weeks, giving it little advantage over the SSRIs. Its main adverse effects include dizziness, headache and light-headedness but it does not increase the sedative effects of alcohol.

Treatment of specific anxiety disorders

Agoraphobia and panic disorder

In agoraphobia, a patient feels anxious about certain situations from which escape may be difficult or where help may not be available should a situational panic attack occur. This usually leads to avoidance of such situations – typically crowded public places (agoraphobia literally means 'fear of the market place').

Panic disorder involves sudden, unexpected, short periods of intense anxiety with a sense of imminent danger and a need to escape. Panic attacks tend to last around 10 minutes but may continue for an hour or more, while the associated severe anxiety symptoms typically include dizziness, palpitations, sweating, nausea, abdominal cramps, breathlessness, chest discomfort and depersonalization.

Should CBT fail to work, SSRIs may be used, their dosages generally slightly higher than those used in depression: paroxetine 10–40 mg daily, citalopram 10–40 mg daily, sertraline 25–150 mg daily and fluoxetine 10–60 mg daily. Unfortunately, the action of SSRIs can be delayed for as long as 6 weeks, with a full response taking up to 12 weeks in many patients.

Up to 40% of panic-disorder patients commencing an SSRI experience an activation syndrome, with increased levels of agitation, and a further 40% relapse when the drug is discontinued. Treatment, therefore, should continue for at least 12 months, at which point the dosage should be tapered slowly downwards by 25% every 2 months to avoid a relapse. Alternatives to SSRIs include TCAs, MAOIs and RIMAs, and benzodiazepines may be used in concordance with current guidelines.

Social phobias and specific phobias

Where CBT fails to ameliorate social phobia, SSRIs, TCAs, MAOIs or RIMAs (or occasionally benzodiazepines) become the drugs of choice; beta blockers (e.g. propranolol 20–60 mg) are sometimes used for symptomatic relief in performance anxiety. However, although specific phobias are treated with CBT, pharmacotherapy is usually inappropriate except in 'once-off' circumstances.

Generalized anxiety disorder

Generalized anxiety disorder involves excessive anxiety lasting at least 6 months and interfering with an individual's ability to cope with everyday demands at home, at work and socially. Symptoms commonly include prominent tension and worry; feelings of apprehension; autonomic arousal symptoms such as tachycardia; muscle-tension; nausea, diarrhoea and abdominal discomfort; tension headaches; difficulty concentrating; sleep disturbance and low mood.

In terms of treatment, CBT is once again the first-line option; severe illness or significant comorbidity may necessitate an SSRI, an SNRI or buspirone. Benzodiazepines with a long half-life may occasionally be used, in accordance with guidelines.

Obsessive-compulsive disorder

Obsessive-compulsive disorder is characterized by at least a two-week period of recurrent, unpleasant, ego-dystonic ruminations that are resisted by the patient and may, in turn, lead to compulsive acts to reduce anxiety. In addition to CBT, management options include SSRIs and clomipramine.

Post-traumatic stress disorder

Post-traumatic stress disorder (PTSD) arises after an exceptionally threatening event outside the range of normal experience. Symptoms typically include a repeated reliving of the trauma, flashbacks, marked irritability, hyperarousal, insomnia and other symptoms. The role of benzodiazepines is particularly limited in PTSD, with SSRIs, MAOIs, RIMAs or valproic acid comprising better options where CBT fails.

Sleep disorders and sexual dysfunction (ICD-10: F51–52. DSM-IV: 302/307)

The ICD-10 divides non-organic sleep disorders into insomnia, hypersomnia, disorders of the sleep–wake cycle, somnambulism, sleep terrors, nightmares and various other ailments. Sexual disorders are categorized into those affecting sexual desire and enjoyment, genital response, inability to experience orgasm, premature ejaculation, non-organic vaginismus and excessive sexual drive. Sexual dysfunction is common in psychiatry, partly due to the side effects of medication, but may be underreported. For example, whereas on self-report questionnaires 15% of patients taking SSRIs admit to sexual dysfunction, this increases to 70% on further questioning. Also of note are the high prolactin levels associated with some antipsychotics. The treatment of sleep disorders and sexual dysfunction are briefly summarized as follows:

Sleep disorders

Insomnia, the most common sleep disorder, may be divided into initial insomnia, middle insomnia and early morning wakening, depending on the timing of the symptoms. As the aetiology may be physical (e.g. pain) or environmental (e.g. noise), it is important to take a detailed history and initiate appropriate pain relief or education regarding sleep hygiene before considering hypnotics.

Although benzodiazepines are sometimes used, newer non-benzodiazepine hypnotics such as zolpidem, zopiclone and zaleplon, are becoming increasingly popular (Table 6.5). Both drug types act rapidly and have minimal hangover effects, however long-term use is not recommended because withdrawal symptoms have been reported. Other drugs with hypnotic properties include promethazine, chlormethiazole and chloral hydrate.

Sexual dysfunction

Management primarily includes education, in addition to pharmacological measures such as sildenafil for erectile dysfunction.

Table 6.5 Drugs with hypnotic properties, their chemical types and half-lives

Drug	*Chemical type*	*Half-life*	*Notes*
Zolpidem	Imidazopyridine	1–3 h	Binds to alpha-1 part of benzodiazepine receptor Reduces sleep latency
Zopiclone	Cyclopyrrolone	3–6 h	Reduces sleep latency Increases sleep length
Zaleplon	Pyrazolopyrimidine	1 h	Fewer side effects

FACILITATING ADHERENCE

Good adherence to medication is a crucial aspect of treatment. Indeed, non-adherence is enormously significant from both the perspective of an individual's quality of life and the overall economic and social implications. For example, one study suggests that full adherence to antipsychotic medication would reduce the personal and financial burden of schizophrenia by 50%. Moreover, Haynes et al. (2002) reported in a Cochrane review meta-analysis that: 'the full benefits of medications cannot be realised at currently achievable levels of adherence. Current methods of improving adherence for chronic health problems are mostly complex and not very effective. Innovations to assist patients to follow medication prescriptions are needed.' The importance of a good therapeutic alliance between clinician and patient cannot be overemphasized; contributory factors for improving adherence include:

- Clear information regarding the purposes and expected outcomes of the medication, including efficacy, tolerability and adverse effects.
- A simple drug regime with clear instructions on the medication container as to how and when the drugs should be taken.
- Ensuring medication is dispensed and collected, enlisting the assistance of community psychiatric nurses, relatives and carers where possible.
- Use of an attractive formulation.
- Monitoring of compliance with regular outpatient feedback sessions and formalized rating of symptoms.
- Facilitation of good insight and positive engagement in therapy.
- Appropriate support for carers and relatives, with adequate psychoeducation to enhance the working alliance and address any ambivalence towards medication.

SUMMARY

This chapter has placed considerable emphasis on the pharmacotherapy of psychological morbidity principally to complement the various psychological approaches outlined in other chapters of the book. It is important to remind ourselves that the appropriate therapy for any given ailment is always a question of emphasis within a multidisciplinary approach, with all appropriate therapeutic options explored for each patient. In this manner, we can hope to ameliorate at least some psychiatric illness and improve quality of life. Perhaps we might even prove Voltaire wrong!

GLOSSARY

Agonist A substance that acts at a cell receptor site and triggers a response.

Agranulocytosis A disorder in which there is severe deficiency of certain types of blood cell due to damage to the bone marrow.

Antagonist A substance that counteracts the effects of an agonist.

Blood–brain barrier A semi-permeable membrane that separates the body's circulating blood from the tissue fluids surrounding the brain cells.

Catatonic Describing a state in which a person becomes mute or stuperose and adopts bizarre postures; a noted feature of schizophrenia.

Depot A means of administration whereby a medication is dissolved in fractionated oil and delivered intramuscularly, allowing slow release over a number of weeks.

Epithelial cell The epithelium is a sheet of tightly bound cells lining any internal or external surface in an organism (e.g. the epidermis of the skin).

Ebstein's anomaly Congenital heart defect affecting the tricuspid valve.

Festinant gait Short, shuffling steps seen in patients with parkinsonism.

Gilles de la Tourette A syndrome involving severe multiple tics and involuntary, obscene speech.

Glaucoma A condition whereby loss of vision occurs due to abnormally high pressure in the eye.

Glomerular filtration Part of the mechanism whereby substances are excreted by the kidney. Such substances pass through a network of capillaries known as the glomerulus and enter the renal tubules.

Half-life The time taken for a drug to drop to half its peak plasma concentration.

Heart block A heart condition in which conduction of electrical impulses from the natural pacemaker is impaired, leading to a slow, inefficient pumping action.

Hyperpyrexia A rise in body temperature above 41 degrees centigrade.

Leucopaenia A reduction in the number of white blood cells.

Monoamine A type of chemical neurotransmitter (e.g. adrenaline, dopamine and serotonin).

Neutropaenia A decrease in the number of neutrophils (a type of white blood cell).

Orthostatic hypotension Low blood pressure found primarily while standing upright.

Paraesthesia Abnormal tingling sensations sometimes referred to as 'pins and needles'.

Parenteral Administered by any route other than the mouth.

Passive diffusion The movement of a substance across a membrane without the help of active chemical transporters.

Phaeochromocytoma A small tumour of the blood vessels in the adrenal gland. By causing the unregulated secretion of adrenaline and noradrenaline, blood pressure may become raised.

Polyurea Production of a large volume of pale, dilute urine.

Topically Administered directly to the part being treated (e.g. to skin or eye).

Torticollis An irresistible and persistent turning of the head to one side due to spasm of the neck muscles.

EXERCISE 6.1

In pairs, role-play part of a session with a client, John, with whom you are working on a psychological intervention for depression. John, who has had many episodes of depression and tried many medications, mentions that he has stopped taking medication. He has questions and concerns about medication, particularly about side effects. He has a scheduled outpatient appointment with his psychiatrist the following day. Work with John to:

1 clarify his questions and concerns
2 plan with him how best he can get his questions addressed at the outpatient psychiatry appointment, using role-play with him where appropriate.

Writing down questions to bring to the appointment, bringing a spouse, friend or other advocate, notebook or tape recorder to the appointment may be helpful to John.

FURTHER READING FOR CLIENTS

Perry, J., Alexander, B., & Liskow, B. (1997). *Psychotropic drug handbook* (Seventh Edition). Washington, DC: American Psychiatric Press.

FURTHER READING FOR PRACTITIONERS

American Psychiatric Association (2001). *Task force report of the APA on the practice of electroconvulsive therapy. Recommendations for treatment, training, and privileging* (Second Edition). Washington, DC: American Psychiatric Press.

Bezchlibnyk-Butler, K. & Jeffries, J. (2003). *Clinical handbook of psychotropic drugs* (Thirteenth Edition). New York: Hogrefe & Huber.

Bradford, D., Stroup, S., & Lieberman, J. (2002). Pharmacological treatments for schizophrenia. In P. Nathan & J. Gorman (Eds), *A guide to treatments that work* (Second Edition, pp. 169–200). New York: Oxford University Press.

Cookson, J., Taylor, D., & Katona, C. (2002). *Use of drugs in psychiatry* (Fifth Edition). London: Gaskell.

Dougherty, D., Rauch, S., & Jenike, M. (2002). Pharmacological treatments of obsessive compulsive disorder. In P. Nathan & J. Gorman (Eds), *A guide to treatments that work* (Second Edition, pp. 387–410). New York: Oxford University Press.

Gelder, M., Mayou, R., & Cowen, P. (2001). *Shorter Oxford textbook of psychiatry*. Oxford: Oxford Medical Publications.

Hersen, M. & Bellack, A. (1999). *Handbook of comparative interventions for adult disorders* (Second Edition). New York: Wiley.

Keck, P. & McElroy, S. (2002). Pharmacological treatment for bipolar disorder. In P. Nathan & J. Gorman (Eds), *A guide to treatments that work* (Second Edition, pp. 277–301). New York: Oxford University Press.

Nathan, P. & Gorman, J. (2002). *A guide to treatments that work* (Second Edition). New York: Oxford University Press.

National Collaboration Centre for Mental Health (2003). *Schizophrenia. Full national clinical guideline on core interventions in primary and secondary care*. London: Royal College of Psychiatrists and British Psychological Society.

Nemeroff, C. & Schatzberg, A. (2002). Pharmacological treatments for unipolar depression. In P. Nathan & J. Gorman (Eds), *A guide to treatments that work* (Second Edition, pp. 229–244). New York: Oxford University Press.

O'Brien, C. & McKay, J. (2002). Pharmacological treatments for substance use disorders. In P. Nathan & J. Gorman (Eds), *A guide to treatments that work* (Second Edition, pp. 125–157). New York: Oxford University Press.

Perry, J., Alexander, B., & Liskow, B. (1997). *Psychotropic drug handbook* (Seventh Edition). Washington, DC: American Psychiatric Press.

Roy-Byrne, P. & Cowley, D. (2002). Pharmcological treamtents for panic disorder, generalized anxiety disorder, specific phobia and social anxiety disorder. In P. Nathan & J. Gorman (Eds), *A guide to treatments that work* (Second Edition, pp. 337–366). New York: Oxford University Press.

Schatzberg, A., Cole, J., & DeBattista, C. (2002). *Manual of clinical psychopharmacology* (Fourth Edition). Washington, DC: American Psychiatric Press.

Taylor, D., Paton, C., & Kerwin, R. (2003). *South London and Maudsley prescribing guidelines*. London: Martin Dunitz.

Tune, L. (2002). Treatments for dementia. In P. Nathan & J. Gorman (Eds), *A guide to treatments that work* (Second Edition, pp. 87–124). New York: Oxford University Press.

World Health Organization (WHO) (1992). *The ICD-10 Classification of Mental and Behavioural Disorders*. Geneva: WHO.

Wright, P., Stern, J., & Phelan, M. (1999). *Core psychiatry*. London: Saunders.

Yehuda, R., Marshall, R., Penkower, A., & Wong, C. (2002). Pharmacological treatments for posttraumatic stress disorder. In P. Nathan & J. Gorman (Eds), *A guide to treatments that work* (Second Edition, pp. 411–446). New York: Oxford University Press.

REFERENCES

American Psychiatric Association (2000). *Diagnostic and statistical manual of the mental disorders* (Fourth Edition-Text Revision) DSM-IV-TR. Washington, DC: APA.

Buchan, H., Johnstone, E., McPherson, K., Palmer, R.L., Crow, T.J., & Brandon, S. (1992). Who benefits from electroconvulsive therapy? *British Journal of Psychiatry*, 160, 349–355.

Greenblatt, M., Grosser, G.H., & Wechsler, H. (1964). Differential response of hospitalised depressed patients to somatic therapy. *American Journal of Psychiatry*, 120, 935–943.

Haynes, R.B., McDonald, H., Garg, A.X., & Montague, P. (2004). Interventions for helping patients to follow prescriptions for medications (Cochrane Review). In: *The Cochrane Library*, Issue 1. Chichester, UK: Wiley.

Johnstone, L. (2003). A shocking treatment. *The Psychologist*, 16, 236–239.

Piccinelli, M. & Wilkinson, G. (1994). Outcome of depression in psychiatric settings. *British Journal of Psychiatry*, 164, 297–304.

Shepherd, M., Watt, D., & Falloon, I. (1989). The natural history of schizophrenia: A five year follow-up study of outcome and prediction in a representative sample of schizophrenics. *Psychological Medicine Monograph Supplement*, 15, 1–46.

World Health Organization (WHO) (1992). *The ICD-10 classification of mental and behavioural disorders*. Geneva: WHO.

Chapter 7

Intake interviews, testing and report writing

Alan Carr and Muireann McNulty

This chapter offers guidelines for conducting intake assessments and report writing.

INTAKE INTERVIEWS

With intake assessments the aim is to both establish a good working alliance with the client and to collect sufficient information to reach a preliminary formulation of the main presenting problems. Careful planning can help the attainment of these two goals. To establish a good working alliance with the client, plan to form a clear contract for assessment at the outset of the intake interview; to work collaboratively with the client during the assessment; and to pace the interview, psychological testing and other procedures to suit the client's readiness and ability to engage fully with the assessment process. To collect sufficient information to draw up a preliminary formulation, plan to cover specific lines of questioning in the intake interview concerning the main presenting problem and its past treatment, the client's personal and family history. Detailed plans for these lines of questioning can be developed in light of the account of the client's problem given by the referring agent in the referring letter or by phone. If you are working in a multi-disciplinary team, consult with colleagues who have had recent contact with the client and read past correspondence and reports available in hospital or agency records to help plan the intake interview. When clients are willing and able, invite them – by post or in the waiting room – to complete and return an intake questionnaire, such as that in Figure 7.1, along with psychometric measures of depression, anxiety, relationship difficulties and so forth if appropriate. Plan your intake interview using information from all of these sources along with available scientific and clinical information about the assessment and treatment of the problems for which the client has been referred.

INTAKE INFORMATION FORM

Please read the information in this box and complete this form before talking to your psychologist. You may ask any questions about this during your first meeting.

Voluntary attendance. Our clinic offers help to people with stress-related problems and other psychological difficulties. Attendance at this clinic is voluntary. You may attend if you wish. If your problems are affecting important family relationships, your partner or other family members are welcome to attend the first appointment.

First appointments. Your first appointment will last about 2 hours. During this meeting you will be invited to outline your current concerns and problems, the things that you have tried to do in the past to solve these, your own developmental history, and your family history. You may also be invited to do some tests of ability or memory and to fill out some questionnaires.

Other appointments. At the end of the first appointment we will let you know if our service can offer you help with the problems that led you to visit us. We will offer you further appointments at times that are convenient to you at that point. If you cannot attend an appointment, please call us at least 2 days before the appointment so we can book in another person.

Confidentiality. In our clinic all staff work as part of a team. The team includes experienced senior psychologists, psychologists in training who work under the supervision of senior psychologists, and professionals in other disciplines such as social work, occupational therapy, and psychiatry. Everything that you say to your psychologist is confidential to our team.

The only circumstances under which we are obliged to give information to other people about your case is where yourself or another person is at risk of serious harm because of your behaviour.

We will not give information about your case to others without your consent.

Annonymized case reports. As a routine part of psychologists' training they are required to write case reports for examination at the university where they are training. All identifying details will be omitted from such reports.

Psychological reports. If you would like a psychological report sent to your family doctor or to some other professional, discuss this with your psychologist.

Please sign the next line to indicate that you consent to the conditions of service outlined in this box.

Signature ____

Please complete this form. The information you give here will be used to help us understand your current living situation, your current concerns and problems, and your personal and family history. If there are any questions that you cannot answer or do not wish to answer for private reasons, please leave the answer boxes blank. Otherwise write your answers in the boxes on the right-hand side of the form or circle the answer that applies to you. Please send this completed questionnaire to the clinic in the enclosed stamped addressed envelope if this has been posted to you.
Thank You.

1	Please put your name and address, telephone number and mobile number in the box opposite.		
2	What is your age?		
3	What is your gender?	Female	Male
4	What is your date of birth?		
5	Who is your family doctor and what is his or her phone number or contact address?		
6	Please sign opposite if you give your consent for me to contact your family doctor and request a summary of your medical history.	Signature ____________________ Date____________	

Figure 7.1 Intake information form.

<table>
<tr><td colspan="7">The following questions are about your current living situation</td></tr>
<tr><td>7</td><td>What is your occupation?</td><td colspan="5"></td></tr>
<tr><td>8</td><td>If you live with a partner or parent, what is your partner or parent's occupation?</td><td colspan="5"></td></tr>
<tr><td>9</td><td>What is your marital status?</td><td>Single</td><td>Married</td><td>In a long-term relationship</td><td>Single and separated or divorced</td><td>Single and widowed</td></tr>
<tr><td>10</td><td>How long you have been in your current marital or family situation?</td><td colspan="5"></td></tr>
<tr><td>11</td><td>If you have had any past long-term relationships or marriages, how long were you in these for?</td><td colspan="5"></td></tr>
<tr><td>12</td><td>How many children have you got and what are the ages of the oldest and youngest child?</td><td colspan="5">No of children_______________
Age of oldest child__________Age of youngest child_________</td></tr>
</table>

	The following questions are about your current concerns and problems		
13	Are you currently concerned about feeling depressed, sad, having a low mood, or little energy?	No	Yes
14	Are you currently concerned about feeling anxious, frightened, panicky, or worrying too much?	No	Yes
15	Are you currently concerned about your sleep pattern?	No	Yes
16	Are you currently worried about your health, because you have aches and pains that have not responded to medical treatment?	No	Yes
17	Are you currently concerned by confusing experiences which other people find difficult to understand?	No	Yes
18	Are you currently concerned about your eating and dieting habits?	No	Yes
19	Are you currently concerned about your use of alcohol or other drugs?	No	Yes
20	Are you currently concerned about your memory or your ability to concentrate?	No	Yes
21	Are you currently concerned about your ability to control your anger?	No	Yes
22	Are you currently concerned about occasional impulses to harm yourself?	No	Yes
23	Are you currently concerned about your performance at work or college?	No	Yes
24	Are you currently concerned about relationship problems with your partner?	No	Yes
25	Are you currently concerned about relationship problems with other family members?	No	Yes
26	Are you currently concerned about medication you are taking for the treatment of any of these problems?	No	Yes
27	Are you currently concerned about counselling or psychotherapy you are receiving for any of these problems?	No	Yes

Continued overleaf

28	Are you currently concerned about involvement with the police, the courts or the judicial system?	No	Yes

29	What are your current top 3 main concerns or problems?	
30	How long you have had these main problems?	
31	What effects have these problems had on your life?	
32	What do you believe caused these problems?	
33	Are you on medication for any of these problems at present?	If so please specify what medication you are taking
34	Are you attending a counsellor or therapist for help with your problems at present?	If so please specify how long you have been attending the counsellor
35	For your main problems that you listed in answer to question 29, what have you found most helpful?	

The following question is about recent life stresses and challenges

36 Circle any of the following events if they have happened to you in the past 6 months:
You yourself suffered a serious illness, injury or assault
A serious illness, injury or assault happened to a close relative
Your parent, child or spouse died
A close family friend or another relative (aunt, cousin, grandparent) died
You had a separation due to marital difficulties
You broke off a steady relationship
You had a serious problem with a close friend or relative
You became unemployed or you were seeking work unsuccessfully for more than one month
You were sacked from your job
You had a major financial crisis
You had problems with the police and a court appearance
Something you valued was lost or stolen
Another major life stress occurred (please specify)________________________

Figure 7.1 Continued.

The following questions ask about your developmental history	
37 List any major stresses or challenges that have occurred in these areas of your life since you were 18 years old: Your work or educational situation Your family life Your relationship with your friends Your personal health	
38 How have you coped with these stresses or challenges?	
39 List the main positive things that have occurred in these areas of your life since you were 18 years old: Your work or educational situation Your family life Your relationship with your friends Your personal health	
40 In your teenage years (11–18) did you face any major stresses or challenges in these areas of your life: Your educational situation Your family life Your relationship with your friends Your personal health?	
41 How did you cope with these stresses or challenges?	
42 In your teenage years (11–18) what were the main positive things that occurred in these areas of your life: Your educational situation Your family life Your relationship with your friends Your personal health?	
43 In your childhood years (0–10) did you face any major stresses or challenges in these areas of your life: Your educational situation Your family life Your relationship with your friends Your personal health?	

Continued overleaf

44	How did you cope with these challenges?	
45	In your childhood years (0–10) what were the main positive things that occurred in these areas of your life: Your educational situation Your family life Your relationship with your friends Your personal health?	
The following questions ask about your current family situation and family history		
46	Currently who are the 3 main people in your family who support you and make dealing with the demands upon you more manageable?	
47	Currently who are the family members with whom you have a particularly stressful relationship?	
48	Has anyone in your family (parents, grandparents, aunts uncles, brothers, sisters, etc.) had difficulties like yours?	
49	Has anyone in your family (parents, grandparents, aunts uncles, brothers, sisters, etc.) had other stress-related difficulties or illnesses?	
50	Are there any other comments about your concerns and situation that you wish to make?	

Figure 7.1 Continued.

CONTRACTING FOR ASSESSMENT

The aim of contracting for assessment is to reach agreement with clients about completing an assessment, which will point to a treatment or case management plan. When contracting for assessment, begin by asking clients what prompted them to look for help and how, in their view, the referral was made. Sometimes clients are the main customers for psychological consultation. They want help with a problem and this has led them to seek the referral for consultation. Here, contracting for assessment is straightforward. Explain what the assessment entails and then proceed with the client's consent and agreement. At other times, clients arrive at an intake assessment at the request of a family member, friend, family doctor, probation officer, or another member of the multi-disciplinary team. In these instances, contracting for assessment is more complex because the referrer, not the client, is the main customer for consultation. In these instances, contracting for assessment is particularly important and failure to do so adequately may lead to the client withdrawing from the assessment before it is over. In such instances, clients may object to answering stressful questions or completing challenging psychological tests because they view these procedures as being forced on them rather than personally chosen. For these cases, once the client has explained his or her understanding of the referral process, explain your understanding of how the referral was made, if this differs from that of the client. When an agreed understanding of the referral route has been established, explain what the assessment involves. Outline the way in which the interviews and testing procedures will be conducted, and the time commitment required. Clarify the limits of confidentiality. Normally, the contents of sessions are confidential unless there is evidence that the client is a serious threat to him or herself or to others. For example, if there is evidence of suicidal intent or violence, confidentiality may be breached. In some instances it may be important to interview not only the client but members of the client's family to obtain collateral information to assist with diagnosis and formulation, or as part of assessment for marital or family therapy. For convenience, all of these items are explained in the top box of the intake form in Figure 7.1.

Devote some time to exploring the pros and cons of completing the assessment. The downside of an assessment is that it involves a significant commitment and answering searching and potentially stressful questions. The benefits include reaching a clearer understanding of one's difficulties and the possibility of identifying solutions to problems of living. Contracting for assessment is complete when clients have been adequately informed about the process and have agreed to complete the assessment. Contracting for assessment within the context of different approaches to psychotherapy is discussed in Chapters 3–5.

INTAKE INTERVIEW SCHEDULE

Intake interviews should cover the following broad areas of inquiry:

- current concerns and problems
- problem and treatment history
- developmental history
- family history
- current risk
- multi-agency involvement.

Current concerns and problems

Begin by inquiring about clients' main concerns and problems. Then ask for an account of the most recent episodes of each of the problems. A description of a problem episode includes an account of what led up to the occurrence of the problem, what happened while the problem was occurring and what happened afterwards. Problem episodes also include accounts of what the client was thinking, feeling, doing and how he or she was interacting with others:

- Questions about what the client was thinking will give information about belief systems, cognitions, cognitive distortions, negative automatic thoughts, conflicts between impulses and injunctions, coping strategies and defence mechanisms.
- Questions about what the client was feeling will give information about affect, emotions, impulses and physiological states.
- Questions about what the client was doing will throw light on typical behaviour patterns.
- Questions about what how the client was interacting with others will give information about transactional patterns, stresses and supports entailed by particular relationships, and patterns of relationships within the client's family, work setting, peer group or the way the client interacts with members of the healthcare system.

If clients reply to invitations to describe problem episodes by giving a general account of what usually happens, invite them to be more specific and to describe for the last time the problem occurred the actual events that occurred in a step-by-step fashion. Ask clients to describe problem episodes as if they were watching a film of the episode happening. Accounts of specific episodes allow us to form more accurate understandings of presenting problems. If clients insist that their problems are chronic and constant rather than episodic, ask them to recount episodes in which their problems deteriorated or improved even marginally on a scale from 1 to 10.

Problems and treatment history

To obtain a succinct history of the course of clients' problems over time, and their response to treatment, ask about the nature, frequency and intensity of the problems starting with the present and working backwards in time to the point where the problems started. Inquire about previous successful and unsuccessful solutions to these problems and the impact of previous episodes of psychological, medical, spiritual or other forms of treatment. Explore clients' views about the causes of these problems and possible solutions that they suspect may be effective in future. In listening to replies to these inquiries and requesting elaboration about the social context within which the problems have been occurring, particular attention should be paid to possible problem-maintaining processes including the following:

- Problematic cognitive factors, including belief systems, attributional styles and cognitive distortions.
- Inadvertent reinforcement of the problem or unsuccessful attempted solutions.
- The use of maladaptive coping strategies.
- The use of immature defence mechanisms.
- Involvement in problematic interaction patterns within the family, workplace, peer group, or treatment system.
- The impact of physical and physiological factors including medication; seasonal mood changes; shift work; sleeping, eating and sexual behaviour patterns; physical illness and immune system functioning.

These factors, which are drawn from CBT, psychodynamic, systemic and biomedical traditions, have been discussed in detail in Chapters 3–6. In tracing the history of the presenting problems, inquire about potential triggering or precipitating factors that preceded the current and past episodes or the problem. Precipitating factors include major stressful life events, a build-up of minor stressful life events, illnesses and injuries, lifecycle transitions and major changes within the family particularly the addition of new family members (e.g. birth of a child or marriage) or loss of a family member (e.g. bereavement or leaving home). These factors have been discussed in detail within the context of the lifecycle in Chapter 1 and with reference to constructing formulations associated with diagnostic syndromes in Chapter 2.

Developmental history

To place the client's difficulties in context it is useful to establish a developmental history. Constructing a lifeline can be helpful in tracing the sequence of significant events with a client's life. Using a large sheet of paper or a white-board, invite the client to collaboratively draw a graphic linear representation of his or her life from the present back to conception, identifying important milestones along the way. Begin with the present. Then ask about significant normative events such as births, adoptions, fostering and deaths within the family; personal and family illnesses, injuries and periods of psychological problems; marriage and separation; current occupation, changes in jobs and periods of unemployment; entering the workforce; experiences in higher education, secondary schooling and primary schooling; family-of-origin experiences in childhood and adolescence; and early family life experiences. When these major markers are placed on the lifeline, start again with the most recent section and fill in periods when the presenting problems were particularly pronounced and when there were periods of remission. Then fill in other significant life events, working from the present to the past. Constructing a lifeline should be informed by the material on the family and personal lifecycles covered in detail in Chapter 1. Lifeline construction affords opportunities for identifying predisposing factors, such as early life adversities, that may have rendered clients vulnerable to developing their current difficulties. However, this procedure can also yield important information on protective factors and personal strengths. Predisposing and protective factors are detailed in Chapter 2.

Family history

Clinical guidelines for constructing a genogram and taking a family history are given in Chapter 5. Inquiries about family membership, structure and development should cover the following areas:

- current household membership
- extended family membership
- other network members
- identifying information, such as names, ages, occupations and locations of important family and network members
- major illnesses and psychosocial problems including hospitalizations, physical and psychological problems and criminality
- major protective factors and strengths of family members
- the major transitions that the family has made through the family lifecycle
- current stage of the lifecycle
- supportive relationships
- stressful relationships
- family factions, triangulation patterns and multi-generational patterns.

In addition to this information about family membership and dynamics, the physical and social context of the client's family should also be assessed. Ask if the client is homeless, which is an increasingly common problem among people with severe psychological problems. If the client is not homeless, ask about the client's accommodation – its proximity to the client's employment and the extended family, the degree of isolation or crowding in the client's home, the quality of living quarters and problems with safety or hygiene. Where the client is homeless or is having financial difficulties that might affect his or her access to accommodation, assess the client's needs and entitlement to benefits, in line with local statutory procedures.

Current risk

In intake interviews it is a statutory duty to assess risk, that is, to determine if clients are a danger to themselves or to other people. The following areas of risk deserve routine consideration:

- suicide risk
- risk to self due to impaired judgement associated with conditions such as psychosis or dementia
- risk to children through impaired parenting capacity, neglect or abuse
- risk of violence to others, including domestic violence or violence to others in the community.

The assessment of suicide risk is described in detail in Chapter 10. The core issue is whether the client shows suicidal intentions (rather than mere ideation) and whether there is a constellation of a significant number of risk factors and few protective factors that make it likely that the client will act on suicidal intentions. Where this is the case, the immediate priority is suicide risk management, described in Chapter 10.

If clients are psychotic or suffering from dementia or some other psychological condition that significantly impairs their capacity to safely care for themselves, then there is a statutory duty to inform the next of kin and arrange a care plan in collaboration with them. Working with people who have psychotic disorders is discussed in Chapter 21 and problems of older adulthood including dementia are covered in Chapter 23.

If the client is a parent then it is important to inquire about his or her capacity to fulfil this role. The key statutory issue is whether the client, along with other adults who collectively have responsibility for parenting the children, is capable of doing so. Do these people collectively have the capacity to meet the children's needs for safety, care and nurturance, control and discipline, and age-appropriate responsibilities and intellectual stimulation? To assess this, conduct a collateral interview with those adults who share responsibility for parenting the client's children. Details of how to conduct this type of assessment are given in the *Handbook of Child and Adolescent Clinical Psychology Second Edition* (Carr, in press).

If the client is at risk of becoming violent towards other adults (such as a spouse, parent, friend, acquaintance or other person) clinicians are responsible for informing the statutory authorities of the risk of violence. If the client is not detained by the statutory authorities, then the clinician has a duty to inform the potential victim of the risk of violence. Assessment of risk of violence is covered in Chapter 24 on anger management.

Co-ordination of multi-agency input

When working with multi-problem clients who are involved with multiple agencies, clarify what other agencies are involved, the duration of their involvement, the role that each of the agencies takes in offering services to the client and the way that multi-agency involvement is co-ordinated. In complex cases with multi-agency involvement, often there is limited co-ordination. Family doctors, psychiatrists, social workers, addiction counsellors, probation officers and other professionals may all be offering services but in an *ad-hoc* manner. In such cases, one of the most useful psychological interventions is to convene a multi-agency meeting with the client and involved professionals, agree on a broad case formulation, a case management plan based on the formulation, and the roles of involved professionals in executing this plan in a co-ordinated way. Clinical guidelines for conducting such network meetings are given in Chapter 5.

FORMULATION AND FEEDBACK

The assessment is complete when the presenting problem and related difficulties are clarified; related predisposing, precipitating, maintaining and protective factors have been identified; a formulation has been constructed; possible goals have been identified; options for case management or treatment have been identified and these have been discussed with the family.

A formulation is a mini-theory that explains why the presenting problems developed, why they persist, what protective factors either prevent them from becoming worse or may be enlisted to solve the presenting problems. Formulations typically integrate information about predisposing, precipitating, maintaining and protective factors. Predisposing factors are those biological or psychological features of the client or negative aspects of the early parent–child relationship or family situation that have rendered the client vulnerable to developing the presenting problems. Precipitating factors are those stressful life events that have led to the onset of the current concerns and problems. Maintaining factors are those biological and psychological characteristics of the client along with patterns of interaction within the client's social system that allow the problem to persist. Protective factors are those biological and psychological characteristics of the client along, with patterns of interaction within the client's social system, which prevent problems from deteriorating and which have positive implications for response to treatment and prognosis.

CBT, psychodynamic, systemic and biomedical formulation models accord specific significance to particular sets of predisposing, precipitating, maintaining and protective factors. Generic CBT, psychodynamic and systemic formulations models are given in Chapters 3, 4 and 5. In Chapters 8–25, formulation models associated with specific problems are presented.

The importance of formulation cannot be overemphasized. It involves linking academic knowledge of theory and research to clinical practice. If the working alliance is the engine that drives the therapeutic process, formulation is the map that provides guidance on what direction to take.

CASE MANAGEMENT OPTIONS

Case management options are derived from the formulation by judging what maintaining factors would have to change in order for the problem to be resolved. Make this judgement on the basis of the literature on effective treatments of similar cases and clinical experience. Most case management options, in order of increasing intensity, fall into the following categories:

- Refer the client back to the referring agent with advice on future management. Such advice may range from reassurance that there is no significant psychological problem to guidance on implementing a psychological intervention programme.
- Offer psychoeducation about the problem and suggest periodic reassessment.
- Refer to another professional within the psychologist's multi-disciplinary team for consultation, for example, social work or physiotherapy.
- Refer to another professional or residential facility outside the multi-disciplinary team.
- Offer focal and circumscribed psychological intervention to the client, such as the programmes described in much of this volume.
- Offer multi-modal intervention in conjunction with other professionals.

A first step in deciding how to proceed beyond assessment is clarifying into which of these categories the case management plan falls. Much of this volume offers guidance on case management plans that fall into the last two categories. A summary of the intake assessment schedule described in this section is given in Figure 7.2. As part of the case management process, it is important to be clear about your own areas of competence and the limits or bounds of that competence. Psychologists are ethically bound to work within the limits of their competence and to refer on to others where they do not possess the competencies necessary to meet the client's needs. With a view to referring on, it is useful to gather information about human and service resources available, including skills and areas of expertise of departmental and multi-disciplinary colleagues, and local and regional services.

Problems and treatment history

- Nature, frequency and intensity of the current problems
- Fluctuations on 10-point scale in recent episodes of chronic problems
- Previous episodes of disorders, precipitating and maintaining factors
- Previous episodes of treatment and helpful aspects of treatment
- Client's views of causes and solutions
- Role of cognitive factors (belief systems, attributional styles and distortions)
- Role of inadvertent reinforcement
- Role of coping strategies
- Role of defence mechanisms
- Role of interaction patterns, chronic stress and support
- Role of physical, physiological and medication factors
- Role of stressful life events
- Role of lifecycle transitions

Developmental history

- Current marital situation and recent changes
- Current work situation and recent changes
- Entering the workforce/unemployment
- Experiences in higher education
- Secondary schooling
- Primary schooling
- Family-of-origin experiences in childhood and adolescence
- Early family life experiences

Family history

- Current household membership
- Extended family and network membership
- Family illnesses, psychosocial and criminal problems
- Family strengths
- Family lifecycle transitions
- Supportive family relationships
- Stressful family relationships
- Family relationship patterns
- Current accommodation or homelessness

Multi-agency input

- Current treatment network membership
- Family doctor, hospital physicians
- Psychiatrists
- Social workers
- Addiction counsellors
- Probation officers
- Patterns of interaction with treatment network

Formulation: Predisposing factors

- Genetic vulnerabilities
- Prenatal and perinatal complications
- Early insults, injuries and illnesses
- Low intelligence
- Difficult temperament
- Neuroticism and negative personality traits
- Low self-esteem
- External locus of control
- Separation from or loss of a parent
- Parental psychopathology
- Insecure attachment to parents
- Family-of-origin disorganization
- Parental marital discord
- Physical and sexual abuse and neglect
- Inadequate early social support network
- Poor premorbid adjustment

Formulation: Precipitating factors

- Major stressful life events
- Build-up of minor stresses
- Loss experiences
- Humiliation
- Illness and injury
- Victimization
- Redundancy
- Financial difficulties
- Imprisonment
- Lifecycle transitions and changes

Formulation: Maintaining factors

- Problematic belief systems
- Low self-efficacy
- Problematic attributional style
- Cognitive distortions
- Inadvertent reinforcement of problem behaviour
- Dysfunctional coping strategies
- Immature defence mechanisms
- Problematic adult attachment styles
- Problematic interaction patterns in marriage and family
- Problematic interaction patterns in social network
- Problematic interaction patterns in the treatment network
- High stress and low support
- Dysregulation of neurotransmitter systems

Formulation: Protective Factors

- Good health
- Good premorbid adjustment
- Average or high intelligence
- Easy temperament in childhood
- No genetic vulnerabilities

Testing • Broad measures • Brief measures • Structured diagnostic interviews • Cognitive tests • Personality inventories • Projective tests **Current risk** • Suicide risk • Risk to self due to impaired judgement (psychosis or dementia) • Risk to children (impaired parenting capacity, neglect or abuse) • Risk of violence (domestic violence or other)	• Positive past response to medication • History of coping well with a similar problem • Psychological mindedness • Extraversion and emotional stability • Conscientiousness and agreeableness • High self-esteem • Internal locus of control • Strong self-efficacy beliefs • Optimistic attributional style • Functional coping strategies • Secure adult attachment style • Mature defence mechanisms • Capacity to maintain a therapeutic alliance • Positive interaction patterns in marriage and family • Positive interaction patterns in social network • Positive interaction patterns in the treatment network • Low stress and high support **Case management options** • Refer back with no action • Psychoeducation periodic reassessment • Refer within team or refer to outside team • Focal treatment or multi-modal treatment

Figure 7.2 Intake assessment.

STRUCTURED INTERVIEWING AND PSYCHOLOGICAL TESTING

Structured assessment instruments such as self-report inventories, clinician rating scales and ability tests may be included in intake assessment procedures. When selecting structured instruments, key concerns are their reliability, validity, sensitivity to change and user-friendliness. For self-report instruments, it is important to have good internal consistency reliability, which shows that all of the items in a scale intercorrelate well and tap into the same construct. Cronbach's alpha, which ranges from 0 to 1, is the most commonly reported index of internal reliability and values above .7 indicate good reliability. For rating scales completed by clinicians based on their observations of clients' behaviour, it is important to have evidence of good inter-rater reliability. Cohen's kappa, which ranges from 0 to 1, is a widely reported index of inter-rater reliability; values above .7 indicate good inter-rater reliability. For self-report inventories and rating scales, good test–retest reliability is also desirable. However, this has to be balanced against the instrument's sensitivity to change. In clinical practice, it is good to use standardized instruments to evaluate symptoms before and after treatment to evaluate treatment effectiveness. Only instruments that are sensitive to change are useful for this purpose.

Instruments with good concurrent criterion and predictive validity are clinically useful. Instruments with good criterion validity can distinguish between known groups. For example, a valid self-report measure of depressed mood can distinguish between people with depression, psychotic disorders and normal controls. Instruments with good predictive validity have been shown to forecast certain types of clinically meaningful outcomes. For example, valid IQ tests partially predict educational and occupational success.

User-friendliness is an important concern because clients are less motivated to complete instruments that are not user friendly. User-friendly assessment instruments do not put excessive demands on clients. Shorter instruments and instruments with items, questions or tasks that are interesting and not objectionable tend to be more user friendly.

Structured assessment instruments fall into the following categories:

- broad measures of general symptoms
- brief measures of symptoms and constructs
- structured diagnostic interviews
- cognitive functioning tests
- personality inventories
- projective tests.

Broad measures of general symptoms

Self-report inventories that cover a broad range of general symptoms are particularly useful when there is a need to screen for a range of psychological problems. The Minnesota Multiphasic Personality Inventory (MMPI-2; Butcher et al., 1989; Graham, 1999; Greene, 2000; Nichols, 2001), now in its second revision, and the Personality Assessment Inventory (PAI; Moorey, 1991, 2003) fall into this category.

The MMPI contains 567 items and takes up to an hour to complete. It yields scores for the following main scales: hypochondriasis, depression, hysteria, psychopathic deviance, paranoia, psychasthenia, schizophrenia, mania, masculinity–femininity and social introversion; it also includes validity scales. A variety of experimental scales have been developed using the MMPI item pool.

In the tradition of the MMPI, the PAI is one of the most important new instruments to be developed for assessing a broad range of symptoms and concerns. The PAI is a 344-item inventory that yields scores on eleven clinical scales (somatic complaints, anxiety, anxiety-related disorders, depression, mania, paranoia, schizophrenia, border-line features, anti-social features, alcohol problems and drug problem), five treatment scales (aggression, suicidal ideation, stress, non-support and treatment rejection), two interpersonal scales (dominance and warmth) and four validity scales (inconsistency, infrequency, positive impression, negative impression).

Briefer scales, which nevertheless aim to evaluate a broad range of symptoms, include the revised Symptom Checklist 90 (SCL-90-R; Derogatis, 1994) and the General Health Questionnaire (GHQ; Goldberg & Williams, 1991). The GHQ was developed in the UK and SCL-90-R was developed in the USA. The SCL-90-R, which contains 90 items, can be completed in 20 minutes. It yields scores for somatization, obsessive-compulsive symptoms, interpersonal sensitivity, depression, anxiety, hostility, phobic anxiety, paranoid ideation and psychoticism. There is a parallel clinician-rated version of the SCL-90-R and briefer 53- and 18-item self-report versions. There are 60-, 30-, 28- and 12-item versions of the GHQ and all contain an overall cut-off score that allows clinicians to reliably distinguish between people whose problems are severe enough to warrant diagnosis and those whose problems are in the normal range. Only the GHQ-28 yields subscale scores; it does this for the following four dimensions: somatic symptoms, anxiety, social dysfunction and severe depression.

Brief measures of symptoms and constructs

Where there are good reasons to believe that a client has a problem in a particular domain, then it is appropriate to use brief, syndrome-specific measures of a circumscribed set of symptoms, such as the Beck Anxiety (BAI; Beck & Steer, 1990) and Depression (BDI-II; Beck, Steer, & Brown, 1996) Inventories. The BAI and BDI-II can be used in cases where depression and anxiety are the symptoms of central concern. For many psychological problems and for particular psychotherapeutic models such as CBT, psychodynamic and systemic models, brief measures of important constructs related to specific problems or particular models are available. These include measures of attributional style, coping strategies, defence mechanisms, stressful life events, social support, marital functioning, family functioning, quality of life and so forth. Many of these measures are listed at the end of other chapters in this volume. Good compendiums of these measures have been published by Fischer and Corcoran (2000) and by Rush et al. (2000).

In addition to using brief, problem-specific or model-specific measures, it is useful to routinely administer a brief general measure of overall functioning to all clients in a service before and after treatment and at follow-up as part of service monitoring and quality assurance practice. In the UK, the Clinical Outcomes in Routine Evaluation (CORE; CORE System Group, 1999) System and the Health of the Nation Outcome Scales (HoNOS; Wing, Curtis, & Beevor, 1996; Wing et al., 2000) are widely used for this purpose and are suitable for clients with a wide range of difficulties. The CORE system contains a self-report, 34-item CORE Outcome Measure that yields scores for subjective well-being, problems and symptoms, personal functioning and current risk to self or others. It also contains a therapy assessment form and end-of-therapy form that allows clinicians to routinely record service quality data focusing on access, appropriateness, acceptability, equity, effectiveness and efficiency. Other CORE instruments have been developed, including an ideograph Goal Attainment and Helpful Aspects of Therapy form. This instrument allows clinicians to refine their therapeutic approach in light of client feedback.

The HoNOS contains twelve scales for rating cases with severe psychological problems. The scales are: (1) overactive, aggressive, disruptive or agitated behaviour; (2) non-accidental self-injury; (3) problem drinking or drug-taking; (4) cognitive problems; (5) physical illness or disability problems; (6) problems with hallucinations and delusions; (7) problems with depressed mood; (8) other mental and behavioural problems; (9) problems with relationships; (10) problems with activities of daily living; (11) problems with living conditions; and (12) problems with occupation and activities. Each scale is scored from 0 = no problem to 4 = severe problem on the basis of all information available during 2 weeks preceding the rating. Versions of the HoNOS have been developed for adults, older adults, children and adolescents; people with intellectual disabilities; people in forensic settings and people with acquired brain injury.

Structured diagnostic interviews

Some of the best-developed structured diagnostic interviews are the Structured Clinical Interviews for DSM-IV-TR Axis I and II Disorders (SCID-I; First, Spitzer, Gibbon, & Williams, 1997a; SCID-II; First, Spitzer, Gibbon, Williams, & Benjamin, 1997b) and the Composite International Diagnostic Interview (CIDI; WHO, 1997), which can be used to derive both DSM and ICD diagnoses. In addition to these omnibus interview schedules covering many disorders, structured interviews have been developed for specific groups of disorders, such as the Anxiety Disorder Interview Schedule for DSM-IV (DiNardow et al., 1994). Other structured interviews of relevance to specific types of psychological problems are listed at the end of other chapters in this volume. In Chapter 2, it was mentioned that structured clinical interviews have been developed to improve the reliability of psychiatric diagnoses, especially in research studies. Structured interviews are not widely used in routine clinical practice by clinical psychologists. This may be partly due to psychologists' awareness of the shortcomings of the DSM and ICD classification systems, as outlined in Chapter 2. It may also be because structured interviews are very time consuming to administer and require a considerable amount of training and practice before they can be used reliably. However, structured interviews can be useful for cases where lack of diagnostic precision may have an important bearing on appropriateness of service provision and outcome.

Cognitive functioning tests

Assessment of general intelligence, verbal and non-verbal intelligence, memory and other cognitive abilities, and academic attainment is necessary when there are reasons to suspect that clients have disabilities in these areas or when an evaluation of fluctuations in cognitive functioning over time is required. Among the more common presentations requiring such assessment are: intellectual disability, specific learning disabilities, traumatic brain injury, cognitive deterioration following chronic drug and alcohol abuse, seizure disorders, dementia and other neurological disorders. The assessment and management of intellectual disability is a specialist area and clinical guidelines for this area of practice are give in O'Reilly et al. (in press). Specialist guidelines for neuropsychological assessment are given in Halligan et al. (2003), Lezak (1995) and Snyder and Nussbaum (1998). For general practice in clinical psychology, guidelines for administering and interpreting tests of cognitive functioning are given in Groth-Marnat (2004) and Dorfman and Hersen (2001). Specific guidelines on the administration and interpretation of the third edition of Wechsler Adult Intelligence Scale (WAIS III; Wechsler, 1999), which is the most widely used measure of adult intelligence, are given in Kaufman and Lichtenberger (1999). In the present volume, assessment of cognitive functioning in older adults is considered in Chapter 23.

Personality tests

Trait theory assumes that cross-situational regularities in personal functioning may best be accounted for by a limited number of dimensions or traits, and that these traits may be reliably and validly assessed by self-report inventories. Usually, self-report personality inventories include validity scales that allow the clinician to check the degree to which respondents have been 'faking good', 'faking bad' or responding randomly. Within the broad tradition of trait theory there has been considerable controversy over the precise number of traits that may appropriately be used to describe personality functioning. At one extreme, Eysenck in the UK argued that three traits (neuroticism, extraversion and psychoticism) could account for most aspects of personality functioning; he then went on to identify the physiological basis for each of the traits. These three traits can be measured by the Revised Eysenck Personality Inventory (EPI-R; Eysenck & Eysenck, 1991). In contrast, Cattell in the USA argued that sixteen traits are required to account for significant areas of personality functioning. These may be assessed using the 16 Personality Factor Inventory, now in its fifth edition (16 PF-5; Cattell, Cattell, & Cattell, 1994). Cattell has shown, through extensive research, how the traits in his model are associated with work practices and relationship styles. Between these three- and sixteen-factor models, Costa and McCrae (1992) have proposed a five-factor model, with each of the five factors having six facets. The factors are neuroticism, extraversion, openness to experience, agreeableness and conscientiousness. The five factors and the six facets associated with each of these can be assessed with the Revised NEO Personality Inventory (NEO-PI-R; Costa & McCrae, 1992). The five-factor model has been used to profile the behaviour of people at work and in relationships over the lifespan and to profile people with personality disorders. Differences in the number of traits in the three models are due to differences in the factor-analytic methods used and the range of items analysed.

The EPI-R, the 16 PF-5 and the NEO-PI-R can all be used to evaluate personality functioning in clinical settings, although these instruments are not widely or routinely used by clinical psychologists in the UK and Ireland. Unlike tests of broad symptoms or psychopathology, such as the MMPI-2, trait-based personality inventories are value neutral; each way of responding suggests its own advantages and disadvantages. Thus, using trait measures may help describe a client's habitual ways of responding to the environment. The fit between the client's traits and the environment can be described in the report.

Projective tests

With projective tests, cross-situational regularities in personal functioning are evaluated by observing and rating clients' responses to relatively ambiguous stimuli presented in a standardized way. Projective testing rests on the assumption that important aspects of personal functioning are revealed in situations where clients respond to relatively ambiguous stimuli. Clients project onto these ambiguous stimuli unconscious habitual modes of functioning. Through validation studies, some evidence has been developed to show that certain patterns of responding on projective tests are associated with certain intrapersonal and interpersonal styles of functioning. The Rorschach (Exner, 2000) and the Thematic Apperception Test (TAT; Murray, 1971) are among the best-developed projective tests. With the TAT, the client is shown a series of pictures and invited to tell stories about them, invented on the spur of the moment. The TAT assesses a variety of needs including the needs for achievement, affiliation and autonomy. With the Rorschach, the stimuli are ink blots and clients comment on how they perceive these. Useful introductory guides to the administration and interpretation of the Rorschach (Rose et al., 2000) and the TAT (Teglasi, 2001) have been developed.

REPORT WRITING

Intake interviews and the results of psychological testing are usually written up as psychological reports and held on clients' clinical files. Report writing is central to the practice of clinical psychology. The limitations of our memories require us to keep detailed accounts of complex information about our clients. An accurate account of information gained in interviews, testing sessions and meetings with other professionals is the basis on which a formulation is constructed and a treatment plan developed. Records also help us to keep track of progress with case management plans. At the end of an episode of consultation, a summary of the episode provides information that may be useful to ourselves or our colleagues in helping clients should they return for a further episode of consultation in the future. During the process of assessment and case management, other members of the professional network, such as colleagues from our team, family doctors, referring agents and other involved professionals, may require verbal or written reports. Clients and members of their family system may also benefit from having written communication about aspects of the consultation process. In some cases it may be necessary to write specialized reports as assignments for clinical psychology training programmes. On an annual basis it may be necessary to write a service report. In this chapter guidelines for writing the following types of reports will be given:

- progress notes
- comprehensive assessment reports
- end-of-episode case summaries
- verbal reports to clients and colleagues
- correspondence to clients and colleagues
- case study reports
- annual service reports.

Psychologists have a duty to their clients to maintain confidentiality and so all reports about clients should be written and managed with this as a central guiding principle. In all circumstances where psychologists wish to exchange information with other members of the client's professional or social network, the client's consent should be sought. Confidentiality may be broken only in circumstances where to maintain confidentiality would place the client or some other person in danger. A guideline for all forms of reports is to always write in such a way that you would be prepared to give your case files or service reports to clients and their families to read.

Progress notes

In making progress notes about clinical cases, five categories of information should always be recorded. These are:

- time
- attendance
- review
- agenda
- plan.

The first letters of these category names form the acronym TARAP. The issues covered by each category will be expanded below.

Time

This category includes the date, day, time and duration of the session. It may be useful to also include the number of the session, particularly if working within a time-limited contract for assessment or intervention. Often in clinical psychology, time-limited contracts of six, ten or twenty sessions are used.

Attendance

The people who attended the session and those who were invited and did not attend should be noted in this category. When the client does not attend a session (referred to sometimes as a 'DNA'), it is important to record what steps were taken to follow up with the client, particularly in cases where there are risks of self-harm.

Review

A review of significant events that may have occurred since the previous session are recorded here. Changes in the presenting problem and factors related to its resolution or maintenance should be reviewed. Inquiries should also routinely be made about completion of assessment tasks such as self-monitoring and treatment tasks. In the case of an initial session, changes that have occurred since the referral was made may be noted.

Agenda

Information about the main content issues and the main processes that occurred may be recorded in this category. Content issues include the topics discussed and the tests administered. Process issues include the quality of the working alliance and the impact of this on the progress of assessment or treatment.

Plan

Future action for clients, network members and the psychologist may be noted in this category. These include assessment or treatment tasks that clients have been invited to complete, assessment procedures or particular therapy-related themes for inclusion on the agenda for the next session and clinical hypotheses requiring further exploration.

The TARAP format for making progress notes is appropriate for assessment and treatment sessions with clients and members of their social systems.

Comprehensive assessment report

A comprehensive assessment report is typically written at the end of the assessment stage. This report represents a summary of information obtained throughout the assessment process, including sessions with the client and review of reports from other professionals. From an integration of this information, the proposed plan for case management is set out. The comprehensive assessment report is written primarily for the psychologist and members of the psychologist's team. All other reports and correspondence are based on this document. Usually it should include the section on the issues listed below.

Demographic information

The client's name, date of birth and address should be given here, along with names, addresses and contact numbers for next of kin where relevant.

Referral information

This section includes the referring agent's name, address and contact number, and the central problems that led to the referral or the principal referral question. It is also useful to include details of significant members of the professional network, such as the name, address and contact numbers of other involved professionals including the family doctor, psychiatrist, social worker, probation officer, addiction counsellor, hostel manager and so forth.

Sources

The sources of information on which the report is based should be listed. These sources include all assessment sessions, with dates and a note of who attended the sessions. If previous reports by physicians, social workers or other professionals were used, these too should be noted.

History of the presenting problem and previous treatment

This section should include an account of how the problem developed and previous episodes of treatment. Note any factors that precipitated episodes of the disorder and what was helpful in previous treatment episodes. The role of other involved professionals may be mentioned here. If medical, psychiatric or social work reports are available salient points from these may be summarized in this section.

Developmental history

Reference should be made to the nature and timing of significant events or abnormalities in physical, cognitive and psychosocial development over the course of the lifecycle. Note possible personal predisposing factors that may have rendered the client vulnerable to the current disorder and any personal strengths that may act as protective factors.

The family history

Family membership, stresses and supports, relationship patterns and significant achievements or difficulties in managing family transitions over the lifecycle should all be mentioned in this section. Note possible social predisposing factors that may have rendered the client vulnerable to their current disorder and any strengths in the client's social network that may act as protective factors.

Psychological testing

If psychological testing has been conducted, it is appropriate to include a section where reference may be made to the results of psychometric assessments of presenting problems and cognitive abilities. In presenting psychological test results include the following information:

- the tests used
- the number and duration of testing sessions
- the impact of co-operation, medication, physical factors (noise, cold, crowding, etc.) and extraneous psychosocial factors (e.g. exhaustion) on the validity of the results
- a list of results and an interpretation of these.

Present the results and their interpretation in a logical, orderly way. For example, divide the results into a subsection for tests of psychosocial functioning (MMPI-2, SCL-90-R, BDA, BDI-II, etc.) and a subsection for results of cognitive tests (WAIS III). Where test results are broadly within the normal range, keep the section on psychological testing brief.

Differential diagnosis and diagnosis

If there has been concern about the differential diagnosis, it is appropriate to include this section. State the main presenting problems, the diagnostic possibilities that were considered and the diagnosis that is best supported by the data gathered during the psychological assessment.

Formulation

A brief restatement of the central problems should be given here, along with an explanation of how they developed based on salient points drawn from previous sections of the report. Reference should be made to predisposing, precipitating and maintaining factors. In addition protective factors that have a bearing on the prognosis should be mentioned. It is important to emphasize the client's strengths and resources, as well as deficits and difficulties.

Recommended case management plan

A prioritized list of options for case management may be listed here. Taking no further action, periodic reassessment, referral to another team member for consultation, referral elsewhere for consultation, focal psychological intervention or multi-modal intervention should all be considered. Where a multimodal intervention programme is central to the management plan, details of the components of the programme and the professionals responsible should be indicated. A key worker responsible for reviewing progress at designated times should be specified.

Signature

Most agencies have a policy about signing reports. Unless there are ethical reasons for not doing so, follow this policy, particularly if you are still in training. If there is no policy in your agency and you are in training, write your name and degrees on one line and underneath Clinical Psychologist in Training (in the UK) or Clinical Psychologist Intern, Extern or Practicum Student (in Canada and the USA). In addition, your supervisor's name, degrees and appointment should be added to the report, which your supervisor should co-sign.

Comprehensive assessment reports are usually written up by the key worker for the case. Under some circumstances it may be useful to use computer-aided systems for report writing. These are available for a variety of structured interviews, cognitive tests and personality tests.

End-of-episode case summary

When clients conclude an episode of treatment or case management, an end-of-episode case summary (or discharge summary) should be written. This report summarizes progress made as a result of implementing the case management plan. An end-of-episode case summary should contain sections on the:

- formulation
- implementation of the case management plan
- outcome.

The formulation outlined in the comprehensive assessment report may be restated in the first section of the end-of-episode case summary. In the second section, a summary of the case management plan that was implemented should be given. It is also useful to note here any co-operation or co-ordination difficulties that occurred and how various resistances within the client's network were managed. In cases that did not respond to treatment, a hypothesis about the reasons for treatment failure should be given. If any new information came to light that led to the original formulation being substantially revised, this should be noted. In the final section of an end-of-episode summary, the degree to which specific treatment goals were met should be noted, along with other positive or negative changes. Follow-up plans for review sessions or relapse management should also be noted.

Verbal reports

During the consultation process it may be necessary to give verbal reports to clients and colleagues in feedback sessions, team meetings and case conferences. In preparing verbal reports, first identify the audience to whom your report will be addressed. Is it a client, a social worker, a physician, a psychiatrist or a mixed group of professionals? Next, clarify the kinds of questions they want answered. Do they want to know if your assessment indicates a client has cognitive deficits? or is at risk for suicide? or has responded to treatment? From your progress notes or the comprehensive assessment report, abstract the points that you are confidently able to make to answer the question. If you are unable to answer the question on the basis of the available information, arrange interviews or testing sessions to obtain such information if this is feasible and within the remit of your professional role.

Then prepare the list of points you wish to make in the meeting to answer the questions you know or guess are of central concern to your audience. Frame the points in language and at a level of technical sophistication that will be optimally intelligible to the audience. So, for example, it will be useful to give detailed psychometric information in a verbal report to a neuropsychologist but of little use to give such information to a surgeon or occupational therapist. In some instances, you will be unable to offer valid information to other professionals. For example, in some cases, suicide risk is difficult to assess confidently whereas in others intelligence is difficult to assess because of co-operation problems. In such instances it is important to report that you are unable to answer the questions posed.

When making a verbal report to any audience state the:

- question you aimed to answer
- source of your information and your confidence in its reliability and validity
- key pieces of information that answer the question (and no more).

If you are presenting information in a team meeting or case conference and do not know all of the participants, it is important to identify yourself as a clinical psychologist (or a clinical psychologist in training working under the supervision of a senior staff member).

If information presented by other professionals in a team meeting or case conference is inconsistent with your findings, think through the possible reasons for the discrepancy between the two sets of information before offering your opinion on this to the team or conference. Discrepancies between professional reports are common. The important issue to resolve is why the discrepancy occurred, not which view is correct and which is incorrect. Discrepancies may be due to the time and place where the assessment was conducted, the assessment or treatment methods used, the informants, the level of co-operation between the client and the professional or a wide range of other factors.

Correspondence with professionals

All correspondence should be written with the concerns of the recipient of the letter in mind. Before writing a letter, clarify what question the recipient would like answered. Common questions are:

- Has the client been placed on the waiting list or have they been assessed?
- Why is the client behaving in an unusual way and what can be done about it?
- Have you been able to help the client manage the problem?
- Should we be co-ordinating our input to this case?

Decide what precise pieces of information the recipient would like abstracted from your case file to answer his or her question. Judge the level of detail and degree of technical sophistication needed. Account should be taken of the recipient's knowledge of developmental psychology, psychometrics, psychotherapy and so forth. If any action will be required on the recipient's part in response to your letter, decide exactly what it is that you are suggesting he or she does to help the client.

Routinely, in most public-service agencies, letters are written to referrers following the receipt of a referral to indicate that the referral has been placed on a waiting list. Letters are also written following a period of assessment to indicate the way the case has been formulated and the recommended case management plan. Finally, letters are also written at the end of an episode of contact to inform the referrer of the outcome of any intervention programme.

Having talked with more than 1000 professional recipients of psychologists' reports on both sides of the Atlantic over the past 25 years, one reasonably valid conclusion may be drawn. As a profession, clinical psychologists' reports are perceived by the referrer to be too long, and often the key information required by the referrer is buried under a mountain of detail, deemed by the referrer to be unnecessary.

When a referral is received, it is sufficient to return a single-sentence letter indicating that the case will be placed on a waiting list and seen within a specified time frame. Following a preliminary interview or series of assessment sessions, it is sufficient to write a brief letter specifying the referral question, the assessment methods used, the formulation and the case management plan. A common mistake is to send referrers (particularly family doctors) unwanted comprehensive assessment reports. It may be useful to conclude letters summarizing preliminary assessments by noting that a comprehensive report is available on request. In closing letters to referrers, it is sufficient to restate the initial question, the formulation, the case management plan, the degree to which it was implemented and the outcome. The text from an end-of-episode case summary may be used as the basis for writing a closing note to a referrer.

Asking other professionals to follow a particular course of action in a letter is more likely to lead to confusion than to co-ordinated action. It is better practice to outline your formulation in a letter and invite other professionals to join you in a meeting to discuss joint action, than to ask them to implement a programme you have already designed.

Correspondence with clients

Letters may be used to help clients remember what was said during a consultation and to highlight key aspects of sessions. Case formulations, test results, instructions for completing specific tasks may all be given in written form.

When writing a letter to a client, first clarify what you want to achieve by writing the letter. Do you want to inform the client or to invite him or her to behave differently? Ideally, what impact would you like the letter to have on the client. Second, guess what is on the client's mind and how the client will be likely to respond to the information or invitation that you offer. In some instances, clients will be likely to receive information positively and respond to invitations to change their behaviour quite flexibly. In other situations, a client's ability level, his or her fear or anger about being negatively labelled by the psychologist, or belief that the invitation in the letter to view the problem differently or behave differently will lead to some negative outcome, may prevent understanding of the information or following through on invitations. The third step in writing letters to clients is to decide how information or invitations should be framed so that they have the desired impact. Where clients have limited verbal or intellectual abilities, use simple language. Where, there is a danger that clients may feel blamed for failing to solve the problem, acknowledge clients' strengths and commitment to change. Where clients fear that looking at the problem differently or behaving differently will lead to negative outcomes, highlight the benefits of accepting the invitation but also the dangers of accepting the invitation without due consideration and deliberation.

When you wish to inform clients about appropriate self-help materials it may be helpful to consult Norcross et al.'s (2000) *Authoritative Guide* (listed at the end of this chapter) and the recommended reading for clients at the end of other chapters in this book.

Case-study reports

In many clinical psychology training programmes, conceptual clinical skills are assessed by case study. Case studies are an opportunity for candidates to demonstrate that they can bring their knowledge of relevant psychological literature to bear on the way in which they conceptualize and manage clinical problems. The precise requirements for writing a case-study report vary from one clinical psychology training programme to another. The guidelines presented here are those used in our doctoral programme in clinical psychology at University College Dublin.

Case studies should be based on clients with whom the candidate has had clinical involvement as the key worker or as a co-worker with another clinician. The scientist–practitioner model should be used; scientific knowledge and systematic investigative and intervention methods must be brought to bear on a specific clinical problem in an interpersonally sensitive way. A knowledge of the relevant literature must be demonstrated. A case study should highlight the candidate's ability to formulate and test clinical hypotheses. The ability to synthesize salient points from a range of investigative procedures into a comprehensive formulation should be clearly shown. A case study should indicate that the candidate can develop and implement treatment programmes and case management plans that follow logically from case formulations. Interpersonal sensitivity and an awareness of process and ethical issues should also be demonstrated in case-study reports.

1. Demographic information about the case and the referral process

- Demographic information
- Referral agent, instigator of the referral and reason for referral
- History of the presenting problem
- Relevant background individual and family psychosocial and medical history
- Previous and current assessment and treatment

2. Review of relevant literature

- Classification, epidemiology, clinical features, course, assessment, treatment and controversial issues
- Reference to ICD and DSM and other relevant classification systems
- Reference to major clinical texts and recent relevant literature (particularly review papers, book chapters, assessment manuals, treatment manuals and handbooks)

3. Preliminary hypotheses and preliminary formulation of problem

- Hypotheses and proposed plan for testing hypotheses
- Preliminary formulation of the problem from a theoretical perspective

4. Assessment

- Procedures used, e.g. interviews, psychometric tests, observation sessions
- Rationale for choice
- Developmental history with particular reference to salient features
- Family history and genogram with particular reference to salient features
- Current cognitive functioning (including a table of test results if cognitive tests were conducted)
- Current psychosocial adjustment (including results of behaviour checklists and personality tests)

5. Formulation

- Implications of data from assessment for preliminary formulation and hypotheses
- Integration of assessment data into a comprehensive formulation highlighting predisposing, precipitating, maintaining and protective factors or other relevant CBT, psychodynamic, systemic or biomedical formulation model

6. Case management

- Consider options for action in the light of formulation (taking no further action; periodic reassessment; referral to another team member for consultation; referral elsewhere for consultation; focal intervention; or multi-modal intervention)
- Choice of option and reason for choice in light of formulation
- Description of programme plan and goals of programme
- Review of progress in the light of goals
- Evaluation of outcome specifying assessment instruments used (graph changes in problems or symptoms if appropriate; at a minimum pre- and post-treatment measures may be used. Single case designs may be used if appropriate)

7. Process issues

- Impact of clinician–client relationship factors on the consultation process
- Impact of interprofessional and interagency relationships on the consultation process

8. Ethical issues

Ethical issues and the way they were managed should be addressed. Common issues include:

- The ability to give informed consent
- Confidentiality of reports
- Risk assessment (suicide, violence, impaired judgement, fitness to parent)
- Right of attorney

9. Summary and conclusions

- Reason for referral
- Summary of assessment and formulation
- Summary of treatment
- Recommendation or future management

10. References and appendices

- No more than 10 references, most of which should be to key review articles, book chapters, manuals, and handbooks should be included as references and these should be in the format used in the *Journal of Consulting and Clinical Psychology*, or the *Irish Journal of Psychology*, which follow the BPS or APA referencing styles
- All relevant test result forms; checklists; reports from other professionals; correspondence; client drawings, etc. should be included as appendices with identifying information deleted

Figure 7.3 Framework for writing a case study.

A case study may focus on describing how assessment procedures were used to resolve a diagnostic issue and arrive at a coherent integrative formulation. In other instances, case studies may show how assessment and formulation led to the development and implementation of a case management or treatment plan. Where candidates had primary responsibility for implementing one aspect of this plan, particular attention may be paid to that in the case report. Where clients with similar problems have received group treatment, an entire group may serve as the focus for the case study. In such instances, a generic formulation of the problem addressed by the group treatment programme may be presented.

A case study should follow the outline structure presented in Figure 7.3 and contain no more than 4000 words (excluding appendices and references). Copies of reports, correspondence and test forms may be included in appendices. Clients' names and other identifying information should be deleted from these documents to preserve confidentiality. Consent for case studies should be obtained at the outset; this issue is covered in the intake form in Figure 7.1. Where the case study format given in Figure 7.3 is clearly unsuitable, candidates may order and organize case material and relevant information from the literature in a way that is most coherent. Psychologists in clinical training usually choose to write up cases where the work proceeded smoothly in accordance with a treatment manual, the client improved and was satisfied with services received; however, it may be more useful to write up work that is more representative of routine practice. Indeed, the purpose of the case study is to demonstrate learning, reflection and professional development, and it is often in difficult work with clients, when things do not go smoothly and when clients are challenging or do not improve that we learn most. Such case studies provide excellent opportunities for reflection and development.

Service reports

On an annual basis, it is useful for clinical psychology service departments to produce reports that describe their performance over the preceding twelve-month period. Such reports are useful for service planning and for keeping managers, service purchasers and funders abreast of departmental performance. Most psychology departments provide consultative and research services to colleagues, as well as clinical services to clients. It is therefore important to include sections on both of these in annual reports. However, here the focus will be on producing that section of the annual report concerned with services to clients. Give a description of the types of services offered, the staff who offer these, the target population for whom the service is intended and the avenues of referral. Then give a short statistical summary of the number and type of cases that received consultation, with a breakdown of the way they were referred, their demographic characteristics, their main diagnoses or presenting problems and the amount of input made to cases in terms of the numbers of hours of clinical contact and the number of hours of administrative time. These data may be routinely recorded for each case using a simple database. It is also useful for annual reports to include data on the response of cases to treatment, with reference to their scores on measures (such as the CORE or HoNOS) that are routinely administered before and after treatment. Mean scores before and after treatment for all cases, or for subgroups of cases, may be given. In addition, the number of cases that showed improvement on these measures may be tabulated. It is also valuable to include information on service users' perspectives, as given for example by the Client Satisfaction with Treatment Scale (Larsen et al., 1979).

SUMMARY

With intake assessments, the aim is both to establish a good working alliance with the client and to collect sufficient information to reach a preliminary formulation of the main presenting problems. Intake interviews should cover the main presenting problem and its past treatment, the client's personal and family history, risk assessment and multi-agency involvement. In certain circumstances it is useful to incorporate structured assessment instruments into the intake evaluation process. Such instruments include broad measures of general symptoms, brief measures of specific sets of symptoms, structured diagnostic interviews, cognitive functioning tests, personality inventories and projective tests. In light of case formulations based on information from tests and intake interviews, case management plans are developed. These plans fall into the following categories: taking no further action, periodic reassessment, referral to another team member for consultation, referral elsewhere for consultation, focal intervention or multi-modal intervention. Intake interviews, test results, formulations and case management plans are usually written up as comprehensive assessment reports and held on clients' clinical files. In routine progress notes, five categories of information may be recorded at the end of each session: time, attendance, review, agenda and plan (TARAP). Throughout case management, progress notes should be recorded following the TARAP system and at the end of a treatment episode, a case summary may be written containing the formulation, a summary of how the plan was implemented and the outcome to which it led.

During the consultation process, and when closing a case at the end of an episode, it may be necessary to keep clients and colleagues informed of progress through verbal or written reports. In preparing such reports or letters, first identify the audience to whom your report will be addressed. Clarify what sort of questions they have. Compose the list of points you wish to make to answer these inquiries. Frame the points in language and at a level of technical sophistication that will be optimally intelligible to the audience.

In clinical psychology training programmes, case-study reports are used to assess conceptual clinical skills. In this chapter, a framework for such reports was outlined. It follows the format of a comprehensive assessment report followed by an end-of-episode summary report, and incorporates a brief literature summary, an explicit preliminary formulation and a section in which process and ethical issues are considered.

To aid service development and provide service funders with accurate information on performance, clinical psychologists may produce annual service reports. Such reports should include a statistical summary of the number and type of cases treated, with a breakdown of the way they were referred, demographic characteristics, diagnoses or presenting problems, amount of input made to cases, response of cases to treatment with reference to scores on psychometric outcome measures, and information on client satisfaction with services provided.

EXERCISE 7.1

Working in pairs, role-play all or part of an intake interview in which one person takes the role of a client with a circumscribed clinical problem. The interviewer should follow the guide in Figure 7.1. After the interview write as brief a comprehensive report as possible and an even briefer letter to the referring family doctor indicating the initial formulation and treatment plan.

FURTHER READING FOR PRACTITIONERS

Dorfman, W. & Hersen, M. (2001). *Understanding psychological assessment: Perspectives on individual differences*. New York: Kluwer Academic–Plenum.

Fischer, J. & Corcoran, K. (2000). *Measures for clinical practice* (Third Edition, Volumes 1 and 2). New York: Free Press.

Groth-Marnat, G. (2004). *Handbook of psychological assessment* (Fourth Edition). New York: Wiley.

Rush, J., Pincus, H. and the Task Force for the Handbook of Psychiatric Measures (2000). *Handbook of psychiatric measures*. Washington, DC: American Psychiatric Association.

FURTHER READING FOR CLIENTS

Norcross, J., Santrock, J., Campbell, L., Smith, T., Sommer, R., & Zukerman, E. (2000). *Authoritative guide to self-help resources in mental health*. New York: Guilford.

REFERENCES

Beck, A. & Steer, R. (1990). *Beck Anxiety Inventory*. San Antonio, TX: Psychological Corporation.

Beck, A., Steer, R., & Brown, G. (1996). *Beck Depression Inventory* (Second Edition; BDI-II). San Antonio, TX: Psychological Corporation.

Butcher, J., Dahlstrom, W., Graham, J., et al. (1989). *Minnesota Multiphasic Personality Inventory – 2 (MMPI–2). Manual for Administration and Scoring*. Minneapolis, MN: University of Minnesota Press.

Carr, A. (in press). *Handbook of child and adolescent clinical psychology: A contextual approach* (Second Edition). London: Brunner-Routledge.

Cattell, R., Cattell, K., & Cattell, H. (1994). *Sixteen Personality Factor* (Fifth Edition; 16PF 5). Champaign, IL: IPAT.

CORE System Group (CSG) (1999). *CORE system user manual*. Leeds: CSG. Online, available: http://www.student.brad.ac.uk/ptwigg/coresite/home.html

Costa, P. & McCrae, R. (1992). *Revised NEO Personality Inventory (NEO-PI-R) and NEO Five-Factor Inventory (NEO-FFI) Professional Manual*. Odessa, FL: Psychological Assessment Resources.

Derogatis, L. (1994). *SCL-90-R and Brief Symptom Inventory Manual*. Minneapolis, MN: National Computer.

DiNardo, P., Brown, T., & Barlow, D. (1994). *Anxiety disorder interview schedule for DSM IV*. San Antonio, TX: Psychological Corporation.

Dorfman, W.I. & Hersen, M. (Eds). (2001). *Understanding psychological assessment: Perspectives on individual differences*. New York: Kluwer Academic–Plenum.

Exner, J. (2000). *Rorschach workbook for the comprehensive system* (Fifth Edition). US: Rorschach Workshop.

Eysenck, H. & Eysenck, S. (1991). *Manual of the Eysenck Personality Questionnaire – Revised*. Sevenoaks, UK: Hodder & Stoughton.

First, M., Spitzer, R., Gibbon, R., & Williams, J. (1997a). Structured Clinical Interview for DSM-IV-TR Axis I Disorders (SCID-I), Clinician Version. Washington, DC: American Psychiatric Press. Online, available: http://www.appi.org

First, M., Spitzer, R., Gibbon, R., Williams, J., & Benjamin, L. (1997b). Structured Clinical Interview for DSM-IV-TR Axis II Personality Disorders (SCID-II). Washington, DC: American Psychiatric Press. Online available: http://www.appi.org

Fischer, J. & Corcoran, K. (2000). *Measures for clinical practice* (Third Edition, Volumes 1 and 2). New York: Free Press.

Goldberg, D. & Williams, P. (1991). *Users guide to the General Health Questionnaire*. Windsor, UK: NFER Nelson.

Graham, J. (1999). *MMPI–2: Assessing personality and psychopathology* (Third Edition). New York: Oxford University Press.

Greene, R. (2000). *MMPI–2: An interpretive manual* (Second Edition). New York: Pearson, Allyn & Bacon.

Groth-Marnat, G. (2004). *Handbook of psychological assessment* (Fourth Edition). New York: Wiley.

Halligan, P., Kischka, U., Marshall, J., & Saunders, C. (2003). *Handbook of clinical neuropsychology*. Oxford: Oxford University Press.

Kaufman, A. & Lichtenberger, E. (1999). *Essentials of WAIS-III assessment*. New York: Wiley.

Larsen, D., Attkinson, C., Hargreaves, W., & Nguyen, T. (1979). Assessment of client/patient satisfaction: Development of a general scale. *Evaluation and Programme Planning*, 2, 197–207.

Lezak, M. (1995). *Neuropsychological assessment* (Third Edition). Oxford: Oxford University Press.

Moorey, L. (1991). *Personality Assessment Inventory*. Odessa, FL: PAR.

Moorey, L. (2003). *Essentials of PAI assessment*. New York: Wiley.

Murray, H. A. (1971). *Thematic apperception test: Manual*. Cambridge, MA: Harvard University Press.

Nichols, D. (2001). *Essentials of MMPI–2 assessment*. New York: Wiley.

Norcross, J., Santrock, J., Campbell, L., Smith, T., Sommer, R., & Zukerman, E. (2000). *Authoritative guide to self-help resources in mental health*. New York: Guilford.

O'Reilly, G., Walsh, P., Carr, A., & McEvoy, J. (in press). *Handbook of intellectual disability and clinical psychology practice*. London: Brunner-Routledge.

Rose, T., Maloney, M., & Kaser-Boyd, N. (2000). *Essentials of Rorschach® assessment*. New York: Wiley.

Rush, J., Pincus, H. and the Task Force for the Handbook of Psychiatric Measures (2000). *Handbook of psychiatric measures*. Washington, DC: American Psychiatric Association.

Snyder, P. & Nussbaum, P. (1998). *Clinical neuropsychology: A pocket handbook for assessment*. Washington, DC: American Psychological Association.

Teglasi, H. (2001). *Essentials of TAT and other storytelling techniques assessment*. New York: Wiley.

Wechsler, D. (1999). *Wechsler Adult Intelligence Scale – Third Edition* (WAIS-III). San Antonio, TX: Psychological Corporation.

Wing, J.K., Curtis, R.H., & Beevor, A.S. (1996). HoNOS: Health of the Nation

Outcome Scales: Report on Research and Development. July 1993 – December 1995. London: Royal College of Psychiatrists. Online, available: http://www.rcpsych.ac.uk/cru/honoscales/what.htm

Wing, J.K., Lelliott, P., & Beevor, A.S. (2000). Progress on HoNOS. *British Journal of Psychiatry*, 176, 392–393.

World Health Organization (WHO) (1997). *Composite International Diagnostic Interview. Version 2*. (CIDI). Geneva: WHO. Online, available: http://www.who.int/msa/cidi/

Section 2

Mood disorders and suicide

Chapter 8

Depression

Alan Carr and Muireann McNulty

CASE EXAMPLE

Ruth, aged forty-two, was referred for treatment of chronic depression. She presented with low mood; diurnal variation in mood; inability to experience pleasure in activities that previously she would have found pleasurable; pessimistic thoughts about the self, the world and the future; excessive guilt about not achieving high standards in all areas of her life; occasional suicidal ideation; loss of concentration and poor memory; loss of energy; loss of libido; early morning waking; hyperphagia involving bingeing on chocolate and restricted physical and social activity. This pattern of symptoms had been present for a couple of months before her first consultation at our clinic. In the preceding twenty years she had had almost annual depressive episodes, although these were not seasonal. The episodes lasted between one and three months. Between episodes she usually had incomplete remission of symptoms. Her energy, libido, concentration and activity levels would return to near normal levels, but she would continue to feel low mood and continue to experience excessive guilt and hold a pessimistic view of the self, the world and the future, although not as extreme as during the depressive episodes. Her early episodes of depression had been precipitated by clearly identifiable and highly significant stressful life events, such as anticipating her final physiotherapy exams, receiving a promotion and the birth of her children. However, later episodes seemed to be precipitated by far less significant events, such as minor disappointments and the routine hassles of everyday life.

Ruth may have been genetically vulnerable to depression; there was a history of mood disorders in the families of both her parents. Her mother and father suffered from depression, as did two aunts on the mother's side and an uncle on the father's side. Ruth may also have been psychologically vulnerable to depression. In childhood she had suffered a number of significant losses as well as having been exposed to chronic intense, violent conflict with her brother. Also, when Ruth was eight, her older sister died. This was a very significant loss because this sister had taken on the role of Ruth's carer when her mother suffered from two episodes of postnatal depression after the birth of Ruth's two younger siblings.

In her childhood Ruth had been a quiet, withdrawn youngster but capable of making and maintaining friendships and of achieving well at school. She found the transition to adolescence difficult and coped with this by bingeing on chocolate, a habit that led to her becoming overweight. She dieted periodically and achieved a normal weight for her height, but weight control became an important difficulty in her life. She graduated from secondary school in the top 5% of her class and gained admission to a highly competitive university-based physiotherapy programme. She was an outstanding student, doing well both academically and clinically, but was overwhelmed by the stress of sitting her final exams and was hospitalized for depression at twenty-two years of age. She was unresponsive to tricyclic antidepressants (TCAs) and monoamine oxidase inhibitors (MAOIs), and was given electroconvulsive therapy (ECT). She recovered from this first episode of depression over a period of four months and went on to complete her final exams at twenty-three years of age.

Throughout her physiotherapy training, her relationship with a boyfriend she had met in her teens deepened and she married him in her mid-twenties. He had qualified as an architect and after a brief period working as a junior partner, left and set up his own practice. David was the same age as Ruth but, unlike her, he was an emotionally lighthearted, gregarious, extraverted person. Over the second half of their twenties and during their early thirties the couple had four children, with the births spaced about two years apart. The children were healthy and well adjusted but Ruth suffered from postnatal depression after each of the births. After the birth of the first child, Ruth gave up her job and never again returned to practice in the public health service as a physiotherapist, although she did on two occasions do periods of part-time private practice. Both of these periods of work were followed by episodes of depression.

Over the twenty-year period from her first episode of depression, Ruth actively engaged in treatment about once every two or three years. However, after her failure to respond to TCAs and MAOIs and her concerns about the side effects of ECT, she refused to consider other pharmacological treatment options. Rather, she had attended a series of psychotherapists, psychologists and psychiatrists and had participated in both individual and group-oriented client-centred and cognitive behaviour therapy (CBT) programmes. She found that psychotherapy helped her to recover from depression but had little effect on residual symptoms she experienced between episodes, or on preventing relapse. She also found that each time she disengaged from therapy she stopped doing the activities and using the coping strategies recommended by the psychotherapists and so she would ultimately relapse.

A preliminary assessment in April 2000 at our clinic led to a syndromal formulation of her disorder, of the type given in the first paragraph. That is, her current episode had been precipitated by a build-up of minor stressful life events. Her current vulnerability to depression stemmed from her experience of multiple previous episodes and from both genetic and early childhood factors. Her low mood; pessimistic, perfectionist and guilt-oriented thinking style; constricted lifestyle and the physiological dysregulation evidenced by her abnormal patterns of sleep, eating and sexual activity were mutually reinforcing and this maintained her depression. On the positive side, there were a number of protective factors in this case. Ruth was very intelligent, she had the capacity to make and maintain friendships, she had a good marriage, good relationships with her four children and had shown in the past that she could use psychotherapy to recover from depression.

On the basis of this formulation, Ruth was offered a contract for ten individual CBT sessions spaced at weekly or fortnightly intervals, which she accepted. In the first four sessions the focus was on monitoring changes in mood and increasing activity levels. Through these interventions Ruth became aware again that engagement in physical and social activities improved her mood, a lesson she had learned in previous episodes of therapy. The pros and cons of Ruth taking selective serotonin reuptake inhibitors (SSRIs) were discussed, but Ruth decided against medication because she thought that this would be an admission that she was powerless to control her own mood. The next four sessions focused on using a daily thought record and learning to 'catch' and challenge negative automatic thoughts and to re-evaluate depressogenic assumptions. In August, before the final two scheduled sessions were convened, therapy ceased due to conflicting holiday arrangements and extra-therapeutic commitments. The plan had been to use these sessions to focus on relapse management,

In late October 2000, Ruth returned for a further episode of therapy. She described how her mood had deteriorated in the preceding two months and this was associated with a reduction in her activity levels and a return to a pessimistic and perfectionist guilt-oriented thinking style. However, prior to returning to therapy, Ruth, after much soul-searching decided to begin a course of pharmacological treatment and arranged for her family doctor to prescribe her SSRIs. It became clear during this interview in October 2000 that Ruth's relapse was in part due to the way she cut herself off from her partner when her mood dropped. Three-column formulations of problematic situations where Ruth's interaction with her partner, David, maintained her low mood and exceptional circumstances in which this was expected to occur but did not were drawn up. These are given in Figures 8.1 and 8.2. The second episode of treatment with Ruth involved both CBT and a systemic approach. Ruth and David were invited to ten conjoint sessions. In the initial session a rationale for couples treatment was offered, since this was new to both of them. Through revisiting formulations of problem and exceptional episodes it became clear to the couple that jointly they had a better chance of defeating depression than leaving Ruth to fight the battle alone. The importance of social support, the value of planning conjoint physical and social activity and the value of jointly challenging pessimistic and perfectionist styles of thinking were all emphasized in this rationale. Throughout the couples therapy, depression (including depressive thinking and all other aspects of the condition) was externalized as a problem the couple had to jointly address.

Psychoeducational material (see, for example, Table 8.4) was presented verbally to the couple over the course of the first three couples sessions and revisited from time to time throughout the therapy. In these three sessions the couple was also invited to plan and complete conjoint mood monitoring and activity-scheduling exercises. They developed a good routine for daily exercise together, weekly joint social outings and mood monitoring, which had an important impact on Ruth's mood. In addition, SSRIs began to take effect. Enactments of support giving and communication skills training were also gradually introduced during the first three sessions.

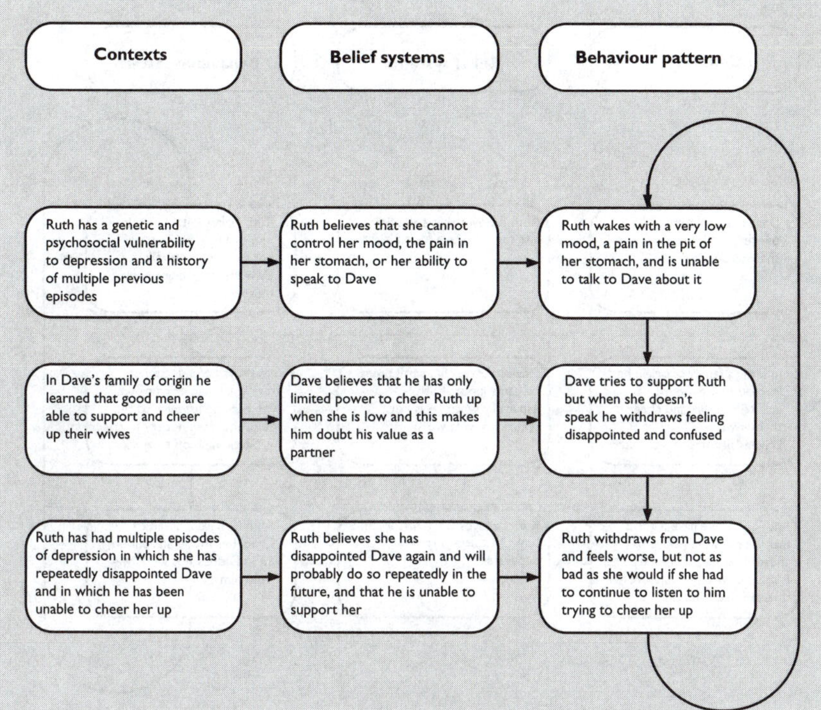

Figure 8.1 Three-column formulation of episodes that strengthen depression.

In sessions four to eight, some part of every session was used primarily as a forum where Ruth could have her viewpoint fully listened to and understood by David, and David would use these communication slots to help Ruth remember particularly happy times in their relationship when her mood had been good. These joint experiences of being understood and remembering happy episodes in their relationship had a particularly strong effect on Ruth's mood. The couple began to incorporate these exercises into their day-to-day lives as a way of jointly combating depression, which they came to see as a 'common enemy'. The externalization intervention begun in the first session began to permeate their way of thinking about depression.

In sessions four to eight, there was also a focus on pessimistic, perfectionist, and catastrophic belief systems. A particularly important aspect of this work involved Ruth's declaration that she was frightened to recover in case it led to the end of her marriage. David and Ruth were

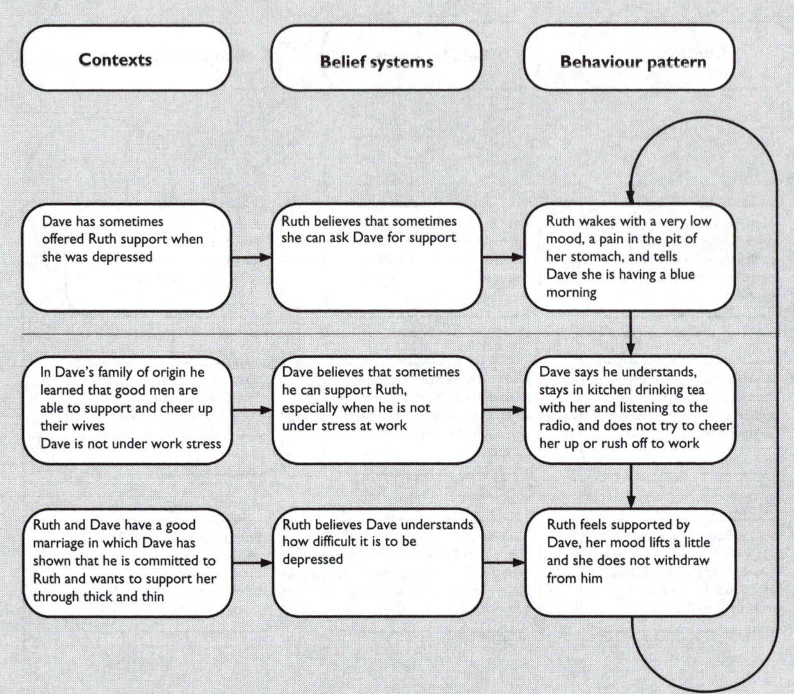

Figure 8.2 Three-column formulation of exceptional episodes that weaken depression.

invited to reflect on how joint participation in therapy and the increasing amount of time they spent talking together outside the sessions affected their attachment to each other. In response they noted that it had drawn them closer together. This observation weakened Ruth's conviction that recovery would lead to the demise of their relationship. Her conviction dropped from 10 to 7 on a 10-point scale. The couple came to see this belief that recovery would lead to separation as 'the voice of depression' trying to prevent them from overcoming it.

The final two sessions were devoted to reviewing how the couple had used therapy to overcome the current episode of depression and anticipating risky situations in which relapses might occur and planning ways of dealing with them. During these sessions, Ruth described how minor decreases in mood due to little disappointments, like not preparing a perfect dinner for guests, could lead to a spiral of negative thinking that in turn would lead to a major drop in mood. She was invited to experiment with using the same process to catch minor improvements in mood and to engage in a spiral of optimistic thinking that would lead to an improvement in mood. This involved her practising with David anticipating a hopeful future by talking and visualizing how they imagined things could work out well in small and realistic ways. The couple rehearsed how they could use this skill and those of joint mood monitoring, activity scheduling and communication to deal with future risky situations. They were also offered open-ended access to occasional booster sessions, since one of Ruth's fears was that if therapy ended it would not be possible to return (she had had this experience with half a dozen health professionals after previous treatment episodes). A year after these two treatment episodes Ruth had suffered no further major relapses, but she and David contacted me periodically to discuss lifecycle transition issues.

CLINICAL FEATURES

Table 8.1 contains diagnostic criteria for episodes of major depression from DSM-IV-TR (APA, 2000a) and ICD-10 (WHO, 1993). A classification of

Table 8.1 Diagnostic criteria for major depression

DSM-IV *Major depressive episode*	*ICD-10* *Depressive episode*
Duration: Symptoms present nearly every day for at least 2 weeks	**Duration**: Symptoms present nearly every day for at least 2 weeks
Key symptoms • Depressed mood • Markedly diminished interest or pleasure in almost all daily activities (anhedonia)	**Key symptoms** • Depressed mood • Loss of interest or pleasure in pleasurable activities • Decreased energy or increased fatigueability
Ancillary symptoms • Fatigue or loss of energy • Change in appetite or weight (increased or decreased) • Insomnia or hypersomnia • Psychomotor retardation or agitation • Low self-esteem or excessive guilt • Poor concentration and indecisiveness • Recurrent thoughts of death, suicidal ideation or suicide attempt	**Ancillary symptoms** • Change in appetite or weight (increased or decreased) • Disturbed sleep • Psychomotor retardation or agitation • Low self-esteem or confidence • Self-reproach or guilt • Reduced concentration and attention • Ideas or acts of self-harm or suicide

Continued overleaf

Table 8.1 Continued

DSM-IV *Major depressive episode*	*ICD-10* *Depressive episode*
Criteria for diagnosis One key symptom and at least five symptoms in total, plus clinically significant distress or impairment in social occupational, educational functioning. Mild, moderate and severe based on number of symptoms and degree of impairment, but no quantity specified	**Criteria for diagnosis** For mild depression, two key and four symptoms in total. For moderate depression, two key and six symptoms in total. For severe depression three key and eight in total
Exclusions Symptoms not due to mixed episode of mania and depression, direct effects of a drug or a general medical condition such as hypothyroidism and not better accounted for by uncomplicated bereavement or psychosis	**Exclusions** No history of manic episodes, not due to substance abuse, an organic disorder or schizophrenia or schizoaffective disorder
Melancholic features One of the following during the most severe period of the current episode: • Loss of pleasure in all or almost all activities • Lack of reactivity to usually pleasurable stimuli And at least three of the following: • Distinct quality of depressed mood • Early morning waking (2 hours before the usual time) • Depression regularly worse in morning • Marked psychomotor retardation or agitation • Significant anorexia or weight loss • Excessive or inappropriate guilt	**Somatic syndrome** Four or the following must be present and this is commonly associated with severe depression: • Loss of interest or pleasure in pleasurable activities • Lack of emotional reactivity • Waking in the morning 2 hours or more before the usual time • Depression worse in the mornings • Psychomotor retardation or agitation • Marked loss of appetite or weight (5% in a month) • Marked loss of libido
Psychotic features One of the following must be present: • Delusions • Hallucinations	**Psychotic symptoms** Any of the following must be present and this is usually associated with severe depression: • Delusions • Hallucinations • Depressive stupor
Catatonic features Two of the following must be present: • Motoric immobility • Excessive motor activity • Extreme negativism • Bizarre postures • Echolalia or echopraxia	
Recurrent depression Two or more major depressive episodes	**Recurrent depression** At least one previous episode of 2 weeks duration

Note: Based on DSM-IV-TR (APA, 2000a) and ICD-10 (WHO, 1993).

the diagnostic and other common clinical features of depression into the domains of mood, behaviour, relationships, somatic state, cognition and perception is given in Table 8.2. The following account of the features of depression draws on extensive literature reviews (Bech, 2000; Gotlib & Hammen, 2002; Joiner & Coyne, 1999; Power, 2004; Williams, Watts, MacLeod & Matthews, 1997).

Loss

When depressive episodes occur, clinical features may be linked by assuming that depressed individuals have usually suffered a loss of some sort. Either a

Table 8.2 Clinical features of depression in adults

Mood	Depressed mood Irritable mood Anxiety and apprehension Distinct quality of depressed mood* Loss of interest in pleasurable activities (anhedonia)* Lack of emotional reactivity*
Behaviour	Psychomotor retardation or agitation* Depressive stupor§
Relationships	Deterioration in family relationships Withdrawal from peer relationships Poor work or educational performance
Somatic state	Fatigue Diminished activity Loss of appetite or overeating Aches and pains Early morning waking* Diurnal variation of mood (worse in morning)* Change in weight* Loss of interest in sex*
Cognition	Negative view of self, world and future Over-general memory Cognitive distortions Inability to concentrate Indecision Suicidal ideation Suicidal intention* Excessive guilt* Mood-congruent delusions§
Perception	Perceptual bias towards negative events Mood-congruent hallucinations§

* These features are associated with melancholic depression and are referred to as vegetative features or the somatic syndrome. §These features occur in psychotic depression.

loss of an important relationship or aspect of a relationship, a loss of some valued attribute such as athletic ability or health, or a loss of status.

Perception

With respect to perception, having suffered a loss, depressed individuals tend to perceive the world as if further losses were probable. Depressed people selectively attend to negative features of the environment and this in turn leads them to engage in depressive cognitions and unrewarding behaviour patterns that further entrench their depressed mood. In severe cases of depression, individuals may report mood-congruent auditory hallucinations. We may assume that this severe perceptual abnormality is present when individuals report hearing voices criticizing them or telling them depressive things. Auditory hallucinations also occur in schizophrenia. However, the hallucinations that occur in schizophrenia are not necessarily mood congruent.

Cognition

With respect to cognition, depressed individuals describe themselves, the world and the future in negative terms. They evaluate themselves as worthless and are critical of their occupations and social accomplishments. Often, this negative self-evaluation or low self-esteem is expressed as guilt for not living up to certain standards or letting others down. They see their world, including family, friends and work or college, as uncontrollable, unrewarding, critical, hostile or apathetic. They describe the future in bleak terms and report little if any hope that things will improve. Where they report extreme hopelessness and this is coupled with excessive guilt for which they believe they should be punished, suicidal ideas or intentions may be reported. Extremely negative thoughts about the self, the world and the future may be woven together in severe cases into depressive delusional systems. In addition to the content of the depressed individual's thought being bleak, they also display logical errors in their thinking and concentration problems. Errors in reasoning are marked by a tendency to maximize the significance and implications of negative events and minimize the significance of positive events. They also have over-general autobiographical memories. That is, they have difficulty remembering specific happy events in detail (which might lighten their mood), but rather remember both positive and negative past episodes in their lives in global over-general ways. In addition, they have concentration and attention problems that lead to difficulties managing occupational, academic or leisure activities demanding sustained attention.

Mood

With respect to affect, low mood is a core feature of depression. Depressed mood is usually reported as a feeling of sadness, loneliness or despair and an inability to experience pleasure when engaging in activities that previously were pleasurable. During an episode of major depression as a person moves from mild, to moderate to severe depression, the increasing number and intensity of the symptoms may lead to intense anxiety. That is, fears are experienced such as 'Will this get worse?' 'Am I stuck in this living hell forever?' 'Will I ever be myself again?' 'Will I be able to prevent myself from committing suicide to escape?' Irritability may also occur, with the person expressing anger at the source of their loss, for example anger at a deceased loved one for abandoning the grieving person or anger at health professionals for being unable to alleviate the depression.

Behaviour

At a behavioural level, depressed individuals may show either reduced and slowed activity levels (psychomotor retardation) or increased but ineffective activity (psychomotor agitation). They may show a failure to engage in activities that would bring them a sense of achievement or connectedness to family or friends. When individuals become immobile, this is referred to as depressive stupor; fortunately, this is rare.

Somatic state

Somatic or vegetative features such as loss of energy, disturbances of sleep and appetite, weight loss, abdominal pains or headaches and diurnal variation in mood are all associated with more severe conditions. A loss of interest in sex, or loss of libido as it is often called, may also occur. These features of depression are consistent with findings that dysregulation of neurophysiological, endocrine and immune functions are associated with depression and that sleep architecture is also affected.

Relationships

At an interpersonal level, depressed individuals report deterioration in their relationships with family, friends, work colleagues and other significant figures in their lives. They describe themselves as lonely and yet unable or unworthy of taking steps to make contact with others.

Self-harm

One complication of depression is self-destructive behaviour. In classifying self-destructive behaviour, a distinction is made between suicidal and parasuicidal behaviour. With suicidal behaviour, the intention to kill oneself is the aim of the self-destructive act. With parasuicide, the person may hope to resolve an interpersonal difficulty by making a self-harming gesture. For example, the person may hope to elicit care, concern or pity. Suicide and self-harm are discussed in detail in Chapter 10.

CLASSIFICATION OF SUBTYPES OF MOOD DISORDERS

Within DSM-IV-TR and ICD-10, distinctions are made between:

- major depression
- bipolar mood disorder
- dysthymia
- cyclothymiacs.

Major depression and bipolar disorder are both episodic mood disorders, with the former being characterized by episodes of low mood, negative cognition, and sleep and appetite disturbance. In addition to the above, bipolar disorder is characterized by episodes of mania in which elation, grandiosity, flight of ideas and expansive behaviour occur. Dysthymia and cyclothymia are non-episodic chronic conditions of at least two years duration, with dysthymia being characterized by depressive symptomatology (at least three symptoms in addition to low mood) and cyclothymia being characterized by similar but less extreme mood fluctuations than bipolar disorder. In the case example that opened the chapter, Ruth showed a clinical picture often called ‘double depression’. That is, her episodes of major depression were superimposed on chronic non-episodic dysthymia. The distinctions between unipolar and bipolar conditions and between recurrent and persistent disorders have replaced distinctions used in earlier classifications systems. These include:

- neurotic and psychotic depression
- endogenous and reactive mood disorders
- overt and masked depression.

Reviews of the classification of mood disorders identify the following reasons for abandoning these earlier distinctions (Farmer & McGuffin, 1989; Kendell, 1976): the neurotic and psychotic distinction, based originally on inferred psychodynamic aetiological factors and differences in observable symptoms, has been discarded because inferred psychodynamic aetiological differences have not been supported by empirical evidence. Having said that, both DSM-IV-TR and ICD-10 have a facility for specifying if a depressive episode is characterized by the presence of psychotic symptoms, including delusions, hallucinations and depressive stupor. The endogenous–reactive distinction has been abandoned because evidence from stressful life event research shows that almost all episodes of depression, regardless of quality or severity, are preceded by stressful life events and in that sense are reactive. However, within DSM-IV-TR and ICD-10 there is a facility for coding whether a depressive episode or disorder is characterized by a cluster of symptoms historically associated with what was termed endogenous depression and now referred to as 'melancholic features' in the DSM and 'somatic features' in the ICD. These features are listed in Table 8.1. The recognition that people with depression may show comorbid axis I or II disorders involving antisocial or troublesome behaviour has rendered the concept of masked depression unnecessary, since the term was often used to classify depressed people who *masked* their low mood with angry outbursts of aggressive, destructive or troublesome behaviour.

EPIDEMIOLOGY

Table 2.2 (p. 56) shows that the current prevalence rate for depression (based on periods from one week to one year) range in round figures from 2–9% for men and 3–14% for women. According to the DSM-IV-TR (APA, 2000a) the lifetime prevalence of major depression is 10–25% for women and 5–12% for men. A number of further findings highlighted in major reviews concerning the epidemiology, aetiology and course of depression deserve mention (Bech, 2000; Craighead, Hart, Wilcoxan, Craighead & Ilardi, 2002; Crits-Cristoph & Barber, 2002; Gotlib & Hammen, 2002; Joiner & Coyne, 1999; Joyce, 2000; Murray & Lopez, 1998; Power, 2004; Segal, Williams & Teasdale, 2002; Williams et al., 1997). The prevalence of depression is increasing in younger cohorts and the age of onset of depression is decreasing, with most cases now occurring in late adolescence and early adulthood.

Comorbidity

Comorbid dysthymia, anxiety disorders, substance-abuse disorders, eating disorders and border-line personality disorder are common in major depression. Depression that occurs with comorbid conditions, particularly personality disorders, dysthymia, and substance-use disorders is less responsive to treatment and so in clinical practice requires more intensive treatment programmes.

Complications

Only 12% of people with depression seek help from a specialist. Up to 15% of people with major depression severe enough to require hospitalization commit suicide. In the year 2000, of all diseases, depression imposed the second largest burden of ill health worldwide.

AETIOLOGY

Risk and protective factors in the aetiology of depression are presented in Table 8.3.

Predisposing factors

Heritability estimates for depression range from 40 to 70% and there is evidence that genes associated with vulnerability to depression are also associated with vulnerability to anxiety disorders and trait neuroticism (Jones, Kent & Craddock, 2002). A concern for many parents with depression is the likelihood that they will pass depression on to their children. If the annual prevalence of depression is taken to be 5% and the chances of first-degree relatives is about three times that of the normal population, then 15% of children born to depressed parents will develop depression and 85% will not. General childhood adversity, adverse early parent–child relationships characterized by poor parental care, and loss of a parent in childhood have all been identified as psychosocial risk factors for depression. Personality traits, notably neuroticism, and cognitive styles, notably a pessimistic attributional style, are risk factors for depression.

Precipitating factors

First episodes of major depression are typically precipitated by major stressful life events, particularly those associated with loss such as separation, divorce bereavement, illness, injury and unemployment. Seasonal depression occurs in winter, probably in response to low levels of sunlight and is marked by hypersomnia, overeating, carbohydrate craving and weight gain. The threshold at which depression can be triggered decreases with second and subsequent episodes, so that for people who have experienced three or more episodes, only minor stresses may precipitate a full-blown major depressive episode. Both cognitive and neurobiological explanations for this have been offered. According to cognitive therapists, small stresses, which lead to small negative mood changes, can give rise to chronic rumination and catastrophizing and precipitate later episodes of depression (Segal et al., 2002). According to neurobiological theorists, multiple episodes of depression, through a

Table 8.3 Risk and protective factors in the aetiology of depression

Risk factors	*Domain*	*Protective factors*
Family history of depression or anxiety Family history of neuroticism Childhood adversity Adverse early parent–child relationships with poor parental care Loss of a parent in childhood Low intelligence or no unique talent	Family-of-origin factors	No family history of depression, anxiety or neuroticism Positive early family-of-origin experiences At least one positive relationship with a supportive adult in childhood High intelligence or a unique talent
Major stressful life events, particularly loss, including separation, divorce, bereavement, illness, injury and unemployment Low levels of sunlight After three or more previous major depressive episodes, minor stressful life events	Precipitating factors	Absence of major stressful life events and losses High levels of sunlight
Three or more previous major depressive episodes	Psychological disorder related factors	Good mental health
Neuroticism and rumination Pessimistic cognitive style Rigid use of few coping skills Poor problem-solving skills	Personality traits and cognitive style	Low neuroticism Optimistic cognitive style Functional coping strategies Good problem solving Learned resourcefulness
Prior episodes of depression produce changes in neurobiological systems that make depression more likely in response to small stresses	Biological factors	Less than three prior episodes of depression
Absence of a confiding relationship Unsupportive marriage	Current family factors	Confiding relationship Supportive marriage
Poor social support network High levels of environmental stress	Wider social system factors	Good social support network Low levels of environmental stress
No treatment or unimodal treatment (psychological or pharmacological only)	Treatment system factors	Multi-modal treatment including brief evidence-based psychological intervention and antidepressant medication

process of kindling, probably render the neurobiological systems that maintain depression more vulnerable to depressogenic changes in response to minor stresses.

Maintaining factors

Depressed mood is maintained by ongoing high levels of environmental stress with demands exceeding personal coping resources, low activity levels, a constricted lifestyle with little positive social interaction, unsupportive relationships with family members (including partners), a depressive cognitive style and probably by dysregulation of neurotransmitter systems in the reward and punishment centres of the brain.

Protective factors

On the positive side, protective factors, particularly in cases where childhood adversity occurred, include at least one positive early relationship with an adult in childhood, high intelligence and a unique talent. Protective factors in adulthood include social support in the form of a confiding relationship, a supportive marriage, a good social support network, learned resourcefulness, well-developed problem-solving skills and functional coping strategies.

Response of acute depression to treatment

About a half to two-thirds of cases of acute depression recover after a course of pharmacological and psychological treatment, compared with about a third of clients who receive a placebo pill (Craighead et al., 2002; Nemeroff & Schatzberg, 2002). The current treatment of choice is a multi-modal programme in which a relatively brief evidence-based psychological therapy is combined with antidepressant medication. Multi-modal programmes are preferred to unimodal programmes because response to treatment is more rapid with a multi-modal approach, and relapse after termination of pharmacological treatment is delayed longer for clients who have received psychological treatment. This is a critical issue since major depression is an episodic disorder and relapse is to be expected.

COURSE

The course of depression in the presence and absence of maintenance therapy has been well documented (APA, 2000b; Judd, 1997; Segal et al., 2002; Weissman et al., 2000). Around 85% of clients experience recurrent episodes of depression and, on average, people with major depression have four episodes of twenty weeks each over the course of their lifetimes. As the condition progresses, the frequency and duration of depressive episodes increases. The relapse rate for those recovering from a first or second episode of depression who are treated with antidepressants and who do not receive psychological or pharmacological maintenance treatment is 20–35%; for those with a history of three or more previous episodes it is 60–80%. Recurrent depression has distinctive features, notably: early morning waking, diurnal variation in mood, lack of responsivity to environmental circumstances and high levels of the stress hormone, cortisol. US and UK treatment outcome studies show that after fourteen to twenty-four months, 50–80% clients who only receive antidepressants relapse, compared with 20–35% of those who also receive CBT. These studies included mixed groups of clients who had experienced one or more episodes of depression. Current maintenance therapies that include continuation of antidepressant pharmacological treatment or psychological maintenance treatment can reduce relapse rates from about 60–80% to about 20–37%. Psychological maintenance treatments include interpersonal therapy and a CBT protocol that includes training in mindfulness meditation skills. For clients with recurrent depression involving three or more episodes, monthly interpersonal therapy sessions over a one-year period or an eight-session course of mindfulness-based cognitive behaviour therapy have been shown to reduce relapse rates from about two-thirds to one-third (Segal et al., 2002; Weissman et al., 2000). For pregnant women, those undergoing surgery, those who cannot tolerate the side effects of antidepressants and those ideologically opposed to medication, psychological maintenance treatment is vital. Altogether, this group constitutes 30–40% of cases.

ASSESSMENT, FORMULATION AND CONTRACTING FOR TREATMENT

In the management of mood problems, the first priority is to assess the risk of self-harm. A structured approach to the assessment and formulation of suicide risk is presented in Chapter 10. Once suicide risk has been managed, the second priority is to clarify the nature and extent of symptomatology. The diagnostic criteria in Table 8.1 and the clinical features in Table 8.2 offer a useful basis for interviewing in this area. Self-report questionnaires and rating scales that can be used to supplement clinical interviewing are listed at the end of this chapter. The third priority is to identify important predisposing, precipitating, maintaining and protective factors listed above, associated with depression. The interview plan in Figure 7.2 (p. 266) can be used for this aspect of the assessment.

Differential diagnosis

When making the differential diagnosis of major depression, the following need to be ruled out: depression due to bipolar disorder (covered in Chapter 9); another psychological problem, such as schizophrenia (covered in Chapter 21); substance abuse (covered in Chapter 20) or a painful or severe medical condition (covered in Chapters 17 and 18). It is particularly important to rule-out bipolar disorder by inquiring about manic or hypomanic episodes, because antidepressants can precipitate episodes of hypomania and lead to a long-term rapid cycling course for people with bipolar disorder.

Formulation

After thorough assessment and diagnosis, a syndromal case formulation may be drawn up that links predisposing, precipitating, maintaining and protective factors to depressive symptomatology, potential treatment goals and possible plans for reaching these. For example, with the case presented at the start of this chapter, a very general formulation was given in the first session of treatment when it was noted that the episode of major depression that led to the referral had been precipitated by a build-up of minor stressful life events. Ruth's vulnerability to depression stemmed from her experience of multiple previous episodes and from both genetic and early childhood factors. Her low mood, pessimistic, perfectionist and guilt-oriented thinking style, constricted lifestyle and the physiological dysregulation evidenced by her abnormal patterns of sleep, eating and sexual activity, were mutually reinforcing and this maintained her depression. On the positive side there were a number of protective factors in this case. Ruth was very intelligent, she had the capacity to make and maintain friendships, she had a good marriage, good relationships with her four children and had shown in the past that she could use psychotherapy to recover from depression. This syndromal formulation might suffice for biomedical treatment but require further refinements to be a reasonable guide for conducting CBT, interpersonal or systemic therapy. For CBT, following the model in Figure 3.2 (p. 79), it would be necessary to supplement the syndromal formulation with an ABC formulation to specify the sort of daily situations (A) that prompted such automatic thoughts (B) along with the emotional, behavioural, and physiological consequences (C) of these and how these feed back into and reinforce core beliefs and assumptions. For interpersonal therapy, an approach to case formulation will be described below. For systemic therapy, problem and exception formulations like those in Figures 8.1 and 8.2, which follow the three-column formulation model described in Chapter 5, may be drawn up.

Contracting for treatment and goal setting

After assessment, present the syndromal formulation to the client in a way that matches the client's readiness and ability to understand it and that highlights the client's strengths. The psychoeducational handout in Table 8.4 may be helpful in giving feedback. This process of giving feedback partially involves socializing the client into a complex biopsychosocial way of conceptualizing mood problems. Some clients will hold implicit unifactorial theories in which they attribute their mood problems exclusively to biological factors ('My doctor said I had a chemical imbalance in my brain') or psychosocial problems ('My counsellor said I was depressed because I was abused as a child'). In most instances, except where pregnancy or medical complications or ethical considerations preclude medication, it is best practice to

Table 8.4 Psychoeducational handout on depression

What is depression?

Depression is a complex condition involving changes in mood, thinking, behaviour, relationships and biological functioning including sleep and appetite.

Vulnerability to depression may be due to genetic factors or early loss experiences or both.

Current episodes of depression arise from big stressful life events or a build-up of small stresses.

These activate the vulnerability that then comes to be maintained by depressed thinking, action and relationships.

Genetic vulnerability may be understood as a nervous system that *goes slow* under pressure and disrupts sleep, appetite and energy. This going-slow process leads to depressed mood.

Early loss-related vulnerability is a set of memories about loss that have been filed away in the mind, but are taken out when a recent loss or stress occurs. The files inform you that more and more losses will occur and this leads to depressed mood.

Overcoming depression involves learning how to control and change patterns of thinking, action and relationships that maintain depression and to keep the number of stresses in your life to manageable proportions.

A diagram of this explanation of depression is presented on the next page.

Somatic state has also been included in the diagram. Antidepressant medication may be used to improve sleep, appetite, and energy levels. Medication takes from 4 to 6 weeks to work fully and speeds up recovery.

Psychological therapy helps you develop the skills to fight depression and prevent or delay relapse.

Two out of three people can benefit from a combined programme of psychological therapy and medication.

If you participate in therapy with your partner, this can offer you both a fresh start, and a way of joining together as a team to defeat depression.

Continued overleaf

Table 8.4 Continued.

If you are worried about your children developing depression the chances of them inheriting a nervous system that goes slow under pressure is only one in five. This is good news, 80% of children of depressed parents do not develop depression. Depression is not inherited, but a nervous system that goes slow under stress is, so this means people with this sort of nervous system have to make sure they do not have too much stress at one time and have a lot of support.

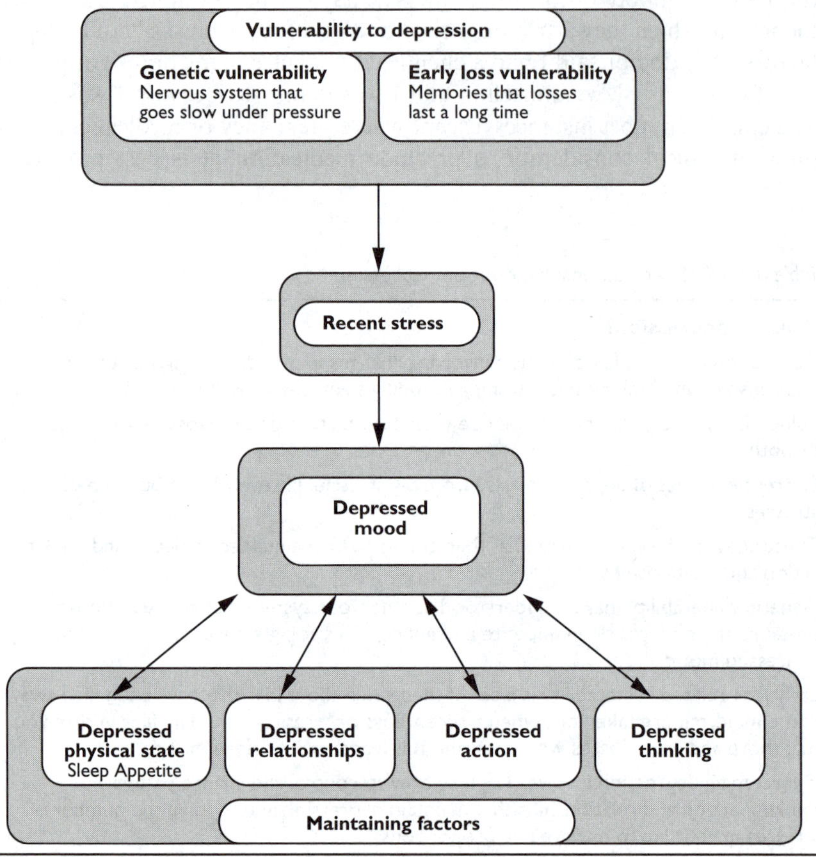

point out that depression involves the dysregulation of both biological and psychological processes and so a multi-modal programme involving both antidepressant medication and psychological therapy is usually the best and most effective treatment. Medication speeds up recovery in the short term. Psychotherapy teaches the skills to prevent relapses. When the client has understood and accepted the formulation, collaboratively explore and identify possible treatment goals. With goal setting, the aim is to define clear, unambiguous, visualizable, measurable, positively stated goals for problem resolution. 'I'd like to feel better' is a vague goal. 'I'd like to have a mood rating of at least 5 on a 10-point scale for at least an hour a day for a full week' is a far more clearly defined goal. In light of specified goals, offer a time-limited contract for therapy specifying scheduling details and client and therapist responsibilities within the therapeutic contract, and a realistic evidence-based statement of the chances that the client will benefit from therapy, along with a statement of the sacrifices the client will have to make in terms of time, energy, financial investment and so forth for the therapy to work. Detailed guidance on contracting for therapy within the context of CBT, psychodynamic and systemic practice models are given in Chapters 3–5.

Acknowledging the inevitability of resistance

Regardless of what psychotherapeutic approach is taken to the treatment of depression, in chronic cases resistance is inevitable and core process issues will emerge. Typically, clients and therapists fall into patterns of interaction in which they adopt polarized roles of helpless victim and overcontrolling or hostile caregiver (McCullough, 2000). This interactional pattern may maintain rather than ameliorate depression. Also, it typically replicates similar patterns that are occurring in the client's current life with significant members of their social network, and patterns from their early childhood (as described in Chapter 4 on psychodynamic therapy). When contracting for any form of psychotherapy, acknowledge the inevitability of these sorts of pattern occurring as a normal part of good therapy. Also make a commitment to the client, and ask the client to make a commitment to you, to try to find ways of collaborating on more equal terms in defeating depression when these transactional patterns emerge. Let the client know that this will usually involve acknowledging that the pattern is happening, and then proceeding to find amicable ways to share responsibility for therapeutic progress more equally without resorting to criticism or cajoling.

TREATMENT OF DEPRESSION

There is good evidence that CBT, interpersonal, and systemic psychological treatment protocols are effective in treating depression (Beach & Gupta, 2003; Byrne et al., in press; Craighead et al., 2002; Gollan et al., 2002; Jones & Asen, 1999; Power, 2004; Shapiro, 1998). There is also good reason to believe that combining antidepressant medication with psychological therapy may lead to more rapid recovery. Practical aspects of using antidepressants are considered in a cursory way at the end of this chapter and are covered in more detail in Chapter 6. The specific guidelines on the application of CBT, psychodynamic and systemic therapy to the treatment of depression should be read in conjunction with the more general and detailed coverage of these approaches to psychotherapy given in Chapters 3–5.

CBT for depression

Beck's cognitive therapy proposes that significant problematic lessons, learned through exposure to early stressful life events, frustration of important needs, and modelling and identification in early family relationships, are encoded in maladaptive schemas (Beck, 1976; Clark, Beck & Alford, 1999). Such schemas are clusters of interconnected core beliefs and assumptions about self and others in significant relationships. For episodes of depression to occur, latent maladaptive schemas are activated in adulthood by schema-related major stressful life events. For example, when a client whose depressive schema entailed the assumption, 'If everyone does not like me, then I am unlovable', passed a friend on the street who did not say hello, he had the automatic thought, 'She really hates me', leading to a drop in mood, which in turn prevented him from going over, greeting his friend warmly and humorously joking about her not saying hello. This, in turn, led to a reduction in the amount of perceived social support available from that friend in future interactions, leaving the client more vulnerable to further distancing and depressive interactions. Within cognitive therapy it is also proposed that, once schemas are activated, people become prone to interpreting ambiguous situations in problematic ways. The various logical errors that they make are referred to as cognitive distortions, some of which are listed in Table 3.2 (p. 69).

The goal of CBT is to help the client first of all monitor mood changes (C) and link them to changes in activating events (A). In the early stages of therapy, the focus is on helping clients re-activate themselves by using behavioural strategies. They include scheduling activities and pleasant events. Once the client is re-activated, the focus of therapy shifts from behavioural to cognitive strategies. Through 'thought catching', clients come to identify the negative automatic thoughts (B) that are elicited by activating events. Clients use the daily thought record to keep track of the way their negative automatic thoughts impact on their mood state. When this skill is learned, clients are shown how to develop alternative, more positive, ways of re-appraising activating events. They also learn to test the relative validity of their negative automatic appraisals of activating events and their more positive re-appraisals by examining the evidence for both. This liberates clients from slavishly interpreting many events in their lives in negative and depressing ways. Instead, they come to gradually interpret more and more minor events in their lives in more positive ways. Each time they do this, their mood improves, or at least does not deteriorate more. Very gradually, they come to see themselves as not totally unworthy, the world as not totally uncontrollable and the future as not totally hopeless. In the later stages of therapy, clients are invited to examine their underlying assumptions and core beliefs and to carefully find evidence to challenge the depressogenic schemas that leave them vulnerable to further episodes of depression. In McCullough's (2000) cognitive behavioural analysis, clients learn to replace ineffective beliefs and coping strategies with more effective alternatives. In all forms of CBT, clients develop strategies for identifying and managing life stresses that might precipitate relapses. In maintenance-oriented mindfulness-based CBT (Segal et al., 2002), clients learn to use meditation to prevent relapse. As part of the therapeutic process, clients may be invited to read books such as David Burns' (1999) *The feeling good handbook* or Paul Gilbert's (2000) *Overcoming depression*, both of which are well-written CBT-based self-help books. Detailed CBT manuals for therapists by McCullough (2000), Moore and Garland (2003), Padesky and Greenberger (1995), and Persons et al. (2001) are also available.

Re-activation using behavioural strategies

After assessment and formulation, much of the first part of CBT focuses on re-activation. For re-activation the overall aim is to help clients become more physically active and to engage in more pleasant events in their daily lives.

Activity scheduling

Begin by helping clients discover the link between physical activity level and mood. Asking depressed clients to remember their moods and the activities associated with them often yields little information because of the tendency for depressed people to remember only negative things in an overly general way. In therapy, the link between activity and mood can be established by asking clients to give a mood rating on a 10-point scale, then engage in a physical activity like pacing up and down the room ten or twenty times until their mood improves by one point on the 10-point scale. Another option is to ask clients to keep a diary for a week and note down each day on an hourly basis the activity they did for that hour and their mood rating on a 10-point scale. By examining this diary, evidence for a link between activity level and mood can be established. Once clients discover the link between activity and mood, invite them to schedule brief periods of daily physical activity and to keep a diary of their mood ratings before and after these activity periods. Review these diaries and use evidence from them to further reinforce clients' acknowledgement of the link between activity and mood and their motivation to exercise daily.

Pleasant event scheduling

In a similar vein, invite clients to list events that have brought them or might in the future bring them high levels of pleasure or a sense of mastery as rated on 10-point scales. Then help clients to schedule some of these activities into their lives, by planning each day to do one or more of these pleasant events at specific times and in specific circumstances. Ask clients to keep a diary of their mood ratings before and after these pleasant events. Review these diaries and use evidence from them to further reinforce clients' acknowledgement of the link between pleasant events and mood and their motivation to do something pleasant every day.

Graded task assignment and self-reward

For activity and pleasant-event scheduling, encourage clients to start with small tasks and gradually assign themselves increasingly more demanding and challenging tasks. Then coach them in using rewarding self-statements to self-reinforce their completion of self-assigned tasks.

Managing insomnia

Sleep difficulties may interfere with the re-activation process. For these, give instructions on sleep hygiene in Table 8.5 (Morin & Espie, 2003). If clients are to be prescribed antidepressants as part of a multi-modal programme and insomnia is a central feature of the depressive presentation, sedative antidepressants taken before retiring may resolve the sleep problem. Where sleep problems do not respond with either of these measures, benzodiazepines may be considered.

Cognitive restructuring using cognitive strategies

Once clients have become re-activated through behavioural interventions, much of the second part of CBT focuses on using cognitive strategies to help them change their depressive thinking routines. Cognitive restructuring involves self-monitoring, thought catching and using a variety of techniques to challenge negative automatic thoughts, cognitive distortions, underlying assumptions and core beliefs.

ABC analysis, thought catching and self-monitoring

Begin with an ABC analysis of a specific situation where a drop in mood (C) occurred on a 10-point scale. Invite clients to pinpoint the activating event (A) that led to the mood change. Then invite clients to guess what they must have told themselves about the activating event for it to lead to a drop in

Table 8.5 Sleep hygiene

Keep a record of the times you spend sleeping each day throughout this programme. This should take account of daytime naps and periods of late night or early morning waking
Set a goal of what 'a good night's sleep' would entail, e.g. 7 hours unbroken sleep
Set regular times for going to bed and rising
Avoid all daytime naps
Make your bedroom quiet, dark and heated to a level that you find comfortable
If you need a clock in your room, use an electric one with a dim display, not a loud-ticking mechanical clock with a bright luminous display, which may keep you awake
For 2 hours before going to bed, avoid vigorous exercise, heavy meals, smoking and all drinks, especially those containing alcohol, caffeine or stimulants
Practise the relaxation, breathing and visualization exercise in Table 3.5 (p. 95) before sleeping, and focus on doing the exercises well, not trying to fall asleep as this may induce sleep-preventing anxiety
Use your bed for sleep and sex only, not for reading, talking on the phone or any other activity associated with wakefulness
If you do not fall asleep within 20 minutes, go to another room and write down any negative racing thoughts and make a commitment to read and challenge them in the morning
Finally, expect this programme to take effect slowly and monitor progress on your daily record of sleep and wakefulness

mood from, say, 5 to 3 on a 10-point scale. Helping clients to articulate these negative self-statements or negative automatic thoughts (B) can be a slow process and may require prompting. But after practising thought catching in therapy sessions in response to minor fluctuations in mood, clients may be invited to regularly monitor significant mood changes that occur each day and for each of these to record the mood change (C), the activating event (A) that preceded the mood change, and the intervening automatic thought (B) or appraisal of the situation that caused the drop in mood. Give clients a three-column ABC daily thought record to use for this self-monitoring task.

Questioning the evidence

When clients have successfully completed a period of self-monitoring using a three-column ABC daily thought record and developed good 'thought-catching' skills, invite them in therapy to list evidence for and against a specific negative automatic thought (B) associated with a specific activating event (A). Questioning the evidence involves inviting clients to distance themselves from the automatic thought or assumption and to accept that a pessimistic interpretation of an activating event is only one possible interpretation of the situation, not a true fact. Distancing sets the stage for stating the evidence for or against the negative automatic thought. The client is invited to state or write down an alternative balanced belief to replace the negative automatic thought or assumption. Once clients have stated or written down the new belief, ask them to rate the degree to which they believe it on a scale from 1 to 10. Also invite them to state or write down the emotion this new belief makes them feel and to rate its intensity on a scale from 1 to 10. Finally, invite them to note if there has been an improvement in their emotional state. This final step offers proof for the effectiveness of the cognitive strategy in improving the client's well-being. A thought record that is specially designed for this technique is contained in Table 3.4 (p. 89). In the first three columns, the activating events (A), negative automatic thoughts (B) and low moods (C) arising from these thoughts are noted. In the next two columns, evidence for and against negative automatic thoughts is given. In the sixth column, an alternative more balanced interpretation of the situation is recorded. Finally, the last column is used to record information about emotional and cognitive changes arising from questioning the evidence for the negative belief. This thought record can be used within therapy sessions to provide focus for questioning the evidence, and as the basis for a homework assignment of using questioning the evidence in their day-to-day lives as a coping strategy.

Behavioural experiments

To generate evidence to test the validity of negative automatic thoughts, underlying assumptions, or core beliefs, invite clients to set up behavioural experiments. In setting these up, collaboratively develop tasks that will have a good chance of refuting the client's negative beliefs and make sure that the client fully understands exactly what they are being invited to do. In the case example at the start of the chapter, Ruth believed that she always forgot important family events and so was a failure as a mother. As a behavioural experiment to test this belief, she put a big poster up in the kitchen to remind her to go to her son's football match on Friday. Afterwards she wrote down exactly what her son did and said. In the session that followed, this experiment was reviewed and led Ruth to believe that under certain circumstances she could remember some important things and that in these situations her child did not behave as if she were a bad mother, but rather a good-enough mother. When setting up these sorts of experiments, invite clients to anticipate possible problems and collaborate on developing a list of strategies to overcome setbacks. Also ask clients to write down the outcome of experiments and whether they supported their negative beliefs or not.

Modifying negative cognitions

There are many ways to modify negative automatic thoughts, cognitive distortions, underlying assumptions and core beliefs. Consider using the following techniques, which are described in Chapter 3, in modifying depressive cognitions: belief surveys, challenging distortions, thinking in shades of grey, reattribution, cost–benefit analysis, focusing on the positive, showing self-compassion, using less extreme language, pie-chart analysis, core belief test and the positive daily log.

Developing effective coping strategies

McCullough (2000) has developed a cognitive behavioural analysis system of psychotherapy in which there is a focus on helping clients develop more effective coping strategies. An underlying assumption of this approach to therapy is that coping strategies used by clients with chronic depression rarely lead to clients having their needs met. Situational analysis is McCullough's main therapeutic technique. Clients are invited in each therapy session to describe problematic or challenging interpersonal situations. For each situation, they must describe in detail: (1) the sequence of events; (2) their interpretation and beliefs about the situation; (3) what exactly they did and said to cope with the situation; (4) the actual outcome specifying what happened, what they thought and what they felt; (5) the desired outcome specifying what they would have liked to have happened and what they would have liked to have thought and felt; and (6) whether the desired outcome was achieved. You may interview clients using this questioning format and also ask clients to keep a record of problematic situations between sessions using these six headings. For each situation, invite clients to consider alternative interpretations of the situation and alternative behavioural coping strategies that they could have used to achieve the outcome they desired rather than the one that actually happened. Finally, invite clients to consider in future how they might apply the lessons learned through analysis of the situation to similar future situations.

Addressing resistance in CBT

Where clients have difficulty following through on any CBT tasks, invite them to recall all the blocks to task completion and then to anticipate possible blocks they might encounter when they attempt such tasks in future. Collaborate with clients in brainstorming coping strategies for overcoming blocks to task completion and then rehearsing these in therapy. For therapists, one of the major challenges in managing resistance effectively is to avoid becoming overly dominant, active or hostile because these interpersonal styles increase clients' tendencies to respond with submissiveness, underactivity and withdrawal. McCullough (2000) argues that therapists should assess the reactions clients elicit in them after the second session using Kiesler's (1987) Impact Message Inventory to make them aware of unhelpful knee-jerk reactions. The management of these reactions should be routinely reviewed in supervision.

Disengagement

In later sessions of CBT, recap lessons learned during therapy about mood management and help clients anticipate and plan how to manage future situations in which there is risk of relapse. For clients who have had three or more episodes of depression, consider offering mindfulness maintenance therapy to further delay or prevent relapses.

CBT-mindfulness maintenance therapy

Mindfulness maintenance therapy is premised on the idea that relapses occur when minor stresses that lead to small initial mood changes are interpreted negatively and result in an avalanche of rumination and catastrophic negative thinking. This, in turn, leads to drastic intensification of depressive mood, and subsequent constriction of activity and dysregulation of neurobiological systems underpinning depression (Segal et al., 2002). The aim of mindfulness-based CBT is to train clients in the mindfulness skills required to nip this process in the bud. Clients learn to decentre or distance themselves from their thinking processes. They learn, 'I am not my thoughts and my thoughts are not the truth or reality; they are simply thoughts'. Ask clients to regularly set aside periods of fifteen to forty-five minutes a day and, during these periods, to practice mindfulness meditations such as those in Tables 8.6 and 8.7. As thought, feelings and bodily sensations arise in these exercises in consciousness, however pleasant or unpleasant, clients acknowledge their occurrence in a welcoming, invitational and friendly way, but then let them go without trying to change or fix them. This mindfulness practice helps clients detach themselves from all types of ideas and sensations that enter consciousness and is helpful in allowing them to let go of depressive thoughts when they arise in response to minor decreases in mood. The attitude of mindfulness prevents clients from getting stuck in vicious cycles of catastrophic thinking central to the depressive experience or in personal battles centred on trying to find evidence for positive interpretations and against negative interpretations of situations, central to routine CBT. In mindfulness-based CBT, there is no attempt to coach clients into stopping or preventing the occurrence of depressive thought or negative affect. Rather, the focus is on helping clients observe these negative thoughts and feelings and then let them pass. Developing this skill requires daily practice of mindfulness exercises such as those in Tables 8.6, 8.7 and 8.8.

A useful conceptual distinction is made in mindfulness-based cognitive therapy between the 'doing' and 'being' mode, which is included in the rationale given for practising mindfulness meditations. When there is a discrepancy between the way our lives are now and the way we would like them to be, we experience negative affect and attempt to reduce this by automatically switching into the doing mode. In this mode we plan ways to reduce the

Table 8.6 Body scan meditation

Lie down on your back in a place where you will not be disturbed or distracted. Allow your eyes to close
Allow your attention to focus on your breathing
Bring your awareness to any sensations you have where your body makes contact with the mat on which you are lying
On each out breath allow yourself to sink a little deeper into the mat
Remind yourself that your intention is not to relax but, as best you can, to bring your attention to focus on each part of your body in turn
Bring your attention to your lower abdomen and notice the sensations that occur as you breathe in and out
Bring your attention to your right leg, down your right leg to your right foot, and out to the toes of the right foot. Focus on each of the toes in turn and notice the quality of sensations you find
Now, as you inhale, imagine your breath passing down into your lungs, through your abdomen down your right leg and into your foot and from there into the toes of your right foot. As you exhale, imagine your breath passing from your toes, into the foot, up the leg into your abdomen, chest and out through your nose. Continue this for a few breaths, breathing down into the toes and back out from the toes
Now, when you are ready for an out breath, let go of awareness of your toes and bring awareness to the sensations in the bottom of your right foot. Notice the sensations in the sole of the foot, the heel where it connects with the mat, and the instep. As you inhale, imagine your breath passing down into your lungs, through your abdomen down your right leg and into your foot. As you exhale, imagine your breath passing from the foot, up the leg into your abdomen, chest and out through your nose. Continue this for a few breaths breathing down into the foot and back out from the foot. Allow the sensations in your foot to be in the foreground of your awareness and your breath to be in the background
Now allow the awareness to expand into the rest of your foot, to the top of the foot, the ankle, the joints and other parts of the foot. Then, as you exhale, let go of awareness of the foot and bring your attention to the lower leg, calf, shin, knee and so forth in turn
Continue to bring awareness and gentle curiosity to the physical sensations in each part of your body in turn . . . to the upper right leg, your left toes, foot, leg, pelvic area, back, abdomen, chest, fingers, hands, arms, shoulders, neck, head and face. As you leave each area, breathe into it as you inhale and then let go of the region as you exhale
When you become aware of tension or any other intense sensation in a particular part of your body, breathe into them and bring your awareness right into the sensation as you inhale and let go or release awareness from the sensation as you exhale
From time to time, the mind will drift away from the breath and the body. This is what the mind naturally does. When this happens, acknowledge it, noticing where the mind has drifted. Gently return you attention to that part of the body you were focusing on before your mind drifted
When you have scanned all parts of the body, spend a few minutes being aware of the body as a whole and of the breath flowing in and out of the body
If you drift into sleep when doing this body scan meditation, you may prefer to do it in a sitting position

Table 8.7 Mindfulness of breathing

Sit in a chair with feet flat on the floor, the spine straight and not resting against the chair back, and the eyes gently closed
Bring awareness to the sensations you feel where your body makes contact with the chair and the floor
Bring awareness to sensations in the lower abdominal wall as the breath moves in and out of the body
Follow with your awareness the changing physical sensations in the abdomen as the breath enters your body as you inhale, the slight pause that may occur before you exhale, the sensations that occur as you exhale, and the slight pause that may occur before you inhale again
There is no need to control your breathing. Just allow it to occur. And in the same way allow your experience to be your experience without trying to control it
From time to time, the mind will drift away from the breath. This is what the mind naturally does. When this happens acknowledge it, noticing where the mind has drifted. Gently return you attention to the abdominal wall again as the breath moves in and out of the body
When you notice your awareness has drifted, congratulate yourself for coming back to being aware of your present experience
When the mind drifts, see these as opportunities to bring patience, gentle curiosity, and kindness to your awareness as you lead it back to focus on the breath
Continue for 15 minutes, using your breath as an anchor to gently reconnect you to the present moment each time your notice your mind has wandered

discrepancy between actual and desired circumstances. However, if reducing this discrepancy is very challenging and beyond our control we become stuck in endless rumination, which in turn intensifies negative affect. This type of experience probably leads to relapse in people with chronic depression. The past, present and future are addressed in different ways in the doing and being modes. In the doing mode, the focus is on the past or the future: rehearsing past attempts to solve similar sorts of problems and anticipating how these might be applied in the future. In contrast, in the being mode, attention is focused on directly experiencing the present moment. The degree of goal-directedness, monitoring and evaluation differs in the doing and being modes. In the doing mode, we monitor and evaluate our performance in achieving the goal of reducing the gap between the actual and desired situation. In contrast, in the being mode, we allow and welcome all experiences equally without evaluation and with wide-ranging curiosity rather than narrowly focused goal-directedness. In the doing and being modes, we have different sorts of relationships with our thoughts and emotions. In the doing mode, thoughts about how to reduce the discrepancy between what is and what ought to be and positive and negative feelings are accorded the status of true reflections of reality. Thus, thoughts are things to be acted on and

Table 8.8 Daily mindfulness

When you are faced with very challenging situations that you cannot control, your mood may drop. If you notice this drop, you may try to improve your mood by looking for ways to control the situation
As you inevitably fail in your attempts to control the uncontrollable, your mood may worsen further; you judge your efforts as ineffective and yourself as incompetent
In these circumstances, practise your mindfulness skills
Acknowledge your drop in mood as an event that occurred, but do not judge it as good or bad
Focus attention on your breathing and, if your mind drifts, to planning ways to control the uncontrollable, acknowledge these thoughts as events and return your awareness to your breathing as your thoughts pass
To be able to do this in times of crisis, practise daily mindfulness
When you wake, before you get out of bed, bring attention to your breathing and observe five mindful breaths
When you change posture, practise mindfulness. As you move from lying down, to standing, to sitting, to walking, be mindful of these changes in posture, bringing awareness to the changing sensations
When there are noticeable changes in your environment, practise mindfulness. When you hear the phone ring, a car horn sound, a door closing, use the sound as a signal to observe five mindful breaths
When you eat, bring awareness to the taste, smell and sensations associated with eating your food
When you do routine activities, practise mindfulness. Bring attention to your sensations at the moment, to the feel of the wind on your face if you are walking, to the feel of the water if you are washing the dishes, to the sensations of standing still if you are queuing
Before you sleep, bring attention to your breathing and observe five mindful breaths

feelings are things to be actively sought out or avoided. In the being mode, thoughts and emotions are accorded a similar status as sounds, sights, smells or bodily sensations. They are accepted as passing events that come to be objects of awareness and then pass out of consciousness. Thoughts are not seen as things to be acted on and feelings are not viewed as things to be prolonged or avoided. Mindfulness skills allow us to switch gear from the doing to the being mode. This gear switching is a core skill for preventing relapses in recurrent depression, since it provides a way out of chronic rumination that often precipitates relapse.

In the mindfulness-based relapse prevention programme, described in detail in Segal et al. (2002), in all eight sessions, clients are instructed in body scan and mindfulness of breathing exercise, similar to those given in Table 8.6 and 8.7. Key points covered by the programme include the following:

- When we are on automatic pilot we are more likely to slip into patterns of thinking that precipitate depression, so practise mindfulness every day.

- Negative emotions arise from negative interpretations and judgements of situations, so allow yourself to acknowledge situations without judging them.
- When practising mindfulness, allow attention to move to positive and negative thoughts, feelings and sensations as they arise, and then gently return attention to breathing.
- Thoughts are not facts and we are not our thoughts, so depressive thinking need not be grounds for despair.
- Know the signs of relapse and plan to practise mindfulness when relapse threatens.

Segal et al. (2002) argue that to effectively deliver a mindfulness-based relapse prevention programme it is important to have developed a mindfulness practice oneself. A good place to start, they suggest, is with Dr Jon Kabat Zinn's (1995) book, *Wherever you go, there you are. Mindfulness meditation in everyday life* or his programme, available on CD, which can be ordered at http://www.stressreductiontapes.com/

Interpersonal therapy

Therapeutic interventions from the psychodynamic tradition have been shown in outcome studies to alleviate depression (Shapiro, 1998). Of the various models from this tradition, interpersonal therapy based on the work of Harry Stack Sullivan (1953) is the best validated (Weissman et al., 2000). In interpersonal therapy (IPT), it is assumed that depression is determined multi-factorially, but that interpersonal difficulties play a central role in the maintenance of depressive symptoms. Four categories of interpersonal difficulty are of central concern in IPT: (1) grief associated with the loss of a loved one; (2) role disputes involving family members, friends or colleagues; (3) role transitions such as starting or ending relationships within the family or work context, moving jobs or houses, graduation, promotion, retirement, or diagnosis of an illness; and (4) interpersonal deficits, particularly poor social skills for making and maintaining relationships. In IPT, in the assessment and formulation stage, pay particular attention to the role of these factors in the maintenance of the current depressive symptoms. Review positive and negative changes in current and past relationships and expectations, satisfaction with, and wishes for these relationships as they relate to the current episode of depression. During feedback of the formulation to the client, highlight the way one or more factors in the four categories listed above appear to maintain the current depression. Then establish a therapeutic contract to address these specific focal interpersonal factors that maintain the symptoms. Set specific attainable goals and specify the duration and frequency of sessions. Usually for IPT, twelve to sixteen sessions are required for treatment to be effective. During the assessment and formulation stage, convey an acknowledgement that it is legitimate to adopt the 'sick role' and that clients do not deserve to be negatively judged for not fulfilling their social roles because of their depressive illness. However, the other side of this 'sick role' framing of depression is that the therapeutic contract is an invitation for clients to take responsibility for recovery from their depressive illness. As part of the therapeutic process they may be invited to read Myrna Weissman's (1995) *Mastering depression: A patient's guide to interpersonal psychotherapy*. In IPT, specific therapeutic strategies are used to help clients address grief, role disputes, role transitions and interpersonal deficits as detailed in Weissman et al.'s (2000) therapy manual.

Grief

Where grief due to complicated bereavement following the death of a loved one is a central factor maintaining depression, the aim of IPT is to facilitate mourning and help the client find relationships and activities to compensate for the loss. To achieve this aim, use the following strategies. Review the onset, nature and course of depressive symptoms. Review in detail the client's relationship with the deceased. Make links between the course of the relationship with the deceased, that person's death and the aftermath of this on the one hand, and the course of the depressive symptoms on the other. Concurrently facilitate the exploration and re-experiencing of feelings associated with the deceased over the course of the relationship. When progress has been made with this grief work, shift the focus onto the future and then explore possible ways of becoming more involved with others. Pace the transition from a focus on mourning the past and anticipating the future to match the degree to which the client has resolved their feelings of grief and their readiness to look to the future.

Role disputes

Marital disharmony or difficulties involving other family members, friends or colleagues are among the more significant role disputes associated with depression. Where role disputes are a central factor maintaining depression, the aim of IPT is to help the client clearly identify the dispute and develop and implement a plan for resolving it. To achieve this aim, use the following strategies. Review the onset, nature and course of depressive symptoms. Identify the current dispute, which may be obvious (e.g. domestic violence) or covertly concealed (e.g. an uneasy feeling about the unspoken possibility of infidelity). Explore the onset and course of the current dispute. Determine the developmental stage of the dispute. If the client believes the dispute is irresolvable, facilitate withdrawal from the relationship in which the dispute is occurring and mourn this loss. If the dispute has reached an impasse, increase disharmony to create movement towards the stage of renegotiation. If it is at the stage where renegotiation is the aim, then facilitate this process by helping partners calmly communicate about it. In facilitating renegotiation, help clients specify the core issue in the dispute and their different expectations and values about this issue. In exploring the present dispute, facilitate framing it in as solvable a way as possible. Then brainstorm multiple options for resolving it. Look at the pros and cons of each. Explore the resources available for resolving the dispute or changing the relationship. Explore the barriers to resolving the conflict by trying to help the client answer these questions: Is the client showing a similar pattern of conflict in this relationship as in others? What assumptions underlie the client's position in this and other similar disputes? What is being gained by not resolving the dispute or what will be lost if it is resolved? Help the client select the best option for resolving the dispute and then plan in detail how to implement and review the impact of this plan.

Role transitions

Starting or ending relationships within the family or work context, moving jobs or houses, graduation, promotion, retirement or diagnosis of an illness are some of the role transitions associated with depression. Where role transitions are a central factor maintaining depression, IPT aims to help the client mourn the loss of the old role, appreciate the benefits of the new one, and develop a sense of mastery concerning the demands of the new role. To achieve this aim use the following strategies. Review the onset, nature and course of depressive symptoms. Relate the depressive symptoms to a recent role change. Review the positive and negative aspects of the new and old roles. Explore and ventilate feelings about the loss of the old role and the process of change from one role to another. Facilitate the development of social support and new skills to help the client manage the demands of the new role.

Social skills deficits

Where depression is maintained by difficulties making and maintaining significant relationships, the aim of IPT is to help clients reduce social isolation and form new relationships. To achieve this aim use the following strategies: Review the onset, nature and course of depressive symptoms. Relate the depressive symptoms to social isolation. Review positive and negative aspects of past relationships, noting in particular repetitive self-defeating patterns that lead to isolation. Discuss the client's positive and negative feelings about the therapist and clarify parallels between the therapeutic relationship and other current relationships in the client's life. The psychodynamic therapy techniques described in Chapter 4 for drawing parallels between the therapeutic relationship and relationships with other significant people in the client's life may be used here.

Specific techniques

In IPT a number of specific techniques are used to implement the strategies outlined above for each of the problem areas. These are:

- exploratory techniques
- clarification
- communication analysis
- encouragement of affect
- use of the therapeutic relationship
- behaviour change techniques.

Exploratory techniques include non-directive exploration and direct elicitation. With non-directive exploration, ask open questions (e.g. How have your been . . .?) and encourage disclosure through maintaining receptive silence; supportive acknowledgement (e.g. saying 'mm', 'hmm' while nodding); and encouraging extension of the topic discussed (e.g. 'Tell me more about that'). While non-directive exploration is largely client-led, direct elicitation is a therapist-led approach to inquiry. With direct elicitation, follow a specific line of questioning to obtain details about a specific issue ('Tell me about . . .?' 'What happened when . . .?' 'Who . . .?' 'What . . .?' 'When . . .?' 'Where . . .?' 'Why . . .?' 'How . . .?') Non-directive exploration is useful to obtain the client's perspective on a situation. Direct elicitation is a useful way to fill in details missing from the account given by the client. Used appropriately, non-directive exploration generates a climate of acceptance and creates an opportunity for clients to take responsibility for making sense of their difficulties. However, used inappropriately with clients who have difficulty verbalizing their difficulties, it can lead to clients feeling despondent because they view the therapy as going nowhere and the therapist as incompetent. Direct elicitation, used appropriately can give clients a sense that the therapist is interested and competent in making sense of their life situation, but used inappropriately it can create an inquisitorial judgemental atmosphere. Skilled therapists balance the use of non-directive exploration and direct elicitation.

Clarification is used to restructure what the client has said so that it makes some implicit belief, assumption, contradiction, inconsistency, or link between ideas, events and emotions clearer to the client. Here are some ways you can clarify. Ask the client to repeat a key phrase or sentence that may highlight an assumption or inconsistency such as 'I left him because I wanted him near me'. Briefly paraphrase and encapsulate key ideas, inconsistencies, or connections in a client's extensive monologue, for example 'From your account of that conversation, it sounds like you wanted him to support you, but you found yourself withdrawing from him'. Point out assumptions implicit in what the client has said, for example, 'It seems that you may hold a belief that you should not ask for support because you may be rejected and you might find this too hard to cope with'. Clarification is used in CBT to pinpoint negative automatic thoughts and assumptions, but then the focus shifts to challenging the validity of these. In IPT, no attempt is made to challenge unhelpful beliefs, inconsistencies and contradictions. Rather, they are simply brought to the client's attention.

Communication analysis is used to help clients identify communication failures and communicate more effectively. Ask clients to select a specific conversation or dispute in which communication failure led to an unsuccessful outcome. Ask clients to reconstruct a verbatim transcript of the conversation in the therapy session. Then ask clients to specify exactly what they hoped to achieve through having the conversation, and what expectations and assumptions they had about the way their verbal and non-verbal communications would be interpreted by the other person. From the account of the actual conversation and the clients' intentions and assumptions, invite clients to pinpoint one or more of the following communication failures: expecting others to know one's needs and wishes, such as needing support, without them being explicitly stated; using indirect or non-verbal communication, such as sulking or self-harm, rather than direct verbal confrontation to communicate complex messages such as 'I'm angry at you because you are not supporting me'; and failing to check that one's understanding was accurate, for example misinterpreting the statement 'I'll be home late today' as meaning 'I don't like you so I'm not coming home early' and then not checking the accuracy of this misinterpretation. When clients identify their communication failures, help them develop ways to communicate their ideas directly and clearly and to check that they have accurately understood others. Communication analysis is central to helping clients deal with role disputes. This is very similar to an individualized version of communication training used in behavioural marital therapy and to assertiveness training.

Encouragement of affect is central to IPT because many depressed clients have difficulty acknowledging, accepting, understanding and regulating their emotions. Where clients are extremely emotionally constricted and are not aware that they may feel anger at the way they are being punitively treated, or affection in response to kindness shown to them by others, help these clients access and express their emotions. Begin by pointing out that, in their situation, specific feelings might be experienced by most people, but it is understandable that such feelings would be suppressed if certain outcomes were feared. Where clients have strong sexual, aggressive or other socially unacceptable emotions and feel guilt because of these, facilitate the acknowledgement, verbal expression and acceptance of these affects within the therapy session. Let clients know that it is acceptable to experience these feelings and that having the feelings does not imply that the client will be driven to act them out uncontrollably. Help clients regulate their emotions in ways that promote the achievement of therapeutic goals. For example, clients who experience anger because of the uncaring way their partners treat them may use this anger as a signal for them to act assertively rather than punish themselves for feeling angry. Such clients may be helped to let their partners know how being treated unkindly hurts them and to ask their partners to treat them in kinder ways.

Use the therapeutic relationship to help clients understand other relationships. Explore clients' positive and negative beliefs, expectations, emotions and behaviour within the therapeutic relationship. Take special care to give clients permission to voice negative feelings and criticisms, however minor, and any possible distortions of the therapeutic relationship. Then draw parallels between the way the client interprets and manages the therapeutic relationship and the way he or she manages other important relationships. Where role disputes are a focus for therapy, use the therapeutic relationship to help clients see how their interactional style prevents them from resolving differences and then help them develop new ways for doing so within the safety of the therapeutic relationship. Where grief and loss are the focus of IPT, point out the clients' tendency to emotionally cut themselves off from others or to develop relationships that mirror the one with the lost person. Where difficulty making and maintaining relationships is the focus for IPT, help clients use the therapeutic relationship as a model for developing other supportive relationships outside therapy. Many of the psychodynamic techniques in Chapter 4 can be used in IPT to encourage the expression of affect and to help clients use the therapeutic relationship as a vehicle for change.

Behaviour change techniques include psychoeducation, decision analysis and role-play. In psychoeducation, give clients information about their condition, factors affecting it and tried and tested ways of managing practical problems associated with it in a way that matches their readiness and ability to understand it. With decision analysis, help clients systematically define their difficulties in solvable terms, generate multiple solutions, explore the pros and cons of these, implement the most feasible solution and modify the solution in light of progress or lack thereof. With role-playing, take the role of a significant person in the client's life and invite the client to use the exercise to demonstrate their usual way of interacting and as a safe forum within which to rehearse alternative and more effective ways of interacting with others. Role-playing may be used to help clients develop communication skills, assertiveness skills or skills for requesting support.

Disengagement

In brief IPT, as the final session approaches facilitate grieving the loss of the therapeutic relationship and the client's recognition of their independent competence in managing depressive illness. If treatment has been ineffective, then acknowledge to the client that IPT was ineffective, just as some anti-depressants are ineffective. Framc this as a limitation of the treatment, not the client.

Maintenance IPT

Where clients have a history of three or more episodes of depression, offering monthly maintenance IPT is appropriate as there is good evidence that this can prevent relapse. In maintenance therapy, invite clients at each session to review the current challenges in their lives. Formulate and address these challenges in terms of grief, role disputes, role transitions, or skills deficits.

Integrative systemic couples therapy for depression

There is evidence from controlled trials for the effectiveness of three different couples-based approaches to the treatment of depression: systemic couples therapy (Jones & Asen, 1999), cognitive behavioural couples therapy (Gollan et al., 2002) and conjoint marital interpersonal therapy (Weissman et al., 2000). This section describes an integrative systemic approach to couples therapy (ISCT) for depression, which draws together key elements from these three empirically supported models of practice and which is consistent with the model of practice described in Chapter 5 (Carr, 2000). Within ISCT it is assumed that in response to stressful life events, psychosocially or biologically vulnerable individuals develop depression, and this comes to be maintained by repetitive patterns of family interaction and associated belief systems (following the three-column model of problem formulation outlined in Chapter 5). The aim of systemic couples therapy is to help couples understand these types of three-column formulations of episodes that strengthen depression and exceptions to these situations, as illustrated in the case example that opened this chapter and the formulations in Figures 8.1 and 8.2. A further aim of therapy is to help couples find new ways of dealing with depression that promote recovery and prevent relapse.

Planning and developing hypotheses

When a client in a marriage or long-term relationship is referred for treatment of depression, it is appropriate to invite the client and their partner to attend an assessment session. The importance of the partner's perspective in giving a fuller account of the difficulties may be offered as a rationale for this joint invitation. In planning what lines of questioning to follow when developing three-column formulations in assessment interviews, a number of hypotheses deserve consideration. These are based on extensive research findings and clinical experience (Bech, 2000; Carr, 2000; Craighead et al., 2002;

Crits-Cristoph & Barber, 2002; Gotlib & Hammen, 2002; Joiner & Coyne, 1999; Jones & Asen, 1999; Joyce, 2000; Murray & Lopez, 1998; Power, 2004; Segal et al., 2002; Williams et al., 1997). What follows are useful hypotheses to consider in cases of depression.

Behaviour patterns

Depression may be strengthened by behaviour patterns that represent unsuccessful attempted solutions for alleviating low mood or depressive behaviour. In these behaviour patterns, couples may become entrenched in rigid roles of care-giving and care-receiving, decomposition, criticism, abuse or mutual distancing.

Belief systems

Partners' roles in rigid behaviour patterns may be maintained by the depressed clients' pessimistic beliefs about powerlessness to change the situation and their partners' construing them as invalids, malingerers, or nuisances to be avoided rather than 'good people with bad problems'. Roles in depression-maintaining behaviour patterns may also be maintained by explicit or implicit beliefs that depression involves some payoff, such as preventing the family from breaking up, communicating to members of the extended family that they are needed as carers, keeping alive the memory of a deceased family member whose death precipitated the depression, regulating the emotional distance or level of intimacy between partners, regulating the power balance within the marriage, providing the depressed person with a break from the demands of ordinary life or providing the depressed person with punishment for past sins.

Precipitating factors

Episodes of depression may be precipitated or exacerbated by major family lifecycle transitions such as births or bereavements, work-related transitions such as redundancy, culture-related stress such as immigration or discrimination, health-related stresses such as diagnosis of a major illness or infertility, or other environmental stresses such as major accidents or natural disasters. Where clients have had many previous episodes of depression, minor stresses may precipitate catastrophic thinking that another episode of depression is about to happen and this may become a self-fulfilling prophecy. Once clients develop depression, referrals for treatment may be precipitated by the increased demands clients place on their families or referrers or by the diminished capacity of families or referrers to cope because of some depletion in the coping resources of families or referring agencies.

Predisposing constitutional, historical and contextual factors

Couples may become entrenched in rigid behaviour patterns and unhelpful belief systems that strengthen depression because of a wide range of predisposing constitutional, historical and contextual factors. These include the presence of a family history and genetic vulnerability to depression or a psychosocial vulnerability associated with early-life loss, trauma, abuse, deprivation or stress, or multiple previous episodes of depression. Clients may also be vulnerable to depression because they have demographic characteristics associated with marital difficulties and depression such as having high stress and low social support, being of lower socioeconomic status, living in urban areas, having married before the age of 20, having had a premarital pregnancy, living alone with young children and being involved in a relationship where partners are from different cultures with differing role expectations.

Protective factors

Exceptions to problematic behaviour patterns may be underpinned by resourceful belief systems and personal strengths. Exceptional patterns probably involve clear communication, good problem solving, a degree of psychological intimacy and power sharing, positive and constructive beliefs about managing relationships, and all of these resources may have their roots in positive early experiences, current involvement in positive social networks and positive demographic profiles. Similarity of cultural values and role expectations, high socioeconomic status, living in a rural area, good mental health, absence of parental divorce, absence of premarital pregnancy and marriage after the age of 30 have all been identified as key factors in positive demographic profiles associated with good adjustment in long-term relationships. The lack of conflict over values associated with similarity of cultural background, the economic resources associated with high socioeconomic status, the community integration associated with rural living, the psychological resources associated with maturity and the model of marital stability offered by non-divorced parents are the more common explanations given for the associations among these factors associated with relationship stability.

Assessment and formulation

Establish a contract for assessment in which it is clear that one to three sessions will be required to develop an understanding of the main problems, suitability for treatment and treatment goals. Individuals who are able to construe couples therapy as an opportunity for making a fresh start are more likely to benefit from treatment, so it is important to find an opportunity in the early sessions to convey this idea. Engagement is a therapeutic priority during the assessment and when resistance occurs during treatment.

Engagement involves developing a relationship with clients within which they feel safe enough to explore new and challenging ways of understanding and managing their lives. Adopt a collaborative, neutral, respectful, curious position. Leave both members of the couple in no doubt that both of their viewpoints are respected as valid. Convey verbally and non-verbally that multiple perspectives on the problem can be safely explored within the therapeutic context.

Begin by inviting partners to describe patterns of interaction that strengthen depression and into which they inadvertently fall. Explore the beliefs that underpin their roles in these patterns and predisposing constitutional, historical and contextual factors that may underpin these beliefs and roles. In a similar vein, inquire about exceptional circumstances that do not strengthen depression, and the beliefs and predisposing strengths associated with these productive patterns of behaviour. Use the hypotheses listed in the previous section and the questioning style described in Chapter 5 to inform this part of the assessment.

To help develop problem and solution formulations, explore the course of past episodes of depression, past episodes of successful and unsuccessful treatment, the roles the couple and others played in these episodes, and the way they made sense of the course of depression and its treatment. Explore the pattern of current family relationships and relationships in the couples' families of origin through genogram construction, as outlined in Chapter 5. Explore links between events and relationships across the family lifecycle and the course of the client's depression and its treatment.

Once problem and exception formulations like those in Figures 8.1 and 8.2 have been developed, discuss the formulations with the couple. Stress the couple's strengths in this feedback process to engender optimism. Match the level of detail in discussing the problem and exception formulations to the couple's ability to understand them and their emotional readiness to accept them. Empathize with each partner's position when outlining their roles in patterns that strengthen depression. Usually, partners are well intentioned but under stress. Without adequate information, they inadvertently contribute to these patterns. In light of this systemic understanding, invite couples to set goals and select directions in which they would like to move to achieve these goals. Help couples set realistic achievable goals. In cases of chronic or severe depression, invite partners to describe the minimal change that would be necessary for them to know that recovery had started.

Treatment

Establish a contract for treatment specifying a limited number of sessions (up to twenty) of set duration but variable spacing. Where one member is housebound or hospitalized, at least some of the later sessions should be conducted on a routine outpatient basis rather than in hospital or in the couple's home. It is also good practice to let the couple know that available evidence suggests two out of three couples benefit from treatment, as discussed in Chapter 5. Mention that in most couples in which one partner has been depressed, the difficulties that this causes lead both partners to consider separation and some couples separate once there is sign of recovery. For this reason, invite couples to make a commitment to remain together for at least six months, so they may have a chance to experience what it would be like to live together once they have used therapy to remove the depression from their relationship. If therapy is unsuccessful (which it will be in a third of cases) or if after six months either partner is still dissatisfied, then separation may be seriously addressed at that point.

Chapter 5 gives a catalogue of many therapeutic techniques used in ISCT, based on extensive reviews of theory, research and practice of couple and family therapy (Carr, 2000). While all of these may be used in the treatment of couples overcoming depression, only techniques that are of specific relevance to mood problems will be mentioned here, specifically:

- scheduling conjoint pleasant events and routines
- externalizing depression and building on exceptions
- enactment
- challenging rigid behaviour patterns
- communication training
- problem-solving training
- creating partner support: remembering pleasant events
- creating partner support: compliments and statements of affection
- creating partner support: writing positive requests for the future
- role reversal
- opening space for recovery and taking it slow.

Scheduling conjoint pleasant events and routines

Early in therapy help couples become re-activated by listing and scheduling regular mutually pleasurable events. These may be graded in demandingness and degree of activity involved. As therapy progresses, invite couples to gradually move from low-activity non-demanding tasks, like watching a sun-set or reading to each other, to higher-activity tasks, like taking a twenty-minute walk together each day or going for a cycle. Physical exercise improves mood so it is important for couples to work towards increasing physical activity over the course of therapy. Often, depression disrupts normal family routines such as times for retiring or waking, mealtimes, times for joint household chores and so forth. Couples may be invited to reconstruct daily schedules and ensure that these include some joint physical activity and some joint periods of supportive conversation and interaction, such as shared mealtimes.

Externalizing depression and building on exceptions

From the outset, refer to depression as a problem distinct from the couple (White & Epston, 1990). Refer to it metaphorically as a negative force in their lives that they must jointly defeat. Refer to the three-column problem formulation (like that in Figure 8.1) as a pattern that strengthens depression. In contrast, refer to the exception formulation (like that in Figure 8.2) as a pattern that weakens depression. Ask the couple to recount in detail multiple instances of exceptional episodes that weakened depression or helped them to defeat depression. Then explore ways that such exceptional behaviour patterns might be reconstructed in the couple's day-to-day lives and ways positive belief systems and strengths may be used. As homework assignments, invite couples to notice the conditions under which exceptions occur or to recreate an exception. As they incorporate more exceptions into their lives that weaken the hold depression has on their relationship, invite them to speculate about what this way of defining themselves says about them as a couple. Then invite them to imagine in the future what their relationship might look like if there were many instances in which they managed to weaken depression.

Enactment

Enactment provides a concrete way of accurately identifying the point at which couples usually get stuck and creates opportunities for exploring new and more effective alternatives for couples to manage their difficulties (Jones & Asen, 1999). Invite the couple to talk to each other about a key issue, solve a problem, make a decision or offer support in their usual way. Then stop talking and leave time and space for the couple to enact their usual routine. Decline invitations to participate in the couple's discussion *during* the enactment. Once the couple become stuck and find that they cannot make any further progress, challenge the rigid behaviour patterns in which the couple are stuck.

Challenging rigid behaviour patterns

Rigid behaviour patterns, particularly those that maintain depression, may be challenged during enactments and at other times using disruption, unbalancing, intensification and boundary making. If one partner speaks far more than another, disrupt these monologues by periodically inviting the less vocal partner to give his or her views on what has been said. With unbalancing, temporarily support one partner's position. For example, with a couple who have difficulty with turn taking you may say to the interrupted wife, 'You have great patience allowing your partner to interrupt so often with such good grace. I'm inviting you to be less polite in future and to notice what happens when you follow through without interruption'. With intensification, invite the couple to persist with a transaction for longer than they normally would, to heighten the emotional tone of the exchange and so open up new possibilities for therapeutic change. For example, you may say to a conflict-avoiding couple 'Even though this discussion may be getting more heated than you would usually let it, I'm inviting you now, to keep going and notice if this helps you find a way forward'. Where the demands of parenting or connections with partners' families of origin leave limited psychological space for the couple, boundary making is an intervention that challenges this state of affairs. With boundary making, invite partners individually or jointly to regulate psychological space within the family so that each member of the couple has enough personal space and there is also adequate space for their relationship. For example, where needs of children or parents are always given higher priority than those of the couple, you may ask provocative metaphorical questions like these: 'Is there a way that you could make these decisions together without taking directions from your children or your parents? Are you married to your mother or your wife? Is your son, your partner, or are you married to your husband?' Lessons learned from challenging rigid behaviour patterns within sessions using these various techniques may be consolidated through homework assignments, such as practising turn taking without interruption for a set period of time each day, continuing a discussion of a specific emotionally laden topic beyond the usual threshold of emotional comfort or setting aside time each day when the couple can be together without interruption from children or parents. Often, challenging rigid behaviour patterns leads on to helping clients develop better communication and problem-solving skills (Jacobson & Christensen, 1998). Let us recap those skills that were previously mentioned in Chapter 5.

Communication training

Communication skills involve fair turn taking; communicating messages clearly, directly and congruently; checking that one has been understood; listening in an empathic manner; paraphrasing partners' messages and checking the accuracy of such paraphrases. Clients' attempts at clear communication may be hindered by making messages too complex or confusing, interrupting before the other person has finished, not listening, failing to summarize what the other person said accurately, attributing negative malicious intentions to the other person, failing to check that the message was accurately sent, failing to check that the message has been accurately received, blaming and sulking.

Problem-solving training

Effective problem solving involves coaching couples to reframe large, complex problems as a series of small, solvable problems. Then for each of these small problems, brainstorm multiple solutions, evaluate the pros and cons of each of these with an eye to past successful and unsuccessful solutions, select the best solution, jointly implement it, review progress and modify the selected solution if it is ineffective or celebrate success if the problem is resolved. Common pitfalls include difficulties reframing big vague problems as small solvable problems, attempting to solve more than one problem at a time and evaluating the pros and cons of solutions before as many solutions as possible have been listed. Couples may be invited to practise communication and problem-solving skills between sessions. As with all homework assignments, agree a convenient time, place and duration for such exercises and design the assignment to maximize the chances of success. Select relatively easy or emotionally undemanding topics as a focus for such tasks initially, before progressing to more challenging topics.

Creating partner support: Remembering pleasant events

People with depression have over-general memories and tend to have difficulty recalling details of autobiographical episodes that might improve their moods and when they do remember details they tend to remember more negative than positive events. Non-depressed partners may help their depressed partners use positive memories to improve their mood by regularly describing in detail pleasant events that they have jointly experienced. In therapy and as a homework assignment invite couples to set aside fifteen minutes a day to jointly remember in detail a positive episode from their lives. This support-building strategy was used in the case example that opened this chapter.

Creating partner support: Compliments and statements of affection

A common depression-maintaining interaction pattern involves the depressed person asking for reassurance (e.g. 'Do you think I'm OK?'), the non-depressed partner offering this (e.g. 'Of course you're OK!') and then the depressed partner discounting the reassurance (e.g. 'You're only saying that to reassure me. You don't mean it'). Coach non-depressed partners to refuse to offer reassurance or evaluative comments on self-critical statements, since any response to such requests will be taken to be insincere and patronizing. Instead, invite them to identify situations when they can congruently compliment their partners for doing something specific well and link these compliments to statements of affection. These statements take the form 'Just now you did ABC. I like the way you did that. That reminds me of how much I care about you'.

Creating partner support: Writing positive requests for the future

Where partners have become embroiled in rigid, hostile or critical behaviour patterns, invite each member of the couple each day to write down every thing their partner does to irritate them immediately without discussion. Ask each partner, on their own in a private place each evening, to review all of the criticisms and complaints that they have written down, but not spoken aloud, about their partners' behaviour in the past day. They should then delete all criticisms that seem trivial. The remainder should be rewritten as positive requests about future activity, rather than negative complaints about past behaviour. For example, 'I hated it when he was complaining about my watching the TV during dinner' may be rewritten as 'I would love tomorrow to talk to you about how my day went during dinner'. All of this reviewing and rewriting is done by each partner alone and privately. For the second part of the task, invite couples to set a fixed time each day to exchange these letters and to respond to those requests within the letters to which they feel it is reasonable to respond within a day of receiving the letter. However, ask couples not to discuss the contents of the letters between sessions because this may lead to them slipping back into destructive behavioural patterns.

Role reversal

Where couples are trapped in rigid care-giving and care-receiving cycles, their roles become so polarized that they may have difficulty empathizing with each other. As a result of this they may have difficulty experiencing the deepening intimacy that follows from empathy. Role reversal is a way of helping couples appreciate and empathize with each other's polarized roles. Invite partners to swap roles. During the exercise, ask depressed partners to act completely rationally and assertively and non-symptomatic partners to fully express the sadness and sense of loss that they have felt since the depression began to destroy the relationship. Partners may need coaching in acting-out these role reversals. Depressed partners may need help in practising assertive responses. Non-depressed partners may require help in expressing the profound sense of loss they experience due to their partner's unavailability. If couples can sustain this reasonably effectively within therapy, they may be invited to practise role reversal as a homework assignment.

Opening space for recovery and taking it slow

Rigid caregiving and receiving cycles can be disrupted by inviting the non-symptomatic partner to open up space for the depressed partner to recover in by reducing the degree to which he or she carries out the depressed partner's household and other duties. This creates opportunities for depressed partners to carry out these duties and show that they are recovering. To prevent depressed partners from feeling overwhelmed by the number of opportunities to show signs of recovery, they may be invited to make haste slowly.

PACING TIMING AND OWNERSHIP IN THERAPY

Whereas early sessions are spaced at weekly or fortnightly intervals, middle sessions may be more widely spaced. Encourage clients to take responsibility for the spacing and pacing of sessions in the middle phase of therapy to fit with their growing sense of ownership of the therapeutic process. Although the agenda for early therapy sessions is determined in large part by the therapist, encourage clients to take responsibility for setting the agenda as therapy progresses. Encourage clients to use sessions for reviewing in step-by-step detail how they managed challenging situations in their day-to-day lives and how they contributed to positive and negative interaction patterns within their relationships. Help clients to incorporate productive ways of managing challenges and positive interaction patterns into their future. Encourage clients to take an active part in designing tasks to be completed between sessions that will help them amplify small positive changes, movement towards goals and use of strengths.

INDIVIDUAL AND FAMILY SESSIONS

It may be appropriate to conduct occasional individual sessions with the depressed client to focus on personal aspects of coping with past and present life stress. It may also be appropriate to include members of the extended family or the professional network in some sessions to address ways in which they may contribute to supporting the couple.

MANAGING RESISTANCE

Clients may have difficulty co-operating because they lack energy or believe they are powerless to continue the battle with depression. In such circumstances, invite couples to take-on tasks in therapy and homework assignments that are less demanding. Ambivalence about change may interfere with couples' attempts to develop new ways of conducting their relationship. Help couples explore the downside to recovery and the catastrophes that may be avoided by not achieving their therapeutic goals. Recovery may alter the distribution of power or the amount of intimacy within relationships beyond tolerable levels. If these fears slow recovery, invite the couple to explore ways to tolerate decreased power, increased autonomy, greater intimacy and so forth.

DISENGAGEMENT

Regularly review progress towards goals and, once significant and sustained progress occurs, help clients understand how they used therapy to resolve their difficulties. Anticipate situations that might lead to future relapses.

Rehearse relapse prevention and management strategies. These strategies will inevitably draw on their understanding of how they used therapy to recover from the current episode of depression. Frame disengagement as the conclusion of an episode in a long-term relationship with a service rather than as the end of treatment, since many mood disorders follow a chronic course.

Biomedical model

The biomedical model assumes that depression arises when people with a genetic vulnerability to mood disorders are exposed to significant life stress (Cookson et al. 2002; Gelder et al. 2001; Perry, Alexander & Liskow, 1997). This vulnerability is probably determined polygenetically and may lead to a reduction in the efficiency with which messages are passed across synapses between neurons in reward and punishment centres of the brain by specific neurotransmitters, notably serotonin and noradrenaline. Antidepressant drugs and electroconvulsive therapy, according to this model, alleviate depression by increasing the efficiency of the connections between neurons. There is little certainty about how this occurs but many working hypotheses. For example, *monoamine oxidase inhibitors* (MAOIs) are thought to prevent the breakdown of neurotransmitters. Other antidepressants are thought to block re-uptake or neurotransmitters. These include tricyclic antidepressants (TCAs), selective serotonin reuptake inhibitors (SSRIs), selective noradrenaline and serotonin reuptake inhibitors (SNRIs); selective noradrenaline reuptake inhibitors (NARIs). It is unclear how *electroconvulsive therapy* (ECT) enhances the efficiency of neurotransmitter functioning by inducing seizures.

Psychoeducation and fostering adherence to medication regime

In practice, multi-modal programmes that include pharmacotherapy and psychotherapy are the treatments of choice for depression. With antidepressant treatment, a low starting dose is prescribed, increased in a stepwise manner as side effects are tolerated with each increased dose, and assessed with the expectation of reaching a therapeutic dose within two weeks and a therapeutic response within six weeks for about two-thirds of clients. Dosages for commonly used antidepressants are given in Chapter 6 and elsewhere (Cookson et al., 2002; Gelder et al., 2001; Perry et al., 1997). The material in Table 8.4 can be used for psychoeducation about depression and also as the rationale for a multi-modal programme. The psychologist and physician should work collaboratively to outline the medication regime briefly and simply, to monitor side effects and to monitor adherence. Explain the side effects of antidepressants and how medication is increased in a stepwise fashion as these side effects are tolerated until the recommended active dose is reached. Review adherence regularly and respond favourably to adherence. Manage non-adherence by exploring obstacles to adherence and problem-solve ways of overcoming these obstacles. Useful advice for clients on antidepressant medication is given in David Burns' (1999) *The feeling good handbook* and in the seventh edition of Perry et al.'s (1997) *Psychotropic drug handbook*. To check for adverse effects particularly when using high doses of antidepressants, electrocardiogram and plasma levels should be monitored. Antidepressants should be continued for at least six months to reduce risk or relapse and then gradually withdrawn over two to four weeks to prevent adverse effects, such as insomnia, anxiety and nausea associated with sudden withdrawal. For recurrent depression where three or more episodes have occurred, pharmacotherapy may be prolonged indefinitely.

Selecting antidepressants

Currently, the evidence suggests that all antidepressants are equally effective, and so decisions about which to use depend on their profile of adverse side effects, toxicity and cost, and on clients' individual reactions to them. Common side effects for TCAs and SSRIs include dry mouth, visual accommodation difficulties, lethargy and tachycardia or hypotension. Contraindications for use include cardiac difficulties and pregnancy. TCAs are the most toxic class of antidepressants and lead to greatest harm following overdose, so are not recommended for impulsive clients with suicidal ideation. Food containing tyramine, such as cheese, cannot be taken when being treated with MAOIs due to a hypertensive response and the risk of subarachnoid haemorrhage. MAOIs are not recommended for impulsive clients who cannot maintain strict dietary control.

Managing non-response to antidepressants

Where no response to a multi-modal programme involving antidepressant treatment and psychotherapy occurs, a second antidepressant of a different class may be tried. If this is ineffective an antidepressant may be augmented with lithium carbonate, a mood-stabilizing drug used for the treatment of bipolar disorder. Other pharmacological approaches to treatment resistant depression are detailed in Chapter 6 and elsewhere (APA, 2000b). ECT is recommended by mainstream psychiatric experts in the US and the UK for cases of severe depression with somatic and psychotic features where there is no response to multi-modal programmes involving psychotherapy and aggressive pharmacotherapy (APA, 2001; Freeman, 1995). However, ECT has serious side effects (notably memory loss), its mode of action is unknown and there is limited evidence for its long-term effectiveness, so many eminent psychologists are critical of its use on ethical grounds (Arscott, 1999; Johnstone, 2000).

SUMMARY

Depression is a syndrome associated with loss, involving low mood and disturbances of behaviour, relationships, somatic state, cognition and perception. Suicidal ideation and self-destructive behaviour are common in depression. Current prevalence rates for depression are about 5% and lifetime prevalence rates are close to 20%. Depression is twice as common in women as men, with most cases occurring in late adolescence and early adulthood. Depression typically occurs when people who are genetically or psychosocially vulnerable due to early trauma or loss are exposed to stressful life events and the condition is maintained by a range of physiological, cognitive, behavioural and interpersonal processes. Low stress and high levels of support are important protective factors in depression. The current treatment of choice is a multimodal programme in which evidence-based psychological and pharmacological interventions are offered in combination. About a half to two-thirds of cases of acute depression recover after such programmes. Multi-modal programmes are preferred because they are more effective in leading to rapid improvement and relapse prevention than uni-modal programmes. Evidence-based psychological therapies for depression include CBT, IPT and couples therapy. With CBT it is assumed that depression is maintained by depressive thinking and behavioural styles. In CBT, through behavioural strategies, clients become re-activated before using cognitive strategies to alter depressive thinking styles. Mindfulness-based meditation may be used to prevent relapse in recurrent depression. In IPT, where it is assumed that depression is maintained by interpersonal factors and deficits, clients are helped to resolve complicated grief reactions, address role disputes and role transitions, and compensate for social skill deficits that maintain their depression. In couples therapy, where it is assumed that relationship factors are central to the maintenance of and recovery from depression, clients and their partners are helped to develop a more supportive relationship and to jointly use a wide range of strategies to manage depression. Pharmacological interventions are based on the assumption that depression is maintained by a reduction in the efficiency with which neurotransmitters such as serotonin and noradrenaline transmit messages across synapses between neurons in the reward and punishment centres of the brain. Antidepressants, according to this model, alleviate depression by increasing the efficiency of the connections between neurons.

EXERCISE 8.1

Working in pairs, and using the case of Ruth discussed in this chapter, role-play part of an individual session with her. Ruth has begun by describing a number of events in the previous week about which she felt stressed, demoralized and inadequate. These included her car breaking down and making her late for an appointment, believing she was over-charged at the garage for the repair, forgetting to buy art supplies for one of her children and missing a parent–teacher meeting. Role-play work with Ruth on using a thought record to catch and challenge negative automatic thoughts she had in these situations. After the role-play, identify three positive aspects of the psychologist's work with Ruth, identifying if possible specific verbal and non-verbal behaviours that were helpful. Identify two specific verbal and non-verbal behaviours that might improve the work. Role-play part of the session again with a view to trying or practising these two specific behaviours.

EXERCISE 8.2

Work in pairs, adopting roles of interviewer and interviewee and reverse roles when the interview is over. The interviewer should invite the interviewee to describe a minor mood problem that he or she had in the past week or two. Collaboratively formulate this minor mood problem from a CBT, IPT or ISCT perspective and work out with the interviewee a way to manage such minor mood problems in future using CBT, IPT or ISCT treatment strategies.

FURTHER READING FOR PRACTITIONERS

Beck, A., Rush, A., Shaw, B., & Emery, G. (1979). *Cognitive therapy of depression*. New York: Guilford Press.

Beck, A.T. (1976). *Cognitive therapy and the emotional disorders*. New York: International University Press.

Jones, E. & Asen, E. (1999). *Systemic couples therapy for depression*. London: Karnac.

McCullough, J. (2000). *Treatment for chronic depression*. New York: Guilford.

McCullough, J. (2001). *Skills training manual for diagnosing and treating chronic depression: Cognitive behavioral analysis system of psychotherapy*. New York: Guilford.

Moore, R. & Garland, A. (2003). *Cognitive therapy for chronic and persistent depression*. Chichester: Wiley.

Morin, C. & Espie, C. (2003). *Insomnia: Psychological assessment and management*. New York: Plenum (comes with a CD).

Padesky, C. & Greenberger, D. (1995). *Clinician's guide to mind over mood*. New York: Guilford.

Persons, J., Davidson, J. & Tomkins, M. (2001). *Essential components of cognitive behaviour therapy for depression*. Washington, DC: American Psychological Association.

Segal, Z., Williams, M. & Teasdale, J. (2002). *Mindfulness-based cognitive therapy for depression*. New York: Guilford.

Weissman, M., Markowitz, J. & Klerman, G. (2000). *Comprehensive guide to interpersonal psychotherapy*. New York: Basic Books.

ASSESSMENT INSTRUMENTS

Bech, P., Stage, K., Nair, V., Larsen, J., Kragh-Sorensen, P. & Gjerris, A. (1997). The Major Depression Rating Scale (MDS). Inter-rater reliability and validity across different settings randomized moclobemide trial. *Journal of Affective Disorders*, 42, 39–48.

Beck, A. & Steer, R. (1988). *Beck Hopelessness Scale*. San Antonio, TX: Psychological Corporation.

Beck, A., Steer, R. & Brown, G. (1996). *Beck Depression Inventory – Second Edition* (BDI-II). San Antonio, TX: Psychological Corporation.

Blackburn, I., Jones, S. & Lewin, R. (1986). Cognitive style in depression. *British Journal of Clinical Psychology*, 25, 241–251. Contains cognitive style test. The scale is on pages 95–100 of Williams, M. (1992). *The psychological treatment of depression* (Second Edition). Routledge: London.

Hamilton, M. (1967). Development of a rating scale for primary depressive illness. *British Journal of Social and Clinical Psychology*, 6, 278–296. Contains the Hamilton Rating Scale – an observer rating scale for severity of depressive symptoms.

Kiesler, D. (1987). *Research manual for the impact message inventory*. Palo Alto, CA: Consulting Psychologist Press.

Rosenbaum, M. (1980). A schedule for assessing self-control behaviours: Preliminary Findings. *Behaviour Therapy*, 11, 109–121. Contains the Self-control Schedule.

Weissman, A. & Beck, A.T. (1978). Development and validation of the Dysfunctional Attitudes Scale. Paper presented at AABT, Chicago. The scale is on pages 100–104 of Williams, M. (1992). *The psychological treatment of depression* (Second Edition). Routledge: London.

VIDEO TRAINING TAPES

Persons, J., Tomkins, M. & Davidson, J. (2001). Cognitive-behaviour therapy for depression. Video series of five tapes. 1. Individualised case formulation and treatment planning. 2. Activity scheduling. 3. Using the thought record. 4. Schema change methods. 5. Structure of the therapy session. Washington, DC: American Psychological Association.

FURTHER READING FOR CLIENTS

Burns, D. (1999). *Feeling good. The new mood therapy*. New York: Avon

Burns, D. (1999). *The feeling good handbook* (Revised Edition). New York: Plume.

Coates, T. & Thoresen, C. (1977). *How to sleep better*. Englewood Cliffs, NJ: Prentice Hall.

Fennell, M. (1999). *Overcoming low self-esteem: A self-help guide using cognitive behavioural techniques*. London: Robinson.

Gilbert, P. (2000). *Overcoming depression: A self-guide using cognitive behavioural techniques*. Revised Edition. London: Robinson.

Greenberger, D. & Padesky, C. (1995). *Mind over mood: Changing how you feel by changing the way you think*. New York: Guilford.

Kabat Zinn, J. (1995). *Wherever you go, there you are. Mindfulness meditation in everyday life*. New York: Hyperion. Mindfulness CDs and tapes are available at: http://www.stressreductiontapes.com/

Lewinsohn, P., Munoz, R., Youngren, M. & Zeiss, A. (1996). *Control your depression*. Englewood Cliffs, NJ: Prentice Hall.

McCullough, J. (2002). *Patient's manual for CBASP*. New York: Guilford.

Weissman, M. (1995). *Mastering depression: A patient's guide to interpersonal psychotherapy*. San Antonio, TX: Psychological Corporation.

REFERENCES

American Psychiatric Association (APA) (2000a). *Diagnostic and statistical manual of the mental disorders* (Fourth Edition-Text Revision) (DSM-IV-TR). Washington, DC: APA.

American Psychiatric Association (APA) (2000b). Practice guidelines for the treatment of patients with major depressive disorder (revision). *Archives of General Psychiatry*, 157, 1–45.

American Psychiatric Association (APA) (2001). *Task force report of the APA on the practice of electroconvulsive therapy. Recommendations for treatment, training, and privileging* (Second Edition). Washington, DC: APA.

Arscott, K. (1999). ECT: The facts psychiatry declines to mention. In C. Newnes, G. Holmes & C. Dunn (Eds.), *This is madness* (pp. 97–118). Ross on Wye, UK: PCCS Books.

Beach, S. & Gupta, M. (2003). Depression. In D. Snyder & M. Whisman (Eds.), *Treating difficult couples. Helping clients with co-existing mental and relationship disorders* (pp. 88–113). New York: Guilford.

Bech, P. (2000). Clinical features of mood disorders and mania. In M. Gelder, J. Lopez-Ibor & N. Andreasen (Eds.), *New Oxford textbook of psychiatry* (Volume 1, Section 4.5.2, pp. 682–688). Oxford: Oxford University Press.

Beck, A. (1976). *Cognitive therapy and the emotional disorders*. New York: International Universities Press.

Burns, D. (1999). *The feeling good handbook* (Revised Edition). New York: Plume.

Byrne, M., Carr, A. & Clarke, M. (in press). Depression and Marriage. *Journal of Marital and Family Therapy*.

Carr, A. (2000). *Family therapy: Concepts, process and practice*. Chichester: Wiley.

Clark, D., Beck, A. & Alford, B. (1999). *Scientific foundations of cognitive theory and therapy for depression*. Chichester: Wiley.

Cookson, J., Taylor, D. & Katona, C. (2002). *Use of drugs in psychiatry* (Fifth Edition). London: Gaskell.

Craighead, E., Hart, A., Wilcoxon Craighead, L. & Ilardi, S. (2002). Psychosocial treatments for major depression. In P. Nathan & J. Gorman (Eds.), *A guide to treatments that work* (Second Edition, pp. 245–262). New York: Oxford University Press.

Crits-Cristoph, P. & Barber, J. (2002). Psychological treatments for personality disorders. In P. Nathan & J. Gorman (Eds.), *A guide to treatments that work* (Second edition, pp. 611–624). New York: Oxford University Press.

Farmer, A. & McGuffin, P. (1989). The classification of depressions: Contemporary confusions revisited. *British Journal of Psychiatry*, 155, 437–443.

Freeman, C. (1995). *The ECT handbook*. London: Gaskell.

Gelder, M., Mayou, R. & Cowen, P. (2001). *Shorter Oxford textbook of psychiatry*. Oxford: Oxford Medical Publications.

Gilbert, P. (2000). *Overcoming depression: A self-guide using cognitive behavioural techniques* (Revised Edition). London: Robinson.

Gollan, J., Friedman, M. & Miller, I. (2002). Couple therapy in the treatment of major depression. In A. Gurman & N. Jacobson (Eds.), *Clinical handbook of couple therapy* (pp. 653–676). New York: Guilford.

Gotlib, I. & Hammen, C. (2002). *Handbook of depression*. New York: Guilford.

Jacobson, N. & Christensen, A. (1998). *Acceptance and change: A therapist's guide to transforming relationships*. New York: Norton.

Johnstone, L. (2000). *Users and abusers of psychiatry*. London: Routledge.

Joiner, T. & Coyne, J. (1999). *The interactional nature of depression*. Washington, DC: APA.

Jones, E. & Asen, E. (1999). *Systemic couples therapy for depression*. London: Karnac.

Jones, I., Kent, L. & Craddock, N. (2002). Genetics of affective disorders. In P. McGuffin, M. Owen & I. Gottesman (Eds.), *Psychiatric genetics and genomics* (pp. 211–246). Oxford: Oxford University Press.

Joyce, P. (2000). Epidemiology of mood disorders. In. M. Gelder, J. Lopez-Ibor & N. Andreasen (Eds.), *New Oxford textbook of psychiatry* (Volume 1, Section 4.5.4, pp. 695–700). Oxford: Oxford University Press.

Judd, L. (1997). The clinical course of unipolar major depressive disorders. *Archives of General Psychiatry*, 54, 989–991.

Kabat Zinn, J. (1995). *Wherever you go, there you are. Mindfulness meditation in everyday life*. New York: Hyperion. Mindfulness CDs and tapes are available at: http://www.stressreductiontapes.com/

Kendell, R. (1976). The classification of depressions: A review of contemporary confusion. *British Journal of Psychiatry*, 129, 15–88.

Kiesler, D. (1987). *Research manual for the impact message inventory*. Palo Alto, CA: Consulting Psychologist Press.

McCullough, J. (2000). *Treatment for chronic depression*. New York: Guilford.

Moore, R. & Garland, A. (2003). *Cognitive therapy for chronic and persistent depression*. Chichester: Wiley.

Morin, C. & Espie, C. (2003). *Insomnia: Psychological assessment and management*. New York: Plenum.

Murray, C. & Lopez, A. (1998). *The global burden of disease: A comprehensive assessment of mortality and disability from disease, injuries and risk factors in 1990 and projected to 2020*. Boston, MA: Harvard University Press.

Nemeroff, C. & Schatzberg, A. (2002). Pharmacological treatment of unipolar depression. In P. Nathan & J. Gorman (Eds.), *A guide to treatments that work* (Second Edition, pp. 229–244). New York: Oxford University Press.

Padesky, C. & Greenberger, D. (1995). *Clinician's guide to mind over mood*. New York: Guilford.

Perry, J., Alexander, B. & Liskow, B. (1997). *Psychotropic drug handbook* (Seventh Edition). Washington, DC: APA.

Persons, J., Davidson, J. & Tomkins, M. (2001). *Essential components of cognitive behaviour therapy for depression.* Washington, DC: American Psychological Association.

Power, M. (2004). *Mood disorders. A handbook of science and practice.* Chichester: Wiley.

Segal, Z., Williams, J. & Teasdale, J. (2002). *Mindfulness-based cognitive therapy for depression.* New York: Guilford.

Shapiro, D.A. (1998). Efficacy of psychodynamic, interpersonal and experiential treatment of depression. In Checkley, S. (Ed), *The management of depression* (pp 142–164). Oxford: Blackwell.

Sullivan, H. (1953). *The interpersonal theory of psychiatry.* New York: Norton.

Weissman, M. (1995). *Mastering depression: A patient's guide to interpersonal psychotherapy.* San Antonio, TX: Psychological Corporation.

Weissman, M., Markowitz, J. & Klerman, G. (2000). *Comprehensive guide to interpersonal psychotherapy.* New York: Basic Books.

White, M. & Epston, D. (1990). *Narrative means to therapeutic ends.* New York: Norton.

Williams, J., Watts, F., MacLeod, C. & Mathews, A. (1997). *Cognitive psychological and emotional disorders* (Second Edition). Chichester: Wiley.

World Health Organization (WHO) (1993). *The ICD-10 classification of mental and behavioural disorders. Diagnostic criteria for research.* Geneva: WHO.

Chapter 9

Bipolar disorder

Dominic Lam and Steve Jones

CASE EXAMPLE

Josephine is thirty years old and currently unemployed. Her mother suffered from depression and her maternal aunt was in and out of hospital for 'some sort of mental disorder'. Her father, a quiet man, ran a small business and was rarely around.

Josephine was an only child and took care of her mother when she was depressed. This led to some isolation from her peers and she therefore became focused on academic achievement, which her mother prized highly. This was reinforced by elevation of her mother's mood when she passed exams for the local independent grammar school. She found that her own mood was generally low during adolescence, with brief peaks when working hard for and passing school exams. She had several undiagnosed episodes of mania with dysphoric symptoms. The first episode started when Josephine left home to go to university. Unused to socializing with people of her own age, she did not fit in and hated her degree course. In particular she struggled with the fact that, although she passed her exams, she was no longer 'top of the class'. Josephine terminated her studies, against her mother's wishes, and worked as a 'temp' doing secretarial work. The following year, she went back to university to continue her degree but remained unhappy there. In her third year of the degree course, Josephine had another episode of depression but was treated by supportive counselling. She managed to finish her course and was awarded a degree with lower-second-class honours, about which her mother was delighted. Josephine started working as a secretary with British Gas. She described her mood at that time as 'up and down', with poor sleep. She found her job unfulfilling but received a lot of support from her mother. She was quickly promoted to be a personal assistant for the manager of the office. After a year, Josephine left the job and joined the Civil Service. It was in her second year with the Civil Service that Josephine became depressed again. She was prescribed Prozac®. Her depression lifted, but the following year Josephine became manic. She spent a lot of money, had arguments with her landlord and flatmates and did not sleep. Five years before presenting to the clinic, Josephine was referred to a psychiatrist and received a diagnosis of bipolar disorder. She was prescribed lithium as a mood stabilizer but unfortunately suffered badly from side effects. She put on a lot of weight and developed psoriasis. Her GP stopped the lithium. Josephine then had a period of instability. She was often absent from work, drank a lot of alcohol, got into debt and was in rent arrears. In the end, she had to leave her job and went into a hostel with staff support during the working hours of 9 a.m. to 5 p.m. At the time of assessment, she had not worked for two years and continued to live in a supported hostel.

CLINICAL FEATURES

Bipolar disorder is characterized by mania/hypomania and depression. In the *Diagnostic and statistical manual of mental disorders* (Fourth Edition, Text Revised) (DSM-IV-TR) (American Psychiatric Association, 2000), bipolar depression has the same diagnostic criteria as unipolar major depression. The client has to have five (or more) of the following symptoms present during the same two-week period, and these symptoms must represent a change from previous functioning: depressed mood, marked diminished interest or pleasure, significant weight loss when not dieting (or weight gain) or decease or increase in appetite, insomnia or hypersomnia, psychomotor agitation or retardation, loss of energy, feelings of worthlessness or excessive guilt, impaired concentration or indecisiveness, recurrent thoughts of death or recurrent suicidal ideation. These symptoms have to be present most of the day and nearly every day. At least one of the symptoms has to be either depressed mood or loss of interest or pleasure. In contrast, the DSM-IV-TR criteria for mania are a distinct period of abnormally and persistently elevated, expansive or irritable mood, lasting for one week. During the period of mood disturbance, three (or more) of the following have to be present to a significant degree: inflated self-esteem or grandiosity, decreased need for sleep (e.g. feel rested after only three hours of sleep), more talkative than usual or pressure of speech, flight of ideas or subjective experience that thoughts are racing, distractibility, increase in goal-directed activity or psychomotor agitation, excessive involvement in pleasurable activities that have a high potential for painful consequences. One of the symptoms has to be either inflated self-esteem or irritability. If irritability is the persistent mood, then four other symptoms have to be present. For a hypomanic episode, the criteria are similar to a manic episode with the exception that the duration is at least four days. If it is the same length of duration as mania, the episode is not severe enough to cause marked impairment in social or occupational functioning. If there are psychotic features or the client has to be admitted to hospital, the episode is mania, not hypomania.

For a mixed episode, the criteria for both a manic episode and for a major depressive episode have to be fulfilled nearly every day for at least a two-week period. Furthermore, the mood disturbance has to be sufficiently severe to cause marked social or occupational impairment or the episode necessitates hospitalization to prevent harm to self or others, or there are psychotic features. Mixed bipolar episodes are rare according to DSM-IV criteria. Rapid cycling is defined as at least four episodes of a mood disturbance in the previous twelve months that meet criteria for a major depression, manic, mixed or hypomanic episode.

There are two subtypes for bipolar illness. For clients to suffer from bipolar I disorder, there has to be at least one manic episode or mixed episode and one major depressive episode. For clients to suffer from bipolar II disorder, there has to be at least one hypomanic episode and one major depressive episode but no manic or mixed episodes. DSM-IV-TR and ICD-10 criteria for manic episodes are presented in Table 9.1.

EPIDEMIOLOGY

Bipolar disorder is relatively common. Prevalence studies in the UK, continental Europe and the US indicate a prevalence rate of 1–1.9% of clients meeting formal diagnostic criteria for bipolar disorder (Bebbington & Ramana, 1995; ten Have et al., 2002; Weissman et al., 1988). Angst and colleagues have argued that, in fact, current diagnostic criteria for bipolar disorder incorrectly exclude people with illnesses that fit within a bipolar spectrum; when these clients are included, prevalence rates increase to around 11% (Angst et al., 2003). This would include clients who experienced symptoms of euphoria, overactivity and irritability for shorter periods than in current DSM-IV criteria, but who exhibited a significant change in functioning. In addition to this being a relatively common illness, by no means all clients meeting criteria for bipolar disorder are involved in psychiatric services. Ten Have and colleagues reported that in their population-based prevalence study, 25.5% of clients with bipolar disorder had never sought any form of professional help (ten Have et al., 2002).

Historically, bipolar disorder was seen as being characterized by periods of

Table 9.1 Diagnostic criteria for manic episode

DSM-IV-TR	*ICD-10*
A. A distinct period of abnormally and persistently elevated, expansive, or irritable mood, lasting at least one week (or any duration if hospitalization is necessary) B. During the period of mood disturbance, three (or more) of the following symptoms have persisted (four if the mood is only irritable) and have been present to a significant degree: • Inflated self-esteem or grandiosity • Decreased need for sleep (e.g. feels rested after only 3 hours of sleep) • More talkative than usual or pressure to keep talking • Flight of ideas or subjective experience that thoughts are racing • Distractibility (i.e. attention too easily drawn to unimportant or irrelevant external stimuli) • Increase in goal-directed activity (socially, at work or school, or sexually) or psychomotor agitation • Excessive involvement in pleasurable activities that have a high potential for painful consequences (engaging in unrestrained buying sprees, sexual indiscretions, or foolish business investments) C. The symptoms do not meet criteria for a mixed episode D. The mood disturbance is sufficiently severe to cause marked impairment in occupational functioning or in usual social activities or relationships with others, or to necessitate hospitalization to prevent harm to self or others, or there are psychotic features E. The symptoms are not due to the direct physiological effects of a substance (e.g. a drug of abuse, a medication, or other treatment) or a general medical condition (e.g. hyperthyroidism) **Note:** Manic-like episodes that are clearly caused by somatic antidepressant treatment (e.g. medication, electroconvulsive therapy, light therapy) should not count toward a diagnosis of bipolar I disorder.	Mood is elevated out of keeping with the individual's circumstances and may vary from carefree joviality to almost uncontrollable excitement. Elation is accompanied by increased energy, resulting in overactivity, pressure of speech, and a decreased need for sleep. Normal social inhibitions are lost, attention cannot be sustained, and there is often marked distractibility. Self-esteem is inflated, and grandiose or over-optimistic ideas are freely expressed Perceptual disorders may occur, such as the appreciation of colours that are especially vivid (and usually beautiful), a preoccupation with fine details of surfaces or textures, and subjective hyperacusis. The individual may embark on extravagant and impractical schemes, spend money recklessly, or become aggressive, amorous, or facetious in inappropriate circumstances. In some manic episodes the mood is irritable and suspicious rather than elated. The first attack occurs most commonly between the ages of 15 and 30 years, but may occur at any age from late childhood to the seventh or eighth decade The episode should last for at least one week and should be severe enough to disrupt ordinary work and social activities more or less completely. The mood change should be accompanied by increased energy and several of the symptoms referred to above (particularly pressure of speech, decreased need for sleep, grandiosity, and excessive optimism)

Note: Adapted from DSM-IV-TR (APA, 2000) and ICD-10 (WHO, 1992).

mania and depression interspersed with periods of 'normality'. Contrary to this view, a review by Solomon and colleagues found that some clients experienced high levels of symptoms in between episodes, and that these individuals are at high risk of relapse and have substantial social problems (Solomon et al., 1995). They reported that a client experiencing recovery from a bipolar mood episode has a 50% risk of a further episode within a year. Furthermore, there is evidence that, if anything, the course of bipolar disorder can become more severe with age (Goodwin & Jamison, 1990), with clients later on in the illness course requiring only relatively modest external stressors to trigger a mood episode (Ambelas, 1987; Post et al., 1986).

Bipolar disorder is associated with high risk of self-harm and suicide. A recent review reported an annual rate of suicide in bipolar clients of 0.4%, which is twenty times higher than in the general population (Tondo et al., 2003). A 34- to 38-year-follow-up study reported a twelve-fold increase in successful suicide attempts, which, although somewhat lower, still represents a substantially elevated risk (Angst, Stassen, Clayton & Angst, 2002). Estimates vary for rates of suicide attempts; 34% of bipolar clients within the Stanley Bipolar Research Network were found to have a history of suicide attempts (Leverich et al., 2003), and a Dutch study found that 20% of its bipolar sample had attempted suicide and 59% experienced suicidal ideation (ten Have et al., 2002). Family studies consistently estimated a higher morbid risk for relatives of bipolar clients to develop the disorder than the general population. However, the ranges vary widely (Gershon et al., 1989). Overall, the findings pointed to a risk of two or three times higher than the general population. Goodwin and Jamison (1990) concluded that unipolar depression is more frequent than bipolar disorder in relatives of bipolar clients. Recently, McGuffin et al. (2003) estimated 85% heritability for bipolar disorder. They found that most of the genetic liability to mania is specific to the manic syndrome, even though there are substantial genetic and non-shared environmental correlations between mania and depression.

COMORBIDITY

A number of comorbid conditions need to be considered with respect to bipolar disorder:

- **Personality disorders**: personality disorders have been estimated to occur in 10–13% of a community sample (Weissman, 1993). Based on structured clinical interview, 29% of a sample of bipolar clients met criteria for a personality disorder, predominantly of the cluster B (dramatic, emotionally erratic) and cluster C (fearful, avoidant) types. The presence of a personality disorder has been associated with more severe residual mood symptoms in adults (George et al., 2003) and adolescents (Kutcher et al., 1990).

- **Substance abuse**: the US Epidemiological Catchment Area study reported that 61% of clients with bipolar I disorder, also met lifetime criteria for substance abuse (Regier et al., 1990). High rates have been reported from numerous studies across a range of different populations in different countries (Cassidy, Ahearn & Carroll, 2001; Strakowski & DelBello, 2000).
- **Panic disorder**: high rates of panic disorder (14–21%) have also been reported amongst clients with bipolar disorder (Chen & Dilsaver, 1995; Savino et al., 1993).

Co-existence of personality disorders, panic disorders and alcohol and drug abuse are again associated with poorer therapeutic outcomes due to more difficulties with therapeutic engagement, higher levels of symptomatology and more frequent hospitalizations. The presence of personality disorder is commonly associated with greater illness severity, including higher risk of self-harm and suicide, and poorer outcome. In addition to consideration of the role of comorbid conditions, there is also the issue of distinguishing bipolar disorder from other disorders. Structured interview approaches indicate that it is possible to reliably diagnose bipolar I and bipolar II disorders (Andreasen et al., 1981; Rice et al., 1992; Simpson et al., 2002). The main diagnosis with which there is significant overlap is schizoaffective disorder. With DSM-IV diagnostic criteria the presence of psychotic symptoms can occur in extremes of mania or depression. The difference between this and schizophrenia-spectrum diagnoses is that such symptoms abate when mood symptoms resolve. Some diagnostic confusion can occur when the mood disorder is itself chronic, as the psychotic symptoms themselves may then appear to be persistent.

ASSESSMENT

A comprehensive assessment is a prerequisite of therapy. There is also an interaction between assessment and therapy processes. In many cases, the information drawn together through a proper assessment will provide the client with his or her first opportunity to understand the relationships between experiences, emotions and behaviour, often previously recalled as separate events. This alone will potentially be therapeutic, as well as enhancing engagement with the therapeutic process. Also, although much of the assessment will occur early in therapy, there will be times later in therapy when opportunities to acquire additional information may occur, such as through meetings with third parties. This interaction between therapy and assessment is a characteristic of successful therapy with bipolar clients.

Individual and family history

The assessment process should begin with an interview designed to elicit information about the history of the individual and his or her family. We know from research that many people with bipolar disorder will have other family members who suffer from affective disorders of various types. Where there has been affective disorder amongst the client's parents, this can clearly have caused disruption during the client's development. Identifying this, and the client's perception of its impact on his or her life, is an important part of assessment. In general, as with other forms of cognitive therapy, the aim of history taking is to get a sense of how the individual has come to his or her own particular beliefs about the world, self and others.

Illness history is also a crucial part of assessment. Many clients will have experience of psychiatric interviews and may not immediately see the relevance of reviewing this area. The key difference for a psychological assessment is that you are working with the client to identify his or her own perception of mood fluctuations, whether or not these amounted to 'psychiatric symptoms' at the time. Once information concerning mood change is collected, it is helpful to lay it out chronologically on a life chart, on which is also included information about life events, medication and occupation/school. The completed life chart, drawn up collaboratively with the client, may show interrelationships between mood and other important factors. This information also serves to illustrate that often mood change occurs within a context, rather than being an event that occurs out of the blue.

A further important issue is that clients will have views about both medication and diagnosis. Clients will often have mixed feelings about the medication that they have been prescribed. Considering these views and feelings in relation to the life chart can prove a useful introduction to later sessions at which adherence issues are discussed. Clients will also vary in their views of their diagnosis. Some people will feel that their diagnosis is a welcome explanation for previously inexplicable symptoms. Many clients will say that having an identified illness for which there is a treatment is a relief, in comparison with a previous fear of undefined 'madness'. However, other clients will see the diagnosis as a label that they do not accept. In both cases, awareness of the client's perception will be key to the development of shared therapy goals and avoiding harmful conflicts within therapy.

Other areas that assessment can usefully address include current mood state, initial information on coping with prodromes, levels of dysfunctional beliefs and experience of stigma. In addition, given the patterns of self-harm and suicide risk, it is important to assess hopelessness and suicidality at assessment and subsequently. Information can also be obtained on the resources at the individual's disposal, both in terms of social skills/performance and sources of professional and informal support. For each of these areas, it is important to use careful questioning within the assessment interview. However, it is usually helpful to combine this with self-report and observer measures to provide a comprehensive picture. Useful measures are considered below.

Self-monitoring

During assessment it is explained that self-monitoring is an important part of treatment. It is emphasized that a lot of the important aspects of therapy will happen between sessions and having information about how clients are feeling and what they are doing between sessions is important in ensuring that they achieve the best possible outcome for the intervention. Initially, clients will complete brief mood and medication adherence measures. As therapy proper progresses, monitoring of activities, mood and thoughts becomes increasingly important.

Standardized measures

There are a number of measures that we have found helpful in initial and ongoing assessment during therapy; these are discussed in turn below. In each case, the information from these measures is used in combination with information from assessment and questioning of the client regarding the issue under consideration.

Current mood state measures

Beck Depression Inventory (Beck & Steer, 1987)

This is a short, self-report measure applicable to adults and adolescents. It includes questions on physical, behavioural and cognitive features of depression. Each item is rated for the preceding week and scored on a three-point scale. Score ranges are: 0–9 asymptomatic, 10–18 mild–moderate depression, 19–29 moderate–severe depression, >29 extremely severe depression.

Beck Hopelessness Scale (Beck & Steer, 1988)

This is again a short, self-report measure. Beck reported that scores 9 or above were significantly predictive of eventual suicide in individuals with suicidal ideas followed up over up to ten years (Beck et al., 1985). Score ranges are: 0–3 normal, 4–8 mild, 9–14 moderate, >14 severe.

Internal States Scale (Bauer et al., 1991)

Individuals rate themselves on a visual analogue scale for sixteen different items that cover: perceived conflict, activation, well-being, depression and global bipolar.

As a general rule, clients are asked to complete this small battery of measures after each therapy session. This allows the therapist and client to develop a database of information tracking a range of aspects of mood over the course of therapy.

Additional useful mood measures

Mania Rating Scale (Bech et al., 1978)

This is an interviewer-rated measure considering eleven features relevant to the possible presence of mania. Each item is rated on a 5-point scale. Score ranges are: 0–5 no mania, 6–9 hypomania, 10–14 probable mania, 15 or more definite mania.

Hamilton Rating Scale for Depression (Hamilton, 1960)

This is generally used as a seventeen-item, observer-rated scale assessing physical, cognitive and behavioural features of depression. Score ranges are: 0–7 no/minimal depression, 8–17 mild, 18–25 moderate, >26 severe depression.

Coping with illness and prodromes

Coping with Prodrome Interview (Lam, Wong & Sham, 2001)

This measure offers open-ended questions, which can provide a helpful initial indication of the individual's approach to mania and depression prodromes. This is usually more helpful than a questionnaire-based approach given the very individual nature of each person's prodromes. This information is then included in the assessment of prodromal coping as part of the cognitive therapy intervention.

Dysfunctional beliefs

Dysfunctional Attitudes Scale (Power et al., 1994)

This self-report measure can provide the clinician with an initial indication of particular patterns of beliefs. It also provides information on sociotropy (dependence on social input) and autonomy (achievement/task focus).

Social functioning

A number of measures of social functioning can be used. Whichever specific measure is selected, in practice we collect this information using a semi-structured interview approach, focusing on the client as an informant.

The Social Performance Schedule (Hurry et al., 1983) has proved a useful indicator of problem behaviours across a comprehensive range of areas of social functioning. This has been used clinically with individuals with bipolar disorder (Lam et al., 1999). Other interviews that measure similar areas of social functioning include the Social Adjustment Scale (Weissman and Bothwell, 1976) and the Social Behaviour Assessment Schedule (Platt et al., 1980).

TREATMENT FOR BIPOLAR DISORDER

Bipolar disorder has a strong genetic component but stress can trigger an onset. It is commonly regarded as sensible to tackle both the stresses affecting clients and the biological aspects of the illness. Hence, therapy with bipolar disorder is often carried out in conjunction with pharmacotherapy. Stress does not have to be an acute, upsetting, life event; it can be a build-up of life's hassles. The way an individual responds can alleviate or exacerbate the stressful situation. Psychotherapy may help clients to examine strategies that help them deal with the stress side of the equation. There are four major approaches to psychotherapy for bipolar disorder: biomedical approaches, cognitive-behavioural treatment (CBT), interpersonal and social rhythm treatment (IPSRT) and family focused treatment (FFT). These approaches will be described below, with particular emphasis on CBT clinical practice with clients with bipolar affective disorder. As psychoeducation is a common part of most treatments, this will be discussed briefly first.

Psychoeducation

Psychoeducation is based on the rationale that treating an illness is not just prescribing medication. Clients need to be educated about the illness to improve medication compliance and hence improve the outcome of treatment. Colom and colleagues reported a randomized controlled study of 120 bipolar clients; the treatment group received medication and twenty sessions of group psychoeducation. The control group received medication and twenty non-structured group sessions (Colom et al., 2003). Group sessions were ninety minutes each and each group consisted of eight to twelve euthymic clients (Young Mania Rating Scale < 6, Hamilton Depression Rating Scale < 8). The therapists' style was directive but also encouraged clients' participation. The psychoeducation group had significantly longer time to relapse than the control group over the twenty-four months of study, although the effect was mainly in the first twelve months; the treatment group had fewer bipolar relapses. However, there was no significant difference between the two groups in number of hospitalizations, even though the psychoeducation group had significantly fewer days in hospital.

Biomedical approaches

The treatment for bipolar disorder since the 1970s has been predominantly pharmacological. There are several pharmacotherapy treatment guidelines for bipolar disorder: the American Psychiatric Association (APA) *Practice guideline for the treatment of patients with bipolar disorder*, Second Edition (APA, 2002), World Federation of Societies of Biological Psychiatry (WFSBP) *Guidelines for biological treatment of bipolar disorders, Part 1: Treatment of bipolar depression* (Grunze et al., 2002) and the *Evidence-based guideline for treating bipolar disorder: recommendations from the British Association for Psychopharmacology* (Goodwin, 2003). Readers are recommended to refer to these guidelines for more details when necessary. This section summarizes their recommendations.

Pharmacotherapy in bipolar disorder can be divided into treatment of acute manic, depressive or mixed episodes, as well as long-term preventive treatment. For severe acute manic or mixed episodes, an antipsychotic or valproate is normally prescribed for their rapid antimanic effects. Generally, atypical antipsychotics are preferred because of their more favourable side-effect profile. For less severe manic episodes, lithium may also be used as a short-term therapeutic agent. If the client is taking antidepressants, these are quickly tapered and discontinued. Benzodiazepines such as clonazepine or lorazepam may also be used for the severe overactive clients. For acute depression, antidepressants, in conjunction with an antimanic agent, (e.g. lithium) are usually prescribed. An antidepressant prescribed alone as a monotherapy is associated with the risk of the client switching from a depressive to manic episode. An antipsychotic may be prescribed for psychotic symptoms. Tricyclic antidepressants carry a greater risk of precipitating a switch to mania compared to other antidepressants, such as selective serotonin reuptake inhibitors (SSRIs). Lamotrigine can be prescribed for bipolar depression if an antidepressant has previously appeared to provoke mood instability. Electroconvulsive therapy (ECT) is also considered for treatment resistant mania or depression and for clients with significant suicide risks.

For long-term treatment, a number of agents are used to prevent relapses, and this requires careful serum level monitoring. Lithium and some antiepilepsy drugs, such as carbamazepine and valproate, are common mood stabilizers. Both lithium and valproate are probably effective in preventing both mania and depression. Lithium is generally considered to be more effective in preventing mania than depression. Either carbamazepine or valproate prescribed alone as monotherapy appear to prevent relapse, although there is still a paucity of data from randomized, placebo-controlled trials (Keck & McElroy, 2002). Carbamazepine has the potential of interacting with a number of drugs and is generally regarded as less effective than lithium.

However, 20–40% of bipolar clients do not appear to benefit from lithium

(Goodwin, 2003; Prien & Potter, 1990). This may be due to difficulties with adherence as well as to limitations in the effectiveness of the medication itself. Lithium has a narrow therapeutic band, meaning that therapeutic and toxic levels of lithium are quite close to each other. Nonadherence rates for lithium have been estimated at between 18 and 53% (Goodwin & Jamison, 1990; Maj, 2003). Although many of these other medications are commonly used in clinical practice, it was recently concluded that 'the only medication with incontrovertible proof of efficacy in multiple maintenance-phase studies is lithium' (Gnanadesikan et al., 2003). Newer mood stabilizers are generally of equivalent efficacy to lithium (Moncrieff, 1995; Solomon et al., 1995). In terms of the newer drugs, olanzapine is more effective in preventing mania whereas lamotrigine has been found to have a long-term role in delaying or preventing the recurrence of depressive episodes (Calabrese, Shelton, Rapport, Kimmel & Elhaj, 2002b). But lithium or sodium divalproex remain the first-line treatment (Calabrese et al., 2002a). Other antipsychotics, such as clozapine and olanzapine, are also used clinically but more research is needed, as the adverse side effects associated with these antipsychotics may outweigh the benefits (Kusumakar, 2002).

Cognitive-behavioural approach

Rationale for the cognitive-behavioural approach

The manifestation of bipolar illness is predominately affective, cognitive and behavioural. Clinically, it has been observed that mania fuels itself and that chaos can lead to more episodes. This suggests that psychotherapy targeting chaos and reducing maladaptive coping can be useful. Some bipolar clients who have frequent relapses often engage in very striving behaviour to 'make up for lost time'. Hence, it is important to promote good routine and to target the extreme striving or goal-attainment beliefs. The early detection of prodromes and good coping strategies during the prodromal phases are also important in addressing the risk of a full-blown episode. Both promoting a good daily routine and the detection and coping with prodromes involve monitoring and regulating. Cognitive therapy is based on the assumption that thinking, mood and behaviour affect each other. Therapists aim to teach clients techniques to monitor, examine and change dysfunctional thinking and behaviour associated with undesirable mood states. Hence, cognitive therapy is well suited to teaching bipolar clients enhanced coping skills.

Two small cognitive therapy (CT) pilot studies (Lam et al., 2000; Scott et al., 2001) have reported encouraging results. Lam et al. (2003) reported a randomized controlled study in which 103 DSM-IV bipolar I clients, suffering from frequent relapses despite the prescription of commonly used mood stabilizers, were randomized into a CT group or a control group. Both groups received mood stabilizers and regular psychiatric follow-up. The CT group received, on average, fourteen sessions of CT during the first six months and two booster sessions in the second six months. Over the twelve-month period, the CT group had significantly fewer bipolar episodes, days in a bipolar episode, and admissions. They also had significantly higher social functioning and showed fewer mood symptoms on the monthly mood questionnaires, as well as less fluctuation in manic symptoms. In a second paper (Lam et al. in press), an additional eighteen months of follow-up data were reported. Over thirty months, the CT group was significantly better in terms of time to relapse. They spent 110 fewer days (CI 32–189 days) in bipolar episodes over the whole thirty months and fifty-four fewer days (CI 3–105 days) in bipolar episodes in total over the last eighteen months. The CT group performed significantly better in mood ratings, social functioning, coping with bipolar prodromes and dysfunctional goal-attainment cognition. The findings indicate that CT specifically designed for relapse prevention in bipolar affective disorder is a useful tool in conjunction with mood stabilizers. However, the effect of relapse prevention was mainly in the first year. It was suggested that the effect of booster sessions or maintenance therapy should be investigated.

Coping with bipolar prodromes

The prodromal period is defined as from the time of the first appearance of symptoms to the time when a full-blown episode is evident. The word 'prodrome' is often used as shorthand for the symptoms at this early stage of an episode. Four retrospective studies have shown that bipolar clients can detect prodromes (Joyce, 1985; Lam & Wong, 1997; Molnar, Feeney & Fava, 1988; Smith & Tarrier, 1992), as has a longitudinal study (Altman, et al., 1992). Most of these studies had small samples. However, despite this, the finding that bipolar clients can detect prodromes seems robust. There is a consensus that each client's pattern or combination of signs and symptoms is unique. Hence, using a checklist to elicit prodromes has the inherent problem of losing some of the more idiosyncratic prodromes. Asking for spontaneous reports of prodromes has the advantage of personalizing the prodromes in the individual's context. Some examples of idiosyncratic prodromes are that *Thought for the day* on Radio 4 seemed to convey a special message to the client, and that the client's family dog became evil.

Studies have found that 25–30% of bipolar clients couldn't detect prodromes of mania whereas only 7.5% could not detect prodromes of depression (Lam & Wong, 1997; Molnar et al., 1988). The high proportion of clients who couldn't detect depression prodromes could be due to its insidious onset. Another problem for many bipolar clients is that some depression prodromes are not qualitatively different from their residual symptoms. This makes the detection of such prodromes more difficult. Across the studies that listed individual prodromes, there was strong agreement about prodromes of mania. Six most often reported prodromes of mania were sleeping less, more goal-directed behaviour, irritability, increased sociability, thoughts starting to race and increased optimism. The most common prodromes of depression reported across studies are loss of interest in activities or people, not able to put worries or anxieties aside, interrupted sleep, and feeling sad or wanting to cry. Clients reported fewer depression prodromes and there seemed to be diversity in the report of prodromal signs and symptoms of depression. Lam et al., 2001 reported that bipolar clients could report mania and depression prodromes reliably eighteen months apart.

The duration of manic or depression prodromal stages varies from individual to individual. However, it is encouraging that most clients have a reasonable prodromal period for early intervention prior to a full-blown episode. For example, Smith and Tarrier (1992) reported that average duration of prodromes of depression was nineteen (SD nineteen) days and average duration of mania prodromes was twenty-nine (SD twenty-eight) days. However, Molnar et al. (1988) reported that mania prodromes lasted on average 20.5 days (range: from one to eighty-four days) whereas average length of depression prodromes was eleven days (ranging from two to thirty-one days).

Ratings of how clients coped with mania prodromes contributed significantly to the clients' level of functioning at baseline after depression and mania symptoms were controlled for statistically (Lam & Wong, 1997). These also predicted clients' manic symptoms eighteen months later and whether clients had relapsed during the eighteen months after the levels of mood symptoms at baseline were controlled for (Lam et al., 2001). The most common good coping strategies for prodromes of mania employed by subjects were: 'modifying high activities and restraining themselves', 'engaging in calming activities', 'taking extra time to rest or sleep' and 'seeing a doctor'. Poor coping strategies included: 'continuing to move about and take on more tasks', 'enjoying the feeling of high', 'going out more and spending money'. It is interesting to note that the spontaneous coping strategies reported by clients are behavioural. The most common coping strategies for depression prodromes were 'getting myself organized and keeping busy', 'getting social support and meeting people', 'distracting from negative thoughts by doing more' and 'recognizing realistic thoughts and evaluating if things are worth worrying about'. Poor coping strategies included 'staying in bed and hoping it would go away', 'doing nothing' and 'taking extra medication, such as lithium or sleeping pills'.

Dysfunctional attitudes

Despite the encouraging outcome in developing CBT for bipolar affective disorder (Lam et al., 1999; Lam et al., 2003; Scott et al., 2001), very little is known about whether there are any differences in dysfunctional attitudes between unipolar clients, bipolar clients and normal controls. The cognitive model for bipolar affective disorder (Lam et al., 1999; Wright & Lam, 2003) postulated high goal striving as a risk factor for bipolar disorder. Scott and colleagues found that euthymic bipolar clients showed significantly higher scores on the Dysfunctional Attitudes Scale (DAS), as well as the 'Need for approval' and 'Perfectionism' subscales than healthy controls (Scott et al., 2001). Lam et al. (in press) in a principal component analysis of the 24-item short DAS of 143 bipolar I clients found three factors: factor 1 'Goal-attainment', factor 2 'Dependency' and factor 3 'Achievement'. No significant differences were found when the validation sample of 143 bipolar I clients was compared with 109 clients suffering from unipolar depression in any of the three factors. When subjects who were likely to be in a major depressive episode were excluded, the scores of bipolar clients were significantly higher than euthymic unipolar clients in factor 1 'Goal-attainment'. Goal-attainment also correlated with the number of past hospitalizations due to manic episodes and to bipolar episodes as a whole.

Clinical practice: Cognitive therapy techniques

Engagement

As with any form of psychological therapy, engagement is crucial for good therapeutic outcomes. For a cognitive therapy approach to bipolar disorder, it is important that the client understands and accepts a version of our basic vulnerability-stress model of bipolar disorder. However, like all other aspects of therapy with this client group, this cannot be achieved in a didactic fashion. Engaging clients with the model needs to be achieved in a collaborative fashion, which makes sense to them in terms of their own individual experience. We normally take several approaches to this in therapy:

WRITTEN INFORMATION

We usually provide the client with written information about cognitive therapy for bipolar disorder and the model on which it is based. This is typically done in the first or second session. The handout which we use has been published elsewhere (Lam et al., 1999). Clients are asked to read this and to feed back on the elements of this information that they find helpful and less helpful. They are given clear permission to disagree with the information where they wish to, so that we can engage in a genuine discussion about the approach.

Two issues can arise, either following discussion of the handout or in assessment generally:

- **Mental health difficulties on a continuum**: some clients do not believe that the diagnosis that they have been given is correct. They may either think that their experiences are just part of who they are and therefore not an illness or sometimes that there is an illness present but not bipolar disorder. Where this issue arises, it is not helpful to get into a debate about the rights and wrongs of diagnosis. Usually it *is* helpful to have a discussion about the psychological approach to mental health/illness that assumes that an individual's propensity for different mental health problems is arrayed across continua. Therefore, if an individual can acknowledge that he or she is having some problems in living and need help with these, it is usually possible to engage in therapy even if the client denies bipolar disorder *per se*.
- **Integrating medical and psychological models of illness**: some clients are overcompliant with a medical model of illness. This means that they see their illness in terms of a chemical imbalance that requires pharmacological correction. This is not surprising, as clients often report that this is the message they have taken from their meetings with their psychiatrists. It can often be helpful in this situation to engage in a discussion about the interaction between psychological and social factors in a wide range of medical problems, including asthma, arthritis and diabetes. This can help the client to see that there is a false dichotomy between medical and psychological aspects of both physical and mental health problems and that optimal outcomes are ensured by an appropriate combination of both approaches.

ENGAGEMENT AS A PROCESS

Engagement is not something that happens in the first few sessions of therapy and is then safely ignored. Although you need to engage clients to begin therapy, you also need to maintain this engagement as therapy continues. For individuals with strong achievement motivation and perfectionism – characteristics of many bipolar clients – the overall cognitive behavioural approach is very helpful in maintaining engagement. Taking a genuinely collaborative problem-solving stance in therapy can help therapists avoid becoming locked into conflicts or battles of wills with the client. It is crucial to respect the client's own perspective even when this does not seem to be correct therapeutically, but also to explore this with Socratic questioning and other cognitive techniques. This balance is important, as in our experience bipolar clients are very alert to when therapists are using questioning in a more directive or didactic way.

LIFE CHARTS AND SHARED ACCOUNT OF SYMPTOM DEVELOPMENT

These are a common part of cognitive behaviour therapy. They are, however, especially crucial for engagement and therapy with bipolar clients. The process of developing and applying life-chart information is dealt with in detail later in the chapter. At this stage, it is useful to highlight that working with the client to generate accounts of the interaction between mood episodes, psychological factors, behaviour, life events, medication and substance use is crucial to engagement. When clients are aware that there is a pattern to their experiences it also indicates that this pattern can potentially be changed. Many individuals will initially see their episodes as coming out of the blue. The realization that this is not the case is often a key moment in engaging clients with the therapeutic intervention.

Goal setting

The setting of agreed goals is a further important part of cognitive therapy. There are a broad range of goals that clients might report and some of the main areas are discussed below. It is important that the therapist and client work together to identify the goals that are important for the client. Therapists therefore need to be alert to goals that are generated for others or because clients 'feel they should'. As with other client groups, unless the bipolar client has ownership of his or her therapy goals, the hard work of therapy will be made substantially more difficult. Areas for goal setting include:

SYMPTOM REDUCTION

Clients will often highlight a desire to learn cognitive therapy techniques to help them to reduce and control symptoms of mania or depression. Sometimes, initial goals are unrealistic, for example, 'to never feel low again' or 'to be happy whatever happens'. Clearly it is important to acknowledge that such goals are understandable but also unrealistic. This can lead onto a discussion of what could be reasonably expected in these areas.

Josephine first stated that she wanted to have a cure for low mood and depression. She has experienced moderate depression for a long time and thought that medication was not helping her. Her aim was to never feel low again and to be just like her uncle Jim, who she identified as the most cheerful member of her extended family. It was necessary to discuss what therapy could realistically help with, and its limitations. Although Josephine found this disappointing initially, she found that she felt quite positive about being 'trusted with the truth' and identified a goal of increasing her control of mood symptoms so that they had less impact on her life.

LIFE GOALS

Although some clients will highlight symptom issues from the outset, others will not. Many people will come to therapy frustrated and upset with the impact that their illness has had on practical aspects of their life. This may be in terms of family relationships, work, study or other areas. This frustration will often be associated with a desire to fix problems totally and immediately. Again, this should be discussed in an open way. With functional goals it will often be important to work out what might be realistically achievable within therapy and then to break down the steps towards such a goal.

Josephine wanted to get back to her post in the Civil Service by the end of therapy. She felt that she had missed out and that she needed to get back into employment and make up for lost time. Given that at assessment she was significantly depressed, had no routine, had alcohol problems and required supported accommodation, this did not seem realistic. There was therefore a discussion about what would need to change for Josephine to achieve this goal. This led to an agreement that such a goal was probably overambitious and to a search for a worthwhile alternative. Eventually, Josephine decided that she wanted to develop her symptom management skills over the course of therapy to the point that she could begin to explore possibilities of part-time voluntary work. This would then allow her to assess further whether her original goal was a reasonable target in the longer term.

Josephine identified a number of other therapy goals. These included understanding triggers for mood episodes, learning cognitive skills to control her mood so that it was less of a roller-coaster, developing a routine, finding a direction in life and finding ways of dealing with the stigma of diagnosis.

Additional goals might be:

MEDICATION ADHERENCE

Evidence to date indicates that cognitive therapy is effective for bipolar disorder in conjunction with appropriate medication. Therefore adherence goals may form part of goal setting. The target here would be to work with clients to identify an optimum system of pharmacological treatment. This involves clients being supported in working actively with their psychiatric team to address limitations of current medications and for clients to have a clear say in their own treatment. In our experience, it is important for clients to identify a prescribing clinician with whom they can develop a collaborative relationship (including use of medication as needed to address prodromal changes).

BUILDING SOCIAL NETWORKS

As indicated in the assessment section above, many bipolar clients, even when remitted, will have some social difficulties. These are often made worse by having a limited social network. Sometimes this network will have been reduced over time as a consequence of episodes of illness. Working with clients to build up a combination of formal and informal support can be important in maintaining therapy gains.

CHALLENGING DYSFUNCTIONAL BELIEFS

There is no evidence that dysfunctional beliefs have a causal role in the onset of bipolar illness. Indeed, they may act as a coping mechanism. However, it is postulated that these beliefs may interact with the illness and predispose bipolar clients to have a more severe course of illness. Clinically, it is observed that clients with highly driven beliefs are more at risk of further episodes, sometimes through lack of routine and structure and at other times through disappointment. These beliefs can be tackled by traditional cognitive therapy techniques. A list of pros and cons of such extreme beliefs can help clients to step back and examine the drawbacks of such beliefs. In doing so, it is important to acknowledge the advantages of having such beliefs. A life chart can also be a very useful tool for both the client and the therapist about past coping behaviour.

In the case of Josephine, the clear advantages of having very high goals and excelling in her studies or job was to get the admiration and respect of friends and family. She was able to produce evidence of making friends who were also 'top drawer'. However, the downside was that she spent so much effort in achieving academically and in her job that she neglected pleasurable and relaxing activities. There was no circle of friends that she could socialize with. She thought that if she was less driven, she could have developed better social skills in her teens. She also thought that the driven behaviour contributed to repeated episodes. She was very disappointed about being off sick. Every time she returned to work she tried to prove to herself and her colleagues that she was back to normal. She overcompensated by plunging into her work as if nothing had happened. Furthermore, she deliberately took on more tasks to prove that she was her 'perfect able self again'. As with challenging dysfunctional beliefs, appealing to pragmatism and carrying out behavioural experiments can sometimes be helpful. In Josephine's case, she was persuaded to set a lower target and examine the outcome. Specifically, she was persuaded to set fewer hours of practising on the computer to prepare herself to get back to work and schedule in breaks. To her surprise, she found that she was able to achieve more by making more reasonable demands on herself.

STRUCTURE AND ROUTINE

Vulnerability–stress models note the importance of structure and routine for individuals with bipolar disorder. The development of structure is an important part of cognitive therapy. Clients record their patterns of activity from early on in therapy, completing an activity schedule that covers

24 hours a day. This is important, as many clients will not have a stable routine when they enter therapy. They may have very erratic sleep patterns and be more active at night than during the day. Working to improve this situation is not as simple as it may first appear. Many individuals with bipolar disorder are highly motivated, driven people. If they feel that they are being asked to engage in behaviour that they see as restrictive or limiting, they will not engage. The information used from the assessment process is employed to look at the extent to which chaos may have been associated with previous mood history. There then follows a baseline period of activity recording to establish current patterns. Normally, clients will also record their mood on the same chart for each day between −10 (lowest ever) and +10 (highest ever). It is then possible in session to review the connections between mood activity and sleep. The process of increasing structure and routine is best done as an experiment to see whether it has an impact on mood and mood stability. When planning this, the therapist is aiming to increase the predictability of key markers in the day, such as sleep, wake and main meal times. It also provides an opportunity to plan for a balance of activities during the week between domestic, leisure and work tasks. Although clients may be initially sceptical about this process, they often find that it has significant benefits. They often report being more productive and creative when their routine is less chaotic. There is also the potential for planning for periods when disruption is unavoidable. For instance, it is important that clients who are going to undertake transatlantic travel plan their activities to allow them to cope with the circadian disruption that this causes. The outcome of this planning is often that individuals are able to cope with a broader range of activities and challenges than when routine seemed more spontaneous.

Josephine had very little in the way of structure and routine. Since she had stopped working, she had spent a lot of time at home. She had lost contact with friends and had decided that she need to avoid all stress. This meant that if she had a disturbed night's sleep, she stayed in bed for all of the next day to compensate. If there were tasks to be done, she put them off indefinitely in case they caused her more pressure. When she began recording her activities, this pattern became apparent. It also became clear that, other than sleeping, her main activities were chores around the house. When the lack of balance and routine was discussed, Josephine acknowledged that she sometimes wanted to do other things but was afraid what would happen if she did. She explained that, prior to her last manic episode, she had worked very hard, taken little sleep and had a very erratic routine. She subsequently decided that she would avoid this but had not been able to come up with an alternative. Some time was therefore spent in working out a reasonable compromise between these two extremes. Elements of a more balanced routine were then introduced over several sessions. Josephine's records indicated that her mood improved and stabilized under this approach. This evidence enabled her to feel confident in engaging with further work on structure and routine, which she continued throughout therapy.

Moderating risky behaviour and avoiding risky situations

A particular important component of cognitive therapy is to examine risky behaviour or situations that led to relapses in the past. This is very idiosyncratic and is best done by going through the life chart. The examination includes any situations that may lead to risky behaviour, such as use of street drugs, excessive alcohol, examinations and work situations that might cause the client to switch into a disorganized routine or a state of sleep deprivation. Work involving long hours and extensive travel requirements can be associated with onset of prodromal symptoms. It is therefore important that the individual acts to moderate these areas as far as is possible. A balanced life style, which involves regular and consistent work hours, often enhances work output and performance in the long run.

Identifying prodromes and coping

To define their pattern of prodromes, clients are simply asked to say, in their experience, what aspects of their behaviour, thinking or mood suggest they are entering a manic or depressive episode. It is important to consider that the symptoms have to be specific and easily detectable. Often, it is helpful to ask clients to anchor their prodromes in a social context, for example in their social interaction with others and comments from other people. Each individual prodromal symptom is written on a piece of paper. Clients are encouraged to sort the pile of paper into three groups: the early, middle and late stages. Most clients find it useful to sort the pile of paper first into early and late stages and the rest go into the middle stage. The therapist and the client then further fine-tune the pattern of prodromes to make sure there is no ambiguity in wording.

Mood states are difficult to gauge. Hence, they are often carefully defined and anchored in the clients' social context if possible. The behaviour linked to the mood state should be mapped out. Often behaviour is easier to monitor. For example, if irritability is a prodromal symptom, the therapist can ask how the irritability shows itself. One client was able to say that he was usually irritable with his wife and picks on her at the very early stage of an episode. As the episode unfolds he is usually irritable with his daughter and, at the final stage, he is irritable with almost anyone. In practice, the last stage of the prodromal phase is almost a full-blown stage for most clients. However, it is important to distinguish it from the full-blown episode. Sometimes clients find the transition into the full-blown stage quite blurry and usually move from the late stage of mania prodromes to a full-blown episode within a day. The prodromal symptoms of these three stages are copied onto a prodromes form. Next, clients are asked to estimate the time intervals they have before the very early stage becomes the middle stage and the middle stage becomes the late stage. The therapist then discusses with the client ways of coping with bipolar prodromes using cognitive and behavioural techniques. The cognitive model of emotional disorder about the way thinking, behaviour and mood can affect each other is used. Some examples of coping strategies of mania prodromes are: avoiding stimulation, engaging in calming activities, resisting the temptation to engage in further goal-directed behaviour and prioritizing tasks. Cognitive behavioural techniques of routine, prioritizing, pleasurable and mastery activities and challenging of negative thoughts have an important part in coping with depression prodromes. During the depression prodromal stage, activating the client's social network for support is important. Social companionship and shared activities can prevent clients from ruminating about their depression leading to an increase in depression symptoms (Lam et al., 2003; Nolen-Hoeksema, 1991). Most clients find it helpful to discuss unrealistic worries with a close other. An empathic confidant can inject some reality into clients' overwhelming and unrealistic worries. Medical appointments and self-medication can be seen as good coping strategies. Making good use of hospital and professional help is part of clients' coping strategies. It is very important for clients to have a mutually respectful and trusting relationship with their psychiatrists. A significant proportion of bipolar clients obtain their medication from general practitioners. It is often helpful for clients to show their key workers or prescribing doctors their record of 'Coping with prodrome form'. It may be a good practice to enclose this record in the discharge report. How early professionals should be called on to help depends on the clients' resources as well as how long the prodromal stages are. Figure 9.1 shows Josephine's 'Coping with Manic Prodromes Form'.

There are several considerations to bear in mind when eliciting prodromes. First, the decision of where the prodromal phases end and a full-blown illness begins can be difficult where onset is more gradual. The onset of mania is often more acute and is less of a problem. However, a depressive episode may gradually become worse over several weeks or months. Second, it is not unusual that some clients suffer from residual symptoms, which may be similar to the prodromal symptoms. Where this is the case, it is even harder to define when residual symptoms change to a prodromal stage. As mentioned above, some clients find it hard to detect prodromes spontaneously, particularly for depression. Consistent with the ethos of monitoring and regulating, therapists should take every opportunity to map out the details of individual patterns of prodromes whenever clients are in a prodromal stage and help clients to practise a more adaptive way of coping. For clients who truly cannot list prodromes spontaneously, it is often helpful to suggest that they should discuss them with close others. As a last resort, a list of common prodromes can be presented to help clients to identify those that are applicable

Name: ___Josephine_________

My very early warning signs of mania are:

1. Waking up early (2 hours)
2. More energetic, e.g. spend an hour tidying my old belongings and want to do more
3. Wanting to spend more time with people (ring up four or five of my friends in a week to arrange meeting them)
4. 'Choppy thoughts' – thoughts jumping about
5. Drinking during the week

Action:

1. Relax by listening to soft music and do housework for half an hour a day maximum
2. Have a relaxing bath and go to bed earlier
3. No drinking during the week or even at the weekend
4. Only go out once during the week and ring two friends in a week

My middle warning signs of mania are:

1. Speaking a lot faster – mum would say slow down
2. Increased spending on clothes and makeup
3. Really wanting to go out – ringing anybody I know
4. Trouble sleeping – only four hours a night
5. Smoking up to 20 a day (normally a packet lasts three to four days)

Action:

1. Time off from studying and do relaxing activities such as walking and listening to soft music and sit by the pond
2. Get medication to help me to sleep
3. No alcohol in the house
4. Make sure I only do the minimal and no extra cleaning
5. Give my credit card to my mum

My late warning signs of mania are:

1. Very irritable – bad language
2. Increased sexual appetite
3. Not going to bed
4. Having such energy that I would scrub the house top to bottom

Action:

1. Give my mobile phone to my parents
2. Cancel my social commitments
3. Do not go out on my own
4. See my psychiatrists and go into hospital

Figure 9.1 Coping with Manic Prodromes Form for Josephine.

to them. However, great care should be taken that these prodromes identified are then elaborated and anchored in the idiosyncratic context. Last, bipolar clients can exhibit frightening psychotic symptoms at an early stage and, as the episode deepens, the psychotic experiences can become increasingly bizarre. Clients often find it helpful to discuss these frightening experiences with someone who is treating them with empathy and understanding. These experiences can be very 'lonely' if clients cannot share them even with their intimate partners or close friends.

In working out coping strategies, it is often a good idea to bear in mind the clients' resources as well as problems. Therapists should rely on Socratic questioning and guided discovery rather than prescribing coping strategies. If therapists rely on persuasion or prescribing coping strategies, clients may find their sense of autonomy offended and hence reject the suggestions. In any case, clients' circumstances are different. Techniques prescribed routinely without taking clients' experience and circumstances into consideration are unlikely to work.

It is not unusual for bipolar clients to like the early stages of mania. They find being more confident, energetic and sociable enjoyable. They might want to pursue certain risky behaviour to get the best out of their high levels of energy. This temptation is understandable, particularly when clients usually suffer from residual symptoms of depression. Therapists should respect the clients' opinions but discuss the pros and cons of certain coping strategies to guide clients to come to a conclusion about whether these strategies are dysfunctional. It often works better if clients can see the pros and cons and then decide on the most appropriate coping strategies.

Dealing with grandiosity

Many of the features of cognitive therapy in bipolar clients are recognizable from work with clients with depression. The issue of grandiosity and the thoughts associated with elevated mood present a different problem, however. Whereas when working with low mood and negative thoughts both therapist and client are working to try to remove unwanted symptoms, with elevated mood and positive thoughts many clients are at best ambivalent at first. Two main approaches are important here:

RETROSPECTIVE EVALUATION OF THOUGHTS AND OUTCOMES

Clients are asked to recall an episode of prodromal hypomanic symptoms. They then recall how they behaved and what they thought in particular situations within this episode. Often, there will be a situation in which the person engaged in risky or impulsive behaviour, which can then be explored for associated thoughts and outcomes. In recalling this, it is important to work with the client to try to identify early changes in thinking and to track these as the situation developed. As clients begin to see such thinking as symptomatic of a particular mood state, rather than 'it's just me', it becomes more likely that they will be able to intervene when such thoughts occur in the future. Another important issue in evaluating such situations is to clarify the outcomes. There is often a tendency for clients to focus on the positive aspects of changed mood and to down-play the immediate and later consequences of their actions. This can again be relevant for clients to make an informed choice about changes that they want to make with respect to their goals.

Josephine recalled a situation when she was a civil servant. After a period of low mood she came to work feeling unusually positive. As she sat at her desk she began to think of ways that the office she worked in could be managed better. As she thought about possible improvements she became more excited and when she finished work for the day she went home to work on a development plan. Josephine mentioned to her manager that she had some good ideas, to which he responded neutrally, with little interest. The following day she informed him that she had developed a three-year plan for the office that she was certain would revolutionize the way it was run and make it a model for other offices in the Civil Service. When he questioned some of her ideas and refused to act immediately on the plan, she responded angrily. She then left work and spent the day at home phoning more senior Civil Service staff in an effort to move her plans forward. She became very angry as she felt that these people were also not recognizing the revolutionary nature of the plan that she had developed. This continued over a period of several days, after which she was called into work and given a formal warning over her behaviour. Soon after this, her mood declined and she experienced an episode of severe depression. In therapy it was important to clarify the true nature of this episode. When Josephine first described it, she mainly recalled feeling positive, excited and full of good ideas. It was only on further discussion that it became clear that the manner in which she had approached her managers and her level of obsession with this particular idea were abnormal for her. She also became aware that she was putting her job at risk as a result of her approach to this and that, given her role within the office, it was not realistic to expect her to be given responsibility for planning its overall strategy.

CHALLENGING THOUGHTS

Once it is agreed that there are episodes where patterns of thinking are symptomatic of mood change towards hypomania, clients can also be asked to work on thought challenges. They will first do this retrospectively, recalling the thoughts they had in specific situations, such as described by Josephine above. They will then work with the therapist to identify alternative more adaptive thoughts – just as when dealing with thoughts associated with depression. The primary difference here is that bipolar clients will only engage with this process once they understand why it might be appropriate to alter what at first glance may feel like ‘good thoughts’.

Delaying tactics

As indicated above, it is extremely helpful to build-up thinking skills when clients are in remission so that they can then draw on them when their mood changes. Clients may come into therapy in elevated mood before it has been possible to establish skilful cognitive approaches to prodromes. In such cases it is very important to avoid getting into battles. If they come in, often after a period of low mood, excited about a good idea, they will not welcome a negative reaction from their therapist. One approach, which was first described by Monica Basco (Basco & Rush, 1996), is the delaying tactic. Here the therapist asks clients to describe the idea that they have. If it appears to be a risky or potentially harmful idea, it is helpful to explore with the clients what they see as the positive and negative aspects of trying to implement the idea. Often, the negative will be around other people being resistant to the new idea. It is also helpful to review whether clients can identify previous periods when they have had ideas that excited them in this way and what the outcomes were. It is important here to take an open-minded approach. Many bipolar clients are creative individuals and some ideas that do not immediately make sense to the therapist may in fact be very positive. The delaying tactic allows for this possibility. Clients will usually be adamant that this plan is a very good one and that it is not associated with any mental health issues. The therapist therefore asks if the client is willing to put the idea to the test. If it is a good idea now, it will be a good idea in a day or two. Clients will normally acknowledge this, and that their patience in fully evaluating their idea might bring others round. It also gives time for mood to change again. Thus, if the evidence accumulates to indicate that the idea has merit, the client gets more support. If it is mood driven, it increases the chances of potential harm being avoided.

Interpersonal and social rhythm therapy

Rationale for social rhythm therapy: Sleep disruptions in bipolar affective disorder

The evidence that bipolar clients experience more life events prior to the onset of an episode than non-psychiatric controls is overwhelming (Bebbington et al., 1993; Johnson and Roberts, 1995; Kennedy et al., 1983; Perris, 1984). However, before an episode, bipolar clients do not experience significantly more life events than clients suffering from schizophrenia (Bebbington et al., 1993; Clancy et al., 1973; Perris, 1984), or unipolar depression (Bebbington et al., 1993; Swann et al., 1990). In fact, Bebbington et al. (1993) reported that psychotically depressed clients experienced more life events than manic clients. Clinically, it is also observed that some bipolar clients develop a manic episode after a couple of sleepless nights due to long distance travelling or jetlag. Hence, it has been postulated (Wehr et al., 1987) that the common path leading to mania is sleep disruption; with disruption of social routines and sleep leading to a state of sleepless hyperactivity. Malkoff-Schwartz and colleagues (Malkoff-Schwartz et al., 1998) tested the role of social-rhythm-disruption events in bipolar disorder. Thirty-nine bipolar clients were monitored in a longitudinal study. Each life event was rated for threat (unpleasantness) and social rhythm disruptions (the extent to which the event disrupts social routine and sleep). Eight weeks prior to manic episodes, significantly more clients had social rhythm disruption events compared to eight-week episode-free periods for the same clients.

IPSRT is based on the theory that overstimulation, which could lead to bipolar episodes, can be addressed by reducing interpersonal stress and adopting regular routines of sleeping, waking, eating, exercise and social interaction, and thus increasing circadian integrity. In a controlled study, IPSRT was compared with a conventional medication clinic approach. Preliminary analysis (Frank, 1999) with a subsample showed that both groups showed comparable changes in symptomatology over a treatment period lasting up to fifty-two weeks. The IPSRT group showed significantly greater stability of routines. In a preliminary report, it was found that IPSRT was superior to intensive clinical management in preventing bipolar depressive symptoms but not manic symptoms. There was no effect in preventing episodes. The final analyses are about to be reported. Another study found family-focused treatment to be tentative and significantly better than individual approach (Rea et al., 2003).

Family-focused treatment

Family functioning, expressed emotion and bipolar affective disorder

Expressed emotion (EE; Leff & Vaughan, 1985) can be seen as an indication of the emotional environment the client lives in, normally at home. It is measured by the Camberwell Family Interview (Vaughan & Leff, 1976), which assesses: criticism, hostility (over-generalization of criticism or rejection), emotional overinvolvement (overprotection or overdevotion) and warmth. Typically, if one relative is rated as high EE, the client is seen as living in a high EE environment. As in research in schizophrenia, high levels of criticism or emotional overinvolvement by parents or spouses lead to poor outcomes in terms of relapses or poor symptomatic outcome in bipolar disorder (Honig et al., 1997; Miklowitz et al., 1988; O'Connell et al., 1991; Priebe et al., 1989).

Family-focused treatment (FFT) was based on the finding that bipolar clients in a high EE environment fared worse than bipolar clients in a low EE environment. Therapy targets families after the client has been stabilized following a hypomanic episode. The programme consists of psychoeducation about bipolar disorder, communication training and problem-solving skills training (Miklowitz, 2002; Miklowitz & Goldstein, 1997). In an intervention study (Miklowitz et al., 2003), 101 bipolar clients were assigned to FFT

(N = 31) or to two family education sessions and follow-up crisis management (CM; N = 70). Survival analysis showed that the FFT group had fewer relapses and longer delays before relapses during the two-year study period than the CM group. The FFT group also showed greater improvements in symptoms. Clients from high EE families benefited most from the FFT.

FFT involves twenty-one sessions over nine months: twelve weekly sessions, six fortnightly sessions, and three monthly sessions. Clients, their partners, siblings, parents and older children may all be included in sessions, although often it is a couple who attends. The programme begins after symptoms have abated and the client is being maintained on mood-stabilizing medication following a hypomanic episode. A contract to complete the programme is framed as an opportunity for the couple to understand bipolar disorder, to accept the concept of vulnerability to relapses, to accept the need for maintenance on mood-stabilizing medication, to distinguish the person from the bipolar disorder, to recognize and cope with stressful situations that may precipitate relapses and to re-establish a supportive relationship after the episode. An assessment of the couple is conducted to determine their understanding of bipolar disorder, their capacity for clear communication, their problem-solving skills and the degree to which they can avoid becoming embroiled in stressful patterns of interaction characterized by either criticism or overinvolvement. A framework for couples assessment is given in Chapter 5.

Following assessment, which may span between two and four sessions, psychoeducation becomes the main focus until about session 10. The couple is given detailed information about the symptoms, course, relapse pattern, probable causes and multi-modal treatment of bipolar disorder. In some couples, the non-symptomatic partner overidentifies the person with the illness, becomes overinvolved and treats the bipolar patient as an invalid. In other couples, the non-symptomatic partner treats the patient in a critical, aggressive way, doubting the reality of the disorder and blaming the patient for acting so irresponsibly. During psychoeducation, the therapist conveys that bipolar disorder is a challenge that the couple must come to understand and cope with together, in the same way that couples manage other medical challenges like diabetes. Adherence to medication regimes and avoidance of major life stresses that might precipitate relapse are given attention during psychoeducation. This information is given within the context of a formulation specific to the client and the couples strengths and vulnerabilities. As part of psychoeducation, the couple write a relapse drill in which they specify the patient's prodromal signs of relapse and a list of 'who will do what' when these occur.

The next seven sessions are devoted to communication enhancement training. Here, couples are coached in how to send clear, unambiguous messages, to make clear statements, to make clear requests, to listen in an active empathic way and to check that accurate understanding has occurred.

Communication enhancement training is offered to couples as a way of avoiding the sorts of relationship tension that can lead to relapses. Where couples have an overly critical or overly involved relational style, and typically engage in communication where there is rapid turn taking and little thought to what is said or the accuracy of what is understood, communication enhancement training can slow this stressful process down.

The next few sessions focus on helping couples identify and define family problems in solvable terms, and then systematically select, plan, implement and evaluate these solutions. Common problems addressed during this part of therapy include how to manage daily or weekly routines, how to manage finances and how to plan leisure time. Problem-solving skills training offers couples a way to reduce stress by making their attempts at solving family problems more predictable, more co-operative and more effective. A detailed account of communication and problem-solving skills training is given in Chapter 5.

In later sessions, the use of communication and problem-solving skills is reviewed, and relapse management is discussed. When reviewing the use of communication and problem-solving skills, the emphasis is on pinpointing and building on the couple's strengths, and treating setbacks as new challenges that may be addressed with the couple's strengths. With relapse management, the focus is on helping couples articulate and 'own' what they have learned about bipolar disorder, the importance of medication adherence, the importance of stress management, the necessity for clear communication and systematic joint problem solving, and how they will recognize and manage prodromal signs associated with relapse. Couples are also referred at the end of therapy to support groups for people with bipolar disorder and their families.

SUMMARY

Bipolar disorder is characterized by mania/hypomania and depression. There are two subtypes: bipolar I disorder, with at least one manic episode or mixed episode and one major depressive episode, and bipolar II, with at least one hypomanic episode and one major depressive episode but no manic or mixed episodes. Bipolar disorder is relatively common, with a prevalence rate of 1–1.9% in Europe and the USA. Although bipolar disorder was historically viewed as a condition with periods of mania and depression interspersed with periods of 'normality', recent evidence suggests that clients experience high levels of symptoms between episodes, are at high risk of relapse and have substantial social problems. A client who has recovered from a bipolar mood episode has a 50% risk of having a further episode within a year, and the course of bipolar disorder can become more severe over time. Bipolar disorder is associated with high risk of self-harm and suicide, with an estimated annual rate of suicide of 0.4% – twenty times higher than in the general population. Family studies indicate a two to three times higher risk for relatives of bipolar clients to develop the disorder than the general population. Common comorbid conditions include personality disorders, particularly in the B and C clusters, alcohol and substance abuse and panic disorder. The presence of personality disorder is commonly associated with greater illness severity, including higher risk of self-harm and suicide and poorer outcome. Co-existence of any of these disorders is associated with poorer therapeutic outcomes, due to more difficulties with therapeutic engagement, higher levels of symptomatology and more frequent hospitalizations. Gathering information from clients during assessment is a prerequisite for treatment planning, as well as an opportunity to come to a shared understanding with clients of how the disorder affects them. A careful interview will cover family history of mental health difficulties and the effects of these on the client, illness history and the relationship between life events and symptoms, and the client's views on diagnosis and medication. Assessment of current mood state, coping with prodromes, levels of dysfunctional beliefs and experience of stigma, hopelessness and suicidality, the client's social skills and sources of professional and informal support may also be made at interview and through the use of self-monitoring forms, standardized self-report and observer measures. Treatment of bipolar disorder typically involves pharmacotherapy, psychoeducation about the interaction of genetic vulnerability and stress in the production of symptoms, and interventions to teach the client to use strategies to cope with stress.

There are three evidence-based psychological treatments for bipolar disorder: complex psychoeducation, cognitive-behavioural treatment (CBT) and family-focused treatment (FFT). Complex psychoeducation incorporates information giving, problem-solving techniques and detection of prodromes. Cognitive-behavioural therapy is based on the assumption that thinking, mood and behaviour affect each other. The therapist aims to teach the client techniques to monitor, examine and change dysfunctional thinking and behaviour associated with undesirable mood states. Initial work on engaging the client is followed by setting and working with cognitive techniques towards goals around symptom reduction, longer-term life goals, medication adherence, building social networks, challenging dysfunctional beliefs, increasing structure and routine, moderating risky behaviours and identifying and responding effectively to prodomes or signs of relapse. FFT is based on the finding that bipolar clients in a family environment of high expressed emotion, an environment characterized by high criticism, hostility and overinvolvement, fare worse than bipolar clients in a low EE environment. After a bipolar episode, families are offered psychoeducation about the illness, communication training and problem-solving skills training.

EXERCISE 9.1: ENGAGEMENT AND GOAL SETTING

Interview in pairs. The client is an individual referred for CBT for bipolar disorder. However, the client's main priority is to 'get well' so as to re-establish a relationship with a partner that broke down six months ago when the client was high. The therapist's task is to assess whether it is possible to agree on symptom and functional goals that would permit engagement with CBT.

This exercise illustrates the process of negotiating the combination of realistic goals as part of the engagement process. It highlights that many clients do not appear at initial sessions with clearly defined symptom goals.

EXERCISE 9.2: WORKING WITH ELEVATED MOOD

Interview in pairs. The therapist has known the client for two or three sessions and, currently, engagement is only partial. As the session progresses, the therapist notices that the client's mood is elevated and the client mentions that he/she has stopped taking lithium. The therapist tries to encourage the client to moderate activity levels, engage in calming activities and re-start lithium. However, the client feels great, thinks he/she is fine and that the current mood change is a great opportunity to make up for lost time.

Illustrate the importance of shared formulation and proper collaborative relationship to achieve change. Feed back to the facilitator on the processes, cognitions and emotions associated with being in the roles of client and therapist.

EXERCISE 9.3: IDENTIFYING PRODROMES

Prodrome card-sort in pairs. The therapist and client brainstorm a list of possible early warning signs for mania. Once all possible signs have been elicited, these are each separately entered onto index cards. The client and therapist work together to identify early, middle and late signs as the client allocates cards to each category. The client is encouraged to estimate the duration of each stage: early, middle and late.

This task illustrates the need to have an in-depth shared knowledge of the client's experience if early warnings signs are to be elicited and ordered in a meaningful manner. The client experience of attempting to order signs is important in understanding why some individuals might not find this easy to do. This also shows how, for most people, early signs are normally relatively mild and changeable, whereas later signs are more severe and require more intensive professional input.

EXERCISE 9.4: DEALING WITH SHAME AND GUILT

Interview in pairs referring to Josephine, presented above. The person in the role of Josephine role-plays feeling low and ashamed because she has not returned to full-time employment. Although she is engaged in a range of activities, she feels a failure and is unsure whether she wishes to continue with therapy. The therapist's role is to employ a cognitive-behavioural approach to help Josephine to see the realistic progress that she has made. This will include discussion on the possibly harmful effects of the achievement driven behaviour and perfectionism, which Josephine has identified previously.

This illustrates the importance of dealing with long-term issues in therapy and avoiding patterns of behaviour that will leave the client vulnerable to increased risk of relapse.

EVIDENCE SUMMARIES

Craighead, E., Miklowitz, D., Frank, E. & Vajk, F. (2002). Psychosocial treatments for bipolar disorder. In P. Nathan & J. Gorman (Eds.), *A guide to treatments that work* (Second Edition, pp. 263–276). New York: Oxford University Press.

Jones, S.H. (2004). A review of psychotherapeutic interventions for bipolar disorder. *Journal of Affective Disorders*, 80, 101–114.

Keck, P. & McElroy, S. (2002). Pharmacological treatment of bipolar disorder. In P. Nathan & J. Gorman (Eds.), *A guide to treatments that work* (Second Edition, pp. 277–300). New York: Oxford University Press.

FURTHER READING FOR PRACTITIONERS

Lam, D., Hayward, P., Bright, J. & Jones, S. (1999). *Cognitive therapy for bipolar disorder*. Chichester, UK: Wiley.

Miklowitz, D. & Goldstein, M. (1997). *Bipolar disorder: A family-focused treatment approach*. New York: Guilford.

Newman, C., Leahy, R., Beck, A., Reilly-Harrington, N. & Gyulai, L. (2002). *Bipolar disorder: A cognitive therapy approach*. Washington, DC: American Psychological Association.

Otto, M., Reilly, N.A., Harrington, N., Kogan, J. et al. (1999). *Cognitive behaviour therapy for bipolar disorder: Treatment manual*. Boston, MA: Massachusetts General Hospital.

Swartz, H., Markowitz, J. & Frank, E. (2002). Interpersonal psychotherapy for unipolar and bipolar disorder. In S. Hofmann & M. Tompson (Eds.), *Treating chronic and severe mental disorders: A handbook of empirically supported interventions* (pp. 131–158). New York: Guilford.

FURTHER READING FOR CLIENTS

Jamison, K. (1995). *An unquiet mind.* London: Picador. Autobiographical account by a psychologist.

Jones, S. H., Hayward, P. & Lam, D.H. (2003). *Coping with bipolar disorder* (Second, Edition). Oxford: Oneworld.

Miklowitz, D.J. (2002). *The bipolar disorder survival guide: What you and your family need to know.* New York: Guilford Press.

ASSESSMENT INSTRUMENTS

Altman, E., Hedeker, D., Janicak, P. et al. (1994). The Clinician Administered Rating Scale for Mania (CARS-M). Development reliability and validity. *Biological Psychiatry*, 36, 124–134.

Bauer, M., Crits-Cristoph, P., Ball, W. & Dewees, E. et al. (1991). Independent assessment of manic and depressive symptoms by self-rating: Scale characteristics and implications for the study of mania. *Archives of General Psychiatry*, 48, 807–812.

Dausch, B., Miklowitz, D., & Richards, J. (1996). A scale for the global assessment of relational functioning. II. Reliability and validity in a sample of families of bipolar patients. *Family Process*, 35, 175–189.

Monk, T., Flaherty, J., Frank, E. et al. (1990). The Social Rhythm Metric: An instrument to quantify the daily rhythms of life. *Journal of Nervous and Mental Diseases*, 178, 120–126.

REFERENCES

Altman, E. S., Rea, M. M., Mintz, J., et al. (1992). Prodromal symptoms and signs of bipolar relapse: A report based on prospectively collected data. *Psychiatry Research*, 41(1), 1–8.

Ambelas, A. (1987). Life events and mania. A special relationship? *British Journal of Psychiatry*, 150, 235–240.

American Psychiatric Association (APA) (2000). *Diagnostic and statistical manual of the mental disorders* (Fourth Edition-Text Revision). Washington, DC: APA.

American Psychiatric Association (APA) (2002). *American Psychiatric Association Practice Guideline for the Treatment of Patients with Bipolar Disorder*. Washington, DC: APA.

Andreasen, N. C. et al. (1981). Reliability of lifetime diagnosis. A multicenter collaborative perspective. *Archives of General Psychiatry*, 38(4), 400–405.

Angst, F., Stassen, H. H., Clayton, P. J. & Angst J. (2002). Mortality of patients with mood disorders: follow-up over 34–38 years. *Journal of Affective Disorders*, 68(2–3), 167–181.

Angst, J., Gamma, A., Benazzi, F., Ajdacic, V., Eich, D. & Roessler, W. (2003). Toward a re-definition of subthreshold bipolarity: Epidemiology and proposed criteria for bipolar-II, minor bipolar disorders and hypomania. *Journal of Affective Disorders*, 73(1–2), 133–146.

Basco, M. R. & Rush, A. J. (1996). *Cognitive-behavioral therapy for bipolar disorder* (pp. xix, 291). New York: The Guilford Press.

Bauer, M. S., Crits-Christoph, P., Ball, W. A., Dewees, E. et al. (1991). Independent assessment of manic and depressive symptoms by self-rating. Scale characteristics and implications for the study of mania. *Archives of General Psychiatry*, 48(9), 807–12.

Bebbington, P. & Ramana, R. (1995). The epidemiology of bipolar affective disorder. *Social Psychiatry & Psychiatric Epidemiology*, 30(6), 279–292.

Bebbington, P. et al. (1993). Life events and psychosis: Initial results from the Camberwell Collaborative Psychosis studies. *British Journal of Psychiatry*, 162, 72–79.

Bech, P. et al. (1978). The Mania Rating Scale: Scale construction and inter-observer agreement. *Neuropharmacology*, 17(6), 430–431.

Beck, A. T. & Steer, R. A. (1987). *Beck Depression Inventory*. San Antonio, TX: The Psychological Corporation/Harcourt Brace.

Beck, A. T. & Steer, R. A. (1988). *Beck Hopelessness Scale*. San Antonio, TX: The Psychological Corporation/Harcourt Brace.

Beck, A. T. et al. (1985). Hopelessness and eventual suicide: A 10-year prospective study of patients hospitalized with suicidal ideation. *American Journal of Psychiatry*, 142(5), 559–563.

Calabrese, J. R., Shelton, M. D., Rapport, D. J. & Kimmel, S. E. (2002a). Bipolar disorders and the effectiveness of novel anticonvulsants. *Journal of Clinical Psychiatry*, 63 (Suppl 3), 5–9.

Calabrese, J. R., Shelton, M. D., Rapport, D. J., Kimmel, S. E. & Elhaj, O. (2002b) Long-term treatment of bipolar disorder with lamotrigine. *Journal of Clinical Psychiatry*, 63 (Suppl 10), 18–22.

Cassidy, F., Ahearn, E. P. & Carroll, B. J. (2001). Substance abuse in bipolar disorder. *Bipolar Disorders*, 3(4), 181–188.

Chen, Y. W. & Dilsaver, S. C. (1995). Comorbidity of panic disorder in bipolar illness: Evidence from the Epidemiologic Catchment Area Survey. *American Journal of Psychiatry*, 152(2), 280–282.

Clancy, J. et al. (1973). The Iowa 500: Precipitating factors in schizophrenia and primary affective disorders. *Comprehensive Psychiatry*, 14, 197–202.

Colom, F. et al. (2003). A randomized trial on the efficacy of group psychoeducation in the prophylaxis of recurrences in bipolar patients whose disease is in remission. *Archives of General Psychiatry*, 60(4), 402–407.

Frank, E. (1999). Interpersonal and social rhythm therapy prevents depressive symptomatology in bipolar 1 patient. *Bipolar Disorder*, 1 (Suppl. 1), 13.

George, E. L., Miklowitz, D. J., Richards, J. A., Simoneau, T. L. & Taylor, D. O. (2003). The comorbidity of bipolar disorders and axis-II personality disorders: Prevalence and clinical correlates. *Bipolar Disorders*, 5(2), 115–122.

Gershon, E. S., Berrettini, W. H., Nurnberger, J. I. & Goldin, L. R. (1989). Genetic studies of affective illness. In J. J. Mann (Ed.), *Models of depressive disorders: Psychological, biological, and genetic perspectives*. The Depressive Illness Series. New York: Plenum.

Gnanadesikan, M., Freeman, M. P. & Gelenberg, A. J. (2003). Alternatives to lithium and divalproex in the maintenance treatment of bipolar disorder. *Bipolar Disorder*, 5(3), 203–216.

Goodwin, F. K. & Jamison, K. (1990). *Manic-depressive illness.* New York: Oxford University Press.

Goodwin, G. M. (2003). Evidence-based guidelines for treating bipolar disorder: Recommendations from the British Association for Psychopharmacology. *Journal of Psychopharmacology*, 17(2), 149–173; discussion 147.

Grunze, H. et al. (2002). World Federation of Societies of Biological Psychiatry (WFSBP) guidelines for biological treatment of bipolar disorders. Part I: Treatment of bipolar depression. *World Journal of Biological Psychiatry*, 3(3), 115–124.

Hamilton, M. (1960). A rating scale for depression. *Journal of Neurology and Psychiatry*, 23, 59–62.

Honig, A., Hofman, A., Rozendaal, N. & Dingemans, P. (1997). Psycho-education in bipolar disorder: Effect on expressed emotion. *Psychiatry Research*, 72(1), 17–22.

Hurry, J., Sturt, E., Bebbington, P. & Tennant, C. (1983). Socio-demographic associations with social disablement in a community sample. *Social Psychiatry*, 18, 113–121.

Johnson, S. L. & Roberts, J. E. (1995). Life events and bipolar disorder: Implications from biological theories. *Psychology Bulletin*, 117(3), 434–449.

Joyce, P. R. (1985). Illness behaviour and rehospitalization in bipolar affective disorder. *Psychological Medicine*, 15(3), 521–525.

Keck, P. E. & McElroy, S. (2002). Carbamazepine and valproate in the maintenance treatment of bipolar disorder. *Journal of Clinical Psychiatry*, 63 (Suppl. 10), 13–17.

Kennedy, S., et al. (1983). Life events precipitating mania. *British Journal of Psychiatry*, 142, 398–403.

Kusumakar, V. (2002). Antidepressants and antipsychotics in the long-term treatment of bipolar disorder. *Journal of Clinical Psychiatry*, 63 (Suppl. 10), 23–28.

Kutcher, S. P., Marton, P. & Korenblum, M. (1990). Adolescent bipolar illness and personality disorder. *Journal of the American Academy of Child & Adolescent Psychiatry*, 29(3), 355–358.

Lam, D., Bright, J. A., Jones, S. et al. (2000). Cognitive therapy for bipolar illness – a pilot study of relapse prevention. *Cognitive Therapy and Research*, 24(5), 503–520.

Lam, D., Hayward, P., Bright, J., et al. (1999). *Cognitive therapy for bipolar disorder: A therapist's guide to concepts, methods and practice*. Chichester, UK: John Wiley & Sons.

Lam, D. H., Watkins, E. R., Hayward, P., Bright, J., Wright, K., Kerr, N., Parr-Davis, G. & Sham, P. (2003). A randomized controlled study of cognitive therapy for relapse prevention for bipolar affective disorder: Outcome of the first year. *Archives of General Psychiatry*, 60(2), 145–152.

Lam, D. & Wong, G. (1997). Prodromes, coping strategies, insight and social functioning in bipolar affective disorders. *Psychological Medicine*, 27(5), 1091–1100.

Lam, D., Wong, G. & Sham, P. (2001). Prodromes, coping strategies and course of illness in bipolar affective disorder – a naturalistic study. *Psychological Medicine*, 31(8), 1397–1402.

Lam, D. et al. (in press). Dysfunctional assumptions in bipolar disorder. *Journal of Affective Disorders*.

Leff, J. & Vaughan, C. (1985). *Expressed emotion in families: Its significance for mental illness*. New York: Guilford Press.

Leverich, G. S., Altshuler, L. L., Frye, M. A., et al. (2003). Factors associated with suicide attempts in 648 patients with bipolar disorder in the Stanley Foundation Bipolar Network. *Journal of Clinical Psychiatry*, 64(5), 506–515.

Maj, M. (2003). The effect of lithium in bipolar disorder: A review of recent research evidence. *Bipolar Disorder*, 5(3), 180–188.

Malkoff-Schwartz, S., Frank, E., Anderson, B., Sherrill, J. T., Siegel, L., Patterson, D. & Kupfer, D. J. (1998). Stressful life events and social rhythm disruption in the onset of manic and depressive bipolar episodes: A preliminary investigation. *Archives of General Psychiatry*, 55(8), 702–707.

McGuffin, P., Rijsdijk, F., Andrew, M., Sham, P., Katz, R. & Cardno, A. (2003). The heritability of bipolar affective disorder and the genetic relationship to unipolar depression. *Archives of General Psychiatry*, 60(5), 497–502.

Miklowitz, D.J. (2002). *The bipolar disorder survival guide: What you and your family need to know*. New York: Guilford Press.

Miklowitz, D. J., George, E. L., Richards, J. A., et al. (2003). A randomized study of family-focused psychoeducation and pharmacotherapy in the outpatient management of bipolar disorder. *Archives of General Psychiatry*, 60(9), 904–912.

Miklowitz, D. J. & Goldstein, M. J. (1997). *Bipolar disorder: A family-focused treatment approach*. New York: Guilford Press.

Miklowitz, D. J., Goldstein, M. J., Nuechterlein, K. H., et al. (1988). Family factors and the course of bipolar affective disorder. *Archives of General Psychiatry*, 45, 225–231.

Molnar, G., Feeney, M. G. & Fava, G. A. (1988). Duration and symptoms of bipolar prodromes. *American Journal of Psychiatry*, 145(12), 1576–1578.

Moncrieff, J. (1995). Lithium revisited: A re-examination of the placebo controlled trials of lithium prophylaxis in manic depressive disorder. *British Journal of Psychiatry*, 167, 569–574.

Nolen-Hoeksema, S. (1991). Responses to depression and their effects on the duration of depressed mood. *Journal of Abnormal Psychology*, 100, 569–582.

O'Connell, R. A., Mayo, J. A., Flatow, L., et al. (1991). Outcome of bipolar disorder on long term treatment with lithium. *British Journal of Psychiatry*, 159, 123–129.

Perris, H. (1984). Life events and depression: Part 2. Results in diagnostic subgroups and in relation to the recurrence of depression. *Journal of Affective Disorders*, 7, 25–36.

Platt, S., Weyman, A., Hirsch, S. R. & Hewett, S. (1980). The Social Behaviour Assessment Schedule (SBAS): Rationale, contents, scoring and reliability of a new interview schedule. *Social Psychiatry*, 15, 43–55.

Post, R. M., Rubinow, D. R. & Ballenger, J. C. (1986). Conditioning and sensitisation in the longitudinal course of affective illness. *British Journal of Psychiatry*, 149, 191–201.

Power, M. J. et al. (1994). The Dysfunctional Attitudes Scale (DAS): A comparison of forms A and B and proposal for a new sub-scaled version. *Journal of Research in Personality*, 28, 263–276.

Priebe, S., Wildgrube, C. & Mueller-Oerlinghausen, B. (1989). Lithium prophylaxis and expressed emotion. *British Journal of Psychiatry*, 154, 396–399.

Prien, R. F. & Potter, W. Z. (1990). NIMH workshop report on treatment of bipolar disorder. *Psychopharmacology Bulletin*, 26(4), 409–427.

Rea, M. M., Tompson, M. C., Miklowitz, D. J., Goldstein, M. J., Hwang, S. & Mintz, J. (2003). Family-focused treatment versus individual treatment for bipolar disorder: Results of a randomized clinical trial. *Journal of Consulting & Clinical Psychology*, 71(3), 482–492.

Regier, D. A., et al. (1990). Comorbidity of mental disorders with alcohol and other drug abuse: Results from the Epidemiologic Catchment Area (ECA) study. *Journal of the American Medical Association*, 264, 2511–2518.

Rice, J. P., Rochberg, N., Endicott, J., et al. (1992). Stability of psychiatric diagnoses. An application to the affective disorders. *Archives of General Psychiatry*, 49(10), 824–830.

Savino, M., Perugi, G., Simonini, E., et al. (1993). Affective comorbidity in panic disorder: Is there a bipolar connection? *Journal of Affective Disorders*, 28(3), 155–163.

Scott, J., Garland, A. & Moorhead, S. (2001). A pilot study of cognitive therapy in bipolar disorders. *Psychological Medicine*, 31(3), 459–467.

Simpson, S. G., McMahon, F. J., McInnis, M. G., MacKinnon, D. F., Edwin, D., Folstein, S. E. & DePaulo, R. (2002). Diagnostic reliability of bipolar II disorder. *Archives of General Psychiatry*, 59(8), 736–740.

Smith, J. A. & Tarrier, N.(1992). Prodromal symptoms in manic depressive psychosis. *Social Psychiatry & Psychiatric Epidemiology*, 27(5), 245–248.

Solomon, D. A., Keitner, G. I., Miller, I. W., et al. (1995). Course of illness and maintenance treatments for patients with bipolar disorder. *Journal of Clinical Psychiatry*, 56(1), 5–13.

Strakowski, S. M. & DelBello, M. P. (2000). The co-occurrence of bipolar and substance use disorders. *Clinical Psychology Review*, 20(2), 191–206.

Swann, A. C., Secunda, S. K., Stokes, P. E., et al. (1990). Stress, depression and mania: Relationship between perceived role of stressful events and clinical and biochemical characteristics. *Acta Psychiatrica Scandinavia*, 81, 389–397.

ten Have, M., Vollebergh, W., Bijl, R. & Nolen, W. A. (2002). Bipolar disorder in the general population in The Netherlands (prevalence, consequences and care utilisation): Results from The Netherlands Mental Health Survey and Incidence Study (NEMESIS). *Journal of Affective Disorders*, 68(2–3), 203–213.

Tondo, L., Isacsson, G. & Baldesserini, R. J. (2003). Suicidal behaviour in bipolar disorder: Risk and prevention. *Central Nervous System Drugs*, 17(7), 491–511.

Vaughan, C. & Leff, J. (1976). The measurement of expressed emotion in the families of schizophrenic patients. *British Journal of Clinical Psychology*, 15, 157–165.

Wehr, T. A., Sack, D. & Rosenthal, N. E. (1987). Sleep reduction as a final common pathway in the genesis of mania. *American Journal of Psychiatry*, 144, 201–204.

Weissman, M. M. (1993). The epidemiology of personality disorders. In R. Michels (Ed.), *Psychiatry*. Philadelphia: Lippincott.

Weissman, M. M. & Bothwell, S. (1976). Assessment of social adjustment by patient self-report. *Archives of General Psychiatry*, 33(9), 1111–1115.

Weissman, M. M., Leaf, P. J.., Tischler, G. L. & Blazer, D. G. (1988). Affective disorders in five United States communities. *Psychological Medicine*, 18(1), 141–153.

World Health Organization (WHO) (1992). *The ICD-10 classification of mental and behavioural disorders*. Geneva: WHO.

Wright, K. & Lam, D. (2003). A cognitive theory for bipolar affective disorder. In M. Power (Ed.), *Mood disorders: A handbook of science and practice* (pp. 235–246). Chichester, UK: Wiley.

Chapter 10

Suicide risk

Alan Carr and Muireann McNulty

CASE EXAMPLE 1

Brian, aged forty-five, was brought by ambulance to the accident and emergency department of a major hospital following an overdose involving a potentially lethal dose of tricyclic antidepressants (TCAs), paracetemol and alcohol. Following emergency medical intervention, psychiatric and psychological assessments were conducted to determine an appropriate short-term risk management plan and to lay the groundwork for a longer-term treatment plan.

The incident

Brian had planned the overdose carefully. He had hoarded the TCAs and paracetemol and checked that the dose was lethal. He arranged his financial affairs so that his wife would be supported adequately following his death and wrote a note explaining that he could no longer bear the humiliation of redundancy or the torment of depression that he had suffered for six months. To take the overdose, he carefully selected the Friday night of a weekend when his wife, Margaret, had arranged to visit her friend in another town. Indeed, the overdose would have been fatal, if Margaret had not returned unexpectedly after midnight on Friday and found Brian unconscious. Margaret's train had been repeatedly delayed and finally cancelled, so she decided to return home and travel to her friend's house early on Saturday morning.

Presentation and recent history

In the assessment interview, it was clear that Brian had intended to end his life. He regretted that he had been unsuccessful. From his perspective, his life had become unbearable. He had suffered from episodes of major depression since his mid-twenties. This had interfered with his career in the IT industry and slowed his promotional progress. He had become embittered by his own sense of personal failure and his distrust of his employers, whom he saw as unfair and vindictive. He was made redundant six months before the overdose and this precipitated an episode of severe depression. Brian was treated with TCAs by his GP. He let his GP know during a routine visit for medication review that he wanted to end his life, but the GP did not judge him to be actively suicidal. Over the following weeks, Brian put his financial affairs in order and made careful arrangements for the potentially fatal overdose at a time when he assumed he would be alone for at least 72 hours.

Personal and family history

Brian came from a well-organized, supportive family of origin. However, there was a history of mood disorders on both his mother and father's side, and one of his uncles had committed suicide. Brian's development was broadly within normal limits until his first episode of depression in his twenties. Fortunately, he responded well to TCAs and between episodes he showed almost complete recovery.

Test results

On the Beck Depression Inventory (BDI), Hopelessness Scale and Suicidal Ideation Questionnaire, all of Brian's scores were in the clinical range. He was deeply depressed, profoundly hopeless and showed strong suicidal intent.

Formulation

It was concluded that Brian was a man in his mid-forties who had attempted suicide by taking a potentially lethal overdose under carefully planned circumstances that precluded discovery and he clearly intended to end his life, a fact he had communicated to his GP some weeks before the attempt. The suicide attempt occurred during an episode of major depression, which had been precipitated by redundancy six months previously. Brian was vulnerable to depression, having had a number of previous episodes and a family history of mood disorders.

Protective factors in this case included, a good relationship with his wife, Margaret, the fact that Brian had responded to treatment with TCAs in the past and the fact that he was a skilled IT professional with reasonable prospects of returning to work once his depression lifted.

Risk assessment

The immediate suicide risk in this case was judged to be high because of the high level of intent, the lethality of the method involved and the severity of the predisposing mood disorder.

Management

A brief period of inpatient treatment on a psychiatric ward at the general hospital was arranged, during which Brian began a multi-modal programme of pharmacological and psychological therapy for his mood disorder and problem-solving therapy focusing on re-entering the workforce. Once his BDI scores dropped into the moderate depression range he was discharged and continued treatment as an outpatient.

CASE EXAMPLE 2

Sandra, aged twenty-two, was brought by her boyfriend in a taxi to the accident and emergency department of a major city centre hospital following an overdose involving a non-lethal dose of benzodiazepines and alcohol. She had also cut her arms with a carpet knife. These injuries were not potentially fatal, as she had not cut her arteries. Following emergency medical intervention, psychiatric and psychological assessments were conducted to determine an appropriate short-term risk management plan and to lay the groundwork for a longer-term treatment plan.

Presentation and recent history

In the assessment interview, it was clear that Sandra had been distressed when she cut her arms and took the overdose but had not intended to end her life. She was relieved that she had been unsuccessful and that her boyfriend Bob had shown concern for her by bringing her to the hospital. The couple had had a series of arguments over the preceding week, culminating in a huge row that evening while both were intoxicated. Sandra suspected that Bob was being unfaithful to her and no longer loved her. She wanted to punish him, so she locked herself in the bathroom, swallowed whatever pills she could find and lay in a bath of warm water after cutting her arms. Sandra expected Bob to break the lock on the door and to be distraught when he found her apparently bleeding to death in the bath. He was upset when he found her and she was relieved, because from her perspective this proved he still cared for her.

Personal and family history

Sandra came from a disorganized family of origin, characterized by physical child abuse, domestic violence, marital discord and inconsistency in parenting style. Sandra ran away from home at age eighteen and led a bohemian lifestyle, never holding a job for more than a couple of months, moving from one accommodation to another, from one stormy relationship to another. She had only been with Bob about four months before her overdose. Sandra had a history of substance abuse and a number of previous minor overdoses. After her last overdose, she had been taken by a friend to the accident and emergency department of her local hospital. Details of the overdose had been taken, her stomach was pumped and she was sent home the following morning without being admitted or referred for psychological assessment. Sandra recalled with great shame overhearing some staff talking about her as an 'attention-seeker' and 'time-waster'. She had also been detoxified on one occasion after a period of heroin use.

Test results

On the Beck Depression Inventory, Sandra's scores were in the moderate range. On the Beck Hopelessness Scale, her scores were not overly elevated. On the Suicidal Ideation Questionnaire, there was evidence for suicidal ideation but not intent. A diagnostic interview confirmed that Sandra met the criteria for borderline personality disorder.

Formulation

It was concluded that Sandra, in her early twenties, was a woman with borderline personality disorder who had engaged in acts of non-lethal self-harm in an attempt to resolve an interpersonal conflict with her partner. The self-harm was impulsive and not carefully planned; Sandra did not intend to end her own life. The self-harm represented a way for Sandra to prevent Bob from leaving her or to check if he really cared about her. Sandra was vulnerable to using impulsive violent acts to solve interpersonal problems, as this was the norm in her disorganized and violent family of origin. Protective factors in this case included the fact that Sandra did not report suicidal intent.

Risk assessment

The immediate suicide risk in this case was judged to be low because of the absence of intent and the low lethality of the method involved. However, the risk of repeated self-harm was judged to be high because of the history of previous attempts, the high level of impulsivity, the presence of borderline personality disorder and the demographic profile (young, single, unemployed female from a violent disorganized family background).

Management

Sandra was offered a programme of outpatient psychological therapy to help her manage her impulsivity and to develop skills for solving interpersonal problems without recourse to self-harm.

SUICIDE AND ATTEMPTED SUICIDE

These two cases occupy different positions on the self-harm continuum. Brian clearly was actively suicidal and fully intended to kill himself, to escape from an intolerable situation. He had taken pains to avoid discovery and planned his suicide to the last detail. He was disappointed when his plan failed. In contrast, Sandra, fearing that Bob would abandon her, used self-harm as a way of preventing this or checking if it was true. She acted impulsively rather than in a planned way and she was not disappointed that her suicide attempt was unsuccessful. This type of attempted suicide is referred to in the literature by a number of terms, including 'deliberate self-harm' and 'parasuicide', and distinguished from suicide in which strong intent was present, illustrated by the case of Brian. Suicide and parasuicide are associated with different clusters of factors, but both also share features and correlates in common (Kerkhof, 2000; Kerkhof & Arensman, 2000; Lonnqvist, 2000a; Sakinofsky, 2000). This chapter considers the epidemiology of suicide and parasuicide and then addresses theoretical perspectives on suicide, risk factors associated with self-harm and approaches to clinical management.

EPIDEMIOLOGY OF SUICIDE AND PARASUICIDE

According to World Health Organization (WHO) statistics in 1995, the annual worldwide incidence of completed suicide was 16 per 100,000 (Lonnqvist, 2000a). The rates in eastern European countries are far higher than those in the UK and Ireland, where the annual incidence is about 10 per 100,000. Suicide rates are higher for males than females, with at ratio of about 3:1. Suicide rates are higher for older rather than younger people, but rates among young adult males in their twenties increased in the 1990s compared to rates in previous decades. According to the WHO study of sixteen European regions for the period 1989–1992, the average annual rate for attempted suicide (or parasuicide) among people over fifteen years was 186 per 100,000 (Kerkoff, 2000; Kerkhof & Arensman, 2000). Rates were higher for females than for males and for younger rather than older people. Lifetime prevalence rates of medically treated attempted suicide are 3% for females and 2% for males. Lifetime prevalence rates for suicidal ideation was found in one US study to be 13.5% (Kessler et al., 1999). Between 30 and 60% of suicide attempters have made previous attempts and 10–15% of suicide attempters eventually die from suicide (Kerkoff, 2000). Between one-third and two-thirds of those who die by suicide have made previous attempts (Sakinofsky, 2000).

THEORETICAL PERSPECTIVES

Within the broad field of suicidology there are multiple theoretical perspectives and research traditions (Bongar, 2002; Hawton & van Heerigan, 2000; Jacobs, 1999). Situational research has aimed to identify the behavioural correlates that distinguish suicidal intent from ideation, such as taking precautions against discovery or method lethality (e.g. Beck & Steer, 1991). Situational research on the precipitants of suicide and self-harm has aimed to identify and classify the life events or seasonal changes associated with suicide attempts (e.g. Chew & McLeary, 1995; Paykel et al., 1975). Situational research on motives has attempted to classify the reasons for self-harm into a limited set of categories such as escape or revenge (Bancroft et al., 1979).

Sociological explanations for suicide have focused on the role of broad societal factors in the economic, religious and familial domains in engendering a sense of alienation in certain demographically defined groups predisposed to suicide (Stack, 2000). Psychological theories and related research programmes have shown how certain personality traits and dispositions, such as hopelessness, lack of positive future thinking, autobiographical memory deficits, impulsivity, rigidity and problem-solving skills deficits can contribute to self-destructive behaviour (McLeod, 2004; Weishaar, 2000; Williams & Pollock, 2000). Psychiatric perspectives on suicide have attempted to establish coherent links between specific syndromes such as depression, substance abuse, schizophrenia and personality disorders on the one hand and suicide on the other (De Hert & Peuskens, 2000; Linehan et al., 2000; Lonnqvist, 2000b; Murphy, 2000). Biomedical explanations of suicide have established the role of genetic factors in predisposing people to self-harm and pinpointed inefficiencies in specific neurotransmitter systems, notably those involving serotonin in cases of suicide (Amsel & Mann, 2000; Roy et al., 2000; Traskman-Bendz & Mann, 2000). Probably integrative approaches that draw together insights from these many traditions offer greatest promise for enhancing clinical practice (van Heeringen et al., 2000).

INTEGRATIVE FRAMEWORK OF RISK AND PROTECTIVE FACTORS

In Table 10.1, findings from a variety of theoretical and research traditions have been integrated into a framework, within which the roles of risk and protective factors may be considered when assessing clinical cases where suicide risk is a central concern. The factors listed in the table are drawn from authoritative literature reviews (Bongar, 2002; Hawton & van Heerigan, 2000; Jacobs, 1999; Lester, 2000; Lonnqvist, 2000a; Maris et al., 2000; McLeod, 2004; Rudd & Joiner, 1998; Rudd et al., 1999). Implicit in this framework is the assumption that when a person has attempted suicide or is contemplating self-harm, suicidal tendencies may vary from vague ideation to specific planned intentions. The lethality of the method may also vary from potentially fatal to less dangerous. Suicide attempts may be precipitated by significant stressful life events, such as bereavement, and there are specific times when suicide is more probable, such as in the spring or at anniversaries of loss experiences. Suicide attempts may be motivated by a variety of intentions, such as escaping from an unbearable psychological state to gaining revenge by inducing guilt. A history of self-harm, specific demographic profiles, negative family of origin experiences and a family history of psychiatric or criminal behaviour are all predisposing risk factors for suicide. These risk factors may operate by contributing to the development of problematic personality trait profiles, involving such traits as hopelessness or impulsivity, or

Table 10.1 Risk and protective factors for suicide

Risk factors	*Domain*	*Protective factors*
Communication of intent prior to act Suicidal intention Advanced detailed planning Precautions against discovery A final act Belief that the act was lethal and irreversible Regret at having survived No attempt to seek help after attempt	Suicidal intention and ideation	Suicidal ideation (not intention)
Availability of or use of lethal method (gun, knife, jumping, hanging, drowning, drugs)	Method lethality	Absence of lethal methods
Loss of partner, family member, friend, key worker or significant other by death, separation, divorce or illness Loss of job, money, prestige, or status Severe personal illness or injury Threat of prosecution or involvement in judicial system Conflict with partner or family members Unwanted pregnancy Exam failure Imitation of other suicides Promotion or increased responsibilities that challenge personal coping resources	Precipitating factors	Resolution of interpersonal conflict with significant other that precipitated suicide Acceptance and mourning of losses that precipitated suicide Physical and psychological distancing from peers or others who precipitated imitative suicide
Spring Anniversary of loss Evening or weekend	Timing factors	Summer or winter Weekdays
Suicide attempted to serve the function of: • escaping an unbearable psychological state or situation involving loss, shame or humiliation • gaining revenge by inducing guilt • inflicting self-punishment • gaining care and attention • sacrificing the self for a greater good	Motivational factors	Capacity to develop non-destructive coping styles or engage in treatment to be better able to: • regulate difficult psychological states • modify painful situations • express anger assertively • resolve conflicts productively

• mourn losses • fulfilling a suicide pact		• manage perfectionist expectations • solicit care and attention from others • cope with family disorganization • manage commitments to others
Previous suicide attempts	Self-harm history	No history of previous suicide attempts
Male Elderly (or in 20s if male) Single, divorced or widowed or living alone Social classes 1 and 5 or unemployed Low educational level Caucasian (not African–American) in US	Demographic factors	Female Young (unless male) Married Social classes 2, 3 or 4 High educational level African–American (not Caucasian) in US
Early life losses, abuse or trauma Family history of suicide attempts Family history of depression Family history of drug and alcohol abuse Family history of assaultive behaviour	Family of origin factors	Positive early family of origin experiences No family history of suicide attempts No family history of depression No family history of drug and alcohol abuse No family history of assaultive behaviour
High level of hopelessness Lack of positive future thinking High level of helplessness High level of perfectionism High level of impulsivity High levels of hostility and aggression Rigid inflexible coping style Poor problem-solving skills Dichotomous black-and-white thinking Over-general autobiographical memory Few reasons for living	Personality factors	Low level of hopelessness Capacity for positive future thinking Low level of helplessness Low level of perfectionism Low level of impulsivity Low levels of hostility and aggression Flexible coping style Good problem-solving skills Capacity to think in shades of grey Accurate autobiographical memory Many reasons for living

Continued overleaf

Table 10.1 Continued

Risk factors	*Domain*	*Protective factors*
Depression Alcohol and drug abuse (overdose or loss of access to substance) Personality disorder (borderline or antisocial) Schizophrenia Multiple comorbid chronic disorders	Psychological disorder-related factors	Good mental health
Chronic illness including epilepsy, cancer, AIDS, stroke, severe disability, severe pain Genetic vulnerability to suicide Serotonin depletion	Biological factors	Good physical health
Marital discord, violence or separation Disorganized, unsupportive family Family has high stress and crowding Family denies seriousness of suicide attempts or threats	Current family factors	Supportive marital relationship Well-organized, supportive family Family has low stress Family accepts seriousness of suicide attempts or threats
Living alone Low social support Low social integration and social isolation Weak religious commitment Criminality Involvement in judicial system Normlessness and lack of commitment to conventional ethical values	Wider social system factors	Living with others High social support High social integration Strong religious commitment Absence of criminality No involvement in judicial system Commitment to conventional ethical values
Poor current therapeutic alliance Previous psychiatric treatment Prior communication of suicidal intent to healthcare professionals Absence of key worker (due to vacation or job transition) Recent discharge from hospital Symptomatic improvement in face of unresolved problems	Treatment system factors	Good current therapeutic alliance Acceptance of no-harm or no-suicide contract Acceptance by next-of-kin of suicide monitoring contract Stable relationship with key worker

psychological disorders such as depression. Biological factors such as severe or chronic illness and serotonin depletion, current family factors such as marital discord, and current social factors such as social isolation may all further erode the coping resources of people with vulnerable personality trait profiles and psychological disorders and so place them at greater risk of suicide. Also, the way engagement occurs between a potentially suicidal client and a treatment system may contribute to the risk of suicide. For example, the risk of suicide may be increased if a poor therapeutic alliance develops.

On the positive side, at each level within the framework there are protective factors that reduce the risk of suicide. Clients who express suicidal ideation and not intention, who have considered non-lethal methods, who have no history of self-harm and who are coping relatively well with recent stressful life events are at lower risk. Specific demographic profiles and personality trait profiles, the absence of psychological disorders, good physical health, a supportive family and social context and good engagement with the treatment system are also all protective factors.

ASSESSMENT OF RISK AND PROTECTIVE FACTORS

Assessment of suicide risk is necessary following attempted suicide, threatened self-harm or in cases of severe depression. Suicide risk assessment involves evaluating the degree to which the risk and protective factors in Table 10.1 are present in a particular case and making a judgement about the probability that a suicide attempt will be made. This is not an exact science. It involves careful interviewing, psychological testing where appropriate, and clinical judgement informed by what is known about risk and protective factors for suicide and parasuicide. Assessment of suicide risk should cover the following domains:

- suicidal ideation and intention
- method lethality
- precipitating factors
- timing factors
- motivation
- history of self-harm
- demographic factors
- family of origin factors
- personality-based factors
- disorder-related factors
- biological factors
- current family factors
- wider social system factors
- treatment system factors.

Suicidal intention and ideation

Suicidal intention can be distinguished from suicidal ideation (Beck & Steer, 1991). Suicidal intention is present when there is evidence of advanced detailed planning, taking precautions against discovery and using a lethal method. The client does not seek help from others to be rescued from self-harm and a final act is carried out, for example, writing a will or suicide note. Usually, those with suicidal intentions communicate this intent to the family doctor, a healthcare professional or significant other prior to acting. When clients are rescued from a suicidal situation, like Brian in the case example that opened this chapter, they express a belief that the act was lethal and irreversible, they regret having survived and they make no attempt to seek help after the attempt.

With suicidal ideation, clients report thinking about self-harm and possibly engaging in impulsive non-lethal self-harm, like Sandra in the second case example. This may involve superficial wrist cutting or a minor overdose. But these clients have no definite clear-cut plans about killing themselves. Suicidal intention and ideation probably reflect two ends of a continuum, with states that approximate suicidal intention reflecting a higher level of risk and those approximating suicidal ideation reflecting a lower level of risk. The absence of suicidal intentions may therefore be considered a protective factor.

Method lethality

The lethality of the method used or threatened is an important factor to consider in assessing risk, with more lethal methods being associated with greater risk in some instances (Bongar, 2002). Using a firearm, a long sharp knife, hanging, jumping from a great height, jumping in front of a high-speed motor vehicle, making a serious attempt at hanging or drowning oneself, and self-poisoning with highly toxic drugs are considered to be more lethal than cutting oneself superficially or overdosing on small amounts of non-prescription drugs. Within this domain, the availability of a lethal method, such as access to a firearm or highly toxic drugs, constitutes an important risk factor for suicide.

Self-harm, particularly superficially cutting of the wrists and arms, should be distinguished from potentially lethal incomplete suicide attempts. Non-lethal self-harm of this sort is sometimes associated with an attempt to relieve tension or gain attention or care following an interpersonal crisis. This type of self-harming is sometimes preceded by a sense of emptiness or depersonalization (a sense of not being oneself). It is common among people with borderline personality disorders (discussed in Chapter 22) with a history of abuse, neglect and repeated parasuicidal episodes, like Sandra. The degree of suicidal intention cannot always be judged from the lethality of the method used. Where clients misunderstand the degree of lethality associated with a particular method, apparently minor parasuicidal gestures may be a significant risk factor for actual suicide. The unavailability of lethal methods, such as firearms and toxic drugs, is an important protective factor. This protective factor may be put in place by inviting family members to remove guns, drugs and other lethal methods from the household or placing clients in a place where they have no access to lethal methods.

Precipitating events

Suicide attempts are commonly precipitated by major stressful life events, especially those involving loss experiences (Paykel et al., 1975). The loss may be of a highly valued person such as a partner, family member or friend. For people with chronic mental health problems, the loss may be of a valued key worker with whom the client had regular supportive contact. Loss may occur through bereavement, illness, temporary or permanent separation or, in the case of marriage, through divorce. Loss of a job, money, prestige or status may also precipitate suicide. Redundancy, which involves all of these, was the precipitating factor in the first case example at the start of the chapter. Involvement in chronic gambling may also lead to some of these losses. Suicide may be precipitated by stresses such as severe personal illness or injury, the threat of prosecution or involvement in the judicial system, conflict with partners or family members, unwanted pregnancy or exam failure. Sometimes apparently positive life events such as promotion or increased responsibilities may precipitate suicide because they involve challenges that exceed clients' personal coping resources. Suicide arising from imitation of others may be precipitated by suicides within the peer group or media coverage of suicides (Schmidtke & Schaller, 2000). Repeated attempted suicide (as distinct from completed suicide) is associated with impulsive separation following romantic relationship difficulties or recent court appearance associated with impulsive or aggressive antisocial behaviour.

Protective factors in this domain include the resolution of interpersonal conflict that precipitated suicide, acceptance and mourning of losses that precipitated suicide and physical and psychological distancing from those who precipitated imitative suicide.

Timing factors

Certain times are associated with greater frequencies of suicide and so may be considered risk factors (Chew & McLeary, 1995). Seasonal studies of suicide consistently show a peak for suicides in the spring, not the winter as one might expect. Suicides may be precipitated by anniversaries of loss experiences, such as a year following a bereavement. Suicides are more commonly committed during the evening or at weekends than during office hours.

Motivation

Suicide is usually perceived by people as the only feasible solution to a difficult problem involving interpersonal loss or conflict. Within this overarching context, the specific reasons why people attempt suicide fall into a limited number of categories (Bancroft et al., 1979). Suicide may be construed as a means of escaping from the psychological pain associated with loss, shame or humiliation. From this perspective, death may be seen as a state that will bring relief from pain. Suicide may alternatively reflect an attempt to obtain revenge; to express aggression; to retaliate or punish a partner, family member or friend for their hostility or for leaving them through death, separation or illness. Here the sentiment is 'You have hurt me, but I will get my revenge by hurting you through killing myself and causing you to feel guilt'. In other instances, suicide represents self-punishment arising from guilt for not living up to perfectionist self-expectations or expectations that people perceive others to have of them. For example, people who become redundant or who have an unplanned pregnancy may judge themselves or anticipate that others will judge them harshly for failing to meet a socioeconomic or moral standard. Suicide may be seen as a way of atoning for such a perceived failure or as a way of escaping from the expected criticism or judgement of others. Attempted suicide may represent a way of obtaining care and attention, particularly for clients who repeatedly make self-harming gestures. People from disorganized conflictual families may view their suicide as a necessary sacrifice that must be made to preserve the integrity of their family. That is, they may fantasize that their suicide will serve as a rallying point that will unite a fragmented family. In some instances, one or more of these motivations for suicide is compounded by forming a suicide pact or promise to jointly commit suicide with others, the fulfilment of this promise becomes another motivation for suicide.

The potential for finding alternative ways of fulfilling the functions of attempted suicide is a protective factor. Thus flexibility about developing new coping styles for solving the problem for which the suicide attempt was a destructive solution places clients at lower risk for suicide. Understanding suicidal motives and the functions that suicidal gestures are intended to fulfil are important in treatment planning. When the functions of an attempted suicide are understood, the treatment plan should help the client find other ways to fulfil these functions. That is, treatment plans should help people find less destructive ways for regulating difficult psychological states, tolerating distress, modifying painful situations, expressing anger assertively, resolving conflicts productively, mourning losses, managing perfectionist expectations, soliciting care and attention from others, coping with family disorganization and managing commitments to others.

Self-harm history

People who have previously attempted suicide are at greater risk than those who have not (Sakinofsky, 2000). Those who have made more suicide attempts and those who have made more lethal attempts are at greater risk. When exploring a history of self-harm, assess what function clients hoped past suicide attempts would fulfil. Also assess whether these functions were fulfilled by non-lethal self-harm or if self-harm would need to be lethal for the function to be fulfilled. In the first case example that opened the chapter, Brian believed that only lethal self-harm could provide an escape for the unbearable psychological pain he was enduring. By contrast, in the second case example, Sandra believed that non-lethal self-harm would lead her partner to demonstrate his care for her. An understanding of the functions of self-harm is important in designing treatment programmes.

Demographic factors

Specific demographic profiles are associated with increased risk of self-harm and suicide (Kerkhof, 2000; Lonnqvist, 2000a). Male clients are at greater risk for completed suicide whereas female clients are at greatest risk of parasuicide. Males tend to use more lethal methods (guns and hanging) whereas females use less lethal methods (cutting or self-poisoning). The risk of suicide increases with advancing age but in recent years there has been a very significant increase in suicide rates among males in their twenties, suggesting that, for males, being in one's twenties is a demographic risk factor for suicide. With respect to marital status, greater suicide risk is associated with being single, divorced or widowed. Membership of social class 5 (unskilled workers with low incomes and educational levels) is a risk factor for completed suicide and repeated parasuicide, whereas membership of social class 1 (professional and higher managerial employees) is a risk factor for completed suicide only. With respect to ethnicity, suicide rates in the US are higher for Caucasian than African–American clients. Protective demographic factors include being female; being younger (unless male); being married; membership of social classes 2, 3 and 4; and, in the US, being African–American.

Family of origin

Early life losses, particularly of parents or primary caregivers through separation or bereavement, and a personal history of child abuse are risk factors for suicide (Bongar, 2002). These early adversities probably render people psychologically vulnerable to depression through providing the basis for the development of depressive schemas, as discussed in Chapter 8. A family history of suicide attempts, depression, drug and alcohol abuse, and assaultive behaviour are also risk factors for suicide. These factors are probably associated with the transmission of both a genetic vulnerability on the one hand and psychological vulnerability on the other. This is because all of these factors constitute childhood environmental adversities and negative models for social problem-solving and coping with life stress. Positive early family of origin experiences, including secure attachments to caregivers and exposure to a consistent authoritative parenting style, are protective factors. So too are the absence of a history of suicide attempts and parental mental health difficulties.

Personality factors

Personality traits and attributes that may be considered risk factors for suicide include hopelessness, lack of positive future thinking, helplessness, perfectionism, impulsivity, hostility and aggression, an inflexible coping style, poor problem-solving skills, dichotomous black-and-white thinking, an over-general autobiographical memory and having few reasons for living (McLeod, 2004; Weishaar, 2000; Williams & Pollock, 2000). People who attempt suicide view themselves as incapable of changing their situation; the future, to them, looks hopeless, they have difficulty anticipating positive future events and they see few good reasons for living. Perfectionism is a risk factor for suicide probably because it leads to heightened self-expectations that may be difficult to achieve. Suicidal clients tend to view complex situations in simplistic black-and-white terms and have difficulties drawing on specific autobiographical memories of successfully solving problems in the past and so have a very limited repertoire of coping strategies to draw upon in flexibly solving complex interpersonal problems. Thus they resort to strategies that may be ineffective. Their aggression and impulsivity may lead them to engage in self-directed aggression with little reflection on other possible alternatives for solving their difficulties. Low levels of hopelessness, helplessness, perfectionism, impulsivity, hostility and aggression are protective factors in this domain. So too are a flexible coping style, good social problem-solving skills, the capacity to think in shades of grey, an accurate autobiographical memory and having many reasons for living.

Disorder-related factors

The presence of depression (discussed in Chapter 8) is the single strongest health-related risk factor for future suicide (Lonnqvist, 2000b). Depression is strongly associated with helplessness and hopelessness, both of which are associated with suicide. Major depression (a recurrent episodic mood disorder) is strongly associated with completed suicide whereas dysthymia (a chronic, milder, non-episodic mood disorder) is associated with repeated suicide attempts. Other disorders that are risk factors for suicide include alcohol and drug abuse (discussed in Chapter 20), antisocial or borderline personality disorders (discussed in Chapter 22) and schizophrenia (discussed in Chapter 21) (De Hert & Peuskens, 2000; Linehan et al., 1983; Murphy, 2000). All of these are more common among impulsive individuals and impulsivity has already been mentioned as a personality-based risk factor for suicide. Increased suicide risk is strongly associated with multiple comorbid chronic psychological and physical disorders. Good mental health is the main protective factor in this domain.

Biological factors

Biological risk factors for suicide include a genetic vulnerability; serotonin depletion in that part of the brain that subserves mood regulation; chronic illness such as epilepsy, cancer, AIDS, stroke; severe disability and severe pain (Roy et al., 2000; Syenager & Stenager, 2000; Traskman-Bendz & Mann, 2000). Evidence from twin studies suggests that some individuals may have a genetic vulnerability to suicidal behaviour (Roy et al., 2000). The vulnerability is probably mediated by a dysregulation of the serotonergic systems in those parts of the brain which subserve mood, aggression and impulsivity. Serotonin depletion in these centres has been found in studies of suicidal clients (Traskman-Bendz & Mann, 2000).

Current family factors

Risk factors associated with the client's current family include marital discord, violence or separation; living in a disorganized unsupportive family; living in a family in which there is high stress and crowding and membership of a family that denies the seriousness of the client's suicide attempts (Bongar, 2002). By contrast, protective factors include being in a supportive marital relationship; membership of a well-organized, supportive family; living with a family that has low stress and membership of a family that accepts the seriousness of the client's suicide attempts or threats.

Wider social system factors

Risk factors within the wider social system include living alone, social isolation, low social support, weak religious commitment and low social integration, which are often associated with minority ethnic status and social isolation (Stack, 2000). These factors may contribute to normlessness and lack of commitment to conventional ethical values. Normlessness may lead to criminal activity, which in turn may lead to involvement in the judicial system, and this may involve loss experiences that precipitate self-harm. Protective factors in this domain include living with others, having a good social support network, social integration, commitment to conventional values and strong religious commitment. Strong religious commitment may operate by increasing the support network available to regular churchgoers, giving clients increased meaning in life, and offering clients a template for moral and healthy lifestyles free from impulsive criminality and alcohol and substance abuse (Carr, 2004).

Treatment system factors

The way engagement occurs between clients and health professionals within the treatment system may place the client at increased risk of self-harm or suicide (Bongar, 2002). Within this context, the treatment system includes current and past health professionals with whom clients have had prior contact, including family doctors, other primary care workers and members of specialist multi-disciplinary mental health teams. Increased suicide risk is associated with clients communicating their suicidal intentions to healthcare professionals. Clients who have a history of previous psychiatric treatment and those recently discharged from hospital are also at increased risk. The risk of suicide is increased in those circumstances where clients have developed a good relationship with a key worker who then becomes unavailable to the client, due to being on leave or changing jobs for example. Suicide risk increases also in situations where clients show symptomatic improvement in the face of unresolved problems. This may occur, for example, when depressed clients respond to antidepressant medication by having increased energy but have not had the opportunity in psychotherapy to explore ways of effectively resolving complex problems of living or coping with challenging life stresses. Failure to form a good therapeutic alliance also places clients at increased risk of suicide since it reduces support and problem-solving resources available to them.

On the positive side, forming a good therapeutic alliance and maintaining a stable therapeutic relationship with a designated key worker are important protective factors within this domain. This creates the context within which clients may engage in a contract to address their life difficulties and psychological disorders that have predisposed them to considering or attempting suicide. The acceptance of a verbal or written contract not to commit suicide during a suicide risk assessment is also a protective factor. The commitment on the part of the client's next-of-kin or family members to monitor the client constantly until all suicidal intention and ideation have abated is a further important protective factor to consider in this domain. This commitment may take the form of an oral or written contract between the clinician and next-of-kin.

CLINICAL MANAGEMENT OF SUICIDE RISK

The overriding objective of assessment and intervention where suicide has been threatened or attempted is to prevent harm, injury or death. For clinical psychologists in training, it is usually appropriate for the assessment to be done by or with a clinical supervisor or another senior experienced member of an adult mental health team to which the trainee psychologist is attached. However, for some psychologists in training, and for many qualified psychologists, circumstances may dictate that they conduct initial suicide risk assessments alone. In such circumstances, conduct the assessment, remain with the client and, as soon as it is practical to do so, contact the supervisor or a senior clinician from your mental health team or agency. Certain broad principles for management, based on the literature and clinical experience, may be followed (Bongar, 2002; Hawton & Catalan, 1987; Jacobs, 1999; Link, 1997; Royal College of Psychiatrists, 1994; Rudd & Joiner, 1998; Rudd et al., 1999).

Immediate comprehensive assessment

In cases where a recent suicide attempt has been made, use the interview schedule in Table 10.2 to assess risk. Obtain a detailed description of the self-destructive behaviour that led to the referral and related suicidal or self-harming intentions. In cases where there has been no recent episode of self-injury but where suicidal ideation is present, use the interview schedule in Table 10.3. Obtain a description of the sequence of events that led up to the current suicidal ideation. In either circumstance, offer immediate consultation. Use the consultation process to develop a comprehensive understanding of the situation surrounding the suicide threat or attempt. During the consultation process, establish or deepen your working alliance with the client. Assess all of the risk and protective factors listed in Table 10.1. Check if the factors were present in the past, the extent to which they were present during the recent episode and whether they are immediately present. Build up a picture of the immediate circumstances surrounding the self-harming episode or suicidal ideation. Clarify if this is an escalation of an entrenched pattern of interaction around previous suicidal ideas, intentions or acts of self-harm. In the recent episode and previous episodes of suicidal ideation or self-harming behaviour, clarify the roles of significant family members, significant members of the client's network and health professionals. The aim here is to obtain a coherent account of how the client came to view his or her life situation as hopeless and selected self-harm as a solution to this experience of hopelessness. Take account of risk and protective factors, listed in Table 10.1, that may have contributed to the sequence of events that led to the client experiencing hopelessness and attempting or considering suicide. Also cover relevant areas for a general intake assessment listed in Figure 7.2 (p. 266), current and past substance abuse and diagnostic criteria for any major psychological disorders relevant to the case, particularly depression (Chapter 8), bipolar disorder (Chapter 9), borderline personality disorder (Chapter 22) and schizophrenia (Chapter 21). At the conclusion of the

Table 10.2 Suicide risk assessment interview – recent episode version

Before you were referred here, what was going wrong in your life?
(probe precipitating life stresses, demographic profile, mental and physical health, significant members of family and social network, involved health professionals, personality disorder)

What expectations did you have of yourself that you could not meet?
(probe perfectionism and high personal standards)

How much hope did you have that things could be better (on a scale of 1 to 10)?
(probe hopelessness)

How much did you believe you could make things in your life better (on a scale of 1 to 10)?
(probe helplessness)

What reasons did you have for living?
(probe reasons for living)

How did you reach the decision to harm yourself and what alternatives did you consider?
(probe problem-solving, inflexibility, black-and-white thinking)

To what extent did you act on impulse, without thinking, when you harmed yourself?
(probe impulsivity, hostility, aggression)

How low was your mood on a scale of 1 to 10?
(probe history of depression)

Had you taken alcohol or something else to make things bearable?
(probe history of drug and alcohol use)

Which was stronger on scales of 1 to 10, your will to live or your will to die?
(probe reasons for living)

Did you hear someone telling you you should harm yourself?
(probe auditory hallucinations associated with schizophrenia or psychotic depression, psychiatric history and treatment compliance)

Had you a plan to harm yourself and what preparations had you made?
(assess impulsive self-harm versus planned self-harm)

How exactly did you harm yourself?
(probe lethality)

When did this happen?
(probe season, day of week, time of day, anniversary reaction)

Did you believe the method of self-harm was lethal and that nothing could be done to save you if your were discovered?
(probe lethality and irreversibility)

Did you let others know about your plan to harm yourself or were you secretive?
(probe precautions against discovery)

Did you write a letter to anyone explaining why you are harming yourself?
(probe details of final acts)

Did you take steps to make a will or put your affairs in order before you harmed yourself?
(probe final act)

What did you hope your family, friends and significant people in your life would think, do and feel when they found you?
(probe motivations for suicide)

What happened afterwards and how did you survive?
(probe precautions against discovery, help seeking, involvement of other health professionals)

Do you regret having survived?
(probe regret)

In what way did you believe that self-harm would solve the difficulties you faced?
(probe problem-solving)

When you look back on that episode, do you think now that there were other things you could have done, besides harming yourself, to deal with the difficulties you faced?
(probe problem-solving)

When you look into the future now, are you hopeful about changing your situation so that it will become more bearable?
(probe hopefulness and optimism)

Are there family members, friends or health professionals that you believe are able and willing to help you solve your current problems?
(probe family, social network, professional network)

Are you willing to promise not to harm yourself between now and the next time we meet and to sign a contract stating this?

Are you willing for your next-of-kin or significant other to witness you signing a contract?

Table 10.3 Suicide risk assessment interview – current state version

What is going wrong in your life right now?
(probe precipitating life stresses, demographic profile, mental and physical health, significant members of family and social network, involved health professionals, personality disorder)

What expectations do you have of yourself that you think you cannot meet?
(probe perfectionism and high personal standards)

How hopeful are you that things will get better (on a scale of 1 to 10)?
(probe hopelessness)

How much do you believe that you can make things in your life better (on a scale of 1 to 10)?
(probe helplessness)

What reasons have you for living?
(probe reasons for living)

How would harming yourself solve the problems you now face and can you see any alternatives right now?
(probe problem-solving, inflexibility, black-and-white thinking)

If you harm yourself in future are you likely to do this impulsively without thinking?
(probe impulsivity, hostility, aggression)

How low is your mood now (on a scale of 1 to 10)?
(probe history of depression)

If you harm yourself, do you expect you may take alcohol or something else to make things bearable?
(probe history and future possibility of drug and alcohol use)

Continued overleaf

Table 10.3 Continued

Which is stronger right now on scales of 1 to 10, your will to live or your will to die? (probe reasons for living)
Do you sometimes hear someone telling you you should harm yourself? (probe auditory hallucinations associated with schizophrenia or psychotic depression, psychiatric history and treatment compliance)
Have you a plan to harm yourself? (assess impulsive self-harm versus planned self-harm)
What preparations have you made to harm yourself?
How exactly will you harm yourself? (probe lethality)
When do you think this will happen? (probe season, day of week, time of day, anniversary reaction)
Do you believe the method of self-harm is lethal and that there will be nothing anyone can do to save you if you are discovered? (probe lethality and irreversibility)
Will you let others know about your plan to harm yourself or will you keep it a secret? (probe precautions against discovery)
Will you write a letter to anyone explaining why you are harming yourself? (probe details of final acts)
Will you take steps to make a will or put your affairs in order before your harm yourself? (probe final act)
What do you hope your family, friends and significant people in your life will think, do and feel when they discover you? (probe motivations for suicide)
If you survive will you regret this? (probe regret)
Are there family members, friends or health professionals that you believe are able and willing to help you solve your current problems? (probe family, social network, professional network)
Are you willing to promise not to harm yourself between now and the next time we meet and to sign a contract stating this?
Are you willing for your next-of-kin or significant other to witness you signing this contract?

interview, integrate the client's story, check its accuracy and agree a plan with the client for discussing this account with the next-of-kin or significant members of the client's network. Obtaining consent to discuss such confidential information with relatives is good ethical practice.

Standardized tests and questionnaires

A number of psychological tests and questionnaires may be helpful in conducting a suicide risk assessment. For assessing suicide intent and ideation, the *Beck Scale for Suicide Ideation* (Beck & Steer, 1991) and the *Adult*

Suicidal Ideation Questionnaire (Reynolds, 1991) are useful adjuncts to a clinical interview, especially where people are reluctant to talk. The *Suicidal Behaviour History Form* (Reynolds & Mazza, 1992) offers a systematic way of obtaining a self-harm history. Other useful standardized assessment instruments for assessing constructs relevant to suicide risk include the *Beck Depression Inventory – II* (Beck et al., 1996), the *Beck Hopelessness Scale* (Beck & Steer, 1988), The *Reasons for Living Inventory* (Linehan et al., 1983) and the *Revised Social Problem Solving Inventory* (D'Zurilla et al., 2001). The hopelessness and depression scales measure two key risk factors, whereas scales for evaluating reasons for living and problem-solving skills throw light on important protective factors.

Collateral interviews

It is useful to conduct at least three different interviews: one with the client, one collateral interview with the next-of-kin or a significant member of the client's family or social network, and a conjoint interview. Clients must give consent for their next-of-kin or significant members of their families or social networks to be involved in the assessment process, except in cases where involuntary detention is being arranged or cases where there is evidence of diminished capacity for rational decision making (discussed below). In the collateral interview, follow a similar line of questioning to that outlined in Tables 10.2 and 10.3. The separate client and collateral interviews provide opportunities to obtain different perspectives on the presence or absence of risk and protective factors. Clients and members of their families or social networks may feel freer to give their frank opinions and views in separate interviews than in conjoint interviews. However, it is also important to conduct a conjoint interview to explore and clarify differences between the client's views and those of their significant others. A clinician who will go on to work individually with the client will probably find it easier to build a therapeutic relation with the client if, from the outset, all conversations with family members are held in the presence of the client. In such situations, it may be preferable to involve another team member in any meetings with the family from which the client is excluded. Also, it is useful to offer the formulation and management plan within the context of a conjoint interview, since the management plan will often involve key responsibilities for the client's significant other.

Contact with other health professionals

Where possible, obtain information relating to risk and protective factors from health professionals who have had previous involvement with the case. Such professionals may include the GP or family doctor, and the psychiatrist or key worker if the client is receiving regular care from a mental health service. Identify people within the client's professional network, family and social network who may be available to help implement a short-term management plan and possibly contribute to a longer-term treatment plan.

Formulation

Draw the information you obtain from the client, the collateral interview and other professionals into a clear formulation on which a short-term management plan may be based. The formulation must logically link together the risk factors identified in the case to explain the occurrence of the episode of self-harming behaviour or suicidal ideation and the current level of risk. It is important to specify predisposing factors and triggering factors that led to an escalation from suicidal ideation to intention, or from suicidal intention to self-injury. The formulation should be specific and pinpoint how specific life circumstances precipitated the specific act of self-harm or suicidal ideation and how a constellation of predisposing risk factors rendered the client vulnerable to the present episode. Examples of formulations are given in each of the cases which opened this chapter.

Judging risk

Clients may be considered a serious immediate suicide risk if they: (1) show suicidal intent as indicated by the presence of most of the factors listed in the first domain of Table 10.1; and (2) plan to use a high lethality method. The greater the number of other risk factors that are present, the greater the risk of immediate suicide. If there is no evidence of suicidal intent and few other risk factors are pinpointed in the assessment, then the risk of immediate suicide is probably low.

Specific predisposing risk factors for suicide risk after attempted suicide

Specific predisposing risk factors for completed suicide following self-harm deserving special weighting are previous suicide attempts, major mental and physical health problems, and being a non-working, single male over 60 who lives alone (Hawton, 2000a, 2000b).

Specific predisposing risk factors for repeated non-fatal self-harm

Another issue requiring assessment is judging the risk of further non-lethal self-harm. Specific predisposing risk factors for this deserving special weighting are previous episodes of self-harm, recent court appearance associated with impulsive or aggressive personality disorder, major mental health problems, and being a young, lower class, unemployed female from an abusive disorganized family background (Hawton, 2000a, 2000b; Kerkhof & Arensman, 2000; Sakinofsky 2000). Many of these factors were present in the second case example presented at the beginning of this chapter.

Short-term management plan

Develop a management plan that specifies the short-term action to be taken in light of the formulation and level of risk. The short-term plan must logically indicate that the changes it involves will probably lower the risk of self-harm. The short-term plan may involve either brief hospitalization or an outpatient care programme. If a short-term outpatient management plan is offered, clients and their next-of-kin or significant members of their families or social networks must sign no-harm and monitoring contracts, like those in Table 10.4, at the conclusion of the initial assessment session and each subsequent session, and give commitments to attend scheduled appointments.

Table 10.4 No-harm and monitoring contracts

No-Harm Contract
I promise that I will not harm myself between now and the next time we meet.
I promise that if I feel an urge to harm myself I will let my next-of-kin or significant other know immediately and will contact the clinic immediately on this number__________
Signed__________(Client)
Witnessed__________(Psychologist)
Witnessed__________(Next-of-kin or significant other)
Date__________

Monitoring Contract
I promise that I will arrange for__________to be under 24-hour observation at my home on the following dates__________
I promise that if there is any sign that he or she has an urge to harm him or herself I will contact the clinic immediately on this number__________
Signed__________(Next-of-kin or significant other)
Witnessed__________(Client)
Witnessed__________(Psychologist)
Date__________

No-harm contracts, monitoring contracts and on-call commitments

For clients, no-harm contracts involve making a commitment not to make further suicide attempts while engaged in treatment. For significant members of the family and social network, the contract involves making a commitment to monitor the client to prevent further self-harm. For clients who have strong suicidal intent, this involves developing a family rota for keeping the client under twenty-four-hour supervision to prevent repeated suicide attempts; agreeing that the person on the rota will only engage in supportive and non-conflictual conversation with the client; and phoning the clinic's twenty-four-hour on-call service as a last resort if strong suicidal ideation and intentions persist. Ideally, the no-harm and monitoring contracts are offered as part of a therapeutic plan in which the client and significant others are given a twenty-four-hour on-call phone number that they can call to contact a member of the treatment team if strong suicidal ideation and intentions persist. If, due to unforeseen circumstances or ill health, you are unable to attend any follow-up appointments with clients at risk of suicide, it is vital to make arrangements for the client to be met by another member of the mental health team or for the appointment to be rescheduled as soon as possible.

Voluntary hospital-based care

If hospitalization is necessary, contact the appropriate psychiatrist or mental health professional. To assist them in conducting a preadmission assessment, brief them on the reasons why you think hospitalization may be necessary. If you are involved in case management following hospitalization, the following points should be borne in mind. The chief concern for hospitalized, suicidal clients is to ensure their safety. This may involve twenty-four-hour constant observation and restricting access to objects (knives, electricity sockets, belts, electric flexes, etc.) and situations (e.g. upper storey open or breakable windows) that may create opportunities for suicide. Making such arrangements typically involves following local procedural guidelines and careful negotiation with nursing staff. Along with ensuring the client's safety, hospitalization should also create a context for developing a plan for solving significant problems associated with suicide risk and treating mental health difficulties. As part of the admission contract, the client, next-of-kin, significant family members or members of the client's social network should be invited to attend a series of sessions aimed at planning ways to modify risk or triggering factors that contributed to the crisis and that, when modified, would create a safe context for discharge from hospital. Thereafter, the protocol outlined above for home-based care should be followed. There is good evidence from a randomized controlled trial that partial hospitalization offered as part of a psychoanalytically oriented treatment programme may effectively reduce suicide attempts for clients with borderline personality disorder (Bateman & Fonagy, 1999, 2001). In those rare instances where such specialist resources are available and hospitalization is required, this is the preferred evidence-based approach.

Involuntary detention

If clients will not accept brief voluntary hospitalization or outpatient care with no-harm and monitoring contracts, and you judge them to be a danger to themselves or others, then follow local procedures to request a statutory assessment for involuntary detention or committal under mental health legislation. Clinical psychologists in training should consult their clinical supervisors about local procedures, as these vary from one jurisdiction to another. Often, very experienced clinicians may help clients accept a voluntary admission as the best course of action and so avoid the necessity of involuntary detention.

Competence and involuntary treatment

When treatment refusal occurs with involuntarily detained clients, the client's competence to accept or refuse treatment will require statutory assessment. Such assessments are conducted under mental health legislation, which varies from one jurisdiction to another. To be competent to accept or refuse treatment, clients must be able to: (1) understand relevant information; (2) believe this information to be true; and (3) weigh-up the pros and cons in a balanced way for accepting or rejecting treatment. Severe depression, delusions, hallucinations, delirium and intellectual disability are examples of psychological factors that may impair a client's competence to make decisions about his or her need for treatment. Psychologists in training should ask their clinical supervisors how to follow local guidelines for referring cases for statutory assessment of competence. To safeguard against unnecessary involuntary detention and treatment, mental health legislation in most jurisdictions includes appeal procedures, which, once again, are usually implemented following local guidelines.

Discharge planning

Following either voluntary or involuntary hospitalization, careful discharge planning is essential. Such plans should involve no-harm contracts with clients and monitoring contracts with relatives or next-of-kin, as described earlier. Clients are at particular risk of suicide just before and after discharge. This is particularly the case with depressed clients who have regained their energy as a result of treatment but still have many unresolved problems.

Long-term planning

Once short-term safety plans have been put in place, develop longer-term plans to treat mental health difficulties and resolve significant problems associated with suicide risk.

Longer-term planning should address clients' needs as identified in the assessment and formulation and should take account of available evidence-based methods for reducing suicide risk. It is useful to routinely include no-harm contracts in longer-term outpatient treatment programmes.

Psychotherapy

Intensive dialectical behaviour therapy (DBT), problem-solving therapy and outreach therapy are the only three outpatient psychological therapy approaches that have been shown to reduce the rate of repeated suicide attempts in controlled trials (Hawton et al., 1998; Heard, 2000; Linehan, 2000). DBT, described in Chapter 22, involves comprehensive overall case management, intensive individual psychotherapy, group-based behavioural problem-solving skills training, mindfulness meditation training and systemic intervention, as appropriate, in the family, social network, health services, social services and judicial system. When the specialist resources for DBT are unavailable, it is probably appropriate to routinely offer problem-solving therapy (described below) coupled with other interventions appropriate for treatment of psychological disorders identified during the risk assessment. Where clients continue to be at reasonably high risk of suicide or fail to attend outpatient appointments, this type of treatment may be offered within the context of an outreach approach. The principles of outreach therapy are to provide ongoing weekly home visits with individual and family-based support, and crisis intervention as required until the risk of suicide reduces.

Problem-solving therapy

In problem-solving therapy (D'Zurilla & Nezu, 1999) work collaboratively with the client and, if appropriate, the next-of-kin and significant family members or members of the client's social network. In light of the formulation, identify key problems that, if solved, would reduce suicide risk. Prioritize these and agree a contract with the client and significant others to work through them in a systematic fashion, one at a time, over a planned number of sessions. For each problem, work to define it in solvable terms. 'Sorting my life out' is a vague problem definition which might be redefined as 'Organizing affordable accommodation and starting to look for a job'. Break big problems into a number of smaller ones, with clearly defined moderately challenging goals. For each of these, with the client and significant other, brainstorm multiple possible solutions. Examine the pros and cons of each, before settling on a preferred solution that is within the client's competence. Then help the client and significant other to write out a step-by-step plan to implement all or part of the preferred solution between one session and the next. If appropriate, role-play and rehearse the plan. Rehearsal may throw light on beliefs and assumptions that may prevent clients from following through on plans. The validity of these problematic beliefs and assumptions may be addressed using cognitive behavioural methods described in Chapter 3. When clients agree to follow through on a plan between one session and the next, always review progress at the next session. If no progress has been made, examine the reasons for this in a non-critical way. Brainstorm ways to overcome obstacles that blocked the implementation of plans between sessions. If appropriate, arrange to phone the client and significant other between sessions to remind them to work on implementing the plan. When each plan is implemented, review how successful it was. If it was successful, help the client and significant other find ways to celebrate success. If it was not successful, modify the plan to increase the chances of success and help the client and significant other list the steps necessary to implement the modified plan with a view to reviewing its impact when implemented. Continue with this systematic problem-solving approach until the problems on the agreed problem-list have been addressed. Throughout the process routinely monitor suicide risk at each session, and help the client make links between reductions in levels of suicidal ideation or intent and success with solving problems on the problem-list.

Pharmacotherapy

Few controlled trials with adequate sample sizes of the effects of pharmacological therapies on repeated suicide have been conducted and much of what we know is based on epidemiological studies of survival rates (Hawton et al., 1998; Verkes & Cowen, 2000). The main findings from these studies are consistent with the view that appropriate pharmacological treatment of a client's psychological disorder may also reduce the risk of repeated suicide attempts in clients with such disorders. For clients with major depression, TCAs and SSRIs may help decrease the probability of multiple suicide attempts. However, since it is easier to overdose on TCAs because of their greater toxicity, SSRIs are the preferred antidepressant for potentially suicidal clients with a diagnosis of major depression. For clients with bipolar disorder, treatment with lithium carbonate reduces the risk of repeated suicide attempts. Clozapine decreases the risk of repeated suicide attempts in clients with a diagnosis of schizophrenia. For clients with personality disorders who have low mood and who have made repeated suicide attempts, SSRIs may help decrease the probability of further self-harm, whereas benzodiazepines may increase the risk of multiple suicide attempts. It is currently best practice to use combined psychological and pharmacological treatment programmes for many psychological problems. Such multi-modal treatment programmes for depression, bipolar disorders, schizophrenia and personality disorders are described in detail in Chapters 8, 9, 21 and 22. When clients at risk of suicide are prescribed medication, the least toxic option should be chosen and, where possible, responsibility for the storage of quantities of medication should be given to family members or significant others, to reduce the opportunities for overdosing. If this is not possible, only small quantities should be prescribed at any one time.

Active follow-up

Clients who attempt or threaten suicide are at risk for not attending follow-up appointment and so an active approach to follow-up is vital (Hawton et al., 1998; Heard, 2000; Linehan, 2000). The client and significant others should be given a definite appointment after the initial consultation, which should be within a couple of days of the first meeting. They should be contacted by phone to remind them about the appointment and to inquire about non-attendance if this occurs. The number, duration and agenda for therapeutic sessions should be made clear to both from the outset and the importance of follow-up for preventing further suicide threats and attempts should be highlighted. Clients at greater risk should be given more frequent appointments. Those who do not attend appointments should be followed up with phone calls or home visits. Document session-to-session changes in suicide risk status by noting the level of intent or ideation.

EFFECTS OF WORKING WITH SUICIDE AND THE IMPORTANCE OF SUPERVISION

Working with suicidal clients is very demanding. They make slow progress and elicit strong countertransference reactions in most clinicians. These reactions typically involve urges to rescue and protect them from the multiple life stresses with which they are having difficulty coping or urges to abandon or persecute them for failing to make therapeutic progress or for repeated suicide attempts despite the clinician's best efforts. In the long term, working with a caseload that includes a number of clients who repeatedly self-harm may make clinicians doubt their own clinical competence and make them question the value of their work. When clinicians ruminate about countertransference reactions and doubts about competence, they have difficulties concentrating on their work and tend to make more mistakes, which in turn confirms their doubts about their competence. All of these intense reactions may 'spill over' into the clinicians' non-professional lives, having a negative impact on relationships with family and friends, on the efficiency with which the immune system functions and on the degree of alcohol and drug use.

Because of the potential negative effects of working with suicidal clients, it is essential to have regular supervision (Fleming & Steen, 2004; Hawkins & Shohet, 2000). Within the supervisory relationship, clinicians have an opportunity to express and explore their countertransference reactions and doubts on the one hand, and check out the validity of their assessments and interventions on the other. The supervisor (or peer supervision group) should offer a safe and supportive context in which this may occur. The supervisory relationship also offers a context within which clinicians may explore ways of balancing their caseloads so that they do not have more self-harming clients than they may adequately cope with. Finally, the supervisory relationship offers a forum for initially addressing immediate reactions to completed suicides. However, for most psychologists in training and qualified psychologists, recovery from a client dying by suicide can best be facilitated through personal grief counselling or psychotherapy.

FAMILY SUPPORT FOLLOWING SUICIDE

When clients commit suicide it may be appropriate in certain circumstances to offer consultation to significant members of their families and social networks (Clark & Goldney, 2000). This may be especially appropriate where you have worked with the client and offer the family and friends of the deceased a clearly formulated explanation of the multiple risk factors present before the suicide. This type of consultation may be helpful in preventing family and friends from holding themselves fully responsible for not preventing the suicide and in facilitating the grief process. It was noted in Chapter 1 that, following bereavement, most people experience some or all of the following grief processes: shock, denial or disbelief, yearning and searching, sadness, anger, anxiety, guilt and bargaining, acceptance. There is not a clear-cut progression through these processes. Rather, at different points in time, one or other process predominates. Consulting to families bereaved by suicide is very demanding clinical work and should be undertaken conjointly with a trusted colleague or in such a way that there are opportunities to prepare and debrief with a supervisor or trusted colleague following such session. Following such consultations, it may be appropriate in some instances to refer bereaved families and friends for grief counselling, as there is some evidence that this may reduce the negative impact of bereavement (Clark & Goldney, 2000).

LEGAL ISSUES AND THE IMPORTANCE OF DOCUMENTATION

In cases of suicide or repeated self-harm, clients' families may take legal action against clinicians or healthcare institutions for malpractice (Bongar, 2002). This may cover charges such as failure to properly assess and diagnose a psychological disorder, failure to take adequate precautions against suicide, inappropriate early release or discharge of the client, failure to involuntarily detain the client under mental health legislation and failure to offer adequate ongoing treatment and risk management following initial assessment. In the event of legal action, contemporaneous notes are central to the defence of the clinician or institution. For this reason, it is particularly important to keep clinical notes and write up a comprehensive assessment report to carefully document the assessment process, the formulation, the initial risk assessment, the short- and long-term management plans, and the ongoing assessment of risk and changes in the client's suicidal risk status from one session to the next. The guidelines in Chapter 7 on report writing and keeping progress notes can be followed for this purpose.

SUMMARY

The annual worldwide incidence of completed suicide is 16 per 100,000. Between 30 and 60% of suicide attempters have made previous attempts. A distinction is made between suicide motivated by a wish to die and self-harm, which may be carried out to achieve other goals. The risk of suicide and repeated self-harm is determined by multiple factors. Chief among these are the degree of suicidal intention and the lethality of the method chosen. Other predisposing risk factors have been identified in the following domains: history of self-harm, demographic profile, family of origin factors, personality-based factors, disorder-related factors, biological factors, current family factors, wider social system factors and treatment system factors. Suicide attempts and acts of self-harm are usually precipitated by stressful life events and challenges that exceed available coping resources at times when clients are particularly vulnerable to suicide. Suicide risk assessments should cover these risk factors and involve interviews with the client, collateral interviews with significant others and conjoint interviews. Involved health professionals should also be contacted. The assessment should lead to a formulation that shows how risk factors explain the occurrence of the episode of self-harming behaviour or suicidal ideation. High suicidal intent and extreme method lethality are indicative of serious immediate suicide risk. Short-term management plans that prevent immediate danger, and longer-term treatment plans that address mental health difficulties and life problems that predisposed the client to suicide, should be drawn up in light of the formulation. Short-term plans may include brief hospital-based care or community-based care. Where people at high risk of suicide refuse hospital admission and treatment, involuntary committal and treatment following statutory assessment under mental health legislation may be appropriate. Evidence-based long-term plans may include combined psychological and pharmacological treatment programmes that include dialectical behaviour therapy (for frequent attempters) or problem-solving therapy offered within the context of an outreach active follow-up model of care. Because of the potential negative effects of working with suicidal clients, it is essential to have regular supervision. Where clients commit suicide, it may be appropriate in certain circumstances to offer consultation to significant members of their families and social networks and to refer for grief counselling. Always carefully document work with clients at risk of suicide because of the risk of litigation.

EXERCISE 10.1

Working in groups of three, assign the roles of client, clinical psychologist and observer. Role-play assessment interviews with Sandra and Brian, the clients introduced at the start of this chapter, changing roles after each interview:

- Assume you are meeting Brian as an inpatient. Assess his level of risk using Table 10.2 and prepare a summary for your supervisor and team. If information from other sources would be helpful, negotiate his permission to contact or meet them.
- Assume you are meeting Sandra at an outpatient appointment 2 weeks after her visit to the accident and emergency department. She reports that everything is fine again, denies the seriousness of the incident and says she and her boyfriend are planning a week's holiday in a month's time. Assess her current level of risk using Table 10.3 and her motivation for psychological treatment.

After each role-play, the observer, 'clinical psychologist' and 'client' give comments on the interview in turn, including at least three positive aspects of the interview they noticed, as well as a maximum of three constructive suggestions for improving the interview.

Discuss the legal and ethical issues raised by the role-plays with Brian and Sandra.

FURTHER READING FOR PRACTITIONERS

Bongar, B. (2002). *The suicidal patient. Clinical and legal standards of care* (Second Edition). Washington, DC: American Psychological Association.

D'Zurilla, T. & Nezu, A. (1999). *Problem solving therapy* (Second Edition). New York: Springer Verlag.

Hawton, K. & Catalan, J. (1987). *Attempted suicide: A practical guide to its nature and management* (Second Edition). Oxford: Oxford Medical Publications.

Jacobs, D. (1999). (Ed). *The Harvard Medical School guide to suicide assessment and intervention*. San Francisco: Jossey Bass.

ASSESSMENT INSTRUMENTS

Beck, A. & Steer, R. (1988). *Beck Hopelessness Scale*. San Antonio, TX: Harcourt Brace.

Beck, A. & Steer, R. (1991). *Beck Scale for Suicide Ideation*. San Antonio, TX: Harcourt Brace. Online. Available at: http://www.psycorp.com

Beck, A., Steer, R. & Brown, G. (1996). *Beck Depression Inventory – Second Edition* (BDI-II). San Antonio, TX: Psychological Corporation.

D'Zurilla, T.J., Nezu, A.M. & Maydeu-Olivares, A. (2001). *Manual for the Social Problem Solving Inventory-Revised*. North Tonawada, NY: Multi-Health Systems.

Linehan, M., Goodstein, J., Nielson, S. & Chiles, J. (1983). Reasons for staying alive when you are thinking of killing yourself. The Reasons for Living Inventory. *Journal of Consulting and Clinical Psychology*, 54, 880–881. Online. Available at: http://www.brtc.psych.washington.edu/framePublications.htm

Reynolds, W. (1991). *Adult Suicidal Ideation Questionnaire. Professional manual*. Odessa, FL: Psychological Assessment Resources.

Reynolds, W. & Mazza, J. (1992). *Suicidal Behaviour History Form: Clinician's guide*. Odessa, FL: Psychological Assessment Resources.

FURTHER READING FOR CLIENTS

Ellis, T. & Newman, C. (1996). *Choosing to live: How to defeat suicide through cognitive therapy*. New York: New Harbinger Publications.

Suicide website with multiple links: http://www.psycom.net/depression.central.suicide. html

REFERENCES

Amsel, L. & Mann, J. (2000). Biological aspects of suicidal behaviour. In. M. Gelder, J. Lopez-Ibor & N. Andreasen (Eds.), *New Oxford textbook of psychiatry* (Volume 1, Section 4.15.3, pp. 1045–1050). Oxford: Oxford University Press.

Bancroft, J., Hawton, K., Simkin, S., Kingston, B., Cumming, C. & Whitwell, D. (1979). The reasons people give for taking overdoses. A further inquiry. *British Journal of Medical Psychology*, 52, 353–365.

Bateman, A. & Fonagy, P. (1999). Effectiveness of partial hospitalization in the treatment of borderline personality disorder. A randomized controlled trial. *American Journal of Psychiatry*, 156, 1563–1569.

Bateman, A. & Fonagy, P. (2001). Treatment of borderline personality disorder with psychoanalytically oriented partial hospitalization. An 18-month follow-up. *American Journal of Psychiatry*, 158, 36–42.

Beck, A. & Steer, R. (1988). *Beck Hopelessness Scale*. San Antonio, TX: Harcourt Brace.

Beck, A. & Steer, R. (1991). *Beck Scale for Suicide Ideation*. San Antonio, TX: Harcourt Brace. Online. Available at: http://www.psycorp.com

Beck, A., Steer, R. & Brown, G. (1996). *Beck Depression Inventory – Second Edition* (BDI-II). San Antonio, TX: Psychological Corporation.

Bongar, B. (2002). *The suicidal patient. Clinical and legal standards of care* (Second Edition). Washington, DC: American Psychological Association.

Carr, A. (2004). *Positive psychology*. London: Brunner-Routledge.

Chew, K. & McLeary, R. (1995). The spring peak in suicides: A cross-national analysis. *Social Science and Medicine*, 40, 223–230.

Clark, S. & Goldney, R. (2000). The impact of suicide on relatives and friends. In K. Hawton & K. van Heeringen (Eds.), *The international handbook of suicide and attempted suicide* (pp. 467–484). Chichester: Wiley.

De Hert, M. & Peuskens, J. (2000). Psychiatric aspects of suicidal behaviour: Schizophrenia. In K. Hawton & K. van Heeringen (Eds.), *The international handbook of suicide and attempted suicide* (pp. 121–134). Chichester: Wiley.

D'Zurilla, T. & Nezu, A. (1999). *Problem solving therapy* (Second Edition). New York: Springer Verlag.

D'Zurilla, T.J., Nezu, A.M. & Maydeu-Olivares, A. (2001). *Manual for the Social Problem Solving Inventory-Revised*. North Tonawada, NY: Multi-Health Systems.

Fleming, I. & Steen, L. (2004). *Supervision and clinical psychology*. London: Brunner-Routledge.

Hawkins, P. & Shohet, R. (2000). *Supervision in the helping professions* (Second Edition). Buckingham, UK: Open University Press.

Hawton, K. (2000a). General hospital management of suicide attempters. In K. Hawton & K. van Heeringen (Eds.), *The international handbook of suicide and attempted suicide* (pp. 519–537). Chichester: Wiley.

Hawton, K. (2000b). Treatment of suicide attempters and prevention of suicide and attempted suicide. In. M. Gelder, J. Lopez-Ibor & N. Andreasen (Eds.), *New Oxford textbook of psychiatry* (Volume 1, Section 4.15.4, pp. 1050–1059). Oxford: Oxford University Press.

Hawton, K., Arensman, E., Townsend, E., Bremmer, S., Feldman, E., Goldney, R., Gunnell, D., Hazell, P., van Heerigen, K., Hourse, A., Owens, D., Sakinofsky, I. & Traskman-Bendz, L. (1998). Deliberate self-harm: Systematic review of efficacy of psychosocial and pharmacological treatments in preventing suicide repetition. *British Medical Journal*, 317, 441–447.

Hawton, K. & Catalan, J. (1987). *Attempted suicide: A practical guide to its nature and management* (Second Edition). Oxford: Oxford Medical Publications.

Hawton, K. & van Heeringen, K. (2000). *The international handbook of suicide and attempted suicide*. Chichester: Wiley.

Heard, H. (2000). Psychotherapeutic approaches to suicidal ideation and behaviour. In K. Hawton & K. van Heeringen (Eds.), *The international handbook of suicide and attempted suicide* (pp. 503–518). Chichester: Wiley.

Jacobs, D. (1999). (Ed). *The Harvard Medical School guide to suicide assessment and intervention*. San Francisco: Jossey Bass.

Kerkhof, A. (2000). Attempted suicide. Patterns and trends. In K. Hawton & K. van Heeringen (Eds.), *The international handbook of suicide and attempted suicide* (pp. 49–64). Chichester: Wiley.

Kerkhof, A. & Arensman, E. (2000). Attempted suicide and deliberate self-harm: Epidemiology and risk factors. In. M. Gelder, J. Lopez-Ibor & N. Andreasen (Eds.),

New Oxford textbook of psychiatry (Volume 1, Section 4.15.2, pp. 1039–1045). Oxford: Oxford University Press.

Kessler, R., Borges, G. & Walters, E. (1999). Prevalence of and risk factors for lifetime suicide attempts in the national comorbidity survey. *Archives of General Psychiatry*, 56, 617–626.

Lester, D. (2000). *Suicide prevention. Resources for the millennium*. Philadelphia, PA: Brunner Routledge.

Linehan, M. (2000). Behavioural treatments of suicidal behaviours. Definitional obfuscation and treatment outcomes. In R. Maris, S. Canetto, J. McIntosh & M. Silverman (Eds.), *Review of suicidology 2000* (pp. 84–111). New York: Guilford Press.

Linehan, M., Goodstein, J., Nielsen, S. & Chiles, J. (1983). Reasons for staying alive when you are thinking of killing yourself. The Reasons for Living Inventory. *Journal of Consulting and Clinical Psychology*, 51, 276–286. Online. Available at: http://www.brtc.psych.washington.edu/framePublications.htm

Linehan, M., Rizvi, S., Welch, S. & Page, B. (2000). Psychiatric aspects of suicidal behaviour: Personality disorders. In K. Hawton & K. van Heeringen (Eds.), *The international handbook of suicide and attempted suicide* (pp. 147–178). Chichester: Wiley.

Link, S. (1997). *Assessing and managing suicide risk*. Leicester: British Psychological Society (Core Miniguide series).

Lonnqvist, J. (2000a). Epidemiology and causes of suicide. In. M. Gelder, J. Lopez-Ibor & N. Andreasen (Eds.), *New Oxford textbook of psychiatry* (Volume 1, Section 4.15.1, pp. 1034–1039). Oxford: Oxford University Press.

Lonnqvist, J. (2000b). Psychiatric aspects of suicidal behaviour: Depression. In K. Hawton & K. van Heeringen (Eds.), *The international handbook of suicide and attempted suicide* (pp. 107–120). Chichester: Wiley.

Maris, R., Canetto, S., McIntosh, J. & Silverman, M. (2000). *Review of suicidology 2000*. New York: Guilford Press.

McLeod, A. (2004). Suicide and attempted suicide. In M. Power (Ed.), *Mood disorders. A handbook of science and practice* (pp. 319–335). Chichester: Wiley.

Murphy, G. (2000). Psychiatric aspects of suicidal behaviour: Substance abuse. In K. Hawton & K. van Heeringen (Eds.), *The international handbook of suicide and attempted suicide* (pp. 135–146). Chichester: Wiley.

Paykel, E., Prusoff, B., & Meyers, J. (1975). Suicide attempts and recent life events. A controlled comparison. *Archives of General Psychiatry*, 32, 327–333.

Reynolds, W. (1991). *Adult Suicidal Ideation Questionnaire. Professional manual*. Odessa, FL: Psychological Assessment Resources.

Reynolds, W. & Mazza, J. (1992). *Suicidal Behaviour History Form: Clinician's guide*. Odessa, FL: Psychological Assessment Resources.

Roy, A., Nielsen, D., Rylander, G. & Sarchiapone, M. (2000). The genetics of suicidal behaviour. In K. Hawton & K. van Heeringen (Eds.), *The international handbook of suicide and attempted suicide* (pp. 209–222). Chichester: Wiley.

Royal College of Psychiatrists (1994). *The general hospital management of adult deliberate self harm*. Council Report CR 32. London: Royal College of Psychiatrists.

Rudd, M. & Joiner, T. (1998). The assessment management and treatment of suicidality; towards clinically informed and balanced standards of care. *Clinical Psychology: Science and Practice*, 5, 135–150.

Rudd, M., Joiner, T., Jobes, D. & King, C. (1999). The outpatient treatment of suicidality: An integration of science and recognition of its limitations. *Professional Psychology: Research and Practice*, 30, 437–446.

Sakinofsky, I. (2000). Repetition of suicidal behaviour. In K. Hawton & K. van Heeringen (Eds.), *The international handbook of suicide and attempted suicide* (pp. 385–404). Chichester: Wiley.

Schmidtke, A. & Schaller, S. (2000). The role of mass media in suicide prevention. In K. Hawton & K. van Heeringen (Eds.), *The international handbook of suicide and attempted suicide* (pp. 675–697). Chichester: Wiley.

Stack, S. (2000). Sociological research into suicide. In D. Lester (Ed.), *Suicide prevention. Resources for the millennium* (pp. 17–29). Philadelphia, PA: Brunner Routledge.

Syenager, E. & Stenager, E. (2000). Physical illness and suicidal behaviour. In K. Hawton & K. van Heeringen (Eds.), *The international handbook of suicide and attempted suicide* (pp. 405–420). Chichester: Wiley.

Traskman-Bendz, L. & Mann, J. (2000). Biological aspects of suicidal behaviour. In K. Hawton & K. van Heeringen (Eds.), *The international handbook of suicide and attempted suicide* (pp. 65–78). Chichester: Wiley.

van Heeringen, K., Hawton, K. & Williams, J. (2000). Pathways to suicide: An integrative approach. In K. Hawton & K. van Heeringen (Eds.), *The international handbook of suicide and attempted suicide* (pp. 223–236). Chichester: Wiley.

Verkes, R. & Cowen, P. (2000). Pharmacotherapy of suicidal ideation and behaviour. In K. Hawton & K. van Heeringen (Eds.), *The international handbook of suicide and attempted suicide* (pp. 487–502). Chichester: Wiley.

Weishaar, M. (2000). Cognitive risk factors in suicide. In R. Maris, S. Canetto, J. McIntosh & M. Silverman (Eds.), *Review of suicidology 2000* (pp. 112–139). New York: Guilford.

Williams, J. & Pollock, L. (2000). The psychology of suicidal behaviour. In K. Hawton & K. van Heeringen (Eds.), *The international handbook of suicide and attempted suicide* (pp. 79–94). Chichester: Wiley.

Section 3

Anxiety disorders

Chapter 11

Generalized anxiety disorder

Adrian Wells and Karin Carter

CASE EXAMPLE

Following consultation with her general practitioner for sleep disturbance and a sense of pervasive anxiety, Joan was referred for clinical assessment with a view to 'stress management training'. At assessment Joan described that she had difficulty relaxing and constantly had something to worry about. She described her recent worries as overwhelming. She was presently concerned about physical symptoms, in particular tingling sensations in her right hand and in her face. Although this was the main worry, she described currently worrying about not being in a relationship, worrying that she was not being supportive enough to her friends and worrying that she could not cope with the stress of work. She reported a diffuse and inconsistent set of somatic symptoms, including muscle tension, aches and pains in her limbs and symptoms of difficulty concentrating, and she described a general feeling of irritability and feeling on edge. Joan traced the onset of the problem back to leaving college nine years ago, and was concerned that her lifestyle at that time may have contributed to her problem. Although she described that she had always had an active mind, her worries had become overwhelming over the past few years. There was no evidence of substance-/alcohol-related problems at the present time.

Following administration of the Structured Clinical Interview for DSM-IV (First et al., 1997), Joan met the diagnostic criteria for generalized anxiety disorder (GAD) with major depressive disorder. Her Beck Depression Inventory score was 21, indicating moderate to severe depressive symptoms. She described a recent onset to her depression and expressed an opinion that this was probably a consequence of the impact that anxiety was having on her life. There was no evidence of suicidality at assessment, although there was some hopelessness concerning her ability to overcome anxiety.

A course of cognitive therapy for GAD based on the metacognitive model was implemented. During the course of treatment the intensity of depressive symptoms was continuously monitored, to determine if a further focused intervention targeted specifically at these symptoms was required. It was not considered necessary to focus on depression independently at the outset because this was not leading to significant cognitive or behavioural impairments, did not constitute a risk, and both therapist and patient agreed that it was probably secondary to GAD.

A course of metacognitive therapy for GAD was implemented and in total ten sessions were delivered. Treatment focused on modifying erroneous negative and positive metacognitive beliefs about worry. In sessions 1 and 2, a case formulation based on the metacognitive model was constructed. Joan was socialized to the model and work commenced on challenging negative metacognitive beliefs concerning uncontrollability. Homework consisted of worry postponement experiments. Sessions 3 and 4 continued work on residual uncontrollability beliefs and began modification of danger-related metacognitions. Homework consisted of loss-of-control worry experiments and a mini-survey to challenge negative beliefs about the abnormality of worry. Sessions 5 and 6 consisted of in-session experiments and verbal re-attribution to challenge specific negative metacognitions. Homework continued with worry postponement experiments when necessary, and increased exposure to worry triggers. Sessions 7 and 8 focused on positive beliefs about worry and challenged them using a combination of verbal methods, the worry contrast technique, and worry modulation experiments for homework. Sessions 9 and 10 focused on assessing and modifying residual metacognitions and on relapse prevention.

Progress throughout treatment was monitored with self-report measures of worry (Anxious Thoughts Inventory, Penn State Worry Questionnaire), model-specific measures (Generalized Anxiety Disorder Scale), and anxiety (Beck Anxiety Inventory) and depression (Beck Depression Inventory (BDI)) symptoms. Ten weekly sessions were completed, at the end of which Joan reported that she was no longer distressed by worry and anxiety. Her sleep had returned to normal and, although she still experienced intermittent somatic symptoms, she did not worry about them. Her mood had improved (post-treatment

BDI = 5) and she had accomplished an important therapeutic goal of challenging her erroneous beliefs about worry and anxiety.

INTRODUCTION

Generalized anxiety disorder (GAD) is a particularly interesting affliction because it is characterized by worry, which is a ubiquitous cognitive activity in psychological disorders. The techniques developed to treat GAD are likely to provide a basis for developing techniques that have broad application across a wide range of disorders.

Worry has been defined as a chain of thoughts that are associated with negative affect and are difficult to control. It is predominantly verbal rather than imaginal in content (Borkovec, Robinson, Pruzinsky & DePree, 1983) and aimed at problem solving. More recently, different worry types have been distinguished in GAD. Type 1 worry refers to worry about non-cognitive events such as finances or physical symptoms, whereas type 2 worry refers to worry about one's own thought processes or worry about worry (Wells, 1994, 1995). As discussed later, this distinction is a key feature of the metacognitive model of GAD. Unfortunately for the practising clinician, worry is not the only variety of intrusive and difficult-to-control thinking that occurs in psychological disorder. Worry must be effectively differentiated from other intrusions such as obsessional thoughts and depressive or obsessional rumination in order to make an accurate diagnosis. Worry has been compared with other types of negative intrusive thoughts such as obsessions (Turner et al., 1992; Wells & Morrison, 1994) and depressive rumination (Papageorgiou & Wells, 1999, 2004) and has been found to have both similarities and differences. One of the key differentiating features diagnostically between worry and obsessions is that obsessions are ego-dystonic in nature. Obsessional thoughts are experienced as senseless, abhorrent and uncharacteristic of the self, whilst worry is not ego-dystonic (uncharacteristic of self) in this way.

THE NATURE OF GAD

Diagnostic features

Until the advent of DSM-III-R (American Psychiatric Association (APA), 1987) GAD was viewed as a residual diagnostic category and not a disorder in its own right. In DSM-III-R, GAD was characterized as a disorder of unrealistic and excessive worry about two or more life circumstances for at least six months. When the person is anxious there is a range of at least six symptoms of motor tension, autonomic hyperactivity and/or vigilance. With the introduction of DSM-IV (APA, 1994) revisions were made to the diagnosis. A new criterion was added, that the individual finds it difficult to control the worry (criterion B), and the symptoms list was modified such that worry is accompanied by at least three symptoms from a list including restlessness, being easily fatigued, difficulty concentrating, irritability, muscle tension and disturbed sleep (criterion C). A diagnosis is made only if the focus of the worry is not confined to features of another axis I disorder, such as having a panic attack in panic disorder or being embarrassed in public in social phobia (criterion D). Individuals must identify that the worry is excessive or report distress due to constant worry, have difficulty controlling worry, or experience related impairment in social, occupational or other important areas of functioning (criterion E). The disturbance is not due to the direct physiological effects of a substance (e.g. drug abuse, medication) or a general medical condition, and does not occur exclusively during a mood disorder, a psychotic disorder or a pervasive developmental disorder (criterion F). Diagnostic criteria for GAD from the World Health Organization (ICD-10; WHO, 1992) and the American Psychiatric Association (DSM-IV; APA, 2000) are given in Table 11.1.

Prevalence and course

GAD is a common emotional disorder seen in primary care settings (Burvill, 1990; Goldberg & Lecrubier, 1995; Wittchen et al., 2002). After major depression, GAD is the next most common emotional disorder in primary care, with a prevalence of 7.9% (Goldberg & Lecrubier, 1995). Approximately 12% of patients attending anxiety clinics meet criteria for GAD (DSM-IV; APA, 1994), and studies show one-year prevalence rates of 1.5–3% and lifetime rates of 5% for the disorder.

GAD is chronic in nature with low remission rates (15% at one year and 25% at two years) and can have an early onset. Yonkers, Warshaw, Massion and Keller (1996) reported age of onset varying between two and sixty-one years with a mean of twenty-one years. Barlow, Blanchard, Vermilyea, Vermilyea and DiNardo (1986) give similar reports of the longstanding nature of the problem. It runs a chronic fluctuating course and affects women twice as much as men (DSM-IV; APA, 1994). In community surveys the prevalence rates for GAD among older adults range from 0.7% to 7.1%, with figures varying depending on case criteria and methodological factors (Stanley & Novy, 2000). Levels of worry, anxiety and depression in older adults with GAD are similar to those of younger adults (Beck et al., 1995). However, there are some differences in worry content across the different age groups, with younger individuals reporting more worries about work and fewer about health than older groups (Molina et al., 1998).

Table 11.1 Diagnostic criteria for generalized anxiety disorder (GAD)

DSM-IV-TR	*ICD-10*
A. Excessive anxiety and worry (apprehensive expectation), occurring more days than not for 6 months about a number of events or activities (such as school or work performance) B. The person finds it difficult to control the worry C. The anxiety or worry is associated with three of the following in adults or one of the following in children for more days than not in the past six months: 1. Restlessness or feeling keyed up or on edge 2. Being easily fatigued 3. Difficulty concentrating or mind going blank 4. Irritability 5. Muscle tension 6. Sleep disturbance D. The focus of the anxiety or worry is not confined to features of an axis I disorder, such as gaining weight (anorexia nervosa) E. The anxiety or physical symptoms cause clinically significant distress or impairment in social, occupational, school and other important area of functioning F. The disturbance is not due to the direct physiological effect of a substance	The essential feature is anxiety, which is generalized and persistent but not restricted to any particular environmental circumstance. The dominant symptoms are highly variable but complaints of continuous feelings of nervousness, trembling, muscular tension, sweating, light-headedness, palpitations, dizziness, and epigastric discomfort are common. Fears that the sufferer or a relative will shortly become ill or have an accident, are often expressed together with a variety of other thoughts and forebodings The sufferer must have the primary symptoms for most days for several weeks at a time, and usually for several months. These symptoms should usually involve elements of: 1. Apprehension (worry about future misfortune, feeling on edge, difficulty in concentrating) 2. Motor tension (restless fidgeting, tension headaches, trembling, inability to relax) 3. Autonomic overactivity (light headedness, sweating, tachycardia, tachypnoea, epigastric discomfort, dizziness, dry mouth) In children, frequent need for reassurance and recurrent somatic complaints may be prominent

Note: Adapted from DSM IV TR (APA, 2000) and ICD 10 (WH0, 1992).

Comorbidity

The degree of comorbidity between GAD and other psychiatric disorders is high. However, recent data suggest that the impact of comorbidity on clinical outcomes is no greater in GAD than in other anxiety disorders (Hunt, 2002). Yonkers et al. (1996) reported that 52% of their GAD sample met criteria for panic disorder or panic with agoraphobia; 32% were socially phobic and 37% met criteria for major depression. Judd et al. (1998) found that major depression (62%) and dysthymia (39%) were the most common comorbidities. Although the magnitude of these overlaps suggest that the DSM-III-R classification may have low integrity, it is possible that this reflects the presence of an underlying and generic vulnerability to psychopathology.

TREATMENT

Psychological therapies

Psychological treatments have consisted of a range of different approaches. Behavioural treatments have focused on the control of anxious symptoms using relaxation methods, and anxiety management approaches have used multi-component approaches combining relaxation, coping techniques and the challenging of negative thoughts (e.g. Butler et al., 1987, 1991). Relaxation-focused treatments have tended to use varieties of applied relaxation, which is introduced in stages and culminates in the acquisition of rapid relaxation skills that are applied in anxiety-provoking situations. Applied relaxation as described by Ost (1987) and progressive plus applied relaxation (Bernstein & Borkovec, 1973) have been used alone or as components of treatment. Cognitive-behavioural approaches have focused to varying degrees on challenging negative thoughts following the methods developed by Beck and associates (Beck et al., 1996), and have varied in the types of thoughts targeted. Some recent treatment approaches have included an exposure component on the conceptual basis that worry may serve as a form of avoidance of distressing emotions associated with other types of thoughts. Exposure has also been used as a means of practising coping skills. For instance Borkovec and colleagues implemented Self-Control Desensitization (SCD) as part of a treatment package (Borkovec et al., 2002). Following the initial learning of relaxation, SCD involves imagining anxious situations and physical reactions, worries, thoughts and images that accompany anxiety. Patients are taught to use their relaxation to counteract anxious responses experienced whilst imagining. SCD involves imagining each situation, thought and sensation as if it were occurring and learning how to let go of these feelings by relaxing mind and body. During SCD, which is administered hierarchically, patients are encouraged to use positive self-statements that have been generated in a coping self-statements part of treatment.

Empirical evaluations show that cognitive-behavioural therapy (CBT) is associated with significant clinical improvement, and treatment gains appear to be maintained at six- and twelve-month follow-up. In one study, there was evidence of maintenance of gains at two years (Borkovec et al., 2002). Cognitive-behavioural treatments appear to be associated with the largest treatment effects when compared with anxiety management, non-directive psychotherapy and psychoanalytic psychotherapy (Durham et al., 1994). Nevertheless, there is room for improvement in outcomes. In a re-analysis of data from six outcome studies published since 1990, Fisher and Durham applied Jacobsen criteria to define recovery rates. The treatments included CBT, behaviour therapy, applied relaxation, cognitive therapy plus relaxation, non-directive therapy, analytic psychotherapy, anxiety management training and combination treatments. Overall, a recovery rate of 40% was found using trait-anxiety as the outcome criterion, with twelve out of twenty treatment conditions associated with modest recovery rates of 30% or less. The two treatments performing best were individual cognitive therapy and applied relaxation, with recovery rates at six-month follow-up of 50–60% (Fisher & Durham, 1999). In a recent study, Ost and Breitholtz (2000) showed that applied relaxation and cognitive therapy were both effective treatments, with 53% and 62% of patients significantly improved on some (but not all) measures at post-treatment. Patients showed little improvement in trait-anxiety and worry. Arntz (2003) compared cognitive therapy with applied relaxation; at post-treatment the percentage improvement in trait-anxiety was only 12.8% following cognitive therapy and 18.1% following applied relaxation. At post-treatment, 35% of cognitive therapy patients and 44% of applied relaxation patients had recovered. At six-month follow-up this had increased to 55% of patients receiving cognitive therapy and 53.3% of those receiving applied relaxation, on the basis of trait-anxiety.

In summary, individual CBT and applied relaxation appear to be the most effective current treatments for GAD. However, there is considerable variability in outcomes across studies, and at best between 50 and 60% of patients can be classified as recovered on the basis of trait-anxiety scores at six-month follow-up. Further research is needed to evaluate the effectiveness of treatments, because reliance on trait-anxiety may not provide a satisfactory indication of what happens to hallmark symptoms of GAD, such as worry. Some trials have relied on advertisements to recruit patients or relied on students as participants (e.g. Borkovec & Costello, 1993; Ladouceur et al., 1999; Ost & Breitholtz, 2000), which may lead to samples that are not representative of community outpatients. It is clear from the evidence currently available that the effectiveness of CBT for GAD has considerable margin for improvement, with treatment effects lagging behind the effects found in the treatment of other anxiety disorders such as panic disorder. One way forward in the development of more effective interventions is to base treatment on individual case formulations that are grounded in empirically tested models of the mechanisms leading to difficult-to-control worry. One such approach based on metacognitive theory will be described in a later section of this chapter.

Pharmacological treatment

Three drug groups have been shown to be beneficial in GAD: benzodiazepines, azapirones and antidepressants. However, a number of issues and limitations need to be considered when evaluating pharmacological approaches.

In particular, few studies have used long-term follow-up evaluations of drug effects, and studies have not tended to assess the impact of treatment on cognitive symptoms of the disorder, namely worry. A further limitation in assessing studies is that earlier studies were conducted on relatively heterogeneous patient samples with diagnoses such as 'anxiety neurosis', which consist of an undifferentiated number of patients probably meeting present criteria for GAD as defined in DSM-IV. Few studies have so far evaluated combined psychological and pharmacological interventions.

Benzodiazepines (such as alprazolam, diazepam and lorazepam) have been found to be effective in GAD (Gale & Oakley-Browne, 2003; Rickels et al., 1993). They are noted for rapid relief of somatic symptoms (over two to nine weeks) compared to symptoms such as worry and irritability. These latter symptoms have been found to be particularly responsive to antidepressant medication (Hoehn-Saric et al., 1988; Rocca et al., 1997). Benzodiazepines have tended to be studied over short periods of time. However, Rickels and Schweitzer (1990) compared a benzodiazepine (clorazepate) with an azapirone (buspirone) over six and forty months follow-up. No differences were found between these treatments at six months. However, by forty months, 60% of participants given the benzodiazepine were experiencing moderate anxiety symptoms compared with 30% in the aspirone group. Benzodiazepines have been associated with increased risk of sedation and dependence (Tyrer, 1990). They may cause adverse effects in neonates if used in late pregnancy or when breast-feeding (Gale & Oakley-Browne, 2003). Rebound anxiety on withdrawal of benzodiazepines has been reported in 15–30% of people (Tyrer, 1990). Brawman-Mintzer (2001) and Connor and Davidson (1998) have recommended gradual tapering of medication and the careful assessment of client suitability before pursuing this treatment.

Buspirone has been found effective in improving symptoms over four to nine weeks compared to placebo (Gould et al., 1997), and appears to be comparable with benzodiazepines. Antidepressants (imipramine, paroxetine and venlafaxine) have been found to improve symptoms over eight to twenty-eight weeks. Antidepressants, benzodiazepines and buspirone appear to produce similar levels of effect (Lydiard, 2000).

Psychological versus drug treatments, and combination approaches

Lindsay et al. (1987) found that CBT, anxiety management and benzodiazepine treatments were comparable after treatment and better than a waiting-list control group. However, at three months only CBT and anxiety management treatments maintained this improvement.

Power, Jerrom, Simpson, Mitchell and Swanson (1989) compared CBT, benzodiazepine and placebo; at post-treatment CBT was superior to the other two conditions. At twelve-month follow-up a smaller proportion of the

CBT group (30%) had sought further treatment than the benzodiazepine (70%) or placebo groups (55%).

Few studies have explored the effects of combining psychological and drug treatments. CBT has been compared with benzodiazepines over a short time period.

Power, Simpson, Swanson and Wallace (1990) compared CBT, benzodiazepines and placebo conditions alone and in combination (CBT plus benzodiazepine, and CBT plus placebo). CBT alone or in combination was superior to diazepam alone or placebo on most measures at post-treatment and at six-month follow-up.

Combined studies can be criticized for their small sample sizes and short duration. The drug treatments have been typically administered in fixed doses, which may mean that optimum treatments have not been delivered. The CBT components have differed across studies in their focus and intensity, and none have been based on GAD-specific models, which were not available at the time.

The metacognitive model of GAD

The metacognitive model (Wells, 1995, 1997) offers a detailed account of the cognitive-behavioural factors in the development and persistence of GAD. It is based on the principle that erroneous metacognitive beliefs about worry are a central cognitive factor in pathological worry.

The metacognitive model is depicted diagrammatically in Figure 11.1. A distinction is made between two types of worry: general worry (type 1), which is similar in content to normal worries, and negative thoughts about worry itself (type 2) or worry about worrying. It is proposed that normal worries develop into GAD when type 2 worrying becomes activated in response to worry and its associated anxiety symptoms. Type 2 worry is the conscious manifestation of underlying negative metacognitive beliefs about worrying. In GAD these negative metacognitive beliefs centre on two themes: (1) beliefs about the uncontrollability of worry; and (2) beliefs about the dangerous consequences of worrying for mental, physical and/or social functioning.

Aside from negative metacognitive beliefs, the model holds that individuals with GAD also have positive metacognitive beliefs about worrying. In particular, they believe that worrying is a helpful coping strategy and that it provides a means of anticipating and avoiding or effectively dealing with potential threats in the future. Beliefs of this kind support sustained type 1 worry as a means of coping in which individuals use worry to 'work-through' problems until they feel able to cope. In the model, positive beliefs are thought to be normal and give rise to the sustained type 1 worry that most people have from time to time. However, it is the development and/or activation of negative metacognitive beliefs and resulting type 2 worry that leads to GAD.

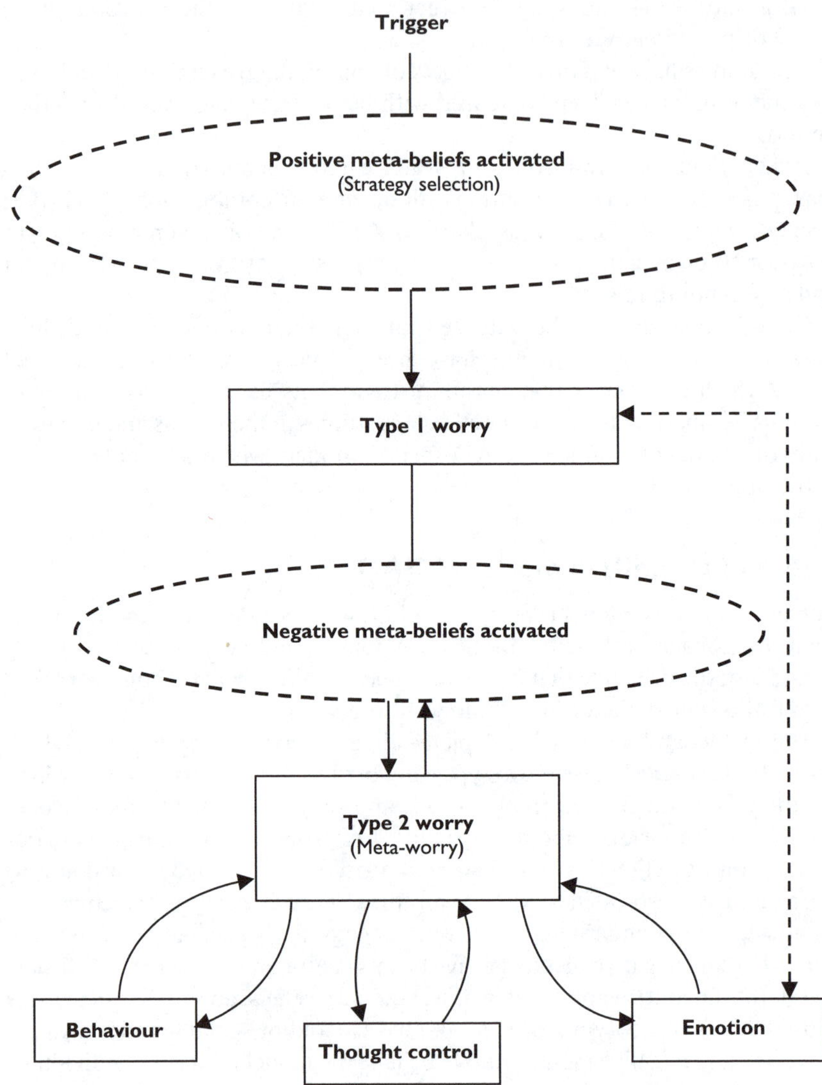

Figure 11.1 The metacognitive model of GAD (reproduced from Wells, 1997).

Having introduced some basic concepts, we now turn to describing the cognitive-behavioural processes as they occur in a typical distressing episode of worry. Referring to Figure 11.1, episodes of pathological worry are often triggered by an intrusive thought, which can be an image or a verbal 'what if . . .' question that has negative implications. For example, a patient described a recent worry episode in which her partner was late arriving home from work and, while listening to the radio, she heard news about a gas explosion; this was accompanied by an image of her husband laying injured in his car. On a different occasion the patient reported that she read in the newspaper that a pupil in a local school had contracted meningitis, this was followed by the intrusive thought 'What if my son caught meningitis?' In each case a negative intrusion acted as the internal trigger for the worry episode that followed. The trigger activates positive metacognitive beliefs about worrying, which supports the use of a worry as a means of contemplating a series of negative outcomes and how to deal with them. This type 1 worrying normally continues until it is displaced by external factors, such as competing demands, or until the person reaches an internal state that signals it is safe to stop worrying. This state is often a sense of knowing that most necessary options have been covered, or an internal 'feeling' that one will be able to cope. However, the individual with GAD activates negative beliefs about worrying and negatively appraises worry and its associated responses during the worry episode. For example, the person thinks that loss of mental control and a mental breakdown is imminent. This leads to an intensification of anxiety depicted by the feedback cycle between type 2 worry and anxiety in Figure 11.1. It also means that it is more difficult to obtain a sense that one will be able to cope.

In Figure 11.1, type 1 worrying can lead to an intensification of anxiety (at least initially) but as the work of type 1 worry is accomplished anxiety can decrease. These processes are depicted by the dotted line linking type 1 worry to emotion. A further process is also important in the model. As worrying is predominantly a verbal conceptual activity that focuses on danger, it may block other processes necessary for emotional processing and the resolution of stress and other emotional reactions. Hence, in Figure 11.1, rather than anxiety alone being represented, the model captures this important factor by specifying a link with 'emotion'. What this means for GAD is that the use of type 1 worry may lead to an increase of other symptoms, such as intrusive thoughts, as symptoms of failed emotional processing following stress. This could in turn strengthen negative beliefs about coping and negative beliefs about the controllability and functioning of one's thinking.

Two other factors contribute to the development and persistence of GAD in the model. These are labelled 'behaviour' and 'thought control' in Figure 11.1. Since people with GAD have disparate beliefs about worry (believing it is helpful but also uncontrollable/dangerous), this leads to unhelpful vacillations in mental control attempts. Individuals will try not to think about topics that may trigger worrying or may try to suppress certain internal triggers. However, once a trigger is experienced the person will activate positive beliefs about the need to worry in order to cope. Thus, there are conflicting motivations to avoid the trigger but to engage the worry if the trigger is encountered. The problem here is that suppression of triggers is not consistently effective and this ineffectiveness can be interpreted as evidence of loss of control thereby strengthening negative metacognitive beliefs. Even when suppression is effective there is a problem in so much that individuals fail to discover that worrying does not lead to catastrophic outcomes such as mental breakdown. The conflicting motivations to disrupt worry once it is activated mean that individuals rarely have experiences of discontinuing their worry episode, which would provide evidence of control (but if successful would not provide evidence that worry is harmless). The individual therefore becomes trapped in the use of a pattern of unhelpful thought control strategies that maintain dysfunctional beliefs about the uncontrollability and/or dangerous consequences of worry. Overt behaviours are also often used to avoid worry and the threat it carries. For example, individuals will seek reassurance from others that there is really nothing to worry about, or seek information to determine that situations are safe and do not necessitate worry. Subtle forms of avoidance are also evident, such as avoiding news items or people that may lead to internal triggers. Problems with behavioural strategies are that some of them increase uncertainty/ambiguity, as is the case when different people offer different or conflicting information. Searching for information as a means of trying to determine that it is not necessary to worry often provides access to a wider range of negative information activating 'what-if?' questions. Avoidance of situations deprives the individual of opportunities to discover that worry is controllable or that worry is not harmful.

A brief review of empirical support for the metacognitive model

Evidence from several sources is supportive of central components of the model. These studies have explored worry in non-patients with high-levels of pathological worry, in non-patients meeting diagnostic criteria for GAD, and patients with GAD.

Borkovec and Roemer (1995) conducted two studies exploring the reasons given for worrying by students, and showed that motivation, preparation and avoidance were the most characteristic reasons given. Individuals meeting criteria for GAD rated using worry for 'distraction from more upsetting things' significantly more than non-anxious subjects. Assuming that these reasons reflect positive attitudes or beliefs about worry these results provide preliminary support for the idea that individuals with problematic worry view worry in positive terms.

More direct evidence for the model and the idea that relationships exist between metacognitive beliefs and worrying comes from studies by Cartwright-Hatton and Wells (1997). We developed the Metacognitions Questionnaire (MCQ) to measure a range of metacognitive dimensions, including positive and negative beliefs about worry and intrusive thoughts. Both positive and negative beliefs about worrying were positively associated with worry in students. Moreover, proneness to pathological worry remained positively associated with positive beliefs about worry, and negative beliefs about worry when trait-anxiety and other metacognitive factors were controlled. In a study of patients with DSM-III-R GAD, obsessive-compulsive disorder (OCD), patients with other anxiety or depressive disorders and non-patients, no differences emerged in positive beliefs about worry, although GAD and OCD patients endorsed significantly higher negative beliefs concerning uncontrollability and danger than the other groups.

In a later study, we (Wells & Papageorgiou, 1998) tested the metacognitive predictors of pathological worry and obsessive-compulsive symptoms whilst controlling for the statistical interdependency of these variables. Both positive beliefs about worry and negative beliefs concerning uncontrollability and danger were independently associated with pathological worry, and negative beliefs made the strongest contribution.

To test the model in the context of DSM-IV GAD, which now includes uncontrollability of worry as a diagnostic criterion, Wells (2005) developed the Meta-worry Questionnaire to assess danger-related appraisals of worry whilst eliminating circularity that would otherwise be caused by retaining uncontrollability appraisals. Negative danger-related appraisals of worry were positively correlated with pathological worry, and ratings were significantly higher in students meeting criteria for DSM-IV GAD than in individuals with somatic anxiety or no anxiety.

Earlier studies of the relationships between type 1 and type 2 worry and pathological worry used the Anxious Thought Inventory (AnTI; Wells, 1994) to assess type 1 and 2 dimensions. Wells and Carter (1999) found that type 1 and type 2 worry were positively correlated with pathological worry and a rating of 'how much is worry a problem for you' in non-patients. However, only type 2 worry, and not type 1, remained as a significant positive predictor of pathological worry when trait-anxiety and overlaps between worry types were statistically controlled. These relationships remained even when the rated uncontrollability of worry was also controlled in subsequent analyses. These results show that irrespective of the frequency of type 1 worries as measured by the AnTI, and of the uncontrollability of worry, type 2 worry is significantly associated with pathological worry.

We (Wells & Carter, 2001) compared patients with a diagnosis of DSM-III-R GAD, with patients with panic disorder, social phobia, depression or non-patient controls, on measures of type 2 worry and metacognitive beliefs. Patients with GAD showed significantly higher negative metacognitive belief and type 2 worry scores than the other groups. In a discriminant function analysis, patients with GAD were significantly discriminated from the other groups in terms of negative metacognitions, whereas the content of type 1 worry was the best discriminator of patients with panic or social phobia.

In a prospective study, Nassif (1999) examined the presence of GAD at time 1 and again at a second time twelve to fifteen weeks later in a sample of students. The level of negative metacognitive beliefs assessed at time 1 was a significant predictor of the presence of GAD at time 2 when the presence of

GAD at time 1 was controlled. These results are consistent with a causal role of negative metacognitions in the development of GAD symptoms.

The model suggests that positive and negative beliefs about worry give rise to conflicting motivations/strategies in regulating negative thinking. A study by Purdon (2000) demonstrated that, during a worry episode, positive and negative beliefs about worry predicted conflicting motivations to engage in or control worrying thoughts.

Finally, in this section the consequences of worry for emotional regulation will be considered. The model gives rise to the hypothesis that worrying can, under some circumstances, cause problems for effective self-regulation. In particular, worrying as a strategy to deal with stress may interfere with processes necessary for effective emotional processing. Symptoms of failed emotional processing include intrusive thoughts, arousal and, clinically, post-traumatic stress disorder. In one study Butler, Wells and Dewick (1995) found that brief periods of worry following exposure to a gruesome film were associated with a significantly higher frequency of intrusive images about the film over a subsequent three-day period compared to brief periods of imagery or 'settling down'. These findings were substantiated and extended in a further study by Wells and Papageorgiou (1995). The Thought Control Questionnaire (TCQ; Wells & Davies, 1994) has been used to explore relationships between the tendency to use worry as a means of coping with distressing thoughts and emotional outcomes. The use of worry as a strategy is positively associated with acute stress disorder and other anxiety disorders (e.g. Warda & Bryant, 1998). In a prospective study, Holeva et al. (2001) demonstrated that the tendency to use worry in the first few weeks after being a victim in a road traffic accident (irrespective of stress symptoms) was associated with a greater incidence of subsequent post-traumatic stress disorder.

ASSESSMENT OF GAD AND WORRY

Two structured interview schedules are useful in the identification and diagnosis of GAD: the Structured Clinical Interview for DSM-IV (SCID; First et al., 1997), and the Anxiety Disorders Interview Schedule (ADIS; DiNardo et al., 1994).

The Generalized Anxiety Disorder Questionnaire (GAD-Q; Roemer, Borkovec, Rosa & Borkovec, 1995) provides a self-report instrument for the identification of GAD that can be scored in accordance with DSM-III-R or DSM-IV criteria. The instrument has been used to identify GAD cases in research on non-patient samples.

Self-report measures of worry used in clinical and research settings are the Penn State Worry Questionnaire (PSWQ; Meyer et al., 1990) and the Anxious Thoughts Inventory (AnTI; Wells, 1994). The PSWQ is a sixteen-item, non-content-based trait measure of the tendency to experience frequent, chronic and difficult to control worry. The AnTI is a twenty-two-item trait scale assessing both content and process dimensions of worry. There are three subscales, which measure social worry, health worry and meta-worry.

The Generalized Anxiety Disorder Scale (GADS; Wells, 1997) has been used in the context of implementing metacognitive therapy for GAD. It provides a multi-component measure of the distress associated with worry, use of coping behaviours, avoidance and maladaptive metacognitive beliefs about worry in the past week. It provides basic information that can be useful in developing a case formulation, and provides an index of the effects of treatment on individual mechanisms central in the formulation. The measure is normally administered at the beginning of each treatment session as a guide to treatment effects and as a means of reducing therapist drift by highlighting target metacognitive beliefs that remain above zero.

In addition to these measures of worry, therapists should use additional measures of anxiety symptoms and mood. We recommend and use the following instruments that are administered at each treatment session: Beck Anxiety Inventory (BAI; Beck et al., 1988), Beck Depression Inventory (BDI; Beck et al., 1961) or Beck Depression Inventory II (BDI-II; Beck & Steer, 1987) and the GADS (Wells, 1997). Additional measures are administered at pretreatment and post-treatment, including: the trait-anxiety subscale of the State-Trait Anxiety Inventory (Spielberger et al., 1983), PSWQ and AnTI.

TREATMENT OF GAD: METACOGNITIVE THERAPY

In the remainder of this chapter, metacognitive therapy will be described and the content of treatment outlined in sufficient detail to serve as an introduction to this treatment approach. For more detail the reader is referred to two references that serve as treatment guides: Wells (1997, Chapter 8) and Wells (2000, Chapter 10). The treatment has been evaluated in an open trial and a randomized trial. The results from these trials conducted with community outpatients with a primary diagnosis of DSM-IV GAD (e.g. Wells & King, 2004), show large improvements in measures of worry, anxiety and depressive symptoms, with post-treatment effect sizes ranging from 1.18 to 2.86. Recovery rates were also high, with 87.5% of patients recovered at post-treatment and 75% at six- and twelve-month follow-up on measures of trait-anxiety in the open trial (see Fisher 2006 for a preliminary analysis of the randomized trial data).

This section will be illustrated with reference to the patient outlined at the beginning of this chapter. Treatment sessions are typically administered once a week for a period of twelve weeks. However, it is common for treatment to be successfully completed in a range of six to twelve sessions, and the number of sessions provided depends on the speed of therapeutic progress. The therapist should consider terminating treatment when the patient consistently shows no conviction in negative and positive beliefs about worry on the GADS and when relapse prevention strategies have been reviewed in therapy and the therapy blueprint is complete. Treatment focuses on modifying negative beliefs about the uncontrollability of worry first, then negative beliefs about the danger of worry, and finally positive beliefs about worry.

Case conceptualization

Treatment begins with case conceptualization, which involves the construction of an idiosyncratic version of Figure 11.1. This is achieved by asking patients about a recent worry episode or exacerbation of worry associated with distress. Questioning about the episode should aim to elicit the triggering thought for worry, anxious symptoms, and negative beliefs about worry. Type 2 worry is typically the situational readout of negative beliefs and so the theme in type 2 worry should mirror negative beliefs. A useful line of questioning is to ask about the content of type 1 worry, then ask about the anxiety symptoms associated with this, and then question the patient about negative thoughts about the anxiety symptoms and worry process itself.

When questioning patients the therapist should determine negative beliefs about uncontrollability and negative beliefs about danger. The uncontrollability beliefs are always present even if implicit in what the patient says. For instance, patients often state that worry is harmful physically or psychologically. In these circumstances, the therapist should question why under such circumstances the patient does not simply stop worrying. This is a direct means of accessing the underlying uncontrollability belief. To determine positive beliefs about worry, the therapist asks about the advantages of worrying. It is important to note that positive beliefs may not be as evident as negative beliefs at the outset of treatment. This is not a problem because treatment focuses initially on challenging negative beliefs about worry. The following example illustrates the line of questioning described above leading to the case formulation in Figure 11.2.

Therapist: Thinking about the last time you had a distressing worry episode, what triggered your worry, a thought, an image, or a situation?

Patient: I was worried about meeting up with my friends and started to think about what I should do when I go out in case I do something to upset them.

Therapist: So what was the first thing that triggered that worry, was it a thought like 'what if I do something wrong?'

Patient: Yes, I had the thought, what if I act badly.

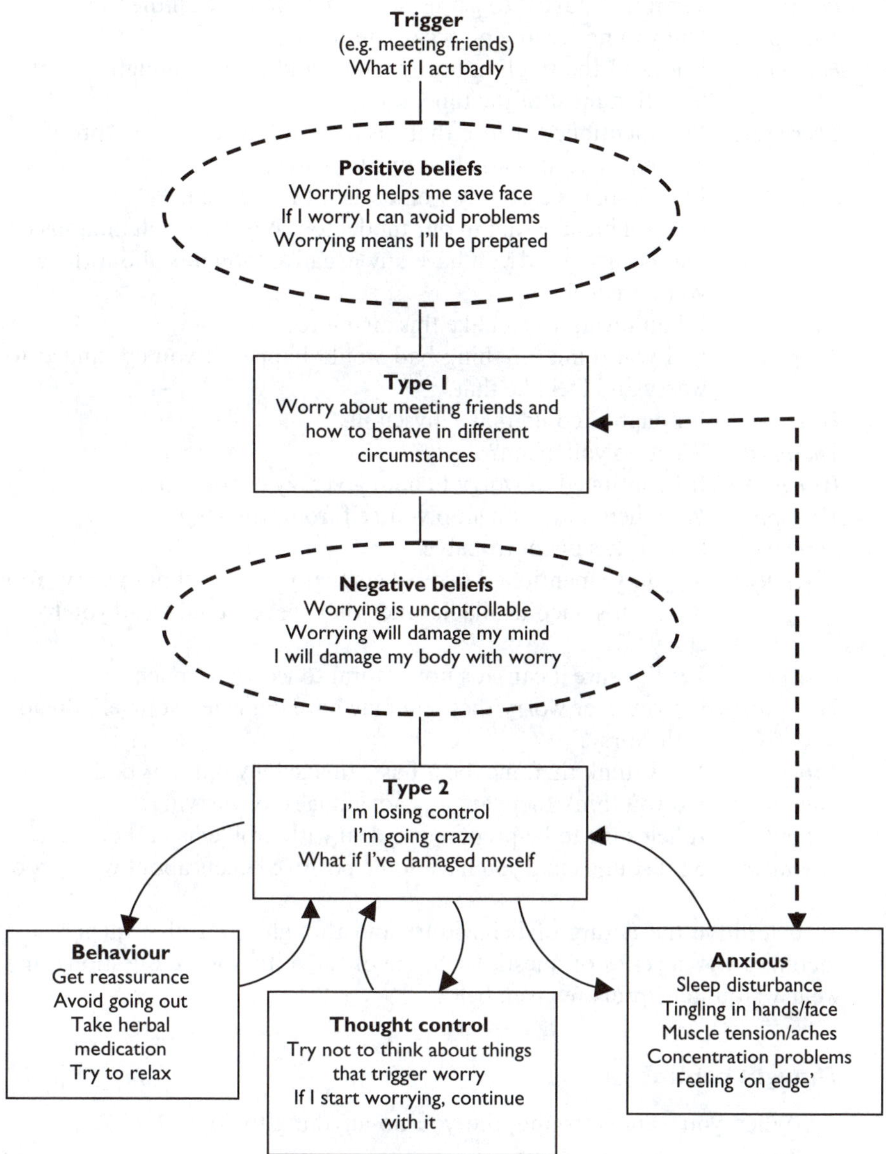

Figure 11.2 An idiosyncratic case conceptualization based on the metacognitive model.

Therapist: OK. Then you started worrying.

Patient: Yes, I was running through what could happen and how I might behave. [Note: this is a Type 1 worry.]

Therapist: It sounds as if you were worrying about acting badly. How did you feel as you thought about those things?

Patient: Terrible, I started to get tense and felt on-edge all the time.
Therapist: Did you notice any physical symptoms?
Patient: I noticed the tingling in my hands and face, although I think I have that most of the time now.
Therapist: You mentioned before that sleep disturbance is also a problem, as is concentration. Is that due to worry?
Patient: I think so, it's certainly worse when I'm worried.
Therapist: OK. I'll include that in our model too. When you felt anxious on that occasion did you have any negative thoughts about the way you were feeling?
Patient: I didn't want to feel like this anymore.
Therapist: Did you think anything bad would happen if you continued to worry and feel like that?
Patient: I thought I could make myself ill.
Therapist: What do you mean?
Patient: If I continued to worry I could go crazy or something.
Therapist: Why then don't you stop yourself from worrying?
Patient: I can't. It's uncontrollable.
Therapist: So you've mentioned two beliefs that you have about worry. You believe it's uncontrollable, and you believe it could lead you to go crazy.
Patient: Yes I'm sure it can, it's not natural to worry so much.
Therapist: Do you ever worry that you may have damaged yourself already with worry?
Patient: Yes, I think that, maybe it has damaged my mind or body.
Therapist: Do you think there are any advantages to worrying?
Patient: It helps me to be prepared to deal with problems in the future.
Therapist: So it sounds like you have some positive beliefs about worry too.

To determine the nature of behaviours and thought control strategies, the therapist asks a series of questions. Some of the initial probe questions that we have found helpful are given below:

Thought control

- When you were worrying, did you do anything to control it? What was that?
- Do you ever try not to think about something in case it triggers worrying?
- When you start worrying, do you need to think it through in order to be OK?
- When you're in the midst of a worry, have you ever decided just to discontinue it?

Behaviour

- Do you avoid situations in order to prevent yourself from worrying?
- Do you rely on other people to stop you worrying (e.g. by asking for reassurance)?
- Do you avoid or search for information in order to prevent worrying?
- Do you do anything to prevent worry and anxiety from harming you?
- Do you do anything to try and relax?

Socialization

Socialization to the model consists of sharing the case formulation with the patient. The therapist proceeds by describing the key elements in the formulation. The central messages to convey are that most people experience worry and that worry only becomes a problem when unhelpful beliefs develop about worry and associated behaviour. The role of beliefs is illustrated by therapist-directed questions, for example:

- If you thought that worrying was only a good thing to do, that it helped you to survive, how much of a problem would worry be?
- If you knew that worrying could be controlled, how much of a problem would you have with worry?

The therapist also helps the patient to see how using unhelpful thought-control strategies can lead to further problems, such as strengthening beliefs about the uncontrollability of worry. This is achieved by questioning patients about how effective their strategies have been to date, and by use of a thought-suppression experiment (e.g. the therapist asks the patient to try not to think about a blue elephant for a period of three minutes). Discussion following the suppression experiment focuses on how effective this was. If it was not effective, and this is typical, then it is evidence of how trying not to think thoughts is counterproductive. If, less typically, it was effective, this can be used a basis to explore why the patient cannot be this effective with worry (i.e. because it is not a consistently effective strategy).

Challenging metacognitive beliefs

Uncontrollability

The first step is challenging of metacognitive beliefs about uncontrollability. Initially, verbal methods are used to explore and weaken these beliefs. Useful questions include:

- If worrying is uncontrollable, how does it ever stop?

- What happens to your worry if suddenly the telephone rings and you have to answer it?
- Have you ever tried to postpone worry until another time?

The therapist obtains a rating in belief about uncontrollability (0–100%) at the beginning and throughout this procedure of reattribution.

At this stage, a worry-postponement experiment is introduced as a means of testing beliefs in uncontrollability as a homework assignment. The therapist introduces this as follows:

> One of the problems is that you are in two minds about worry. You believe you should engage with it in order to cope, but also that it is uncontrollable and dangerous. So you oscillate between attempting to avoid worry but not interrupting it once it starts. This means you cannot find out the truth about worry. I would like you to try an experiment for homework. When you notice yourself worrying I would like you to say to yourself 'Stop, I'm worrying again. I won't complete this now. I'll do it later'. I would then like you to set aside 15 minutes at the end of the day, say between 6 p.m. and 6.15 p.m., when you can sit down and work through your worry. But you don't need to use that time if by then you don't feel the need. In fact, most people find that they don't use it.

At this stage the therapist is careful to point out the difference between thought suppression and worry postponement:

> I don't want you to confuse this technique with the idea of trying not to think a thought. I'm not asking you to use the blue elephant strategy. You may have a worry, such as worry about your physical health, and that thought can stay in your mind, you are not trying to blank it out. You are deciding to postpone more detailed thinking about it. Can you see the difference?

In the next session, the results of the experiment are discussed and belief in uncontrollability re-rated. The therapist then introduces further discussion of the evidence and counter-evidence for the belief that worry is uncontrollable and then introduces the 'loss of control experiment'. This is conducted in-session and subsequently applied as a modified postponed worry experiment for homework. An example of the therapist dialogue for the loss of control experiment is as follows:

> I'd like you to try an experiment right now. We have reviewed evidence that worry is not uncontrollable, and you have started to believe that you do have some control. But it is important to put this to the test. I'd like to try and push the limits of worry, to see if you can lose control of the

activity. Can you think of a worry that you have had in the last week or that you are having at the present time? I would like you to start worrying about that, worry as much as you can, really go for it, and see if you can lose control of the activity.

Following this exercise, beliefs in uncontrollability should be re-rated. Some patients find the experiment unhelpful and disqualify the exercise by stating that it was not a real or significant worry. This is to be expected, but this is the first stage of the procedure, the more powerful stages are to follow. Next, the patient is asked to run the experiment for homework, which consists of continuing with worry postponement but using the allotted postponed worry time to try and lose control of the worry experienced earlier in the day. Once this has been practised a couple of times the patient is encouraged to try and lose control of worry during a naturally occurring worry episode rather than postponing the activity.

Danger-related metacognitions

Once belief in uncontrollability is at zero, treatment focuses on modifying metacognitive beliefs concerning the dangers of worrying. The three broad classes of danger are: physical (e.g. 'worrying can damage my body'), psychological (e.g. 'worrying can make me lose my mind') and social (e.g. 'worrying is abnormal and will lead people to reject me'). Often, in appraising the harmful effects of worry, patients equate worry with stress and, because they have been led to believe stress is harmful, they assume worry must also be harmful. We will see later that strategies of questioning the mechanism for worry effects, education and decoupling can be used to deal with this issue.

The dissonance technique

Initial weakening of metacognitions concerning danger (or positive beliefs – it can go either way) can be obtained by emphasizing the dissonance that exists between the patient's negative and positive beliefs about worry. Here, the therapist aims to show how believing that worrying is a helpful coping strategy conflicts with negative beliefs about worry. The patient is then invited to accept either the positive or negative belief or to revise beliefs to make them more parsimonious. The following transcript illustrates this process:

Therapist: On the one hand you believe that worry helps you be prepared, yet on the other you think it could cause mental breakdown, is that right?

Patient: Yes, well stress is a bad thing for health, and I know worry gives me symptoms.

Therapist: So you are in two minds about worry. But how can worry help you be prepared if it can also make you lose your mind. Isn't there a conflict in what you believe?

Patient: Yes, I'd not thought of it that way before, maybe worry isn't so good after all then.

Therapist: Or maybe worry isn't harmful.

Patient: I'd like to think that, but I'm sure it's not good.

Therapist: OK, so it sounds as if you are beginning to doubt how good worry is.

Patient: Yes, I suppose so.

Therapist: We will come back to positive beliefs later in therapy. Right now though, how much do you believe worry could cause a mental breakdown?

Patient: I'm sure it could, I believe it 60%.

Therapist: Let's take a look at that belief in more detail.

Five verbal techniques for challenging danger metacognitions

Five overlapping techniques will be considered here, these we will refer to as: (1) questioning the evidence; (2) questioning the mechanism plus education; (3) questioning the normality of worry; (4) reviewing counter-evidence; and (5) decoupling. The aim is not to obtain a definitive challenge to the patient's negative belief with every question but to apply the questions and techniques fluidly.

QUESTIONING THE EVIDENCE

- What is the evidence that you have that worry causes (e.g. physical illness)?
- How long have you been a worrier . . . why hasn't the problem (e.g. going crazy) happened yet?

The evidence that the patient has to support the view that worry is dangerous should be explored. This exploration can provide entry points for re-framing experiences and modifying knowledge by education and the strategies that are described below. The type of evidence frequently cited is that worry causes bodily symptoms, that stress is thought to be harmful, and that someone known to the patient had a 'nervous breakdown' and that person was a worrier. In each case it is useful to question how the patient knows that it is worry that causes these events, perhaps it is some third factor that causes both worry and these events, or some of these events may cause worry (i.e. bodily symptoms may cause worry, harmful events may cause worry).

The patient should be asked why it is, given the length of time he or she has been worrying, that negative consequences have not yet occurred. This is an unpredictable strategy, but interesting none the less, because some patients state that a catastrophe has happened already and that is why they are seeking treatment. This type of response can be dealt with by bringing the patient back to the main belief that was the focus of evaluation at the outset. It is useful to help the patient to see that they are seeking treatment for worry, which is unpleasant, but this does not in itself mean that worry causes more serious problems.

QUESTIONING THE MECHANISM PLUS EDUCATION

- What is the mechanism that leads worry to have this effect?
- How does worry do that?

The mechanism by which worry has negative personal consequences should be questioned. Patients vary in their knowledge of mechanisms that they believe underlie the harmful effects of worrying. For some, worry is equated with anxiety/stress and is therefore seen as negative. Others believe that worry has specific effects, such as raising blood pressure, which in turn is damaging. Answers to this question can be corrected by providing new information about the effects of stress and worry. For example, concerns about raised blood pressure can be allayed by asking the patient what their blood pressure is. If it is normal, this provides evidence that, despite worrying, there is no effect on this dimension. A distinction can also be made between periodically elevated blood pressure related to worry and the chronically elevated type associated with poor health outcomes. Stress and anxiety experiences can be re-framed in terms of the flight and fight survival response and patients can be helped to see how anxiety has survival value. The therapist can ask the question: 'Is it likely that humankind would have evolved from stressful early environments if worry and stress caused death, illness or mental breakdown?' Some patients believe that worry puts a strain on the heart, and could lead to a heart attack. Here the therapist should explore if the patient knows what is done to re-start a heart following a heart attack. One procedure is the injection of adrenaline into the heart muscle and it is adrenaline that is released when anxious and worried. This scenario is used to show how worry/stress effects on physiology are not harmful.

QUESTIONING THE NORMALITY OF WORRY

- How many people would you estimate worry in your street?
- And how many have had a mental breakdown?

By questioning the pervasiveness of worry, it is possible to follow-up with questions concerning the distribution of negative outcomes to show that there is significantly more worry than feared outcomes. In addition, the therapist can present evidence that worry is a normal activity that most people engage in. This procedure should be followed up with a mini-survey to assess the prevalence and nature of worry (see later).

REVIEWING THE COUNTER-EVIDENCE

- Can you think of evidence that worry is not harmful?

This strategy is best placed after those described above as a means of consolidating the new information learned as a result of those procedures. Typically, the therapist will be required to help the patient generate a list of counter-evidence, an example follows:

- Worry is normal and most people have it.
- Worry and stress are not the same thing.
- Worry is a component of anxiety and anxiety can have survival value.
- I have been a worrier for years and nothing bad has happened.
- I know other people who worry more than me and they are OK.
- People in worrying situations don't go crazy due to worry (e.g. people in war).
- I've tried to lose control of my mind with worry and I found I couldn't.
- My doctor says that my blood pressure is normal.

DECOUPLING

For some patients, worry is treated as synonymous with stress or synonymous with mental illness. It is necessary to decouple these concepts to challenge danger-related metacognitions. One way that we have found useful to decouple the worry and stress concept is to view stress as a consequence of demands on the individual, whereas worry can be seen as a response to stress. This is generally consistent with the patient's positive worry beliefs in which worry is seen as a coping strategy, therefore it is not synonymous with stress. The issue of equating worry with mental illness can be more problematic to deal with. Some patients view their need for treatment as evidence that they are already mentally abnormal. To deal with this we have found it beneficial to equate GAD with specific phobias, such as a spider phobia. One way to look at GAD is as a specific fear of worrying because of the belief that something bad will happen if a big worry is encountered. This is very much like having a fear of spiders because of the belief that something bad will happen if exposed to one. The patient can then be asked if they would consider a spider phobia to be a mental illness, to which the typical response is no. Another useful strategy is to ask patients to describe what they mean by mental illness, and list the attributes/symptoms of such in collaboration with the therapist. The symptoms can then be compared against those accompanying GAD with the aim of showing a discrepancy suggesting that mental illness and GAD are not equivalent.

Behavioural experiments

Various experiments involving the manipulation of worry can be used to challenge belief in danger-related metacognitions. The use of verbal procedures (above) should be followed by behavioural experiments to test – unambiguously – predictions concerning the dangerous consequences of worrying. In-session experiments consist of asking patients to engage in a period of intense worry to determine if it culminates in a predicted negative outcome. The validity of such experiments can be increased by introducing strategies that combine exposure to bodily symptoms with intense worry. For example, one patient predicted that worrying would put his mind under stress and he would lose touch with reality. To test this, we asked him to worry intensely, but he reported that this wasn't a good test because he didn't have the feeling that things around him were unreal. We decided to induce the feelings of unreality by asking him to stare at his reflection in a mirror and once the feeling occurred to engage in intense worrying to see if this made it worse. To his surprise he discovered that as he worried the feeling of unreality decreased. The experiment was repeated using hyperventilation to induce perceptual disturbances, and this was combined with intense worry. The patient discovered that worrying had no effect on these symptoms.

Experiments of this kind are consolidated through homework assignments in which patients are asked to practise pushing worry *in situ* when worry episodes actually occur, in order to test negative predictions.

For some patients, a key belief concerns the negative social consequences of worrying, such that it may lead to rejection. Experiments can be devised in which the patient is encouraged to disclose to other people, for example friends/colleagues, that they have been worrying and to observe the reactions obtained. Before doing this, the therapist and patient work together to establish the type of reaction that would be expected if revealing signs of worry lead to rejection. The occurrence of these reactions can then be objectively assessed.

Mini-surveys can offer an effective means of normalizing worry and providing a basis for challenging negative beliefs about its dangerous consequences. The patient is asked to briefly question four or five people about their own experience of worry. Questions pertinent to the patient's negative beliefs can be incorporated in the interview. For example, a patient believed that worrying was abnormal and that her worry was more serious than other people's. She asked the following questions of her friends and husband:

- How often do you worry?
- Do you ever find it difficult to control your worry?
- Do you ever think that you worry too much about things?

She discovered that everyone she interviewed said that they worried and had difficulty controlling worry, and most of the people interviewed said that they sometimes worried too much. To her surprise she found that one person whom she assumed was not a worrier actually worried more than she did herself. When asked what conclusions she drew from this exercise she stated: 'Worry is normal then, and actually my worry isn't much different from anyone else's'.

Modifying positive metacognitive beliefs

In the last third of treatment attention shifts to focusing on modifying positive beliefs about worry as a means of setting the foundations for increased flexibility in cognitive strategies for dealing with threat.

The range and strength of positive beliefs varies across cases, and these are tackled using verbal reattribution methods involving: (1) questioning the evidence; (2) reviewing the counter-evidence; (3) use of the mismatch technique; and (4) worry-modulation experiments.

Questioning the evidence and reviewing counter-evidence needs little further discussion as these techniques were described previously to challenge negative beliefs about worry. The mismatch technique (Wells, 1997) consists of asking a patient to write out a detailed summary of a recent worry narrative. The events in the narrative are then compared with the events that actually happened in the worried-about situation. This strategy can be performed retrospectively for a situation that has been encountered or prospectively for a situation that has been avoided or has not yet been encountered. In this latter case, the worry narrative is written and then the patient enters the situation and a narrative of what actually transpired in the situation is then written. The worry narrative is then compared with the factual narrative and the mismatch between them is emphasized. In this way the patient can be helped to see how worrying distorts reality and, as such, cannot provide an effective means of anticipating and coping with real events.

Worry-modulation experiments (Wells, 1997) involve asking patients to engage in activities normally associated with worrying while deliberately increasing and then decreasing the intensity of worry. If the patient prediction concerning the benefits of worry are correct then it should be possible to detect evidence of better performance/coping on the occasions when worry was increased, and a decline in performance when it was decreased. Patients typically discover that, contrary to predictions, performance is unaltered or it actually feels easier under no-worry conditions.

Strategy shifts

In the last couple of sessions of treatment, the therapist introduces alternative strategies for dealing with and thinking about threat. Since many patients have been worriers for most of their lives, there can be a degree of inflexibility or rigidity in styles of processing. The therapist introduces the notion that it is possible to think about threats or distressing events in different ways. One strategy is to encourage patients to use different endings for 'what if . . .' -related negative thoughts and other negative intrusions when they occur. For example, patients can be asked to practise finishing intrusions with positive images instead of engaging the normal verbal catastrophizing process of type 1 worry. Any reluctance to do this can be indicative of residual or undetected metacognitive beliefs that should be targeted prior to termination of treatment. For instance, some patients hold superstitious-like beliefs about the dangers of thinking positively. Some alternative strategies have already been practised during the course of treatment, one of these is to make a decision not to engage in worry or extended analysis on a topic in response to intrusions.

Relapse prevention

In the last two sessions, relapse prevention focuses on reviewing the patient's level of belief in metacognitions and determining if there is residual avoidance of situations that might trigger worrying. Evidence of remaining problems in these areas requires that the therapist revisit them to further modify belief level and avoidance.

The therapist works in collaboration with the patient to write a summary of the information learned during treatment. This summary forms the basis of the therapy blueprint that the patient can use for reference in the future. The blueprint consists of a copy of the formulation, a description of the factors maintaining GAD and a listing of the main negative and positive worry beliefs. The evidence counteracting each belief is documented and a summary of alternative strategies for dealing with worrying thoughts is written out as a series of alternative plans.

Applying metacognitive therapy to other disorders

The approach to GAD described here is grounded in a general metacognitive theory of the maintenance and treatment of psychological disorders. GAD represents some of the core basic psychological processes and factors that are conceptualized as underpinning most forms of psychopathology and emotional vulnerability. The techniques and conceptual framework described here have also been adapted and applied in conceptualizing and treating post-traumatic stress disorder, obsessive-compulsive disorder and depression, and in developing a brief treatment of social phobia (Wells, 2000; Wells & Papageorgiou, 2001, 2004; Wells & Sembi, 2004a, 2004b).

CONCLUSION

GAD is a chronic and lifelong condition if untreated. It is one of the most common anxiety disorders and is of special interest as a potential marker for basic pathological processes associated with psychological vulnerability. The disorder has proven to be difficult to treat effectively. Cognitive-behavioural interventions are the most efficacious, producing at best approximately 50–60% recovery rates, although metacognitive therapy is particularly encouraging. Pharmacological approaches also appear to be effective, but relapse appears to be a problem following discontinuation of medication and some treatments run the risk of significant side effects, particularly dependency with benzodiazepines. Few studies have evaluated the impact of psychological or drug treatments on the worry component of the disorder, which prevents conclusions being drawn about the effects of treatments on a central and arguably most important feature of the disorder.

The metacognitive model of GAD provides the most comprehensive model supported by an empirical literature, and provides a means of conceptualizing and treating cases that could improve clinical outcomes. This treatment approach is relatively new and evaluations of its effects are ongoing. The model itself is based on the principle that maladaptive metacognitive beliefs and the consequences of behavioural regulation of thoughts lead to the development and persistence of GAD. Of particular importance are erroneous negative beliefs about worry in the areas of uncontrollability and danger/consequences of the activity.

Metacognitive therapy based on the model follows a sequence that can be implemented within twelve weekly sessions. A range of strategies have been developed and/or applied to modifying maladaptive negative and positive metacognitive beliefs, and unhelpful coping behaviours.

Metacognitive theory and therapy has applications outside the realm of treating GAD, and offers the possibility that metacognitive treatment techniques may be effectively applied to problems of repetitive, persistent and difficult-to-control thinking processes across a range of disorders.

EXERCISE 11.1

Using the case example of Joan presented above and Figure 11.2, divide into groups of three and assign roles of clinical psychologist, client and observer. Role-play the following, alternating roles after each one:

- Socializing Joan into the model and communicating the ideas that worry is normal and that the problem in GAD lies in certain positive and negative beliefs held about worry.
- Challenging Joan's uncontrollability metacognitive beliefs about worry, including some gentle questioning of these beliefs, working through a thought-suppression experiment and agreeing a worry-postponement homework task.
- Challenging Joan's danger-related metacognitive beliefs about worry by

focusing on the dissonance between her positive and negative beliefs about worry, and two of the five verbal techniques for challenging danger-related metacognitiions outlined in the text: questioning the evidence, questioning the mechanism plus education, questioning the normality of worry, reviewing the counter-evidence and decoupling.

- Challenging Joan's danger-related metacognitive beliefs about worry by working collaboratively with her to design a relevant behavioural experiment. Take a record of Joan's predictions before the experiment.
- Challenging Joan's positive metacognitive beliefs about worry with two of the verbal strategies outlined in the text: questioning the evidence, reviewing the counter-evidence, using the mismatch technique and worry-modulation experiments.

EVIDENCE SUMMARIES

Barlow, D., Raffa, S., & Cohen, E. (2002). Psychosocial treatments for panic disorders, phobias, and generalized anxiety disorder. In P. Nathan & J. Gorman (Eds.), *A guide to treatments that work* (Second edition, pp. 301–336). New York: Oxford University Press.

Fisher, P.L. (2006). The efficacy of psychological treatments for generalised anxiety disorder. In G.C.L. Davey & A. Wells (Eds.), *Worry and its psychological disorders: Theory, assessment and treatment* (pp. 359–377). Chichester, UK: Wiley.

Roy-Byrne, P. & Cowley, D. (2002). Pharmacological treatment of panic disorder, generalized anxiety disorder, specific phobia and social anxiety disorder. In P. Nathan & J. Gorman (Eds.), *A guide to treatments that work* (Second edition, pp. 337–366). New York: Oxford University Press.

FURTHER READING FOR PRACTITIONERS

Andrews, G., Creamer, M., Crino, R., Hunt, C., Lampe, L., & Page, A. (2003). *The treatment of anxiety disorders. Clinician's guides and patient manuals* (Second Edition, chapters 20–23). Cambridge: Cambridge University Press.

Brown, T., O'Leary, T., & Barlow, D. (2001). Generalized anxiety disorder. In D. Barlow (Ed.), *Handbook of psychological disorders: A step-by-step manual* (pp. 154–208). New York: Guilford.

Wells, A. (1997). *Cognitive therapy of anxiety disorders: A practice manual and conceptual guide*. Chichester, UK: Wiley.

Wells, A. (2000). *Emotional disorders and metacognition: Innovative cognitive therapy*. Chichester, UK: Wiley.

FURTHER READING FOR CLIENTS

Barlow, D. & Rapee, R. (1991). *Mastering stress: A lifestyle approach*. Dallas, TX: American Health Publishing Co.

Bourne, E. (1995). *The anxiety and phobia workbook*. Oakland, CA: New Harbinger.

ASSESSMENT INSTRUMENTS

Beck, A. (1990). *Beck Anxiety Inventory*. San Antonio, TX: Psychological Corporation.

Beck, A.T., Epstein, N., Brown, G., & Steer, R.A. (1988). An inventory for measuring clinical anxiety psychometric properties. *Journal of Consulting and Clinical Psychology*, 56, 893–897.

Cartwright-Hatton, S. & Wells, A. (1997). Beliefs about worry and intrusions: The Metacognitions Questionnaire and its correlates. *Journal of Anxiety Disorders*, 11, 279–296.

DiNardo, P., Brown, T., & Barlow, D. (1994). *Anxiety Disorder Interview Schedule for DSM-IV*. San Antonio, TX: Psychological Corporation.

Lovibund, P. & Lovibund, S. (1995). The structure of negative emotional states: Comparison of the Depression and Anxiety Stress Scales (DASS) with the Beck Anxiety and Depression Inventories. *Behaviour Research and Therapy*, 33, 335–343.

Marks, I. & Matthew, A. (1979). Brief standard self-rating for phobic patients. *Behaviour Research and Therapy*, 17, 263–267.

Meyer, T., Miller, M., Metzger, R., & Borkovec, T. (1990). Development and validation of the Penn State Worry Questionnaire. *Behaviour Research and Therapy*, 28, 487–495.

Roemer, L., Borkovec, M., Rosa, P. & Borkovec, T.D. (1995). A self-diagnostic measure of generalized anxiety disorder. *Journal of Behaviour Therapy and Experimental Psychiatry*, 26, 345–350.

Snaith, R., Baugh, S., Clayden, A., Hussain, A., & Sipple, M. (1982). The Clinical Anxiety Scale: An instrument derived from the Hamilton Anxiety Scale. *British Journal of Psychiatry*, 141, 518–523.

Spielberger, C., Gorsuch, R., & Lushene, R. (1987). *The State-trait Anxiety Inventory*. Windsor, UK: NFER Nelson.

Spielberger, C.D., Gorsuch, R.L., Lushene, R., Vagg, P.R., & Jacobs, G.A. (1983). *Manual for the Stait-Trait Anxiety Inventory*. Palo Alto, CA: Consulting Psychology Press.

Wells, A. (1994). A multidimensional measure of worry. Development and preliminary validation of the Anxious Thoughts Inventory. *Anxiety Stress and Coping*, 6, 289–299.

Wells, A. (1997). *Cognitive therapy of anxiety disorders: A practice manual and conceptual guide*. Chichester, UK: Wiley.

Wells, A. & Cartwright-Hatton, S. (2004). A short form of the metacognitions questionnaire: Properties of the MCQ-30. *Behaviour Research and Therapy*, 42, 385–396.

Zung, W. (1971). A rating instrument for anxiety disorders. *Psychosomatics*, 12, 371–379.

REFERENCES

American Psychiatric Association (APA) (1987). *Diagnostic and statistical manual of mental disorders* (Third Edition-revised text). Washington, DC: APA.

American Psychiatric Association (APA) (1994). *Diagnostic and statistical manual of mental disorders* (Fourth Edition). Washington, DC: APA.

American Psychiatric Association (APA) (2000). *Diagnostic and statistical manual of mental disorders* (Fourth Edition – revised text). Washington, DC: APA.

Arntz, A. (2003). Cognitive therapy versus applied relaxation as treatment of generalized anxiety disorder. *Behaviour Research and Therapy*, 41, 633–646.

Barlow, D.H., Blanchard, E.B., Vermilyea, J.A., Vermilyea, D.B., & DiNardo, P.A. (1986). Generalized anxiety and generalized anxiety disorder: Description and reconceptualisation. *American Journal of Psychiatry*, 143, 40–44.

Beck, A.T., Emery, G., & Greenberg, R. L. (1996) Cognitive therapy for evaluation anxieties. In C. G. Lindemann (Ed.), *Handbook of the treatment of the anxiety disorders* (Second Edition, pp. 235–260). Northvale, NJ: Jason Aronson.

Beck, A.T., Epstein, N., Brown, G., & Steer, R.A. (1988). An inventory for measuring clinical anxiety: Psychometric properties. *Journal of Consulting and Clinical Psychology*, 56, 893–897.

Beck, A.T. & Steer, R.A. (1987). *Manual for the revised Beck Depression Inventory*. San Antonio, TX: Psychological Corporation.

Beck, A.T., Ward, C.H., Mendelson, M., Mock, J., & Erbaugh, J. (1961). An inventory for measuring depression. *Archives of General Psychiatry*, 4, 561–571.

Beck, J.G., Stanley, M.A., & Zebb, B.J. (1995). Psychometric properties of the Penn State Worry Questionnaire in older adults. *Journal of Clinical Geropsychology*, 1(1), 33–42.

Bernstein, D.A. & Borkovec, T.D. (1973). *Progressive relaxation training*. Champaign, IL: Research Press.

Borkovec, T.D. & Costello, E. (1993). Efficacy of applied relaxation and cognitive-behavioural therapy in the treatment of generalized anxiety disorder. *Journal of Consulting and Clinical Psychology*, 61, 611–619.

Borkovec, T.D., Newman, M.G., Pincus, A.L., & Lytle, R. (2002). A component analysis of cognitive-behavioural therapy for generalized anxiety disorder and the role of interpersonal problems. *Journal of Consulting and Clinical Psychology*, 70, 288–298.

Borkovec, T.D., Robinson, E., Pruzinsky, T., & DePree, J.A. (1983). Preliminary exploration of worry: Some characteristics and processes. *Behaviour Research and Therapy*, 21, 9–16.

Borkovec, T.D. & Roemer, L. (1995). Perceived functions of worry among generalized anxiety disorder subjects: Distraction from more emotionally distressing topics? *Behavior Therapy and Experimental Psychiatry*, 26, 25–30.

Brawman-Mintzer, O. (2001). Pharmacologic treatment of generalized anxiety disorder. In O. Brawman-Mintzer (Ed.), *The psychiatric clinics of North America:*

Generalized anxiety disorder (pp. 119–137, Vol. 24(1)). Philadelphia: W.B. Saunders Co.

Burvill, P.W. (1990). The epidemiology of psychological disorders in general medical settings. In N. Sartorius, D. Goldberg, G. De Girolamo, E. Costa, J. Silva, Y. Lecrubier, & H.-U. Wittchen (Eds.), *Psychological disorders in general medical settings*. Toronto: Hogrefe & Huber.

Butler, G., Cullington, A., Hibbert, G., Klimes, I., & Gelder, M. (1987). Anxiety management for persistent generalized anxiety disorder. *British Journal of Psychiatry*, 151, 535–542.

Butler, G., Fennell, M., Robson, P., & Gelder, M. (1991). Comparison of behaviour therapy and cognitive behaviour therapy in the treatment of generalized anxiety disorder. *Journal of Consulting and Clinical Psychology*, 59, 167–175.

Butler, G., Wells, A., & Dewick, H. (1995). Differential effects of worry and imagery after exposure to a stressful stimulus: A pilot study. *Behavioural and Cognitive Psychotherapy*, 23, 45–56.

Cartwright-Hatton, S. & Wells, A. (1997). Beliefs about worry and intrusions: The metacognitions questionnaire and its correlates. *Journal of Anxiety Disorders*, 11, 279–296.

Connor, K.M. & Davidson, J.R.T. (1998). Biology and drug therapy of GAD. *Biological Psychiatry*, 44, 1286–1294.

DiNardo, P., Brown, T., & Barlow, D.H. (1994). *Anxiety Disorder Interview Schedule for DSM-IV*. San Antonio, TX: Psychological Corporation.

Durham, R.C., Murphy, T., Allan, T., Rochard, K., Treliving, L.R., & Fenton, G.W. (1994). Cognitive therapy, analytic psychotherapy and anxiety management for generalized anxiety disorder. *British Journal of Psychiatry*, 165, 315–323.

First, M.B., Spitzer, R.L., Gibbon, M., & Williams, J.B.W. (1997). *Structured Clinical Interview for DSM-IV axis I disorders – patient edition* (SCID-I/P, version 2.0, 4/97 revision). Biometrics Research Department, New York State Psychiatric Institute, New York.

Fisher, P.L. (2006). The efficacy of psychological treatments for generalised anxiety disorder. In G.C.L. Davey & A. Wells (Eds.), *Worry and its psychological disorders: Theory, assessment and treatment* (pp. 359–377). Chichester, UK: Wiley.

Fisher, P.L. & Durham. R.C. (1999). Recovery rates in generalized anxiety following psychological therapy: An analysis of clinical significant change in the STAI-T across outcome studies since 1990. *Psychological Medicine*, 29, 1425–1434.

Gale, C. & Oakley-Browne, M. (2003). Generalised anxiety disorder. *Clinical Evidence*, 10, 1–18.

Goldberg, D.P. & Lecrubier, Y. (1995). Form and frequency of mental disorders across centres. In T. B. Ustun & N. Sartorius (Eds.), *Mental illness in general health care: An international study*. New York: Wiley.

Gould, R.A., Otto, M.W., Pollack, M.H., & Yap, L. (1997). Cognitive-behavioral and pharmacological treatment of generalized anxiety disorder: A preliminary meta-analysis. *Behavior Therapy*, 28, 285–305.

Hoehn-Saric, R., McLeod, D.R., & Zimmerli, W.D. (1988). Differential effects of alprazolam and imipramine in generalized anxiety disorder: Somatic versus psychic symptoms. *Journal of Clinical Psychiatry*, 49, 293–301.

Holeva, V., Tarrier, N., & Wells, A. (2001). Prevalence and predictors of acute stress disorder and PTSD following road traffic accidents: Thought control strategies and social support. *Behavior Therapy*, 32, 65–84.

Hunt, C.J. (2002). The current status of the diagnostic validity and treatment of generalized anxiety disorder. *Current Opinion in Psychiatry*, 15, 157–162.

Judd, L.L., Kessler, R.C., & Paulus, M.P. (1998). Comorbidity as a fundamental feature of generalized anxiety disorders: Results from the National Comorbidity Survey (NCS). *Acta Psychiatrica Scandinavica*, 393, 6–11.

Ladouceur, R., Dugas, M.J., Freeston, M.H., Rheaume, J., Blais, F., Boisvert, J.M., Gagnon, F., & Thibodeau, N. (1999). Specificity of generalized anxiety disorder symptoms and processes. *Behavior Therapy*, 30, 191–207.

Lindsay, W.R., Gamsu, C.V., McLaughlin, E. et al. (1987). A controlled trial of treatments for generalized anxiety. *British Journal of Clinical Psychology*, 26, 3–15.

Lydiard, R.B. (2000). An overview of generalized anxiety disorder: Disease state-appropriate therapy. *Clinical Therapeutics*, 22 (Suppl A), 3–19.

Meyer, T., Miller, M., Metzger, R., & Borkovec, T. (1990). Development and validation of the Penn State Worry Questionnaire. *Behaviour Research and Therapy*, 28, 487–495.

Molina, S., Borkovec, T.D., Peasley, C., & Person, D. (1998). Content analysis of worrisome streams of consciousness in anxious and dysphoric participants. *Cognitive Therapy and Research*, 22(2), 109–123.

Nassif, Y. (1999). *Predictors of pathological worry*. MPhil thesis. University of Manchester, UK.

Ost, L. (1987). Applied relaxation: Description of a coping technique and review of controlled studies. *Behaviour Research and Therapy*, 25, 397–409.

Ost, L. & Breitholz, E. (2000). Applied relaxation versus cognitive therapy in the treatment of generalized anxiety disorder. *Behaviour Research and Therapy*, 38, 777–790.

Papageorgiou, C. & Wells, A. (1999). Process and metacognitive dimensions of depressive and anxious thoughts and relationships with emotional intensity. *Clinical Psychology and Psychotherapy*, 6, 156–162.

Papageorgiou, C. & Wells, A. (2004). Nature, functions and beliefs about depressive rumination. In C. Papageorgiou & A. Wells (Eds.), *Depressive rumination: Nature, theory and treatment* (pp. 3–20). Chichester, UK: Wiley.

Power, K.G., Jerrom, D.W.A., Simpson, R.J., Mitchell, M.J., & Swanson, V. (1989). A controlled comparison of cognitive behaviour therapy, diazepam and placebo in the management of generalised anxiety. *Behavioural Psychotherapy*, 17, 1–14.

Power, K.G., Simpson, R.J., Swanson, V., & Wallace, B. (1990). A controlled comparison of cognitive-behaviour therapy, diazepam and placebo, alone and in combination, for the treatment of generalized anxiety disorder. *Journal of Anxiety Disorders*, 4, 267–292.

Purdon, C. (2000). *Metacognition and the persistence of worry*. Paper presented at the annual conference of the British Association of Behavioural and Cognitive Psychotherapy, Institute of Education, London, UK.

Rickels, K., Downing, R., Schweitzer, E., & Hassman, H. (1993). Antidepressants for the treatment of generalized anxiety disorder: A placebo controlled comparison of imipramine, trazodone, and diazepam. *Archives of General Psychiatry*, 50, 884–895.

Rickels, K. & Schweitzer, E. (1990). The clinical course and long term management of generalized anxiety disorder. *Journal of Clinical Psychopharmacology*, 10, 101–110.

Rocca, P., Fonzo, V., Scotta, M., Zanalda, E., & Ravizza, L. (1997). Paroxetine efficacy in the treatment of generalized anxiety disorder. *Acta Psychiatrica Scandinavica*, 95, 444–450.

Roemer, L., Borkovec, M., Rosa, P., & Borkovec, T.D. (1995). (GAD-Q) A self-diagnostic measure of generalized anxiety disorder. *Journal of Behaviour Therapy and Experimental Psychiatry*, 26, 345–350.

Spielberger, C.D., Gorsuch, R.L., Lushene, R., Vagg, P.R., & Jacobs, G.A. (1983). *Manual for the State-Trait Anxiety Inventory*. Palo Alto, CA: Consulting Psychology Press.

Spitzer, R.L. & Williams, J.B.W. (1986). *Structured Clinical Interview for DSM-III-R (SCID)*. New York: New York State Psychiatric Institute, Biometrics Research.

Stanley, M.A. & Novy, D.M. (2000). Cognitive-behavior therapy for generalized anxiety in late life: An evaluative overview. *Journal of Anxiety Disorders. Special Issue: Anxiety in the elderly*, 14(2), 191–207.

Turner, S.M., Beidel, D.C., & Stanley, M.A. (1992). Are obsessional thoughts and worry different cognitive phenomena? *Clinical Psychology Review*, 12(2), 257–270.

Tyrer, P. (1990). Current problems with benzodiazepines. In: D. Wheatly (Ed.), *The anxiolytic jungle: Where next?* (pp. 23–47). Chichester, UK: Wiley.

Warda, G. & Bryant, R.A. (1998). Thought control strategies in acute stress disorder. *Behaviour Research and Therapy*, 36, 1171–1175.

Wells, A. (1994). A multidimensional measure of worry: Development and preliminary validation of the Anxious Thoughts Inventory. *Anxiety, Stress and Coping*, 6, 289–299.

Wells, A. (1995). Metacognition and worry: A cognitive model of generalized anxiety disorder. *Behavioural and Cognitive Psychotherapy*, 23, 301–320.

Wells, A. (1997). *Cognitive therapy of anxiety disorders: A practice manual and conceptual guide*. Chichester, UK: Wiley.

Wells, A. (2000). *Emotional disorders and metacognition: Innovative cognitive therapy*. Chichester, UK: Wiley.

Wells, A. (2005). The metacognitive model of GAD: Assessment of meta-worry and relationship with DSM-IV generalized anxiety disorder. *Cognitive Therapy and Research*, 29, 107–121.

Wells, A. & Carter, K. (1999). Preliminary tests of a cognitive model of GAD. *Behaviour Research and Therapy*, 37, 585–594.

Wells, A. & Carter, K. (2001). Further tests of a cognitive model of generalized anxiety disorder: Metacognitions and worry in GAD, panic disorder, social phobia, depression and non-patients. *Behavior Therapy*, 32, 85–102.

Wells, A. & Cartwright-Hatton, S. (2004). A short form of the metacognitions questionnaire: Properties of the MCQ-30. *Behaviour Research and Therapy*, 42, 385–396.

Wells, A. & Davies, M. (1994). The Thought Control Questionnaire: A measure of individual differences in the control of unwanted thoughts. *Behaviour Research and Therapy*, 32, 871–878.

Wells, A. & King, P. (2004). Metacognitive therapy for generalized anxiety disorder: A open trial. Submitted for publication.

Wells, A. & Morrison, T. (1994). Qualitative dimensions of normal worry and normal intrusive thoughts: A comparative study. *Behaviour Research and Therapy*, 32, 867–870.

Wells, A. & Papageorgiou, C. (1995). Worry and the incubation of intrusive images following stress. *Behaviour Research and Therapy*, 33, 579–583.

Wells, A. & Papageorgiou, C. (1998). Relationships between worry, obsessive-compulsive symptoms, and metacognitive beliefs. *Behaviour Research and Therapy*, 36, 899–913.

Wells, A. & Papageorgiou, C. (2001). Brief cognitive therapy of social phobia: A case series. *Behaviour Research and Therapy*, 39, 713–720.

Wells, A. & Papageorgiou, C. (2004). Metacognitive therapy for depressive rumination. In C. Papageorgiou & A. Wells (Eds.), *Depressive rumination: Nature, theory and treatment* (pp. 259–274). Chichester, UK: Wiley.

Wells, A. & Sembi, S. (2004a). Treating PTSD with metacognitive-focused therapy: a core treatment manual. *Cognitive and Behavioral Practice*, 11, 365–377.

Wells, A. & Sembi, S. (2004b). Metacognitive therapy for PTSD: A preliminary investigation of a new brief treatment. *Journal of Behavior Therapy and Experimental Psychiatry*, 35, 307–318.

Wittchen, H.-U., Kessler, R.C., Beesdo, K., Krause, P., Hoefler, M., & Hoyer, J. (2002). Generalized anxiety and depression in primary care: Prevalence, recognition, and management. *Journal of Clinical Psychiatry. Special Issue: Generalized anxiety disorder: New trends in diagnosis, management, and treatment*, 63 (Suppl. 8), 24–34.

World Health Organization (WHO) (1992). *The ICD-10 classification of mental and behavioural disorders. Clinical descriptions and diagnostic guidelines*. Geneva: WHO.

Yonkers, K.A., Washaw, M.G., Massion, A.O., & Keller, M.B. (1996). Phenomenology and course of generalized anxiety disorder. *British Journal of Psychiatry*, 168, 308–313.

Chapter 12

Panic disorder and agoraphobia

Steven Taylor and Gordon J. G. Asmundson

CASE EXAMPLE

Lisa was a twenty-three-year-old undergraduate science student who presented to student counselling services because of recurrent panic attacks. The first attack had occurred about three months earlier, in the midst of a stressful series of university exams. Lisa had been quite anxious about the exams and had been staying up late studying. She had also been drinking a lot of coffee. Her first attack occurred the morning before the first of her exams. She suddenly felt queasy and light-headed and her surroundings seemed vaguely unreal. She broke into a cold sweat and her heart pounded like a hammer in her chest. Lisa thought she was about to die. Twenty minutes later the attack passed, leaving Lisa weak and exhausted. She attributed the attack to stress, lack of sleep and too much coffee. Accordingly, she cut down on coffee and tried to get more rest.

Two weeks later Lisa's exams were over but she continued to have panic attacks, regardless of whether she was feeling stressed or drinking coffee. Lisa started having panic attacks in supermarkets, while travelling on crowded trains and when in crowded bars. Each time, she felt dizzy, her heart pounded wildly, her surroundings seemed unreal and she thought she was going to die. The panic attacks were truly terrifying and so Lisa started avoiding situations in which the attacks seemed likely to occur. Twice she went to the hospital Accident and Emergency department for help. Each time the attending physician gave her a physical examination but could find nothing wrong. Lisa was told that the attacks were due to stress and that she should try to relax. She was also given a small supply of 1-mg tablets of lorazepam, which she was told to take whenever she felt panicky. Lisa took the tablets but continued to worry a great deal about her panics. 'Why,' she thought to herself, 'should I be panicking when I'm not feeling stressed?' At times Lisa worried that she might have a fatal brain disease – possibly 'mad cow' disease. Lisa feared she might suddenly drop dead from the disease.

CLINICAL FEATURES AND CLASSIFICATION

Panic attacks and panic disorder

Panic disorder is characterized by recurrent, unexpected panic attacks (American Psychiatric Association (APA), 2000; World Health Organization (WHO), 1992). Table 12.1 lists the defining features of these attacks. The panic attacks can be either full-blown (i.e. having four or more of the symptoms in Table 12.1) or they may be limited-symptom panics (three or fewer symptoms).

To diagnose panic disorder, at least one of the full-blown attacks must be followed by a month or more of either: (1) persistent concern about having more attacks; (2) worry about the implications or consequences of the attacks; or (3) behavioural changes as a result of the attacks (e.g. avoidance of work or school activities). The attacks must not stem solely from the direct effects of illicit substance use, medication or a general medical condition (e.g. hyperthyroidism, vestibular dysfunction) and should not be better explained by another mental disorder (e.g. such as social phobia for panic attacks that occur solely in social situations).

Panic subtypes

The panic attacks found in panic disorder should be distinguished from panic reactions that are triggered by exposure to actual life-threatening situations (e.g. panicking when you notice a poisonous spider crawling up your arm). Panic disorder is defined by panics that occur in the absence of real danger. Three types of panic attack are seen in panic disorder (and, less commonly, in other anxiety disorders):

- *Unexpected panics*: these are not associated with a trigger that the person can identify; these attacks seem to come 'out of the blue'.
- *Situationally bound panics*: these are panics that almost invariably occur when exposed to a situational trigger.
- *Situationally predisposed panics*: these are attacks that often, but not invariably, occur when the person is exposed to a situational trigger.

Notice that Lisa, the patient described in the opening vignette, suffered from

Table 12.1 Panic attack: Definition and criteria

DSM-IV-TR	*ICD-10*
A panic attack is a discrete period of intense fear or discomfort in the absence of real danger that develops abruptly, reaches a peak within 10 minutes, and is accompanied by four or more of the following symptoms: 1. Palpitations, pounding heart, or accelerated heart rate 2. Sweating 3. Trembling or shaking 4. Sensations of shortness of breath or smothering 5. Feeling of choking 6. Chest pain or discomfort 7. Nausea or abdominal distress 8. Feeling dizzy, unsteady, light-headed, or faint 9. Derealization (feelings of unreality) or depersonalization (being detached from oneself) 10. Fear of losing control or going crazy 11. Fear of dying 12. Paraesthesias (numbness or tingling sensations) 13. Chills or hot flushes	The dominant symptoms of a panic attack vary from person to person but sudden onset of palpitations, chest pain, choking sensations, dizziness, and feelings of unreality (depersonalization or derealization) are common There is also, almost invariably, a secondary fear of dying, losing control, or going mad Individual attacks usually only last for minutes An individual in a panic attack often experiences a crescendo of fear and autonomic symptoms which result in a hurried exit from wherever he or she may be If this occurs in a specific situation, such as on a bus or in a crowd, the patient may subsequently avoid that situation Frequent and unpredictable panic attacks produce a fear of being alone or going into public places

Note: Adapted from DSM-IV-TR (APA, 2000) and ICD-10 (WH0, 1992).

unexpected panics and situationally bound panics. The vignette describes full-blown panics, although it is likely that she also had milder, limited symptom attacks.

Agoraphobia

Agoraphobia is characterized by anxiety about being in places or situations from which escape might be difficult (or embarrassing) or in which help may not be available in the event of having a panic attack or panic-like symptoms (e.g. fear of having a sudden attack of dizziness or a sudden attack of diarrhoea) (APA, 2000). Agoraphobia usually develops as a consequence of panic attacks (Ballenger & Fyer, 1996). People with agoraphobia tend to fear and avoid a wide range of situations, including being alone outside the home, being at home alone, crowds, bridges, elevators and travelling by car, bus, train, or aeroplane. Often, the person is better able to endure these situations when with a trusted companion, such as a parent or spouse. Lisa was diagnosed as having panic disorder with agoraphobia.

EPIDEMIOLOGY

Prevalence, onset and course

The lifetime prevalence rates for unexpected panic attacks and agoraphobia are approximately 4% and 9%, respectively (Wittchen et al., 1998). Most epidemiological studies suggest that the lifetime prevalence of panic disorder (with or without agoraphobia) is 1% to 2% (Reed & Wittchen, 1998; Weissman et al., 1997). Weissman and colleagues (1997) have demonstrated that, despite some minor variation, lifetime prevalence rates are generally consistent around the world. Panic disorder with agoraphobia is more common than panic disorder without agoraphobia in clinical samples. In fact, in clinical settings, over 95% of people with agoraphobia also have a current or past history of panic disorder (APA, 2000).

Age of onset for panic disorder is bimodally distributed, typically developing between fifteen and nineteen years or between twenty-five and thirty years (Ballenger & Fyer, 1996). Women are diagnosed with panic disorder more than twice as often as men (Weissman et al., 1997). Women are more likely than men to have panic disorder with agoraphobia, and panic disordered men are more likely to try to 'self-medicate' by abusing alcohol (Yonkers et al., 1998). Panic disorder may wax and wane over time but, if left untreated, the typical course is chronic (APA, 2000).

Comorbidity

Panic disorder (with or without agoraphobia) is commonly comorbid with other anxiety disorders, mood disorders, somatoform and pain-related disorders, substance-use disorders (particularly alcohol abuse and dependence) and personality disorders. The most common comorbid anxiety disorders are social phobia and generalized anxiety disorder (15% to 30%) followed by specific phobia (2% to 20%), obsessive-compulsive disorder (10%) and post-traumatic stress disorder (2% to 10%) (APA, 2000). The most parsimonious explanation of high comorbidity between panic disorder and the other anxiety disorders is that they share a common diathesis.

Major depression occurs in up to 65% of patients with panic disorder at some point in their lives. In about two-thirds of these cases, depression develops along with, or secondary to, panic disorder (APA, 2000). In these cases, depression might be a demoralized response to the impairments and suffering imposed by panic disorder.

Hypochondriasis has been diagnosed in approximately 20% of panic-disorder patients attending general medical clinics, and in almost 50% of those attending anxiety disorders clinics (Noyes, 2001). Acute and chronic musculoskeletal pain is reported, respectively, by about 85% and 40% of panic disorder patients attending anxiety disorders clinics (Asmundson et al., 2000). Irritable bowel syndrome, a condition characterized by persistent abdominal pain and defecation difficulties, co-occurs in 17% to 41% of treatment-seeking panic-disorder patients (Lydiard et al., 1994; Noyes et al., 1990). Emerging evidence suggests that comorbidity between panic disorder and both somatoform and pain-related disorders may be best explained by a shared diathesis model (Asmundson & Taylor, 1996; Asmundson et al., 2001).

Panic disorder can be precipitated by the use of psychoactive substances such as caffeine, amphetamines, cocaine, marijuana or alcohol (Ballenger & Fyer, 1996). Alcohol has been identified as playing a precipitating, maintaining and aggravating role in panic disorder. The six-month prevalence of alcohol abuse or dependence in panic disorder has been reported to be 40% in men and 13% in women (Leon et al., 1995). These rates are higher than those observed in people with other anxiety disorders and those with no anxiety disorder (Leon et al., 1995). Although heavy drinking can precede panic disorder, alcohol problems can emerge or worsen after panic disorder arises, apparently as a means of self-medication (Bibb & Chambless, 1986).

Compared to the general population, panic-disordered patients are more likely to have co-occurring avoidant, dependant or histrionic personality disorders (Taylor & Livesley, 1995). These disorders are also commonly comorbid with other anxiety disorders and with mood disorders (APA, 2000). Personality problems often remain even when panic disorder is successfully treated (Mavissakalian & Hamann, 1992). Reasons for comorbidity between panic and personality disorders are currently unclear, but again a common diathesis has been suggested as causal. Tyrer, for example, proposed a more general neurotic syndrome that runs in families, characterized by fluctuating symptoms of anxiety, including panic and agoraphobia, and depression, with features of dependent and obsessive-compulsive personality disorder (Tyrer, 1985). While this hypothesized syndrome helps explain the frequent comorbidity of panic disorder and other DSM-IV axis I and II disorders, it does not explain why people with the general neurotic syndrome do or do not develop panic attacks or agoraphobia.

The reader will notice that our opening vignette (Lisa) describes a case of panic disorder and agoraphobia without other comorbid disorders. We deliberately chose a simple case so we could highlight the interventions used in panic disorder and agoraphobia. For details on the treatment of more complex cases, see Taylor (2000).

DIFFERENTIAL DIAGNOSIS

Panic disorder is not diagnosed if panics are the direct physiological result of acute intoxication or withdrawal from a substance (e.g. intoxication of caffeine, amphetamines or cocaine; withdrawal from alcohol, barbiturates or benzodiazepines). Panic disorder is also not diagnosed if the attacks are entirely due to a general medical condition (e.g. entirely due to hyperthyroidism, hyperparathyroidism, phaeochromocytoma, vestibular dysfunctions, seizure disorders or cardiac conditions) (APA, 2000). Panics arising from these sources may be best treated with approaches other than those described in this chapter. Thus, differential diagnosis plays an important role for planning appropriate treatment.

Panic disorder is diagnosed if the attacks continue even when the precipitant is no longer present (e.g. when the patient is no longer intoxicated with, or in withdrawal from, a psychoactive substance). Panic disorder is also diagnosed if the attacks cannot be entirely explained by the effects of a drug or a general medical condition. Drugs or medical conditions can trigger or worsen panic disorder. To illustrate, if Lisa found that she panics more frequently or more severely when she drinks a lot of coffee, she would still be diagnosed with panic disorder because caffeine consumption is insufficient to explain her panic disorder.

Panic disorder is not diagnosed if the attacks are better accounted for by another psychiatric disorder, such as another anxiety disorder. To illustrate, a person might seem to have recurrent, unexpected panic attacks. But on further inquiry it might be found that the person has a specific phobia and is subject to recurrent, unexpected exposures to the phobic stimulus (e.g. a person with dog phobia who had had a number of unexpected encounters with large, snapping dogs). Here, the attacks only appear unexpected; the attacks are actually cued panics triggered by unexpected exposure to the phobic object.

Recall that Lisa had a medical evaluation when she presented to the emergency department. No medical conditions or psychiatric disorders were identified that could account for her recurrent panic attacks. Therefore, differential diagnoses were ruled out.

AETIOLOGY

Cognitive approaches

In what is probably the most influential and widely cited psychological model of panic, Clark (1986) proposed that panic attacks arise from a tendency to catastrophically misinterpret arousal-related sensations, alternatively referred to as high anxiety sensitivity (e.g. misinterpreting palpitations as a sign of impending cardiac arrest; misinterpreting dizziness as a sign that one is about to go crazy; misinterpreting chest tightness and shortness of breath as an indication that one is about to suffocate). Anxiety sensitivity, measured with the Anxiety Sensitivity Index (Reiss et al., 1986) has three factors: fear of somatic symptoms, fear of psychological symptoms and fear of publicly observable anxiety reactions (Taylor, 1999). While there is some evidence of modest heritability of anxiety sensitivity in women (Jang et al., 1999), environmental factors have an important influence on the development of anxiety sensitivity (Taylor, 2000). Other contemporary cognitive models (e.g. Bouton et al., 2001) similarly emphasize the role of fear of arousal-related sensations in causing panic. Clark's model and similar approaches are supported by a good deal of empirical research, and have led to a highly effective form of treatment (for reviews, see McNally, 1994; Taylor, 1999, 2000).

To illustrate the cognitive processes proposed by Clark, consider the panic attack reported by Lisa, which is illustrated in Figure 12.1. Feeling fatigued from a long day of studying, Lisa went into a supermarket to shop for dinner. Suddenly she noticed that her surroundings seemed 'weird and unreal, like being on drugs' (derealization). Fluorescent lighting (as commonly used in supermarkets) combined with fatigue is a common but harmless way of inducing derealization (see Taylor, 2000). Not knowing this, Lisa appraised the derealization as strange and threatening ('Things seem weird. Something terrible is happening'). As a result, she became anxiously aroused and therefore experienced a range of arousal-related (but harmless) sensations (palpitations, dizziness, trembling). These sensations, along with derealization, were catastrophically interpreted by Lisa ('There's something wrong with my brain – maybe I have mad cow disease!! Maybe I'm about to die!!'). These thoughts were clearly alarming, which led to more anxious arousal and to more intense

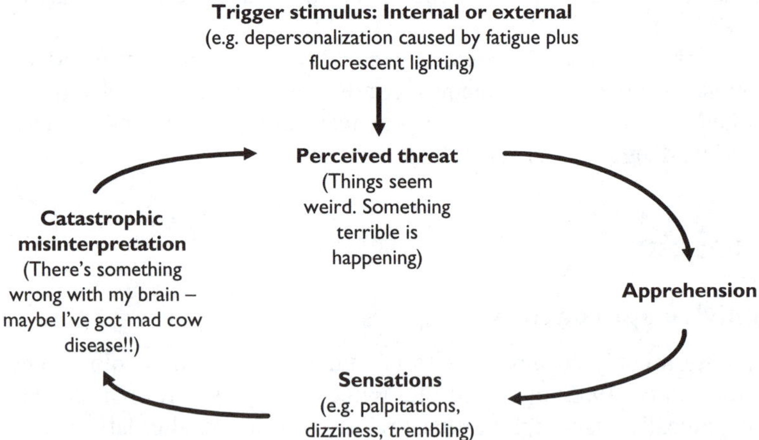

Figure 12.1 An illustration of the cognitive model with one of Lisa's panic attacks.

arousal-related sensations. The rapidly increasing severity of sensations further convinced Lisa that something calamitous was happening. Thus, a vicious cycle of arousal sensations and catastrophic thoughts unfolded, culminating in a panic attack. This is shown in Figure 12.1. Although the example illustrates one of Lisa's panics, note that the vicious cycle model in Figure 12.1 is a general one; it was developed to account for panic attacks in general (for people with panic disorder), rather than simply the example shown in Figure 12.1. For people with panic disorder, the attacks seem unexpected because they fail to identify the external or internal triggering stimulus.

Clark's model is based on several assumptions. First, while recognizing that a person's initial panic attack may be caused by various factors (e.g. drug-related autonomic surges), it assumes that people prone to panic disorder have an enduring tendency to catastrophically misinterpret benign arousal sensations. Lisa's first panic may have been triggered by a combination of stress, fatigue and excessive caffeine consumption, but her subsequent panics were unrelated to stress or caffeine.

The second assumption is that misinterpretations can occur at the conscious and unconscious level (Clark, 1988). Nocturnal (sleep) panics are explained by positing that people monitor their internal and external environment even while they are sleeping, and therefore some form of catastrophic misinterpretation can occur while the person is asleep. To explain this concept to patients (or to sceptical trainees), one can ask them whether they ever wake up at night when they need to go to the bathroom. In our experience, all patients and clinical trainees readily acknowledge that they indeed, do wake up. We then ask them how they know to wake up. The answer, of course, is that the brain, at some level, is monitoring bodily sensations (in this case bladder distension). Detection of bladder distension causes the person to awaken. Similarly, panic patients who are terrified of sensations like skipped heartbeats or shortness of breath will detect these sensations while asleep, and thereby awaken and panic (see Taylor, 2000, for a further discussion of nocturnal panic).

The third assumption is that the vicious cycle of panic can be entered at any point. The cycle can be initiated by a contextual trigger, for example, such as fatigue and lighting induced derealization in the case of Lisa, or simply by having catastrophic thoughts about bodily sensations. Fourth, physiological changes are viewed as one of several components in a process, rather than as a pathogenic mechanism.

Cognitive models can also account for agoraphobia. Agoraphobia has long been regarded as a product of operant conditioning (Marks, 1987). As noted above, it most often develops as a consequence of panic attacks. These attacks typically occur in particular situations (e.g. when in a queue in a shop, when driving) and serve to motivate the person to avoid or escape these situations. The avoidance and escape behaviours are negatively reinforced by the reduction of aversive autonomic arousal and other anxiety-related sensations. Cognitive factors, such as expectations that an attack will be imminent and harmful, and that coping will be ineffective, play a significant role by influencing and maintaining avoidance behaviour (Taylor, 2000).

Biological models

Evidence suggests that several neurotransmitter systems, involving neurotransmitters or neuromodulators such as serotonin, noradrenaline, adenosine, γ-aminobutyric acid and cholecystokinin-4, play a role in panic disorder (McNally, 1994). Various brain structures in the limbic system and associated regions have also been implicated. Contemporary biological models emphasize the amygdala, a limbic structure that appears to be involved in co-ordinating the different neurotransmitters involved in anxiety disorders (Goddard & Charney, 1997). Today, there is no single, leading biological model of panic. However, there are a number of useful models that guide research and clinical practice. Among the most promising is the neuroanatomical hypothesis proposed by Gorman and colleagues (2000). This hypothesis is useful for several reasons. First, it integrates a wide range of findings, including animal research and studies of humans. Second, it provides a unifying framework for understanding why panic disorder is associated with so many biological dysregularities, such as abnormalities in neurotransmitter systems and irregularities on various indices of autonomic functioning (e.g. Wilhelm et al., 2001; Yeragani et al., 2000). Third, the model accounts for much of the treatment-outcome data, which show that pharmacological and psychological therapies are both effective treatments. Fourth, it can subsume Clark's (1986, 1988) cognitive model of panic.

Gorman et al.'s (2000) neuroanatomical hypothesis begins with the observation that there is a remarkable similarity between the physiological and behavioural consequences of panic attacks in humans and the conditioned fear responses in animals. Similarities include autonomic arousal, fear evoked by specific cues (contextual fear) and avoidance of these cues. Animal research suggests that conditioned fear responses are mediated by a 'fear network' in the brain, consisting of the amygdala and its afferent and efferent projections, particularly its connections with the hippocampus, medial prefrontal cortex, hypothalamus and brainstem. Animal studies also show that activation of this network produces biological and behavioural reactions that are similar to those associated with panic attacks. Thus, Gorman and colleagues (2000) posit that a similar network is involved in panic disorder.

The fear network consists of a complex matrix of interconnections, implicating a number of brain structures and neurotransmitter systems (LeDoux, 1998). Sensory input passes through the anterior thalamus to the lateral nucleus of the amygdala. Input is then transferred to the central nucleus of the amygdala, which co-ordinates autonomic and behavioural responses. Direct sensory input to the amygdala from brainstem structures and the sensory thalamus enables a rapid response to potentially threatening stimuli. In addition, there are reciprocal connections between the amygdala and the prefrontal cortex, insula, and primary somatosensory cortex.

According to Gorman and colleagues (2000), panic attacks arise from excessive activation of the fear network. In other words, the fear network becomes sensitized (conditioned) to respond to noxious stimuli such as internal stimuli (bodily sensations) and external stimuli (contexts or situations) that the person associates with panic. Sensitization of the network may be manifested by the strengthening of various projections from the central nucleus of the amygdala to brainstem sites (such as the locus ceruleus, periaqueductal grey region and hypothalamus). The network could be over-activated if brainstem inputs to the amygdala are dysregulated.

Autonomic activation (e.g. increased respiration and heart rate) and neuroendocrine activation (e.g. increased cortisol secretion) do not occur in all panic attacks. And a variety of biological agents with diverse physiological properties can trigger panic attacks in people with panic disorder (e.g. sodium lactate, yohimbine, CO_2, caffeine, cholecystokinin-4) (McNally, 1994). Therefore, it is unlikely that a single brainstem dysregulation is responsible for panic or, in turn, that brainstem dysregulation is the only way of producing an over-active fear network.

Accordingly, Gorman and colleagues (2000) suggested that there are various ways of activating the fear network, in addition to the above-mentioned mechanism. For example, the amygdala receives input from cortical regions involved in the processing and evaluation of sensory information. Therefore, a neurocognitive deficit in these cortico-amygdala pathways could result in the catastrophic misinterpretation of sensory information (i.e. misinterpretation of bodily sensations), leading to an inappropriate activation of the fear network. Notice that this pathway resembles the cognitive model of panic, described earlier in this chapter. Thus, Gorman and colleagues' (2000) model integrates the cognitive model and places it in a neuroanatomical context.

Medications, particularly selective serotonin reuptake inhibitors (SSRIs), are thought to desensitize the fear network. This may happen in a number of ways. For example, SSRIs increase serotonergic transmission in the brain (Blier et al., 1987). Serotonergic neurons originate in the brainstem raphe and project throughout the central nervous system (Tork & Hornung, 1990). Some of these projections have inhibitory influences. Also, SSRIs may directly inhibit activity of the lateral nucleus of the amygdala (Stutzman & LeDoux, 1999). Effective psychological therapies are thought to reduce contextual fear and catastrophic misinterpretations at the level of the medial prefrontal cortex and hippocampus.

Gorman et al.'s (2000) neuroanatomical hypothesis is elegant and comprehensive, and it has the ability to incorporate Clark's (1986) cognitive model. However, the Gorman hypothesis, like all models of panic, is a work in progress, and will need to be modified as new findings emerge.

Psychodynamic models

The most promising psychodynamic models for understanding panic disorder are those that focus specifically on this disorder. Rather than review all the models, we will summarize the model developed by the Cornell Panic-Anxiety Study Group (Milrod et al., 1997; Shear et al., 1993) because it has led to a treatment that, at least on the basis of initial findings, looks promising. According to the Cornell group, people at risk for panic disorder have: (1) a neurophysiological vulnerability to panic attacks; and/or (2) multiple experiences of developmental trauma. These factors lead the child to become frightened of unfamiliar situations and to become excessively dependent on the primary caregiver to provide a sense of safety. The caregiver is unable to always provide support, so the child develops a fearful dependency. This leads to the development of unconscious conflicts about dependency (independence versus reliance on others) and anger (expression versus inhibition). The dependency conflict is said to express itself in a number of ways. Some panic-vulnerable people are sensitive to separation and overly reliant on others, while others are sensitive to suffocation and overly reliant on a sense of independence. These conflicts can activate conscious or unconscious fantasies of catastrophic danger, which can trigger panic attacks. In addition, the conflicts evoke aversive emotions, such as anxiety, anger and guilt. The otherwise benign arousal sensations accompanying these emotions can become the focus of 'conscious as well as unconscious cognitive catastrophizing' (Shear et al., 1993, p. 862), thereby leading to panic attacks. Thus, again we see that something similar to Clark's (1986) model finds its way into other models of panic.

ASSESSMENT

The most comprehensive and accurate diagnostic information emerges when the clinician uses open-ended questions and empathic listening, combined with structured inquiry about specific events and symptoms (APA, 1995). An example of one of the most useful structured interviews is the Structured Clinical Interview for DSM-IV (SCID-IV; First et al., 1996). A complete assessment for panic disorder also includes a general medical evaluation (APA, 1995), which involves a medical history, review of organ systems, physical examination and blood tests. A general medical evaluation is important for identifying general medical conditions that mimic or exacerbate panic attacks or panic-like symptoms (e.g. seizure disorders, cardiac conditions, phaeochromocytoma). These disorders should be investigated and treated before contemplating a course of panic disorder treatment.

Although these medical mimics are rare, they are important to rule out. Over the past fifteen years the first author has encountered three cases of medical mimics. Two were seizure disorders misdiagnosed as panic disorder. To illustrate, one patient was referred by her primary care physician with what seemed to be classic panic attacks. As part of the assessment, the CBT practitioner (ST) asked the patient to describe how a typical panic attack unfolded for her. The attacks seemed like real panics. But then the practitioner asked the patient to describe what happens just before the panics erupted. The patient replied, 'I hear a voice, telling me I'm bad'. The panics were apparently triggered by this distressing hallucination. When asked whether she had ever told her doctor about the hallucinations she said, 'No, because he never asked me'. A neurological referral was sought to investigate what appeared to be complex partial seizures.

Another example of a medical mimic involved a psychiatry resident who was using CBT to treat another case of what appeared to be classic panic disorder. Treatment was moderately successful; the patient was no longer panicking, but remained anxious. A further medical evaluation revealed that she, in fact, had phaeochromocytoma, not panic disorder. In other words, a sufficient medical evaluation had not been conducted before commencing CBT.

We present these examples to highlight the importance of conducting a thorough medical evaluation to rule-out medical mimics before contemplating a course of CBT. Medical mimics are rare, but the consequences of misdiagnosis can be harmful for the patient and embarrassing for the clinician. Consider, for example, a patient with a seizure disorder who has been misdiagnosed as having panic disorder. Voluntary hyperventilation (e.g. two minute of rapid, deep breathing) is commonly used as an interoceptive exposure exercise to teach panic patients that arousal-related sensations like palpitations, dizziness and breathlessness are harmless. But hyperventilation can trigger seizures in people with seizure disorders and thus it is important to rule out seizure disorder before using interventions such as hyperventilation.

Once a diagnosis of panic disorder (with or without agoraphobia) has been established, then the diagnostic information can be usefully supplemented by short self-report questionnaires. Areas to assess include the severity of panic-related symptoms, with the Panic Attacks Symptom Questionnaire, (PASQ; Clum et al., 1990), panic-related cognitions, with the Agoraphobic Cognitions Questionnaire (ACQ; Chambless et al., 1984) and the Body Sensations Questionnaire (BSQ; Chambless, 1988), as well as other variables (see Chapter 9 of Taylor (2000), for a detailed review). For example, the Anxiety Sensitivity Index (Peterson & Reiss, 1992) is a useful short questionnaire that can be used to gauge the severity of the patient's fear of bodily sensations. Scores on this scale can be used to assess whether treatment is altering the patient's tendency to catastrophically misinterpret bodily sensations. This scale has good reliability and validity, is sensitive to treatment-related effects and its post-treatment scores predict who is likely to relapse after panic treatment (Taylor, 1999).

A useful questionnaire to monitor panic symptoms and treatment progress is the Panic and Agoraphobia Scale (Bandelow, 1995). This thirteen-item scale was designed as a short, sensitive measure for treatment outcome studies. The patient is asked to rate the past-week frequency and/or severity of the following: (1) panic attacks; (2) agoraphobia; (3) anticipatory anxiety (i.e. worry about having a panic attack); (4) panic-related disability in various areas of functioning; and (5) worry about the health-related implications of panic (e.g. worry that panic attacks will lead to a heart attack). The Panic and Agoraphobia Scale has good reliability and validity and is sensitive in detecting treatment-related change (Bandelow et al., 1995, 1998).

To gain more detailed information on panic attacks, clinicians and clinical researchers are increasingly including some form of prospective monitoring in their assessment batteries (Shear & Maser, 1994). The most widely used are the panic attack records. The patient is provided with a definition of a panic attack and then given a pad of panic attack records that can be readily carried in a purse or pocket. The patient is instructed to carry the records at all times and to complete one record (sheet) for each full-blown or limited symptom attack, soon after the attack occurs. Variants on the panic diaries developed by Barlow and colleagues (e.g. Rapee et al., 1990) are among the most informative and easy to use. A version is shown in Figure 12.2, which shows details of one of Lisa's panic attacks. These records are then reviewed during treatment sessions to glean information about the links among beliefs, bodily sensations, and safety behaviours, and to assess treatment progress.

Lisa reported that the panic attack summarized in Figure 12.2 occurred when she was in a local supermarket. As she walked down the aisle she looked at the long rows of fluorescent lights and then began to feel mildly derealized. Upon noticing this sensation she increasingly feared that she had a brain disease that might strike her dead. This frightened her greatly and led to an increase in the intensity of arousal sensations (as described in the cognitive model of panic; see Figure 12.1). In an effort to reduce the intensity of the feared derealization, she averted her gaze from the lights, and began studiously pouring over her shopping list. This avoidance behaviour calmed her down and reduced the feared derealization to the point that she was able quickly leave the supermarket (without her groceries).

The panic attack record serves as a useful aide-mémoire to help patients recall the details and circumstances of their panic attacks. Lisa's example shows how the panic attack record helped her recall that she used distraction as an avoidance behaviour. Armed with this information, the therapist could set up exposure exercises to help Lisa learn whether distraction was essential to protecting her from what she perceived to be the harmful consequences of derealization.

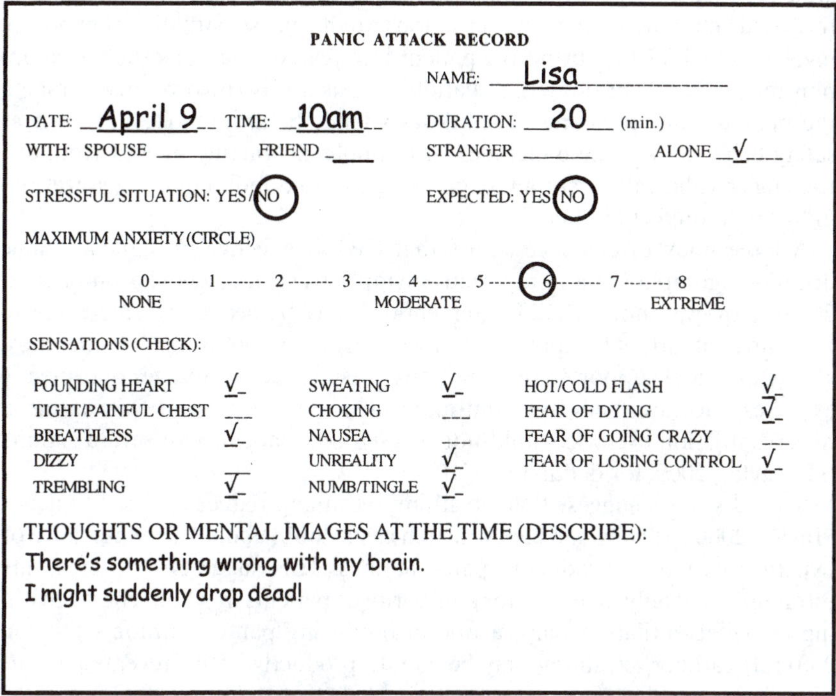

PANIC ATTACK RECORD

NAME: Lisa

DATE: April 9 TIME: 10am DURATION: 20 (min.)

WITH: SPOUSE ___ FRIEND ___ STRANGER ___ ALONE √

STRESSFUL SITUATION: YES/NO (NO circled) EXPECTED: YES/NO (NO circled)

MAXIMUM ANXIETY (CIRCLE)

0 -------- 1 -------- 2 -------- 3 -------- 4 -------- 5 -------- 6 (circled) -------- 7 -------- 8

NONE MODERATE EXTREME

SENSATIONS (CHECK):

POUNDING HEART	√	SWEATING	√	HOT/COLD FLASH	√
TIGHT/PAINFUL CHEST	___	CHOKING	___	FEAR OF DYING	√
BREATHLESS	√	NAUSEA	___	FEAR OF GOING CRAZY	___
DIZZY		UNREALITY	√	FEAR OF LOSING CONTROL	√
TREMBLING	√	NUMB/TINGLE	√		

THOUGHTS OR MENTAL IMAGES AT THE TIME (DESCRIBE):

There's something wrong with my brain.

I might suddenly drop dead!

Figure 12.2 A completed panic attack record for Lisa.

TREATMENT

The remaining sections of this chapter review the major treatments for panic disorder, with particular attention to cognitive-behaviour therapy (CBT) because this is among the most effective and enduring. Space limitations prevent us from comprehensively reviewing each treatment. For an extended discussion, particularly on the nuts and bolts of CBT, see Taylor (2000).

Cognitive-behavioural therapy

CBT treatment packages include a number of components, such as psychoeducation (e.g. information about the cognitive model of panic), breathing retraining, cognitive restructuring, relaxation exercises, interoceptive exposure and situational exposure. Breathing retraining involves teaching the patient to breathe with the diaphragm rather than with the chest muscles. Cognitive restructuring focuses on challenging patient's beliefs about the dangerousness of bodily sensations (e.g. challenging a belief that palpitations lead to heart attacks). Interoceptive exposure involves inducing feared bodily sensations to further teach patients that the sensations are harmless. Situational exposure involves activities that bring the patient into feared situations such as shopping malls, bridges or tunnels. Situational exposure also involves discouraging the patient from engaging in subtle avoidance behaviours (also known as safety behaviours). These include, for example, distracting oneself from distressing (but harmless) stimuli (e.g. trying to avoid looking at derealization-inducing fluorescent lights).

A large body of evidence shows that CBT is effective in reducing panic disorder, agoraphobia and associated symptoms such as depression (Taylor, 2000). However, not all CBT interventions may be necessary. Interoceptive exposure, situational exposure and cognitive restructuring are the most widely used and supported interventions. Despite the advantages of exposure exercises, they are medically contraindicated in some cases. For example, a hyperventilation exercise would not be used in a patient with severe asthma (see Taylor, 2000, for details).

Several studies suggest that breathing retraining reduces panic frequency (Taylor, 2000). However, recent research casts doubt about the importance of hyperventilation in producing panic attacks. This suggests that breathing retraining may only be useful for a minority of patients in whom chest breathing or hyperventilation plays a role in producing panic symptoms (Taylor, 2001). Breathing retraining may be counterproductive if it prevents patients from learning that their catastrophic beliefs are unfounded. Given these concerns, breathing retraining should be used sparingly in the treatment of panic disorder. If used at all, the clinician should ensure that the patient understands that breathing exercises are used to remove unpleasant but harmless sensations. Similarly, relaxation training is not always necessary. Interoceptive exposure and cognitive restructuring are important for helping patients learn that the sensations are not dangerous.

CBT can be augmented by involving the patient's spouse in treatment (Taylor, 2000). This can be done either by inviting the spouse (with the patient's permission) to serve as a coach or therapist's aid in conducting situational exposure exercises. Alternatively, couples therapy can be incorporated into treatment when there is evidence of relationship problems. This may be particularly important when relationship problems interfere with the treatment of panic and agoraphobia (e.g. when there is evidence that the spouse is interfering with treatment, such as criticizing the patient as being 'weak' for seeking treatment for panic from a mental health professional).

There are several detailed manuals for teaching clinicians how to do CBT for panic disorder (e.g. Craske & Barlow, 2000). However, there is no substitute for apprenticeship training, where the trainee learns first-hand how to do this therapy from an experienced CBT practitioner. The following example of the interventions used with Lisa should give readers a taste of what is involved in CBT for panic disorder and agoraphobia, at least for a simple case in which there was no other complicating (comorbid) disorders.

The goals of CBT treatment may be summarized as: (1) the reduction or elimination of panic attacks; (2) the reduction or elimination of avoidance behaviour; and (3) the reduction of the vulnerability to developing further panic attacks or agoraphobia (Andrews et al., 2003).

Case example: Lisa's treatment

Before starting treatment, the CBT practitioner collected detailed information about Lisa's panic attacks. The most useful information came from the panic attack records (see Figure 12.2 for an example). The information gleaned from these records enabled the clinician to develop a working hypothesis of the sorts of beliefs and associated catastrophic misinterpretations that seem to play a role in Lisa's problems. The assessment suggested that Lisa harboured the following beliefs:

- Lethal brain diseases, like mad cow disease, are lurking everywhere.
- These diseases can strike people down unexpectedly.
- The first signs of these diseases are unusual perceptual experiences.

How did these beliefs arise? An assessment of Lisa's history of panic disorder and her early experiences indicated that she had long been exposed to information about lethal viral diseases. Her father worked in the health sciences and often held court over family meals, regaling the family with tales of exotic diseases that he had encountered or heard about in his line of work. During the year before Lisa's first panic attack, she read many newspaper accounts of lethal diseases threatening the community. The list included sudden acute respiratory syndrome (SARS), West Nile virus, monkey pox and bovine spongiform encephalopathy (BSE; 'mad cow' disease). Her early exposure to tales of deadly diseases, combined with the recent media reports of such diseases, heightened Lisa's concerns and led her to become vigilant for any signs that she might be afflicted with a serious disease. Thus, her learning history and recent experiences set her up to misinterpret benign sensations, such as derealization induced by fatigue and fluorescent lighting.

Furnished with this information, the clinician implemented treatment as follows. First, the formulation was shared with Lisa. This was done for the purpose of psychoeducation, and Lisa's feedback was also elicited to identify any flaws in the formulation. Lisa agreed with the formulation; it fit well with her experience. As part of psychoeducation, the vicious cycle model (Figure 12.1) was also shared with Lisa, to show her how unexpected sensations (e.g. derealization unexpectedly triggered by fatigue and fluorescent lighting) could lead to catastrophic misinterpretation and the spiral into panic. Because the sensations occurred unexpectedly, the panic attacks seemed (to Lisa) to occur unexpectedly. For Lisa, this information was valuable; it made her panics more understandable and predictable, and less frightening.

Contrast this education with the information Lisa received from the Accident and Emergency department. There she was told that there was nothing wrong with her health and that her panics were simply due to stress. The information from the Accident and Emergency doctors was not helpful because it didn't tell Lisa how her panics could be caused by something as benign as stress. She left Accident and Emergency feeling confused and unconvinced. In contrast, the information she received from the CBT practitioner gave her a clear, concrete explanation of how and why her panics arose. And importantly, the explanation suggested some ways that she could overcome her panic attacks.

Cognitive restructuring exercises were also used to help Lisa realistically appraise the probability of succumbing to a lethal condition such as mad cow disease. She realized that she would need to accept that there were no guarantees that she would ever be completely free from danger; living in the world involves the acceptance of risk. Lisa realized that she calmly accepted many risks in her daily life, such as driving and crossing streets (which lead to many more fatalities than mad cow disease). She was also encouraged, with the therapist's help, to generate a list of benign things that induce derealization (e.g. fatigue, lighting, cold medications, stress). This lead to a discussion of the probability that her next bout of derealization would indicate mad cow disease instead of some benign cause. Through this discussion Lisa realized that the odds were exceeding low – in fact, almost zero – that her next episode of derealization would be a harbinger of mad cow disease.

Although these discussions were therapeutic, the CBT practitioner next suggested to Lisa that they needed to go further, to strongly prove to her that everyday causes of derealization were harmless. The therapist asked her how they could do that. In other words, the therapist initiated a careful line of questioning to help Lisa problem-solve; to think of ways of overcoming her fear of derealization. This type of questioning is a form of Socratic dialogue, commonly used in CBT for panic disorder (and other emotional disorders). Socratic dialogue encourages patients to become their own therapist, and thereby encourages and prepares them to solve emotional problems in their daily lives (for an extended discussion of Socratic dialogue, see Taylor, 2000, Chapter 12).

Through this line of questioning, Lisa realized that interoceptive exposure would be useful in proving to herself that derealization was harmless. Several five-minute exercises were used; staring at a fluorescent light, staring at a spot on the wall and looking through a book on visual illusions that induced perceptual distortions. When practising these exercises, Lisa was encouraged to notice any perceptual aberrations, and to not distract herself from them, or to use any other form of avoidance. The goal was for Lisa to learn that derealization does not have any harmful consequences, such as death.

Initially, Lisa felt anxious during these exercises, and even had a mild panic attack while leafing through the book on visual illusions. The therapist reframed the panic attack as an important learning experience. Lisa was encouraged to reflect on what led her to panic while looking at the book. She realized that one of the illusions triggered the false sensation of shimmering and colour. This was a visual illusion that she had not previously experienced. She catastrophically misinterpreted this 'new' perceptual aberration, and thereby panicked. Armed with this important piece of information, Lisa and her therapist realized that she should be exposed to a wide range of illusion-inducing stimuli, to limit the chances that she would catastrophically misinterpret any 'new' illusions in the future. Accordingly, additional interoceptive exercises were added; staring at her hand for five to ten minutes, staring at her face in a mirror and staring at, and then looking away from, brightly coloured objects (to induce visual after-images). Lisa's anxiety gradually abated over the course of four 50-minute sessions of these exercises. The frequency of panic attacks in her daily life similarly abated.

Lisa and her therapist then designed and implemented a series of situational exposure exercises (set as 'homework' assignments in between treatment sessions) to reduce her agoraphobia. The exercises were implemented in a gradual, step-by-step fashion, beginning with the easiest exercise. Lisa began by returning to the supermarket in which she had panicked in the past. The initial goal was to enter the supermarket in the morning on a weekday, when the store was uncrowded. She spent 30 minutes shopping for a few small items, while also being mindful of the fluorescent lighting. Once this task no longer evoked anxiety, Lisa returned to the supermarket at a busier time of day (in the early evening after work). Once this was mastered she went to the supermarket at a very busy time (Saturday morning). Each time she shopped for a few small items and deliberately paid attention to the fluorescent lighting. Similar graduated exposure exercises were planned and conducted for the other situations that she feared and avoided, such as travelling by train and entering crowded bars. Situational exposure was conducted over eight weeks. By that time her agoraphobia was substantially reduced, although there were some residual symptoms (e.g. she continued to feel anxious in crowded, stuffy trains). Lisa was encouraged to continually practice, as needed, the situational exposure exercises.

The formal course of therapy (twelve weeks) ended with a discussion of three topics: (1) a review of the progress made in treatment, including a review of the interventions she found to be most useful; (2) a discussion of the symptoms that remained to be addressed, and the development of a plan how to address them (e.g. ongoing situational exposure to crowded, stuffy trains); and (3) the development of a plan for relapse prevention. The latter began by asking Lisa to try to think of what conditions might lead her to panic in the future. After some thought she realized that she might panic if something happened that induced strong perceptual aberrations. A list of examples was generated, including the following: a bout of influenza might lead to light-headedness and dizziness; cold medications could induce depersonalization; anaesthetic for surgery or dental procedures could induce faintness and weird bodily feelings. Lisa was asked to write down a written plan of how she would deal with panic attacks in the future, such as those triggered by these examples. Lisa's plan consisted of the following. If she panicked in the future, she would: (1) analyse the situation to identify the feared sensations and the catastrophic misinterpretation; (2) implement interoceptive exercises to induce and become accustomed to the feared sensations; (3) implement situational exposure exercises if she was beginning to develop agoraphobia; and (4) if these don't work, then she should telephone her therapist for some booster sessions.

Couples-based approaches

Partner-assisted CBT has been shown in a series of treatment outcome studies to be as effective as individual CBT. Clinically, it is worth considering a couples-based approach when there are marital difficulties or where partners are inadvertently reinforcing patient's symptoms (Byrne, Carr & Clark, 2004). In partner-assisted CBT, the patient's partner is coached in: (1) avoiding inadvertently reinforcing catastrophic thinking and agoraphobic avoidance behaviours through excessive care-taking; (2) actively reinforcing the development of anxiety management skills and the completion of exposure-based homework assignments; and (3) couples-based communication and problem-solving skills.

Other psychosocial interventions

Several other approaches have been used in the treatment of panic disorder, including psychodynamic psychotherapies (Milrod et al., 2000; Wiborg & Dahl, 1996), hypnosis (e.g. Stafrace, 1994) and mindfulness meditation (Miller et al., 1995). Unlike CBT, support for these treatments is limited largely to case studies and uncontrolled trials. Hypnosis appears to be of limited value in treating panic disorder, and may be no better than placebo (Taylor, 2000). Another form of psychotherapy for panic disorder, called emotion-focused psychotherapy, has been found to be less effective than either CBT or imipramine, and is no more effective than placebo (Shear et al., 2001). An intervention that looks more promising is mindfulness meditation (e.g. Miller et al., 1995), although further evaluation is required. Uncontrolled studies have yielded encouraging findings for psychodynamic psychotherapies modified to specifically focus on panic symptoms (Milrod et al., 2000; Wiborg & Dahl, 1996). However, none has been extensively evaluated as panic treatments, and none has been compared to empirically supported treatments like CBT or SSRIs.

Pharmacotherapies

Controlled studies show that effective anti-panic medications include tricyclic antidepressants (e.g. imipramine), monoamine oxidase inhibitors (MAOIs; e.g. phenelzine), benzodiazepines (e.g. alprazolam, clonazepam, lorazepam) and SSRIs (e.g. fluvoxamine, fluoxetine, paroxetine, sertraline). These treatments have broadly similar efficacy, although there is some evidence that SSRIs tend to be most effective (Boyer, 1995; Taylor, 2000). The trade names of many drugs vary across countries, so in this chapter we list only their generic names. The typical dose ranges of the commonly used medications are as follows:

- imipramine: 50–300 mg/day
- phenelzine: 45–90 mg/day
- alprazolam: 2–10 mg/day
- clonazepam: 1–3 mg/day
- lorazepam: 2–6 mg/day
- fluvoxamine: 50–300 mg/day
- fluoxetine: 20–80 mg/day
- paroxetine: 10–50 mg/day
- sertraline: 50–200 mg/day.

The medications differ in their side effects and contraindications. Anticholinergic effects (blurred vision, dry mouth) are common problems with tricyclics. The latter medications are also contraindicated in patients with particular comorbid cardiac disorders (Simon & Pollack, 2000). Dietary restrictions (i.e. abstaining from foods containing tyramine) are a limitation of many MAOIs (Stein & Stahl, 2000). Sedation, impaired motor co-ordination and addiction are concerns with benzodiazepines (Barbone et al., 1998). To illustrate the latter problems, one of the first author's patients (suffering from panic disorder and agoraphobia) reported that, prior to commencing CBT, he had tried alprazolam (prescribed by his family doctor). He felt greatly relaxed by the medication and he felt like he could resume formerly avoided activities, such as entering supermarkets and driving. Unfortunately, however, alprazolam impaired his driving skills (and his ability to judge that his skills were impaired). In the initial weeks on alprazolam he ventured out driving, only to have a rear-end collision when he failed to notice that the car ahead of him had stopped at a traffic light. He was not injured in the accident but it reinforced his fear of driving, and also made him afraid to take alprazolam.

When efficacy and side effects are considered together, SSRIs emerge as the most promising drug treatments for panic disorder. However, even SSRIs have side effects, with the most troublesome being a short-term increase in arousal-related sensations (the 'jitteriness syndrome'; Pohl et al., 1988). To overcome this problem, SSRIs can be started at a low dose (5–10 mg/day for paroxetine; 12.5–25 mg/day for sertraline) and then increased gradually (up to 10–50 mg/day for paroxetine; up to 25–200 mg/day for sertraline). The choice of SSRI is determined on the basis of several factors, including side effects, patient preference and the patient's history of responding (or not responding) to particular agents (Simon & Pollack, 2000).

For drug refractory patients or patients who are unable to tolerate SSRI side effects, combination medications are sometimes used. SSRIs, for example, can be augmented with benzodiazepines (Uhlenhuth et al., 1999). The latter are used to dampen the side effects of SSRIs. Despite some positive preliminary reports supporting this strategy, its value in the treatment of panic disorder remains to be properly evaluated. An alternative strategy is to change the patient's medication. Some of the newer, non-SSRI antidepressants could be considered, such as venlafaxine, nefazodone or gabapentin (Simon & Pollack, 2000). A concern with using these newer medications to treat panic disorder is that there are few data to guide the clinician. Another approach to the drug refractory patient is to use a psychosocial treatment, such as CBT as an alternative or adjunctive intervention.

How effective are medications compared to CBT? A small but growing literature suggests that the efficacy of CBT is equal to or greater than that of alprazolam, imipramine and possibly SSRIs at post-treatment (Barlow et al., 2000; Taylor, 2000). Follow-up studies suggest that the effects of CBT may be more enduring than the effects of medication (see Taylor, 2000, for a review). This is probably because CBT, unlike pharmacotherapies, teaches patients skills for coping with, and overcoming, panic disorder and agoraphobia. These skills can be used as needed after the formal course of therapy ends.

Combining CBT with drug treatments

Simultaneous treatments

Clinical lore holds that the optimal treatment consists of drugs combined with some form of psychosocial intervention (Alexander, 1991; Fahy et al., 1992). This view arose from observations that even the most effective drugs and the most effective psychosocial interventions do not eliminate panic disorder in all cases. It was thought that combination treatments might be a way to improve treatment outcome. The available evidence provides mixed support for this view. Evidence suggests that the efficacy of CBT is not improved when it is combined with either diazepam or alprazolam (Taylor, 2000). In fact, some studies have found that the efficacy of situational exposure is worse when alprazolam is added (Echeburúa et al., 1993; Marks et al., 1993).

Several studies have compared CBT to CBT plus imipramine. The results have also been mixed. Adding imipramine in the range of 150–300 mg/day to either situational exposure or CBT sometimes improves treatment outcome in the short term, provided that patients are able to tolerate the dose (Barlow et al., 2000; Taylor, 2000). Any advantage of combined treatment tends to be lost at follow-up. Similarly, studies of combining CBT with SSRIs (fluvoxamine or paroxetine) have produced mixed results, with some studies finding the combination is no better than CBT alone (Sharp et al., 1996), others finding that the combination is most effective (de Beurs et al., 1995; Oehrberg et al., 1995) and yet others finding the combination to be most effective in some symptom domains but not others (Stein et al., 2000). Methodological limitations of these studies might account for the inconsistent findings (Taylor, 2000).

Thus, it remains unclear whether treatment outcome is enhanced by combining CBT with SSRIs. Gorman et al.'s (2000) neuroanatomical hypothesis, with its dual emphasis on cortical and serotonergic mechanisms, suggests that combined treatment ought to be superior to either CBT alone or SSRIs alone. However, pharmacotherapies such as SSRIs could undermine the patient's confidence in implementing CBT, particularly if patients attribute their gains to medications rather than to their own efforts at using the skills learned in CBT (Basoglu et al., 1994; Brown & Barlow, 1995).

Sequential treatments

A more promising type of combined therapy is a sequential approach, where patients are treated with pharmacotherapy during the acute phase and are then treated with CBT as the medication is phased out. Several studies have shown that adding CBT during the tapering period for alprazolam and clonazepam reduces the relapse rate associated with these drugs (e.g. Bruce et al., 1999; Otto et al., 1993). It remains to be demonstrated that CBT can reduce relapse when patients are tapered off other anti-panic drugs, such as SSRIs. However, there is no reason to expect that CBT would not be helpful in these cases.

A similar sequential approach can be used with treatment of non-responders. CBT has been shown to be effective for medication-refractory patients (Biondi & Picardi, 2003; Heldt et al., 2003) and SSRIs can be successful with patients who have failed to fully respond to CBT (Kampman et al., 2002). The clinician could therefore start with one of these treatments (drugs or CBT), and if the patient does not respond then change to the other treatment. Patients who initially respond to drugs, however, may still require CBT during the drug tapering phase in order to reduce the risk of relapse.

SUMMARY

Panic disorder, with or without agoraphobia, is a common condition, with a lifetime prevalence up to 2%. Treatment planning typically begins with a thorough assessment, including a medical history, a structured diagnostic interview and prospective monitoring of symptoms. Based on contemporary biological and cognitive-behavioural models, there are several treatment options. These include various pharmacotherapies, particularly SSRIs, and psychosocial interventions, particularly CBT. Preliminary evidence suggests that treatments that combine SSRIs and CBT may be somewhat more effective than either treatment alone, at least in the short term and in some symptom domains. Evidence suggests that the effects of CBT may be more enduring than those of medications. This is probably because CBT, unlike pharmacotherapies, teaches patients skills for coping with, and overcoming, panic disorder and agoraphobia. These skills can be used as needed after the formal course of therapy ends. There are several detailed manuals for teaching clinicians how to do CBT for panic disorder. But there is no substitute for apprenticeship training, where one learns how to do this therapy first-hand from an experienced CBT practitioner.

EXERCISE 12.1

Divide into groups of three. Using the case of Lisa above, assign roles of client, therapist and observer. Rotate roles through the following role-plays:

- Initial session where you meet Lisa for assessment of presenting problem.
- Second session during which you discuss with Lisa a formulation of her difficulties.
- Second session during which you provide psychoeducation; discuss with Lisa the vicious cycle of misinterpretation of symptoms and escalation of panic, and outline the cognitive-behavioural treatment approach.
- Later session during which you complete the thought record (see Chapter 3) with Lisa for one of her recent panic attacks.

FURTHER READING FOR PRACTITIONERS

Andrews, G., Creamer, M., Crino, R., Hunt, C., Lampe, L., & Page, A. (2003). *The treatment of anxiety disorders: Clinician guides and patient manuals*. Cambridge: Cambridge University Press.

Craske, M. G. & Barlow, D. H. (2000). *Master your anxiety and panic: Therapist guide* (Third Edition). New York: Graywind.

Taylor, S. (2000). *Understanding and treating panic disorder: Cognitive-behavioural approaches*. Chichester, UK: Wiley.

Wells, A. (1997). *Cognitive therapy of anxiety disorders: A practice manual and conceptual guide*. Chichester, UK: Wiley.

FURTHER READING FOR CLIENTS

Craske, M. G. & Barlow, D. H. (2000). *Master your anxiety and panic: Client workbook* (Third Edition). New York: Graywind.

Kennerly, H. (1997). *Overcoming anxiety: A self-help guide using cognitive-behavioural techniques*. London: Robinson.

Wilson, R. R. (1996). *Don't panic: Taking control of anxiety attacks*. New York: HarperPerennial.

Zuercher-White, E. (1998). *An end to panic* (Second Edition). Oakland, CA: New Harbinger.

ASSESSMENT INSTRUMENTS

Bandelow, B. (1995). Assessing the efficacy of treatments for panic disorder and agoraphobia: II. The Panic and Agoraphobia Scale. *International Clinical Psychopharmacology*, 10, 73–81.

Chambless, D. (1988). Body Sensations Questionnaire. In M. Hersen & A. Bellack (Eds.), *Dictionary of behavioural assessment techniques* (pp. 85–86). New York: Pergamon.

Chambless, D., Caputo, G. Bright, P., & Gallagher, R. (1984). Assessment of fear in agoraphobics: the Body Sensations Questionnaire and the Agoraphobic Cognitions Questionnaire. *Journal of Consulting and Clinical Psychology*, 52, 1090–1097.

Chambless, D., Caputo, G., Jasin, S., Gracely, E., & Williams, C. (1985). The Mobility Inventory for Agoraphobia. *Behaviour Research and Therapy*, 23, 35–44.

Clum, G., Broyles, S., Borden, J., & Watkins, P. (1990). Validity and reliability of the panic attack symptoms and cognitions questionnaires. Special Issue DSM IV and the psychology literature. *Journal of Psychopathology and Behavioural Assessment*, 12, 233–245.

DiNardo, P., Brown, T., & Barlow, D. (1994). *Anxiety Disorder Interview Schedule for DSM-IV*. San Antonio, TX: Psychological Corporation.

Peterson, R. & Reiss, S. (1992). *Anxiety Sensitivity Index Manual* (Second Edition-Revised). Worthington, OH: International Diagnostic Services.

Rapee, R., Craske, M., Brown, T., & Barlow, D. (1995). Measurement of perceived control over anxiety related events. *Behaviour Therapy*, 27, 279–293.

Scupi, B., Maser, J., & Uhde, T. (1992). The National Institute of Mental Health Panic Questionnaire: An instrument for assessing the clinical characteristics of panic disorder. *Journal of Nervous and Mental Disease*, 180, 566–572.

REFERENCES

Alexander, P. E. (1991). Management of panic disorders. *Journal of Psychoactive Drugs*, 23, 329–333.

American Psychiatric Association (APA) (1995). Practice guidelines for psychiatric evaluation of adults. *American Journal of Psychiatry*, 152 (Suppl. 11), 63–80.

American Psychiatric Association (APA) (2000). *Diagnostic and statistical manual of mental disorders* (Fourth Edition-Text Revision, DSM-IV-TR). Washington, DC: APA.

Andrews, G., Creamer, M., Crino, R., Hunt, C., Lampe, L., & Page, A. (2003). *The treatment of anxiety disorders: Clinician guides and patient manuals*. Cambridge: Cambridge University Press.

Asmundson, G. J. G. & Taylor, S. (1996). Role of anxiety sensitivity in pain-related fear and avoidance. *Journal of Behavioral Medicine*, 19, 573–582.

Asmundson, G. J. G., Walker, J. R., Furer, P., & Kjernisted, K. (2000). *Beyond anxiety: A preliminary look at acute and chronic pain in individuals seeking treatment for anxiety disorders*. Paper presented at the 20th annual meeting of the Anxiety Disorders Association of America, Washington DC.

Asmundson, G. J. G., Wright, K. D., Taylor, S., & Cox, B. J. (2001). Future directions and challenges in assessment, treatment, and investigation of health anxiety. In G. J. G. Asmundson, S. Taylor, & B. J. Cox (Eds.), *Health anxiety: Clinical and research perspectives on hypochondriasis and related disorders* (pp. 365–381). Chichester, UK: Wiley.

Ballenger, J. C. & Fyer, A. J. (1996). Panic disorder and agoraphobia. In T. A. Widiger, A. J. Frances, H. A., Pincus, R. Ross, M. B. First & W. W. Davis (Eds.), *DSM-IV sourcebook* (Vol. 2, pp. 411–471). Washington: APA.

Bandelow, B. (1995). Assessing the efficacy of treatments for panic disorder and agoraphobia. II. The Panic and Agoraphobia Scale. *International Clinical Psychopharmacology*, 10, 73–81.

Bandelow, B., Brunner, E., Broocks, A., Beinroth, D., Hajak, G., Pralle, L., & Rüther, E. (1998). The use of the Panic and Agoraphobia Scale in a clinical trial. *Psychiatry Research*, 77, 43–49.

Bandelow, B., Hajak, G., Holzrichter, S., Kunert, H. J., & Rüther, E. (1995). Assessing the efficacy of treatments for panic disorder and agoraphobia. I. Methodological problems. *International Clinical Psychopharmacology*, 10, 83–93.

Barbone, F., McMahon, A. D., & Davey, P. G. (1998). Association of road-traffic accidents with benzodiazepine use. *Lancet*, 352, 1331–1336.

Barlow, D. H., Gorman, J. M., Shear, M. K., & Woods, S. W. (2000). Cognitive-behavioral therapy, imipramine, or their combination for panic disorder: A randomized controlled trial. *Journal of the American Medical Association*, 283, 2529–2536.

Basoglu, M., Marks, I. M., Kiliç, C., Brewin, C.R., & Swinson, R. P. (1994). Alprazolam and exposure for panic disorder with agoraphobia: Attribution of improvement to medication predicts subsequent relapse. *British Journal of Psychiatry*, 164, 652–659.

Bibb, J. & Chambless, D. L. (1986). Alcohol use and abuse among diagnosed agoraphobics. *Behaviour Research and Therapy*, 24, 49–58.

Biondi, M. & Picardi, A. (2003). Increased probability of remaining in remission from panic disorder with agoraphobia after drug treatment in patients who received concurrent cognitive-behavioural therapy: A follow-up study. *Psychotherapy and Psychosomatics*, 72, 34–42.

Blier, P., DeMontigny, C., & Chaput, Y. (1987). Modifications of the serotonin system by antidepressant treatments: Implications for the therapeutic response in major depression. *Journal of Clinical Psychopharmacology*, 7, 24S–35S.

Bouton, M. E., Mineka, S., & Barlow, D. H. (2001). A modern learning theory perspective on the etiology of panic disorder. *Psychological Review*, 108, 4–32.

Boyer, W. (1995). Serotonin uptake inhibitors are superior to imipramine and alprazolam in alleviating panic attacks: A meta-analysis. *International Clinical Psychopharmacology*, 10, 45–49.

Brown, T. A., & Barlow, D. H. (1995). Long-term outcome in cognitive-behavioral treatment of panic disorder: Clinical predictors and alternative strategies for assessment. *Journal of Consulting and Clinical Psychology*, 63, 754–765.

Bruce, T. J., Spiegel, D. A., & Hegel, M. T. (1999). Cognitive-behavioral therapy helps prevent relapse and recurrence of panic disorder following alprazolam discontinuation: A long-term follow-up of the Peoria and Dartmouth studies. *Journal of Consulting and Clinical Psychology*, 67, 151–156.

Byrne, M., Carr, A., & Clarke, M. (2004). The efficacy of couples-based interventions for panic disorder with agoraphobia. *Journal of Family Therapy*, 26, 105–125.

Chambless, D. L. (1988). Body sensations questionnaire. In M. Hersen & A. Bellack, (Eds.), *Dictionary of behavioral assessment techniques* (pp. 85–86). New York: Pergamon.

Chambless, D. L., Caputo, G. C., Bright, P., & Gallagher, R. (1985). Assessment of fear in agoraphobics: the Body Sensations Questionnaire and the Agoraphobic Cognitions Questionnaire. *Journal of Consulting and Clinical Psychology*, 52, 1090–1097.

Clark, D. M. (1986). A cognitive approach to panic. *Behaviour Research and Therapy*, 24, 461–470.

Clark, D. M. (1988). A cognitive model of panic attacks. In S. Rachman & J. D. Maser (Eds.), *Panic: Psychological perspectives* (pp. 71–89). Hillsdale, NJ: Lawrence Erlbaum Associates.

Clum, G. A., Broyles, S., Borden, J., & Watkins, P. L. (1990). Validity and reliability of the panic attack symptoms and cognitions questionnaires. Special Issue: DSM-IV and the psychology literature. *Journal of Psychopathology and Behavioral Assessment*, 12, 233–245.

Craske, M. G. & Barlow, D. H. (2000). *Master your anxiety and panic: Client workbook* (Third edition). New York: Graywind.

de Beurs, E., van Balkom, A. J. L. M., Lange, A., Koele, P., & van Dyck, R. (1995). Treatment of panic disorder with agoraphobia: Comparison of fluvoxamine, placebo, and psychological panic management combined with exposure and of exposure in vivo alone. *American Journal of Psychiatry*, 152, 683–691.

Echeburúa, E., De Corral, P., Bajos, E. G., & Borda, M. (1993). Interactions between self-exposure and alprazolam in the treatment of agoraphobia without current panic: An exploratory study. *Behavioural and Cognitive Psychotherapy*, 21, 219–238.

Fahy, T. J., O'Rourke, D., Brophy, J., Schazmann, W., & Sciascia, S. (1992). The Galway study of panic disorder I: Clomipramine and lofepramine in DSM III-R panic disorder: A placebo controlled trial. *Journal of Affective Disorders*, 25, 63–76.

First, M. B., Spitzer, R. L., Gibbon, M., & Williams, J. B. W. (1996). *Structured clinical interview for DSM-IV axis I – patient edition*. New York: Biometrics Research Department, New York State Psychiatric Institute.

Goddard, A. W. & Charney, D. S. (1997). Toward an integrated neurobiology of panic disorder. *Journal of Clinical Psychiatry*, 58 (Suppl. 2), 4–12.

Gorman, J., Kent, J. M., Sullivan, G. M., & Coplan, J. D. (2000). Neuroanatomical hypothesis of panic disorder, revised. *American Journal of Psychiatry*, 157, 493–505.

Heldt, E., Manfro, G. G., Kipper, L., Blaya, C., Maltz, S., Isolan, L., Hirakata, V. N., & Otto, M. W. (2003). Treating medication-resistant panic disorder: Predictors and outcome of cognitive-behavior therapy in a Brazilian public hospital. *Psychotherapy and Psychosomatics*, 72, 43–48.

Jang, K. L., Stein, M. B., Taylor, S., & Livesley, W. J. (1999). Gender differences in the aetiology of anxiety sensitivity: A twin study. *Journal of Gender Specific Medicine*, 2, 39–44.

Kampman, M., Keijsers, G. P., Hoogduin, C. A., & Hendriks, G. J. (2002). A randomized, double-blind, placebo-controlled study of the effects of adjunctive paroxetine in panic disorder patients unsuccessfully treated with cognitive-behavioral therapy alone. *Journal of Clinical Psychiatry*, 63, 772–777.

LeDoux, J. E. (1998). *The emotional brain*. New York: Simon and Schuster.

Leon, A. C., Portera, L., & Weissman, M. M. (1995). The social costs of anxiety disorders. *British Journal of Psychiatry*, 166 (Suppl. 27), 19–22.

Lydiard, R. B., Greenwald, S., Weissman, M. M., Johnson, J., Drossman, D. A., & Ballenger, J. C. (1994). Panic disorder and gastrointestinal symptoms: Findings from the NIMH Epidemiologic Catchment Area project. *American Journal of Psychiatry*, 151, 64–70.

Marks, I. M. (1987). *Fears, phobias, and rituals*. New York: Oxford University Press.

Marks, I. M., Swinson, R. P., Basoglu, M., Kuch, K., Noshirvani, H., O'Sullivan, G., Lelliott, P. T., Kirby, M., McNamee, G., Sengun, S., & Wickwire, K. (1993). Alprazolam and exposure alone and combined in panic disorder with agoraphobia: A controlled study in London and Toronto. *British Journal of Psychiatry*, 162, 776–787.

Mavissakalian, M. & Hamann, M. S. (1992). DSM-III personality characteristics of panic disorder with agoraphobia patients in stable remission. *Comprehensive Psychiatry*, 33, 305–309.

McNally, R. J. (1994). *Panic disorder: A critical analysis*. New York: Guilford.

Miller, J. J., Fletcher, K., & Kabat-Zinn, J. (1995). Three-year follow-up and clinical implications of a mindfulness meditation-based stress reduction intervention in the treatment of anxiety disorders. *General Hospital Psychiatry*, 17, 192–200.

Milrod, B. L., Busch, F. N., Cooper, A. M., & Shapiro, T. (1997). *Manual of panic-focused psychodynamic psychotherapy*. Washington, DC: APA.

Milrod, B., Busch, F., Leon, A. C., Shapiro, T., Aronson, A., Roiphe, J., Rudden, M., Singer, M., Goldman, H., Richter, D., & Shear, M. K. (2000). Open trial of psychodynamic psychotherapy for panic disorder: A pilot study. *American Journal of Psychiatry*, 157, 1878–1880.

Noyes, R., Jr. (2001). Hypochondriasis: Boundaries and comorbidities. In G. J. G. Asmundson, S. Taylor, & B. J. Cox (Eds.), *Health anxiety: Clinical and research perspectives on hypochondriasis and related conditions* (pp.132–160). Chichester, UK: Wiley.

Noyes, R., Jr., Cook, B., Garvey, M., & Summers, R. (1990). Reduction of gastrointestinal symptoms with treatment for panic disorder. *Psychosomatics*, 31, 75–79.

Oehrberg, S., Christiansen, P. E., & Behnke, K. (1995). Paroxetine in the treatment of panic disorder: A randomized double-blind placebo-controlled study. *British Journal of Psychiatry*, 167, 374–379.

Otto, M. W., Pollack, M. H., Sachs, G. S., Reiter, S. R., Meltzer-Brody, S., & Rosenbaum, J. F. (1993). Discontinuation of benzodiazepine treatment: Efficacy of cognitive-behavior therapy for patients with panic disorder. *American Journal of Psychiatry*, 150, 1485–1490.

Peterson, R. A. & Reiss, S. (1992). *Anxiety Sensitivity Index Manual (Second Edition)*. Worthington, OH: International Diagnostic Systems.

Pohl, R., Yergani, V., Balon, R., & Lycaki, H. (1988). The jitteriness syndrome in panic disorder patients treated with antidepressants. *Journal of Clinical Psychiatry*, 49, 100–104.

Rapee, R. M., Craske, M. G., & Barlow, D. H. (1990). Subject-described features of panic attacks using self-monitoring. *Journal of Anxiety Disorders*, 4, 171–181.

Reed, V., & Wittchen, H. U. (1998). DSM-IV panic attacks and panic disorder in a community sample of adolescents and young adults: How specific are panic attacks? *Journal of Psychiatric Research*, 32, 335–345.

Reiss, S., Peterson, R. A., Gursky, M. & McNally, R. J. (1986). Anxiety sensitivity, anxiety frequency, and the prediction of fearfulness. *Behaviour Research and Therapy*, 24, 1–8.

Sharp, D. M., Power, K. G., Simpson, R. J., Swanson, V., Moodie, E., Anstee, J. A., & Ashford, J. J. (1996). Fluvoxamine, placebo, and cognitive behaviour therapy used alone and in combination in the treatment of panic disorder and agoraphobia. *Journal of Anxiety Disorders*, 10, 219–242.

Shear, M. K., Cooper, A. M., Klerman, G. L., Busch, F. N., & Shapiro, T. (1993). A psychodynamic model of panic disorder. *American Journal of Psychiatry*, 150, 859–866.

Shear, M. K., Houck, P., Greeno, C., & Masters, S. (2001). Emotion-focused psychotherapy for patients with panic disorder. *American Journal of Psychiatry*, 158, 1993–1998.

Shear, M. K. & Maser, J. D. (1994). Standardized assessment for panic disorder research: A conference report. *Archives of General Psychiatry*, 51, 346–354.

Simon, N. M. & Pollack, M. H. (2000). The current status of the treatment of panic disorder: Pharmacotherapy and cognitive-behavioral therapy. *Psychiatric Annals*, 30, 689–696.

Stafrace, S. (1994). Hypnosis in the treatment of panic disorder with agoraphobia. *Australian Journal of Clinical Hypnosis*, 22, 73–86.

Stein, D. J. & Stahl, S. (2000). Serotonin and anxiety: Current models. *International Clinical Psychopharmacology*, 15 (Suppl. 2), S1–S6.

Stein, M. B., Norton, G. R., Walker, J. R., Chartier, M. J., & Graham, R. (2000). Do SSRIs enhance the efficacy of very brief cognitive behavioral therapy for panic disorder? A pilot study. *Psychiatry Research*, 94, 191–200.

Stutzman, G. E. & LeDoux, J. E. (1999). GABAergic antagonists block the inhibitory effects of serotonin in the lateral amygdala: A mechanism for modulation of sensory inputs related to fear conditioning. *Journal of Neuroscience*, 19, RC8.

Taylor, S. (1999). *Anxiety sensitivity*. Mahwah, NJ: Lawrence Erlbaum Associates.

Taylor, S. (2000). *Understanding and treating panic disorder: Cognitive-behavioural approaches*. New York: Wiley.

Taylor, S. (2001). Breathing retraining in the treatment of panic disorder: Efficacy, caveats, and indications. *Scandinavian Journal of Behavior Therapy*, 30, 1–8.

Taylor, S. & Livesley, W. J. (1995). The influence of personality on the clinical course of neurosis. *Current Opinion in Psychiatry*, 8, 93–97.

Tork, I. & Hornung, J. P. (1990). Raphe nuclei and the serotonergic system. In G. Paxinos (Ed.), *The human nervous system* (pp. 1001–1022). San Diego: Academic.

Tyrer, P. (1985). Neurosis divisible? *Lancet*, i, 685–688.

Uhlenhuth, E. H., Balter, M. B., Ban, T. A., & Yang, K. (1999). International study of expert judgment on therapeutic use of benzodiazepines and other psychotherapeutic medications: IV. Treatments in recommendations for the pharmacotherapy of anxiety disorders. *Depression and Anxiety*, 9, 107–116.

Weissman, M. M., Bland, R. C., Canino, G. J., Faravelli, C., Greenwald, S., Hai-Gwo, H., Joyce, P. R., Karam, E. G., Lee, C. K., Lellouch, J., Lepine, J. P., Newman, S. C., Oakley-Browne, M. A., Rubio-Stipec, M., Wells, J. E., Wickramarante, P. J., Wittchen, H. U., & Yeh, E. K. (1997). The cross-national epidemiology of panic disorder. *Archives of General Psychiatry*, 54, 305–309.

Wiborg, I. M. & Dahl, A. A. (1996). Does brief dynamic psychotherapy reduce the relapse rate of panic disorder? *Archives of General Psychiatry*, 53, 689–694.

Wilhelm, F. H., Trabert, W., & Roth, W. T. (2001). Physiological instability in panic disorder and generalized anxiety disorder. *Biological Psychiatry*, 49, 596–605.

Wittchen, H. U., Reed, V., & Kessler, R. C. (1998). The relationship of agoraphobia and panic in a community sample of adolescents and young adults. *Archives of General Psychiatry*, 55, 1017–1024.

World Health Organization (WHO) (1992). *The ICD-10 classification of mental and behavioural disorders: Clinical descriptions and diagnostic guidelines*. Geneva: WHO.

Yeragani, V. K., Pohl, R., Jampala, V. C., Balon, R., Ramesh, C., & Srinivasan, K. (2000). Increased QT variability in patients with panic disorder and depression. *Psychiatry Research*, 93, 225–235.

Yonkers, K. A., Zlotnick, C., Allsworth, J., Warshaw, M., Shea, T., & Keller, M. B. (1998). Is the course of panic disorder the same in women and men? *American Journal of Psychiatry*, 155, 596–602.

Chapter 13

Obsessive-compulsive disorder

Padmal de Silva

CASE EXAMPLE

Gill is a twenty-four-year-old woman who was referred because of obsessive-compulsive problems. She was worried about contamination by 'dirt' and 'germs', and engaged in excessive handwashing and cleaning. Any object touched by others – except a few family members and close friends – worried her, and she would try to avoid coming into contact with such items. If, however, she did touch any of these objects (which included telephones, door handles, chairs in offices, others' clothes, etc.) she would feel very anxious and would wash excessively. She would use large amounts of soap and detergents, and wash her hands repeatedly until she felt clean. She would also often wash her arms and face in the same way. A bath would take a long time, as she was determined to cleanse herself thoroughly. In the office where she worked as a part-time secretary, Gill would go to the washroom at least ten times a day to wash her hands. She sought help when she found that her problems seriously interfered with normal living, and when family and friends began to comment on her peculiar behaviour.

Gill had always been anxious. However, the fear of dirt and germs did not appear as a problem until she was in her mid-teens. The problem was minimal at first, but gradually became worse. The terminal illness of an aunt when Gill was twenty-two caused a major escalation. She felt 'affected by germs' whenever she visited her aunt in hospital, and would have a thorough wash, if not a bath, after each visit.

Gill was unable to specify what the germs were that she was afraid of. She felt germs were associated with illness and with dirt, and anything dirty needed to be avoided. She felt that, if she did not cleanse herself after coming into contact with germs/dirt, she would develop a serious illness – which was unspecified. She also felt that she would inadvertently spread the germs and cause harm to others.

CLINICAL FEATURES AND CLASSIFICATION

Obsessive-compulsive disorder is one of several anxiety disorders. The phenomena of obsessive-compulsive disorder are so striking that they are very well described and recognized (see de Silva, 2003; de Silva & Rachman, 2004; Emmelkamp, 1982; Rachman & Hodgson, 1980).

Defining features of obsessive-compulsive disorder

The American Psychiatric Association's (APA's) *Diagnostic and statistical manual of mental disorders*, Fourth Edition – Text Revision, (DSM-IV-TR; APA, 2000) and the World Health Organization's (WHO's) *International classification of diseases*, Tenth Edition (ICD-10; WHO, 1992) criteria for obsessive-compulsive disorder are presented in Table 13.1.

Obsessions

Obsessions are unwanted and intrusive thoughts, impulses or images, or combinations of them, which are generally resisted. They are also recognized to be of internal origin (Rachman & Hodgson, 1980). Some clinical examples are:

- A young woman had the recurrent intrusive thought that she has a terminal illness.
- A man had the recurrent intrusive doubt that he may cause a serious fire or other disaster through negligence.
- A young married woman had the recurrent intrusive impulse to strangle small children and animals. This would be followed by the thought/doubt that she may actually have done this.
- A man had the recurrent intrusive impulse to shout obscenities during prayer or a church service.
- A young man had recurrent intrusive images of himself violently attacking his elderly parents. He also had the thought that he might actually commit this act. This experience included images of the victims, of blood flowing and of injuries caused.

The contents of obsessions are usually associated with contamination, violence and aggression, harm, disease, orderliness, sex, and religion, although obsessions that relate to seemingly trivial matters can also occur (Khanna &

Table 13.1 Diagnostic criteria for obsessive-compulsive disorder (OCD)

DSM-IV-TR	*ICD-10*
A. Either obsessions or compulsions Obsessions are defined by 1, 2, 3, and 4: 1. Recurrent or persistent thoughts impulses or images that are experienced as intrusive or inappropriate and cause marked anxiety or distress 2. The thoughts, images or impulse are not excessive worries about real-life problems 3. The person attempts to ignore or suppress these thoughts, impulses or images or to neutralize them with some other thought or action 4. The person recognizes that the thoughts images or impulses are the product of his or her own mind (and not imposed from without as in thought insertion) Compulsions are defined by 1 and 2: 1. Repetitive behaviours (e.g. hand washing, ordering, checking) or mental acts (e.g. praying, counting, repeating words silently) that the person feels driven to performing in response to an obsession or according to rules that must be applied rigidly 2. The behaviours or mental acts are aimed at preventing or reducing distress or preventing some dreaded event or situation. However, these behaviours or mental acts either are not connected in a realistic way with what they are designed to neutralize or prevent or are clearly excessive B. The person has at one time recognized that the obsessions or compulsions are unreasonable; this condition does not apply to children C. The obsessions or compulsions cause considerable distress, are time consuming (more than 1 hour a day), and impair social and academic functioning D. The content of the obsessions and compulsions is unrelated to another disorder if one is present E. The disorder is not due to a medical condition or the effects of a drug	The essential feature of this disorder is recurrent obsessional thoughts or compulsive acts Obsessional thoughts are ideas, images or impulses that enter the individual's mind again and again in a stereotyped form. They are invariably distressing either because they are violent or obscene or because they are senseless and the sufferer often tries unsuccessfully to resist them. They are recognized as the individual's own thoughts even though they are repugnant and/or involuntary Compulsive acts or rituals are stereotyped behaviours that are repeated again and again. They are not inherently enjoyable nor do they result in the completion of inherently useful tasks. The individual views them as preventing some objectively unlikely event often involving harm to, or caused by, himself or herself. Usually this behaviour is recognized as pointless and repeated attempts are made to resist it Autonomic anxiety symptoms are often present but distressing feelings of internal or psychic tension without obvious autonomic arousal are also common Depressive symptoms commonly accompany the condition For a definite diagnosis obsessional symptoms or compulsive acts or both must be present on most days for at last two successive weeks and be a source of distress or interference with activities. The obsessional symptoms should have the following characteristics: 1. They must be recognized as the individual's own thoughts or impulses 2. There must be at least one thought or act that is still resisted unsuccessfully 3. The thought of carrying out of the act must not be inherently pleasurable 4. The thoughts, images or impulses must be unpleasantly repetitive

Note: Adapted from DSM-IV-TR (APA, 2000) and ICD-10 (WHO, 1992).

Channabasavanna, 1988; Rachman, 2003; Rachman & Hodgson, 1980; Rasmussen & Tsuang, 1986). It is also worth noting that most normal persons also have such unwanted, intrusive cognitions, but they are less intense and less frequent, and neither disabling nor unduly distressing (Rachman, 2003; Rachman & de Silva, 1978; Salkovskis & Harrison, 1984).

Compulsions

Compulsions are repetitive and seemingly purposeful behaviours, preceded or accompanied by a subjective sense of compulsion, and generally resisted by the person. They are performed according to certain rules or in a stereotyped fashion. Despite the resistance, these behaviours are actively carried out by the person.

Common compulsions are ritualistic behaviours involving checking and washing/cleaning. Other compulsive behaviours include doing things in a certain stereotyped way, ordering inanimate objects and doing things in a strictly rigid sequence. Sometimes a certain special number is involved, in that the behaviour has to be carried out that number of times. Clinical examples include:

- A young woman who felt contaminated by germs and dirt every time she touched door handles, money and so on, and washed her hands thoroughly and repeatedly in an elaborate ritual.
- A young man who had to check repeatedly that he had correctly locked the door, windows, drawers, cupboards and so on every time he left his house.
- A man who opened letters he had written and sealed to make sure that he had written the correct things. Thus he would rip open the envelope, re-read the letter and put into a new envelope several times before eventually posting it.
- A young man who silently uttered a string of words each time he heard or read about any disaster or accident.
- A woman who complained that every time she entered a room, she had to touch the four corners of it, starting from the left.

As can be seen in the above examples, compulsions can be overt (e.g. hand washing) or covert (e.g. silently uttering a set of words).

Relationship between obsessions and compulsions

To examine the relationship between the two sets of phenomena, it will be useful to consider the events that might be present in an episode of obsessive-compulsive experience and their relationships. Table 13.2 attempts to present such a sequence.

Table 13.2 Possible sequence of events in an obsessive-compulsive experience

(a) Trigger	*(b) Obsession*	*(c) Discomfort*	*(d) Compulsive urge*	*(e) Compulsive behaviour*	*(f) Discomfort reduction*
External/ internal None	Thought/ doubt/ image/ impulse None	+	+ –	Overt/ covert None	+ –

+ = yes; – = no.

Thus, an obsession may arise with or without a trigger, which in turn can be external (e.g. sight of knife: doubt, 'Did I stab someone?') or internal (e.g. remembering a meeting with someone: thought, 'I am taller than he, am I not?'). The obsession can take the form of a thought, image or impulse, or a combination of these. The obsession usually leads to discomfort/anxiety/ distress. This could lead to an urge to engage in certain compulsive behaviour or ritual, and this can be either overt (e.g. washing) or covert (such as counting backwards in silence). Carrying out this compulsive behaviour would, normally, lead to a reduction of discomfort, although there can be exceptions (see Beech, 1971).

A compulsive urge can sometimes arise without a preceding obsession. Consider a man who accidentally touches a part of the wall of a public toilet and immediately rushes into a washing ritual. This is particularly so with long-standing compulsive behaviours that have, over the years, acquired a habit-like quality.

Thus obsessions and compulsions can take place in the absence of each other, although in practice they are commonly found to occur together.

Other major features

Avoidance

An important feature of obsessive-compulsive disorder that does not appear in the scheme proposed (Table 13.2) is avoidance. Many obsessive-compulsive clients have avoidance, which can be almost like phobic avoidance in some cases (e.g. Jakes, 1996; Rachman & Hodgson, 1980). The avoidance behaviour concerns stimuli, and sometimes behaviours, that can potentially trigger the obsession or compulsion. Those with contamination/washing/cleaning type problems, like Gill in the case study given above, strive to avoid what they believe to be dirty or contaminating. Those with checking rituals may avoid situations that lead to repeated checking.

Fears of disaster

Clients not infrequently report a fear of disastrous consequences if they neglect their compulsive behaviour. The reason often given for carrying out the compulsion is that the behaviour wards off some danger, usually to the client in person, or to someone he or she loves. In some cases the feared disaster and the action intended to ward it off are closely related, such as infection by germs and handwashing, but this is not always the case.

Resistance

Resistance to the obsession and compulsion has been considered traditionally as a central feature in obsessive-compulsive disorder. Aubrey Lewis (1936), for example, considered it to be its cardinal feature. More recent empirical work suggests that this is not entirely correct (e.g. Stern & Cobb, 1978). Although obsessions and compulsions are mostly resisted, in some clients there is no strong resistance.

Reassurance seeking

Many obsessive-compulsive clients resort to reassurance seeking, usually from family members. Often, obsessional thoughts such as 'Am I an evil person?' or 'Do I need to check the taps again?' lead to the client asking for reassurance. When reassurance is given, the client feels relief from discomfort, although it is often short-lived and the request for reassurance is repeated.

Disruption

When obsessive-compulsive clients engage in their compulsion they feel a need to carry it out precisely as they feel it ought to be done. If the behaviour is disrupted by an external event or another unwanted thought, the ritual is considered invalidated and may need to be re-started. For long and complicated compulsive rituals, this can be extremely time consuming (de Silva & Rachman, 2004).

Ruminations

A rumination is a somewhat complex phenomenon sometimes found in obsessive-compulsive disorder. The client attempts to think through a question or topic, such as 'Is there a life after death?' or 'Am I genetically abnormal?' and this thinking is inconclusive, prolonged and frustrating. The client does this compulsively, and the compulsion is often triggered by the appearance of the relevant obsessional thought (de Silva, 2003).

EPIDEMIOLOGY

Prevalence

Obsessive-compulsive disorder is relatively rare, but not as rare as it was once thought to be. Studies have shown that, among psychiatric outpatients, less than 1% suffer from this disorder. The figure among inpatients is higher, but is certainly under 5%. There are, however, problems with figures such as these since diagnostic practices are not consistent across clinics and hospitals.

The occurrence of the disorder in the general population was, until recently, estimated to be about 0.05% – that is, one out of every two thousand. More recent findings from a systematic survey in selected catchment areas in the United States suggest a much higher figure (Karno, Golding, Sorenson & Burman, 1988); a lifetime prevalence of 3% was found in Baltimore. In other words, three out of every hundred persons interviewed had the disorder at some point in their life. The figure was 2.6% in New Haven, Connecticut, and 1.9% in St Louis. This study also investigated the six-month prevalence rate – that is, how many had the disorder in the six months prior to being interviewed by the researchers. The figures were: 2.4% in Baltimore, 1.4% in New Haven and 1.3% in St Louis. A similar investigation carried out in Edmonton, Canada, showed a lifetime prevalence of 3% and a six-month prevalence of 1.6% (Bland, Orn & Newman, 1988). A cross-national collaborative study, using similar methods in seven countries, estimated that the lifetime prevalence was 2% (Weissman et al., 1994). Many authorities argue that these figures err on the side of overestimation but, even allowing for this, they show that obsessive-compulsive disorder is more common in the general population than had been suspected. These issues are discussed more fully by Krochmalik and Menzies (2003).

Course of the disorder

In roughly half of all cases, the problems begin and develop gradually. Among those with an acute onset, there is a preponderance of washers and cleaners over checkers. Generally, the course of the disorder shows some fluctuation. There may be periods when the problem is clearly present and active, followed by relatively good periods. These relatively good periods are, however, not fully symptom-free in most cases. In some, perhaps about half, there is steady worsening of the disorder. Also, when the person is under stress, the chances of obsessions and compulsions reappearing, or getting worse, are increased (Rachman & Hodgson, 1980; Rasmussen & Eisen, 1992; Rasmussen & Tsuang, 1986).

COMORBID AND RELATED CONDITIONS TO CONSIDER IN DIFFERENTIAL DIAGNOSIS

Depression

There is a clear relationship between obsessive-compulsive disorder and depression (Rachman & Hodgson, 1980). This can take several forms. First, some people develop obsessions when they become depressed; in such cases the obsessions are essentially secondary to the depression, and usually clear up when the depression lifts. Second, many obsessive-compulsive clients tend to have a past history of depression. Third, some of these clients become depressed subsequent to the onset of their disorder, and may have episodes of depression. When depressed, the symptoms of obsessive-compulsive disorder tend to get worse. Research has also shown that clients who are very depressed might not respond well to the standard cognitive-behavioural treatment of the obsessive-compulsive disorder. In such cases, the depression needs to be treated before improvement can be expected in the obsessive-compulsive symptoms (de Silva & Rachman, 2004).

Schizophrenia

According to one view, the relationship between obsessive-compulsive disorder and schizophrenia is limited, because psychosis is categorically different from normal and neurotic functioning. In schizophrenia, stereotyped behaviour, which may appear like compulsive behaviour, is sometimes evident. While in the early stages of schizophrenic illness, obsessions and compulsions may appear occasionally; these are short-lived. Complaints by schizophrenic clients about thoughts that they wished they did not have can bear a superficial similarity to obsessions, but these are usually thoughts that they believe to have been put into their minds by external forces, human or otherwise. This feature distinguishes them from obsessional thoughts, which the clients recognize as their own. In fact, obsessive-compulsive clients are sometimes diagnosed (or misdiagnosed) as schizophrenic. This is largely because of the superficial similarity between obsessions and the delusions (intensely held, personal false beliefs) that clients with schizophrenia commonly hold. Ordinarily, the two phenomena can be distinguished from each other. A schizophrenic delusion is an intensely held belief – that is, the client has no insight that it is false (for example, a client really believes that his enemies are sending radio waves to harm him), whereas an obsession is experienced as ego-dystonic – that is, not in keeping with one's own beliefs and thoughts – and is seen as unwanted. In other words, obsessive-compulsive clients have insight; they know that their obsessional beliefs, for example that some disaster is about to happen to their loved ones, are really not valid. Although obessive-compulsive clients act on their belief by performing compulsive behaviour or avoiding certain things, there is the recognition, if not at the time of the behaviour then a few hours later, that it is ultimately irrational. Admittedly there are exceptions, but they are very small in number. The DSM-IV of the American Psychiatric Association (APA, 1994) refers to those 'with poor insight'. These are clients who, for most of the time during the current episode of the disorder, do not recognize that their obsessions or compulsions are irrational or excessive. In this minority of clients, the obsessional belief is held with some tenacity. Some writers have commented on such strongly held beliefs in obsessive-compulsive clients and described them as 'overvalued ideas' (e.g. Foa, 1979). Recent studies investigating this issue appear to show that some of the schizophrenia-like features (schizoid features) are found more commonly in obsessive-compulsive disorder than in other anxiety disorders (e.g. Enright & Beech, 1990).

Another view of the relationship between obsessive-compulsive disorder and schizophrenia is that psychosis, normal functioning and neurotic functioning are on a continuum, and that the differences between delusions, overvalued ideas, obsessions and 'normal' beliefs are dimensional rather than categorical (Garety & Hemsley, 1994). The traditional conceptualization of a delusion as a false belief held with strong conviction, a belief not shared by the majority in the culture and not amenable to argument or contrary evidence, has been challenged by recent research suggesting that none of these characteristics applies to all cases (Fulford & Gipps, 2004). This view, outlined further in Chapter 21, proposes that delusions are on a continuum with ordinary beliefs, with which they share characteristics; the differences between delusions and ordinary beliefs are dimensional, not categorical.

Phobias

Sometimes obsessive-compulsive disorders are confused with phobias. Phobias are characterized by anxiety, and most obsessive-compulsive clients experience a lot of anxiety. In both, there is avoidance behaviour. It is certainly the case that some obsessive-compulsive clients have some phobic characteristics, particularly those with concerns about contamination.

However, the two disorders are different in some important ways (Enright & Beech, 1997; Jakes, 1996). The ritualistic behaviour of the obsessive-compulsive client is absent in the phobic. Many of the former describe their feeling when affected by an obsession or exposed to a triggering situation, such as contact with dirt, not so much as 'fear' but as 'discomfort', 'uneasiness' or 'disgust'. A further important difference is that individuals with a phobia can usually, if they successfully avoid the object or situation they are afraid of, feel safe and be unaffected by the problem in their day-to-day life. Someone with a phobia of elevators, for example, will avoid using elevators and be able to lead a perfectly happy life as long as he or she is not forced to use an elevator; and someone with a phobia of spiders can lead a normal life as long as he or she avoids encounters with spiders. In contrast, obsessive-compulsive clients cannot escape from their problems as easily; even if they keep away from things that trigger their obsessions or compulsive urges, they do not feel free. For example, a woman with this disorder may totally avoid knives, scissors and other sharp objects, which she fears she may use to attack people, but still frequently worry that she may commit these acts, or indeed even wonder whether she has actually attacked someone.

Eating disorders

Anorexia nervosa has been described by some writers as a form of obsessive-compulsive disorder. The single-minded determination to lose weight and the incessant preoccupation with food, weight, body size and shape that these clients display have been given as evidence for this. Anorexics are commonly described as 'obsessed with thinness'. They are certainly preoccupied with their weight, size and eating. However, anorexia nervosa is a separate disorder, not part of an obsessive-compulsive illness, although there is some relationship between the two and a small proportion of females with obsessive-compulsive disorder have a past history of anorexia nervosa. Among anorexics, a sizeable subgroup have obsessions and/or compulsions, some of them quite marked. It appears that, in these clients, the two disorders co-exist. Sometimes, the symptoms of the two disorders influence each other and get intertwined – that is, certain behaviour assumes significance in both disorders.

In bulimia nervosa the client has recurrent episodes of binge eating, followed by self-induced vomiting and/or laxative abuse. The urge to engage in binge eating is described by some of these clients as having a compulsive quality, although the nature of the behaviour is by no means senseless. As with anorexics, some bulimics also have concomitant obsessive-compulsive problems, some features of which may become closely related to the eating disorder. For example, a young woman with a history of both disorders reported that when she binged on chocolate bars she felt compelled to eat 24 bars at a time, neither more nor less, and the binge had to be uninterrupted. If the chocolates got 'contaminated' by the smell of another food, then the binging episode had to be restarted.

These issues are discussed more fully in de Silva (1993) and Shafran (2002).

Post-traumatic stress disorder

The psychological effects of severe traumatic experiences have been known and recorded for a long time, but it is only in recent years that the diagnostic category of post-traumatic stress disorder has been officially recognized. Essentially, this refers to a psychological disorder that some people develop after exposure to a traumatic event (for example, war, earthquakes and fires, violence, serious motor accidents). The main features are the persistent re-experiencing of the traumatic event, for example, recurrent intrusive memories or recurrent dreams, avoidance of reminders of the event and increased arousal, as reflected by sleep difficulties, poor concentration, and so on. Large numbers of war veterans have been treated for this disorder in the United States and elsewhere, and there is an active and still growing interest in this area.

The recurrent, intrusive thoughts and images that occur in this disorder are very much like some of the obsessions experienced by clients with obsessive-compulsive disorder. This is particularly so for the very vivid intrusive images. For example, a former soldier now suffering from post-traumatic stress disorder had the recurrent image of bloated and charred bodies. It is also not uncommon for sufferers to have intrusive thoughts other than memories of the event (e.g. 'Why did it have to happen to me?' 'Am I really safe now?'). Some also report cognitive compulsions, such as compulsively saying 'No it wasn't my fault', or compulsively going over the incident. In a small number of clients with this disorder, overt compulsive rituals are found. One, a 46-year-old man who was subjected to a particularly vicious act of violence, developed rituals of repeatedly checking door and window locks. A young woman who was seriously sexually assaulted while on holiday, began to compulsively wash herself in order to 'become clean'.

While the overlap of some of the features of obsessive-compulsive disorder and post-traumatic disorder is clear, are the two related? There are certainly instances in which a trauma victim has developed obsessions and/or compulsions to the degree that one can describe him or her as suffering from obsessive-compulsive disorder (see de Silva & Marks, 2001). It is also clear that a small number of obsessive-compulsive clients have a history of traumatic or disturbing experiences. However, the two disorders are different entities, and the majority of clients with obsessive-compulsive disorder do not have a history of trauma. Similarly, the majority of clients who suffer from post-traumatic disorder do not develop full-blown obsessive-compulsive disorder. A small number do, and may have both disorders concurrently.

Gilles de la Tourette syndrome

This condition is characterized by multiple tics, including vocal tics, which may take the form of swear words or obscenities. Some authors have emphasized the similarities between the Tourette syndrome and some aspects of obsessive-compulsive disorder (e.g. Steingard & Dillon-Stout, 1992). However, the tics in the Tourette syndrome are different from true compulsions – they are purposeless and involuntary, unlike compulsions. Nor can they be easily delayed, reshaped or substituted, again unlike compulsions. Another difference is that the treatment methods that are successful with obsessive-compulsive disorder are of little use with clients with Tourette syndrome.

It has been reported that some clients with this syndrome also have obsessive-compulsive symptoms, particularly younger clients (Como, 1995). In some studies, first-degree relatives of people with Tourette syndrome have been reported to have a higher incidence of obsessive-compulsive disorder than the general population. Despite these apparent associations, however, the vast majority of clients with obsessive-compulsive disorder do not have Gilles de la Tourette syndrome.

Body dysmorphic disorder

The disorder, which used to be called 'dysmorphophobia', is characterized by excessive concern and preoccupation with imagined defects in bodily appearance. The common complaints are about the face or head (for example, shape of nose, mouth, eyebrows or jaws). Less commonly, the person may be overconcerned with some other part of the body (such as hands, feet, breasts or genitals). The repetitive thoughts may resemble obsessions, and the person usually engages in extensive checking behaviour, especially in the mirror. Reassurance seeking is also common. In some cases, the conviction that there is a physical abnormality leads to social avoidance.

Despite the repetitive thoughts and checking, body dysmorphic disorder is quite distinct from obsessive-compulsive disorder. It is not considered to be an anxiety disorder at all. On the other hand, a significant minority of clients with body dysmorphic disorder have comorbid obsessive-compulsive disorder (see Hollander & Benzaquen, 1997; Veale, 2003). Indeed, over-valued ideas, described in DSM-IV as 'an unreasonable and sustained belief that is maintained with less than delusional intensity (i.e. the person is able to acknowledge the possibility that the belief may or may not be true). The belief is not one that is ordinarily accepted by other members of the person's culture or subculture' (APA, 1994), are seen by some as a common factor in both obsessive-compulsive disorder and body dysmorphic disorder, as well as occurring in a range of other mental health problems, including anorexia nervosa, social phobia, avoidant personality disorder, morbid jealousy and paranoid delusions.

Brain damage

Symptoms similar to obsessions and compulsions can result from brain damage caused by injury or neurological disease: the client may engage in repetitive acts or express repetitive ideas. The appearance of obsessive-compulsive-type symptoms in certain organic conditions (for example, encephalitis lethargica) has been recognized for many decades. These symptoms are usually accompanied by other signs of brain damage, such as deficits in memory and learning ability. Furthermore, repetitive acts and ideas of these clients are different from obsessions and compulsions in that they lack intellectual content and intentionality, and have a mechanical or primitive quality. Studies undertaken to investigate the neurological and neuropsychological features of obsessive-compulsive clients have not, up to now, produced consistent or clear-cut results. There are, however, interesting findings that have potential relevance to our understanding of obsessive-compulsive disorder. These are discussed in detail by Frampton (2003) and Tallis (1995).

Obsessive-compulsive personality disorder

Persons with obsessional personality features to a degree that seriously affects their life and functioning are sometimes clinically described as suffering from an obsessive-compulsive personality disorder, (see DSM-IV; APA, 1994). In these clients, the main features are long-standing personality traits, such as excessive rigidity and perfectionism, and undue preoccupation with details, indecisiveness, and so on, and not episodes of illness. These features are well established by early adulthood. In addition, these people tend to show a lack of, or limited, ability to express, warm and tender emotions. They do not necessarily have, or develop, true obsessions and compulsions. In clinical practice, such clients are encountered only rarely and, when they do come for help, it is usually because of a depressive or other illness. Sometimes a client may display features of this disorder as well as obsessive-compulsive disorder. In such cases a dual diagnosis is given.

AETIOLOGY

There are various models and theories about the origins of obsessive-compulsive disorder.

The psychoanalytic view

Historically, the oldest theoretical account is the psychoanalytic one. In this view, obsessions and compulsions are seen as symptoms of some deeper problem in the person's unconscious mind. Certain memories, desires and conflicts are kept out of consciousness, or repressed, because they would otherwise cause anxiety. These repressed elements may later manifest themselves as neurotic symptoms. Fixation (or 'getting stuck') at a particular stage of development, caused by various factors during one's formative years, determines the nature of the neurotic symptoms that appear in this way in later life. Obsessive-compulsive disorder is linked in this way to the stage of development that is called, in this theory, the 'anal-sadistic stage', in which toilet training is a major feature. Anger and aggression are also associated with this stage of the child's development. Certain experiences during this phase, including desires, impulses, conflicts and frustrations, can make one vulnerable to obsessive-compulsive disorder, and to obsessive-compulsive personality features, in later years. The compulsive acts, obsessional thoughts, and so on are seen as defensive reactions that suppress the real, hidden anxieties.

There are many versions of the psychoanalytic theory of obsessive-compulsive disorder, including some recent contributions. Some of them have led to interesting and extensive theoretical discussion. However, there is little evidence to support the psychoanalytic theory in its various forms. It is also a theory that cannot easily be tested (Jakes, 1996).

The learning view

The other classical theory that attempts to explain obsessive-compulsive disorder is the learning view (Jakes, 1996; Rachman & Hodgson, 1980). This considers neurotic disorders, and many other behavioural problems, to be predominantly acquired or learned. Individuals may learn, through association with a painful or terrifying experience, to become anxious about certain things that are really harmless. They may also learn that certain behaviour reduces anxiety, and this then becomes strengthened. In this case, the compulsive behaviour, because it reduces anxiety, becomes established and strengthened; the individual thus engages in this behaviour as a habitual way of reducing or preventing anxiety.

There is no doubt that, in most cases, the carrying-out of the compulsive behaviour indeed reduces anxiety or discomfort (Rachman & Hodgson, 1980). The discomfort coming from one's own obsessions, or from various events and objects around one, is generally reduced by the performance of the rituals. So, the compulsive behaviour is maintained because it is an effective way of reducing discomfort. Another piece of evidence that gives some support to the learning view comes from animal studies. In certain experimental settings, animals placed in aversive or painful situations are seen to engage in previously learned anxiety-reducing behaviour in a stereotyped, repetitive way, even though this behaviour does not lead to any relief or escape from the current situation (see Wolpe, 1958, for a discussion of this work). This suggests that, in stressful situations, previously useful anxiety-reducing behaviour may be rigidly resorted to even though it has no logical relationship to the present stress. The seemingly senseless ritualistic behaviour of some obsessive-compulsive clients may be seen as a similar phenomenon.

However, the learning view has difficulty in providing a comprehensive explanation of these problems. The majority of clients with obsessive-compulsive disorder do not recall any initial painful experience or experiences as the starting point of their problems; that is, there is often no clear direct learning experience. Also, the theory gives no explanation as to why only certain kinds of things, for example, dirt, germs and so on, commonly become the subject of concern and lead to obsessions and compulsions. It also fails to explain the origin of the obsessions themselves, particularly those that are senseless (for example, order, patterns, symmetry, and so on) and those that, although meaningful, have no relevance to the person's history or present life.

Cognitive-behavioural view

The older learning view has been complemented in recent years by views taking into account cognitive factors. The present cognitive-behavioural theory is best represented by Salkovskis (1999; Salkovskis & McGuire, 2003). In this view, early experiences can make one vulnerable to the disorder, and certain critical incidents are seen as triggering off the disorder. Both these classes of factor contribute to assumptions and beliefs that play a key part in obsessive-compulsive disorder. These include beliefs such as 'not preventing a disaster is as bad as causing it' and 'better to be safe now than be sorry later'. In clients with the disorder, unwanted intrusive cognitions, which most people experience, are interpreted as significant. The random thought 'I may harm someone', for example, can lead to the person feeling that he or she is an evil person (see Rachman, 2003). This leads to the thought becoming a recurrent obsession, and also to a need to engage in a behaviour, internal or external – even both – to neutralize the obsession when it occurs. Thus cleaning, washing and other compulsions are generated. The carrying-out of the compulsion reduces discomfort, but this is only a temporary relief.

The cognitive-behavioural account gives a more sophisticated theory than the original learning view, and offers a plausible explanation in most cases. It has also led to a treatment approach that includes specific cognitive work, in addition to the behavioural techniques derived from the learning approach.

Biological causation

In the past two decades, it has been suggested by several authors that obsessive-compulsive disorder is caused by a biological disturbance (e.g. Zohar & Insel, 1987). The biological theory proposes that the disorder is caused by a biochemical imbalance in the brain; in particular, it is claimed that obsessive-compulsive disorder arises because of an inadequate supply of serotonin (see Chapter 6). This theory originally emerged from the finding that an antidepressive drug, clomipramine, which blocks the natural loss of serotonin, can produce therapeutic effects in these clients.

The biological theory has gained some support, but also has its critics. Therapeutic effects of equal or greater magnitude than those produced by clomipramine or similar drugs have been achieved through purely psychological treatment methods – when the serotonin level is ignored. There is no evidence that people suffering from obsessive-compulsive disorder have serotonin levels that differ from those of people suffering from other comparable psychological disorders, especially other anxiety disorders, or levels that differ from people free of any such disorder. Furthermore, there is no relationship between the amount of clomipramine absorbed and the degree of therapeutic change. Even with high doses of the drug, and hence high levels of serotonin, relatively few clients are clear of obsessive-compulsive symptoms and some clients simply do not improve. It has also been found that a client's initial response to clomipramine does not provide a good basis for predicting the longer term effects of this medication. Additionally, on present evidence, the most effective anti-obsessive drug is clomipramine, which is more effective than comparable drugs that are superior boosters of serotonin levels.

Another criticism of the biological theory is that the attempt to decide the cause of a disorder from a therapeutic effect is risky. For example, the fact that aspirin relieves a headache tells us little about the cause of the headache, and it certainly does not tell us that the headache occurred because the person was short of aspirin. The fact that clomipramine often reduces obsessive-compulsive symptoms does not mean that the disorder was caused by a shortage of clomipramine, or of the serotonin that it bolsters.

Other approaches

Some writers (e.g. Reed, 1985) have offered the view that obsessive-compulsive clients' problems are the result of a cognitive defect – that is, a deficit in their thinking or thinking style. The well-known difficulty of many obsessive-compulsive clients in making decisions is often cited as evidence of this. There are also some experimental results that show certain thinking patterns in most of these clients. However, the available evidence does not support the view that a cognitive defect or a particular cognitive style is the explanation of this disorder. While some cognitive features, such as need for certainty, perfectionism, tendency to suppress unwanted thoughts, etc. are commonly found in obsessive-compulsive clients, these features are easily accommodated within the cognitive-behavioural theory (see Rachman, 2003; Salkovskis & McGuire, 2003).

ASSESSMENT

Clinical interview

The clinical interview is the main data source in the assessment. Obsessive-compulsive clients are usually co-operative and give a good account of the difficulties as they see them. One problem is that – unlike many other groups of clients – they may talk too much and give too many details, so that the main thrust of the interview can get affected and the whole process delayed or derailed. Some tend to take a very long time giving answers because of their own doubts about what to say; others check with the interviewer repeatedly about previous answers, to make sure they did not give wrong details. In trying to maintain a structure and keep to an agenda in the interview, it may be helpful to enlist the client's help in managing the time in the meeting, bringing the client's attention to the agenda to be covered and the limited time available. Alternatively, the assessor may respond to the client's need to tell his or her story more slowly and carefully, and conduct the assessment over a number of interview appointments. Additional details may be discouraged when clearly irrelevant, at least in the initial interview. Detailed discussions of interviewing obsessive-compulsive clients are found in, among others, Turner and Beidel (1988).

Areas of enquiry during interview

The interview should aim to get information about what the main problems are, when and where they occur, how they affect the client's life and work, how the client's family is affected and, of course, the history. The sequence of events suggested in Table 13.2 would be a useful basis on which to make specific enquiries about the phenomena themselves, with regard to each problem area. For obsessions, it is important to ask why the client is worried about their occurrence. What does the client think it signifies? Does the client attempt to dismiss or suppress the obsession? For compulsive behaviour, the time taken for the rituals and the number of times they are repeated must be enquired about. The degree of disability has to be assessed in different areas of life, such as work, leisure, family and sex. The role of anxiety/discomfort is an important aspect that will have bearing on therapy. What brings on anxiety/discomfort? What compulsive activity brings it down? What is the client's appraisal of the problem behaviour? Does the client believe that unless the compulsion is carried out some unpleasant consequences will occur? Does the client feel a special responsibility to avoid such harm/disaster by personally carrying out the ritual? Are there other ways in which the client can reduce anxiety, such as asking for reassurance from a family member or getting someone else to do some of the checking? The nature and extent of avoidance needs to be gone into fully, as does the presence or absence of identifiable triggers. An assessment of mood, if necessary using a depression scale, should be undertaken. The impact of mood on the obsessions/compulsions, and vice versa, should also be examined.

The stimuli/situations that cause problems or are avoided have to be explored in detail. A list of such situations may be constructed, graded in terms of how much discomfort they arouse as estimated by the client. This is broadly similar to a fear hierarchy used with phobic clients in desensitization (Wolpe, 1958, 1991) – that is, it will include diverse situations that have a basic discomfort-arousing quality (for example, contamination) in common. The clients' urge to engage in a compulsive behaviour may also be rated for each situation. The client's ratings of discomfort and compulsive urge are best done on a simple numerical scale, for example from 0 to 100 (see below).

An example of a hierarchy of problem situations is given in Table 13.3.

Key informants

An interview with a key person in the client's life, usually parent or spouse, will help in getting a valuable complementary account of the problems. The time taken by rituals, the number of times a ritual is performed per day, the specific situations and the stimuli that provoke problem behaviours, the extent of avoidance and of reassurance-seeking, and the degree to which the immediate family has been drawn into, and are affected by, the client's obsessive-compulsive problems can usually be elucidated by such an informant.

Diagnostic interviews

Two widely used diagnostic interviews can help in the assessment. One is the Standard Clinical Interview for DSM, Axis I (SCID-I; First et al., 1995). This is intended to be administered by trained clinicians. The second is the Anxiety Disorders Interview Schedule (ADIS; Di Nardo et al., 1994). This provides an assessment of anxiety disorders, common comorbid conditions and those disorders that are commonly assessed to screen participants for research trials. This is also designed to be used by trained clinicians.

Table 13.3 An example of a hierarchy of problem situations of an obsessive-compulsive client

Items	*Discomfort 0–100*	*Compulsive urge*[1] *0–100*
Using a public toilet	100	100
Touching the inside of the kitchen waste bin	95	90
Touching the outside of the kitchen waste bin	70	75
Touching papers/documents handled by others	–	–
Shaking hands with a stranger	65	55
Using a public telephone	60	50
Touching door handles in a busy office	55	45
Bumping into a stranger	55	50
Touching money given by a cashier in a supermarket	50	35

[1] The strength of the urge to engage in strenuous hand-washing after the activity concerned.

Daily records/diaries

A fairly simple assessment technique is to ask the client to keep a daily diary of relevant cognitions and behaviours, with details of time, circumstances, and so on. This is particularly valuable as a source of baseline data. Many obsessive-compulsive clients keep meticulous and detailed diaries when asked to. To avoid being given hundreds of pages, the clinician may supply a structured format, concentrating on a few relevant headings. An example of a daily record sheet used for this purpose is given in Figure 13.1.

Date:______ Target[1]: ____

Time	Frequency[2]	Highest discomfort[3]	Highest compulsive urge[4]	Details and comments[5]
Before 7 a.m.				
7–10 a.m.				
10 a.m.– 1 p.m.				
1–4 p.m.				
4–7 p.m.				
7–10 p.m.				
After 10 p.m.				

Figure 13.1 An example of a daily record sheet.

[1] The particular obsession or compulsion to be monitored.
[2] How many times it happened in each time period.
[3,4] Rated on a 0–100 scale; give the highest felt during the time period.
[5] Details of what happened: when, where, what was the trigger, how long taken, number of repetitions, and so on, of the *worst* episode.

Questionnaires, inventories and rating scales

Several instruments are available for assessment of obsessive-compulsive clients. These are not intended to be substitutes for clinical assessment. They supplement interview assessment and also provide quantified scores.

Compulsive Activity Checklist

This instrument is used both for self-rating by the client and for rating by the therapist (Marks et al., 1977). It consists of thirty-eight specific activities (for example, having a bath or shower, touching door handles). Each activity is rated on a four-point scale of severity. A total score is obtained by adding the individual score items. What is more important, however, is the identification of the activities that cause real difficulty for the client. A shorter version of this instrument has also been reported (Steketee & Freund, 1993).

Maudsley Obsessional-Compulsive Inventory

The Maudsley Obsessional-Compulsive Inventory (MOCI) is easy and quick to administer, being made up of thirty items with 'true'/'false' answers (Hodgson & Rachman, 1977; Rachman & Hodgson, 1980). In addition to a global score, it gives four subscores: checking, washing/cleaning, slowness/repetitiveness and doubting/conscientiousness. Unfortunately, the inventory has only two items covering thoughts (obsessions) and it assesses extent of the problem, as opposed to degree of disability or severity of the problem. However, it does differentiate between obsessive-compulsive clients and those with other anxiety disorders. On the whole, the MOCI is a useful and easy-to-use instrument, and can be easily included in the routine assessment procedure. It is particularly useful for monitoring change with therapy. A revised version of this instrument is currently being developed.

Padua Inventory

The Padua Inventory was developed in Italy (Sanvio, 1988). It consists of sixty items, using five-point ratings, and is designed to evaluate a range of clinical obsessions and compulsions. It has four subscales: contamination, checking, impaired control of mental activities, and urges and worries over losing control of motor behaviour. Completion time is about thirty minutes. It may be used to determine the severity of obsessive-compulsive disorder and to monitor response to treatment.

Obsessive-Compulsive Inventory

This was developed by Foa and colleagues (Foa, Kozak, Salkovskis, Coles & Amir, 1998), and consists of forty-two items. It contains seven subscales: washing, checking, doubting, ordering, obsessing, hoarding and mental neutralizing. For each item, four-point rating scales (0–4) are used for frequency and for distress.

Yale-Brown Obsessive-Compulsive Scale

The Yale-Brown Obsessive-Compulsive Scale (Y-BOCS) is a comprehensive interview instrument that is widely used in the United States (Goodman et al., 1989a; Goodman et al., 1989b). It allows the clinician to estimate the severity of the disorder, particularly the extent to which the disorder affects the person's life. Completion time is about thirty minutes. It is useful as a screening instrument for obsessive-compulsive disorder and as an instrument to monitor progress in treatment. Self-report versions, both paper-and-pencil (Steketee, Front & Bogart, 1996) and computerized (Rosenfeld et al., 1992), take about fifteen minutes to complete.

Behavioural tests

Behavioural tests are perhaps the most useful and most direct assessment method available. Simple behavioural tests can be carried out in a clinical interview setting; for example, asking clients to touch a 'contaminating' object, observing the reaction and degree of avoidance, and getting a self-rated measure of discomfort and of urge to wash (see below). This should be done for selected target problems – usually ones that cause the greatest difficulty to the client. More structured and better planned behavioural tests will attempt to sample the relevant problems more fully. Such a planned assessment will ideally include systematic manipulation of several variables, including presence or absence of trigger, different triggers, permission to engage in compulsive behaviour, presence and absence of family, and so on.

Behavioural tests carried out in the home environment by the client can also be used and provide valuable information.

Naturalistic observation

Observation of the client in the natural environment can throw valuable light on the nature of the problems but this is usually difficult in practice. However, if there are problems in specific situations (such as excessive checking at work, avoidance of any contact with people in public transport), direct observation by the clinician in the target situations should be seriously considered. More usually, the client and the key informants are relied on to supply details of what happens in such situations.

Numerical self-ratings

In behavioural tests, as indeed in interview assessment and diary-keeping, the client should be asked to give his or her subjective reactions (de Silva & Rachman, 2004; Rachman & Hodgson, 1980). A 0–100 scale, similar to a 'fear thermometer', is relatively easy to use for these purposes. Clients will rate their discomfort (a more neutral term than 'anxiety') and – where relevant – the strength of the urge to engage in a compulsive behaviour. These simple self-rating measures are easy for clients to learn and use, and add a useful dimension to self-reports. The discomfort ratings are particularly useful in preparing hierarchies of difficult situations.

Case study: Gill

To return now to the case study given at the beginning of this chapter, Gill was assessed by the clinician in two sessions. She clearly satisfied the diagnostic criteria for obsessive-compulsive disorder, with mild dysphoria but no significant depression. On the MOCI she scored 20, with a subscale score of 10 for washing/cleaning. This was her major problem, and it had begun to affect her functioning at home and at work. Her partner was also interviewed, with Gill's agreement, and he confirmed her difficulties. In exploring Gill's cognitions, it became clear that she had an exaggerated idea that dirt and germs were present almost everywhere, especially on things other people had touched. She believed that she needed to get rid of the dirt and the germs. If she did not, she feared she would remain in a state of discomfort and distress, unable to relax. She also had the idea that she might catch an illness of some sort as a result of the dirt/germs. This was, however, only a vague belief.

Gill and the clinician were able to construct a hierarchy of problem situations. This was done on the basis of the discomfort ratings she gave for these (see Table 13.3).

It was also established at interview that Gill was motivated to get over her problems and to be able to live normally again. Her partner, John, was keen to help her get over the problems.

TREATMENT

This section discusses the treatment of obsessive-compulsive disorder. The focus will be on cognitive-behavioural treatment for those with overt compulsive behaviours, as in the case study. Brief comments will be made on other applications at the end of the chapter.

The main elements of cognitive-behavioural therapy for these clients are exposure and response prevention. This is usually accompanied with cognitive elements, thus earning the description cognitive-behavioural therapy. The early successful behavioural treatment relied largely on exposure and response prevention (e.g. Meyer, 1966; Rachman & Hodgson, 1980) and the outcome literature on this is impressive (see Foa et al., 1998; Kyrios, 2003). The addition of the cognitive elements has led to further development and refinement (Marks, 2003).

Elements of therapy: Behavioural aspects

Exposure refers to exposing the client to stimuli or situations that provoke the compulsive urge. Thus, someone whose rituals are based on the belief that he or she will be contaminated by coming into contact with dustbins and kitchen floors will be asked to touch these objects repeatedly and thoroughly. This may seem to be an exaggerated act but it is useful in that it provokes the compulsion, usually via a strong feeling of discomfort.

Response prevention requires clients to refrain from engaging in their usual compulsive behaviour. After touching the dustbin, for example, a client may wish immediately to decontaminate him- or herself by washing but is asked to refrain from this – usually for several hours.

In addition to exposure and response prevention, modelling is sometimes included in the treatment programme. This involves the therapist demonstrating to the client how to engage in exposure. It has the effect of encouraging and persuading the client to engage in exposure, which he may initially be reluctant to undertake.

Rationale

The rationale for this standard treatment package comes from both animal studies and clinical/experimental investigations. The blocking of avoidance responses has been shown to lead to the reduction of these responses in animal studies (e.g. Baum, 1970). Similarly, early studies by Maier and Klee (1945) and Maier (1949) have shown how manually guiding rats towards a previously avoided situation was successful in eliminating established stereotyped responses. Meyer's pioneering use of this form of therapy was based on the assumption that prolonged prevention of the ritual would lead to changes in the client's expectancies and thus in the strength of the urge to ritualize (Meyer, 1966). A series of studies carried out at the Maudsley Hospital has shown that:

- Typically, an obsessive-compulsive client with rituals experiences discomfort and a strong urge to ritualize when provoked by exposure to the trigger stimulus or situation.

- When the client engages in the compulsive behaviour, such as hand-washing, the discomfort and the compulsive urge both diminish.
- When the discomfort and the urge to engage in the compulsive behaviour are provoked but the client refrains from carrying out the response, the urge and the discomfort still dissipate, but much more slowly.

This spontaneous decay of the compulsive urges and associated discomfort may be regarded as the main cornerstone of response prevention therapy (de Silva et al., 2003; Rachman et al., 1976). With repeated sessions, there is a cumulative effect leading to progressively less discomfort and urge to engage in compulsive behaviour and, more markedly, progressively quicker dissipation of these (Likierman & Rachman, 1980).

Implementation of therapy

To carry out this treatment package, the therapist has to get a clear idea as to what stimuli or cues trigger the compulsions. A comprehensive assessment will elicit this information. A hierarchy of these stimuli/situations will need to be prepared (see Table 13.2). Therapy begins with a clear explanation of the rationale of therapy and a statement of the requirements to be fulfilled by the client. The difficulty the client may experience in complying should be acknowledged, but he or she should be supportively persuaded to go through with the therapy. The treatment is never imposed on an unwilling client.

Explaining the rationale

How should the rationale of therapy be explained? The relationship between discomfort arising from the stimuli in question and the compulsion should be explained, using examples from the client's own account, such as:

> As you have noticed yourself, when you touch money you feel you have become contaminated. So you feel quite anxious and – naturally – you feel a strong need to wash your hands, which you then do. This clearly helps you at the time, but it also strengthens the link between touching money and washing, doesn't it? Washing makes you feel relieved and so you want to wash every time you touch money.

How the therapy aims to break this relationship is then explained:

> The treatment programme is intended to break this relationship, and for this we would want you to touch money and other worrying things but not wash, perhaps for several hours. You will, of course, feel quite dirty and quite anxious, but after some time you will begin to feel better. It is

important that we do it this way, for within a few days you will be able to break the link between money and washing. We'll help you with this as much as we can. I shall touch the money with you, and I shall stay without washing my hands, just as you will.

Graded or rapid exposure?

There is no need, as in systemic desensitization, to work gradually from the least to the most anxiety-arousing situation in a series of graded steps. It is expedient to concentrate on situations/items that are high on the list and to go for lower items only as part of generalization training. However, it may be necessary to begin working at a somewhat lower level in the hierarchy if the client is unable to co-operate with a programme that commences with a very high-anxiety situation. In practice, the best strategy is to start at the highest level the client is willing to try.

Issues in exposure

The exposure can lead to practical difficulties. The client may touch only a 'safe corner' of the contaminating stimulus, or touch it with only the back of the hand. A client who is required to carry a contaminating item might carry it wrapped in several handkerchiefs, which makes the item, to the client, not so bad. Efforts must be made to ensure that there is full and clear exposure; use of exaggerated exposure, such as thoroughly touching inside and outside a dustbin, rubbing the hands hard on the floor several times, rubbing the now contaminated hands on one's face, hair or clothes, usually guarantees effective exposure. The use of modelling is valuable here. The point is that the exposure exercise should lead to a substantial degree of discomfort and a substantially high urge to engage in the compulsion. Clearly it has to be more than nominal.

The practice of exposure too can be diverse. It can be a time-limited exposure to a situation (for example, getting a client to touch an animal he or she considers contaminating) or it can be continuous (getting the client to carry a small packet of dog hair in his or her pocket all the time). It is possible to expose the client to several stimuli at the same time, together or in close succession. In an intensive programme for a client with a disabling range of difficult stimuli, such a multiple-exposure programme may be desirable.

Issues in response prevention

The most important aspect of this package, in terms of practical issues, is response prevention. On the one hand, this may require direct and close supervision of the client for two to three hours – even twenty-four hours in some programmes (e.g. Sturgis & Meyer, 1981). On the other hand, a well-motivated client with a clear commitment to therapy can be expected to co-operate fully so that such supervisory measures may not always be necessary (Emmelkamp, 1982). It is important to discuss with the client the difficulties that this phase of therapy brings. For example, the client may carry out an unnoticeable, abbreviated ritual to bring down discomfort, or may happily survive even a relatively long response prevention period with the internal resolve that he or she will, at the end of it, carry out the necessary ritual. These expedients are not unusual and the therapist needs to discuss them, and how they can be controlled, with the client (de Silva & Rachman, 2004).

It is necessary to make clear that while in some programmes the response prevention is specific and time-limited, for example the client is exposed to a contaminating object and then not allowed to clean or wash for a limited period of two hours or so, in others it is general and relatively unlimited, for example, the client is prevented from engaging in any of his target behaviours for the whole duration of the intensive treatment period. Foa and Tillmanns (1980) describe a programme where washing of any sort is banned, except for a quick supervised shower followed by recontamination, in the initial phase of therapy. The latter seems to be the more desirable in general, but would require a great deal of motivation from the client and/or facilities for full supervision. In practice, the important factor is to ensure that the target response doe not occur for a period long enough to bring down the urge to engage in the behaviour and the associated discomfort (Rachman et al., 1976; Sturgis & Meyer, 1981). Hence it is important to monitor the strength of the urge carefully.

Elements of therapy: Cognitive aspects

The cognitive-behavioural approach includes cognitive elements as well as behavioural ones. The cognitions of the client that may contribute to the problem behaviour are explored and, where necessary, re-structured. Many clients have inflated risk appraisals – that is, they believe that there is a greater risk (of danger, harm, things going wrong, etc.) than the situation warrants. The therapy needs to include steps to modify these, by, for example, working on probability estimates. With those whose problems include compulsive checking as a major feature, an inflated sense of responsibility tends to be a significant factor, and will need focused cognitive work. The modification of cognitions may require behavioural experiments, and indeed exposure and response prevention tasks can be construed as elaborate experiments.

The use of cognitive work with those who have overt compulsive rituals are discussed in Salkovskis (1999) and Salkovskis and McGuire (2003). Marks (2003) has provided a good overview.

Cognitive work has a particular role to play in the treatment of clients who have distressing obsessions as their main problem. Some of them also have internal neutralizing rituals. The cognitive therapy for these include educating the client that attempts to suppress or dismiss an obsessional cognition only serve to increase the chances of its recurrence. Thought suppression experiments may be carried out to demonstrate this. The client's appraisal of the thought as signifying something negative about himself ('I am an awful person, otherwise why would I get these thoughts of violence'), is also explored and modified. There is much new work in this field and promising results have been reported by, among others, Freeston, Rheaume and Ladouceur (1996) and Rachman (2003). A review of some of this work is provided by de Silva (2003).

It must be noted that early treatment techniques for obsessional thoughts, such as thought-stopping (Wolpe, 1958) and satiation/habituation training (Rachman, 1976), have not been shown to be particularly effective and are seldom used now.

Clinician's role

After the assessment, the clinician draws up the treatment programme in collaboration with the client, and will usually carry out the first few therapy sessions. However, the client is asked to carry out additional exposure and response prevention sessions at home. For this, the involvement of a family member as a co-therapist is desirable. The clinician will continue to play a role, doing cognitive work as necessary and reviewing progress, discussing difficulties and suggesting changes, but the actual exposure and response prevention tasks are carried out by the client, with a co-therapist as necessary.

Case example: Gill

Much of Gill's treatment was behavioural, although in therapy sessions some cognitions that were relevant to the compulsions were explored and she was encouraged to modify them. The exposure and response prevention was carried out initially in the clinic setting, with response prevention periods of two and half hours. Much extra work was undertaken by Gill at home, with the help and encouragement of her partner. The targets were chosen from a hierarchy of situations she had constructed with the clinician (Table 13.3). In homework sessions, Gill kept a record of each task undertaken, using a record sheet provided for this purpose (see Figure 13.2).

Gill made rapid progress and was able, within three weeks, to refrain from compulsive washing in most situations. She was seen three and six months later for follow-up, and she had maintained her gains. Gill and her partner had, by then, also decided to start a family, as she no longer felt that dirt and germs would be a problem in looking after a baby.

Date: _______ Target[1]: ______________________________

Task[2]	
Time	
Any help[3]	
Discomfort felt[4]	
Urge to ritualize[5]	
Outcome[6]	

Figure 13.2 Record sheet for treatment session.

[1] The particular compulsion treated.
[2] Specific tasks undertaken.
[3] Was a co-therapist involved? Who?
[4,5] Rated on a 0–100 scale.
[6] Details of what happened.

Group approaches

The individual treatment approach described in this chapter is the most widely used and is the best established, in terms of evidence, for these problems. There are also reports of the use of group approaches, but the evidence for these is still limited (e.g. Krone, Hilme & Nesse, 1991; van Oppen, Steketee, McCorkle & Pato, 1997). In busy clinical settings, a group approach may be considered as an economical alternative to individual therapy.

The marital system and obsessive-compulsive disorder

In many cases, partners and other family members of people with obsessive-compulsive disorder accommodate to their symptoms and this both maintains the symptoms of obsessive-compulsive disorder and reduces the quality of marital and family relationships. In turn, this may lead to stress that exacerbates the symptoms of obsessive-compulsive disorder (Steketee, 1997).

For example, non-anxious partners may engage in cleaning or checking rituals or provide frequent reassurance to attempt to alleviate their partner's anxiety and, when their efforts do not yield long-term anxiety-reducing benefits for their partner, they may develop a conflictual, hostile or distant relationship with the partner. This observation has, in part, provided a rational for spouse-assisted exposure and response prevention (ERP), and other systemically based treatment programmes for obsessive-compulsive disorder (Baucom, Stanton & Epstein, 2003; Craske & Zoellner,1995). With spouse-assisted ERP, the patient and spouse are engaged in conjoint psycho-education about obsessive-compulsive disorder and given the rationale for ERP. The non-anxious partner is directed to stop accommodating to the anxious partner's need to check, clean, provide reassurance or engage in other rituals related to obsessive-compulsive disorder. He or she is also directed to avoid becoming involved in arguments about the illogical nature of the partner's obsessional beliefs. Couples jointly attend ERP sessions and, afterwards, jointly complete ERP homework assignments. In these assignments the non-anxious partner supports and reinforces the anxious partner to expose him- or herself to anxiety-provoking stimuli and to prevent reducing anxiety by engaging in compulsive rituals. Couples in which one partner has obsessive-compulsive disorder that has gone untreated for some time may require marital therapy, as described in Chapter 5, to help revitalize the quality of their relationship once the obsessive-compulsive disorder symptoms begin to abate.

Biological approaches

The role of medication needs to be noted briefly. In recent years, many psychiatrists have reported the use of antidepressants, especially clomipramine and drugs of the selective serotonin reuptake inhibitor (SSRI) type, such as fluoxetine, fluvoxamine and paroxetine, for clients with obsessive-compulsive disorder. Some clients do respond to these medications but there is the problem of relapse when the drug is withdrawn. Sometimes combined therapy including medication and cognitive-behavioural treatment is used, especially when the client also has significant depression. Starting with medication may also be considered for clients who find it difficult to accept a cognitive-behavioural treatment programme. In the use of drugs, a small dose is used at the start, building up to an effective dosage.

The literature on the pharmacotherapy for obsessive-compulsive disorder is already quite large, and is growing. There are several good reviews of this field, including McDonough (2003) and Simos (2002).

Another biological treatment for this disorder that was used fairly widely many decades ago is neurosurgery. Refined neurosurgical techniques are sometimes used, but this approach is limited to those with intractable obsessive-compulsive disorder. This is to be seen as an intervention of last resort and, even in this limited usage, caution is needed. A review of this area is available in Jenike (2000).

SUMMARY

Obsessive-compulsive disorder is a relatively common anxiety disorder, with distinctive features. Much progress has been made in the clinical management of this disorder in recent decades. Effective psychological treatment is now available for clients with obsessive-compulsive disorder. The cognitive-behavioural approach has a good evidence base and is clearly the treatment of choice. A careful and detailed assessment is needed before a treatment package is planned. A collaborative approach, where the client takes an active role in the planning of implementation of therapy, is recommended. In some cases pharmacological treatment is useful, but the long-term efficacy of this approach is still open to dispute. Within the cognitive-behavioural approach, there have been valuable and promising new developments in the last few years, especially with regard to the cognitive aspects of therapy. The next decade or so likely to produce further developments along these lines.

EXERCISE 13.1

Allocate the roles of Gill, the therapist and observer. Role-play the assessment interview of Gill, as given in the case study:

1 To establish the nature and extent of the problem.
2 To explore Gill's cognitions that are relevant to her washing/cleaning compulsions.

Role-play a session with Gill to explain the rationale for the exposure and response prevention treatment.

EXERCISE 13.2

In small groups of about five people:

1 Discuss the treatment of clients who present with obsessions, with no overt compulsions; generate ideas on treatment options, based on the literature.
2 Discuss the role of medication.

FURTHER READING FOR CLIENTS

de Silva, P. & Rachman, S. (2004). *Obsessive-compulsive disorder: The facts*, Third Edition. Oxford: Oxford University Press.

Foa, E. B. & Wilson, R. (1991). *S. T. O. P obsessing! How to overcome your obsessions and compulsions*. New York: Bantam Books.

Hill, F. (2000). *Understanding obsessive-compulsive disorder*. London: Mind.

Steketee, G. & White, K. (1991). *When once is not enough: Help for obsessive-compulsives*. Oakland, CA: New Harbinger Publications.

Toates, F. & Coschug-Toates, O. (2002). *Obsessive-compulsive disorder*, Second Edition. London: Class Publishing.

FURTHER READING FOR PRACTITIONERS

Jakes, I. (1996). *Theoretical approaches to obsessive-compulsive disorder*. Cambridge: Cambridge University Press.

Menzies, R. G. & de Silva, P. (Eds) (2003). *Obsessive-compulsive disorder: Theory, research and treatment*. Chichester, UK: Wiley.

Rachman, S. (2003). *The treatment of obsessions*. Oxford: Oxford University Press.

Swinson, R. P., Antony, M. M., Rachman, S. & Richter, M. A. (1998). *Obsessive-compulsive disorder: Theory, research, and treatment*. New York: Guilford Press.

ASSESSMENT INSTRUMENTS

Di Nardo, P. A., Brown, T. A. & Barlow, D. H. (1994). *Anxiety Disorders Interview Schedule for DSM IV*. Albany, NY: Graywind.

First, M. B., Spitzer, R. L., Gibbon, M. & Williams, J. B. W. (1995). *Structured Clinical Interview for DSM IV Axis I Disorders* (SCID-1/D, version 20). New York: Biometrics Research Department, New York Psychiatric Institute.

Foa, E. B., Kozak, M. J., Salkovskis, P. M., Coles, M. E. & Amir, N. (1998). The validation of a new obsessive-compulsive disorder scale: the Obsessive-Compulsive Inventory. *Psychological Assessment*, 10, 206–214.

Goodman, W. K., Price, L. H., Rasmussen, S. A., Mazure, D. D., Delgado, L., Heninger, G. R. & Charney, D. S. (1989). The Yale–Brown Obsessive-Compulsive Scale: Part II, Validity. *Archives of General Psychiatry*, 46, 1012–1016.

Goodman, W. K., Price, L. H., Rasmussen, S. A., Mazure, D., Fleischmann, R. L., Hill, C. L., Heninger, G. R. & Charney, D. S. (1989). The Yale-Brown Obsessive-Compulsive Scale: Part I, Development, use and reliability. *Archives of General Psychiatry*, 46, 1006–1011.

Hodgson, R. J. & Rachman, S. (1977). Obsessional compulsive complaints. *Behaviour Research and Therapy*, 15, 389–395.

Marks, I. M., Hallam, R. S., Connolly, J. & Philpott, R. (1977). *Nursing in behavioural psychotherapy*. London: Royal College of Nursing.

Sanavio, E. (1988). Obsessions and compulsions: The Padua Inventory. *Behaviour Research and Therapy*, 26, 169–177.

Steketee, G. S. & Freund, B. (1993). Compulsive Activity Checklist (CAC): Further psychometric analyses and revision. *Behavioural Psychotherapy*, 21, 13–25.

REFERENCES

American Psychiatric Association (APA) (1994). *Diagnosis and statistical manual of mental disorders*, Fourth Edition. Washington, DC: APA.

American Psychiatric Association (APA) (2000). *Diagnostic and statistical manual of the mental disorders* (Fourth Edition-Text Revision, DSM-IV-TR). Washington, DC: APA.

Baucom, D., Stanton, S. & Epstein, N. (2003). Anxiety disorders. In D. Snyder & M. Whisman (Eds.), *Treating difficult couples: Helping clients with co-existing mental and relationship disorders* (pp. 57–87). New York: Guilford.

Baum, M. (1970). Extinction of avoidance responding through response prevention (flooding). *Psychological Bulletin*, 74, 276–284.

Beech, H. R. (1971). Ritualistic activity in obsessional patients. *Journal of Psychosomatic Research*, 15, 417–422.

Bland, R. C., Orn, H. & Newman, S. C. (1988). Lifetime prevalence of psychiatric disorders in Edmonton. *Acta Psychiatrica Scandanavia*, 77 (Suppl. 338), 24–32.

Como, P. (1995). Obsessive-compulsive disorder in Tourettes syndrome. In W. J. Wiener & A. E Lang (Eds.), *Behavioral neurology of movements disorders* (pp. 281–291). New York: Raven Press.

Craske, M. & Zoellner, L. (1995). Anxiety disorders: The role of marital therapy. In N. Jacobson & A. Gurman (Eds.), *Clinical handbook of couple therapy* (pp. 394–411). New York: Guilford.

de Silva, P. (1993). Anorexia nervosa and obsessive-compulsive disorder. *Neuropsychiatric de l' Enfance*, 41, 269–272.

de Silva, P. (2003). The phenomenology of OCD. In R. G. Menzies & P. de Silva (Eds.), *Obsessive-compulsive disorder: Theory, research and treatment* (pp. 21–36). Chichester, UK: Wiley.

de Silva, P. & Marks, M. (2001). Traumatic experiences, post-traumatic stress disorder and obsessive-compulsive disorder. *International Journal of Psychiatry*, 13, 172–180.

de Silva, P., Menzies, R. G. & Shafran, R. (2003). Spontaneous decay of compulsive urges: The case of covert compulsions. *Behaviour Research and Therapy*, 41, 129–137.

de Silva, P. & Rachman, S. (2004). *Obsessive-compulsive disorder: The facts*, Third Edition. Oxford: Oxford University Press.

Di Nardo, P., Brown, T. A. & Barlow, D. H. (1994). *Anxiety Disorders Interview Schedule for DSM-IV (ADIS-IV)*. Albany, NY: Graywind.

Emmelkamp, P. M. G. (1982). *Phobic and obsessive-compulsive disorders: Theory, research and practice*. New York: Plenum.

Enright, S. J. & Beech, A. R. (1990). Obsessional states: Anxiety disorders or schizotypes? An information processing and personality assessment. *Psychological Medicine*, 20, 621–627.

Enright, S. J. & Beech, A. R. (1997). Schizotypes and obsessive-compulsive disorder. In G. Claridge (Ed.) *Schizotypes: Implications for illness and health* (pp. 202–223). New York: Oxford University Press.

First, M. B., Spitzer, R. L., Gibbon, M. & Williams, J. B. W. (1995). *Structured Clinical Interview for DSM-IV Axis I Disorders* (SCID I/D, Version 20). New York: Biometrics Research Department, New York Psychiatric Institute.

Foa, E. B. (1979). Failure in treating obsessive-compulsives. *Behaviour and Research and Therapy*, 17, 169–176.

Foa, E. B., Franklin, M. A. & Kozak, M. J. (1998). Psychological treatment for obsessive-compulsive disorders. In R. P. Swinton, M. M. Antony, S. Rachman & M. A. Richter (Eds.) *Obsessive-compulsive disorder: Theory, research, and treatment* (pp. 258–276). New York: Guilford.

Foa, E. B., Kozak, M. J., Salkovskis, P. M, Coles, M. E. & Amir, N. (1998). The validation of a new obsessive-compulsive disorder scale: The Obsessive-Compulsive Inventory. *Psychological Assessment*, 10, 206–214.

Foa, E. B. & Tillmanns, A. (1980). The treatment of obsessive-compulsive neurosis. In A. Goldstein & E. B. Foa (Eds.) *Handbook of behavioral interventions: A clinical guide* (pp. 229–251). New York: Wiley.

Frampton, I. (2003). Neuropsychological models of OCD. In R. G. Menzies & P. de Silva (Eds.) *Obsessive-compulsive disorder: Theory, research and treatment* (pp. 39–58). Chichester, UK: Wiley.

Freeston, M., Rheaume, J. & Ladouceur, R. (1996). Correcting faulty appraisals of obsessional thoughts. *Behaviour Research and Therapy*, 34, 433–446.

Fulford K. W. M. & Gipps, R. G. T. (2004). Understanding the clinical concept of delusion: from an estranged to an engaged epistemology. *International Review of Psychiatry*, 16, 225–235.

Garety, P. A. & Hemsley, D. R. (1994). *Delusions: Investigations into the psychology of delusional reasoning*. Maudsley Monograph. Oxford: Oxford University Press.

Goodman, W. K., Price, L. H., Rasmussen, S. A., Mazure, D., Delgado, P., Heninger, G. R. & Charney, D. S. (1989a). The Yale–Brown Obsessive-Compulsive Scale: Part II, Validity. *Archives of General Psychiatry*, 46, 1012–1016.

Goodman, W. K., Price, L. H., Rasmussen, S. A., Mazure, D., Fleischmann, R. L., Hill, C. L., Heninger, G. R. & Charney, D. S. (1989b). The Yale–Brown Obsessive-Compulsive Scale: Part I, Development, use and reliability. *Archives of General Psychiatry*, 46, 1006–1011.

Hill, F. (2000). *Understanding obsessive-compulsive disorder*. London: Mind.

Hodgson, R. J. & Rachman, S. (1977). Obsessional compulsive complaints. *Behaviour Research and Therapy*, 15, 389–395.

Hollander, E. & Benzaquen, S. (1997). The obsessive-compulsive spectrum disorders. *International Review of Psychiatry*, 9, 99–110.

Jakes, I. (1996). *Theoretical approaches to obsessive-compulsive disorder*. Cambridge: Cambridge University Press.

Jenike, M. A. (2000). Neurosurgical treatment of obsessive-compulsive disorder. In W. K. Goodman, M. W. Rudorfer & J. D. Maser (Eds.) *Obsessive-compulsive disorder: Contemporary issues in treatment* (pp. 457–482). Mahwah, NJ: Lawrence Erlbaum Associates.

Karno, M., Golding, J. M., Sorenson, S. B. & Burman, M. A. (1988). The epidemiology of obsessive-compulsive disorder in five US communities. *Archives of General Psychiatry*, 45, 1094–1099.

Khanna, S. & Channabasavanna, S. M. (1988). Phenomenology of obsessions in obsessive-compulsive disorder. *Psychopathology*, 21, 12–18.

Krochmalik, A. & Menzies, R. G. (2003). The classification and diagnosis of OCD. In R. G. Menzies & P. de Silva (Eds.) *Obsessive-compulsive disorder: Theory, research and treatment* (pp. 3–20). Chichester, UK: Wiley.

Krone, K. P., Himle, J. A. & Nesse, R. M. (1991). A standardized behavioural group treatment programme for obsessive-compulsive disorder: Preliminary outcomes. *Behaviour Research and Therapy*, 29, 627–632.

Kyrios, M. (2003). Exposure and response prevention for OCD. In R. G. Menzies & P. de Silva (Eds.) *Obsessive-compulsive disorder: Theory, research and treatment* (pp. 259–274). Chichester, UK: Wiley.

Lewis, A. (1936). Problems of obsessional illness. *Proceedings of the Royal Society of Medicine*, 29, 235–336.

Likierman, H. & Rachman, S. (1980). Spontaneous decay of compulsive urges: Cumulative effects. *Behaviour Research and Therapy*, 18, 387–394.

Maier, N. R. F. (1949). *Frustration*. New York: McGraw-Hill.

Maier, N. R. F. & Klee, J. B. (1945). Studies of abnormal behaviour in the rat XVII: Guidance versus trial and error in the alteration of habits and fixations. *Journal of Psychology*, 19, 133–163.

Marks, I. M., Hallam, R. S., Connolly, J. & Philpott, R. (1977). *Nursing in behavioural psychotherapy*. London: Royal College of Nursing.

Marks, M. (2003). Cognitive therapy for OCD. In R. G. Menzies & P. de Silva (Eds.) *Obsessive-compulsive disorder: Theory, research and treatment* (pp. 275–290). Chichester, UK: Wiley.

McDonough, M (2003). Pharmacological and neurosurgical treatment of OCD. In R. G. Menzies & P. de Silva (Eds.) *Obsessive-compulsive disorder: Theory, research and treatment* (pp. 291–310). Chichester, UK: Wiley.

Meyer, V. (1966). Modification of expectations in cases with obsessional rituals. *Behaviour Research and Therapy*, 4, 273–280.

Rachman, S. (1976). The modification of obsessions: A new formulation. *Behaviour Research and Therapy*, 14, 437–443.

Rachman, S. (1997). A cognitive theory of obsessions. *Behaviour Research and Therapy*, 35, 793–803.

Rachman, S. (2003). *The treatment of obsessions*. Oxford: Oxford University Press.

Rachman, S. & de Silva, P. (1978). Normal and abnormal obsessions. *Behaviour Research and Therapy*, 16, 445–453.

Rachman, S., de Silva, P. & Roper, G. (1976). The spontaneous decay of compulsive urges. *Behaviour Research and Therapy*, 14, 445–453.

Rachman, S. & Hodgson R. J. (1980). *Obsessions and compulsions*. Englewood Cliffs, NJ: Prentice Hall.

Rasmussen, S. A. & Eisen, J. L. (1992). The epidemiology and clinical features of compulsive disorder. *Psychiatric Clinics of North America*, 15, 743–758.

Rasmussen, S. A. & Tsuang, M. (1986). Clinical characteristics and family history in DSM III obsessive-compulsive disorder. *American Journal of Psychiatry*, 143, 317–322.

Reed, G. (1985). *Obsessional experience and compulsive behaviour: A cognitive-structural approach*. London: Academic Press.

Rosenfeld, R., Dar, R., Anderson, D. et al. (1992). A computer-administered version of the Yale–Brown Obsessive Compulsive Scale. *Psychological Assessment, 4*, 329–332.

Salkovskis, P. M. (1999). Understanding and treating obsessive-compulsive disorder. *Behaviour Research and Therapy*, 37, 529–552.

Salkovskis, P. M. & Harrison, J. (1984). Abnormal and normal obsessions: A replication. *Behaviour Research and Therapy*, 22, 549–552.

Salkovskis, P. M. & McGuire, J. (2003). Cognitive-behavioural therapy of OCD. In R. G. Menzies & P. de Silva (Eds.), *Obsessive-compulsive disorder: Theory, research and treatment* (pp. 59–78). Chichester, UK: Wiley.

Sanavio, E. (1988). Obsessions and compulsions: The Padua Inventory. *Behaviour Research and Therapy*, 26, 169–177.

Shafran, R. (2002). Eating disorders and obsessive-compulsive disorder. In R. O. Frost & G. Steketee (Eds.), *Cognitive approaches to obsessions and compulsions: Theory, assessment and treatment* (pp. 215–231). Amsterdam: Pergamon.

Simos, G. (2002). Medication effects on obsessions and compulsions. In R.O. Frost & G. Steketee (Eds.), *Cognitive approaches to obsessions and compulsions: Theory, assessment and treatment* (pp. 435–453). Amsterdam: Pergamon.

Steingard, R. & Dillon-Stout, D. (1992). Tourette syndrome and obsessive-compulsive disorder: Clinical aspects. *Psychiatric Clinics of North America*, 15, 849–860.

Steketee, G. (1997). Disability and family burden in obsessive-compulsive disorder. *Canadian Journal of Psychiatry*, 42, 919–928.

Steketee, G. & Freund, K. (1993). Compulsion Activity Checklist (CAC): Further psychometric analyses and revision. *Behavioural Psychotherapy*, 21, 13–25.

Steketee, G., Front, R. & Bogart, K. (1996). The Yale–Brown Obsessive Compulsive Scale: interview vs. self-report. *Behaviour Research and Therapy, 34*, 675–685.

Steketee, G. & White, K. (1991). *When once is not enough: Help for obsessive-compulsives*. Oakland, CA: New Harbinger.

Stern, R. & Cobb, J. (1978). Phenomenology of obsessive-compulsive neurosis. *British Journal of Psychiatry*, 132, 233–239.

Sturgis, E. T. & Meyer, V. (1981). Obsessive-compulsive disorders. In S. M. Turner, R. S. Calhoun & H. E. Adams (Eds.), *Handbook of clinical behavior therapy*. New York: Wiley.

Tallis, F. (1995). *Obsessive-compulsive disorder: A cognitive and neuropsychological perspective*. Chichester, UK: Wiley.

Toates, F. & Coschug-Toates, O. (2002). *Obsessive-compulsive disorder*, Second Edition, London: Class Publishing.

Turner, S. M. & Beidel, D. C. (1988). *Treating obsessive-compulsive disorder*. New York: Pergamon.

van Oppen, P., Steketee, G., McCorkle, B. H. & Pato, M. (1997). Group and multi-family behavioural treatment for obsessive-compulsive disorder: A pilot study. *Journal of Anxiety Disorders*, 11, 431–446.

Veale, D. (2002). Over-valued ideas: A conceptual analysis. *Behaviour Research and Therapy*, 40, 383–400.

Veale, D. (2003). The obsessive-compulsive spectrum and body dysmorphic disorder.

In R. G. Menzies & P. de Silva (Eds.), *Obsessive-compulsive disorder: Theory, research and treatment* (pp. 221–238). Chichester, UK: Wiley.

Weissman, M. M., Bland, R. C., Canino, G. J. et al. (1994). The cross national epidemiology of obsessive-compulsive disorder. *Journal of Clinical Psychiatry*, 55 (Suppl. 3), 5–10.

Wolpe, J. (1958) *Psychotherapy by reciprocal inhibition*. Stanford, CA: Stanford University Press.

Wolpe, J. R. (1991). *The practice of behavior therapy*, Fourth Edition. New York: Pergamon.

World Health Organization (WHO) (1992). *The ICD-10 classification of mental and behavioural disorders. Clinical descriptions and diagnostic guidelines*. Geneva: WHO. Available at: http://www.informatik.fh-luebeck.de/icd/welcome.html

Zohar, J. & Insel, T. R. (1987). Obsessive-compulsive disorder: Psychological approaches to diagnosis, treatment and psychopathology. *Biological Psychiatry*, 22, 667–787.

Chapter 14

Post-traumatic stress disorder

Mark Creamer and Jessica Carty

CASE EXAMPLE

Matt, who was twenty-eight years old and married with two children, presented for treatment twelve months post-trauma. He had previously resisted treatment but agreed to seek help after punching a wall during an argument with his wife.

History of presenting complaint: Following an argument in a bar, Matt was attacked by three men while walking alone in a nearby street. They punched and kicked him repeatedly about his head and body. One of the men pulled a knife and threatened to kill him before leaving him lying in the street. Matt feared for his life throughout the incident, stating that he believed he was going to die and that he would never see his wife or children again. He was not intoxicated at the time of the attack, having consumed only a single drink. He reported symptoms of extreme fear and high arousal (heart racing, sweating) during the incident. Sometime later a passing motorist saw him and called an ambulance.

Matt remained overnight in the hospital but did not sustain any permanent injuries from the attack. On his return home, he became fearful of leaving the house and did not go outside for over a week. During this time, he was required to repeat the story for police statements. Each retelling was accompanied by high physiological arousal and intense feelings of fear and anger. Since then, he has refused to discuss the incident or his reactions with anyone (including his wife). He is a builder and was off work for several weeks as a result of his injuries. Since returning to work, his performance has been patchy; he is often late, takes longer to complete tasks and feels that he is generally 'not coping' with work. He reports that his social life is now virtually non-existent and he has given up many activities (including playing soccer and coaching a basketball team) that were previously important to him. He noted that he is constantly irritable with others.

Mental state: Matt presented as a casually dressed man of average intelligence who initially appeared defensive and tense. His responses were brief and contained little personal information. During the interview he became more relaxed and eventually spoke openly about his history and current problems. His affect varied from flat to angry, raising his voice when talking about the effect the incident had had on his life. He showed little insight and was unable to understand why he had not recovered from the event, seeing it as a sign of weakness. Equally, he was highly motivated to work on his problems saying that he would 'do anything' to get back to the way he was prior to the assault.

During the interview, Matt reported several symptoms typical of post-traumatic stress disorder (PTSD). He was troubled by vivid intrusive images, notably faces of the men and the knife, and occasional nightmares (although these had reduced in frequency). He was easily distressed and angered by similar incidents reported in the media, and was upset by memories of his inability to defend himself during the attack. He avoided talking about the incident, tried to block thoughts from his mind and had significantly changed his lifestyle to avoid potential reminders. Previously very sociable, he had become withdrawn and avoided social activities, saying that they no longer held any enjoyment for him. He complained of feeling tense and agitated, reporting that he would 'explode' in response to minor frustrations. His sleep had become very disturbed, dropping from seven to eight hours per night before the incident to four to five hours. He complained of problems with memory and decision making, and stated that he was unable to concentrate sufficiently to read books or focus on television programmes. He talked of being hypervigilant and 'jumpy' when away from home, particularly when out at night (which he tried to avoid if at all possible). His alcohol consumption had increased significantly to regular consumption of five or six standard drinks each evening. The course of symptoms over the previous twelve months had been relatively stable, with a slight reduction in intrusive symptoms accompanied by an increase in avoidance and general arousal.

A brief interview with Matt's partner confirmed the above story. She emphasized his short temper, social withdrawal and emotional numbing. In particular, she was worried about his anger.

History: There was no evidence of significant prior psychiatric or medical history. The oldest of three children, Matt's childhood was relatively stable and he always had several friends. He described his mother as a friendly, quiet women. His father drank fairly heavily and would often become verbally aggressive, although not physically violent. He reported that his family did not discuss problems but just 'got on with things'. He left school at fifteen to pursue a building apprenticeship. He had worked successfully as a builder for thirteen years, a position he had enjoyed prior to the trauma. He had been married five years ago and he and his wife have two children (aged two and four).

Premorbid personality: Matt described himself as being a happy and sociable person prior to the trauma. He had always been confident in his own ability, particularly in areas requiring physical strength and stamina. Not particularly psychologically minded, his habitual style of coping with stress appeared to be one of avoidance and denial.

Formulation: Matt meets criteria for a diagnosis of chronic PTSD, with evidence of a traumatic experience, several re-experiencing symptoms, widespread avoidance and numbing, and persistent hyperarousal. The anger and substance use are complicating features and both are probably impeding the recovery process. Despite an absence of prior trauma history or psychiatric problems, there appears to be a history of familial substance abuse (his father) and a habitual pattern of coping with stress by avoidance and denial. Although these strategies have worked well in the past, they have prevented Matt from integrating this experience and moving on. The traumatic memories remain unchanged and continue to invade consciousness, causing frequent distress. His attempts to deal with the memories by increased avoidance, denial and emotional numbing have resulted in social and occupational problems.

Course of treatment: All sessions were audiotaped and Matt was asked to listen to the tape at least once between sessions. Treatment comprised one 50-minute session per week for nine weeks, followed by three follow-up sessions at fortnightly and then monthly intervals.

Initial sessions were devoted to developing rapport, establishing the credibility of the therapist, discussing what treatment would involve and attempting to allay Matt's concerns about the process. Psychoeducation about PTSD, including the rationale for treatment, was conducted and reinforced using prepared handouts. Several symptom management strategies were introduced over the initial sessions, with a focus on regular aerobic exercise, breathing control techniques, some simple self-statements and scheduling pleasant activities. Matt was asked to keep a diary of his alcohol consumption, which, in itself, reduced his intake dramatically. By about session 4, a good therapeutic relationship had been established and Matt was feeling much more in control of his symptoms. He was working hard at treatment and felt ready to tackle the traumatic memories. A hierarchy of avoided situations and activities was developed collaboratively for *in vivo* exposure homework over the coming weeks.

Sessions 5, 6 and 7 comprised predominantly imaginal exposure to the feared memories of the assault. The process was graded, with Matt allowed to skip the worst aspects (and keep his eyes open, talk in the past tense, etc.) in earlier sessions but not in later sessions. Subjective units of distress (SUDS) were taken throughout to monitor habituation. A separate tape was used to record these exposure components and Matt was instructed to listen to it daily. Although a very distressing process for him, Matt was able to acknowledge the anxiety reduction and felt very proud at having 'confronted the skeletons in the closet'.

Distorted and/or unhelpful cognitions that emerged during the imaginal exposure were noted. When possible, these were discussed (with a view to reformulating them) during the same session, with instructions to think through the issue during the week. A more structured approach to cognitive restructuring was briefly introduced in session 7 to address the key cognition that had not resolved during the imaginal exposure: that Matt was a weak failure for not defending himself more and fighting back. Sessions 8 and 9 were devoted primarily to cognitive restructuring, helping Matt to identify and challenge key negative cognitions associated with the assault and its aftermath. Eventually, these cognitions were replaced with more realistic, rational, and adaptive alternatives. Throughout the second half of treatment, Matt continued *in vivo* exposure, with each therapy session beginning with a review of his progress in that area.

Session 10 was devoted to relapse prevention: providing education about the likely future course of the disorder, helping Matt to identify high-risk times and generating a clear plan to deal with any symptom recurrence. Sessions 11 and 12 were largely devoted to reviews of progress in the intervening period, as well as to addressing minor issues that arose.

Matt responded extremely well to treatment. Objective symptom measures administered weekly illustrated a sizeable drop after week 1, with a general trend towards continued improvement through to session 8. Gains on these measures were maintained through to the final follow-up session. Subjective reports from Matt and his wife revealed improvements in mood, social and occupational functioning, and in family relationships, as well as significant reductions in anger and substance use.

CLINICAL FEATURES AND DIAGNOSIS

The clinical picture of PTSD is characterized by three core symptom groups: intrusion, avoidance and arousal. Diagnostic criteria for PTSD according to DSM-IV and ICD-10 classification systems are given in Table 14.1. In terms

Table 14.1 Diagnostic criteria for post-traumatic stress disorder (PTSD)

DSM-IV-TR	*ICD-10*
A. The person has been exposed to a traumatic event in which both of the following were present: 1. The person experienced, witnessed, or was confronted with an event that involved actual or threatened death or serious injury of self or others 2. The person's response involved intense fear, helplessness or horror or in the case of children disorganized behaviour	This arises as a delayed and/or protracted response to a stressful event or situation of an exceptionally threatening or catastrophic nature, which is likely to cause pervasive distress to almost anyone (e.g. natural or man-made disaster, combat, serious accident, witnessing the violent death of others, being a victim of rape, torture, terrorism or another crime)
B. The traumatic event is persistently re-experienced in one or more of the following ways 1. Recurrent and intrusive distressing recollections of the event including thoughts, images, or in children repetitive play in which the themes of the trauma are re-enacted 2. Recurrent distressing dreams of the event or in children the dreams may have unrecognizable fearful content 3. Acting or feeling as if the traumatic event were recurring (including hallucinations, illusions and dissociative flashbacks, or in children re-enactments)	Typical symptoms include episodes of repeated reliving of the trauma in intrusive memories (flashbacks) or dreams, occurring against the persisting background of a sense of numbness and emotional blunting, detachment from other people, unresponsiveness to surroundings, anhedonia, and avoidance of activities and situations reminiscent of the trauma. Commonly there is a fear and avoidance of cues that remind the sufferer of the original trauma. Rarely there may be dramatic acute bursts of fear, panic, or aggression triggered by stimuli arousing a sudden recollection and/or re-enactment of the trauma

Continued overleaf

Table 14.1 Continued

DSM-IV-TR	*ICD-10*
4. Intense psychological distress to exposure to internal or external cues that symbolize the traumatic event 5.Physiological reactivity to exposure to internal or external cues that symbolize the traumatic event	There is usually a state of autonomic hyperarousal with hypervigilance, enhanced startle reaction, and insomnia. Anxiety and depression are commonly associated with the above symptoms and signs and suicidal ideation is not infrequent. Excessive use of alcohol and drugs may be a complicating factor
C. Persistent avoidance of stimuli associated with the trauma and numbing of general responsiveness as indicated by three of the following: 1. Avoidance of thought feelings or conversations associated with the trauma 2. Avoidance of activities, places or people that arouse recollection of the trauma 3. Inability to recall an important aspect of the trauma 4. Markedly diminished interest or participation in significant activities 5. Feeling of detachment or estrangement from others 6. Restricted range of affect 7. Sense of foreshortened future	The disorder may be diagnosed if it occurs within six months of the trauma. In addition there must be repetitive intrusive recollection or re-enactment of the event in memories, daytime imagery or dreams. Conspicuous emotional detachment, numbing of feeling, and avoidance of stimuli that might arouse recollection of the trauma are often present but are not essential for the diagnosis. The autonomic disturbances, mood disorder, and behavioural abnormalities all contribute to the diagnosis but are not of prime importance
D. Persistent symptoms of increased arousal as indicated by two of the following: 1. Sleep difficulties 2. Irritability or outbursts of anger 3. Difficulty concentrating 4. Hypervigilance 5. Exaggerated startle response E. Duration of disturbance longer than 1 month	
F. The disturbance causes clinically significant distress and impairment of social or academic functioning	

Note: Adapted from DSM IV TR (APA, 2000) and ICD 10 (WHO, 1992).

of a formal DSM-IV diagnosis, the first criterion to be met is experience of a traumatic event (criterion A1), with the current wording emphasizing physical threat to self or others during the experience. In addition, the person's reaction must involve 'intense fear, helplessness or horror' (criterion A2). Although the DSM does not specify when this must occur, clinical experience suggests that, in some cases, this reaction may occur some time after the initial trauma.

The B criteria represent the re-experiencing symptoms that characterize post-traumatic stress: the person remains haunted by the traumatic memories. The five symptoms described in the DSM-IV comprise: recurrent, intrusive, distressing memories, images and perceptions (B1); nightmares (B2); 'flashbacks' or a feeling that the event is happening again (B3); psychological distress on reminders (B4); and physiological reactivity when reminded of the trauma (B5). At least one symptom from this cluster is required for a diagnosis.

The intrusive symptoms are extremely distressing. The C criteria of avoidance and numbing are conceptualized as attempts to prevent activation of the traumatic memories and to avoid the associated distress. The first two C criteria relate to active avoidance, with something of a phobic quality: avoidance of thoughts, feelings and conversations associated with the trauma (C1); and avoidance of activities, places, or people that arouse recollections of the trauma (C2). The remaining five C criteria, often referred to as emotional numbing, may be described as a more passive form of avoidance. These symptoms comprise psychogenic amnesia for all or part of the event (C3); loss of interest in normal activities (C4); estrangement from significant others (C5); flattened affect (C6); and a sense of foreshortened future (C7). While the DSM-IV includes active and passive avoidance within the same symptom cluster, there is increasing evidence that the two may represent separate constructs (King, Leskin, King & Weathers, 1998) and that the presence of numbing symptoms may distinguish PTSD from more common but less pathological trauma responses (Foa et al., 1995). Three symptoms from this cluster are required for a diagnosis.

The D criteria represent persistently increased arousal, with the following five symptoms identified in the DSM-IV: sleep disturbance (D1); anger and irritability (D2); concentration problems (D3); hypervigilance (D4); and exaggerated startle response (D5). Two symptoms from this cluster are required for a diagnosis. DSM-IV requires the presence of symptoms from criteria B, C and D for at least one month (criterion E), and they must cause significant distress or functional impairment (criterion F). The disorder is considered acute if symptoms have lasted for less than three months and chronic if they have persisted for longer. DSM-IV also allows for a delayed PTSD subtype if symptom onset is at least six months post-trauma.

A related diagnosis, acute stress disorder (ASD), was introduced in DSM-IV to describe a post-trauma reaction that has been present for more than two days but less than the four weeks required for a PTSD diagnosis. ASD criteria require at least one symptom from each of the PTSD re-experiencing, avoidance and hyperarousal clusters. The ASD diagnosis, however, also places considerable emphasis on dissociation during, or immediately following, the event, with a requirement for three of five possible symptoms (numb, dazed, derealization, depersonalization, dissociative amnesia). Although the ASD diagnosis was designed to predict the subsequent development of PTSD and facilitate access to early treatment, it has been criticized for confused criteria and a lack of empirical support (Bryant & Harvey, 1997; Marshall et al., 1999). Research on 'complex PTSD' or 'complicated PTSD' began in the 1990s (Roth, Newman, Pelcovitz, van der Kolk & Mandel, 1997), looking at enduring maladaptive effects on personality following sustained and severe trauma, such as experienced by people in concentration camps, prostitution brothels, and by those who experience long-term domestic violence and child sexual abuse. While the proposed new diagnostic category was not included in DSM-IV, ICD-10 includes a similar diagnostic category of 'enduring personality change after catastrophic experience'.

COMORBIDITY

Comorbidity is the norm rather than the exception in chronic PTSD with 80–85% meeting criteria for at least one other psychiatric diagnosis (Creamer et al., 2001; Kessler et al., 1995). Depression, substance-use disorders and other anxiety disorders (notably panic and social phobia) are very common. Guilt is frequently reported by trauma survivors and somatic symptoms (including gastrointestinal problems, aches and pains, cardiovascular symptoms, psychosexual difficulties and poor health behaviour) may also be present. It is important to note that many of these disorders frequently constitute the primary diagnosis following traumatic exposure and clinicians should be careful not to diagnose all psychological responses to traumatic events as PTSD, especially when an alternative diagnosis may be more appropriate.

EPIDEMIOLOGY AND COURSE

Recent epidemiological studies indicate that experience of trauma is relatively common, with around 60% of the general population having experienced a criterion A1 event (Creamer et al., 2001; Kessler et al., 1995). The subsequent prevalence of PTSD varies considerably according to event type; rape is consistently associated with the highest rates, while rates are generally lowest following natural disasters and accidents.

Estimates of lifetime PTSD prevalence within the general community vary from a low of 1% (Helzer et al., 1987) to around 10% for women and 5% for men (Kessler et al., 1995). Lifetime prevalence rates, however, may be somewhat misleading; around half those people who develop PTSD will recover over the first 12 months regardless of treatment (Kessler et al., 1995). Twelve-month prevalence rates vary across studies and across cultures, from 1.3% in Australia (Creamer et al., 2001) to 3.9% in the United States (Kessler et al., 1999). Data from several sources (e.g. Kessler et al., 1995; Solomon, 1989) suggest that individuals who still meet PTSD criteria at around six months post-trauma are likely (in the absence of effective treatment) to show a chronic course, with symptoms lasting for many decades.

TREATMENT OUTCOME STUDIES

Recent years have seen an increase in the number of high-quality randomized controlled trials (RCTs) investigating psychological treatments for PTSD. Excellent reviews of the literature appear elsewhere (Creamer & O'Donnell, 2002; Foa et al., 2000) and only a brief review will be provided here.

Cognitive-behavioural approaches

The strongest evidence base in the treatment of PTSD exists for cognitive-behavioural approaches, with particular reference to anxiety management (or stress inoculation training; SIT), prolonged exposure (PE) and cognitive therapy (CT, or cognitive processing therapy; CPT). Although routinely provided together in routine clinical practice, a trend in recent research has been attempts to dismantle the primary active components (SIT, PE and CT) to determine the specific contribution of each to overall efficacy. In a comparison of PE, SIT and combined PE/SIT (Foa, Dancu, Hembree, Jaycox, Meadows & Street, 1999a), all three active treatments reduced PTSD severity relative to the waiting-list condition but did not differ significantly from each other (although in the intent-to-treat sample PE was superior to both SIT and PE/SIT). These results were slightly at odds with an earlier study by the same group (Foa, Rothbaum, Riggs & Murdock, 1991), which found PE to be superior to SIT at follow-up.

Several studies have sought to compare PE, CT and (in some studies) combined PE/CT in the treatment of PTSD (Bryant et al., 2003; Marks et al., 1998; Resick et al., 2002; Tarrier et al., 1999). In all studies, these approaches have been shown to be superior to waiting-list controls or supportive counselling, although there is little to suggest reliable differences in outcome between these two therapeutic approaches. In summary, however, prolonged exposure and cognitive therapy have both been demonstrated as highly effective treatments for PTSD. The evidence base for these two approaches is far stronger than for any other psychological treatment.

Other psychological approaches

Several other non-drug treatments have been proposed for the treatment of PTSD. Regrettably, few of those have an adequate theoretical basis and even fewer have been the subject of controlled clinical research. An exception to the latter is eye movement desensitization and reprocessing (EMDR; Shapiro, 2001). Recent reviews of the EMDR research (e.g. Davidson & Parker, 2001) have concluded that the procedure does produce significant benefits for some people. However, several studies suggest that CBT is superior in the treatment of PTSD and concerns have been raised about the maintenance of treatment effects following EMDR (Devilly & Spence, 1999; Taylor, 2003). In summary, while EMDR appears to be useful for some patients, it is not superior to other exposure techniques and there is ample evidence to suggest that the eye movements are unnecessary.

Although brief psychodynamic approaches have a well-developed theoretical basis, only one controlled study has appeared in the literature (Brom et al., 1989). This study reported improvements in PTSD symptoms following brief psychodynamic therapy, although treatment effects were smaller than those obtained for desensitization. A vast array of other techniques has been proposed, many as 'one-session' cures for PTSD. In the absence of either a strong theoretical basis or objective empirical support, most of these do not justify attention in this review and clinicians should exercise great caution when considering such approaches. Nevertheless, it is possible that some will prove to be useful interventions and controlled clinical trials are clearly required.

Debriefing

Psychological debriefing (PD) or critical incident stress debriefing (CISD) is an acute intervention directed at the entire trauma-exposed population. It aims rapidly to restore normal functioning and to reduce the incidence and severity of traumatic stress cases by intervening before disorders develop. Debriefing was originally designed to be part of a larger process of critical incident stress management (CISM), which included components such as pre-incident intervention, individual crisis intervention, follow-up and referral to other sources (Mitchell & Everly, 1995). Examples included CISM programmes for emergency workers or bank personnel, who would receive CISD or PD following traumas that were certainly unpleasant but largely predictable in the course of this work, and which did not, therefore, damage fundamental belief systems. Systematic reviews of the research literature on psychological debriefing (e.g. Rose & Bisson, 1998) generally conclude that the practice is, at best, inert and at worst dangerous (Mayou et al., 2000). However, the RCTs on which these conclusions are based bear little resemblance to the way PD is carried out in routine practice. The RCTs, for example, generally focus on civilian populations, follow unexpected trauma that may have shattered fundamental beliefs about the self and the world, use single-session, individual debriefings in the absence of on-going organizational support structures; that is, CISD in isolation, rather than CISD in its intended context of CISM.

Unfortunately, research purporting to support the use of debriefing is usually methodologically flawed, much of it using quasi-experimental designs, rather than RCT, due to the ethical difficulty of withholding debriefing to people exposed to traumatic events, Studies have used non-manualized programmes, with facilitators who were untrained, applying debriefing to populations that were inappropriate, outside the time periods during which debriefing is recommended, with outcome measures that were symptom-based, without measures based on social or occupational functioning (Humphries & Carr, 2001). Thus, the results are hard to interpret (e.g. Everly et al., 1999).

It is important to note that debriefing is generally well received by participants, who tend to see the process as very helpful. There is little doubt that the opportunity to chat informally with friends or colleagues after a shared stressful experience has been an almost universal approach to dealing with frightening and upsetting events throughout human history. There is, perhaps, now a danger of 'throwing the baby out with the bath water' in declaring the whole process invalid. However, the data suggest that single-session debriefings should probably not be used with isolated civilians following unexpected acts of violence or serious accidents. Further, the use of debriefing in other settings should be a clinical decision in each case (not an automatic, compulsory process). Routine interventions in the acute aftermath of trauma should probably be restricted to information, facilitating the use of naturally occurring support networks, and screening for high-risk survivors (Bisson, 2003).

Group treatments

Group treatments have a long history in PTSD, albeit with a distinct lack of empirical support. Early approaches to PTSD group treatments evolved from veteran 'rap groups' and sought to provide a therapeutic, non-judgemental environment within which individuals who share a similar traumatic history can validate each others' experiences while cultivating supportive interpersonal relationships. Several papers have reported data from naturalistic studies of group treatments with veteran populations. Although most have been discouraging, with little treatment gain or even a deterioration (Johnson et al., 1996; Solomon et al., 1992), recent reports from CBT programmes with a strong outpatient focus have provided cause for cautious optimism (Creamer et al., 1999). These studies do not constitute randomized controlled trials and, therefore, must be interpreted cautiously.

A recently published study represents the only RCT of group treatment for PTSD in veterans to have appeared in the literature (Schnurr et al., 2003). This study randomly assigned 360 male Vietnam veterans to receive either 'trauma-focused' psychotherapy or a 'present-centred' comparison treatment that avoided any focus on the traumatic experiences. Cohorts of six veterans per group received weekly treatment for thirty weeks, followed by five, monthly booster sessions. Both groups improved significantly from intake to post-treatment, with gains maintained at follow-up. While average improvement was modest, around 40% of participants showed clinically significant change. Contrary to expectations, no overall differences were found between treatment conditions. Importantly, however, analyses suggested that those who received an 'adequate' dose of trauma focus treatment (attending at least 80% of sessions) did respond slightly better than those in the control condition. While the results are modestly encouraging, the treatment gains were considerably less than those achieved using individual treatment in civilian populations. While group interventions may have some benefits (for example, providing support and a sense of belonging), there is little to recommend them at this stage as a treatment of choice for PTSD.

Marital and family therapy

Despite the obvious impact of PTSD on the family of the sufferer, few controlled studies have investigated marital and family interventions. A recent review (Riggs, 2000) identifies two basic approaches differentiated according to their therapeutic approach and treatment outcome goals. Systemic treatments address disruption to family relationships caused by the trauma. This approach seeks to reduce relationship distress and improve family functioning through conflict reduction and increased communication. Support treatments, on the other hand, emphasize the role of partner and family support in trauma recovery and symptom reduction. These approaches emphasize psychoeducation and skills training interventions. In the majority of cases (with the possible exception of treating traumatized children), marital and family therapy in PTSD should be considered secondary to treatment targeted directly at the post-trauma symptoms.

Pharmacotherapy

Comprehensive reviews of pharmacological treatments for PTSD are available elsewhere (e.g. Albucher & Liberzon, 2002; Davidson, 2000; Foa et al., 2000) and, again, only a brief summary will be provided here. At present, PTSD-specific drugs have yet to be developed and the field has been restricted to medications developed originally for other conditions, such as anxiety and depression.

New-generation antidepressants, notably the selective serotonin reuptake inhibitors (SSRIs), have emerged recently as the first-line drug treatment for PTSD. Based on positive outcomes reported by the two largest randomized controlled trials (Brady et al., 2000; Davidson, Rothbaum, van der Kolk, Sikes & Farfel, 2001), the US Food and Drug Administration (FDA) registered sertraline in 2001 as the first approved drug treatment for PTSD. Since then, paroxetine has also been approved. Other new drugs, such as trazadone and nefazadone (serotonergic antidepressants with both SSRI and 5-HT_2 blockade properties) and venlafaxine (a serotonin and noradrenaline reuptake inhibitor) also have potential, although they have yet to be tested in controlled trials.

The dietary restrictions associated with the older monoamine oxidase inhibitors (MAOIs) have been largely overcome by their replacements, the reversible inhibitors of monoamine oxidase type A (RIMAs), such as moclobemide. Although no randomized controlled trials exist for PTSD, this medication looks promising because it has less effect on sexual functioning than the SSRIs. The tricyclic antidepressants have produced mixed, and generally moderate, results in randomized and open trials. Although benzodiazepines continue to be widely used (and may certainly have short-term benefits for sedation), trials suggest that they are no better than placebo in reducing core PTSD symptoms, and they may even impede recovery when used in the first few weeks following the trauma (Gelpin et al., 1996). Preliminary research suggests that anti-adrenergic agents such as clonidine and propranolol may be useful in the very acute stages of traumatic stress (Friedman et al., 1993; Pitman et al., 2002). Several other classes of medication have been used in the treatment of PTSD, although none has been adequately evaluated at this stage. At the time of writing, particular interest is being devoted to the new generation of atypical antipsychotic medications, although it remains to be seen whether they will prove beneficial in the treatment of PTSD.

Expert consensus (Foa et al., 1999b) suggests that chronic PTSD may require a higher dosage and longer treatment phase than other disorders. Once a good treatment response has been achieved, medication should normally continue for twelve to twenty-four months (or at least twenty-four months if the disorder is chronic with residual symptoms). At present, only one randomized controlled trial has addressed cessation of medication in PTSD (Davidson et al., 2001); not surprisingly, relapse rates were high.

In summary, pharmacological interventions are likely to be useful for many patients with PTSD. Although empirical data are lacking, pharmacotherapy would routinely be combined with psychological interventions in clinical practice in order to optimize treatment response and to minimize relapse on cessation.

ASSESSMENT

In most clinical settings, an unstructured interview comprises the primary assessment strategy. In PTSD, however, there may sometimes be a need for objective assessment that will stand up to more rigorous scrutiny. Regardless of the process, the clinician must remain sensitive to the mental state of the client and maintain a balance between providing empathetic and caring support to a distressed victim while obtaining reliable and objective information. For a comprehensive overview of assessment issues in PTSD, see Simon (1995) or Wilson and Keane (1997).

The development of a successful treatment plan with realistic goals requires a comprehensive assessment of the patient's pre-trauma history, the trauma itself, current psychosocial functioning, presence and course of PTSD symptoms, and possible comorbid conditions. Attention should be directed towards key issues such as prior mental health problems (especially depression; see Ozer, Best, Lipsey & Weiss, 2003), prior treatment experience, and pre-trauma coping strategies. While it is inappropriate to assume the existence of prior trauma on the basis of symptom profile, the clinician is advised to keep the possibility in mind; clients may be unwilling to disclose information regarding prior trauma within the first session. Good social support is associated with recovery (Brewin, Andrews & Valentine, 2000; Ozer et al., 2003) and, therefore, the client's support network should be examined. If social support is lacking, clinicians may consider providing a skills-development, problem-solving approach in the initial stages of treatment. An evaluation of the client's occupational functioning (in the broadest sense) is important also; structure provided by daily routines often helps to restore a sense of control.

There is currently no agreed 'gold standard' against which to make a PTSD diagnosis. Rather, clinicians should adopt a multi-faceted approach incorporating information from a variety of sources. In clinical settings, this may comprise unstructured psychiatric interviews (to collect the above information), structured clinical interviews, self-report inventories and (where possible) informant reports. In research contexts, the addition of psychophysiological measures (such as heart rate, electromyogram (EMG), galvanic skin response (GSR), skin temperature, etc.) may provide an extra degree of objectivity, which is rarely practical in clinical settings.

Structured clinical interviews

Structured clinical interviews provide the optimal strategy for making a reliable clinical diagnosis and an indication of symptom severity. For a competent, well-trained clinician, these measures combine a standardized and objective instrument with an element of clinical judgement. The questions directly address PTSD symptoms and an objective scale determines whether each is sufficiently severe to meet criteria.

The Clinician Administered PTSD Scale (CAPS; Blake et al., 1995; Weathers et al., 2001) is a psychometrically robust instrument designed to overcome many of the limitations of other structured PTSD interviews. Each symptom is assessed for intensity and frequency and, where possible, is behaviourally defined. Although the CAPS is highly recommended in research settings, it is a little complex for use in routine clinical practice. Several other well-validated structured PTSD interviews, which are briefer and simpler to administer, are appropriate in this context (see Weiss, 1997, for a review). Two that are strongly recommended include the PTSD Symptom Scale

Interview (PSS-I; Foa et al., 1993) and the Structured Interview for PTSD (SIP; Davidson et al., 1997).

Self-report measures

Several comprehensive reviews of self-report PTSD symptom measures exist (e.g. Norris & Riad, 1997; Solomon et al., 1996). The best scales are psychometrically robust, relatively non-intrusive and often (although not always) reasonably inexpensive. Although these measures have the potential to assess the client's own perception of his or her symptoms without influence from the interviewer, they are easy to fake and thus pose a risk of symptom exaggeration or minimization. Accordingly, it is not appropriate to rely on self-report measures as the only (or even the primary) diagnostic tool. Rather, they provide a useful means of screening clients for more intensive interview procedures, or to assess symptom change as a function of treatment through repeated administration.

Although several established scales that have been around for decades continue to be popular among clinicians and researchers, the diagnostic criteria have evolved in recent years and it is recommended that more contemporary scales be adopted where possible. The PTSD Checklist (PCL; Weathers et al., 1993) covers the seventeen DSM PTSD symptoms, with each rated on a five-point scale from 'not at all' to 'extremely'. The scale takes only five minutes to complete and possesses excellent psychometric qualities (Blanchard et al., 1996; Forbes et al., 2001). A score of 50 is recommended as the diagnostic cutoff. The self-report version of PSS structured interview (PSS-SR; Falsetti et al., 1993) is similar to the PCL, while the Davidson Trauma Scale (DTS; Zlotnick et al., 1996) allows for both frequency and intensity ratings. In the final analysis, there is probably little to choose between these scales; any would be a useful addition for clinicians and researchers alike.

Symptom exaggeration and malingering

Perhaps more than any other disorder, symptom exaggeration and malingering can be issues in PTSD. Although there has been debate regarding the ease with which symptoms can be fabricated or exaggerated, and the extent to which this occurs (Frueh et al., 2000; Resnick, 1995), clinicians should remain aware of the possibility. Unless the person is a very good actor, credible descriptions of PTSD symptoms are difficult to produce. Thus, clinicians should not be satisfied with a simple 'yes/no' response, but should request further detail (e.g. 'Tell me about the last time you experienced that – what was it like?'). Other issues that may alert caution in the clinician include endorsement of all seventeen PTSD symptoms, a history of occupational and social instability, emphasis on re-experiencing (rather than avoidance and numbing) symptoms, and lack of sexual dysfunction or sleep disturbance. The clinician should remain alert for PTSD symptoms that are directly observable during the interview (e.g. hypervigilance and flattened affect) and to contradictions in the patient's reports (e.g. complete inability to work but retention of an active social life). Informant interviews, especially a spouse or partner, can further illuminate the validity of a patient's report. In the final analysis, a thorough knowledge of the disorder and comprehensive assessment, incorporating standardized instruments where possible, will minimize inaccuracies. However, unless we assume that everyone with PTSD is malingering until proved otherwise, even the best clinicians can sometimes be deceived.

TREATMENT

Cognitive-behavioural treatment of PTSD

The major stages of CBT treatment for PTSD involve: stabilization and engagement, psychoeducation, anxiety management, prolonged exposure, cognitive restructuring, and relapse prevention and maintenance. While interventions are generally presented in that order, clinicians should remain flexible and integrate components where appropriate (e.g. exposure and cognitive restructuring). Treatment sessions are usually taped to enable clients to review and consolidate the information. It is suggested that two tapes, with one reserved exclusively for exposure, are used for each client. Regular homework tasks are a central feature of treatment, a fact that should be made clear to clients from the outset of treatment. A detailed practical description of each stage is beyond the scope of this chapter and interested readers are referred to specialist texts (such as Andrews et al., 2003; Foa & Rothbaum, 1998).

Stabilization and engagement in treatment

Individuals with PTSD often present for treatment in crisis, particularly in the acute aftermath of trauma. Stabilization of life crises, and bringing substance use under control, is essential prior to the commencement of PTSD-specific interventions. Clients will not be able to focus on trauma recovery until fundamental issues such as suicidal behaviour, major psychosocial crisis and personal safety are recognized and addressed.

Engaging patients in treatment may be particularly challenging, especially in chronic PTSD. Thus, it is essential that clinicians spend adequate time in the early treatment phase developing rapport and a strong relationship with the client. The advantage of the following treatment model is that the early stages, such as psychoeducation and symptom management, are relatively non-threatening, allowing the clinician to demonstrate his or her knowledge, credibility and non-judgemental approach. Thus, the therapeutic relationship is able to develop while still covering important ground.

Psychoeducation

Psychoeducation aims to help the client understand common trauma reactions and to provide a rationale for treatment. The sudden onset of symptoms can be extremely frightening, especially for someone without a prior psychiatric history, and concern about symptoms is a strong predictor of subsequent adjustment (Halligan et al., 2003). Secondary distress, possibly including denial, avoidance and withdrawal, may arise as a consequence of such beliefs and impede recovery.

Although the frequently used phrase, 'normal reactions in a normal person to an abnormal event' is generally inappropriate and may sound dismissive of the client's distress, the concept is important and other phrases may be useful (e.g. 'although the problems you have told me about are very unpleasant, they are part of a common human response to life-threatening events and will decline'). The therapist should talk through the symptoms and provide a rationale for their appearance, possibly based around the notion of survival value (see, for example, Foa & Rothbaum, 1998). Written handouts are a useful accompaniment, providing concrete validation that the survivor's personal experience and responses are not unique.

Symptom management

Most clients with PTSD present feeling frightened, vulnerable and out of control. Symptom management does not address the underlying causes of PTSD but helps the client regain a sense of control. A range of strategies in the physical, cognitive and behavioural domains may be offered. It is important not to overwhelm the patient with too many strategies but, rather, to select the most appropriate for each case. In standard stress inoculation models, a rationale and description of the strategy is provided before it is modelled and practised during the session. Any problems or misunderstandings should be discussed as they arise. The clinician should also emphasize the importance of practising the skill (often several times a day) in non-stressful environments before attempting to use it to control anxiety in a difficult (especially trauma-related) situation (Meichenbaum, 1985).

A first step often involves introducing the concept of subjective units of distress (SUDs). This, 'fear thermometer' is used by clients to rate their current level of anxiety or distress on a scale of 0 ('perfectly relaxed and calm') to 100 ('the worst imaginable anxiety and distress'). SUDs allow the client to self-monitor the effects of anxiety-management interventions, providing a more objective measure of efficacy. As SUDs are also a vital component of subsequent exposure treatment, introducing them at this stage allows the patient to practise rating his or her own anxiety before being asked to do so during the difficult exposure phase.

Physiological arousal is a fundamental feature of traumatic stress. Physically oriented strategies are an ideal starting point while the patient is still feeling vulnerable, as they not only produce rapid results but are also non-threatening, easy to learn and have a straightforward rationale (in terms of a fight–flight response). Moreover, clinical evidence suggests that effective arousal strategies improve self-efficacy and expectations of recovery. Regular aerobic exercise, advice concerning diet (including reduction in stimulants such as nicotine and caffeine) and getting enough rest can do much to reduce arousal. A simple controlled breathing strategy is usually a good first step and some clients will benefit from progressive muscle relaxation.

While cognitive interventions are routinely used in anxiety management to reduce arousal, they have a second possible role in PTSD by providing some degree of control over intrusive memories and ruminations. The clinician must be careful not to send a contradictory message here: thinking about the trauma is not unhealthy and, indeed, will be central to later treatment. However, it is important that the client feels a sense of control over the thoughts such that they do not dominate every waking hour.

Distraction techniques can be used both to reduce arousal and to control intrusive memories. This approach can include anything from counting backwards from 100 in 7s to asking patients to describe their current surroundings in intricate detail (the latter being especially useful for patients who tend to dissociate). Clients should also be helped to engage in more natural forms of distraction such as involvement in crafts, games and other creative activities (rather than passive strategies such as reading or watching TV).

Guided self-dialogue is routinely used in the early stages of treatment. The client is helped to generate, and to write out on a card to be carried with them, coping statements for use in difficult situations. Such statements (from Meichenbaum, 1985) are useful approaching the situation (e.g. 'don't focus on how bad I feel: think about what I can do about it'), entering the situation (e.g. 'one step at a time; I can handle this'), coping with feelings of anxiety and distress as they arise (e.g. 'I expect my fear to rise, but I can keep it manageable'), and positive reinforcement after the event (e.g. 'I did it – I got through it; each time it will be easier'). Statements relating specifically to the trauma are also useful (e.g. 'I'm safe now').

Behaviourally oriented anxiety management techniques usually involve scheduling activities and structuring a daily routine. Encouraging people to resume a normal routine as quickly as reasonably possible following a trauma is often beneficial (although they should be discouraged from throwing themselves into work to avoid unpleasant memories). Pleasant activities should also be incorporated into a daily plan (as in the treatment of depression), as the core symptoms of PTSD are likely to produce anhedonia and loss of interest. The client should be encouraged to undertake activities with family and friends to reduce social withdrawal and to maintain healthy relationships.

It is recommended that one or two interventions from each of the physical, cognitive and behavioural domains be provided to the patient over the first few weeks. It is important that some progress is made in symptom management before commencing exposure, as the client's ability to manage arousal and distress will become vital during the next stage of treatment.

Exposure

Providing an opportunity to confront the traumatic memories is the most empirically supported component of all successful PTSD treatments. Excellent descriptions of exposure treatment in PTSD are provided elsewhere (e.g. Foa & Rothbaum, 1998; Lyons & Keane, 1989) and only a brief overview of the technique follows.

Background issues

In vivo exposure is generally considered to be more effective than imaginal exposure in treating the anxiety disorders. While it is neither possible nor desirable to actually relive the trauma, a hierarchy of external cues (feared and avoided situations, activities, etc.) can be generated with the client. This hierarchy should be worked through progressively as homework between sessions (with assistance from a friend and/or the therapist from time to time if necessary). As the primary feared stimulus to be confronted is the traumatic memory, however, the majority of exposure work will involve imaginal exposure.

Exposure targets should be graded according to the level of fear they provoke and each confronted in turn. With *in vivo* exposure this is relatively straightforward – a list of feared situations is generated and rank ordered. Likewise, individuals who have suffered multiple traumas (e.g. emergency workers) may rate the severity of each event for imaginal exposure and, again, each can be confronted in turn. Grading imaginal exposure within a single event is a little more difficult. While it is generally best to move to the most powerful memories as quickly as reasonably possible, several strategies may be adopted to titrate the exposure if necessary to ensure the client is not overwhelmed by emotion. If necessary, for example, clients may skip over the most difficult aspects of the event in early sessions, but not later sessions; they may be allowed to keep their eyes open in early sessions, closing them during later exposures to increase the vividness of the imagery; they may recount the event in past tense during early sessions (e.g. 'I saw him coming towards me') but move to the present tense in later sessions ('I can see him coming towards me'). The clinician can use these strategies to grade exposure levels, maintaining arousal at levels that are sufficiently high to be optimally therapeutic, yet low enough to manage.

The session should be prolonged until anxiety has reduced substantially – ideally by about 50%. Arousal levels routinely rise during exposure before they start to drop and premature termination of exposure may incubate or worsen the anxiety response. In clinical practice, it is not always possible to prolong the session long enough for the anxiety to reduce by half. At the very least, however, a significant reduction must take place before the session is terminated, even if this means prolonging the session longer than usual.

Each item on the hierarchy needs to be repeated until it evokes minimal anxiety. This repetition may occur within a single session, within multiple sessions or between sessions.

Finally, exposure needs to be functional, which means that the affective components of the memory must be accessed along with the stimulus material. Individuals with PTSD become adept at telling their story in a detached, unemotional manner, accessing only part of the traumatic memory network. This process is not likely to be therapeutic. However, a few probing questions are generally sufficient to access the accompanying affect, allowing habituation to occur.

The process

The following provides a brief outline of the key stages required to conduct exposure in PTSD. First, the client is given a detailed rationale for exposure based around habituation or emotional processing models (in lay terms) and often incorporating the use of metaphors to explain the process (see Andrews et al., 2003; Foa & Rothbaum, 1998). Second, the concept of SUDs is reviewed. Third, a hierarchy of feared external and internal stimuli is constructed. It is often useful to generate two separate lists, one comprising potential targets for *in vivo* exposure and the other (in the case of multiple trauma) a list of events for imaginal exposure. Each item on the hierarchy is rated using SUDs for the predicted fear associated with confronting that situation, activity or memory. Fourth, the therapist works with the client to generate specific homework assignments from the *in vivo* hierarchy for the client to practice every day over the coming days. Specificity is important: client and therapist should agree on exactly what will be done, where, how often and so on. It is important to start with a relatively easy item, ensuring success on the first trial. Each item is repeated until it evokes only minimal anxiety before the client continues down the list. Each treatment session should commence with a review of the client's homework and the identification of subsequent targets.

In imaginal exposure, the client repeatedly describes the traumatic experience in detail, continuing until the event is over and a point of safety reached. SUDs are taken at regular intervals (every few minutes). Although, as noted above, some grading may be possible, all aspects of the traumatic memory must be confronted before treatment can be considered complete. As the SUDs gradually reduce over repeated sessions, attention is increasingly directed towards the most distressing elements of the memory (or 'hot spots').

These elements may become the primary focus of later sessions during which it is important to maximize the cues in all sensory modalities (sights, smells, etc.). Elements of cognitive restructuring are routinely incorporated towards the end of each session as new information emerges during the exposure. Adequate time should be allocated at the end of the session to discuss the experience.

Repeated exposure to the traumatic memory is best achieved by taping the session and instructing the client to listen to the tape daily at home. Obviously, this component may not be appropriate in all cases. At the very least, it is important to provide clear structure and guidelines for homework and to ensure that support is available should the experience prove too distressing. The therapist may also suggest that the client write in detail about the incident. This process, outlined by Resick and Schnick (1993), involves a hand-written (preliminary research suggests that type-written may be less effective; Brewin & Lennard, 1999), detailed account of the event including as many sensory details as possible. The client should either rewrite the episode every day or read previous accounts at least once, continuing the process until SUDs levels are relatively low throughout (e.g. a maximum of 30).

Finally, the client's understanding of his or her experience should be considered. A key to recovery may be the ability to answer fundamental questions about what happened and why it happened (Figley, 1985). Many survivors have confused, fragmented memories of the trauma, making it difficult to process the experience and move on. Thus, therapists should look for opportunities to fill in these gaps and to assist the client make sense of the experience.

Potential problems

If the above procedure is followed in the context of a good therapeutic relationship, few problems are likely to be encountered. Nevertheless, exposure can be a powerful experience, involving high levels of emotion for both the therapist and client. It is vital that clinicians communicate confidence in their ability to cope and help the client manage whatever emerges during the session. Ideally, anxiety should be allowed to habituate of its own accord during exposure; however, arousal reduction techniques may be used if the client's distress levels become intolerable or if insufficient habituation has occurred over a reasonable period (e.g. 60 minutes).

If problems arise, they are likely to be associated with either under- or over-engagement with the memory. A failure to engage effectively with the memory will be associated with poor outcome. Foa and Rothbaum (1998) suggest that asking clients to recount the most difficult aspects using a 'slow motion strategy for thoughts, feelings and physical sensations' may help to maintain full engagement. Likewise, reassurances of safety by the therapist and making the distinction between experiencing the trauma itself and reliving the memory are also useful. Equally, over-engagement may also be counter-therapeutic. It is not possible to modify the traumatic memory network effectively and incorporate new information while experiencing a flashback. The therapist should, therefore, make every effort to bring the client back to the 'here and now' before proceeding with exposure. Instructions to open their eyes, look around, feel the chair, describe the room, and so on are all useful grounding strategies to use in such situations. It should be emphasized that this type of over-engagement is a rare occurrence if exposure is conducted carefully according to the above guidelines.

Contraindications for exposure are basically common sense. Timing is important: does the client feel sufficiently in control (having mastered some key symptom-management strategies) and is rapport adequate? Acute life crises, current substance abuse, severe psychiatric comorbidity and a history of treatment non-compliance should all suggest caution in the use of exposure. While the possibility of iatrogenic effects with exposure – as with any other potent intervention – should not be ignored, the likelihood of adverse reactions can be minimized by sensible clinical practice.

Cognitive restructuring

Cognitive restructuring techniques, based on the work of Beck and colleagues (Beck et al., 1979), have been used to directly address dysfunctional thoughts and beliefs about the world, other people or themselves that have arisen from, or been strengthened by, the traumatic experience. Developed specifically for PTSD, cognitive processing therapy (CPT; Resick & Schnicke, 1993) involves cognitive restructuring with reference to five primary themes: safety, trust, power, self-esteem and intimacy. Similarly, Foa and Rothbaum (1998) have identified several core dysfunctional beliefs associated with PTSD: pre-trauma beliefs about the self and the world; beliefs about reactions or behaviour during the trauma; beliefs about the symptoms of PTSD; and beliefs about the reactions of others.

The therapist helps the client to identify these negative automatic thoughts and dysfunctional beliefs following the trauma. They are subsequently treated as hypotheses rather than facts, which are challenged and replaced with more balanced and rational alternatives. This is an active and rigorous process: it is not sufficient simply to replace the maladaptive cognitions with an adaptive alternative; the individual must make an effort to really understand why the thought is based on faulty logic. Many trauma survivors seek unrealistic assurances (e.g. that they will never experience such an event again) and try to replace the distress-producing thoughts with beliefs that are blatantly untrue. The therapist may need to help the client realistically evaluate the potential risks and to focus on learning to accept the uncertainty.

The timing of cognitive restructuring in PTSD is important. Although exposure work is routinely commenced before cognitive interventions, in practice the two are intertwined. Exposure often helps to integrate the fragmented traumatic memory, revealing information that casts a new perspective on the event. Cognitive restructuring can facilitate the processing of this perspective. Indeed, it may be postulated that the processing of new information comprises the real therapeutic mechanism of exposure treatment. Therapists should be prepared, therefore, to do at least some of the cognitive restructuring work in the same sessions as exposure when target thoughts and beliefs are activated.

Guilt deserves special mention in this context. Clinicians are advised not to immediately dispute guilt-related cognitions, even if they appear highly irrational. Unlike fear or sadness, survivors may be less likely to discuss feelings of guilt with support networks (who would often respond instantly with reassurances). Thus, the client may benefit from the opportunity to simply ventilate the guilt in a reassuring and supportive environment. If guilt feelings do not resolve, however, cognitive restructuring may be indicated. The client is assisted in identifying the discrepancies between value judgements made on the basis of the context and available information during the trauma, and those made within the current context of acceptable behaviour and with the benefit of hindsight. It is often useful to distinguish guilt about a specific behaviour or action (which may be quite healthy) from characterological guilt, which is potentially much more problematic (e.g. 'I am a terrible, worthless person for behaving that way'). In such cases, the therapist needs to highlight the logical errors inherent in global self-rating, distinguishing between a bad, or unwise, behaviour and a bad person. This is particularly important when working with someone who did, undeniably, 'do something bad' during the traumatic event. It is counter-therapeutic to pretend that it did not happen or that it was an acceptable way to behave. Rather, the clinician should assist the client to understand that it is illogical and unhelpful to generalize from a single mistake or negative act to rate their whole selves. Useful clinical advice on managing guilt in PTSD has been published elsewhere (e.g. Kubany & Watson, 2003).

Relapse prevention and maintenance

For acute PTSD presentations with little premorbid psychopathology or comorbidity, a return to normal functioning with a low chance of relapse may be possible. Even in such cases, however, and certainly in more chronic and complex cases, it is likely that some vulnerability will remain. Relapse may be triggered during periods of high stress or exposure to (or hearing about) other traumatic events. Clients need to be prepared for, and have strategies to deal with, such situations. In more severe cases, ongoing support from a mental health professional or counselling agency may be required.

Relapse prevention normally involves several steps. First, the client should be informed that distress will occasionally occur when confronted with reminders and that this is a normal part of traumatic stress reactions. Provided they are not too severe and do not last too long, an ability to accept such lapses philosophically will indicate effective recovery. Second, it is important to identify situations that may provoke a relapse, such as trauma reminders, hearing about or experiencing another trauma and times of high-stress. The therapist and client should develop a written plan to cope with lapses. Who can the client call (and what are the phone numbers)? What physical, cognitive and behavioural coping strategies have they found useful and could use at such times? The written plan should include also expectations of recovery, perhaps in the form of self-statements (e.g. 'I expect to be upset when reminded of what happened, but that's OK. It's a perfectly normal reaction and I can cope with it. It will pass. Now, what strategies can I use to take control and help myself feel better?'). It is important that the client tries to remain positive and is willing to seek professional help if necessary.

The duration and timing of treatment

A multitude of factors determine the duration of PTSD treatment. In the best-case scenario (e.g. treatment initiated within a few weeks of a single incident trauma, good pre-trauma functioning, strong support networks), it should be possible to cover the above treatment plan in around six sessions. Several studies of early intervention using such approaches (e.g. Bryant et al., 1998; Foa et al., 1995a) have used four to six sessions, although these sessions were of one-and-a-half hours' duration. Indeed it is advisable to schedule 90-minute sessions when conducting the exposure components of treatment in PTSD to ensure sufficient time for the anxiety to habituate.

The more complex the presentation, the more time will be required for each component of treatment, although the general format and structure of the intervention will remain largely the same. In cases with high levels of comorbidity and psychosocial dysfunction, those issues may be addressed before, after or even in the midst of the suggested treatment plan.

Managing comorbidity

Comorbidity, usually in the form of substance-use disorders or depression, is the norm rather than the exception in chronic PTSD. The appropriate management of comorbid conditions is an important factor in treatment. Unfortunately, due to a lack of solid empirical evidence, therapeutic decisions regarding the management of comorbidity in the context of PTSD treatment are generally based on informed clinical judgement. With regard to depression, clinical experience suggests that mild depression is likely to resolve with improvement in PTSD and unlikely to interfere significantly with treatment. More severe depression, however, may impact negatively on the treatment process and should be addressed prior to (or, at least, in conjunction with) a focus on PTSD. Evidence-based psychological or pharmacological interventions may be useful and may have additional advantages in providing some amelioration of core PTSD symptoms.

There is a larger body of literature in the area of substance use and PTSD. Alcohol (or other substance) misuse is usually conceptualized as a maladaptive attempt to manage trauma-related intrusion and arousal symptoms. As such, it is seen as being a component of the numbing and avoidance symptoms and any attempts to remove this 'crutch' should be accompanied (or preceded) by the provision of alternative and more appropriate coping strategies. Clinicians disagree on the best treatment approach. Some argue that substance abuse will decline with PTSD symptom improvement, indicating the need to treat core PTSD symptomatology first. Others believe that substance abuse must be addressed first, partly because it may exacerbate (or even cause) some of the PTSD symptoms and partly because a period of sobriety is required before traumatic memories can be adequately processed. At the very least, substance abuse must be under control to the extent that the person can attend treatment without being intoxicated and can deal with the increase in emotional distress that will be part of treatment without resort to drugs or alcohol as a means of coping. Contemporary opinion, however, is that the two should be treated concurrently (Najavits, 2003; Ouimette & Brown, 2003) and the early stages of PTSD treatment should proceed in conjunction with substance-abuse interventions. There is significant overlap in areas of psychoeducation and symptom management skills, and change in one area may facilitate change in the other. It is unlikely, however, that the intensive stages of exposure and cognitive restructuring will be effective in the context of ongoing substance abuse.

EMDR: Rationale and clinical practice

The mechanisms underlying EMDR are unknown and few attempts have been made to generate and test models to explain the processes by which change may occur. Nevertheless, it has been proposed that, when a person experiences a traumatic event with high states of anxiety and terror, routine information processing in the brain may be blocked (van der Kolk et al., 1996). The traumatic experience is then not integrated into the ordinary explicit memory networks of semantic and autobiographical information, which are predominantly in the left hemisphere. Instead, fragments of traumatic memory, such as tastes, sounds, images, physical sensations and smells are stored in a separate traumatic memory network, predominantly in the right hemisphere, and not available for verbal processing. External cues that are similar to some aspect of the trauma can trigger the entire traumatic memory network so that a person may feel the anxiety and terror of the trauma again or may re-experience bodily sensations associated with the trauma. For example, when Matt saw or had to handle kitchen knives, or was aware of groups of people standing close behind him, he became very anxious and felt threatened and angry. His muscles tensed, particularly those in his arms and his palms began to sweat.

In EMDR, a client is encouraged to pick and then focus on a part of the traumatic memory. This target, usually an image, becomes the access point for the traumatic memory network. While focusing on the target, the clinician moves his or her fingers back and forth in front of the client's eyes, asking the client to follow the movements with his or her eyes; alternatively, the clinician may use hand tapping or bilateral sound stimulation. While the precise mechanism of action of EMDR is unclear, it is hypothesized that, just as the eye movements that occur during REM sleep facilitate the processing and integration of events of the day, in a similar way the eye movements and other bilateral stimulation in EMDR accelerate information processing. This allows information from the traumatic memory to be integrated with the ordinary memory network to yield new understanding and insight of the trauma that are less distressing. The client can watch the traumatic image but know that it happened in the past and is not happening in the present. The traumatic image becomes increasingly less vivid and upsetting, although it is still remembered.

EMDR is conducted in a series of eight stages. A more detailed description is provided by Shapiro (2001), while Parnell (1999) describes using EMDR with adult clients who have experienced childhood abuse who may meet criteria for complex PTSD. First, a history is taken from the client. Next, the client is prepared for EMDR with detailed information about the process involved, what to expect, how to stay safe in the process and how to stop the process if he or she is uncomfortable. The third stage is an assessment, during which the client is asked to focus on a target and eye movement or other stimulation is conducted. The client is asked about the target picture or image and the associated negative cognition, or belief about the self that is associated with the picture but is held in the present. For example, Matt might describe being surrounded by the men with the image of the knife being held at his throat. His negative cognition might be 'I am vulnerable and unsafe'. Following this, the therapist asks the client for a cognition that he would like to believe about himself now when bringing up the image. This positive cognition is rated for how valid or true it feels now, on a scale of one (not true) to seven (true). For Matt, this might be 'I am safe', with a rating of only two. The client is next asked for the associated emotion and to rate this in SUDs on a scale of zero to ten. Matt felt tense and anxious, with a rating of eight. Finally, the client is asked to locate any associated body sensations, which for Matt might include sweating palms and tension in his arms. The fourth stage is the desensitization phase, during which the clinician works with the client on a target, using bilateral stimulation, looking for signs of a client's emotional shift. Some clients like to verbalize their stream of thought or images during the focusing, making it easier to identify a shift in emotion. Others who remain quiet will indicate this shift non-verbally. After an obvious shift or alternatively after about 25 saccades, or movements of eyes from left to right, or equivalent aural or tapping stimulation, the clinician checks how the client is doing and what is coming up for him or her, as well as checking SUDs. New images, sensations or emotions may then become the target for further desensitization work. Desensitization continues until SUDs have decreased to zero or one. This is a sign to continue to the fifth stage, installing positive cognitions. The client is encouraged to focus on the target image, think about the positive cognition and say how true or valid it feels now. Matt might re-rate the validity of the positive cognition as six. The image and positive cognition are held in mind during a further series of eye movements to 'install the cognitions'. The sixth stage is a body scan, where the client is encouraged to notice any bodily sensations that come up when the target image is focused on. Any positive sensations may then be amplified with further eye movements, while negative sensations need further desensitization, as they may be a sign of further unprocessed memories held in the body memory. The penultimate stage is closure, or preparing the client to end the session, perhaps by noting all the good work done by the client in the session, using relaxation techniques or meditation. The final stage is re-evaluation, which occurs at the start of the next session, when the clinician asks the client about images and sensations that came up since the last session.

Couples therapy and trauma

For clients for whom PTSD has a significant impact on their marital or romantic relationships, and for clients who are involved in relationships that lead to PTSD, couples therapy may be an important component in a multi-modal treatment programme that also involves individual CBT.

Complex PTSD may have a significant impact on relationships in couples where one partner is a survivor of child sexual abuse (Compton & Follette, 2003). Preliminary evidence points to the effectiveness of emotionally focused couples therapy, described in Chapter 5, as an adjunct to individual CBT for such cases (Johnson & Makinen, 2003). With emotionally focused couples therapy, it is assumed that traumatized partners have difficulty developing secure attachments to their partners, and having their attachment needs met, because they lack internal working models of others as 'a secure base'. Rather, they oscillate between viewing their partners as a source of safety and security to which they cling on the one hand, and as a threatening source of anxiety, related to expectations of hurt and abandonment on the other. These problematic internal working models of others lead traumatized people to develop destructive interaction patterns with their partners. These interaction patterns prevent them from having their attachment needs met. Often, these patterns are characterized by periods of intense closeness followed by periods of distancing following outbursts of extreme anger. These outbursts usually occur because, commonly for survivors of child sexual abuse, even minor indications of loss of closeness are cues for traumatic memories of hurt, betrayal and abandonment. In emotionally focused couples therapy, couples learn to recognize their problematic interaction patterns, the cues that precipitate trauma-related intrusions and angry outbursts, and subsequent distancing. They also learn to distinguish between primary emotions, such as the need for belonging, and secondary emotions, such as anger, which arise from frustration of such attachment needs. Finally, couples are helped to find ways to express primary emotions and to practise using these ways to meet each other's attachment needs. This gradual process of finding ways to trust, to talk about and tolerate minor indications of loss of closeness; and to tolerate experiencing traumatic intrusions without expressing extreme anger is central to the use of emotionally focused couples therapy to help couples where one member is a survivor of CSA with complex PTSD. Substance abuse (discussed in Chapter 20), self-harm (discussed in Chapters 10 and 22) and domestic violence are common comorbid problems in these couples and may also require a couple-based approach to treatment.

SUMMARY

Post-traumatic stress disorder is a relatively new diagnosis and there is much still to learn about the aetiology, assessment and management of this complex condition. Equally, there has been an enormous increase in the quantity of research output over the last decade and considerable progress has been made. The last five years, in particular, have seen a growth in the number of well-conducted, treatment outcome studies such that there is now a strong evidence base from which to recommend cognitive-behavioural interventions as the psychological treatment of choice for PTSD. It is to be hoped that the next decade will see further development and refinement of effective treatments to better manage the mental health effects of trauma and to reduce the human and financial costs associated with post-traumatic mental health problems.

EXERCISE 14.1

Divide into groups of three. Assign roles of psychologist, client and observer. Changing roles after each role-play, role-play the following scenarios:

1 Part of an early session with Matt where Matt is encouraged to describe his current symptoms and distress, and the psychologist engages in psychoeducation with him.
2 Part of a session where the psychologist works with Matt to develop a

hierarchy of external cues and feared situations for *in vivo* and imaginal exposure.

3 Part of a session during which the psychologist asks Matt about the meaning of the event, and works to identify with him the negative automatic thoughts and dysfunctional beliefs about the trauma.

FURTHER READING FOR CLIENTS

Allen, J. (1999). *Coping with trauma: A guide to self understanding*. Washington, DC: American Psychiatric Press.

Herbert, C. & Wetmore, A. (1999). *Overcoming traumatic stress: A self-help guide using cognitive behavioural techniques*. London: Robinson.

Matsakis, A. (1996). *I can't get over it: A handbook for trauma survivors* (Second Edition). Oakland, CA: New Harbinger Publications.

Rosenbloom, D., Williams, M. & Watkins, B. (1999). *Life after trauma: A workbook for healing*. New York: Guilford.

EVIDENCE SUMMARIES

Foa, E. B., Keane, T. M., & Friedman, M. J. (2000). *Effective treatments for PTSD*. New York: Guilford Press.

Keane, T. (1998). Psychological and behavioural treatments for post-traumatic stress disorder. In P. Nathan & J. Gorman (Eds.), *A guide to treatments that work* (pp. 398–407). New York: Oxford University Press.

National Institute for Clinical Excellence (2005). Management of post-traumatic stress disorder in adults in primary, secondary and community care. Available online at: www.nice.org.uk/page.aspx?0=248114

Stein, D. J., Ipser, J. C. & Seedat, S. (2006). Pharmacotherapy for post traumatic stress disorder (PTSD). *The Cochrane Database of Systematic Reviews* 2006, Issue I. Art No.: CD002795. DOI:10.1002/14651858. CD002795.pub2. Available at: http://tinyurl.com/8tvda

FURTHER READING FOR PRACTITIONERS

Andrews, G., Creamer, M., Crino, R., Hunt, C., Lampe, L. & Page, A. (2003). *The treatment of anxiety disorders. Clinician's guides and patient manuals* (Second Edition, chapters 24–27). Cambridge: Cambridge University Press.

Resick, P. & Calhoun, K. (2001). Posttraumatic stress disorder. In D. Barlow (Ed.), *Handbook of psychological disorders: A step-by-step manual* (pp. 60–113). New York: Guilford.

Shapiro, F. (2001). *Eye movement desensitization and reprocessing. Basis principles, protocols and procedures*. New York: Guilford.

ASSESSMENT INSTRUMENTS

Blake, D., Weathers, F., Nagy, L., Kaloupek, D., Klauminzer, G., Charney, D. & Keane, T. (1995). The development of a clinician administered PTSD scale. *Journal of Traumatic Stress*, 8, 75–90.

Blanchard, E., Jones-Alexander, J., Buckely, T. et al. (1996). Psychometric properties of The PTSD Checklist (PCL). *Behaviour Research and Therapy*, 34, 669–679.

Briere, J. (1995). *Trauma symptom inventory (TSI). Professional manual.* Odessa, FL: PAR.

Davidson, J., Malik, M. & Travers, J. (1997). Structured interview for PTSD (SIP): Psychometric validation for DSM-IV criteria. *Depression and Anxiety*, 5, 127–129.

Falsetti, S. A., Resnick, H. S., Resick, P. A. & Kilpatrick, D. G. (1993). The modified PTSD Symptom Scale: A brief self report measure of posttraumatic stress disorder. *The Behavior Therapist*, 16, 161–162.

Foa, E. (1995). *Posttraumatic stress diagnostic scale: Manual.* Minnesota, MN: National Computer Systems. Self-report and interview versions are available.

Foa, E. B., Riggs, D. S., Dancu, C. V. & Rothbaum, B. O. (1993). Reliability and validity of a brief instrument for assessing post-traumatic stress disorder. *Journal of Traumatic Stress*, 6(4), 459–473.

Lauterbach, D. & Vrana, S. (1996). Three studies on the reliability and validity of a self-report measure of post traumatic stress disorder. *Assessment*, 3, 17–25. Contains the Purdue PTSD scale.

Lyons, J. & Keane, T. (1992). Keane PTSD Scale: MMPI and MMPI-2 update. *Journal of Traumatic Stress*, 5, 111–117.

Norris, F. & Perilla, J. (1996). Revised Civilian Mississippi Scale for PTSD: Reliability, validity and cross-language stability. *Journal of Traumatic Stress*, 9, 285–298.

Weathers, F. W., Keane, T. M. & Davidson, J. (2001). Clinician-administered PTSD scale: A review of the first ten years of research. *Depression and Anxiety*, 13(3), 132–156.

Weathers, F. W., Litz, B. T., Herman, D. S., Huska, J. A. & Keane, T. M. (1993). *The PTSD Checklist (PCL): Reliability, validity, and diagnostic utility*. Paper presented at the 9th Annual Conference of the ISTSS, San Antonio.

Weiss, D. & Marmar, C. (1997). The Impact of Events Scale – Revised. In J. Wilson & T. Keane (Eds.), *Assessing psychological trauma and PTSD* (pp. 399–411). New York: Guilford.

Zlotnick, C., Davidson, J., Shea, M. & Pearlstein, T. (1996). Validation of the Davison Trauma Scale in a sample of survivors of childhood sexual abuse. *Journal of Nervous and Mental Disease*, 184, 255–257.

TRAINING VIDEO

Creamer, M., Forbes, D., Phelps, A. & Humphreys, L. (2004). *Treating traumatic stress: Conducting Imaginal Exposure in PTSD – Clinician's Manual and Training Video*. Australian Centre for Posttraumatic Mental Health. University of Melbourne. Online. Available at: http://www.acpmh.unimelb.edu.au

Shapiro, F. *EMDR for trauma*. Washington, DC: American Psychological Association. Online. Available at: http://www.apa.org

REFERENCES

Albucher, R. C. & Liberzon, I. (2002). Psychopharmacological treatment in PTSD: A critical review. *Journal of Psychiatric Research*, 36(6), 355–367.

American Psychiatric Association (APA) (2000). *Diagnostic and statistical manual of the mental disorders* (Fourth Edition-Text Revision). Washington, DC: APA.

Andrews, G., Creamer, M., Crino, R., Hunt, C., Lampe, L. & Page, A. (2003). The treatment of anxiety disorders: Clinician guides and patient manuals (Second Edition). New York: Cambridge University Press.

Beck, A. T., Rush, A. J., Shaw, B. F. & Emery, G. (1979). *Cognitive therapy of depression*. New York: Guilford Press.

Bisson, J. I. (2003). Single-session early psychological interventions following traumatic events. *Clinical Psychology Review*, 23(3), 481–499.

Blake, D. D., Weathers, F., Nagy, L. M. et al. (1995). The development of a clinician administered PTSD scale. *Journal of Traumatic Stress*, 8(1), 75–90.

Blanchard, E. B., Jones Alexander, J., Buckley, T. C. & Forneris, C. A. (1996). Psychometric properties of the PTSD Checklist (PCL). *Behaviour Research and Therapy*, 34(8), 669–673.

Brady, K., Pearlstein, T., Asnis, G. M., Baker, D., Rothbaum, B., Sikes, C. R. et al. (2000). Efficacy and safety of sertraline treatment of posttraumatic stress disorder: A randomised controlled trial. *Journal of the American Medical Association*, 283(14), 1837–1844.

Brewin, C. R., Andrews, B. & Valentine, J. D. (2000). Meta-analysis of risk factors for posttraumatic stress disorder in trauma-exposed adults. *Journal of Consulting and Clinical Psychology*, 68(5), 748–766.

Brewin, C. R. & Lennard, H. (1999). Effects of mode of writing on emotional narratives. *Journal of Traumatic Stress*, 12(2), 355–361.

Brom, D., Kleber, R. J. & Defares, P. B. (1989). Brief psychotherapy for posttraumatic stress disorders. *Journal of Consulting and Clinical Psychology*, 57(5), 607–612.

Bryant, R. A. & Harvey, A. G. (1997). Acute stress disorder; a critical review of diagnostic issues. *Clinical Psychology Review*, 17(7), 757–773.

Bryant, R. A., Harvey, A. G., Dang, S. T., Sackville, T. & Basten, C. (1998). Treatment of acute stress disorder: A comparison of cognitive-behavioural therapy and supportive counselling. *Journal of Consulting and Clinical Psychology*, 66(5), 862–866.

Bryant, R. A., Moulds, M. L., Guthrie, R. M., Dang, S. T. & Nixon, R. D. V. (2003). Imaginal exposure alone and imaginal exposure with cognitive restructuring in treatment of posttraumatic stress disorder. *Journal of Consulting & Clinical Psychology*, 71(4), 706–712.

Compton, J. & Follette, V. (2002). Couple therapy when a partner has a history of child sexual abuse. In A. Gurman & N. Jacobson (Eds.), *Clinical handbook of couple therapy* (Third Edition, pp. 466–487). New York: Guilford.

Creamer, M., Burgess, P. & McFarlane, A. C. (2001). Post-traumatic stress disorder:

Findings from the Australian National Survey of Mental Health and Well-being. *Psychological Medicine*, 31(7), 1237–1247.

Creamer, M., Morris, P., Biddle, D. & Elliott, P. (1999). Treatment outcome in Australian veterans with combat-related posttraumatic stress disorder: A cause for cautious optimism? *Journal of Traumatic Stress*, 12(4), 545–558.

Creamer, M. & O'Donnell, M. (2002). Post-traumatic stress disorder. *Current Opinion in Psychiatry*, 15(2), 163–168.

Davidson, J. (2000). Pharmacotherapy of posttraumatic stress disorder: Treatment options, long-term follow-up, and predictors of outcome. *Journal of Clinical Psychiatry*, 61(Suppl 5), 52–59.

Davidson, J., Malik, M. & Travers, J. (1997). Structured interview for PTSD (SIP): Psychometric validation for DSM-IV criteria. *Depression and Anxiety*, 5, 127–129.

Davidson, J., Pearlstein, T., Londborg, P. et al. (2001). Efficacy of sertraline in preventing relapse of posttraumatic stress disorder: Results of a 28-week double-blind, placebo-controlled study. *American Journal of Psychiatry*, 158(12), 1974–1981.

Davidson, J., Rothbaum, B. O., van der Kolk, B. A., Sikes, C. R. & Farfel, G. M. (2001). Multicenter, double-blind comparison of sertraline and placebo in the treatment of posttraumatic stress disorder. *Archives of General Psychiatry*, 58(5), 485–492.

Davidson, P. R. & Parker, K. C. (2001). Eye movement desensitization and reprocessing (EMDR): a meta-analysis. *Journal of Consulting & Clinical Psychology*, 69(2), 305–316.

Devilly, G. J. & Spence, S. H. (1999). The relative efficacy and treatment distress of EMDR and a cognitive-behavior trauma treatment protocol in the amelioration of posttraumatic stress disorder. *Journal of Anxiety Disorders*, 13(1–2), 131–157.

Everly, G. S., Boyle, S. H. & Lating, J. M. (1999). The effectiveness of psychological debriefing with vicarious trauma: A meta-analysis. *Stress Medicine*, 15(4), 229–233.

Falsetti, S. A., Resnick, H. S., Resick, P. A. & Kilpatrick, D. G. (1993). The modified PTSD Symptom Scale: A brief self report measure of posttraumatic stress disorder. *The Behavior Therapist*, 16, 161–162.

Figley, C. R. (1985). *Trauma and its wake*. New York: Brunner/Mazel.

Foa, E. B., Dancu, C. V., Hembree, E. A., Jaycox, L. H., Meadows, E. A. & Street, G. P. (1999a). A comparison of exposure therapy, stress inoculation training, and their combination for reducing posttraumatic stress disorder in female assault victims. *Journal of Consulting and Clinical Psychology*, 67(2), 194–200.

Foa, E. B., Davidson, J., Frances, A., Culpepper, L., Ross, R. & Ross, D. (1999b). The expert consensus guideline series: Treatment of posttraumatic stress disorder. *Journal of Clinical Psychiatry*, 60(Suppl 16), 4–76.

Foa, E. B., Hearst Ikeda, D. & Perry, K. J. (1995a). Evaluation of a brief cognitive-behavioral program for the prevention of chronic PTSD in recent assault victims. *Journal of Consulting and Clinical Psychology*, 63(6), 948–955.

Foa, E. B., Keane, T. M. & Friedman, M. J. (2000). *Effective treatments for PTSD*. New York: Guilford Press.

Foa, E. B., Riggs, D. S., Dancu, C. V. & Rothbaum, B. O. (1993). Reliability and validity of a brief instrument for assessing post-traumatic stress disorder. *Journal of Traumatic Stress*, 6(4), 459–473.

Foa, E. B., Riggs, D. S. & Gershuny, B. S. (1995b). Arousal, numbing, and intrusion: Symptom structure of PTSD following assault. *American Journal of Psychiatry*, 152(1), 116–120.

Foa, E. B. & Rothbaum, B. O. (1998). *Treating the trauma of rape: Cognitive-behavioral therapy for PTSD*. New York: Guilford Press.

Foa, E. B., Rothbaum, B. O., Riggs, D. S. & Murdock, T. B. (1991). Treatment of posttraumatic stress disorder in rape victims: A comparison between cognitive-behavioral procedures and counseling. *Journal of Consulting and Clinical Psychology*, 59(5), 715–723.

Forbes, D., Creamer, M. & Biddle, D. (2001). The validity of the PTSD checklist as a measure of symptomatic change in combat-related PTSD. *Behaviour Research and Therapy*, 39(8), 977–986.

Friedman, M. J., Charney, D. S. & Southwick, S. M. (1993). Pharmacotherapy for recently evacuated military casualties. *Military Medicine*, 158(7), 493–497.

Frueh, B. C., Hammer, M. B., Cahill, S. P., Gold, P. B. & Hamlin, K. (2000). Apparent symptom overreporting in combat veterans evaluated for PTSD. *Clinical Psychological Review*, 20, 853–885.

Gelpin, E., Bonne, O., Peri, T. & Brandes, D. (1996). Treatment of recent trauma survivors with benzodiazepines: A prospective study. *Journal of Clinical Psychiatry*, 57(9), 390–394.

Glass, S. (2002). Couple therapy after the trauma of infidelity. In A. Gurman & N. Jacobson (Eds.), *Clinical handbook of couple therapy* (Third Edition, pp. 488–507). New York: Guilford Press.

Halligan, S. L., Michael, T., Clark, D. M. & Ehlers, A. (2003). Posttraumatic stress disorder following assault: The role of cognitive processing, trauma memory, and appraisals. *Journal of Consulting and Clinical Psychology*, 71(3), 419–431.

Helzer, J. E., Robins, L. N. & McEvoy, L. (1987). Post-traumatic stress disorder in the general population: Findings of the Epidemiologic Catchment Area survey. *New England Journal of Medicine*, 317, 1630–1634.

Holtzworth-Munroe, A., Meehan, J., Rehman, U. & Marshall, A. (2002), Intimate partner violence: An introduction for couple therapists. In A. Gurman & N. Jacobson (Eds.), *Clinical handbook of couple therapy* (Third Edition, pp. 441–465). New York: Guilford.

Humphries, C. & Carr, A. (2001). The short term effectiveness of critical incident stress debriefing. *Irish Journal of Psychology*, 22, 188–197.

Johnson, D. R., Rosenheck, R., Fontana, A., Lubin, H., Charney, D. & Southwick, S. (1996). Outcome of intensive inpatient treatment for combat-related post-traumatic stress disorder. *American Journal of Psychiatry*, 153, 771–777.

Johnson, S. & Makinen, J. (2003). Posttraumatic stress. In D. Snydeer & M. Wishman (Eds.), *Treating difficult couples: Helping couples with co-existing mental and relationship disorders* (pp. 308–329). New York: Guilford Press.

Kessler, R. C., Sonnega, A., Hughes, M. & Nelson, C. B. (1995). Posttraumatic stress disorder in the national comorbidity survey. *Archives of General Psychiatry*, 52, 1048–1060.

Kessler, R. C., Zhao, S., Katz, S. J. et al. (1999). Past-year use of outpatient services for psychiatric problems in the National Comorbidity Survey. *American Journal of Psychiatry*, 156, 115–123.

King, D. W., Leskin, G. A., King, L. A. & Weathers, F. W. (1998). Confirmatory factor analysis of the clinician-administered PTSD Scale: Evidence for the dimensionality of posttraumatic stress disorder. *Psychological Assessment*, 10(2), 90–96.

Kubany, E. S. & Watson, S. B. (2003). Guilt: Elaboration of a multidimensional model. *Psychological Record*, 53(1), 51–90.

Lyons, J. & Keane, T. (1989). Implosive therapy for the treatment of combat-related PTSD. *Journal of Traumatic Stress*, 2, 137–152.

Marks, I., Lovell, K., Noshirvani, H., Livanou, M. & Thrasher, S. (1998). Treatment of posttraumatic stress disorder by exposure and/or cognitive restructuring: A controlled study. *Archives of General Psychiatry*, 55(4), 317–325.

Marshall, R. D., Spitzer, R. & Liebowitz, M. R. (1999). Review and critique of the new DSM-IV diagnosis of acute stress disorder. *American Journal of Psychiatry*, 156(11), 1677–1685.

Mayou, R. A., Ehlers, A. & Hobbs, M. (2000). Psychological debriefing for road traffic accident victims: Three-year follow-up of a randomised controlled trial. *British Journal of Psychiatry*, 176, 589–593.

Meichenbaum, D. (1985). *Stress inoculation training*. New York: Pergamon Press.

Mitchell, J. T. & Everly, G. S. (1995). *The critical incident stress debriefing (CISD) and the prevention of work-related traumatic stress among high risk occupation groups*. New York: Plenum Press.

Najavits, L. M. (2003). Seeking safety: A treatment manual for PTSD and substance abuse. *Psychotherapy Research*, 13(1), 125–126.

Norris, F. H. & Riad, J. K. (1997). Standardized self-report measures of civilian trauma and posttraumatic stress disorder. In J. P. Wilson & T. M. Keane (Eds.), *Assessing psychological trauma and PTSD* (pp. 7–42). New York: Guilford Press.

Ouimette, P. & Brown, P. J. (2003). *Trauma and substance abuse: Causes, consequences, and treatment of comorbid disorders*. Washington, DC: American Psychological Association.

Ozer, E. J., Best, S. R., Lipsey, T. L. & Weiss, D. S. (2003). Predictors of posttraumatic stress disorder and symptoms in adults: A meta-analysis. *Psychological Bulletin*, 129(1), 52–73.

Parnell, L. (1999). *EMDR in the treatment of adults abused as children*. New York: W. W. Norton.

Pitman, R. K., Sanders, K. M., Zusman, R. M. et al. (2002). Pilot study of secondary prevention of posttraumatic stress disorder with propranolol. *Biological Psychiatry*, 51(2), 189–192.

Resick, P. A., Nishith, P., Weaver, T. L., Astin, M. C. & Feuer, C. A. (2002). A comparison of cognitive-processing therapy with prolonged exposure and a waiting condition for the treatment of chronic posttraumatic stress disorder in female rape victims. *Journal of Consulting and Clinical Psychology*, 70(4), 867–879.

Resick, P. A. & Schnicke, M. K. (1993). *Cognitive processing therapy for sexual assault victims: A treatment manual*. Newbury Park, CA: Sage Publications.

Resnick, P. J. (1995). Guidelines for the evaluation of malingering in posttraumatic stress disorder. In R. I. Simon (Ed.), *Posttraumatic stress disorder in litigation: Guidelines for forensic assessment* (pp. 117–134). Washington, DC: American Psychiatric Press.

Riggs, D. S. (2000). Marital and family therapy. In E. B. Foa, T. M. Keane & M. J. Friedman (Eds.), *Effective treatments for PTSD: practice guidelines from the International Society for Traumatic Stress Studies* (pp. 280–301). New York: Guilford.

Rose, S. & Bisson, J. (1998). Brief early psychological interventions following trauma: A systematic review of the literature. *Journal of Traumatic Stress*, 11(4), 697–710.

Roth, S., Newman, E., Pelcovitz, D., van der Kolk, B. & Mandel, F. S. (1997). Complex PTSD in victims exposed to sexual and physical abuse: Results from the DSM-IV field trial for posttraumatic stress disorder. *Journal of Traumatic Stress*, 10, 539–555.

Schnurr, P. P., Friedman, M. J., Foy, D. W. et al. (2003). Randomised trial of trauma-focused group therapy for posttraumatic stress disorder – Results from a department of Veterans Affairs Cooperative Study. *Archives of General Psychiatry*, 60(5), 481–489.

Shapiro, F. (2001). *Eye movement desensitization and reprocessing: Basic principles, protocols, and procedures* (Second Edition). New York: Guilford.

Simon, R. I. (1995). *Posttraumatic stress disorder in litigation*. Washington, DC: American Psychiatric Press.

Solomon, S., Keane, T., Newman, E. & Kaloupek, D. (1996). Choosing self-report measures and structured interviews. In E. B. Carlson (Ed.), *Trauma research methodology* (pp. 56–81). Lutherville, MD: Sidran Press.

Solomon, Z. (1989). Psychological sequelae of war: A 3-year prospective study of Israeli combat stress reaction casualties. *Journal of Nervous and Mental Disease*, 177(6), 342–346.

Solomon, Z., Shalev, A., Spiro, S. E. et al. (1992). Negative psychometric outcomes: Self-report measures and a follow-up telephone survey. *Journal of Traumatic Stress*, 5(2), 225–246.

Tarrier, N., Sommerfield, C., Pilgrim, H. & Humphreys, L. (1999). Cognitive therapy or imaginal exposure in the treatment of post-traumatic stress disorder. Twelve-month follow-up. *British Journal of Psychiatry*, 175, 571–575.

Taylor, S. (2003). Outcome predictors for three PTSD treatments: Exposure therapy, EMDR, and relaxation training. *Journal of Cognitive Psychotherapy. Special Issue on Posttraumatic Stress Disorder*, 17(2), 149–161.

Van der Kolk, B., McFarlane, A. C. & Weisaeth, L. (Eds.) (1996). Traumatic stress. New York: Guilford Press.

Weathers, F. W., Keane, T. M. & Davidson, J. (2001). Clinician-administered PTSD scale: A review of the first ten years of research. *Depression and Anxiety*, 13(3), 132–156.

Weathers, F. W., Litz, B. T., Herman, D. S., Huska, J. A. & Keane, T. M. (1993). *The PTSD Checklist (PCL): Reliability, validity, and diagnostic utility*. Paper presented at the 9th Annual Conference of the ISTSS, San Antonio.

Weiss, D. (1997). Structured clinical interview techniques. In J. Wilson & T. Keane (Eds.), *Assessing psychological trauma and PTSD* (pp. 493–511). New York: Guilford Press.

Wilson, J.-P. & Keane, T.-M. (1997). *Assessing psychological trauma and PTSD*. New York: Guilford Press.

World Health Organization (WHO) (1992). *The ICD-10 classification of mental and behavioural disorders. Clinical descriptions and diagnostic guidelines*. Geneva: WHO. Online. Available at: http://www.informatik.fh-luebeck.de/icd/welcome.html

Zlotnick, C., Davidson, J., Shea, M. T. & Pearlstein, T. (1996). Validation of the Davidson Trauma Scale in a sample of survivors of childhood sexual abuse. *Journal of Nervous and Mental Disease*, 184(4), 255–257.

Chapter 15

The clinical management of social anxiety disorder

Tony Bates

CASE EXAMPLE

As each social event drew near, Richard's panic steadily increased. Anticipating an encounter was almost as painful as the event itself. Conscious of his potential to go red with embarrassment and let himself down in front of others, he endured meeting people only by virtually holding his breath. He made frequent visits to the bathroom to check his face for signs of blushing in the mirror and – if he thought he saw the slightest evidence of raised colour – he splashed his face with cold water and verbally attacked himself in the harshest way: 'What the hell is wrong with you? . . . You're so *stupid*!' A safe corner of the room, or remaining near a quiet relative, offered temporary refuge, but inwardly there was really nowhere to hide. Afterwards, the onslaught of self-attacking continued for days as he obsessed about every aspect of the encounter. At thirty-four years old, this was a problem he had been growing into, rather than out of, since he was fourteen years of age.

He remembered when it had first begun: the night he stood on stage in the school concert in front of his classmates and completely forgot his lines. 'Oh you should have seen your face, you were *so* red' was the only feedback he heard. It was a memory and an experience that had become frozen in his mind and which he seemed destined to repeat. With each new encounter, the audience was different, but his physical sensations remained the same. Why had it meant so much? Why had he walked out of school three days later never to set foot in a classroom again, moving from one menial job to another, from continent to continent?

Growing up as a somewhat anonymous child, one of seven children born to hard-pressed parents, he had managed to carve a niche for himself and cope. His father's constant reference to him as 'brainless' had nurtured seeds of self-doubt and perhaps his 'failure' on stage represented proof that his father was right. And yet he distinctly remembered his friendships, achievements and self-confidence on the football field and how all that changed after he left school. Each job provoked increasing degrees of fear and despair.

By twenty-four Richard had become quite suicidal but chanced on a magazine article that suggested psychologists could help a person to overcome blushing. His initial euphoria that a professional could help him quickly gave way to an even deeper sense of despair, as the individual he consulted offered neither warmth nor empathy, but discharged him after six unsuccessful sessions with the ominous verdict 'I would be very worried about you'. Later on, participation in the programme described below finally restored to him a sense of dignity and confidence in social situations but only after living into his thirties a life that became increasingly curtailed by fear and hiding. Like many others with social phobia, his existence was a miserable half-life in a safe but lonely hell.

CLINICAL FEATURES

Social phobia is an anxiety disorder that is characterized by 'a marked and persistent fear of social or performance situations' (American Psychiatric Association (APA), 1994, p. 411) due to the individual's belief that he or she will act in a way that will result in embarrassment, ridicule or rejection by others. Feared situations are avoided where possible or endured with significant discomfort. Sufferers are distinguished on the basis of their being afraid of specific performance situations (e.g. speaking, writing, eating in public) or frightened generally by social encounters where their vulnerabilities and inadequacies may become apparent to others. Whilst these concerns are common and not in themselves pathological, a diagnosis of social phobia is given when these fears significantly hinder a person's daily life on a consistent basis. The presence of a clinically significant impairment is necessary to distinguish it from normal social anxiety, which itself has an important function of alerting people to signs of social threat (Buss, 1996) and contributing to the motivation to prepare and adapt to challenging performances and encounters (Rothbart & Ahadi, 1994). The key to distinguishing this disorder from normal anxiety is the presence of an 'involuntary impairment' (Klein, 1999, p. 424). This denotes an individual's awareness of his or her problems as significant, accompanied by an inability to resolve or regulate the distress these problems cause. Social life is increasingly impaired by repeated refusals to meet and interact with others; career opportunities and promotions may be declined due to the increased social exposure involved. Attendance at family celebrations may prove so uncomfortable that events like a child's first communion, graduation ceremonies and family weddings may be avoided rather than risk the horror of marring the event by some humiliating display of anxiety. Diagnostic criteria for social phobia established by the World Health Organization (ICD-10; WHO, 1992) and the APA (DSM-IV; APA, 1994) are presented in Table 15.1.

Table 15.1 Diagnostic criteria for social phobia

DSM-IV-TR	*ICD-10*
A. A marked or persistent fear of one or more social or performance situations in which the person is exposed to unfamiliar people or to possible scrutiny by others. The individual fears that he or she will act in a way that will be humiliating or embarrassing. In children the child must have the capacity for age-appropriate relationships with familiar people and the anxiety occurs in peer-group settings	Social phobias are centred around a fear of scrutiny by other people in comparatively small groups (as opposed to crowds) leading to avoidance of social situations. They may be discrete (i.e. restricted to eating in public, to public speaking, or to encounters with the opposite sex) or diffuse, involving almost all social situations outside the family circle
B. Exposure to the feared social situation produces an immediate anxiety response, which may take the form of a panic attack or, in children, may involve crying, tantrums, freezing or shrinking from social situations with unfamiliar people	All of the following should be fulfilled for a definite diagnosis: 1. The psychological or autonomic symptoms must be primarily manifestations of anxiety and not secondary to other symptoms such as delusions or obsessional thoughts 2. The anxiety must be restricted to or predominate in particular social situations 3. Avoidance of the phobic situations must be a prominent feature
C. The person recognizes that the fear is excessive or unreasonable, although this feature may be absent in children	
D. The feared social situations are avoided or endured with intense anxiety or distress	
E. The avoidance or anxiety interferes significantly with personal, social or academic functioning	
F. If under 18 years of age the duration is at least 6 months	
G. The anxiety and avoidance is not better accounted for by another disorder	
H. The fear is not related to a general medical or psychological condition such as Parkinson's disease or stuttering	

Note: Adapted from DSM-IV-TR (APA, 2000) and ICD-10 (WHO, 1992).

EPIDEMIOLOGY

Epidemiological studies have suggested a high incidence of social phobia in the general population. In their meticulous survey of the twelve-month and lifetime prevalence of DSM-III-R psychiatric disorders in the US, which involved structured clinical interviews with over 8000 respondents, Kessler et al. (1994) found a twelve-month prevalence of 7.9% and a lifetime prevalence of 13.3% for social phobia. These results established this disorder as the third most common in the US, after major depression (17% lifetime prevalence) and alcohol dependence (14%). Of particular concern was the finding in a later study that social phobia was a 'chronic unremittent disorder' (De Wit et al., 1999, p. 569) with the median length of suffering being reported as twenty-five years. The onset of social phobia is typically in the mid-teens to early twenties, with earlier onset common. Regier, Rae, Narrow, Kaelber & Schatzberg (1998) found a mean onset age of 11.5 years. Onset after age twenty-five is relatively uncommon (Magee et al., 1996; Schneier et al., 1992). In terms of clinical presentation, a recent study found that the average age at which professional help was sought was thirty years old (Rapee, 1995).

Both clinical and epidemiological studies have noted different patterns of onset and recovery among different subtypes of this disorder. For example, distinctions have been made between individuals with fears limited to public speaking and individuals with fears of most social situations (Kessler et al., 1998). Those with fears of most social situations tend to have an earlier age of onset (Heimberg et al., 1990b), a history of childhood shyness (Stemberger et al., 1995) and they have a poorer prognosis than those with speaking-only or 'specific' social phobias. Specific or circumscribed social anxiety was found by Stemberger to be associated with traumatic experiences usually arising in early teens. In general, however, the differentiation of categorical subtypes of social anxiety disorder has failed to hold up in research (Furmark et al., 2000). Rather, social anxiety disorder in a community more likely exists along a continuum of severity.

COMORBIDITY

Axis I disorders

People with social anxiety disorder are more than likely to have at least one comorbid condition (Lepine & Pelissolo, 1998; Merikangas & Angst, 1995). The most likely Axis I disorder to coexist with social phobia is major depression, present in over one in every four sufferers (Regier et al., 1998; Schneier et al., 1992) followed by panic disorder (Stein et al., 1989), agoraphobia (Goisman et al., 1995), generalized anxiety disorder (Borkovec et al., 1995;

Mennin et al., 2000) substance abuse disorders (Dilsaver, Qamar & del Medico, 1992; Page & Andrews, 1996) and eating disorders (Bulik et al., 1997). Social phobia has been found to precede mood, substance abuse and eating disorders. The presence of psychiatric comorbidity has been found to be associated with a poorer prognosis (Davidson et al., 1993) or at least to slow recovery time. In 72% of individuals with both social phobia and depression, social phobia was found to precede depression, whereas only 5% had depression first (Regier et al., 1998). A diagnosis of major depression has been found to follow the onset of social phobia by an average of 13.2 years, but it has also been found that social phobia may be a secondary condition that remits naturally when the episode of depression has been resolved (Stein et al., 1990).

Social anxiety disorder and avoidant personality disorder

It was not until the publication of DSM-III in 1980 that the diagnoses of social phobia and avoidant personality disorder first appeared. Prior to this, in the first and second editions of the DSM, social fears were categorized with other anxiety disorders and, reflecting the prominence of psychodynamic thinking at the time, viewed as projections of underlying conflicts onto social situations (Alden & Crozier, 2001). Social phobia was first classified as a disorder in the DSM-III when an individual consistently experienced a disabling phobic reaction to specific social situations, with the four most common situations identified as: 'speaking or performing in public, using public lavatories, eating in public, and writing in the presence of others' (APA, 1980, p. 324). In contrast, a diagnosis of avoidant personality disorder was made when there was evidence of a pervasive pattern of social inhibition, feelings of inadequacy and hypersensitivity to negative evaluation. Strongly influenced by the work of Theodore Millon's biosocial learning theory (1969, 1981), avoidant personality disorder described a behaviour pattern resulting from an anxious child being subjected to persistent experiences of depreciation, which in turn resulted in an *active-detached* coping style. In the DSM-III the diagnosis of social phobia was made only if avoidant personality disorder could be excluded.

Clinical experience following the publication of DSM-III failed to support this distinction of social phobia as an anxiety disorder with clearly circumscribed phobic reactions to discrete social situations. The majority of clients seeking help for social anxiety described more pervasive difficulties and yet did not necessarily merit the more disabling diagnosis of avoidant personality disorder, but with a strong clinical overlap, which made clear differentiation difficult. The criteria were therefore amended in the edition of DSM-III-R published in 1987 and a new subtype of social phobia, 'generalized' social phobia was added to the category, which was applied to individuals for whom 'the phobic situation includes most social situations' (APA, 1987, p. 243). With this revision, avoidant personality was dropped as an exclusion criterion, which could now exist as a comorbid diagnosis. Since this generalized subtype of social phobia was described as having a chronic course, with onset in late childhood or early adolescence, the distinction between it and avoidant personality disorder became increasingly blurred. Whatever distinction there was seemed to reflect more a severity of dysfunction rather than any qualitative difference (Widiger, 1992).

Rather than clarify the distinction between these two disorders, the publication of DSM-IV (APA, 1994) further revised the criteria for generalized anxiety in a manner that suggested even greater overlap with avoidant personality disorder. For example, the DSM-III-R diagnostic criterion 'is reticent in social situations because of a fear of saying something inappropriate or foolish, or of being unable to answer a question' (APA, 1987, p. 353) was replaced by 'is inhibited in new interpersonal situations because of feelings of inadequacy' (APA, 1994, p. 665). Greater emphasis was given in the DSM-IV to underlying and enduring personality factors that contributed to social anxiety, e.g. the persistent negative image of self as 'socially inept, personally unappealing, or inferior to others' (APA, 1994, p. 665) that led to 'frequently lifelong' (APA, 1994, p. 414) social phobia. To reflect this revised conception of social phobia as an enduring pervasive difficulty, rather than an irrational fear of some specific activity or situation, the preferred term 'social anxiety disorder' was introduced (APA, 1994, p. 411). In practice, the terms social phobia and generalized social anxiety disorder are used interchangeably in the literature and their usage in this chapter is consistent with this convention.

The debate as to whether generalized social anxiety reflects primarily a disorder of anxiety or of personality continues and remains unresolved (Widiger, 2001). However, the constant revisions of social anxiety have implications for treatment. The consensus would appear to be that a treatment that focuses exclusively on the regulation of distressing symptoms is inadequate. Effective therapy needs to address underlying issues of vulnerability, insecurity, self-consciousness and the individuals' image of themselves as socially incompetent. The cognitive model of social phobia proposed by Clark and Wells (1995) provides a systematic comprehensive treatment approach that addresses both the distressing symptoms that constitute this syndrome and the underlying vulnerabilities that account for its persistence and intractability.

THEORIES OF SOCIAL ANXIETY DISORDER

The cognitive model of social anxiety disorder

Key sources for a detailed account of the cognitive model of social anxiety disorder and its therapeutic applications are Clark and Wells (1995), Wells

(1998), Bates and Clark (1998), and Clark (2001). The development of this model was prompted by a number of puzzling features in respect to social phobia (Butler, 1985, 1989). In contrast to other phobic reactions that tended to habituate in response to prolonged, repeated exposures, social phobia often persisted and became more intense despite countless, unavoidable social encounters where feared catastrophes repeatedly failed to occur (Butler, 1985). Also, neither social skills training nor relaxation training appeared to reduce social phobia, despite earlier assumptions that deficits in social skills (van Dyck, 1996), and inability to control increased arousal in social situations were critical to the maintenance of this disorder. These anomalies were addressed in the seminal work of Clark and Wells (1995), who focused on key processes that are activated for social phobics when they enter a feared situation, and on the safety strategies they adopt to prevent their particular feared catastrophe from happening. These 'safety behaviours', which assume a vital role for sufferers since they are believed to be their only protection from certain humiliation and rejection, are ultimately self-defeating. They prevent individuals from ever experiencing direct or unmediated 'exposure' to social situations and discovering that their negative predictions of themselves and others are biased, if not completely untrue. Underlying assumptions regarding other's intolerance of vulnerability can more easily be tested when safety behaviours are dropped. Relaxation exercises undertaken to regulate anxiety may fail to deliver their desired effect because they unwittingly reinforce the self-focused attention and self-consciousness that are central to the problem of social anxiety disorder.

Before describing the assessment, formulation and clinical interventions for this disorder, a more detailed exposition of the theoretical model is presented. Figure 15.1 outlines a number of processes that are activated when an individual with social anxiety disorder enters a feared social situation. In common with other people, social phobics have a strong desire to make a good impression on others and achieve acceptance and a sense of belonging within groups. However, underlying beliefs and assumptions they hold about themselves and others seriously limit their confidence in being able to achieve this goal. Clark (2001) describes three categories of assumption that can be activated in feared situations: (1) *Excessively high standards for social performance*, e.g. 'I must sound interesting and intelligent', 'I must not seem in any way odd or different'; (2) *Conditional beliefs regarding the consequences of acting in certain ways*, e.g. 'If I appear in any way anxious people will see me as incompetent', 'If I appear to blush or shake, people will think I'm weird'; and (3) *Unconditional negative beliefs about the self*, e.g. 'I am boring/stupid/odd/', 'I am damaged'.

The threat of being exposed or betrayed, by some outward manifestation of vulnerability such as shakiness or blushing, or by failing to reach the high expectations that others are believed to hold for any type of social performance, naturally arouses fear and dread when the social phobic confronts

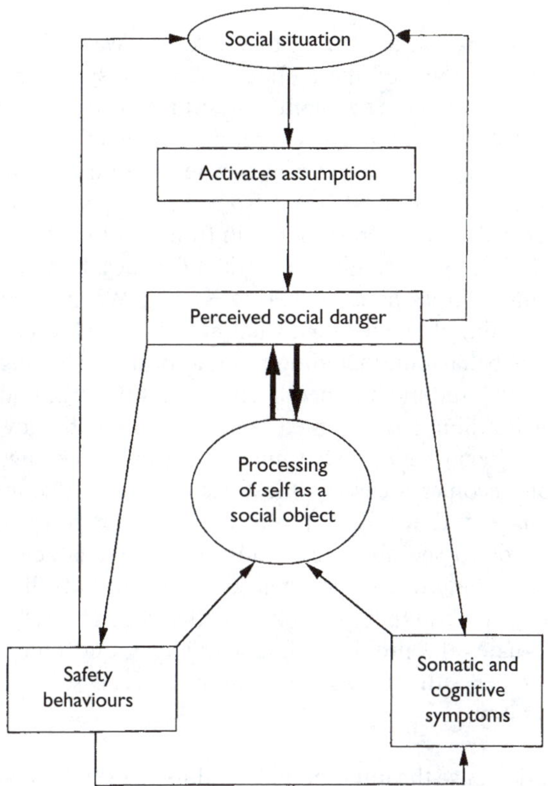

Figure 15.1 Clark and Wells 1995 cognitive model of the processes that occur when a socially phobic individual enters a feared social situation (reproduced by kind permission).

the prospect of a social encounter. Fears may become highly focused or may remain unclear (e.g. 'I will blush in some extreme way', 'I will appear odd') but will always centre on themes of behaving in some unacceptable way that will be perceived by others as grounds for a diminution of their respect, if not for outright ridicule. Whilst many writers identified these concerns as fundamental to social anxiety, the unique contribution of the cognitive model was to identify a number of processes that occur when the individual becomes seduced by these fears, which in turn prevent them from discovering how unfounded they are. Three processes that contribute, to the vicious cycle of anxiety of social phobia and to its persistence, are the shift of attention in social situations to a negative image of self, the safety strategies adopted to prevent this self from being exposed, and the manner in which the strategies process social events prior to, and following, the encounter.

Negative image of self

A critical feature of social phobia, according to Clark and Wells (1995), is the shift in attention in the mind of the sufferer to bodily symptoms of anxiety; this shift is activated when the encounter or performance is perceived as holding danger. On the basis of these symptoms, sufferers' awareness becomes dominated by an image of themselves as they fear they might appear to others. This social self-image is constructed from the perspective of the observer. One man described how, when standing in front of other clients to give a talk that he would later have to give to work colleagues, he was convinced that he was coming across as a 'gibbering wreck'. When asked to elaborate on this image of himself, he detailed what he considered to be very frightening features of his behaviour, including talking too fast, shaking his head uncontrollably, shifting and moving nervously around the room, all of which were compelling for him but completely at variance with how he appeared to his audience. Regardless of what may in fact be happening, the social phobic's attention becomes focused almost exclusively on this nightmare of how he or she imagines they might appear. Fleeting attention to their internal state of arousal or to the audience, whose behaviour is generally neutral or ambiguous, serve only to confirm their worst fear of how they are being perceived and further lock-in their self-focused attention. This sets up a vicious cycle that perpetuates the problem of social anxiety and reinforces their perception of the social situation as threatening. Clark describes this dilemma in the following way:

> They [social phobics] . . . use the internal information made accessible by self-monitoring to infer how they appear to other people and what other people are thinking of them. In this way they become trapped in a closed system in which most of their evidence for their fears is self-generated and disconfirmatory evidence (such as other people's *positive* responses) becomes inaccessible or is ignored.
>
> (Clark, 2001, p. 408, italics added)

Safety behaviours

Safety behaviours are behavioural and internal mental processes employed by socially anxious individuals to prevent some specific feared outcome from occurring (one example would be covering one's face to conceal possible blushing; another would be concentrating internally on what one has just said and checking to see if what one is about to say next follows logically, to prevent the nightmare of sounding illogical and incoherent). Because of the energy and concentration they require, these strategies more often serve to heighten anxiety, increase self-focused attention and reinforce the perception of a particular social situation as dangerous. Salkovskis (1996) noted that when situations do not turn out as predicted, success is often attributed to these behaviours and not to the sufferer's mistaken predictions. Safety behaviours, far from serving to make social situations safer, contribute significantly to perpetuation of the sufferer's beliefs that the world is a dangerous and unforgiving place and that if one were to 'be oneself' (i.e. to drop safety strategies), rejection would inevitably follow. One woman in our group-based treatment programme adamantly refused to leave her home (or answer the door) without spending the best part of an hour meticulously layering on make-up to conceal her blushing. When she ventured outside and related in a normal relaxed way to others, she attributed the success of the meeting completely to the protective power of her make-up in concealing from others 'the person she really was'.

Safety behaviours may appear to relax someone sufficiently so they can engage successfully with others but there is another aspect to safety behaviours, noted by Clark (2001), which is their potential to create the impression of 'odd' behaviour in the social phobic and invite the somewhat 'perplexed' attention of others. The client who was terrified of others seeing his underarm perspiration and wore a jacket over his shirt, under an overcoat, in summertime, presented in our clinic with a red sweaty face, which looked most uncomfortable. His flustered appearance may well have given the impression of an individual without appropriate social skills, and suggested that some social skill training in the correct dress code for a hot summer day might have been indicated. However, it was not any lack of social skill but rather his attachment to a specific safety behaviour that created the impression of someone 'odd'. Similarly, an individual who couldn't bear that others might see any evidence in his eyes of 'nervousness', avoided eye contact and created a negative impression of being hostile and unfriendly. It is important to bear in mind that it may be the impact of the individual's safety behaviours rather than specific social skill deficits that account for the negative impression he or she creates in feared social situations. This may explain why the earlier popularity of social skill training with this population failed to achieve its intended effect (Heimberg, 1989; Marzillier et al., 1976). In running a dedicated programme for social phobia, our clinic's secretarial staff have naturally had to process a large number of enquiries for help from individuals we later ascertained were quite distressed and eager to secure some effective therapy. We have been repeatedly struck by the number of times different front-line staff have commented on how these individuals seemed so 'unfriendly' or so 'cold and demanding'. Clearly, the caller's embarrassment at having to contact a hospital and risk being identified as someone with social phobia had provoked the use of safety behaviours which may have concealed their anxiety but did little for their public personas.

Pre- and post-mortems

Facing the imminent prospect of a social encounter or performance, individuals with social anxiety disorder can become intensely anxious. Typically, they review a host of memories of previous encounters where they perceived themselves to have failed to control their anxiety and are convinced that these negative experiences will be repeated yet again. Clark and Wells (1995) have highlighted the destructive effects of this negative anticipatory processing, which either has the effect of making them withdraw from the social event or of inducing in them a high state of arousal and self-focused attention by the time they confront it. Their mind is likely to be dominated by the expectation of failure and their processing is so biased that they fail to notice what in fact transpires in the encounter, e.g. being received positively by others. Similarly, when the event is over, they engage in destructive 'post-mortems' where their ruminations are focused exclusively on how they may have let themselves down. Clark (2001) has described the abiding sense of shame most social phobics can experience long after a social event, regardless of how well they may have managed it. In this way, there is a tendency to accumulate evidence from each encounter, which serves to reinforce their deeper assumptions of being socially incompetent. This feature of the disorder has important clinical implications. Clients may have positive experiences in simulated social encounters in the context of a therapy session (and acknowledge their achievement at the time) but, a few days later, their report of what transpired has become distorted out of all recognition as a result of endless post-mortems. Any course of therapy needs to include a functional analysis of this aspect of social phobia. Individuals need to understand their attachment to this behaviour as a safety strategy, which they believe will protect them from making embarrassing mistakes in social situations, but also to become aware of how anticipation and post-mortems severely undermine their confidence to perform successfully socially.

ASSESSMENT

The socially phobic individual is very likely to postpone seeking help because the professional consultation is itself a social situation that involves exposure and embarrassment as much as any other. Sensitivity to these fears prepares the clinician for any off-putting behaviours (e.g. a dismissive attitude, ambivalence regarding commitment to change) that may simply be an expression of safety behaviours that are being employed to disguise or minimize the true extent of the individual's anxiety. Assessment questionnaires can offer the client a safe way of detailing the extent of their specific symptoms and their distress in social situations. Table 15.2 identifies specific instruments that have frequently been used in empirical studies and which have been found particularly helpful in monitoring response to a cognitive treatment approach in a community-based adult mental health setting (Cormack, 2000; Rohan, 1997).

Table 15.2 Useful assessment instruments in the treatment of social anxiety disorder

Fear of Negative Evaluation Scale (FNE)

The FNE (Watson & Friend, 1969) is a 30-item true–false inventory that assesses an individual's expectation of being negatively evaluated by others. It has a long history of use in social phobia research and its use in ongoing studies is considered to be of importance by Heimberg et al. (1988). Watson and Friend reported a Kuder Richardson-20 reliability coefficient of 0.94 and a test–retest reliability coefficient of 0.78, after a one-month interval. In terms of validity, Smith and Sarason (1975) found that individuals with high FNE scores rated themselves more highly as likely to receive negative feedback from others than those with low FNE scores, and an earlier study found that high scorers on the FNE avoided social comparison information that they found threatening (Friend & Gilbert, 1973). A briefer form of this scale was developed by Leary (1983) and a revised longer 39-item version (FNE-R) has been produced by Watson and Friend (1998). This revised scale uses a Likert scale (0–4) in place of the true–false rating and adds nine new items to the 30 included in the original version

Social Phobia Scale (SPS)

The Social Phobia Scale (Mattick & Clark, unpublished) is a 20-item scale that uses a Likert (0–4) scale to assess the degree of anxiety an individual experiences in situations where they are being observed by others. Internal consistency was reported by the authors to exceed 0.88 and test–re-test reliability was reported at 0.91 after one month and 0.93 after three months. Rohan (1997), using an Irish sample, reported a Cronbach's alpha reliability coefficient of 0.89. Mattick and Clark (unpublished) reported significant positive correlations with other standardized anxiety measures ($r = 0.54$) and with the SIAS ($r = 0.71$). Heimberg et al. (1992) found the SPS correlated significantly with a performance anxiety measure, and McNeil et al. (1995) found that this scale had good discriminative validity

Social Interaction Anxiety Scale (SIAS)

The Social Interaction Anxiety Scale (Mattick & Clark, unpublished) is a 20-item scale, developed as a companion to the SPS scale. Using a Likert scale (0–4) it was designed to measure anxiety in a broad range of social situations. Internal consistency was reported to exceed alpha = 0.88 and test–re-test reliability was 0.93 based on a social phobia sample. Heimberg et al. (1988) found this scale correlated highly with other measures of social interaction and McNeil et al. (1995) established that it had good discriminative validity

Social Cognition Questionnaire (SCQ)

This 21-item scale, developed by Wells, Stopa and Clark (unpublished) measures the frequency of negative cognitions activated in social situations (1 = thought never occurs, 5 = always occurs when nervous) and the degree of belief in these cognitions (0 = no belief in thought, 100 = completely convinced thought is true). Factor analysis with non-anxious subjects identified three dimensions: negative self-evaluative beliefs, fear of performance failure and showing anxiety, and fear of negative evaluation and attracting attention (Wells, 1997). Stopa (1995) reported a test–re-test reliability of 0.79 and significant correlations of 0.59 with the FNE. Rohan (1997) reported a Cronbach's alpha reliability coefficient of 0.87 for the frequency scale and 0.91 for the belief scale with socially phobic subjects

A review of the clients' self-ratings on these scales highlights key difficulties they routinely experience in social situations at a cognitive, affective, physiological and behavioural level. Feedback to clients concerning highly scored items can convey a recognition of, and empathy for, their predicament and helps to move the discussion towards a more precise formulation of the sequence of events that unfold in threatening social encounters. At the close of this assessment session, information can be summarized under the following headings: feared situations, negative thoughts (worst fears), level of anxiety and depression, and safety behaviours.

In addition to the above information, assessment should consider the key event(s) in the client's life that marked the onset of their difficulties. Other issues that can be explored include the following: the consequences of social anxiety on the client's quality of life and relationships with others; the presence of comorbid problems such as depression, alcohol abuse or social isolation; the specific goals the client might wish to pursue if he or she were free of this problem; and the client's perception of how therapy may help to overcome his or her difficulty. A review of the client's interpersonal or systemic context is important to identify resources that can be drawn on in recovery, and any factors that may sabotage attempts to become more socially confident.

CLINICAL INTERVENTIONS FOR SOCIAL PHOBIA

Early behavioural interventions with social phobics focused on encouraging exposure to social situations in the hope that habituation would occur and that non-phobic behaviours would be reinforced by positive reactions from others (McNeil et al., 2001). Overall, this approach showed success for sufferers in repeated trials (Fava, Grandi & Canestrari, 1989) but concern was raised in respect to the long-term benefit of exposure alone (Heimberg & Juster, 1995) and more recent approaches have combined behavioural and cognitive approaches. In these cognitive-behavioural approaches, exposure is seen as a critical means of bringing new information to bear on unhelpful assumptions and biases that serve to repeatedly create experiences of social discomfort.

Cognitive-behavioural intervention for social phobia

CBT proceeds by working collaboratively with clients to elucidate and formulate the different mechanisms that are keeping them entrenched in their predicament, employing different methods to encourage alternative ways of thinking and behaving, and modifying key deeper beliefs and assumptions (Beck et al., 1985). In this way, the cognitive approach seeks to bring about a transformation of meaning (Power & Brewin, 1997) whereby the individual perceives his or her anxiety symptoms as a reflection of vulnerability that potentially can bring them closer to others rather than alienate them. Learning to accept anxiety as part of any social encounter and shifting their attention to others, confident of the value of what they have to give and of the likelihood of a positive response, becomes the goal of treatment for social phobics. The cognitive model of Clark and Wells (1995) adapts these broad principles to the problem of social phobia through a series of specific steps designed to address different but inter-related aspects of this disorder.

The remainder of this chapter focuses on clinical interventions with the socially anxious client. Since the dominant model of treatment under consideration in this chapter is the model proposed by Clark and Wells, a detailed step-by-step outline of this approach is described, in respect to individual therapy. Briefer consideration is then given to group-based cognitive therapy and to the interpersonal, psychodynamic and psychopharmacological approaches to treatments of social phobia.

Building a formulation of the client's unique experience of social anxiety

Once a therapeutic agenda has been agreed, the therapist and client can work collaboratively to draw out an idiosyncratic formulation of the client's experience, guided by the generic model outlined in Figure 15.1. Focusing on a recent 'typical' episode of social anxiety, the client is asked to describe the circumstances that provoked anxiety and the specific fears that were activated. 'What was it exactly that you feared you would do?' 'What did you imagine the consequences of your behaviour would be?' At this point, clients can usefully be asked 'What happened next?', whereupon they may recount the specific symptoms they noticed, e.g. heart beating faster, face growing hot, a tightening sensation in their neck. Specific safety behaviours employed can be identified by asking 'When you feared you might do X (specify their particular fear) did you do anything to prevent this from happening?' or 'What did you do to ensure your discomfort would not become apparent to others in that situation?' The shift of attention to that negative construction of themselves that they feared might be apparent to others can be identified by asking: 'When you became self-conscious, did you have a picture in your mind of how you imagined you looked to others?' Hackman, Clark and McManus (2000) have reported the frequency with which these spontaneously occurring images of self in social phobia are tied to early memories of traumatic social experiences. Clark (2000) suggests it is helpful to note this association with earlier traumas with clients and thereby suggest that their negative impressions of self may be tied more to the past than to the present.

Self-monitoring homework exercises initiated from the very beginning of therapy identify key components of anxiety episodes and draw the client into the collaborative process of evolving a formulation of their difficulties. Table

Table 15.3 Sample homework record of reactions to typical feared social situations

Feared situation	*Perceived physical symptoms*	*Negative thoughts*	*Safety behaviours*
Being introduced to stranger in a bar	Heart beating rapidly	Oh my God, this is awful	Avoid eye contact, hunch shoulders Try to look 'cool'
Talking to my neighbour	Shaky voice Hot feeling	How can I stop this person from seeing what a basket case I am	Cover face with hands Look away
Standing at supermarket checkout	Abnormal breathing Nervous Palpitations	I'm going to shake from head to toe and then panic and have to run out, and leave my shopping, and have everyone staring at me	Tense up muscles to steady myself Try to block out thoughts of self and think of good things

15.3 is an example of a completed assignment where the client monitored her reaction to social situations that triggered anxiety and recorded her symptoms (which she imagined were apparent to others), her negative thoughts and the safety behaviours she employed to protect her worst fear from happening.

Causal lines between different components of clients' experience can be drawn by asking such questions as 'When you noticed you were becoming hot and shaky, what effect did that have on the image of yourself you feared others would see?' or 'When you were trying hard not to appear anxious, were you feeling more or less comfortable in the situation?' It is important to draw out collaboratively with each client the way different aspects of the experience are interlinked to generate the vicious cycle of anxiety that constitutes that person's distress in social situations.

The example in Figure 15.2 concerns Eva, aged thirty-six years, who presented with an eighteen-year history of generalized social phobia. The specific event around which the formulation was derived was the occasion of her making a presentation to her work colleagues, where she feared being unable to control her anxiety and inevitably having to disclose that she was socially phobic, before walking away in disgrace. She described how her attention was divided equally between the image of herself standing before them, tense and awkward, her hands shaking uncontrollably, and the image of the audience to whom she was speaking. Her symptoms and her safety behaviours drew her

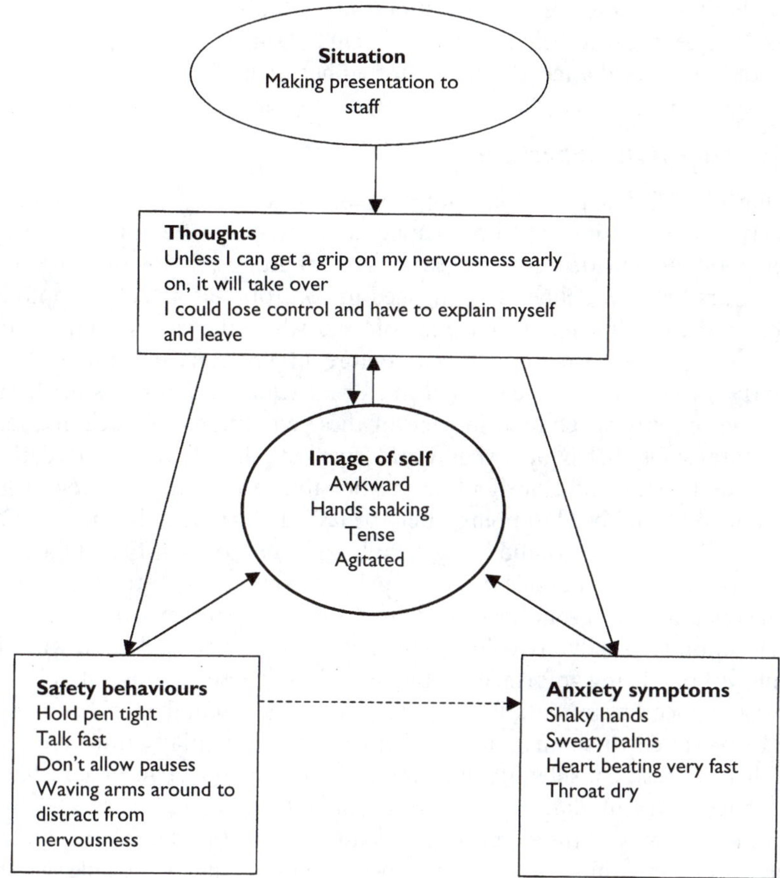

Figure 15.2 Idiosyncratic formulation of the experience of a woman with social anxiety, making a presentation to her staff.

attention back to herself and resulted in increasing efforts to hide her vulnerability at all costs. The more she engaged her safety behaviours to protect her from exposure, the more compelled she felt to keep doing this at all costs. The deeper issue of the assumptions that predisposed her to repeated episodes of this nature would be addressed later (see below), but this provisional formulation was sufficient to move therapy to the next stage of reconstructing her social self-image in situations such as the one she recounted.

A successful formulation, one that 'fits' a client's experience, can itself be a powerful intervention. It shifts the client's perspective from feeling shame for failing to negotiate everyday social situations to an appreciation of how he or she routinely construes social situations as threatening and how the understandable protective manoeuvres he or she employs serve only to intensify his or her fears and increase self-consciousness. It also provides direction for the subsequent safety behaviour experiments designed to break the vicious cycle of self-focused attention and distorted negative self-appraisal.

Safety behaviour experiment

Having identified a provisional formulation of a typical episode of social anxiety, clients are invited to participate in a role-play of a feared situation where they can be videoed under two sets of conditions, first with their safety behaviours 'on', i.e. deliberately engaged to control their anxiety symptoms, and then with their safety behaviours 'off', i.e. where they let go controls and risk allowing the worst to happen. Before filming this experiment, it is important to clarify (on the basis of the formulation) and, if necessary, practice, what exactly is required in each of these conditions. If 'speaking fast' constitutes safety behaviour, what would 'speaking slowly' involve? If 'curling up and making myself as insignificant as possible' was a safety strategy, what would its opposite be? Dropping safety behaviours can be quite an alarming prospect for some clients and it is generally sufficient to identify and focus on two or three critical manoeuvres for the video experiment. If the feared situation concerns one-to-one social encounters, a naive 'stooge' from within the organization is usually invited to participate in a brief conversation with the client without being informed of the specific purpose of this role-play. If the fear concerns presentations or performances, a number of volunteers can be recruited to simulate an 'audience' that is potentially threatening to the client. These considerations increase the likelihood of feedback that is spontaneous, truthful and credible to the individual.

In the first part of the experiment, clients are asked to engage their safety behaviours and monitor their inner experience as closely as possible. After a short period the role-play is interrupted and the client is asked to describe how they felt during the exercise and how they imagined they came across to others. Each of their descriptive words is rated on a 1–10 scale (e.g. 'How anxious/stupid/incoherent did you feel (1–10)?', 'How anxious/stupid/incoherent did you feel you appeared to X?' 'How would you rate your performance overall?'). These ratings are elicited out of hearing of the audience, who will be asked for their feedback when the behavioural experiment is completed. In the second part of the exercise, clients continue their conversation/presentation, but 'drop' their safety behaviours and shift their attention to their 'audience'. Similar ratings are taken with this segment and both sets of ratings are compared. Two important insights often emerge from these comparisons: on the one hand, clients can see how their anxiety is greater when safety behaviours are engaged; on the other hand, they can see that their evaluation of how they appear to others is based on inner anxiety cues rather than any objective evidence. The more they *feel* anxious the more they *think* their anxiety is apparent to others.

Feedback from the listener(s) can have a striking impact on clients and reveal the inaccuracies in their own estimate of how they appear to others. From the perspective of the listener, clients' behaviour generally seems more anxious when they are trying to hide their nervousness than when they risk being more present and open with the audience. However, even when clients appear anxious to the listener, it is generally much less apparent than they had predicted. Furthermore, it can come as a surprise to clients to learn that – contrary to impressing the listener as 'anxious' or 'stupid' – the impact of their use of safety behaviours is to appear 'distant', 'disinterested', or 'unfriendly'.

Video feedback is employed in this model because of its unique potential for offering clients feedback on their observable self in social situations. In their single-case study detailing the process of reconstructing the social self-image of a socially phobic woman, Lynn (Bates & Clark, 1998), scores on the social cognition questionnaire showed a dramatic shift after Lynn watched a video conversation that had been staged between her and a psychiatric registrar. This feedback more than any other revealed to her how distorted her evaluation was of her presentation:

> The discrepancy between the video image and the much more negative self-image she had of herself was striking and made a strong impact on her. Even those moments where she appeared slightly awkward or uneasy were not nearly as obvious in Lynn's own judgement as she had predicted. Furthermore, she saw that many of her apparent social difficulties were merely the observable effects of her safety behaviours and she saw how these disappeared in the second part of the experiment when she 'dropped' these behaviours.
>
> (Bates & Clark, 1998, pp. 296–297)

Clark (2001) highlights the need for care and preparation in having clients watch a video replay of themselves. The risk they run is of re-experiencing feelings they had in the role-play while viewing the video and processing themselves through the 'lens' of these feelings. To minimize this risk, clients can be assigned homework after the role-play session and asked to write out their predictions of what they will see when they watch the video, operationalizing their 'felt sense' of how they will appear, and rating each of their predictions on a 1–10 scale. When they eventually view the recording, they are advised to watch themselves as though they are watching a stranger, focusing on observable behaviours and evaluating these objectively.

Shifting attention and testing negative predictions

The next task for clients is to practise shifting their attention to the situation they find threatening and to begin to process actual feedback from others.

Given that their fears very likely include some concern about the negative impact of making even a minor social 'error', they are encouraged to experiment with 'breaking their own rules' and observe what happens. A client with a fear of drying up in the middle of a presentation deliberately allowed herself to pause momentarily mid-sentence, on a number of occasions during her talk. She discovered that such supposed misdemeanours went unnoticed, and from the feedback of her audience learned that her slowing down improved the impact of her presentation style. Repeated experiments such as these serve to modify beliefs regarding 'dangers' in social situations and help the client construct a more accurate image of their own performance. Since socially phobic individuals often harbour excessively high standards for social performance, these behavioural experiments help them realize the extent to which other people can accept a wide variation of standards that fall short of perfection.

Modifying dysfunctional assumptions

As clients experience a greater freedom to 'be themselves' and take risks to relate to others in a more spontaneous way, therapy may become attentive to critical early experiences that have contributed to fears of being ridiculed and rejected. Childhood experiences and traumatic memories that left them feeling inadequate and ashamed become the appropriate focus of later sessions. As these experiences are re-visited, clients become able to identify the core beliefs and the assumptions these gave rise to, and to weave these into a more comprehensive, developmental formulation of their social anxiety disorder. Eva, whose provisional formulation is outlined in Figure 15.2, described an early family experience that had a direct bearing on her later difficulties in social encounters. She grew up in a family where there were constant injunctions to eat right, look right and act right. 'Either you do it perfectly or not at all' was the family motto. Another dominant memory was constantly trying to cover up for any minor shortcomings because the consequence of being found out was a pressure to 'justify' oneself to others. 'Don't disclose anything to anyone because it will be held against you' seemed to capture the essence of her experience. Both of these assumptions were activated in social situations where her performance might fall short. Her reluctance to show initiative at work unless she could 'do it perfectly' often resulted in her opting out, or remaining silent at meetings where she had an important contribution to make. In addition, her anxiety in these situations was aggravated by her assumption that any evidence of anxiety would require her to make a full disclosure of her inner insecurities, which in turn would leave her very vulnerable to invasive enquiries about her emotional life at work. Eva had never felt right in exercising her boundaries and was hampered by her belief 'If I do something inappropriate, I owe it to others to explain and justify the reasons why'. Towards the close of therapy, she modified this assumption to 'It's OK just to have a position, and not always justify my position'. Homework was assigned to encourage her to test this new belief in the context of her episodes of social anxiety. Not only did she allow herself to 'just do what has to be done' rather than 'do it perfectly', she practised owning and disclosing normal anxiety at staff meetings without explaining the reasons why. Gradually, she became less troubled by signs of anxiety, comfortable in the knowledge that such experiences are universal and do not require inappropriate personal disclosures.

Therapy could now re-visit Eva's goals for her life, which she had outlined in the opening session when she was asked what she might want to do differently if she was not hampered by social phobia. Her improved self-understanding and an appreciation of her courage and resilience in confronting her fears enabled her to set new goals and leave therapy confident that they were within her reach. Whilst her feelings and felt sense of how she performed had previously determined her image of self and her behaviour in social situations, her changing appraisal of herself and others could begin to transform her behaviours and feelings in each encounter.

Recovery blueprint

The final phase of this therapeutic approach is to have the client write out a summary of the critical insights and strategies they will take from therapy and identify some immediate and long-term goals they wish to pursue. Standard questions that might be included in a recovery blueprint are set out in Table 15.4. This exercise is given as a written homework assignment in the penultimate session. In our group programmes we have structured our last meetings around each member of the group reading aloud their personal blueprint. Particular emphasis is given to the unique personal strengths they displayed in the course of therapy and how these might serve as important resources for them in months ahead. The inevitability of setbacks is also discussed in individual and group therapy and access to emotional and social support is explored.

Table 15.4 Developing a personal recovery blueprint

What are key fears/predictions that are activated when I enter a social situation?
What have I learned about these fears?
How do I contribute to keeping myself anxious when I enter feared situations?
How might I behave differently in feared situations to reduce my anxiety?
What goals can I set for myself in the weeks ahead?
What strengths/supports do I have to draw on to achieve these goals?

Evidence in support of the Cognitive Model of Social Anxiety Disorder

The Clark and Wells model (1995) outlined above proposes a number of testable hypotheses that have been subjected to a wealth of experimental studies, which are reviewed by Clark (2001). Overall, there is consistent support for specific features of their model, although analogue studies with high and low socially anxious non-clients are the sole source of support in respect to some of their hypotheses. These findings need to be confirmed with clients through systematic comparison of relevant variables with non-clients. What does emerge from a number of studies with clients is that their reported anxiety in social situations is highly correlated with self-focused attention (Bruch et al., 1989; Mellings & Alden, 2000; Saboonchi et al., 1999). In addition, social phobics are clearly impaired in their processing of external cues when anxious (Chen et al., 2002) and consistently generate distorted observer-perspective images of themselves, which appear most often to be a reactivation of early images of themselves that were provoked by early traumatic experiences (Hackman et al., 2000). Because these images may reflect unprocessed traumatic experiences, and because the attention of the client is self-focused in anxious situations, they are seldom updated in the light of positive encounters and so continue to reoccur. The potential for safety behaviours to increase anxiety has been demonstrated consistently through comparing self-ratings of anxiety when they drop these safety strategies with conditions where they do not (Morgan & Raffle, 1999; Wells et al., 1995). The negative impact of safety behaviours in contaminating the impression the socially anxious individual creates on others has been shown in several studies (Alden & Bieling, 1998; Alden & Wallace, 1995; Curtis & Miller, 1986).

Evidence for the effectiveness of this approach is still at a preliminary stage. Clark (1999) reported substantial improvement in fifteen consecutively referred clients with social phobia, who were given up to sixteen sessions of treatment. Scores on the Fear of Negative Evaluation scale (FNE) showed a mean reduction of 11 points at post-treatment and a reduction of 15 points at follow-up, with pre- and post-effect sizes being 2.7 and 3.7, respectively. In a single-case report, Bates and Clark (1998) found reductions of 21 and 22 points, respectively, at post-treatment and six-month follow-up. Striking reductions in the frequency and degree of belief in negative social cognitions, levels of depression and anxiety, and use of safety behaviours were also noted. Wells and colleagues (1995) found that dropping safety behaviours and shifting to externally focused attention significantly enhanced exposure to feared social situations. The effectiveness of the inclusion of video feedback in eliciting the correction of distorted negative impressions of self was supported by a recent study, which emphasized the importance of cognitive preparation with clients before watching video playback (Harvey et al., 2000).

Two unpublished studies demonstrated the effectiveness of this model when applied in group settings (Cormack, 2000, Rohan, 1997). In the first of these studies (Rohan, 1997), fourteen clients took part in an eight-week group therapy programme and were compared with fifteen waiting-list controls. The study yielded significant cognitive, affective and behavioural change in the treatment group with notable reductions in FNE scores and in the frequency of negative cognitions experienced in socially feared situations, and in the level of distress in response to them. Significant reductions were noted in avoidance behaviours from pre- to post-treatment, compared with the control group whose avoidance behaviours increased during the same time period. A subsequent study (Cormack, 2000) in the same setting investigated whether varying the length of treatment (i.e. twelve or sixteen weeks) would impact on outcome and whether any benefits experienced would continue to be evident at six-month follow-up. The fifteen participants in both conditions also rated the importance of various 'curative factors' (Yalom, 1995) in these groups. This study confirmed positive changes in FNE, Social Phobia Scale (SPS), and Social Interaction Anxiety Scale (SIAS) scores at post-treatment and at follow-up. Qualitative feedback from the two groups and a comparative analysis of the progress of six group programmes ($n = 39$), based on the Clark and Wells model, suggested that group cohesiveness may exert a strong influence on the degree to which groups benefit from this model. This factor may have accounted for variations in post-treatment scores on the FNE across the six groups, which varied from an increase in scores of 4 points in the case of one eight-week group to a reduction of 12–14 points in two twelve-week groups. Later groups incorporated the use of both the original and revised editions of the FNE and the author recommended this strategy in any future research. The forced choice required in the original form of the FNE may not always accurately assess the degree of change, whereas the 4-point Likert scale in the revised edition allows more scope for the participant to report the degree of change, if any, in respect to individual items. The latter revised scale showed significant and substantial improvement in five of the six groups included in the author's review.

Whilst the above model emphasizes a core cognitive process whereby an individual becomes focused on an erroneous construction of self, based on the interplay of anxiety symptoms and reactivation of memories of early experiences of shame and humiliation, earlier cognitive-behavioural models had shown improvements through combining a range of conventional cognitive and behavioural interventions. Controlled trials involving exposure and cognitive restructuring techniques have indicated that each of these interventions has a specific effect in social phobia, and that the combination of techniques were superior to exposure alone (Butler et al., 1984, Heimberg et al., 1990a, Mattick & Peters, 1998). In a meta-analysis of ten outcome studies using cognitive-behavioural techniques, Feske and Chambless (1995) reported that improvement was a function of change on cognitive measures of anxiety. Effect sizes for these studies were 0.98 and 0.75 for changes on the FNE, suggesting significant benefit for the sample, but with room for improvement. Research to date has been characterized by findings that only 38% of participants (Mattick & Peters, 1998) to 65% (Heimberg et al., 1990a) achieved high end-state functioning. This limited success for traditional CBT approaches prompted Clark and Wells to develop a more integrated theory-driven treatment. Although results are as yet insufficient to establish its merit, preliminary findings are very promising and the imminent publication of controlled studies is eagerly awaited.

Cognitive-behavioural group therapy

A group-based cognitive behavioural treatment (CBGT) protocol has been developed and refined by Heimberg and associates over the past two decades. Rapee and Heimberg (1997) outline a comprehensive explanatory framework for the aetiology and maintenance of social phobia that informs this treatment approach. They propose that individuals with social anxiety have childhood histories characterized by overintrusive or overprotective parents who undermine the child's confidence to deal with social challenges. These parents also model a fear of other people and instil in the child a heightened sense that the approval of others matters. Social situations in later life provoke expectations of a negative outcome, which set in motions a vicious cycle of anxiety very similar to what Clark and Wells (1995) described.

CBGT is a structured, manualized approach that aims to disrupt the cycle of social anxiety through exposure (both in group sessions and in the client's natural environment) and cognitive restructuring. The programme is offered to six clients who meet for weekly sessions lasting approximately 2.5 hours, over a period of twelve weeks. For a detailed description of this approach, the reader is referred to Coles, Hart and Heimberg (2001), Heimberg and Becker (2003) or Heimberg and Juster (1995). This model of treatment has been the focus of several studies and found consistently to produce substantial improvement in clients. For example, in a comparison study with educational-supportive group therapy (ES), 75% of CBGT clients were improved compared to 40% of ES clients (Heimberg et al., 1990a). At six-month follow-up, 80% of CBGT clients as compared to 47% ES clients showed improvement. Comparisons between this treatment offered in a group (CBGT) versus individual basis (ICBT), revealed significant improvement in both conditions and no significant difference between the two (Lucas & Telch, 1993). However, an index of cost-effectiveness showed that CGTB was three times more cost-effective than ICBT.

Interpersonal and psychodynamic approaches

Interpersonal psychotherapy (ITP) is based on the premise that emotional disorders reflect specific difficulties in the individual's interpersonal and social context. Developed initially with depressed clients and found to be effective with this population (Elkin et al., 1989; Weissman et al., 1979), it aims to reduce distressing symptoms through improving interpersonal functioning. A modified version of this therapeutic approach for social phobia (Lipsitz et al., 1999) was offered to nine clients in an uncontrolled trial. Following treatment, 78% of the sample was judged by observers to have gained significantly. Therapy comprised an assessment of core interpersonal difficulties and their modification through various techniques, which included exploration and expression of feelings related to social situations, communication training and role-play. Clinician and client ratings of improvement were also found to be significant. Clearly, further controlled studies with larger samples are required to confirm the potential value of this approach. In common with many of the humanistic approaches, IPT offers valuable interventions that may well help the client's general social functioning, but it lacks a coherent theoretical formulation of this chronic and unremitting disorder.

In her review of interpersonal and developmental perspectives on social anxiety, Alden (2002) concluded that there is consistent evidence to support the proposal that early interpersonal experiences contribute to later patterns of social anxiety. These studies locate the pathogenesis of these difficulties in an interaction of innate temperament and family experience that either fails to help children overcome their innate shyness and timidity or magnifies their fears through overprotection, excessive control or the expression of strong negative emotion in response to childhood timidity.

Gilbert and Trower (2001) propose a model of social phobia that combines psychobiological and psychodynamic components within the framework of evolutionary theory. These authors suggest that social anxiety evolved originally as a natural behavioural defence where aggression and physical harm were possible. A key element in activating social anxiety is the perception people hold of their ranking in social relationships. If socially anxious individuals believe they are inferior to others, who have superior qualities, they find themselves 'on the horns of a dilemma' (Gilbert & Trower, 2001, p. 269). If they engage in a conversation, or risk exposure in any way, they may face the possibility of rejection or shame by others. If they do not engage, they continue to be vulnerable in social situations by being viewed by others as shy and uninteresting. The safety strategies that are activated, such as submissiveness, self-consciousness and avoidance are intended to limit the potential damage that can result from negative evaluation. The problems of socially anxious individuals become compounded when their estimate of their own attractiveness to others is very poorly developed and their theory of mind is biased in terms of being more likely to view others' intentions towards them as hostile. Alternatively, if people see themselves as accepted by others who care about them, they feel relatively safe and their information processing is more accurate. Trower and Gilbert (1989) propose that socially anxious individuals overuse their defensive or *agonic systems* and underuse their safety or *hedonic systems* in interacting with others. Support for this formulation was reported by Hope, Sigler, Penn and Meier (1998) and by Walters and Hope (1998). How relationships are classified in the mind of an individual, his or her evaluation of others' expectations, and his or her fear of deception by others are key factors that influence which system is activated. The therapeutic implications of this model do not contradict cognitive-behavioural approaches but extend them by helping people to appreciate the underlying reasons for their symptoms and to view them as the excessive intrusion of normal submissive defences into normal potentially rewarding social interactions.

Pharmacotherapy for social phobia

Irreversible monoamine oxidase inhibiters (MAOIs) have been shown in repeated research trials to be effective for social phobia (Blanco, Schneier & Liebowitz, 2002). At present, phenelzine is the best established treatment for this condition, having proved itself to have an early onset of action and potent short-term effects superior to beta-blockers, benzodiazepines and CBGT. However, CBGT proved to be the more effective long-term solution for social phobia; phenelzine was associated with a high relapse risk when discontinued. In a recent study, Heimberg et al. (1998) compared phenelzine, placebo, an educational supportive group and twelve-week CBT. Phenelzine and CBT were both superior to the other conditions, with the MAOI showing superiority to CBT on some measures. Although this drug has repeatedly proved itself to be beneficial, its main disadvantages are its side-effect profile, the dietary restrictions it requires of users and the high risk of relapse on discontinuation.

Beta-blockers emerged in the 1950s and were observed to be effective in decreasing autonomic manifestations of anxiety, including tachycardia, tremor, sweating, blushing and dry mouth. They have been commonly used by individuals with non-generalized performance anxiety and have been noted to be especially popular among musicians. They have the advantage over benzodiazepines of rarely impairing concentration or coordination. However, in a controlled clinical trial they were less effective than behaviour therapy and failed to prove themselves superior to placebos (Turner et al., 1994).

The success of selective serotonin reuptake inhibitors (SSRIs) for depression has prompted research on their applications to social phobia. Paroxetine was the first SSRI to be given approval by the US Food and Drug Administration (FDA) in the treatment of social phobia. In a multi-centre, double-blind, placebo-controlled study (n = 323), Baldwin et al. (1999) showed improvement in 66% treated with paroxetine compared to 32% in the placebo group. Another study (Van Ameringen et al. 2001) found sertraline to be effective for 53% of the treated sample (n = 204) compared to 29% in the control sample at the end of 20 weeks. Overall, early research suggests that SSRIs may prove to be as effective as MAOIs without the complication of adverse side-effects.

Newer medications, such as pregabalin, a derivative of the neurotransmitter GABA, and the developing class of neuropeptides are regarded as exciting innovations in the field and studies regarding their effectiveness are eagerly awaited (Hood & Nutt, 2002).

Research currently does not easily shed light on the question of who would be most likely to benefit from what treatment or whether a combination of drug and non-drug treatments would increase benefit to the social phobic. A concern that arises, in terms of a cognitive formulation, is whether the use of any medication might be incorporated by sufferers as part of their repertoire of safety behaviours and thereby contribute to the maintenance of the underlying problem. It is hard to deny that some medications work, at least in the short term, but their mechanisms of actions are poorly understood and their capacity to help socially phobic individuals make sense to themselves of their condition is limited.

SUMMARY

This chapter has presented an overview of the classification, aetiology, assessment and treatment options in respect to social phobia. It highlights the new integrated cognitive model proposed by Clark and Wells (1985). Evidence in support of the theoretical premises of this approach is encouraging and although its treatment effectiveness in large-scale controlled studies has yet to be demonstrated, early results with individuals and groups are very promising. Other cognitive-behavioural approaches have also shown the efficacy of specific interventions for social phobics. There is also a wealth of understanding from interpersonal and evolutionary theory and research, which can complement CBT and deepen its therapeutic impact in the clinical environment. Medication is likely to become an increasing focus of interest as an alternative intervention, but the primarily psychological and social origin of this disorder suggests that a structured psychotherapy model of intervention provides the most obvious possibility of an enduring recovery.

EXERCISE 15.1

Divide into groups of three and assign roles of clinical psychologist, Eva and observer (see Figure 15.2). Prepare and then role-play part of a session where the psychologist works with Eva and alternate roles after each of the following scenarios:

1 Build an individualized formulation of Eva's difficulty by asking her to describe in detail a recent social situation in which she felt anxious.
2 Review homework Eva completed in which she identified the feared

social situation, the perceived physical symptoms, her negative thoughts and safety behaviours. The therapist should try to help Eva to make connections between physical, cognitive and behavioural aspects of the situation.

3 Design a role-play experiment with Eva. The experiment is in two parts, the first in which she uses her safety behaviours in a situation and the second in which she gives up her safety behaviour. Explain to her that the role-play will be taped so that you and she can review it after and the reasons for this. Help her to identify what exactly the safety behaviours are that she will be using in part 1 of the experiment, for example avoiding eye contact. Help her also to define the behaviours she will use in part 2, for example, making eye contact.

After the role-plays, give feedback to the person who was in the role of the psychologist, including at least three positive aspects of their behaviour in the role, and no more than two suggestions for behaviours to change.

EVIDENCE SUMMARIES

Barlow, D., Raffa, S. & Cohen, E. (2002). Psychosocial treatments for panic disorders, phobias and generalized anxiety disorder. In P. Nathan & J. Gorman (Eds.), *A guide to treatments that work* (Second Edition, pp. 301–336). New York: Oxford University Press.

Roy-Byrne, P. & Cowley, D. (2002). Pharmacological treatment of panic disorder, generalized anxiety disorder, specific phobia and social anxiety disorder. In P. Nathan & J. Gorman (Eds.), *A guide to treatments that work* (Second Edition, pp. 337–366). New York: Oxford University Press.

FURTHER READING FOR PRACTITIONERS

Andrews, G., Creamer, M., Crino, R., Hunt, C., Lampe, L. & Page, A. (2003). *The treatment of anxiety disorders. Clinician's guides and patient manuals* (Second Edition, chapters 8–11). Cambridge: Cambridge University Press.

Wells, A. (1997). *Cognitive therapy of anxiety disorders. A practice manual and conceptual guide*. Chichester, UK: Wiley.

FURTHER READING FOR CLIENTS

Rapee, R. (1997). *Overcoming shyness and social phobia: A step-by-step guide*. Killara, NSW: Lifestyle Press.

Zimbardo, P. (1987). *Shyness*. Reading, MA: Addison Wesley.

ASSESSMENT INSTRUMENTS

DiNardo, P., Brown, T. & Barlow, D. (1994). *Anxiety Disorder Interview Schedule for DSM IV*. San Antonio, TX: Psychological Corporation.

Liebowitz, M. (1987). Social phobia. *Modern Problems in Pharmacopsychiatry*, 22, 141–173. Contains the Social Anxiety Scale.

Mattick, R. & Clarke, J. (1998). Development and validation of measures of social phobia scrutiny fear and social interaction anxiety. *Behaviour Research and Therapy*, 36, 455–470. Contains the Social Phobia Scale and the Social Interaction Anxiety Scale.

Turner, S., Beidel, D., Dancu, C. & Stanley, M. (1989). An empirically derived inventory to measure social fears and anxiety: The Social Phobia and Anxiety Inventory. *Psychological Assessment*, 1, 35–40.

Watson, D. & Friend, R. (1969). Measurement of social-evaluative anxiety. *Journal of Consulting and Clinical Psychology*, 33, 448–457. Contrains the Fear of Negative Evaluation Scale.

Wells, A. (1997). Social Cognitions Questionnaire. In A. Wells. (1997), *Cognitive therapy of anxiety disorders. A practice manual and conceptual guide* (pp. 28–30). Chichester, UK: Wiley.

REFERENCES

Alden, L. E. (2002). Interpersonal perspectives on social phobia. In W. R. Crozier & L. E. Alden (Eds.), *International handbook of social anxiety: Concepts, research and interventions relating to the self and shyness* (pp. 381–404). New York: John Wiley & Sons.

Alden, L. E. & Bieling, P. (1998). Interpersonal consequences of the pursuit of safety. *Behaviour Research and Therapy*, 36, 53–65.

Alden, L. E. & Crozier, R. W. (2001). Social anxiety as a clinical condition. In W. R. Crozier & L. E. Alden (Eds.), *International handbook of social anxiety: Concepts, research and interventions relating to the self and shyness* (pp. 327–334). New York: John Wiley & Sons.

Alden, L. E. & Wallace, S. T. (1995). Social phobia and social appraisal in successful and unsuccessful social interactions. *Behaviour Research and Therapy*, 33, 945–957.

American Psychiatric Association (APA) (1980). *Diagnostic and statistical manual of mental disorders* (Third Edition). Washington, DC: APA.

American Psychiatric Association (APA) (1987). *Diagnostic and statistical manual of mental disorders* (Third Edition, revised). Washington, DC: APA.

American Psychiatric Association (APA) (1994). *Diagnostic and statistical manual of mental disorders* (Third Edition, revised). Washington, DC: APA.

Baldwin, D., Bobes, J. & Stein, D. J. et al. (1999). Paroxetine in social phobia/social anxiety disorder: Randomised, double-blind, placebo-controlled study. *British Journal of Psychiatry*, 175, 120–126.

Bates, A. & Clark, D. M. (1998). A new cognitive treatment for social phobia: A single-case study. *Journal of Cognitive Psychotherapy*, 12(4), 289–322.

Beck, A. T., Emery, G. & Greenberg, R. L. (1985). *Anxiety disorders and phobias: A cognitive perspective*. New York: Basic Books.

Blanco, C., Schneier, F. R. & Liebowitz, M. R. (2002). Pharmacotherapy for social phobia. In E. Hollander & D. J. Stein (Eds.), *Textbook of anxiety disorders* (pp. 309–322). Washington, DC: American Psychiatric Publishing.

Borkovec, T. D., Abel, J. L. & Newman, H. (1995). Effects of psychotherapy on comorbid conditions in generalised anxiety disorder. *Journal of Consulting and Clinical Psychology*, 63, 479–483.

Bruch, M. A., Heimberg, R. G., Berger, P. A. & Collins, T. M. (1989). Social phobia and perception of early parental and personal characteristics. *Anxiety Research*, 12, 57–65.

Bulik, C. M., Sullivan, P. F. & Fear J. L. et al. (1997). Eating disorders and antecedent anxiety disorders: A controlled study. *Acta Psychiatrica Scandinavica*, 96, 101–107.

Buss, D. M. (1996). Social adaption and the five major factors of personality. In J. S. Wiggins (Ed.), *The five-factor model of personality. Theoretical perspectives* (pp. 180–207). New York: Guilford Press.

Butler, G. (1985). Exposure as a treatment for social phobia: Some instructive difficulties. *Behaviour Research and Therapy*, 23, 651–657.

Butler, G. (1989). Issues in the application of cognitive and behavioural strategies to the treatment of social phobia. *Clinical Psychology Review*, 9, 91–106.

Butler, G. et al. (1984). Exposure and anxiety management in the treatment of social phobia. *Journal of Consulting and Clinical Psychology*, 59, 167–175.

Chen, Y. P., Ehlers, A., Clark, D. M. & Mansell, W. (2002). Patients with generalized social phobia direct their attention away from faces. *Behaviour, Research and Therapy*, 40, 677–687.

Clark, D. M. (1999). Anxiety disorders: why they persist and how to treat them. *Behaviour Research and Therapy*, 37, S5–S27.

Clark, D. M. (2000). Cognitive behaviour therapy for anxiety disorders. In M. G. Gelder, J. Lopez-Ibor & N. N. Anderson (Eds.), *New Oxford textbook of psychiatry* (pp. 405–430). Oxford: Oxford University Press.

Clark, D. M. (2001). A cognitive perspective on social phobia. In W. R. Crozier & L. E. Alden (Eds.), *International handbook of social anxiety: Concepts, research and interventions relating to the self and shyness* (pp. 405–430). New York: John Wiley & Sons.

Clark, D. M. & Wells, A. (1995). A cognitive model of social phobia. In R. Heimberg, M. Leibowitz, D. A. Hope, & F. R. Schneier (Eds.), *Social phobia: Diagnosis, assessment and treatment* (pp. 69–93). New York: Guilford Press.

Coles, M. E., Hart, T. A. & Heimberg, R. G. (2001). Cognitive-behavioral group treatment for social phobia. In W. R. Crozier & L. E. Alden (Eds.), *International handbook of social anxiety: Concepts, research and interventions relating to the self and shyness* (pp. 449–469). New York: John Wiley & Sons.

Cormack, C. (2000). *An evaluation of the immediate and long-term effects of a cognitive-behavioural group therapy programme*. D. Clin. Psych thesis in Clinical Psychology, University College Dublin.

Curtis, R. C. & Miller, K. (1986). Believing another likes or dislikes you: Behaviours making the beliefs come true. *Journal of Personality and Social Psychology*, 51, 284–290.

Davidson, J. R. T. et al. (1993). Treatment of social phobia with clonazepam and placebo. *Journal of Clinical Psychopharmacology*, 13(6), 423–428.

De Wit, D. J., Ogborne, A., Offord, D. R. & MacDonald, K. (1999). Antecedents of the risk of recovery from DSM-III-R social phobia. *Psychological Medicine*, 29, 569–582.

Dilsaver, S. C., Qamar, A. B. & Del Medico, V. J. (1992). Secondary social phobia in patients with major depression. *Psychiatry Research*, 44, 33–40.

Elkin, I., Shea, M. T. & Watkins, J. T. et al. (1989). National Institute of Mental Health Treatment of Depression Collaborative Research Program: General effectiveness of treatments. *Archive of General Psychiatry*, 46, 971–982.

Fava, G. A., Grandi, S. & Canestrari, R. (1989). Treatment of social phobia by homework exposure. *Psychotherapy & Psychosomatics*, 52, 209–213.

Feske, U. & Chambless, D. (1995). Cognitive behavioral versus exposure only treatment for social phobia: a meta-analysis. *Behavior Therapy*, 26, 695–720.

Furmark, T., Tillfors, M. & Stattin, H. (2000). Social phobia subtypes in the general population revealed by cluster analysis. *Psychological Medicine*, 30, 1335–1344.

Gilbert, P. & Trower, P. (2001). Evolution and process in social anxiety. In W. R. Crozier & L. E. Alden (Eds.), *International handbook of social anxiety: Concepts, research and interventions relating to the self and shyness* (pp. 259–279). New York: John Wiley & Sons.

Goisman, R. M., Goldenberg, I. & Vasile, R. G. et al. (1995). Comorbidity of anxiety disorders in a multicenter anxiety study. *Comprehensive Psychiatry*, 36, 303–311.

Hackmann, A., Clark, D. M. & McManus, F. (2000). Recurrent images and early memories in social phobia. *Behaviour Research and Therapy*, 38, 1183–1192.

Heimberg, R. G. (1989). Cognitive and behavioural treatments for social phobia: A critical analysis. *Clinical Psychology Review*, 9, 107–128.

Heimberg, R. G. & Becker, R.E. (2003). Cognitive-behavioral group therapy for social phobia. *Journal of Contemporary Psychotherapy*, 33(2), 147–148.

Heimberg, R. G., Dodge, C. S., Hope, D. A., Kennedy, C. R., Zollo, L. J. & Becker, R. E. (1990a). Cognitive behavioural group treatment for social phobia: A comparison with a credible placebo control. *Cognitive Therapy and Research*, 14(1), 1–23.

Heimberg, R. G., Hope, D. A., Rapee, R. M. & Bruch, M. A. (1988). The validity of the Social Avoidance and Distress Scale and the Fear of Negative Evaluation Scale with social phobia patients. *Behaviour Research and Therapy*, 26, 407–410.

Heimberg, R. G., Hope, D. A., Dodge, C. S. & Becker, R. E. (1990b). DSM-III-R subtypes of social phobia: Comparison of generalized social phobics and public speaking phobics. *Journal of Nervous and Mental Disease*, 178, 172–179.

Heimberg, R. G. & Juster, H. R. (1995). Cognitive-behavioural treatments: Literature review. In R. G. Heimberg, M. R. Liebowitz & D. A. Hope et al. (Eds.), *Social phobia: Diagnosis, assessment, and treatment* (pp. 261–309). New York: Guilford Press.

Heimberg, R. G., Liebowitz, M. R. & Hope, D. A. et al. (1998). Cognitive behavioural group therapy versus phenelzine in social phobia: 12-week outcome. *Archive of General Psychiatry*, 55, 1133–1141.

Heimberg, R. G., Mueller, G., Holt, C. S., Hope, D. A. & Liebowitz, M. R. (1992). Assessment of anxiety in social interaction and being observed by others: The Social Interaction Anxiety Scale and the Social Phobia Scale. *Behaviour Research and Therapy*, 23, 53–73.

Hood, S. D. & Nutt, D. J. (2002). Psychopharmacological treatments: An overview. In W. R. Crozier & L. E. Alden (Eds.), *International handbook of social anxiety: Concepts, research and interventions relating to self and shyness* (pp. 471–504). New York: John Wiley & Sons.

Hope, D. A., Sigler, K. D., Penn, D. L. & Meier, V. (1998). Social anxiety, recall of interpersonal information and social impact on others. *Journal of Cognitive Psychotherapy*, 12, 303–322.

Kessler, R. C., McGonagle, K. A., Zhao, S. et al. (1994). Lifetime and 12-month prevalence of DSM-III-R psychiatric disorders in the United States: Results from the National Comorbidity Survey. *Archives of General Psychiatry*, 51, 8–19.

Kessler, R. C., Stein, M. B. & Berglund, P. (1998). Social phobia subtypes in the National Comorbidity Survey. *American Journal of Psychiatry*, 155, 613–619.

Klein, D. F. (1999). Harmful dysfunction, disorder, disease, illness and evolution. *Journal of Abnormal Psychology*, 108, 421–429.

Leary, M. R. (1983). A brief version of the Fear of Negative Evaluation Scale. *Personality and Social Psychology Bulletin*, 9(3), 371–375.

Lepine, J. P. & Pelissolo, A. (1998). Social phobia and alcoholism: A complex relationship. *Journal of Affective Disorders*, 50 (Suppl 1), S23–S28.

Lipsitz, J. D., Markowitz, J. C., Cherry, S. & Fyer, A. J. (1999). Open trial of interpersonal psychotherapy for the treatment of social phobia. *American Journal of Psychiatry*, 156(11), 1814–1816.

Lucas, R. A. & Telch, M. J. (1993). *Group versus individual treatment of social phobia.* Paper presented at the annual meeting of the Association for Advancement of Behavior Therapy, Atlanta, GA.

Magee, W. J., Eaton, W. W., Wittchen, H. U., McGonagle, K. A. & Kessler, R. C. (1996). Agrophobia, simple phobia and social phobia in the national Comorbidity Survey. *Archives of General Psychiatry*, 53, 159–168.

Marzillier, J. S., Lambert, C. & Kellet, J. (1976). A controlled evaluation of systematic desensitization and social skills training for socially inadequate psychiatric patients. *Behaviour Research and Therapy*, 14, 225–238.

Mattick, R. P. & Peters, L. (1998). Treatment of severe social phobia: Effects of guided exposure with and without cognitive restructuring. *Journal of Consulting and Clinical Psychology*, 56, 251–260.

McNeil, D. W., Lejuez, C. W. & Sorell, J. T. (2001). Behavioural theories of social phobia: Contributions of basic behavioural principals. In S. G. Hofmann & P. M. DiBartolo (Eds.), *From social anxiety to social phobia: Multiple perspectives* (pp. 235–253). Needham Heights, MA: Allyn & Bacon.

McNeil, D. W., Ries, B. J. & Turk, C. L. (1995). Behavioural assessment: Self-report, physiology, and overt behaviour. In R. G. Heimberg, M. R. Liebowitz, D. A. Hope & F. R. Schneier (Eds.), *Social phobia diagnosis assessment and treatment* (pp. 202–231). New York: Guilford Press.

Mellings, T. M. B. & Alden, L. E. (2000). Cognitive processes in social anxiety: The effects of self-focus, rumination and anticipatory processing. *Behaviour Research and Therapy*, 38, 243–257.

Mennin, D. S., Heimberg, R. G. & Jack, M. S. (2000). Comorbid generalized anxiety disorder in primary social phobia: Symptom severity, functional impairment, and treatment response. *Journal of Anxiety Disorders*, 14, 325–343.

Merikangas, K. R. & Angst, J. (1995). Comorbidity and social phobia: Evidence from clinical, epidemiologic, and genetic studies. *European Archive of Clinical Neuroscience*, 244, 297–303.

Millon, T. (1969). *Modern psychopathology: A biosocial approach to maladaptive learning and functioning*. Philadelphia: W.B. Saunders.

Millon, T. (1981). *Disorders of personality. DSM-III: Axis II*. New York: Wiley.

Morgan, H. & Raffle, C. (1999). Does reducing safety behaviours improve treatment response in patients with social phobia? *Australian and New Zealand Journal of Psychiatry*, 33, 243–257.

Page, A. C. & Andrews, G. (1996). Do specific anxiety disorders show specific drug problems? *Australian and New Zealand Journal of Psychiatry*, 30, 410–414.

Power, M. J. & Brewin, C. R. (Eds.). (1997). *The transformation of meaning in psychological therapies: Integrating theory and practice*. New York: Wiley.

Rapee, R. M. (1995). Descriptive psychopathology of social phobia. In R. G. Heimberg, M. R. Liebowitz, D. A. Hope & F. R. Schneier (Eds.), *Social phobia diagnosis assessment and treatment* (pp. 41–66). New York: Guilford.

Rapee, R. M. & Heimberg, R. G. A. (1997). Cognitive-behavioral model of anxiety in social phobia. *Behaviour Research and Therapy*, 35(8), 741–756.

Regier, D. A., Rae, D. S., Narrow, W. E., Kaelber, C. T. & Schatzberg, A. F. (1998). Prevalence of anxiety disorders and their comorbidity with mood and addictive disorders. *British Journal of Psychiatry*, 173, 24–28.

Rohan, N. (1997). *An evaluation of the cognitive model of social phobia as applied in a group setting*. M. Psych. Sc thesis, University College Dublin, Dublin.

Rothbart, M. K. & Ahadi, S. A. (1994). Temperament and the development of personality. *Journal of Abnormal Psychology*, 103, 55–66.

Saboonchi, F., Lundh, L. G. & Ost, L. G. (1999). Perfectionism and self-consciousness in social phobia and panic disorder with agoraphobia. *Behaviour Research and Therapy*, 37, 799–808.

Salkovskis, P. M. (1996). The cognitive approach to anxiety: Threat beliefs, safety-seeking behaviour and the special case of health anxiety and obsessions. In P. M. Salkovskis (Ed.), *Frontiers of cognitive therapy* (pp. 48–74). New York: Guilford Press.

Schneier, F. R., Johnson, J., Hornig, C. D., Liebowitz, M. R. & Weissman, M. M. (1992). Social phobia: Comorbidity and morbidity in a epidemiological sample. *Archives of General Psychiatry*, 49, 282–288.

Smith, R. E. & Sarason, I. G. (1975). Social anxiety and the evaluation of negative inter-personal feedback. *Journal of Consulting and Clinical Psychology*, 48, 176–185.

Stein, M. B., Shea, C. A. & Uhde, T. W. (1989). Social phobic symptoms in patients with panic disorder: Practical and theoretical implications. *American Journal of Psychiatry*, 146, 235–238.

Stemberger, R. T., Turner, S. M., Beidel, D. C. & Calhoun, D. S. (1995). Social phobia: an analysis of possible developmental factors. *Journal of Abnormal Psychology*, 104, 526–531.

Stopa, L. (1995). *Cognitive processes in social anxiety*. D. Phil. thesis, Oxford University.

Trower, P. & Gilbert, P. (1989). New theoretical conceptions of social anxiety and social phobia. *Clinical Psychology Review. Special Issue: Social phobia*, 9(1), 19–35.

Turner, S. M., Beidel D. C. & Jacob, R. G. (1994). Social Phobia: A comparison of behaviour therapy and antenolol. *Journal of Consulting and Clinical Psychology*, 62, 350–358.

Van Ameringen, M. A. et al. (2001). Steraline treatment of generalized social phobia: A 20-week, double-blind, placebo-controlled study. *American Journal of Psychiatry*, 158(2), 275–281.

van Dyck, R. (1996). Non-drug treatment for social phobia. *International Clinical Psychopharmacology*, 11, 65–70.

Walters, K. S. & Hope, D. A. (1998). Analysis of social behaviour in individuals with social phobia and non anxious participants using a psychobiological model. *Behavioural Therapy*, 29, 387–407.

Watson, D. & Friend, R. (1969). Measurement of social evaluative anxiety. *Journal of Consulting and Clinical Psychology*, 33, 448–457.

Watson, D. & Friend, R. (1998). *The Fear of Negative Evaluation Questionnaire-Revised.* Department of Psychiatry, University of Oxford/Warneford Hospital, Oxford.

Weissman, M. M., Prusoff, B. A. & Dimascio, A. et al. (1979). The efficacy of drugs psychotherapy in the treatment of acute depressive episodes. *American Journal of Psychiatry*, 136, 555–558.

Wells, A. (1997). *Cognitive therapy of anxiety disorders. A practice manual and conceptual guide*. Chichester, UK: Wiley.

Wells, A. (1998). Cognitive therapy of social phobia. In N. Tarrier, A. Wells & G. Haddock (Eds.), *Treating complex cases* (pp. 1–26). Chichester, UK: Wiley.

Wells, A., Clark, D. M., Salkovkis, P., Ludgate, J., Hackman, A. & Gelder, M. G. (1995). Social phobia: The role of in-situation safety behaviours in maintaining anxiety and negative beliefs. *Behaviour Research and Therapy*, 26, 153–161.

Widiger, T. A. (1992). Generalised social phobia versus avoidant personality disorder: A commentary on three studies. *Journal of Abnormal Psychology*, 101, 340–343.

Widiger, T. A. (2001). Social anxiety, social phobia, and avoidant personality. In W. R. Crozier & L. E. Alden (Eds.), *International handbook of social anxiety: Concepts, research and interventions relating to the self and shyness* (pp. 336–356). New York: John Wiley & Sons.

World Health Organization (WHO) (1992). *The ICD-10 classification of mental and behavioural disorders. Diagnostic criteria for research.* Geneva: WHO.

Yalom, I. D. (1995). *The theory and practice of group psychotherapy* (Fourth Edition). New York: Basic Books.

Section 4

Physical health problems

Chapter 16

Health anxiety: Hypochondriasis and somatization

John R. Walker and Patricia Furer

CASE EXAMPLE

Maria, a forty-seven-year-old high-school teacher, came to the clinic after reading a newspaper article describing health anxiety. For years she had scrutinized her body constantly, afraid she would miss an early sign of cancer and suddenly find herself with advanced, untreatable cancer. She felt overwhelmed by everyday experiences with illness or death and, when she was struggling with a specific worry, she was distracted from her work. As a child, Maria had had many difficult experiences with illness and death. When she was nine she had to stand by the open coffin of an aunt who was murdered by a family member. At fifteen she lost two close friends, one to cancer and the other killed in a car accident. Even as a child she worried about having a serious disease and she could remember being afraid she would find blood in her urine and her stool. Whenever she experienced a new symptom, she could concentrate on nothing else until she felt reassured it was not serious. At the same time, she dreaded visits to the doctor and worried that the examination and tests would confirm her worst fears. One year before she came to the clinic, her mother died of colon cancer after a long and painful illness. Maria felt almost paralysed by her intense health worries.

HEALTH ANXIETY

Many people experience anxiety concerning their own health or the health of loved ones. The anxiety and worry are often triggered by bothersome physical symptoms or by experiences such as finding a breast lump or feeling a skipped heart beat. They may also be triggered by stories about health in the community or the media, or by coping with an illness in a loved one. Health anxiety may be quite mild and transient, or it may be severe and chronic. Often the anxiety level fluctuates. Some individuals fear one specific illness or body symptom; others fear many. Conviction that one actually has a serious disease may be a part of the picture and both fear of illness and disease conviction range along a continuum of severity. Health anxiety is often associated with excessive focus on bodily symptoms, checking for symptoms and signs related to health concerns, frequent efforts to obtain reassurance, and high levels of worry. These individuals may have histories of frequent health service utilization, or they may avoid healthcare professionals because they fear being diagnosed with a serious disease or because they are dissatisfied with previous healthcare experiences.

Health anxiety is the central feature of hypochondriasis and is significant in other somatoform disorders and in somatization in general. It is often seen in other clinical conditions, including anxiety and depressive disorders.

CLASSIFICATION OF HEALTH ANXIETY AND SOMATIZATION

The most widely used classification systems for mental health disorders are the DSM-IV-TR (American Psychiatric Association (APA), 2000) and the ICD-10 (World Health Organization (WHO), 1992). In both the DSM-IV-TR and ICD-10, problems involving health anxiety and/or somatization are generally classified as somatoform disorders. The common feature of the somatoform disorders is the presence of physical symptoms that suggest a general medical condition, but are not fully explained by a diagnosed medical condition, by the direct effects of a substance, or by another mental disorder (e.g. panic disorder). The symptoms must cause clinically significant distress or impairment in social, occupational, or other areas of functioning. Unlike in DSM-IV-TR factitious disorders and malingering, the physical symptoms are not deliberately produced. A somatoform disorder can be diagnosed even when a person does have an identified medical problem if the worry and fear are inordinate for that health problem. For example, a person with high blood pressure may be extremely anxious about this and may check his or her blood pressure many times a day. DSM-IV-TR and ICD-10 diagnostic criteria for hypochondriasis and somatization disorder are presented in Tables 16.1 and 16.2, respectively.

According to the DSM-IV-TR system, the somatoform disorders that involve significant health anxiety and/or somatization include hypochondriasis, somatization disorder, undifferentiated somatoform disorder and pain disorder. The DSM-IV-TR criteria for diagnosis of somatization disorder are very stringent: a history of many physical complaints, beginning before age thirty, that continue over several years and that result in treatment being sought or in significant impairment in functioning; and an extensive pattern

Table 16.1 Diagnostic criteria for hypochondriasis

DSM-IV-TR	*ICD-10*
A. Preoccupation with fears of having, or the idea that one has, a serious disease based on the person's misinterpretation of bodily symptoms B. The preoccupation persists despite appropriate medical evaluation and reassurance C. The belief in criterion A is not of delusional intensity (as in delusional disorder, somatic type) and is not restricted to a circumscribed concern about appearance (as in body dysmorphic disorder) D. The preoccupation causes clinically significant distress or impairment in social, occupational, or other important areas of functioning E. The duration of the disturbance is at least 6 months F. The preoccupation is not better accounted for by generalized anxiety disorder, obsessive-compulsive disorder, panic disorder, a major depressive episode, separation anxiety, or another somatoform disorder *Specify* if: **With poor insight:** if, for most of the time during the current episode, the person does not recognize that the concern about having a serious illness is excessive or unreasonable *Reprinted with permission from the Diagnostic and Statistical Manual of Mental Disorders, fourth Edition. Copyright 1994 American Psychiatric Association*	For a definite diagnosis, both of the following should be present: 1. Persistent belief in the presence of at least one serious physical illness underlying the presenting symptom or symptoms, even though repeated investigations and examinations have identified no adequate physical explanation, or a persistent preoccupation with a presumed deformity or disfigurement 2. Persistent refusal to accept the advice and reassurance of several different doctors that there is no physical illness of abnormality underlying the symptoms Includes: body dysmorphic disorder, dysmorphophobia (non-delusional) hypochondriacal neurosis, hypochondriasis, nosophobia.

Note: Adapted from DSM-IV-TR (APA, 2000) and ICD-10 (WHO, 1992).

of physical symptoms including at least four pain symptoms (related to four different sites or functions), two gastrointestinal symptoms, one sexual symptom and one pseudoneurological symptom. The criteria for undifferentiated somatoform disorder are similar to those for somatization disorder but are less stringent: only one or more physical problem lasting at least six months needs to be reported.

Table 16.2 Diagnostic criteria for somatization

DSM-IV-TR	*ICD-10*
A. A history of many physical complaints beginning before age 30 years that occur over a period of several years and result in treatment being sought or significant impairment in social, occupational, or other important areas of functioning B. Each of the following criteria must have been met, with individual symptoms occurring at any time during the course of the disturbance: 1. Four pain symptoms: a history of pain related to at least four different sites or functions (e.g. head, abdomen, back, joints, extremities, chest, rectum, during menstruation, during sexual intercourse, or during urination) 2. Two gastrointestinal symptoms: a history of at least two gastrointestinal symptoms other than pain (e.g. nausea, bloating, vomiting other than during pregnancy, diarrhoea, or intolerance of several different foods) 3. One sexual symptom: a history of at least one sexual or reproductive symptom other than pain (e.g. sexual indifference, erectile or ejaculatory dysfunction, irregular menses, excessive menstrual bleeding, vomiting throughout pregnancy) 4. One pseudoneurological symptom: a history of at least one symptom or deficit suggesting a neurological condition not limited to pain (conversion symptoms such as impaired co-ordination or balance, paralysis or localized weakness, difficulty swallowing or lump in throat, aphonia, urinary retention, hallucinations, loss of touch or pain sensation, double vision, blindness, deafness, seizures; dissociative symptoms such as amnesia; or loss of consciousness other than fainting) C. Either (1) or (2): 1. After appropriate investigation, each of the symptoms in criterion B cannot be fully explained by a known general medical condition or the direct effects of a substance (e.g. a drug of abuse, a medication)	A definite diagnosis requires the presence of all of the following: 1. At least 2 years of multiple and variable physical symptoms for which no adequate physical explanation has been found 2. Persistent refusal to accept the advice or reassurance of several doctors that there is no physical explanation for the symptoms 3. Some degree of impairment of social and family functioning attributable to the nature of the symptoms and resulting behaviour

2. When there is a related general medical condition, the physical complaints or resulting social or occupational impairment are in excess of what would be expected from the history, physical examination, or laboratory findings

D. The symptoms are not intentionally feigned or produced (as in factitious disorder or malingering)

Note: Adapted from DSM-IV-TR (APA, 2000) and ICD-10 (WHO, 1992).

The ICD-10 criteria for somatization disorder are simpler and require the presence of:

> (a) at least 2 years of multiple and variable physical symptoms for which no adequate physical explanation has been found; (b) persistent refusal to accept the advice or reassurance of several doctors that there is no physical explanation for the symptoms; and (c) some degree of impairment of social and family functioning attributable to the nature of the symptoms and resulting behaviour. (WHO, 1993, p. 163)

ICD-10 also allows for the diagnosis of undifferentiated somatoform disorder in cases where the full criteria for somatization disorder are not met.

The DSM-IV-TR criteria for a diagnosis of hypochondriasis are that the individual must report significant fears of having, or the idea that he or she currently has, a serious disease, based on a misinterpretation of bodily symptoms. This preoccupation must persist for at least six months, even with appropriate medical evaluation and reassurance, and must cause clinically significant distress or impairment in social, occupational, or other important areas of functioning.

The ICD-10 criteria for hypochondriacal disorder differ significantly from the DSM-IV-TR criteria. ICD-10 requires the presence of:

> (a) persistent belief in the presence of at least one serious physical illness underlying the presenting symptom or symptoms, even though repeated investigations and examinations have identified no adequate physical explanation, or a persistent preoccupation with a presumed deformity or disfigurement; and (b) persistent refusal to accept the advice and reassurance of several different doctors that there is no physical illness or abnormality underlying the symptoms. *Includes:* body dysmorphic disorder, dysmorphophobia (nondelusional), hypochondriacal neurosis, nosophobia [disease phobia]. (WHO, 1993, p. 165)

The most notable difference between these two diagnostic systems is the inclusion of body dysmorphic disorder in ICD-10 hypochondriacal disorder. This is considered to be a separate diagnosis in DSM-IV. The different views of hypochondriasis in the two major diagnostic systems may result in difficulty comparing results in studies using the different criteria.

What's in a term?

It has been a challenge to find terms acceptable to both clinicians and clients for the phenomena observed in the somatoform disorders in general and hypochondriasis in particular. Berrios (2001) reviewed the history of the term 'hypochondriasis'. Use of the term 'hypochondriac', in the sense we use it now, began in the 1600s. As Berrios notes, the name had negative connotations even then. Certainly, clients today do not like being labelled a 'hypochondriac'; this description implies to them that 'the symptoms are all in your head'. While clients may jokingly acknowledge that family members tell them they are hypochondriacs, they would prefer that this label not appear in consultation reports concerning their treatment. A number of alternative terms have been considered for problems with hypochondriasis. In our clinic, instead of 'hypochondriasis', we use 'intense illness worry' and 'health anxiety', and these terms seem to be well accepted by clients.

Terms used for problems with somatization include 'medically unexplained physical symptoms' (Melville, 1987) and 'functional somatic symptoms' (Kellner, 1987). One can imagine the challenges of informing a client she has 'medically unexplained symptoms' or that perhaps she has a psychiatric diagnosis such as undifferentiated somatoform disorder. She is likely to respond with frustration and disappointment and perhaps by continuing to seek medical opinions.

EPIDEMIOLOGY

Hypochondriasis and other somatoform disorders have not usually been included in large-scale epidemiological studies of mental disorders in the community. However, research in the area of health anxiety is slowly developing and there are now a few interesting studies examining the frequency of these problems in a variety of populations.

In one study focused specifically on somatoform disorders, Faravelli et al. (1997) conducted a structured interview with 673 randomly selected residents in Florence, Italy. They found one-year prevalence rates of 4.5% for hypochondriasis, 0.7% for somatoform disorder, 13.8% for undifferentiated somatoform disorder, 0.6% for somatoform pain disorder and 0.3% for conversion disorder. This study was unique in that the clinical interviewers were physicians with extensive access to health information on the participants.

Noyes and colleagues (2000) describe a survey of illness fears in a random sample of 500 residents of the midwest United States. Respondents were asked a series of fourteen questions about fears of illness, medical care, blood, or needles, and fear of aging or death. Five per cent of respondents reported much more nervousness than most people in relation to at least four of six illness/injury items, 4% indicated that such fears interfered with obtaining medical care and 5% reported some negative effect of these fears on their life.

Prevalence estimates of hypochondriasis in primary care populations range from 0.8% (Gureje et al., 1997; using ICD-10 criteria) to 3% (Escobar et al., 1998; DSM-IV criteria) to 8% (Kirmayer & Robbins, 1991; DSM-III criteria). Good reviews of the epidemiology of hypochondriasis in medical settings are provided by Noyes (2001) and by Asmundson et al. (2001).

ASSESSMENT APPROACHES TO HEALTH ANXIETY

Clinician evaluation and self-report instruments are the central strategies in a comprehensive assessment of health anxiety. The material below focuses on the assessment of hypochondriasis but many of the strategies and tools can be applied to individuals with other forms or degrees of health anxiety.

The assessment interview

Structured interviews are the research standard in diagnosing somatoform disorders. The Structured Clinical Interview for DSM-IV axis I disorders (SCID-Version 2) is a popular clinician measure. The Composite International Diagnostic Interview (CIDI), which was developed for use by trained non-clinician interviewers (WHO, 1991), can be used with both ICD-10 and DSM-IV criteria.

Structured diagnostic interviews may not be practical in a clinical setting and, furthermore, the somatoform disorder sections of the SCID and the CIDI are not extensive. Table 16.3 provides questions we have used with health anxiety, both for establishing diagnoses and for assessing potential treatment targets. Before initiating a discussion of health anxiety it is important to review the status of the client's health and history of health problems.

Providing clients with examples of some of these items can be helpful: you may, for example, want to ask specifically whether a client ever probes his or her body for lumps or how often he or she checks for moles. Clients may be embarrassed by their behaviours and may not volunteer information about them unless the clinician asks specific questions in a relaxed and non-judgemental way. The more detail you can obtain about the individual's health anxiety, and the accompanying fears and behaviours, the easier it will be to plan effective interventions.

Table 16.3 Interview questions for health anxiety

Topics	*Suggested interview questions*
General questions about health worries	• Are you worried about your health? Could you tell me about that? • Do family members or friends say that you worry too much about your health? • Does your doctor say you worry too much about your health? • Which illnesses do you worry about? • Do you worry a lot about death and dying? • What seems to set off an episode of worry about your health? Bodily symptoms? News stories about disease? Illness in a friend or family member?
Extent of difficulty with illness worries	• In the last 12 months, how many months did you worry a lot about having or getting a serious illness? • How much did these worries interfere with your life or activities?
Effects of help seeking	• Have you seen a doctor to check about this illness or symptom? • Have you had any tests or examinations for this problem? • Have you ever been afraid to go to the doctor because you were worried that he or she might find a serious problem? • Have you seen other healthcare providers about this problem? • How effective was the care you received?
Response to the doctor's evaluation	• Were you satisfied with how the doctor handled your health concerns? • Do you think the doctor was mistaken? • Are you worried that the doctor may have missed a serious health problem? • Even though the doctor reassured you, did you later start worrying again about your health?
Checking and reassurance seeking	• Do you check your body to see if you are healthy or to see if there is something wrong? If yes, how do you do that? How often? • Do you check your bodily fluids to see if something is wrong? (I mean things like checking your urine or stool.) If yes, how often? • Do you talk to your family and friends about your bodily symptoms to get their reactions? If yes, how often? • Do you spend time reading about health problems or looking up medical information on the internet? If yes, how much time?
Avoidance	• Are there things you feel uncomfortable doing because of your health worries? • Are you bothered by things that remind you of sickness and death? Do you avoid some of those things?

Case formulation is an essential step in developing an effective treatment plan. In pulling together the information from the assessment, a thorough review of the client's history, including potential predisposing, precipitating and perpetuating factors, is critical. Many individuals report an extensive history of difficult life experiences of illness and death, often dating from childhood. Unresolved grief is also common. The onset or exacerbation of the disorder at a stressful time in the person's life is typical. Once the disorder becomes well established, perpetuating factors often make it difficult to break out of the pattern of excessive worry about health and disability. A thorough understanding of these factors will help in developing an intervention that fits the individual.

Self-report measures of health anxiety

A number of self-report instruments provide useful information about health anxiety. For comprehensive reviews of assessment strategies and questionnaire measures for health anxiety, somatization and hypochondriasis, we recommend Stewart and Watt (2001), Warwick (1995) and Speckens (2001). Measures of hypochondriasis that we typically use are the Illness Attitude Scales (IAS; Kellner, 1986, 1987) and the Whiteley Index (Pilowsky, 1967).

The IAS includes twenty-seven items measuring fears, beliefs and attitudes about health and illness. Items are rated on a five-point scale and nine scale scores may be calculated. This instrument has adequate test–re-test reliability and good discriminative validity, and successfully identifies patients diagnosed with hypochondriasis. The internal consistency of the nine scales may, however, be problematic. Recent evaluations of the factor structure of the IAS (Stewart & Watt, 2001) suggest that the most robust factors are: worry about illness and pain, disease conviction, health habits and symptom interference with lifestyle.

The fourteen-item Whiteley Index has been used for many years and has good test–re-test reliability. It is also useful in identifying possible cases of hypochondriasis but may lack discriminative validity (e.g. it may not distinguish well between individuals with hypochondriasis and panic disorder). Traditionally, it has been used with true–false responses but more recently it has been used with a five-point Likert rating scale (Barsky et al., 1992). This measure yields three factors: disease fear, disease conviction and bodily preoccupation.

The Health Anxiety Questionnaire (Lucock & Morley, 1996) and the newer Health Anxiety Inventory (Salkovskis et al., 2002) are broader in focus than the IAS and Whiteley Index, and assess a range of health anxiety, not only hypochondriasis. These instruments may thus be particularly useful in assessing health anxiety in community and primary care samples and in broader clinical populations. We typically supplement the health anxiety measures with several brief self-report questionnaires targeting other issues: the Beck

Depression and Anxiety Inventories (Beck, 1996; Beck et al., 1988) and the Symptom Checklist 90 Revised (SCL-90R; Derogatis, 1975). Comorbid disorders are very common with the somatoform disorders so it is helpful to assess and monitor symptoms of anxiety and depression. The SCL-90R is useful as a broad measure of distress that inquires about a range of health and mental health issues, and includes a useful somatization subscale that assesses symptoms such as headaches, dizziness, stomach pain and back pain.

Diagnostic challenges: Comorbidity

One of the challenges facing clinicians working in the area of health anxiety is whether, in fact, there is organic disease to account for a client's somatic symptoms. Conscientious communication with the client's family physician or other medical consultants is important. By the time clients come to us, they have typically had extensive contact with the healthcare system but they continue to be highly anxious about their health. It is common for a person to have excessive medical investigations that reveal no disease while problems with severe health anxiety go untreated. Even when no organic cause for physical symptoms has been found, we acknowledge to the client that it is possible a significant illness may reveal itself on any day. The problem of health anxiety exists even for people who have severe illness, and the issues tackled in treatment of health anxiety are important for people, whether or not they have a life-threatening illness; one might call this an *agnostic approach*. Our goal over the course of treatment is to help clients become good consumers of health care so that should a health problem requiring treatment arise, clients will deal with this appropriately.

Other diagnostic challenges arise out of the substantial overlap between health anxiety and other disorders with prominent symptoms of anxiety and depression. For example, hypochondriasis, panic disorder, generalized anxiety disorder (GAD) and obsessive-compulsive disorder share common features and are frequently comorbid. The clinician must determine which diagnoses best represent a client's concerns and which problems to target first in treatment. Detailed information about the diagnostic overlap and comorbidity between health anxiety and other disorders is provided by Noyes (2001), and Fava and Mangelli (2001).

TREATMENT OF HEALTH ANXIETY

Cognitive behaviour therapy for somatization

The application of cognitive behaviour therapy (CBT) to somatization was described initially by Salkovskis (1989) and later by Sharpe et al. (1992). The extensive literature that has developed in this area has been reviewed by

Kroenke and Swindle (2000) and Looper and Kirmayer (2002). Two studies are described below as examples. Speckens et al. (1995) described a clinical trial comparing CBT with optimized medical care in a general medical outpatient clinic of a teaching hospital in the Netherlands. Patients were asked to complete a general health questionnaire and a checklist of somatic symptoms. Of the patients with medically unexplained symptoms, thirty-nine were assigned to the CBT condition and forty to the control condition of optimized medical care. CBT was carried out individually in the clinic over a range of six to sixteen sessions. For the optimized medical care condition, the quality of care was enhanced with additional training for the primary care physicians in detection and management of psychiatric disorders (ninety minutes every three months). At six months, those in the CBT condition had a higher recovery rate, lower intensity of symptoms, less disturbed sleep, reduced illness behaviour, and improved social functioning and recreation. The differences between the groups were maintained at twelve-month follow-up.

Lidbeck (1997, 2003) described a randomized study of group therapy for somatization problems in primary care. A limited form of CBT was delivered by a mental health professional. The treatment included relaxation training, education about psychological and physiological stress symptoms, and cognitive restructuring. Compared to the waiting-list control condition, the active treatment clients showed a modest decrease in measures of illness beliefs and hypochondriacal concerns. These changes were maintained at six-month and eighteen-month follow-up assessments.

Cognitive behaviour therapy for hypochondriasis

The number of studies reported in this area, particularly the number of controlled trials, has been modest, although results to this point are promising. The treatment strategies have been drawn from previous work on anxiety disorders, particularly panic disorder, obsessive-compulsive disorder, and generalized anxiety disorder.

The pioneers in the area of CBT and hypochondriasis have been the group at Oxford University (including Salkovskis, Warwick, Clark and others). Their procedures are summarized in Warwick and Marks (1988), Warwick et al. (1996), Clark et al. (1998), and, more recently, by Warwick and Salkovskis (2001). This group has incorporated a broad range of cognitive and behavioural procedures commonly used with anxiety disorders, including education about the problem (participants are given an individualized written formulation of their problem from a cognitive behavioural framework); education on the meaning of previous symptoms, medical interventions and medical opinions; induction of symptoms through bodily focusing; use of diaries to record negative thoughts and rational responses; behavioural experiments to clarify the development of symptoms; response prevention for bodily checking and reassurance seeking; the participation in treatment of significant others involved in providing reassurance; and exposure to previously avoided illness-related situations. The results of their initial randomized trial with thirty-two participants (Warwick et al., 1996) suggested that individual cognitive behavioural therapy for hypochondriasis was superior to a waiting-list control condition and that treatment gains were maintained at a three-month follow-up. In a second randomized trial (with forty-eight participants), Clark et al. (1998) compared two clients in active treatments and one in a waiting-list condition. Both individual CBT and a behavioural stress management intervention were found to be effective and superior to the waiting-list condition. The two treatments were equivalent at one-year follow-up.

Bouman and Visser (1998) compared two interventions using random assignment of eighteen participants to either a behavioural or a cognitive treatment. The behavioural treatment involved response prevention and exposure to previously avoided situations or bodily sensations. The cognitive treatment emphasized Beck's approach to cognitive intervention (Beck & Emery, 1985). No differences were found between the two approaches. Visser and Bouman (2001) conducted a larger (n = 78) randomized trial comparing separate behavioural and cognitive treatments to a waiting-list control condition. Both active treatments were found to be equally effective. There was no improvement in the waiting-list condition. The finding of clinically significant improvements with primarily behavioural and primarily cognitive treatments suggests that the procedures involved in cognitive behaviour therapy are robust and may not be degraded by small changes in procedure.

A recent study by Barsky and Ahern (2004) provides a larger randomized trial comparing individual CBT to a 'usual medical care' control condition. The CBT sample comprised 102 individuals, eighty-five of whom were assigned to the control condition. Half of the total sample met DSM-IV criteria for hypochondriasis and the other half had subsyndromal hypochondriasis. The CBT involved six standardized sessions focusing on the patients' amplification of somatic symptoms and misattribution of these symptoms to serious disease. This protocol appears to emphasize cognitive interventions and does not incorporate exposure to illness fears. The results of this study suggested that the brief CBT intervention was significantly superior to the control condition in reducing hypochondriacal concerns and behaviours as assessed six months' post-treatment. These gains were maintained at twelve-month follow-up.

The procedures used in individual CBT for hypochondriasis are described in more detail by Furer et al. (2001), Sharpe et al. (1992), Taylor and Asmunsdson (2004), and Warwick and Salkovskis (2001). Preliminary trials of group cognitive educational treatment for hypochondriasis suggest this may also be helpful (Bouman, 2002).

Pharmacotherapy for somatization and hypochondriasis

Early descriptions of pharmacological treatments of hypochondriasis were not optimistic. More recently, a number of case reports describe more favourable results with hypochondriasis with and without delusional psychotic features (reviewed by Enns et al., 2001). To date, there have been only three reports of open-label trials of treatment of hypochondriasis, all with generally positive effects (Fallon et al., 1993; Kjernisted et al., 2002; Wesner & Noyes, 1991). Open-trial evaluations of antidepressants with somatoform disorder have also been reported with generally favourable results (Menza et al., 2001; Noyes et al., 1998). Only a single randomized placebo-controlled trial for hypochondriasis has been reported, with eight of twelve patients who received fluoxetine being classed as responders as compared to four of eight on placebo over a twelve-week trial. The sample size in this study was small and statistical comparison did not reveal a statistically significant difference between medication and placebo (Fallon et al., 1996).

In spite of the limited research on pharmacological treatment and the absence of information on long-term outcome, this is the most widely available treatment and probably the most frequently used with hypochondriasis and other somatoform disorders (Escobar, 1996). Enns et al. (2001) point out that many of these individuals have comorbid anxiety or depressive disorders, and these pharmacological treatments (usually selective serotonin reuptake inhibitors or serotonin–norepinephrine reuptake inhibitors) have been effective in these disorders.

Clearly, it is desirable for the specialist in cognitive behaviour therapy to have a good working knowledge of common pharmacological treatments for health anxiety. This is necessary to provide information about treatment options and to be able to provide good support and information to individuals who are concurrently receiving pharmacological treatment. The clinician can encourage appropriate compliance with medication and assist the client in troubleshooting any problems. Many clients' symptoms fluctuate because of inconsistency in taking medication, and others misinterpret the significance of medication side effects (such as sexual difficulties) common with many antidepressants. Some clients benefit from additional support and education if they decide to gradually discontinue medication treatment (in consultation with the prescribing physician) after a significant period of few symptoms activity (Whittal et al., 2001).

A SPECIFIC APPROACH TO COGNITIVE BEHAVIOURAL TREATMENT

Our clinical service is based in the outpatient anxiety disorders programme of a teaching hospital. Over the years, we became aware that clients with various anxiety disorders were also having difficulty with health anxiety (Furer et al., 1997). For some of these individuals, the health concerns were severe, persistent and required specific intervention. Our approach incorporates findings from the research summarized above, and our experience in treating panic disorder, generalized anxiety disorder, obsessive-compulsive disorder and death anxiety. As we refined our approach, we placed increasing emphasis on the role of exposure to illness worries and to illness-related situations, and introduced exposure strategies early in the treatment. Preliminary results with this treatment programme are promising and a controlled trial is underway. The programme can be administered in either group or individual treatment format. Components may be implemented on a flexible basis using the cognitive and behavioural assessment and case formulation. The following treatment description focuses on the application of this approach in hypochondriasis. A similar treatment approach applies to other somatoform disorders. In every case, we adapt the approach to target the problems identified in the assessment and case formulation.

Some aspects of the problem may cause particular interference and disability. In planning treatment, these may warrant attention first. The client (or therapist) may identify priorities that influence the initial treatment goals. On the other hand, the clinician may see some areas where improvement is likely to come quickly, and may provide encouragement to the client so he or she can persist through the more difficult areas of the treatment (such as facing the reality of illness and death). The components of treatment are described individually, but we typically implement more than one component simultaneously. We often emphasize response prevention early in treatment because this frequently results in a relatively rapid decrease in anxiety if checking and reassurance seeking are prominent. We might also concurrently introduce activities that improve the enjoyment of life. A treatment manual for the client (Furer & Walker, 1998) provides educational material about the problem, descriptions of the treatment components, clinically based examples and detailed homework assignments. A typical session involves introduction and discussion of new material, review of previous homework and preparation of homework assignments for the coming week.

The primary treatment strategies covered in the programme are: (1) educational material describing a CBT model of health anxiety; (2) response prevention; (3) exposure to illness worries; (4) establishing personal goals and enhancing life satisfaction; (5) strategies for overcoming avoidance of illness-related situations; (6) methods of coping with fear of death; (7) cognitive reappraisal; and (8) relapse prevention.

Cognitive behavioural model of health anxiety

It is critical to provide individuals with an explanation of how health anxiety may have developed and how CBT can be useful. Clients are often receptive to an explanation of health anxiety that suggests there are common triggers for worries about health. These triggers may include bodily symptoms or changes in physiological function that are interpreted as signs of serious disease. Health worries may also be provoked by external triggers, such as reading or hearing about illness. Checking the body for signs and symptoms and seeking reassurance about one's health are behaviours that may develop as strategies to cope with anxiety. Avoidance of illness and death-related situations may also begin as attempts to reduce fear. Over time, these strategies increase health anxiety.

Many clients are already aware, to some degree, of how their thoughts and their reactions to body sensations can increase and maintain their health fears. We ask our clients to observe the impact of focusing on their body symptoms by having them experiment with deliberately attending to a specific body sensation. Clients experience how this can quickly increase the intensity of a sensation and the sense of alarm. Constant attention to body sensations can result in exceptional skill at detecting even minor changes in the body, triggering further anxiety. Clients need to understand how bodily checking, reassurance seeking and avoidance of illness and death-related situations can increase this anxiety.

Carefully reviewing the components of the model (Figure 16.1) with examples from the individual's experience are essential to the educational process. This provides a new perspective on health anxiety and an explanation of approaches to breaking the pattern of anxiety.

In the case example outlined on p. 593, Maria identified several internal and external triggers for her health anxiety. The most significant internal trigger was seeing something red (that looked like blood or was blood) in her throat, nose, urine or stool. Other triggers included new physical symptoms, such as a rash or a lump, and media stories about illnesses (external triggers). Bodily sensations when she was anxious were muscle tension, headaches and fatigue. Catastrophic cognitions included 'Blood in my urine means I have cancer and will die' and 'I can't enjoy life if there is any chance I have cancer'. Checking behaviours were prominent in Maria's daily routine. She went to the toilet frequently to check her stool and urine for blood. She often found herself in front of a mirror, examining the back of her throat and her nose for signs of blood and she would ask her husband to check her symptoms. Maria checked the internet for information about symptoms and found frightening descriptions of diseases involving these symptoms.

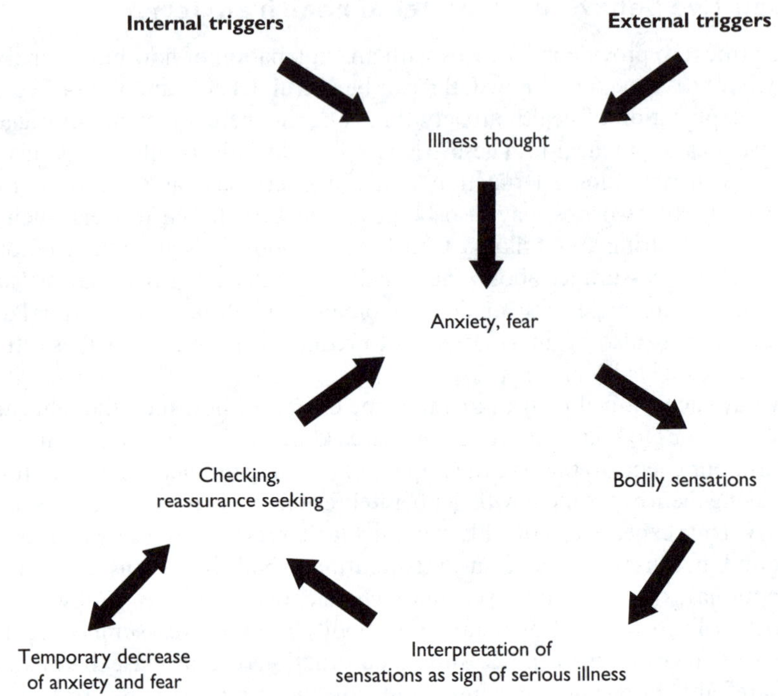

Figure 16.1 Health anxiety: Cognitive behavioural model (© 2004 by Patricia Furer and John Walker).

Response prevention

In the same way that bodily checking and reassurance seeking play a critical role in obsessive-compulsive disorder, these behaviours are often prominent in health anxiety and hypochondriasis. Typical examples of checking behaviours include probing the body for lumps, checking the skin for moles or changes in the moles, monitoring pulse rate and blood pressure, checking for weight loss, monitoring pain levels or unusual bodily sensations and frequent breast self-examinations. Reassurance-seeking strategies may include asking a family member, friend, or healthcare provider about symptoms, and researching symptoms or diseases in medical textbooks or on the internet. Excessive or stereotyped use of health foods, vitamin supplements and other unusual health-related behaviours may also be potential targets for change. Some individuals may have difficulty identifying ways in which they check their bodies or obtain reassurance because these behaviours are so automatic or routine. The clinician should explore this area thoroughly, keeping in mind that, to the client, these may be private and embarrassing behaviours.

Once checking and reassurance-seeking behaviours are identified, clients are asked to monitor them, using a diary. The goals of monitoring include identifying a baseline frequency of the behaviours and developing behaviour analysis skills. Clients record the situation, their anxious thoughts and their initial anxiety level (on a scale of 0 to 10). They then provide a detailed description of the checking/reassurance-seeking behaviour, and record their subsequent anxiety level (to determine whether the behaviour increases or decreases anxiety). Some clients report immediate anxiety reduction but, generally, this is short-lived; the anxiety rebounds and the individual may then engage in the behaviour again. Interestingly, many individuals describe either no anxiety reduction or even an increase in anxiety related to checking and reassurance seeking. However, they may believe that checking is a preventive strategy, that is, 'If I don't check my moles today then I will be even more worried about them tomorrow, so I'd better check.' Understanding the pattern of anxiety in relation to checking and reassurance seeking will help in planning the response prevention approach. If the client has many checking or reassurance-seeking behaviours, we may focus on only three or four behaviours at first to facilitate monitoring.

Maria monitored various checking behaviours daily for several weeks. She recorded how often and for how long she checked her urine and stool for signs of blood. She also monitored the frequency of her nasal and throat checks (duration was not monitored because these checks took less than thirty seconds). We asked Maria to record the frequency and triggers of any other bodily checking that she noticed such as probing her abdomen for lumps. She monitored her reassurance-seeking behaviours a few weeks later, as they were not as troublesome.

Once the diaries have revealed patterns of checking and reassurance seeking, clients select several behaviours they wish to decrease. We discuss various approaches to response prevention, including postponing the target behaviours, gradually decreasing their frequency, or simply stopping the behaviour altogether (Foa & Wilson, 2001). Response prevention homework is determined between the client and therapist. It is critical that the client decide on a response prevention assignment he or she feels able to implement successfully. We inform clients that they may experience a temporary increase in anxiety as they work on decreasing their checking or reassurance-seeking behaviours. This increased anxiety is generally short-lived. Many clients are surprised by how quickly they can reduce their focus on their bodies and health anxiety, using response prevention.

One of the challenges here is helping individuals determine whether their health-monitoring behaviours are reasonable and healthy or whether they are excessive and detrimental. For example, some physicians recommend monthly breast self-examination as a preventive healthcare strategy. This is a clear directive and most women would agree that daily examinations are not helpful or necessary, and would likely increase worry about breast health.

Other healthcare recommendations are not as specific. For example, physicians recommend that people be aware of their moles and report any significant changes. Does this mean daily checking? Is monthly or bimonthly monitoring reasonable? If a person notes a change, do they need to report immediately to their physician's office or can they wait until their next regular visit? These are some of the issues to be discussed in treatment to establish reasonable frequencies.

Response prevention is an important strategy throughout treatment. For example, when the client begins working on facing feared situations in the exposure component of the programme, it is important to ensure that the checking and reassurance-seeking behaviours are kept under control. For some clients, the urge to check their bodies for symptoms will increase again when they are, for example, visiting a cancer-care ward as part of their exposure homework.

Exposure to illness worries

Many individuals with health anxiety or hypochondriasis worry that if illness is not already present, it will soon develop. Some are afraid their worrying will make it more likely they will develop the illness ('I have to stop worrying or I will give myself cancer'). These worries often are present even when the client is not experiencing somatic symptoms and when disease conviction is low. We target these fears of developing a serious illness using both imaginal and *in vivo* exposure. These strategies draw on approaches that are helpful in working with generalized anxiety disorder (GAD; Dugas et al., 2003; Ladouceur et al., 2000) and obsessive-compulsive disorder (Foa & Wilson, 2001; McLean et al., 2001).

An imaginal exposure strategy we have found particularly useful is having clients write a narrative describing in detail their worries and fears about developing or having a particular illness. Clients typically write two or three *illness stories* targeting their major health worries. We encourage clients to make the story as real and emotionally evocative as possible as they imagine their worst fears coming true. The illness story includes the bodily feelings and possible signs of illness that trigger the worry, as well as the doubts about whether to seek medical attention and whether there was anything they could have done to prevent the illness. Clients are encouraged to describe the stages of the illness and their worries at each point along the way, including being extremely ill, dependent on others, and facing death. Clients also include their worries about how their illness and death would affect loved ones. The experience of writing this narrative is often very emotional and intense, and in itself serves as an exposure exercise. The following story details one of Maria's worst fears: developing skin cancer.

I was checking out my moles as I usually do. To my horror I discovered that one of the moles has changed dramatically. It is no longer circular, but a strange irregular shape and it has grown larger than I remember it being. The usual brown colour is now splotchy, with different shades of brown and black. I touch the mole and it doesn't hurt, but it feels slightly raised and bumpy. I have been panicking all day, but I am too afraid to call Dr Carter. If this is cancer, all my most horrible worries will have finally come true. The mere thought of having cancer or dying sends me into a terrible state of crying and anxiety.

My husband, Bob, finally makes me call and I have an appointment with the doctor. Dr Carter agrees that the mole is highly suspicious and I am to see a dermatologist. Even though she didn't say it, I could tell from the look on her face that it is very serious. I can't get the thought of having skin cancer out of my mind, even though it hasn't been confirmed yet. I can't eat, relax, sleep or even breathe very well because all this stress is making my asthma worse. What did I do to deserve this? Will I need chemo and radiation? Melanoma is usually fatal. I can't die because I can't imagine what it would be like not to be able to play with my dogs and hold hands with Bob. If I die, will I know I am dead? Will I be very upset and lonely? I can't imagine just ceasing to be.

I go to the dermatologist and he confirms everything. I do have melanoma and it is at an advanced stage. He makes an appointment for me at the Cancer Centre. I am so upset, I am crying through the entire appointment. Not only do I have melanoma but it is at an advanced stage which, to me, pretty much guarantees I am going to die. When I tell Bob, he begins to cry, which is very unlike him. Seeing him so upset sends me into an uncontrollable, inconsolable fit of anger and crying. I can't die because I love my family too much. I can't imagine being dead and Bob moving on with another woman (even though he should). I am worried that the sheer stress of the next few months and years might be too much for him and maybe he will break up with me. He swore that he would be with me through everything, but this is too much to ask of him.

I'm going to be so sick from the treatment but it might not make any difference. I go ahead with the treatment because I'm too scared to die, but if I am ultimately going to die, my final months will be full of sickness and pain. This is just too much to bear.

The chemo started today. I am now terribly sick from my first infusion. I keep throwing up even though there is nothing left to throw up and all the retching is making my stomach and head hurt. Bob is taking care of me the best he can, but it breaks my heart knowing I will likely die and I won't be able to see or touch him again. So, I'm trying to distance myself from him but he won't let me. He has caught on to my plan.

I'm starting to have problems walking and I stumble a lot and speech is becoming increasingly difficult. If I'm going to die, why do I have to suffer like this? Today I have my first radiation treatment. I feel so very tired and the area that was radiated is already red and itchy. Between the fatigue of radiation and the vomiting from the chemo, I feel like I am dying already. The doctors say there hasn't been much improvement despite all the chemo I've received so far, but they are still hoping. My eyes and fingernails are starting to take on a yellowish cast. My family is trying to keep my spirits up and they are trying to be hopeful but I can't focus on anything other than my horrible side effects and my ultimate fate.

I've finished all the chemo and the radiation, and still no improvement. I have now been admitted to the palliative service at the hospital. I have extreme difficulty doing anything for myself now because my brain has been taken over by cancer. It is so hard to face my family and see the sorrow and pain in their eyes. How could this have happened to me? There had to have been an earlier sign than just the mole being different. How could I have missed it? Why can't the doctors do anything more for me? What if I start to die and my family isn't around?

I think today is the day I am going to die. I feel a tremendous amount of anxiety and fear. I hope my family senses this because I have lost the ability to tell them. I can only blink my eyes now and I find it difficult to understand what everyone says sometimes. I am struggling to stay awake now. I feel like I am going to sleep. I am fighting it because I am afraid I will never wake up and I will never see my family again. Bob is holding my hand and stroking my forehead. As I try to vomit, I end up aspirating and suddenly I feel like I am having a terrible asthma attack and I absolutely cannot breathe. My family is panicking, the nurses rush in, and I struggle to keep my eyes open . . . I finally close my eyes and I am gone.

We ask clients to read their illness stories repeatedly (either out loud or to themselves) and to use the story to assist them in imagining that the feared events are actually happening. Some clients prefer to make an audiotape of their narratives. In group treatment, it can be very useful to have group members share their illness stories in session for additional exposure practice (both for themselves and the other group members). As with all exposure exercises, it is important that the client is aware there may be a temporary increase in anxiety as they think about difficult issues they may have avoided for a long time. The anxiety will then decline and the health concerns will become less anxiety evoking. The purpose of the exercise is not to mechanically read or listen to a story but, rather, to use the narrative to stimulate the imagination in this very difficult situation. We continue the exposure practice over several weeks and clients develop new narratives as their anxiety with the initial story decreases.

Some clients are puzzled that we ask them to focus on their fears using this exposure strategy, when they already obsess about their health. It is important to make the distinction between facing fears in a planned way and worrying about health and disease in an uncontrolled fashion. Often, individuals will try manoeuvres to eliminate the worry and to convince themselves that their worst fears will not come true. Individuals will often try to 'get the worry out of their mind', or to escape from their fear by using distraction or avoidance. The approach of facing fears directly with exposure is quite different. Exposure involves a planned, systematic strategy of scheduling time to face fears and worries. The goal is to take control of the worrying rather than having the worry come unexpectedly. This increases clients' confidence in the ability to handle fears. Repeatedly facing the thoughts of illness and death, and accepting the reality that these things do happen, allows the individual to face even difficult and unpleasant possibilities more calmly.

Establishing goals and enhancing life satisfaction

Shifting the focus from death and dying to life and living can go a long way to reducing anxiety and worry. We take a two-pronged approach to facilitate this shift. First, clients identify a list of goals, beginning with their life goals. Identifying concrete and specific broad goals can assist in the development of more immediate goals. Clients are prompted to consider what they would want out of life if they were not hampered by health anxiety. They then work on developing clear, behaviourally based, medium-term and short-term goals that will help them achieve their life goals. The medium-term goals are those the client could work on within a year, and the short-term goals could be targeted within three months. We encourage clients to set goals that involve moving ahead with activities in spite of anxiety.

For some individuals, the task of developing goals, especially long-term goals, is very challenging. Some clients have completely ceased thinking about the future, as they are sure they will soon be very ill or dying. Working first on short-term goals can be more productive with these individuals. For example, if clients are sure they will be dead in a year, we encourage them to think about what they would like to do and accomplish during this year (for example, spend more time with friends on a weekly basis and travel to their hometown to visit relatives). Clients are often surprised by what they can accomplish, as they work on these immediate goals. This may facilitate the development of long-term goals.

> Maria's goals included improving her relationship with her partner and learning how to manage conflict between them more productively, interacting more with her co-workers, spending more time with her family, and developing a healthier lifestyle. Other goals focused on reducing health anxiety and included being able to attend prayers for her mother, visiting friends who were ill and being able to have a medical test without calling the laboratory daily to inquire about the results.

A second strategy to help clients focus on living is to work on building life satisfaction. Clients are asked to keep track of activities that give them a sense of pleasure or satisfaction. Many clients are surprised to find that small things in life give them pleasure, for example, a phone call to a friend or spending time with a young relative. Some individuals find it helpful to think about what kinds of things they used to enjoy as children or as young adults. We then ask clients to consider whether they have enough fun in their lives and, if not, to schedule more daily activities that give them satisfaction or pleasure. Increasing pleasurable activities often has a quick and significant impact on their fears about health and dying.

> Maria found that going on regular dates with her husband had the dual effect of increasing the amount of fun she was having and improving their relationship. Maria also focused on making time for her artistic endeavours that gave her a strong sense of personal satisfaction.

Overcoming avoidance of illness-related situations

Many individuals cope with their health anxiety by avoiding situations that cause them fear or discomfort, such as going to funerals, visiting friends and family who are seriously ill or dying, writing a will, going to the doctor, reading articles about illness and death and doing monthly breast self-examinations. We discuss the short-term and long-term effects of avoiding these situations, and highlight the erosion of self-confidence and gradual increase in avoidance. We encourage clients to face their fears daily in a systematic and repeated fashion, and emphasize the importance of not engaging in bodily checking or reassurance seeking when practising exposure.

Targets for exposure are selected from the client's list of short-term goals. If the goal is too difficult or too large, it is broken down into smaller, more manageable steps that can be practised regularly. Each step is practised consistently until the anxiety is at a low or moderate level, before moving on to the next step. We encourage clients to spend at least thirty to sixty minutes per day practising. Each week, clients plan out homework exposure exercises, using a daily assignment log, and track their success in attempting and/or completing these assignments.

Some of the same behaviours that are avoided and are targets for exposure for some clients serve as checking or reassurance-seeking behaviours for other clients (and then we encourage response prevention). For example, some individuals avoid reading newspaper stories with health information, while others spend hours scouring the newspaper and the internet for health information as a way to check out their symptoms, to reassure themselves that they are healthy, or to be vigilant for signs of danger.

Exposure exercises may also involve exposure to bodily symptoms. Sensations that may trigger anxiety and fear include dizziness, difficulty breathing, changes in heart rate, lumps, skin rashes and pain. We help clients identify sensations that trigger anxiety and activities they avoid. Then, we encourage them to deliberately engage in physical activities that cause these sensations. For example, aerobic exercise, such as brisk walking, dancing, climbing stairs, swimming or jogging, increases both heart rate and breathing rate and can therefore be used as an exposure strategy for these physical symptoms. Deliberate hyperventilation (also used in exposure treatment of panic disorder) is an excellent strategy for producing shortness of breath, tingling of the extremities and lightheadedness. The client and therapist hyperventilate together during the session and then focus on the resulting sensations. We then observe how these unpleasant sensations dissipate. If the sensations produced by hyperventilation are similar to those that distress the client, we will ask him or her to hyperventilate once or twice a day to practise that exposure.

For bodily sensations that are difficult to produce deliberately (such as a rash, a headache or a lump), imaginal exposure strategies are helpful. As with the illness stories, clients are asked to describe in vivid terms the body symptom they fear, the worries and doubts they experience when they have this symptom, and the catastrophic consequences they worry about. For some clients, the body symptom and illness stories are quite different, with the former tapping into fears about discomfort or disability related to the physical symptom itself rather than fears about serious disease or death. For other clients, the stories are very similar. As with the illness stories, the body symptom stories are reviewed for at least thirty minutes to stimulate imaginal exposure over a number of days until there is a considerable reduction in the anxiety about the symptom.

Maria found that regular practice visiting the hospital where her mother received her cancer treatment was challenging. It paid off by giving her the freedom to visit the hospital with minimal anxiety. Maria also practised spending time with friends who had serious health problems. An interesting exposure task that was helpful for Maria was regularly eating beets so she could practise having red colour in her stool. Being careful not to check her stool during this practice was an important treatment component.

Coping with fear of death

For many individuals with health anxiety, fear of death is a central concern. It is important to address two main areas in dealing with fear of death. The first involves increasing appreciation and enjoyment of life and the second is to work on accepting the reality of death.

Avoiding the issue of death seems to work for most people most of the time, and allows them to get on with their lives. At times, however, the usual ways of coping with fears of death break down. People may be constantly preoccupied with fears of death, illness, accident, injury and harm. These fears create intense distress, limit pleasure and satisfaction in life, disrupt close relationships, distract from working effectively and consume enormous amounts of energy. Many clients try hard not to think about death and try to avoid things that remind them of death. Other clients take the approach that if they take very good care of themselves or are very cautious about their health, then they will be able to postpone the time when they have to deal with their own illness and death. Sometimes they also want to identify any problem early so they can be rescued by the healthcare system before the problem becomes too serious. This approach denies the reality that while most of us will live to a ripe old age (and have a lot of potential time to enjoy life), death can come at any time and in many unexpected ways.

By directly facing fears of death and dying, and by accepting the inevitability of serious illness and death, the anxiety, distress, and loss of satisfaction caused by fear of death can be reduced. We ask clients to consider any ways in which they may avoid thoughts or experiences related to death. Areas of avoidance can be addressed using the same exposure strategies outlined in the previous section. We also encourage clients to identify their anxious thoughts about death and to develop coping thoughts that can assist them in managing their fears (as outlined in the cognitive reappraisal section below).

When clients' fear of death is prominent, we ask them to complete several helpful exposure assignments: (1) making or updating a will; (2) discussing wishes for funeral arrangements with a family member; and (3) writing their own obituary. We provide reading material on making a will, information from a non-profit funeral-planning organization and several sample obituaries. The obituary should reflect an early death rather than a death late in life. Articles, books and movies about coping with death are also very helpful in facilitating exposure. We realize family members may be uncomfortable with these assignments, reflecting the discomfort with death that exists in our culture.

> One exposure exercise that seemed helpful for Maria was cutting out and saving newspaper obituaries of people her age. Initially, this task produced substantial anxiety but, with repeated practice, she was able to calmly face obituaries and stories about death.

Cognitive reappraisal

When we began working with individuals with health anxiety, we encouraged work on identifying catastrophic thoughts and developing coping thoughts quite early in the therapy. However, we have found it beneficial to emphasize exposure and response prevention first and to focus on cognitive techniques later in the programme. Providing exposure and response prevention experiences early in treatment seems to result in significant change in cognition. Later in treatment, we encourage clients to identify any illness-related thoughts that remain troubling. We have found the following exercise to be useful:

1 List the most common catastrophic thoughts you have about illness.
2 For each thought, note:

   a When does this thought tend to come to you?
   b What is the probability this negative event will happen? In considering this, if you have had this negative thought before, how often has the negative outcome happened in the past? How often does this negative event happen to other people of your age? Do not ask whether this negative event will happen in your lifetime (we are all likely to have serious illnesses in our lifetime). How likely is it that it will happen today? This year?
   c If it did happen, how would you cope with it? Negative events happen to people throughout their lifetime – often not when they are worrying about them but at an unexpected time.
   d This negative or catastrophic thought will occur again in the future. What are some coping thoughts you could use when this negative or catastrophic thought happens again?

Question 2b deals with the probability of the negative event's occurring. Most people have limited information on the probability of the illnesses they fear. However, rather than using probability figures to reassure people that their worse fears will not come true, we emphasize the importance of learning to tolerate uncertainty. All of us will have to face illness at various points in our life and death is a certainty. We will not know in advance, however, what challenges we will have to face, so it is important to live life to the fullest until the time comes that we have to cope with illness and death. Question 2c relates to the client's understanding of people's ability to cope with illness and death. We emphasize that people are generally able to cope with these challenges with dignity, even though anxiety about illness and death is a normal part of the coping process. Clients complete a self-monitoring diary to keep track of their anxious thoughts and ways to cope.

Maria's coping thoughts to help her deal with blood in her urine included: 'The blood may be a sign of cancer, but it may also be a kidney stone. I will just try drinking more water and see how it works out.' A coping thought she developed to cope with a small lump she found at the back of her neck was: 'It may be cancer but I have had lumps like this before and they were not cancer. I will just check it once per month until my next doctor's visit and show it to my doctor then.'

Relapse prevention

Most people recovering from problems with health anxiety experience periods of increased symptoms even after significant progress. Many find these setbacks extremely upsetting, feeling that their work and effort were for nothing, and they may lose confidence in their coping strategies. At times, clients feel the entire approach they have been taking in therapy is wrong and they must find a new way to deal with the problem. Others may become discouraged and feel that nothing will ever help with the problem.

We encourage clients to have realistic expectations about the role that anxiety plays in each of our lives. Sickness and death are normal parts of life and we will be confronted by this many times as the years go on. It is normal to think about these issues and to be apprehensive when facing illness or death.

Certain experiences are often related to setbacks:

- a new physical symptom or the return of a previous symptom
- a situation related to illness or death that has been avoided for a long time
- serious illness, either in the client or someone close to him or her
- the loss of someone close (this can be through death, life changes, moves to other cities, etc.)
- threat to an important relationship or the end of an important relationship
- increased life stress.

A helpful approach for clients is to prepare for the inevitability of setbacks and to develop coping strategies. When clients experience an increase in anxiety, we encourage them to continue applying the coping strategies they have learned and to keep working toward their goals. At times, it may be helpful to go back to an easier level in working on goals, in order to rebuild confidence. We recommend the following process in dealing with a setback:

1 Analyse the situation(s) before the setback. In most cases you can identify important factors related to the setback. Understanding this can give you more sense of control.
2 Review the coping strategies you have been using. Were you rusty in using some of your coping strategies? Did you let some bad habits develop? Are there some additional coping strategies that would be helpful now?
3 Are you checking your body more frequently now? Are you asking others for reassurance about your symptoms more often? If you are, work on decreasing these behaviours because, in the long run, checking and reassurance seeking will make anxiety *worse*.
4 If you are having difficulty getting over the effects of a setback, consider getting support from a therapist or a group you have worked with before. A setback is a good time to make sure you have solid support from family and friends, if possible.

The difference between having occasional worries and fears in difficult circumstances and having a problem with intense health anxiety is knowing how to cope effectively. Thoughts about illness and death do not have to cause a major disruption in life. Thinking about these issues in a constructive way is part of a healthy approach to life.

Relationships with primary care providers and medical specialists

Individuals with somatoform disorders are often seen regularly by a primary care physician and by several other medical specialists. They are frequently receiving some form of pharmacological treatment for symptom relief. All aspects of the treatment (including CBT) are more likely to be successful if there is effective communication among the health professionals involved. Our programme emphasizes providing information concerning treatment recommendations to primary care physicians when they are involved in the treatment. Generally, this information is welcomed by the primary care provider and other medical specialists.

In CBT for hypochondriasis and other somatoform disorders, clients are typically encouraged to limit their use of health services in reassurance seeking and to care for themselves in dealing with non-urgent symptoms (e.g. back pain, headaches or cold symptoms) for several weeks before seeking medical consultation. Most clients are able to manage this. If the response of another healthcare provider begins to feed into a pattern of reassurance seeking or excessive use of healthcare services, however, it may be helpful to discuss recommendations concerning treatment with that provider. We contact the other professional with a brief letter (and a follow-up telephone contact if necessary) outlining our suggestions, framed as recommendations to the client (rather than directives to the physician). The letter generally closes by indicating that we would be happy to provide further information and would value any recommendations from the primary care provider.

SUMMARY

Health anxiety is a common problem that can be triggered by physical symptoms, personal health experiences and the health experiences of others. It is often accompanied by excessive bodily checking and seeking reassurance. Health anxiety, hypochondriasis and somatization may cause significant distress and interference with daily functioning. Historically, hypochondriasis and the other somatoform disorders were viewed as being resistant to treatment. However, research over the last fifteen years suggests that CBT is often helpful. With more understanding of the extent of this problem in the community and more optimism about treatment, we have entered a period of steadily expanding knowledge in this area.

EXERCISE 16.1: SKILLS BUILDING

One advantage clinicians have in understanding health anxiety is that we have all had to deal with illness and death in our own lives. Usually, younger clinicians will have fewer of these experiences than older individuals. Here are some exercises to broaden experience in this area:

1 Develop a narrative describing an intense experience in this area, including your thoughts, emotions, bodily sensations and behaviours. What were your responses before, during and after the experience? As examples, consider unpleasant medical or dental experiences, serious illness or death in someone close, being with someone through the process of death, or being present at a peaceful death.
2 Many people have had limited experiences with medical procedures, illness and death. You may broaden your experiences in these areas by reading some of the excellent material available in these areas. Elizabeth Kübler-Ross has written extensively, and has edited an excellent series of

accounts from individuals, family members and friends, about coming to terms with death (Kübler-Ross, 1975). Sherwin Nuland is a professor who focuses on surgery and the history of medicine. His book, *How we die* (1994), provides detailed medical accounts and first-person accounts of how people die from common causes such as cancer, heart disease, Alzheimer's disease, accidents and crime. Although the content is difficult, the presentation is compassionate. Cancer, heart disease and neurological diseases are commonly feared. There are many excellent first-person and family accounts of dealing with these kinds of chronic illness. (These materials may also be useful for clients.)

3 Individuals experiencing health anxiety are often exposed to uncomfortable tests and medical procedures (e.g. Margolis, 2001; Segen & Stauffer, 1998). Review descriptions of these procedures and imagine your reactions as you experience these tests yourself.
4 Consider broadening your experiences related to medical procedures, illness and death by arranging to observe medical procedures (if you work frequently in an area) or visiting a palliative care unit. If these opportunities are not available, speak to a friend or family member about their experiences (including thoughts and emotions).
5 Think of a client you have seen or you might see. List some of the exposure experiences available in your community (including exposure through the use of television or videotapes) for themes related to illness and death.
6 You have just found out you have only twelve months to live. For about six months of this time you will be experiencing some symptoms but you will be able to continue with many normal life activities. After this, your health will be more uncertain and it is not clear how much energy you will have. Write a description of your thoughts and emotions in this situation and consider how you would like to spend your remaining time. Write an obituary for your local newspaper. Write a plan for your funeral arrangements. Focus on your thoughts and emotions. This project works best if you continue your journaling over a number of days.

EVIDENCE SUMMARIES

Simon, G. (2002). Management of somatoform and factitious disorders. In P. Nathan & J. Gorman (Eds.), *A guide to treatments that work* (Second Edition, pp. 447–463). New York: Oxford University Press.

FURTHER READING FOR PRACTITIONERS

Furer, P., Walker, J. & Freeston, M. (2001). Integrated approach to cognitive behavioural therapy for intense illness worries. In G. Asmundson, S. Taylor &

B. Cox (Eds.), *Health anxiety: Clinical and research perspectives on hypochondriasis and related conditions* (pp. 161–192). Chichester, UK: Wiley.

Kellner, R. (1986). *Somatization and hypochondriasis*. New York: Praeger.

Kirmayer, L. & Robbins, J. (1991). *Current concepts of somatization: Research and clinical perspectives*. Washington, DC: American Psychiatric Press.

Kübler-Ross, E. (Ed.) (1975). *Death: The final stage of growth*. New York: Touchstone.

Nuland, S. (1994). *How we die*. New York: Alfred A. Knopf.

Salkovskis, P. (1989). Somatic problems. In K. Hawton, P. Salkovskis, J. Kirke & D. Clark (Eds.), *Cognitive therapy for psychiatric problems: A practical guide* (pp. 235–276). Oxford: Oxford University Press.

Segen, J. & Stauffer, J. (1998). *The patient's guide to medical tests: Everything you need to know about the tests your doctor prescribes*. New York: Facts on File, Inc.

Taylor, S. & Asmundson, G. J. G. (2004). *Treating health anxiety: A cognitive-behavioral approach*. New York: Guilford Press.

Wells, A. (1997). *Cognitive therapy of anxiety disorders. A practice manual and conceptual guide* (chapter 6). Chichester, UK: Wiley.

ASSESSMENT TOOLS

Barsky, A., Cleary, P., Wyshak, G., Spitzer, R., Williams, J. & Klerman, G. (1992). A structured diagnostic interview for hypochondriasis. A proposed criterion standard. *The Journal of Nervous and Mental Disease*, 180, 20–27.

Barsky, A., Wyshak, G. & Klerman, G. (1986). DSM III hypochdriasis in medical outpatients. *Archives of General Psychiatry*, 43, 493–500. Contains the Somatic Symptom Inventory, which measures hypochondriasis using SCL-90-R and MMPI-2 items.

Barsky, A., Wyshak, G. & Klerman, G. (1990). The Somatosensory Amplification Scale and its relationship to hyochondriasis. *Journal of Psychiatric Research*, 24, 323–334.

Escobar, J., Rubio-Stiper, M., Canino, G. & Karno, M. (1989). Somatic Symptom Index (SSI): A new abridged somatization construct. *Journal of Nervous and Mental Disease*, 177, 1140–1146.

Janca, A., Burke, J., Isaac, M. et al. (1995). The World Health Organization Somatoform Disorders Schedule: A preliminary report on design and reliability. *European Psychiatry*, 10, 373–378.

Kellner, R. (1986). *Somatization and hypochondriasis*. New York: Praeger. Contains the Illness Attitudes Scale.

Kellner, R. (1987). *Abridged Manual of the Illness Attitude Scale*. Department of Psychiatry, School of Medicine, University of Mexico, Albuquerque.

Lucock, M. & Morley, S. (1996). The Health Anxiety Questionnaire. *British Journal of Health Anxiety*, 1, 137–150.

Pilowsky, I. & Spence, N. (1994). *Manual for the Illness Behaviour Questionnaire* (Third Edition). Available from The Department of Psychiatry, University of Adelaide, Adelaide, South Australia.

Rief, W., Hiller, W. & Margraf, J. (1998). Cognitive aspects of hypochondriasis and the somatization syndrome. *Journal of Abnormal Psychology*, 107, 587–595.

Robbins, J. & Kimayer, L. (1991). Attributions of common somatic symptoms. *Psychological Medicine*, 21, 311–313. Contains the Symptom Interpretation Questionnaire.

REFERENCES

American Psychiatric Association (APA) (2000). *Diagnostic and statistical manual of mental disorders* (Fourth Edition, Text Revision). Washington, DC: APA.

Asmundson, G. J. G., Taylor, S., Sevgur, S. & Cox, B. J. (2001). Health anxiety: Classification and clinical features. In G. Asmundson, S. Taylor & B. Cox (Eds.), *Health anxiety: Clinical and research perspectives on hypochondriasis and related conditions* (pp. 3–21). Chichester, UK: Wiley.

Barsky, A. J. & Ahern, D. K. (2004). Cognitive behavior therapy for hypochondriasis. A randomized controlled trial. *Journal of the American Medical Association*, 291, 1464–1470.

Barsky, A. J., Cleary, P. D., Wyshak, G., Spitzer, R. L., Williams, J. B. & Klerman, G. L. (1992). A structured diagnostic interview for hypochondriasis: A proposed criterion standard. *The Journal of Nervous and Mental Disease*, 180, 20–27.

Beck, A. T. (1996). *BDI-II*. San Antonio, TX: The Psychological Corporation.

Beck, A. T. & Emery, G. (1985). *Anxiety disorders and phobias*. New York: Basic Books.

Beck, A.T., Epstein, N., Brown, G. & Steer, R. A. (1988). An inventory for measuring clinical anxiety: Psychometric properties. *Journal of Consulting and Clinical Psychology*, 56, 893–897.

Berrios, G. (2001). Hypochondriasis: History of the concept. In V. Starcevic & D. R. Lipsitt (Eds.), *Hypochondriasis: Modern perspectives on an ancient malady* (pp. 3–20). Oxford: Oxford University Press.

Bouman, T. K. (2002). A community-based psychoeducational group approach to hypochondriasis. *Psychotherapy and Psychosomatics*, 71, 326–332.

Bouman, T. K. & Visser, S. (1998). Cognitive and behavioural treatment of hypochondriasis. *Psychotherapy and Psychosomatics*, 67, 214–221.

Clark, D. M., Salkovskis, P. M., Hackmann, A., Wells, A., Fennell, M., Ludgate, J., Ahmad, S., Richards, H. C. & Gelder, M. (1998). Two psychological treatments for hypochondriasis. *British Journal of Psychiatry*, 173, 218–225.

Derogatis, L. R. (1975). *SCL-90-R: Administration, scoring and procedures manual II for the revised version and other instruments of the psychopathology rating scale series*. Towson, MD: Clinical Psychometric Research.

Dugas, M. J., Ladouceur, R., Leger, E., Freeston, M. H., Langlois, F., Provencher, M. D. & Boisvert, J. M. (2003). Group cognitive-behavioral therapy for generalized anxiety disorder: Treatment outcome and long-term follow-up. *Journal of Consulting and Clinical Psychology*, 71, 821–825.

Enns, M. W., Kjernisted, K. & Lander, M. (2001). Pharmacological management of hypochondriasis and related disorders. In G. Asmundson, S. Taylor & B. Cox (Eds.), *Health anxiety: Clinical and research perspectives on hypochondriasis and related conditions* (pp. 193–219). Chichester, UK: Wiley.

Escobar, J. L. (1996). Overview of somatization: Diagnosis, epidemiology, and management. *Psychopharmacology Bulletin*, 32, 589–596.

Escobar, J. I., Gara, M., Waitzkin, H., Silver, R. C., Holman, A. & Compton, W. (1998). DSM-IV hypochondriasis in primary care. *General Hospital Psychiatry*, 20, 155–159.

Fallon, B. A., Liebowitz, M. R., Salman, E., Schneier, F. R., Jusino, C., Hollander, E. & Klein, D. F. (1993). Fluoxetine for hypochondriacal patients without major depression. *Journal of Clinical Psychopharmacology*, 13, 438–441.

Fallon, B. A., Schneier, F. R., Marshall, R., Campeas, R., Vermes, D., Goetz, D. & Liebowitz, M. R. (1996). The pharmacotherapy of hypochondriasis. *Psychopharmacology Bulletin*, 32, 607–611.

Faravelli, C., Salvatori, S., Galassi, F., Aiazzi, L., Drei, C. & Cabras, P. (1997). Epidemiology of somatoform disorders: A community survey in Florence. *Social Psychiatry and Psychiatric Epidemiology*, 32, 24–29.

Fava, G. A. & Mangelli, L. (2001). Hypochondriasis and anxiety disorders. In V. Starcevic & D. R. Lipsitt (Eds.), *Hypochondriasis: Modern perspectives on an ancient malady* (pp. 89–102). Oxford: Oxford University Press.

Foa, E. B. & Wilson, R. (2001). *Stop obsessing: How to overcome your obsessions and compulsions*. New York: Bantam.

Furer, P. & Walker, J. R. (1998). *Intense illness worry: Client treatment manual*. University of Manitoba, Canada.

Furer, P. & Walker, J. (2004). *Interview questions for health anxiety*. University of Manitoba, Canada.

Furer, P., Walker, J. R., Chartier, M. J. & Stein, M. B. (1997). Hypochondriacal concerns and somatization in panic disorder. *Depression and Anxiety*, 6, 78–85.

Furer, P., Walker, J. R. & Freeston, M. (2001). Approach to integrated cognitive-behavior therapy for intense illness worries. In G. Asmundson, S. Taylor, and B. Cox (Eds.), *Health anxiety: Clinical and research perspectives on hypochondriasis and related conditions* (pp. 161–192). Chichester, UK: Wiley.

Kellner, R. (1986). *Somatization and hypochondriasis*. Westport, CT: Praeger-Greenwood.

Kellner, R. (1987). Hypochondriasis and somatization. *Journal of the American Medical Association*, 258, 2718–2722.

Kirmayer, L. J. & Robbins, J. M. (1991). Three forms of somatization in primary care: Prevalence, co-occurrence, and sociodemographic characteristics. *Journal of Nervous and Mental Disease*, 179, 647–655.

Kjernisted, K. D., Enns, M. W. & Lander, M. (2002). An open-label clinical trial of nefazodone in hypochondriasis. *Psychosomatics*, 43, 290–294.

Kroenke, K. & Swindle, R. (2000). Cognitive-behavioral therapy for somatization and symptom syndromes: A critical review of controlled clinical trials. *Psychotherapy and Psychosomatics*, 69, 205–215.

Kübler-Ross, E. (Ed.) (1975). *Death: The final stage of growth*. Touchstone: New York.

Ladouceur, R., Dugas, M. J., Freeston, M. H., Leger, E., Gagnon, F. & Thibodeau, N. (2000). Efficacy of a cognitive-behavioral treatment for generalized anxiety disorder: Evaluation in a controlled clinical trial. *Journal of Consulting and Clinical Psychology*, 68, 957–964.

Lidbeck, J. (1997). Group therapy for somatization disorders in general practice:

Effectiveness of a short cognitive-behavioural treatment model. *Acta Psychiatrica Scandinavica*, 96, 14–24.

Lidbeck, J. (2003). Group therapy for somatization disorders in primary care: Maintenance of treatment goals of short cognitive-behavioural treatment one-and-a-half-year follow-up. *Acta Psychiatrica Scandinavica*, 107, 449–456.

Looper, K. J. & Kirmayer, L. J. (2002). Behavioral medicine approaches to somatoform disorders. *Journal of Consulting and Clinical Psychology*, 70, 810–827.

Lucock, M. P. & Morley, S. (1996). The Health Anxiety Questionnaire. *British Journal of Health Psychology*, 1, 137–150.

Margolis, S. (Ed.). (2001). *The Johns Hopkins Consumer Guide to Medical Tests*. New York: Rebus, Inc.

McLean, P. D., Whittal, M. L., Thordarson, D. S., Taylor, S., Sochting, I., Koch, W. J., Paterson, R. & Anderson, K. W. (2001). Cognitive versus behaviour therapy in the group treatment of obsessive-compulsive disorder. *Journal of Consulting and Clinical Psychology*, 69, 205–214.

Melville, D. I. (1987). Descriptive clinical research and medically unexplained physical symptoms. *Journal of Psychosomatic Research*, 31, 359–365.

Menza, M., Lauritano, M., Allen, L., Warman, M., Ostella, F., Hamer, R. M. & Escobar, J. (2001). Treatment of somatization disorder with nefazodone: A prospective, open-label study. *Annals of Clinical Psychiatry*, 13, 153–158.

Noyes, R. Jr. (2001). Epidemiology of hypochondriasis. In V. Starcevic & D. R. Lipsitt (Eds.), *Hypochondriasis: Modern perspectives on an ancient malady* (pp. 127–154). Oxford: Oxford University Press.

Noyes, R. Jr., Happel, R. L., Muller, B. A., Holt, C. S., Kathol, R. G., Sieren, L. R. & Amos, J. J. (1998). Fluvoxamine for somatoform disorders: An open trial. *General Hospital Psychiatry*, 20, 339–344.

Noyes, R. Jr., Hartz, A. J., Doebbeling, C. C., Malis, R. W., Happel, R. L., Werner, L. A. & Yagla, S. J. (2000). Illness fears in the general population. *Psychosomatic Medicine*, 62, 318–325.

Nuland, S. (1994). *How we die*. New York: Alfred A. Knopf.

Pilowsky, I. (1967). Dimensions of hypochondriasis. *British Journal of Psychiatry*, 113, 89–93.

Salkovskis, P. M. (1989). Somatic problems. In H. Hawton, P. M. Salkovskis, J. Kirk & D. M. Clark (Eds.), *Cognitive behaviour therapy for psychiatric problems: A practical guide* (pp. 235–276). Oxford: Oxford University Press.

Salkovskis, P. M., Rimes, K. A., Warwick, H. M. & Clark, D. M. (2002). The Health Anxiety Inventory: Development and validation of scales for the measurement of health anxiety and hypochondriasis. *Psychological Medicine*, 32, 843–853.

Segen, J. & Stauffer, J. (1998). *The patient's guide to medical tests: Everything you need to know about the tests your doctor prescribes*. New York: Facts on File, Inc.

Sharpe, M., Peveler, R. & Mayou, R. (1992). The psychological treatment of patients with functional somatic symptoms: A practical guide. *Journal of Psychosomatic Research*, 36, 515–529.

Speckens, A. E. (2001). Assessment of hypochondriasis. In V. Starcevic & D. R. Lipsitt (Eds.), *Hypochondriasis: Modern perspectives on an ancient malady* (pp. 61–88). Oxford: Oxford University Press.

Speckens, A. E., van Hemert, A. M., Spinhoven, P., Hawton, K. E., Bolk, J. H. & Rooijmans, H. G. (1995). Cognitive behavioural therapy for medically unexplained physical symptoms: A randomised controlled trial. *British Medical Journal*, 311, 1328–1332.

Stewart, S. H. & Watt, M. C. (2001). Assessment of health anxiety. In G. Asmundson, S. Taylor & B. Cox (Eds.), *Health anxiety: Clinical and research perspectives on hypochondriasis and related conditions* (pp. 95–131). Chichester, UK: Wiley.

Taylor, S. & Asmundson, G. (2004). *Treating health anxiety: A cognitive-behavioural approach*. New York: Guilford.

Visser, S. & Bouman, T. K. (2001). The treatment of hypochondriasis: Exposure plus response prevention vs. cognitive therapy. *Behaviour Research and Therapy*, 39, 423–442.

Warwick, H. M. (1995). Assessment of hypochondriasis. *Behaviour Research and Therapy*, 33, 845–853.

Warwick, H. M. C., Clark, D. M., Cobb, A. M. & Salkovskis, P. M. (1996). A controlled trial of cognitive-behavioural treatment of hypochondriasis. *British Journal of Psychiatry*, 169, 189–195.

Warwick, H. M. C. & Marks, I. M. (1988). Behavioural treatment of illness phobia and hypochondriasis: A pilot study of 17 cases. *British Journal of Psychiatry*, 152, 239–241.

Warwick, H. M. C. & Salkovskis, P. M. (2001). Cognitive-behavioral treatment of hypochondriasis. In V. Starcevic & D. R. Lipsitt (Eds.), *Hypochondriasis: Modern perspectives on an ancient malady* (pp. 314–328). Oxford: Oxford University Press.

Wesner, R. B. & Noyes, R. Jr. (1991). Imipramine: An effective treatment for illness phobia. *Journal of Affective Disorders*, 22, 43–48.

Whittal, M. L., Otto, M. W. & Hong, J. J. (2001). Cognitive-behavior therapy for discontinuation of SSRI treatment of panic disorder: A case series. *Behaviour Research and Therapy*, 39, 939–945.

World Health Organization (WHO) (1991). *Composite international diagnostic interview (CIDI)*. Geneva: WHO.

World Health Organization (WHO) (1992). *The ICD-10 classification of mental and behavioural disorders. Clinical descriptions and diagnostic guidelines*. Geneva: WHO. Online. Available at: http://www.informatik.fh-luebeck.de/icd/welcome.html

World Health Organization (WHO) (1993). *The ICD-10 classification of mental and behavioural disorders: Diagnostic criteria for research*. Geneva: WHO.

Chapter 17

Coping with chronic pain[1]

Dennis C. Turk and Tasha M. Burwinkle

CASE EXAMPLE

Mary was a sixty-four-year-old married woman and mother of three adult children. She presented to the clinic following referral from a back specialist who had treated her for several years. He did not recommend any further medical treatment and encouraged Mary to exercise, particularly to swim to strengthen her back muscles, and to attend for psychological assessment.

Mary presented as a pleasant and friendly woman. Describing chronic pain in her lower back over the previous ten years, she was at times tearful and admitted to low mood and occasional passive suicidal ideation. Due to her strong religious faith, she said she would never harm herself but, looking to the future, she despaired at the thought of never getting respite from the pain. The pain began initially during her second pregnancy (aged twenty-four) and had flared up intermittently during the next thirty years. In the last ten years it had never remitted, being at best a dull ache but at worst a severe and shooting pain that sent Mary to her bed to rest on hot pads. She explained that exercising was impossible, as it always involved some slight pulling or twisting that exacerbated her pain. Mary also complained of intermittent pain in her head, with tingling pain and occasional dizziness. This had been extensively assessed and no physical cause established; she was prescribed some analgesics for this pain, which she would take, go to bed with the curtains drawn and wait for the worst pain to pass. Mary desperately wanted

1 Preparation of this chapter was supported in part by grants from the National Institute of Arthritis and Musculoskeletal and Skin Diseases (AR/AI44724, AR47298) and the National Institute of Child Health and Human Development/National Center for Medical Rehabilitation Research (HD33989) awarded to the first author.

relief and felt hurt about the referral for psychological assessment. She saw it as a sign that her physician did not believe her accounts of her pain, had lost interest in helping her and was unfairly saying that her pain was 'all in [her] head'.

Mary's husband retired ten years ago from running his own successful business, a business that kept him extremely busy throughout his working life. He had looked forward to spending his retirement travelling with Mary or sailing with her at his local club. He was supportive, if demoralized, by her frequent episodes of pain, particularly if such pain disrupted holidays or planned social events. In fact, due to the difficulties of Mary being in pain on previous holidays, the couple no longer planned any trips, nor did Mary go sailing with him any more. He offered her extensive practical support on a daily basis, acting as a porter for her as Mary would not lift shopping bags, chairs or even a coffee pot for fear of worsening her pain. He often felt guilty about going sailing while leaving her at home in pain, and consequently did not go out as often as he planned.

Mary had given up her job after the birth of her first child. She described her adult life as being devoted to her children, with whom she had good relationships and whom she missed a great deal since they left home. They in turn noticed that conversations with Mary were increasingly dominated by her accounts of her most recent pains and frustrations. They were sympathetic and concerned, and when she was in bed with pain made a special effort to call and visit her more. Mary valued contact with her children. She was particularly frustrated that her preparations for family gatherings invariably led to bouts of acute pain so that her own and the family's enjoyment of such events were reduced.

Although Mary had a wide circle of friends, she was gradually less involved with them as she stopped sailing or attending social outings. Preoccupied by her pain, she was less and less interested in others' lives or pursuits. As her children became more involved with building their careers and relationships, her friends called on her less and less, and she gave up more activities, Mary felt more alone with her pain, more depressed and hopeless.

CLINICAL FEATURES OF CHRONIC PAIN

Pain is the most frequent reason for physician consultation in the United States (Abbott & Fraser, 1998) with nearly one-half of those who seek treatment reporting that their primary symptom is pain. Examination of the largest categories of chronic pain syndromes reveals that the vast majority suffer from symptoms that are unrelated to identifiable pathology but rather symptoms present at specific body locations such as low back pain and headache or widespread pain (e.g. fibromyalgia syndrome (FMS)) (Frolund & Frolund, 1986).

Diagnostic criteria for pain disorder from fourth edition of the *Diagnostic and Statistical Manual* (DSM-IV; APA, 1994) and from tenth edition of the *International Classification of Diseases* (ICD-10; WHO, 1992) are given in Table 17.1. Pain disorder, according to the DSM-IV, involves pain in one or

Table 17.1 Diagnostic criteria for pain disorder

DSM-IV-TR	*ICD-10*
A. Pain in one or more anatomical sites is the predominant focus of the clinical presentation and is of sufficient severity to warrant clinical attention B. The pain causes clinically significant distress of impairment in social, occupational, or other important areas of functioning C. Psychological factors are judged to have an important role in the onset, severity, exacerbation, or maintenance of the pain D. The symptom or deficit is not intentionally produced or feigned E. The pain is not better accounted for by a mood, anxiety, or psychotic disorder and does not meet criteria for dyspareunia Acute specifier if duration is less that 6 months Chronic if 6 months or longer	**Persistent Somatoform Pain Disorder** The predominant complaint is of persistent, severe and distressing pain, which cannot be explained fully by a physiological process or a physical disorder. Pain occurs in association with emotional conflict or psychosocial problems that are sufficient to allow the conclusion that they are the main causative influences. The result is usually a marked increase in support and attention, either personal or medical Pain presumed to be of psychogenic origin occurring during the course of depressive disorder or schizophrenia should not be included here. Pain due to known or inferred psychophysiological mechanisms such as muscle tension pain or migraine, but still believed to have a psychogenic cause, should be coded by the use of F54 (psychological or behavioural factors associated with disorders or diseases classified elsewhere), plus an additional code from elsewhere in ICD-10 (e.g. migraine, G43-) Includes: • Psychalgia • Psychogenic backache or headache • Somatoform pain disorder

Note: Adapted from DSM-IV-TR (APA, 2000) and ICD-10 (WHO, 1992).

more anatomical sites as the predominant focus of the clinical presentation and of sufficient severity to warrant clinical attention. The pain causes clinically significant distress of impairment in social, occupational or other important areas of functioning. Psychological factors are judged to have an important role in the onset, severity, exacerbation or maintenance of the pain. The symptom or deficit is not intentionally produced or feigned. The pain is not better accounted for by a mood, anxiety, or psychotic disorder and does not meet criteria for dyspareunia. Pain that persists for less than six months is specified as 'acute', while pain that lasts longer than six months is specified as 'chronic'.

Despite the soaring cost of treating people with chronic pain, relief for many pain sufferers remains elusive and total elimination of pain is rare, hence the phrase 'chronic pain'. Although there have been phenomenal advances in the knowledge of neurophysiology, anatomy and biochemistry, along with the development of potent analgesic medications and other innovative medical and surgical interventions, pain and disability as problems have not been eliminated for a significant portion of the population. Nevertheless, there has been progress in the treatment of chronic pain from the biopsychosocial perspective, which has helped people cope with their pain experience when it cannot be eliminated. The purpose of this chapter, then, is to provide information about conceptual models, assessment, and intervention strategies for people with chronic pain with an emphasis on the role of psychological factors and treatment that addresses psychosocial and behavioural contributors to the pain experience.

CLASSIFICATION OF PAIN

Acute pain

From our earliest experiences, we become familiar with the pain of a cut, sunburn, or bruised knee. In these instances, the pain is *acute*. That is, it is self-limiting and will remit on its own, without the need of treatment by a healthcare professional, in a reasonably short period of time (usually hours, days, or a few weeks). Rarely are there any long-term consequences following acute pain episodes.

In acute pain, *nociception* (activation of sensory conduction in nerve fibres that transmit information about tissue damage from the periphery to brain via the spinal cord) acts as a warning signal directing concentration and demanding attention in order to prevent further damage and to expedite the healing process. For example, when we place our hands on a hot stove, we quickly remove it to avoid tissue being damaged. Pain also signals that an injury or disease state is present as in the case of a broken leg or inflamed appendix. In these instances, pain serves an important, protective function informing us that steps should be taken to prevent additional problems and, if necessary, seek medical attention.

Recurrent acute pain

A number of pain diagnoses and syndromes (e.g. migraine, rheumatoid arthritis, tic doloureux) are characterized by pain episodes that alternate with pain-free periods, often in an unpredictable fashion. For example, migraine may last for several hours and then remit even without any treatment, or the episode might be prevented or aborted with pharmacological agents. The migraine sufferer may be headache-free for days or weeks only to have another migraine episode. After the headache has run its course the person will again be headache free until stricken by yet another episode. Migraine and conditions with similar episodic characteristics may be viewed as *recurrent acute pain*. In the case of recurrent acute pain conditions, the role of pain is unclear as there are rarely any protective actions that can be taken, nor is there any identifiable tissue damage that might initiate the episode. Thus, in both recurrent acute pain and, as we shall see, chronic pain, the symptom may serve no useful purpose.

Chronic pain

Chronic pain persists and can last for months, years and even decades beyond any period for which healing of the initial injury might be expected. As is the case in recurrent acute pain, in chronic pain syndromes (e.g. osteoarthritis; FMS) the pain does not appear to have any obvious useful function. Pain that is chronic or recurrent significantly compromises quality of life and, if unremitting, may actually produce physical harm by suppressing the immune system (Liebeskind, 1991).

Often, the underlying cause for patients' chronic pain cannot be determined using currently available imaging and laboratory methods. There have been some suggestions regarding alterations within the nervous system where prolonged pain leads to neurophysiological changes and increased sensitivity within the central nervous system (CNS) that perpetuate the experience of pain even when the initial cause has resolved (Coderre et al., 1993). To complicate matters, the diagnosis and treatment of chronic pain is often based solely on a client's subjective report of pain. Patients' perception of pain and the presence of behaviours connoting pain ('pain behaviours'), however, are not necessarily proportional to the amount of tissue pathology or the pain and disability reported. For example, for some people with rheumatoid arthritis, laboratory values and imaging studies reveal inflammation that might contribute to reports of severe pain. However, many other individuals who show similar signs of disease activity do not report persistent, severe symptoms. In this case it is unclear why two people with the same physical findings respond so differently; one reports being incapacitated by pain whereas the other reports no pain whatsoever. Obviously, something other than physical pathology is influencing the reports of pain.

EPIDEMIOLOGY OF CHRONIC PAIN

Precise estimates of the prevalence of chronic pain syndromes are difficult to ascertain. In the US, for example, there may be over 30 million people with chronic or recurrent painful conditions (Joranson & Lietman, 1994). Data obtained from an American survey of pain specialists suggest that approximately 2.9 million (1.1% of the population) are treated annually by health-care professionals specializing in chronic pain (Marketdata Enterprises, 1995). In the US, 17% of patients treated in primary care report persistent pain (Gureje, 1998). These figures, however, do not include treatment by medical specialists who do not consider themselves pain specialists, nor does it include visits to practitioners of complementary and alternative medicine, or self-medication using over-the-counter pharmacological preparations or nutritional supplements.

Pain medications are the second most prescribed drugs (after cardiac–renal dugs) during visits to physicians' offices and accident and emergency rooms (Schappert, 1998), accounting for 12% of all medication prescribed during ambulatory office visits (National Ambulatory Medical Care Survey, 1998). Data from the third National Health and Nutrition Examination Survey (NHANES), conducted between 1988 and 1994, indicated that 9% of American adults were prescribed analgesic medication in the month prior to the survey; of these, 69% were prescribed non-steroidal anti-inflammatory drugs (NSAIDs) and 36.5% (6.21 million) opioids (Paulose-Ram et al., 2003). Pharmaceutical industry data indicate that over 312 million prescriptions for opioid medications were written in the US in the year 2000, approximately one prescription for every man, woman and child (Merck, personal communication, November 2001). The number of people taking non-prescription analgesics, however, far exceeds these figures: NHANES data indicate that approximately 76% of American adults consumed non-prescription analgesic medication in the month prior to the survey (Paulose-Ram et al., 2003). It is perhaps not surprising, then, that there are currently over 170 non-prescription products containing analgesics either alone or in combination with other medications available for purchase by the US public (*Physicians' desk reference for nonprescription drugs and dietary supplements*, 2001).

The costs of managing chronic pain are astronomical, involving not only health care but also indirect costs such as lost time at work, lost tax revenue, legal services, and disability compensation. Some data also suggest that Americans spend as much money on complementary and alternative medicine (e.g. acupuncture, spinal manipulation, nutritional supplements) as they do on conventional medical care (Eisenberg et al., 1998). Although the many medical and alternative treatments make it difficult to derive exact figures, estimates of the total annual costs of chronic pain (including treatment, lost work days, disability payments, legal fees) in the US range from $150 to $215 billion (United States Bureau of the Census, 1996; National Research Council, 2001). Cousins (1995) suggested that the costs of health care for patients with chronic pain internationally might exceed the combined costs of treating patients with coronary artery disease, cancer and Aids.

THEORIES OF CHRONIC PAIN

A number of models have been postulated to conceptualize the chronic pain experience. Single-factor models (including the biomedical model, psychogenic model, motivational model and behavioural models) focus on a particular cause of the symptoms reported. Multidimensional models (gate control theory, biopsychosocial model) emphasize the contributions of a range of factors that influence individuals' experiences and reports of pain.

Single-factor models of chronic pain

Biomedical model of chronic pain

The traditional biomedical view of pain assumes that reports of pain must be related, in a proportionate manner, with a specific physical cause. As a consequence, the extent of pain should be directly associated with the amount of detectable neurophysiological perturbations. Healthcare providers often undertake Herculean efforts (frequently at great expense) attempting to establish the specific link between tissue damage and the severity of pain. The expectation is that once the physical cause has been identified, appropriate treatment will follow. Treatment will then focus on eliminating the putative cause(s) of the pain, or chemically (e.g. oral medication, regional anaesthesia, implantable drug delivery systems), surgically (e.g. laminectomy) or electrically (e.g. transcutaneous electrical nerve stimulation, spinal cord stimulation) disrupting the pain pathways in the nervous system.

Several perplexing features of chronic pain do not fit neatly within the traditional biomedical model, with its suggestion of an isomorphic relationship between pathology and symptoms. In addition to the observation of individual differences in responding to the same physical pathology, a particular conundrum is the fact that pain may be reported even in the absence of identified pathological process. It is estimated that one-third to one-half of all visits to primary care physicians are prompted by symptoms for which no biomedical causes can be detected (Kroenke & Mangelsdorff, 1989). For example, in 80% to 85% of the cases, the cause of back pain is unknown (Deyo, 1986). Conversely, imaging studies using computed tomography (CT) scans and magnetic resonance imaging (MRIs) have observed the presence of significant pathology in up to 35% of *asymptomatic* people (e.g. Jensen et al., 1994; Wiesel et al., 1984). Similarly, asymptomatic individuals may have significant degrees of degeneration and, more importantly, a similar prevalence of disk herniation that is comparable to symptomatic people (Boos et al., 1995), yet report no pain. Thus, some people report severe pain with *no* identifiable pathology, whereas others with demonstrable pathology *may not complain* of any pain. Such observations suggest that the biomedical model may be insufficient to describe chronic pain.

Psychogenic model of chronic pain

As is frequently the case in medicine, when physical explanations seem inadequate or when the results of treatment are inconsistent, reports of pain are attributed to a psychological aetiology (and thus are 'psychogenic'). Assessment based on the psychogenic perspective is directed towards identifying the psychopathological tendencies or personality factors that instigate and maintain the reported pain. Traditional psychological measures such as the Minnesota Multiphasic Personality Inventory (MMPI) and the Symptom Checklist-90 (SCL-90; Derogatis, 1983) are commonly used to evaluate chronic pain sufferers (Piotrowski, 1997). Elevated patterns of scores on such instruments are considered to support the notion of psychogenic pain, despite the fact that these instruments were not standardized on medical samples. This is a significant problem since items related to physical symptoms, such as the presence of pain in the back of the neck, the ability to work, feelings of weakness, and beliefs regarding health status in comparison with friends, can be affected by disease status and medication, resulting in misleading elevations in scores. It is assumed that reports of pain will cease once the psychogenic mechanisms are resolved. Treatment is geared towards helping clients gain 'insight' into the underlying maladaptive psychological contributors (e.g. Beutler et al., 1986; Grzesiak et al., 1996).

Empirical evidence supporting the psychogenic view is scarce. A number of chronic pain sufferers do not exhibit significant psychopathology. Furthermore, insight-oriented psychotherapy has not been shown to be effective in reducing symptoms for the majority of clients with chronic pain. Studies suggest that the emotional distress observed in persons with chronic pain more typically occurs in *response to* the persistence of pain and not as a causal agent (e.g. Okifuji et al., 2000; Rudy et al., 1988) and may resolve once pain is adequately treated (Wallis et al., 1997). The psychogenic model has thus come under scrutiny and may be flawed in its view of chronic pain.

Motivational model of chronic pain

The motivational model suggests that reports of pain in the absence of or in excess of physical pathology are attributed to the individual's desire to obtain some benefit such as attention, time off from undesirable activities or financial compensation – *secondary gains*. In contrast to the psychogenic model, in the motivational view, a high degree of discrepancy between what the client says about his or her pain and disability and performance on more objective assessment of physical functioning are taken as evidence that the client is *consciously* exaggerating or fabricating his or her symptoms to obtain a desired outcome (e.g. malingering).

Assessment of clients using the motivational model focuses on identifying discrepancies between what clients say they are capable of doing and what they actually can do, through repeated performance of functional capacity testing, or through surveillance. Thus, a client who states that he cannot lift weights over 10 lbs and who refuses to attempt to lift during a functional capacity evaluation might be videotaped lifting groceries out of a car. The report of the inability to lift, in the light of the observation of lifting groceries, is viewed as proof of dissimulation, even though these inconsistencies fail to consider the limited ability of people to accurately estimate the capacity and the refusal to perform associated with fear of injury, re-injury, or exacerbation of pain (e.g. Lenthem et al., 1983; Vlaeyen et al., 1995).

The treatment of pain from the motivational perspective is simple – denial of disability payments, with the assumption that this will lead inevitably to resolution of the symptoms. Although this view is prevalent, especially among third-party payers, there is little evidence of dramatic cure of pain following denial of disability (Mendelson, 1982).

Behavioural conceptualizations of chronic pain

Three major principles of learning contribute to our understanding of the acquisition of adaptive as well as dysfunctional behaviours associated with pain. These principles are well known in the general psychology literature and are applicable in the context of chronic pain.

Classical (respondent) conditioning

In the classical (or respondent) conditioning model, if a nociceptive stimulus is repeatedly paired with a neutral stimulus, the neutral stimulus will come to elicit a pain response. For example, a patient who received a painful treatment from a physical therapist (PT) may become *conditioned* to experience a negative emotional response to the presence of the PT, to the treatment room and to any stimulus associated with nociceptive stimuli. The negative emotional reaction may lead to tensing of muscles and this may in turn exacerbate pain, thereby reinforcing the association between the presence of the PT and pain.

Once a pain problem persists, fear of motor activities that the client expects to result in pain may develop and motivate avoidance of activity. Avoidance of pain is a powerful rationale for reduction of activity, where muscle soreness associated with exercise functions as a justification for further avoidance. Although it may be useful to reduce movement in the acute stage, limitation of activities can be chronically maintained not only by pain but also by *anticipatory* fear that has been acquired through the mechanism of classical conditioning. In this way, it is the anticipation that motivates a conscious decision to avoid specific behaviours, situations, or stimuli.

In chronic pain, many activities that were neutral or even pleasurable may come to elicit or exacerbate pain and are thus experienced as aversive and actively avoided. Over time, a growing number of stimuli (e.g. activities and exercises) may be expected to elicit or exacerbate pain and will be avoided (a process known as *stimulus generalization*). Thus, the anticipatory fear of pain and restriction of activity, and not just the actual nociception, may contribute to disability. Anticipatory fear can also elicit physiological reactivity that may aggravate pain. Thus, conditioning may directly increase nociceptive stimulation and pain.

So long as activity avoidance succeeds in preventing pain initiation or exacerbation, the conviction that pain sufferers hold that they remain inactive is difficult to modify. Treatment of pain from the classical conditioning model includes repeatedly engaging in behaviour – *exposure* – that produces progressively less pain than was predicted (corrective feedback), which is then followed by reductions in anticipatory fear and anxiety associated with the activity (Fordyce et al., 1982; Vlaeyen et al., 1995). Such transformations add support to the importance of quota-based physical exercise programmes, with clients progressively increasing their activity levels despite fear of injury and discomfort associated with use of deconditioned muscles (Dolce et al., 1986).

Operant conditioning – contingencies of reinforcement

A new era in thinking about pain began in 1976 with Fordyce's extension of operant conditioning to chronic pain. This view proposes that acute pain behaviours (such as avoidance of activity to protect a painful area from additional pain) may come under the control of external contingencies of reinforcement (responses increase or decrease as a function of their reinforcing consequences) and thus develop into a chronic pain problem. Overt pain behaviours include verbal reports, paralinguistic vocalizations (e.g. sighs, moans), motor activity, facial expressions, body postures and gesturing (e.g. limping, rubbing a painful body part, grimacing), functional limitations (reclining for extensive periods of time, inactivity) and behaviours designed to reduce pain (e.g. taking medication, use of the healthcare system). These behaviours may be positively reinforced directly (e.g. attention from a spouse or healthcare provider, monetary compensation, avoidance of undesirable activity). Pain behaviours may also be maintained by the escape from noxious stimulation by the use of drugs or rest, or the avoidance of undesirable activities such as work. In addition, 'well behaviours' (e.g. activity, working) may not be positively reinforcing and the more rewarding pain behaviours may, therefore, be maintained.

We can consider an example to illustrate the role of operant conditioning. When a back pain sufferer's pain flares up, she may lie down and hold her back. Her husband may observe her behaviour and infer that she is experiencing pain. He may respond by offering to rub her back. This response may positively reward the woman and her pain behaviours (i.e. lying down) may be repeated even in the absence of pain. The husband might also reinforce her pain behaviours by permitting her to avoid undesirable activities (such as suggesting they cancel evening plans, which she may have preferred to avoid anyway). In these situations, her husband providing extra attention and comfort and the opportunity to avoid an undesirable social obligation rewards and maintains her pain behaviours by the learned consequences.

Figure 17.1 summarizes the mechanisms and consequences involved in operant conditioning. The operant learning paradigm does not uncover the aetiology of pain but focuses primarily on the maintenance of pain behaviours and deficiency in well behaviours. Adjustment of reinforcement schedules will probably modify the probability of recurrence of pain behaviours and well behaviours.

It is important to emphasize that pain sufferers do not necessarily intentionally communicate pain to obtain attention or avoid undesirable activities. This is more likely the result of a gradual process of the shaping of behaviour that neither pain sufferer nor her significant others recognize. Thus, a person's response to life stressors, as well as how others respond to the pain sufferer, can influence the experience of pain in many ways, but are not the cause of the pain condition.

Social learning processes

From the Social Learning perspective the acquisition of pain behaviours may occur by means of observational learning and modelling processes. That is, people can acquire behavioural responses that were not previously in their repertoire by the observation of others, particularly those whom they view as being similar to themselves.

Children, for example, develop attitudes about health, health care, and the perception and interpretation of symptoms and physiological processes from their parents and others they confront in their social environment. They learn how others respond to injury and disease and thus may be more or less likely

Schedule	Consequences	Probability of the behaviour recurring
Positive reinforcement	Reward the behaviour	More likely
Negative reinforcement	Prevent or withdraw, avoidance	More likely
Punishment	With negative emotions and much attention	More likely
Punishment	With little attention, ignoring the behaviour	Less likely
Neglect	Prevent or withdraw positive results	Less likely

Figure 17.1 Consequences of operant conditioning.

to ignore or over-respond to symptoms they experience based on behaviours modelled in childhood. For example, children of chronic pain clients may make more pain-related responses during stressful times or exhibit greater illness behaviours (e.g. complaining, days absent, visit to school nurse) than children of healthy parents based on what they observed and learned at home (Richard, 1988).

Expectancies and actual behavioural responses to nociceptive stimulation are based, at least partially, on prior social learning history. Models can influence the expression, localization, and methods of coping with pain (Craig, 1986). Even physiological responses may be conditioned during observation of others in pain (Vaughan & Lanzetta, 1980). Complicating the issue is that how people interpret, respond to, and cope with illness is largely culturally determined. This may contribute to the marked variability in response to objectively similar degrees of physical pathology noted by healthcare providers.

Multidimensional models of chronic pain

While the biomedical, psychogenic, motivational and behavioural views are single-factor conceptualizations that ascribe pain to either physical or psychological factors, it may be that both physical and psychological components interact to create and influence the experience of pain. Thus, several efforts have been made to integrate physical, psychosocial and behavioural factors within multidimensional models.

Gate control theory

The first attempt to develop an integrative model designed to address the problems created by one-dimensional models and to integrate physiological and psychological factors was the gate control theory (GCT) proposed by Melzack and Wall (1965) (Figure 17.2). Perhaps the most important contribution of the GCT is the way it changed thinking about pain perception. In this model, Melzack and Wall postulated that three systems were related to the processing of nociceptive stimulation – sensory-discriminative, motivational-affective, and cognitive-evaluative – all of which contribute to the subjective experience of pain. Melzack and Wall emphasized the CNS mechanisms and provided a physiological basis for the role of psychological factors in chronic pain.

From the GCT perspective, the experience of pain consists of an ongoing sequence of activities, largely reflexive in nature at the outset, but modifiable even in the earliest stages by a variety of excitatory and inhibitory influences (physiological and psychological), and by the integration of ascending and descending nervous system activity. The process results in overt expressions communicating pain and strategies by the person to terminate the

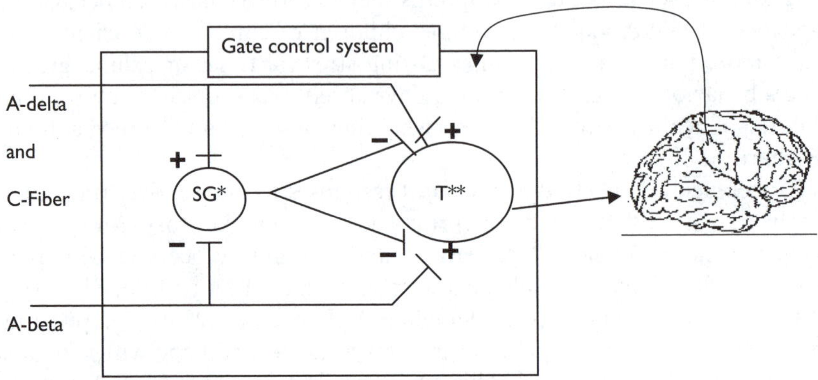

Figure 17.2 Gate control model of pain.

pain. In addition, considerable potential for shaping the pain experience is implied because the GCT invokes continuous interaction of multiple systems (sensory-physiological, affect, cognition and, ultimately, behaviour).

The GCT describes the integration of peripheral stimuli with cortical variables, such as mood and anxiety, in the perception of pain. This model contradicts the notion that pain is either somatic or psychogenic and instead postulates that both factors have either potentiating or moderating effects on pain perception. In this model, for example, pain is not understood to be the result of depression or vice versa, but rather the two are seen as evolving simultaneously. Any significant change in mood or pain will necessarily alter each other.

The GCT emphasizes the integration of psychological variables such as past experience, attention, and other cognitive activities into research and therapy on pain. Prior to this formulation, psychological processes were largely dismissed as reactions to pain. This new model suggested that cutting nerves and pathways was inadequate because a host of other factors modulated the input. Perhaps the major contribution of the GCT was that it highlighted the central nervous system as an essential component in pain processes and perception.

Despite challenges to the postulated anatomy and neurophysiology, the GCT has proved remarkably resilient. It provides a powerful summary of the phenomena observed in the spinal cord and brain, and can explain many of the most mysterious and puzzling problems encountered in the clinic. The GCT has had enormous heuristic value in stimulating further research in the basic science of pain mechanisms as well as in spurring new clinical treatments. After the GCT was first described, in 1965, no one could try to explain pain exclusively in terms of peripheral factors.

A number of authors have extended the GCT to integrate more detailed psychological contributions, which has lead to the presentation of heuristic biopsychosocial or biobehavioural models of pain (e.g. Turk 1996; Turk & Flor, 1999). These conceptual models emphasize the important contributions and the mediating and modulation role of a range of cognitive, affective, and behavioural variables. Before describing these models it is important to focus on the psychology of pain.

Psychology of pain

Emotional distress is common in people with chronic pain. People with chronic and recurrent acute pain often feel rejected by the medical system, believing that they are blamed or labelled as symptom magnifiers and complainers by their physicians, family members, friends, and employers when their pain condition does not respond to treatment. They may see multiple physicians and undergo numerous laboratory tests and imaging procedures in an effort to have their pain diagnosed and successfully treated. As treatments expected to alleviate pain are proven ineffective, patients may lose faith and become frustrated and irritated with the medical system. As their pain persists, they may be unable to work, have financial difficulties, difficulty performing everyday activities, sleep disturbance, or treatment-related complications. They may be fearful and have inadequate or maladaptive support systems and other coping resources available to them. These consequences of chronic pain can result in depression, anger, anxiety, self-preoccupation or isolation – in one word, demoralization.

Biomedical factors, in the majority of cases, appear to instigate the initial report of pain. Over time, however, psychosocial and behavioural factors (such as those described above) may serve to maintain and exacerbate the level of pain, influence adjustment, and contribute to excessive disability. Following from this view, pain that persists over time should not be viewed as solely physical or purely psychological; the experience of pain is maintained by an interdependent set of biomedical, psychosocial, and behavioural factors.

Healthcare providers need to consider not only the physical basis of pain but also patients' mood, fears, expectancies, coping resources, and the response of significant others, including themselves. Regardless of whether there is an identifiable physical basis for the reported pain, both psychosocial and behavioural factors will interact to influence the nature, severity, and persistence of pain and disability. We can extend the discussion of the psychology of pain by examining some specific affective and cognitive factors that are particularly important in understanding chronic pain sufferers, and their experiences.

AFFECTIVE FACTORS

Pain is ultimately a subjective, private experience but it is invariably described in terms of sensory and affective properties. As defined by the International

Association for the Study of Pain: '[Pain] is unquestionably a sensation in a part or parts of the body but it is also always unpleasant and therefore also an emotional experience' (Merskey, 1986). The affective components of pain include many different emotions, but they are primarily negative emotions. Depression and anxiety have received the greatest amount of attention, however, anger has received considerable interest as a significant emotion in chronic pain clients.

Depression Studies suggest that 40–50% of chronic pain clients suffer from significant depression (Banks & Kerns, 1996). As noted previously, in the majority of cases, depression appears to be reactive, although some have suggested that chronic pain is a form of 'masked depression', whereby clients feel it is more acceptable to complain of pain than to acknowledge that they are depressed.

Although a large number of pain patients are depressed, why is it that they are not *all* depressed? Turk and colleagues (Okifuji et al., 2000; Turk et al., 1995) determined that individuals' appraisals of the effects of the pain on their lives and of their ability to exert control over the pain and their lives mediated the pain-depression relationship. That is, those patients who believed that they could continue to function and maintain control despite their pain did not become depressed.

Anxiety Anxiety is a prevalent emotion observed in chronic pain sufferers. In the absence of physical pathology to explain their pain they become fearful. The fear relates to activities that they anticipate will increase their pain or exacerbate whatever physical factors might be contributing to the pain. These fears may contribute to inactivity and greater disability. In addition to fear of movement, people with persistent pain may be anxious about the meaning of their symptoms for the future – will their pain increase, will their physical capacity diminish, will they have progressive disability and ultimately end up in a wheelchair or bed-ridden? In addition to these sources of fear, pain sufferers may fear that on the one hand people will not believe that they are suffering and on the other they may be told that they are beyond help and will 'just have to learn to live with it'. All of these fears will contribute to increased muscle tension and physiological arousal that may exacerbate and maintain pain.

Anger Anger has been widely observed in people with chronic pain (Schwartz et al., 1991), with up to 53% of clients reporting 'bottled up anger' (Pilowsky & Spence, 1976). Even though chronic pain clients might present an image of themselves as even-tempered, Corbishley et al. (1990) found that 88% acknowledged their feelings of anger when these were explicitly sought. This is perhaps not surprising, given the frustrations related to persistence of symptoms, limited information on aetiology and repeated treatment failures along with anger toward others (employers, insurance companies, the health-care system, family members) and anger towards themselves, perhaps, for their inability to alleviate their symptoms and to move on with their lives.

Although the effects of anger and frustration on magnification of pain and treatment acceptance has not received much attention, Kerns, Rosenberg and Jacob (1994) noted that the internalization of angry feelings was related to measures of pain intensity, perceived interference and reported frequency of pain behaviours. Furthermore, Summers et al. (1991) found that anger and hostility were powerful predictors of pain severity in people with spinal cord injuries. It is thus reasonable to expect that the presence of anger may serve as a complicating factor, increasing autonomic arousal and blocking motivation and acceptance of treatments oriented towards rehabilitation and disability management rather than cure, which are often the only treatments available for chronic pain (Fernandez & Turk, 1995).

It is important to be aware of the significant role of negative mood in chronic pain clients because it is likely to affect treatment motivation and adherence to treatment recommendations. For example, clients who are anxious may fear engaging in what they perceive as demanding activities; clients who are depressed and who feel helpless may have little initiative to comply; and clients who are angry with the healthcare system are not likely to be motivated to respond to recommendations from yet another healthcare professional.

COGNITIVE FACTORS

A great deal of research has been directed toward identifying cognitive factors that contribute to pain and disability. These studies have consistently demonstrated that clients' attitudes, beliefs and expectancies about their plight, themselves, their coping resources and the healthcare system affect reports of pain, activity, disability, and response to treatment.

Beliefs about pain People respond to medical conditions in part based on their subjective ideas about illness and their symptoms. Studies have shown that clients who attribute their pain to a worsening of their underlying disease experience more pain despite comparable levels of disease progression (e.g. Spiegel & Bloom, 1983). Because behaviour and emotions are influenced by interpretations of events (rather than solely by objective characteristics of the event itself), when pain is interpreted as signifying ongoing tissue damage or a progressive disease, it is likely to produce considerably more suffering and behavioural dysfunction than if it is viewed as being the result of a stable problem that is expected to improve.

We can consider the case of a man who wakes up one morning with a headache to illustrate the important role of cognitive processes in affect and behaviour related to noxious sensations. Very different responses would be expected if he attributed the headache to excessive alcohol intake or a brain tumour. Thus, although the amount of nociceptive input in the two cases may be equivalent, the emotional and behavioural responses would vary in nature and intensity. If the interpretation is that the headache is related to excessive alcohol, there might be little emotional arousal. The man might take some over-the-counter analgesics, a hot shower, and relax for a few hours. On the other hand, interpretation of the headache as indicative of a brain tumour is highly likely to create significant worry and might result in a call to a neurologist.

Beliefs about the meaning of pain and one's ability to function despite discomfort are important aspects of expectations about pain. For example, a cognitive representation that one has a very serious, debilitating condition, that disability is a necessary aspect of pain, that activity is dangerous, and that pain is an acceptable excuse for neglecting responsibilities, will likely result in maladaptive responses and greater disability.

Once beliefs and expectancies are formed they become stable and rigid and become relatively impervious to modification. Pain sufferers tend to avoid experiences that could invalidate their beliefs (disconfirmations) and guide their behaviour in accordance with these beliefs, even in situations where these beliefs are no longer valid. It is thus essential for people with chronic pain to develop adaptive beliefs about the relationships among impairment, pain, suffering, and disability, and to de-emphasize the role of experienced pain in their regulation of functioning. In fact, results from numerous treatment outcome studies have shown that changes in pain level do not parallel changes in other variables of interest, including activity level, medication use, return to work, rated ability to cope with pain, and pursuit of further treatment (see Turk, 2002a). If healthcare providers hope to achieve better outcomes and to reduce their frustration about patients' lack of adherence to their advice, then they need to learn about, attend to and address patients' beliefs and expectancies within this therapeutic context.

Self-efficacy Self-efficacy is a personal expectation that is particularly important in people with chronic pain. A self-efficacy expectation is defined as a personal conviction that one can successfully execute a course of action (perform required behaviours) to produce a desired outcome in a given situation (Bandura, 1977). Given sufficient motivation to engage in a behaviour, it is a person's self-efficacy beliefs that determine the choice of activities that he or she will initiate, the amount of effort that will be expended, and how long the individual will persist in the face of obstacles and aversive experiences. In this way, self-efficacy plays an important role in therapeutic change.

Efficacy judgements are based on four sources of information regarding one's capabilities, listed in descending order of effects (Bandura, 1977): one's own past performance at the task or similar tasks, the performance accomplishments of others who are perceived to be similar to oneself, verbal persuasion by others that one is capable and perception of one's own state of physiological arousal, which is in turn partly determined by prior efficacy estimation. Performance mastery can then be created by encouraging people to undertake subtasks that are initially attainable but become increasingly difficult, and subsequently approaching the desired level of performance (Dolce et al., 1986). It is important to remember that coping behaviours are influenced by the person's beliefs that the demands of a situation do not exceed their coping resources. For example, Council et al. (1988) asked clients to rate their self-efficacy as well as expectancy of pain related to performance during movement tasks. Clients' performance levels were highly related to their self-efficacy expectations, which in turn appeared to be determined by their expectancies regarding levels of pain that would be experienced.

Catastrophic thinking Distorted thinking can contribute to the maintenance and exacerbation of pain (Turk & Rudy, 1986). A particularly potent and pernicious thinking style that has been observed in chronic pain clients is catastrophizing (Sullivan et al., 2001). Catastrophizing – experiencing extremely negative thoughts about one's plight and interpreting even minor problems as major catastrophes – appears to be a powerful way of thinking that greatly influences pain and disability. Research has indicated that catastrophizing and adaptive coping strategies are important in determining one's reaction to pain (e.g. Sullivan et al., 2001). People who spontaneously used more catastrophizing thoughts reported more pain than those who did not catastrophize in several acute and chronic pain studies.

Coping Self-regulation of pain and its effects depends on the person's specific ways of dealing with pain, adjusting to pain and reducing or minimizing pain and distress caused by pain; in other words, their coping strategies (DeGood & Tait, 2001). Coping strategies act to alter both the perception of intensity of pain and one's ability to manage or tolerate pain and to continue everyday activities, and they can be assessed in terms of overt and covert behaviours. Overt, behavioural coping strategies include rest, medication, and use of relaxation among others. Covert coping strategies include various means of distracting oneself from pain, reassuring oneself that the pain will diminish, seeking information, and problem solving, to list some of the most prominent.

Studies have found active coping strategies (efforts to function in spite of pain or to distract oneself from pain, such as activity and ignoring pain) to be associated with adaptive functioning, and passive coping strategies (depending on others for help in pain control, restricted activities, avoiding activities because of fear of pain/injury, self-medication, alcohol) to be related to greater pain and depression (Boothby et al., 1999). However, beyond this, there is no evidence supporting the greater effectiveness of any one active coping strategy compared to any other (Turk et al., 1983). It seems more likely that different strategies will be more effective than others for some people at some times but not necessarily for all people all of the time. Regardless of the type of coping strategy, if clients are instructed in the use of adaptive coping strategies, their rating of intensity of pain decreases and tolerance of pain increases (Boothby et al., 1999).

Biopsychosocial model of pain

Given our discussion of the psychological factors that have been implicated as playing a role in pain, we can now consider how these factors can be integrated within a multidimensional model of pain. An integrative model of chronic and acute recurrent pain needs to incorporate the mutual interrelationships among physical, psychosocial, and behavioural factors, and the changes that occur among these relationships over time. A model that focuses on only one of these sets of factors will inevitably be incomplete.

Although the GCT model proposed by Melzack and Wall (1965) introduced the role of psychological factors in the maintenance of pain symptoms, it focused primarily on the basic anatomy and neurophysiology of pain. The biopsychosocial model, in contrast, focuses primarily on the psychological and cognitive-behavioural components of pain, and views illness as a dynamic and reciprocal interaction between biological, psychological, and socio-cultural variables that shape the person's response to pain (Turk, 1996; Turk & Flor, 1999).

The conceptual view of the biopsychosocial model is depicted in Figure 17.3. The biopsychosocial model presumes some form of physical pathology or at least physical changes in the muscles, joints, or nerves that generate nociceptive input to the brain. At the periphery, nociceptive fibres transmit sensations that may or may not be interpreted as pain. Such sensation is not yet considered pain until subjected to higher order psychological and mental processing that involves perception, appraisal, and behaviour. Perception involves the interpretation of nociceptive input and identifies the type of pain (e.g. sharp, burning and punishing). Appraisal involves the meaning that is attributed to the pain and influences subsequent behaviours. A person may choose to ignore the pain and continue working, walking, socializing and engaging in previous levels of activity (Linton & Buer, 1995) or may choose to leave work, refrain from all activity and assume the sick role. In turn, this interpersonal role is shaped by responses from significant others that may promote either the healthy response or the sick role. The biopsychosocial model has been instrumental in the development of cognitive-behavioural treatment approaches for chronic pain, including assessment and intervention. In the remainder of this chapter we will describe assessment and treatment based on the multidimensional model with an emphasis on psychological factors (for extended discussions of medically based assessment and treatment, see Turk & Melzack, 2001 and Loeser et al., 2001).

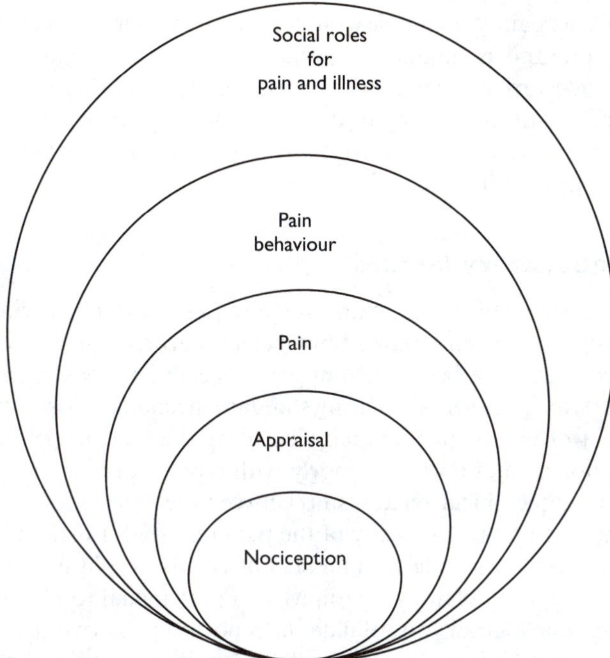

Figure 17.3 Biopsychosocial model of pain.

ASSESSMENT

To understand and appropriately treat a client whose primary symptom is pain begins with a comprehensive history and physical examination. Clients are usually asked to describe the characteristics (e.g. stabbing, burning), location, and severity of their pain. Physical examination procedures and sophisticated laboratory and imaging techniques are readily available for use in detecting organic pathology. Although the assessment of pain may at first seem to be quite an easy task, it is complicated by the psychological, social, and behavioural characteristics of the person. Thus, in addition to this standard medical approach, an adequate pain assessment also requires evaluation of the myriad psychosocial and behavioural factors that influence the subjective report.

Quantifying pain severity

Because there is no 'pain thermometer' that can provide an objective quantification of the amount or severity of pain experienced by a client, this can be assessed only indirectly, based on a client's overt communication, both verbal and behavioural. However, even a client's communications make pain assessment difficult, as pain is a complex, subjective phenomenon comprised of a range of factors and is uniquely experienced by each individual. As noted previously, wide variability in pain severity, quality and impact may be noted in reports of clients attempting to describe what appear to be objectively identical phenomena. Client's descriptions of pain are also coloured by cultural and sociological influences.

Physical and laboratory factors

Routine clinical assessment of chronic pain patients relies primarily on clinical judgements, although agreement among physicians is surprisingly low. Poor interobserver agreements have been noted in physical examinations of spinal motion and muscle strength, even when using standard mechanical assessment devices. Assessment of pain is further complicated by the fact that physical and laboratory abnormalities correlate poorly with reports of pain severity, such that there is no direct linear relationship between the amount of detectable physical pathology and the intensity of the pain reported. Furthermore, as we mentioned earlier, for significant numbers of clients no physical pathology can be identified using plain radiographs, computed axial tomography (CAT) scans or electromyography to validate the report of pain severity.

Because of these issues, it is often not possible to make any precise pathological diagnosis or even to identify an adequate anatomical or physiological origin for the pain. Despite these limitations, however, the patient's history and physical examination remain the basis of medical diagnosis, and may be the best defence against overinterpreting results from sophisticated imaging procedures. Physicians must therefore be cautious not to overinterpret either the presence or absence of objective findings. An extensive literature is available focusing on physical assessment, radiographic and laboratory assessment procedures to determine the physical basis of pain and the extent of impairments in adults (see Turk & Melzack, 2001).

Psychosocial contributions

Based on the multidimensional perspective, healthcare providers need to search not only for the physical source of the pain through examination and diagnostic tests but also the client's mood, fears, expectancies, coping efforts, resources, responses of significant others, and the impact of pain on the clients' lives. In short, the healthcare provider must evaluate the whole client. Regardless of whether an organic basis for the pain can be documented or whether psychosocial problems preceded or resulted from the pain, the evaluation process can be helpful in identifying how biomedical, psychosocial, and behavioural factors interact to influence the nature, severity, and persistence of pain and disability.

Evaluating the client with chronic pain

Turk and Meichenbaum (1984) suggested that three central questions should guide assessment of people who report pain:

1 What is the extent of the client's disease or injury (physical impairment)?
2 What is the magnitude of the illness? That is, to what extent is the client suffering, disabled, and unable to enjoy usual activities?
3 Does the individual's behaviour seem appropriate to the disease or injury or is there any evidence of amplification of symptoms for any of a variety of psychological or social reasons or purposes?

We will focus on the second two questions, specifically, the extent of the client's disability, and behavioural influences on the client's pain, distress and suffering. Evaluating these variables begins with gathering information from the client, via clinical interview and through standard assessment instruments.

Interview

When conducting an interview with chronic pain clients, the healthcare professional should focus not simply on factual information but on clients' and significant others' specific thoughts (e.g. expectations, meaning of symptoms) and feelings, and should observe specific behaviours. Pain sufferers' beliefs about the cause of symptoms, their trajectory, and beneficial treatments will have important influences on emotional adjustment, and adherence to therapeutic interventions. A habitual pattern of maladaptive thoughts may contribute to a sense of hopelessness, dysphoria, and unwillingness to engage in activity. The interviewer should determine both the client's and the significant others' expectancies, and goals for treatment. An expectation that pain will be eliminated completely may be unrealistic and will have to be addressed to prevent discouragement when this outcome does not occur.

Attention should focus on the client's reports of specific thoughts, behaviours, emotions, and physiological responses that precede, accompany, and follow pain episodes or exacerbation, as well as the environmental conditions and consequences associated with cognitive, emotional and behavioural responses in these situations. During the interview, the clinician should attend to the temporal association of these cognitive, affective and behavioural events, their specificity versus generality across situations, and the frequency of their occurrence, to establish salient features of the target situations, including the controlling variables. The interviewer seeks information that will assist in the development of potential alternate responses, appropriate goals for the client, and possible reinforcers for these alternatives.

Table 17.2 contains a list of salient points that can be stated as questions worthy of considering with clients who report persistent or recurring pain.

Table 17.2 Screening questions*

1. Has the client's pain persisted for three months or longer despite appropriate interventions and in the absence of progressive disease? [Yes]

2. Does the client repeatedly and excessively use the healthcare system, persist in seeking invasive investigations or treatments after being informed these are inappropriate, or use opioid or sedative-hypnotic medications or alcohol in a pattern of concern to the client's physician (e.g. escalating use)? [Yes]

3. Does the client come in requesting specific opioid medication (e.g. dilaudid, oxycontin)? [Yes]

4. Does the client have unrealistic expectations of the healthcare providers or the treatment offered ('Total elimination of pain and related symptoms') [Yes]

5. Does the client have a history of substance abuse or is he or she currently abusing mind-altering substances? [Yes] Clients can be asked, 'Have you ever found yourself taking more medication than was prescribed or have you used alcohol because your pain was so bad?' or 'Is anyone in your family concerned about the amount of medication you take?'

6. Does the client display large number of pain behaviours that appear exaggerated (e.g. grimacing, rigid or guarded posture)? [Yes]

7. Does the client have litigation pending? [Yes]

8. Is the client seeking or receiving disability compensation? [Yes]

9. Does the client have any other family members who had or currently suffer from chronic pain conditions? [Yes]

10. Does the client demonstrate excessive depression or anxiety? [Yes]. Straightforward questions such as, 'Have you been feeling down?' or 'What effect has your pain had on your mood?' can clarify whether this area is in need of more detailed evaluation.

11. Can the client identify a significant or several stressful life events prior to symptom onset or exacerbation? [Yes]

12. If married or living with a partner, does the client indicate a high degree of interpersonal conflict? [Yes]

13. Has the client given up many activities (recreational, social, familial, in addition to occupational and work activities) due to pain? [Yes]

14. Does the client have any plans for renewed or increased activities if pain is reduced? [No]

15. Was the client employed prior to pain onset? [No] If yes, does he or she wish to return to that job or any job? [No]

16. Does the client believe that he or she will ever be able to resume normal life and normal functioning? [No]

* If a combination of more than 6 'Yes' to the first 13 questions and 'No' to the last 3 questions below, or if general concerns in any one area, consider referral for psychological assessment.

When a number of these questions are endorsed, referral for more thorough evaluation by pain specialists should be considered. Generally, a referral for evaluation may be indicated where disability greatly exceeds what would be expected based on physical findings alone, when clients make excessive demands on the healthcare system, when the client persists in seeking medical tests and treatments when these are not indicated, when clients display significant emotional distress (e.g. depression or anxiety), or when the client displays evidence of addictive behaviours or continual non-adherence to the prescribed regimen. Table 17.3 contains a detailed outline of the areas that should be addressed in a more extensive psychological interview.

Table 17.3 Areas addressed in psychological interviews

Experience of pain and related symptoms
Location and description of pain (e.g. 'sharp', 'burning')
Onset and progression
Perception of cause (e.g. trauma, virus, stress)
What have they been told about their symptoms and condition? Do they believe that what they have been told is accurate?
Exacerbating and relieving factors (e.g. exercise, relaxation, stress, massage).
'What makes your pain worse?' 'What makes your pain better?'
Pattern of symptoms (e.g. symptoms worse certain times of day or following activity or stress)
Sleep habits (e.g. difficulty falling asleep or maintaining sleep, sleep hygiene)
Thoughts, feelings and behaviours that precede, accompany and follow fluctuations in symptoms

Treatments received and currently receiving
Medication (prescribed and over-the-counter). How helpful have these been?
Pattern of medication use (as-needed or time-contingent), changes in quantity or schedule
Physical modalities (e.g. physical therapy). How helpful have these been?
Exercise (e.g. Do they participate in a regular exercise routine?)
Is there evidence of deactivation and avoidance of activity due to fear of pain or exacerbation of injury? Has the pattern changed (increased, decreased)?
Complementary and alternative (e.g. chiropractic manipulation, relaxation training).
How helpful have these been?
Which treatments have they found the most helpful?
Compliance/adherence with recommendations of healthcare providers
Attitudes towards previous healthcare providers

Compensation/litigation
Current disability status (e.g. receiving or seeking disability, amount, per cent of former job income, expected duration of support)
Current or planned litigation (e.g. 'Have you hired an attorney')

Activity
Typical daily routine ('How much time do you spend sitting, standing, lying down?')
Changes in activities and responsibilities (both positive and obligatory) due to symptoms ('What activities did you use to engage in prior to your symptoms?' 'How has this changed since your symptoms began?')
Changes in significant other's activities and responsibilities due to client's symptoms

Continued overleaf

Table 17.3 Continued

Activities that client avoids because of symptoms
Activities continued despite symptoms
Pattern of activity and pacing of activity (can use activity diaries that ask clients to record their pattern of daily activities [time spent sitting, standing, walking, and reclining] for several days or weeks)

Responses by client and significant others
Client's behaviour when pain increases or flares up ('What do you do when your pain is bothering you?' 'Can others tell when your pain is bothering you?' 'How do they know?'
Significant others' responses to behavioural expressions of pain ('How can significant others tell when your pain is bad?' 'What do your significant others do when they can tell your pain is bothering you?' 'Are you satisfied with their responses?')
What does the client do when pain is not bothering him or her (uptime activities)?
Significant other's response when client is active ('How does your significant other respond to your engaging in activities?')
Impact of symptoms on interpersonal, family, marital, and sexual relations (e.g. changes in desire, frequency or enjoyment)

Coping
How does the client try to cope with his or her symptoms? (e.g., 'What do you do when your pain worsens?' 'How helpful are these efforts?').
Does client view himself or herself as having any role in symptom management? ('What role?')
Current life stresses
Pleasant activities ('What do you enjoy doing?')

Educational and vocational history
Level of education completed (any special training)
How long at most recent job?
How satisfied is the client with most recent job and supervisor?
What is liked least about most recent job?
Would the client like to return to most recent job?
If not what type of work is preferred?
Current work status (including homemaking activities)
Vocation and vocational plans

Social history
Relationships with family of origin
History of pain or disability in family members
History of substance abuse in family members
History of, or current physical, emotional, and sexual abuse
Was the client a witness to abuse of someone else?
Marital history and current status?
Quality of current marital and family relations

Alcohol and substance use
Current and history of alcohol use (quantity, frequency)
History and current use of illicit psychoactive drugs
History and current use of prescribed psychoactive medications
Consider the CAGE questions as a quick screen for alcohol dependence (Mayfield, McLeod & Hall, 1987)
Depending on response consider other instruments for alcohol and substance abuse (Allen & Litten, 1998)

Psychological dysfunction
Current psychological symptoms/diagnosis (depression including suicidal ideation, anxiety disorders, somatization, post-traumatic stress disorder)
Depending on responses, consider conducting formal SCID (American Psychiatric Association, 1997)
Is the client currently receiving treatment for psychological symptoms? If yes, what treatments (e.g. psychotherapy or psychiatric medications). How helpful?
History of psychiatric disorders and treatment, including family counselling
Family history of psychiatric disorders

Concerns and expectations
Client concerns/fears (e.g. Does the client believe s/he has serious physical problems that have not been identified? Or that symptoms will become progressively worse and client will become more disabled and more dependent? Does the client worry that he or she will be told the symptoms are all psychological?)
Explanatory models ('What have you been told is the cause of your symptoms?' 'Does this explanation make sense?' 'What do you think is the cause of your pain now?')
Expectations regarding the future and regarding treatment (will get better, worse, never change)
Attitude toward rehabilitation versus 'cure'
Treatment goals

Clients with chronic pain problems often consume a variety of medications. It is important to discuss a client's medications during the interview, as many pain medications (particularly opioids) are associated with side effects that may mimic emotional distress. A cautious clinical psychologist, for example, should be familiar with side effects that result in fatigue, sleep difficulties, and mood changes to avoid misdiagnosis of depression. A general understanding of commonly used medications for chronic pain is important. During the interview, potential psychological dependence on pain-relieving medications should be evaluated. We have included a list of some of the most commonly prescribed medications taken by chronic pain sufferers, their dosages, and side effects in Tables 17.4 to 17.6.

Assessment instruments

In addition to interviews, a number of assessment instruments designed to evaluate clients' attitudes, beliefs, and expectancies about themselves, their symptoms, and the healthcare system have been developed (see Table 17.7 for a description of some of the most commonly used). Standardized instruments have advantages over semi-structured and unstructured interviews. They are easy to administer, require less time, assess a wide range of behaviours, obtain information about behaviours that may be private (sexual relations) or unobservable (thoughts, emotional arousal) and, most importantly, can be submitted to analyses that permit determination of their reliability and validity. These instruments should not be viewed as alternatives to interviews;

Table 17.4 Non-opioid analgesics

Drug/drug class	*Trade name*	*Average analgesic dose (dosage interval; h)*	*Common side effects**
Ibuprofen	Motrin, Advil, Rufen, Nuprin, Medipren, others	200–400 mg (4–6)	1,4,5,8,9,10,14,18,19,20,21
Naproxen	Naprosyn, Naprolyn	500 mg initial, 250 mg subsequent (6–8)	1,4,5,8,9,10,14,18,19,20,21
Naproxen sodium	Anaprox	550 mg initial, 275 mg subsequent (6–8)	1,4,5,7,9,11,12,13,15,22,23,24,25, 26,27,28,29
Naproxen sodium OTC	Aleve	220 mg (8–12)	1,2,4,5,9,11,13,16,19
Fenoprofen	Nalfon	200 mg (4–6)	1,4,5,8,9,10,14,18,19,20,21
Ketoprofen	Orudis	25–50 mg (6–8)	3,7,9,10,13,28
Ketoprofen OTC	Actron, Orudis-K+	12.5–25 mg (4–6)	3,7,9,10,13,28
Oxaprozin	Daypro	600 mg (12–24)	1,2,4,5,9,11,13,16,19
Indomethacin	Indocin, Indocin SR, Indochron E-R	25mg (8–12)	1,4,5,7,9,10,15,16,18,19,22
Sulindac	Clinoril	150 mg (12)	1,4,5,8,9,10,14,18,19,20,21
Etodolac	Lodine	300–400 mg (8–12)	1,4,5,8,9,10,14,18,19,20,21
Ketorolac	Toradol	30–60 mg or 30 mg initial, 15–30 subsequent (6)	1,4,5,9,10,14,19,20,21,30
Tolmetin	Tolectin	200–600 mg (8)	1,4,5,8,9,10,14,18,19,20,21
Mefenamic acid	Ponstel	500 mg initial, 250 mg subsequent (6)	1,4,5,8,9,10,14,18,19,20,21
Diclofenac potassium	Cataflam	50 mg (8)	1,3,7,12,15

Meloxicam	Mobic	7.5–15 mg (24)	1,4,7,9,10,12,22,23,28,30
Piroxicam	Feldene	20–40 mg (24)	1,2,4,5,9,15,30
Nabumetone	Relafen	1000 mg initial, 500–750 subsequent (8–12)	1,4,5,8,9,10,14,18,19,20,21
Cox-2 inhibitors			
Celecoxib	Celebrex	200–400 mg (12–24)	1,4,6,7,8,9
Rofecoxib	Vioxx	12.5–50 mg (24)	1,14
Valdecoxib	Bextra	10–20 mg (12–24)	1,2,4,9
Other non-opiods			
Paracetamol (acetaminophen)	Numerous	500–1000 mg (4–6)	Varies, depending on brand name
Salicylates			
Aspirin	Numerous	500–1000 mg (4–6)	2,3,7,17
Diflunisal	Dolobid	1000 mg initial, 500 mg subsequent (8–12)	1,3,4,7,9,12,15,16,22
Salts (choline magnesium trisalicylate)	Trilisate, Tricosal	1000–1500 mg (12)	1,2,4,5,9,10,11,13,15,16,17,19
Paracetamol (acetaminophen)	Numerous	500–1000 mg (4–6)	Varies, depending on brand name

Note: 1, nausea; 2, upset stomach; 3, ulcers, bleeding; 4, diarrhoea; 5, constipation; 6, indigestion; 7, stomach/abdominal pain; 8, gas; 9, headache; 10, dizziness; 11, heartburn; 12, rash; 13, drowsiness; 14, weakness; 15, tinnitus; 16, vomiting; 17, Reye syndrome; 18, depression; 19, fatigue; 20, dry mouth; 21, irregular menstrual periods; 22, dyspepsia; 23, flu-like symptoms; 24, back pain; 25, rhinitis; 26, sinusitis; 27, urinary tract infection; 28, oedema; 29, dyspnoea; 30, flatulence.

* When prevalence data was available, common side effects are those which affect > 1% of patients taking the drug.

Table 17.5 Opioid analgesics

Drug/drug class	*Trade name*	*Average analgesic dosage (dosage interval; h)*	*Common side effects**
Opioids			
Codeine		30–60 mg	3,4,6,8,10,11,12,14,15,16,17,18,19,20
Oxycodone	Oxycontin	5–20 mg	1,2,4,5,6,21,22,23,24,25,26
Meperidine	Demerol	50–300 mg	1,2,4,5,6,8,9,13,16,18,19,21,22,23,24,25,26,29
Propoxyphene	Darvon	65–130 mg	4,5,6,13,21,22,23,26,29
Hydrocodone		5–10 mg	2,4,5,6,12,17,22,27,28,30,31,32
Tramadol	Ultram	50–100 mg (4–6)	4,5,6,22,23,24,25,30
Pentazocine	Talwin	50 mg	4,5,6,13,14,15,16,17,19,21,22,23,25,26,27,29
Morphine sulphate		30 mg	4,5,6,12,13,14,17,19,20,21,22,23,24,25,26,27,30,31
Hydromorphine	Dilaudid	7.5 mg	2,4,5,6,21,22,27,28,30,31,32
Methadone		5–10 mg	2,6,24,26,27,29,31
Levorphanol	Levo-Dromoran	1–4 mg	4,5,6,12,22,24,25,27,33,34
Oxymorphone		5 mg	4,5,6,12,22,24,25,27,33,34
Nalbuphine	Nubain	10 mg	4,5,21,22,23,24,25
Butorphanol	Stadol	2 mg	4,5,6,13,22,24,25,29,31,35
Buprenorphine	Buprenex	0.4 mg	4,5,23,25

Note: Range of dosage related to moderate vs. severe pain: 1, shortness of breath; 2, difficulty breathing; 3, stomach bleeding; 4, nausea; 5, vomiting; 6, constipation; 7, tachycardia; 8, bradycardia; 9, palpitation; 10, kidney damage; 11, liver damage; 12, itching; 13, rash; 14, blurred vision; 15, disorientation; 16, hallucinations; 17, depression; 18, agitation; 19, tremors; 20, seizures; 21, sedation; 22, dizziness; 23, headache; 24, dry mouth; 25, sweating; 26, weakness; 27, urinary difficulty; 28, mood changes; 29, euphoria; 30, anxiety; 31, drowsiness; 32, restlessness; 33, fatigue; 34, muscle twitches; 35, insomnia.

* [illegible]

Table 17.6 Co-analgesics: Administered to enhance the effects of opioids or NSAIDs, or counteract side effects of analgesics

Drug/drug class (trade name)	*Used for*	*Notes*	*Common side effects*
Tricyclic antidepressants			
Amitrptyline (Elavil), desipramine, imipramine, nortriptyline (Pamelor)	Treatment of neuropathic pain; promotes sleep	Administered at lower doses (25–100 mg/day) than recommended antidepressant doses (150–300 mg/day)	1,5,10,13,19,20,31,32,33,34,35
SSRI antidepressants			
Fluoxetine (Prozac), Paroxetine (Paxil), Citalopram (Celexa), Escitalopram (Lexapro)	Treatment of concurrent depression associated with chronic pain		1,4,9,19,35,36,37,39
Antiepileptic drugs			
Gabapentin (Neurontin), carbamazepine (Tegretol), oxycarbazapine (Trileptal), pregabalin (Lyrica), topiramate (Topamax), sodium valproate (Depacon), tiagabine (Gabitril), levetiracetam (Keppra), phenytoin (Dilantin), lamotrigine (Lamictal), zonisimade (Zonegran)	Treatment of neuropathic pain/ neuralgias, diabetic neuropathy, migraine prophylaxis; anti-seizure properties	Can be combined with TCAs if TCA is inadequate to manage pain	2,12,19,35
Local anaesthetics			
Lidocaine, prolocaine	Acute pain management, Post-herpetic neuralgia	Administered topically via cream or patches	12

Continued overleaf

Table 17.6 Continued

Drug/drug class (trade name)	*Used for*	*Notes*	*Common side effects*
Glucocorticoids			
Dexamethasone	Acute/chronic cancer pain		Chronic use produces weight gain, osteoporosis, Cushing's syndrome, proximal myopathy, psychosis Should not be used with NSAIDs
Carisoprodol (SOMA), tizanidine (Zanaflex)	Temporary relief of acute muscle injuries	Should be used only for a few days Carisoprodol often causes dependence	1,5,9,10,13,14,19,20
Antispasmodil agents			
Baclofen	Prevents muscle spasms		1,8,10,13,14
Antihistamines			
Hydroxyzine (Vistaril, Atarax)	Aids sleep, counteracts itching		2,9,10,13,20
Benzodiazepines			
Diazepam (Valium), lorazepam (Ativan), clonazepam (Klonopin)	Treatment of acute anxiety or muscle spasm associated with acute pain		10,13,39,40
Caffeine	Uterine cramping, episiotomy pain, dental pain, headaches, other pain syndromes	Increases analgesia when given with aspirin-like drugs	31,36,39,42

Topical agents			
Capsaicin	Peripheral neuropathic pain, arthritic pain	Topical administration; must be applied 3–4 times daily	43
Dextroamphetamine	Postoperative period Counteracts opioid sedation	May produce additive analgesia when combined with opioids	
Phenothiazines			
Chlorpromazine (Thorazine), fluphenazine (Permitil, Prolixin), prochlorperazine (Compazine)	Antiemitics and antipsychotic agents		Prolonged use can lead to tardive dyskinesia, extrapyramidal manifestations

Note: 1, nausea; 2, upset stomach; 3, ulcers, bleeding; 4, diarrhoea; 5, constipation; 6, indigestion; 7, stomach/abdominal pain; 8, gas; 9, headache; 10, dizziness; 11, heartburn; 12, rash; 13, drowsiness; 14, weakness; 15, tinnitus; 16, vomiting; 17, Reye syndrome; 18, depression; 19, fatigue; 20, dry mouth; 21, irregular menstrual periods; 22, dyspepsia; 23, flu-like symptoms; 24, back pain; 25, rhinitis; 26, sinusitis; 27, urinary tract infection; 28, oedema; 29, dyspnoea; 30, flatulence; 31, anxiety; 32, sun sensitivity; 33, restlessness; 34, urinary difficulty; 35, weight gain; 36, agitation; 37, sexual dysfunction; 38, sleep disturbances; 39, vivid dreams; 40, clumsiness; 41, slurred speech; 42, irritability; 43; skin irritation.

* When prevalence data was available, common side effects are those which affect > 1% of patients taking the drug.

Table 17.7 Commonly used self-report measures to assess pain and pain-related constructs

	Domains assessed	*No. of items*	*Scoring*
Generic pain questionnaires			
McGill Pain Questionnaire (MPQ), Melzack (1975)		20	78 pain-related words grouped in 20 subclasses; respondents rank words according to pain intensity; calculates sensory, affective, evaluative, and miscellaneous scores, and a total score ('Pain Rating Index')
Vanderbilt Pain Management Inventory (VPMI), Brown & Nicassio (1987)	Active and passive coping strategies specifically relevant to chronic pain	19	Calculates 2 scales: Active Coping and Passive Coping
Physical functioning questionnaires			
Pain Disability Index (PDI), Pollard (1984)	Measure disability due to pain (degree to which clients believe pain interferes with family/home responsibilities, recreation, social activities, occupation, sexual behaviour, self-care, life support activity)	7	Derives a total score
Oswestry Disability Scale, Fairbank, Couper, Davies, & O'Brien (1980)	Measures disability		Derives a total score
Functional Independence Measure (FIM), Keith, Granger, Hamilton, & Sherwin (1987)	Measures physical and cognitive ability, estimates burden of care	18	Items cover independence in self-care, sphincter control, mobility, locomotion, communication, and social cognition. Score ranges from 1 (total assistance) to 7 (complete independence)

Pain condition-specific measures			
Migraine Disability Assessment Scale (MIDAS), Stewart, Lipton, Whyte, Kolodner Liberman, & Sawyer (1999)	Impact of headaches on daily function	5	Derives four scores: Grade I, little or no disability; Grade II, mild disability; Grade III, moderate disability; Grade IV, severe disability
Neuropathic Pain Scale (NPS), Galer & Jensen (1997)	Assesses qualities of neuropathic pain: sharpness, heat/cold, dullness, intensity, unpleasantness, and surface vs. deep pain	10	Derives total score
Psychosocial pain measures			
Chronic Pain Coping Inventory (CPCI), Jensen, Turner, Romano, & Strom (1995)	Illness and well-focused coping strategies	64	Calculates 8 subscales: Guarding, Resting, Asking for Assistance, Relaxation, Task Persistence, Exercising/Stretching, Coping Self-Statements, Seeking Social Support
Chronic Illness Problem Inventory (CIPI), Kames, Naliboff, Heinrich, & Schag (1984)	Assesses behavioural problems associated with a variety of chronic illnesses	65	Calculates 18 scales: Activities of Daily Living, Inactivity, Social Activity, Family/Friends contact, Employment, Sleep, Eating, Finances, Medication, Cognition, Physical Appearance, Body Deterioration, Sex, Assertion, Medical Interaction, Marital Overprotection, Marital Difficulty, and Nonmarital Relationships
Vanderbilt Multidimensional Pain Coping Inventory (VCPMI), Smith, Wallston, Dwyer, & Dowdy (1997)	Revised VPMI: assesses ways of coping with pain	49	Calculates 9 subscales: Planful Problem-Solving, Positive Reappraisal, Distraction, Confrontative Coping, Distancing/Denial, Stoicism, Use of Religion, Self-Blame, Self-Isolation

Continued overleaf

Table 17.7 Continued

	Domains assessed	*No. of items*	*Scoring*
Coping Strategies Questionnaire (CSQ), Rosenstiel & Keefe (1983)	Assesses specific coping strategies (six cognitive coping strategies; 1 behavioural coping strategy)		Calculates 7 subscales: Diverting Attention, Reinterpreting Pain, Coping Self-Statements, Ignoring Pain, Praying or Hoping, Catastrophizing, and Increasing Activity
Fear-Avoidance Beliefs Questionnaire (FABQ), Waddell, Newton, Henderson, Somerville, & Main (1993)	Evaluates clients' beliefs about how physical activity and work may affect their back pain	16	Calculates two scales: Fear-avoidance beliefs related to work, and Fear-avoidance beliefs about physical activity in general
Fear of Pain Questionnaire-III (FPQ-III), McNeil & Rainwater (1998)	Measures pain anxiety/fear of pain	30	Calculates three scales: Fear of Severe Pain, Fear of Minor Pain, Fear of Medical Pain
Illness Behavior Inventory, Turkat & Pettegrew (1983)	Measures illness behaviours	20	Calculates two scales: Work-Related Illness Behaviour (9 items) and Social Illness Behaviour (11 items)
Millon Behavioral Health Inventory (MBHI), Millon, Green, & Meagher (1983)	Evaluates psychological functioning of medical clients	150	Calculates 8 scales that assess dimensions of styles of relating to healthcare providers (e.g. Cooperative, Forceful), 6 scales that assess major psychological stressors (e.g. Future Despair, Social Alienation) and 6 scales that assess probable response to illness (e.g. G.I. Susceptibility) and treatment interventions (e.g. pain treatment responsivity)

Descriptor Differential Scale of Pain Intensity (DDS-I), Gracley & Kwilosz (1988)	Assesses intensity of pain	12	Derives a total score of pain intensity
Pain-O-Meter (POM) Affective subscale, Gaston-Johansson (1996)	Measures pain affect	14	Derives total Affective scale score
Pain Beliefs and Perceptions Inventory (PBAPI), Williams & Thorn (1989)	Measures pain beliefs	16	Calculates three dimensions: Self-Blame, Mystery (i.e. perception of pain as mysterious), and Stability (i.e. beliefs about the stability of pain over time)
Pain Stages of Change Questionnaire (PSOCQ), Kerns, Rosenberg, Jamison, Caudill, & Hayuthornwaite (1997)	Measures conditions that are relevant for a clients' readiness for change	30	Derives 4 stages of self-management: Precontemplation, Contemplation, Action, and Maintenance
Survey of Pain Attitudes (SOPA), Jensen, Karoly, & Huger (1987)	Measures beliefs about pain	57	Derives 7 dimensions: Control, Disability, Harm, Emotion, Medication, Solicitude, and Medical Cure
Pain Anxiety Symptoms Scale (PASS), McCracken, Zayfert, & Gross (1992)	Assesses fear of pain across cognitive, psychological, and behavioural domains	53	Calculates 4 subscales: Fear of Pain, Cognitive Anxiety, Somatic Anxiety, and Fear and Avoidance
Pain Beliefs Questionnaire (PBQ), Edwards, Pearce, Turner-Stokes, & Jones (1992)	Assesses beliefs about pain	12	Calculates 2 subscales: Organic Beliefs (8 items) and Psychological Beliefs (4 items)
Symptom Checklist-90 Revised (SCL-90R), Derogatis (1983)	Measures presence and intensity of symptoms: depression, somatization, anxiety, hostility, obsessive-compulsive, interpersonal sensitivity, phobic anxiety, paranoid ideation, psychoticism	90	Calculates 3 global indices of distress (Global Severity Index, Positive Symptom Distress Index, and Positive Symptom Total score); domains most relevant for chronic pain are depression, anxiety, and somatization
Pain Catastrophizing Scale (PCS), Sullivan, Bishop, & Pivik (1995)	Examines components of catastrophizing	13	Calculates three components: Rumination, Magnification, and Helplessness

Continued overleaf

Table 17.7 Continued

	Domains assessed	*No. of items*	*Scoring*
Multidimensional/Health-Related Quality of Life Measures			
SF-36, Ware & Sherbourne (1992)		36	Calculate mental health and physical health scores; higher scores = better health status
West Haven-Yale Multidimensional Pain Inventory (WHYMPI), Kerns, Turk, & Rudy (1985)	Measures pain severity, interference, support, life control, affective distress, others' responses to pain behaviours, and frequency of performance on 18 common activities	52	Higher scores on each scale reflect higher levels of that dimension; scores can be used to classify clients as 'dysfunctional', 'interpersonally distressed' or 'adaptive copers'
Sickness Impact Profile (SIP), Bergner, Bobbitt, Carter, & Gibson (1981)	Measures ambulation, mobility, body care, social interaction, communication, alertness, sleep and rest, eating, work, home management, recreation and pastime activities, and emotional behaviour	136	Calculate overall dysfunction score, and summary scores of physical and psychosocial dysfunction; Range of scores = 0% to 100% dysfunction

rather, they may suggest issues to be addressed in more depth during an interview or investigated with other measures.

General ratings of pain

Self-report measures of pain often ask clients to quantify their pain by providing a single, general rating of pain: 'Is your usual level of pain "mild", "moderate", or "severe"?' or 'Rate your typical pain on a scale from 0 to 10 where 0 equals no pain and 10 is the worst pain you can imagine'. More valid information may be obtained by asking about current level of pain or pain over the past week and by having clients maintain regular diaries of pain intensity with ratings recorded several times each day (for example at meals and bedtime) for several days or weeks. A number of simple methods can be used to evaluate current pain intensity – numerical scale, descriptive ratings scales, and visual analogue scales.

Assessment of function

Poor reliability and questionable validity of physical examination measures has led to the development of self-report functional status measures that seek to quantify symptoms, function and behaviour directly, rather than inferring them. Self-report measures have been developed to assess peoples' reports of their abilities to engage in a range of functional activities, such as the ability to walk up stairs, to sit for specific periods of time, to lift specific weights, to perform activities of daily living, as well as the severity of the pain experienced on the performance of these activities.

Assessment of coping and psychosocial adaptation to pain

Historically, psychological measures that are designed to evaluate psychopathological tendencies have been used to identify specific individual differences associated with reports of pain, even though these measures were usually not developed for or standardized on samples of medical clients. As stated previously, it is possible that responses by medical clients may be distorted as a function of the disease or the medications that they take. For example, common measures of depression ask clients about their appetites, sleep patterns, and fatigue. Since disease status and medication can affect responses to such items, clients' scores may be elevated, distorting the meaning of the responses.

More recently, a number of measures have been developed for use specifically with pain clients. Instruments have been developed to assess psychological distress, the impact of pain on clients' lives, feeling of control, coping behaviours and attitudes about disease, pain and healthcare providers and the client's plight (Turk & Melzack, 1992, 2001).

Assessment of overt expressions of pain

Clients display a broad range of responses that communicate to others that they are experiencing pain, distress and suffering – pain behaviours. Some of these may be controllable by the person whereas others are not. Although there is no one-to-one relationship between these pain behaviours and self-report of pain, they are at least modestly correlated.

A number of different observational procedures have been developed to quantify pain behaviours. Several investigators using the Pain Behavior Checklist (Turk et al., 1985) have found a significant association between these self-reports and behavioural observations. Behavioural observation scales can be used by clients' significant others as well. Healthcare providers can use observational methods to systematically quantify various pain behaviours and note the factors that increase or decrease them. For example, observing the client in the waiting room, while being interviewed, or during a structured series of physical tasks.

Uses of the healthcare system and analgesic medication are other ways to assess pain behaviours (see Table 17.6). Clients can record the times when they take medication over a specified interval such as a week. Diaries not only provide information about the frequency and quantity of medication but may also permit identification of the antecedent and consequent events of medication use. Antecedent events might include stress, boredom, or activity. Examination of antecedents is useful in identifying patterns of medication use that may be associated with factors other than pain per se. Similarly, patterns of response to the use of analgesic may be identified. Does the client receive attention and sympathy whenever he or she is observed by significant others taking medication? That is, do significant others provide positive reinforcement for the taking of analgesic medication and thereby unwittingly increase medication use?

TREATMENT OF CHRONIC PAIN

Cognitive-behavioural model for the treatment of chronic pain

The cognitive-behavioural model (CBM) has become the most commonly accepted model for the psychological treatment of chronic pain clients (Morely et al., 1999). The CBM perspective suggests that behaviours and emotions are influenced by interpretations of events, and emphasis is placed on how peoples' idiosyncratic attitudes, beliefs, and unique representations filter and interact reciprocally with physical, cognitive, affective, and behavioural factors. CBM incorporates many of the psychological variables previously described; namely, anticipation, avoidance, and contingencies of reinforcement, but suggests that cognitive factors rather than conditioning factors are of central importance. The cognitive-behavioural (CB) approach suggests that conditioned reactions are largely self-activated on the basis of learned expectations rather than automatically evoked. The critical factor for CB, therefore, is that people learn to predict events and to summon appropriate reactions. It is the person's processing of information that results in anticipatory anxiety and avoidance.

Assumptions of the cognitive-behavioural approach

Five central assumptions characterize the CB approach. The first assumption is that all people are active processors of information rather than passive reactors to environmental contingencies. People attempt to make sense of the stimuli from the external environment by filtering information through organizing attitudes derived from their prior learning histories and by general strategies that guide the processing of information. People's responses (overt as well as covert) are based on these appraisals and subsequent expectations and are not totally dependent on the actual consequences of their behaviours (i.e. positive and negative reinforcements and punishments).

A second assumption of the CB approach is that one's thoughts (e.g. appraisals, attributions and expectations) can elicit or modulate affect and physiological arousal, both of which may serve as impetuses for behaviour. Conversely, affect, physiology and behaviour can instigate or influence one's thinking processes. Thus, this cycle demonstrates the interaction of thoughts, feelings, physiological activity and behaviour.

The third assumption of the CB perspective is that behaviour is reciprocally determined by both the environment and the person. People not only respond to their environment but also elicit environmental responses by their behaviour. In a very real sense, people create their environments. The person who becomes aware of a physical event (symptoms) and decides the symptom requires attention from a healthcare provider initiates a differing set of circumstances than a person with the same symptom who chooses to self-medicate or to ignore the symptoms.

A fourth assumption is that if people have learned maladaptive ways of thinking, feeling, and responding, then successful interventions designed to alter behaviour should focus on these maladaptive thoughts, feelings, physiology, and behaviours, and not on one to the exclusion of the others. There is no expectancy that changing only thoughts, or feelings, or behaviours will necessarily result in changes in the other two areas.

The final assumption is that people are, and should be considered, active agents of change of their maladaptive modes of responding. Chronic pain sufferers, no matter how severe, despite their common beliefs to the contrary, are not helpless pawns of fate. They can and should become instrumental in learning and carrying out more effective modes of responding to their environment and their plight.

From the CB perspective, people with pain are viewed as having negative expectations about their own ability to control certain motor skills when in pain. Moreover, pain clients tend to believe they have limited ability to exert any control over their pain. Such negative, maladaptive appraisals about the situation and personal efficacy may reinforce the experience of demoralization, inactivity, and over-reaction to nociceptive stimulation. These cognitive appraisals and expectations are postulated as having an effect on behaviour leading to reduced efforts and activity, which may contribute to increased psychological distress (helplessness) and subsequent physical limitations. If one accepts that pain is a complex, subjective phenomenon that is uniquely experienced by each person, then knowledge about idiosyncratic beliefs, appraisals, and coping repertoires becomes critical for optimal treatment planning, and for accurately evaluating treatment outcome.

Pain sufferers' beliefs, appraisals, and expectations about pain, their ability to cope, social supports, their disorder, the medicolegal system, the healthcare system, and their employers are all important because they may facilitate or disrupt the sufferer's sense of control. These factors also influence clients' investment in treatment, acceptance of responsibility, perceptions of disability, adherence to treatment recommendations, support from significant others, expectancies for treatment, and acceptance of treatment rationale.

Cognitive interpretations also affect how clients present symptoms to others, including healthcare providers. Overt communication of pain, suffering and distress will enlist responses that may reinforce pain behaviours and impressions about the seriousness, severity and uncontrollability of pain. That is, complaints of pain may induce physicians to prescribe more potent medications, order additional diagnostic tests, and, in some cases, perform surgery (Turk & Okifuji, 1997). Significant others may express sympathy, excuse the pain sufferer from responsibilities, and encourage passivity, thereby fostering further physical deconditioning. It should be obvious that the CB perspective integrates the operant conditioning emphasis on external reinforcement and respondent view of conditioned avoidance within the framework of information processing.

People with persistent pain often have negative expectations about their own ability and responsibility to exert any control over their pain. Moreover, they often view themselves as helpless. Such negative, maladaptive appraisals about their condition, situation, and their personal efficacy in controlling their pain and problems associated with pain reinforce their experience of demoralization, inactivity, and over-reaction to nociceptive stimulation. These cognitive appraisals are posited as having an effect on behaviour, leading to reduced effort, reduce perseverance in the face of difficulty, reduced activity, and increased psychological distress.

Mary, for example, had a long-standing sense of herself as both physically and emotionally fragile and needing special care and protection. When she felt pain, she believed that continuing to move was potentially physically damaging and would thus lead to more pain. She felt powerless to help herself beyond resting, remaining still and taking analgesic medications, the only safe and effective ways she knew to cope with her pain. The effects of these coping strategies were to reduce her activity level and social outlets. They limited the possibility of being distracted from pain, reduced access to positive reinforcement of well behaviours and convinced her that she had almost no ability to decrease pain. She believed that significant others could and should help her bear the pain, by sitting with her, listening to her, and offering sympathy and understanding, as she had cared for her children for years when they were ill or upset. She thus attributed most of the responsibility for pain management to others: doctors, family members, and friends. Since doctors in particular were in her words 'writing [her] off' after numerous unsuccessful investigations and procedures, she felt angry at professionals generally and sceptical in particular about psychological input.

The CB perspective on pain management focuses on providing the client with techniques to gain a sense of control over the effects of pain on his or her life as well as actually modifying the affective, behavioural, cognitive, and sensory facets of the experience. For Mary, the treatment aimed to show her that she could affect her pain experience. Behavioural experiments help to show pain sufferers that they are capable of more than they assumed, increasing their sense of personal competence. Cognitive techniques (e.g. self-monitoring to identify relationship among thoughts, mood, and behaviour; distraction using imagery and problem solving; described below) help to place affective, behavioural, cognitive, and sensory responses under the person's control.

The assumption is that long-term maintenance of behavioural changes will occur only if the pain sufferer has learned to attribute success to his or her own efforts. There are suggestions that these treatments can result in changes of beliefs about pain, coping style, and reported pain severity, as well as direct behaviour changes. Treatment that results in increases in perceived control over pain and decreased catastrophizing also results in decreases in pain severity and functional disability. When successful rehabilitation occurs there is a major shift from beliefs about helplessness and passivity to resourcefulness and ability to function regardless of pain, and from an illness conviction to a rehabilitation conviction (Jensen, Turner, & Romano, 1994; Tota-Faucette, Gil, Williams, Keefe, & Goli, 1993).

Components of cognitive-behavioural therapy

CBT comprises four interrelated components: (1) reconceptualization; (2) skills acquisition; (3) skills consolidation; and (4) generalization and maintenance. We briefly describe each below but for more detail the reader should see Turk et al. (1983) and Turk (1997, 2002b).

Reconceptualization

The CB therapist is concerned not only with the role that clients' thoughts play in contributing to disability and to the maintenance and exacerbations of symptoms, but also with the nature and adequacy of the client's behavioural repertoire. The strategic plan of a CB intervention then is to facilitate a client's reconceptualization of his or her plight. The benefits of reconceptualization are that it provides a more benign view of the problem than the client's original view, it translates physical and psychological symptoms from vague, uncontrollable problems into specific, addressable problems, and it focuses on solutions to problems that should foster hope and expectancy for success.

It is hard for many people with persistent pain to accept that their thoughts and emotions can actually affect their bodies. To convince them of this fact, it is useful to have them self-monitor the thoughts and feelings that precede, accompany, and follow a pain episode or pain flare-up. When clients monitor their thoughts, a number of thoughts and beliefs that might lead to increased muscle tension and increased emotional distress are frequently identified. For example, Mary thought, 'I feel as though I can't take it any more', 'I can't do anything when my pain is bad', and 'I don't see how this pain is ever going to get better'.

Daily diaries are useful diagnostically and clinically. They have the potential of demonstrating to both clinician and client the patterns of maladaptive thinking and pain behaviours that may be contributing to the client's pain experience. In a diary, pain sufferers can record when their pain was particularly severe, what the situation was at the time of the pain (including what they thought about and felt prior to the exacerbation of pain or pain episode), during the episode, and after the episode as well as what they tried to do to help alter the pain experienced. Examination of these diaries can lead to identification of maladaptive patterns of thoughts, feelings, behaviours and pain flare-ups. From Mary's diary, she realized that pain was worst in the evening and at weekends, periods when she had too much time on her hands and missed her children most.

Once specific associations of thoughts, emotions, and pain are identified, the client can consider alternative thoughts and strategies that might be used in similar circumstances. He or she can try these alternative thoughts and record the effects. The crucial element in the successful treatment is bringing about a shift in the client's repertoire from well-established, habitual, and automatic but ineffective responses towards systematic problem solving and planning, control of affect, behavioural persistence, or disengagement when appropriate.

Reconceptualization goes on throughout treatment and involves reorienting the client from his or her belief that symptoms or physical impairment are an overwhelming, all-encompassing sensory experience resulting solely from tissue pathology and that he or she is helpless to do anything about them to a concept that symptoms and impairments can be differentiated and systematically modified and controlled by the sufferers themselves. Part of reonceptualization is a method called 'cognitive restructuring'. Like reconceptualization, cognitive restructuring is designed to make clients aware of the role thoughts and emotions play in potentiating and maintaining stress and physical symptoms. With this method, the CB therapist elicits the client's thoughts, feelings, and interpretations of events; gathers evidence for or against such interpretations; identifies habitual self-statements, images and appraisals; tests the validity of these interpretations; identifies automatic thoughts that set up an escalating stream of negative, catastrophizing ideation and helps examine how such habitual thoughts exacerbate stress and interfere with performance of adaptive coping responses.

Steps in cognitive restructuring include: identifying clients' maladaptive thoughts during problematic situations (e.g. during pain exacerbations, stressful events), introduction and practice of coping thoughts, shifting from self-defeating to coping thoughts, introduction and practice of positive or reinforcing thoughts, and finally, home practice and follow-up. Using these steps, the clinical psychologist encourages the clients to test the adaptiveness (not the so-called rationality) of individual thoughts, beliefs, expectations, and predictions. One thought that was worked on extensively with Mary was the belief that 'moving when in pain causes damage and more pain'. Mary conducted a cost–benefit analysis of this belief, as well as of an alternative belief that 'moving when in pain is helpful and can reduce pain'. She agreed to gather evidence for and against the belief, by reviewing initially times in the past when she had moved and had not moved when in pain. Initially very sceptical about the alternative belief, Mary agreed to engage in a specific activity while in pain, walking with a friend for 10 minutes during the day. Before the activity, she rated how much she believed this new belief, and rated it again after the walking over a three-week period, as well as rating pain intensity at intervals throughout the day. She was surprised to realize that her pain ratings did not increase following walking and, if anything, reduced slightly, and thus her belief in the idea that moving is helpful and can reduce pain increased over a number of weeks.

With cognitive restructuring, clients may be asked to relive in their mind's eye one or more recent experiences of stress as if they were running a movie in slow motion in their mind, eliciting thoughts and feelings around specific events and responses (termed 'imagery recall'). A number of questions might be used to guide the client, such as 'Is there anything common about these situations?', 'What thoughts and feelings preceded, accompanied and followed the situation?', 'How did you cope with the situation?', and 'How did it resolve?' Through self-monitoring, the clinical psychologist helps clients identify when they are becoming stressed, assists them to become aware of low-intensity cues, then examines the contribution of their thoughts and de-automatizes the connection between events and arousal or distress. For example, a recent conflict with a spouse might be examined to determine whether the client's getting upset had any effect both on the physical and psychological symptoms experienced. Mary recognized that preparations for family events were a stress trigger and that she had many anxious thoughts and images of the event going badly, being blamed by the family and feeling like a failure. To reduce her anxiety about this happening, she worked furiously to prepare food and clean the home, and her anxiety and associated muscle tension exacerbated pain. Using a thought record to explore the thought 'It's my fault if this party is a flop', she identified the new belief that she and the family shared responsibility for the event going well.

Treatment is viewed as a collaborative process by which the clinical psychologist carefully elicits the troublesome thoughts and concerns of clients, acknowledges their bothersome nature, and then constructs an atmosphere in which the client can critically challenge the validity of his or her own beliefs. Rather than suggesting alternative thoughts, the clinical psychologist attempts to elicit competing thoughts from the client and then reinforces the adaptive nature of these alternatives. Clients have well learned and frequently rehearsed thoughts about their condition. Only after repetitions and practice in cuing competent interpretations and evaluations will clients come to change their conceptualizations.

Because significant others may contribute to unwittingly undermining clients' changing conceptualizations, the clinical psychologist should attempt to ascertain how significant others respond to the client and when their manner of response is an inappropriate attempt to help the client alter these. This may be accomplished by encouraging the client to discuss the responses of significant others openly. It may be desirable to have the client practice how he or she will conduct this discussion with the clinical psychologist.

Throughout treatment it is important to permit and even to urge clients to express their concerns, fears, and frustrations, as well as their anger directed towards the healthcare system, insurance companies, employers, social system, family, fate, and perhaps themselves. During the reconceptualization process, symptoms are explained briefly within the context of the role of stress on physical functioning. Caution should be exercised in suggesting that psychological factors or psychiatric illness play a causal role in symptoms. For many clients, such suggestions imply that they are imaging or exaggerating symptoms, are at fault for being ill, or are going 'crazy.' Common ground can be established by discussing the role of *stress* in medical conditions.

The reconceptualization process can be enriched through educating the client about common cognitive errors made by pain clients. A list of common cognitive errors is listed in Table 17.8.

Once cognitive errors that contribute to pain perception, emotional distress, and disability are identified they become the target of intervention. Clients are usually asked to generate alternative, adaptive ways of thinking and

Table 17.8 Common thinking errors observed in chronic pain clients

Overgeneralization: Extrapolation from the occurrence of a specific event or situation to a large range of possible situations. For example, 'This coping strategy didn't work, so none of them will work'

Catastrophizing: Focusing exclusively on the worst possibility regardless of its likelihood of occurrence. For example, 'This pain in my back means my condition is degenerating and my whole body is falling apart.' Several acute and chronic pain studies have demonstrated that individuals who spontaneously utilize fewer catastrophizing self-statements reported more pain than those who did not catastrophize

All-or-none thinking: Considering only the extreme 'best' or 'worst' interpretation of a situation without regard to the full range of alternatives. For example, 'If I am not feeling perfectly well, I cannot enjoy anything'

Jumping to conclusions: Accepting an arbitrary interpretation without a rational evaluation of its likelihood. For example, 'The doctor is avoiding me because he thinks I am a hopeless case'

Selective attention: Selectively attending to negative aspects of a situation while ignoring any positive things. For example, 'Physical exercises only serve to make me feel worse that I already do'

Negative predictions: Assuming the worst. For example, 'I know this coping technique will not work' or 'If I lose my hearing as a result of chemotherapy my husband will no longer find me attractive'

Mind-reading: Instead of finding out what people are thinking, making assumptions. For example, 'My family does not talk to me about my pain because they don't care about me'

responding to minimize stress and dysfunction (for example, 'I'll just take one day at a time', 'I'll try to relax and calm myself down', 'Getting angry doesn't accomplish anything, I'll try to explain how I feel'). Clients will usually be asked to practise these at home and to review these during therapy sessions.

The clinical psychologist's skills and the relationship that is established between the clinical psychologist and client grease the gears of treatment; without a satisfactory therapeutic alliance, treatment will grind to a halt. Treatment should not be viewed as a rigid process with fixed techniques. There is a need to individualize the treatment programme for specific clients; however, the CB rationale described above remains constant.

Skills acquisition and consolidation

Cognitive and behavioural treatment makes use of a whole range of techniques and procedures designed to bring about alterations in clients' perceptions of their situation, their mood, their behaviour, and their abilities to modify these psychological processes. Techniques such as progressive relaxation training, problem-solving training, distraction skills training, and communication skills training to name only a few, have all been incorporated within the general CB framework.

RELAXATION

Perhaps the most common and practical techniques to control pain are controlled breathing and deep muscle relaxation. Relaxation can be used for its direct effects on specific muscles, for reduction of generalized arousal, for its cognitive effects (as a distraction or attention diversion strategy), and for its value in increasing the client's sense of control and self-efficacy. Relaxation skills are generic and a wide range of different techniques (for example, biofeedback, imagery, controlled breathing) is geared towards assisting clients to learn how to deal with stress and, in particular, how to reduce site-specific muscular hyperarousal.

One type of relaxation technique known as progressive muscle-tension-reduction relaxation is useful because: (1) it has face validity; (2) it is a concrete procedure and thus easy to recall and practice at home; and (3) it is less prone than passive relaxation techniques to failure due to distraction by symptoms or cognitive intrusions. The idea behind progressive muscle relaxation is that if muscle tension results in increased symptoms, it can be reasoned that the converse – muscle relaxation – leads to symptom reduction. With progressive muscle relaxation, the CB therapist first induces a state of relaxation, with controlled breathing. The therapist then instructs the client to tense and relax specific muscle groups in a sequential fashion. Clients can learn how to practise progressive muscle relaxation at home, giving them a skill they can use on their own to decrease pain symptoms. Clients are told that relaxation is a skill and, like any skill, requires a good deal of practice.

Following each session, clients can be given specific home practice assignments to perform, self-monitor, and record. At the beginning of each subsequent session, the clinical psychologist reviews the self-monitored practice charts with the client to identify problems and to reinforce effort as well as success. After the clients have become proficient in relaxation, it is useful to have them imagine themselves in various stress or conflict situations and to visualize themselves employing the relaxation skills in those situations. In subsequent sessions, the clinical psychologist teaches clients that one can relax not only by tensing and releasing muscle groups, as in progressive relaxation or by means of some passive activities such as controlled breathing, but also by means of absorbing activities such as physical activity (for example, walking, swimming), hobbies (knitting, gardening), and so forth.

Where pain is due to muscle spasm, muscle relaxation procedures may be effective in reducing pain by decreasing or preventing this process. Engaging in muscle relaxation may also reduce the anxiety and distress that accompany persistent pain or trigger pain episodes. Relaxation can improve sleep, which may have secondary benefits; it is much easier to cope when rested than fatigued due to lack of sleep. Muscle relaxation may also serve to distract the client from noxious sensations.

It is helpful to begin relaxation exercises early in treatment because they can be readily learned by almost all clients and they can quickly give the client a sense of self-efficacy in the management of their symptoms. There are many types of relaxation and no one 'best' approach has been demonstrated to be more effective than any other. The client can learn different approaches in order to find one that is most useful. Regardless of the type of relaxation used, the clinical psychologist should discuss with clients how to identify bodily signs of physical tenseness, the stress–tension cycle, how occupying one's attention can short-circuit stress, how relaxation can reduce anxiety because it enables clients to exert control, how relaxation and tension are incompatible states and, finally, how unwinding after stressful experiences can be therapeutic.

Mary learned some relaxation techniques and used them for a half-hour before going to bed at night. She found her ability to fall asleep improved and her sleep was less interrupted. This had a positive effect on her confidence in the clinical psychologist and in psychological treatment. More well rested, she also increased her ability to bear pain.

PROBLEM SOLVING

Problem solving consists of six steps. Each step is related to specific questions or actions: (1) problem identification (What is the concern?); (2) goal selection (What do I want?); (3) generation of alternatives (What can I do?); (4) decision making (What is my decision?); (5) implementation (Do it!); and (6) evaluation (Did it work? If not recycle).

An important first step is to identify the situations that are associated with pain. The use of self-monitoring can help to identify the links between thoughts, feelings, and pain, and thereby identify the problem. Once a set of problems has been identified, the client can begin to enumerate a set of solutions. Clients then evaluate the likely outcomes of implementing each possible solution. Clients may then try their strategies and evaluate the outcome. If they are not satisfied with the first strategy they can review the other options that they generated and decide to try another possible solution. By using problem-solving strategies, for example, an individual is able to target the situations that trigger the muscle tension associated with the pain. After using successful problem-solving approaches, an individual can build confidence in his or her ability to handle stressful situations. Regarding Mary's anxiety about family gatherings and precipitating further acute pain episodes, she identified a number of possible solutions: asking another family member to host the event, hosting the event at a commercial venue, getting caterers to provide the food in her home, asking her children to prepare or buy some of the food, reducing the ambitiousness and laboriousness of the dishes she was preparing, asking her children to help her clean and prepare the house, reducing her standards for pre-party cleaning and decorating, hosting the venue outdoors buffet/picnic-style. Mary decided that she really liked to host family events. She agreed to share the food preparation with her children and to hold the event outdoors with disposable plates and glasses. The event went off well, with family members appreciating the new informality of the event and enjoying themselves. Although Mary experienced some pain, she was able to stay at the party and enjoyed the event.

DISTRACTION

People who have persistent pain often try to distract themselves by reading books, watching television, engaging in hobbies, or listening to music. Using thoughts and imagination can also help people distract themselves from their bodies and pain. The idea behind cognitive distraction is that taking one's mind off of pain by attending to something else may lead to reduced perceptions of pain and reduce levels of stress arousal. For this reason, cognitive distraction techniques are best used during pain episodes where the client experiences an exacerbation of symptoms.

An example of cognitive distraction is when a clinical psychologist asks a client to close his or her eyes and to focus attention on some part of his or her body. The clinical psychologist then notes some ambient sound, such as the ventilation system, and suggests that while attending to his or her body, the client was not aware of the sound of the air conditioning. The clinical psychologist calls attention to the sound of ventilation but then reminds the client that he or she has stopped focusing on his or her body. The clinical psychologist also might call the client's attention to some part of the body that he or she was not attending to, such as the gentle pressure of a watch on the wrist. The point is that there is environmental (internal and external) input that remains out of conscious attention until it is focused on directly.

Different cognitive coping strategies that have been studied in the literature can be classified into five different groups: (1) focusing on the environment rather than on the body; (2) neutral images; (3) dramatized images where the painful part was included in the image (e.g. imaging that one is a spy who has been wounded but is trying to escape); (4) pleasant images; and (5) rhythmic activity (e.g. singing a song). Each of these different strategies has been shown to be effective for mild to moderate pain. Fernandez and Turk (1989) concluded that no one coping strategy was consistently more effective than any other; however, the imagery strategies as a set seem to be more effective than those that did not include any imagery.

Mary was instructed in and tried all five types of distraction strategies. She found singing songs from musicals helpful. She discovered that talking on the telephone about subjects apart from her pain was also distracting and she found it helpful to imagine pleasant scenarios, such as lying on a beach or travelling to exotic locations.

Imagery is a useful strategy for helping clients to relax and distract themselves from pain. It is important to customize any images to clients by asking them to identify specific situations that they find pleasant and engaging. A detailed image can then be created. When clients are feeling pain or are experiencing pain exacerbation, they can use imagery to redirect their attention away from their pain. It seems that the most successful images are those that involve all of the senses – vision, sound, touch, smell, and taste; thus clients should be encouraged to use images that evoke these various senses. Some people, however, may have difficulty generating a particularly vivid visual image and may find it helpful to listen to a taped description or buy a poster on which they can focus their attention as a way of assisting their imagination.

The more success in making use of a skill, the greater the feeling of self-control, which can serve to decrease muscle tension, reduce production of stress hormones and lower pain severity. Imagery and other cognitive coping strategies are usually combined with other techniques, such as cognitive restructuring, relaxation and problem solving, and would not be suggested as the sole treatment approach for dealing with persistent pain.

ASSERTIVENESS AND COMMUNICATION SKILLS TRAINING

Assertiveness training is often an important intervention for enabling clients to re-establish their roles, particularly within the family, and thus to regain a sense of self-esteem and potency. Through role-playing (described below) of existing tension-producing interpersonal transactions, the client and clinical psychologist can identify and modify maladaptive thoughts, feelings, and communication deficiencies underlying non-assertiveness, while practising more adaptive alternatives. Clients may find assertiveness training useful in addressing reactions from family members and healthcare providers who may be opposing their self-management objectives.

Mary worked with the clinical psychologist on asking her husband and children for time and attention at times when she was well, for example coming with her to a movie she particularly wanted to see or discussing and taking seriously her plans for taking an evening class in Feng Shui.

Biofeedback

Biofeedback has been used to treat a number of chronic pain states such as headaches, back pain, and pain associated with temporomandibular disorders. Biofeedback procedures teach individuals to exert control over physiological processes, such as muscle tension, of which they have only marginal awareness. When a client undergoes biofeedback, he or she is connected to equipment that records physiological responses such as skin conductance, respiration, heart rate, skin temperature, and muscle tension. The client sits in front of a monitor that displays the results from all the recordings. The biofeedback equipment converts the readings of physiological responses into visual or auditory signals that the individual uses as the basis for developing voluntary control of the physiological response. The physiological information is *fed back* to the client so that he or she can learn about physiological activity and try to alter it by thoughts or breathing.

As individuals achieve success controlling physiological activity, they can practise the techniques that they have learned in different situations without needing to use the biofeedback apparatus. With practice, most people can learn to control voluntarily important physiological functions that may be associated directly with pain and stress. As with imagery, biofeedback is usually used in conjunction with other modalities such as cognitive restructuring.

Exercise and activity pacing

Physical exercise and activities are important not only to building muscle strength, flexibility, and endurance, but also in bolstering a person's sense of control over his or her physical functioning. People with chronic pain conditions should begin physical exercises at a level that is reasonably comfortable and gradually increase the levels of activity. It is important for people with chronic pain to learn to pace their activities and rest only after attaining the specified activity rather than the experience of pain, and they should be reminded that hurt and harm are not equivalent. Clients may be reluctant to perform some activities (perhaps due to fear of further injury or pain), and a clinical psychologist or physical therapist should address these fears or worries. It is also helpful to keep charts of the activities so that progress can be monitored. Then each day a recording can be made of the amount of the specific activity (e.g. walking distance, number of sit-ups) that was achieved for that day. In time, the benefits of exercise will be evident not only in the recordings on paper, but also in feeling physically and emotionally more healthy.

As mentioned above, Mary initially agreed to walk for ten minutes a day despite any pain experienced. She began walking with a friend because she realized that she did not feel her pain as badly when around other people. She gradually increased the duration of her walking to forty minutes five times a week. Reluctant to try swimming because of prior experiences of pain after it, she tried for a while but soon gave it up as she admitted that she disliked the water.

Role-playing and role reversal

Role-playing is useful not only in the rehearsal of new skills but also in the identification of potential problem areas that may require special attention. Most typically, the client is asked to identify and participate in a role-play situation indicative of a particular problematic area for the client. In this way the client can rehearse potential responses in specific problem situations. In a variation on role-playing – role reversal – the client is asked to role-play a situation in which the clinical psychologist and the client reverse roles. Clients are instructed that it is their job to assume the role of the clinical psychologist, and the clinical psychologist will assume the role of another person with a similar physical diagnosis to the client who has not received the specific skills training. It is known from research on attitude change that when people have to improvise (as in role-playing or role reversal), they generate exactly the kinds of arguments, illustrations, and motivating appeals that they regard as most salient and convincing. These exercises contribute to self-persuasion as well as permit the clinical psychologist to determine areas of confusion and potential difficulties. Mary swapped roles with the clinical psychologist to discuss the idea that when pain was really bad, she needed to lie down and could not be expected to continue with normal chores and responsibilities. She engaged in some very encouraging and empathic conversation, where she acknowledged how hard it must be but pointed out the benefits of keeping busy and active and the costs of staying in bed.

Home assignments and practice

Home assignments are especially useful both for assessing and treating chronic pain clients and they provide important feedback to both clients and clinical psychologists. The idea behind home assignments is that clients can practise skills learned during therapy sessions in real-world situations. They can then return to the clinical psychologist and report on any progress or obstacles (which can then be examined and become a focus for problem solving). The purpose of home assignments is that they are able: to assess various areas of the client's life and how these influence or are affected by the pain problem, to assess responses of others to the client, to help clients become more aware of factors that exacerbate pain, to help clients identify maladaptive responses to pain, to remind clients that they can achieve their goals, to identify obstacles to self-management, and to assist the clinical team in evaluating progress and modifying goals.

Home assignments and practice should be mutually agreed upon, as reluctance from the client may lead to non-completion of assignments. During treatment, each task is targeted toward observable and manageable tasks, starting with those that are most readily achievable and progressing to more difficult ones. The purposes of graded tasks are to enhance clients' sense of competence and to reinforce their continued efforts. Successful completion of these assignments can be reinforced and maladaptive patterns that inhibit rehabilitation can be identified and addressed directly.

Preparation for generalization and maintenance

To maximize the likelihood of maintenance and generalization of treatment gains, cognitive-behavioural clinical psychologists focus on the cognitive activity of clients as they are confronted with problems throughout treatment (e.g. failure to achieve specified goals, plateaus in progress on physical exercises, recurrent stresses). These events are employed as opportunities to assist clients to learn how to handle such setbacks and lapses because they are probably inevitable and will occur once treatment is terminated.

It is helpful to assist clients to anticipate future problems, stress and symptom-exacerbating events and to plan coping and response techniques before these problems occur (e.g. relapse prevention). Clients are helped to identify high-risk situations (non-supportive spouse, conflict with child) and the types of coping and behavioural responses that may be necessary for successful coping. The benefit of relapse prevention is that it gives the client the understanding that minor setbacks are to be expected but that they do not signal total failure.

In the final stage of treatment, discussion is focused on possible ways of predicting and avoiding difficult and problematic situations in general, as well as specific ones identified during treatment. It is important to note that not all possible problematic circumstances can be anticipated. Rather, the goal during this phase, as for the entire treatment strategy, is to enable clients to develop a problem-solving perspective so that they believe that they have the skills and competencies within their repertoires to respond in an appropriate way to problems as they arise. In this manner, attempts are made to help clients learn to anticipate future difficulties, develop plans for adaptive responding and adjust their behaviour accordingly.

During the final sessions with pain clients, all aspects of the treatment should be reviewed. Clients should be engaged in discussions of what they have learned and how they have changed from the onset of treatment; there should be recognition of how the client's own efforts contributed to the positive changes. The clinical psychologist is also encouraged to use client self-monitoring charts to foster self-reinforcement of accomplishments. The goal is for clients to no longer view themselves as *patients* but as *competent people* who happen to have some physical symptoms and discomfort.

SUMMARY

From the pain sufferer's point of view, pain connotes distress and is a plea for assistance. The subjective experience includes an urge to escape from the cause or, if that is not possible, to obtain relief. It is the overwhelming desire to terminate it that gives pain its power. Pain has many dimensions, including sensory and affective components, location, intensity, time course, and the memories, meaning, and anticipated consequences that it elicits. It has become abundantly clear that no isomorphic relationship exists between tissue damage, nociception, and pain report. The more recent conceptualizations view pain as a perceptual process resulting from the nociceptive input, which is modulated on a number of different levels in the CNS. In this chapter, conceptual models were presented to explain the subjective experience of pain.

As was noted, the current state of knowledge suggests that pain must be viewed as a complex phenomenon that incorporates physical, psychosocial, and behavioural factors. Failure to incorporate each of these factors will lead to an incomplete understanding. It is wise to recall John Bonica's comment in the preface to the first edition (1954/1990) of his volume, *The management of pain*, and repeated in the second edition some 36 years later:

> The crucial role of psychological and environmental factors in causing pain in a significant number of patients only recently received attention. As a consequence, there has emerged a sketch plan of pain apparatus with its receptors, conducting fibers, and its standard function that is to be applicable to all circumstances. But . . . in so doing, medicine has overlooked the fact that the activity of this apparatus is subject to a constantly changing influence of the mind. (p. 12)

EXERCISE 17.1

Develop a written diagrammatic formulation of Mary's pain, including predisposing factors, triggers, or precipitating factors, personal, familial and social perpetuating or maintaining factors, personal resources, including positive coping strategies, family, and social resources.

EXERCISE 17.2

Develop a plan for your first post-assessment session with Mary, including review of the CB model and how her situation may be seen within this model.

EXERCISE 17.3

Work in groups of three and assign roles of Mary, the clinical psychologist and an observer. Role-play a fifteen-minute segment of a session with Mary during which you:

1 Introduce her to the idea of relaxation, demonstrate and teach (a part of) a relaxation technique and agree homework with her.
2 Introduce her to a thought record and identify a maladaptive thought from a recent pain episode.
3 Work with Mary to look for evidence for and against a maladaptive pain-related thought and generate an alternative thought.
4 Conduct a cost–benefit analysis for the maladaptive and alternative thought.

After the role-plays, debrief. Describe your experience in the various roles. Identify at least three positive specific behavioural aspects of the clinical psychologist's work with Mary. Identify no more than two specific behavioural ways that the clinical psychologist might act to improve the session for Mary.

EVIDENCE SUMMARIES

Gatchel, R. & Turk, D. (1999). *Psychosocial factors in pain: Critical perspectives.* New York: Guilford Press.

FURTHER READING FOR PRACTITIONERS

Gatchel, R. & Turk, D. (1996). *Psychological approaches to pain management. A practitioner's handbook.* New York: Guilford Press.

ASSESSMENT INSTRUMENTS

These are listed in Table 17.7.

TRAINING VIDEO

Gatchel, R. (2001). *Pain management.* Washington, DC: American Psychological Association. Online. Available at: http://www.apa.org

REFERENCES

Abbott, F.V. & Fraser, M.I. (1998). Use and abuse of over-the-counter analgesic agents. *Journal Psychiatry and Neuroscience*, 23, 13–34.

Allen, J.P. & Litten, R.Z. (1998). Screening instruments and biochemical screening. In A.W. Graham, T.K. Schultz & Wilford, B.B. (Eds.), *Principles of addiction medicine* (pp. 263–272). Arlington, VA: American Society of Addiction Medicine.

American Psychiatric Association (APA) (1994). *Diagnostic and statistical manual of the mental disorders* (Fourth Edition). Washington, DC: APA.

American Psychiatric Association (APA) (1997). *User's guide for the Structured Clinical Interview for DSM-IV axis I disorders SCID-1: Clinician version*. Washington, DC: APA.

American Psychiatric Association (APA) (2000). *Diagnostic and statistical manual of the mental disorders* (Fourth Edition, text revision). Washington, DC: APA.

Bandura, A. (1977). Self-efficacy: Toward a unifying theory of behavior change. *Psychological Review*, 84, 191–215.

Banks, S.M. & Kerns, R.D. (1996). Explaining high rates of depression in chronic pain: A diathesis-stress framework. *Psychological Bulletin*, 119, 95–110.

Bergner, M., Bobbitt, R., Carter, W. & Gilson, B. (1981). The Sickness Impact Profile: Development and final revision of a health status measure. *Medical Care*, 19, 787–805.

Beutler, L., Engle, D., Oro'-Beutler, M., Daldrup, R. & Meredith, K. (1986). Inability to express intense affect: A common link between depression and pain? *Journal of Counseling and Clinical Psychology*, 54, 752–759.

Bonica, J.J. (1954/1990). *The management of pain* (First/Second Editions). Philadelphia: Lea & Febiger.

Boos, N., Rieder, R., Schade, V., Spratt, K.F., Semmer, N. & Aebi, M. (1995). The diagnostic accuracy of magnetic resonance imaging, work perception, and psychosocial factors in identifying symptomatic disc herniations. *Spine*, 20, 2613–2625.

Boothby, J.L., Thorn, B.E., Stroud, M.W. & Jensen, M.P. (1999). Coping with pain. In R.J. Gatchel & D.C. Turk (Eds.), *Psychosocial factors in pain: Critical perspectives* (pp. 243–259). New York: Guilford Press.

Brown, G.K. & Nicassio, P.M. (1987). Development of a questionnaire for the assessment of active and passive coping strategies in chronic pain patients. *Pain*, 31, 53–63.

Coderre, T.J., Katz, J., Vaccarino, A.L. & Melzack, R. (1993). Contribution of central neuroplasticity to pathological pain: Review of clinical and experimental evidence. *Pain*, 52, 259–285.

Corbishley, M., Hendrickson, R., Beutler L. & Engle, D. (1990). Behavior, affect, and cognition among psychogenic pain patients in group expressive psychotherapy. *Journal of Pain and Symptom Management*, 5, 241–248.

Council, J., Ahern, D., Follick, M. & Cline, C.L. (1988). Expectancies and functional impairment in chronic low back pain, *Pain*, 33, 323–331.

Cousins, M.J. (1995). Foreword. In W.E. Fordyce (Ed.), *Back pain in the workplace. Management of disability in nonspecific conditions. Task Force Report*. Seattle: IASP Press, p. ix.

Craig, K.D. (1986). Social modeling influences: Pain in context. In R.A. Sternbach (Ed.), *The psychology of pain* (Second Edition, pp. 67–95). New York: Raven Press.

DeGood, D.E. & Tait, R. (2001). Assessment of pain beliefs, coping, and self-efficacy. In D.C. Turk & R. Melzack (Eds.), *Handbook of pain assessment* (Second Edition, pp. 320–345). New York: Guilford Press.

Derogatis, L. (1983). *The SCL-90R manual-II: Administration, scoring and procedures*. Towson, MD: Clinical Psychometric Research.

Deyo, R.A. (1986). Early diagnostic evaluation of low back pain. *Journal of General Internal Medicine*, 1, 328–338.

Dolce, J.J., Crocker, M.F., Moletteire, C. & Doleys, D.M. (1986). Exercise quotas, anticipatory concern, and self-efficacy expectations in chronic pain: A preliminary report. *Pain*, 24, 365–372.

Edwards, L.C., Pearce, S.A., Turner-Stokes, L. & Jones, A. (1992). The Pain Beliefs Questionnaire: An investigation of beliefs in the causes and consequences of pain. *Pain*, 51, 267–272.

Eisenberg, D.M., Davis, R.B. & Ettner, S.L. (1998). Trends in alternative medicine use in the United States, 1900–1997: Result of a follow-up survey. *Journal of the American Medical Association*, 280, 1569–1575.

Fairbank, J.C., Couper, J., Davies, J.B. & O'Brien, J.P. (1980). The Oswestry low backpain disability questionnaire. *Physiotherapy*, 66, 271–273.

Fernandez, E. & Turk, D.C. (1989). The utility of cognitive coping strategies for altering pain perception: A meta-analysis. *Pain*, 38, 125–135.

Fernandez, E. & Turk, D.C. (1995). The scope and significance of anger in the experience of chronic pain. *Pain*, 61, 165–175.

Fordyce, W. E. (1976). *Behavioral methods in chronic pain and illness*. St Louis: CV Mosby.

Fordyce, W.E., Shelton, J.L. & Dundore, D.E. (1982). The modification of avoidance learning in pain behaviors. *Journal of Behavioral Medicine*, 5, 405–414.

Frolund, F. & Frolund, C. (1986). Pain in general practice. *Scandinavian Journal of Primary Healthcare*, 4, 97–100.

Galer, B.S. & Jensen, M.P. (1997). Development and preliminary validation of a pain measure specific to neuropathic pain: The Neuropathic Pain Scale. *Neurology*, 48, 332–338.

Gaston-Johansson, F. (1996). Measurement of pain: The psychometric properties of the Pain O'Meter, a simple, inexpensive pain assessment tool that could change health care practice. *Journal of Pain and Symptom Management*, 12, 172–181.

Gracley, R.H. & Kwilosz, D.M. (1988). The Descriptor Differential Scale: Applying psychophysical principles to clinical pain assessment. *Pain*, 35, 279–288.

Grzesiak, R.C., Ury, G.M. & Dworkin, R.H. (1996). Psychodynamic psychotherapy with chronic pain patients. In R.J. Gatchel & D.C. Turk (Eds.), *Psychological approaches to pain management: A practitioner's handbook* (pp. 148–178). New York: Guilford Press.

Gureje, O. (1998). Persistent pain and well-being: a World Health Organization study in primary care. *Journal of the American Medical Association*, 280, 147–151.

Jensen, M. C., Brant-Zawadzki, M., Obuchowski, N., Modic, M.T. & Malkasian Ross, J.S. (1994). Magnetic resonance imaging of the lumbar spine in people without back pain. *New England Journal of Medicine*, 331, 69–73.

Jensen, M.P., Karoly, P. & Huger, R. (1987). The development and preliminary validation of an instrument to assess patient's attitudes toward pain. *Journal of Psychosomatic Research*, 31, 393–400.

Jensen, M.P., Turner, J.A. & Romano, J.M. (1994). Correlates of improvement in multidisciplinary treatment of chronic pain. *Journal of Consulting and Clinical Psychology*, 62, 172–179.

Jensen, M.P., Turner, J.A., Romano, J.M. & Strom, S.E. (1995). The Chronic Pain Coping Inventory: Development and preliminary validation. *Pain*, 60, 203–216.

Joranson, D.E. & Lietman, R. (1994). *The McNeil national pain survey*. New York: Louis Harris and Associates.

Kames, L.D., Naliboff, B.D., Heinrich, R.L. & Schag, C.C. (1984). The Chronic Illness Problem Inventory: Problem-oriented psychosocial assessment of patients with chronic illness. *International Journal of Psychiatry in Medicine*, 14, 65–75.

Keith, R.A., Granger, C.V., Hamiilton, B.B. & Sherwin, F.S. (1987). The Functional Independence Measure: A new tool for rehabilitation. In M.G. Eisenberg (Ed.), *Advances in clinical rehabilitation* (pp. 6–18). New York: Springer.

Kerns, R.D., Rosenberg, R. & Jacob, M. (1994). Anger expression and chronic pain. *Journal of Behavioral Medicine*, 17, 57–67.

Kerns, R.D. Rosenberg, R., Jamison, R.N., Caudill, M.A. & Hayuthornwaite, J. (1997). Readiness to adopt a self-management approach to chronic pain: The Pain Stages of Change Questionniare (PSOCQ). *Pain*, 72, 227–234.

Kerns, R.D., Turk, D.C. & Rudy, T.E. (1985). The West Haven-Yale Multidimensional Pain Inventory (WHYMPI). *Pain*, 23, 345–356.

Kroenke, K. & Mangelsdorff, A. (1989). Common symptoms in ambulatory care: Incidence, evaluation, therapy, and outcome. *American Journal of Medicine*, 86, 262–266.

Lenthem, J., Slade, P.O., Troup, J.P.G. & Bentley, G. (1983). Outline of a fear-avoidance model of exaggerated pain perception. *Behaviour Research and Therapy*, 21, 401–408.

Liebeskind, J.C. (1991). Pain can kill. *Pain*, 44, 3–4.

Linton, S.J. & Buer, N. (1995). Working despite pain: Factors associated with work attendance versus dysfunction. *International Journal of Behavioral Medicine*, 2, 252–262.

Loeser, J.D., Butler, S.D., Chapman, C.R. & Turk, D.C. (Eds.) (2001). *Bonica's management of pain* (Third Edition). Philadelphia: Lippincott Williams & Wilkins.

MarketData Enterprises (1995). *Chronic pain management programs: A market analysis*. Valley Stream, New York: MarketData Enterprises.

Mayfield, D., McLead, G. & Hall, P. (1987). The CAGE questionnaire. *American Journal of Psychiatry*, 131, 1121–1123.

McCracken, L.M., Zayfert, C. & Gross, R.T. (1992). The Pain Anxiety Symptoms Scale: Development and validation of a scale to measure fear of pain. *Pain*, 50, 67–73.

McNeil, D.W. & Rainwater, A.J. III. (1998). Development of the Fear of Pain Questionnaire-III. *Journal of Behavioral Medicine*, 21, 389–410.

Melzack, R. (1975). The McGill Pain Questionnaire: Major properties and scoring methods. *Pain*, 1, 277–299.

Melzack, R. & Wall, P. D. (1965). Pain mechanisms: A new theory. *Science*, 150, 971–979.

Mendelson, G. (1982). Not 'cured by a verdict.' *Medical Journal of Australia*, 2, 132–134.

Merskey, H, (1986). International Association for the Study of Pain: Classification of chronic pain. Descriptions of chronic pain syndromes and definitions of pain terms. *Pain*, 3, S1–226.

Millon, T., Green, C. & Meagher, R. (1983). *Millon Behavioral Health Inventory Manual* (Third Edition). Minneapolis, MN: National Computer Systems.

Morley, S., Eccleston, C. & Williams, A. (1999). Systematic review and meta-analysis of randomized controlled trials of cognitive-behaviour therapy and behavior therapy for chronic pain in adults, excluding headache. *Pain*, 80, 1–13.

National Ambulatory Medical Care Survey (1998). *National Center for Health Statistics*. Washington, DC: Department of Health and Human Services.

National Research Council (2001). *Musculoskeletal disorders and the workplace*. Washington, DC: National Academy Press.

Okifuji, A., Turk D.C. & Sherman, J.J. (2000). Evaluation of the relationship between depression and fibromyalgia syndrome: Why aren't all patients depressed? *Journal of Rheumatology*, 27, 212–219.

Paulose-Ram, R., Hirsch, R. & Dillon, C. (2003). Prescription and non-prescription analgesic use among the US adult population: Results from the third National Health and Nutrition Examination Survey (NHANES III). *Pharmacoepidemiology Drug Safety*, 112, 15–26.

Physicians' desk reference for nonprescription drugs and dietary supplements (Twenty-second Edition) (2001). Montvale, NJ: Medical Economics Company Inc.

Pilowsky, I. & Spence, N. (1976). Pain, anger, and illness behaviour. *Journal of Psychosomatic Research*, 20, 411–416.

Piotrowski, C. (1997). Assessment of pain: A survey of practicing clinicians. *Perceptual and Motor Skills*, 86, 181–182.

Pollard, C.A. (1984). Preliminary validity study of the Pain Disability Index. *Perceptual and Motor Skills*, 59, 974.

Richard, K. (1988). The occurrence of maladaptive health-related behaviors and teacher-related conduct problems in children of chronic low back pain patients. *Journal of Behavioral Medicine*, 11, 107–116.

Rosenstiel, A.K. & Keefe, F.J. (1983). The use of coping strategies in chronic low back pain patients: Relationship to patient characteristics and current adjustment. *Pain*, 17, 33–44.

Rudy, T.E., Kerns, R.D. & Turk, D.C. (1988). Chronic pain and depression: Toward a cognitive-behavioral mediational model. *Pain*, 35, 129–140.

Schwartz, L., Slater, M., Birchler, G. & Atkinson, J.H. (1991). Depression in spouses of chronic pain patients: The role of patient pain and anger, and marital satisfaction. *Pain*, 44, 61–67.

Smith, C.A., Wallston, K.A., Dwyer, K.A. & Dowdy, S.W. (1997). Beyond good and bad coping: A multidimensional examination of coping with pain in persons with rheumatoid arthritis. *Annals of Behavioral Medicine*, 19, 11–21.

Spiegel, D. & Bloom, J.R. (1983). Pain in metastatic breast cancer. *Cancer*, 52, 341–345.

Stewart, W.F., Lipton, R.B., Whyte, J., Kolodner, K., Liberman, J.N. & Sawyer, J. (1999). An international study to assess reliability of the Migraine Disability Assessment (MIDAS) score. *Neurology*, 53, 988–994.

Sullivan, M.J.L., Bishop, S. & Pivik, J. (1995). The Pain Catastrophizing Scale: Development and validation. *Psychological Assessment*, 7, 524–532.

Sullivan, M.J.L., Thorn, B., Haythornthwaite, J.A., Keefe, F., Martin, M., Bradley,

L.A. & Lefebvre, J.C. (2001). Theoretical perspectives on the relation between catastrophizing and pain. *Clinical Journal of Pain*, 15, 52–64.

Summers, J. D., Rapoff, M. A., Varghese, G., Porter, K. & Palmer, R.E. (1991). Psychosocial factors in chronic spinal cord injury pain. *Pain*, 47, 183–189.

Tota-Faucette, M.E., Gil, K.M., Williams, D.A., Keefe, F.J. & Goli, V. (1993). Predictors of response to pain management treatment. The role of family environment and changes in cognitive processes. *Clinical Journal of Pain*, 9, 115–123.

Turk, D.C. (1996). Biopsychosocial perspective on chronic pain. In R.J. Gatchel & D.C. Turk (Eds.), *Psychological approaches to pain management: A practitioner's handbook* (pp. 3–30). New York: Guilford Press.

Turk, D.C. (1997). Psychological aspects of pain. In P. Bakule (Ed.), *Expert pain management* (pp. 124–178). Springhouse, PA: Springhouse Corporation.

Turk, D.C. (2002a). Clinical effectiveness and cost effectiveness of treatments for chronic pain patients. *Clinical Journal of Pain*, 18, 355–365.

Turk, D.C. (2002b). A cognitive-behavioral perspective on treatment of chronic pain patients. In D.C. Turk & R.J. Gatchel (Eds.), *Psychological approaches to pain management: A practitioner's handbook*. (Second Edition, pp. 138–158). New York: Guilford Press.

Turk, D.C. & Flor, H. (1999). Chronic pain: A biobehavioral perspective. In R.J. Gatchel & D.C. Turk (Eds.), *Psychosocial factors in pain: Critical perspectives*. (pp. 18–34). New York: Guilford Press.

Turk, D.C. & Meichenbaum, D. (1984). A cognitive-behavioral approach to pain management. In P.D. Wall & R. Melzack (Eds.), *Textbook of pain* (pp. 787–794). New York: Churchill-Livingstone.

Turk, D.C., Meichenbaum, D. & Genest, M. (1983). *Pain and behavioral medicine: A cognitive-behavioral perspective*. New York: Guilford.

Turk, D.C. & Melzack, R. (1992). *Handbook of pain assessment*. New York: Guilford Press.

Turk, D.C. & Melzack, R. (2001). *Handbook of pain assessment*. (Second Edition), New York: Guilford Press.

Turk, D.C. & Okifuji, A. (1997). What factors affect physicians' decisions to prescribe opioids for chronic non-cancer pain patients? *Clinical Journal of Pain*, 13, 330–336.

Turk, D.C., Okifuji, A. & Scharff, L. (1995). Chronic pain and depression: Role of perceived impact and perceived control in different age cohorts. *Pain*, 61, 93–101.

Turk, D.C. & Rudy, T.E. (1986). Assessment of cognitive factors in chronic pain: A worthwhile enterprise? *Journal of Consulting and Clinical Psychology*, 54, 760–768.

Turk, D.C., Wack, J. T. & Kerns, R.D. (1985). An empirical examination of the 'pain behavior' construct. *Journal of Behavioral Medicine*, 9, 119–130.

Turkat, I.D. & Pettegrew, L.S. (1983). Development and validation of the Illness Behavior Inventory. *Journal of Behavioral Assessment*, 5, 35–47.

United States Bureau of the Census (1996). *Statistical Abstract of the United States: 1996* (116th Edition) Washington, DC: US Bureau of the Census.

Vaughan, K.B. & Lanzetta, J.T. (1980). Vicarious instigation and conditioning of facial expressive and autonomic responses to a model's expressive display of pain. *Journal of Personality and Social Psychology*, 38, 909–923.

Vlaeyen, J.W., Kole-Snijders, A.M., Boeren, R.B. et al. (1995). Fear of movement/(re)injury in chronic low back pain and its relation to behavioral performance. *Pain*, 62, 363–372.

Waddell, G., Newton, M., Henderson, I., Somerville, D. & Main, C.J. (1993). A Fear-Avoidance Beliefs Questionnaire (FABQ) and the role of fear-avoidance beliefs in chronic low back pain and disability. *Pain*, 52, 157–168.

Wallis, B.J., Lord, S.M. & Bogduk, N. (1997). Resolution of psychological distress of whiplash patients following treatment by radiofrequency neurotomy: A randomised, double-blind, placebo-controlled trial. *Pain*, 73, 15–22.

Ware, J.E. & Sherbourne, C.D. (1992). The MOS 36-item Short Form Health Survey (SF-36). *Medical Care*, 30, 473–481.

Wiesel, S.W., Tsourmas, N., Feffer, H.L., Citrin, C.M. & Patronas, N. (1984). A study of computer-assisted tomography. I. The incidence of positive CAT scans in an asymptomatic group of patients. *Spine*, 9, 549–551.

Williams, D.A. & Thorn, B.E. (1989). An empirical assessment of pain beliefs. *Pain*, 36, 351–358.

World Health Organization (WHO) (1992). *The ICD-10 classification of mental and behavioural disorders. Clinical descriptions and diagnostic guidelines.* Geneva: WHO. Online. Available at: http://www.informatik.fh-luebeck.de/icd/welcome.html

Chapter 18

Psychological assessment and treatment in cancer care

Craig A. White

Dedication

I would like to dedicate this chapter to my brother-in-law, Andrew, who died on 24 July 2003, aged thirty-seven years, seven weeks after being diagnosed with advanced renal cancer.

CASE EXAMPLE

Joe was a forty-two-year-old man with advanced metastatic cancer who was referred to the author for opinion on managing panic and anxiety. He was an inpatient within the local hospice and his anxiety had been managed by benzodiazepines. He had been reviewed by a consultant psychiatrist who had recommended the addition of amitryptiline at night. The duration of assessment was limited due to his physical health status but concentrated on a review of his nursing notes, discussion with several members of nursing staff and discussion with him about a recent problem episode. He was encouraged to talk about his thoughts and feelings when experiencing panic and asked about the presence of any images. Information was collected on his family and personal history and his sisters were interviewed. He talked about a distressing image when he had been at home on the day of his father's death some years previously. Staff were encouraged to assess the personal significance of this in further detail.

INTRODUCTION

This chapter outlines information that can be used to assist with the phases of assessment, formulation and intervention with common psychological problems and disorders that present among people who have been diagnosed with cancer. The headings used reflect the sequential phases that are applied by clinical psychologists in their approach to clinical practice.

These sections are presented after an initial overview of cancer, its treatment and the psychosocial impact of cancer. The emphasis is on those elements of clinical practice that are particular to the psychological assessment, formulation and psychological care of people with cancer. The content and clinical processes that are covered in other chapters will also be of relevance in considering the needs of those who present for psychological assessment and therapy relating to their experience of cancer.

EPIDEMIOLOGY: INCIDENCE AND TREATMENTS

Cancer is a generic term that relates to over 100 different diseases, each characterized by a process where cells develop and grow in an unregulated manner, forming a tumour. Tumours invade surrounding normal tissues and often spread to other organs within the body. Cancer is a major cause of morbidity in the UK. It is estimated that around 2% (1.2 million people) from the UK population are living with cancer at any one time. For men, lung cancer is the most common diagnosis, followed by prostate cancer. Breast cancer is the most common cancer affecting women, followed by colorectal cancer and lung cancer (Cancer Research UK, 2003). The main treatment modalities for cancer are surgery, chemotherapy, immunotherapy, radiotherapy and hormone therapy. Because cancer is a range of illnesses and diseases, each with a different aetiology, treatment regime and prognosis, it is often associated with unique psychological concerns or problems.

Consider a patient who has experienced breast cancer in the context of adequate personal and supportive care resources, who experiences her care and treatment without major problems with side effects. She will have experienced an entirely different set of thoughts and feelings to a patient with head and neck cancer with few supportive relationships and a past history of alcohol abuse. Such differences in psychological experiences would become more apparent if the latter patient had also experienced a range of disfiguring surgical treatments and was been told that his or her overall treatment was no longer curative. As is the case with all physical illnesses, the psychological variability between patients with very similar illness characteristics can be significant. These two contrasting examples highlight that, with cancer in particular, there are very different psychological issues that confront people depending on the primary site of their cancer, the extent of spread and treatment intent. Past life history and current personal and social resources are also very likely to have a bearing upon the precise interaction between cancer and the person with cancer.

CANCER AND PSYCHOLOGICAL DISTRESS

Increasing medical advances mean that more people are cured of cancer than ever before. As a consequence, people with cancer are now tending to live longer than used to be the case (even when cancer treatment is being given without curative intent). These changing circumstances mean cancer is increasingly being conceptualized as a chronic illness. Almost everyone who is told that they have cancer will experience a period of shock and psychological distress. For the majority of patients, this will be a self-limiting experience, one that does not cause any lasting psychological problems and that can be understood as part of a normal adjustment reaction. Some people will experience more severe distress. Currently available estimates suggest that this severity of distress will apply to around 25% of people who have cancer (Derogatis et al., 1983), although there are some cancer sites where this figure is higher (Zabora et al., 2001). Patients with this level of distress are more likely to be experiencing psychological problems that interfere significantly with their quality of life and ability to function on a day-to-day basis. Distress is more common in younger patients, patients who are single by virtue of separation, divorce or being widowed, patients living alone, patients with children aged under 21 years of age, patients experiencing economic adversity, patients with a perceived lack of social support, patients with poor marital or family functioning and in patients with a history of psychiatric problems, experience of cumulative stressful life events and a history of alcohol or other substance abuse. More severe distress is more likely at the time of diagnosis or recurrence, at advanced stages of cancer, in the presence of a poorer prognosis and when someone is experiencing more treatment side effects. The presence of symptoms such as lymphoedema, pain or fatigue also increases the risk of such distress (National Breast Cancer Centre and National Cancer Control Initiative, 2003).

Clinically significant psychological problems usually occur as part of an adjustment disorder, major depressive disorder or one of the anxiety disorders (White & Macleod, 2002). Although incidence figures vary in accordance with the way in which symptoms are assessed, it is thought that around 10–15% of patients will experience a significant depressive episode that is triggered by cancer. There has been an increased interest in viewing cancer as a trigger for post-traumatic stress symptoms (Smith et al., 1999). Although prevalence estimates have tended to depend on the assessment methodologies used, it is thought that in the region of 5–19% of people with cancer experience symptoms to meet the criteria for PTSD approximately six months after diagnosis and 3–22% in terms of lifetime diagnosis (Kangas et al., 2002). The precise figures also differ in accordance with the way in which the diagnosis is made.

Many patients have to face treatment regimes that are difficult to tolerate and which require frequent hospital visits and levels of motivation that can be difficult to generate or sustain. Some patients will experience anxiety, depression or trauma symptoms that although not experienced at sufficient severity to warrant a diagnosis, can cause problems. Indeed, non-physical treatment side effects such as anger, anxiety or apprehension are often rated by patients as being more severe than physical side effects such as nausea or hair loss (Coates et al., 1983). Some patients may drop out of chemotherapy because of psychological problems (Gilbar & De-Nour, 1989; Watson, 2000). Some treatment procedures (e.g. bone marrow transplantation) result in psychological problems because of the particular demands that they involve (e.g. prolonged exposure to isolation). Chemotherapy is more challenging for patients with fears of needles and radiotherapy can be distressing for people who have fears of enclosed places. Advances in drug therapies have resulted in a reduction in the incidence of nausea and vomiting associated with chemotherapy. However, conditioned nausea and vomiting do still occur (particularly among those with an anxious disposition) and aversions to food or to other elements of the cancer experience can also develop. Even after the end of treatment, patients' lives may be affected throughout the follow-up period, as they attend appointments to determine whether the cancer has returned.

Progress in cancer genetics has resulted in increased awareness of the possibility of negative psychological reactions to increased genetic predisposition for cancer (Cull et al., 1999; Hopwood, 1997). Researchers have examined the way in which patients manage uncertainty about this, make decisions about treatment (e.g. risk reducing mastectomy) and how, in some cases, beliefs about genetic risk of cancer can precipitate or mediate psychological problems. Although people who have had cancer may feel relieved that their active treatment has ended, they may experience fear and anxiety about the uncertainty associated with the future (Dunkel-Schetter et al., 1992). Fear of recurrence is thought to be almost universally present (O'Neill et al., 1999), although it is more likely to be experienced on a continuum (as with other fears and anxiety). There are also undoubtedly some patients who have to address these issues more directly as a result of the initial pathological staging of their tumour and/or by virtue of knowledge about increased genetic risk. Beliefs about the likelihood of cancer recurrence are thought to be very significantly influenced by exposure to information within the popular press and media (Lee-Jones et al., 1997).

Some cancers and treatment regimes are associated with neuropsychological sequelae. Treatments can have an impact on sexual functioning (e.g. hormonal therapies or surgically induced damage to pelvic autonomic nerves). Quality of relationship is an important correlate of sexual functioning (Weijmar Schultz et al., 1990). Radiotherapy and chemotherapy can be associated with reduced sexual desire, related particularly to the occurrence of physical side effects such as fatigue, constipation or weight changes that reduce the extent to which an individual feels 'sexual'. Fatigue is one of the most common unrelieved symptoms in cancer patients and is a major factor affecting quality of life, both during and following treatment. Fatigue associated with cancer is generally more severe and persistent than 'everyday' fatigue and tends to persist even in the presence of adequate amounts of sleep and rest. For some cancer survivors, fatigue does not decline to premorbid levels following treatment and can become chronic. In an attempt to standardize the definition for and improve the recognition of cancer-related fatigue, diagnostic criteria for cancer-related fatigue (CRF) have been proposed. Studies that have used these criteria have reported prevalence estimates of 17 and 21% (Cella et al., 2001; Sadler et al., 2001). Fatigue is often associated with psychological morbidity, sleep problems and reduced activity levels.

Given the many psychological consequences of cancer and cancer treatment, it is not surprising that clinical psychologists are often considered to be essential core members of the multi-disciplinary team in cancer and palliative medicine teams. Although this chapter focuses on the way in which clinical psychology can be applied to the assessment, formulation and intervention elements of clinic work, clinical and other applied psychologists can also make a valuable contribution in teaching psychological care skills to colleagues (e.g. communication skills training; Fallowfield et al., 2002).

TREATMENT OUTCOME: DOES PSYCHOLOGICAL INTERVENTION INFLUENCE SURVIVAL?

In the context of a growing interest in the effects of psychosocial factors on health and illness over the past two decades, there have been various attempts to examine the influence of psychosocial factors on mortality and the potential benefits of psychological intervention on survival. Spiegel's well-known study of group therapy for women with metastatic breast cancer reported a significantly longer survival time (36.3 months for group members vs. 18.9 months for no-treatment controls). This has led to a great deal of interest in the effect of group therapies on morbidity and mortality. Studies of the effect of group interventions on these variables are inconsistent, with some showing improved survival time and immunological response for cancer group members (Fawzy et al., 1995; Spiegel et al., 1989), but others failing to demonstrate such a connection (Cunningham et al., 1998; Edelman et al., 1999; Goodwin et al., 2001; Ilnyckyj et al., 1994; Schrock et al., 1999). This debate is ongoing (Sampson, 2002; Spiegel, 2001) and further research to address these issues is being carried out (Cunningham & Edmonds, 2002; Kissane et al., 2001). Walker et al. (2000) has reported that a relaxation-based intervention prolonged survival. Patients may request psychological intervention when they wish to prolong their survival. There is no place within ethical psychotherapy practice for offering interventions that aim to prolong survival by directly influencing disease-specific biological processes. This is not to say that psychotherapy might not have a positive impact on treatment adherence or mood. It has also been suggested that psychotherapy may have an impact by influencing host defences or the amelioration of chemotherapy-induced immunosuppression. Walker et al. (1999) showed that greater mood disturbance is associated with poorer response to chemotherapy. Watson et al. (1999) demonstrated that high helpless/hopelessness scores on the Mental Adjustment to Cancer Scale are associated with a moderately detrimental effect on survival. It is possible that psychotherapy targeted at helplessness and/or hopelessness might produce modest survival benefits.

ASSESSMENT

Assessing a person with cancer for psychological problems may require some changes from assessments carried out in general clinical psychology practice settings with physically healthy people.

Starting the assessment process

Clinical psychologists who are not used to working with people with cancer may find initial exposure to working in this area difficult and emotionally challenging, particularly if their involvement relates to the care of someone with an advanced and incurable cancer. Psychologists may struggle with their own beliefs about mortality, with concepts of 'justice' and 'fairness' in the world, particularly when first starting work in this area. It is important to be able to discuss any related concerns and problems with an experienced supervisor and to ensure adequate self-care opportunities.

The process of assessment can be therapeutic, particularly with patients who have not had an opportunity to talk about their cancer experiences. The psychologist should aim to balance supportive-expressive and problem-focused content within the assessment and allow for the validation of the emotional impact of cancer-related events. Many patients will not have had the opportunity to tell their 'cancer story', that is to talk about their cancer experiences from the time when they first presented with symptoms. The pacing and content of assessment needs to be implemented with this delicate balance in mind. Psychologists should not underestimate the therapeutic value that can be gained from an assessment that has been sensitively conducted.

If all assessment contact is in the presence of a relative then it is common for patients to censor what they disclose for fear of causing further distress to the relative whom they know is already distressed by what they have been experiencing. Assessments should therefore always include time when individuals with cancer are able to speak with a clinical psychologist on their own.

The content of assessment

Some common areas should be routinely addressed as part of a specialist psychological assessment of someone with cancer. These are screening for the presence or absence of symptoms and listening for themes that have been outlined in the initial section of this chapter. Assessing for the presence or absence of psychological symptoms is similar to work in mainstream practice, although it is important to be aware that there are some cancers and cancer treatments that result in psychological symptoms that would otherwise be assumed to be mediated by non-disease-related factors. It is important for subsequent case formulation and treatment planning to understand if a symptom is related to cancer and its treatment or to other factors.

For example, a patient who has a biochemically mediated anxiety reaction is unlikely to benefit from strategies designed to reduce autonomic arousal or challenge thoughts relating to panic. Assessment content should always therefore include a component that asks about cancer type, chemotherapy regime and a full list of medications that have been taken.

Brennan (2001) has outlined a very useful way of conceptualizing the themes that are commonly reflected among the thoughts of people with cancer. He proposes ways in which these might influence negative and positive patterns of adjustment to cancer, based on a social cognitive transition model. During the process of psychological assessment, information can be elicited about these cognitive themes. They are highly likely to be important both in formulating the contributors to common patterns of adjustment and in planning intervention strategies that might be subsequently implemented. Information could be elicited using specific questioning designed to facilitate reporting of the issues within the model. There are, of course, times when patients will disclose information relating to these themes without the need for prompting, allowing information to be collated according to themes at a later point.

Meaning is a concept that has relevance from a number of perspectives in understanding the psychology of cancer. Cancer challenges people's views of the world as meaningful, purposeful and coherent; 'What it all means' is a common focus of thinking. Cancer results in changes in anticipated life trajectory. For some people, this leads to a revision of priorities in life and the establishment of new motivational structures. Other people find that this can become a factor that dominates their day-to-day thoughts and causes hopelessness. Useful questions include, 'Sometimes cancer leads to changes in the way people think about what they want from life and how they will approach each day. Have you experienced this?' Coward (1997) has suggested that the experiences associated with cancer result in 'severe spiritual disequibilrium' and that process of searching for meaning is a response to this state. Lepore and Helgeson (1998) suggested that 'integrating the cancer experience into (their) pre-existing mental models should promote psychological adjustment'. O'Connor, Wicker and Germino (1990) defined the process of searching for meaning as '. . . questions about the personal significance of a life circumstance, such as cancer, in order to give the experience purpose and to place it in the context of a total life pattern'.

While some patients are able to retain feelings of self-control and worth throughout their cancer experiences, for a substantial minority of others loss of control becomes a significant issue influencing adjustment (Osowiecki & Compas, 1998). Asking the following may be helpful, 'How much control have you felt that you have had in terms of your cancer experiences?' Like many other physical illnesses, cancer has an impact on the nature of the significant emotional attachments that people with cancer have with others in their lives. The social and family support that is experienced by some patients can act as a significant personal resource; for others, the lack of such support leads to feelings of isolation and loneliness. Useful questions include, 'Has cancer had an effect on your relationships with other people? How have your relationships with other people affected how you have been feeling about cancer?' Some relatives of patients with cancer become more distressed than the patient, something that should be borne in mind when conducting an initial assessment.

Assessment of psychosocial aspects of problems related to cancer should aim to be sensitive to issues such as the site of the patient's cancer, the person's previous life experiences (particularly family and personal experience of cancer), treatment regime, experiences following diagnosis and unique hurdles associated with cancer. Having knowledge of the main tumour site should immediately lead to thoughts about some of the potential issues that will have been concerning the patient.

Beginning an assessment with an invitation to outline personal experiences relating to the sequence of cancer-related events provides the psychologist with a way of identifying clues to thoughts, feelings, coping strategies, family relationships, inner conflicts, critical incidents and contextual information that can be used for planning further psychological assessment content. The sequence of events leading to the confirmation of a cancer diagnosis will often be significant, particularly if there have been actual or perceived delays. It is important to ask people if there are key phrases that they recall from outpatient consultations around the time of diagnosis, for example by asking 'What sticks in your mind most about your initial contact with the clinic?' The way in which the news about cancer was given to a patient will be significant and should be assessed. This can become very significant in terms of beliefs about staff sensitivity and support (crucial when it comes to later efforts to access support) and the fact that distress in the early weeks post-diagnosis is predictive of later levels of distress. Patients should be asked about their relationships with doctors and nurses, for example, 'How do you feel about the doctors and nurses that have been involved with your cancer care?' Most patients want to be fully informed about their care and treatment (Jenkins et al., 2001). Satisfaction with information also is a very significant determinant of overall psychosocial adjustment, particularly during the early stages of cancer care and treatment. Ensuring that patients are asked about their current level of understanding of their cancer and treatment can reveal misconceptions and informational needs that then become a key factor in subsequent intervention.

Cancer can result in recall of a number of memories of physical illness within families, and thus the following questions may be helpful, 'Do you find that you get unwanted thoughts about cancer? Have you experienced more memories of times that you or your loved ones have been ill?' (Brewin et al., 1998). Images often have their origins in life events such as a relative with cancer, witnessing another patient on a ward with the same cancer and/or re-experiencing actual events such as the recall of statements that have been made by medical or nursing staff. The occurrence and frequency of intrusive memories and thoughts about cancer experiences should be assessed. It is crucial to take time to explore any images and in particular to consider any personally salient fears or concerns reflected within them.

It is important to assess beliefs about the causes of cancer and predicted consequences of the disease. The content of such beliefs will depend on the exposure a person has had to cancer-related information, for example through the media or through experiences of friends or family members who had cancer.

Ask the patient, 'What was your experience of cancer before you were diagnosed?' and 'Has this influenced the way you think or feel in any way?' Therapists should ask what patients think and feel about the reactions of relatives to their cancer, especially to what degree they feel they have to manage this in addition to their own problems. Criticism by spouses has been shown to moderate the relationship between intrusive thoughts and distress (Manne, 1999). This is one of the reasons why therapists should determine the impact of cancer diagnosis on the behaviour of spouses.

There are some patients who survive by developing a global avoidance strategy. This can make assessment difficult (as this involves reversal of avoidance). Avoidance is often a key maintaining factor for problems associated with anxiety and depression. It should be distinguished from denial, as the concepts used in formulation and the strategies that are used to manage each are different. Avoidant patients differ from those in denial because they know that they have cancer and choose not to think about this. This can usually easily be determined by asking patients 'What is your understanding of what disease you have?' or in some cases the more direct 'Do you think you have cancer?'

A small proportion of cancer patients will have had the experience of anxiety and depressive symptoms prior to their diagnosis. With patients who have a positive prior psychological history, assessment should aim to determine which cancer-related psychological problems are related to pre-morbid problems and which have been specifically triggered or exacerbated by the experience of cancer ('Of all of these problems we have been talking about, which do you see as being a result of the cancer?', 'Are there any of these problems that have become worse because of the cancer?'). Katz et al. (1995) stated that 'the integration of the illness into the self-concept without undue loss of self-esteem may protect those with serious medical illnesses from clinical depression'. Information should be obtained on a patient's self-esteem as this can be vitally important in conceptualizing psychological reactions to cancer. It can be done by asking screening questions such as 'How do you feel about yourself compared to other people?' or 'Do you ever feel worthless?' Knowledge about the presence of worthlessness is often very helpful in distinguishing depression from normal sadness.

Having someone who is physically ill within the family can have a significant impact on one or more members of the immediate and extended family (Kissane et al., 1994). In most cases, families act as a helpful resource to support and assist a family member with cancer (Xiaolian et al., 2002). Indeed, families are often very involved with decision-making about treatment and tend to provide emotional support throughout the duration of a physical illness affecting a family member. All assessments should at the very least include an assessment of the composition of the family using a family tree. The important assessment elements relate to the level of knowledge, support and involvement that each member of a family has with the index patient who has cancer. There are usually some members of the family who have more frequent contact with the person being assessed, who demonstrate greater empathy and understanding, who offer more practical support and in whom the patient will find it easier to confide. Each family member will also have his or her own understanding of the index patient's experience of cancer and, while it will not always be possible to speak with each member of the family at the same time, it is important to gather as much information as possible about different perspectives. Clinicians should consider the impact of cancer on each family member. The assessment process will need to take account of the age and developmental stages of the constituent family members (Veach & Nicholas, 1998). Family 'myths' are also an important part of the assessment process. These often influence and may mirror beliefs shared by the patient. This is sometimes referred to as the 'family world view' or the 'family paradigm'. In general, families (as with individuals) tend to cope with conflict or problem situations in similar ways throughout life. This is usually by directly confronting the situation in some way or by avoiding the situation. Family members can be asked, 'Which of these styles would have best characterized your way of resolving problems when you were growing up?' and asked to provide examples of the ways in which other people might perceive their family to have reacted to other significant events.

When screening suggests that there may be family issues influencing presentation, family members' experiences of cancer need to be assessed. A patient who has had the experience of both of their parents, siblings and a brother-in-law die as a result of cancer will have a very different understanding of the impact of cancer than someone who has not had such an experience of cancer. It is, of course, also possible that individuals will have been exposed to illnesses other than cancer and that this experience within their family unit will have some bearing on understanding their and the family's psychological experience of cancer. Families may express their thoughts about the most appropriate way in which to meet the needs of family members who have cancer, for example saying. 'We don't think that you should tell him that it has spread to his liver'; clinical colleagues will often look to clinical psychologists for advice on how best to manage these situations.

Clinicians may not come into contact with all members of the family at the one time, as might traditionally be the case in an outpatient family therapy clinic. It might take some weeks to build up a picture of how a particular family has responded to illness. Psychologists should determine the ways in which families have addressed problems in the past as this may lead to the identification of successful strategies or assist the therapist in recognizing characteristic problems and/or responses to problems within the family system. Clinical staff who work in inpatient settings are in the unique position of being able to meet many family members in the course of their involvement with inpatient care. They often make observations that can be useful in conceptualizing family response to illness.

Sources of information

Assessments should aim to incorporate a range of sources of information on the content areas that have been referred to. Questioning within a consulting room or at the bedside can be complemented by review of medical and nursing notes, interview of clinical colleagues, observations, the completion of self-report questionnaires and also of diaries. As with clinical psychology practice in general, there are many self-report measures that have been developed for use with people who have cancer. Some of the more commonly available measures will be briefly described, with some information on the circumstances in which they might be an appropriate component of an assessment.

The Mental Adjustment to Cancer Scale (MACS) (Watson et al., 1988) is a forty-item scale measuring coping styles used by people with cancer.

Respondents are asked to rate the degree to which statements apply to them (using a scale that varies from 'Definitely does not apply to me' to 'Definitely applies to me'). The MACS takes approximately ten minutes to complete and provides scores on five subscales. The subscales are: Fighting spirit, Helpless/hopeless, Anxious preoccupation, Fatalistic and Avoidance. A shorter version of this measure is also available (Watson et al., 1994). Osborne, Ellsworth, Kissane, Burke and Hopper (1999) suggested that the MACS may be measuring six independent constructs: Positive orientation to illness, Minimizing the illness, Fatalism (revised from the original MAC development work), Loss of control, Angst and Helplessness/hopelessness.

The Cancer Behavior Inventory (Merluzzi & Martinez-Sanchez, 1997a) assesses self-efficacy for coping with cancer. The brief version has twelve items and the longer version has thirty-six items. Respondents are required to rate the degree to which they feel confident in their ability to accomplish the behaviour being asked about.

The Functional Assessment of Chronic Illness Therapy and EORTC Quality of Life Questionnaires (Sprangers et al., 1998, 1999) are commonly used to assess quality of life among people with cancer and have the advantage of having good normative data and versions that are specific to tumour types and to cancer specific issues.

Clinical psychologists who intend to work regularly in this area should familiarize themselves with the range of measures that are available, e.g. Cancer Coping Questionnaire (Moorey et al., 2003) or the Cancer Worries Inventory (D'Errico et al., 1999). The Sexual Self Schema Scale (Andersen et al., 1999; Cyranowski & Andersen, 1998) has been used in studies of sexual responsiveness in gynaecological cancers and can be useful when sexual problems require assessment. It consists of a list of adjectives for which respondents indicate the degree to which the term describes them (on a 7-point scale ranging from 0, not at all descriptive, to 7, very much descriptive of me). The items that comprise the Sexual Self Schema Scale are embedded within the larger list of adjectives. Andersen et al. (1997) and Yurek, Farrar and Anderson (2000) have found that the sexual self-schema of their samples of women cancer patients accounted for significant amounts of variation in sexual responsiveness.

The Life Attitude Profile-Revised (LAP-R) has been hypothesized to have six subscales named as: Purpose, Coherence, Choice/responsibleness, Death acceptance, Existential vacuum and Goal seeking. Reker (1994) has suggested that composite scores can be computed for 'Personal Meaning Index' and 'Existential Transcendence' scales. This measure has been used in some work that has examined global meaning with regard to the presence of distress, quality of life and intrusive thoughts (Vickberg et al., 2000). The introduction of this theme within assessments can provide a way of asking about spirituality and religion. In addition to providing a useful way of identifying issues that can then form the basis for further assessment, self-report questionnaires can provide a means of quantifying symptoms and evaluating the impact of psychological intervention. White (2004) provides a review of some of the measures that have been used to assess meaning.

Using diaries for assessment

Using diaries and written records to collect information for review (see Schumacher et al., 2002 for experiences with a cancer pain diary) can help a patient recognize links between two or more variables, for example variables identified at interview and/or variables identified by other staff. The inclusion of an element of assessment that involves writing in greater detail about thoughts and feelings can also be therapeutic in itself (Stanton et al., 2002) and may help the patient clarify concerns.

FORMULATION

Following assessment, information needs to be synthesized into an explanation of the psychological factors and processes that are thought to account for the onset, maintenance and expression of the problems. Some of the many issues and factors that could be outlined within a case formulation and that are more commonly encountered within psychosocial oncology practice will be outlined in this section. Faulkener and Maguire (1994) have suggested that psychosocial adjustment to cancer is associated with six hurdles: managing uncertainty about the future, searching for meaning, dealing with a loss of control, having a need for openness, having needs for emotional support and having needs for medical support. They suggest that a failure to deal with these results in psychosocial problems. It can be useful in constructing a formulation to think about the extent to which these hurdles have been successfully surmounted. Using information from the assessment, a case formulation should offer an account of the psychological reasons why some hurdles are more of a challenge than others.

When information has been elicited on the presence, frequency and severity of psychological problems, the role of biomedical factors within the case conceptualization may be clearer. In some circumstances, this will be clearly apparent to a clinical psychologist with some knowledge about the common pharmacological and oncological contributors to psychological symptoms. Colleagues in oncology and palliative medicine will usually have considered these issues prior to referral or request for advice. In cases of doubt it is useful to discuss the potential biomedical mediators within the multidisciplinary team. The practice of clinical psychology in cancer care settings often results in clinicians being involved on a shorter-term basis than might be the case within adult clinical psychology practice. This can be because therapists are engaged in the delivery of brief interventions designed to address a problem that has not generalized to other life domains or when it is more appropriate to restrict therapeutic focus purely to symptom change (e.g. when patients are transferred to other care settings and continued psychological therapy is not possible). White (2001) has used the term 'problem level formulation' as a way of illustrating this level of work, as distinct from a 'case level formulation'. The following sections will outline some common themes often seen when formulating problems at both levels within psychosocial oncology.

Patients' perception of the severity and course of their cancer has a crucial role in determining their psychological responses. In most cases, patient perceptions are accurate and reflect what they have been told by their oncologists. However, there are some patients who have unrealistic perceptions, for example overly optimistic or inappropriately pessimistic views regarding their illness and its treatment. This can lead to problems, particularly when it becomes clear that their perception of their cancer is at odds with information from other sources (e.g. when they develop problems with functional abilities due to spread of their cancer). Expectations tend to influence emotional reactions in response to new events. When cancer recurs, patients who did not expect recurrence tend to be more distressed than those who at some level did expect it. When patient expectations and perceptions are included within a formulation, it is important to outline the hypothesized contributors to the perception (e.g. a longstanding avoidant coping style or the presence of severe distress at the time of information provision). Information on the range of internal (e.g. physical symptoms, memory of prior illness) and external (e.g. hospital attendance, comment by family member) triggering factors should be considered for each of the presenting problems within a formulation. Patients with a greater perception of discrepancies between actual experiences and ideal aspects of their self-concept tend to be more depressed (Heidrich et al., 1994).

The stage of an individual patient's 'cancer journey' will be important because the type of psychological problems experienced will depend on this. Patients (particularly those with higher risks toward vulnerability) are more at risk when the illness is diagnosed, during the early months of treatment, when all treatment has ended or when a recurrence or spread of the cancer is discovered. Patients within the first few weeks of their chemotherapy are likely to have formulations that include the presence of physical side effects, personal experiences of coping with treatment demands and emotions relating to considering whether the treatment is working. The concept of problematic re-entry to a pre-morbid lifestyle (Cella & Tross, 1986) can be used to conceptualize obstacles for patients who have psychological problems after treatment has ended (Arai et al., 1996).

All relevant aspects of the patient's current and past life experiences in relation to their cancer (e.g. how cancer-related problems link with events such as prior abuse or current problems with social isolation) should be included where this adds explanatory value. These experiences need not be events that have been experienced personally but can be experiences that have been observed. The presence or absence of adequate levels of social support often moderates the expression or severity of a psychological problem. Patients with high levels of trait anxiety may experience heightened sensitivity to somatic symptoms. Cameron, Leventhal and Love (1998) have suggested that this phenomenon may be a result of trait anxiety fuelling perception of heightened risk for illness, that this results in the formation of unhelpful illness representations, which in turn impact on coping and related behaviours. Cancer patients with high levels of trait anxiety are also likely to have higher levels of cancer worry and higher estimations of the likelihood of recurrence. Dispositional optimism should be incorporated into case level formulations as this can significantly buffer the levels of distress experienced by patients in response to cancer-related events (Epping-Jordan et al., 1999). The predominant coping pattern preferred by the patient should be outlined, as it may be that there is a restricted pattern of coping where patients rely on one strategy for all problems, as opposed to varying the strategy depending on the demands of the situation. Escape-avoidance coping has been consistently shown to be associated with distress (Dunkel-Schetter et al., 1992; McCaul et al., 1999) whereas emotionally expressive coping has been shown to have benefits (Stanton et al., 2000). Although the literature in this area tends to give the impression that coping style is consistent across time and problems domains, this is not the case.

A helpless response to the diagnosis is predictive of later affective disorder (Parle et al., 1996) and for patients with affective disorder, cognitive, behavioural, environmental and physical elements of helplessness need to be outlined. Patients who believe that they have been successful in resolving concerns are less likely to experience significant affective disorder. Conversely, having a low level of confidence in one's ability to resolve concerns may be a primary maintaining factor in depression and helplessness. The psychological effects of cancer and cancer treatments may also result in the patient becoming more avoidant in their thinking about illness, having greater illness concerns and diminished capacity to work (Cella and Tross, 1986).

A cancer diagnosis challenges a patient's core beliefs and assumptions about themselves and the world in which they live. Cella, Mahon and Donovan (1990) have suggested that more 'rigid' assumptions are likely to shatter. Patients who report prior beliefs with marked conviction ('I was sure that I was a healthy person', 'I was always in control of the way I reacted to life events') often experience more distress from having their assumptive world shattered. Lepore and Hegelson (1998) suggest that the integration of cancer into pre-existing mental models should promote psychological adjustment and that intrusions are markers of incomplete information processing. Patients who experience the same intrusive memory (e.g. of a relative's prior illness) for a few months are more likely to experience greater depressive symptoms. Patients who engage in greater levels of avoidance of memories experience greater anxiety. The occurrence of intrusive memories is often related to the reactivation of traumatic memories that have been incompletely processed. In such cases the problems lies with assimilation or accommodation of cancer-related experiences to existing schema about illness, cancer, self, their own mortality, the regulation of emotion or other personally salient schemata. A formulation should try to explain the process by which a patient's experience of cancer has been integrated (or not) with pre-existing mental models and outline how any intrusive thoughts or memories have been triggered and are being maintained. When patients have had past psychological problems that resurface or are exacerbated by the cancer diagnosis, this should be made clear in the formulation. Some people report a number of 'benefits' that they think about in relation to their cancer experiences (see Thornton, 2002, for a review). This information should be incorporated into the formulation as a positive 'buffer' of problem severity or frequency.

A psychodynamic perspective contributes to understanding the psychological impact of cancer by emphasizing the potential challenge to one's sense of self and the threat to the ego (Backman, 1989a). Early childhood experiences that define one's self can generate core conflicts that may be triggered by cancer. It is important to think about events within a patient's early personal history that may resurface during cancer treatment and/or have the potential to influence reactions to cancer experiences. Some patients, by virtue of being in the patient 'role', might come to be especially distressed in dependent situations or vulnerable to conflict with authority figures. Issues relating to separation, abandonment or mistrust can influence the psychological experiences of some patients. When defences such as denial, regression, repression of affect or intellectualization break down, patients become emotionally overwhelmed and unable to cope proactively (Backman, 1989b). For patients who have had early experiences when they have been unable to trust parents or significant adults within their lives, delays in diagnosis and/or problems with the provision of information about their disease and/or care may be particularly difficult.

Complex consequences can develop when family members have differing thoughts about cancer and the most appropriate responses to the psychological needs of the index patient. Misunderstandings that are the product of such differing views of physical illness can contribute to distress or, in some cases, to major family conflict. Family members might also have different feelings about the way in which the index patient responds to his or her illness. Most families will respond to the initial challenge of cancer within the family by gaining mastery of the situation at the initial phases. Some families have difficulty modifying their initial response to the illness when the acute phase has passed (Kreutzer et al., 2002). It is important to track responses within the family, with particular emphasis on the extent to which these responses seem to take account of changes in illness course, treatment or prognosis.

There tends to be a great variability in the knowledge and skill level of clinical colleagues when it comes to the psychological care of people with cancer and thus the concept of psychological case formulation and links with therapy may need a greater level of attention to explanation than, for example, would be necessary within a community mental health team.

PSYCHOLOGICAL INTERVENTIONS

Having completed an assessment of the problems and processes that are relevant in understanding an individual patient's experience of cancer and linked these in a formulation that accounts for the onset, maintenance and manifestation of presenting problems, clinical psychologists can begin to plan an intervention. As with general practice, a range of psychological models and constructs can be used to intervene. There is evidence to support the application of a range of interventions (Fawzy, 1999; Fawzy et al., 1995). Many of these target similar psychological processes, although they may do so using different strategies and in a way that emphasizes different processes of change. This section is divided into two: first, the range of processes that are commonly influenced by psychological therapy in cancer care settings are outlined; second, the main schools of psychological therapy are outlined, with guidance on how they might be used to address psychological problems in cancer care.

In practice, most clinicians will tailor their application of psychotherapy with people with cancer to take account of the presenting problems, and the treatment plan will include elements of educational, supportive, expressive or existential interventions. In this respect, psychotherapy with cancer patients illustrates the way in which differing therapeutic modalities can be tailored to the presenting problems and issues facing the person who is physically ill. Barrowclough (1999) and Burton and Watson (1998) provide helpful overviews of how psychological interventions can be applied in cancer settings.

The establishment of a psychotherapeutic relationship with someone who has a life-threatening or incurable disease can be overwhelming for clinicians (Anderson & Barret, 2001). Some clinical psychologists that I have supervised struggle to apply procedural elements of psychotherapy with people who have cancer, reporting that they are concerned that this might seem irrelevant or insensitive to the degree of life threat and/or the nature of the issues relating to impending death for patients with incurable disease. Although clinical psychologists are used to talking about issues that result in heightened levels of affect, when someone is dying it may seem insensitive to introduce issues such as defence mechanisms, conflicts, automatic thoughts or interpersonal relationships. Some report that they feel that simply 'being with' a dying person is more rewarding and less dismissive of the patient's plight. While facilitating emotional expression is important, therapists should not underestimate the value of pursuing a more 'active' approach to therapy, and should try not to let their own assumptions and issues about death and dying get in the way of more active parts of treatment. Experienced psychologists tend to incorporate such countertransference reactions into their intervention plans and know that they can significantly enhance the quality of life of someone with an incurable disease by balancing the supportive, expressive and problem-focused modes within therapy. Chochinov (2001) has developed what he calls 'dignity psychotherapy' to focus directly on the personal significance of death. This provides yet another way in which psychologists can integrate another dimension to their work with people with progressive, incurable disease.

Processes targeted in psychological interventions

Tackling avoidant behaviour and thinking

As with many presentations in adult clinical psychology practice, avoidance is often a significant maintaining factor for many cancer-related psychological problems. It may involve avoidance of people, situations or appointments and frequently extends to the avoidance of talking about cancer within sessions. Interventions should therefore target both the nature of the fears and thoughts about coping ability. All psychological interventions target this, although they differ in the extent to which they explicity emphasize this. Psychodynamically focused therapeutic sessions might reverse avoidance by focusing on emotionally charged material in transference and countertransference and tackle avoidance by making interpretations relating to defence mechanisms. This enables patients to gain insight into avoidance. Cognitive psychotherapy would tend to be more explicit about the role of avoidance and may set up behavioural experiments that show patients how avoidance reinforces their symptoms and demonstrate the benefits of alternatives to avoidance.

Avoidance is usually mediated by intermediate beliefs about the predicted consequences of not avoiding, for example the idea, 'If I talk about cancer then I will be overwhelmed'. Patients are often very reluctant to give up their avoidance behaviour and often need to be offered an explanation of why avoidance should be addressed, such as 'You seem to be reluctant to spend any time at the day hospice because you have been thinking that everyone will start to speak to you about death'. This may involve exploring advantages and disadvantages of the strategy and testing out the effects of dropping avoidance for a period of time:

Therapist: This is certainly a common experience of many of my patients. They would rather avoid everything to do with cancer than have the unpleasant feelings associated with facing up to whatever it is that they are avoiding.

Patient: My view is why feel bad if you can avoid it.

Therapist: I would agree with you. Avoidance certainly makes you feel better at the time. But some people find that avoidance does not work in the long run or that it gets more and more difficult to avoid unpleasant feelings.

Patient: It seems to work for me.

Therapist: It may be that there is no downside to your avoidance, in which case this may have nothing to do with the agitation and unpleasant thoughts you were telling me about. On the other hand it may be that it is the avoidance that is making things more difficult and we may need to work on helping you to reverse it.

Patient: I can see that it might be a problem.

Therapist: Do you find that there is any change in how often you have to push the thoughts out of your mind or how often you have to make an effort to avoid reminders of cancer?

Patient: I am not sure.

Therapist: Given the fact that your avoidance could be crucial in keeping your problems going, would you consider monitoring this for a week to see when and how often you have to do this?

Patient: If you can show me how to do that and you think it might help me.

This patient returned to the next session having discovered that she was having to engage in significant effort to avoid reminders of cancer. This was used to discuss the advantages and disadvantages of avoidance and to try out alternative strategies to address her urge to avoid unpleasant reminders. Modification of intermediate beliefs ('If I get frightening memories then I should block them from my mind') about avoidance can be combined with behavioural experiments designed to evaluate the emotional, cognitive and behavioural consequences of engagement with cancer stimuli. Patients should be advised to keep note of the advantages of reversing cognitive and behavioural avoidance. Reversal of cognitive avoidance is essential for patients who are experiencing problems related to intrusive memories, flashbacks and nightmares. Patients often find it easier to consider this if intrusive phenomena are normalized. Therapists may need to help patients address problematic meta-cognitions that influence cognitive and behavioural avoidance. Avoidance is often reinforced by the avoidance behaviours displayed by cancer care staff, who may themselves promote avoidance in their interactions with patients and have their own problems that relate to exposure to distress.

Facilitating control

Many psychological problems associated with cancer can be minimized if people can control the impact of the disease and treatment on their lives. The very process of engagement within psychological therapy (irrespective of psychotherapeutic orientation) provides patients with the experience that they may be able to exert some control over the problems that have resulted in their presentation for help. Group psychotherapeutic approaches also enable participants to learn more about the ways in which others have developed control over their problems.

To this end, the use of weekly activity schedules can be implemented during assessment and linked with intervention. Forward planning can be used to enable people to pre-empt problems associated with treatment by scheduling activities around treatment days. There may be occasions when a patient has to be in isolation, for example, because of an immunocompromised state or because of radioactivity (in the case of brachytherapy). The use of an activity schedule can be helpful and provide the patient with a structure to buffer the negative emotions that exposure to these scenarios can cause. Patients can be encouraged to keep written records of their fatigue and daily activity levels. These can be used to plan responses to fatigue and to schedule appropriate amounts of rest. The Multidimensional Fatigue Inventory (Smets et al., 1995) can be used to monitor outcome. Patients may have difficulty accepting the need for rest and the limitations that accompany a diagnosis. This can often be addressed by enabling them to set more achievable goals and changing the thoughts that make activity more difficult at times of diminished energy.

The following extract outlines how planning activities was discussed with a patient with metastatic ovarian cancer who was struggling to cope with weakness during a course of chemotherapy:

Therapist: You feel that there is nothing you can do, that the chemotherapy takes control over your routine?

Patient: It seems to get in the way of anything I try to do.

Therapist: Do you remember using the activity diary when we first met?

Patient: The thing on the grid?

Therapist: Yes.

Patient: Yes.

Therapist: I wondered if we could use it again, this time to try to work round the chemotherapy. You know when you have to come for it and now that you have been in twice we could probably work out when you were feeling at your worst and work around it.

Patient: I see. Keeping a note of what I do again.

Therapist: The main thing will be to make a plan, keeping a note of what you do will be a good idea though, as you can check out how the plan goes.

Patient: Right.
Therapist: When do you get the chemotherapy again?
Patient: I come in on Friday morning.
Therapist: What do you think then about beginning to make the plan from Saturday to Thursday? We can meet up again next Friday to see how you got on.
Patient: Just the idea of doing something to try to break the monotony helps . . .
Therapist: Good. Let's start with Saturday morning and what you usually like to do on a Saturday?
Patient: I usually try to get out to the supermarket for 8.30, for it opening, to miss the rush.
Therapist: When was the last time that you did that?
Patient: A month ago.
Therapist: How realistic is it, based on the past two chemo visits, that you will be able to do that on Saturday?
Patient: Mmm, I would like to be able to get it done, but I need to sleep.
Therapist: That's what this planning will be about, being realistic about what you can achieve. This way you can feel that you have achieved something. Before you were getting down because you did not achieve anything, mainly because your plan was not sensitive to the temporary changes in your life.
Patient: I see.
Therapist: Is there another shop that you could go to? Or could you go at another time? Or day?

Enhancing social, partner and family support

Given the pivotal role of social, partner and family support, the formulation for some patients will outline the central negative influence of a lack of a social network or adequate social, partner or family support. Here the therapist's role is to facilitate changes within the patient's environment; in the case of more prolonged therapeutic contacts, the psychologist will also become part of a supportive framework. Patients must first be helped to determine the main reasons why there is diminished social support. This could relate to hopelessness, procrastination, a lack of opportunity to socialize or anxiety. Diminished support may relate to individual family members feeling threatened as a result of the cancer diagnosis and/or having developed psychological problems that require intervention in their own right. Friends and relatives may avoid patients, resulting in less social support being available. When relatives are uncertain about how best to help the patient, therapists can arrange to provide advice on practical strategies and on how to overcome some of the obstacles to providing support. Significant others may need help to evaluate beliefs about the consequences of expressing negative emotion for example with ideas, such as, 'If I talk to her about her cancer, then I will make things worse'. The management of communication problems that have been triggered by the cancer is generally easier than scenarios in which communication problems are a longstanding feature of the patient's life and cancer is just another example of how it can become manifest.

Patients may have held beliefs about the support that they thought that they would have received from friends and family and become depressed when this does not materialize. Support may be withdrawn prematurely and/or be provided when it is not needed. Patients who are making predictions about the unrewarding nature of social interaction can be encouraged to identify and evaluate these thoughts and, if appropriate, evaluate them using a behavioural experiment. Some patients find that they have no idea what they will say to other people who ask about their cancer and may need assistance both in evaluating their predictions about this and developing skills to confidently manage these interactions. After spending time in session on skills training or role-playing things they can say to others, patients may go on to try out these new skills while in hospital or at a daycare facility:

Therapist: So you have very few contacts with other people at the moment?

Patient: I suppose so. That's why they want me to go to the day centre.

Therapist: Has that always been the case, that you don't tend to see too many people during the week?

Patient: No, I used to fill my week without a problem.

Therapist: What sorts of things filled your week that you don't have happening now?

Patient: I had my visits to the church lunches on a Tuesday, my sister visited on a Wednesday, I did some voluntary work on a Friday and Saturday was always my day for seeing the family.

Therapist: When was the last time that your week had this normal pattern for you?

Patient: Let me see, must have been about two weeks before the surgery, Yes, that would be the last time I had a 'normal' week for me.

Therapist: What would you see as being the main things that have interfered with you being in touch with other people like you used to be?

Patient: I don't know.

Therapist: Let's look at it another way. What would need to happen for you to have a week that was more like the ones that you used to have?

Patient: It would need to be two months' time. That's how long the doctor said it would be before I had fully recovered.

Therapist: That's certainly one way of looking at it. Can you think of any disadvantages of relying on the passage of time alone?

Patient: I get very low with no one around.

Therapist: That's what I was thinking too. Your depression does seem to relate to having few contacts at the moment. Is there any way that you could have contact with the people from your normal week but not have to go out and about to see them all?

Patient: I couldn't ask them to all come and see me.

Therapist: Could you ask some of, or even one of them, if they would like to come for a visit?

Patient: Yes, maybe they are waiting to be asked.

Handling uncertainty

The uncertainty associated with a cancer diagnosis triggers powerful emotional responses. All psychological therapies focus on enabling patients to articulate and express these. They differ slightly in the ways in which they might address this process. Psychodynamic and supportive-expressive psychological therapies help patients express and tolerate the powerful emotions linked with uncertainty. In some circumstances, the main vehicle of therapeutic change relates to the support and nurturance that the psychologist provides in enabling patients to 'stay with' this powerful emotion, contrasted with the pervasive avoidance that is often reflected in the responses of society and significant others. There is a huge variability in the psychosocial correlates of uncertainty. Some patients interpret this as a positive reason to 'live for the moment' and others tend to respond to uncertainty with hopelessness and fear. Some patients can accept the uncertainty associated with the course of their disease. They interpret this as an inevitability that cannot be avoided and are able to keep their thinking focused on what is known to them, without becoming preoccupied with 'what ifs'.

The way in which cancer services are delivered can worsen problems with uncertainty. Waiting for test results, how appointments are scheduled and the way in which information is provided to patients (as 'indirect' psychological intervention components) can all be modified with good result to minimize the problems of those struggling with uncertainty. Therapists should consider environmental and situational strategies as first-line intervention strategies. Cognitive intervention strategies for uncertainty begin by enabling patients to understand that it is not the uncertainty that is mediating their problems, but that it is their thoughts and beliefs about uncertainty that are causing difficulty. Life is always full of uncertainties but most of the time we choose to avoid thinking about this. The following extract illustrates how cognitive interventions can be used to enable patients to build a new way of viewing the uncertainties associated with cancer:

Therapist: The last panic attack was in the clinic?

Patient: Yes.

Therapist: That was the time that you were having thoughts that you were going to go mad and end up in a local psychiatric hospital?

Patient: I couldn't stand not knowing. The uncertainty was unbearable.

Therapist: This is perhaps something else that we could work on by looking at your thoughts, your thoughts about uncertainty and your ability to deal with it.

Patient: I need certainty.

Therapist: What would you like to have certainty about?

Patient: That the cancer will not come back.

Therapist: You want to be told for certain that the cancer will never return?

Patient: I know, I know I can't have that. That would solve the panic though.

Therapist: What is it about knowing it wouldn't come back that would help you feel less panicky?

Patient: I would know that I could control things again.

Therapist: What sort of things?

Patient: Well, I could still work, could still see my children and have some sort of life.

Therapist: Is it that you think that this is not going to happen, being with your children and having some sort of life?

Patient: When I feel panicky, yes.

Therapist: So, you think about the fact that you cannot be certain about the cancer coming back, this then leads you to feel panicky?

Patient: I just think, I can't deal with the uncertainty, it is going to drive me mad. It will all come back, I know it will.

Therapist: So your awareness of the uncertainty leads you to think things will go out of control, that the cancer will come back. Feeling more in control you think might help you to feel less panicked about it?

Patient: Yes.

Therapist: Perhaps we could also put together an action plan of all of the things you could do if the cancer were to come back. This might mean that you have less need to keep going over this possibility in your mind.

Patient: Not just yet, if I can feel more in control then I think I could just about face this.

Therapist: I agree, let's spend our next session on that topic, helping you to feel more in control and able to deal with the uncertainties in life.

Specific treatment modalities

Cognitive-behavioural and problem-solving approaches

Cognitive-behavioural interventions and therapies have been shown to be effective when applied to the psychosocial issues and problems experienced by cancer patients (Fawzy et al., 1995, Meyer & Mark, 1995). Moorey and Greer

(2002) have published guidance on the application of cognitive-behavioural psychotherapy with people who have cancer. Cognitive-behaviourally based interventions such as adjuvant psychological therapy have been shown to improve anxiety and depressive symptoms (Greer et al., 1992; Greer & Moorey, 1997) and be superior to supportive counselling (Moorey et al., 1998). Problem-solving therapy has been shown to be effective in reducing cancer-related distress and improving quality of life (Nezu et al., 2003). Some interventions, although not strictly cognitive-behavioural therapy, incorporate cognitive and behavioural strategies as part of a package of psychoeducation. There is good evidence of their application to depression (Barsevick et al., 2002) and pain (Devine, 2003) in cancer. Most cognitive-behavioural approaches to psychosocial morbidity in cancer are characterized by short-term approaches, consisting of time-limited interventions that enable patients to acquire strategies to regulate their feelings and behaviour in relation to cancer and its impact on their lives. They aim to enhance confidence with ability to cope with the hurdles which cancer can present and successfully manage the practical aspects of living with cancer.

In some circumstances, it may be necessary to devote more therapy time to the coverage of existential themes, particularly when working with those patients who have advanced disease. Kissane et al. (1997) outline details of this in an approach that they called cognitive-existential therapy. Concentrating on emotional expression as a therapeutic component is an important part of cognitive-behaviour therapy, especially with regard to 'realistic' thoughts and in the presence of avoidant coping. Cognitive-behavioural therapies can also be delivered in a group format for cancer patients (Bottomley, 1996). Supportive expressive psychotherapy has traditionally been delivered in this format and will be considered next.

Supportive expressive psychotherapy

Supportive expressive therapy has been traditionally delivered in a group and in the context of evaluating the impact of participation in such groups on survival. One of the major goals of this modality is to enable individuals to express a wide range of positive and negative emotions. Based on the premise that most people tend to avoid the fear and anxiety associated with the possibility of death, supportive expressive therapy enables someone to express and tolerate the affect associated with thoughts of death and dying. This has been referred to as 'detoxifying death' (Spiegel & Classen, 2000). It has been suggested that therapy with this focus may be more appropriate for patients with advanced cancer. The therapy consists of the building of bonds between participants, facilitating emotional expression, assisting with the redefinition of life priorities, enabling increased access to the support of family and friends, improving doctor–patient relationships and improving coping skills.

Interventions that focus on family dynamics

Family therapy has traditionally been applied to the psychosocial needs of families with a physically ill child (Finney & Bonner 1993; Wood, 1994), to the needs of families with children who have emotional and behavioural problems (Cottrell & Boston, 2002) and to the needs of families with adults who have mental health problems (Barrett et al., 1996), although this has been changing over the past two decades (Doherty et al., 1994; Speice et al., 2000). In psychosocial oncology, most family-oriented interventions seek to enhance communication and facilitate relationships that are sensitive to the emotional and psychological dimensions of the family member with cancer. Treatment goals often involve enabling patients to tackle avoidance of communication, particularly on emotionally charged topics such as death. Therapeutic work may focus on enabling families to ensure that cancer does not become a dominant feature in influencing all relationships and responses to everyday events. Families often find it useful to focus on the identification of shared assets and to engage in a process whereby they begin to prioritize the problems that face them or consider how they might have untapped resources that could be used to address problems. The majority of families are able to maintain a degree of stability, ensuring that the non-medical needs of the family are addressed. However, therapeutic time may need to be devoted to reinforcing the non-medical needs of the index patient (and possibly those of key family members, especially those of young children). This is particularly the case when a conceptualization reveals that families have been neglecting the well-being of individual family members or of the family as a whole.

Interventions with a psychodynamic focus

In psychodynamic therapies, a major goal is to enable patients to experience and express distressing emotions within a non-judgemental, supportive relationship. The therapist also helps patients to explore underlying conflicts, and understand their expression within current relationships. The aims when using a psychodynamic approach to psychological therapy with people who have cancer is to move patients from rigid, limiting defences to proactive, positive coping efforts. As with all psychodynamically based interventions in general adult practice, the therapeutic relationship with the person who has cancer is key to the process. The clinical psychologist working within this framework works towards enabling a patient to have deep trust within the therapeutic relationship, feeling able to let defences down and to open up and allow emotional exploration. Psychodynamic psychotherapy highlights unresolved childhood conflicts. This can help patients understand the role that these conflicts play in current relationships. This way, the patient can gather and experience appropriate support and re-establish a sense of personal control. Patients may transfer old feelings and ways of relating that were established with parents, causing distortions and conflict. Cancer (like any physical illness) can often foster dependency on the therapist. Patients can idealize their clinical psychologist as the 'only one who understands'. Patients may become extremely angry when the nurturance they seek is not provided and will often resist the therapist's efforts to guide or explore their psychological experience of cancer, particularly when there are unresolved authority issues.

Some patients project the anger that they have about the diagnosis and course of their cancer onto the therapist. The opportunity to work through these issues, to accept mature relationship boundaries, to face dependency needs or work with, not against, an authority figure can provide significant opportunities for emotional growth (Stoute, Shapiro & Viederman, 1996). Therapists also develop countertransference feelings, that is, emotional responses to the patient that may be rooted in the therapist's own needs and conflicts. The therapist may feel out of control and helpless to impact the illness. He or she may be uncomfortable in relation to signs of medical illness (e.g. scars and disfigurement), may fear loss and sadness if the patient dies, and may struggle with a need to nurture the patient and foster an unhealthy dependency. A psychologist may use his or her own defences to cope with these feelings, which will then influence the therapeutic relationship. The therapist pays attention to the patient's deepest unexpressed feelings, to help him or her understand and process those feelings. When the patient does not need to expend emotional energy defending against feelings, he or she is better able to cope with illness-related distress.

EXERCISE 18.1: DEVELOPING SKILLS IN THE MANAGEMENT OF CANCER-RELATED MORBIDITY

You have been asked to assess a forty-two-year-old patient with colorectal cancer who is 'struggling'. You have been told that this patient is significantly depressed and anxious and has frequently been saying to staff that 'You would feel like this if your life was threatened. Leave me alone'.

Split into groups of three and assign the roles of clinical psychologist, patient and observer. In roles, begin the process of assessment with this patient, paying particular attention to: (1) how you explain the process of assessment; (2) the main content areas that you cover; and (3) how assessment process and content might need to take account of this repeated statement that the patient's distress reflects the reality of his or her situation.

EXERCISE 18.2: DEVELOPING SKILLS IN THE MANAGEMENT OF CANCER-RELATED MORBIDITY

You have completed an assessment of a fifty-six-year-old woman with an incurable brain tumour who is on high doses of steroid medications. She lives alone and is very preoccupied about how long she will have left to live and feeling 'useless' as a person. She avoids thinking or talking about her cancer diagnosis and is very irritable with ward staff. You are told that she appears most irritable when her elderly parents visit. What further information might you wish to gather? What emerging hypotheses do you have that could be incorporated within the case formulation?

EXERCISE 18.3: DEVELOPING SKILLS IN THE MANAGEMENT OF CANCER-RELATED MORBIDITY

Consider some of the common emotional reactions to cancer (e.g. anxiety, panic, anger and sadness) and outline the ways in which some of the main psychotherapeutic schools of thought might conceptualize these experiences. Discuss in small groups the psychological processes that will be important in providing guidance on the management of each of these reactions.

FURTHER READING FOR PRACTITIONERS AND EVIDENCE SUMMARIES

Antoni, M. (2003). *Stress management intervention for women with breast cancer*. Washington, DC: American Psychological Association.

Baum, A. & Ndersen, B. (2001). *Psychosocial interventions for cancer*. Washington, DC: American Psychological Association.

Moorey, S. & Greer, S. (2002). *Cognitive behaviour therapy for people with cancer*. Oxford: Oxford University Press.

White, C. (2001). *Cognitive behaviour therapy for chronic medical problems*. Chichester, UK: Wiley.

FURTHER READING FOR CLIENTS

Antoni, M. (2003). *Stress management intervention for women with breast cancer. Participants workbook*. Washington, DC: American Psychological Association.

ASSESSMENT INSTRUMENTS

Derogatis, L. & Lopez, M. (1986). *Psychosocial Adjustment To Illness Scale (PAIS & PAIS-SR). Administration scoring and procedures manual.* Baltimore, MD: Clinical Psychometric Research.

Merluzzi, T. & Martinez-Sanchez, M. (1997). Assessment of self-efficacy and coping with cancer: Development and validation of the Cancer Behaviour Inventory. *Health Psychology*, 16, 163–170.

Watson, M., Greet, S., Young, J. et al. (1988). Development of a questionnaire measure of adjustment to cancer: The MAC scale. *Psychological Medicine*, 18, 203–209.

Weinman, J., Petrie, K., Moss-Morris, R. & Horne, R. (1996). The Illness Perception Questionnaire: A new method for assessing the cognitive representation of illness. *Psychology and Health*, 11, 431–455.

Weinman, J., Wright, S. & Johnson, M. (1995). *Measures in health psychology: A user's portfolio*. Windsor, UK: NFER Nelson.

REFERENCES

Andersen, B. L., Cyranowski, J. M. & Espindle, D. (1999). Men's Sexual Self-Schema. *Journal of Personality and Social Psychology*, 76, 645–661.

Andersen, B. L., Woods, X. A. & Copeland, L. J. (1997). Sexual Self Schema and Sexual Morbidity Among Gynaecologic Cancer Survivors. *Journal of Consulting and Clinical Psychology*, 65, 221–229.

Anderson, J. R. & Barret, R. L. (Eds.). (2001). *Ethics in HIV-related psychotherapy: Clinical decision making in complex cases*. Washington, DC: American Psychological Association.

Arai, Y., Kawakita, M., Hida, S., Terachi, T., Okada, Y. & Yoshida, O. (1996). Psychological aspects in long term survivors of testicular cancer. *The Journal of Urology*, 155, 574–578.

Backman, M.E. (1989a). Challenges to the self. In M. E. Backman (Ed.), *The Psychology of the physically ill patient: A clinician's guide* (pp. 15–22). New York: Plenum Press.

Backman, M.E. (1989b). Psychosocial issues and medical illness. In M. E. Backman (Ed.), *The psychology of the physically ill patient: A clinician's guide* (pp. 7–14). New York: Plenum Press.

Barrett, P. M., Dadds, M. R. & Rapee, R. M. (1996). Family treatment of childhood anxiety: A controlled trial. *Journal of Consulting and Clinical Psychology*, 64(2), 333–342.

Barrowclough, J. (1999). *Cancer and emotion. An introduction to psycho-oncology*. Chichester, UK: John Wiley & Sons.

Barsevick, A. M., Sweeney, C., Haney, E. & Chung, E. (2002). A systematic qualitative analysis of psychoeducational interventions for depression in patients with cancer. *Oncology Nursing Forum*, 29, 73–87.

Bottomley, A. (1996). Group cognitive behavioural therapy: An intervention for cancer patients. *International Journal of Palliative Nursing*, 2, 131–137.

Brennan, J. (2001). Adjustment to cancer – coping or personal transition? *Psycho-Oncology*, 10, 1–18.

Brewin, C., Watson, M., McCarthy, S., Hyman, P. & Dayson, D. (1998). Memory processes and the course of anxiety and depression in cancer patients, *Psychological Medicine*, 28, 219–224.

Burton, M. & Watson, M. (1998). *Counselling people with cancer*. Chichester, UK: John Wiley & Sons.

Cameron, L. D., Leventhal, H. & Love, R. R. (1998). Trait anxiety, symptom perceptions, and illness-related responses among women with breast cancer in remission during a tamoxifen clinical trial. *Health Psychology*, 17, 459–469.

Cancer Research UK (2003). *Scientific yearbook 2002/3*. London: Cancer Research UK.

Cella, D., Davis, K., Breitbart, W. & Curt, G. (2001). Cancer-related fatigue: Prevalence of proposed diagnostic criteria in a United States sample of cancer survivors. *Journal of Clinical Oncology*, 19(14), 3385–3391.

Cella, D. F., Mahon, S. M. & Donovan, M. I. (1990). Cancer recurrence as a traumatic event. *Behavioural Medicine*, 16(1), 15–22.

Cella, D. F. & Tross, S. (1986). Psychological adjustment to survival from Hodgkin's disease. *Journal of Consulting and Clinical Psychology*, 54, 616–622.

Chochinov, H. M. (2001). Dignity-conserving care – a new model for palliative care: Helping the patient feel valued. *Journal of the American Medical Association*, 287(17), 2253–2260.

Coates, A., Abraham, S., Kaye, S. B., Sowerbutts, T., Frewin, C., Rox, R. M. & Tattersal, M. H. N. (1983). On the receiving end – patient perception of the side effects of cancer chemotherapy. *European Journal of Cancer and Clinical Oncology*, 19, 203–208.

Cottrell, D. & Boston, P. (2002). Practitioner review: The effectiveness of systemic family therapy for children and adolescents. *Journal of Child Psychology & Psychiatry & Allied Disciplines*, 43(5), 573–586.

Coward, D. D. (1997). Constructing meaning from the experience of cancer. *Seminars in Oncology Nursing*, 13, 248–251.

Cull, A., Anderson, E. D. C., Campbell, S., Mackay, J., Smyth, E. & Steel, M. (1999). The impact of genetic counselling about breast cancer risk on women's risk perceptions and levels of distress. *British Journal of Cancer*, 79(3/4), 501–508.

Cunningham, A. J. & Edmonds, C. (2002). Group psychosocial support in metastatic breast cancer (letter). *New England Journal of Medicine*, 346(16), 1247–1248.

Cunningham, A. J., Edmonds, C. V. I., Jenkins, G. P., Pollack, H., Lockwood, G. A. & Warr D (1998). A randomized controlled trial of the effects of group psychological therapy on survival in women with metastatic breast cancer. *Psycho-Oncology*, 7, 508–517.

Cyranowski, J. M. & Andersen, B. L. (2000). Evidence of self-schematic cognitive processing in women with differing sexual self-views. *Journal of Social and Clinical Psychology*, 19(4), 519–543.

D'Errico, G. M., Galassi, J. P., Schanberg, R. & Ware, W. B. (1999). Development and validation of the cancer worries inventory: A measure of illness-related cognitions. *Journal of Psychosocial Oncology*, 17, 119–137.

Derogatis, L. R., Morrow, G. R., Fetting, J., Penman, D., Piasetsky, S., Schmale, A. M., Henrichs, M. & Carnicke, C. L. M. (1983). The prevalence of psychiatric disorders among cancer patients. *Journal of the American Medical Association*, 249, 751–757.

Devine, E. C. (2003). Meta-analysis of the effect of psychoeducational interventions of pain in adults with cancer. *Oncology Nursing Forum*, 30, 75–89.

Doherty, W. J., McDaniel, S. H. & Hepworth, J. (1994). Medical family therapy: An emerging arena for family therapy. *Journal of Family Therapy*, 16, 31–46.

Dunkel-Schetter, C., Feinstein, L. G., Taylor, S. E. & Falke, R. L. (1992). Patterns of coping with cancer. *Health Psychology*, 11(2), 79–87.

Edelman, S., Lemon, J., Bell, D. R. & Kidman, A. D. (1999). Effects of group CBP on the survival time of patients with metastatic breast cancer. *Psycho-Oncology*, 8, 474–481.

Epping-Jordan, J. E., Compas, B. E., Osowiecki, D. M., Oppedisano, G., Gergardt, C., Primo, K. & Krag, D. N. (1999). Psychological adjustment in breast cancer: Processes of emotional distress. *Health Psychology*, 18(4), 315–326.

Fallowfield, L., Jenkins, V., Farewell, V., Saul, J., Duffy, A. & Eves, R. (2002). Efficacy of a Cancer Research UK communication skills training model for oncologists: A randomised controlled trial. *The Lancet*, 359, 650–656.

Faulkener, A. & Maguire, P. (1994). *Talking to cancer patients and their families*. Oxford: Oxford Medical Publications.

Fawzy, F. I. (1999). Psychosocial interventions for patients with cancer: What works and what doesn't. *European Journal of Cancer*, 35, 1559–1564.

Fawzy, F. I., Fawzy, N. W., Arndt, L. A. & Pasnau, R. O. (1995). Critical review of psychosocial interventions in cancer care. *Archives of General Psychiatry*, 52(2), 100–113.

Finney, J.W. & Bonner, M.J. (1993). The influence of behavioural family intervention on the health of chronically ill children. *Behaviour Change*, 9, 157–170.

Gilbar, O. & De-Nour, K. (1989). Adjustment to illness and dropout of chemotherapy. *Journal of Psychosomatic Research*, 33, 1–5.

Goodwin, P. J., Leszcz, M., Ennis, M. et al. (2001). The effect of group psychosocial support on survival in metastatic breast cancer. *New England Journal of Medicine*, 345(24), 1719–1726.

Greer, S. & Moorey, S. (1997). Adjuvant psychological therapy for cancer patients. *Palliative Medicine*, 11, 240–244.

Greer, S., Moorey, S., Baruch, J. D., R., Watson, M., Robertson, B. M., Mason, A., Rowden, L., Law, M. G. & Bliss, J. M. (1992). Adjuvant psychological therapy for patients with cancer: a prospective randomised trial. *British Medical Journal*, 304, 675–680.

Heidrich, S. M., Forsthoff, C. A. & Ward, S. E. (1994). Psychological adjustment in adults with cancer: the self as mediator. *Health Psychology*, 13(4), 346–353.

Hopwood, P. (1997). Psychological issues in cancer genetics: Current research and future priorities. *Patient Education and Counselling*, 32, 19–31.

Ilnyckyj, A., Farber, J., Cheang, J. & Weinerman, B. H. (1994). A randomized controlled trial of psychotherapeutic intervention in cancer patients. *Annals of the Royal College of Physicians and Surgeons of Canada*, 27, 93–96.

Jenkins, V., Fallowfield, L. & Saul, J. (2001). Information needs of patients with cancer: results from a large study in UK cancer centres. *British Journal of Cancer*, 84, 48–51.

Kangas, M., Henry, J. L. & Bryant, R. A. (2002). Posttraumatic stress disorder following cancer. A conceptual and empirical review. *Clinical Psychology Review*, 22, 499–524.

Katz, M. R., Rodin, G. & Devins, D. (1995). Self esteem and cancer. *Canadian Journal of Psychiatry*, 40, 608–615.

Kissane, D. W., Bloch, S., Clarke, D. M. & Smith, G. C. (2001). *Australian RCT of group therapy for breast cancer*. Paper presented at the American Psychiatric Association Annual Meeting, New Orleans.

Kissane, D. W., Bloch, S., Miach, P., Smith, G. C., Seddon, A. & Keks, N. (1997). Cognitive-existential group therapy for patients with primary breast cancer-techniques and themes. *Psycho-Oncology*, 6, 25–33.

Kissane, D. W. et al. (1994). Psychological morbidity in the families of patients with cancer. *Psycho-Oncology*, 3, 47–56.

Kreutzer, J. S., Kolakowsky-Hayner, S. A., Demm, S. R. & Meade, M. A. (2002). A structured approach to family intervention after brain injury. *Journal of Head Trauma Rehabilitation*, 17(4), 349–367.

Lee-Jones, C., Humphris, G., Dixon, R. & Bebbington Hatcher, M. (1997). Fear of cancer recurrence – a literature review and proposed cognitive formulation to explain exacerbation of recurrence fears. *Psycho-Oncology*, 6, 95–105.

Lepore, S. J. & Helgeson, V. S. (1998). Social constraints, intrusive thoughts and mental health after prostate cancer. *Journal of Social and Clinical Psychology*, 17, 89–106.

Manne, S. L. (1999). Intrusive thoughts and psychological distress among cancer patients: The role of spouse avoidance and criticism. *Journal of Consulting and Clinical Psychology*, 67, 539–546.

McCaul, K. D., Sandgren, A. K., King, B., O'Donnell, S., Bransetter, A. & Foreman, G. (1999). Coping and adjustment to breast cancer. *Psycho-Oncology*, 8, 230–236.

Merluzzi, T. V. & Martinez-Sanchez, M. A. M. (1997). Assessment of self efficacy and coping with cancer: Development and validation of the cancer behaviour inventory. *Health Psychology*, 16, 163–170.

Meyer, T. J. & Mark, M. M. (1995). Effects of Psychosocial interventions with adult cancer patients: A meta-analysis of randomized experiments. *Health Psychology*, 14(2), 101–108.

Moorey, S., Frampton, M. & Greer, S. (2003). The cancer coping questionnaire: a self-rating scale for measuring the impact of adjuvant psychological therapy on coping behaviour. *Psycho-Oncology*, 12(4), 331–344.

Moorey, S. & Greer, S. (2002). *Cognitive behaviour therapy for cancer patients*. Oxford: Oxford Medical Publications.

Moorey, S., Greer, S., Bliss, J. & Law, M. (1998). A comparison of adjuvant psychological therapy and supportive counselling in patients with cancer. *Psycho-Oncology*, 7, 218–228.

National Breast Cancer Centre and National Cancer Control Initiative (2003). *Clinical practice guidelines for the psychosocial care of people with cancer*. Camperdown, NSW: National Breast Cancer Centre.

Nezu, A. M., Nezu, C. M., Felgoise, S. H., McClure, K. S. & Houts, P. S. (2003). Project Genesis: assessing the efficacy of problem-solving therapy for distressed adult cancer patients. *Journal of Consulting and Clinical Psychology*, 71(6), 1036–1048.

O'Connor, A. P., Wicker, C. A. & Germino, B. B. (1990). Understanding the cancer patient's search for meaning. *Cancer Nursing*, 13(3), 167–175.

O'Neill, M. P. (1975). Psychological aspects of cancer recovery. *Cancer*, 36, 271–273.

Osborne, R. H., Elsworth, G. R., Kissane, D. W., Burke, S. A. & Hopper, J. L. (1999). The Mental Adjustment to Cancer (MAC) Scale: Replication and refinement in 632 breast cancer patients. *Psychological Medicine*, 29, 1335–1345.

Osowiecki, D. & Compas, B. E. (1998). Psychological adjustment to cancer: Control beliefs and coping in adult cancer patients. *Cognitive Therapy and Research*, 22, 483–499.

Parle, M., Jones, M., & Maguire, P. (1996). Maladaptive coping and affective disorders among cancer patients. *Psychological Medicine*, 26, 735–744.

Reker, G. T. (1994). Logotheory and logotherapy: Challenges, opportunities, and some empirical findings. *International Forum for Logotherapy*, 17(1), 47–55.

Sadler, I. J., Jacobsen, P. B., Booth-Jones, M., Belanger, H., Weitzner, M. A. & Field, K. K. (2001). Preliminary evaluation of a clinical syndrome approach to assessing cancer-related fatigue. *Journal of Pain and Symptom Management*, 23(5), 406–416.

Sampson, W. (2002). Controversies in cancer and the mind: Effects of psychosocial support. *Seminars in Oncology*, 29(6), 595–600.

Schrock, D., Palmer, R. F. & Taylor, B. (1999). Effects of a psychosocial intervention on survival among patients with stage 1 breast and prostate cancer: A matched case-control study. *Alternative Therapies and Health Medicine*, 5, 49–55.

Schumacher, K. L., Koresawa, S., West, C., Dodd, M., S.M., P., Tripathy, D., Koo, P. & Miaskowski, C. (2002). The usefulness of a daily pain management diary for outpatients with cancer-related pain. *Oncology Nursing Forum*, 29, 1304–1313.

Smets, E. M. A., Garssen, B., Bonke, B. & de Haes, J. C. J. M. (1995). The multidimensional fatigue inventory (MFI) psychometric qualities of an instrument to assess fatigue. *Journal of Psychosomatic Research*, 39(5), 315–325.

Smith, M. Y., Redd, W. H., Peyser, C. & Vogi, D. (1999). Post-traumatic stress disorder in cancer: A review. *Psycho-Oncology*, 8(6), 521–537.

Somerfield, M. R., Stefanek, M. E., Smith, T. J. & Padberg, J. J. (1999). A systems model for adaptation to somatic distress among cancer survivors. *Psycho-Oncology*, 8(4), 334–343.

Speice, J., Harkness, J., Laneri, H., Frankel, R., Roter, D., Kornblith, A. B., Ahles, T., Winer, E., Fleishman, S., Luber, P., Zevon, M., McQuellon, R., Trief, P., Finkel, J., Spira, J., Greenberg, D., Rowland, J. & Holland, J. C. (2000). Involving family members in cancer care: Focus group considerations of patients and oncological providers. *Psycho-Oncology*, 9, 101–112.

Spiegel, D. (2001). Mind matters: Group therapy and survival in breast cancer (editorial). *New England Journal of Medicine*, 345, 1767–1768.

Spiegel, D. & Classen, C. (2000). *Group therapy for cancer patients*. New York: Basic Books.

Spiegel, D., Bloom, J. R., Kraemer, H. C. & Gottheil, E. (1989). Effect of psychosocial treatment on survival of patients with metastatic breast cancer. *The Lancet*, 14, 888–891.

Sprangers, M. A. G., Cull, A., Groenvold, K., Bjordal, K., Blazeby, J. & Aaronson, N. K. (1998). The European Organisation for Research and Treatment of Cancer approach to developing questionnaire modules: an update and overview. *Quality of Life Research*, 7, 291–300.

Sprangers, M. A. G., te Velde, A. & Aaronson, N. K. (1999). The construction and testing of the EORTC colorectal cancer-specific Quality of Life Questionnaire Module (QLQ-CR38). *European Journal of Cancer*, 35, 238–247.

Stanton, A. L., Cameron, C. L., Bishop, M., Collins, C. A. Kirk, S. B., Lisa, A. & Twillman, R. (2000). Emotionally expressive coping predicts psychological and physical adjustment to breast cancer. *Journal of Consulting and Clinical Psychology*, 68, 875–882.

Stanton, A. L., Danoff-Burg, S., Sworowski, L. A., Collins, C. A., Branstetter, A. D., Rodriguez-Hanley, A., Kirk, S. B. & Austenfeld, J. L. (2002). Randomized controlled trial of written emotional expression and benefit finding in breast cancer patients. *Journal of Clinical Oncology*, 20, 4160–4168.

Thornton, A. A. (2002). Perceiving benefits in the cancer experience. *Journal of Clinical Psychology in Medical Settings*, 9, 153–165.

Veach, T. A. & Nicholas, D. R. (1998). Understanding families of adults with cancer: combining the clinical course of cancer and stages of family development. *Journal of Counseling and Development*, 76, 144–156.

Vickberg, S. M. J., Bovbjerg, D. H., DuHamel, K. N., Currie, V. & Redd, W. H. (2000). Intrusive thoughts and psychological distress among breast cancer survivors: Global meaning as a possible protective factor. *Behavioral Medicine*, 25, 152–160.

Walker, L. G. et al. (1999). Psychological, clinical and pathological effects of relaxation training and guided imagery during primary chemotherapy. *British Journal of Cancer*, 80, 262–268.

Walker, L. G., Ratcliffe, M. A. & Dawson, A. A. (2000). Relaxation and hypnotherapy: Long term effects on the survival of patients with lymphoma. *Psycho-Oncology*, 9, 355–356.

Watson, M. (2000). What to do when a depressed or anxious cancer patient refuses further treatment. *Drug Benefit Trends*, 12, 5–9.

Watson, M., Greer, S., Young, J., Inayat, Q., Burgess, C. & Robertson, B. (1988). Development of a questionnaire measure of adjustment to cancer: The MAC scale. *Psychological Medicine*, 18, 203–209.

Watson, M., Haviland, J. S., Greer, S., Davidson, J. & Bliss, J. M. (1999). Influence of psychological response on survival in breast cancer: a population-based cohort study. *Lancet*, 354(9187), 1331–1336.

Watson, M., Law, M., dos Santos, M., Greer, S., Baruch, J. & Bliss, J. (1994). The Mini-MAC: Further development of the Mental Adjustment to Cancer Scale. *Journal of Psychosocial Oncology*, 12(3), 33–46.

Weijmar Schultz, W.C., van de Wiel, H.B., Bouma, J. et al. (1990). Psychosexual functioning after the treatment of cancer of the vulva. A longitudinal study. *Cancer*, 66(2), 402–407.

White, C.A. (2001). *Cognitive behaviour therapy for chronic medical problems. A guide to assessment and treatment in practice*. Chichester, UK: John Wiley & Sons.

White, C.A. (2004). The measurement of meaning in psychosocial oncology. *Psycho-Oncology*, 13(7), 468–481.

White, C.A. & Macleod, U. (2002). *Cancer in ABC of Psychological Medicine*. London: BMJ Books.

Wood, B.L. (1994). One articulation of the structural family therapy model: A biobehavioural family model of chronic illness in children. *Journal of Family Therapy*, 16, 53–72.

Xiaolian, J., Chaiwan, S., Panuthai, S., Yiang, C., Lei, Y. & Jiping, Li (2002). Family support and self-care behavior of Chinese chronic obstructive pulmonary disease patients. *Nursing & Health Sciences*, 4(1–2), 41–49.

Yurek, D., Farrar, W. & Andersen, B. L. (2000). Breast cancer surgery: Comparing surgical groups and determining individual differences in post operative sexuality and body change stress. *Journal of Consulting and Clinical Psychology*, 68, 697–709.

Zabora, J., BrintzenhofeSzoc, K., Jacobsen, P., Curbow, B., Piantodosi, S., Hooker, C., Owens, A. & Derogatis, L. (2001). A new psychosocial screening instrument for use with cancer patients. *Psychosomatics*, 42, 241–246.

ACKNOWLEDGEMENT

Parts of this chapter are based on joint work to be published in White, C.A. & Trief, P. (2005). Psychotherapy for medical patients. In G. O. Gabbard, J. Beck & J. Holmes (Eds.), *Oxford textbook of psychotherapy* (pp. 393–409). Oxford: Oxford University Press.

Chapter 19

Eating disorders

Alan Carr and Muireann McNulty

In our Western industrial culture, where food is plentiful, it is ironic that self-starvation and a pattern of bingeing and purging are major problems, particularly for young women. These two eating disorders – bulimia and anorexia nervosa – are addressed in this chapter. First, a case study illustrating the central clinical features of bulimia and an account of a client's progress through a psychological treatment programme is given. This is followed by a succinct account of the clinical features, epidemiology, course and aetiology of bulimia and anorexia. The use of motivational interviewing to engage clients with eating disorders in assessment and treatment is then outlined. An account is given of the assessment of eating disorders along with detailed guidelines for the evidence-based treatment of bulimia with cognitive-behaviour therapy (CBT) and interpersonal therapy (IPT). Two biomedical interventions are also mentioned: inpatient weight restoration programmes for emaciated clients with anorexia and the use of antidepressants in the treatment of bulimia.

CASE EXAMPLE

Linda was a twenty-seven-year-old woman referred for psychological intervention by her GP because of binge eating, purging and low self-esteem. At interview, she was appreciative of the chance to talk and eager to get help. Initially quite nervous, she responded well to invitations to tell her story and gave a clear outline of her current problems and experiences growing up. She was tearful and frustrated when talking about her problems with food. She also showed a wry sense of humour, pointing out the darkly funny side of her purging behaviour.

Linda admitted to feeling disgusted with her body, describing herself as fat and ugly. In childhood, she had been described as 'plump' and 'cute', but since adolescence she had felt deeply unhappy about her weight and shape. For at least ten years, she wanted to be three dress sizes smaller or 25 pounds lighter. She avoided looking at herself in mirrors and tried to hide her body from the gaze of others. Everyday she vowed anew to lose weight, berating herself for her 'failures' of the day before. She did not eat breakfast, drank several cups of black coffee throughout the day at her telesales job, and ate salad or fruit at lunchtime. At the office where she worked, there were frequently biscuits and chocolates available to staff. As the day wore on, Linda found herself increasingly pre-occupied with not eating these, so that it became hard to concentrate on her work. Often in the late afternoon she would eat some of this food, which only seemed to increase both her guilt and her urge to eat. Once at home, she cooked a low-fat, low-calorie, small-portioned dinner for herself, but was quickly hungry again. Her boyfriend would eat a regular-sized meal and then either play computer games or go out with his friends. Alone, Linda watched television and her cravings intensified. She became restless and unable to concentrate on anything other than her fantasies of forbidden foods and her struggles not to eat. Usually, late in the evening, she would go to a nearby shop to buy 'forbidden' foods, including salty snacks, ice-cream and cake, and return home to eat them quickly, in an almost trance-like state. Immediately she would feel relief from tension and anxiety, but soon after would feel remorse and guilt, leading her to either purge or use laxatives. She went to bed in a state of deep disappointment with herself and renewed disgust at her body and lack of 'will power'.

Linda was the second oldest of four children, with a sister a year-and-a-half older than her. Her younger sister was born eleven months after her, followed by her brother four years later. Her parents owned their own grocery business, working long hours to support the family. Linda described her mother as 'probably overwhelmed' by the demands of her daughers, born so quickly after each other. To ease the pressure on her mother, Linda and her younger sister spent a lot of time with her grandparents from the time her younger sister was born. She described herself as very close to them, admitting they fussed over her and spoiled her with attention and food treats. She was deeply upset by their deaths, within months of each other, when she was twelve years old. Linda and her sisters were sent to an expensive private school, where they were less well off than the other students. Aware that affording the fees was quite a sacrifice for her parents, she worked hard and her grades were average.

She thought her parents sent her there to appease their conscience about how little time they had to spend with their children. She regretted that they did not have more interest in how she was coping or achieving at school.

Linda had had two romantic relationships. The first was while at school. She thought she was so flattered that her boyfriend wanted to date her that she probably was too accommodating towards him and regretted having a sexual relationship with him. After five months, she realized that he was seeing another girl at the same time, a fact that apparently many of her friends knew. In the last two years, Linda met Pete, who worked as an accountancy technician, and they had lived together for about nine months. Linda thought she probably was too 'motherly' towards Pete, cooking and cleaning for both of them, but she also felt guilty that she would not let him look at her body and that she was only rarely interested in sex. She also thought she was 'too nice' at work, not standing up for herself and letting others take advantage of her. Her two goals for treatment were to 'sort out' her problems with food and to improve her self-esteem.

The above information was gathered from Linda over three assessment sessions, during which she also completed the Eating Disorder Inventory (Garner, 2005). Between sessions she kept a food diary and mood rating form. At her fourth and fifth sessions, an individualized formulation was developed with Linda, based on the cognitive-behavioural model presented in Figure 19.1 (see p. 727). Linda identified strongly with the model and expressed high motivation for treatment. She was offered fifteen sessions of cognitive-behavioural therapy (CBT) focused on bulimia. Low self-esteem and low mood was also discussed with Linda, both as responses to eating and body image concerns and as related to her feelings about the loss of her grandparents and what she missed from her parents in her growing-up years. Linda agreed to work on eating issues first. After her fifteen sessions of CBT for bulimia, she would review with the psychologist her mood, self-esteem and motivation for further work on these areas.

Over the next four sessions, Linda was presented again with the CBT model and encouraged to resume a regular eating pattern of three meals and two snacks a day, to refrain from purging and to complete self-monitoring forms for eating. This was very challenging for Linda. She felt ashamed to write down what she ate during a binge, fearing the psychologist would judge her as 'a pig' and 'stupid'. She was certain

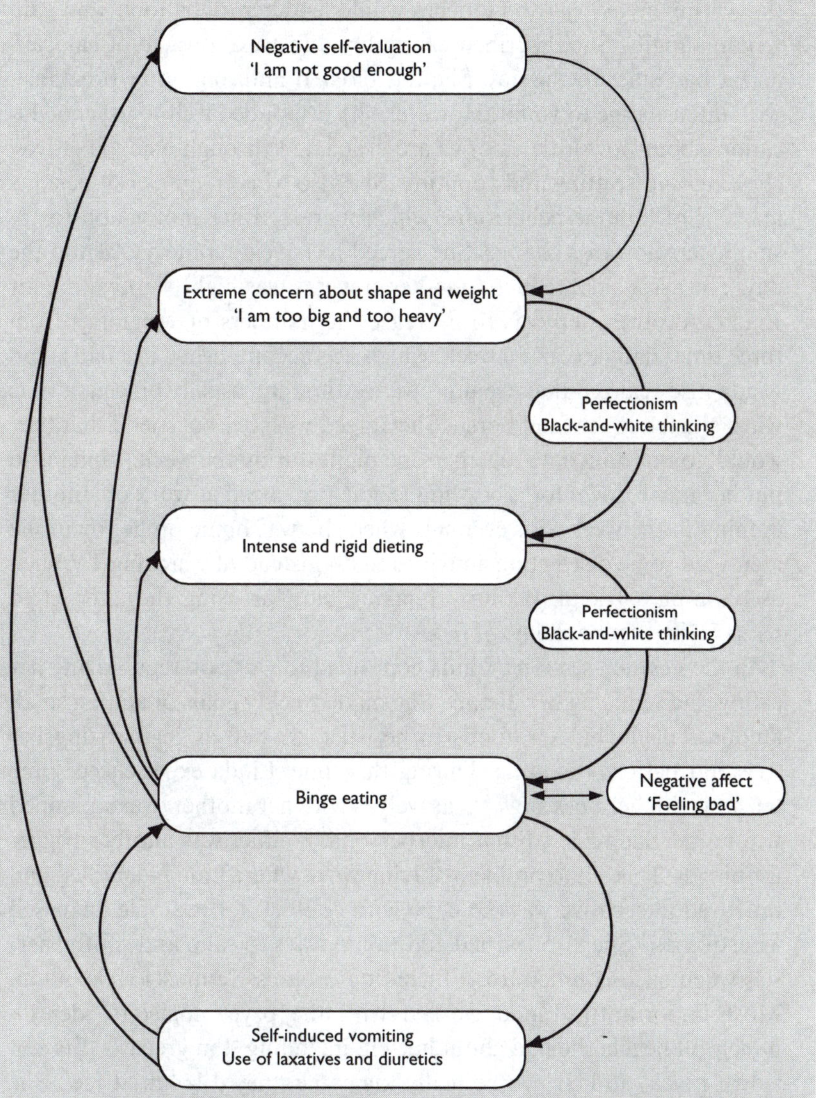

Figure 19.1 CBT model of the maintenance of bulimia nervosa (adapted from Fairburn, 1997).

that eating breakfasts and lunches would lead her to 'balloon' and gain weight rapidly. She described eating breakfast as 'a waste of calories' and a bad start to the day. She felt bloated and 'big' after breakfast, with intense urge to vomit. However, she responded well to psychoeducation about how little calories are evacuated through using laxatives, chewing-and-spitting and vomiting. She also worked on a cost–benefits analysis of bulimic behaviours, which increased her motivation to try small steps towards change. She agreed to try eating more often in the day. The associated reduction in her cravings was highly motivating for Linda. Another step was to decrease the numbers of weighings from three times daily to once a week, which was accomplished in small steps. Linda also realized that evenings were a time she usually binged, a time when she felt lonely and bored. She agreed with her boyfriend that they would go out on a date together one night during the week. Linda also put her name down for a bowling league organized at work on another evening in the week. For evenings when she was home on her own, she identified some distracting activities to do instead of watching TV, such as phoning a friend, taking a relaxing bath or using the internet to research her next holiday.

In the next ten sessions, Linda continued to work on regularizing her eating and reducing her dieting. She made weekly goals of adding small amounts of 'forbidden' foods to her diet, as well as regularizing her weekend pattern of eating. During this time, Linda experienced some tension with her boss at work, as well as with her mother over a planned trip home. She realized that interpersonal conflict was another trigger for binges. This led to problem-solving work where Linda identified and practised alternative ways to cope with conflict, for example increased assertiveness. She also learned additional ways to calm and soothe herself when such conflict arose, including progressive muscle relaxation. Most importantly, Linda worked with the psychologist to identify unhelpful beliefs she had about herself, including 'I'm greedy', 'I'm not worth much' and 'If people really knew me, they'd laugh at me'. She reviewed the evidence for and against these beliefs and conducted some experiments to test them out. For example, she predicted that if she gave her view at work, others would be dismissive or ridicule her. She agreed to try giving her view at a meeting with her boss and was surprised by his positive response to her suggestion. Through this work Linda identified a related belief that her needs were too much for others to cope with. This belief was harder to work on, but Linda made small steps in making requests of people who she trusted, including the psychologist by asking to change the appointment time to a time that suited her better.

The last four sessions involved summarizing and consolidating what Linda learned and making a plan for relapse prevention. She identified her triggers and ways of coping with cravings and difficult feelings. She worked to reframe her thinking about 'slips' and to identify ways to both monitor and reinforce her own progress. Linda attended a follow-up session six weeks later, at which she reported overall good maintenance of gains. She decided that she did not want to do more work on self-esteem or mood at that time.

CLINICAL FEATURES

Historically, anorexia nervosa was first described in modern medical literature by Charles Lasègue in France in 1873 and by Sir William Gull in the UK in 1874, and it was Gull who first used the term 'anorexia nervosa' (Gull, 1873; Lasègue, 1874; Mount Sinai, 1965). Both Lasègue and Gull described anorexia as a condition characterized by emaciation, an inadequate and unhealthy pattern of eating and an excessive concern with the control of body weight and shape. Attempts at subclassifying anorexia led to the establishment of bulimia nervosa by Gerard Russell (1979) in the UK as an eating disorder with a different clinical picture than anorexia nervosa. In the classification of eating disorders in both DSM-IV-TR (APA, 2000a) and ICD-10 (WHO, 1992), this distinction between anorexia nervosa and bulimia nervosa is a central organizing principle, with the former being characterized primarily by weight loss and the latter by a cyclical pattern of bingeing and purging. Diagnostic criteria from both systems for these disorders are set out in Tables 19.1 and 19.2. The distinction made between anorexia nervosa and bulimia nervosa, while descriptively useful, does not take full account of variations in eating problems seen in clinical practice. Many anorexic clients present with bulimic symptoms and many bulimic clients develop anorexia. For this reason, in DSM-IV-TR, a distinction is made between two subtypes of anorexia: the restricting type and the binge-purge type. In an appendix, DSM-IV-TR also contains a new, and less well validated, category of binge-eating disorder, which refers to bingeing in the absence of the compensatory purging which occurs in bulimia (Spitzer et al., 1992). Some, but not all, people with this diagnosis are obese.

Eating disorders are characterized by distinctive clinical features in the

Table 19.1 Diagnostic criteria for anorexia nervosa

DSM-IV-TR	*ICD-10*
A. Refusal to maintain body weight at or above a minimally normal weight for age and height (weight loss or failure to gain weight in a growth period leading to body weight less than 85% of that expected) B. Intense fear of gaining weight or becoming fat even though under weight C. Disturbance in the way in which one's body weight or shape is experienced, undue influence of body weight or shape on self-evaluation, or denial of seriousness of the current low body weight D. In postmenarcheal females, amenorrhoea (the absence of at least three consecutive menstrual cycles) Specify restricting type or binge-eating-purging type	For a definitive diagnosis the following are required: A. Body weight is maintained at least 15% below that expected (either lost or never achieved) or a Quetelet's body mass index of 17.5 or less (BMI = weight (kg)/height $(m)^2$) Prepubertal patients may show failure to make the expected weight gain during the period of growth B. The weight loss is self-induced by the avoidance of fattening foods, self-induced vomiting, self-induced purging, excessive exercise, use of appetite suppressants or diuretics C. There is a body image distortion in the form of a specific psychopathology whereby a dread of fatness persists as an intrusive, overvalued idea and the patient imposes a low weight threshold on him- or herself D. A widespread endocrine disorder involving the hypothalamic–pituitary–gonadal axis is manifest in women as amenorrhoea and in men as a loss of sexual interest and potency. There may also be elevated levels of growth hormone, raised cortisol levels, changes in the peripheral metabolism of the thyroid hormone and abnormalities of insulin secretion E. If the onset is prepubertal, the sequence of pubertal events is delayed or arrested (growth ceases; in girls breast do not develop and there is a primary amenorrhoea; in boys the genitals remain juvenile). With recovery, puberty is often completed normally but the menarche is late

Note: Adapted from DSM-IV-TR (APA, 2000a), ICD-10 (WHO, 1992).

Table 19.2 Diagnostic criteria for bulimia nervosa

DSM-IV-TR	*ICD-10*
A. Recurrent episodes of binge eating. An episode of binge eating is characterized by both of the following: 1. Eating in a discrete period of time (e.g. within a 2-hour period), an amount of food that is definitely larger than most people would eat during a similar period of time and under similar circumstances 2. A sense of lack of control over eating during the episode (e.g. a feeling that one cannot stop eating or control what or how much one is eating) B. Recurrent inappropriate compensatory behaviour in order to prevent weight gain, such as self-induced vomiting; misuse of laxatives, diuretics, enemas or other medications; fasting or excessive exercise C. The binge eating and inappropriate compensatory behaviours both occur, on average, at least twice a week for 3 months D. Self-evaluation is unduly influenced by body shape and weight E. The disturbance does not occur exclusively during episodes of anorexia nervosa Specify purging or non-purging type	For a definitive diagnosis all of the following are required: A. There is a persistent pre-occupation with eating and an irresistible craving for food; the patient succumbs to episodes of overeating in which large amounts of food are consumed in short periods of time B. The patient attempts to counteract the fattening effects of food by one or more of the following: self-induced vomiting; purgative abuse; alternating periods of starvation; use of drugs such as appetite suppressants, thyroid preparations or diuretics. When bulimia occurs in diabetic patients they may choose to neglect their insulin treatment C. The psychopathology consists of a morbid dread of fatness and the patient sets herself or himself a sharply defined weight threshold, well below the pre-morbid weight that constitutes the optimum or healthy weight in the opinion of the physician. There is often but not always a history of an earlier episode of anorexia nervosa, the interval between the two disorders ranging from a few months to several years. This earlier episode may have been fully expressed or may have assumed minor cryptic form with a moderate loss of weight and/or a transient phase of amenorrhoea

Note: Adapted from DSM-IV-TR (APA, 2000a) and ICD-10 (WHO, 1992).

domains of behaviour, perception, cognition, emotion, social adjustment and physical health.

Behaviour

At a behavioural level, restrictive eating is typical of anorexia. Clients report low calorific intake and eating low-calorie foods over a significant time period. They may cook for the family but not eat meals they prepare. Clients with anorexia present as thin or emaciated. They may wear baggy clothes to conceal the extent of their weight loss. By contrast, clients with bulimia are typically of normal weight. A cycle of restrictive eating, bingeing and compensatory behaviours is typical of bulimia. These compensatory behaviours may include vomiting, using diuretics and laxatives or excessive exercising. Usually, particular types of situation that are interpreted as threatening or stressful lead to a negative mood state and it is these that precipitate a bout of bingeing. Such situations include interpersonal conflicts, isolation and small violations of a strict diet, such as eating a square of chocolate; bingeing may also arise from alcohol intoxication. While bingeing brings immediate relief, it also leads to physical discomfort and to guilt for not adhering to a strict diet. Purging relieves both guilt and physical discomfort but may also induce shame and fear of negative consequences of the binge-purge cycle. Relatives who live with bulimic clients may describe aspects of their behaviour that aim to conceal their vomiting and excessive exercise as secretive. In addition to abnormal eating patterns, clients with eating disorders – especially bulimia – may display a variety of self-destructive behaviours, including self-injurious behaviour, suicide attempts and drug abuse. These self-destructive behaviours are often construed as self-punishments for not living up to perfectionistic standards or attempts to escape from conflicts associated with self-worth and individuation.

Perception

With respect to perception, in most clinical cases of eating disorder there is a distortion of body image. The client perceives the body or parts of the body such as the stomach, buttocks, thighs and so forth to be larger than they are.

Cognition

With respect to cognition, there is a preoccupation with food that is a consequence of dietary restraint. Low self-esteem and low self-efficacy are also common. Thus, many clients with eating disorders view themselves as worthless and powerless, and see achieving a slim body shape and low body weight through dietary restraint as the route to an increased sense of control over their lives and increased self-worth. This process is often compounded by perfectionist tendencies and a wish to attain exceptionally high standards. In bulimia, the repeated failure to sustain low-calorie intake leads to further self-criticism and low self-esteem and also strengths the belief in lack of control. In anorexia, starvation directly affects cognitive processes. There is an increasing rigidity and inflexibility in thinking style and a gradual reduction in the capacity to concentrate. In all eating disorders, there may be conflict concerning dependence and maturity. On the one hand there may be a fear of maturity and independence. On the other there may be a wish to escape from parental control and the lack of autonomy and privacy that this entails.

Emotion

Clients with eating disorders report an intense fear of fatness and depressed or irritable mood arising from dietary restraint. In bulimia, low mood may arise from binge eating and the sense of failure that this entails. In anorexia, low mood may arise from a failure to live up to perfectionist standards.

Social adjustment

Withdrawal from peer relationships, deterioration in family relationships and poor educational or vocational performance may all occur as a result of eating problems.

Physical health

The health complications of anorexia involve an endocrine disorder affecting the hypothalamic–pituitary–gonadal axis. This leads to amenorrhoea; starvation symptomatology such as reduced metabolic rate, bradycardia, hypotension, hypothermia, and anaemia; lanugo hair on the back; delayed gastric emptying; electrolyte abnormalities; renal dysfunction and zinc deficiency. In bulimia, erosion of dental enamel may occur due to vomiting. Lesions on the back of the dominant hand may develop if the hand is used to initiate vomiting. With both anorexia and bulimia, a particularly serious concern is that the client may develop electrolyte abnormalities that may lead to a fatal arrhythmia.

EPIDEMIOLOGY, COURSE AND OUTCOME

Anorexia nervosa and bulimia nervosa are most common among female adolescents and young women (Hoek, & Van Hoeken, 2003; Masjuan et al., 2003; Palmer, 2000; van Hoeken et al., 2003). About 1–2% of the adolescent and young adult female population suffer from eating disorders. Anorexia is less common than bulimia. The prevalence of anorexia nervosa among adolescent and young adult women is about 0.3%, and the condition is rare in young men. The prevalence of bulimia is about 1% and 0.7% for young women and men, respectively. The peak age of onset for anorexia and bulimia is during mid to late adolescence. Community studies show that, contrary to earlier data from clinical studies, there is not a significant relationship between eating disorders and social class. Since 1960 there has been an increase in the incidence of eating disorders in the UK and the US. While eating disorders may be more common in Western industrialized countries, there is growing evidence of eating disorders in non-Westernized cultures. In clinical rather than community populations, anorexia nervosa is commonly comorbid with mood and obsessive-compulsive disorders, while bulimia nervosa is relatively commonly comorbid with drug abuse and borderline personality disorder,

The outcome for eating disorders is poor but early intervention and evidence-based treatment can improve outcome (APA, 2000b; National Institute for Clinical Excellence (NICE), 2004; Steinhausen, 2002; Stice, 2002). For anorexia nervosa, about half of all cases have a good outcome, a third have moderate outcome and a fifth have a poor outcome. At twenty years follow-up, the mortality rate is about 6% (with a range from 0 to 21% across studies). Poor prognosis is associated with lower weight, a more chronic condition, the absence of a clear precipitating stressful life event, bulimic symptoms, comorbid obsessive-compulsive disorder, problematic family relationships, dropping out of treatment and lower social class. For bulimia nervosa, about half of all cases have a good outcome, a quarter have a moderate outcome and the remaining quarter have a poor outcome. Poor prognosis in bulimia is associated with later onset, a more chronic condition, more frequent bingeing and vomiting, greater body dissatisfaction, higher perfectionism, comorbid substance abuse, impulsive personality disorders and lower social class.

AETIOLOGICAL FACTORS

Under normal circumstances, when people are hungry, they eat until they have the experience of 'being full' and most of the time their weight is remarkably stable, as if homostatically governed. When people try to slim through restrained eating, they experience hunger, negative affect and become preoccupied with food. In response to these negative experiences, most people give up dieting and return to their usual eating habits and normal body weight. People who develop anorexia, however, redouble their efforts to maintain a pattern of restrained eating when they experience hunger, negative affect and intense food pre-occupation. In contrast, people who develop bulimia, engage in bingeing and later in compensatory purging. A variety of aetiological factors contribute to the development and maintenance of these eating disorders. These include genetic, temperamental, socio-cultural, personality, biomedical, cognitive-behavioural and interpersonal factors, all of which are addressed below.

Genetic factors

Evidence from twin and family studies show unequivocally that genetic predisposing factors contribute moderately to the aetiology of eating disorders (Eley et al., 2002).

Temperamental factors

Collier and Treasure (2004), on the basis of available evidence, propose that genetic factors contribute to temperamental dispositions that underpin the development of personality traits associated with eating disorders. These may be conceptualized as falling along a continuum from restrictive-anorexia-like disorders to disinhibited-bulimic-like disorders. The predisposing personality traits of perfectionism, harm avoidance and depression may place people at risk for developing both restrained-anorexic-like and disinhibited-bulimic-like eating disorders. Compulsivity and inflexibility may be the personality traits that place people at specific risk for developing restricting-anorexia-like disorders. Impulsivity and novelty seeking may be the personality traits that place people at specific risk for developing disinhibited-bulimia-like eating disorders. The assumption in this proposal is that the biological basis for each of these personality traits is polygenetically determined, and that through interaction with the environment the traits develop and predispose the person to developing an eating disorder. Thus, central to this hypothesis is the assumption that environmental factors play a key role in the aetiology of eating disorders.

Sociocultural factors

Epidemiological studies consistently show that eating disorders are more prevalent in Western societies where food is plentiful, thinness is valued and dieting is promoted (Nasser & Katzman, 2003; Szmukler & Patton, 1995). Also, since 1960, there has been a concurrent increase in the idealization of thinness and the promotion of dieting on the one hand and the prevalence of eating disorders on the other. This has been most pronounced in the case of bulimia. Furthermore, eating disorders are more prevalent among groups exposed to greater pressure to achieve the slim aesthetic ideal, such as dancers. Finally, the prevalence of eating disorders is higher in ethnic groups that move from a culture that does not idealize the thin female form to cultures that do engage in such idealization. While these findings point to the importance of sociocultural factors in predisposing individuals to developing eating problems, not all dieters develop anorexia or bulimia. Precipitating factors such as stressful life events and the presence of other individual psychological or family factors probably contribute to the development of eating disorders.

Life stresses and personality factors

There is some evidence that life stress, the absence of social support, negative affectivity, the internalization of a thin ideal body image and possibly other variables cumulatively predispose people to developing eating disorders

(Serpell & Troop, 2003; Stice, 2002). Serpell and Troup (2003) propose that four background predisposing personality factors render people vulnerable to developing eating disorders: (1) childhood helplessness; (2) childhood adversity; (3) low self-esteem; and (4) rigid perfectionism. In response to sociocultural pressures for thinness, these four factors give rise to four intermediate predisposing factors: (1) dietary restraint; (2) low shape and weight-based self-esteem; (3) disgust of food and food-related body stimuli; and (4) bodily shame. When stressful life events that involve managing complex interpersonal situations and relationships arise in people who have these vulnerability factors, an eating disorder may occur. These include problematic parent–child relationships, body weight teasing, peer group experiences and life events (Klump et al., 2002).

Biomedical factors

Evidence from studies of people with anorexia and participants in starvation laboratory experiments show that the neuroendocrine abnormalities and changes in gastric functioning that arise from experimentally induced starvation are similar to those observed in clients with anorexia (Frichter & Pirke, 1995; Singh 2002). The evidence also shows that more pronounced changes occur in anorexia compared with bulimia. Most of the starvation-related neuroendocrine changes occur in the hypothalamic–pituitary–gonadal axis, which governs reproductive functioning; the hypothalamic–pituitary–adrenal axis and the hypothalamic–pituitary–thyroid axis, which governs mood, appetite, arousal and other vegetative functions. There is also evidence that starvation leads to delayed gastric emptying and that this reduces hunger perception. One implication of starvation theories is that a distinction should be made between re-feeding programmes that initially aim to reverse the starvation process in anorexia by helping clients regain weight to help them become accessible to psychological therapy, and later therapy that aims to help clients maintain normal body weight and eating patterns.

With bulimia, one hypothesis is that bulimia is an expression of a mood disorder (Singh, 2002). Depression is often present in the family histories of people with eating disorders, along with other mood regulation difficulties such as substance abuse and borderline personality disorder. If bulimia is fundamentally a mood disorder, the biomedical hypothesis is that it is associated with a deregulation of neurotransmitters, notably serotonin, in those centres of the brain that govern mood and appetite. This theory has led to controlled trials of antidepressants. Both selective serotonin reuptake inhibitors (SSRIs) and tricyclic antidepressants (TCAs) have been found to lead to short-term improvements in bulimia but have no impact on anorexia nervosa (Wilson & Fairburn, 2002; Zhy & Walsh, 2002).

Cognitive-behavioural maintaining factors

Cognitive-behavioural models of anorexia and bulimia argue that certain people are rendered vulnerable to eating disorders because of personal and environmental predisposing factors, and once an eating disorder is precipitated by life stresses, cognitive and behavioural factors maintain the disorder (Shafran & de Silva, 2003). Predisposing factors, such as those listed in Table 19.3, contribute to the development of negative beliefs such as 'I am worthless', 'I am unlovable' or 'I am unattractive'. These core beliefs lead to the development of assumptions such as 'I must be thin to be attractive, successful or happy', 'I must do everything perfectly, for people to love me' or 'I must punish myself to be good'. Although these beliefs and assumptions develop during childhood, they do not have a significant effect on the client's life until they are activated by a series of critical stressful demands of adolescence and early adulthood. These precipitating factors include pressures to become emotionally and vocationally independent and competent, and pressures to be socially acceptable and thin. Once core beliefs and assumptions have been activated, in specific day-to-day trigger situations, they give rise to negative automatic thoughts conducive to dieting. For example, when dressing or looking in the mirror, the client may think 'I'm too heavy, too fat and too ugly'; or when hungry or eating the client may think 'I'm not in control'. These negative automatic thoughts typically involve cognitive distortions such as those listed in Table 19.4. These distorted negative automatic thoughts maintain restrained eating in both anorexia and bulimia. With anorexia, restrained eating is also maintained by the sense of control, self-worth and 'being special' that comes from achieving a thin body shape. Avoidance

Table 19.3 Predisposing vulnerability factors for eating disorders

Stress and support. Early life stress and lack of support including abuse and other family adversities are vulnerability factors for eating disorders
Self-esteem. Low self-esteem generally and low self-esteem associated with weight and shape specifically are risk factors for eating disorders
Emotions. Depression and anxiety are vulnerability factors for eating disorders. People with anorexia tend to be alexithymic (have difficulty putting emotions into words) and in both anorexia and bulimia restrained eating or bingeing are ways of avoiding or regulating negative emotions
Perfectionism. Perfectionism, obsessionality, compulsivity, inflexibility and related disorders such as OCD or OCD personality disorder are vulnerability factors for anorexia
Impulsivity. Impulsivity and related disorders such as substance abuse or borderline personality disorder are vulnerability factors for bulimia
Psychological disorders. A personal and/or family history of eating disorders and other psychological disorders are vulnerability factors for eating disorders
Thin ideal. Family, peer group and societal pressures to be thin are vulnerability factors for eating disorders

OCD, obsessive-compulsive disorder.

Table 19.4 Cognitive distortions

All or nothing thinking. Thinking in extreme categorical terms, for example 'If I'm not in complete control, then I have no control whatsoever'
Selective abstraction. Selectively focusing on a small aspect of a situation and drawing conclusions from this, for example 'I will only be good if I am thin and nothing else matters'
Overgeneralization. Generalizing from one instance to all possible instances, for example 'I ate too much last night, so I will always eat too much'
Magnification. Exaggerating the significance of an event, for example 'I gained a pound, so I know that I will never be able to wear a mini-skirt again'
Personalization. Attributing negative feeling of others to the self, for example 'If people see me, I will ruin their day because I'm fat'
Emotional reasoning. Taking feelings as facts, for example 'I feel fat so I am fat'

of fatness also maintains restrained eating, although the margin of safety required to avoid fatness increases as the disorder progresses. Furthermore, the process of starvation induces cognitive inflexibility, which strengthens the cognitive distortions, such as black-and-white thinking, which characterizes the thinking of clients with anorexia, which in turn maintains dietary restriction. Family and peer-group approval for thinness also reinforce dietary restraint. In bulimia, a different pattern occurs. After a period of restraint certain stressful trigger situations lead to binge eating, which in turn triggers guilt for over-eating and related negative automatic thoughts about shape and weight, which in turn leads to compensatory vomiting, laxative use and other forms of purging, and a commitment to redouble dietary restraint. Fairburn's formulation (1997) of this process is given below in the section on CBT for bulimia. A behavioural pattern of weighing and checking the size of body parts increases the salience of perceived deficits in body weight and shape (in the case of bulimia) and perceived thinness (in the case of anorexia) which in turn increases motivation for restrained eating. For young adults with bulimia, cognitive-behavioural therapy is the treatment of choice (Wilson & Fairburn, 2002). This therapy, described below, helps clients to map out the binge-purge cycle, to monitor eating patterns and related cognitions and contingencies, and to use cognitive and behavioural strategies to disrupt the cycle and manage relapses. There is also some evidence for the effectiveness of CBT for anorexia.

Interpersonal maintaining factors

In interpersonal therapy (IPT) for bulimia, it is assumed that the four categories of interpersonal difficulties listed in Table 19.5 maintain eating disorders: grief, role disputes, role transitions and interpersonal deficits, a position supported by a growing body of evidence (Wilfley, Stein & Welch, 2003). Interpersonal therapy, which is an effective treatment for bulimia, alleviates the

Table 19.5 Interpersonal maintaining factors

Grief. Associated with the loss of a loved one
Role disputes. Involving family members, friends or colleagues
Role transitions. Such as starting or ending relationships within the family or work context, moving jobs or house, graduation, promotion, retirement, or diagnosis of an illness
Interpersonal deficits. Particularly poor social skills for making and maintaining relationships

condition by helping clients resolve problems that maintain the pattern of bingeing and purging in these areas (Wilson & Fairburn, 2002). A detailed account of IPT for bulimia is given below.

ENGAGEMENT

To benefit from assessment and treatment, clients with eating disorders need to engage effectively with services and establish a good working alliance with clinicians providing that service. This is often challenging because of the ambivalence many clients with eating disorders have about seeking treatment. For this reason, special attention needs to be devoted to the process of engagement. A useful approach is motivational interviewing, which is based on the transtheoretical stages of change model.

Stages of change

In the transtheoretical stages of change model distinctions are made between the stages of precontemplation, contemplation, preparation, action and maintenance (Miller & Rollnick, 2002; Prochaska & Velicer, 1997a, 1997b; Treasure & Bauer, 2003). Clients at the precontemplation stage deny that they have a problem and usually have come for assessment at the request of a family member or concerned person. Their aim in seeking consultation is to prevent the family member or concerned person from nagging them about their eating pattern or weight. Those at the contemplation stage accept that there is a problem but are ambivalent about resolving it. People in these early stages of change require an opportunity to discuss whether or not they think they have a significant problem and, if they agree that they do, it is useful to discuss the costs and benefits of trying to change. Some of the costs and benefits of eating disorders are given in Table 19.6. Offering clients at the precontemplation or contemplation stages advice on how to change may lead to resistance or treatment drop-out. Clients at the preparation stage have accepted that they have an eating disorder and want to make effective plans to overcome it. Those at the action stage are currently trying to overcome their disorder. Those at the maintenance stage have overcome the disorder but

Table 19.6 Costs and benefits of eating disorders

Disorder	*Costs*	*Benefits*
Anorexia	Hunger Tiredness Low mood Poor concentration Sensitivity to cold Sleep disturbances Weak bladder Constipation Periods stop and infertility occurs Excessive body hair growth Swelling of ankles Thin bones Anaemia Stunted growth	Slim shape Low weight Approval from others Sense of being in control Sense of being special
Bulimia	Hunger Tiredness Low or irritable mood Dental problems – erosion of tooth enamel Mouth ulcers Throat haemorrhages Chronic hoarseness Swollen cheeks Acid reflux and chronic regurgitation of food Diarrhoea or constipation Dry hair and bloodshot eyes Oedema Electrolyte imbalance Irregular heart beats (arrhythmia) leading to palpitations, chest pain and fits	The prospect of a slim shape The prospect of a low weight The prospect of approval from others Sense of being in control

require help with relapse prevention and management. To maximize their chances of success, clients at the preparation, action and maintenance stages require evidence-based treatments that involve planning and implementing strategies to overcome eating problems. At intake interviews the majority of clients are in precontemplation or contemplation stages of change. Thus, most clients who come to psychologists either deny that there is a problem or are ambivalent about resolving their eating problems. On the one hand, they wish to feel better and healthier, or to appease the concerned family member who has arranged the appointment. On the other hand, they may wish to retain what they view as the benefits of their disorder, including in anorexia, a slim shape, low weight and approval from others; and in bulimia the prospect of these factors. Both anorexia and bulimia may also involve a tenuous sense of being in control or of being special for engaging in restrained eating.

Motivational interviewing

Clients in precontemplation and contemplation stages of change may benefit from motivational interviewing, which helps people move from precontemplation and contemplation to preparation, action and maintenance stages of change (Miller & Rollnick, 2002). There are six key aspects to motivational interviewing: (1) understand the client's frame of reference; (2) express acceptance and affirmation of clients and their frames of reference; (3) when summarizing and feeding back what clients have said, give prominence to statements that indicated that they recognize that they have a problem that they may wish to change, and give less emphasis to statements about maintaining the status quo; (4) use questions that elicit emotive statements from clients in which they recognize that they have problem about which they are concerned, which they believe they can change and which they intend to change; (5) match interventions to the stage of change and do not jump ahead of the client, by, for example, proceeding to preparation when the client is still at contemplation and needs to explore the pros and cons of change; (6) affirm the client's freedom of choice and self-direction. Motivational interviewing works by reducing the sort of resistance elicited by confrontation, and by fostering a strong therapeutic alliance through collaboration.

ASSESSMENT

Alongside the process of engagement and establishment of a therapeutic alliance, comprehensive assessment should be conducted. Assessment should be carried out by a multi-disciplinary team and cover the client's physical, nutritional and psychological state (APA, 2000b; Bell et al., 2001; NICE, 2004; Royal College of Psychiatrists, 2002). Assessment should include individual interviews with clients and collateral or conjoint interviews with partners, parents or concerned others. Assessment interviews may cover the circumstances of referral; the primary concerns of the client and of the concerned person if such a person prompted the referral; the client's current daily eating, starving, bingeing and exercising patterns and cognitions related to these; history of dieting, weight and menstruation; use of diuretics; medical, psychological and social history; history of previous psychological and psychiatric treatment for eating disorders and other disorders; history and current status of possible comorbid disorders including depression, anxiety, obsessive-compulsive disorder, drug and alcohol abuse, borderline personality disorder; and possible predisposing, precipitating and maintaining factors relevant to the eating disorder. Where appropriate, dietary histories may be taken in conjoint interviews with a nutritionist.

A full medical examination should routinely be conducted to assess current health, medical risk and inpatient care needs. Criteria for inpatient care are described below. Height and weight measurements may taken to determine body mass index (BMI). BMI is calculated by dividing the weight in kilograms by the height in metres squared. A normal BMI falls between about 19 and 25. Precautions must be taken to ensure that adolescents do not artificially increase their weight by putting weights in their pockets or by drinking excess fluid prior to weighing.

Some psychometric instruments that may be useful in the assessment of clients with eating disorders are listed at the end of the chapter. Of these, the Eating Disorder Examination (Cooper & Fairburn, 1987) is considered the diagnostic gold standard and the third edition of the Eating Disorder Inventory (Garner, 2005) is the most comprehensive and best-validated self-report psychological assessment instrument for assessing eating pathology and related psychological traits.

On the basis of the assessment, a preliminary formulation may be drawn up. This should link predisposing, precipitating and maintaining factors to the abnormal eating pattern and specify protective factors that may be drawn on during treatment. For both CBT (Fairburn, 1997; Fairburn et al., 1993) and IPT (Wilfley et al., 2003) of bulimia, quite specific formulation models have been developed and sharing such formulations with clients is central to the treatment process. Both therapy protocols have been found to be effective in about two-thirds of cases (Wilson & Fairburn, 2002).

TREATMENT

Cognitive-behavioural treatment of bulimia

Manualized CBT, typically conducted over ten to twenty sessions, aims to disrupt the binge-purge cycle and modify the belief systems that underpin this cycle (Fairburn, 1997; Fairburn et al., 1993). In the first stage, the client is helped to understand the cognitive-behavioural view on the maintenance of bulimia and the implications of this for resolving the eating problems. Behavioural techniques are employed to help the client begin to replace the binge-eating pattern with a more normal eating pattern. In the second stage, attempts are made to establish healthy eating habits with a particular focus on eliminating dieting. It is during this stage that clients learn to challenge the beliefs and values concerning shape, weight and self-worth that are maintaining their eating disorder. Maintenance of therapeutic gains and relapse prevention are the focus of the third stage of therapy.

Stage 1: Rationale for CBT treatment of bulimia and addressing binge eating

The two main goals of the first stage are to establish the rationale for a CBT approach to treatment and to replace binge eating with a regular eating pattern. The psychologist initially develops therapeutic relationships with the client through the process of history taking, presenting a CBT formulation of the client's binge-purge cycle, and offering a contract for treatment. This stage spans eight weekly sessions, some of which may be conducted conjointly with the client's concerned family members and some with the client alone. With history taking, in addition to the areas outlined previously in the section on assessment, detailed information is gathered on the client's attitudes to shape and weight (including the importance attached to shape and weight, desired weight and cognitive, emotional and behavioural reactions to comments about shape and weight); eating habits (including daily eating pattern, dieting and bingeing); weight control methods (including self-induced vomiting; use of laxatives, purgatives and diuretics; and exercise); and current medical status particularly the status of the client's electrolytes.

Rationale and formulation

In presenting the formulation, the model presented in Figure 19.1 is used. Usually, binge eating is presented as the central concern. The client wishes to stop bingeing but feels out of control. With this in mind, certain key points should be made in presenting the formulation. First, dieting maintains binge eating because it leads to feelings of intense hunger and negative affect. Second, this negative affect is intensified in specific trigger situations. Clients interpret these trigger situations (such as noticing that they are not slim) in a negative way (due to perfectionism, black-and-white thinking or other cognitive distortions) and these negative appraisals intensify negative mood states. For example, they may think 'I want to be slim, I never will be, I feel terrible, eating is the only thing that will comfort me'. Binge eating is a short-term way of improving the negative mood states associated with these negative automatic thoughts. Third, vomiting and purging also maintain binge eating because clients hold the mistaken belief that these are effective methods for calorie control; the act of vomiting brings relief because of these erroneous beliefs. For example, a client may hold the following beliefs 'I've stuffed myself and I will get very fat unless I get this food out of my system now. I must be perfectly thin or I'm no good, I feel completely guilty for having eaten so much and having no will power, so I'll vomit. That's a relief, now that I've vomited. I will diet from now on'. Fourth, the belief that high self-worth will arise from a slim shape and low weight promotes extreme dieting, in part because clients adopt a perfectionistic thinking style and tend to think in black-and-white terms. For example, clients may hold beliefs such as 'I must be the perfect shape otherwise no one will like me' or 'Either I'm thin or I'm fat, good or bad, there is no middle ground'. Fifth, over-concern about shape and weight is linked to longstanding negative self-evaluation. This may include beliefs that the client has little intrinsic worth as a person and has very little power to change this, except through maintaining a slim shape and low weight. While these five general issues should be addressed in presenting the formulation, it should be customized in each case to the unique circumstances and beliefs of the client in question. It is useful to draw the formulation, as given in Figure 19.1, for the client and parents working from the bottom of the diagram (the bingeing and vomiting cycle) upwards. The formulation may be revisited regularly throughout the process of treatment.

When clients understand this CBT formulation they may be offered a contract for treatment. The client is informed that the treatment will span about twenty sessions; that it is likely to be effective in about two out of three cases, and so is not a guaranteed cure; that the client will be invited to complete tasks between sessions and that a strong commitment to therapy and to following through on therapeutic tasks is essential for success. The treatment tasks aim to break the cycles contained in the formulation model in Figure 19.1. Clients may be told that initially treatment will focus on their central concerns, the behaviour pattern of bingeing and vomiting at the bottom of Figure 19.1, but for treatment to be effective, later they must focus on dieting. In particular they must address clients' beliefs about themselves, their weight, and their shape that underpin chronic dieting, since chronic dieting sets the stage for bingeing.

Self-monitoring

The first treatment task is to complete self-monitoring sheets on which clients record exactly what they eat each day, the time when it is eaten, the place, whether the client considered the episode of eating to be a binge, whether it was followed by vomiting or laxative use, and the overall circumstances and context under which the eating occurred. A self-monitoring form is presented in Table 19.7. The second session, and all subsequent sessions, begins with a review of self-monitoring forms. In the final column of the self-monitoring form, clients record the situation and their thoughts about it. By regularly reviewing this material throughout treatment, clients may be helped to identify negative automatic thoughts, cognitive distortions, assumptions and core beliefs that underpin their eating disorder.

Weekly weighing

The second task is for clients to agree to weekly rather than daily weighing. They should weigh themselves once, and once only, each week throughout treatment on a morning of their choice. When clients are weighing themselves

Table 19.7 Self-monitoring form for bulimia

<table>
<tr><td colspan="7">To understand your eating habits, it is important for you to keep a detailed daily record of everything you eat and drink and the related circumstances.
In the first column write down the time of day, e.g. 9.15 a.m.
In the second column write down what you ate and drank, e.g. 3 slices of toast and marmalade and 3 cups of coffee with milk and two sugars.
In the third column write down where you ate them, e.g. In the kitchen.
In the fourth column put an X if you think this was bingeing (eating too much)
In the fifth column put an X if you vomited after you ate the food.
In the sixth column put a D if you took a diuretic, put an L if you took a laxative, put an E if you did some exercise to burn off the food you ate.
In the seventh column write down you comments on the situation and what you were thinking, e.g. I was upset because I thought I looked fat in the mirror in my school uniform. I said this to my mum and she started to argue with me. I thought 'I'm so fat. No one understands me and no one likes me.' Then I ate a lot to make me feel better. Then I made myself sick. I felt a bit of relief then.
Also in the seventh column write down your weight on the one morning a week you weigh yourself.
Complete this form every day and bring all the forms you complete to every meeting to review with your therapist.</td></tr>
<tr><td colspan="7">Date</td></tr>
<tr><td>Time</td><td>Food and drink consumed</td><td>Place</td><td>Binge</td><td>Vomit</td><td>Laxative/ diuretic/ exercise</td><td>The situation and what you thought</td></tr>
<tr><td></td><td></td><td></td><td></td><td></td><td></td><td></td></tr>
<tr><td></td><td></td><td></td><td></td><td></td><td></td><td></td></tr>
<tr><td></td><td></td><td></td><td></td><td></td><td></td><td></td></tr>
<tr><td></td><td></td><td></td><td></td><td></td><td></td><td></td></tr>
<tr><td></td><td></td><td></td><td></td><td></td><td></td><td></td></tr>
<tr><td></td><td></td><td></td><td></td><td></td><td></td><td></td></tr>
<tr><td></td><td></td><td></td><td></td><td></td><td></td><td></td></tr>
<tr><td></td><td></td><td></td><td></td><td></td><td></td><td></td></tr>
</table>

many times each day, this new weighing pattern may be introduced gradually. In this form of treatment, the therapist weighs the client only during the initial assessment interview and at the end of treatment, to avoid the therapy becoming over-focused on weight-related issues.

Reading self-help books

The third task is for the client and parents to read CBT bulimia self-help books, such as those listed at the end of the chapter. This process should continue throughout treatment. Detailed instructions on understanding eating disorders, completing self-monitoring and all other CBT tasks are given in these self-help books.

Psychoeducation

Psychoeducation about bulimia is also covered in the first stage of treatment. This should be given orally and appropriate chapters of self-help books should be given as homework assignments. Clients are informed about how to calculate the body mass index (BMI) and, using BMI norms, to set a weight goal that does not involve dieting. Psychoeducation also covers the physical consequences of bingeing and vomiting; the ineffectiveness of vomiting, laxative and diuretic use as means of weight control and the fact that dieting inevitably leads to intense hunger, loss of control and bingeing. The negative consequences of bingeing, vomiting and using purgatives that should be stressed include electrolyte imbalance, salivary gland enlargement (leading to a chubby face), erosion of dental enamel, intermittent oedema and menstruation irregularities. Other negative consequences of bulimia are listed in Table 19.6.

Prescribing a regular eating pattern

Clients should be given the following advice on eating habits. First, eat three meals per day, and two or three planned snacks, spaced no more than three hours apart. Meals should not be followed by vomiting, the use of diuretics, purgatives or intense exercise, and other unplanned eating should be avoided. Where eating habits are severely disturbed, this regular pattern should be introduced gradually. This task aims to both regularize eating habits and shows clients that the eating pattern does not result in weight gain.

Stimulus control

Stimulus-control techniques may be introduced to help clients adhere to a regular eating pattern. These include not engaging in other activities (such as watching TV) while eating; and savouring their food; confining eating to one place and formalizing the eating process by setting the table, etc.; limiting the supply of food available while eating by putting out the required amount and putting the packet away before the meal starts; practising leaving food on the plate; throwing away left-overs; keeping as little 'danger food', such as chocolate, in the house as possible; planning shopping lists when not hungry and sticking to them; and avoiding finishing food on plates of other family members.

Planning alternatives to bingeing and vomiting

Clients may be invited to predict trigger situations where they are at risk of bingeing and vomiting, and to develop lists of alternative behaviours in which they can engage to avoid bingeing and vomiting. Such behaviours may include talking to a partner or parent, phoning a friend, playing music, taking gentle exercise or having a bath.

Managing vomiting

To reduce the frequency of vomiting, clients may be invited to select meals or snacks that induce a lower urge to vomit, and to carefully plan to engage in distracting activities for an hour following eating to avoid vomiting.

Managing laxative and diuretic use

To reduce the frequency of laxative and diuretic use, the ineffectiveness of these drugs in preventing food absorption should be explained. Then clients may be invited to discard their supply of such drugs in one step or a series of gradual steps. Sometimes there is a brief temporary rebound effect after ceasing diuretic use during which weight increases, and clients should be warned of this.

Stage 2: Reducing dieting, improving problem solving and challenging cognitive distortions

Throughout stages 2 and 3, processes begun in stage 1 are continued. The three main goals of the second stage, which spans about eight weeks, are to reduce dieting; improve problem-solving skills; and challenge beliefs about shape, weight and self-worth that maintain the eating disorder.

Reducing dieting

With bulimia, most clients practise three types of dieting: (1) abstaining from eating for long periods of time; (2) avoiding specific 'forbidden' foods; and (3) restricting the amount of food eaten. Clients attempt to follow strict rules about when to eat, which forbidden foods to avoid and how much to eat. Following these rules leads to intense hunger. In stressful trigger situations, this hunger leads to bingeing, which is interpreted as evidence of poor self-control and low self-worth rather than unrealistic dietary rules. A central strategy for resolving bulimia, therefore, is reducing or eliminating dieting. In stage 1, the prescription of a regular eating pattern of three meals and two snacks a day with intervals no longer than three hours, addressed the first type of dieting, that is, avoiding eating for long time periods.

To address the second type of dieting, clients may be invited to visit a supermarket, identify and list all the 'forbidden' foods they can see, and then classify these into four categories from the least to the most forbidden. Over the following weeks, the client – alone or with parents – is invited to plan and eat meals or snacks in which these forbidden foods are incorporated in small or normal amounts into the meals, starting with the least forbidden and working gradually towards the most forbidden foods. These meals or snacks containing forbidden foods should only be planned for low-stress periods when the client is likely to experience a high degree of self-control. This gradual and graded introduction of forbidden foods into the client's diet should be continued until the client no longer feels anxious about eating them. After that, clients may return to a narrower diet that may not often include them. In some situations, clients may be so anxious about eating certain foods because they fear over-eating or vomiting that desensitization should be conducted in the clinic using an exposure and response prevention format. These sessions should be carefully planned. The meal or snack containing the forbidden food is eaten early in the session and the client is helped by the therapist for the remainder of the session to cope with the urges to overeat the forbidden food or to vomit. For clients with strong food avoidance, a number of such sessions may be necessary.

To address the third type of dieting – restrictive dieting – the client should be helped to move from a restricted diet to a diet containing 1500 calories per day. Inspection of self-monitoring sheets will indicate current calorific intake and this information may be used to plan a gradual increase in food consumption. Clients may also be invited to eat a more varied diet.

Problem solving

To deal with problematic situations, especially trigger situations that precede bingeing, clients may be coached in using systematic problem-solving skills. Invite clients to first break big, vague problems into many smaller, specific problems to be tackled one at a time. Second, define each of these in solvable terms. Third, focus on solving the specific problem at hand, not attacking the person or people involved in the problem, or simply leaving the problem unresolved. Fourth, generate many possible solutions to the problem in hand. Fifth, when all solutions are generated, examine the pros and cons of each, and select the best. Sixth, implement this solution, review progress and modify the solution if it is not working. Finally, repeat this sequence as often as is necessary to solve the problem and celebrate success. Inspection of self-monitoring forms will usually show that many binge-triggering situations involve difficult interpersonal problems. Through addressing these in therapy sessions as they arise, clients gradually learn systematic problem-solving skills.

Cognitive restructuring

From the formulation in Figure 19.1 it is clear that dieting and the bingeing and vomiting cycle are driven by negative mood states that arise from negative beliefs about shape and weight (such as 'I'm too big and too heavy') and negative self-evaluative beliefs (such as 'I'm not good enough' or 'I've no self-control'). In specific triggering situations, these beliefs give rise to specific negative automatic thoughts, which are typically distorted by a range of cognitive processes of which perfectionism and black-and-white thinking are often the most salient. For example, when a client notices that her weight has increased by two pounds as she steps on the scales she may have the negative automatic thought 'I'm a tub of lard!' This negative automatic thought is underpinned by the core beliefs 'I'm no good' and 'I'm too fat'. This negative automatic thought is also underpinned by perfectionism insofar as only perfection is acceptable, and by black-and-white thinking, insofar as the thought does not reflect the fact that a minor gain in weight has occurred, but rather that the client is either 'a tub or lard' or not.

With cognitive restructuring, the first step is for the client to write down the actual situation and the specific negative automatic thought that occurred in the situation (not a summary or rephrasing of it). These thoughts may be identified in the final columns of self-monitoring sheets within and outside treatment sessions. The following situations usually elicit relevant automatic thoughts: looking in a mirror, weighing themselves, reacting to a comment about their appearance or appetite, situations where urges to binge or vomit occur, or seeing themselves in a swimming costume or tight clothes. The following is an example of a situation and the negative automatic thought: 'I stepped on the scales on Tuesday morning and was 8 stone 2 when I should have been 8 stone. I thought "I'm a tub of lard! I'm really fat!" '.

The second step in cognitive restructuring is to accurately list the evidence that supports the thought. For example, 'My weight increased by two pounds over a period of 10 days'.

The third step is to help clients list arguments or evidence that cast doubt on the validity of the negative automatic thought. Here Socratic questioning may be used: 'How would you know if any person was fat?', 'What clothes size do you have to have to be fat?', 'Would you judge someone in your class at school who was 8 stone 2 pounds to be fat?', 'Are you applying one set of standards to yourself and another set to other people?', 'Have you gained two pounds because your body has accumulated more fat due to over-eating or because you are retaining fluid due to being in the premenstrual stage of your monthly cycle?' Clients may be taught to recognize the cognitive distortions listed earlier in the section on CBT theories of eating disorders and invited to identify which of these are present in their negative automatic thoughts.

The fourth and final step of cognitive restructuring is to help clients reach a reasoned conclusion, which they may then use to guide their behaviour as an alternative to the negative automatic thought. For example, 'I put on two pounds but my weight is within the normal range'.

It is not essential for clients to fully accept the validity of their reasoned conclusion. The point is, that they become aware through repeatedly challenging their negative automatic thoughts in therapy sessions and as homework that they have a limited number of such thoughts which drive their dieting, bingeing and vomiting behaviour, and that these thoughts are not absolutely true. Also, the negative automatic thoughts become less automatic and more conscious as clients become more practiced at challenging them.

As more examples of negative automatic thoughts are addressed in therapy, certain extreme, rigid underlying assumptions, of which clients are usually not conscious, and which they hold with great tenacity become clear. Examples include: 'If I am thin and light, then I will be loved by others, happy, successful and worthwhile', 'If I am fat and heavy, I will be abandoned by others, a failure, sad and worthless', 'If I have self-control I am strong, good and a success', 'If I show any sign of lack of control, I am completely powerless, bad and a failure'. These underlying assumptions may tentatively be suggested to clients and they may be challenged using the four steps for cognitive restructuring outlined above. In addition, clients may be invited to complete behavioural experiments, to disconfirm their beliefs that they will be ostracized if others see their bodies. For example, clients may be invited to wear more close-fitting clothes, to go to exercise classes where they wear leotards, or to go swimming. Clients often have a safety behaviour of wearing clothes that are nearer the size they want to be, rather than the size they currently are, for example wearing a size 12 because it is nearer the size 10 they want to be, even though a size 14 would be a better fit now. Their rationale or negative automatic thoughts may be that the sensation of tightness in their clothes warns them of the need to diet and lose weight, helping them 'keep control'; they fear that if they wore a bigger size there would be fewer bodily cues of fatness, they would exercise fewer weight-control measures, grow larger and thus be unhappier. Experiencing the discomfort of tight-fitting clothes throughout the day, particularly after eating, fuels pressure to diet, thus feeding into the negative cycle presented in Figure 19.1. As a behavioural experiment, clients may be encouraged to give up this safety behaviour by wearing better-fitting, more comfortable clothes, which paradoxically reduces subjective feelings of fatness and pressures to diet, helping them get out of the negative cycle of bingeing and purging.

Stage 3: Relapse prevention

Throughout stage 3, processes begun in stages 1 and 2 are continued. The main goal of the third stage, which involves three fortnightly sessions, is relapse prevention. A distinction should be made between a complete relapse (a rare event) and a minor lapse or slip (which is a common event). Bingeing as a response to stress may be described as the client's Achilles heel. Clients' mastery of bulimia is strengthened by coping well with slips, where they occasionally binge in response to stress. To equip them to cope with slips, clients may be invited to predict the sorts of situations that might trigger such slips, and to develop plans for managing lapses when they occur. Such plans should include acknowledging that the temporary slip is not a permanent relapse; that a slip is an opportunity for gaining strength rather than a sign of weakness; that planning regular daily eating patterns with three meals, two snacks and no dieting is crucial for success; that problem-solving skills should be used to address complex social problems that trigger urges to binge; that negative automatic thoughts and assumptions must be continually challenged and that parental support is essential for the client's success. The client should be given a homework assignment of writing out a plan to manage lapses and this plan should be reviewed in the final session.

Interpersonal therapy for bulimia

Interpersonal therapy (IPT) based on the work of Harry Stack Sullivan (1953) and originally developed as a treatment for depression has been shown to be an effective treatment for bulimia (Weissman, et al., 2000, Chapter 21; Wilfley et al., 2003; Wilson & Fairburn, 2002). In interpersonal therapy (IPT) it is assumed that bulimia is multi-factorially determined, but that the four categories of interpersonal difficulty listed in Table 19.5 play a central role in precipitating the onset of the disorder and maintaining bulimic symptoms. IPT aims to help clients resolve interpersonal problems that maintain their eating disorders. IPT has a slower impact than CBT on bulimic symptoms but is as effective in the long-term. This is not surprising, because CBT directly targets eating behaviour and related cognitions, early in treatment. In contrast, IPT targets relationship difficulties, which are more complex and slower to change, and only when these begin to change do changes in eating patterns occur.

IPT for bulimia involves twenty sessions conducted over a period of four to five months. IPT has three stages. In the first stage, which spans four sessions, the client is engaged in treatment, current interpersonal problems are identified and a treatment contract is established.

In the middle stage, which spans about a dozen sessions, the core interpersonal problem that maintains the eating disorders is addressed. In the final stage, which spans about four sessions, gains made are consolidated and clients are helped to prepare to continue the work after termination of therapy.

Stage 1: Diagnosis, formulation and contracting

In the first stage, an assessment is conducted over four sessions and clients are given a diagnosis and assigned to the sick role. This role defines clients as needing help, exempts them from social pressures and elicits their co-operation in the recovery process. Many clients with eating disorders adopt excessive caretaking responsibilities with a self-sacrificing disregard for their own welfare to obtain the approval of others. The sick role provides a legitimate way to curtail this. Clients may be advised to focus their energy on recovery rather than on meeting the needs of others. To generate hope, clients may be informed that bulimia is a known syndrome defined by DSM-IV or ICD-10 criteria (listed in Table 19.2) that responds well to psychotherapy. Clients are informed that the binge-purge cycle and related beliefs and attitudes are typically maintained by interpersonal factors, and identifying and modifying these leads to resolution of the disorder. The therapist then conducts a review of the client's past and current social functioning and intimate relationships. For each significant person in the client's social network, an interpersonal inventory is taken. Information is obtained on frequency and duration of contact, regular activities that occur within these relationships, satisfactory and unsatisfactory aspects of these relationships and aspects of the relationships that the client would like to change. In addition, the therapist takes a history of significant life events, transitions, changes and stresses and related fluctuations in mood, self-esteem, relationships and bulimic symptoms. The therapist then links the onset and maintenance of the eating disorder to one (or in some cases two) of the four key areas in Table 19.5 (grief, role disputes, role transitions and interpersonal deficits). This interpersonal formulation provides a basis for setting goals, which involve resolving specific interpersonal difficulties, and establishing a treatment contract to work towards these goals.

Stage 2: Resolving interpersonal difficulties associated with bulimia

In the intermediated phase, specific strategies may be used to help clients achieve the goals from their interpersonal formulation of eating disorder. Progress towards interpersonal goals is reviewed at each session, but not changes in bulimic symptoms, weight or shape. The therapeutic positioning in IPT is one of warmth, empathy and respect. Therapeutic conversations focus on specific incidents relevant to achieving interpersonal goals rather than on generalities. In enquiring about specific incidents, therapists facilitate the expression of affect, particularly affects that are avoided or unacknowledged. A central principle for practising IPT with bulimic clients is to minimize and avoid discussion of bulimic symptoms. If clients bring these up, they are acknowledged but the therapist redirects the conversation to the key unresolved interpersonal issue and related goals that are the focus of treatment. Little time is spent discussing eating habits, vomiting, weighing or body shape. Specific strategies are used to address goals in each of the four key areas listed in Table 19.5.

Grief

Where grief due to complicated bereavement following the death of a loved one is a central factor maintaining depression, the aim of IPT is to facilitate mourning and help the client find relationships and activities to compensate for the loss. To achieve this aim the following strategies may be used. Link the course of the relationship with the deceased, their death and the aftermath of this on the one hand and the course of the bulimic symptoms on the other. Concurrently facilitate the exploration and re-experiencing of feelings associated with the deceased over the course of the relationship. When progress has been made with this grief work, shift the focus onto the future and then explore possible ways of becoming more involved with others. Pace this transition to match the degree to which the client has resolved his or her feelings of grief and is ready to look to the future.

Role disputes

Marital disharmony or difficulties involving other family members, friends or colleagues are among the more significant role disputes associated with bulimia. Where role disputes are a central factor maintaining bulimia, the aim of IPT is to help the client clearly identify the dispute and develop and implement a plan for resolving it. To achieve this aim the following strategies may be used. Link the current dispute to bulimic symptoms. The dispute may be overt (e.g. domestic violence) or covert (e.g. an uneasy feeling about the unspoken possibility of infidelity). Explore the onset and course of the current dispute and determine the current developmental stage of the dispute. If the client believes the dispute is irresolvable, facilitate withdrawal from this relationship and mourning of this loss. If the dispute has reached an impasse, increase disharmony in order to create movement towards the stage of renegotiation. If it is at the stage where renegotiation is the aim, then facilitate this process by helping partners communicate calmly about it. In facilitating renegotiation, help clients specify the core issue in the dispute, and their different expectations and values about this issue. In exploring the present dispute, facilitate framing it in as solvable a way as possible. Then brainstorm multiple options for resolving it. Look at the pros and cons of each. Explore the resources available for resolving the dispute or changing the relationship. Explore the barriers to resolving the conflict by trying to help the client answer these questions: 'In this and other relationships, is the client showing a similar pattern or style of conflict?', 'What assumptions underlie the client's position in this and other similar disputes?', 'What is being gained by not resolving the dispute or what will be lost if it is resolved?' Help the client select the best option for resolving the dispute and then plan in detail how to implement and review the impact of this plan.

Role transitions

Starting or ending relationships within the family or work context, moving jobs or houses, graduation, promotion, retirement or diagnosis of an illness are some of the role transitions associated with bulimia. Where role transitions are a central factor maintaining bulimia, IPT aims to help the client mourn the loss of the old role, appreciate the benefits of the new one and develop a sense of mastery of the demands of the new role. To achieve this aim, the following strategies may be adopted. Relate the bulimic symptoms to a recent role change. Review the positive and negative aspects of the new and old roles. Explore and ventilate feelings about the loss of the old role and the process of change from one role to another. Facilitate the development of social supports and new skills to help the client manage the demands of the new role.

Social skills deficits

Where bulimia is maintained by difficulties making and maintaining significant relationships, the aim of IPT is to help clients reduce social isolation and form new relationships. To achieve this aim, the following strategies may be used. Relate the bulimic symptoms to social isolation. Review positive and negative aspects of past relationships, noting in particular repetitive self-defeating patterns that lead to isolation. Discuss the client's positive and negative feelings about the therapist and clarify parallels between the therapeutic relationship and other current relationships in the client's life. The psychodynamic therapy techniques described in Chapter 4 for drawing parallels between the therapeutic relationship and relationships with other significant people may be used here.

Stage 3: Disengagement

In the last four sessions the therapist ask clients to describe how they have achieved their therapeutic goals. The therapist helps clients develop a detailed understanding of how they have achieved the improvements they have shown and explores ways of consolidating these gains. The therapist also helps clients develop strategies for maintaining improvements in the identified interpersonal problem areas, preventing relapse if dietary restriction recurs, and identifying further work that needs to be pursued independently by the client when therapy has finished. The client's feelings about termination of the therapeutic relationship are also explored in the final stage of IPT.

A more detailed account of specific IPT therapy strategies and skills is given in Chapter 8 in the section on IPT for depression.

Psychotherapy for anorexia

In contrast to the good evidence base for CBT and IPT as effective treatments for bulimia, the evidence base for the psychotherapeutic treatment of anorexia is sparse (Wilson & Fairburn, 2002). There is some evidence from a couple of small controlled trials for the efficacy of CBT (Waller & Kennerley, 2003), cognitive analytic therapy (Tanner & Connan, 2003), and focal psychodynamic psychotherapy of the type described in Chapter 4 (Eisler et al., 1997) with adult anorexic clients. In practice, assessment of clients with anorexia following the guidelines given above and careful case formulation where predisposing, precipitating and maintaining factors are specified provides a basis for rational treatment of anorexia following the principles of CBT or IPT outlined above for bulimia. In high-risk cases of anorexia, inpatient weight restoration, described below, may be required.

Systemic interventions

There is good evidence for the efficacy of family therapy with young adolescents with anorexia but family therapy is not effective with adult clients (Eisler et al., 2003). However, it is important, when providing therapy for young adults with eating disorders, to take account of the extraordinary strain the disorder places on partners and parents (Nielsen & Bará-Carril, 2003). There are good ethical grounds and precedents in the treatment of psychosis for providing a psychoeducational family support group service for parents and partners of clients with eating disorders and for disseminating family support materials such as Janet Treasure's (1997) *Anorexia nervosa. A survival guide for families friends and sufferers*. Family members may also benefit from membership of carer support groups.

Biomedical practices and eating disorders

The two evidence-based biomedical practices routinely used in the treatment of eating disorders are inpatient re-feeding and weight restoration programmes for anorexic clients, and antidepressant medication for clients with bulimia (Wilson & Fairburn, 2002).

Inpatient re-feeding and weight restoration programmes

The treatment of clients with anorexia should begin with inpatient care to address physical complications of starvation in severe cases with high medical risk. This should be followed up with outpatient psychotherapy. In lower-risk cases, treatment may begin with outpatient therapy. Following a thorough medical examination, a decision on inpatient treatment may be made. Where any of the following features are present, inpatient treatment is indicated (APA, 2000b; NICE, 2004; Royal College of Psychiatrists, 2002; Winston & Webster, 2003):

- a BMI of 13.5 or less, or a rapid fall in weight of more than 20% in six months
- bradycardia (less than forty beats per minute)
- hypotension (blood pressure less than 90/60 mmHg if over sixteen years; 80/50 mmHg if under sixteen years)
- orthostatic drop greater than 10–20 mmHg
- severe dehydration
- hypoglycaemia
- poor diabetic control
- severe electrolyte imbalance (e.g. $K^+ < 2.5$ mmol/L; $Na^+ < 130$ mmol/L)
- petechial rash and significant platelet suppression
- organ compromise – hepatic, renal, bone marrow
- uncontrolled vomiting
- gastrointestinal bleeding
- self-injurious or suicidal behaviour
- severe depression or obsessive-compulsive disorder
- low motivation for treatment and lack of insight
- lack of response to outpatient treatment
- intolerable family situation (highly critical, abusive or collusive family)
- unsupportive social situation (social isolation).

Historically, highly restrictive, authoritarian behavioural weight restoration was common practice but there is now good evidence that relatively lenient collaborative programmes can be as effective in helping clients gain weight (Palmer, 2000; Winston & Webster, 2003). Typically, a plan for hospital admission and weight restoration is agreed between the client, a member of the client's family, the psychologist or other professional conducting outpatient therapy, the psychiatrist or other physician responsible for the inpatient unit and a key worker, often a nurse, who will be responsible for implementing the re-feeding programme. A target plateau BMI of 20–25 is agreed as the overall weight restoration goal. Intermediate weight-gain goals, of 0.5 to 1.0 kg per week, are set. A balanced diet and gradually increasing daily calorific intake is agreed. Clients who are severely emaciated may need to begin with a calorie count as low as 1500 calories a day to reduce the chances for stomach pain and bloating, fluid retention, and heart failure. Gradually, daily calorific intake is increased to as many as 3500 calories a day. Small, frequent meals are preferable to large, infrequent meals, because of delayed gastric emptying associated with anorexia. Dietary supplements may be required. Zinc supplementation has been shown to help increase body mass and, in some units, calcium, multi-vitamins and oral phosphates are routinely given. Nasogastric tube or intravenous feeding is rarely required unless the client's condition is life threatening. Over-zealous administration of glucose solutions can trigger *re-feeding syndrome*, in which phosphate levels drop severely and causes hypophosphataemia. Symptoms include irritability, muscle weakness, bleeding from the mouth, disturbed heart rhythms, seizures and coma. During inpatient re-feeding programmes, clients are initially confined to bed, usually in a private room, and their mealtimes and toilet visits are strictly supervised by the key worker. However, in lenient programmes there is no restriction on visitors or on access to books or TV. As weight restoration progresses, clients are permitted to take some gentle exercise each day, to leave their room for increasingly longer periods, and supervision of mealtimes and toilet visits is relaxed. During mealtime, discussion of eating disorders is usually avoided.

Daily or thrice weekly weighing routines may be established on the ward. Key workers without specialist training may require considerable support in dealing with clients with eating disorders. Helping them to avoid the pitfalls of being either too punitive or too protective is essential since such attitudes may simply replicate family responses to the condition and further maintaining the client's eating problems. Staff need to be briefed on weight targets, mealtime routines and specific limits that must be kept. For mealtime routines, at the outset, the client may be given a set time period, such as an hour, within which to consume a meal, otherwise finishing the meal may be supervised by a nurse. In supervising eating, staff sit with clients and sympathetically but firmly insist that they eat. The over-riding position taken by staff is one of supporting the client in her fight against the disorder.

Antidepressant medication for bulimia

There is good evidence that antidepressants, both tricyclic antidepressants (TCAs) and selective serotonin reuptake inhibitors (SSRIs), can lead to short-term reductions in bulimic symptoms for most clients, but total remission occurs in under a third of cases (Bruna & Fogteloo, 2003). In contrast, remission occurs in about 50% of bulimic clients treated with CBT or IPT. Fluoxetine, the most studied antidepressant for bulimic clients, is effective in a daily dose of 60 mg. This is three times the advised dose for depression, suggesting that the mode of action may be different in bulimia. Results of randomized controlled trials with a variety of medications do not support the use of psychopharmacological interventions for anorexia nervosa (Wilson & Fairburn, 2002).

Other biomedical issues

Eating disorders involve multiple medical risks, not all of which are associated with chronic high-risk cases (NICE, 2004). In primary care, subthreshold cases of anorexia with diabetes or pregnant clients require careful monitoring and intervention.

SERVICE ORGANIZATION

Guidelines on service provision for people with eating disorders have been developed by various professional groups (APA, 2000b; Bell et al., 2001; NICE, 2004; Royal College of Psychiatrists, 2002). These guidelines contain proposal for service development and organization. Early screening and intervention for older adolescents and young women with eating disorders in primary care may prevent the later development of chronic eating disorders and so is strongly advised. There is a consensus that a stepped-care approach to treatment is appropriate for eating disorders with circumscribed initial intervention being offered first, and only if this is unsuccessful is more intensive intervention provided. Subthreshold cases of eating disorders may benefit from self-help bibliotherapy or CD-ROM-based programmes using the self-help materials listed at the end of the chapter coupled with minimal supportive counselling or participation in a self-help group, of which there are many. Clients who do not respond to this approach may benefit from locally provided specialist outpatient psychological intervention of the type described in this chapter. The effective provision of specialist psychological therapy involves therapists receiving regular case supervision. Where cases do not respond to psychological therapy, antidepressant treatment for bulimia is appropriate, but antidepressant treatment is not effective with anorexia. High-risk cases with multiple medical complications require hospitalization and a weight restoration re-feeding programme such as that described above. Optimally, this is provided at a regional specialist unit staffed by a multi-disciplinary team. Chronic complex cases may require long-term outpatient care and attendance at a local day hospital. Services should be organized according to a hub and spoke model, with a regional 'hub' specialist centre with inpatient facilities of at least six beds and a full multi-disciplinary team for a population of 1 million, with a 'spoke' specialist outpatient eating disorder service for every locality of 30,000 people (Richards, 2003).

SUMMARY

Anorexia nervosa and bulimia are the two main eating disorders seen in clinical practice, with the former being characterized primarily by weight loss and the latter by a cyclical pattern of bingeing and purging. Both eating disorders are most common among female adolescents and young women. About 1–2% of the adolescent and young adult female population suffer from eating disorders. In clinical populations, comorbid mood disorders and obsessive-compulsive disorders are common in cases of anorexia; for bulimia, comorbid drug abuse and borderline personality disorder are relatively common. About half of all cases of anorexia nervosa have a good outcome, a third have a moderate outcome and a fifth have a poor outcome. At twenty years follow-up, the mortality rate is about 6%. For bulimia nervosa, about half of all cases have a good outcome, a quarter have a moderate outcome and the remaining quarter have a poor outcome. A variety of genetic, temperamental, sociocultural, personality, biomedical, cognitive-behavioural and interpersonal factors contribute to the development and maintenance of eating disorders. Because of their ambivalence about resolving their eating problems, motivational interviewing is a useful intervention to help clients with eating disorders engage in assessment and treatment. Assessment should be carried out by a multi-disciplinary team and cover current and past physical, nutritional and psychological state.

On the basis of the assessment, a preliminary formulation may be drawn up. This should link predisposing, precipitating and maintaining factors to the abnormal eating pattern and specify protective factors that may be drawn on during treatment. Evidence-based intervention for bulimia includes either manualized CBT or IPT conducted over about twenty sessions. CBT, aims to disrupt the binge-purge cycle and modify the belief systems that underpin this cycle. IPT aims to help clients resolve interpersonal difficulties that maintain their eating disorder. Antidepressants, notably fluoxetine, are effective with a proportion of bulimic clients and may be used where psychotherapy has been ineffective or is unavailable. In contrast to the good evidence base for the treatment of bulimia, the evidence base for the psychotherapeutic treatment of anorexia is sparse. In high-risk cases of anorexia, inpatient weight restoration is essential, followed by formulation-driven CBT or IPT.

EXERCISE 19.1

Divide into groups of three and assign roles of Linda, the psychologist and an observer. Role-play with Linda the following parts of sessions, rotating roles after each role-play. The observer's role is to listen attentively and after the role-play to give feedback to the psychologist on three specific and behavioural aspects of what he or she did well and at most two suggestions of things to do differently:

1 Session 5, in which Linda and the psychologist collaboratively develop an individualized formulation with Linda.
2 Session 7, in which Linda and the psychologist discuss the CBT formulation (see Figure 19.1) and work towards setting some goals for regularizing eating habits.
3 Session 13, in which Linda and the psychologist look at evidence for and against Linda's belief that, if others knew her better, they would laugh at her.

EXERCISE 19.2

In either a diagram or a paragraph, formulate Linda's difficulties with three models: CBT, interpersonal therapy and systemic. In small groups, discuss the merits of each formulation and treatment approach.

FURTHER READING FOR PRACTITIONERS

Bell, L., Clare, L. & Thorn. (2001). *Service guidelines for people with eating disorders. Division of clinical psychology occasional paper no. 3.* Leicester: British Psychological Society.

Garner, D. & Garfinkle, P. (1997). *Handbook of treatment for eating disorders* (Second Edition). New York: Guilford Press.

Palmer, B. (2000). *Helping people with eating disorders.* Chichester, UK: Wiley.

Schmidt, U. & Treasure, J. (1997). *Clinician's guide to getting better bit(e) by bit(e).* Hove, UK: Psychology Press.

Treasure, J., Schmidt, U. & van Furth, E. (2003). *Handbook of eating disorders* (Second Edition). Chichester, UK: Wiley.

FURTHER READING FOR CLIENTS

Cooper, M., Todd, G. & Wells, A. (2000). *Bulimia nervosa – a cognitive therapy programme for clients.* London: Jessica Kingsley.

Cooper, P. J. (1995). *Bulimia nervosa: A guide to recovery.* London: Robinson Publishing.

Crisp, A., Joughin, N., Halek, C. & Bower, C. (1996). *Anorexia nervosa: The wish to change. Self-help and discovery, the thirty steps* (Second Edition). Hove, UK: Psychology Press.

Fairburn, C. (1995). *Overcoming binge eating.* New York: Guilford Press.

Freeman, C. (2001). *Overcoming anorexia nervosa.* London: Constable Robinson.

Schmidt, U. & Treasure, J. (1993). *Getting better bit(e) by bit(e)*. Hove, UK: Psychology Press.

Treasure, J. (1997). *Anorexia nervosa. A survival guide for families, friends and sufferers*. Hove, UK: Psychology Press.

Williams, C., Schmidt, U. & Aubin, S. (2005). *Overcoming bulimia. A self-help CBT CD-ROM*. Online. Available at: http://www.calipso.co.uk University of Leeds Media Innovations Ltd, 3 Gemini Business Park, Sheepscar Way, Leeds LS7 3JB. Tel: +44–113–262–1600. Website: http://www.calipso.co.uk

ASSESSMENT INSTRUMENTS

Cooper, P. J., Taylor, M., Cooper, Z. & Fairburn, C. (1987). The development and validation of the Body Shape Questionnaire. *International Journal of Eating Disorders*, 6, 485–494.

Cooper, Z. & Fairburn, C. (1987). The Eating Disorder Examination. A semi-structured interview for the assessment of the specific psychopathology of eating disorders. *International Journal of Eating Disorders*, 6, 1–8.

Fairburn, C. & Beglin, S. (1994). Assessment of Eating Disorders. Interview or self-report questionnaire. *International Journal of Eating Disorders*, 16, 363–370. Contains self-report version of EDE.

Fichter, M., Elton, M., Engel, K. et al. (1990). The Structured Interview for Anorexia and Bulimia Nervosa (SIAB): Development and characteristics of a (semi-) standardized instrument. In M. Fichter (Ed.), *Bulimia nervosa: Basic research diagnosis and therapy* (pp. 57–70). Chichester, UK: Wiley.

Garner, D. (2005). *Eating disorder inventory – 3*. Odessa, FL: Psychological Assessment Resources.

Garner, D., Olmsted, M., Bohr, Y. & Garfinkle, P. (1982). The Eating Attitudes Test, psychometric features and clinical correlates. *Psychological Medicine*, 12, 871–878.

Henderson, M. & Freeman, C. (1987). A self-rating scale for bulimia: the 'BITE'. *British Journal of Psychiatry*, 150, 18–24.

Mintz, L., O'Halloran, M., Mulholland, A. & Schneider, P. (1997). Questionnaire for eating disorder diagnoses. Reliability and validity of operationalising DSM-IV criteria into a self-report format. *Journal of Counselling Psychology*, 44, 63–71.

Morgan, A. & Hayward, A. (1988). Clinical assessment of anorexia nervosa: The Morgan–Russell outcome assessment schedule. *British Journal of Psychiatry*, 152, 367–371.

Plamer, R., Christie, M., Cordle, C., Davies, D. & Kerrick, J. (1987). The Clinical Eating Disorder Rating Instrument (CEDRI): A preliminary description. *International Journal of Eating Disorders*, 6, 9–16.

Slade, P. & Dewey, M. (1986). Development and preliminary validation of SCANS: A screening instrument for identifying individuals at risk of developing anorexia and bulimia nervosa. *International Journal of Eating Disorders*, 5, 517–538.

Slade, P., Dewey, M., Kiemle, G. & Newton, T. (1990). Update on SCANS: A screening instrument for identifying individuals at risk of developing an eating disorder. *International Journal of Eating Disorders*, 9, 583–584.

Slade, P., Dewey, M., Newton, T., Brodie, D. & Kiemle, G. (1990). Development and preliminary validation of the body satisfaction scale (BSS). *Psychology and Health*, 4, 213–220.

Stunkard, A. & Messick, S. (1985). The Three Factor Eating Questionnaire. To measure dietary restraint, disinhibition and hunger. *Journal of Psychosomatic Research*, 29, 71–83. Eating Inventory is available from San Antonio, TX: Psychological Corporation.

Thelen, M., Farmer, J., Wonderlich, S. & Smith, M. (1991). A revision of the bulimia test: The BULIT-R. *Psychological Assessment*, 3, 119–124.

Williams, G. & Power, K. (1996). *Stirling Eating Disorder Scales*. San Antonio, TX: Psychological Corporation.

Williams, G., Power, K., Miller, H., Freeman, C., Yellowlees, A., Dowds, T., Walker, M. & Parry-Jones, W. (1994). Development and validation of the Stirling Eating Disorder Scales. *International Journal of Eating Disorders*, 16, 35–43.

WEBSITES

Eating Disorders Association: http://www.edauk.com/
Eating Disorders Resources: http://edr.org.uk/
Eating Disorders Shared Awareness: http://eating-disorder.com
Bodywhys Online: An Irish site for eating disorders: http://www.bodywhys.ie

REFERENCES

American Psychiatric Association (APA) (2000a). *Diagnostic and statistical manual of the mental disorders (Fourth Edition-Text Revision, DSM-IV-TR)*. Washington, DC: APA.

American Psychiatric Association (APA) (2000b). Practice guidelines for the treatment of eating disorders (revision). American Psychiatric Association Work Group on Eating Disorders. *American Journal of Psychiatry*, 157, 1–39.

Bell, L., Clare, L. & Thorn. (2001). *Service guidelines for people with eating disorders. Division of clinical psychology occasional paper no. 3*. Leicester, UK: British Psychological Society.

Bruna, T. & Fogteloo, J. (2003). Drug treatment. In J. Treasure, U. Schmidt & E. van Furth (Eds.), *Handbook of eating disorders* (Second Edition, pp. 333–348). Chichester, UK: Wiley.

Collier, D. & Treasure, J. (2004). The aetiology of eating disorders. *British Journal of Psychiatry*, 185, 363–365.

Cooper, Z. & Fairburn, C. (1987). The Eating Disorder Examination. A semi-structured interview for the assessment of the specific psychopathology of eating disorders. *International Journal of Eating Disorders*, 6, 1–8.

Eisler, I., Dare, C., Russell, G., Szmukler, G., Le Grange, D. & Dodge, E. (1997). Family and individual therapy in anorexia nervosa: A 5-year follow-up. *Archives of General Psychiatry*, 54, 1025–1030.

Eisler, I., le Grange, D. & Aisen, A. (2003). Family Interventions. In J. Treasure, U.

Schmidt & E. van Furth (Eds.), *Handbook of eating disorders* (Second Edition, pp. 291–310). Chichester, UK: Wiley.

Eley, T., Collier, D. & McGuffin, P. (2002). Anxiety and eating disorders. In P. McGuffin, M. Owen & I. Gottesman (Eds.), *Psychiatric genetics and genomics* (pp. 303–340). Oxford: Oxford University Press.

Fairburn, C. (1997). Eating disorders. In D. Clark & C. Fairburn (Eds.), *The science and practice of cognitive behaviour therapy* (pp. 209–241). Oxford: Oxford University Press.

Fairburn, C.G., Marcus, M.D. & Wilson, G.T. (1993). Cognitive behaviour therapy for binge eating and bulimia nervosa: A comprehensive treatment manual. In C.G. Fairburn & G.T. Wilson (Eds.), *Binge eating: Nature, assessment, and treatment* (pp. 361–404). New York: Guilford Press.

Frichter, M. & Pirke, K. (1995). Starvation models and eating disorders. In G. Szmukler, C. Dare & J. Treasure (Eds.), *Handbook of eating disorders* (pp. 83–108). Chichester, UK: Wiley.

Garner, D. (2005). *Eating disorder inventory – 3*. Odessa, FL: Psychological Assessment Resources.

Gull, W. (1874). Anorexia nervosa (apesia hysterica, anorexia hysterica). *Transactions of the Clinical Society of London*, 7, 22–28.

Hoek, H. & Van Hoeken, D. (2003). Review of the prevalence and incidence of eating disorders. *International Journal of Eating Disorders*, 34, 383–396.

Klump, K., Wonderlich, S., Lehoux, P., Lilenfeld, L. & Bulik, C. (2002). Does environment matter? A review of non-shared environment and eating disorders. *International Journal of Eating Disorders*, 31, 118–135.

Lasègue, E. (1873). De l'anorexie hysterique. *Archives Generales de Medicine*, 21, 385–403.

Masjuan, M., Aranda, F. & Raich, R. (2003). Bulimia nervosa and personality disorders: A review of the literature. *Journal of Clinical and Health Psychology*, 3, 335–349.

Miller, W. & Rollnick. S. (2002). *Motivational interviewing* (Second Edition). New York: Guilford Press.

Mount Sinai (1965). *Evolution of psychosomatic concepts – anorexia nervosa: A paradigm. The International Psychoanalytic Library (no. 65)*. London: Hogarth Press.

Nasser, M. & Katzman, N. (2003). Sociocultural theories of eating disorders. In J. Treasure, U. Schmidt & E. van Furth (Eds.), *Handbook of eating disorders* (Second Edition, pp.139–150). Chichester, UK: Wiley.

National Institute for Clinical Excellence (NICE) (2004). *Eating disorders: Core Interventions in the treatment and management of anorexia nervosa, bulimia nervosa and related disorders. A national clinical practice guideline*. London: NICE. Online. Available at: http://www.nice.org.uk/page.aspx?o=101243

Nielsen, S. & Bará-Carril, N. (2003). Family, burden of care and social consequences. In J. Treasure, U. Schmidt & E. van Furth (Eds.), *Handbook of eating disorders* (Second Edition, pp. 191–217). Chichester, UK: Wiley.

Palmer, B. (2000). *Helping people with eating disorders*. Chichester, UK: Wiley.

Prochaska, J. & Velicer, W. (1997a). The transtheoratical model of health behaviour change. *American Journal of Health Promotion*, 12, 38–48.

Prochaska, J. & Velicer, W. (1997b). Misinterpretations and misapplications of the transtheoratical model. *American Journal of Health Promotion*, 12, 11–12.

Richards, L. (2003). Eating disorder services. In J. Treasure, U. Schmidt & E. van Furth (Eds.), *Handbook of eating disorders* (Second Edition, pp. 325–332). Chichester, UK: Wiley.

Royal College of Psychiatrists (2002). *Guidelines for the nutritional management of anorexia nervosa. A report of the Eating Disorders Special Interest Group*. London: Royal College of Psychiatrists.

Russell, G. (1979). Bulimia nervosa: An ominous variant of anorexia nervosa? *Psychological Medicine*, 9, 429–448.

Serpell, L. & Troup, N. (2003). Sociocultural theories of eating disorders. In J. Treasure, U. Schmidt & E. van Furth (Eds.), *Handbook of eating disorders* (Second Edition, pp. 151–167). Chichester, UK: Wiley.

Shafran, R. & de Silva, P. (2003). Cognitive behavioural models. In J. Treasure, U. Schmidt & E. van Furth (Eds.), *Handbook of eating disorders* (Second Edition, pp. 121–138). Chichester: Wiley.

Singh, A. (2002). Recent and conceptualized basic research activities for eating disorder: A review and future directions. *International Medical Journal*, 9, 83–85.

Spitzer, R., Marcus, M., Walsh, B. et al. (1992). Binge eating disorder: A multi-site field trial of the diagnostic criteria. *International Journal of Eating Disorders*, 11, 191–203.

Steinhausen, J. (2002). The outcome of anorexia nervosa in the 20th century. *American Journal of Psychiatry*, 159, 1284–1293.

Stice, E. (2002). Risk and maintenance factors for eating pathology. A meta-analytic review. *Psychological Bulletin*, 128(5), 825–848.

Sullivan, H. S. (1953). *The interpersonal theory of psychiatry*. New York: Norton.

Szmukler, G. & Patton, G. (1995). Sociocultural models of eating disorder. In G. Szmukler, C. Dare & J. Treasure (Eds.), *Handbook of eating disorders* (pp. 177–194). Chichester, UK: Wiley.

Tanner, C. & Connan, F. (2003). Cognitive analytic therapy. In J. Treasure, U. Schmidt & E. van Furth (Eds.), *Handbook of eating disorders* (Second Edition, pp. 279–290). Chichester, UK: Wiley.

Treasure, J. (1997). *Anorexia nervosa. A survival guide for families friends and sufferers.* Hove, UK: Psychology Press.

Treasure, J. & Bauer, B. (2003). Assessment and motivation. In J. Treasure, U. Schmidt & E. van Furth (Eds.), *Handbook of eating disorders* (Second Edition, pp. 219–211). Chichester, UK: Wiley.

van Hoeken, D., Seidell, J. & Hoek, H. (2003). Epidemiology. In J. Treasure, U. Schmidt & E. van Furth (Eds.), *Handbook of eating disorders* (Second Edition, pp. 11–34). Chichester, UK: Wiley.

Waller, G. & Kennerley, H. (2003). Cognitive behavioural treatments. In J. Treasure, U. Schmidt & E. van Furth (Eds.), *Handbook of eating disorders* (Second Edition, pp. 233–252). Chichester, UK: Wiley.

Weissman, M., Markowitz, J. & Klerman, G. (2000). *Comprehensive guide to interpersonal psychotherapy*. New York: Basic Books.

Wilfley, D., Stein, R. & Welch, R. (2003). Interpersonal psychotherapy. In J. Treasure, U. Schmidt & E. van Furth (Eds.), *Handbook of eating disorders* (Second Edition, pp. 253–270). Chichester, UK: Wiley.

Wilson, T. & Fairburn, C. (2002). Treatments for eating disorder. In P. Nathan &

J. Gorman (Eds.), *A guide to treatments that work* (Second Edition, pp. 559–592). New York: Oxford University Press.

Winston, A. & Webster, P. (2003). Inpatient treatment. In J. Treasure, U. Schmidt & E. van Furth (Eds.), *Handbook of eating disorders* (Second Edition, pp. 349–367). Chichester, UK: Wiley.

World Health Organization (WHO) (1992). *The ICD-10 classification of mental and behavioural disorders. Clinical descriptions and diagnostic guidelines.* Geneva: WHO.

Zhy, A. & Walsh, T. (2002). In review: Pharmacologic treatment of eating disorders. *Canadian Journal of Psychiatry*, 47, 227–234.

Chapter 20

Alcohol and other substance-use problems

Barbara S. McCrady

CASE EXAMPLE

Paula was a thirty-eight-year-old executive who had been married for two years to Bruce, a fifty-three-year-old independent construction contractor. Paula sought treatment for her drinking, which had become increasingly problematic over the past eight years. Paula and Bruce drank together every day, typically splitting three or four bottles of wine each evening. They had a number of friends, with whom they socialized and travelled, who were all equally heavy drinkers. Recently, Paula became a born-again Christian and experienced a deep sense of conflict between her religious practices and her heavy drinking. This sense of conflict was her primary motivation for seeking help. Bruce wanted to be involved with treatment as well, saying that he would do whatever was necessary to help her.

Paula was the oldest of three, having a younger brother and sister. Her parents were divorced and she had no contact with her mother. Her father, a retired electrician, was a life-long heavy drinker who was terminally ill with lung cancer. He lived nearby and Paula saw him virtually every day, helping him with meals and the care of his home. Her siblings lived several hundred miles away and she had sporadic contact with them. Her sister was married, had children, and was functioning well; her brother was married as well, but was a heavy drinker.

Paula was a highly successful financial analyst with a large company based in New York City. She worked very long hours (sixty to eighty hours in a typical week), travelled frequently, and attended numerous business-related functions. Paula was the first in her family to complete college, and took great pride in her personal and financial success.

Paula started drinking at the age of twelve, and drank regularly throughout high school and college. She stated that she always had been able to drink more than her friends and said she had always believed that she was different because of her ability to drink so much. Although always a heavy drinker, her daily drinking began at about the age of thirty, coincident with her taking her present job. She reported that she was usually exhausted when she arrived home, and that she had a great deal of difficulty 'turning off' her work. Alcohol provided a means to unwind. When she and Bruce met, they began to drink together, and the amounts increased over time to her present level of seven to twelve drinks per day. Since she began drinking every day she had never tried to cut down or stop, but reported no withdrawal symptoms in the mornings and no medical problems related to her drinking. She did, however, have behavioural tolerance to alcohol as well as blackouts, which were a source of great concern when they occurred after a work function. She felt utterly out of control of her drinking and could not imagine how she would be able to change, but felt strongly that she needed to try.

Paula also smoked a pack of cigarettes per day and wanted to stop, for both health and religious reasons. She also reported long-term feelings of sadness and inadequacy, and had been prescribed fluoxetine approximately six months before seeking treatment for her drinking, 40 mg per day. She felt that the medication had been somewhat helpful in that she did not become as deeply depressed as she had before beginning the medication, but said that she still did not feel 'happy'.

Paula and Bruce had a strong and loving relationship. He described himself as incredibly lucky to have found Paula; Paula said that she 'adored' Bruce and found him a source of strength and stability in her life. They described a passionate sexual relationship, laughed easily and listened carefully to each other during treatment sessions.

I treated Paula and Bruce using Alcohol Behavioral Couple Therapy (ABCT; Epstein & McCrady, 2002), a treatment that combines cognitive-behavioural coping skills training with interventions to help the partner learn how to respond differently to drinking and to abstinence and interventions to enhance the couple's relationship. Treatment followed a structured treatment manual, which allowed for up to twenty sessions of treatment over a six-month period.

Paula and Bruce responded well to the treatment. They attended regularly for the first three months and gradually reduced the frequency and amount that they drank. At first, Paula found it difficult to attain complete abstinence and we had regular conversations about when she thought she would be ready to abstain. During the treatment she was dealing with the continued failing health of her father, a reorganization at her job that meant she would have very different responsibilities and Bruce's ex-wife's announcement that she did not want to have their sons live with her any more, leading Paula and Bruce to make plans to have the boys move in with them. About three months into treatment, Paula and Bruce travelled to visit Paula's brother. His drinking had become more severe and she was deeply disturbed by his deterioration, as well as the chaos in his home. She helped him enter a detoxification programme and, on returning home, decided that she was ready to discontinue drinking, in which she was successful.

During treatment, we devoted a good deal of time to developing strategies to help Paula avoid drinking in work-related situations, while travelling and when she and Bruce socialized with friends. Over time, they began to spend more time with friends met through the church and less time with their former drinking friends. They also began to develop new rituals to be together in the evening without drinking, including listening to mood music, filling their porch with scented candles and preparing various flavoured ice-tea drinks to share. Paula also struggled with her complex feelings about her father, a combination of resentment, sadness and feelings of obligation, as well as her ambivalence about becoming a full-time stepmother. She abstained for the second three months of treatment and, in our follow-ups with her over the next year, we learned that she and Bruce both remained abstinent throughout.

INTRODUCTORY COMMENTS

Paula illustrates many aspects of working with individuals with alcohol and other substance-use disorders. These problems affect individuals of all social and economic circumstances; affect both men and women; are often characterized by complex comorbidities with other social, psychological or medical conditions; and are supported by an individual's social system and psychological needs. Treatment requires a delicate balancing of movement towards change with recognition that change is a process that occurs over time. Many clients respond well to treatment and make changes in their lives that are sustained over time.

This chapter starts with an overview of alcohol and drug problems. The bulk of the chapter focuses on assessment, case conceptualization, the process of decision making at each step in treatment, the selection of treatment modalities and implementation of specific treatment techniques. A wealth of research provides the empirical underpinnings for the chapter, and in the chapter I will show developing clinicians how to translate that knowledge into clinical practice with individual clients.

CLINICAL FEATURES OF ALCOHOL AND OTHER SUBSTANCE-USE DISORDERS, AND CLASSIFICATION OF SUBTYPES

The continuum of use

There are a number of ways to think about alcohol and drug use and abuse. The perspective taken in this chapter is a substance problems perspective (Institute of Medicine, 1990). The perspective is functional and focuses on the problem consequences of use as the key factor determining whether an individual needs to change. The perspective is atheoretical, saying nothing about the aetiology or course of the substance-use problem, and allows for multiple explanations of aetiology. The substance-use problems perspective views use as occurring along a continuum (illustrated in Figure 20.1). At one end of the continuum is the large proportion of the population that does not use a specific substance at all. This proportion varies by substance, country, gender, race and age, and is lower for alcohol than any other drug of abuse. Further along the continuum are individuals who use the substance occasionally and without problems. Although the possibility of problem consequences exists for these individuals, their risk is low. Still further along the continuum are more frequent or heavier users. Although not perhaps experiencing problems, such individuals are at risk for problems because of their pattern of use. Furthest along the continuum are those who experience occasional problems from their use and those who meet criteria for abuse or dependence on the substance. Viewing use on a continuum recognizes that there are gradations of problems, and that the boundaries between problem and non-problem use are blurred rather than sharp and distinct.

Although the substance problems perspective will be used throughout this chapter, alternative models are quite prominent. In the classic disease model, for example, Jellinek (1960) described several 'species' of alcoholism, viewing 'gamma' alcoholism as a disease characterized by inability to abstain and loss of control. The contemporary medical model (McLellan et al., 2000) views alcohol and other substance-use disorders as medical diseases, characterized by a defined set of symptoms, a specific aetiology, predictable course and responsive to specific treatments. Although a full discussion of these alternative models is beyond the scope of this chapter, the interested reader is referred to the Institute of Medicine (1990) report.

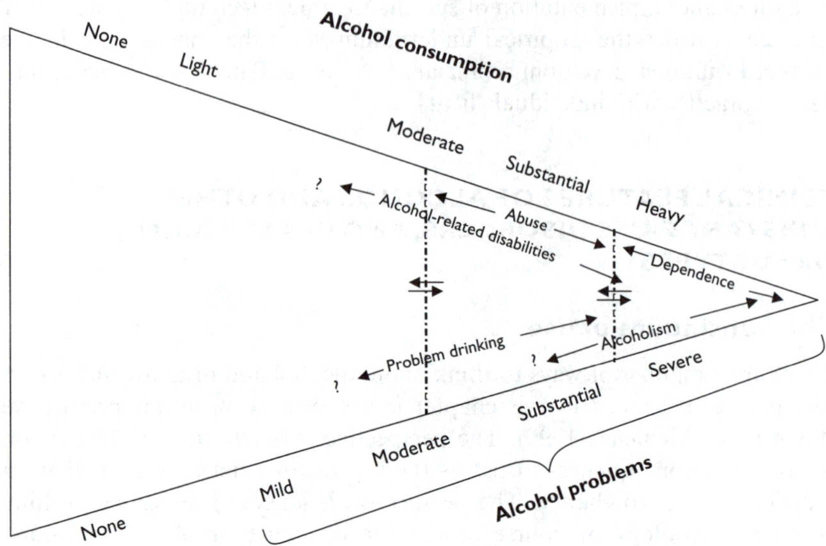

Figure 20.1 A terminological map (from the report of the Institute of Medicine, 1990, p. 30). 'The triangle represents the population of the United States. The alcohol consumption of the population ranges from none to heavy (along the upper side of the triangle) and the problems experienced in association with alcohol consumption range from none to severe (along the lower side of the triangle). The two-way arrows and the dotted lines indicate that, both from an individual and a population perspective, consumption levels and the degree of problems vary from time to time. The scope of terms that are often used to refer to individuals and groups according to their consumption levels and the degree of their problems are illustrated: question marks indicate that the lower boundary for many of the terms is uncertain.' (Institute of Medicine, 1990, p. 30)

Diagnostic features of substance-use disorders

Although viewing alcohol and drug problems along a continuum is helpful in planning treatment and helping the client accept the need for change, knowledge of formal diagnostic criteria is important to communicate among health and mental health professionals, as well as to define specific populations for studies of aetiology, course and treatment. The *Diagnostic and statistical manual of mental disorders* (Fourth Edition, Text Revision; DSM-IV-TR; American Psychiatric Association (APA), 2000) and the *International classification of diseases* (Tenth Edition; ICD-10; World Health Organization (WHO), 1992) define two major substance-related disorders. Criteria for the diagnosis of substance-use disorders are summarized in Table 20.1. These criteria are applied uniformly to all classes of substances of abuse, with variability in criteria only because either the tolerance or withdrawal criterion does not apply to some substances. Classes of substances include: alcohol;

Table 20.1 Diagnostic criteria for alcohol and drug abuse and dependence

DSM-IV-TR	*ICD-10*
Substance abuse A. A maladaptive pattern of alcohol or substance-use leading to clinically significant impairment or distress as manifested by one or more of the following occurring within a 12-month period: 1. Recurrent alcohol or substance abuse resulting in a failure to fulfil major obligations at work, school or home 2. Recurrent alcohol or substance abuse in situations in which it is physically hazardous 3. Recurrent alcohol or substance-related legal problems 4. Continued alcohol or substance-use despite having persistent or recurrent social or interpersonal problems caused by or exacerbated by the effects of the substance B. The symptoms have never met the criteria for substance dependence for this type of substance	**Harmful use** A pattern of alcohol or psychoactive substance abuse that is causing harm to health The damage may be physical (as in cases of hepatitis from the self-administration of injected drugs) or mental (e.g. episodes of depressive disorder secondary to heavy consumption of alcohol) The fact that pattern of use of alcohol or a particular substance is disapproved of by a culture or may have led to socially negative consequences, such as arrest or marital arguments is not in itself evidence of harmful use
Substance dependence A maladaptive pattern of alcohol or substance abuse, leading to clinically significant impairment or distress, as manifested by three or more of the following occurring at any time in the same 12-month period: 1. Tolerance defined by either: (a) a need for markedly increased amounts of the substance to achieve intoxication (b) markedly diminished effect with continued use of the same amount of the substance 2. Withdrawal as manifested by either of the following: (a) the characteristic withdrawal syndrome for the substance (b) the same substance is taken to relieve or avoid withdrawal symptoms 3. The substance is taken in larger amounts over a longer period than was intended	**Dependence syndrome** A cluster of physiological, behavioural and cognitive phenomena in which the use of alcohol or a substance or a class of substances takes on a much higher priority than other behaviours that once had greater value Three or more of the following in a 12-month period: 1. A strong desire or sense of compulsion to take alcohol or the substance 2. Difficulty in controlling drinking or substance-taking behaviour in terms of onset, termination or levels of use 3. A physiological withdrawal state when drinking or substance-use has ceased or been reduced as evidenced by: the characteristic withdrawal syndrome for alcohol or the substance; use of alcohol or the substance to avoid withdrawal symptoms

Continued overleaf

Table 20.1 continued

DSM-IV-TR	*ICD-10*
4. There is a persistent desire or unsuccessful efforts to cut down or control alcohol or substance-use 5. A great deal of time is spent in activities necessary to obtain alcohol or the substance, use the substance or recover from its effects 6. Important social, occupational or recreational activities are given up or reduced because of alcohol or substance-use 7. The alcohol or substance-use is continued despite knowledge of having a persistent or recurrent physical or psychological problem that is likely to have been caused or exacerbated by alcohol or the substance Specify with or without physiological dependence	4. Evidence of tolerance such that increased doses of alcohol or the substance are required in order to achieve the effects originally produced by lower doses 5. Progressive neglect of alternative pleasures or interests because of drinking or psychoactive substance-use, increased amount of time necessary to obtain or take alcohol or the substance or to recover from its effects 6. Persisting with drinking or substance-use despite clear evidence of overtly harmful consequences, such as harm to the liver through excessive drinking, depressive mood states consequent to periods of heavy substance abuse, or drug-related impairment of cognitive functioning

Note: Adapted from DSM-IV-TR (APA, 2000) and ICD-10 (WHO, 1992).

amphetamines-like compounds; caffeine; cannabis; cocaine; hallucinogens; inhalants; nicotine; opioids; phencyclidine and sedative, hypnotic or anxiolytic agents.

Comorbid disorders

Alcohol and other drug-use disorders are complex and individuals with these problems often have a number of other problems as well. For heavier and longer-term users, medical sequelae of use are common. Medical problems are specific to different drugs. Alcohol has the most pervasive medical consequences, affecting every organ system in the body. The medical complications from chronic use of other drugs are less pervasive and are related partly to the mode of administration of the drug (e.g. inhalation or injection). Table 20.2 summarizes these effects.

In addition to medical complications, alcohol and drug-use disorders occur in conjunction with many other psychological disorders. Among persons diagnosed with an alcohol-use disorder, 37% will meet criteria for another Axis I disorder (Rosenthal & Westreich, 1999). The most common diagnoses are mood and anxiety disorders, with comorbid post-traumatic stress disorder (PTSD) being particularly elevated. Axis II disorders also are common,

Table 20.2 Medical consequences of heavy use of alcohol or other drugs[1]

	Central nervous system	*Gastrointestinal*	*Cardiovascular*	*Endocrine and reproduction*	*Pulmonary*	*Other*
Alcohol[1]	Wernicke's encephalopathy Korsakoff's psychosis Cerebellar ataxia Alcoholic dementia Polyneuropathy	Fatty liver Alcoholic hepatitis Cirrhosis Pancreatitis Gastritis	Cardiomyopathy Arrhythmias Hypertension Increased cholesterol	Hypoglycaemia (acute exposure) Hyperglycaemia (chronic exposure) Osteoporosis Menstrual cycle irregularity Decreased testosterone		
Cannabis	Impaired ability to focus attention		Acute risk of myocardial infarction after use		Chronic bronchitis Increased risk of lung cancer	Reduced immune response – susceptibility to infection
Hallucinogens	Psychosis Flashbacks					Risk of accidental injury
Inhalants	Peripheral neuropathies Cortical or cerebellar atrophy	Liver damage Sudden death from suffocation	Sudden death from heart failure			Kidney damage Hearing loss Bone marrow damage
Nicotine	Stroke	Aortic aneurysm		Increased risk of uterine cancer Reduced fertility Impotence Low birth weight Sudden infant death syndrome	Cancer of mouth, throat, lungs Chronic obstructive pulmonary disorder	Poor wound healing

Continued overleaf

Table 20.2 continued

	Central nervous system	*Gastrointestinal*	*Cardiovascular*	*Endocrine and reproduction*	*Pulmonary*	*Other*
Opioids		Chronic liver disease (hepatitis B & C)	Pericardial infection Collapsed veins	Obstetric complications	Pneumonia	Overdose Infectious diseases (HIV, tuberculosis) Abcesses Cellulitis
Phencyclidine	Seizures Coma Psychosis Memory loss	Nausea and vomiting	Hypotension			Violence or suicidality
Sedative, hypnotic or anxiolytic agents	Depression of central nervous system Confusion Anterograde amnesia				Respiratory depression	
Stimulants, including amphet-amines and cocaine	Symptoms like movement disorder Seizures Hyperthermia Respiratory paralysis Cerebral infarction (stroke)	Nausea, vomiting, diarrhoea Severe anorexia Malnutrition	Tachycardia Hypertension Arrhythmias Cardiomyopathy Myocardial infarction (heart attack)	Spontaneous abortion Neonatal cerebral infarction Sudden infant death syndrome	Chronic cough (if smoked)	Inflammation and atrophy of nasal mucosa

[1] Taken from chapters in McCrady & Epstein (1999) and pages on specific drugs of abuse accessed from http://www.drugabuse.gov/Infofax/infofaxindex.html
Note: Effects differ for different specific inhalants.

with rates reported up to almost 33% (Rosenthal & Westreich, 1999); antisocial personality disorder is the most common Axis II disorder.

Substance-use disorders are also associated with interpersonal and social problems. Rates of divorce are high, children of substance-abusing parents are at increased risk for substance-use disorders as well as both externalizing (e.g. conduct disorder) and internalizing disorders (such as mood or anxiety disorders); spouses experience elevated rates of anxiety and depression, and intact relationships are characterized by distress and, often, domestic violence (Caetano et al., 2001; McCrady et al., 1998). Substance use also results in a variety of social problems. Individuals have legal problems from driving under the influence, disorderly conduct, drug distribution and other illegal activities because of the need to obtain money to acquire drugs. Given the high cost of purchase of large amounts of alcohol or most drugs, many individuals experience financial problems because they have diverted funds from daily needs to drugs or alcohol. Occupational disruption may occur, with loss of job or demotion to less demanding and less lucrative positions. Severe and chronic problems may result in unemployment and, at times, homelessness. Thus, the clinician working with an individual with a substance-use disorder must assess each client along multiple dimensions and be prepared to develop a comprehensive treatment plan that addresses the multiple needs that these clients present.

Subtypes

Given the complexity and heterogeneity of individuals with substance-use disorders, researchers have attempted to develop meaningful systems to subtype substance abusers into homogeneous subgroups. Clients have been subtyped using uni-dimensional and multi-dimensional schemes (Epstein et al., 2002). The subtyping approach with the best empirical support is the type A/B approach, originally developed on an alcohol-dependent population by Babor et al. (1992). Later research has provided support for the same subtyping scheme with individuals diagnosed with cocaine dependence (Ball, Carroll, Babor & Rounsaville, 1995). In this scheme, compared to type A alcoholics or cocaine users, individuals classified as type B have an earlier onset for their problems; more pre-morbid risk factors, such as a family history of substance-use disorder or behavioural problems in childhood; more adult antisocial characteristics; more comorbid disorders, such as problems with anxiety and depression; and more severe substance-use problems. Generally, type B individuals have a poorer outcome than type A individuals (Litt et al., 1992; Morgenstern et al., 1998).

EPIDEMIOLOGY AND COURSE

Prevalence

Rates of substance abuse and dependence vary by country, sex, age and racial/ethnic background. Across cultures, rates of abuse and dependence on alcohol are higher for males (12.35% in the US) than females (4.87%; Grant et al., 2004), and rates of abuse and dependence decrease with age, both because of mortality and because of natural maturing out of abuse patterns. Table 20.3 summarizes rates of abuse and dependence in the United States.

Course and outcomes of treated and untreated substance-use disorders

Long-term outcomes

Four pathways characterize individuals with alcohol and other substance-use disorders over time: complete remission, continued problem use, alternating periods of remission and relapse, and death. There is good evidence that many individuals with alcohol-use disorders will resolve their problems without treatment, with two Canadian surveys (reported in Sobell et al., 1996) finding that 77% of those in remission had achieved remission without formal treatment. Longitudinal studies of untreated populations find that the majority of individuals with some alcohol-related problems do not show these problems at follow-ups ranging from four to twenty-seven years (Cahalan et al., 1969; Kerr et al., 2002). Remission to non-problem drinking status is particularly common among youthful drinkers exhibiting some problems associated with their use. Remission status may be to either abstinence or non-problem drinking. Some evidence suggests that individuals with more severe drinking problems remit to abstinence, while those with less severe problems remit to non-problem drinking (Vaillant, 1995).

Among those receiving treatment, remission rates from alcohol problems are higher, averaging about 4.8% per year, compared to 3% per year among untreated individuals (Finney et al., 1999). An analysis of the outcomes of treatment from several large-scale treatment studies suggests that 25% of individuals will remain abstinent from alcohol one year after treatment; 10% will engage in moderate but controlled drinking and, even though continuing to drink and perhaps experiencing problems from drinking, other clients will reduce their drinking frequency by 87% and drinking problems by 60% (Miller et al., 2001).

Long-term, prospective data on recovery from other drug problems without treatment are lacking. Reviews of longitudinal studies of treated populations suggest that annualized recovery rates are lower for opiate than alcohol dependence, and average about 3.7% per year (Finney et al., 1999). It also is

Table 20.3 Illicit drug use in lifetime, past year, and past month among persons aged 12 or older: percentages, 2002[1]

Drug	*Time period*		
	Life time	*Past year*	*Past month*
Any illicit drug[2]	46.0	14.9	8.3
Marijuana and hashish	40.4	11.0	6.2
Cocaine:	14.4	2.5	0.9
Crack	3.6	0.7	0.2
Heroin	1.6	0.2	0.1
Hallucinogens:	14.6	2.0	0.5
LSD	10.4	0.4	0.0
PCP	3.2	0.1	0.0
Ecstasy	4.3	1.3	0.3
Inhalants	9.7	0.9	0.3
Non-medical use of any psychotherapeutic[3]	19.8	6.2	2.6
Pain relievers	12.6	4.7	1.9
Tranquillizers	8.2	2.1	0.8
Stimulants:	9.0	1.4	0.5
Methamphetamine	5.3	0.7	0.3
Sedatives	4.2	0.4	0.2
Any illicit drug other than marijuana[2]	29.9	8.7	3.7

[1] This table is in the public domain, and was obtained from SAMHSA, Office of Applied Studies, National Survey on Drug Use and Health, 2002, http://oas.samhsa.gov/nhsda/2k2nsduh/Results/2k2Results.htm#toc

[2] Any illicit drug includes marijuana/hashish, cocaine (including crack), heroin, hallucinogens, inhalants or any prescription-type psychotherapeutic used non-medically.
Any illicit drug other than marijuana includes cocaine (including crack), heroin, hallucinogens, inhalants or any prescription-type psychotherapeutic used non-medically.

[3] Non-medical use of any prescription-type pain reliever, tranquillizer, stimulant or sedative; does not include over-the-counter drugs.

more difficult to provide stable estimates of abstinence rates, as reported rates have ranged from 10% to as high as 65% (Finney et al., 1999).

Response to specific treatments

Literally thousands of treatment outcome studies have evaluated the outcomes of specific treatment programmes and models, and hundreds of studies have used randomized clinical trials methodologies to compare the effectiveness of well-defined treatments to either treatment as usual or to minimal interventions and to assess the relative effectiveness of different treatments. Several major conclusions can be drawn from these studies. First, there is fairly good evidence that treatment can increase the chances of successful resolution of a drinking or drug problem over self-directed change efforts.

Second, it appears that there is not a single best treatment for alcohol or other substance-use disorders. Third, there is evidence for the effectiveness of several different treatments. Fourth, despite the strong intuitive appeal of patient-treatment matching approaches, empirical evidence to guide clinicians in tailoring treatment to individual patients is largely absent.

Miller and colleagues (e.g. Miller & Wilbourne, 2002) have conducted a number of meta-analyses of the psychosocial alcohol treatment literature. From their reviews, they have identified several treatments with strong evidence for effectiveness, including several forms of cognitive-behavioural treatment, brief treatments with a motivational focus, behavioural couple therapy and case management. Most recently, controlled studies of treatment designed to enhance involvement with twelve-step recovery programmes (such as Alcoholics Anonymous; AA) have reported outcomes equivalent to those of other treatments with demonstrable effectiveness, so it is reasonable to include such treatments among those with empirical support. Effective pharmacotherapies for alcohol-use disorders include disulfiram, naltrexone, nalmefene and acamprosate.

Effective treatments for other substance-use disorders also have been identified. For those with heroin dependence, methadone maintenance has the strongest evidence for effectiveness. Opiate antagonist treatment (e.g. naltrexone) and long-term therapeutic communities also are highly effective, but compliance typically is low with both forms of treatment. Demonstrably effective treatments for cocaine dependence include drug counselling that combines cognitive-behavioural coping skills training with twelve-step programme involvement (Crits-Cristoph et al., 1999) and the Community Reinforcement Approach with vouchers (Higgins et al., 2000). Studies of treatments for marijuana dependence are less common but current evidence supports the use of cognitive-behavioural treatments with a relapse prevention focus as well as motivational enhancement therapy with vouchers (Budney et al., 2000). Effective pharmacotherapies are lacking for cocaine and marijuana dependence.

Intensity, duration and level of care

Considerable controversy surrounds issues related to the intensity and duration of treatment. Traditional views suggested that treatment needed to remove substance-users from their usual environment to be able to break through their denial, motivate them to desire change, help them focus on recovery and re-form their identities as individuals with a life-long disease. So-called 'Minnesota Model' programmes, developed originally in the state of Minnesota in the US, but now in existence in a number of Western countries, exemplify this treatment model.

Controlled research, however, has challenged this model. Early research in the UK examined the assumption of the need for intensive treatment.

Edwards and colleagues (Edwards et al., 1977) randomly assigned alcohol-dependent men to comprehensive assessment plus access to a full complement of treatment services, or to comprehensive assessment plus directive advice to stop drinking without formal treatment. Overall outcomes a year after treatment were comparable for the two groups, although subgroup analyses suggested that those with more severe alcohol dependence fared better in the treatment than the advice condition, with no differences in outcome for those with less severe problems (Orford et al., 1976). A number of other studies with alcohol-dependent populations have found no differences in outcomes for residential compared to various forms of outpatient treatment (reviewed in Miller & Hester, 1986). The most recent research examined matching of patients to level of care, finding that patients with severe alcohol dependence responded more favourably to residential treatment, while those with less severe problems responded better to ambulatory treatment (Rychtarik et al., 2000).

Findings from research on length of treatment also are complex. Correlational studies consistently report a positive correlation between more treatment sessions or longer attachment to treatment and positive outcomes of treatment. However, most randomized clinical trials comparing treatments of different duration have found no differences in outcome for different lengths of treatment.

Clinical applications of the complex set of findings about treatment intensity and duration have been integrated in two related models. Stepped-care models (e.g. Sobell & Sobell, 2000) suggest that, whenever possible, treatment should be initiated at the least intensive level of care, which would be ambulatory treatment of short duration. Response to treatment would be evaluated continuously, and decisions about longer duration or more intensive treatment would be made based on the client's initial response. An alternative model, developed by the American Society of Addiction Medicine (ASAM, 1991) suggests use of multiple dimensions of functioning to make decisions about initial level of care as well as to make decisions about changes in level of care. Dimensions of client functioning to consider include severity of physiological dependence, relapse potential, severity of medical and psychiatric complications or co-occurring disorders, motivation and the nature of the recovery environment. Combining these six dimensions allows the clinician to select among treatments ranging from brief interventions at one end of the continuum to medically supervised inpatient treatment at the other end. The ASAM system is quite elaborate and beyond the scope of this chapter.

Treatment goals (abstinence versus moderation)

Although less controversial in European countries, selection of treatment goals has been a topic of considerable controversy in the US, and the proliferation of Alcoholics Anonymous (Mäkelä et al., 1996) and Minnesota model programmes in European countries suggests that issues around selection of treatment goals will challenge clinicians across countries and cultures. Given that virtually all of this discussion has focused on alcohol rather than other drug use, the discussion here focuses only on drinking-related goals.

Early and conventional thought promoted the view that abstinence was the only safe and appropriate goal for the treatment of alcohol dependence, and moderated drinking outcomes were thought to be impossible or improbable. Several decades of research challenge these assumptions, with many studies demonstrating moderate drinking as an outcome for at least some of those with alcohol dependence (e.g. Helzer et al., 1985; Vaillant, 1995). European studies have found that when clients are given the opportunity to select treatment goals they often select goals appropriate to the severity of their alcohol dependence, and that as many as half of clients will change their goals over time (Ojehegan & Berglund, 1989; Orford & Keddie, 1986). Less evidence directs clinicians to demonstrably effective treatments to effect moderate drinking outcomes, but there is good evidence that those with less severe dependence, a history of successful control over drinking, lack of a family history of alcohol dependence, lack of medical complications or history of withdrawal syndrome, and being female all are associated with greater probability of success with controlled drinking (Rosenberg, 1993). Clinical application of this research is discussed later in the chapter in the section on treatment engagement.

A BIOPSYCHOSOCIAL MODEL TO GUIDE TREATMENT PLANNING AND IMPLEMENTATION

Substance-use disorders are influenced by and influence multiple systems, ranging from the individual to the larger society. The treatment model that guides the remainder of this chapter is based on the assumption that there are multiple aetiologies for substance-use disorders, multiple factors maintaining use and multiple pathways to successful change. Adopting a multi-perspectival approach is more difficult and challenging, particularly for the beginning clinician, than simply adopting a unitary model that provides a common conceptualization and treatment for all clients. However, the more complex approach gives the clinician more options for treatment engagement and implementation.

Such an approach requires an initial case conceptualization. A functional analytic approach allows the clinician to integrate information about environmental, cognitive, physiological, affective and behavioural elements that maintain drinking or drug use. Figure 20.2 provides a schematic of a functional analysis. Drinking or drug use is assumed to occur in response to stimuli in the external environment. These stimuli may derive from habitual

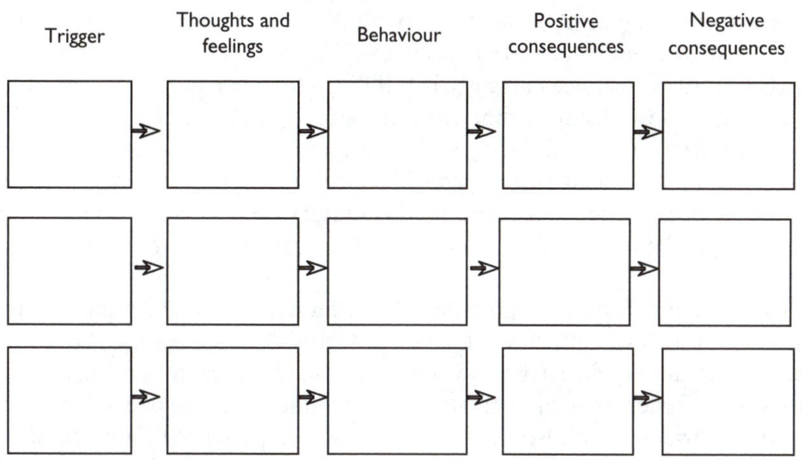

Figure 20.2 Functional analysis.

and reinforced patterns of use (such as drinking in a pub with fellow workers at the end of the day), the individual's own psychological vulnerabilities (such as experiencing depression after a perceived failure), the dependence-inducing qualities of the drug (such as drinking at certain times of the day to avoid withdrawal symptoms) or from interpersonal difficulties with family or friends. Considering multiple systems of influence beyond the individual is central to case conceptualization.

The second step in a functional analysis requires an assessment and understanding of internal reactions to environmental stimuli. These reactions may be cognitive, affective or physiological. In assessing internal reactions, the clinician can identify patterns of alcohol or other drug withdrawal, repeated patterns of affective responses, common cognitions that occur across multiple situations, and specific expectancies about the anticipated impact of the alcohol or drug. Key to the assessment of internal variables is the understanding of common patterns of response to multiple situations.

The third element in functional analysis is assessment and understanding of the individual's behavioural repertoire. Clients use substances in a specific and patterned manner, and a careful assessment of quantity and frequency of use provides the clinician with a good understanding of the extent and severity of physiological dependence. In addition to the client's use pattern, it is important to the client's behavioural coping repertoire to understand the types of behavioural deficits and excesses that will need to be a focus of treatment.

The fourth aspect of a functional analysis is the consideration of positive and negative consequences of use. Positive consequences that occur in close proximity to use are assumed to help maintain the use pattern. These consequences may be physiological, cognitive, affective and/or interpersonal. Careful assessment of positive consequences also helps the clinician identify needs that the substance currently is fulfilling. Negative consequences of use often occur more distal in time from the use. Negative consequences often form the core of motivation to seek treatment, but clients who have been coerced into treatment often have difficulty identifying or acknowledging negative consequences. Over time, even voluntary clients may begin to minimize or forget the negative consequences that formed their original motivation to change.

The functional analysis provides a current view of factors maintaining substance-use. The influence of historical and developmental factors also needs to be understood. Clients with a positive family history of alcohol- or drug-use disorders may have greater genetic vulnerability to dependence on a specific substance and also have been exposed to parental models of use to cope with problems. Given the high comorbidities between substance-use and other psychiatric disorders, the offspring of substance abusers may have grown up in households with inconsistent discipline, inconsistent affectional attachments and limited stability and predictability in their family or origin. Women with substance-use disorders have an elevated rate of childhood and adult physical and sexual abuse. These historical factors can be viewed as experiences that have shaped the way the individual responds cognitively, affectively and behaviourally to current situations in their lives, and provides a context for clients to understand their patterns of maladaptive responding.

Finally, clinicians must consider other psychological, medical and social conditions that are complicating the client's life. These complicating conditions may make it difficult for a client to comply with treatment or to make progress in dealing with the substance abuse. Appropriate assessment of multiple dimensions of functioning facilitates treatment planning and co-ordination of services to help clients deal with the myriad of life problems that they are experiencing and facilitate their involvement with and ability to benefit from substance-abuse treatment.

Societal context of use

Societal norms about alcohol and drug use vary with country, subculture and proximal social group. Use of licit drugs is influenced as well by advertising and media portrayals of use. Laws regulating access to substances as well as legal penalties for use, acquisition, sales and distribution of substances also affect use patterns. In the US, alcohol use is portrayed in as much as 64% of television shows (Wallack et al., 1990), and 86% of British soap operas contain references to alcohol (verbal or visual), at the rate of one reference every 3.5 minutes (Furnham et al., 1997). Additionally, the alcohol industry spends billions of dollars advertising their products, approximately $1.6 billion in 2002 (Mothers Against Drunk Driving; MADD, 2004). Advertisers attempt to create product recognition and product preference as well as associations between alcohol use and desirable attributes such as youth, physical prowess or sexual appeal. Research suggests that these efforts are successful, in that even in middle childhood children have positive expectancies about the effects of alcohol (Dunn & Ynigues, 1999).

In most countries, other drugs are either regulated or illegal, and the massive societal visibility of these drugs is absent. But, within certain cultural and economic groups, drugs have a cachet in the local community that makes them visible and attractive even though illegal, and drug dealers may be high-status individuals in the subculture. Efforts to decriminalize some drugs, such as marijuana in the Netherlands, have been promoted as a way to decrease the attractiveness of these drugs in specific subcultures.

Individuals tend to use alcohol and drugs in patterns similar to those in their proximal social and family group. Heavy drinkers have a concentration of heavy drinkers in their social networks (McCrady, 2004); drug-using women often are in relationships with drug-using men. Teens typically are part of peer groups with similar patterns of use. Although in the past it was thought that peers could be a 'good influence' or 'bad influence' on a youth, more recent work suggests that adolescents seek out like-using peers as friends, and that use patterns evolve in the group (Donohew et al., 1999).

During the resolution of substance-use disorders, changes in the individual's social network form an important aspect of recovery (reviewed in McCrady, 2004). Individuals are at higher risk for relapse if they have even one member of their immediate social network who uses the same drugs, and successful recovery from alcohol-use disorders is associated with changes in the social network so that there are more abstainers/recovering alcoholics in the network, and more friends in general.

Family and other interpersonal factors maintaining use

Alcohol and other drug use develops in a familial context, and successful resolution of problems also may occur in a familial context. Families have multiple influences on use patterns. During development, adolescents are less likely to develop alcohol or drug-use problems if they have parents who are warm, nurturing and non-confrontational; provide consistent and firm discipline; monitor their child's behaviour; advocate for their child outside of their home and provide a religious context (Bry & Slechta, 2000). Conversely, some families experience multiple psychological, social and substance problems across generations, and the children are at very high risk for developing substance-use or other externalizing disorders themselves (Loukas et al., 2003).

For those with established substance-use disorders, the family may play a central role in the maintenance of use. Familial interactions may serve as antecedents to use, and may include family members using the same drugs, encouraging each other to use, attempting to control the individual's use, as well as typical family problems that are managed poorly or not at all when the individual is using actively. Families also may provide consequences that help to maintain the use. They may provide deliberate or inadvertent reinforcement for continued use, or they may shield the user from negative consequences of use that could otherwise motivate the user to change.

Psychological aspects of use

There are multiple psychological aspects of use that clinicians should consider. As noted, comorbidities are high between substance-use and other psychological disorders, and these other problems may require additional psychological or pharmacotherapeutic interventions. There also may be intimate interrelationships between the substance-use and the other disorder, such as the person with social phobia who drinks heavily to interact in social situations, or the depressed individual who uses cocaine to feel energized.

Cognitions about substance-use and the effects of the substances are a second important psychological factor to consider. Heavy users tend to have more positive expectancies about the effects of use than light or non-users. Those with substance-use disorders may believe that they have no control over their use and attribute their use to external and stable factors such as family history. If they are to achieve abstinence, they may be vulnerable to the abstinence violation effect (AVE; Marlatt & Gordon, 1986), which would lead to binge or heavy drinking post-relapse. Substance users also may have low self-efficacy about their ability to cope with high-risk situations without use. Higher self-efficacy has been associated with better treatment outcomes (Vielva & Iraugi, 2001), although very high self-efficacy may be associated with poor outcomes as it reflects an unrealistic appraisal of the challenges associated with abstinence.

Affect regulation is an important part of substance-use. Individuals use substances both to attenuate negative affect and to enhance positive experiences. Those who use for both reasons are at the highest risk for the development of substance-use disorders (Labouvie & Bates, 2002), and relapses occur in response to negative and positive emotions (Marlatt & Gordon, 1986).

Motivation is a key psychological variable to understand in treating those with substance-use disorders. Although motivation was historically considered as a trait that was relatively immune to therapeutic influence, contemporary perspectives view motivation as a state that is influenced by life experiences and therapeutic influence (e.g. Miller & Rollnick, 2002). Motivation and problem recognition are best viewed along a continuum, ranging from viewing one's substance-use as non-problematic (sometimes called the 'precontemplation stage') to considering the possibility of use as a problem ('contemplation'), to determining use is problematic and preparing to change ('preparation' or 'determination'), to active change ('action')

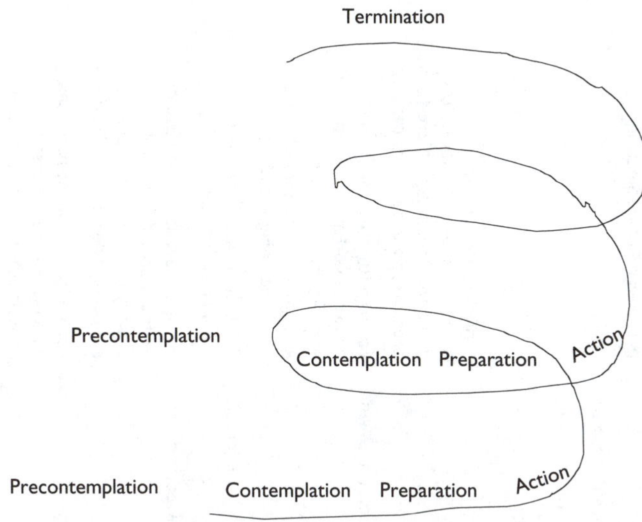

Figure 20.3 A spiral model of the stages of change (from Prochaska, DiClemente & Norcross, 1992).

(Prochaska et al., 1992). Figure 20.3 illustrates this continuum. Perceptions of positive and negative consequences vary with an individual's level of readiness to change, with a perception of more positive consequences and less negative consequences among those least ready to change, and a reversal among those starting to change (Cunningham et al., 1997). Greater commitment to abstinence is associated with a greater probability of success in treatment (Hall et al., 1991).

Biological aspects of use, abuse, dependence and medical complications

Psychoactive substances have characteristic physiological effects. Table 20.4, adapted from the US National Institute on Drug Abuse (NIDA) website, summarizes the effects of different substances. Many, although not all, drugs create physical dependence. Cessation of use or a sudden reduction in use can precipitate a characteristic pattern of withdrawal. Withdrawal from alcohol or minor tranquillizers with long half-lives (e.g. Valium, Librium) is most dangerous and may be life-threatening. Withdrawal symptoms are summarized in Table 20.5. A number of signs suggest that a client may be physically dependent. Daily use, using regularly or intermittently throughout the day, and morning use all suggest physical dependence. If a client reports awakening during the night with fears, trembling or nausea, or experiences such symptoms upon first awakening, these are also suggestive of dependence on alcohol. Further, in a client who is physically dependent on alcohol, cessation or a

Table 20.4 Effects of drugs, commercial and street names, and routes of administration[1] for commonly abused drugs

Substance: Category and name	*Examples of commercial and street names*	*How administered**	*Intoxication effects*
Cannabinoids			Euphoria, slowed thinking and reaction time, confusion, impaired balance and co-ordination
Hashish	Boom, chronic, gangster, hash, hash oil, hemp	Swallowed, smoked	
Marijuana	Blunt, dope, ganja, grass, herb, joints, Mary Jane, pot, reefer, sinsemilla, skunk, weed	Swallowed, smoked	
Depressants			Reduced anxiety; feeling of well-being; lowered inhibitions; slowed pulse and breathing; lowered blood pressure; poor concentration
Barbiturates	Amytal, Nembutal, Seconal, Phenobarbital; barbs, reds, red birds, phennies, tooies, yellows, yellow jackets	Injected, swallowed	For barbiturates – sedation, drowsiness/depression, unusual excitement, fever, irritability, poor judgement, slurred speech, dizziness, life-threatening withdrawal
Benzodiazepines (other than flunitrazepam)	Ativan, Halcion, Librium, Valium, Xanax; candy, downers, sleeping pills, tranks	Swallowed, injected	For benzodiazepines – sedation, drowsiness/dizziness
Flunitrazepam**	Rohypnol; forget-me pill, Mexican Valium, R2, Roche, roofies, roofinol, rope, rophies	Swallowed, snorted	For flunitrazepam – visual and gastrointestinal disturbances, urinary retention, memory loss for the time under the drug's effects
GHB**	Gamma-hydroxybutyrate; G, Georgia home boy, grievous bodily harm, liquid ecstasy	Swallowed	For GHB – drowsiness, nausea/vomiting, headache, loss of consciousness, loss of reflexes, seizures, coma, death

Methaqualone	Quaalude, Sopor, Parest; ludes, mandrex, quad, quay	Injected, swallowed	For methaqualone – euphoria/ depression, poor reflexes, slurred speech, coma
Dissociative anaesthetics			Increased heart rate and blood pressure, impaired motor function
Ketamine	Ketalar SV; cat Valiums, K, Special K, vitamin K	Injected, snorted, smoked	For ketamine – at high doses – delirium, depression, respiratory depression and arrest
PCP and analogues	Phencyclidine; angel dust, boat, hog, love boat, peace pill	Injected, swallowed, smoked	For PCP and analogues – possible decrease in blood pressure and heart rate, panic, aggression, violence
Hallucinogens			Altered states of perception and feeling; nausea
LSD	Lysergic acid diethylamide; acid, blotter, boomers, cubes, microdot, yellow sunshines	Swallowed, absorbed through mouth tissues	For LSD and mescaline – increased body temperature, heart rate, blood pressure; loss of appetite, sleeplessness, numbness, weakness, tremors For LSD – persistent mental disorders
Mescaline	Buttons, cactus, mesc, peyote	Swallowed, smoked	For psilocybin – nervousness, paranoia
Psilocybin	Magic mushroom, purple passion, shrooms	Swallowed	
Opioids and morphine derivatives			Pain relief, euphoria, drowsiness
Codeine	Empirin with Codeine, Fiorinal with Codeine, Robitussin A-C, Tylenol with Codeine; Captain Cody, Cody, schoolboy; (with glutethimide) doors & fours, loads, pancakes and syrup	Injected, swallowed	Also, for codeine – less analgesia, sedation, and respiratory depression than morphine

Continued overleaf

Table 20.4 continued

Substance: Category and name	*Examples of commercial and street names*	*How administered**	*Intoxication effects*
Fentanyl and fentanyl analogues	Actiq, Duragesic, Sublimaze; Apache, China girl, China white, dance fever, friend, goodfella, jackpot, murder 8, TNT, Tango and Cash	Injected, smoked, snorted	
Heroin	diacetylmorphine; brown sugar, dope, H, horse, junk, skag, skunk, smack, white horse	Injected, smoked, snorted	For heroin – staggering gait
Morphine	Roxanol, Duramorph; M, Miss Emma, monkey, white stuff	Injected, swallowed, smoked	
Opium	Laudanum, paregoric; big O, black stuff, block, gum, hop	Swallowed, smoked	
Oxycodone HCl	Oxycontin; Oxy, O.C., killer	Swallowed, snorted, injected	
Hydrocodone bitartrate, acetaminophen (paracetamol)	Vicodin; vike, Watson-387	Swallowed	
Stimulants			Increased heart rate, blood pressure, metabolism; feelings of exhilaration, energy, increased mental alertness
Amphetamine	Biphetamine, Dexedrine; bennies, black beauties, crosses, hearts, LA turnaround, speed, truck drivers, uppers	Injected, swallowed, smoked, snorted	Also, for amphetamine – rapid breathing/tremor, loss of co-ordination; irritability, anxiousness, restlessness, delirium, panic, paranoia, impulsive behaviour, aggressiveness, tolerance, addiction, psychosis

Cocaine	Cocaine hydrochloride; blow, bump, C, candy, Charlie, coke, crack, flake, rock, snow, toot	Injected, smoked, snorted	For cocaine – increased temperature
MDMA (methylenedioxymethamphetamine)	Adam, clarity, ecstasy, Eve, lover's speed, peace, STP, X, XTC	Swallowed	For MDMA – mild hallucinogenic effects, increased tactile sensitivity, empathic feelings/impaired memory and learning, hyperthermia, cardiac toxicity, renal failure, liver toxicity
Methamphetamine	Desoxyn; chalk, crank, crystal, fire, glass, go fast, ice, meth, speed	Injected, swallowed, smoked, snorted	For methamphetamine – aggression, violence, psychotic behaviour
Methylphenidate (safe and effective for treatment of ADHD)	Ritalin; JIF, MPH, R-ball, Skippy, the smart drug, vitamin R	Injected, swallowed, snorted	
Nicotine	Cigarettes, cigars, smokeless tobacco, snuff, spit tobacco, bidis, chew	Smoked, snorted, taken in snuff and spit tobacco	
Other Compounds			
Inhalants	Solvents (paint thinners, gasoline, glues), gases (butane, propane, aerosol propellants, nitrous oxide), nitrites (isoamyl, isobutyl, cyclohexyl); laughing gas, poppers, snappers, whippets	Inhaled through nose or mouth	Stimulation, loss of inhibition; headache; nausea or vomiting; slurred speech, loss of motor co-ordination; wheezing

* Taking drugs by injection can increase the risk of infection through needle contamination with staphylococci, HIV, hepatitis and other organisms. **Associated with sexual assaults.

[1] Adapted from the National Institute on Drug Abuse website: http://www.nida.nih.gov/DrugPages/DrugsofAbuse.html

Table 20.5 Withdrawal symptoms

	Alcohol	*Sedatives and hypnotics*	*Opiates*	*Stimulants*
Anxiety	X	X	X	
Sleep disturbance	X	X	X	X
Irritability	X	X		
Tremors	X	X		
Sweating	X		X	
Nausea and other gastrointestinal distress	X	X	X	
Elevated blood pressure and pulse	X	X		
Seizures	X	X		
Disorientation/confusion	X	X		
Hallucinations	X	X		
Muscle pain		X	X	
Fever			X	
Runny eyes and nose			X	
Depression				X
Fatigue				X
Loss of appetite				X
Onset from last dose	5–12 hours	12–20 hours	6–8 hours	

substantial decrease in use will result in the appearance of minor withdrawal symptoms such as tremulousness, nausea, vomiting, difficulty sleeping, irritability, anxiety and elevations in pulse, blood pressure and temperature. Such symptoms usually begin within 5–12 hours. More severe withdrawal symptoms, such as seizures, delirium or hallucinations may also occur, usually within 24–72 hours of the cessation of drinking.

Medical complications are summarized earlier in the chapter (see p. 772) and in Table 20.2.

ENGAGEMENT

Successful treatment requires a client! The first challenge for the clinician is to engage the client in the process of change. Change may occur in the context of therapy but change also occurs through self-directed change efforts, the use of bibliotherapy, self-help groups, prayer and meditation, supervised medical care, health and exercise programmes, and other unique and idiosyncratic means (Fletcher, 2001). It is important for clinicians to recognize that there are multiple routes to successful change, with therapy being only one of these routes. Treatment engagement and its converse – 'resistance', non-compliance, or early treatment dropout – are poorly understood topics. When clients will not seek treatment or do not comply with the demands of treatment, it is tempting to label such clients as 'unmotivated' or 'not ready to change'. Contemporary views of motivation, as described in the previous section, however, would suggest several alternative explanations. For example, clients may not perceive their drinking or drug use as problematic (being in the 'precontemplation' stage), or they may be concerned about their use but believe that their self-directed efforts will result in successful change. For these clients, efforts are best directed at helping them recognize the extent and severity of their problems, or encouraging the use of formal assistance if self-directed efforts have failed. Clients also may have different treatment goals than the clinician or treatment programme, or may have a different model of change than that espoused by the treatment programme. For these clients, the value of working with and building on their motivation becomes particularly important. Three specific approaches to treatment engagement are: (1) individually focused approaches such as motivational interviewing; (2) interventions that involve persons in the individual's social network; and (3) coerced treatment entry.

Individual engagement approaches

Early research (Chafetz et al., 1962) found that clients are more likely to enter treatment if their immediate needs are met. Chafetz's research, conducted in the emergency room of an inner-city hospital, focused on immediate needs, such as new eye-glasses. More recently, harm reduction approaches (e.g. Marlatt, 1996) in the Netherlands have taken the same approach – to respond to the specific needs of substance abusers for clean needles, health care, etc. as a way both to reduce the harm associated with continued use and to help them develop a positive relationship with a treatment agency. Individual clinicians can learn from these research efforts, by recognizing the importance of listening carefully to the client's presenting concerns and crafting a treatment plan that addresses their concerns early in treatment. At times, direct treatment of the substance abuse may occur in a second phase of treatment, after the client has experienced the therapist as responsive to the client's own needs and concerns.

A second important engagement strategy focuses on the match between client and programme goals. Mismatches may occur in at least two ways – around drinking/drug use goals and around treatment philosophy. Most often, clients enter treatment with a less restrictive goal than the clinician or treatment programme which may be advocating complete abstinence from all substances. Clinicians may use moderation strategically as a treatment goal. To facilitate engagement, clinicians may work with clients towards a moderate drinking goal either as an end goal of treatment or as a strategic intermediate step on the way to helping the client become willing to work towards abstinence. In the latter strategy, the clinician may educate the client about the appropriateness of moderation versus abstinence as a goal, based on the client's individual history and characteristics, agree to work towards moderation, but also suggest that the clinician and client might revisit drinking goals as treatment progresses. The term 'harm reduction' has been used broadly to describe strategies designed to reduce harm associated with alcohol or drug use, and working with clients around self-selected goals is one example of a harm reduction approach (Marlatt, 1996).

Clients may see themselves and the change process in a different light from the clinician. In the US, the heavy emphasis on the disease model, AA and working the Twelve Steps is integral to most treatment programmes, but may be a deterrent to treatment for some individuals. Research on successful self-changers (e.g. Ludwig, 1985) suggests that some individuals find the emphasis on powerlessness and reliance on others or a higher power to be inimical to their self-perception, and dogged adherence to these principles in therapy may drive the client away. Clinicians should enquire into and then listen carefully to a client's views about therapy and the change process. If the clinician's approach to therapy is radically different from the client's and the clinician cannot see a way to accommodate or build on the client's views, a referral to another clinician may be appropriate.

Motivational interviewing (MI) has been developed as another means to enhance client motivation. Based originally on Rogerian counselling principles of unconditional positive regard, reflective listening and empathy, MI has evolved into a rather specific approach to clinical interactions. Early research (Miller et al., 1993) suggested that confrontational styles in therapy with alcoholics lead to client resistance and statements against positive change efforts. In contrast, a supportive, empathic style tends to elicit more change statements. Miller and Rollnick (2002) have emphasized three aspects of the 'spirit' of motivational interviewing. These include: (1) collaboration rather than confrontation – viewing the clinical experience as a partnership between client and clinician; (2) evocation rather than education – helping to draw out the client's intrinsic motivation and resources for change; (3) autonomy rather than authority – respecting the client's own ability to change and right to make decisions about what and how to change. Miller and Rollnick also describe four major therapeutic principles to carry out the spirit of MI: (1) expression of empathy through active listening, understanding and accepting the ambivalence that people feel about change, and use of reflective statements to communicate this empathy; (2) developing a discrepancy with the client between his or her present situation and goals and aspirations; (3) rolling with the resistance that clients present for changing, rather than providing argumentation in favour of change; and (4) supporting self-efficacy to help the client see that he or she is able to change.

Involvement of the social network

A second approach to treatment engagement is through the user's social network. Members of the social network can be taught how to respond to alcohol or drug use in ways that increase the experience of negative consequences of use, to concomitantly support and reinforce help-seeking or change, and to engage in better self-care while the person continues to use or have difficulties. The earliest approach to social network involvement was proposed by Johnson (1980), who suggested an 'intervention' to develop a 'family surround' to motivate an alcoholic family member to seek treatment. The intervention approach is popular and visible among addictions treatment professionals, and involves extended preparation with the clinician of the family or concerned others, followed by a meeting with the user, the family and the clinician. The family is helped to identify and list specific and observable negative consequences of the use (e.g. 'We had to move out of our house because you could not pay the rent' rather than 'You're irresponsible'). They are then coached in how to provide feedback to the user about these observed consequences, and also arrange for treatment to begin immediately after the intervention. Generally, the user is brought to the intervention unaware of the goal of the meeting, and is provided intensive and extensive feedback, coupled with specific requests to seek treatment. Research suggests that most families who initially plan to do an intervention will not follow through (approximately 70–80%), but if they do complete the intervention, the user usually seeks help (Miller et al., 1999).

A second family-based approach was originally developed in parallel by Thomas and Santa (1982) (Unilateral Family Therapy) and by Azrin and his associates (Sisson & Azrin, 1986) as an extension of the Community Reinforcement Approach to treatment. In the most recent research, the Community Reinforcement Approach and Family Training (CRAFT) model (Miller et al., 1999) has been found to be effective in motivating persons with alcohol and other drug dependence to seek treatment, with 60–67% of users seeking treatment after a family member participated in CRAFT. The CRAFT model includes education and exercises to help the family member decrease protection from negative consequences of use, increase requests for change, increase support for change and engage in self-care as well as protection from potential violence.

Coerced treatment

Many clients enter alcohol or drug treatment as an express requirement from an external agent, such as the courts, an employer or a social service agency. Although the clinician has not participated in creating the coercion, clinicians must know how to respond to and engage coerced clients in treatment. Treatment attendance is often quite good with coerced clients (Gregoire & Burke, 2004) and often these clients are motivated to change, but at times cognitive and behavioural change is more difficult to effect. Clinicians can use many of the engagement strategies described above (such as meeting client needs, development of mutually negotiated treatment goals and application of motivational interviewing techniques) to facilitate psychological involvement in the therapy. At the same time, however, clinicians must have a clear contract and agreement among the clinician, client and referring agent about the limits of confidentiality, the kind of information that the clinician must provide to the agent requiring the treatment, and the required length and/or intensity of treatment.

ASSESSMENT

Client assessment occurs both at the beginning and throughout treatment. Although the clinician must collect certain kinds of information to facilitate treatment decision making and to satisfy record keeping and other external requirements, 'data collection' should be construed as a therapeutic activity, and information should be collected in an empathic and respectful manner that fosters engagement with treatment.

The types of and formats for collecting information may be dictated in part by requirements of the treatment agency, source of payment for the treatment, clinician time and client reading ability. Typically, self-report questionnaires represent one of the easiest ways to collect large amounts of client information but clients with reading difficulties or a high level of ambivalence about treatment may be deterred by too many forms. Assessment should address multiple areas of life functioning and provide the clinician with sufficient information to develop an initial treatment plan to address immediate needs for medical or acute psychiatric care, detoxification and attention to pressing social needs (such as housing), as well as information to develop a case formulation and change plan. Assessment should address substance-use, other psychological problems, cognitive and affective factors related to the substance-use, the client's social environment and client strengths – both individual and in their social network.

Substance use

A clinical interview can be used to assess drinking and drug-use history and client perceptions of his or her current substance-use patterns. An outline of major topics to cover in the clinical interview is listed in Table 20.6. Typically, we use a hand-held breathalyser at the beginning of each session to assess current blood alcohol level (BAL), and a urine drug tester to screen for

Table 20.6 Topics to cover in initial clinical interview (both partners present)

Initial orientation
Introductions
Breathalyser reading
Brief questionnaires

Initial assessment
Presenting problems
Role of drinking/drug use in presenting problems

Other concerns
How the drinking has affected the partner
How the drinking has affected the relationship

Drinking/drug-use assessment
Identified patient
- Quantity, frequency, pattern of drinking
- Last drink/drug use
- Length of drinking/drug problem
- Negative consequences of drinking/drug use
- DSM-IV symptoms
- Assessment of need for detoxification

Partner
- Quantity, frequency, pattern of drinking
- Last drink/drug use
- Length of drinking/drug problem
- Negative consequences of drinking/drug use
- DSM-IV symptoms
- Assessment of need for detoxification

Assessment of other problems
Psychotic symptoms
Depression
Anxiety
Organic brain syndromes/cognitive impairment
Health status

Assessment of domestic violence
This assessment is done privately with each partner alone

Review of Conflict Tactics Scale
Identification of episodes of physical aggression
Determination of level of harm/injury from aggression
Assessment of individual's sense of safety in couples therapy

major drugs of abuse. In addition to the clinical interview, two structured interviews may be helpful in completing a standardized assessment. The Timeline Followback Interview (TLFB; Sobell, Maisto, Sobell, Cooper & Saunders, 1980) is designed to assess drinking and drug-use behaviour on each day in a set window of time before treatment and provides information about quantity, frequency and pattern of drinking. The alcohol and drug sections of the Structured Clinical Interview for DSM-IV (SCID; Spitzer et al., 1996) provide standardized information to establish a formal diagnosis. Self-report measures can be used to assess severity of alcohol dependence (Alcohol Dependence Scale (ADS); Skinner & Allen, 1982) or drug dependence (Severity of Dependence Scale; Gossop et al., 1995) and negative consequences of drinking or drug use (e.g. the Drinker Inventory of Consequences; Miller et al., 1995; the Inventory of Drug Consequences; Tonigan & Miller, 2002).

Assessment also should include a formal assessment of the need for detoxification. If a client is physically dependent on alcohol or drugs then he or she will experience withdrawal symptoms when decreasing or stopping drinking. Signs of withdrawal are summarized in Table 20.5. Assessment of physiological dependence can be accomplished using the SCID, a clinical interview to assess patterns of use that might be indicative of dependence, or the use of a checklist such as the Clinical Institute Withdrawal Assessment for Alcohol (Sullivan et al., 1989).

If a client has not used alcohol or drugs for several days prior to initial clinical contact and is not showing signs of withdrawal, then concerns about withdrawal are not relevant. If the client has stopped using alcohol or an opiate within the last three days, or long-acting tranquillizers within the last two weeks, the clinician needs to enquire about and observe for signs of withdrawal. If currently using, the clinician must rely on history, pattern of use, and the results of previous attempts to stop using to determine if detoxification will be necessary.

On-going assessment of substance-use can be achieved using daily self-recording cards (Figure 20.4), which are used throughout the treatment to record drinks, drug use and urges to drink or use drugs. By reviewing the information the client records and discussing events associated with drinking or drinking urges, the clinician can develop a clearer picture of drinking antecedents and consequences. Self-recording cards also allow the clinician to track progress through treatment in terms of quantity and frequency of drinking as well as frequency and intensity of urges to drink.

Specific assessment of high-risk situations associated with drinking or drug use also is an important component of the substance-use assessment. Two assessment techniques can be used to identify antecedents to drinking. A self-report questionnaire, the Drinking Patterns Questionnaire (DPQ; Zitter & McCrady, 1979; also adapted for drugs), lists potential environmental, cognitive, affective, interpersonal and intrapersonal antecedents to drinking

Urges			Drinks/drugs				
Time	Strength (1–7)	Trigger?	Time	Type	Amount	% Alcohol	Trigger?

Relationship satisfaction: 1 2 3 4 5 6 7

Worst ever — Greatest ever

Figure 20.4 Client self-recording card.

or drug use. The Inventory of Drinking Situations (IDS; Annis, 1982), a shorter measure that assesses situations in which a client drinks heavily, also can be used.

Other psychological problems

The clinician can draw from a wide variety of structured measures and interviews to assess life problems separate from drinking or drug use. Assessment may range from unstructured interviews to the use of simple problem checklists to formal interviewing techniques. The Addiction Severity Index (ASI; McLellan et al., 1992) is a widely used measure of client functioning across multiple domains of functioning, including medical, psychiatric, social, family, legal, occupational and alcohol/drug use. The ASI can be administered as an interview in about forty-five minutes, and computer-assisted interview versions are available. The ASI, however, does not provide diagnostic information for any psychological disorders and the cautious clinician should use formal screening questions to assess for the possible presence of other psychological disorders (Zimmerman, 1994). Brief symptom checklists such as the SCL-90R or shorter versions of the SCL-90 (Derogatis & Savitz, 2000) may be used to screen for other types of psychological distress. Checklists also may be used to monitor specific areas, such as the Beck Depression and Beck Anxiety Inventories (Beck 1990; Beck et al., 1996). Completion of such measures, however, at the beginning of treatment, may provide an overestimate of the client's level of distress, as responses will be affected by current substance-use and withdrawal symptoms. The SCID (Spitzer et al., 1996) provides structured diagnostic modules to assess symptoms of a variety of Axis I and Axis II disorders. Self-report instruments such as the Millon inventories (Millon, 1997) also may be used to assess for other psychological disorders.

Cognitive and affective factors related to use

Assessment of motivation should consider multiple aspects of motivation, such as: (a) the reasons, both internal and external, why the client is seeking treatment; (b) the client's treatment goals in terms of drinking, drug use and other areas; (c) the client's stage of readiness to change; and (d) the degree to which the client perceives negative consequences of his/her current drinking or drug-use pattern and potential positive consequences of change. Clinical interviewing provides information about reasons for seeking treatment, and drinking goals can be assessed either by asking the client directly or through a simple goal choice list (Table 20.7). The University of Rhode Island Change Assessment scale (URICA; McConnaughy et al., 1983) and the Readiness to Change Questionnaire (Rollnick, Heather, Gold & Hall, 1992) both measure stage of change. Perception of negative consequences of drinking and positive consequences of change also can be assessed through the clinical interview, through the development of a decisional balance sheet with the client (Figure 20.5), or with a questionnaire such as the Alcohol and Drug Consequences Questionnaire (Cunningham et al., 1997).

Assessment of expectancies can focus on both anticipated physical, psychological, emotional and interpersonal positive consequences of use and anticipated negative consequences. The Alcohol Expectancy Questionnaire

Table 20.7 Assessment of drinking goals (from Hall et al., 1991)

Assessment of Drinking Goal

We would like to know the one goal you have chosen for yourself about drinking at this time. Please read the goals listed below and choose the *ONE* goal that best represents your goal at this time by checking the box next to the goal and by filling in any blanks as indicated for that goal.

- ❑ I have decided not to change my pattern of drinking.
- ❑ I have decided to cut down on my drinking and drink in a more controlled manner – to be in control of how often I drink and how much I drink. I would like to limit myself to no more than_______drinks (upper limit amount) per_______(time period).
- ❑ I have decided to stop drinking completely for a period of time, after which I will make a new decision about whether I will drink again. For me, the period of time I want to stop drinking is for_______________________________(time).
- ❑ I have decided to stop drinking regularly, but would like to have an occasional drink when I really have the urge.
- ❑ I have decided to quit drinking once and for all, even though I realize I may slip up and drink once in a while.
- ❑ I have decided to quit drinking once and for all, to be totally abstinent, and to never drink alcohol ever again for the rest of my life.
- ❑ None of this applies exactly to me. My own goal is_______________________

	Not Drinking	Drinking
Pros		
Cons		

Figure 20.5 Decisional balance sheet.

(Brown et al., 1987) assesses anticipated benefits of drinking; comparable forms have been developed to assess anticipated positive consequences of use of cocaine (Jaffe & Kilbey, 1994). There is some evidence that negative expectancies also are strong predictors of outcome, and the Negative Alcohol Expectancy Questionnaire provides a measure of such expectancies (Jones & McMahon, 1994).

Self-efficacy is the degree of confidence that an individual has about his or her ability to cope with specific situations related to a problem behaviour. However, global measures of self-efficacy may provide the clinician with an overall sense of the client's confidence about change. Use of a simple Likert rating scale (0–100) in response to the question 'How confident are you about your ability to succeed in treatment', can provide such a rough gauge. A more detailed self-efficacy measure, the Situational Confidence Questionnaire (Annis, 1982) assesses client confidence in coping with a variety of use situations. Alternatively, an individualized self-efficacy scale, constructed from a client-generated list of high-risk situations for use, has been shown to predict relapse situations after alcohol treatment (Miller et al., 1994).

Social environment

Drinking and drug use often occur in a social–interpersonal context. Clinical interviewing can be used to identify major persons with whom the client drinks or uses drugs. The Important People Interview (Zywiak et al., 2002) provides a systematic approach to identifying key members of the client's social environment, each individual's importance to the client, their alcohol and drug-use patterns, and the degree to which the client perceives members of the social network as supportive or not supportive of help-seeking and change. Self-report questionnaires, such as the Family Environment Scale (Moos et al., 1990) may be used to assess family functioning and, for couples, the Areas of Change Questionnaire (Margolin et al., 1983) and the Dyadic Adjustment Scale (Spanier, 1976) are excellent self-report measures of relationship problems and satisfaction. The Modified Conflict Tactics Scale (Pan et al., 1994) assesses relationship conflict, including physical violence.

Client strengths

Some client strengths will become apparent in the course of the assessment described above, such as the identification of positive members of the client's social network. Unfortunately, though, the absence of problems in an area does not necessarily imply an area of strength. The clinician should make the assessment of positive coping skills an explicit part of treatment. Asking a client how he or she had coped with challenging or difficult situations provides some insight into client strengths, as does an assessment of concrete client strengths such as occupational skills, job stability or economic resources. Self-report questionnaires can be used to assess coping with alcohol-related situations (e.g. the Coping Behaviours Questionnaire; Litman et al., 1983) or general coping skills (e.g. the Revised Ways of Coping Questionnaire; Folkman et al., 1986). Some role-play scenarios have been standardized to assess skills to cope with high-risk situations, but these are time-consuming to administer and to rate and have limited utility in clinical practice.

Treatment planning

Decision making about need for and setting for detoxification

If the client needs detoxification, four alternatives are available, although the availability of each will vary with geographic location and client resources: inpatient or partial hospital medical detoxification, inpatient non-medical detoxification or outpatient medical detoxification. Inpatient, medically assisted detoxification is essential if the client has a history of or is showing signs of disorientation, delirium, hallucinations or seizures during withdrawal. If the client does not believe that he or she can stop drinking without being physically removed from the alcohol-using environment, but does not show any major withdrawal signs, is in good health and does not abuse other drugs, a social setting detoxification from alcohol might be appropriate. Detoxification could be initiated on a partial hospital or outpatient basis if the client has some social support for change. The choice between these two latter settings would be determined by how much support the person will need during withdrawal and whether a structured programme will be needed after detoxification. If the client will need a fairly structured programme, then the partial hospital would be the preferred setting for detoxification.

Level of care decision making for treatment

A number of settings are available for the provision of alcohol or drug treatment. These include inpatient or residential settings, therapeutic communities, partial hospitals, outpatient clinics and halfway houses. Self-help groups also are widely available. Rational models to determine level of care have been proposed, with those proposed by insurance companies and by the American Society of Addiction Medicine (ASAM, 1991) being most visible. ASAM has proposed a multi-dimensional decision-making model for selecting initial and continuing level of care. The criteria include: need for supervised withdrawal, medical conditions that might require monitoring, comorbid psychiatric conditions, motivation for change and degree of treatment acceptance or resistance, relapse potential and the nature of the individual's social environment in recommending an initial level of care. Assessment and decision making according to the ASAM criteria require fairly extensive training and experience, and computer-based models for decision making are being tested. In general, the ASAM criteria point to higher levels of care for clients who are more impaired in terms of their substance abuse, medical or psychiatric conditions, lower in motivation and with a poorer recovery environment. Less restrictive levels of care are deemed more appropriate with less impaired clients and those with greater motivation and better recovery environments. The full criteria for each level of care are described in detail in ASAM (1991).

Alternatively, stepped-care models (Breslin et al., 1997) suggest brief interventions as the modal initial approach to treatment, with decisions about more intensive and/or longer treatments being made based on the client's initial response to the treatment. Although such models are appealing as economically conservative and maintaining the principle of least restrictive level of care, they may not take sufficient account of the complex problems and situations experienced by many clients with substance-use disorders.

Decision making about drinking/use goals

As noted earlier in the chapter, traditional approaches to alcohol treatment have suggested that abstinence is the only appropriate drinking goal, because alcoholism has been viewed as a progressive disease that can be arrested with abstinence but not cured. Behavioural clinicians have examined alternatives to abstinence and have developed a number of strategies to teach clients how to drink moderately. Although better accepted as a goal for individuals with alcohol abuse (rather than dependence), moderation training continues to be controversial, particularly in the US, and the clinician who elects to provide such treatment may be vulnerable to criticism from the traditional, mainstream alcoholism-treatment community. There is little documentation of successful use of moderation goals to treat clients with problems with drugs other than alcohol.

I have argued in favour of abstinence as my preference for a treatment goal (e.g. McCrady, 1992; Nathan & McCrady, 1987) and continue to view it as such. Abstinence is clearly defined, is in accord with usual clinical practice in the US and several other countries, and there is no risk of alcohol-related consequences for the abstaining client. Also, agreeing readily to a controlled drinking goal may reinforce a client's distorted view that alcohol is important and necessary to his or her daily functioning.

Under certain circumstances, however, a reduced drinking goal may be appropriate. Moderation may be used as a provisional goal to engage a client in treatment or may be used when the client will not agree to abstinence but does want assistance to change. A moderate drinking goal is also more appropriate if a client shows few signs of alcohol dependence or withdrawal, has a history of being able to drink in moderation, does not have medical or psychological problems that would be exacerbated by continued drinking, is younger, and does not have a family history of alcoholism (Rosenberg, 1993). With a moderation goal, a period of initial abstinence (at least thirty days) makes it easier for the client to then drink moderately. In selecting a moderation goal, the clinician should be careful to discuss and document the discussion of current and potential negative consequences of excessive drinking, and should help the client make an informed and thoughtful choice in selecting a treatment goal. The clinician should also view the drinking goal selected at the start of treatment (abstinence or moderation) as a tentative goal that may be re-evaluated as therapy progresses.

Case formulation and the treatment plan

The case formulation integrates the various sources of assessment data into an initial working understanding of the client that then leads to an initial and comprehensive treatment plan. Case formulation considers biological, psychological and social interpersonal factors in both the development and maintenance of the substance-use, and the interrelationships among these factors. Case formulation is more art than science, but several principles can guide the case formulation. First, case formulation should be parsimonious, using the least number of variables to explain observed behaviour and problems. Second, case formulation should focus more on current factors maintaining problem patterns of substance-use than historical factors. Third, case formulation is best considered as a series of hypotheses to be tested through interventions in the therapy, rather than as a fixed formulation. Fourth, a careful functional analysis of specific substance-use situations can help the clinician identify major and frequent high-risk situations (through identification of triggers for use), dysfunctional cognitions and cognitive schemas, types of negative affect that create the most vulnerability for the client, (examination of thoughts and feelings in response to triggers), gaps in coping skills (examination of behavioural responses to triggers), the kinds of needs that substance-use may be fulfilling (examination of positive consequences of use), and potential sources of motivation that may be capitalized on in the treatment (examination of negative consequences of use).

TREATMENT

Individual aspects

Treatment may be provided in an individual, couple, family or group modality, or may combine different treatment modalities. Treatment may also be based in one or more theoretical models for understanding substance-use, abuse and dependence. As noted above, treatments based in disease model, cognitive-behavioural and family systems approaches all have empirical support for their effectiveness. The balance of this chapter will focus primarily on treatments based on a cognitive-behavioural model of treatment, but readers are encouraged to learn about and develop skills and appreciation for alternative approaches as well, in order to match treatment model to client needs.

Treatment follows a logical sequence, although the needs of clients will dictate the pacing of therapy as well as, to some extent, the ordering of treatment. Client needs and concerns should drive the treatment, rather than rigid adherence to a specific treatment protocol. However, clinicians should use treatment interventions with empirical support for effectiveness, even if delivered in a flexible manner that is adapted to the individual client.

Following assessment, the early part of treatment focuses on establishing a therapeutic alliance, mutually agreeing on treatment goals and a treatment plan, and attending to motivation. After an overall treatment plan is agreed on, the early focus of treatment most typically is on helping the client to achieve his or her specified goals related to substance-use. The focus, then, is on the development both of skills to attain or maintain sobriety or moderate use, and on accessing social supports for abstinence or moderate use. As the client begins to achieve some success with drinking or drug-use goals, therapy moves gradually to focusing on more general life problems and circumstances. Throughout therapy the clinician should be monitoring alcohol and/or drug use, monitoring other major targets of treatment (e.g. depression, relationship unhappiness), and providing the client with sufficient time in sessions to discuss problems of current concern. Figure 20.6 provides an outline for a typical CBT treatment session.

- Checking in
- Breathalyser or urine drug screen
- Overview of session plan for the day
- Review of self-recording cards and graphing results
- Discussion of any problem days
- Review of other homework
- Teaching of new skill or follow-up on skill training from previous session
- Anticipation of high-risk situations for the week
- Assignment of homework

Figure 20.6 Outline of CBT treatment session.

Treatment contract

The treatment contract represents the formal commitment to treatment from both the client and the clinician. Review of the treatment contract communicates to the client that the clinician is serious about the treatment and is making a commitment of his or her time and expertise to the client, with the expectation that the client is making a similarly serious commitment to the treatment. Client responsibilities are outlined, such as on-time attendance at sessions, notifying the therapist of possible missed sessions or lateness, completion of assigned homework outside of treatment and agreement to discuss possible changes in intentions related to treatment. Clinician responsibilities include on-time attendance at sessions, being available (within reason) to re-schedule sessions, provision of appropriate clinical coverage when the clinician is not available, and provision of the most effective treatment available.

In addition to these formal commitments, the treatment contract may include information about treatment goals, frequency of sessions, fees and payment schedules, use of audio- or videotapes and limits on confidentiality.

Development of therapeutic alliance

The clinician is working to develop and maintain a positive therapeutic alliance from the initial contact with a client all the way through to the last treatment session. Respect must be communicated for the client, his or her particular life circumstances and goals, and the challenges that the client experiences in acknowledging and changing substance-use patterns. Many clients with substance-use disorders have engaged in behaviours that clinicians find disturbing and that run counter to the clinician's values or mores. Working with these clients requires that the clinician learn to separate clients from their substance-related behaviour, and to find aspects with which to form an empathic bond. The client who gets his grandfather with Alzheimer's disease to sign over his assets to the client, who then uses the money to buy drugs;

the client who kills her child when she drives while intoxicated; the client who beats his wife when high, each present challenges to the clinician's compassion. But those same clients may experience deep remorse or shame for their behaviour, may feel desperate and unable to see a pathway out of addiction, or may bear scars from their own abusive parent, all of which provide the clinician with an initial link around which to form an empathic bond.

Beginning clinicians with limited experience with alcohol or drug dependence may consider a self-change project of their own to develop a better sense of empathy for the challenges that clients experience. The clinician may select a behaviour of their own to reduce or stop, and then try to follow through with a behaviour change programme of their own. The behaviour could be a consummatory behaviour such as eating a specific type of food (cookies, chocolate), drinking specific beverages (coffee, tea), or reducing or giving up another behaviour that has negative consequences for the clinician (a student in one of my classes gave up purchasing shoes!). The clinician should commit to maintaining the behaviour change project for at least twelve weeks, and keep a journal of the experience of trying to give up something that he or she has found pleasurable even though problematic. Completion of such an exercise will provide the clinician with important insights into the challenges of changing a substance-use disorder, and will make the empathic connection and understanding of the client's challenges easier.

Several aspects of the therapeutic alliance are important and relate positively to retention in treatment, including: (1) communicating accurate empathy and positive regard for the client; (2) listening carefully to the client to understand his or her experience rather than simply forcing the client into the therapist's therapeutic model; (3) using open-ended questions; (4) avoiding arguments with the client; (5) providing sufficient structure and direction to the therapy without being excessively structured or controlling; (6) providing therapy in a flexible manner that connects to the client's concerns; and (7) conveying competence and commitment to helping the client (Raytek et al., 1999).

Treatment rationale and psychoeducation about CBT model

Cognitive-behavioural treatment is less familiar to clients than either twelve-step-based models or psychodynamic approaches. Both of the latter two approaches are portrayed widely in the media and in dramas on television and in the cinema, and clients come to therapy with expectations quite different from CBT. The therapist should provide a rationale that addresses several key points: (1) drinking or drug use may develop for many reasons but the key to change is in understanding what maintains use in the present; (2) substance-use occurs in response to situations in the individual's environment; (3) the individual's reactions to events, in terms of thoughts and feelings, will determine whether he or she uses substances or responds differently to a situation; (4) treatment will help the client have a better understanding of the situations, thoughts and feelings that lead to use, and will provide alternative ways to cope; (5) treatment is an active process that requires effort and commitment on the part of the client, including willingness to try new skills and perspectives, and to carry out tasks between sessions; (6) acquisition of new skills is a gradual process that is likely to include 'mistakes' along the way.

Skills to attain and maintain sobriety

Early in therapy, the client needs concrete skills to be able to maintain abstinence or reduced drinking. Often, concrete therapeutic tasks and 'prescriptions' are helpful. Self-recording helps the client track drinking and drug use as well as urges to use. Additionally, the client should record the situation associated with urges or substance-use. The therapist should collect the self-recording cards each week and create a graph of drinking, drug-use days or money spent on drugs, as well as number and intensity of urges. The self-recording cards thus provide a way to track progress in treatment, and help the client become more aware of triggers for use. In addition, the process of self-recording may enhance awareness of use and provide an incentive for the client to avoid use.

After identifying major triggers for use through interviewing, questionnaires and self-recording cards, the therapist and client can develop a 'high-risk hierarchy' of use-related situations (Figure 20.7). The client rates each

My hierarchy of risky situations

Many things happen that increase the desire to drink or use drugs. This is a list of situations that are difficult for me to handle without using alcohol or drugs. They are rated for difficulty, with 100 being the most difficult to 0 being the easiest to handle without using.

Situation	Difficulty (0–100)

Figure 20.7 High-risk hierarchy worksheet.

situation for difficulty, and then begins to develop change plans based on the hierarchy. Stimulus control procedures may be used for many environmental triggers. From a theoretical perspective, stimulus control is intended to change the cues for use to decrease both classically and operantly conditioned responses. In practice, clients are taught three alternatives for dealing with use-related stimuli: (1) avoid them; (2) rearrange them; or (3) respond differently to the same stimulus. Self-management planning sheets (Figure 20.8) can be used to help the client brainstorm ideas for managing environmental cues. The therapist should work through a self-management plan with the client, and then have the client implement the plan during the week and also work out additional self-management plans on his or her own between therapy sessions. Common areas to focus for self-management planning include: major drinking/drug-use environments (bars, neighbourhoods where drugs are sold), presence of alcohol or drugs in the home, specific times of the day when use occurs (first thing in the morning, after work), specific activities associated with use (drinking during meal preparations) and specific people. Twelve-step groups focus on similar issues and encourage users to avoid 'people, places and things' associated with use. Attendance at twelve-step group meetings can serve as a behavioural alternative to substance-use environments and spending time with substance-using friends or acquaintances.

As the client learns to restructure the environment to support change, he or she also is faced with the experience of urges or cravings for use. Urges can be understood as conditioned responses to internal and external cues for use, and may vary in intensity and frequency both within and across clients. Some clients are very aware of their urges to use; others report use without any awareness of a desire to use. Most commonly, clients experience frequent

Trigger	Plan	Pluses	Minuses	How hard
1.				
2.				

Figure 20.8 Self-management planning sheet.

and intense urges to use in the early part of treatment, particularly if newly abstinent. Urges decrease over time, although they can continue episodically for months or years after initial abstinence. The clinician can elicit the client's understanding of urges but should help the client understand that urges are responses to triggers, and that they are time-limited. As with any conditioned response, if the individual does not act on the urge, the urge will abate over time.

There is a range of alternatives to cope with urges. Behaviourally, clients may use distraction techniques (such as getting involved with an absorbing activity), leave the environment that is cuing the urge, or reach out to others for social support to deal with the urge. Cognitively, some clients find imagery helpful to deal with urges (e.g. Marlatt & Gordon, 1986). 'Urge surfing' evokes the image of the urge as a wave, and the client as the surfer riding the wave to the shore. Alternatively, clients may use more active imagery, such as karate chopping the urge like a block of wood. Most important is that the clinician address urges directly, help the client find coping strategies that are individually relevant and helpful, and have the client practise these strategies in their everyday life.

A third important aspect of attaining and maintaining abstinence is the ability to recognize cognitions about the substance that may lead to use. Clients hold a set of 'irrational' beliefs related to their drug or drugs of choice that focus on the positive consequences of use. Research on successful self-changers has found that individuals abstinent from alcohol think primarily of the negative consequences of using, or quickly think past the positive to the negative consequences of using (Ludwig, 1985). The functional analysis provides an initial way to identify automatic and positive thoughts about the substance and completion of several behaviour chains will help the client become more aware of these cognitions. Common thoughts include, 'I'll just have one', 'If I drink I'll have more fun', 'This time will be different', 'I deserve a reward – I've been good lately', 'I'll feel better if I just smoke one rock'. Two approaches may help clients with these thoughts. First, clients may be taught cognitive-restructuring techniques to challenge their thoughts. They must learn to recognize such thoughts as dysfunctional or irrational rather than true and accurate beliefs, and then develop alternative, more accurate and perhaps rational thoughts (see Figure 20.9 for a sample worksheet). Sample responses might be, 'I usually have more than I plan to, I don't want to risk it', 'How many times do I have to beat my head against the same wall before I realize that I keep getting in trouble', 'I can find much better rewards that won't get me in trouble', 'I might feel better for the moment, but the risks are just too great'.

A second approach to dealing with automatic positive thoughts is to identify negative consequences of use as well as positive consequences of not using, and help the client rehearse these consequences in high-risk situations. The clinician can help the client construct a simple index card (see Figure 20.10

Handling my negative thoughts

It is easy to have positive thoughts about alcohol or drugs, or to forget the harm that using them has caused me. It is important that I am aware of these thoughts and that I know how to counter them.

I also have other kinds of thoughts that lead me to feeling badly. Some of these thoughts are irrational thinking, and it is important that I can recognize and think through these thoughts more logically.

An irrational thought about alcohol or drugs:
A more rational way to think:
An irrational thought about alcohol or drugs:
A more rational way to think:
An irrational thought:
A more rational way to think:
An irrational thought:
A more rational way to think:

Figure 20.9 Dysfunctional thoughts worksheet.

Bad things about drinking/using drugs	**Good things about not drinking/using drugs**
I feel sick	I wake up with a clear head
I look bad	I look forward to the day
I get into trouble with the law	I feel in control of myself
I have injured my wife when I was high	My hands are steady and my eyes are clear
I keep losing jobs	I am starting to rebuild a relationship with my wife
I don't respect myself	I'm a better role model for my kids
	I have a decent enough job

Figure 20.10 Sample decisional-balance index card.

for a sample card) with a list of 'reasons to stay sober' and 'reasons not to use', and assign frequent daily review of the card as homework. Pairing the review with a high-frequency activity, such as looking in the mirror; drinking coffee, tea or another preferred beverage; or smoking cigarettes, will help the client remember to review the card. Over time, homework can hone in more specifically on rehearsal of the card in high-risk situations.

A fourth important set of skills is the ability to refuse offers of alcohol or drugs from others. Early in therapy, clients usually find it easiest to avoid heavy users and those who push alcohol or drugs, but inevitably the client will experience offers of alcohol or drugs. Drink refusal is a skill that can be learned readily with practice through role plays in the therapy session and *in vivo* practice between sessions. The high-risk hierarchy and functional analysis can be used to identify particularly challenging situations or persons for refusing drinks or drugs. The clinician also should help clients consider their relationship to the person offering substances, as the degree of intimacy of the relationship and the frequency with which the client interacts with an individual may determine the approach to refusal. Thus, for casual acquaintances who are seen infrequently, the client may be most comfortable with a 'social lie', such as 'I can't have anything to drink right now because I'm on medication (or on a diet)'. However, for persons with whom the client interacts on a regular basis, a more candid and direct statement of the client's goals makes future interactions easier, such as 'I've decided that alcohol was harming me so I'm not going to drink' or 'I've decided to focus on my health and am trying to change my diet and exercise regularly from now on, and alcohol doesn't fit into my plan'. For any drink refusal situation, there are several important components to an effective response: (1) starting with the word 'no' to indicate refusal of the drink or drug; (2) suggesting an alternative, such as, 'Do you have any juices?'; (3) being consistent in refusing, even in the face of pressure; (4) communicating confidence by looking the person in the eye, using a firm tone of voice, and confident body posture; (5) when appropriate, indicating an intent to continue to abstain; (6) if necessary, changing the topic of conversation or leaving the situation.

Maintaining motivation and dealing with ambivalence

Even the most motivated client has moments of ambivalence about change. Continued ambivalence may come from several sources, including uncertainty about the long-term benefits of change, a sense of loss of the positive aspects associated with using the substance, lack of self-efficacy about maintaining change, social pressure to resume use, or reactance against pressure to abstain from the therapist or others in the client's social network. As described above, review of an index card that contains a list of positive reasons for change and negative consequences of continued use, may be helpful. If lack of self-efficacy seems to be contributing to flagging motivation, the clinician should consider whether he or she is asking the client to makes changes that are too difficult for the client, and should help the client set smaller goals with a high likelihood of success. Continued use of the techniques of motivational interviewing, particularly 'rolling with resistance' at times when the client expresses ambivalence about change, may be effective.

Developing social supports for sobriety

A considerable body of research (see McCrady, 2004) points to the importance of the social network in the long-term maintenance of change in substance-use disorders. Clients who use alcohol heavily, or who use illicit drugs, are often part of a social network of heavy users of similar substances. Alcohol or drugs may be integral to these friendships and family interactions, alcohol or drugs may be a central focus of social events, the client's abstinence or moderate use may be disruptive to the usual interactions in these social units and the client may experience intense pressure to continue to use. However, most clients have members of their social network who are abstainers or moderate users, as well as individuals who support them strongly in their efforts to change. To foster positive social support, three steps may be helpful: (1) identification of key members of the social network, followed by a discussion of each person's alcohol or drug use and the degree of support they may provide for the client's goals; (2) discussion of ways to increase interactions with the most supportive members of the social network; and (3) discussion of ways to meet people and access social networks supportive of abstinence. Clients may find potential support by cultivating new friendships with persons at work or in their neighbourhood, through involvement in clubs that have a service or social focus that does not involve alcohol or drugs (such as a hiking club), through involvement with religious or spiritual activities, or through recreational programmes. Finding new friends is not simple, nor is dealing with social pressure, particularly from intimate others and close family members, but research suggests that having even one member of the social network who uses and actively encourages use will place the client at higher risk of relapse (reviewed in McCrady, 2004), so the effort is important to successful change.

Involvement with self-help groups

One particularly positive source of social support for change is self-help groups. Alcoholics Anonymous is widely available, with more than 87,000 meetings in more than 150 countries (reviewed in McCrady et al., 2003); Narcotics Anonymous is somewhat less widespread but is also fairly widely available. Other self-help groups, such as SMART Recovery or Women for Sobriety (reviewed in McCrady et al., 2003), have fewer groups and a less international focus but may be appealing to clients who are particularly uncomfortable with twelve-step programmes. There are several advantages to self-help group involvement, including the opportunity to interact with people dealing with similar problems, having role models for successful change, getting concrete guidance and support for change, learning specific skills and attitudes to support sobriety, meeting abstainers who may provide new sources of friendship, having time-structuring activities that do not involve substance-use and, for the twelve-step programmes, a deepening of spirituality and faith.

Clinicians may foster client involvement in self-help groups by linking involvement to specific client goals or aspects of the treatment plan, such as the need to find sources of social support for abstinence. Education about self-help groups is important to getting clients involved, and the clinician should be knowledgeable about the format of group meetings, requirements for attendance (for example, the only requirement for membership in AA is a desire to stop drinking), and the basic principles of the programme. Clinicians should have meeting schedules available to help clients select meetings that are most convenient for them, and should encourage clients to try several different meetings before deciding whether or not a self-help group will be a part of their recovery plan. Ideally, the clinician might be able to link the client up with a current member of the self-help group to accompany the client to an initial meeting, but such an arrangement is not always feasible. Clinicians also should provide ample opportunities within the treatment session to discuss the client's experience at the meetings, to answer questions, respond to ambivalence and to support continued efforts at attendance. The clinician should be keenly aware of how difficult it is for many clients when they first go to a self-help group meeting, as they may experience substantial social anxiety, fear that they will have to talk, fear that they will see someone they know, fear that they will feel confronted with the seriousness of their own problems by being at the meeting, and anxiety about the many unknowns of the situation.

Communication skills

A range of communication skills can support successful change. Some of these are directly related to the substance-use, such as the ability to discuss past use and receive feedback and, at times, criticism from others about past alcohol or drug use; the ability to request support from others and the ability to explain to others the reasons that the client is attempting to change. More general communication skills include skills in giving and receiving positive and negative feedback, conflict resolution skills and general social skills in social interaction. Therapists can teach communication skills through discussion, problem-solving and role-play rehearsal in the therapy sessions. Two important keys to communication skills training are a focus on expectancies and beliefs, and identification and rehearsal of effective communication techniques. A detailed description of techniques to teach communication skills is beyond the scope of this chapter, and the reader is referred to Monti, Kadden, Rohsenow, Cooney and Abrams (2002) for specific therapeutic techniques.

Developing alternatives to use

When the client becomes fairly proficient at avoiding alcohol or drug use on a daily basis, and is receiving some support from his or her social environment for these changes, the first phase of therapy may be considered complete. The second part of therapy involves an active focus on developing longer-term alternatives to using alcohol or drugs. Two sources of information will help the clinician identify needs that alcohol or drugs have been serving for the client: high-risk situations identified on the functional analysis, and positive consequences of use, also identified from the functional analysis. Clients may use alcohol or drugs for fun, to deal with uncomfortable social situations, to cope with negative affect, to shut down negative thinking or as a tool to retaliate when angry.

There are both common and specific skills to help clients develop alternative means to obtain the same desirable effects in their lives without alcohol or drugs. First, the clinician and client may develop a list of major anticipated positive consequence for using substances. The alternatives planning worksheet provided in Figure 20.11 may be used as a starting point. After the client has listed some of the positive consequences desired from alcohol or

Alternative to using alcohol or drugs

Alcohol and drugs have given me pleasure or helped me cope with some difficulties in my life. Now that I don't want to use alcohol or drugs, I need other ways to fulfil these needs. Here are my ideas:

A positive effect of alcohol or drugs	**Another way to fill my need**

Figure 20.11 Alternatives planning worksheet.

drugs, brain-storming and problem solving may be used to come up with viable alternatives. For example, identifying pleasurable activities that do not involve substances, improving social skills to converse with others without the aid of alcohol or a drug and focusing on positive lifestyle choices around substances, exercise and diet can all provide positive alternatives to use.

The clinician may want to focus more intensively on skills to cope with negative emotions, including anxiety, depression and anger. After the client has been abstinent for several weeks, the clinician may want to again assess the client for the presence of a major mood or anxiety disorder, as substance-related mood disturbances should have abated, and continuing difficulties with intense anxiety or depression could be markers of an additional disorder that would merit separate psychological or pharmacological intervention. However, clients tend to have had years of experience damping-down negative feelings with psychoactive substances, and often find even the relatively normal experiences of anxiety and depression, which are part of the human condition, difficult to cope with. Both cognitive and behavioural techniques may be helpful. Cognitive reframing may help clients realize that they are experiencing normal but perhaps unfamiliar emotions, and that if they allow themselves to experience these emotions they will become more familiar with them over time. A second cognitive intervention is to identify negative thoughts that accompany the negative feelings, and then teach clients to identify the more irrational or dysfunctional aspects of these thoughts and challenge them through cognitive disputation techniques (e.g. Young et al., 2001).

Behavioural techniques also are helpful in dealing with negative affect. Accessing enjoyable situations and activities is one way to counter depressive affect, and Lewinsohn has developed a comprehensive programme to cope with depression through involvement with reinforcing activities (see, for example, Lewinsohn, Muñoz, Youngren & Zeiss, 1986). Additionally, progressive relaxation, meditation and breathing techniques can all be helpful to clients struggling with anxiety. Each behavioural and cognitive technique reviewed here may take considerable time for a client to learn and the attraction of psychoactive substances as a quicker 'fix' to cope with negative affect is always something that the clinician and client must be aware of and deal with.

Relapse prevention

A final important part of treatment that may be a focus of both individual and family-involved sessions is relapse prevention. Relapse is a major concern in the treatment of substance-use disorders, and return to use or problem use is the norm, with, on average, only 35% of treated patients maintaining continuous abstinence or non-problem use a year after treatment (Miller et al., 2001). Relapse prevention involves educating clients to the possibility of relapse, focusing therapy to try to avoid relapse and preparing the client to manage if relapses occur. Marlatt and Gordon (1986) originally conceptualized relapse as a somewhat linear process, triggered by exposure to a high-risk situation and mediated by cognitive and behavioural coping responses. More recently, Witkiewitz and Marlatt (2004) have suggested an updated model of the relapse process that views high-risk situations as contextual factors that influence the probability of relapse, and that there are both distal factors that create a higher or lower predisposition to relapse and more proximal risk factors that serve as immediate precipitants to relapse. They describe a dynamic interaction among risk factors, cognitive processes, physiological and affective states, and coping behaviours, with feedback loops among these factors that influence the subsequent level of risk for use. Their updated relapse prevention model helps to explain how, in some circumstances, apparently minor events may trigger a severe and extended relapse, while, in other circumstances, what looks like a very risky situation is handled with little fuss or difficulty.

In many ways, all of cognitive-behavioural treatment is relapse prevention treatment, as the clinician focuses on identification of high-risk situations, development of cognitive and behavioural coping skills, and enhancement of self-efficacy through successful experience. However, the clinician also may focus more specifically on relapse prevention through a series of treatment strategies. Introducing the idea that the client may be vulnerable to relapse is an important starting point for targeted relapse prevention interventions. Clients may be reluctant to consider the possibility of future 'failure' but the therapist may allay some concern by using the analogy of the fire drill – no-one hopes for or expects a fire in a building but if a fire does occur, having fire extinguishers, escape routes, a fire department and established procedures is certainly preferable to perishing!

After helping the client accept the rationale for preparing for relapse, the clinician may help the client identify possible warning signs for impending relapse. Discussion of past relapses after a period of abstinence may provide some warning signs; giving up the use of key skills and attitudes acquired during therapy may be identified as another warning sign. The client and therapist may then work together to develop short-term and longer-term strategies should relapse warning signs occur. Strategies may range from review of materials from treatment, to calling the therapist, to re-instituting previously successful strategies, to attendance at self-help group meetings, to discussing concerns with a trusted member of the client's social network. Figure 20.12 provides a sample worksheet.

The third target for relapse prevention interventions is preparing the client for how best to respond should a relapse occur. A first challenge for the clinician is to help the client define what would constitute a relapse. Marlatt and Gordon (1986) discussed three types of relapses: 'lapses', which were limited episodes of use; 'prolapses', which were episodes of use from which the client learned; and 'relapses', which were returns to problem use. Providing clients with these distinctions may be helpful, but since the clinician's goal is

Relapse warning signs worksheet

Some signs that I may be heading towards a relapse, and what I might do:

Warning sign	What to do

Figure 20.12 Relapse warning signs worksheet.

that clients make any drinking or drug use either a 'lapse' or a 'prolapse', these distinctions may be unnecessary and the term 'lapse' might be easiest for clients to use. For clients with a goal of abstinence, any use of the substance that is the target of abstinence (alcohol, another drug or all psychoactive substances) might be considered a lapse, regardless of the extent or severity. For clients with a goal of moderate use, use beyond an agreed-upon level of use should be considered a lapse. Should a lapse occur, Marlatt and Gordon (1986) recommended that clients take several steps: (1) leave the situation; (2) delay any further use for at least a few hours; (3) take time to identify the internal and external circumstances that led to the use; (4) accept that use occurred but not think of it as a irretrievable failure; (5) get help if needed; (6) make a commitment to returning to the goal the next day. The therapist may provide the client with a list of these principles, and telephone numbers to use in an emergency.

Marital/family therapy aspects

Rationale

Involving families in alcohol or drug treatment increases the likelihood that the user will have a positive outcome (reviewed in Epstein & McCrady, 2002; McCrady, 2004). Drinking and drug use develop in an interpersonal context, patterns of use are maintained in part by interpersonal interactions and families are deeply affected by an individual's alcohol or drug dependence. Families play an important role in helping individuals recognize that they have a drinking or drug problem and that they need to change (Room, Greenfield & Weisner, 1991) and individuals who have resolved their drinking problems cite their spouses as the most important source of support in maintaining change. Families can contribute to the recovery process during treatment and they too need to learn how to adjust to recovery and relapses.

A number of models have been proposed to explain the functioning of families of alcoholics and drug users, and these models provide the basis for very different models of treatment engagement for family members. There is substantial evidence that the experience and behaviour of families affected by alcohol or drug use can best be understood within a stress and coping framework (Orford et al., 1998). Families are faced with an unpredictable set of behaviours and multiple stressors associated with the user's behaviour, such as the economic impact on the family, the heightened risk of family violence and the emotional toll of worry, anger and sadness. Families utilize a range of ways to attempt to cope with these stressors, and often show the ill effects in greater levels of depression, anxiety and psychosomatic symptoms. Coping behaviours can be classified into three major types – tolerant coping, withdrawal coping and engaged coping (Orford et al., 1998). In addition to the effects on family members, the interpersonal relationships of alcohol and drug users often are characterized by discord, poor communication and problem-solving skills, elevated rates of domestic violence and a variety of specific family problems (e.g. financial, sexual, parenting) (Epstein & McCrady, 2002).

Cognitive-behavioural treatment that involves the family derives directly from the stress and coping model of family adjustment and the observed behavioural deficits in familial relationships. Family-involved cognitive-behavioural treatments for adults (e.g. Alcohol Behavioral Couple Therapy; ABCT) typically have focused on the primary intimate relationship; treatment for adolescents has involved whole families as much as possible. ABCT includes three major components: (1) interventions to help the drinker stop drinking and maintain abstinence; (2) interventions to help the partner learn to cope differently with drinking situations and to support abstinence; and (3) interventions to improve the couple's relationship. A full ABCT treatment involves the partner throughout the assessment and treatment programme, but various models of partner- or family-involved treatment may be adapted from ABCT to suit the needs of individual clients and circumstances.

Therapeutic contract and issues in therapeutic alliance with couples

If both partners participate in treatment together, the therapist must deal with the unique challenges of the therapeutic contract and therapeutic alliance. In the therapeutic contract, expectations for each partner's involvement in therapy should be clarified, as must matters of confidentiality if the therapist holds both individual and couple therapy sessions. Each partner should be expected to keep monitoring cards (see Figure 20.13 for a sample monitoring card for the partner) and to complete other homework assignments. Both partners should come to sessions free of alcohol and other drugs. The therapist should clarify in advance whether a session will be held if only one partner can attend.

The therapeutic alliance with couples presents additional challenges, as the therapist needs to establish three alliances – with the user, with the partner and with the relationship. The alliance with the user needs to communicate respect for the user as a person, facilitate involvement, decrease defensiveness and engage the user in a change process. The alliance with the partner needs to recognize the difficult experiences of the partner, minimize the partner's sense of guilt or responsibility for either the use or for the outcome of treatment, and engage the partner in changing. The alliance with the relationship should communicate equal respect and support for both partners, and minimize the therapist's position as favouring one or the other partner. Unfortunately, these three alliances at times come into conflict. Partners may find the motivational interviewing style frustrating when they want the therapist to support them strongly in pushing the user to change. Partners also, at times, view the functional analysis and identification of high-risk situations as supporting 'excuses' for using. Education about the treatment model and supporting the partner through reflective listening may obviate some of the partner's frustration. Conversely, although the presence of a supportive partner is clearly associated with positive treatment outcomes, for some couples the therapist may feel that continuing in the relationship is dysfunctional for the partner and that a separation might be the best course for the partner. In couple therapy, the therapist typically should maintain a neutral stance and not advocate either for separation or continuing the relationship, but rather should help the couple explore their options. Referring the partner to sepa-

Day	Date	Drinking	Drug use		Urge intensity	Relationship satisfaction
		No L M H	No L M H		0 1 2 3 4 5 6 7	0 1 2 3 4 5 6 7
		No L M H	No L M H		0 1 2 3 4 5 6 7	0 1 2 3 4 5 6 7
		No L M H	No L M H		0 1 2 3 4 5 6 7	0 1 2 3 4 5 6 7
		No L M H	No L M H		0 1 2 3 4 5 6 7	0 1 2 3 4 5 6 7
		No L M H	No L M H		0 1 2 3 4 5 6 7	0 1 2 3 4 5 6 7
		No L M H	No L M H		0 1 2 3 4 5 6 7	0 1 2 3 4 5 6 7

Note: Use the reverse side of the card to track behaviours you are learning to change.
L = light; M = moderate; H = heavy.

Figure 20.13 Sample partner monitoring card.

rate individual therapy may provide him or her with an outlet for discussing decisions about continuing the relationship with a clinician who does not have an alliance to the user as well. There are no easy answers to any of these dilemmas, but the therapist who is cognisant of these multiple relationships will be more effective at negotiating them and making decisions that maximize benefit for everyone involved with the treatment.

Changing partner cues for use

The behaviours of the partner can be conceptualized within the functional analytic framework. Partners engage in behaviours that may serve as cues or triggers for drinking or drug use, even when these behaviours are intended to help the user avoid alcohol or drug use. Several types of partner behaviours may serve as triggers – drinking or drug use by the partner, shared celebratory situations, attempts to control the user, attempting to influence the user through repeated attempts at verbal persuasion (also know as 'nagging'), attempts to discuss problems in the relationship or relationship conflicts.

Three interventions may be used to target partner behaviours. First are the assessment process and the functional analysis. Clients will be identifying high-risk situations as they occur and recording these on their cards. The therapist should discuss these situations with the couple, and partner actions may be identified that contributed to an urge to use or actual use. By linking the partner's actions to the functional analysis, the therapist can emphasize both that there is a connection between the partner's actions and urges or use, and that the client's thoughts and feelings in response to these actions are what determine whether or not he/she drinks or uses drugs, rather than that the partner 'makes' the user relapse or experience urges. The therapist also should note, however, that the partner's actions may increase or decrease the user's desire to use. The therapist may also use a self-report measure of spouse coping, such as The Coping Questionnaire (Orford et al., 1998) to develop a better understanding of characteristic ways that the partner has responded in the past.

Following the assessment of partner triggers and coping, cognitive-behavioural techniques may be used to help the partner change behaviours that serve as cues to use. Self-management planning sheets (see Figure 20.8) may be used to brainstorm ways to handle situations differently, and both partners should be involved with the discussion. The partner may address a range of situations using self-management planning, such as drinking in the presence of the client if the client is attempting to abstain from alcohol or what to do in situations that involve alcohol or drugs.

A third important set of interventions around partner triggers is communication skills. Partner verbal behaviour often serves as a trigger for use, particularly expressions of doubt about the user's intentions, expressions of anger or hurt about past situations, or attempts to control the user when the partner is fearful about possible use. The therapist should work closely with the couple to help them articulate exactly what kinds of communication are particularly disturbing to the client, and to brainstorm together about other ways for the partner to communicate opinions and feelings that are easier to hear. The therapist should not communicate that the partner should be silent about his or her feelings, but rather that there are more and less effective ways to communicate. The therapist should focus on direct, assertive communication in which the partner expresses and owns the feelings, and is behaviourally specific rather than globally critical of the user. Role-playing of discussions about partner concerns is particularly important and powerful.

Family reinforcement for abstinence

Family members can provide both real and symbolic support to the user for change, and these behaviours may provide reinforcement for continued abstinence. Reinforcers may be provided through verbal or other kinds of behaviours, and should be contingent on abstinence or staying within a moderate use goal for the day. Partners often are reluctant to express positive comments about changes in the user's behaviour, as they may view the client as only doing what 'should be' done. They also may be distrustful that changes will persist, as they may have experienced many episodes of short-term sobriety in the past, only to be disappointed when a relapse occurs. The therapist can respond to these concerns by supporting and being respectful of the concerns, but also explaining that change is most successful when an individual experiences many rewards for the new behaviours. Thus, although the partner may not believe that a week of abstinence is terribly impressive, it usually has required effort on the part of the client to achieve the abstinence, and some expression of recognition of the effort and success may feel good to the client. The client and partner should work together to identify expressions of support that both are experienced as supportive and that the partner is willing to use.

Partners also may engage in other behaviours to express support and reinforce the client's abstinence. These may be simple gestures of kindness, such as making a cup of tea for the client, or providing a brief massage, and should in fact not be large, time-consuming, or expensive gestures. Instead, the therapist should help the couple identify a number of small actions that the partner could use as expressions of support for days when the client is abstinent.

Decreasing family reinforcement for use

Despite the many negative consequences that families experience as a result of the client's substance-use, family members may reinforce continued use. Examples of family reinforcers include: sharing enjoyable times primarily when the client is using, providing the user with more attention and concern when using than when sober, avoiding discussing negative topics or maintaining a neutral tone when the client has been using alcohol or drugs and expressing more negative emotions and opinions when the client is abstinent. The types of intervention to provide are similar to those for partner triggers for using. Awareness of partner patterns of reinforcement can be enhanced through the functional analysis of drinking or drug-use situations, with the therapist paying particular attention to positive consequences of use that the client identifies. Emphasizing the inadvertent but still unhelpful nature of the reinforcement may facilitate the partner being willing to change some of these actions. Finally, use of self-management sheets and problem solving may yield alternative behaviours that would decrease reinforcement for use.

Two types of partner reinforcers for use are particularly challenging for the therapist. A first type of behaviour is partner actions that protect the client from negative consequences of use, such as injury, loss of job or humiliation. Partners are understandably reluctant to let the client be harmed physically as a consequence of use, but often go beyond simple protection to creating a positive experience. For example, if the user has a history of passing out and vomiting after a drinking binge, the partner might want to place the client in a posture that will prevent choking on the vomit, but should not go beyond that to helping the person into bed, cleaning them up if they have vomited or providing soothing food and beverages the next day. A second type of partner action that is both a trigger and a reinforcer for use is the partner's own alcohol or drug use. For couples that use substances together, change in one partner is particularly challenging if the other person plans to continue to use. Couples are then confronted with decisions about whether or not to keep alcohol or drugs in their home and what kinds of social and recreational activities will accommodate both of their goals. A frank discussion, creative brainstorming and development of concrete plans for shared time and recreation that does not involve use may all be valuable, but very different patterns of alcohol or drug use between intimate partners may contribute to on-going tension in the relationship.

Use of family to maintain client treatment engagement

In addition to reinforcement for abstinence, family members may reinforce specific treatment-related activities. O'Farrell and Fals-Stewart (2000) use a daily 'sobriety contract' between the client and partner. If the client is taking disulfiram or other medication to prevent substance-use, the medication may be taken in the presence of the partner. If the client is not using medication, the client expresses his or her intent to remain abstinent that day, and the partner expresses verbal support for the client's abstinence. A number of other approaches to family reinforcement for treatment engagement have been used. For example, Ahles et al. (1983) developed behavioural contracts between family members and alcoholics for the family to provide a weekly reinforcer, desired by the client, for attendance at aftercare sessions following inpatient alcoholism treatment. Patients who had the family contracts attended significantly more aftercare sessions than patients without the family contracts.

Linking family to social supports for themselves

As described at the beginning of this section, family members may be profoundly affected by the client's alcohol or drug use, and may experience a range of negative emotions as well as ambivalence about the relationship. Additionally, if the client is not successful in achieving treatment goals, some partners may be thinking about whether or not to continue the relationship, as well as how to protect themselves and their children physically, emotionally and financially. The clinician working with the drinker or drug user may experience an impossible conflict between the goals of the client to remain in the family and the needs of other family members. Providing a referral to another competent practitioner who is knowledgeable about substance-use disorders may help the partner sort through his or her emotions and make decisions about the best courses of action.

An additional source of support may come from self-help groups for families, such as Al-Anon or Nar-Anon. Like AA and NA, these family support groups are free of charge and members are persons affected by someone else's alcohol or drug-use disorder. The programmes derive from a disease model of addiction, and the twelve-step framework is used to help members recover. Family members are seen as having a disease as well, which most commonly is termed 'co-dependence'. The focus of Al-Anon and Nar-Anon meetings is support for the individual family member's recovery, and the programme emphasizes the family member's powerlessness over the addiction. The message of powerlessness is different from cognitive-behavioural models, which state that the actions of the family may influence the user, so families who are actively involved with ABCT may experience a contradiction between the two models. For some families, however, hearing the experiences of others who have coped with alcohol or drug dependence in their families and learning how others have coped provides a sense of relief and support that cannot be matched in the therapy session.

Role of family in relapse prevention and dealing with slips

Relapse prevention that involves a family member is very similar to the approach to relapse prevention described earlier in the chapter, including preparing family members for the possibility of relapse, educating them about the value of preparedness, identifying warning signs for relapse and providing a concrete set of steps to take should a relapse occur. The therapist and couple should work together to identify specific actions that the family member may take if warning signs occur, as well as actions in the case of relapse. Most important is that the actions are agreed to by both the client and the partner, and that they have written agreements about what to do.

Pharmacotherapies

Medications play an important role in detoxification and the maintenance of patients with long-term heroin dependence; the role of medications in the long-term maintenance of change in clients with other substance-use disorders is less prominent. Medications also play an important role in the treatment of substance-related medical conditions and comorbid psychiatric disorders, but these are beyond the scope of this chapter. Medications commonly are used for detoxification from certain drugs of abuse, to deal with cravings, to substitute for the substance of abuse or to create immediate and adverse effects from use of the substance of abuse. Almost all studies of pharmacotherapies for substance-use disorders have been conducted in conjunction with psychological counselling, and there is little evidence, other than in the management of acute conditions, that medication alone is an effective treatment for any substance-use disorder. Although medications must only be prescribed and monitored by qualified medical personnel, and medical personnel must make decisions about the appropriate level of care for specific medications, clinicians should be familiar with medications, the role for medications in treatment, and should have relationships with appropriately qualified medical personnel for referral. Table 20.8 summarizes medications approved for use in the treatment of substance-use disorders in the United States.

Medications for detoxification

Decision making about the need for detoxification is described earlier in the chapter. Medications may be used to manage withdrawal from substances of abuse that create physiological dependence, including opiates, alcohol and sedative-hypnotic drugs. Detoxification may be effected on an inpatient or ambulatory basis, depending on the severity of the physiological dependence and the general medical condition of the patient.

Several major approaches are used to manage opioid withdrawal (see O'Connor et al., 2003), including slow methadone detoxification on inpatient (over a one- to two-week period) or ambulatory basis (up to six months), clonidine (approximately a ten-day detoxification) or combining clonidine and naltrexone.

Alcohol withdrawal (see Mayo-Smith, 2003) typically is accomplished by substituting a long-acting tranquillizer, most commonly a benzodiazepine, for the short-acting tranquillizer, alcohol. Doses are tapered over several days until the patient is no longer taking the medication. If patients are being

Table 20.8 Pharmacological treatments for substance-use disorders

Indicated use	*Medication (generic/trade)*	*Typical dosage*	*Side effects*	*Contraindications*
Withdrawal – opiate	Methadone	Up to 20 mg first 24 hours; tapering by 5 mg/day for 5–6 days in inpatients; may taper 5%/day in outpatients		
	Clonidine (Catapres)	0–0.2 mg tid or qid, up to 1–2 mg/day; tapering over 6–10 days	Sedation, drowsiness, fatigue Dry mouth	
Withdrawal – alcohol, uncomplicated	Chlordiazepoxide (Librium) or other long-acting benzodiazepine *or* Lorazepam (Ativan) or other short-acting benzodiazepine	Chlordiazepoxide: Up to 300 mg first day; halved each day for about 3 days Lorazepam		Selection of medication based on setting for detoxification, liver involvement
Withdrawal – alcohol, complicated (delirium tremens)	Haloperidol (Haldol)	0.5–2.0 mg intramuscularly every 2 hours until symptoms abate (up to 5 doses)		
Withdrawal – sedative/Hypnotics	Tapering of drug of abuse over 6–12 weeks Phenobarbital substitution (severe dependence only) Carbamazapine substitution (benzodiazepines)	Dependent on specific drug of abuse		

Cravings	Naltrexone (Revia)	50 mg/day	Abdominal discomfort Headaches	Use of IV heroin in past 3 days, acute hepatitis, liver failure, other acute liver dysfunction
Opiate substitution therapy	Methadone	60 to greater than 100 mg/day		
	Levo-alpha-acetylmethadol (LAAM)	20–120 mg every other day		Hepatic failure
	Buprenorphine (Buprenex)	8 mg/day	Sedation Nausea Dizziness/vertigo	Compromised respiratory function Recent use of CNS/respiratory Demonstrated sensitivity to the drug Safety not established for pregnancy
Alcohol sensitizing agent	Disulfiram (Antabuse)	250 mg/day	Hepatitis Skin eruptions Drowsiness Impotence Headache	Recent use of alcohol-containing product Severe heart disease Psychosis Sensitivity to thiuram derivatives/history of rubber contact dermatitis Safety not established for pregnancy-use if benefits outweigh risks

medicated for alcohol withdrawal, they should not be consuming any alcohol because of the possibility of synergistic sedative effects of combining alcohol and tranquillizers. Other medications are used to manage alcohol withdrawal only if patients are disoriented and hallucinating. Then, small doses of haloperidol are most commonly used to control these symptoms.

Patients who are dependent on sedative-hypnotic drugs, such as benzodiazepines or barbiturates, experience difficult and prolonged withdrawal syndromes. Withdrawal is managed either by gradually tapering the dose of the drug of abuse or by substituting another cross-tolerant medication and gradually tapering the dose (see Dickinson et al., 2003).

Medications to deal with cravings

Opiate antagonist drugs bind to opiate receptor sites and therefore prevent the binding of opiates to those sites. Naltrexone completely blocks the binding of heroin to opiate receptor sites, and therefore blocks the reinforcing properties of heroin in patients taking naltrexone. Despite the positive pharmacological effects of naltrexone in the treatment of opiate dependence, it has not become a commonly used pharmacotherapy because compliance with the medication is extremely poor; with retention rates of only 20–30% over a six-month period (see Stine et al., 2003).

Both naltrexone (Revia®) and nalmefene (Revex®) have been studied for the treatment of alcohol dependence, and naltrexone has reasonably good data supporting its effectiveness (see Kranzler & Jaffe, 2003). In the treatment of alcohol dependence, naltrexone appears to affect cravings for alcohol and decrease the reinforcing properties of alcohol, and is effective primarily in decreasing the probability of heavy drinking if a patient consumes an alcoholic beverage. Naltrexone appears to be particularly effective with patients who are fully compliant with taking the medication, those who experience strong cravings for use, and those with a positive family history of alcohol dependence.

Opioid substitution therapy

The most common pharmacological treatment of opiate dependence is methadone maintenance therapy. Methadone is an opiate, and methadone maintenance thus is a treatment that substitutes the use of a regulated, carefully dosed, carefully controlled opiate for unregulated and illicit use of opiates. That methadone maintenance keeps patients physiologically dependent on an opiate has elicited negative reactions from the lay public, some patients, and health and mental health professionals with limited training in the treatment of substance-use disorders. Despite what are perhaps moral judgements against the long-term use of methadone, evidence is consistent in showing that patients with a history of opiate dependence of a year or more are very unlikely to effect a long-term, drug-free recovery, but do respond positively to methadone and are able to stabilize their lives and function with the medication (see Payte et al., 2003 for a review). The use of methadone has been highly regulated, clinics to dispense methadone must follow strict regulations in the US, and most patients take the medication only at the methadone clinic. The daily trips to the methadone clinic impose a substantial burden on those patients who may be indigent and have difficulties with transportation and on fully employed patients who then have to co-ordinate their daily medications with their work schedules.

Two more recent medications have been developed that avoid some of the inconvenience associated with methadone maintenance. Levo-alpha-acetylmethadol (LAAM) is a derivative of methadone but has a slower onset of effect and longer duration of action. Patients may be impatient when first started on LAAM as they wait for the effects. Because of LAAM's slower onset of action, patients are sometimes first stabilized on methadone before switching to LAAM. LAAM is then given three times a week, with a slightly larger dose on Fridays to carry the patient through the weekend. Buprenorphine is a partial opioid agonist that also has opiate antagonist effects. Although used in injectable form for a number of years, it only has been available in pill form in the US since 2002, and models for office-based management of opiate-dependent patients on buprenorphine are being promulgated (see, for example, Saxon, 2003).

Alcohol-sensitizing agents

The purpose of alcohol-sensitizing agents is to make the use of alcohol physically unpleasant or even toxic. Disulfiram (Antabuse®) has been approved for use since the 1940s, although data on the effectiveness of the medication are limited. Disulfiram works by inhibiting the action of aldehyde dehydrogenase, resulting in an accumulation of acetaldehyde in the body if a person drinks while on disulfiram. The alcohol–disulfiram reaction is extremely uncomfortable and may include flushing, increased heart rate, heart palpitations, decreased blood pressure, nausea, vomiting, shortness of breath and dizziness (see Kranzler & Jaffe, 2003). The medication may be indicated for patients who want to abstain from the use of alcohol but are having difficulty in doing so. Clinicians may suggest that a patient be evaluated for disulfiram if they have difficulty with impulsive drinking, and may help the patient use the medication particularly in anticipation of high-risk situations. Additionally, as noted above, contracts to have the medication administered by a family member may increase compliance and also provide reassurance to the family member that the patient is complying with the prescribed medication.

Patients must not be given disulfiram without their full knowledge and consent, despite the suggestion of some spouses that they slip the medication into the patient's morning juice. Patients must learn to monitor all substances that they consume for the presence of alcohol, and must avoid many common cough and cold medications, mouthwashes, aftershaves and foods prepared with alcohol.

SUMMARY

Alcohol and other substance-use disorders present some of the most fascinating challenges to clinicians – they are complex, require knowledge of physiology, individual psychology, interpersonal relationships and the larger social environment. Although sometimes maddeningly difficult to treat, the rewards are great as the clinician has the unusual opportunity to participate in someone's finding and building a new life.

EXERCISE 20.1: SKILLS BUILDING

There are many ways to develop skills in the treatment of substance-use disorders, as well as a subjective understanding of the challenges involved. The beginning clinician is encouraged to develop his or her own self-change project (described in detail on p. 805) to learn the challenges of giving up a behaviour that has many desirable aspects. At a minimum, as part of the self-change exercise, the clinician should use daily self-monitoring cards, conduct a functional analysis of the target behaviour, complete a decisional matrix about continuing versus discontinuing the behaviour, complete several self-management plans and try to identify alternatives to the target behaviour. Keeping a journal of the experience provides an additional level of reflection, as well as a record of the clinician's experience.

EXERCISE 20.2: FORMING A BOND

As noted, clients with substance-use disorders have often engaged in behaviour that is upsetting and difficult to understand, and the clinician may feel challenged to find qualities around which to form an empathic bond with a client. The following may help to develop empathy with substance-abusing clients:

1 Interview several persons with long-term recovery from a substance-use disorder. Ask them about their active use, the period of recovery and their current functioning.
2 Keep a journal for a week. For every person encountered, attempt to identify three qualities around which the clinician could form a bond with the individual. The journal could include family members, co-

workers or classmates, clients, friends, service people and anyone else encountered even casually in the course of the week.

EXERCISE 20.3: MODELS OF TREATMENT

Clinicians also may use a number of approaches to learn more about models of treatment. Anyone working with clients with substance-use disorders should have some knowledge of and exposure to self-help group meetings, including twelve-step groups such as AA and NA. The beginning clinician should attend at least four to six meetings, preferably of different types and in different locations, to develop a reasonable understanding of the structure and atmosphere of the meetings. In addition, clinicians should obtain experience with using structured treatment manuals, and should treat several clients strictly 'by the book'. Although in on-going clinical practice it is not uncommon for clinicians to be somewhat selective in how they use treatment manuals, having experience with using a manual from beginning to end provides invaluable experience to draw upon for later treatment planning.

SUGGESTED TREATMENT MANUALS

An excellent source for treatment manuals and other materials related to substance abuse is the National Institute on Drug Abuse (NIDA) Toolbox, which can be viewed at: http://www.nida.nih.gov/TB/Clinical/ClinicalToolbox.html. The toolbox can be obtained from NIDA for a small shipping fee and includes the following materials:

1 Treatment manuals: *A cognitive-behavioral approach: Treating cocaine addiction; A community reinforcement plus vouchers approach: Treating cocaine addiction*; and *An individual drug counseling approach to treat cocaine addiction: The collaborative cocaine treatment study Model.*
2 Research reports: *Anabolic steroid abuse, Cocaine abuse and addiction, Methamphetamine abuse* (available in English and Spanish), *Nicotine addiction, Inhalant abuse* and *Heroin abuse and addiction.*
3 Additional publications: *Approaches to drug abuse counseling, Principles of drug addiction treatment, NIDA publications catalog*, NIDA web page flyer and ordering information for other NIDA materials.
4 Other materials: *Commonly abused drugs chart*, other flyers and brochures.

Several manuals for the treatment of alcohol-use disorders are available through the National Institute on Alcohol Abuse and Alcoholism, and can be viewed at: http://www.niaaa.nih.gov/publications/guides.htm. Three excellent treatment manuals came out of the Project MATCH research programme, including: *Twelve-step facilitation therapy manual, Motivational enhancement therapy manual* and *Cognitive-behavioral coping skills therapy manual*.

FURTHER READING FOR PRACTITIONERS

American Society of Addiction Medicine (ASAM) (1991). *Patient placement criteria for the treatment of psychoactive substance-use disorders*. Washington, DC: ASAM.

Dickinson, W. E., Mayo-Smith, M. F. & Eickelberg, S. J. (2003). Management of sedative-hypnotic intoxication and withdrawal. In: A. W. Graham, T. K. Schultz, M. F. Mayo-Smith, R. K. Ries, & B. B. Wilford (Eds.), *Principles of addiction medicine* (Third Edition, pp. 633–652). Chevy Chase, MD: American Society of Addiction Medicine.

Epstein, E.E. & McCrady, B.S. (2002). Marital therapy in the treatment of alcohol problems. In: A. S. Gurman & N. A. Jacobson (Eds.), *Clinical handbook of marital therapy* (Third Edition, pp. 597–628). New York: Guilford Press.

Fletcher, A. M. (2001). *Sober for good: New solutions for drinking problems. Advice from those who have succeeded*. New York: Houghton Mifflin.

Hester, R. & Miller, W. (2003). *Handbook of alcoholism treatment approaches: Effective alternatives* (Third Edition). Boston, MA: Allyn & Bacon.

Institute of Medicine (1990). *Broadening the base of treatment for alcohol problems*. Washington, DC: National Academy Press.

Jellinek, E M. (1960). *The disease concept of alcoholism*. New Brunswick, NJ: Hillhouse Press.

Kranzler, H. R. & Jaffe, J. H. (2003). Pharmacologic interventions for alcoholism. In: A. W. Graham, T. K. Schultz, M. F. Mayo-Smith, R. K. Ries & B. B. Wilford (Eds.), *Principles of addiction medicine* (Third Edition, pp. 701–720). Chevy Chase, MD: American Society of Addiction Medicine.

Mäkelä, K. et al. (1996). *Alcoholics Anonymous as a mutual-help movement: A study in eight societies*. Madison, WI: University of Wisconsin Press.

Marlatt, G. A. & Donovan, D. (2005). *Relapse prevention* (Second Edition). New York: Guilford Press.

Mayo-Smith, M. F. (2003). Management of alcohol intoxication and withdrawal. In: A. W. Graham, T. K. Schultz, M. F. Mayo-Smith, R. K. Ries & B. B. Wilford (Eds.), *Principles of addiction medicine* (Third Edition, pp. 621–632). Chevy Chase, MD: American Society of Addiction Medicine, Inc.

McCrady, B. S. (2004). To have but one true friend: Implications for practice of research on alcohol use disorders and social networks. *Psychology of Addictive Behaviors*, 18(2), 113–121.

McCrady, B. S. & Epstein, E. E. (1999). *Addictions: A comprehensive guidebook*. New York: Oxford University Press.

McCrady, B. S., Horvath, A. T., & Delaney, S. I. (2003). Self-help groups. In: R. K. Hester & W. R. Miller (Eds.), *Handbook of alcoholism treatment approaches. Effective alternatives* (Third Edition, pp. 165–187). Boston: Allyn & Bacon.

McLellan, A. T., Lewis, D. C., O'Brien, C. P. & Kleber, H. D. (2000). Drug dependence, a chronic medical illness: Implications for treatment, insurance, and outcomes evaluation. *JAMA*, 284, 1689–1695.

Meyers, R. & Smith, J. (1995). *Clinical guide to alcohol treatment. The community reinforcement approach*. New York: Guilford Press.

Miller, W. R., Meyers, R. J. & Tonigan, J. S. (1999). Engaging the unmotivated in treatment for alcohol problems: A comparison of three strategies for intervention through family members. *Journal of Consulting and Clinical Psychology*, 67, 688–697.

Miller, W. R. & Rollnick. S. (2002). *Motivational interviewing: Preparing people for change*. New York: Guilford Press.

Miller, W. R., Walters, S. T. & Bennett, M.E. (2001). How effective is alcoholism treatment in the United States? *Journal of Studies on Alcohol*, 62, 211–220.

Miller, W. R., Zweben, A., DiClemente, C. & Rychtarik, R. (1995). *Motivational Enhancement Therapy Manual*. Rockville, MD: National Institute on Alcohol Abuse and Alcoholism.

Monti, P. M., Kadden, R. M., Rohsenow, D. J., Cooney, N. L. & Abrams, D. B. (2002). *Treating alcohol dependence: A coping skills training guide* (Second Edition). New York: Guilford Press.

O'Connor, P. G., Kosten, T. R. & Stine, S. M. (2003). Management of opioid intoxication and withdrawal. In: A. W. Graham, T. K. Schultz, M. F. Mayo-Smith, R. K. Ries & B. B. Wilford (Eds.), *Principles of addiction medicine* (Third Edition, pp. 651–667). Chevy Chase, MD: American Society of Addiction Medicine.

Payte, J. T., Zweben, J. E. & Martin, J. (2003). Opioid maintenance treatment. In: A. W. Graham, T. K. Schultz, M. F. Mayo-Smith, R. K. Ries & B. B. Wilford (Eds.), *Principles of addiction medicine* (Third Edition, pp. 751–766). Chevy Chase, MD: American Society of Addiction Medicine.

Prochaska, J. O., DiClemente, C. C. & Norcross, J. C. (2001). In search of how people change. Applications to addictive behaviors. *American Psychologist*, 47, 1102–1114.

Rosenberg, H. (1993). Prediction of controlled drinking by alcoholics and problem drinkers. *Psychological Bulletin*, 113, 129–139.

Skinner, H. & Allen, B. A. (1982). Alcohol dependence syndrome: Measurement and validation. *Journal of Abnormal Psychology*, 91, 199–209.

Stine, S. M., Greenwald, M. K. & Kosten, T. R. (2003). Pharmacologic interventions for opioid addiction. In: A. W. Graham, T. K. Schultz, M. F. Mayo-Smith, R. K. Ries & B. B. Wilford (Eds.), *Principles of addiction medicine* (Third Edition, pp. 735–748). Chevy Chase, MD: American Society of Addiction Medicine.

EVIDENCE SUMMARIES

Finney, J. & Moos, R. (2002). Psychosocial treatments for substance alcohol use disorders. In P. Nathan & J. Gorman (Eds.), *A guide to treatments that work* (Second Edition, pp. 157–168). New York: Oxford University Press.

O'Brien, C. & McKay, J. (2002). Pharmacological treatments for substance-use disorders. In P. Nathan & J. Gorman (Eds.), *A guide to treatments that work* (Second Edition, pp. 125–156). New York: Oxford University Press.

FURTHER READING FOR CLIENTS

Alcoholics Anonymous (1976). *Alcoholics Anonymous* (Third Edition). Alcoholics Anonymous.

Colclough, B. (1993). *Tomorrow I'll be different. The effective way to stop drinking.* London: Viking.

Ellis, A. & Velton, E. (1992). *When AA doesn't work for You.* Fort Lee, NJ: Barricade Books. An alternative self-help guide for people who cannot accept AA's insistence on spiritual commitment; based on the principles of cognitive therapy.

Miller, W. & Munzo, R. (1982) *How to control your drinking.* Albuquerque, NM: University of New Mexico Press.

Tyrer, P. (1986). *How to stop taking tranquilizers.* London: Sheldon Press.

Trickett, S. (1986). *Coming off tranquilizers.* New York: Thorsons.

ASSESSMENT INSTRUMENTS

Annis, H. M. (1982). *Inventory of drinking situations (IDS-100).* Toronto, Canada: Addiction Research Foundation of Toronto.

Brown, S. A., Christiansen, B. A. & Goldman, M. S. (1987). The Alcohol Expectancy Questionnaire: An instrument for the assessment of adolescent and adult alcohol expectancies. *Journal of Studies on Alcohol*, 48, 483–491.

Cunningham, J. A., Sobell, L. C., Gavin, D. R., Sobell, M. B. & Breslin, F. C. (1997). Assessing motivation for change: Preliminary development and evaluation of a scale measuring the costs and benefits of changing alcohol or drug use. *Psychology of Addictive Behaviors*, 11, 107–114.

Derogatis, L. R. & Savitz, K. L. (2000). The SCL-90-R and Brief Symptom Inventory (BSI) in primary care. In: M E. Maruish (Ed.), *Handbook of psychological assessment in primary care settings* (pp. 297–334). Mahwah, NJ: Lawrence Erlbaum Associates.

Gossop, M., Darke, S., Griffiths, P., Hando, J., Powis, B., Hall, W. & Strang, J. (1995). The Severity of Dependence Scale (SDS): Psychometric properties of the SDS in English and Australian samples of heroin, cocaine and amphetamine users. *Addiction*, 90, 607–614.

Hall, S. M., Havassy, B. E. & Wasserman, D. A. (1991). Effects of commitment to abstinence, positive moods, stress, and coping on relapse to cocaine use. *Journal of Consulting and Clinical Psychology*, 59, 526–532.

Jaffe, A. J. & Kilbey, M. M. (1994). The Cocaine Expectancy Questionnaire (CEQ): Construction and predictive utility. *Psychological Assessment*, 6, 18–26.

Jones, A. (1995). Measuring ethanol in saliva with the QED Enzymatic Test Device, Comparison of results with blood- and breath-alcohol concentrations. *Journal of Analytical Toxicology*, 19, 1690–1694.

Litman, G., Stapleton, J., Oppenheim, A. N. & Peleg, M. (1983). An instrument for measuring coping behaviours in hospitalized alcoholics: Implications for relapse prevention and treatment. *British Journal of Addiction*, 78, 269–276.

Margolin, G., Talovic, S. & Weinstein, C. D. (1983). Areas of Change Questionnaire: A practical approach to marital assessment. *Journal of Consulting and Clinical Psychology*, 51, 921–931.

Mayfield, D., McLeod, G. & Hall, P. (1974). The CAGE Questionnaire. Validation of a new alcoholism screening instrument. *American Journal of Psychiatry*, 131, 1121–1123.

McConnaughy, E A., Prochaska, J. O. & Velicer, W. F. (1983). Stages of change in psychotherapy: Measurement and sample profiles. *Psychotherapy: Theory, Research and Practice*, 20, 368–375.

McLellan, A. T., Kushner, H., Metzger, D. et al. (1992). The fifth edition of the Addiction Severity Index. *Journal of Substance Abuse Treatment*, 9, 199–213.

Miller, W. R., Tonigan, J. S. & Longabaugh, R. (1995). *The Drinker Inventory of Consequences (DrInC): An instrument for assessing adverse consequences of alcohol abuse*. Rockville, MD: National Institute on Alcohol Abuse and Alcoholism.

Millon, T. (1997). *The Millon inventories: Clinical and personality assessment*. New York: Guilford Press.

Monti, P. (1997). *Coping with Alcohol Relevant Situations Test (CARS)*. Providence, RI: Centre for Alcohol and Addiction Studies, Brown University.

Orford, J., Natera, G., Davies, J., Nava, A., Mora, J., Rigby, K., Bradbury, C., Bowie, N., Copello, A. & Velleman, R. (1998). Tolerate, engage or withdraw: A study of the structure of families coping with alcohol and drug problems in South West England and Mexico City. *Addiction*, 93, 1799–1813.

Pan, H. S., Neidig, P. H. & O'Leary, K. D. (1994). Male–female and aggressor–victim differences in the factor structure of the Modified Conflict Tactics Scale. *Journal of Interpersonal Violence*, 9, 366–382.

Rollnick, S., Heather, N., Gold, R. & Hall, W. (1992). Development of a short 'Readiness to Change' Questionnaire for use in brief opportunistic interventions. *British Journal of Addictions*, 87, 743–754.

Saxon, A. J. (2003). Special issues in office-based opioid treatment. In: A. W. Graham, T. K. Schultz, M. F. Mayo-Smith, R. K. Ries & B. B. Wilford (Eds.), *Principles of addiction medicine* (Third Edition, pp. 767–783). Chevy Chase, MD: American Society of Addiction Medicine.

Selzer, M. (1971). The Michigan Alcohol Screening test: The quest for a new diagnostic instrument. *American Journal of Psychiatry*, 127, 1653–1658.

Skinner, H. & Allen, B. (1982). Alcohol Dependence Syndrome: Measurement and validation. *Journal of Abnormal Psychology*, 91, 199–209. (Contains the Alcohol Dependence Scale.)

Sobell, M. B., Maisto, S. A., Sobell, L. C., Cooper, T. & Saunders, B. (1980). Developing a prototype for evaluating alcohol treatment effectiveness. In: L. C. Sobell, M. B. Sobell & E. Ward (Eds.), *Evaluating alcohol treatment effectiveness: Recent advances*. New York: Pergamon Press.

Sobell, L. & Sobell, M. (1992). Timeline follow-back: A technique for assessing self-reported ethanol consumption. In: J. Allen & R. Litten (Eds.), *Measuring alcohol consumption: Psychosocial and biochemical methods* (pp. 41–72). Totowa, NJ: Humana Press. E-mail:sobell@cps.nova.edu

Spanier, G. (1976). Measuring dyadic adjustment: New scales for assessing the quality of marriage and similar dyads. *Journal of Marriage and the Family*, 38, 15–28.

Spitzer, R. L., Williams, J. B. W., Gibbon, M. & First, M. B. (1996). *Structured Clinical Interview for DSM-IV-Patient Edition (with Psychotic Screen – Version 1.0)*. Washington, DC: American Psychiatric Press.

Sullivan, J. T., Sykora, K., Schneiderman, J. et al. (1989). Assessment of alcohol withdrawal: The revised Clinical Institute Withdrawal Assessment for Alcohol scale (CIWA-Ar). *British Journal of Addiction*, 84, 1353–1357.

Tonigan, J. & Miller, W. (1993). Assessment and validation of the Drinker Inventory of Consequences: A multi-site outpatient and aftercare clinical sample of problem drinker. *Alcoholism: Clinical and Experimental Research*, 17, 513.

Tonigan, J. S. & Miller, W. R. (2002). The Inventory of Drug Use Consequences (InDUC): Test–retest stability and sensitivity to detect change. *Psychology of Addictive Behaviors*, 16, 165–168.

Willoughby. F. & Edens, J. (1996). The construct validity and predictive validity of the Stages of Change Scale for alcoholics. *Journal of Substance Abuse*, 8, 275–291. Contains a measure of stages of change.

Zimmerman, M. (1994). *Interview guide for evaluating DSM-IV psychiatric disorders and the mental status examination*. East Greenwich, RI: Psych Products Press.

Zitter, R. & McCrady, B. S. (1979). *The Drinking Patterns Questionnaire*. Unpublished questionnaire, Brown University.

REFERENCES

Ahles, T. A., Schlundt, D. G., Prue, D. M. & Rychtarik, R. G. (1983). Impact of aftercare arrangements on the maintenance of treatment success in abusive drinkers. *Addictive Behaviors*, 8, 53–58.

American Psychiatric Association (2000). *Diagnostic and statistical manual of mental disorders, fourth edition, text revision*. Washington, DC: American Psychiatric Association.

American Society of Addiction Medicine (ASAM) (1991). *Patient placement criteria for the treatment of psychoactive substance-use disorders*. Washington, DC: ASAM.

Annis, H. M. (1982). *Inventory of Drinking Situations (IDS-100)*. Toronto, Canada: Addiction Research Foundation of Toronto.

Babor, T. F., Hofmann, M., DelBoca, F. K. et al. (1992). Types of alcoholics: I. Evidence for an empirically derived typology based on indicators of vulnerability and severity. *Archives of General Psychiatry*, 49, 599–608.

Ball, S. A., Carroll, K. M,. Babor, T. F. & Rounsaville, B. J. (1995). Subtypes of cocaine abusers: Support for a type A-Type B distinction. *Journal of Consulting and Clinical Psychology*, 63, 115–124.

Beck, A. (1990). *Beck Anxiety Inventory*. San Antonio, TX: Psychological Corporation.

Beck, A., Steer, R. & Brown, G. (1996). *Beck Depression Inventory* (Second Edition). San Antonio, TX: Psychological Corporation.

Breslin, F. C., Sobell, M. B., Sobell, L. C., Buchan, G. & Cunningham, J. A. (1997). Toward a stepped care approach to treating problem drinkers: The predictive utility of within-treatment variables and therapist prognostic ratings. *Addiction*, 92, 1479–1489.

Brown, S. A., Christiansen, B. A. & Goldman, M. S. (1987). The Alcohol Expectancy Questionnaire: An instrument for the assessment of adolescent and adult alcohol expectancies. *Journal of Studies on Alcohol*, 48, 483–491.

Bry, B. H. & Slechta, C. (2000). Research evidence for home-based, school, and community interventions. In: N. Boyd-Franklin & B. H. Bry (Eds.), *Reaching out in family therapy. Home-based, school, and community interventions*. New York: Guilford Press.

Budney, A. J., Higgins, S. T., Radonovich, K. J. & Novy, P. L. (2000). Adding voucher-based incentives to coping skills and motivational enhancement improves outcomes during treatment for marijuana dependence. *Journal of Consulting and Clinical Psychology*, 68, 1051–1061.

Caetano, R., Schafer, J. & Cunradi, C. B. (2001). Alcohol-related intimate partner violence among White, Black, and Hispanic couples in the United States. *Alcohol Health and Research World*, 25(1), 58–65.

Cahalan, D., Cisin, I.H. & Crossley, H.M. (1969). American drinking practices: A national study of drinking behavior and attitudes. *Monographs of the Rutgers Center of Alcohol Studies*, 6, 260.

Chafetz, M,. Blane, H., Abram, H., Golner, J., Lacy, E., McCourt, W., Clark, E. & Meyers, W. (1962). Establishing treatment relations with alcoholics. *Journal of Nervous & Mental Disease*, 134, 395–409.

Crits-Christoph, P., Siqueland, L., Blaine, J., Frank, A., Luborsky, L., Onken, L. S., Muenz, L. R, Thase, M. E., Weiss, R. D., Gastfriend, D. R., Woody, G. E., Barber, J. P., Butler, S. F., Daley, D., Salloum, I., Bishop, S., Najavits, L. M., Lis, J., Mercer, D., Griffin, M. L., Moras, K. & Beck, A. T. (1999). Psychosocial treatments for cocaine dependence: National Institute on Drug Abuse Collaborative Cocaine Treatment Study. *Archives of General Psychiatry*, 56, 493–502.

Cunningham, J. A., Sobell, L. C., Gavin, D. R., Sobell, M. B. & Breslin, F. C. (1997). Assessing motivation for change: Preliminary development and evaluation of a scale measuring the costs and benefits of changing alcohol or drug use. *Psychology of Addictive Behaviors*, 11, 107–114.

Derogatis, L. R. & Savitz, K. L. (2000). The SCL-90-R and Brief Symptom Inventory (BSI) in primary care. In: M E. Maruish (Ed). *Handbook of psychological assessment in primary care settings* (pp. 297–334). Mahwah, NJ: Lawrence Erlbaum Associates.

Dickinson, W. E., Mayo-Smith, M. F. & Eickelberg, S. J. (2003). Management of sedative-hypnotic intoxication and withdrawal. In: A. W. Graham, T. K. Schultz, M. F. Mayo-Smith, R. K. Ries & B. B. Wilford (Eds.), *Principles of addiction medicine* (Third Edition, pp. 633–652). Chevy Chase, MD: American Society of Addiction Medicine.

Donohew, L, Clayton, R. R., Skinner, W. F. & Colon, S. (1999). Peer networks and sensation seeking: Some implications for primary socialization theory. *Substance Use and Misuse*, 34, 1013–1023.

Dunn, M. E. & Yniguez, R. M. (1999). Experimental demonstration of the influence of alcohol advertising on the activation of alcohol expectancies in memory among fourth- and fifth- grade children. *Experimental and Clinical Psychopharmacology*, 7, 473–483.

Edwards, G. et al. (1977). Alcoholism: A controlled trial of treatment and advice. *Journal of Studies on Alcohol*, 38, 1004–1031.

Epstein, E. E., Labouvie, E., McCrady, B. S., Jensen, N. K. & Hayaki, J. (2002). A multi-site study of alcohol subtypes: Classification and overlap of unidimensional and multidimensional typologies. *Addiction*, 97, 1041–1053.

Epstein, E.E. & McCrady, B.S. (2002). Marital therapy in the treatment of alcohol problems. In: A. S. Gurman & N. A. Jacobson (Eds.), *Clinical handbook of marital therapy* (Third Edition, pp. 597–628). New York: Guilford Press.

Finney, J., Moos, R. & Timko, C. (1999). The course of treated and untreated substance-use disorders. In: McCrady, B. S. & Epstein, E. E. (1999). *Addictions: A comprehensive guidebook* (pp. 30–49). New York: Oxford University Press.

Fletcher, A. M. (2001). *Sober for good: New solutions for drinking problems. Advice from those who have succeeded.* New York : Houghton Mifflin.

Folkman, S., Lazarus, R., Dunkel-Schetter, C., DeLongis, A. & Gruen, R. (1986). Dynamics of a stressful encounter: Cognitive appraisal, coping, and encounter outcomes. *Journal of Personality and Social Psychology*, 50, 992–1003.

Furnham, A., Ingle, H., Gunter, B. & McClelland, A. (1997). A content analysis of alcohol portrayal and drinking in British television soap operas. *Health Education Research*, 12, 519–529.

Gossop, M., Darke, S., Griffiths, P., Hando, J., Powis, B., Hall & Strang, J. (1995). The Severity of Dependence Scale (SDS): Psychometric properties of the SDS in English and Australian samples of heroin, cocaine and amphetamine users. *Addiction*, 90, 607–614.

Grant, B. F., Dawson, D. A., Stinson, F. S., Chou, S. P., Dufour, M. C. & Pickering, R. P. (2004). The 12-month prevalence and trends in DSM-IV alcohol abuse and dependence: United States, 1991–1992 and 2001–2002. *Drug and Alcohol Dependence*, 74, 223–234.

Gregoire, T. K. & Burke, A. C. (2004). The relationship of legal coercion to readiness to change among adults with alcohol and other drug problems. *Journal of Substance Abuse Treatment*, 26, 35–41.

Hall, S. M., Havassy, B. E. & Wasserman, D. A. (1991). Effects of commitment to abstinence, positive moods, stress, and coping on relapse to cocaine use. *Journal of Consulting and Clinical Psychology*, 59, 526–532.

Helzer, J. E. et al. (1985). The extent of long-term moderate drinking among alcoholics discharged from medical and psychiatric treatment facilities. *New England Journal of Medicine*, 312, 1678–1682.

Higgins, S. T., Wong, C. J., Badger, G. J., Ogden, D. E. H. & Dantona, R. L. (2000). Contingent reinforcement increases cocaine abstinence during outpatient treatment and 1 year of follow-up. *Journal of Consulting and Clinical Psychology*, 68, 64–72.

Institute of Medicine (1990). *Broadening the base of treatment for alcohol problems.* Washington, DC: National Academy Press.

Jaffe, A. J. & Kilbey, M. M. (1994). The Cocaine Expectancy Questionnaire (CEQ): Construction and predictive utility. *Psychological Assessment*, 6, 18–26.

Jellinek, E M. (1960). *The disease concept of alcoholism.* New Brunswick, NJ: Hillhouse Press.

Johnson, V E. (1980). *I'll quit tomorrow* (Revised Edition). San Francisco: Harper & Row.

Jones, B. T. & McMahon, J. (1994). Negative alcohol expectancy predicts post-treatment abstinence survivorship: The whether, when and why of relapse to a first drink. *Addiction*, 89, 1653–1665.

Kerr, W. C., Fillmore, K. M. & Bostrom, A. (2002). Stability of alcohol consumption over time: Evidence from three longitudinal surveys from the United States. *Journal of Studies on Alcohol*, 63, 325–333.

Kranzler, H. R. & Jaffe, J. H. (2003). Pharmacologic interventions for alcoholism. In:

A. W. Graham, T. K. Schultz, M. F. Mayo-Smith, R. K. Ries & B. B. Wilford (Eds.), *Principles of addiction medicine* (Third Edition, pp. 701–720). Chevy Chase, MD: American Society of Addiction Medicine.

Labouvie, E. & Bates, M. E. (2002). Reasons for alcohol use in young adulthood: Validation of a three-dimensional measure. *Journal of Studies on Alcohol*, 63, 145–155.

Lewinsohn, P. M., Muñoz, R. F., Youngren, M. A. & Zeiss, A. M. (1986). *Control your depression*. New York: Simon & Schuster.

Litman, G., Stapleton, J., Oppenheim, A. N. & Peleg, M. (1983). An instrument for measuring coping behaviours in hospitalized alcoholics: Implications for relapse prevention and treatment. *British Journal of Addiction*, 78, 269–276.

Litt, M. D., Babor, T. F., DelBoca, F. K. et al. (1992). Types of alcoholics: II. Application of an empirically derived typology to treatment matching. *Archives of General Psychiatry*, 49, 609–614.

Loukas, A., Zucker, R. A., Fitzgerald, H. E. & Krull, J. L. (2003). Developmental trajectories of disruptive behavior problems among sons of alcoholics: Effects of parent psychopathology, family conflict, and child undercontrol. *Journal of Abnormal Psychology*, 112, 119–131.

Ludwig, A. (1985). Cognitive processes associated with 'spontaneous' recovery from alcoholism. *Journal of Studies on Alcohol*, 46, 53–58.

Mäkelä, K. et al. (1996). *Alcoholics Anonymous as a mutual-help movement: A study in eight societies*. Madison, WI: University of Wisconsin Press.

Margolin, G., Talovic, S. & Weinstein, C. D. (1983). Areas of Change Questionnaire: A practical approach to marital assessment. *Journal of Consulting and Clinical Psychology*, 51, 921–931.

Marlatt, G. A. (1996). Harm reduction: Come as you are. *Addictive Behaviors*, 21, 779–788.

Marlatt, G. A. & Gordon, J. (1986). *Relapse prevention*. New York: Guilford Press.

Mayo-Smith, M. F. (2003). Management of alcohol intoxication and withdrawal. In: A. W. Graham, T. K. Schultz, M. F. Mayo-Smith, R. K. Ries & B. B. Wilford (Eds.), *Principles of addiction medicine* (Third Edition, pp. 621–632). Chevy Chase, MD: American Society of Addiction Medicine.

McConnaughy, E A., Prochaska, J. O. & Velicer, W. F. (1983). Stages of change in psychotherapy: Measurement and sample profiles. *Psychotherapy: Theory, Research and Practice*, 20, 368–375.

McCrady, B. S. (1992). A reply to Peele: Is this how you treat your friends? *Addictive Behaviors*, 17, 67–72.

McCrady, B. S. (2004). To have but one true friend: Implications for practice of research on alcohol use disorders and social networks. *Psychology of Addictive Behaviors*, 18(2), 113–121.

McCrady, B. S. & Epstein, E. E. (1999). *Addictions: A comprehensive guidebook*. New York: Oxford University Press.

McCrady, B. S., Epstein, E. E. & Kahler, C. (1998). Families of alcoholics. In N. Singh (Ed.), *Comprehensive clinical psychology: Volume 9. Applications in diverse populations* (pp. 199–218). Oxford: Elsevier Science.

McCrady, B. S., Horvath, A. T. & Delaney, S. I. (2003). Self-help groups. In: R. K. Hester & W. R. Miller (Eds.), *Handbook of alcoholism treatment approaches. Effective alternatives* (Third Edition, pp. 165–187). Boston: Allyn & Bacon.

McLellan, A. T., Kushner, H., Metzger, D., Peters, R. et al. (1992). The fifth edition of the Addiction Severity Index. *Journal of Substance Abuse Treatment*, 9, 199–213.

McLellan, A. T., Lewis, D. C., O'Brien, C. P. & Kleber, H. D. (2000). Drug dependence, a chronic medical illness: Implications for treatment, insurance, and outcomes evaluation. *JAMA*, 284, 1689–1695.

Miller, K. J., McCrady, B. S., Abrams, D. B. & Labouvie, E. W. (1994). Taking an individualized approach to the assessment of self-efficacy and the prediction of alcoholic relapse. *Journal of Psychopathology & Behavioral Assessment*, 16, 111–120.

Miller, W. R., Benefield, R. G. & Tonigan, J. S. (1993). Enhancing motivation for change in problem drinking: A controlled comparison of two therapist styles. *Journal of Consulting and Clinical Psychology*, 61, 455–461.

Miller, W. R., Meyers, R. J. & Tonigan, J. S. (1999). Engaging the unmotivated in treatment for alcohol problems: A comparison of three strategies for intervention through family members. *Journal of Consulting and Clinical Psychology*, 67, 688–697.

Miller, W. R. & Rollnick. S. (2002). *Motivational interviewing: Preparing people for change*. New York: Guilford Press.

Miller, W. R., Tonigan, J. S. & Longabaugh, R. (1995). *The Drinker Inventory of Consequences (DrInC): An instrument for assessing adverse consequences of alcohol abuse*. Rockville, MD: National Institute on Alcohol Abuse and Alcoholism.

Miller, W. R., Walters, S. T. & Bennett, M.E. (2001). How effective is alcoholism treatment in the United States? *Journal of Studies on Alcohol*, 62, 211–220.

Miller, W. R. & Wilbourne, P. L. (2002). Mesa Grande: A methodological analysis of clinical trials of treatment for alcohol use disorders. *Addiction*, 97, 265–277.

Millon, T. (1997). *The Millon inventories: Clinical and personality assessment*. New York: Guilford Press.

Monti, P. M., Kadden, R. M., Rohsenow, D. J., Cooney, N. L. & Abrams, D. B. (2002). *Treating alcohol dependence: A coping skills training guide* (Second Edition). New York: Guilford Press.

Moos, R., Finney, J. & Cronkite, R. (1990). *Alcoholism treatment: Context, process, and outcome*. New York: Oxford.

Morgenstern, J., Kahler, C W. & Epstein, E (1998). Do treatment process factors mediate the relationship between Type A–Type B and outcome in 12-Step oriented substance abuse treatment? *Addiction*, 93, 1765–1776.

Mothers Against Drunk Driving (MADD) (2004). Online. Available at: http://www.madd.org/stats/0,1056,1777,00.html [accessed 3 June 2004].

Nathan, P. E. & McCrady, B. S. (1987). Bases for the use of abstinence as a goal in the behavioral treatment of alcohol abusers. *Drugs and Society*, 1, 109–131.

O'Connor, P. G., Kosten, T. R. & Stine, S. M. (2003). Management of opioid intoxication and withdrawal. In: A. W. Graham, T. K. Schultz, M. F. Mayo-Smith, R. K. Ries & B. B. Wilford (Eds.), *Principles of addiction medicine* (Third Edition, pp. 651–667). Chevy Chase, MD: American Society of Addiction Medicine, Inc.

Ojehagen, A. & Berglund, M. (1989). Changes of drinking goals in a two-year out-patient alcoholic treatment program. *Addictive Behaviors*, 14, 1–9.

O'Farrell, T. J. & Fals-Stewart, W. (2000). Behavioral couples therapy for alcoholism and drug abuse. *Journal of Substance Abuse Treatment*, 18, 51–54.

Orford, J. & Keddie, A. (1986). Abstinence or controlled drinking in clinical practice: A test of the dependence and persuasion hypotheses. *British Journal of Addiction*, 81, 495–504.

Orford, J., Natera, G., Davies, J., Nava, A., Mora, J., Rigby, K., Bradbury, C., Bowie, N., Copello, A. & Velleman, R. (1998). Tolerate, engage or withdraw: A study of the structure of families coping with alcohol and drug problems in South West England and Mexico City. *Addiction*, 93, 1799–1813.

Orford, J., Oppenheimer, E. & Edwards, G. (1976). Abstinence or control: The outcome for excessive drinkers two years after consultation. *Behaviour Research and Therapy*, 14, 409–418.

Pan, H. S., Neidig, P. H. & O'Leary, K. D. (1994). Male-female and aggressor-victim differences in the factor structure of the Modified Conflict Tactics Scale. *Journal of Interpersonal Violence*, 9, 366–382.

Payte, J. T., Zweben, J. E. & Martin, J. (2003). Opioid maintenance treatment. In: A. W. Graham, T. K. Schultz, M. F. Mayo-Smith, R. K. Ries & B. B. Wilford (Eds.), *Principles of addiction medicine* (Third Edition, pp. 751–766). Chevy Chase, MD: American Society of Addiction Medicine.

Prochaska, J. O., DiClemente, C. C. & Norcross, J. C. (1992). In search of how people change. Applications to addictive behaviors. *American Psychologist*, 47, 1102–1114.

Rollnick, S., Heather, N., Gold, R. & Hall, W. (1992). Development of a short 'Readiness to Change' Questionnaire for use in brief opportunistic interventions. *British Journal of Addictions*, 87, 743–754.

Room, R., Greenfield, T. K. & Weisner, C. (1991). 'People who might have liked you to drink less': Changing responses to drinking by U.S. family members and friends, 1979–1990. *Contemporary Drug Problems*, 18, 573–595.

Rosenberg, H. (1993). Prediction of controlled drinking by alcoholics and problem drinkers. *Psychological Bulletin*, 113, 129–139.

Rosenthal, R. N. & Westreich, L. (1999). Treatment of persons with dual diagnoses of substance-use disorder and other psychological problems. In B. S. McCrady & E. E. Epstein (Eds.) *Addictions: A comprehensive guidebook* (pp. 439–476). London: Oxford University Press.

Rychtarik, R. G., Connors, G. J., Whitney, R. B., McGillicuddy, N. B., Fitterling, J. M. & Wirtz, P. W. (2000). Treatment settings for persons with alcoholism: Evidence for matching clients to inpatient versus outpatient care. *Journal of Consulting and Clinical Psychology*, 68, 277–289.

Saxon, A. J. (2003). Special issues in office-based opioid treatment. In: A. W. Graham, T. K. Schultz, M. F. Mayo-Smith, R. K. Ries & B. B. Wilford (Eds.), *Principles of addiction medicine* (Third Edition, pp. 767–783). Chevy Chase, MD: American Society of Addiction Medicine, Inc.

Sisson, R. W. & Azrin, N. H. (1986). Family-member involvement to initiate and promote treatment of problem drinkers. *Journal of Behavior Therapy and Experimental Psychiatry*, 17, 15–21.

Skinner, H. & Allen, B. A. (1982). Alcohol dependence syndrome: Measurement and validation. *Journal of Abnormal Psychology*, 91, 199–209.

Sobell, L. C., Cunningham, J. A. & Sobell, M. B. (1996). Recovery from alcohol problems with and without treatment: Prevalence in two population surveys. *American Journal of Public Health*, 86, 966–972.

Sobell, M. B., Maisto, S. A., Sobell, L. C., Cooper, T. & Saunders, B. (1980). Developing a prototype for evaluating alcohol treatment effectiveness. In: L. C. Sobell, M. B. Sobell & E. Ward (Eds.), *Evaluating alcohol treatment effectiveness: Recent advances*. New York: Pergamon Press.

Sobell, M. B. & Sobell, L C. (2000). Stepped care as a heuristic approach to the treatment of alcohol problems. *Journal of Consulting and Clinical Psychology*, 68, 573–579.

Spanier, G. (1976). Measuring dyadic adjustment: New scales for assessing the quality of marriage and similar dyads. *Journal of Marriage and the Family*, 38, 15–28.

Spitzer, R. L., Williams, J. B. W., Gibbon, M. & First, M. B. (1996). *Structured Clinical Interview for DSM-IV-Patient Edition (with Psychotic Screen – Version 1.0)*. Washington, DC: American Psychiatric Press.

Stine, S. M., Greenwald, M. K. & Kosten, T. R. (2003). Pharmacologic interventions for opioid addiction. In: A. W. Graham, T. K. Schultz, M. F. Mayo-Smith, R. K. Ries & B. B. Wilford (Eds.), *Principles of addiction medicine* (Third Edition, pp. 735–748). Chevy Chase, MD: American Society of Addiction Medicine.

Sullivan, J. T., Sykora, K., Schneiderman, J. et al. (1989). Assessment of alcohol withdrawal: The revised Clinical Institute Withdrawal Assessment for Alcohol Scale (CIWA-Ar). *British Journal of Addiction*, 84, 1353–1357.

Thomas, E J. & Santa, C.A. (1982). Unilateral family therapy for alcohol abuse: A working conception. *American Journal of Family Therapy*, 10, 49–58.

Tonigan, J. S. & Miller, W. R. (2002). The Inventory of Drug Use Consequences (InDUC): Test–retest stability and sensitivity to detect change. *Psychology of Addictive Behaviors*, 16, 165–168.

Vaillant, G. E. (1995). *The natural history of alcoholism revisited*. Cambridge, MA: Harvard University Press.

Vielva, I. & Iraugi, I. (2001). Cognitive and behavioural factors as predictors of abstinence following treatment for alcohol dependence. *Addiction*, 96, 297–303.

Wallack, L., Grube, J. W., Madden, P. A. & Breed, W. (1990). Portrayals of alcohol on prime-time television. *Journal of Studies on Alcohol*, 51, 428–437.

World Health Organization (WHO) (1992). *The ICD-10 classification of mental and behavioural disorders. Clinical descriptions and diagnostic guidelines*. Geneva: WHO. Online. Available at http://www.informatik.fh-luebeck.de/icd/welcome.html

Young, J. E., Weinberger, A. D. & Beck, A. T. (2001). Cognitive therapy for depression. In: D. H. Barlow (Ed.), *Clinical handbook of psychological disorders: A step-by-step treatment manual* (*Third Edition*, pp. 264–308). New York: Guilford Press.

Zimmerman, M. (1994). *Interview guide for evaluating DSM-IV psychiatric disorders and the mental status examination*. East Greenwich, RI: Psych Products Press.

Zitter, R. & McCrady, B. S. (1979). *The Drinking Patterns Questionnaire*. Unpublished questionnaire. Providence, RI: Brown University.

Zywiak, W. H., Longabaugh, R. & Wirtz, P. W. (2002). Decomposing the relationships between pretreatment social network characteristics and alcohol treatment outcome. *Journal of Studies on Alcohol*, 63, 114–121.

Section 5

Other psychological difficulties

Chapter 21

Schizophrenia

Elizabeth Kuipers, Emmanuelle Peters and Paul Bebbington

> I know that there is a secret government cell that monitors everything that I do or say. I have got used to this. I am a survivor. But what really annoys me is that because they are watching me, they are also watching anyone I have a relationship with. That's not right. That makes me really angry. No-one should have to put up with that sort of invasion (thirty-four-year-old man with medication-resistant paranoid delusions)

CASE EXAMPLE

John has a fifteen-year history of delusional beliefs, dating back to when he lost consciousness in a car accident. He believes that during this time he had an implant placed in his head, which allowed government surveillance to start. He feels this has since continued unabated. He has got used to it but it makes him very angry. Current evidence within the last year that it is ongoing is provided by a woman in a crowd saying to him 'We're still watching' and another man who looked at him strangely.

John had a normal upbringing and supportive parents. He dropped out of education in his late teens and took large quantities of street drugs, including cannabis. He had the car accident at this time. He has now had several episodes of illness, and four hospital admissions. At times in the past he has felt suicidal, and made a serious attempt in the last year.

CLINICAL FEATURES AND CLASSIFICATION

Schizophrenia is defined as (World Health Organization (WHO) 2001, p. 33):

> A severe disorder that typically begins in late adolescence or early adulthood. It is characterised by fundamental distortions in thinking and perception, and by inappropriate emotions. The disturbance involves the most basic functions that give the normal person a feeling of individuality, uniqueness and self-direction. Behaviour may be seriously disturbed during some phases of the disorder, leading to adverse social consequences. Strong belief in ideas that are false and without any basis in reality (delusions) is another feature of this disorder.

The diagnosis of schizophrenia has itself generated controversy and there is still argument about whether the category has any reliability or validity (Bentall, 1990a; Boyle, 1990). To be useful, a diagnosis should clarify causation and predict treatment and outcome; it has been argued that as a diagnostic class schizophrenia has failed to do this. Moreover, it has been felt strongly that the diagnosis has added to feelings of shame and stigma in users (May, 2000), without helping to clarify causes or improve treatments. On the other hand, diagnostic systems can be seen to be summarizing a set of complex difficulties, enabling clinicians to communicate and – for some users and carers – it can be helpful to find they are not the only person to be dealing with these kinds of problem (Kinderman & Cooke 2000). The DSM-IV and ICD-10 diagnostic criteria for schizophrenia are presented in Table 21.1.

However, although the terminology is still used, the argument that it is better to try and understand single symptoms, not diagnostic categories, has been largely won (Bentall, 1990b; van Os et al., 1999). A symptom-based approach has been particularly helpful in developing some of the psychological treatments described later, particularly the treatment of delusions and hallucinations.

Although schizophrenia can thus be seen as a failed category, covering disparate processes and with no necessary or sufficient indicators, it does retain heuristic value as a focus for the examination of interesting processes, and for the delivery of treatments. Most of the refinement of the concept of schizophrenia occurred over perhaps a century and a half, with important contributions from a group of German-speaking psychiatrists working in the first half of the twentieth century (Kraepelin, Bleuler, Jaspers, the Schneiders; see Berrios, 1996). It was conceived as an underlying *process*, which manifested itself not only in those relatively dramatic ('positive') symptoms that are used to identify it, but also in more insidiously developing dysfunctions, the so-called negative symptoms.

The positive symptoms of schizophrenia can be roughly defined as unusual beliefs (delusions) and anomalous experiences (perceptual abnormalities, hallucinations and certain disorders of the experience of mental events). Like schizophrenia itself, the concept of delusion is a very difficult one: mental health professionals are generally able to agree when a delusion is present but the concept cannot be defined in an unequivocal way. It is classically said to

Table 21.1 Diagnostic criteria for schizophrenia

DSM-IV-TR	*ICD-10*
A. Characteristic symptoms. Two or more of the following, each present for a significant portion of time during a 1-month period (or less if successfully treated): 1. delusions 2. hallucinations 3. disorganized speech (e.g. frequent derailment or incoherence) 4. grossly disorganized or catatonic behaviour 5. negative symptoms, affective flattening, alogia or avolition Only one criterion A symptom required if delusions are bizarre or hallucinations consist of a voice keeping up a running commentary on the person's behaviour or thoughts or two or more voices conversing with each other B. Social/occupational dysfunction. For a significant portion of the time since the onset of the disturbance, one or more major areas of functioning such as work, interpersonal relations, or self-care are markedly below the level achieved prior to onset or with children a failure to achieve the expected level of interpersonal, academic or occupational achievement C. Duration. Continuous signs of the disturbance persist for at least *6 months* D. Not due to schizoaffective or mood disorder E. Not due to substance use or general medical condition F. If there is autism or a pervasive developmental disorder, then prominent delusions and hallucinations of 1 month's duration must be present	A minimum of one very clear symptom (or two or more of less clear cut) belong to any one of the groups (a) to (d) and at least two of the symptoms (e) to (h) should have been present most of the time during a period of *1 month* or more: (a) thought echo, thought insertion or withdrawal and thought broadcasting (b) delusions of control, influence, or passivity, clearly referred to body of limb movements or specific thoughts (c) hallucinatory voices giving a running commentary on the patient's behaviour, or discussing the patient among themselves, or other types of hallucinatory voice coming from some part of the body (d) persistent delusions of other kinds that are culturally inappropriate and completely impossible, such as religious or political identity, or superhuman powers and abilities (e) persistent hallucinations in any modality, when accompanied either by fleeting or half-formed delusions without clear affective content, or by persistent overvalued ideas, or when occurring every day for weeks or months on end (f) breaks or interpolations in the train of thought, resulting in incoherence or irrelevant speech or neologisms (g) catatonic behaviour, such as excitement, posturing, or waxy flexibility, negativism, mutism or stupor (h) negative symptoms such as marked apathy, paucity of speech, and blunting or incongruity of emotional responses, usually result in social withdrawal and lowering of social performance (i) a significant and consistent change in the overall quality of some aspects of personal behaviour, manifest as loss of interest, aimlessness, idleness a self-absorbed attitude and social withdrawal

Note: Adapted from DSM-IV-TR (APA, 2000) and ICD-10 (WHO, 1992b).

be a false belief, outwith the ordinary beliefs of the subject's cultural group, held with inordinate conviction and not amenable to argument or the presentation of contrary evidence. However, with the possible exception of the assertion that it is a belief, none of the defining features adheres in all cases (Gipps & Fulford, 2004). It may be better to conceive of delusions as sharing characteristics with ordinary beliefs and differing from them in dimensional rather than categorical ways – by being held with more conviction, or by leading to greater preoccupation and distress for example (Garety & Hemsley, 1994). This links in with the modern view of psychosis itself as representing extreme forms of processes that are quite widely spread in the general population (Johns et al., 2002; Peters et al., 1999a; Verdoux et al., 2003).

Delusions have traditionally been classified in terms of the themes represented in their content, although we must admit that this procedure has resulted in some classes that have the quality of an afterthought. Some delusions are essentially explanations of anomalous experiences that are intrinsically compelling, while others seem to arise out of combinations of types of abnormalities of the thinking process.

As virtually all delusions have considerable elements of self-reference, the delusion of reference can be seen as an archetype. Delusions are *powerful ideas*, and would be much less so if their meaning were not self-directed. Many delusions of reference also have a persecutory theme, although some have grandiose or depressive components. Thus themes in delusional thinking often overlap in a way that makes classification imperfect.

A number of subtypes of delusions of reference/persecution have been described: delusional misinterpretation is an example, in which self-referential meaning is attached to objects and actions. It includes the so-called de Clerambault's syndrome in which subjects imagine that they are the object of a secret and denied passion on the part of some unattainable person. A wide range of circumstances is then held to confirm the belief. Other subtypes include delusions of surveillance, of misidentification, of conspiracy, of accusation (e.g. of homosexuality) and of quotation of ideas. Delusions of misrecognition include two that are mirror images, the Capgras syndrome and the Fregoli syndrome. In the former, sufferers insist that their relatives or friends have been replaced by doubles, in the latter, that the people surrounding them are in fact their relatives and friends in disguise.

Other delusions are unified by a clear link to abnormal affect. The affects include jealousy, depression and mania. These delusions have non-delusional equivalents, which shade into them. Depressive delusions can include themes of reference, guilt, poverty, catastrophe and hypochondriasis, while manic delusions have themes of assistance, grandiose ability, grandiose identity and sometimes of reference and of persecution.

Finally, there are a number of delusions with more disparate themes. Thus some people have convictions that their appearance is abnormal in some way, others insist they are pregnant despite every evidence to the contrary, yet others think they give off an unpleasant odour. One interesting type is the delusion of depersonalization, which again has a non-delusional equivalent that psychopathologists were wont to distinguish very firmly from it. People who suffer from delusions of depersonalization do not merely feel *as if* they are unreal, but that in some sense they *are* unreal. In extreme cases they will claim that parts of them are missing, e.g. 'I have no brain'. Where most delusions are concerned with social improbabilities (e.g. 'The IRA is persecuting me'), fantastic delusions are characterized by themes that it is hard to imagine anyone would believe: 'I have been magicked out of a black hole in the Andromeda galaxy'.

Another descriptive attribute of delusions concerns whether they are explanatory or not. Most delusions represent clear attempts to explain some state of affairs, whether this is a social context, a sensation or an anomalous mental experience. Psychopathologists have traditionally distinguished these 'ordinary' delusions from so-called 'primary delusions', which appear to spring from nowhere. Three types of primary delusion have been described. The primacy of the first type is somewhat dubious, as it is the sudden clarification that occurs when someone is suffering from *delusional mood*. This is an unpleasant experience whereby sufferers feel their surroundings have become imbued with an atmosphere of vague and perplexing self-referential threat. This is resolved when its meaning suddenly becomes clear through a delusional explanation. Another type, Schneider's two-element *delusional perception*, comprises a *normal* perception, image or memory that is suddenly transformed by the emergence of a formulated delusion. Finally, *autochthonous delusions* appear to emerge fully formed out of the blue with a sense of instant realization. It is possible that the difference between the last two is merely that in delusional perception, the normal perception acquires significance from the delusion formation and thus just happens to be remembered as significant. However, some authorities have been sceptical about the reality of primary delusions (Garety & Hemsley, 1994), seeing them all as secondary explanation of unusual perceptual states.

A range of *anomalous experience* may be involved in psychosis, from perceptual anomalies to full-blown hallucinations and disorders of the experience of thought. The latter (see Table 21.2) are a particularly interesting group of phenomena, as we shall see. The loss of the sense of possession characteristic of thought insertion can also occur with related mental contents. Thus some people with psychotic disorders lose this sense in relation to the mental representation of particular actions, such that they feel alien, the results of outside agency. 'Something has taken over my voice', 'My hand writes but it isn't me that's doing it' (Blakemore et al., 2003). Loss of possession may also occur with feelings and emotions. A number of terms have been applied to these phenomena: will replacement, made actions, made emotions, etc. The term 'delusions of possession' refers only to the explanatory delusion that almost invariable accompanies these compelling experiences.

The concept of hallucination is dependent on the process of external projection and on the availability in principle of consensual verification. The brain relies on being able to construct a distinction in awareness between what is external and what is internal. Hallucinations represents a failure of this mechanism where what is normally internal is projected, and perceived, externally. This can be identified because humans provide each other with a consensus about what is 'out there'. Where external projection flouts the consensus, a hallucination may be inferred, by others if not always by the sufferer. Hallucinations have been described in all modalities (auditory, visual, olfactory, gustatory, tactile and interceptive or somatic), but not all the supposed types are equally open to consensual verification. This is clearly the case for auditory, visual and olfactory hallucinations, but becomes less so for taste and touch, and internal bodily sensations cannot be verified at all. It is possible to test the assertion 'this coffee tastes of marzipan' but not 'my mouth is full of the taste of aluminium'. Likewise, it is possible to falsify a statement like 'the woman from the pub just touched me on the shoulder', but not 'I just felt as if I had been touched on the shoulder'. In most cases, what are described as hallucinations of touch, taste and somatic sensation are actually and improperly inferred from the oddity of the description of the sensation and the delusional elaborations that may go with it: 'The people behind it all use the television mast to send the rays giving me these hot feelings shooting up my legs'.

A large number of people with psychotic disorders experience auditory and visual hallucinations, especially the former. Auditory hallucinations are of particular interest because they seem to reflect combinations of abnormal psychological *processes* in a way that link them to the sorts of thought disorder described above. These processes include loudness, external projection and the loss of the sense of possession of the mental content.

Another process that may unify several types of psychopathology, both neurotic and psychotic, is the distortion of the emotional component of mental events. Examples include dulled and heightened perception. In the former, typical of depressed mood, colours, sounds, tastes, lose their savour and meaning and become dull. People with elevated mood often describe the particular acuteness and beauty of visual and musical experience. Depersonalization and derealization, not normally regarded as psychotic phenomena, seem also to be related to the detachment of the emotional component of perception. Depressed people sometimes feel they have lost their emotions. By this, they mean that they retain knowledge of their feelings for the people close to them, but somehow have lost the emotional meaning of that knowledge: 'I know I love them, I just can't feel it' (the paradox here is that the loss of feeling is felt). The emotional component of the process of person recognition can also be lost, as in the Capgras syndrome, while in the Fregoli syndrome it is heightened. Neurological conditions suggest that facial recognition is dependent on connections between the fusiform gyrus and the amygdala, and it is possible that malfunctions of amygdalar connections may underlie several of these functional types of psychopathology. The future of psychopathological studies is likely to lie in more detailed analysis of process, as a number of authors have suggested (Kapur, 2003; Ramachandran & Blakeslee, 1998). This may then be linked into other approaches (genetic, neuroimaging, psychological processes at other levels) to understanding the multiple pathways that contribute to the emergence of the symptoms of schizophrenia. Useful further sources of descriptions of psychotic psychopathology can be found in the SCAN glossary (WHO, 1992b), in Garety and Hemsley (1994) and in Berrios (1996).

EPIDEMIOLOGY

Schizophrenia is diagnosed about equally in men and women, typically in late adolescence and early adulthood, although the onset in women is usually a few years later and women tend to have a better outcome (Peters 2000; WHO 2001). About 1% of the population will receive this diagnosis during their lifetime, with a point prevalence of 0.4%. It has been ranked the third most disabling condition by the general population (Ustun et al., 1999), and is also associated with high economic costs to society, because of lost potential earnings and costs of care (WHO, 2001). Worldwide, schizophrenia falls in the top ten disorders causing disability and accounts for between 1.5% and 2.6% of healthcare expenditure in developed countries. Rates of unemployment of 79% have been reported across six sites in Europe for people with this diagnosis (Thornicroft et al., 2004). Ten per cent of people with schizophrenia will commit suicide (Caldwell & Gottesman, 1990; Heila & Lonnqvist, 2003), and 30% will attempt it (Radomsky et al., 1999; WHO 2001). Around 5% of homicides in the UK will be committed by people with schizophrenia (National Confidential Inquiry 2001; reviewed by Taylor & Estroff 2003).

COURSE

With recent advances in medication and psychosocial care, it is now thought that up to 50% of those developing these kinds of problems can expect a good recovery (WHO, 2001), with a better outcome in developing countries. Long-term studies suggest around a third may recover completely, symptomatically and socially (Kinderman & Cooke, 2000; WHO, 2001). For others, problems can be variable. About a quarter of individuals will have only one episode. The remaining three quarters can be vulnerable to relapses in which acute 'positive' symptoms, such as distressing delusional ideas or hallucinations, recur, together with varying degrees of social difficulties. Some may also have residual positive symptoms that continue to cause problems. On the other hand, some with these symptoms manage to function well, having satisfying relationships and occupational success. For another group, residual symptoms are mainly 'negative', such as loss of interest and motivation, with difficulties in initiating activities or enjoying them. These problems are particularly likely to lead to feelings of poor quality of life and continued difficulties in social functioning, and are also particularly likely to impact on others, such as carers (Scazufca & Kuipers, 1996; Thornicroft et al., 2004).

ASSESSMENT

The main psychiatric assessments of schizophrenia tend to measure the severity or frequency of the main clinical features highlighted above. They are almost always based on interviews rather than self-report, since lack of insight is traditionally seen to be central to the disorder (David, 1990). Most include both items rated from the information elicited from the respondent, and others rated on the basis of observation during the interview. Their administration can range from twenty minutes to several hours, depending on how symptomatic the individual is. The most widely used measures include: the Present State Examination (PSE; Wing et al., 1974), now incorporated in the Schedules for Clinical Assessment in Neuropsychiatry (SCAN; WHO, 1992a); the Brief Psychiatric Rating Scale (BPRS; Overall & Gorham, 1962); the Scale for the Assessment of Positive Symptoms (SAPS; Andreasen, 1984a); the Scale for the Assessment of Negative Symptoms (SANS; Andreasen, 1984b); the Positive and Negative Symptom Scale (PANSS; Kay et al., 1987, 1988, 1989); the Krawiecka Scale (also known as the Manchester Scale and the KGV; Hyde, 1989; Krawiecka et al., 1977) and the Comprehensive Psychiatric Rating Scale (CPRS; Asberg et al., 1978; Jacobsson et al., 1978).

Each of these scales has advantages and disadvantages, and the appropriateness of their use will depend on the purpose of the assessment (see Barnes & Nelson, 1994). For instance, the PSE/SCAN will enable a reliable classification of syndromes but is not very useful for looking at change over time. The BPRS is better for the detection of change, but reliability and validity are poorer. The PANSS is used extensively in research but the interview is not user-friendly for clinical purposes. The SAPS and SANS are the most thorough in terms of positive and negative symptoms, but do not include other areas of psychopathology that may be relevant clinically, such as disorganization or emotional problems.

The recent symptom approach has also led to the emergence of a number of self-report scales and interviews concentrating on single symptom dimensions. The most widely used currently is the Psychotic Symptom Rating Scales (PSYRATS; Haddock et al., 1999), a semi-structured interview measuring psychological dimensions, rather than categorical types, of delusions and hallucinations. The Personal Questionnaires (PQs; Brett-Jones et al., 1987; Garety, 1985) also assess psychological dimensions such as conviction, preoccupation and distress for delusions, and frequency, intensity and distress for hallucinations. PQs differ from other questionnaire forms in that they are devised for each individual, using that person's words to describe their beliefs, experiences or feelings.

Other measures to assess delusions include the Maudsley Assessment of Delusions Schedule (MADS; Buchanan et al., 1993), the Delusions-Symptoms-States Inventory – Revised (DSSI-R; Foulds & Bedford, 1975), the Brown Assessment of Beliefs Scale (BABS; Eisen et al., 1998), and the Peters et al. Delusions Inventory (PDI; Peters, Joseph & Garety, 1999b; Peters et al., 2004). Other measures to assess hallucinations include the Auditory Hallucinations Record Form (Slade, 1972) and Self-Report Form (Hustig & Hafner, 1990), the Mental Health Research Institute Unusual Perceptions Schedule (MUPS; Carter et al., 1995), the Structured Interview for Assessing Perceptual Anomalies (SIAPA; Bunney et al., 1999); and the Cardiff Anomalous Perceptions Scale (CAPS; Bell et al., 2005). An important dimension of hallucinations consists of the beliefs people hold about their voices (Chadwick & Birchwood, 1994), and the Beliefs about Voices Questionnaire – Revised (BAVQ-R; Chadwick et al., 2000) and the Cognitive Assessment of Voices Interview Schedule (Chadwick et al., 1996) assess this dimension specifically. Two further measures are worth mentioning: the La Trobe University 'Coping with Auditory Hallucinations' Interview Schedule (Farhall & Gehrke, 1997) and the 'Interview with a person who hears voices' (Romme & Escher, 2000).

Thought disorder has not received as much attention as delusions and hallucinations in the research literature, and this is reflected by the smaller number of scales available, namely: the Scale for the Assessment of Thought, Language and Communication (Andreasen, 1986) and the Comprehensive Index of Positive Thought Disorder (Marengo et al., 1986). Similarly, apart from the general psychiatric measures mentioned above, such as the SANS and the PANSS, there are few specific negative symptoms scales. One notable exception includes the Subjective Experience of Negative Symptoms Scale (SENS; Selten et al., 1993), which is a self-rating scale based on the SANS items, and measures awareness of negative symptoms plus associated disruption and distress. Otherwise, clinical researchers have used assessment tools measuring social functioning and quality of life, both related to negative symptoms. Social functioning scales include the Social Behaviour Scale (Wykes & Sturt, 1986), the Social Functioning Scale (Birchwood et al., 1990), the Global Assessment of Functioning Scale (GAF; APA 1987) and an adapted version of the GAF, the Social and Occupational Functioning Assessment Scale (SOFAS; Goldman et al., 1992). Quality-of-life scales are numerous but tend to be too lengthy for use with psychosis populations.

Again, one exception is the Manchester Short Assessment of Quality of Life (MANSA; Priebe et al., 1999).

Lastly, there is an increasing emphasis on detecting schizophrenia early, to reduce the length of time individuals are left with an untreated psychosis (the so-called 'duration of untreated psychosis' or DUP) and to accelerate access to care (McGorry, 1998). As a result, a number of assessment tools have been devised to identify prodromal patients, or individuals with an 'at-risk mental state'. The most well-known include the Comprehensive Assessment of At Risk Mental States (CAARMS; Yung et al., 2005), the Structured Interview for Prodromal Syndromes (SIPS; Miller et al., 1999, 2002), the Bonn Scale for the Assessment of Basic Symptoms (Gross et al., 1987; Klosterkutter et al., 2001) and the Wisconsin Manual for Assessing Psychotic-like Experiences (Kwapil et al., 1999). In addition, a couple of measures have been developed for use in epidemiological studies looking at the incidence of psychosis in the general population. The Psychosis Screening Questionnaire (PSQ; Bebbington & Nayani, 1995) is a very brief screening interview to ascertain the presence of hypomania, thought insertion, paranoia, strange experiences and hallucinations. The Community Assessment of Psychic Experiences (CAPE; Stefanis et al., 2002) is a forty-item self-report instrument based on the PDI but with added questions on hallucinations, negative symptoms and depression. Each item assesses both frequency of the experience and associated distress.

TREATMENT

Biomedical approaches

Typically, people with these diagnoses need a range of treatments, regularly reviewed. Current treatments and their effectiveness will now be described. The first line of treatment is almost always medication, which is based on a group of drugs with related effects, the neuroleptics (Table 21.3). These were first introduced in the 1950s, and contributed to a revolution in the care of people with schizophrenia. They enabled many sufferers to live in the community rather than the large mental hospitals of the period. Neuroleptics have multiple effects on neural transmitter substances, although they all share a common action in reducing cerebral dopamine transmission. This tallies with a generally accepted view that anomalous dopamine function is central to the emergence of the symptoms of schizophrenia (Kapur, 2003).

Dopamine transmission is characteristic of neurons that link the mid-brain with the cerebral cortex, but is also seen in other neural tracks in the brain. As a result, medications capable of treating the positive symptoms of schizophrenia have also the capacity to induce side effects, in particular, movement disorders including dystonia and parkinsonism. Sexual function may also be

Table 21.2 Anomalous experiences of thought

Thought insertion: a bad name. The essence of the symptom is the loss of the sense of possession of the thought. The idea of insertion is a secondary delusional elaboration, made likely by the oddity of the central experience

Thought broadcast: again, a bad name because it connotes an action rather than a passive experience. The essence of the symptom is that people experience their thoughts as being unbounded by their sense of their inner world. They may then worry that their thoughts are available to other people, that their thoughts can be read, which is a delusional elaboration

Thought block: again, passive, and therefore unlike the common experience in states of anxiety or tiredness where we lose the train of our thoughts. In thought block, the train of thought stops suddenly and then it resumes. There is no desperate searching for the lost thought content, and both the cessation and the resumption are passively experienced

Thought withdrawal: in some cases this can be regarded as present if people interpret thought block as due to the removal of thoughts by some other agent, and as such it is a delusional explanation. However, in other individuals the withdrawal is described as actually felt, experienced

Thought echo: a good name, as the experience has some cardinal features of an ordinary echo. Thus the original thought is owned, but the person lacks the sense of possession over the repetition of the thought. However, they share the same modality, i.e. thought, just as in an ordinary echo, the original and the repeat are both sounds

Thought commentary: rare but interesting. The person possesses one set of thoughts but lacks a sense of possession over a second stream of thoughts that are essentially commentary on the first. It must be emphasized that this second element is experienced as thought, not as a voice

Gedankenlautwerden (loud thoughts): people experience their thoughts as having the quality of loudness. They have a sense of possession of the thoughts, and the thoughts are experienced as being within internal subjective reality

impaired because reduced dopamine transmission in the hypothalamus increases the production of the hormone prolactin.

After its introduction, neuroleptic treatment had a dramatic effect on many people suffering from psychosis, but was not successful in all cases. This led to a tendency towards the use of greater doses and, in the 1960s and 1970s, psychiatric wards were often full of people marked out by disorders of movement. In the 1970s clozapine was introduced, which controlled positive symptoms very effectively without producing movement disorders. However, it was withdrawn in the UK and the USA, although not in every European country, because it sometimes caused severe illness, even death, by destroying white cells (agranulocytosis). It was launched again in the late 1980s under strictly controlled conditions, whereby prescription was dependent on a weekly blood count carried out by the pharmaceutical company. This appeared to be a breakthrough, helping many people with persistent positive symptoms to improve considerably and, in some cases, become symptom free.

Clozapine did have other side effects, notably weight gain, epilepsy and hypersalivation (leading classically to a wet morning pillow).

Clozapine was followed by other new drugs with a reduced propensity to produce movement disorder in doses that seemed effective in controlling symptoms. Because their mechanism of action appeared somewhat different from the earlier neuroleptics, these were termed atypical neuroleptics, even though the term probably under-states the differences between individual neuroleptic drugs and over-states the differences between the atypical and the 'conventional' (older) neuroleptics (Table 21.3). The atypical neuroleptics appear no more effective in treating the symptoms of schizophrenia than their older counterparts. However, a reduction in movement disorders is a particularly desirable objective, as these are uniformly disliked by sufferers and are a persistent cause of people declining to continue with medication; in turn, discontinuation of medication is associated with a more than doubling of relapse rates.

Because the atypical neuroleptics remain under licence, they are far more expensive than the older drugs. However, not surprisingly, they have been strongly marketed by the pharmaceutical companies that produce them. Thus there is a trade-off between expensive drugs with an apparently superior side-effect profile and very cheap drugs with more side effects.

The neuroleptic drugs were reviewed in the UK as part of the National

Table 21.3 Equivalent daily dose ranges for antipsychotic medication

Drug	*Low*	*Medium*	*High*
Typicals			
Chlorpromazine	200 mg or less	201 mg–400 mg	>400 mg
Thioridazine	200 mg or less	201 mg–400 mg	>400 mg
Fluphenazine	4 mg or less	5 mg–8 mg	>8 mg
Trifluoperazine	10 mg or less	11 mg–20 mg	>20 mg
Flupenthizol	6 mg or less	7 mg–12 mg	>12 mg
Zuclopenthizol	50 mg or less	51 mg–100 mg	>100 mg
Haloperidol	5 mg or less	6 mg–10 mg	>10 mg
Droperidol	8 mg or less	9 mg–16 mg	>16 mg
Sulpiride	400 mg or less	401 mg–800 mg	>800 mg
Pimozide	4 mg or less	5 mg–8 mg	>8 mg
Loxapine	20 mg or less	21 mg–40 mg	>40 mg
Atypicals			
Zotepine	150 mg or less	151 mg–300 mg	>300 mg
Olanzapine	10 mg or less	11 mg–20 mg	>20 mg
Amisulpride	800 mg or less	801 mg–1200 mg	>1200 mg
Risperidone	4 mg or less	5 mg–8 mg	>8 mg
Clozapine	300 mg or less	301 mg–600 mg	>600 mg
Quetiapine	300 mg or less	301 mg–600 mg	>600 mg

Institute for Clinical Excellence (NICE) guidelines on the management of schizophrenia (NICE, 2003). NICE offers the following advice (paraphrased):

- Where patients cannot express a preference, an atypical drug should be chosen.
- The relative or carer should be contacted if the patient cannot give informed consent.
- Drug treatment should form only part of a comprehensive package of care.
- Drug treatment should normally be the outcome of a process of negotiation between prescriber and patient.
- The dose range should lie between 300 mg and 1000 mg of chlorpromazine equivalents (see Table 21.3).
- Rapid progress to a very large dose ('rapid neurolepticization') should be avoided.
- Atypicals should be prescribed for people with side effects or a history of side effects when on conventional neuroleptics.
- The choice of medication should not be changed if the patient is well managed on a conventional neuroleptic without side effects.
- Polypharmacy (the use of more than one neuroleptic drug) should be strongly avoided.
- Weight gain and the emergence of diabetes must be monitored.

These recommendations now look slightly dated – they were taken verbatim from a Health Technology Assessment carried out by NICE in 2001 and under-state the dangers of the side effects of the newer drugs. Olanzapine, in particular, can be associated with very large weight gain, which can be very damaging to the self-esteem of the young adults who are often started on it; it is also associated with raised rates of diabetes. In addition, some of the drugs have effects on the heart rhythm and may impair sexual function. The US Food and Drugs Administration (FDA) now advises that anyone who is a candidate for olanzapine, risperidone or quetiapine and is obese, or has a family history of obesity or diabetes, should undergo fasting glucose testing. Moreover, the charge that the beneficial side-effects profile of the atypical drugs may partly come about because they were compared with rather large doses of the older drugs has never been adequately rebutted (Geddes et al., 2000). Good practice would seem to dictate careful dosing, whether using conventional or atypical antipsychotic drugs.

In addition to the normal route of administration of these drugs by mouth, some are available as a depot (long-lasting) injection. This carries the advantage that patients only have to make the decision to take their medication at set intervals of 2–4 weeks. This makes continuation more likely. However, the injection causes pain at the site of administration and many patients therefore refuse to take drugs in this way. The new long-acting version of the atypical drug risperidone is less painful because it is not oil based, but experience with this is so far limited.

Finally, other types of medication are used in the treatment of schizophrenia. Many sufferers experience exacerbations of their positive symptoms when they are particularly highly aroused, and this arousal can be temporarily allayed using a benzodiazepine (e.g. diazepam, lorazepam). Others may have marked depressive symptoms from time to time, and may merit treatment with one of the range of antidepressive drugs.

Medication is something that should ideally be agreed by a process of informed negotiation between the patient and the prescribing clinician. In an emergency this may be difficult, but it should be initiated as soon as possible after the emergency has resolved.

Psychological therapies

Evidence for efficacy: Family interventions and cognitive-behavioural therapy

Family interventions (FI) were one of the earliest psychosocial approaches to schizophrenia. They were developed from theoretical work in the 1960s examining factors that influenced course and outcome in schizophrenia. Later on, in the 1990s, research on single symptoms led to treatments that adapted the successful use of cognitive-behavioural therapy (CBT) with anxiety and depression, to the more complex problems of psychosis. These two therapies have recently been endorsed by the NICE guidelines (2003) as effective, particularly for people with persistent positive symptoms and a relapsing course. For FI the meta-analysis evaluated eighteen randomized controlled trials (n = 1458). It found that FI improved outcome, particularly relapse rates, both during treatment and up to fifteen months afterwards. The evidence was strongest for interventions that included the user (NICE, 2003, p. 106).

For CBT, the meta-analysis included thirteen randomized controlled trials (n = 1297) and found good evidence that it reduced symptoms in people with schizophrenia at up to a year of follow-up. The evidence was stronger for those with persistent rather than acute symptoms (NICE, 2003, p. 96).

For both FI and CBT, treatments that are of at least six months duration and include at least ten sessions were recommended. Both of these evidence-based approaches will be discussed in some detail.

Social skills training and cognitive remediation therapy

Other psychological treatments in the literature include social skills, or assertiveness, training and cognitive remediation. Social skills training has a long literature from the 1960s (Ayllon & Azrin, 1965). However, its effectiveness was queried by Shepherd (1978), who pointed out that such skills do not tend to generalize for people diagnosed with schizophrenia; this opinion effectively arrested its use in the UK. The meta-analysis from the NICE guidelines (2003) (nine randomized controlled trials; $n = 436$), confirmed this view. It found no evidence for the effectiveness of social skills training as a discrete intervention (NICE, 2003, p. 116), and its clinical use is not currently recommended. For this reason it will not be described further.

Cognitive remediation therapy (CRT) has impeccable credentials as a theoretically driven intervention. It is well attested that there are cognitive deficits associated with a diagnosis of schizophrenia, particularly in attention and working memory, and that these are associated with poor social outcomes and negative symptoms (Wykes, 1994). Techniques derived from laboratory work suggest that errorless learning, scaffolding and verbalizing instructions should be particularly useful in improving these difficulties, trying directly to 'remediate' or correct these cognitive processes (Wykes & Van der Gaag, 2001). Brenner et al. (1994) developed integrated psychological therapies (IPT) based on these kinds of techniques. Computerized tasks have also been used (reviewed by Suslow et al., 2001). Unfortunately, despite these promising beginnings, there have been relatively few well-conducted clinical trials and the published studies report inconsistent findings. The NICE guidelines (2003) meta-analysis (seven randomized controlled trials; $n = 295$) found no consistent evidence that cognitive remediation improved outcomes in the targeted cognitive functions or in terms of core symptoms, and concluded that there was insufficient evidence to recommend its clinical use at present (NICE, 2003, p. 99). One study that did seem to show some clinical changes (Wykes et al., 1999) seemed to do so mainly via improvements in self-esteem, which in itself is an important outcome. It is entirely plausible that these approaches could indeed improve motivation and so reduce both positive and negative symptoms but at present this pathway has not been evaluated. As these interventions lack an evidence base at present, they will not be further described either, but have been recently elaborated (Wykes & Reeder, 2005).

Family interventions in schizophrenia

These were driven theoretically by early research on the importance of family factors in predicting outcome for people with schizophrenia living with carers. This research was started in the late 1950s and 1960s (Brown & Rutter, 1966) and has now provided impressive evidence that attributes of carers' reactions to the stress of providing this kind of care predict different outcomes for the person diagnosed with schizophrenia.

Specifically, those going back to live in settings characterized as high in levels of criticism or over-involvement (high in expressed emotion; EE), are more likely to relapse with another episode of schizophrenia than those returning to live in calmer, more tolerant, low EE environments. Using an aggregate analysis, Bebbington and Kuipers (1994) examined data from twenty-five studies available at that time (n = 1346) and found that 52% of carers had high levels of EE. The relapse rate associated with returning to live in this setting was 50% for high EE and 21% for low EE families. Butzlaff and Hooley (1998) did a meta-analysis of twenty-seven studies, and found very similar rates. There are now over thirty studies of this effect, including in non-Western cultures such as Japan (Mino et al., 1997).

Because different family affective reactions to caregiving appeared to have such strong effects on outcome, these initial findings led directly to the development of interventions designed specifically to help reduce high EE reactions in carers, and thus to improve levels of distress in carers and the likelihood of relapse in those they were caring for. As already discussed, the review in the NICE guidelines (2003) has shown that these kinds of intervention are successful, particularly in reducing relapse rates, and are now recommended. EE has been defined as an appraisal by carers of the difficulties of the caring role (Scazufca & Kuipers, 1996) and has also begun to be understood in terms of carers' attributions (Barrowclough & Parle, 1997). These translations of EE into normal psychological processes have helped to improve and refine the kinds of interventions that are helpful, and our understanding of the processes that need to be changed in order to reduce the likelihood of a further episode (relapse).

It has also been argued that all families suffer from stigma and the 'burden' of care (Lefley, 1989, 2003) and that interventions should not be limited to a subgroup with particular difficulties (Birchwood & Smith, 1987). It has now been shown that EE and the 'burden' of care are associated, such that ratings of the impact of care could be used as a proxy measure of EE (Scazufca & Kuipers, 1996, 1998). However, it is also the case that reducing this burden of care by focusing on the needs of relatives (Barrowclough et al., 1999; Szmukler et al., 2003) does not tend to reduce carer distress. This underlines the importance of assessing carefully the needs of every participant in a family setting, as suggested by Barrowclough et al. (1998), who have developed a relatives' version of needs assessment; it cannot be assumed that change can occur without the whole system adjusting. This may explain the NICE guideline (2003) findings that FI was more effective when the whole family was involved.

Finally, while the interventions have focused on families, family carers are not alone in their affective responses to the demands of caring; staff carers have also been shown to have similar attitudes, particularly criticism (Kuipers & Moore, 1995). Although fewer interventions have been attempted with formal carers (Willetts & Leff, 1997), there is no theoretical reason why such interventions should not be at least considered for individuals not living with informal carers, but in hostels or secure settings (Ball et al., 1992; Moore & Kuipers, 1999).

Family assessments

Although the research has developed from the literature on EE, rating this in routine clinical settings is not really feasible. The five-minute speech sample (FMSS; Amato, 1993) has been developed as a shorter way of accessing these family reactions, but it still requires some knowledge of EE, and raters need to be trained. Questionnaire methods that focus on the impact of care on relatives, for instance, the Experience of Care Inventory (ECI; Szmukler, Burgess, Herman, Benson & Colusa, 1996) and the Relatives' Cardinal Needs Schedule mentioned above (Barrowclough et al., 1998), are alternative ways of quantifying initial difficulties. As it is also known that high levels of burden are associated with high EE and with distress, another more straightforward clinical approach is to look directly at relatives' own levels of depression, using the Beck Depression Inventory (Beck & Steer, 1987). For instance, reducing carer depression directly has been found feasible for those caring for people with Alzheimer's disease (Marriott et al., 2000).

Specific family interventions

The kinds of interventions found helpful for families have been discussed in several published manuals over the last nearly twenty years (Anderson et al., 1986; Barrowclough & Tarrier, 1992; Falloon et al., 1984; Kuipers et al., 1992, 2002). All are characterized, to a differing extent, by the following features:

- engaging with the family and improving listening and negotiating skills
- offering specific advice and information about diagnosis, medication and the problems that carers are likely to face
- a problem-solving approach to immediate and identified difficulties that all family members have to cope with
- identifying, normalizing and cognitively reappraising the emotional and behavioural impact of problems
- encouraging medication adherence in those with the diagnosis.

Attempts have been made to focus on the specific requirements that help families to change, but so far the results have been rather limited. So-called 'psychoeducation' on its own is not helpful, and this finding is reiterated by the meta-analysis of the NICE guidelines (2003), which updates and refines the earlier and more positive Cochrane review of Pekkala & Merinder (2001). The NICE guidelines reviewed ten studies (n = 1070) and found limited evidence that psychoeducation produced benefits, and no evidence that it reduced outcomes such as relapse rates. It nevertheless recommends as good practice that easily accessible information should be available. While this is undoubtedly true, it seems to be the case clinically that offering information is only part of an effective intervention; it is likely to improve optimism and help understanding of some terminology but, on its own, it will not change attitudes or behaviour. Answering questions seems a helpful strategy, together with backing answers up with written information and access to organizations such as RETHINK (http://www.rethink.org/). This charity provides national helplines and local resources such as supported accommodation, work schemes, respite care and relative education and support groups.

To carry out this kind of FI (Kuipers et al., 2002), it is important that the clinician organizes appropriate initial training, managerial support and access to expert or peer supervision. This kind of work is demanding with this population and should not be undertaken without support. Given the needs of people with these diagnoses, FI should be seen as part of a team approach to the illness. Support and monitoring needs to be available in case of changes in mental state. Medication needs to be reviewed and adjusted, particularly if there are unacceptable side effects. Opportunities for appropriate occupation and activity need to be provided as does crisis support. Whole-team training is one model sometimes used and this can be incorporated into specialist teams, for instance those providing early intervention (Kuipers et al., 2004). However, these requirements demand resources and prioritizing in busy NHS settings, and this partly accounts for the difficulties that prevent such evidence-based interventions from becoming widely available so far (Fadden, 1997; Kuipers 2000). This may now change, given the strictures of the current NICE guidelines (2003).

Co-therapy

It is suggested that any family work is done with pairs of professionals. Even a family of two, a carer and the person with schizophrenia, requires more input than can easily be provided through individual work. It is also important to be able to balance sometimes competing demands from different family members, and this is more feasible with co-therapists. Furthermore, two therapists may provide an important model of how to co-operate, to treat each other with respect even when views differ, to listen carefully while the other is talking and to repeat and clarify what the other person is saying. Some families will have lost these communication skills in the stress of the caregiving situation and modelling is a particularly useful way of relearning these.

Frequency of family sessions

It is not clear how intense family sessions need to be. The NICE guideline evidence is best for longer-term courses of treatment (more than ten sessions, over six months or more). This suggests that fortnightly, reducing to monthly, is a reasonable aim. Families may be difficult to engage at non-crisis times (Szmukler et al., 2003) and many of the research trials focused more productively on interventions that began at a time of crisis, such as an admission, or shortly after a relapse. These times have the benefit of making it clear that there are indeed problems (otherwise this can be denied or minimized by at least someone in the family), and this can be a catalyst for change.

While families have to be engaged in sessions, and no psychological treatment can be delivered that does not engage participants, the overall structure of sessions can be kept broadly the same. Initially, there will be issues about when, where and who is included. Visits based at home for about an hour with whoever is willing to attend usually allow more family members to engage, are less demanding of them and are more likely to be successful. They are, of course, tremendously time-consuming for staff, which has been another cause of limited service implementation. Within the bounds of safety and practicality, therapist flexibility is usually the key here.

Structure of sessions

All sessions should try to focus on listening to everyone's point of view, deciding an agenda that prioritizes a single problem, facilitating the discussion so that there is some negotiated problem solving and setting a very small piece of homework based on the decisions made in the meeting. This begins the process of getting everyone to try things just a bit differently. The content of the discussion can be prosaic, almost trivial, or more serious; who buys the cat food, what time someone gets up in the morning, who takes responsibility for doing the washing up, who picks up the five-year-old son from school. However, by looking at these details, the emotional issues that have prevented their solution are immediately raised. New information can be introduced, emotions can be normalized and contained, situations can be reappraised and new solutions can be found. This process focuses on the present: it helps to solve current difficulties, rather than avoiding them, and we know that high EE is related to avoidance coping (Raune, Kuipers & Bebbington, 2004; Scazufca & Kuipers, 1996). Further, it allows discussion, while preventing arguments and promoting negotiation; it suggests that even intractable situations may start to shift; it begins to engender optimism, seeing positives in how things are now, instead of the despair and pessimism associated with high EE, high levels of burden and long-term problems.

Focus on one problem

Ideally, only one problem should be focused on in each session. Families often feel overwhelmed by problems, and this can also be overwhelming for therapists. One problem per session, mutually prioritized and agreed on, with an agenda set, makes the situation a little more manageable, and also breaks problems down into tasks that can be started on. Initially the chosen problems may be entirely practical, as above. While these are being looked at, therapists can also seek to improve communication skills.

Improving communication

This requires the encouragement of listening, asking individuals to take turns in speaking, and checking whether comments have been heard. It is also crucial that, right from the first session, the two therapists work together to interrupt negative comments that emerge; the session must not just be a facilitated opportunity for relatives to criticize each other. If this starts to happen, it must be looked at and an attempt made to bring out the more positive emotions underlying even the most devastating negative remarks. This is called 'positive reframing'. It is also helpful to ensure that people talk directly to each other, not about each other (which after all mimics third-person auditory hallucinations). Talking to each other directly about the problems is more likely to help develop a solution, and limits the opportunity to allocate blame.

Positive reframing

In this example, the father has just made an overtly negative comment about his daughter, and this must be immediately interrupted, with an attempt to reframe the emotions more positively and attempt some more direct solution:

Mr S: I just hate her sometimes.
Therapist 1: Can I just interrupt here? (*defusing negativity in session*)
Therapist 1: Mary, did you hear what your father just said?
Mary: Yes.
Therapist 1: How did that make you feel? *(checking emotional impact)*
Mary: I know he can't stand it when I get so upset with the voices and start shouting.
Therapist 1: Is that right Mr S?
Mr S: Yes. It makes me feel so helpless. God knows I've tried everything, and she doesn't take any notice of what I say, yet there she is shouting at night and keeping us all awake. I can't take much more of it.
Therapist 1: So you would really like to help. Did you know that Mary? (*positive reframing*)
Mary: Yes, I suppose I do know it sometimes. I know he wants to make me better . . .
Therapist 1: But it has been very difficult to find anything that works, hasn't it? That is very upsetting for all of you. We can see that. Can we try something else?

Therapist 1: Mr S would you please ask Mary directly what you could do that would be helpful, when she is shouting at night? *(defusing and problem solving)*

Mr S: I've tried all this.

Therapist 1: Yes, I'm sure, but now, could we just look at it now?

Mr S: All right, Mary, what could I do?

Mary: Well you could just come and put your arm round me, and try to get me to lie down again. I sometimes just need someone to calm me down a bit.

Therapist 1: Could you try that at all? Would it be very difficult at night? Would it take long?

Mr S: Well we're all awake anyway, yes I could perhaps give it a go.

Therapist 2: And that might make you feel a bit better Mary? Perhaps if you could both try this out, we can see next time how you both felt, find out if it makes any difference. *(homework)*

More general emotional issues

Later on in sessions, other emotional issues can be agreed as the main aim of the session. These can range from anger, frustration, grief, guilt, despair and isolation to stigma. All family members, including the person with the diagnosis, may feel upset at times. At a later stage of therapy these more general issues can be brought out:

- Thinking how to help the person with schizophrenia become more independent so that they can manage things in a more adult way despite their problems.
- Giving parents 'permission' to take time off from the caring role to look after themselves; this also allows them to adopt a different perspective on the family's problems.
- Persuading family members to face up to the losses that may have occurred with the onset of schizophrenia; lost prospects, relationships, changed opportunities, difficulties concentrating and worries over how long recovery is taking, while still being able to be positive about the ill person.
- Focusing on how they and other family members are managing to cope with these problems and what can be done in the next few days to maximize these good parts.

In this example, a mother and her daughter were trying to negotiate (rather than shout at each other) about money, and how much the mother could be expected to give to her daughter, and in what way. This emphasizes how to be caring in a more reciprocal way, not just doing as one person requires.

Therapist 1: It sounds as if it you are both trying to negotiate about this, but it is difficult. How could you both do this so that neither of you feels resentful?*(problem solving)*

Mother: If J worked out a budget plan, so that she had some money left over, then if she had a particular need for something, I would feel that was a reasonable request.

J: I need to have a say in things, you buy stuff for me but I don't want that, I want to be able to decide.

Therapist 2: So what would make that easier for you J?*(checking emotional impact)*

J: She buys stuff so as not to give me the money, in case I buy vodka with it, but then I don't want that.

Therapist 1: No that's clear, but you did manage to do something together at the weekend, something your mum paid for, was it the video, how did that work? *(containing and rechannelling negative emotion)*

J: I chose the video and mum paid for it.

Therapist 1: Did you mind that Mrs M? (*checking emotional impact with mother*)

Mother: No I enjoyed it. We don't do things together enough. It was good. I don't mind that sort of money.

Therapist 1: So you paid, J chose it and you both liked the time together. That sounds like a success. Is that right, that there are times that things can be sorted out between you both, and you both feel good about it? Perhaps we can use that idea again to find some way of you both negotiating about money next time. *(reinforcing positives)*

Both therapists are trying here to help the family members find positives in what they do; trying to help them focus on what does work, on how the family is beginning to solve problems and on how this can make them both feel a bit less upset with each other, and sometimes even enjoy each other's company again.

Although these kinds of change can look small, the aim in each session is to find something that can be managed successfully, and to try to build on the strengths of the family to improve optimism and some sense that things can begin to change. Each family will have its own priorities and needs and, by taking these seriously and trying to help everyone to change the way problems are solved slightly, therapists can begin the cycle of helping family members deal differently with the range of problems they may have.

Cognitive-behavioural therapy

CBT for psychosis developed from the single-symptom research espoused by Bentall (1999), and also from a range of studies that have helped to emphasize the continuum between 'normality' and the more unusual experiences often found in people with a diagnosis of schizophrenia, e.g. delusional ideas and hallucinations. These studies show that there is such a continuum and that even the more unusual and positive symptoms of schizophrenia do not themselves define the clinical population but overlap with it (Morrison & Peterson 2003; van Os et al., 1999). This research also emphasized that what characterizes clinical populations is not the conviction with which a delusional idea is held but the distress it engenders, either to the individual or to others (Peters et al., 1999a, 1999b). This has enabled the CBT approaches developed successfully for depression and anxiety to be adapted for this population.

Another strand of research has helped to elucidate that reasoning biases and memory distortions can also contribute to the development and maintenance of delusional thinking. Garety and Hemsley (1994) identified a tendency for people with delusions to use limited evidence, the 'jumping to conclusions' reasoning bias, which has since been confirmed by other groups (Dudley et al., 1997a, 1997b). There is also a tendency for those with paranoid delusional ideas to externalize their attributions for events, in contrast to those with depression, who tend to internalize them (Kinderman & Bentall, 2000). Frith has suggested that hallucinations may reflect a poorer ability to self-monitor thoughts (1992), and there is evidence for this (Brébion et al. 2000; Johns et al., 2002). Hemsley (1998) has discussed the loss of a 'sense of self' due to information-processing deficits; distortions in memory have been found in those convinced of abduction by aliens (Clancy et al., 2002). This has led to new models for psychosis that are informing treatment approaches. These posit that it is not the unusual experiences themselves that are problematic but the appraisal of them as external and anxiety provoking, which then turns them into symptoms (Garety et al., 2001; Morrison & Peterson, 2003).

This focus on appraisal has been particularly helpful in helping people with schizophrenia make sense of their unusual experiences, reintegrate them, and react and cope with them differently to reduce distress.

Assessments

The two most important areas for working psychologically with individuals with psychosis consist of the distressing experiences they bring to the therapy, and the sense they make of them, i.e. what 'model' or perspective they have about their experiences. From the start of the assessment it is vital to use the person's own terminology for their psychotic experiences, rather than using psychiatric jargon such as 'voices' or 'delusions': so, for instance, the person may not recognize that he or she is 'hearing voices' if what is actually being heard is Uncle Bob talking, or spirits accompanied by their visual apparition. Words such as 'schizophrenia' or 'mental illness' can be offensive and should not be used unless a client is happy with an explanation in terms of a medical model.

Throughout the assessment, it is crucial to remember that the ultimate goal of the therapist is to try to understand, rather than to try to make clients change their mind by challenging the reality of their voices and delusions. In contrast to challenge, empathy with the distress caused by the experiences is an important therapeutic tool in early stages of assessment and engagement.

The 'funnel' method of assessment is a useful model to follow. In the first instance, an overview assessment of distressing experiences is carried out, which might include positive and negative symptoms as well as emotional disorders. Once specific problems have been identified, those problems can then be assessed in more depth.

For hallucinations, a useful place to start is by identifying the physical characteristics of the voices (although note that hallucinations in other modalities are also common: visions, somatic and tactile hallucinations). Important factors include the frequency, duration, loudness, number, location and type of the voices. The content of the voices should be identified, although some clients may not be ready to disclose this until trust in the therapist has been established, for instance if it is shaming or dangerous. The PSYRATS (Haddock et al., 1999), or Chadwick et al.'s (1996) 'Interview with a person who hears voices', can be a useful guide for this part of the assessment. An ABC assessment will also be helpful, i.e. identifying antecedents or triggers, and consequences. Triggers can be both environmental (where, when, etc.) and internal or emotional (e.g. anxiety). Consequences to look out for should be both behavioural and emotional, as well as the general impact on functioning. It is important to identify the extent to which people resist or comply with their voices, especially in the case of command hallucinations. Voice diaries can be useful for identifying the ABCs outside of the sessions.

It is also crucial to assess the beliefs people hold about their voices (Chadwick & Birchwood, 1994), since much of the CBT work will attempt to modify these beliefs to reduce emotional distress and enhance feelings of control, rather than the frequency of hallucinations *per se*. Crucial dimensions include identity ('Who are they?' 'Are they beneficial or harmful?'), the perceived cause ('What causes them?'), their power ('How powerful are they?') and control ('How much control does the client have over the voices?' 'How much control do the voices have over the client?'). The type of relationship the person has with his or her voices is also a key feature (Birchwood, Meaden, Trower, Gilbert & Plaistow, 2000). Again, useful guides for the cognitive and interpersonal aspects of voices include Chadwick et al.'s (1996) 'Interview with a person who hears voices' and the PSYRATS, as well as Chadwick et al.'s (1996) Cognitive Assessment of Voices Interview Schedule.

It is important to view delusions as lying on more than one dimension, rather than being all-or-nothing false beliefs (Garety & Hemsley, 1987; Peters et al., 1999a). Once the content and number of delusions have been identified, the crucial dimensions to assess consist of conviction ('How much do they believe it?'), preoccupation ('How much time do they think about it?'), distress ('How upsetting are the beliefs?') and disability ('What impact does it have on their lives?'). The PSYRATS covers these dimensions or, alternatively, patients can be asked to rate conviction, preoccupation and distress on 0–100% or any kind of Likert scale on a session-by-session basis.

As with voices, delusions are often inextricably linked with emotional factors (Freeman & Garety, 2003) and potential maintenance factors, such as safety behaviours, should also be identified. Delusions, especially those of a persecutory or grandiose nature, can be linked with self-esteem and such associations should be explored before attempting to modify the beliefs. The links may either be direct (i.e. reflecting low self-esteem; Freeman et al., 1998) or indirect (i.e. protecting against low self-esteem; Bentall et al., 2001). Lastly, it can be useful to assess cognitive flexibility about delusions (i.e. the extent to which the client is willing to entertain the idea that there may be an alternative explanation, even if alternative explanations are not actually available to the client), since there is some preliminary evidence that flexibility is associated with good CBT outcome (Garety et al., 1997).

Frequency of sessions

The NICE guidelines recommend at least six months, or more than ten sessions of treatment. Weekly or fortnightly is often the preferred time interval, usually in an outpatient or community team setting for about an hour.

Specific interventions for CBT for psychosis

There are now several manuals written about this (e.g. Chadwick et al., 1996; Fowler et al., 1995; Kingdon & Turkington, 1991; Morrison, 2001; Nelson, 1997) and some opportunities for qualified clinicians to obtain training in these particular interventions. The following discussion is based primarily on Fowler et al. (1995).

As with all intervention with this client group, it should not be done in a vacuum. People with these diagnoses are likely to have multiple needs and care should normally be given alongside the involvement of a team of mental health specialists (e.g. a community mental health team or continuing care team) with regular reviews and monitoring of mental state. CBT is almost always given as an adjunct to medication. Therapists should ensure that they receive training and ongoing supervision in these approaches.

ENGAGEMENT

One of the most important issues in offering treatment to people with psychosis is the fact that we know that they may have particular difficulties in engaging in therapy. By definition, they are likely to have paranoid ideas (the most common positive symptom) and this may include being suspicious of the therapist. People with psychosis are more likely to have small social networks (Creswell et al., 1992) and we know that increased social isolation is associated with poor insight (White et al., 2000). They may also have a number of cognitive problems with attention, concentration and memory. Moreover, they may have reasoning biases that may make them more likely to have selective attention, to use limited evidence and attribute events externally. Given the stigma still associated with these diagnoses, many people will have experienced considerable loss (Rooke & Birchwood, 1998) and even trauma (Mueser et al., 1998b), and some of this may be ongoing. The diagnosis is also associated with poverty and reduced work and social opportunities (Thornicroft et al., 2004).

For all of these reasons, therapists should focus on reducing distress and be very sensitive during sessions to the impact of any discussion. It is important that sessions are not aversive, as this may increase anxiety and bring on acute symptoms. Instead, therapists should be aiming at calm sessions, which maximize cognitive capacity for more flexible thinking and encourage the consideration of alternatives (Freeman and Garety, 2003). Sessions may need to be short and activities may need to be varied (going for a walk mid-session, having a cigarette break). It can be useful to check in session for any suspiciousness and to try to deal with it immediately, by clarifying what the problem is and being reassuring where possible. Fostering a collaborative therapeutic style is essential from the beginning of any session, while being very flexible and tolerant of rapid changes in mental state. Unlike some other therapeutic situations, the therapist may have to be much more prepared to take responsibility for the session, and for apologizing if things are misinterpreted. We have found that even after a long initial assessment, which is part of the engagement process, therapists often have to spend time in each session making sure the person feels able to continue the work, and is not feeling upset or mistrustful for any reason.

ENHANCING COPING RESPONSES

It has been known for some time that individuals with these diagnoses do have coping responses (Falloon & Talbot, 1981), but that these may be suboptimal. Typically, people cope with distressing ideas or voices by social withdrawal, the avoidance of stressful situations and safety behaviours such as staying indoors or wearing particular clothing, e.g. to keep off harmful 'lasers'. Sometimes people use alcohol, cannabis or crack cocaine to try to improve mood, to 'drown out' voices or just to relax. Unfortunately, the latest research, particularly on cannabis use, suggests that many of these substances can make unusual experiences worse (Arsenault et al., 2004).

It is usually most helpful to try to ask clients to monitor their distressing symptoms, and also to note their activity, their mood and their situation, before and after symptoms start. Often, this monitoring on its own will help to show there is in fact a pattern to experiences that can seem uncontrollable, and the monitoring can usually suggest that there are at least some times, or situations, when symptoms are not so likely, or not so distressing. These can then be enhanced.

If the person cannot manage this kind of monitoring, even with adapted forms that allow for poor literacy, limited concentration or motivation, experiences of that day or the day before can be asked about in session in some detail. This is another way of providing some of the same information, which can then be tried out in homework sessions, e.g. 'If you try not to sit in a darkened room all afternoon, but listen to the radio and speak to someone else in your hostel, does this make the voices less likely to start?'

Improving coping responses would typically be attempted as part of the initial assessment of difficulties, and also as part of engagement. By itself, enhancing coping is likely to lead only to temporary relief from the distress of symptoms, but it is always worth trying out alternative coping strategies. This is because it can make a dramatic difference for some people, and even a small and temporary change can suggest that progress is possible, and foster therapeutic optimism.

SHARING A FORMULATION

Although there is as yet no systematic evidence for this, we have found in our practice that it is a useful exercise, after the initial stage of assessment and some immediate help with coping responses, to try to draw all the information together and to collaborate with clients in drawing out a model of factors that have led up to their current problems. Usually, this is best done in the form of a diagram of the sorts of early difficulty, such as being taken into care, poor parenting or a specific life event, that have contributed to emotional changes, poor self-esteem or feelings of vulnerability. The feelings of vulnerability can then be seen by the patient as something that feeds into critical voices. Voices may also be associated in the model with times of low mood and isolation. The consequences of voices for this individual might then be to make them feel suicidal and desperate for the voices to stop. This can then, of course, make the voices worse. It is useful, while doing this, to involve clients in writing this out for themselves if possible or, if not, to make use of their words and incorporate their descriptions. Once this kind of model is drawn, it is also helpful to consider alternative routes. Does it help, for example, at the stage of low mood, if the client distracts him- or herself by going out for a walk? Once the voices start, how can the client calm down and feel less panicky? Can the client at this stage think about the voices as part of his or her own distress and deal with them directly, or does this have to wait for a later stage of therapy? A clear model, constructed together, which clients can then take home and think about, is a way of helping them to understand and make sense of their difficulties. It is also the beginning of a collaborative decision about how to intervene.

MODIFYING DELUSIONAL BELIEFS

Once delusional beliefs have been assessed in some detail, the therapist is in a position to decide with the client how to engineer change. The way various personal experiences (antecedents, cues, cognitions and emotions) may have led to an externalizing appraisal or a symptom such as a delusional belief can be laid out in a diagram. This model can then be used as a basis for reconsidering, for instance, the evidence for a delusional belief. Describing this as *challenging* delusional ideas is incorrect. Rather, at this stage, the process is one of considering impartially how the person uses the evidence for his or her beliefs, and whether there may be aspects that they have not been able to consider beforehand.

While not always possible, reality testing can be considered. Not all situations are amenable to reality testing, 'The pyramids are held up by ancient races who are trying to harm me', but sometimes the *consequences* of even this kind of belief can be tested. A process of Socratic questioning, querying what might be happening in an interested rather than aggressive way, is the best approach. At this stage, therapists must also be prepared to have their own beliefs tested; theoretically an experiment can go both ways. It is very important before any reality test is carried out that the results and what they might mean are gone through in detail beforehand.

For instance, if the therapist and client agree to use a tape recorder to demonstrate the voices, what will it mean if the tape plays silence? Does it mean the tape was faulty, the machine was faulty or that the person is 'mad' (an unattractive and stigmatizing assertion for many)? Or might it mean that voices, although heard as being in the outside world, are not in fact available to others, and might this be reassuring?

Likewise, if the therapist and client agree to test out the latter's telepathic or clairvoyant abilities, what will it mean if the experiment demonstrates that the client is devoid of such abilities? Will the results be easily dismissed as a consequence of fatigue or other environmental factors? Will it have the unfortunate consequence of shaming the individual, or further compromising an already low self-esteem? Or will it be a relief and a mitigation of the client's sense of responsibility for negative events in the world? It is also important to tease out the function and context of behaviours associated with delusions, since one person's maladaptive 'safety behaviour' can be another's helpful 'coping strategy'. For instance, someone who believes that people in parked cars are spying on him or her is likely to benefit from going back to check whether or not the parked car is still there after a period of time, since this will act as reality-checking. In contrast, someone who believes specific letters in number plates have a threatening meaning is unlikely to benefit from checking cars at his or her destination, since this is a safety behaviour that prevents the disconfirmation of the belief (i.e. nothing bad happened *because* I checked the number plates).

CASE EXAMPLE: COURSE OF TREATMENT

When seen initially, John was stable on medication and just wanted to use sessions to talk things through. He was not prepared to see anyone junior, or to take part in formal assessments. He easily became extremely angry about the way the government was treating him. The initial session was spent in engaging him and deciding on an agreed agenda, which, because of his conditions, was quite limited and had to focus on dealing with current issues. It was established early in the sessions that if he started shouting, I would ask him to take a pause and lower his voice. This happened in the first few sessions but not afterwards. John wished to be seen infrequently but consistently over a year at times that were mutually agreeable. He was keen to continue in higher education and has been studying for courses. He successfully passed an AS level during this time.

John still believes with 100% conviction that he is being monitored. However, the distress that this causes has declined. He now says that it is manageable. A key intervention was for me to say that obviously I would be being monitored too, but that I did not find this a problem; it was a risk I was prepared to take but I felt it would not cause me difficulties. This helped John to reduce his own anxiety and anger.

A key formulation has been that there was a series of phone calls that John *knows* (100% conviction) triggered the surveillance unit to monitor him via the gadget in his head. He agrees with the therapist that, although there was a sequence of calls, if he could think his appraisal of being monitored might have another explanation, he would feel very relieved. We have drawn out the two models and their different conclusions. We are working on whether there is any way to explore this kind of alternative way of thinking.

At the moment, his distress levels are reduced, from 80% down to

20%, and he is functioning well, with a successful relationship and plans for the future. He continues to take medication (risperidone) and finds it helpful. He has remained under the care of his local community mental health team while having psychological treatment, and is seen regularly by his psychiatrist and care co-ordinator.

Modifying beliefs about hallucinations

It has been found that although improving coping can temporarily help with hallucinations such as voices, they are more likely to decline in frequency if the underlying beliefs that fuel them are tackled (Kuipers et al., 1998; Trower et al., 2004).

Coping with voices

Coping responses are worth trying to provide even a limited degree of relief, particularly if the voices are loud and the content distressing. Anything that uses the parts of the mouth concerned with speech seems to interfere directly with voices and are reasonably easy to try out. Activities such as humming, chewing gum, reading or singing out loud (not necessarily loudly) or talking to someone have all been found helpful by some service users. The fact that auditory hallucinations have been found to recruit the same areas of the brain, Broca's area, as speech (Maguire et al., 1993) can be discussed, as it suggests that voices might be a form of internal speech. Sometimes, voices or visual hallucinations can be understood as old memories, e.g. of a dead parent, remembered rather than in the present, although still threatening or unpleasant.

For some people, voices represent their own poor self-esteem, or other negative or traumatic incidents in their past, such as being bullied at school. Linking voices to understandable parts of the client's history can be reassuring and may facilitate interventions to reduce negative effects. While it may not always help, it is worth doing this kind of work if at all possible, as it is likely to prevent future episodes.

Modifying the beliefs that individuals hold about the power of their voices can be an extremely useful therapeutic strategy. For instance, voices often threaten to harm the person if he or she disobeys them in some way or talks about them to third parties, such as the therapist. Behavioural experiments can be devised collaboratively with the client to test out the power of the voices, either during or between sessions. Realizing that the voices alone cannot carry out their threats can lead to a sharp drop in anxiety, which may then lead to a reduction in their frequency.

Increasing the *perceived control* that people have over their voices can

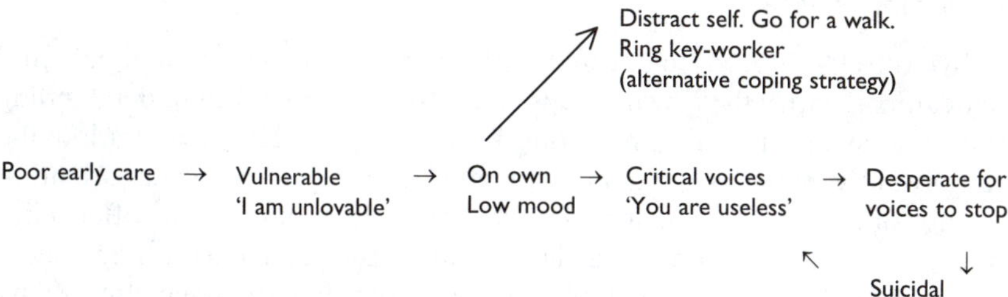

Figure 21.1 Possible model of factors associated with voices.

also be extremely therapeutic. A cognitive shift in perceived control is often obtained as a result of the implementation of coping strategies. A few individuals may even be able to induce their voices, which paradoxically reduces their hold over the person as they now feel in control of their onset. Other people, oddly, find that they can strike a 'deal' with their voices: for instance they agree to give the voices their undivided attention at a pre-arranged time of the day, while in return the voices agree to leave them alone for the rest of the day. For many clients, therapeutic work with voices will centre on reality testing. Clients are encouraged to consider that what they can hear is not actually coming from people around them but in fact originates from themselves/their mind/overactive imagination/illness (or whatever model the person finds least distressing). Being able to distinguish real speech from hallucinations correctly is likely to lead to a reduction in anxiety, since this means the client is not in immediate danger (if the voices are threatening) or that they are not being insulted in public (if the voices are disparaging). Again, a reduction in anxiety may in itself lead to a reduction in the frequency of the voices.

Improving self-esteem

Low self-esteem is common in psychosis (Freeman et al., 1998), as are rates of comorbid depression and anxiety. If self-esteem seems to be the main problem, it may be worth trying to improve it, using the same sort of methods as in depression. Hall and Tarrier (2003, 2004) describe in detail one such set of interventions, encouraging the person to write down and evaluate the evidence for two positives about themselves each week for five weeks. Chadwick (2003) discusses using a 'two chair method' to enable the person to experience not just their usual negative self but a positive self in the other chair. These kinds of intervention can be helpfully incorporated into the model already described. If the low self-esteem predates the first episode of psychosis, a life review can be helpful (Young, 1990). Even if the low self-esteem is subsequent to episodes, recasting someone as a survivor not a victim, thus re-evaluating life events, can also be useful.

Recognizing relapse

Birchwood et al. (1989) pioneered early work on helping individuals and their carers identify their own 'relapse signatures' as an aid to understanding prodromal symptoms and preventing future relapses. This involves looking carefully at the patterns apparent before a relapse, paying particular attention to symptoms that are non-specific but extremely common and often idiosyncratic. For one person, a headache and a feeling of unease might be a precursor to more serious symptoms of paranoia. For someone else, feeling very tired and socially avoidant might indicate the early stages of voices recurring. Helping individuals to identify these early signs and then to consider the interventions that they could institute to reduce their impact can be empowering, and may also prevent a relapse or reduce its impact. A crisis card system that enables people to specify their preferred interventions before an acute stage is reached and insight is lost, has been shown to reduce subsequent admissions (Sutherby et al., 1999).

Community psychiatric services

Community mental health teams

The course of schizophrenia and the effectiveness of treatment are such that most people are able to live at home for much, if not all, of the time. This is particularly so if they can be supported by services designed to meet their individual needs. In many Western countries, community psychiatric services have been set up to target the problems of people with severe and enduring mental illness, a category that includes many with schizophrenia. While it is generally agreed that this is the best contribution to the amelioration of the course of the disorder, the optimal configuration of services is not finally established (Bebbington et al., 2002).

It is now generally accepted that continuous and effective care is best delivered by cohesive teams of workers, involving collaboration between different clinical disciplines in a manner that allows pooling of skills. Generic multi-disciplinary community mental health teams (CMHTs) are increasingly the basis of community mental health services, particularly in the UK. These usually serve defined geographic areas (sectors or GP catchment areas) to make clear which patients are their responsibility. Tyrer (2000) has listed the features that facilitate the effective function of CMHTs: skill sharing, co-ordination, flexible hours of work, good liaison, assertive but flexible contracts, links with designated hospital beds and the development of specific referral criteria. CMHTs usually cover the needs of all adults (aged 18–65) with severe mental illness in given sectors.

Tyrer et al. (2000) reviewed randomized controlled trials of management by CMHTs, comparing them with services that did not involve integrated community teams. Team management seems to be better for patients' satisfaction and acceptance of treatment, and to result in fewer suicides. There was, however, no clear benefit for overall clinical and social outcomes. The advantages are likely to arise from flexibility and continuity of care. However, even well-equipped CMHTs are likely to fail some patients with serious clinical and social needs (Melzer, Hale, Malik, Hogman & Wood, 1991). This has led to the idea of specialist community teams to deal with patients who are particularly hard to help, and to provide a rapid response to crises. Teams like this were adopted by the Department of Health (DoH) in England and Wales in its strategic plan (DoH 2001).

Assertive community treatment

Assertive community treatment (ACT) was developed in the mid-West of the USA in the 1970s (Marx et al., 1973; Stein & Test, 1980). As Marshall and Creed (2000) note, so-called ACT teams have actually been used for a number of purposes: to facilitate the discharge of long-term patients, as an alternative to admission for acutely ill patients and as a mechanism for keeping vulnerable patients with longstanding illness in the community. However, Marshall and Creed (2000) argue that the type of ACT most likely to become widespread is the last of these.

This form of ACT has been shown effective in the USA and in Australia (Hoult, Reynolds, Charbonneau-Powis, Weekes & Biggs, 1983; Stein & Test, 1980). Marshall and Lockwood (2000) have made a systematic review of randomized controlled trials of ACT. Overall, it was able to save one admission for every ten patients treated. There was a 42% reduction in time spent in hospital and an increase in engagements with services. There was, however, no evidence of cost-saving or of improvement in psychiatric and social functioning. Residential stability may have been improved.

In the UK, the government response to ACT has been enthusiastic and, as a result, there are now over twenty ACT teams in London alone (Wright et al., 2003). There is, however, considerable dispute over whether ACT has been exported successfully into the UK. Five randomized controlled trials (RCTs) of ACT were carried out in the UK in the 1990s (Bebbington et al., 2002); their results were disappointing. While the number of patients remaining in contact with services increased, they did not deliver improvements in social or clinical outcome, despite a possible increase in costs. Some of the studies failed to increase quality of life or patient satisfaction. Marshall and Creed (2000) have argued that these experimental services lacked essential characteristics of ACT as developed in the US, and that this may explain the poor results. They regard these British services merely as *intensive case management* (ICM). According to Teague et al. (1998), the characteristics that define ACT are assertive outreach, case-sharing, small caseloads, dedicated psychiatric time, twenty-four-hour cover, a community location and a team leader who is an active member of the team.

Mueser and his colleagues (1998a) are less convinced that there is much difference between ACT and ICM. Wright et al. (2003) have applied measures of ACT orthodoxy to purported assertive outreach teams in London, and found quite a lot of variation in their practice. Thus we do not really know yet whether the ACT model is exportable to a British context, where privacy and freedom from intrusion is valued and the provision of CMHTs may in any case already meet the needs of an appreciable number of the difficult-to-help patients who are the natural clientele of ACT. It is probably naïve to expect social treatments to be infinitely transferable to novel settings: the jury remains out on whether ACT would add to the British mental health service firmament. The recent results of the REACT study from north London confirm this view. A total of 251 people with severe mental illness (SMI) were randomly allocated either to a form of ACT faithful to the key features described by Teague et al. (1998) or to non-specialist community teams. No differences in inpatient bed use, clinical or social outcomes were found, but those receiving ACT were better engaged and more satisfied with services (Killaspy et al., 2006).

Crisis resolution teams

Although it was clearly possible to close the large old mental hospitals and move their inmates into the community, we do not know to what extent *acute* psychiatric beds can be substituted by management in the community. Closing acute beds without alternative provision leads, in the view of one eminent commentator, to an inefficient and profligate service (Tyrer, 1988).

Few CMHTs have the resources to visit acutely ill patients on a daily basis, and would therefore be unable to replace the need for an episode of inpatient care. However, a better resourced specialist team might be able to take on this function, at least for some acutely ill patients. On this premise, crisis resolution teams (CRTs – sometimes known as *home treatment teams*), which are generally available twenty-four-hours a day, assess and manage acutely ill patients in their homes. The pioneering work of Stein and Test (1980), and of Hoult et al. (1983), has interestingly served as the model for CRT as well as for ACT. Those studies provided promising evidence of effective substitution of community- for hospital-based care, with an overall reduction in bed use and improved satisfaction among both patients and their carers. There have now been some investigations of teams like this in the UK, although Kluiter (1997) has been critical of the evidence base overall. The large Islington studies provide better evidence of bed reduction and possibly improved patient satisfaction in both historically controlled and randomized controlled trials (Johnson et al., 2005a, 2005b). The exact place of CRTs in an overall service context remains to be established, although the British government has made them an instrument of its mental health policy. When they work well, CRTs can be effective in improving the maintenance of people with schizophrenia in the community, and seem to reduce costs by reducing the need for inpatient beds. They do not seem to have effects on social or clinical functioning.

Thus the best way to configure services to maximize the benefit for people with schizophrenia and other longstanding severe mental illnesses remains uncertain. Some of the functions of both ACT and CRT might be adequately placed within the CMHT structure rather than in specialist teams as it has been argued that the introduction of specialist teams might reduce the functioning and morale of CMHTs.

Managing people with a dual diagnosis

A major difficulty in providing services for people with schizophrenia is the issue of *dual diagnosis* of severe mental disorder and substance abuse. The prevalence of substance abuse in most US community samples of individuals with psychosis runs between 30% and 50% (Mueser et al., 1990). The frequency of dual diagnosis obviously varies geographically according to local attitudes towards substances of potential misuse. Dual diagnosis leads to greater inpatient service use, poorer adherence to treatment, more frequent violent behaviour and more severe clinical and social problems (Bartels et al., 1993; Scott et al., 1998).

There has been a major investment in attempts to help people with dual diagnosis in the US over the 1990s (Osher & Drake, 1996); much less research has been done on the other side of the Atlantic. In the British system we might choose to provide treatment wholly within generic CMHTs, wholly within addiction services or by close liaison between these two sorts of team. There are, however, difficulties with all these approaches: CMHT staff are sometimes not totally sympathetic to the problems of substance abuse, while staff in addiction services often lack the confidence to manage psychosis. The US experience has led to an advocacy of specialist dual-diagnosis teams, with staff being trained in the skills to deal with both sets of problems.

Community dual-diagnosis teams often share principles with ACT. In the initial phase of treatment there may be a focus on engagement rather than the problem of abuse. Later, addiction techniques are used, such as motivational interviewing, education about the effects of substance abuse, and relapse prevention and containment. Well-known examples of specialist services in the US include the 'continuous treatment teams' developed in New Hampshire (Drake et al., 1996). There is initial evidence that teams of this sort can improve outcome, variously measured. Preliminary reports from the New Hampshire RCT show reductions in hospitalization, improvement in functioning and greater degrees of abstinence at three-year follow-up.

In Western Europe, there is less separation between addiction services and community psychiatric services, so it is unclear whether specialist dual-diagnosis teams would be the best way forward. It may be better to train specialist workers with protected caseloads to operate within CMHTs.

Early intervention services

In the past ten or fifteen years a new sort of specialist team has been developed to deal specifically with the problems of people in the early stages of schizophrenia. These are *early intervention services*, which have stimulated great interest in developed countries among clinicians, researchers and service planners alike. They are justified on the basis of recent claims that vigorous and appropriately targeted intervention during the early stage of illness may improve overall prognosis.

Among the best-established early intervention services are the EPPIC programme in Melbourne (McGorry et al., 1996) and the North Birmingham service (Spencer, Birchwood & McGovern, 2001). Their rationale is that effective intervention and good engagement with services at an early stage may attenuate the medium- and long-term consequences of psychosis and reduce stigma.

Early intervention strategies vary in the stage of illness targeted. Sometimes the focus is the detection of the prodromal stage of illness and prevention of progression to acute schizophrenia (McGlashan et al., 2003; McGorry et al., 2002; Morrison et al., 2002). For others, e.g. the TIPS project in Scandinavia, the main aim is to detect and treat psychosis earlier through measures such as public education, enhanced links with primary care and with agencies working with young people (Johannessen et al., 2001). A third category of intervention focuses on the stage following initial presentation to mental health services with symptoms of psychotic illness. This last type seeks to promote good early recovery, to reduce the frequency and impact of relapse, and to maintain good mental health and social functioning.

Several observations and aspirations underpin the argument for specialist teams of this sort. First, some research on the course of schizophrenia suggests a characteristic period of early decline and increasing social disability (McGlashan & Johannessen, 1996). This is at least partly based on the evidence that the longer the duration of untreated psychosis (DUP) the poorer the outcome. While some studies find that DUP can consistently predict outcome (e.g. Harrigan et al., 2003) others dispute this. However, stepwise increases in disability and a slower and less complete response to drug treatment have been reported after the first few relapses (Lieberman et al., 1996). It has thus been suggested that the first few years of illness constitute a 'critical period', followed by a plateau of much greater stability in functioning (Birchwood et al., 1998). Neurodevelopmental explanations for this remain contentious, and psychosocial accounts in terms of the extent of early damage to identity, social development and social networks are also plausible.

Thus effective intervention during this putative critical period *might* improve long-term prognosis.

Second, initial experiences of contact with services are often aversive to patients and carers alike, especially when they involve compulsory treatment. This threatens long-term engagement with services and treatment adherence, so that there is a good case for making early treatment as acceptable to clients as possible, and for paying great attention to engagement and the development of a good therapeutic alliance at this stage.

Third, secondary morbidity, including substance misuse and depression, are frequent at this stage of the illness (Addington et al., 1998; Cantwell et al., 1999) and the risk of suicide is at its highest (Power et al., 2003). A further aim for first episode services is therefore to reduce secondary morbidity (McGorry & Yung, 2003).

Despite the importance of the suggestion that the prognosis of schizophrenia can be ameliorated by specialist early psychosis services, direct evidence remains limited and ambiguous. Results of a number of case series or studies with non-equivalent control groups have been reported. The Swedish Parachute Study is investigating outcomes from seventeen clinics across Sweden that have implemented a programme based on low-dose medication, continuity of contact for five years with a specialist team, rapid response in crisis, and access to a crisis home. Initial one-year results suggest greater satisfaction and less inpatient service use in the intervention group than in two control groups, one historical and one prospective, but important study limitations are reliance on routinely collected data and major differences in sampling frame and recruitment criteria between intervention and control groups (Culberg et al., 2002). In the EPPIC programme in Melbourne, comparisons were made of symptomatic and functional outcomes between a small cohort of first-episode clients receiving care from the fully established service and matched historical controls who had been assessed at an early stage of the service's development when it was a primarily a specialist inpatient service (McGorry et al., 1996). Outcomes were better for the later cohort cared for by the fully developed community service. Malla et al. (2002) investigated outcomes from a modified ACT programme catering for first-episode clients, including intensive contact with families and groups for patients focusing on re-establishing regular activities and networks, resuming work or education and cognitively oriented skills training. At one year, admission had been avoided for almost half of the small series investigated, and 70% were assessed as completely in remission. However, no control group was included in the study.

Recently, management of early psychosis by dedicated specialist teams has been investigated in four randomized controlled trials. In Denmark, the OPUS study is an investigation of modified ACT, with a strong emphasis on family intervention, psychoeducation and social skills training (Jorgensen et al., 2000). One-year outcomes suggest reduced symptoms, greater satisfaction, greater likelihood of being engaged in education or training, and lower hospital bed use in the intervention group than in control subjects receiving standard treatment from a community mental health centre (Nordentoft, 2003). The LEO trial in south London has also evaluated modified ACT delivered by a dedicated early psychosis team in combination with a specialist inpatient unit. This was compared with standard care involving local sector community mental health teams. Results suggest increased engagement with services, lower inpatient bed use and better social functioning among the group receiving the specialist team intervention (Craig et al., 2004; Garety et al., 2006). COAST (Croydon Outreach and Assertive Support Team) evaluated an RCT of whole-team training in a specialist early intervention team, which offered a range of optimal treatments including low-dose atypicals, CBT and FI for psychosis when indicated, and a range of vocational and occupational help, compared to standard care in a comparable local team. Clients in both teams improved significantly over the year of evaluation, but not because of the intervention. There was only some slight evidence of less bed use and better carer quality of life in COAST. These last results suggest that people need high-quality interventions at whatever stage they present to services (Kuipers et al., 2004). Finally, Morrison et al. (2004) report on an Early Detection and Intervention Evaluation (EDIE) study in which fifty-eight people in a prodromal stage were randomly allocated to CBT ($n = 37$) or treatment as usual (TAU) ($n = 23$). CBT was offered for six months and the cohort was followed up for twelve months. Overall, the transition rate for psychosis was low (12%) but significantly less in the CBT group (2/37). The intervention also significantly improved positive symptoms of psychosis. The authors note that CBT was well accepted by people in this prodromal period.

Thus, there is a theoretical basis and some initial evidence for the suggestion that specialist early psychosis services may improve some outcomes, either at a prodromal stage or following initial presentation to services with a psychosis. However, the evidence is not overwhelming, as intervention may delay rather than prevent psychosis, and several of the relevant studies have important methodological flaws. The Department of Health in the UK has responded by earmarking funds for the introduction of dedicated early intervention services (EIS) across the country. Although welcomed by some, this policy has also encountered substantial scepticism because of doubts regarding the robustness of the evidence and the perceived disadvantages of separate early intervention teams (Curtis, 2003; Pelosi, 2003). Critics suggest that dedicating high levels of resource to such services may distract from the task of providing high-quality and well-funded care for people with psychotic illness throughout the course of their illnesses. Being left with seeing only patients whose illnesses are well-established may demoralize generic community mental health teams (CMHTs). With the recent introduction of CRTs and assertive outreach teams, the network of potential specialist services in UK catchment areas is becoming increasingly complex and, especially for service planners in areas where the incidence of psychosis is relatively low, the introduction of a further specialist team may create unduly fragmented and unmanageable local service systems. The fact that early psychosis services often serve relatively large catchment areas also deprives people with first-episode psychosis of the advantages of sectorized care (Thornicroft et al., 1995). These include services provided from bases that are accessible and local, and close links between sector teams, primary care teams and other relevant services within the small areas they serve. These doubts regarding specialist early psychosis services suggest an alternative route to improved care for this group. This is the augmentation of CMHT services to include early psychosis workers, who remain within generic sector teams but have protected time, training and supervision for the management of people with early psychosis. This is the model currently being adopted in much of the state of Victoria, Australia, where the EPPIC service is based, as policy makers have not thus far been persuaded that full-scale specialist services are an affordable and cost-effective measure throughout the state (Yung et al., 2003).

SUMMARY

As can be seen, schizophrenia is now a focus of therapeutic optimism and of a variety of new approaches – individual, family centred and organizational – to try and alleviate the stress and distress associated with the diagnosis, and to reduce later difficulties. This is a real change in the way such problems are viewed. Psychological theorizing has helped to change old perceptions of such problems as immutable into perceptions that help can be offered. Seeing schizophrenia as a set of difficulties that may be quantitatively but not qualitatively different from other psychological problems has been enormously productive, and is set to continue.

EXERCISE 21.1

Divide into three groups: observer, clinical psychologist and client. Using the case example of John from this chapter, role-play a session during which you and John collaboratively develop a formulation of his current difficulties, based on a stress-vulnerability model and identifying John's current and past stressors. Rotate roles and continue to role-play a session where John is distressed about being looked at strangely by a man in the supermarket. Identify the antecedents (A), John's beliefs (B) and his consequent (C) feelings and behaviour in the situation. Work with John to begin to consider whether there are any alternative explanations for this belief. Alternate roles and continue the role-play. Work with John on one of the following:

- generate evidence for both his current and the alternative beliefs
- identify some behavioural experiment that John might do to test the alternative beliefs
- identify with John the advantages and disadvantages of the existing and alternative beliefs, while referring back to your joint formulation.

FURTHER READINGS FOR CLIENTS

Bernheim, K., Lewine, R. & Beale, C. (1982). *The caring family: Living with mental illness*. New York: Random House.

Keefe, R. & Harvey, P. (1994). *Understanding schizophrenia: A guide to the new research on causes and treatment*. New York: Free Press.

Kuipers, E. & Bebbington, P.E. (2005). *Living with mental illness*. (Third Edition). London: Souvenir Press.

Marsh, D. & Dickens, R. (1998). *How to cope with mental illness in your family: A self-care guide for siblings, offspring and parents*. New York: Tarcher/Putnam.

Mueser, K. & Gingerich, S. (1994). *Coping with schizophrenia: A guide for families*. Oakland, CA: New Harbinger.

Sheehan, S. (1982). *Is there no place on earth for me?* Boston, MA: Houghton Mifflin.

Torrey, E.F. (1995). *Surviving schizophrenia: A manual for families, consumers and providers*. New York: Harper Perrenial.

Vine, P. (1982). *Families in pain*. New York: Pantheon.

Wasow, M. (1982). *Coping with schizophrenia*. Palo Alto, CA: Science and Behaviour Books.

FURTHER READINGS FOR PRACTITIONERS

Birchwood, M. & Tarrier, N. (1994). *Psychological management of schizophrenia*. Chichester, UK: Wiley.

Brenner, H., Roder, V., Hodel, B., Kienzle, N., Reed, D. & Liberman, R. (1994). *Integrated psychological therapy for schizophrenic patients*. Toronto: Hogrefe & Huber.

Chadwick, P., Birchwood, M. & Trower, P. (1996). *Cognitive therapy for delusions, voices and paranoia*. Chichester, UK: Wiley.

Falloon, I., Laporta, M., Fadden, G. & Graham-Hole, V. (1993). *Managing stress in families*. London: Routledge.

Fowler, D., Garety, P. & Kuipers, L. (1995). *Cognitive behavioral psychotherapy: A rationale, theory and practice*. Chichester, UK: John Wiley & Sons.

Haddock, G. & Slade, P. (1996). *Cognitive-behavioural interventions with psychotic disorders*. London: Routledge.

Hogarty, G. (2002). *Personal therapy for schizophrenia and related disorders*. New York: Guilford.

Kuipers, E., Leff, J. & Lam, D. (2002). *Family work for schizophrenia* (Second Edition). London: Gaskell.

Liberman, R., DeRisi, W. & Mueser, K. (1989). *Social skills training for psychiatric patients*. New York: Pergamon.

Truscott, F. (2002). My experience of mental illness. *Clinical Psychology*, 11, 36–39.

ASSESSMENT INSTRUMENTS

Diagnosis

First, M., Spitzer, R., Gibbon, R. & Williams, J. (2001). *Structured Clinical Interview for DSM-IV-TR Axis I Disorders – Patient Edition (SCID-I/P, 2001 revision) Research Version*. New York: Biometrics Research Department, New York State Psychiatric Institute. 10 51, Riverside Drive Unit 60, New York 10032. Online. Available at: http://www.scid4.org/ or http://cpmcnet.columbia.edu/dept/scid/. Computer Assisted SCID available at: http://www.mhs.com/

Psychiatric symptoms

Andreason, N.C. (1983). *Scales for the Assessment of Positive Symptoms (SAPS)*. Iowa City: University of Iowa.

Andreason, N.C. (1983). *Scale for the Assessment of Negative Symptoms (SANS)*. Iowa City: University of Iowa.

Kay, S., Opler, L. & Fiszbein, A. (1994). *Positive and Negative Syndrome Scale Manual*. North Tonawanda, NY: Multihealth Systems. Online. Available at: http://www.hhs.com.

Overall, J. & Gorham, D. (1988). The Brief Psychiatric Rating Scale: Recent developments in ascertainment and scaling. *Psychopharmacology Bulletin*, 24, 97–99.

Rhoades, M. & Overall, J. (1988). The semistructured BPRS Interview and Rating Guide. *Schizophrenia Bulletin*, 24, 101–104.

Tres, K., Bellenis, C., Brownlow, J., Livinston, G. & Leff, J. (1987). Present State Examination Change Rating Scale. *British Journal of Psychiatry*, 150, 201–207.

Wing, J., Cooper, J. & Sartorius, N (1974). *Measurement and classification of psychiatric symptoms*. Cambridge, UK: Cambridge University Press. Contains the Present State Examination.

Features of symptoms

Brett-Jones, J., Garety, P. & Hemsley, D. (1987). Measuring delusional experiences: A method and its application. *British Journal of Clinical Psychology*, 26, 257–265.

Chadwick, P. & Birchwood, M. (1996). The omnipotence of voices; II. The Beliefs About Voices Questionnaire (BAVQ). *British Journal of Psychiatry*, 166, 773–776.

Haddock, G., McCarron, J. & Tarrier, N. (1999). Scales to measure dimensions of hallucinations and delusions. The Psychotic Symptom Rating Scale. *Psychological Medicine*, 29, 879–889.

Insight

Amador, X.F., Strauss, D.H., Yale, S., Gorman, J.M. & Endicott, J. (1993). The assessment of insight in psychosis. *American Journal of Psychiatry*, 150, 873–879.

Birchwood, M., Smith, J., Drury, V., Healy, J. & Slade, M. (1994). A self-report insight scale for psychosis: Reliability, validity and sensitivity to change. *Acta Psychiatrica Scandinavica*, 89, 62–67.

Social adjustment

Baker, R. & Hall, J. (1983). REHAB: Rehabilitation evaluation. Aberdeen: Vine Publishing.

Birchwood, M., Smith, J., Cochrane, R., Wetton, S. & Copestake, S. (1990). The Social Functioning Scale: The development and validation of a new scale of social adjustment for use in family intervention programmes with schizophrenic patients. *British Journal of Psychiatry*, 157, 853–859.

Clifford, P. (1986). *Community Placement Questionnaire*. London: National Unit for Psychiatric Research and Development.

Mullhall, D. (1990). *Functional performance record*. Windsor: NFER.

Rosen, A., Hadzi-Pavloic, D. & Parker, G. (1989). The Life Skills Profile: A measure assessing function and disability in schizophrenia. *Schizophrenia Bulletin*, 15, 325–337.

Schooler, N., Hogarty, G. & Weissman, M. (1979). Social Adjustment Scale II (SAS-II). In W. Hargreaves, C. Atkinson & J. Sorenson (Eds.), *Resource materials for community mental health programme evaluations* (DHEW Publication No. (ADM) 79–328, pp. 290–303). Rockville, MD: National Institute of Mental Health.

Wallace, C., Liberman, R., Tauber, R. & Wallace, J. (2000). The Independent Living Skills Survey: A comprehensive measure of the community functioning of severely and persistently mentally ill individuals. *Schizophrenia Bulletin*, 26, 631–658.

Wykes, T. & Sturt, E. (1986). The measurement of social behaviour in psychiatric patients: An assessment of the reliability and validity of the SS schedule. *British Journal of Psychiatry*, 148, 1–11. Contains the Social Behaviour Schedule.

Family functioning

Amato, A.M. (1993). *Manual for coding expressed emotion from the five-minute speech sample*. Los Angeles, CA: UCLA Family Project.

Barrowclough, C., Marshall, M., Lockwood, A., Quinn, J. & Sellwood, W. (1998). Assessing relatives' needs for psychosocial interventions in schizophrenia: A relatives' version of the Cardinal Needs Schedule (RCNS). *Psychological Medicine*, 28(3), 531–542.

Fadden, G., Kuipers, L. & Bebbington, P. (1987). The burden of care: The impact of functional psychiatric illness on the patient's family. *British Journal of Psychiatry*, 150, 285–292.

REFERENCES

Addington, D., Addington, J. & Patten, S. (1998). Depression in people with first episode schizophrenia. *British Journal of Psychiatry*, 172, Suppl. 33, 90–92.

Amato, A.M. (1993). *Manual for coding expressed emotion from the five-minute speech sample*. Los Angeles, CA: UCLA Family Project.

American Psychiatric Association (APA) (1987). *Diagnostic and statistical manual of mental disorders (DSM-III-R)*, (Third Edition – Revised). Washington, DC: APA.

American Psychiatric Association (APA) (2000). *Diagnostic and statistical manual of the mental disorders* (Fourth Edition, text revision). Washington, DC: APA.

Anderson, C.M., Reiss, D.J. & Hogarty, G.E. (1986). *Schizophrenia and the family*. New York: Guilford Press.

Andreasen, N. (1984a). *Scale for the Assessment of Positive Symptoms* (SAPS). Iowa City: University of Iowa, Department of Psychiatry.

Andreasen, N. (1984b). *Scale for the Assessment of Negative Symptoms* (SANS). Iowa City: University of Iowa, Department of Psychiatry.

Andreasen, N. (1986). Scale for the assessment of thought, language and communication. *Schizophrenia Bulletin*, 12, 473–482.

Arsenault, L., Cannon, M., Witten, J. & Murray, R. (2004). Causal association between cannabis and psychosis: Examination of the evidence. *British Journal of Psychiatry*, 184, 110–117.

Asberg, M., Montgomery, S., Perris, C., Schalling, D. & Sedvall, G. (1978). The comprehensive psychopathological rating scale. *Acta Psychiatrica Scandinavica*, Suppl 271, 5–27.

Ayllon, T. & Azrin, N.H. (1965). The measurement and reinforcement of behaviour of psychotics. *Journal of Experimental Analysis of Behavior*, 8, 357–383.

Ball, R.A., Moore, E. & Kuipers, L. (1992). EE in community care staff: A comparison of two hostels. *Social Psychiatry and Psychiatric Epidemiology*, 27, 35–39.

Barnes, T.R.E & Nelson, H. (1994). *The assessment of psychoses. A practical handbook*. London: Chapman & Hall Medical.

Barrowclough, C., Marshall, M., Lockwood, A., Quinn, J. & Sellwood, W. (1998). Assessing relatives' needs for psychosocial interventions in schizophrenia: A relatives' version of the Cardinal Needs Schedule (RCNS). *Psychological Medicine*. 28(3), 531–542.

Barrowclough, C. & Parle, M. (1997). Appraisal, psychological adjustment and expressed emotion in relatives of patients suffering from schizophrenia. *British Journal of Psychiatry*, 171, 26–30.

Barrowclough, C. & Tarrier, N. (1992). *Families of schizophrenic patients: Cognitive behavioural intervention*. London: Chapman & Hall.

Barrowclough, C., Tarrier, N., Lewis, S., Sellwood, W., Mainwaring, J., Quinn, J. & Hamlin, C. (1999). Randomised controlled effectiveness trial of a needs-based psychosocial intervention service for carers of people with schizophrenia. *British Journal of Psychiatry*, 174, 505–511.

Bartels, S.J., Teague, G.B., Drake, R.E., Clark, R.E., Bush, P.W. & Noordsy, D.L. (1993). Substance abuse in schizophrenia: Service utilization and costs. *Journal of Nervous and Mental Disease*, 181, 227–232.

Bebbington, P. & Kuipers, L. (1994). The predictive utility of EE in schizophrenia: An aggregate analysis. *Psychological Medicine*, 24, 707–718.

Bebbington, P. & Nayani, T. (1995). The Psychosis Screening Questionnaire. *International Journal of Methods in Psychiatric Research*, 5, 11–19.

Bebbington, P.E., Johnson, S. & Thornicroft, G. (2002). Community mental health care: pitfalls and promises. In N. Sartorius, W. Gaebel, JJ. López-Ibor & M. Maj (Eds.), *Psychiatry in society*. Chichester, UK, Wiley.

Beck, A.T. & Steer, R.A. (1987). *The BDI manual*. San Antonio, TX: The Psychological Corporation.

Bell, V., Ellis, H., & Halligan, P.W. (2006). *The Cardiff Anomalous Perception Scale* (CAPS). A new validated measure of anomalous perceptual experience. Schizophrenia Bulletin, 32, 366–377.

Bentall, R.P. (1990a). The syndromes and symptoms of psychosis: Or why you can't play 'twenty questions' with the concept of schizophrenia and hope to win. In R.P. Bentall (Ed.), *Reconstructing schizophrenia*. Florence, KY: Taylor & Frances/Routledge.

Bentall, R.P. (1990b). The illusion of reality: A review and integration of psychological research on hallucinations. *Psychological Bulletin*, 107(1), 82–95.

Bentall, R.P. (1999). Commentary on Garety & Freeman III: Three psychological investigators and an elephant. *British Journal of Clinical Psychology*, 38, 323–327.

Bentall, R.P., Corcoran, R., Howard, R., Blackwood, N. & Kinderman, P. (2001). Persecutory delusions: A review and theoretical integration. *Clinical Psychology Review*, 21, 1143–1192.

Berrios, G.E. (1996). *The history of mental symptoms: Descriptive psychopathology since the nineteenth century*. Cambridge: Cambridge University Press.

Birchwood, M., Meaden, A., Trower, P., Gilbert, P. & Plaistow, J. (2000). The power and omnipotence of voices: Subordination and entrapment by voices and significant others. *Psychological Medicine*, 30, 337–344.

Birchwood, M. & Smith, J. (1987). Schizophrenia in the family. In J. Orford (Ed.), *Coping with disorder in the family* (pp. 7–36). London: Croom-Helm.

Birchwood, M., Smith, J., Cochrane, R., Wetton, S. & Copestake, S. (1990). The Social Functioning Scale. The development and validation of a new scale of social adjustment for use in family intervention programmes with schizophrenic patients. *British Journal of Psychiatry*, 157, 853–859.

Birchwood M., Smith, J., Macmillan, F., Hogg, B., Prasad, R., Harvey, C. & Bering S. (1989). Predicting relapse in schizophrenia: The development and implementation of an early signs monitoring system using patients and families as observers, a preliminary investigation. *Psychological Medicine*, 19(3), 649–656.

Birchwood, M., Todd, P. & Jackson, C. (1998). Early intervention in psychosis: The critical period hypothesis. *British Journal of Psychiatry*, 172, Suppl. 33, 53–59.

Blakemore, S.J., Sarfati, Y., Bazin, N. & Decety, J. (2003). The detection of intentional contingencies in simple animations in patents with delusions of persecution. *Psychological Medicine*, 33, 1433–1441.

Boyle, M. (1990). *Schizophrenia*: A scientific delusion? London: Routledge.

Brébion, G., Amador, Z., David, A., Malaspina, D., Sharif, Z. & Gorman, J.M. (2000). Positive symptomatology and source-monitoring failure in schizophrenia – an analysis of symptom-specific effects. *Psychiatry Research*, 95, 119–131.

Brenner, H., Roder, V., Hodel, B., Kienzle, N., Reed, D. & Liberman, R. (1994). *Integrated psychological therapy for schizophrenia patients (IPT)*. Goettingen, Germany: Hogrefe & Huber Publishers.

Brett-Jones, J., Garety, P.A. & Hemsley, D. (1987). Measuring delusional experiences: A method and its application. *British Journal of Clinical Psychology*, 26, 257–265.

Brown, G. W., & Rutter, M. (1966). The measurement of family activities and relationships: A methodological study. *Human Relations*, 19(3), 241–263.

Buchanan, A., Reed, A., Wessely, S., Garety, P., Taylor, P., Grubin, D. & Dunn, G. (1993). Acting on delusions. II: The phenomenological correlates of acting on delusions. *British Journal of Psychiatry*, 163, 77–81.

Bunney, W., Hetrick, W., Bunney, B., Patterson, J., Jin, Y., Potkin, S. & Sandman, C. (1999). *Structured Interview for Assessing Perceptual Anomalies (SIAPA). Schizophrenia Bulletin*, 25, 577–592.

Butzlaff, R.L. & Hooley, J.M. (1998). Expressed emotion and psychiatric relapse: A meta-analysis. *Archives of General Psychiatry*, 55(6), 547–552.

Caldwell, C.B. & Gottesman, I.I. (1990). Schizophrenics kill themselves too: A review of risk factors for suicide. *Schizophrenia Bulletin*, 16(4), 571–589.

Cantwell, R., Brewin, J., Glazebrook C. et al. (1999). Prevalence of substance misuse in first episode psychosis. *British Journal of Psychiatry*, 174, 150–153.

Carter, D., Mackinnon, A., Howard, S., Zeegers, T. & Copolov, D.L. (1995). The development and reliability of the Mental Health Research Institute unusual perceptions schedule (MUPS): An instrument to record auditory hallucinatory experience. *Schizophrenia Research*, 16, 157–165.

Chadwick, P. (2003). Two chairs, self-schemata and a person based approach to psychosis. *Behavioural and Cognitive Psychotherapy*, 31, 439–449.

Chadwick, P. & Birchwood, M. (1994). The omnipotence of voices: A cognitive approach to auditory hallucinations. *British Journal of Psychiatry*, 164, 190–201.

Chadwick, P., Birchwood, M. & Trower, P. (1996). *Cognitive therapy for delusions, voices and paranoia*. Chichester, UK: John Wiley & Sons.

Chadwick, P., Lees, S. & Birchwood, M. (2000). The revised Beliefs About Voices Questionnaire (BAVQ-R). *British Journal of Psychiatry*, 177, 229–232.

Clancy, S.A., McNally, R.J., Schacter, D.L. & Lenzenweger, M.R. (2002) Memory distortion in people reporting abduction by aliens. *Journal of Abnormal Psychology*, 111(3), 455–461.

Craig, T.K.J., Garety, P., Power, P., Rahaman, N., Colbert, S., Fornells-Ambrojo, M. & Dunn, G. (2004). The Lambeth Early Onset (LEO) Team: Randomized controlled trial of the effectiveness of specialized care for early psychosis. *British Medical Journal*, 329, 1067–1073.

Cresswell, C.M., Kuipers, L. & Power, M.S. (1992). Social networks and support in long term psychiatric patients. *Psychological Medicine*, 22, 1019–1026.

Culberg, J., Levander, S., Holmqvist, R. et al. (2002). One year outcome in first episode psychosis patients in the Swedish Parachute Study. *Acta Psychiatrica Scandinavica*, 106, 276–285.

Curtis, D. (2003). Innovations in service provision need evidence not opinion. *British Medical Journal*, 327, 322–335.

David, A.S. (1990). Insight to psychosis. *British Journal of Psychiatry*, 156, 798–808.

Department of Health (DoH) (2001). Early intervention in psychosis. In *The mental health policy implementation guide*. London: DoH.

Drake, R.E., Mueser, K.T., Clark, R.E. et al. (1996). The course, treatment and outcome of substance disorder in persons with severe mental illness. *American Journal of Orthopsychiatry*, 66, 42–51.

Dudley, R. E. J., John, C. H., Young, A. W. & Over, D. E. (1997a). Normal and abnormal reasoning in people with delusions. *British Journal of Clinical Psychology*, 36, 243–258.

Dudley, R. E. J., John, C. H., Young, A. W. & Over, D. E. (1997b). The effect of self-referent material on the reasoning of people with delusions. *British Journal of Clinical Psychology*, 36, 575–584.

Eisen, J., Phillips, K., Baer, L., Beer, D., Atala, K. & Rasmussen, S. (1998). The Brown Assessment of Beliefs Scale: Reliability and validity. *American Journal of Psychiatry*, 155, 102–108.

Fadden, G. (1997). Implementation of family interventions in routine clinical practice following staff training programmes: A major cause for concern. *Journal of Mental Health*, 6, 599–612.

Falloon, I.R.H., Boyd, J.L. & McGill, C.W. (1984). *Family care of schizophrenia*. New York: Guilford Press.

Falloon, I. & Talbot, R. (1981). Persistent auditory hallucinations: Coping mechanisms and implications for management. *Psychological Medicine*, 11, 329–339.

Farhall, J. & Gehrke, M. (1997). Coping with hallucinations: Exploring stress and coping framework. *British Journal of Clinical Psychology*, 36, 259–261.

Foulds, G.A. & Bedford, A. (1975). Hierarchy of classes of personal illness. *Psychological Medicine*, 5, 181–192.

Fowler, D., Garety, P. & Kuipers, L. (1995). *Cognitive behavioral psychotherapy: A rationale, theory and practice*. Chichester, UK: John Wiley & Sons.

Freeman, D. & Garety, P.A. (2003). Connecting neurosis and psychosis: The direct influence of emotion on delusions and hallucinations. *Behaviour Research and Therapy*, 41, 923–947.

Freeman, D., Garety, P., Fowler, D., Kuipers, E., Dunn, G., Bebbington, P. & Hadley, C. (1998). The London–East Anglia randomised controlled trial of cognitive-behaviour therapy for psychosis IV: Self esteem and persecutory delusions. *British Journal of Clinical Psychology*, 37, 415–430.

Frith, C.D. (1992). *The cognitive neuropsychology of schizophrenia*. Hove, UK: Lawrence Erlbaum Associates.

Garety, P.A. (1985). Delusions: Problems of definition and measurement. *British Journal of Medical Psychology*, 58, 25–34.

Garety, P.A., Craig, T.K.J., Dunn, G., Fornells-Ambrojo, M., Colbert, S., Rahaman, N., Read, J. & Power, P. (2006). Specialised care for early psychosis: Symptoms, social functioning and patient satisfaction: Randomised controlled trial. *British Journal of Psychiatry*, 188, 37–45.

Garety, P. A., Fowler, D., Kuipers, E., Freeman, D., Dunn, G., Bebbington, P., Hadley, C. & Jones, S. (1997). London–East Anglia randomised controlled trial of cognitive-behavioural therapy for psychosis. II: Predictors of outcome. *British Journal of Psychiatry*, 171, 420–426.

Garety, P.A. & Hemsley, D.R. (1987). Characteristics of delusional experience. *European Archives of Psychiatry and Neurological Science*, 236, 294–298.

Garety, P.A. & Hemsley, D.R. (1994). *Delusions: Investigations into the psychology of delusional reasoning*. Maudsley Monograph. Oxford: Oxford University Press.

Garety, P.A., Kuipers, E., Fowler, D., Freeman, D. & Bebbington, P. (2001). A cognitive model of the positive symptoms of psychosis. *Psychological Medicine*, 31, 189–195.

Geddes, J., Freemantle, N., Harrison, P. & Bebbington, P. for the National Schizophrenia

Guideline Development Group (2000). Atypical antipsychotics in the treatment of schizophrenia: Systematic overview and meta-regression analysis. *British Medical Journal*, 321, 1371–1376.

Gipps, R.G.T. & Fulford, K.W.M. (2004). Understanding the clinical concept of delusion: From an estranged to an engaged epistemology. *International Review of Psychiatry*, 16(3), 225–235.

Goldman, H.H., Skodol, A.E. & Lave, T.R. (1992). Revising axis V for DSM-IV: A review of measures of social functioning. *American Journal of Psychiatry*, 149, 1148–1156.

Gross, G., Huber, G., Klosterkotter, J. & Linz, M. (1987). *Bonner Skala fur die Beurteilung von Basissymptomen*. Berlin: Springer-Verlag.

Haddock, G., McCarron, J., Tarrier, N. & Faragher, E.B. (1999). Scales to measure dimensions of hallucinations and delusions: The psychotic symptom rating scales (PSYRATS). *Psychological Medicine*, 29, 879–889.

Hall, P.L. & Tarrier, N. (2003). The cognitive-behavioural treatment to improve low self-esteem in psychotic patients: A pilot study. *Behaviour Research and Therapy*, 41, 317–332.

Hall, P.L. & Tarrier, N. (2004). Short term durability of a cognitive behavioural intervention in psychosis: Effects from a pilot study. *Behavioural and Cognitive Psychotherapy*, 32, 117–121.

Harrigan, S.M., McGorry, P.D. & Krstev, H. (2003). Does treatment delay in first-episode psychosis really matter? *Psychological Medicine*, 33, 97–110.

Heila, J. & Lonnqvist, J. (2003). The clinical epidemiology of suicide in schizophrenia. In R. Murray et al. (Eds.), *The epidemiology of schizophrenia*. Cambridge: Cambridge University Press.

Hemsley, D.R. (1998). The disruption of the 'sense of self' in schizophrenia: Potential links with disturbances of information processing. *British Journal of Medical Psychology*, 71, 115–124.

Hoult, J., Reynolds, I., Charbonneau-Powis, M., Weekes, P. & Briggs, J. (1983). Psychiatric hospital versus community treatment: The results of a randomized trial. *Australian and New Zealand Journal of Psychiatry*, 101, 160–167.

Hustig, H.H. & Hafner, R.J. (1990). Persistent auditory hallucinations and their relationship to delusions and mood. *Journal of Neurology and Mental Disorders*, 178, 264–267.

Hyde, C. (1989). The Manchester Scale: A standardised psychiatric assessment for rating chronic psychotic patients. *British Journal of Psychiatry*, 155, Suppl. 7, 45–47.

Jacobsson, L., Von Knorring, L., Mattsson, B., Perris, C., Edenius, B., Kettner, B., Magnusson, K. & Villemoes, P. (1978). The comprehensive psychopathological rating scale – CPRS – inpatients with schizophrenic symptoms. *Acta Psychiatrica Scandinavica*, (Suppl) 271, 39–44.

Johannessen, J. O., McGlashan, T. H., Larsen, T. K., et al. (2001). Early detection strategies for untreated first-episode psychosis. *Schizophrenia Research*, 51, 39–46.

Johns, L.C., Nazroo, J.Y., Bebbington, P. & Kuipers, E. (2002). Occurrence of hallucinatory experiences in a community sample and ethnic variations. *British Journal of Psychiatry*, 180, 174–178.

Johnson, S., Nolan, F., Hoult J. et al. (2005a). Outcomes of crises before and after introduction of a crisis resolution team. *British Journal of Psychiatry*, 187(1), 68–75.

Johnson, S., Nolan, F., Pilling, S., Sandor, A., Hoult, J., McKenzie, N., White, I.R., Thompson, M. & Bebbington, P.E. (2005b). Randomised controlled trial of care by a crisis resolution team: The North Islington Crisis Study. *British Medical Journal*, 331, 599–602.

Jorgensen, P., Nordentoft, M., Abel, M. et al. (2000). Early detection and assertive community treatment of young psychotics: the Opus Study – Rationale and design of the trial. *Social Psychiatry and Psychiatric Epidemiology*, 35, 283–287.

Kapur, S. (2003). Psychosis as a state of aberrant salience: A framework linking biology, phenomenology, and pharmacology in schizophrenia. *American Journal of Psychiatry*, 160, 13–23.

Kay, S., Fiszbein, A. & Opler, L. (1987). The Positive and Negative Syndrome Scale (PANSS) for Schizophrenia. *Schizophrenia Bulletin*, 13, 261–275.

Kay, S., Opler, L. Lindenmayer, J-P (1988). Reliability and validity of the Positive and Negative Syndrome Scale for schizophrenics. *Psychiatry Research*, 23, 99–110.

Kay, S., Opler, L. Lindenmayer, J-P (1989). The Positive and Negative Syndrome Scale (PANSS): Rationale and Standardisation. *British Journal of Psychiatry*, 155, Suppl. 7, 59–65.

Killaspy, H., King, M., Bebbington, P.E., Blizard, R., Johnson, I.S., McCrone, P., Nolan, F. & Pilling, S. (2006). The REACT study: A randomised evaluation of assertive community treatment in North London. *British Medical Journal*, online.

Kinderman, P. & Bentall, R.P. (2000). Self-discrepancies and causal attributions: Studies of hypothesized relationships. *British Journal of Clinical Psychology*, 39(3), 255–273.

Kinderman, P. & Cooke, A. (2000). *Understanding mental illness: Recent advances in understanding mental illness and psychotic experiences*. A report by the BPS. Leicester: British Psychological Society.

Kingdon, D.G. & Turkington, D. (1991). *Cognitive-behavioral therapy of schizophrenia*. Hove, UK: Lawrence Erlbaum Associates.

Klosterkotter, J., Hellmich, M., Steinmeyer, E.M. & Schultze-Lutter, F. (2001). Diagnosing schizophrenia in the initial prodromal phase. *Archives of General Psychiatry*, 58, 158–164.

Kluiter, H. (1997). In-patient treatment and care arrangements to replace it or avoid it – searching for an evidence based balance. *Current Opinions in Psychiatry*, 10, 160–167.

Krawiecka, M., Goldberg, D. & Vaughan, M. (1977). A Standardised Psychiatric Assessment Scale for Rating Chronic Psychotic Patients. *Acta Psychiatrica Scandinavica*, 55, 299–308.

Kuipers, E. (2000). Psychological treatment of psychosis. Evidence based but unavailable? *Psychiatric Rehabilitation Skills*, 4, 249–258.

Kuipers, E., Fowler, D., Garety, P., Chisholm, D., Freeman, D., Dunn, G., Bebbington, P. & Hadley, C. (1998). The London–East Anglia randomised controlled trial of cognitive behaviour therapy for psychosis III: Follow up and economic evaluation at 18 months. *British Journal of Psychiatry*, 173, 69–74.

Kuipers, E., Holloway, F., Rabe-Hesketh, S. & Tennakoon, L. (2004) An RCT of early intervention in psychosis: Croydon Outreach and Assertive Support Team (COAST). *Social Psychiatry and Psychiatric Epidemiology*, 39, 358–363.

Kuipers, E., Leff, J. & Lam, D. (1992). *Family work for schizophrenia: A practical guide*. London: Gaskell Press. (2nd Edition, 2002).

Kuipers, E. & Moore, E. (1995). Expressed emotion and staff client relationships. Implications for the community care of the severely mental ill. *International Journal of Mental Health*, 24(3), 13–26.

Kwapil, T.R., Chapman, L.J. & Chapman, J. (1999). Validity and usefulness of the Wisconsin Manual for Assessing Psychotic-like Experiences. *Schizophrenia Bulletin*, 25, 363–375.

Lefley, H.P. (1989). Family burden and family stigma in major mental illness. *American Psychologist*, 44, 556–560.

Lefley, H.P. (2003). Changing caregiving needs as persons with schizophrenia grow older. In C.I. Cohen (Ed.), *Schizophrenia into later life: Treatment, research and policy* (pp. 251–268). Washington, DC: American Psychiatric Publishing.

Lieberman, J., Koreen, A., Chakos, M. et al. (1996). Factors influencing treatment response and outcome of first-episode schizophrenia: Implications for understanding the pathophysiology of schizophrenia. *Journal of Clinical Psychiatry*, Suppl. 9, 5–9.

Maguire, P.K., Shah, G.M. & Murray, R.M. (1993). Increased blood flow in Broca's area during auditory hallucinations in schizophrenia. *Lancet*, 342 (8873), 703–706.

Malla, A.K., Norman, R.M.G., Manchanda, R., McLean, T.S., Harricharan, R., Cortese, L., Townsend, L.A. & Scholten, D.J. (2002). Status of patients with first-episode psychosis after one year of phase-specific community-oriented treatment. *American Psychiatric Association*, 58 (4), 458–463.

Marengo, J., Harrow, M., Lanin-Kettering, I. & Wilson, A. (1986). Comprehensive index of thought disorder. *Schizophrenia Bulletin*, 12, 497–509.

Marriott, A., Donaldson, C., Tarrier, N. & Burns, A. (2000). Effectiveness of cognitive-behavioural family intervention in reducing the burden of care in carers of patients with Alzheimer's disease. *British Journal of Psychiatry*, 176, 557–562.

Marshall, M. & Creed, F (2000). Assertive community treatment – is it the future of community care in the UK? *International Review of Psychiatry*, 12, 191–196.

Marshall, M. & Lockwood, A. (2000). *Assertive community treatment for severe mental disorders*. Cochrane Library: Schizophrenia Group.

Marx, A., Stein, L. & Test, M. (1973). Extrahospital management of severe mental illness. *Archives of General Psychiatry*, 29, 505–511.

May, R. (2000). Routes to recovery from psychosis: The roots of a clinical psychologist. *Clinical Psychology Forum*, 146, 6–10.

McGlashan, T. & Johannessen, J. (1996). Early detection and intervention with schizophrenia: Rationale. *Schizophrenia Bulletin*, 22, 201–222.

McGlashan, T., Zipursky, R., Perkins, D. et al. (2003). The PRIME North American randomized double-blind clinical trial of olanzepine versus placebo in patients at risk of being prodromally symptomatic for schizophrenia. I: Study rationale and design. *Schizophrenia Research*, 61, 7–18.

McGorry, P. (1998). Preventive strategies in early psychosis: Verging on reality. *British Journal of Psychiatry*, 172 (Suppl. 33), 1–2.

McGorry, P., Edwards, J., Mihalopoulos, C. et al. (1996). EPPIC: An evolving system of early detection and optimal management. *Schizophrenia Bulletin*, 22, 305–326.

McGorry, P. & Yung, A. (2003). Early intervention in psychosis: An overdue reform. *Australian and New Zealand Journal of Psychiatry*, 37, 393–398.

McGorry, P., Yung A., Phillips L. et al. (2002). Randomized controlled trial of interventions designed to reduce the risk of progression to first-episode psychosis in a clinical sample with subthreshold symptoms. *Archives of General Psychiatry*, 59, 921–928.

Melzer, D., Hale, A., Malik, S.J., Hogman, G.A. & Wood, S. (1991). Community care for patients with schizophrenia one year after hospital discharge. *British Medical Journal*, 303, 1023–1026.

Miller, T.J., McGlashan, T.H., Rosen, J.L., Somjee, L., Markovich, P.J., Stein, K. & Woods, S.W. (2002). Prospective diagnosis of the initial prodrome for schizophrenia based on the Structured Interview for Prodromal Syndromes: Preliminary evidence of interrater reliability and predictive validity. *American Journal of Psychiatry*, 159, 863–865.

Miller, T.J., McGlashan, T.H., Woods, S.W., Stein, K., Driesen, N., Corcoran, C.M., Hoffman, R. & Davidson, L. (1999). Symptom assessment in schizophrenic prodromal states. *Psychiatric Quarterly*, 70, 273–287.

Mino, Y., Inoue, S., Tanaka, S. & Tsuda, T. (1997). Expressed emotion among families and course of schizophrenia in Japan: A 2-year cohort study. *Schizophrenia Research*, 24, 333–339.

Moore, E. & Kuipers, E. (1999.) The measurement of EE: The use of short speech samples. *British Journal of Clinical Psychology*, 38, 345–355.

Moore, E., Yates, M., Mallindine, C., Ryan, S., Jackson, S., Chinnon, N., Kuipers, E. & Hammond, S. (2002). Expressed emotion in relationships between staff and patients in forensic services: Changes in relationship status at 12 month follow-up. *Legal and Criminological Psychology*, 7, 203–218.

Morrison, A., Bentall, R., French, P. et al. (2002). Randomised controlled trial of early detection and cognitive therapy for preventing transition to psychosis in high-risk individuals: Study design and interim analysis of transition rate and psychological risk factors. *British Journal of Psychiatry*, 181, 78s.

Morrison, A., French, P., Walford, L., Lewis, S.W., Kilcommons, A., Green, J., Parker, S. & Bentall, R. (2004). Cognitive therapy for the prevention of psychosis in people at ultra-high risk. *British Journal of Psychiatry*, 185, 291–297.

Morrison, A. & Petersen, T. (2003). Trauma, metacognition and predisposition to hallucinations in non-patients. *Behavioural and Cognitive Psychotherapy*, 31, 235–246.

Mueser, K., Bond, G., Drake, R. & Resnick, S. (1998a). Models of community care for severe mental illness: A review of research on case management. *Schizophrenia Bulletin*, 24, 37–74.

Mueser, K.T., Goodman, L.B.., Trumbetta, S.L., Rosenberg, S.D., Osher F.C., Vidaver, R., Auciello, P. & Foy, D.W. (1998b). Trauma and posttraumatic stress disorder in severe mental illness. *Journal of Consulting and Clinical Psychology*, 66(3): 493–499.

Mueser, K.T., Yarnold, P.R., Levinson, D.F., Singh, H., Bellack, A.S., Kee, K., Morrison, R.L. & Yadalam, K.G. (1990). Prevalence of substance abuse in schizophrenia: Demographic and clinical correlates. *Schizophrenia Bulletin*, 16, 31–56.

National Institute for Clinical Excellence (NICE) (2003). *Schizophrenia: Full national clinical guideline on core interventions in primary and secondary care*. London: Gaskell Press.

Nelson, H. (1997). *Cognitive behavioural therapy with schizophrenia. A Practice Manual*. Thornes Publishers.

Nordentoft, M. (2003). Early detection in psychosis. Abstract for presentation at 2nd Nordic Psychiatry Conference, Reykjavik. *Icelandic Medical Journal*, Suppl. 48, 13.

Osher, F.C. & Drake, R.E. (1996). Reversing a history of unmet needs: Approaches to care for persons with co-occurring addictive and mental disorders. *American Journal of Orthopsychiatry*, 66, 4–11.

Overall, J. & Gorham, D. (1962). The brief psychiatric rating scale. *Psychological Reports*, 10, 799–812.

Pekkala, E. & Merinder, L. (2001). *Psychoeducation for schizophrenia* (Cochrane Review). Oxford: The Cochrane Library, Issue 4.

Pelosi, A. (2003). Is early intervention for psychosis a waste of valuable resources? *British Journal of Psychiatry*, 182, 196–197.

Peters, E.R. (2000). Women and psychosis. In J. Ussher (Ed.), *Women's health: Contemporary international perspectives*. Leicester: BPS Books.

Peters, E.R., Day, S., McKenna, J. & Orbach, G. (1999a). The incidence of delusional ideation in religious and psychotic populations. *British Journal of Clinical Psychology*, 38, 83–96.

Peters, E.R., Joseph, S., Day, S. & Garety, P.A. (2004). Measuring delusional ideation: The 21-item PDI (Peters et al. Delusions Inventory). *Schizophrenia Bulletin*, 30(4), 1005–1022.

Peters, E.R., Joseph, S. & Garety, P.A. (1999b). The assessment of delusions in normal and psychotic populations: Introducing the PDI (Peters et al. Delusions Inventory). *Schizophrenia Bulletin*, 25, 553–576.

Power, P.J.R., Bell, R.J., Mills, R., Herrman-Doig, T., Davern, M., Henry, L., Yuen, H.P., Khademy-Deljo, A. & McGorry, P.D. (2003). Suicide prevention in first episode psychosis: The development of a randomised controlled trial of cognitive therapy for acutely suicidal patients with early psychosis. *Australian and New Zealand Journal of Psychiatry*, 37, 414–420.

Priebe, S., Huxley, P., Knight, S. & Evans, S. (1999). Application and results of the Manchester Short Assessment of Quality of Life (MANSA). *International Journal of Social Psychiatry*, 45, 7–12.

Radomsky, E.D., Haas, G.L., Mann, J.J. & Sweeney, J.A. (1999). Suicidal behavior in patients with schizophrenia and other psychotic disorders. *American Journal of Psychiatry*, 156(10), 1590–1595.

Ramachandran, V.S. & Blakeslee, S. (1998). *Phantoms in the brain: Human nature and the architecture of the mind*. London: Fourth Estate.

Raune, D., Kuipers, E. & Bebbington, P. (2004). EE at first episode psychosis: Investigating a carer appraisal model. *British Journal of Psychiatry*, 184, 321–326.

Romme, M. & Escher, S. (2000). *Making sense of voices. A guide for mental health professionals working with voice-hearers*. London: Mind Publications.

Rooke, O. & Birchwood, M. (1998). Loss, humiliation and entrapment as appraisals of schizophrenic illness: A prospective study of depressed and non-depressed patients. *British Journal of Clinical Psychology*, 37(3), 259–268.

Scazufca, M. & Kuipers, E. (1996). Links between EE and burden of care in relatives of patients with schizophrenia. *British Journal of Psychiatry*, 168, 580–587.

Scazufca, M. & Kuipers, E. (1998). Stability of EE in relatives of those with schizophrenia, and its relationship with burden of care and perception of patients' social function. *Psychological Medicine*, 28, 453–461.

Scott, H., Johnson, S., Menezes, P., Thornicroft, G., Marshall, J., Bindman, J., Bebbington, P. & Kuipers, E. (1998). Substance abuse and risk of aggression and offending among the severely mentally ill. *British Journal of Psychiatry*, 172, 345–350.

Selten, J. P., Sijben, N. E., van den Bosch, R.J., Omloo-Visser, J. & Warmerdam, H. (1993). The subjective experience of negative symptoms: A self-rating scale. *Comprehensive Psychiatry*, 34(3), 192–197.

Shepherd, G. (1978). Social skills training: The generalisation problem – some further data. *Behavioural Research and Therapy*, 16, 297–299.

Slade, P.D. (1972). The effects of systematic desensitization on auditory hallucinations. *Behavioural Research Therapy*, 10, 85–91.

Spencer, E., Birchwood, M. & McGovern, D. (2001). Management of first-episode psychosis. *Advances in Psychiatric Treatment*, 7, 133–140.

Stefanis, N.C., Hanssen, M., Smirnis, N.K., Avramopoulos, D.A., Evdokimidis, I.K., Stefanis, C.N., Verdoux, H. & Van Os, J. (2002). Evidence that three dimensions of psychosis have a distribution in the general population. *Psychological Medicine*, 32, 347–358.

Stein, L. & Test, M. (1980). Alternatives to mental hospital treatment. I. Conceptual model, treatment program, and clinical evaluation. *Archives of General Psychiatry*, 37, 392–393.

Suslow, T., Schonuer, K. & Arolt, V. (2001). Attention training in the cognitive rehabilitation of schizophrenia patients: A review of efficacy studies. *Acta Psychiatrica Scandinavica*, 103, 15–23.

Sutherby, K., Szmukler, G.I., Halpern, A., Alexander, M., Thornicroft, G., Johnson, C. & Wright, S. (1999). A study of 'crisis cards' in a community psychiatric service. *Acta Psychiatrica Scandinavica*, 100(1), 56–61.

Szmuckler, G.T., Burgess, P., Herman, H., Benson, A. & Colusa, S. (1996). Caring for relatives with serious mental illness: The development of the 'Experience of Caregiving Inventory'. *Social Psychiatry and Psychiatric Epidemiology*, 31, 137–148.

Szmuckler, G., Kuipers, E., Joyce, J., Harris, T., Leese, M., Maphosa, W. & Staples, E. (2003). An exploratory randomised controlled trial of a support programme for carers of patients with a psychosis. *Social Psychiatry and Psychiatric Epidemiology*, 38, 411–418.

Taylor, P.J. & Estroff, S.E. (2003). Schizophrenia and violence. In S.R. Hirsch & D Weinberger (Eds.), *Schizophrenia* (Second Edition). Oxford: Blackwell.

Teague, G.B., Bond, G.R. & Drake, R.E. (1998). Program fidelity in assertive community treatment: Development and use of a measure. *American Journal of Orthopsychiatry*, 68, 216–232.

Thornicroft, G., Strathdee, G. & Johnson, S. (1995). The case for catchment areas for mental health services. *Psychiatric Bulletin*, 19, 343–345.

Thornicroft, G., Tansella, M., Becker, T., Knapp, M., Leese, M., Schene, A., Vazquez-Barquero, J.L. & the EPSILON Study Group (2004). The personal impact of schizophrenia in Europe. *Schizophrenia Research*, 69, 125–132.

Trower, P., Birchwood, M., Meaden, A., Byrne, S., Nelson, A. & Ross, K. (2004).

Cognitive therapy for command hallucinations: Randomised controlled trial. *British Journal of Psychiatry* 184(4), 312–320.

Tyrer, P. (1988). Cost-effective or profligate community psychiatry? *British Journal of Psychiatry*, 172, 1–3.

Tyrer, P. (2000). The future of the community mental health team. *International Review of Psychiatry*, 12, 219–225.

Tyrer, P., Coid, J., Simmonds, S., Joseph, P. & Marriott, S. (2000). *Community mental health team management for those with severe mental illnesses and disordered personality*. Oxford: The Cochrane Library.

Ustun, T.B., Rehm, J., Chatterji, S., Saxena, S., Trotter, R., Room, R. & Bickenbach, J. (1999). Multiple-informant ranking of the disabling effects of different health conditions in 14 countries. WHO/NIH Joint Project CAR Study Group. *Lancet*, 354 (9173), 111–115.

Van Os, J., Gilvarry, C., Bale, R., van Horn, E., Tattan, T., White, I. & Murray, R. (1999). A comparison of the utility of dimensional and categorical representations of psychosis. *Psychological Medicine*, 29, 595–606.

Verdoux, H., Husky, M., Tournier, M., Sorbara, F. & Swendsen, J.D. (2003). Social environments and daily life occurrence of psychotic symptoms – an experience sampling test in a non-clinical population. *Social Psychiatry and Psychiatric Epidemiology*, 38, 654–661.

White, R., Bebbington, P., Pearson, J., Johnson, S. & Ellis, D. (2000). The social context of insight in schizophrenia. *Social Psychiatry and Psychiatric Epidemiology*, 35, 500–507.

Willetts, L.E. & Leff, J (1997). Expressed emotion and schizophrenia: The efficacy of a staff training programme. *Journal of Advanced Nursing*, 26, 1125–1133.

Wing, J.K., Cooper, J.E. & Sartorius, N. (1974). *Measurement and classification of psychiatric symptoms*. Cambridge: Cambridge University Press.

World Health Organization (WHO) (1992a). *SCAN: Schedules for Clinical Assessment in Neuropsychiatry*. Geneva: WHO.

World Health Organization (WHO) (1992b). *The ICD-10 classification of mental and behavioural disorders. Clinical descriptions and diagnostic guidelines*. Geneva: WHO.

World Health Organization (WHO) (2001). *World Health Report, mental health; new understandings, new hope*. Geneva: WHO.

Wright, C., Burns, T., James, P., Billings, J., Johnson, S., Muijen, M., Priebe, S., Ryrie, I., Watts, J. & White I. (2003). Assertive outreach teams in London: Models of operation. Pan-London Assertive Outreach Study, Part 1. *British Journal of Psychiatry*, 183, 132–138.

Wykes, T. (1994). Predicting symptomatic and behavioural outcomes of community care. *British Journal of Psychiatry*, 165, 486–492.

Wykes, T. & Reeder, C. (2005). Cognitive remediation therapy for schizophrenia. Theory and practice. Hove, UK/New York: Routledge (Taylor & Francis Group).

Wykes, T., Reeder, C., Corner, J., Williams, C. & Everitt, B. (1999). The effects of neurocognitive remediation on executive processing in patients with schizophrenia. *Schizophrenia Bulletin*, 25(2) 291–307.

Wykes, T. & Sturt, E. (1986). The measurement of social behaviour in psychiatric patients: An assessment of the reliability and validity of the SBS schedule. *British Journal of Psychiatry*, 148, 1–11.

Wykes, T. & Van Der Gaag, M. (2001). Is it time to develop a new cognitive therapy for psychosis – cognitive remediation therapy (CRT)? *Clinical Psychology Review*, 21, 1227–1256.

Young, J. (1990). *Cognitive therapy for personality disorder*. Sarasota, FL: Professional Resource Exchange.

Yung, A. R., Organ, B. A. & Harris, M. G. (2003). Management of early psychosis in a generic adult mental health service. *Australian and New Zealand Journal of Psychiatry*, 37, 429–436.

Yung, A.R., Yuen, H.P., McGorry, P.D. et al. (2005). Mapping the onset of psychosis – the Comprehensive Assessment of At Risk Mental States. *The Australian and New Zealand Journal of Psychiatry*, 39(11–12), 964–971.

Chapter 22

Borderline personality disorder

Janice R. Kuo, Kathryn E. Korslund and Marsha M. Linehan

CASE EXAMPLE

Jamie was a thirty-three-year-old single, Caucasian female living in a suburban area. Her father contacted the therapist saying that Jamie's previous therapist did not feel qualified to treat her for her parasuicidal behaviour (i.e. deliberate self-harm intended to cause acute injury with or without intent to die) and that this therapist was terrified Jamie would kill herself. Jamie was a college graduate and, at the beginning of treatment, was working in advertising. At age sixteen, she was diagnosed with major depression with suicidal ideation and at age twenty-one she was hospitalized for a suicide attempt and continuing suicide ideation. A year prior to receiving treatment with us, Jamie was hospitalized for twelve weeks. Most of her friends were no longer interested in friendship after that. At the start of treatment, Jamie was cutting herself at least once weekly. At her first session she reported that she was 'addicted' to cutting herself, saying that she enjoyed watching the blood drops as she cut. At the start of treatment, Jamie had a history of three suicide attempts (two overdoses, one attempt to stab herself to death), and multiple instances of self-cutting and infliction of burns. Jamie met criteria for a DSM-IV diagnosis of borderline personality disorder (BPD) (meeting eight out of the nine diagnostic criteria), obsessive-compulsive disorder, panic disorder with agoraphobia and major depression. Her panic attacks were particularly distressing to her, as she invariably sobbed uncontrollably during each panic episode. She felt humiliated by the sobbing, running out of groups whenever she would start to cry or felt like crying. Ordinarily, whenever a panic attack started Jamie would call one of her parents for coaching and soothing. Not infrequently, one of them would go and pick her up or, if she were at her own apartment, would go over to her apartment to help calm her down. Her mother's response vacillated between giving her over-simplistic suggestions (just smile) to lying down on the bed with her and handing her tissues. At the start of treatment, Jamie had also just broken up with her former fiancé and boyfriend of four years and complained that she was always attracted to the wrong men.

Jamie is a client who met criteria for borderline personality disorder (BPD) and was treated by the third author with dialectical behaviour therapy (DBT) in the Behavioral Research and Therapy Clinics at the University of Washington. Jamie is typical of BPD clients coming into treatment with multiple diagnoses and a high number of suicidal behaviours. The case example follows Jamie through one year of treatment and highlights the basic structure, modes, and strategies utilized in standard DBT. Readers new to DBT may not initially understand the rationale and strategies illustrated in the case. The remainder of the chapter however, will describe DBT in detail and refer to the case example to facilitate understanding of the treatment and ultimately provide the reader with a comprehensive orientation to DBT.

CLINICAL FEATURES OF BORDERLINE PERSONALITY DISORDER

BPD is a life-threatening disorder characterized by severe cognitive, behavioural and emotional dysregulation. Although the prevalence of BPD in the general population is between 0.2% and 1.8% (Linehan, 1993a), up to 40% of high utilizers of inpatient mental health care services are diagnosed with BPD (Geller, 1986; Linehan, 1993a). The implications of these statistics are compelling in view of the extremely high lifetime prevalence of self-injurious acts (up to 75%) (Clarkin et al., 1983) and completed suicide (approximately 10%; Frances et al., 1986; McGlashan, 1986; Paris, 2003; Paris et al., 1987). Furthermore, research has shown that participants meeting all nine criteria of BPD have a suicide rate of 33% (Stone et al., 1987). When the DSM-III was developed in 1980, BPD included an eight-item criteria set, with one or two items in each of the following domains: affect instability, impulsive actions, unstable interpersonal relationships, psychotic-like cognitions, social maladjustment, and unstable identity (Skodol et al., 2002b). More recent modifications to the criteria (seen in the DSM-IV; American Psychological Association (APA), 1994) involved changing the 'unstable identity' criterion to capture instability of self-image, and adding a ninth criterion: 'transient, stress-related severe dissociative symptoms or paranoid ideation'. Diagnostic characteristics of BPD as outlined in DSM-IV (APA, 1994, 2000) and ICD-10 (WHO, 1992) are presented in Table 22.1.

AETIOLOGY

Biological factors

Although not well understood, the aetiology of BPD probably includes biological dysfunctions as well as environmental factors. Biological factors have not been definitively identified, although a growing body of research has found strong associations between neurochemical factors and some of the criterion behaviours for BPD. For example, impulsive aggression has been found to be associated with reduced serotonergic activity (Coccaro et al., 1989; Siever & Trestman 1993) and some research has demonstrated a link between affective instability and noradrenergic activity (Skodol et al., 2002c). A relationship between increased dopaminergic activity and psychotic symptoms in personality disorder individuals have also been identified, suggesting that hyperactive dopamine activity may contribute to the paranoid thinking experienced in this group (Siever et al., 1991).

Structural and physiological aberrations and their correlation with emotion dysregulation have also been identified. There is substantial neuroimaging research indicating that the amygdala mediates emotional responses (Irwin, Davidson, Lowe, Mock, Sorenson & Turski, 1996; Morris, et al., 1996) and studies have found amygdala hyperreactivity in individuals with BPD (Herpertz et al., 2001). Furthermore, structural and functional disturbances of the prefrontal cortex (De la Fuente et al., 1997; Goyer, et al., 1994) and reduction in frontal and orbitofrontal lobe volumes (Lyoo et al., 1998; Tebartz et al., 2003) have been documented in individuals with BPD. These disturbances indicate that a weakening of prefrontal inhibitory control may contribute to the hyperactivity in the amygdala.

More recently, psychophysiological research has suggested that reduced basal parasympathetic activity (termed 'vagal tone') may be a marker of trait-like emotional sensitivity (Beauchaine, 2001; Porges et al., 1994). Research has indicated that various disorders of emotion dysregulation (e.g. generalized anxiety disorder (GAD), panic disorder, depression) including BPD, are characterized by attenuated basal vagal tone (Beauchaine, 2001; Kuo et al., 2003).

Environmental factors

A number of environmental factors have also been proposed as important in the development of BPD. Linehan's (1993a) Biosocial Theory states that the criterion behaviours for BPD represent a pervasive dysfunction of the

Table 22.1 Diagnostic criteria for borderline personality disorder

DSM-IV-TR	*ICD-10*
A pervasive pattern of instability of interpersonal relationships, self-image, and affects, and marked impulsivity beginning by early adulthood and present in a variety of contexts, as indicated by five (or more) of the following: 1. Frantic efforts to avoid real or imagined abandonment. **Note:** Do not include suicidal or self-mutilating behaviour covered in criterion 5 2. A pattern of unstable and intense interpersonal relationships characterized by alternating between extremes of idealization and devaluation 3. Identity disturbance: markedly and persistently unstable self-image or sense of self 4. Impulsivity in at least two areas that are potentially self-damaging (e.g. spending, sex, substance abuse, reckless driving, binge eating) **Note:** Do not include suicidal or self-mutilating behaviour covered in criterion 5 5. Recurrent suicidal behaviour, gestures, threats or self-mutilating behaviour 6. Affective instability due to a marked reactivity of mood (e.g. intense episodic dysphoria, irritability, or anxiety usually lasting a few hours and only rarely more than a few days) 7. Chronic feelings of emptiness 8. Inappropriate, intense anger or difficulty controlling anger (e.g. frequent displays of temper, constant anger, recurrent physical fights) 9. Transient, stress-related paranoid ideation or severe dissociative symptoms	**Emotionally unstable personality disorder, borderline type** Several of the characteristics of emotional instability are present; in addition, the patient's own self-image, aims and internal preferences (including sexual) are often unclear or disturbed. There are usually chronic feelings of emptiness. A liability to become involved in intense and unstable relationships may cause repeated emotional crises and may be associated with excessive efforts to avoid abandonment and a series of suicidal threats or acts of self-harm (although these may occur without obvious precipitants)

Note: Adapted from DSM-IV-TR (APA, 2000) and ICD-10 (WHO, 1992).

emotion regulation system, caused jointly by biological vulnerability to high emotionality and an invalidating environment. According to Linehan (1993a), the invalidating environment: (1) chronically and inadvertently negates, rejects or dismisses an individual's behaviour and emotional expression; (2) punishes emotional displays and intermittently reinforces emotional escalation; and (3) over-simplifies ease of problem solving and meeting goals.

Table 22.2 Structured interviews for borderline personality disorder

Structured interview	*Reference*
Diagnostic Interview for Borderlines (DIB)	Gunderson, Kolb & Austin, 1981
Diagnostic Interview for DSM-IV Personality Disorders (DIPD-IV)	Zanarini, Frankenburg, Chauncey & Gunderson, 1987
Structured Clinical Interview for DSM-IV Axis II Personality Disorders (SCID-II)	First, Spitzer, Gibbon & Williams, 1997
International Personality Disorder Examination (IPDE)	Loranger et al., 1994
Structured Interview for DSM-IV Personality (SIDP-IV)	Pfohl, Blum & Zimmerman, 1997
Personality Disorder Interview-IV (PDI-IV)	Widiger, Mangine, Corbitt, Ellis & Thomas, 1995
Zanarini Rating Scale for Borderline Personality Disorder (ZAN-BPD)	Zanarini, 2003

A substantial amount of research has found evidence for such an environment, with a high percentage of individuals with BPD reporting a number of adverse childhood events. Experiences of neglect, physical and childhood abuse are reported by a high percentage of individuals with BPD (Links et al., 1988; Zanarini et al., 1989; Zanarini et al., 1997). Of these events, childhood sexual abuse appears to be the most prominent, being reported by 40–71% of inpatients with BPD (Zanarini et al., 1989, 1997). Unfortunately, there is very little prospective research and the retrospective data is unreliable.

Genetic influence

The genetic factors underlying BPD have only recently begun to be investigated. Several studies have provided evidence of a familial component of BPD (Loranger, Oldham & Tulis, 1982; Zanarini et al., 1988) and one twin study (Torgerson et al., 2000) has investigated the concordance of 'definite' BPD (i.e. the required number of criteria were fulfilled) and 'broad' BPD (i.e. one or two short of meeting full criteria). In the monozygotic pairs, the concordance was 35% and 38% for definite and broad BPD, respectively, and in the dizygotic pairs, the concordance was 7% and 11% for definite and broad BPD, respectively. These data provide preliminary evidence for a potential genetic component underlying BPD. Recently, four factors of emotion dysregulation on personality disorder traits have been identified: emotion dysregulation, unstable cognitive functioning, unstable self, and unstable interpersonal relationships. These factors reflect many of BPD criteria, and genetic investigators estimate heritability of the group of characteristics at 47% (Skodol et al., 2002b, 2002c).

COURSE OF BPD

The data on the course of BPD and its chronicity is mixed. Recent research has suggested that the onset of BPD typically is in late childhood (Zanarini et al., 2001). Two large-scale studies have reported that remission of criterion behaviours is common. The larger of these followed the natural course of BPD and found that approximately 75% of individuals with BPD who were hospitalized at the beginning of the study remitted at the end of a six-year follow-up (Zanarini et al., 2003a). However, other studies consistently indicate that the diagnosis of BPD is chronic, although the number of individuals who continue to meet diagnostic criteria slowly decreases over the life span. Two to three years after index assessment, 60 to 70% of individuals with BPD continue to meet criteria and little change in level of functioning over two to five years following an index assessment is common (Barasch et al., 1985; Dahl, 1986; Richman & Charles, 1976). Four to seven years after index assessment, 57 to 67% continue to meet criteria (Kullgren, 1992; Pope et al., 1983) and an average of fifteen years after index assessment, 25 to 44% continue to meet criteria (McGlashan, 1986; Paris et al., 1987).

COMORBIDITY

BPD is commonly comorbid with a variety of DSM-IV axis I disorders, most notably substance abuse, panic disorder (PD), eating disorders, post-traumatic stress disorder (PTSD) and major depressive disorder (MDD; for a review, see Skodol et al., 2002b). Within substance abuse populations, comorbidity with BPD ranges from 5.2% to 32% (Brooner et al., 1997; Weiss, et al., 1993) and 39.2% of individuals with BPD met criteria for at least one mood disorder (31.3% major depression, 16% dysthymia, 9.2 bipolar I, and 4.1% bipolar II). Among individuals with BPD selected for current parasuicide (i.e. either a recent suicide attempt or a recent intentional self-injury), up to 75% met criteria for MDD, 51.1% met criteria for PTSD, and 40.2% met criteria for panic disorder (Linehan, Comtois, Murray-George, Whiteside & Levensky, 2002).

BPD has also demonstrated high comorbidity rates with other axis II personality disorders. Grilo, Anez and McGlashen (2002) examined comorbidity rates of BPD with other PD. Of one hundred outpatients assessed, the thirty-four individuals with BPD had significantly higher rates of personality disorders than the sixty-six individuals without BPD. The BPD group was found to have significantly higher comorbidity rates for antisocial, avoidant and depressive PD. Linehan et al. (2002) found that, in a BPD sample with current parasuicide, 20.8% met criteria for avoidant personality disorder, 8.9% met criteria for antisocial personality disorder and 7.9% met criteria for obsessive-compulsive personality disorder.

TREATMENT RESPONSE

It is estimated that 97% of individuals with BPD seeking treatment in the US receive outpatient treatment from approximately six therapists each (Perry et al., 1990; Skodol et al., 1983). Of this group, 95% receive individual therapy, 56% receive group therapy, 42% receive family or couples therapy, 37% are in day treatment, 2% in psychiatric hospitalization and 24% are treated in a halfway house. Several authors have suggested that the outpatient services available for this group do not match well with their needs, which may account for poor treatment compliance and subsequent hospitalization (Rascati, 1990; Swigar et al., 1991). Furthermore, research has indicated that treatment as it is usually administered in the community (treatment-as-usual; TAU) may have less than promising results (Skodol et al., 2002a). Even among individuals with BPD who receive high amounts of psychosocial treatments and/or pharmacotherapy, there is likely to be severe impairment in global satisfaction, social adjustment and overall functioning (Skodol et al., 2002a). However, recent developments have seen the emergence of important advancements in BPD treatment.

Empirically supported treatments

Currently, two treatments for BPD have demonstrated empirical support. Of these two, dialectical behaviour therapy (DBT) is the most researched and best supported treatment. DBT is based on both a motivational and capability deficit model of BPD, proposing that: (1) individuals with BPD lack important interpersonal, self-regulation (e.g. emotion regulation) and distress tolerance skills; and (2) personal and environmental factors both inhibit the use of coping strategies the individual does have, and reinforces dysfunctional behaviours. To date, seven randomized controlled trials (RCTs) and six non-randomised controlled studies have supported the efficacy of DBT as compared with a variety of control conditions (for a review, see Lieb et al., 2004). In the first of these RCTs, DBT subjects were significantly less likely to engage in parasuicidal behaviour during the treatment year, reported fewer episodes of parasuicidal behaviour at each assessment point, had less medically severe parasuicidal behaviour over the year, were less likely to drop out of treatment and improved more on scores of global as well as social adjustment (Linehan et al., 1991). In general, suicidal behaviours reduced significantly in all seven trials and were significantly lower in DBT than in an array of control conditions in five of the seven trials.

The second treatment that has demonstrated to be efficacious in BPD is Bateman and Fonagy's psychodynamic long-term partial hospitalization programme (Bateman & Fonagy, 1999, 2001). This treatment shares some features with DBT, in that both treatments are highly structured, multi-modal approaches that allow frequent accessibility with therapists, directly target behaviours that interfere with therapy, emphasize current emotional experiences, and balance the use of validation and change. The results suggest that individuals in the partial hospital condition had a decrease in suicidal and self-injurious acts, reduced inpatient days and better social and interpersonal function. However, it should be noted that this approach has not yet been replicated in a second trial.

Cognitive therapy

Recently, researchers have begun to develop and apply cognitive treatment approaches to BPD. Of these approaches, Beck's treatment is focused on restructuring cognitions and developing more adaptive world views in individuals with BPD (Freeman & Davis, 2003); however, the development of this treatment is still in its infancy and data on its efficacy have not been published. Young (1983, 1990; Young & Swift, 1988) and Pretzer (1990) address some of the difficulties encountered when applying the standard cognitive approach to the BPD population and therefore modified the traditional techniques. Young has developed a schema-based cognitive theory proposing that early maladaptive schemas result in maladaptive behaviours, and that such maladaptive behaviours serve to reinforce and strengthen the pathogenic schemata. Young's therapy approach (schema-therapy) focuses on challenging and modifying these early maladaptive schemas. Pretzer's approach has modified standard cognitive therapy to target difficulties often encountered in clients with BPD, such as establishing a collaborative therapeutic relationship, maintaining a focused treatment and improving homework compliance. To date, there are no published data on the efficacy of Beck's, Young's or Pretzer's approaches.

Family therapy

There is one comprehensive family therapy approach to BPD that involves components of systems, dynamic and other theories and practices (Glick et al., 1995). Glick et al.'s (1995) approach involves working collaboratively with the family to develop a therapeutic alliance ('joining'), and to provide information on the symptoms, diagnosis, treatment and prognosis of BPD (Glick et al., 1995). BPD symptoms are reframed in terms of family dynamics, emphasizing the positive aspects of the family's motivation to help the 'identified patient'. Similar to psychodynamic approaches (Gunderson, 1989; Kernberg, 1984), this treatment focuses on therapeutic transference and attends to familial over-involvement and abuse/neglect. Currently, there are no data investigating the efficacy of this treatment approach.

Pharmacotherapy

Individuals with BPD frequently utilize pharmacotherapy. Although there is no identified 'BPD drug', studies have indicated that several psychotropic agents may be associated with improved global functioning, depression, psychotic symptoms and aggressive behaviours (Dimeff et al., 1999; Gardner & Cowdry, 1989). Results from placebo-controlled trials found that pharmacotherapy is effective in BPD in targeting its specific dimensions such as cognitive-perceptual symptoms, emotion dysregulation or impulsive-behavioural dyscontrol (Schmahl & Bohus, 2001; Soloff, 2000). Specifically, low-dose neuroleptics such as haloperidol (although with mixed results) (Soloff, 2000; Soloff et al., 1989), clozapine (Chengapa et al., 1999; Frankenburg & Zanarini, 1993), risperidone (Rocca et al., 2002), and olanzapine (Schulz et al., 1999) have been shown to be effective in decreasing suspiciousness, paranoid ideation, ideas of reference, stress-related hallucinations, anxiety, impulsivity and rejection sensitivity. Selective serotonin reuptake inhibitors (SSRIs) have been shown to be effective in decreasing rapid mood shifts, anger, and anxiety (Coccaro & Kavoussi, 1997; Markovitz, 1995; Rinne et al., 2002). Although tricyclic antidepressants (TCAs) and monoamine oxidase inhibitors (MAOIs) have been shown to be moderately effective (TCAs even showing evidence of detrimental effects; Moleman et al., 1999), the potential of over-dose and difficulties in management of these medications have led clinicians to choose SSRIs as the first medication of choice. Recent findings with omega-3 fatty acids have been particularly compelling. Zanarini and Frankenburg (2003) found that this treatment was comparable to mood stabilizers and achieved lower attrition rates due to the low side effects.

A note of caution is needed when considering the use of pharmacotherapy for the BPD population. Individuals meeting criteria for BPD are generally non-compliant with treatment regimens, may experience unexpected unwanted effects and may overdose on prescribed drugs. Therefore, careful monitoring of pharmacotherapy is necessary in this group. For those interested in principles of prescribing, Soloff (2000) presents a BPD medication algorithm based on a behaviourally-specific approach. However, currently there are no data supporting the effectiveness of this algorithm.

ASSESSMENT OF BPD

The need to assess BPD in clinical care settings cannot be over-emphasized. It is often the case that treatment providers deal with clinical cases that are progressively difficult to treat, only to find later that their clients meet criteria for BPD. The various ways to assess BPD vary in ease of administration, diagnostic validity and treatment utility. A number of both BPD and general personality questionnaires can be used for initial diagnostic screening. We suggest beginning with self-report screening measures and, if the client meets criteria, a structured interview should follow. However, even reliable self-report screening measures are high in sensitivity but lack specificity (Hyler, Skodol, Kellman, Oldham & Rosnick, 1990). Therefore, for a valid diagnosis, we recommend the practitioner follow the screen with a diagnostic interview. A recently developed self-report questionnaire, the McLean Screening Instrument of BPD (MSI-BPD) (Zanarini et al., 2003b), has been shown to have good sensitivity and specificity for identifying individuals meeting criteria for BPD.

Of the diagnostic interviews, it cannot be determined which most validly assesses the BPD diagnosis (Kaye & Shea, 2000). See Table 22.2 for the most commonly used interviews.

TREATMENT OF BPD WITH DIALECTICAL BEHAVIOUR THERAPY

Rationale for dialectical behaviour therapy

The biosocial theory

Dialectical behaviour therapy (DBT) is a behavioural approach to treating BPD based on a dialectical philosophy that integrates traditional, cognitive-behavioural change-based interventions and more acceptance-based approaches derived primarily from Zen practice. Specific treatment interventions in DBT are guided by a theory of BPD that incorporates the dialectical transaction over time between biological and environmental factors (Linehan, 1993a).

Linehan's (1993a) biosocial theory posits that BPD is primarily a dysfunction of the emotion regulation system. Specifically, BPD is the consequence of a biological vulnerability to high emotionality paired with an inability to modulate emotions. As a result, individuals with BPD experience extreme intense emotional reactions but lack the skills necessary to regulate these reactions. Furthermore, individuals 'adopt' the invalidating environment, learning to invalidate or reject their own private experiences, search the environment for cues on how to respond and oscillate between extreme emotional expression and inhibition.

Linehan's theory proposes that BPD criterion behaviours are either a direct outcome of, or function to modulate unwanted emotional experiences (Linehan, 1993a; McMain et al., 2001). As illustrated in Figure 22.1, Linehan defines emotional vulnerability as high sensitivity (quick responses) and reactivity (strong responses) to emotional stimuli, and a delayed return to emotional baseline. The sequelae of this high emotionality leaves individuals with the inability to regulate physiological arousal, and they keep attention fixed on emotional stimuli, distort information processing, act impulsively,

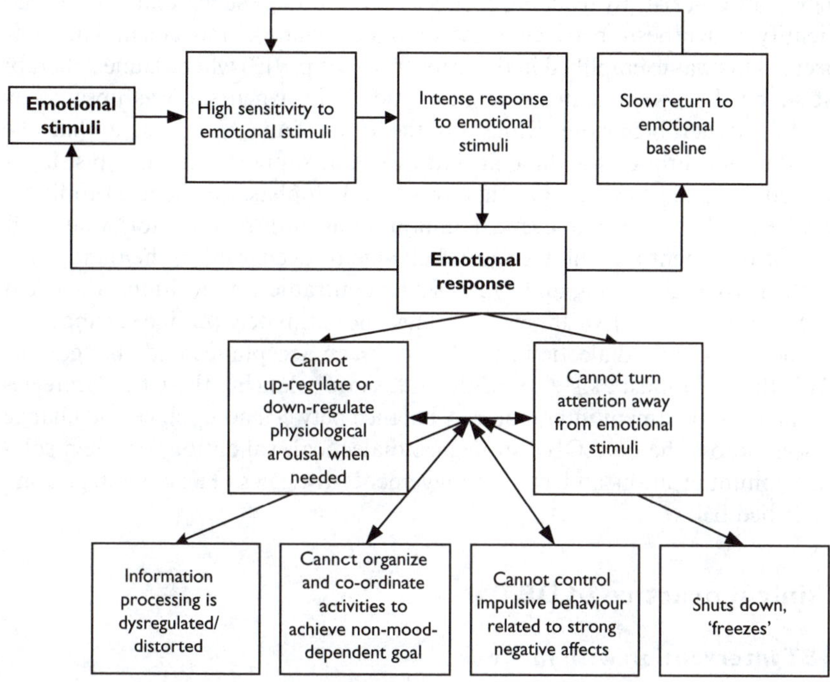

Figure 22.1 Linehan's emotional dysregulation schemas.

'freeze' and have difficulty inhibiting mood-dependent impulsive behaviour and organizing behaviour in the service of non-mood dependent goals (Linehan, 1993a). A hallmark of this theory is the notion that emotion dysregulation is pervasive across the entire emotional system (including both positive and negative emotions), and the physiological, expressive, subjective and action-oriented components of emotions. In addition, dysregulation occurs across varied environmental contexts.

Philosophical basis: Dialectics

DBT adopts a dialectical world view that reflects an ever-changing, transactional process in which each action leads to a *re*action (its opposite), its resolution of which is a synthesis of both positions. From this perspective, everything in the universe is interrelated, oppositional and in polarity. The essence of dialectics is that there is a known sequence of thesis–antithesis–synthesis, embodying not a static relation of events but rather a complex interplay inherent in the nature of truth, or competing truths. Reality is an activity, not an event; movement rather than repose. The dialectical world view is translated into therapy by teaching clients that multiple tensions will inevitably co-exist. By teaching clients to acknowledge such polarizations and identify a synthesis between these extremes, change, movement and flow occur. This was exemplified in the transcript (see p. 913) where Jamie's therapist stated that, when Jamie's parents' 'moved in' when she was upset, they reinforced her behaviour while, on the other hand, Jamie said that she couldn't get through the difficult times without support. The therapist highlighted the dialectical tension that arose, and emphasized the need to find a synthesis. The model of dialectical thinking constantly searches for 'what is left out' of treatment and allows natural change to occur within the therapeutic context. By highlighting and synthesizing contradictory positions, the client and therapist can arrive at new meanings and ultimately produce change.

The over-riding dialectic in DBT is between acceptance and change. The DBT therapist must master the difficult task of balancing these two strategies within each treatment interaction. A balance between acceptance and change is seen across the core DBT strategies: dialectical, validation, problem solving, communication and case management strategies. These strategies are described below.

Clinical practice of DBT

DBT intervention with Jamie

Jamie came to the first session with her parents who were extremely worried that she was going to kill herself. Jamie also wanted them there because she was having trouble remembering things and wanted them to help her. The therapist conducted a behavioural assessment of Jamie's problem behaviours and helped her determine what her goals were for therapy. Jamie reported that she was 'a mess', and that her goal for therapy was to stop having panic attacks and become a 'normal' person. Throughout the session, the therapist highlighted the over-riding dialectic in DBT of balancing acceptance with change by validating the difficulty of Jamie's situation, while also communicating the necessity for change in order for her to reach her goals. The therapist oriented Jamie and her parents to the theory, rationale and structure of DBT. Additionally, the therapist employed various DBT commitment strategies to obtain and strengthen her commitment to stay alive, stay in therapy and stop cutting herself.

At the second session, the therapist oriented Jamie to the diary card, which allowed her to track and monitor her problem behaviours during the week. While reviewing the diary card at the third session, Jamie reported that her urges to self-injure and commit suicide had increased over the week and were currently very high (5 on a 5-point scale). Upon assessment of suicide risk, Jamie indicated that, if she were to kill herself, she would use a gun, cut herself or overdose. The therapist then assessed Jamie's access to lethal means, discovering that Jamie did not have a gun but did have both sharp knives and a lethal quantity of prescription medications. In taking her history of suicidal behaviour, it was clear to the therapist that Jamie had a definite pattern of impulsive behaviours and, thus, there was a risk that she would impulsively overdose on her medications. Jamie, on the other had, was unwilling to do anything to make herself safer. She viewed suicide as a way out of misery and did not want her ability to kill herself limited in any way. The therapist walked Jamie through an analysis of the pros and cons of committing suicide and highlighted that there was no evidence that a person's life would be better after suicide. In this conversation, Jamie indicated that she believed in reincarnation and was worried that, if she killed herself, she would come back only to suffer again. The therapist capitalized on this worry to strengthen Jamie's fears of committing suicide. This particular argument worked at getting her to let go of the idea that she had to hold on tightly to lethal means during the next week. After much discussion, Jamie agreed to give her medications to her father, who would keep them and give her non-lethal amounts as needed. Jamie further agreed to call her therapist that evening to verify that she had indeed given the medications to her family. At the conclusion of the session, Jamie was still expressing significant hopelessness and misery and was ambivalent about life and death. Before leaving the session, the therapist spent time troubleshooting problems that might arise in keeping Jamie's commitment to staying alive until the next session. In particular, they created a crisis plan that included using a variety of specific crisis survival skills and problem-solving strategies and, if they did not work, calling the therapist for coaching.

DBT hierarchically targets life-threatening behaviours, therapy-interfering behaviours and quality-of-life-interfering behaviours. Therefore, Jamie's treatment targets focused on her current suicide ideation, pattern of cutting, panic attacks and distress over attending a skills group and various situations at work. The therapist personalized Jamie's diary card by adding panic as a field, and the frequency and intensity of panic attacks and parasuicide acts were monitored throughout the week. Each time Jamie cut herself or experienced a panic attack, a detailed chain analysis was conducted to determine the events that triggered and followed the panic episode. A number of chain analyses revealed that Jamie's panic attacks were followed by an intense fear of losing control, and, when experiencing this loss of control, she would cut herself to regulate her emotions. The therapist highlighted the problematic behaviours in this chain and, in sessions, exposed her to the cues triggering the panic attacks. Initially, it was very difficult for the therapist to determine what the cue was but, after several chain analyses, it was apparent that the experience of shame was the usual cue. Therefore, the therapist did formal exposure sessions to shame-evoking cues. During these sessions, Jamie's anxiety would initially increase and the therapist would instruct her to pay attention to the physiological sensations that accompanied the anxiety and shame until the anxiety went down. If Jamie called the therapist during a panic attack, the therapist would coach her in the exposure procedure until the panic subsided. During panic episodes where Jamie could not comply with any exposure directions she was directed to fill a large bowl with ice water and put her face in the ice water for 30 seconds. This ordinarily had the immediate effect of reducing arousal, after which she could follow the exposure procedures. As Jamie's sense of control over her own emotions went up, her intense urges to commit suicide started to come down.

As the panic attacks went down, reports of 'rage attacks' typically directed at her mother emerged. In these Jamie would scream at her parents, stomp around the house, slam doors and hit her mother. Her mother would pull back and leave her alone following these episodes and her father would respond by hugging Jamie hard to stop her and then would walk her to her room and soothe her while sitting on her bed. The therapist feared that the parents' reactions to Jamie's attacks might be reinforcing them. This was a difficult point to get through to Jamie as she could not separate the concept of reinforcement from the concept of unconscious intent. After much discussion this point was made and Jamie asked the therapist to explain it to her parents. At a family session the therapist, Jamie, and her parents devised a plan where, if Jamie attacked either parent, or broke anything in the house during a rage episode, she would get in her car immediately, go back to her apartment and stay there for at least an hour. Under no circumstances was either parent to soothe her nor back off from Jamie. After much sobbing, Jamie agreed to the plan. The contingency was designed to capitalize on both extinction and punishment. That the behaviour at home stopped after one episode suggested that it was the punishment value of the contingency that was working. If it had been extinction, one would have expected the behaviour to escalate before it went down. By this time, Jamie's panic attacks were subsiding but she had been fired from her job for crying and staying at home (she had stayed home from work every time she thought she would cry). Therefore, her parents were assisting her financially.

Jamie found a new job as an editorial assistant. Her pattern of morning vomiting and frequent sick days at new jobs continued, however. To explain her absences from her new job, Jamie told her new boss that she had tried to kill herself previously and had been diagnosed as borderline personality disorder. She quickly became too ashamed of her emotional state to go near her boss and the quality of her work began to deteriorate, primarily from her excessive worry about what her boss was thinking of her. Within a short period of time, she was laid off.

Jamie then decided not only did she pick the wrong men, but the wrong jobs, and was therefore fatally flawed. She quickly got a new job and the treatment plan shifted to a focus on viewing ruminating and worrying as emotional escape behaviours, functioning similarly to cutting, thinking about being dead, attacking her parents and staying home from work. This rationale made sense to Jamie and she began refocusing attention on the physiological sensations of emotions whenever she was starting to ruminate or think about suicide. Jamie had also learned the principles of reinforcement. Although she was afraid she would vomit on the bus to work, she did not want to reinforce getting sick by staying at home. On her own, she decided to go to work and bring a container (for vomit) with her on the bus.

With self-injury extinguished and panic attacks and rage episodes now almost completely gone, therapy also focused on developing a new social support system with people who didn't know she had been hospitalized. She joined a rowing club and began rowing every morning and most evenings. She gradually began building a new network of friends. She also gained an enormous sense of mastery from rowing and began feeling that she indeed could take care of herself. She also began tentatively dating.

At this time, Jamie's suicide ideation and negative emotions significantly decreased and she was actively confronting her fears. She still easily felt overwhelmed and out of control, but did not experience panic attacks. Sessions mainly addressed difficulties with anger, shame and interpersonal relationships. By the tenth month of therapy, Jamie's previously dysregulated behaviours were under her control, signalling that she was ready for stage 2 of DBT.

In stage 2, treatment focused on exposure to trauma events, particularly Jamie's shame about being a 'mental patient'. Three months into stage 2, Jamie showed signs of significant progress and expressed a desire to take a break from therapy. By now she was still had the same job and developed new abilities to cope. Her rage had decreased but she was still looking to get into a relationship with someone. She terminated after approximately one year of treatment.

Below is a transcript from a session when Jamie was two months into therapy. It represents actual examples and techniques that were used in stage 1, when Jamie expressed frequent and intense parasuicidal ideation and urges. This transcript was chosen to illustrate several basic DBT strategies.

The session begins with reviewing the diary card. In DBT, the purpose of the diary card is to monitor information about the client's targeted behaviours that have occurred during the previous week. For example, the card indicates whether or not a parasuicidal act has occurred, or if a client engaged in skilful behaviours. Additional information is also collected, such as the client's use of medications and his or her urges to quit therapy at pre- and post-session. Diary cards enable the therapist to track the client's behaviour between sessions and also serve to structure the targets of each therapy session.

Therapist: Did you engage in any self-harm since I saw you last week?
Jamie: No.
Therapist: How about your urges to harm yourself?
Jamie: Probably a five. (*out of five*)
Therapist: When? Today?
Jamie: Yesterday and today.
Therapist: Oh, so they have started to go back up again?
Jamie: Um hmm.
Therapist: We have to talk about that don't we? OK, and how about your suicide ideation yesterday and today?
Jamie: Five.
Therapist: And what would you say your mood swings have been?
Jamie: Five.
Therapist: OK, so coming down the hall today, while you were sitting out there waiting for me, what was your urge to harm?
Jamie: Five.
Therapist: You were actually thinking about harming yourself?
Jamie: Um hmm.
Therapist: OK. And how about your urge to quit therapy?
Jamie: A five.
Therapist: (*surprised laugh*) You are mad at me I take it.
(*therapist uses level 3 validation by articulating the unarticulated*)
Therapist: And how about your urge to kill yourself?
Jamie: A five.
Therapist: Well, we ought to talk about the urge to quit therapy for sure because that's new. Have you ever given a five before? I don't think so in the whole time I have known you. OK, what's on your agenda?
Jamie: Hopelessness.
Therapist: You would like to get that to go down?
Jamie: Um hmm.
(*the therapist sets the agenda according to the DBT target hierarchy by first attending to suicide and life-threatening behaviours, followed by any behaviours that interfere with therapy*)
Therapist: All right. So when did you have the panic attack?

(*the therapist is addressing a panic attack the client experienced in the week prior*)

Jamie: It started during group.

Therapist: That's when you started crying, during group?

(*Jamie nods*)

Therapist: So what we ought to work on is how that happened.

Jamie: I know how it happened.

Therapist: Well, how we are going to make it *not* happen? Because this is almost identical to what happened to you at work. So the good news is that it is happening right in front of us so we can work on it.

(*the therapist highlights that, when out-of-session dysfunctional behaviour occurs in session, it is a prime opportunity to work on decreasing those behaviours and learn more adaptive behaviours. The therapist targeted crying because of its functional relationship to higher order targets, namely, that crying at work often served as a precursor to Jamie leaving work and, ultimately quitting her job*)

Therapist: (*going over diary card*) OK, so we have urges to self-harm, urges to commit suicide and urges to avoid, because you have lots of urges to avoid. OK, so that's the order. And then emotions I put down are panic, sadness, shame, anger, fear and anxiousness. Because don't you think fear, anxiousness and panic are different?

Jamie: Um hmm.

Therapist: And then, do you know what the 'r' means over here?

Jamie: No.

Therapist: OK, what that means is that I want you to start working on reinforcing yourself, doing something that reinforces you when you have a day when you have a lot to do and are skilful doing it. Because what we are going to work on is learn how to self reinforce. Now see the bottom? What we are trying to do is increase your belief or sense that you can control your emotions, your behaviour and your thoughts. So zero is I am completely out of control, and a five is I am in very good control, I am where I want to be. Normal control.

Jamie: So zero is bad and five is good.

Therapist: Right. We don't want to say good and bad, we say zero is none and five is adequate.

(*the therapist replaces judgemental words with non-judgemental words. Increased awareness and subsequent replacement of judgements is typically emphasized in DBT mindfulness skills. Individuals with BPD are often judgemental of themselves and others in both positive and negative terms. In mindfulness, the client is *encouraged to take a non-judgemental stance, seeing everything simply as it is*)

Jamie: OK.

Therapist: OK, so um, the fact that you want to quit therapy sounds like you are angry with me. Is that true?
(*prolonged silence*)

Jamie: (*coughs*) I just don't get why my parents can't be involved because we are a close-knit family.

Therapist: What do you mean they can't be involved?

Jamie: Sounds like you are, you know, shutting me out from my parents.

Therapist: How so?

Jamie: Because you say they reinforce me. You know I needed them there last night and you made it sound like it was a bad thing. I can't do it alone.

Therapist: That's true. (*the therapist validates the fact that Jamie can't do it alone*) So let's talk about what I did and see whether we agree. What did I say?

Jamie: You said for my parents to go home. You make it sound like any interaction with them is like meddling or going to ruin therapy or something.

Therapist: Let me just tell you how I think about it OK? My perspective has been that when you get really upset, panic or emotional, your parents move in very close. What I would rather see is your parents moving in very close before you get really upset or when you are recently happy. So what happened last night was that you stormed out of group and then your parents moved in, and so in effect there was no consequence for you avoiding. So what I would rather have is you staying in group the whole time, then your parents move in big time. But the facts are last night you were not alone, you were at group, and you could have stayed. You were actually not alone at all and you left.

Jamie: Oh.

Therapist: So my worry is that if, whenever you leave, your parents come in and are soothing, then in effect there is really not a consequence. In effect, the consequence is that your parents become closer to you the more upset you get and that's never a good situation for everyone. This is really not unique to you. I would say this about anyone in this kind of situation.
(*the therapist presents didactic information on the principles of reinforcement. She highlights that, when Jamie's parents move in close after she engages in dysfunctional behaviours, Jamie is reinforced for the dysfunctional behaviour. Specifically, the therapist emphasizes that, after leaving group early, the client's parents attended to her, thereby reinforcing her behaviour of leaving group*)

Jamie: Well, when you are upset you need people.

Therapist: I don't know that you do. I think that when you are upset . . .

Jamie: I *do* need people.

Therapist: You *think* you need people.

Jamie: No, I *do* need people.

Therapist: Need them for what?

Jamie: For support.

Therapist: And why do you need support?

Jamie: Because I am feeling really bad and I don't want to be alone. And I am afraid that I might do something.

Therapist: Right. But the point is that you were not alone, you left your group. You could have come back to group.

Jamie: I didn't want to come back to that fucking group!

Therapist: This is true, you didn't want to. But that is where the problem is. Leaving the group is just like leaving work. And that's where the problem has been at work. So what I am trying to help you do is not leave. But if whenever you leave, someone comes along and soothes you, then there is really very little I can say that can possibly . . .

Jamie: I was going to leave whether anyone was there or not.

Therapist: The point I am making is that . . . I am not talking about intent OK? I am just talking about the consequence of leaving, where, when you get upset, your parents get closer. This is never a good idea. It puts you in a very difficult hot spot.

Jamie: (*crying*) So I am just supposed to sit there and be upset alone. The kind of upset that I get is despair.

Therapist: That's sort of the dialectic. That's what we have to solve . . . the dialectic of how, for you, to have enough help for when you need help, and also how to have it so you don't get reinforced. And the two of us have to figure it out. Because your point is very good when it comes to you needing help. And my point is very good in that reinforcement will cause you difficulties in the long run. This is a perfect case when you had help available and you chose not to take it.

(*the therapist highlights the dialectic of needing help and support on the one hand, and how dysfunctional behaviours should not get reinforced on the other hand. The therapist emphasizes the truth in both positions and invites the client to join in and make a collaborative effort on how to get support without reinforcing dysfunctional behaviour. The therapist also weaves in the use of validation, agreeing that needing help is perfectly reasonable*)

Jamie: I didn't have help available; it was group, that's not help.

Therapist: Certainly it is. And after group you could have talked to one of the group leaders.

Jamie: I am not going to sit there and cry in front of group the whole time and get nothing done.

Therapist: This is what you and I have to work on. Solving this particular problem because this is the problem you also had at work. So why don't we move back and see what happened and see if we can figure out other ways for you to cope with it.

(*the therapist sets the stage for conducting a chain analysis on what went wrong while the client was in group, and how the client might have been able to cope with things differently. Again, the therapist emphasizes the importance of dealing with this behaviour because it shows up in the client's everyday life*)

Overview of DBT treatment

The DBT model combines both a motivational and capability deficit model of behavioural dysfunction, necessitating interventions to address both motivational and skills deficits. However, it is very difficult for therapists working with suicidal individuals with BPD to manage crises while simultaneously shaping new, skilful behaviours and reducing incentives to engage in dysfunctional behaviours. Consequently, DBT addresses skill-building and motivational issues separately. Individual therapy focuses on highlighting contingencies of behaviour and devising systems of contingency management to increase adaptive function and decrease maladaptive behaviours. Individual therapy also focuses on skills generalization (e.g. through between-session telephone consultation or other programmed activities), while a separate skills training group teaches clients new skilful behaviour. Standard outpatient DBT includes four primary treatment modes (individual psychotherapy, telephone consultation, skills training, therapists' consultation meeting) in addition to uncontrolled ancillary treatments such as pharmacotherapy and acute inpatient psychiatric services.

DBT addresses five functions, each of which is related to the treatment modes reviewed above. Each mode emphasizes one or more of the following functions: (1) enhance capabilities; (2) improve motivational factors; (3) assure generalization to natural environment; (4) enhance therapist capabilities and motivation to treat effectively; and (5) structure the environment. Enhancing capabilities is targeted both in individual sessions and in a skills group, and consists of skills training and psychoeducation. Improving motivational factors is typically targeted in individual psychotherapy by applying reinforcement contingencies and exposure-based procedures. Once these behaviours are acquired in the therapy room, the therapist works to help these behaviours generalize to the client's natural environment. This can be done through a variety of ways, such as after-hours and crisis phone coaching, case management and e-mail consultation. As clients with BPD are notoriously difficult to treat, therapist capabilities and motivation to treat this group are also addressed. Through close supervision and use of the consultation team (reviewed later), the acquisition and generalization of the behaviours necessary for effective treatment application are targeted. Lastly, structuring the environment includes careful arrangement of administrative interactions, case management, and family interventions. The details underlying these five functions are described below.

DBT: Structuring the treatment frame

DBT is designed to treat individuals with BPD at all levels of severity and complexity, and is conceptualized as occurring in stages. The overarching goal is for the client to have a life worth living, and each treatment stage sets the client on the appropriate path to attain this goal. The levels of disorder in DBT are defined as: level 1 (behavioural dyscontrol); level 2 (quiet desperation); level 3 (problems in living); and level 4 (incompleteness). All the research to date has focused on severely and multiply disordered individuals with BPD in level 1, or on axis I eating disorders at level 3.

Pre-treatment: Orienting and commitment

The aim of pre-treatment sessions is for the client and therapist to arrive at a mutual agreement to work with one another. Together, the client and therapist negotiate a common set of expectancies to guide the initial steps of therapy. A description of DBT and the biosocial theory is presented, and the client and therapist discuss how much change is expected, the goals of treatment and any preconceptions the client may have about treatment. When needed, the therapist attempts to modify the client's dysfunctional beliefs regarding therapy. Strategies used in commitment and orienting are described later and are among the most important strategies during this phase of treatment.

Stage 1: Attaining basic capabilities

In Stage 1, the therapist's primary goal is to decrease severe behavioural dyscontrol and establish behavioural control. The focus of this stage is to prevent out-of-control behaviours (e.g. behaviours due to the criterion behaviours of BPD, or severity due to comorbid disorders) and stabilize the client. Clients are in stage 1 when their general level of functioning is low and work on the targets and goals of therapy are hampered until out-of-control behaviours are under control. An example of this includes a client who is highly suicidal, with comorbid diagnoses of post-traumatic stress disorder (PTSD) and major depression. The first goal for this client would be to eliminate/reduce suicidal behaviours, as targeting PTSD and major depression would be futile with a dead client. The primary targets of stage 1 are (hierarchically), to decrease life-threatening behaviours, to decrease therapy-interfering behaviours, to decrease severe quality-of-life-interfering behaviours and to increase behavioural skills. The amount of time required to get clients out of stage 1 may vary, but clients who are highly suicidal and severely dysfunctional at the start of treatment can be expected to make significant progress after one year of treatment.

Suicidal and life-threatening behaviours

Any indication of imminent suicide, self-injury, homicide or significant aggression that poses serious threat must be explicitly addressed as a first priority. Significant increases in suicide or aggressive ideation/communication and associated mood changes also need to be attended to. In general, the hierarchical arrangement of targets is as follows: imminent threat, behaviours that occurred since the previous session and increases in urges or suicide ideation. This hierarchy is used to set the session agenda. As illustrated in the transcript (see p. 911), diary cards are very useful in stage 1, as they enable the therapist to monitor parasuicidal behaviours. It is relatively easy for therapists to forget to inquire about suicidal behaviours at every session. Additionally, therapists might make assumptions that the client is not currently at high risk. However, with a high-risk population such as BPD, careful monitoring of these behaviours is integral to treatment. Diary cards allow the therapist to continuously track these behaviours without relying on his or her memory or depending on the client's verbal report. In the case where a therapist is not aware of new or increased parasuicidal or life-threatening behaviour, the diary card will prevent him or her from making the detrimental mistake of failing to intervene.

Therapy-interfering behaviours

The second target of stage 1 is to keep the client and therapist engaged collaboratively in the therapy. Therapy-interfering behaviours are important to address because these behaviours decrease the therapist's motivation to treat the client and also interfere with the client's full participation of therapy. Even the most efficacious of treatments may be 'diluted' if the therapist is burned out or the client is not fully participating or at session to receive the treatment. Examples of behaviours that are considered therapy-interfering are non-collaborative behaviours, non-compliance and sporadic session attendance. It should be noted that therapy-interfering behaviours can occur on the part of the client or therapist. Therapy-interfering behaviours on the part of the client also include behaviours that burn-out the therapist (e.g. behaviours that reduce the therapist's motivation to treat a client). Therapy-interfering behaviours on the part of the therapist include behaviours that unbalance therapy (e.g. extreme acceptance or change, flexibility or rigidity) and disrespectful behaviours (e.g. accepting telephone calls in session, forgetting important facts about the client's life). Therapy-interfering behaviours are addressed directly and consistently; they are dealt with in the therapy session, and also at the consultation team meeting.

Quality-of-life-interfering behaviours

The third target is to reduce behavioural patterns that seriously impair the possibility of having a reasonable quality of life. Examples of these include high-risk sexual behaviour, extreme financial difficulties and criminal behaviours. The goal here is for the client to achieve a stable lifestyle that meets reasonable standards for safety and adequate functioning.

Behavioural skills

The fourth target is to increase skill acquisition and skill strength. These include mindfulness, interpersonal effectiveness, emotion regulation, distress tolerance and self-management skills. The individual therapist monitors the acquisition of the skills over time and assists the client in applying the skills to his or her daily life. Of these skills, mindfulness is the centre of DBT. Mindfulness has to do with the quality of both awareness and participation that a person brings to everyday living. It's a way of living awake, with one's eyes wide open. Unlike standard behaviour and cognitive therapies that emphasize change, a major part of mindfulness is learning to bear pain skillfully. Mindfulness was adapted from Eastern practices and involves acceptance of the world as it is, embracing the notion that everything is as it should be at this moment. Approaching life with this attitude is the epitome of radically accepting oneself, other people and the universe.

Interpersonal effectiveness skills involve helping clients decide what they want in difficult situations, and how to obtain their objective with others while maintaining a positive relationship and self-respect. Emotion-regulation skills target the reduction of emotional distress through increasing positive events and mastery and decreasing negative events. Distress tolerance skills teach clients how to get through difficult situations without engaging in behaviours that make them worse. Finally, self-management skills pervade the other skills and include the knowledge of fundamental principles of learning and behaviour change, the ability to set realistic goals, the ability to conduct one's own behaviour analysis, and the ability to implement contingency management plans.

Stage 2: Post-traumatic stress reduction

The transition from stage 1 to stage 2 occurs only when targeted stage 1 behaviours are under control and the client can refrain from severely dysfunctional behaviours. The primary goal of stage 2 is to move the client from a place of quiet desperation to emotional experiencing. The main target is to decrease post-traumatic stress responses (e.g. distortion or denial of trauma, avoidance of traumatic cues), with an emphasis on accepting and changing current patterns using exposure and cognitive modification.

Stage 3: Resolving problems in living and increasing respect for self

In the third stage, the goal is to target the client's problems in living and experience ordinary happiness and unhappiness. The primary targets are to increase the client's respect for him- or herself and decrease the individual's problems in living. At stage 3, it is important for the therapist to appropriately reinforce the client's attempt to self-validate, self-care and problem solve.

Stage 4: Attaining the freedom and capacity for joy

In the fourth and final stage, the goal is to bring the client from a place of incompleteness to a capacity for freedom. The client is supported in making meaning and experiencing joy. Although most individuals are content with level 3 functioning, this stage is for individuals who still experience some residual incompleteness. This is done by expanding awareness (of self, the past to the present and of the self to other) and finding spiritual fulfilment. By this stage, clients benefit most by engaging in insight-oriented psychotherapy, experiential treatments and finding spiritual meaning.

Structuring the agreements of treatment

DBT requires clear and informed agreements before beginning any treatment mode. At pre-treatment, three primary agreements are sought between the client and the therapist. In standard stage 1 DBT, the client agrees to stay in therapy for a specified period of time (typically, six months to one year), attend the scheduled therapy sessions, work towards changing the targeted behaviours, work on therapy-interfering behaviour, participate in skills training and pay agreed-upon fees. The therapist agrees to make every reasonable effort to conduct competent and effective therapy, obey ethical and professional guidelines, respect the integrity and rights of the clients, maintain confidentiality and obtain consultation when needed. Finally, the therapist must agree to be available to the client for weekly therapy sessions, phone consultations and provide therapy back-up when away.

Functions and modes of treatment

Individual therapy

The focus of individual therapy is contingent on the treatment target hierarchy described earlier. The amount of session time dedicated to any one target is determined by the client's behaviours since the previous session, and any immediate problems that occur in session. Although more than one target may be relevant in the session (e.g. the client engaged in parasuicidal behaviour and is engaging in therapy-interfering behaviour), the higher-priority target takes precedence.

The use of diary cards is extremely helpful in determining the foci of the sessions. These cards are filled out by the clients during the week, and monitor the occurrence of daily parasuicidal behaviour, suicidal ideation, urges to parasuicide, 'misery', use of illicit drugs and prescribed drugs and use of behavioural skills. As illustrated in the case example, diary cards may be personalized to suit the current needs of the client. For each session, the therapist begins by reviewing the diary card and, by doing so, effectively structures the focus of the therapy session.

Skills training

Skills training occurs as a separate mode but concurrently with individual therapy. The rationale for this is that managing crisis-generating behaviours and the contingencies related to implementation of new skills is difficult to address within the framework of individual therapy. Consequently, a separate DBT skills training mode was developed to focus on skill acquisition and strengthening. Typically, skills training occurs weekly for 2–2½ hours and is held in a group setting. The goal of skills training is to teach skilful behaviours to replace problem behaviours and strengthen these new, effective behaviours.

Skills training is distinct from individual sessions in that the format is highly structured. The first half of skills training is devoted to homework review, during which clients discuss the skills practised in the previous week and receive feedback on skills they need. The second half of skills group is primarily didactic and follows a psychoeducational format. The target hierarchy for skills training differs from that of individual therapy. The targets are to teach new skills, decrease behaviour that, if not addressed, would destroy the group (e.g. setting fire to the clinic) and decrease therapy-interfering behaviour. This hierarchy supports the function associated with the mode, namely to enhance behavioural capability through acquisition of skills. If crisis behaviours occur in group, the client is instructed to call his or her therapist or directly address it with the primary therapist at the next session.

Telephone crisis consultation

Telephone calls between sessions are considered an integral part of DBT. These phone consultations serve three purposes: (1) to provide skills coaching outside of the skills group and generalize these skills to the client's daily life; (2) to provide emergency crisis intervention; and (3) to provide opportunities to immediately repair a therapeutic relationship. The focus of the phone conversations is contingent on the nature of the call. In most situations the phone call focuses on skills coaching. However, if more complex problems are presented, the focus is on helping the client determine what the problem is, ameliorating and tolerating distress, and inhibiting dysfunctional problem-solving behaviours until the next session. If extensive problem solving is required, it is targeted in the next therapy session. The final purpose of telephone calls is relationship repair. Individuals with BPD often experience delayed emotional reactions to interactions occurring in the therapy sessions. However, waiting a week before dealing with emotions related to the therapy relationship may lead to premature termination from therapy, at worst, or unnecessary agony, at best. Thus, telephone contact can be used to sooth and reassure the client that the relationship is not ruptured.

DBT therapeutic strategies

DBT therapeutic strategies refer to the role and focus of the therapist, as well as a co-ordinated set of procedures that serve to achieve the specific treatment goals. The DBT therapeutic strategies include dialectical strategies, core strategies of validation and problem solving, stylistic strategies, case management strategies and integrated strategies.

Dialectical strategies

The dialectical strategies permeate the application of all other DBT strategies. The dysregulated emotions and behaviours characteristic of individuals with BPD can be viewed as failures of dialectical synthesis, producing extreme and often polarized experiencing of the world. The overarching goal of DBT is to replace these extreme patterns with dialectical ones. This is accomplished by eliciting opposites in emotional states, thinking styles and behavioural patterns, and by facilitating opportunities for growth through synthesis. The dialectical strategies used in DBT serve to highlight these tensions and to provide the necessary conditions for eventual resolution through synthesis.

One way that synthesis is promoted is through balancing the therapeutic style and treatment strategies. The therapist balances nurturing of the client as he or she is in the moment with a benevolent demanding for change and applies a balance of acceptance-oriented and problem-solving strategies. The therapist does this using a 'forward-back movement' in response to the client.

To use a metaphor, it is like trying to help someone wiggle down a pipe; first move this way and then that way. Mindfulness is especially crucial here, as this entails a moment-to-moment analysis of where the client is at, and how to respond effectively.

Another strategy is the use of paradox. The purpose of entering the paradox is to teach the client to tolerate ambiguity. Oppositions are highlighted such that the client experiences a 'both and' as opposed to an 'either or' perspective. For example, in the case of Jamie, the therapist emphasized that her (Jamie's) need for parental support was valid while simultaneously noting that the dysfunctional behaviours reinforced by her parents were not helpful. Rather than seeing one as true and the other false, both are true. It is through the awareness of both ends of the dilemma that a resolving synthesis emerges where change can occur. The use of metaphor and playing devil's advocate are prominent in traditional psychotherapy interventions (Levitt et al., 2000; Rasmussen, 2000). In DBT, the trick is to use metaphors spontaneously. When playing devil's advocate, the therapist presents a propositional statement that is an extreme version of the client's dysfunctional beliefs, and then plays the role of devil's advocate to counter the client's attempts to disprove the extreme statement. Playing devil's advocate is commonly used in commitment sessions, but can be integrated in typical sessions as well.

Extending is a translation of a technique used in Aikido, a Japanese martial art (Saposnek, 1980). The idea of extending refers to taking the client more seriously than he or she intends. The purpose of this technique is to allow the client's problematic position to go to its natural conclusion, while the therapist joins in with it, so it goes a bit further. By doing so, the client experiences a sense of imbalance, which allows the therapist to shift the client away from the problematic position without the use of confrontation. For example, a client may say, 'You are a horrible therapist, I'm going to write a complaint about you', with little intent of writing a complaint but with the expectation that the therapist will focus on repairing any damage to the therapy relationship to prevent the client from writing the letter. A therapist using extending, however, may suggest spending the session helping the client to write the letter because it is the therapist's job to help the client to be as effective as possible. Another strategy is to invoke clients to use 'wise mind'. This strategy is taught with the DBT core mindfulness skills, and encourages clients to find a place within themselves wherein lies inherent wisdom. Finally, making 'lemonade out of lemons' is a strategy based on a genuine belief that whatever life presents truly can be changed into something positive and that the client can play an integral part in making the change. An example of this is when a client tells the therapist that he or she has an angry employer who makes work difficult. The therapist may respond by saying, 'Too fabulous. A perfect opportunity for you to practise your skills'. When using these dialectical strategies, the therapist allows natural change to occur and remembers that, when change is a loss, validate.

Core strategies

Validation

Validation strategies are the most reflective of the acceptance strategies, whereas problem-solving strategies are the most reflective of the change strategies. Validation, according to the *Oxford English Dictionary*, is 'the action of validating or making valid . . . a strengthening, reinforcement, confirming; an establishing or ratifying as valid' (Simpson & Weiner, 1989). In DBT, validation serves as an acceptance strategy to balance change. In addition, it strengthens clinical progress, the client's ability to self-validate strengthens the therapeutic relationship and provides feedback. When using validation, it is important for the therapist to use it appropriately. It does not mean 'making' something valid, nor does it mean validating that which is invalid. Therefore, therapists need to be mindful of validating only the valid, so as to avoid reinforcing dysfunctional behaviours.

Validation in DBT can occur at any one of six levels. Each level is more complete than the previous one and depends on one or more of the previous levels. The levels of validation can be divided into emotional validation strategies, behavioural validation strategies, cognitive validation strategies and cheerleading strategies.

Level 1 validation refers to listening to and observing what the client is saying, feeling and doing in addition to an active effort to understand what is being said and observed. Put simply, the therapist is interested in the client. At level 1, the therapist maintains the dialectical tension of listening and observing on the one hand, while filtering what is seen and heard through the lenses of theory and previous behaviours of the client, on the other hand. The second level of validation is the accurate reflection of the client's feelings, thoughts, assumptions, and behaviours. Validation at this level authenticates the meaning of the client's words and the individual as to who he or she actually is. In level 3 validation, the therapist 'reads' the client's behaviour and figures out what the client is feeling, and what he or she is wishing for or thinking. The therapist conveys an intuitive understanding of the client, sometimes knowing her better than she knows herself. For example, in Jamie's interaction with her therapist, when she marked her urge to quit therapy as a five, her therapist employed a level 3 validation by suggesting that Jamie was upset with her. At level 4, validation is based on the notion that all behaviour is caused and thus, in principle, is understandable. The therapist acknowledges that the client's behaviour makes perfect sense given his or her experience, physiology and life to date. For example, if a client who was a victim of childhood sexual abuse expresses discomfort with having a male therapist, the therapist might say, 'It makes sense that you would feel that way, given your childhood experiences'. At level 5, the therapist communicates that the client's behaviour is justifiable, reasonable, well grounded, meaningful and/or efficacious in terms of current events, normal biological functioning and/or the client's ultimate life goals. The therapist looks for all the relevant facts in the client's current environment to communicate that the response is understandable. In level 6, the therapist expresses radical genuineness by recognizing the client as he or she is, seeing and responding to his or her strengths, while maintaining an empathic understanding of the client's difficulties. Referring to the previous example, the therapist might use a level 6 validation by saying, 'A man may not understand your experience as well as a woman understands'. It is the opposite of treating the client in a condescending manner or as overly fragile. Finally, a special type of validation is cheerleading, where the therapist validates the ability of the client to overcome difficulties and build a life worth living. The task here is to balance validation of the difficulties of making progress while simultaneously instilling hope and confidence that the client can change.

Problem solving

Although validation strategies are crucial in DBT, exclusive focus on validation can be equally problematic as its absence. Encouraging individuals who have excruciatingly painful life experiences to accept their current situation offers little solace. DBT employs problem-solving strategies as the core strategy for change. The process of change is especially difficult for individuals with BPD; therefore, the therapist needs to master the art of weaving validation strategies while encouraging active problem solving. DBT divides the problem-solving strategies into a two-stage process. The first focuses on understanding and accepting the problem at hand, and the second focuses on generating alternate solutions.

PROBLEM ASSESSMENT

Behavioural analysis The targets of conducting a behavioural analysis are to identify: (1) the problem behaviour; (2) the prompting event that led to the behaviour; (3) what prevents its resolution; and (4) what aids are available for solving it.

Conducting a behavioural analysis begins with defining the problem in terms of behaviour and then conducting a moment-to-moment examination of the chain of events leading up to and following the problematic behaviour; this is termed a 'chain analysis'. The overall goal of a chain analysis is to determine the function of the problem behaviour. The term 'behaviour' is used to refer to anything a person does, public or private, including thinking, feeling and acting. It is helpful to define the problem as a behavioural excess (i.e. unwanted behaviour), behavioural deficit (i.e. desired or missing behaviour), or faulty stimulus control (i.e. where the behaviour occurs in the wrong situation or fails to occur in the right situation). Useful questions to ask here are:

- Are ineffective behaviours being reinforced, and are effective behaviours followed by aversive outcomes?
- Does the client have the necessary behavioural skills to regulate his or her emotions, respond skilfully to conflict, and manage his or her own behaviour?
- Are there patterns of avoidance, or are effective behaviours inhibited by unwarranted fears or guilt?
- Is the client unaware of the contingencies operating on his or her environment, or are effective behaviours inhibited by faulty beliefs or assumptions?

A pictorial display of a chain analysis is represented in Figure 22.2. A chain analysis always begins with identifying the 'prompting event', a specific environmental event that triggered the problem behaviour. This may be difficult, as clients are often unable to identify anything in the environment that led to the problem behaviour. Next, the therapist identifies the vulnerability factors and the relevant 'links' in the chain. Vulnerability factors are contextual factors giving prompting event more power (e.g. lack of sleep, stressful day at work) and links in the chain refer to all the subsequent environmental and behavioural events that occurred after the prompting event. Questions such as, 'What happened next?' or 'How did you get from there to there?' are often used here. After identifying the relevant links leading up to the problem behaviour, it is important to pinpoint the environmental and behavioural consequences that are maintaining the problem behaviour. Having a substantial foundation on the principles of learning is crucial in determining the potential variables that are maintaining or influencing the behaviour (for a review of learning and behaviour theory, see Pierce & Cheney, 2004). The final step in the behavioural analysis is to develop and test hypotheses about the events that triggered and maintain the problem behaviour.

Solution analysis Once the problem has been identified and analysed, the therapist works with the client to find alternative solutions that will lead to more adaptive and skilful behaviours. The client's goals, needs, and desires should be in the forefront of the therapist's mind while possible solutions are generated. Finally, a solution is chosen to implement. Once the client and

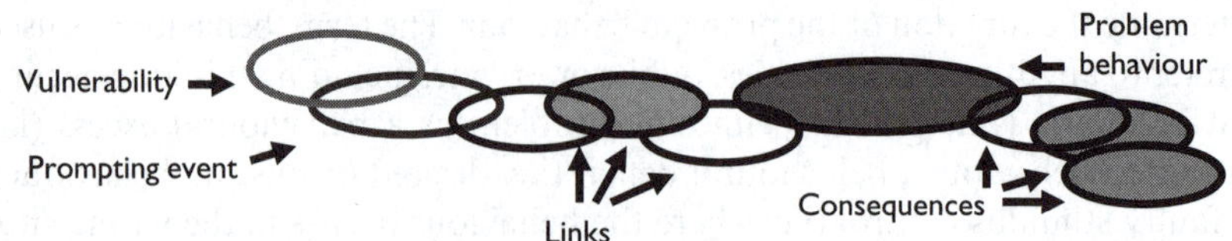

Figure 22.2 Chain analysis illustration.

therapist have agreed upon a solution, they collaboratively troubleshoot the possible obstacles that are likely to occur when trying to implement the solution. Together, they 'brainstorm' alternative behaviours or strategies that will surpass the obstacle and lead to the desired goal.

Change procedures

One of the assumptions underlying DBT is that clients are doing the best they can. Thus, dysfunctional solutions to problems in living require a fine-tuning in clients' problem-solving skills. The factors that interfere with effective problem-solving include: (1) the behavioural skill is not in the client's repertoire; (2) the behaviour is too low in the client's response hierarchy; (3) the behaviour is interfered with by dysfunctional behaviours that are higher in the client's behavioural hierarchy; or (4) the behaviour is inhibited by faulty beliefs and assumptions or by efforts to avoid unpleasant emotions. The DBT problem-solving procedures outlined below are taken directly from the cognitive and behavioural treatment literature and are viewed as the primary vehicles of change.

SKILLS TRAINING

Skills training is called for when a solution requires skills that are not currently in the individual's behavioural repertoire, or when the client has the necessary behaviours but cannot integrate its use effectively. Skills training incorporates three procedures: (1) skills acquisition; (2) skills strengthening; and (3) skills generalization. In skills acquisition, the therapist provides didactic instruction to the client on the necessary skill, and then models it. The new skill is strengthened through behavioural rehearsal and natural and arbitrary reinforcement. Finally, skill generalization occurs through consulting with the client between sessions (e.g. on the phone), providing session tapes for review *in vivo*, giving behavioural homework assignments and changing the environment (e.g. getting family and significant others involved with therapy groups).

CONTINGENCY MANAGEMENT

Contingency management requires therapists to organize their behaviour so that adaptive, skilful behaviours of the client are reinforced, while unskilful or maladaptive behaviours are extinguished or punished. The four strategies used in contingency management are positive reinforcement, negative reinforcement, extinction and punishment. The general rule is as follows: When the goal is to strengthen the client's behaviour, a positive consequence is added, or something experienced as aversive is removed. When the goal is to weaken a behaviour, reinforcers must be withheld and an aversive experience is maintained. When extinguishing maladaptive behaviours, it is important for the therapist to find another skilful response to reinforce. The idea here is for the client to 'reverse' his or her behavioural hierarchy such that high-probability maladaptive behaviours become lower in the hierarchy, and low-probability skilful behaviours move higher up in the hierarchy. When the goal is to suppress a behaviour, an aversive consequence is added (e.g. withdrawing warmth) or a positive consequence is removed.

COGNITIVE MODIFICATION

When adaptive behaviour is inhibited and maladaptive behaviour is facilitated by cognitions and cognitive styles, cognitive modification procedures are employed. These procedures include contingency clarification and cognitive restructuring. Although the direct cognitive restructuring procedures (Beck et al., 1979; Ellis, 1962, 1973) are used here, contingency clarification is more commonly used. In contingency clarification, the therapist clarifies current contingencies (e.g. highlighting consequences as they occur) and future contingencies by providing realistic information. For example, in the case of Jamie, the therapist highlighted a current contingency by explaining to Jamie that her parents were reinforcing her dysfunctional behaviour.

EXPOSURE

All of the change procedures in DBT can be conceptualized as exposure strategies. Therapeutic exposure procedures are used informally throughout the whole of therapy and formally in stage 2, where the client is systematically exposed to cues of previous traumatic events. Most of these strategies have been derived from standard exposure principles employed by other treatment researchers (Foa & Kozack, 1986). The purpose of these strategies is to recondition dysfunctional associations that develop between stimuli (respondent conditioning) or between a stimulus and a response (operant conditioning). For example, parasuicidal behaviours may be a result of respondent conditioning (e.g. associated with attention from loved ones) or operant conditioning (e.g. parasuicidal behaviour is followed by relief). The exposure procedure begins with orienting the client by reviewing the research on exposure and predicting that the client will feel worse before feeling better. Next, the therapist provides a non-reinforced exposure and blocks the action tendencies associated with the problem emotion (e.g. lowering eyes and head when experiencing shame). Finally, the client's control over aversive events is enhanced through opposite action. Opposite action in DBT refers to: (1) identifying the client's action urge when presented with the relevant cue (e.g. negative emotion prompts urge to avoid/dissociate); and (2) practising the opposite action of the urge (e.g. instead of dissociating, the client mindfully experiences the negative emotion). See the DBT *Skills manual* for a more detailed description of opposite action (Linehan, 1993b).

Stylistic strategies

The stylistic strategies in DBT define *how* to apply the treatment strategies. The DBT therapist balances two quite different styles of communication: irreverent communication and reciprocal communication. Irreverent communication is similar to the style advocated by Whitaker (1975) in his writings on strategic therapy, whereas reciprocal communication is similar to the communication style advocated in client-centred therapy. The two strategies are carefully balanced, with each being woven into a single, stylistic fabric.

Irreverent communication

Irreverent communication refers to reframing the client's communication in an unorthodox, offbeat manner. This stylistic strategy is highly useful when the client is immovable or when the therapist and client are 'stuck'. It often has an offbeat flavour and uses logic to weave a web from which the client cannot escape. For instance, if a client says 'I am going to kill myself', the therapist might reply with 'I thought you agreed not to drop out of therapy'. Irreverent communication also uses a confrontational tone and, in a sense, calls the client's bluff. For example, if a client says 'I'm quitting therapy', the therapist might respond with 'Would you like a referral?' The trick here is to carefully time the bluff with the simultaneous provision of a safety net, and leave the client a way out.

Reciprocal communication

Responsiveness, self-disclosure, warm engagement and genuineness are the basic guidelines of reciprocal communication. Self-involving (disclosure of immediate, personal reactions to the client) and personal self-disclosure (disclosure of facts about the therapist) are both used. An example of a self-involving self-disclosure is when a therapist responds to a client who consistently shows up late by saying, 'When you show up late, I feel like you are not taking treatment seriously'. When using reciprocal communication, the therapist's responses are always laced with warmth and genuineness, conveying the message that the therapist and client are both equals within the interpersonal relationship.

Case management strategies

The therapist moves into case management strategies when there are problems in the client's environment that interfere with his or her functioning or progress. Case management strategies refer to how the therapist interacts with others about the client. Typically, the DBT therapist favours teaching clients to interact with others about themselves, but some exceptions are made. Three case management strategies are used: consultant-to-the-client strategy, environmental intervention, and the consultation/supervision team meeting.

Consultant-to-the-client

The role of the DBT therapist is to consult with the client about how to manage his or her social/professional network. It is *not* to consult with the network about how to manage the client. The therapist does not intervene to adjust environments for the sake of his or her client, nor does he or she consult with other professionals about how to treat the client unless the client is present. The consultant-to-client strategy is the preferred case management strategy and perhaps the most innovative aspect of DBT. Its purpose is to help clients learn to manage their own lives, conveying that they are capable of performing interventions on their own behalf.

Environmental intervention

Although DBT is oriented towards teaching the client how to interact effectively with his or her environment, there are times when intervention by the therapist is needed. This occurs when the short-term gain is worth the long-term loss in learning. Some examples of a condition mandating environmental intervention is when the client is unable to act on his or her own behalf and the outcome is very important, or when the client is a minor.

Therapist supervision/consultation meeting

Crisis-generating behaviours and intense emotions of individuals with BPD can make this group extremely difficult to treat. Thus, therapist supervision and consultation are integral to DBT. From this perspective, therapists apply DBT to the client and the supervisor and consultation group apply DBT to the therapist. The overarching purpose of consultation-to-the therapist is to hold the therapist within the treatment frame, utilizing a dialectical approach of balancing acceptance and change. One of the most difficult aspects of DBT is that many clients reinforce their therapists for doing ineffective therapy, and punish therapists for doing the treatment effectively. Therefore, consultation-to-the-therapist balances this out by providing support for applying the treatment effectively.

There are three primary functions of consultation-to-the-therapist. First, the supervisor and consultation team help keep the therapist in the therapeutic relationship by cheerleading and supporting the therapist. Second, the supervisor or consultation team balances the therapist in his or her interactions with the client. The team moves close to the therapist, helping him or her maintain a strong position, or the team may move away from the therapist, which helps the therapist move close to the client to maintain balance. Third, the team provides the context for the treatment in two forms. In one form, DBT is viewed as a transactional relationship between the community of clients with BPD and a community of mental health professionals. The over-riding essence of the consultation meeting is that the entire team is treating the client. Another form in which the team provides treatment is by increasing the competencies of the therapist. From this perspective, the team works together to ensure that the therapist is administering the best treatment possible.

Integrative strategies for use with specific problems

Linehan et al. (1999) adapted standard DBT for women with BPD and substance dependence (DBT-S). Modifications of the treatment hierarchy were made such that strategies targeting substance abuse and behaviours functionally related to substance abuse were added. In addition, attachment strategies were employed to keep clients in therapy, and replacement medications were used for individuals with stimulant or opiate dependence. Findings suggest that DBT-S has been effective in targeting parasuicide, abstinence, treatment retention, social and global adjustment, and state and trait anger.

DBT has also been adapted to antisocial behaviours such that the foci are on life-threatening behaviours (both suicidal and homicidal), behaviours that interfere with the treatment programme, and the therapist's motivation. McCann et al. (2000) tailored standard DBT by expanding the domain of life-threatening behaviours to include homicide and interpersonal violence, and targeting the emotional insensitivity of antisocial individuals. A 'graduate' level skills group was also developed to increase empathy for victims and prevent relapse of violent behaviour. This approach has shown to decrease levels of maladaptive coping and increase levels of adaptive coping.

DBT has also been modified for eating disorders, particularly for binge-eating disorder (BED). Wiser and Telch (1999) adapted standard DBT to treat this population by conceptualizing BED as a maladaptive, yet momentarily effective method of emotion regulation and distress tolerance. Therefore, the modified DBT treatment includes mindfulness, emotion regulation and distress tolerance skills to equip BED individuals with the skills needed when they experience the urge to binge. A recent emergence of studies investigating the efficacy of DBT for BED suggest that DBT is effective in reducing binge eating and eating pathology (Telch et al., 2000, 2001).

SUMMARY

BPD is a potentially life-threatening disorder involving dysregulation of cognitions, behaviour and emotions. While the prevalence of BPD is between 0.2 and 1.8%, clients with BPD are high users of mental health services and about 10% complete suicide. BPD is associated with biological dysfunction; there is evidence of changes to the neurochemistry and structures of the brains of clients with BPD, as well as preliminary evidence of a genetic component to BPD. Psychosocial theories suggest that some biological vulnerability, for example high emotionality, interacts with an early invalidating environment to produce the dysregulation seen in BPD; research supporting this view includes the high rates of abuse and adverse life events in childhood reported by clients with BPD.

BPD typically has onset in late childhood. The course of BPD is disputed, with some studies reporting that fewer clients continue to meet criteria over time while others suggest that BPD is chronic. BPD is commonly comorbid with other disorders, including the DSM-IV axis I panic, eating, post-traumatic stress and major depressive disorders, and the axis II disorders, particularly antisocial, avoidant and depressive personality disorders. Clients with BPD typically have severe impairments in social adjustment and overall functioning. They often have difficulty adhering to treatment contracts and routine outpatient treatment frequently ends prematurely or is interrupted by the client dropping out or being readmitted to a hospital. Empirically supported treatments include DBT and psychodynamic long-term partial hospitalization, both highly structured, multi-modal treatments that allow the client frequent access to the therapist, directly target behaviours that interfere with therapy, emphasize current emotional experiences and balance the use of validation and change.

Dialectical behaviour therapy is a comprehensive treatment that incorporates a unique blend of Eastern teachings to promote acceptance, with behavioural principles used to promote change. It embodies a dialectical philosophy, reflecting a transactional process between inherent opposites, where resolution is borne out of a synthesis of both positions. From a dialectical perspective, the therapeutic relationship is the context in which a more accurate world view and resulting set of behaviours is fostered. DBT emphasizes the interplay between extensive validation and problem-solving techniques, and provides explicit guidelines and formal targeting strategies to yield a structured treatment package for both the client and the therapist. To date, a growing body of research provides empirical support for the effectiveness of DBT in BPD and, more recently, for other disorders.

EXERCISE 22.1

Using the example of Jamie in the chapter, or of a client with whom you are all familiar, divide into groups of three. Assign roles of clinical psychologist, client and observer.

1 Pick two therapeutic strategies of potential benefit to your client from the description of DBT above, for example validation, problem solving, behavioural analysis. Role-play a ten-minute section of the session where you try to use the strategies with the client.
2 Pick two skills that may be of use to the client and role-play a ten-minute part of the session where the therapist works with the client on skills acquisition, skills strengthening or skills generalization.

After each role-play, exchange feedback and ask the observer for feedback. Be encouraging and respectful of your colleagues and offer constructive suggestions.

EVIDENCE SUMMARIES

Crits-Cristoph, P. & Barber, J. (2002). Psychological treatments for personality disorders. In P. Nathan & J. Gorman (Eds.), *A guide to treatments that work* (Second Edition, pp. 611–624). New York: Oxford University Press.

Koenigsberg, H., Woo-Ming, A. & Siever, L. (2002). Pharmacological treatments for personality disorders. In P. Nathan & J. Gorman (Eds.), *A guide to treatments that work* (Second Edition, pp. 625–643). New York: Oxford University Press.

FURTHER READING FOR PRACTITIONERS

Gunderson, J. (2001). *Borderline personality disorder: A clinical guide*. Washington, DC: American Psychiatric Press.

Linehan, M. (1993). *Cognitive-behavioural treatment of borderline personality disorder*. New York: Guilford Press.

Linehan, M. (1993). *Skills training manual for treating borderline personality disorder*. New York: Guilford Press.

Linehan, M. & Dimeff, A. (1997). *Dialectical behaviour therapy manual of treatment interventions for drug abusers with borderline personality disorder*. Seattle: University of Washington Press.

McCullough, L., Kuhn, N., Andrews, S., Kaplan, A., Wolfe, J. & Lanza, C (2003). *Treating affect phobia: A therapist manual for short-term dynamic psychotherapy*. New York: Guilford Press.

Young, J. (1999). *Cognitive therapy for personality disorders: A schema focused approach* (Third Edition). Saratosa, FL: Professional Resource Press.

VIDEOS

Linehan, M. M. (1995). *Understanding borderline personality disorder: The dialectical approach*. New York: Guilford Press.

Linehan, M. M. (1995). *Treating borderline personality disorder: The dialectical approach*. New York: Guilford Press.

Linehan, M.M., Dimeff, L., Waltz, J. & Koerner, K. (2000). *DBT skills training video: Opposite action*. Seattle: The Behavioural Technology Transfer Group.

ASSESSMENT INSTRUMENTS

First, M., Spitzer, R., Gibbon M. & Williams, J. (1997). *Structured Clinical Interview for DSM-IV Personality Disorders, (SCID-II)*. Washington, DC: American Psychiatric Press. Online. Available at: http://cpmcnet.columbia.edu/dept/scid/ Computer Assisted SCID available at: http://www.mhs.com/ or e-mail Jodi Douglass (jodi.d@mhs.com) Tel: +1–416–492–2627; fax: 1–416–492–3343. PO Box 950, North Tonawanda, NY, 14120–0950, USA.

Loranger, A. (1999). International Personality Disorder Examination (IPDE). Odessa, FL: PAR. Online: Available at: http://www.parinc.com/product.cfm?ProductID=164

Pfohl, B., Blum, N. & Zimmerman, M. (1997). Structured Interview for DSM IV Personality, Washington, DC: American Psychiatric Association. Online. Available at: http://www.appa.org or e-mail bruce_p@compuserve.com

Assessment instruments developed by Marsha Linehan and colleagues

The following assessment instruments are available at http://www.brtc.psych.washington.edu/framePublications.html

- Reasons for Living Scale (RFL)
- Suicide Attempt – Self Injury Interview (SASII)
- Lifetime Parasuicide Count (LPC)
- Suicidal Behaviours Questionnaire (SBQ)
- Treatment History Interview (THI)
- Social History Interview (SHI)
- Substance Abuse History Interview (SAHI)
- Demographic Data Scale (DDS)
- Parental Anger Test

REFERENCES

American Psychiatric Association (APA) (1994). *Diagnostic and statistical manual of the mental disorders (Fourth Edition, DSM-IV)*. Washington, DC: APA.

American Psychiatric Association (APA) (2000). *Diagnostic and statistical manual of the mental disorders (Fourth Edition-Text Revision, DSM-IV-TR)*. Washington, DC: APA.

Barasch, A., Frances, A. J. & Hurt, S. W. (1985). Stability and distinctness of borderline personality disorder. *American Journal of Psychiatry*, 142, 1484–1486.

Bateman, A. & Fonagy, P. (1999). Effectiveness of partial hospitalization in the treatment of borderline personality disorder: A randomized controlled trial. *American Journal of Psychiatry*, 156, 1563–1569.

Bateman, A. & Fonagy, P. (2001). Treatment of borderline personality disorder with psychoanalytically oriented partial hospitalization: An 18-month follow-up. *American Journal of Psychiatry*, 158, 36–52.

Beauchaine, T. (2001). Vagal tone, development, and Gray's motivational theory: Toward an integrated model of autonomic nervous system functioning in psychopathology. *Developmental Psychopathology*, 13, 183–214.

Beck, A. T., Rush, A. J., Shaw, B. F. & Emery, G. (1979). *Cognitive therapy of depression*. New York: Guilford Press.

Brooner, R. K., King, V. L., Kidorf, M., Schmidt, C. W. & Bigelow, G. E. (1997). Psychiatric and substance use comorbidity among treatment-seeking opioid abusers. *Archives of General Psychiatry*, 54, 71–80.

Chengappa, K., Ebeling, T., Kang, J., Levine, J. & Parepally, H. (1999). Clozapine reduces severe self-mutilation and aggression in psychotic patients with borderline personality disorder. *Journal of Clinical Psychiatry*, 60, 477–484.

Clarkin, J., Widiger, T., Frances, A., Hurt, S. & Gilmore, M. (1983). Prototypic typology and the borderline personality disorder. *Journal of Abnormal Psychology*, 92, 263–275.

Coccaro, E. & Kavoussi, R. (1997). Fluoxetine and impulsive aggressive behaviour in personality-disordered subjects. *Archives of General Psychiatry*, 54, 1081–1088.

Coccaro, E., Siever, L., Klar, H. T., et al. (1989). Serotonergic studies in patients with affective and personality disorders: Correlates with suicidal and impulsive aggressive behaviour. *Archives of General Psychiatry*, 46, 587–599.

Dahl, A. A. (1986). Prognosis of the borderline disorders. *Psychopathology*, 19, 68–79.

De la Fuente, M., Goldman, S., Stanus, E. et al. (1997). Brain glucose metabolism in borderline personality disorder. *Journal of Psychiatry Research*, 31, 531–541.

Dimeff, L. A., McDavid, J. & Linehan, M. M. (1999). Pharmacotherapy for borderline personality disorder: A review of the literature and recommendations for treatment. *Journal of Clinical Psychology in Medical Settings*, 6, 113–138.

Ellis, A. (1962). *Reason and emotion in psychotherapy*. New York: Lyle Stuart.

Ellis, A. (1973). *Humanistic psychotherapy: The rational-emotive approach*. New York: Julian Press.

First, M., Spitzer, R., Gibbon, R., Williams, J. & Benjamin, L. (1997). *Structured Clinical Interview for DSM-IV-TR Axis II Personality Disorders (SCID-II)*. Washington, DC: Psychiatric Press.

Foa, E. B. & Kozak, M. J. (1986). Emotional processing of fear: Exposure to corrective information. *Psychological Bulletin*, 99, 20–35.

Frances, A., Fyer, M. & Clarkin, J. (1986). Personality and suicide. *Annals of the New York Academy of Sciences*, 487, 281–293.

Frankenburg, F. & Zanarini, M. (1993). Clozapine treatment of borderline patients: A preliminary study. *Comprehensive Psychiatry*, 34, 402–405.

Freeman, A. & Davis, D. (2003). *Cognitive therapy of personality disorders* (Second Edition). New York: Guilford Press.

Gardner, D. L. & Cowdry, R. W. (1989). Pharmacotherapy of borderline personality disorder: A review. *Psychopharmacology Bulletin*, 25, 515–523.

Geller, J. (1986). In again, out again: Preliminary evaluation of a state hospital's worst recidivists. *Hospital Community Psychiatry*, 37, 386–390.

Glick, I., Dulit, R., Wachter, E. & Clarkin, J. (1995). The family, family therapy, and borderline personality disorder. *The Journal of Psychotherapy Practice and Research*, 4, 237–246.

Goyer, P., Andreason, P., Semple, W. et al. (1994). Positron-emission tomography and personality disorders. *Neuropsychopharmacology*, 10, 21–28.

Grilo, C., Anez, L. & McGlashan, T. (2002). DSM-IV Axis II comorbidity with borderline personality disorder in monolingual Hispanic psychiatric outpatients. *Journal of Nervous and Mental Disease*, 190, 324–330.

Gunderson, J. (1989). *Borderline personality disorder, in treatments of psychiatric disorders: A task force report of the American Psychiatric Association* (pp. 2749–2759). Washington, DC: American Psychiatric Association.

Gunderson, J., Kolb, J. & Austin, V. (1981). The diagnostic interview for borderline patients. *American Journal of Psychiatry*, 138, 896–903.

Herpertz, S. C., Dietrich, T.M., Wenning, B., Krings, T., Erberich, S. G., Willmes, K., Thron, A. & Sass, H. (2001). Evidence of abnormal amygdala functioning in borderline personality disorder: A functional MRI study. *Biological Psychiatry*, 50, 292–298.

Hyler, S., Skodol, A., Kellman, H., Oldham, J. & Rosnick, L. (1990). Validity of the personality diagnostic questionnaire-Revised: Comparison with two semi structured interviews. *American Journal of Psychiatry*, 147, 1043–1048.

Irwin, W., Davidson, R. J., Lowe, M. J., Mock, B. J., Sorenson, J. A. & Turski, P. A. (1996). Human amygdala activation detected with echo-planar functional magnetic resonance imaging. *Neuroreport*, 7, 1765–1769.

Kaye, A. & Shea, M. (2000). Personality disorders, personality traits, and defense mechanisms. In Task Force for the Handbook of Psychiatric Measures (Eds.), *Handbook of psychiatric measures* (pp. 713–749). Washington DC: American Psychiatric Association.

Kernberg, O. (1984). *Severe personality disorders: Psychotherapeutic strategies*. New Haven, CT: Yale University Press.

Kullgren, G. (1992). Personality disorders among psychiatric inpatients. *Nordisk Psykiastrisktidsskrift*, 46, 27–32.

Kuo J., Shaw-Welch, S. & Linehan, M. (2003). *Biological markers of emotion dysregulation in borderline personality disorder*. Poster presented at the 37th Association for Advancement of Behavior Therapy, Boston, MA.

Levitt, H., Korman, Y. & Angus, L. (2000). A metaphor analysis in treatments of depression: Metaphor as a marker of change. *Counseling Psychology Quarterly*, 13(1), 23–35.

Lieb, K., Zanarini, M. C., Linehan, M. M. & Bohus, M. (2004). Seminar section: borderline personality disorder. *The Lancet*, 364, 453–461.

Linehan, M. M. (1993a). *Cognitive-behavioural treatment of borderline personality disorder*. New York: Guilford Press.

Linehan, M. M. (1993b). *The skills training manual for treating borderline personality disorder*. New York: Guilford Press.

Linehan, M. M., Armstrong, H. E., Suarez, A., Allmon, D. & Heard, H.L. (1991). Cognitive-behavioural treatment of chronically parasuicidal borderline patients. *Archives of General Psychiatry*, 48, 1060–1064.

Linehan, M., Comtois, K., Murray-Gregory, A., Whiteside, U. & Levensky, E. (2002). *University of Washington treatment study for borderline personality disorder: DBT versus non-behavioural treatment by experts in the community*. Symposium presented at the Association for the Advancement of Behavior Therapy, Reno, NV.

Linehan, M., Schmidt, H., Dimeff, L., Craft, J., Kanter, J. & Comtois, K. (1999): Dialectical behaviour therapy for patients with borderline personality disorder and drug-dependence. *American Journal on Addictions*, 8, 279–292.

Links, P. S., Steiner, M., Offord, D. R. & Eppel, A. (1988). Characteristics of borderline personality disorder: A Canadian study. *Canadian Journal of Psychiatry*, 33, 336–340.

Loranger, A., Oldham, J. & Tulis, E. (1982). Familial transmission of DSM-III borderline personality disorder. *Archives of General Psychiatry*, 39, 795–799.

Loranger, A., Sartorius, N., Andreoli, A. S., et al. (1994). The International Personality Disorder Examination: The World Health Organization/Alcohol, Drug Abuse, and Mental Health Administration international pilot study of personality disorders. *Archives of General Psychiatry*, 51, 215–224.

Lyoo, I., Han, M. & Cho, D. (1998). A brain MRI study in subjects with borderline personality disorder. *Journal of Affective Disorders*, 50, 235–243.

Markovitz, P. (1995). Pharmacotherapy of impulsivity, aggression, and related disorders. In E. Hollander & D. J. Stein (Eds.), *Impulsivity and aggression* (pp. 263–287). Chichester, UK: John Wiley & Sons.

McCann R., Ball, E. & Ivanoff, A. (2000). DBT with an inpatient forensic population: The CMHIP forensic model. *Cognitive Behavioral Practice*, 7, 447–456.

McGlashan, T. H. (1986). The Chestnut Lodge follow-up study. III: Long-term outcome of borderline personalities. *Archives of General Psychiatry*, 43, 20–30.

McMain, S., Korman, L. & Dimeff, L. (2001). Dialectical behaviour therapy and the treatment of emotion dysregulation. *In Session: Psychotherapy in Practice*, 57, 183–196.

Moleman, P., Van Dam, K. & Dings, V. (1999). *Treatment of personality disorders* (pp. 207–227). Dordrecht, Netherlands: Kluwer Academic Publishers.

Morris, J. S., Frith, C. D., Perrett, D. I., Rowland, D., Young, A. W., Calder, A. J. & Dolan, R. J. (1996). A differential neural response in the human amygdala to fearful and happy facial expressions. *Nature*, 383, 812–815.

Paris, J. (2003). *Managing chronic suicidality in BPD*. Symposium presented at the International Society for the Study of Personality Disorders, Florence, Italy.

Paris, J., Brown, R. & Nowlis, D. (1987). Long-term follow-up of borderline patients in a general hospital. *Comprehensive Psychiatry*, 28, 530–535.

Perry, J., Herman, J., van der Kolk, B. & Hoke, L. (1990). Psychotherapy and psychological trauma in borderline personality disorder. *Psychiatric Annals*, 20, 33–43.

Pfohl, B., Blum, N. & Zimmerman, M. (1997). *Structured Interview for DSM-IV Personality*. Washington, DC: American Psychiatric Press.

Pierce, W. D. & Cheney, C. D. (2004). *Behavior analysis and learning*. Mahwah, NJ: Lawrence Erlbaum Associates.

Pope, H. G., Jonas, J. M., Hudson, J. I., Cohen, B. M. & Gunderson, J. G. (1983). The validity of DSM-III borderline personality disorder: A phenomenologic, family history, treatment response, and long term follow-up study. *Archives of General Psychiatry*, 40, 23–30.

Porges, S. W., Doussard-Roosevelt, J. A. & Maiti, A. K. (1994). Vagal tone and the physiological regulation of emotion. *Monographs of the Society for Research in Child Development*, 59, 167–186.

Pretzer, J. (1990). Borderline personality disorder. In A. Freeman, J. Pretzer, B. Fleming & K. M. Simon (Eds.), *Clinical applications of cognitive therapy* (pp. 181–202). New York: Plenum Press.

Rascati, J. (1990). Managed care and the discharge dilemma: Commentary. *Psychiatry*, 53, 124–126.

Rasmussen, B. (2000). Poetic truths and clinical reality: Client experiences of the use of metaphor by therapists. *Smith College Studies in Social Work*, 70(2), 355–373.

Richman, J. & Charles, E. (1976). Patient dissatisfaction and attempted suicide. *Community Mental Health Journal*, 12, 301–305.

Rinne T, van den Brink, W., Wouters, L. & van Dyck, R. (2002). SSRI treatment of borderline personality disorder: A randomized, placebo-controlled clinical trial for female patients with borderline personality disorder. *American Journal of Psychiatry*, 15, 2048–2054.

Rocca, P., Marchiaro, L., Cocuzza, E. & Bogetto, F.. (2002). Treatment of borderline personality disorder with risperidone. *Journal of Clinical Psychiatry*, 63, 241–244.

Saposnek, D. T. (1980). Aikido: A model for brief strategic therapy. *Family Process*, 19, 227–238.

Schmahl, C. & Bohus, M. (2001). Symptomorientierte Pharmakotherapie bei Borderline-Persönlichkeitsstörung. *Fortschritte der Neurologie, Psychiatrie*, 69, 310–321.

Schulz, S., Camlin, K., Berry, S. & Jesberger, J. (1999). Olanzapine safety and efficacy in patients with borderline personality disorder and comorbid dysthymia. *Biological Psychiatry*, 46, 1429–1435.

Siever, L., Amin, F., Coccaro, E. et al. (1991). Plasma homovanillic acid in schizotypcal personality disorder patients and controls. *American Journal of Psychiatry*, 148, 1246–1248.

Siever, L. & Trestman, R. (1993). The serotonin system and aggressive personality disorder. *International Journal of Clinical Psychoharmacology*, 8 (suppl 2), 33–39.

Simpson, J. A. & Weiner, E. S. (1989). *Oxford English dictionary* (Second Edition). Oxford: Oxford University Press.

Skodol, A., Buckley, P. & Charles, E. (1983). Is there a characteristic pattern to the treatment history of clinic outpatients with borderline personality? *Journal of Nervous and Mental Diseases*, 171, 405–410.

Skodol, A., Gunderson, J., McGlashan, et al. (2002a). Functional impairment in patients with schizotypcal, borderline, avoidant, or obsessive-compulsive personality disorder. *American Journal of Psychiatry*, 159, 276–283.

Skodol, A., Gunderson, J., Pfohl, B., Widiger, T., Livesley, J. & Siever, L. (2002b). The borderline diagnosis I: Psychopathology, Comorbidity, and Personality Structure. *Biological Psychiatry*, 51, 936–950.

Skodol, A., Siever, L., Livesley, W., Gunderson, J., Pfohl, B. & Widiger, T. (2002c). The borderline diagnosis II: Biology, genetic, and clcinical course. *Biological Psychiatry*, 51, 951–963.

Soloff, P. H. (2000). Psychopharmacology of borderline personality disorder. *Psychiatric Clinics of North America*, 23, 169–192.

Soloff, P. H., George, A., Nathan, R. S. et al. (1989). Amitriptyline versus haloperidol in borderlines: Final outcomes and predictors of response. *Journal of Clinical Psychopharmacology*, 9, 238–246.

Stone, M., Hurt, S. & Stone, D. (1987). The PI 500: Long-term follow-up of borderline inpatients meeting DSM-III criteria. I: Global outcome. *Journal of Personality Disorders*, 1, 291–298.

Swigar, M. E., Astrachan, B. M., Levine, M. A., Mayfield, V. & Radovich, C. (1991). Single and repeated admissions to a mental health center. *The International Journal of Social Psychiatry*, 37, 259–266.

Tebartz van Elst, L., Hesslinger, B., Thiel, T. et al. (2003). Subtle Prefrontal Neuropathology in a pilot magnetic resonance spectroscopy study in patients with borderline personality disorder: A volumetric magnetic resonance imaging study. *Biological Psychiatry*, 54, 163–171.

Telch, C., Agras, W. & Linehan, M. (2000). Group dialectical behaviour therapy for binge-eating disorder: A preliminary, uncontrolled trial. *Behavior Therapy*, 31, 569–582.

Telch, C., Agras, W. & Linehan, M. (2001). Dialectical behaviour therapy for binge eating disorder. *Journal of Consulting and Clinical Psychology*, 69(6), 1061–1065.

Torgersen, S., Lygren, S., Per A. et al. (2000). A twin study of personality disorders. *Comprehensive Psychiatry*, 42, US-425.

Weiss, R. D., Mirin, S. M., Griffin, M. L. et al. (1993). Personality disorders in cocaine dependence. *Comprehensive Psychiatry*, 34, 145–149.

Whitaker, C. (1975). Psychotherapy of the absurd: With special emphasis on the psychotherapy of aggression. *Family Process*, 14, 1–16.

Widiger, T., Mangine, S., Corbitt, E., Ellis, C. & Thomas, G. (1995). *Personality Disorder Interview-IV: A Semi-structured interview for the assessment of personality disorders*. Odessa, FL: Psychological Assessment Resources.

Wiser, S. & Telch C. (1999). Dialectical behaviour therapy for binge-eating disorder. *Journal of Clinical Psychology*, 55, 755–768.

World Health Organization (WHO) (1992). *The ICD-10 classification of mental and behavioural disorders. Diagnostic criteria for research*. Geneva: WHO.

Young, J. (1983). *Borderline personality: Cognitive theory and treatment*. Paper presented at the annual meeting of the American Psychological Association, Anaheim, CA.

Young, J.E. (1990). *Cognitive therapy for personality disorders: A schema-focused approach*. Sarasota, FL: Professional Resources Exchange.

Young, J. & Swift, W. (1988). Schema-focused cognitive therapy for personality disorders: Part I. *International Cognitive Therapy Newsletter*, 4, 13–14.

Zanarini, M. (2003). Zanarini Rating Scale for Borderline Personality Disorder (ZAN-BPD): A continuous measure of DSM-IV borderline psychopathology. *Journal of Personality Disorders*, 17(3) 233–242.

Zanarini M. & Frankenburg F. (2003). Omega-3 fatty acid treatment of women with borderline personality disorder: A double-blind, placebo-controlled pilot study. *American Journal of Psychiatry*, 160, 167–169.

Zanarini, M., Frankenburg, F., Chauncey, D. & Gunderson, J. (1987). The Diagnostic

Interview for Personality Disorders: Interrater and test-retest reliability. *Comprehensive Psychiatry*, 28, 467–480.

Zanarini, M., Frankenburg, F., Hennen, J., Silk, K. (2003a). The longtitudinal course of borderline psychopathology: 6-year prospective follow-up of the phenomenology of borderline personality disorder. *American Journal of Psychiatry*, 160, 274–283.

Zanarini, M., Frankenburg, F., Khera, G. & Bleichmar, J. (2001). Treatment histories of borderline inpatients. *Comprehensive Psychiatry*, 42, 144–150.

Zanarini, M., Gunderson, J., Marino, M., Schwartz, E. & Frankenburg, F. (1988). DSM-III disorders in the families of borderline outpatients. *Journal of Personality Disorders*, 2, 292–302.

Zanarini, M., Gunderson, J., Marino, M., Schwartz, E. & Frankenburg, F. (1989). Childhood experiences of borderline patients. *Comprehensive Psychiatry*, 30, 18–25.

Zanarini, M., Vujanovic, A., Parachini, E., Boulanger, J., Frankenburg, F. & Hennen, J. (2003b). A screening measure for BPD: The McLean Screening Instrument for Borderline Personality Disorder (MSI-BPD). *Journal of Personality Disorders*, 17(6), 568–573.

Zanarini, M., Williams, A., Lewis, R. & Reich, R. (1997). Reported pathological childhood experiences associated with the development of borderline personality disorder. *American Journal of Psychiatry*, 146, 490–495.

ACKNOWLEDGEMENT

Writing of this manuscript was partially supported by grants MH34486 from the National Institute on Mental Health and DAO8674 from the National Institute on Drug Abuse, Bethesda, MD.

Chapter 23

Psychological problems of older people

Bob Woods and Carolien Lamers

CASE EXAMPLE

Mr Bill Jones is 83 and has been referred to the memory clinic by his GP, who reports that Mr Jones complains about forgetting people's names and that he needs reminding by his wife to complete tasks. He gets annoyed with himself when he cannot find things he is looking for. He goes out much less now, as most of the close friends he used to socialize with have passed away.

On the face of it, perhaps, this is a fairly typical 'older adult' referral. Is Mr Jones one of the 20+% of his age group developing a dementia? Will this be confirmed by a neuropsychological assessment? How will Mr Jones adjust to such a diagnosis? Is this what he suspects is the problem when he presents himself at the clinic? Will Mrs Jones slip effortlessly into a caregiving role? What will be the implications for their lives together?

However, a cursory glance at the literature on the psychology of ageing gives pause for thought. Surely, changes in memory and other cognitive functions are to be expected as one ages? Is it not possible that Mr Jones is simply reacting to 'normal' age-related changes? The key initial question for the clinical psychologist in this case then becomes: How can cognitive changes associated with a dementia be distinguished from normal ageing? Note that it is *change* in functioning that is of importance, which leaves the additional quandary of estimating change when there is no documented baseline level.

COGNITIVE CHANGES AND NORMAL AGEING – AN OVERVIEW

Most studies of cognitive ageing compare groups of younger and older people; they provide cross-sectional information regarding age differences rather than indicating the nature and extent of changes with age. Longitudinal studies of ageing tend to show much less extensive decline than cross-sectional studies. Cohort effects, related to the time in history when the person was born, are thought to account for a large proportion of age differences (Schaie, 1996); these may relate to early experiences, in education and nutrition, for example. Stability across much of the lifespan appears to be the norm, rather than a decline from age twenty. For example, Deary, Whalley, Lemmon, Crawford and Starr (2000) assessed a sample of 101 people sixty-six years after they were assessed at age eleven, using the identical IQ test. They found that scores *increased* over this time, but that a person's scores at age eleven and at age seventy-seven were highly correlated.

Groups of older people in longitudinal studies do show changes in cognition (e.g. Cullum et al., 2000), with increased variance reflecting probable variability in rates of individual change. There is some support from Schaie's longitudinal studies that 'crystallized' abilities (e.g. verbal ability) show change later than 'fluid' abilities (such as spatial ability and perceptual speed), although individual patterns of change are diverse (Schaie, 1990). Salthouse (2000) suggests that an age-related reduction in speed of processing could be the fundamental cognitive change with age. Baltes and Baltes (1990) provide a model of successful ageing, which can be applied to conceptualizing the way in which many older people maintain good cognitive function, despite changes occurring at a neurophysiological level. The Selective Optimization with Compensation (SOC) model suggests that older people ageing successfully select their goals carefully, focusing on the areas of most importance or interest to themselves; optimize goal-relevant means, perhaps by practising more or devoting more time and energy to a task than previously; and compensate for areas of lost function using substitute means. Thus, in particular domains – chess, bridge, an Open University degree, musical performance, wisdom – the person may maintain and develop function, despite experiencing age-related changes. Schaie (1996) comments that in his large-scale longitudinal study assessing five areas of cognitive function, most people showed decline in one area by age sixty, but that virtually no-one had declined in all five areas even by age eighty-eight (p. 355). Cognitive decline with age is not a uniform or a universal phenomenon.

In considering the reasons why, on average, groups of older people show reduced scores on cognitive tests, there is no doubt that health problems are the major factor. For example, vascular disease has been shown in a large scale study of older men (Elwood et al., 2002) to be related to the equivalent of five years of 'normal' age change. Diabetes (Holland & Rabbitt, 1991) and sensory problems have also been shown to be related to cognitive loss, with even mild hearing and visual impairment reducing performance (Rabbitt, 1988). Lifestyle may also have an influence, with those involved in activities that are complex and intellectually stimulating being said to show less decline (Schaie, 1996, p. 356).

ASSESSMENT

Assessment is the first step in any work to be undertaken with a client. In a crisis or emergency, assessments can be quick and instantaneous, but will need to be followed up systematically. To offer a client any type of intervention, be it individual or family therapy, memory retraining or counselling, one needs to have some idea about the nature of the needs and issues encountered by the client and associated support systems. An intervention is likely to be more effective when the client's perception of his or her difficulties, the impact these might have on their lives and their family, and their concerns for the future are taken into consideration. Due to the complex interplay of physical, psychological and social factors in older adulthood, a multidisciplinary assessment will often be required in order to ensure a holistic and comprehensive intervention package is provided.

Pre-assessment phase

Before commencing any type of formal assessment, a rapport must be established with the client. This stage of the contact will endeavour to establish their perceptions about the referral. The client might not be aware of any problems or may feel that the caregivers are over-concerned and exaggerating the problems. Through careful interviewing one can begin to establish the nature and level of awareness. The client may be aware of the difficulties but understands them as signs of old age or in the light of other important life events. Often the client will express some concerns about what might lie ahead if they were to admit to any difficulties. Statements like 'I was afraid I would be put away' might be heard. Others will have a clear concern about the nature of their problems and possible origin and the treatment that may be required.

In any event, explaining the nature of the contact and the plan for the next few sessions can be helpful. The client can experience the boundaries of the involvement and the intentions of the professionals being set out as helpful and reassuring. The professional can find explaining the limitations of confidentiality, in terms of risks involving the safety of the client or others, more difficult. The perceived risk to the therapeutic relationship can be seen as an obstacle. However, in order to avoid potentially more difficult situations at a later stage, these limitations to confidentiality need to be pointed out.

Mr and Mrs Jones are initially seen together in the clinic. Mrs Jones is a lively, talkative woman, some fifteen years younger than her husband. Mr Jones seems hesitant to talk about his difficulties but his wife quickly fills in the gaps; Mr Jones looks uncomfortable and embarrassed as a litany of his memory failures is recounted. The history of the memory problems is raised; Mrs Jones says 'he was never any good with names', but it appears that over the last twelve months she has noticed a worsening of the problems.

Did anything else change at that time? Mrs Jones describes how just over a year ago they lost a daughter, who had become progressively frail over a two-year period with cancer. However, although Mr Jones and his daughter were close, she feels it has had little impact on him, and he never mentions her.

Interviewed alone, it is clear Mr Jones is slightly hard of hearing. He has not considered a hearing aid, as wearing one would be too embarrassing, he says. When asked about his memory problems, he motions to the chair vacated by his wife: 'you'll have to ask her about all that', he says. He makes it clear that it is his wife who has initiated the referral. He sounds sad as he talks about the friends he has lost, and becomes tearful when his daughter is mentioned. He remarks how unfair that one relatively young should die, whilst he has to go on living.

Pre-diagnostic counselling

Undertaking pre-assessment and pre-diagnostic counselling has become almost routine in other parts of the health service, e.g. in cancer and HIV/AIDS services. Clients will be informed about the intention behind the assessment and discussions will be held about the consequences of a likely positive outcome. It is considered to be a patient's right to be informed regarding investigations and findings. However, there appears to be a different attitude towards older people. Particularly when the client is suspected of having cognitive impairment, the assumption can be made that the person is not aware of what is going on and that they will not understand or remember the impact of the assessments and diagnosis. Sometimes the assumption is made that sharing a diagnosis might distress the patient and exacerbate or even trigger an episode of depression or suicide. The client's caregivers may raise or share this anxiety themselves. However, studies asking people (including caregivers) if they would like to be informed about certain conditions clearly indicate that people want to be informed if the illness involves them (Erde et al., 1988; Maguire et al., 1996; Rimmer, 1993).

The move towards engaging clients with cognitive impairment fully in decision making has been encouraged by Kitwood's person-centred care approach, which argues that attending to the whole person is essential to enable the person to make the fullest use of his or her abilities and to remain a social being (Kitwood, 1997).

Pre-diagnostic counselling plays a major role in the assessment process for clients with suspected dementia. Clients who have an awareness and insight into their changing faculties can understandably be anxious and might have a desire to hide, ignore or deny any difficulties (Keady & Nolan, 1994). When the client presents for an assessment, it is possible that the first symptoms have existed for several months. 'Early' diagnosis is often recommended, but it can be difficult for a primary care worker to raise concerns that they or a carer might have about the abilities of a client if the person themself is not making any overt complaints. Assessment and diagnosis need to be 'timely', offered when the client is prepared to engage at some level with the process (Woods et al., 2003). The client's beliefs that the symptoms are part of old age and growing older need to be discussed in a sensitive manner, and alternative possibilities raised.

Establishing the client's understanding of the experienced problems and identifying previously adopted coping mechanisms will inform further action. Their anxieties may be fuelled by previous experiences of people with similar conditions or symptoms. Explanations about the possible origins of cognitive impairment can begin to guide the client through the maze of assessments. The possibility of a deteriorating condition like a dementia syndrome should be considered and discussed as openly as possible. To actually use the words that might constitute a diagnosis should be attempted. Very often it is the professionals themselves who are uneasy about this. It can be a relief to clients when the condition they have been worried about is openly discussed. The containment of the client's anxiety until the assessment process is completed is the aim.

> Mr Jones does not know what is wrong with him. He feels he lacks energy and cannot be bothered doing things. If he only had the energy to remember things, he would be much better. He wonders whether this could all be related to old age. When the procedure of assessment is explained to him, he asks whether he might have Alzheimer's. He is slightly worried, as his mother had become rather confused in old age. He says he is the sort of person who would want to know what is wrong with him.

Assurances can seldom be given at an early stage. An openness of approach aims to avoid the development of suspicion and indicate to clients that their concerns will be given serious consideration. The professional needs to be prepared to accept the fact that after pre-diagnostic counselling the client may decide that he/she does not want to continue with the assessment. Only under exceptional circumstances might there be a need to invoke the relevant legislation (in the UK, the Mental Health Act), typically if one is aware of a risk to self or others. Another possibility is that the person does not object to the assessment but does not want to be informed of a possible diagnosis. It is important to clarify at this point whether the client gives consent that other people could be informed.

Health assessment

There is a high comorbidity of a range of physical illnesses in later life, which could contribute to the cognitive problems and mood changes. It is therefore important to ensure that a comprehensive physical examination has taken place, whether by the GP or, where appropriate, by a specialist such as a neurologist, geriatrician or psychiatrist. A range of blood tests is usually carried out to exclude common conditions. For example, low iron levels, vitamin deficiencies, over or under active thyroid, and infections can be diagnosed and treated or further investigated if necessary. Other investigations like X-rays, EEG, ECG, CT scan or MRI scan might be considered, usually depending on the findings of neurological investigations, the presenting problems and their history.

Mr Jones' medical history shows that he has had raised blood pressure for many years, for which he receives medication, and that he recently has developed diabetes, which is controlled through diet.

These findings will need to be taken into consideration when a diagnosis is made.

Mood assessment

Mr Jones is asked about his appetite and his sleep; he eats well but his regular nightmares lead to sleepless nights. He has been reliant on benzodiazepines to help him sleep for many years. The nightmares have become worse over the last few years and concern his wartime experiences, when he was a prisoner of war in the Far East. Since the loss of his old friends, who went back to his army days, he has not been able to mention these; it is not a topic of discussion favoured by his wife, who tells him 'it was a long time ago'.

At this point, the careful neuropsychological assessment, which seemed the most likely response to the initial referral, is put on hold. The priority is to evaluate Mr Jones' mood and affect, the likelihood of a grief reaction and the possibility of PTSD. If these factors turn out not to be contributory to his presentation then there are medical factors (hearing, hypertension, diabetes and benzodiazepine use) to consider. On the social front, there appears to be some tension in the relationship with Mrs Jones, and a reduction in his social network that may well be relevant.

In fact, it is this combination and interaction of biological, social and psychological factors that is the hallmark of work with older adults. Formulations need to reflect the multi-factorial nature of older adult presentations, and assessment and interventions need to be based on this premise.

DEPRESSION AND ANXIETY IN LATER LIFE

Prevalence

Depression and anxiety are common psychological disorders in late life. Reported prevalence rates vary from study to study, and reflect differences in criteria and measures as well as between populations. A typical estimate, from an urban community sample (Lindesay et al. 1989), is of 4.3% of over 65s having severe depression and 13.5% having a mild/moderate form of the disorder; 3.7% with generalized anxiety and 10% with phobic anxiety (with some comorbidity between anxiety and depression).

It is important to emphasize that the rates of depressive disorder in older people living in the community are no greater than those of younger age groups (Henderson, 1994). The incorrect assumption that the weight of loss and adversity faced by older people must inevitably lead to depression is potentially harmful to older people. It may lead to depression and anxiety not being recognized, acknowledged and appropriately treated. It may set limits to therapeutic aspirations, if depression is accepted as part of the natural state of late life. In fact, gerontological studies suggest that typically older people maintain life satisfaction and well-being, in the face of losses and life events and difficult life circumstances (e.g. Windle & Woods, 2004). The key role of psychological resources is apparent in this research, with those individuals with a stronger sense of control, mastery or resilience emerging as better equipped to deal with problems encountered in later life.

Life events

Clinical studies indicate that the onset of depression is associated with higher rates of life events and difficulties during the preceding year (Kraaij & de Wilde, 2001; Lam et al., 1987; Murphy, 1982), as with younger people. Again, it is important to note that many older people experience similar life events without developing depression. Davies (1996) suggests that, perhaps counter-intuitively, older people experience fewer adverse life events than younger people; however, they also enjoy fewer desirable events.

Life events that threaten the person's social roles and social identity are especially difficult; they reduce the potential for the person to exert control in areas of life of particular salience and importance. Kuypers and Bengtson (1973) postulate, in their Social Breakdown Theory, that older people have an ill-defined role in society and that the lack of a positive reference group can potentially decrease their abilities to cope in a constructive manner. Retirement provides a good example; if work was fundamental to the person's sense of worth and identity, this will be more difficult. For many people, a sense of control is important – if the retirement was planned for and anticipated, than it is likely to be less problematic than if it was unexpected and involuntary. Many people find retirement a relief from the demands of work, which can be monotonous, physically challenging or even damaging to health. The impact of retirement on finances will increasingly be a major issue for retirees, with financial security in late life challenged by changes in policies on pensions.

Bereavement

Compared to younger people, older adults tend to have fewer severe grief reactions. They report lower levels of distress and mental health problems following a bereavement, although there may be more of an impact on physical health (e.g. Breckenridge et al., 1986; McKiernan, 1996). One factor in this intergenerational difference is that most bereavements experienced by older people are of other older people, and so are less likely to be perceived as 'untimely'. However, the death of an adult child remains difficult for older people, perhaps because this departs from the developmental expectation. When the death is expected, as in a terminal illness, younger people often benefit from this period of anticipatory mourning, and show a less severe grief reaction. This does not seem to be the case for older people, who may be exhausted after a prolonged period of caregiving, or for whom the death is no less unexpected, despite the presence of chronic illness (McKiernan, 1996).

Grief is, of course, a normal process in response to loss. The question arises as to when does grief become 'abnormal' or, perhaps, when is psychological intervention required? There is now acceptance that 'stage theories' of grief, which prescribe a particular sequence of tasks for the grief process, whilst being a useful reminder of the range of emotions and reactions often encountered, do not represent a required way of coping; there is, in fact, wide variation in normal grieving (Stroebe & Stroebe, 1991). Nor can a specific time period be specified. Later adjustment difficulties can be predicted by certain indicators a few months after the bereavement; these include negative self-image and low self-esteem, negative cognitions such as self-blame and guilt and a continued impact on day-to-day living (McKiernan, 1996).

Mr Jones is asked about the loss of his daughter in more detail. He bursts into tears again and explains how much he misses her and how special their relationship had been. He finds it hard to discuss his feelings with his wife, afraid of upsetting her as well. He feels he should be stronger but has no energy or interest in anything. He feels he cannot focus on anything as his thoughts drift back to images of his daughter in the final stages of her illness. He blames himself for not doing more to help her previously.

Health and mood

The most common adversities in later life relate to health problems, and severe illness in the past year is one of the life events shown by Kraaij and de Wilde (2001) to be related to depressive symptoms in late life. Depression and physical health have a complex relationship. Symptoms of depression (slowness, lethargy, loss of energy, loss of appetite and difficulty in sleeping) may in fact be a manifestation of physical health difficulties (a problem with some self-report depression scales, which include several such somatic items); or a person may complain of physical symptoms but in fact be depressed or, typically, a person may have a combination of physical health and psychological difficulties. Some common health problems in older people (especially Parkinson's and stroke) are known to be associated with depression (Laidlaw et al., 2003), with as many as a fifth of stroke patients being depressed six months post-stroke (Skilbeck, 1996). It is sometimes argued that the mood disorder arises directly from the changes associated with the disorder, however, from a psychological perspective, the person's mood needs to be understood in relation to the dynamics of the process of adjustment. Dent et al. (1999) suggest it is the level of disability that is the key factor, rather than the specific disorder, which mediates the occurrence of depression. The extent to which the person feels control over the health problem (is it perceived as life-threatening?), the extent to which it threatens the person's body image (e.g. a limb amputation) and interferes with valued roles will also be relevant in assessing the person's psychological reaction to the difficulty.

Cognitive impairment and mood

It has been long established that depression and anxiety are themselves associated with cognitive impairments; it would seem evident that difficulties with motivation, concentration, sustained attention and speed of response could be associated with mood disorders. Beyond this level of explanation, there are strong suggestions that the observed impairments might also reflect cerebral changes. Thus, Cervilla and Prince (1997) suggest that cognitive impairment is a pathway to depression in late life distinct from that mediated by life events and social adversity. For example, Pearlson et al. (1989) showed that on CT scanning, depressed patients with and without cognitive impairment could be distinguished, with the former group being closer to, but distinct from patients with dementia; vascular changes are often implicated as being responsible for the structural change observed. There are some suggestions that cognitive impairments do not necessarily recover when the depressed mood returns to normal (Abas et al., 1990). Beats, Sahakian and Levy (1996) suggest that disruption to 'fronto-subcortical neural circuitry' underlies cognitive impairments in depression. However, the exact nature of the cognitive changes is not agreed, and shows variation from sample to sample and task to task (Poon, 1992). In Beats et al.'s study, depressed patients were shown to be particularly sensitive to failure on the first trial of a problem solving task, to which they showed a catastrophic response; a successful first attempt, on the other hand, was associated with relatively efficient problem-solving. An interaction between depressive cognitive style and performance does, then, appear to be evident. These considerations emphasize the futility of pursuing 'depression vs. dementia' referrals through assessment of cognitive impairment. Thus the question in relation to Mr Jones is how best to understand and offer help with the multiple problems he is experiencing, not to make a differential diagnosis.

Post-traumatic stress disorder

Traumatic and difficult events earlier in life have an important influence on older people, just as they do on younger adults (Kraaij & de Wilde, 2001). Childhood sexual abuse, exposure to traumatic incidents in war-time, rape, involvement in life-threatening accidents and so on, may all have ramifications in later life. As many as 16% of Second World War veterans have been reported as showing symptoms of post-traumatic stress disorder (PTSD; Bonwick & Morris, 1996), with even higher rates amongst prisoners of war (e.g. 30% of British Far-East POWs; Neal et al., 1995). Much depends on the specific experiences of combat or imprisonment. Whilst some older people will have had the symptoms of PTSD ever since the traumatic event, for others the memories seem to re-emerge. Perhaps the stress has been contained for many years, with the person coping by remaining busy and occupied. Retirement or ill-health leads to more inactivity, more time to think, perhaps a life review process; or anniversaries of events provide graphic reminders of events long forgotten. For some, the memories surface through nightmares initially, rather than day-time intrusive thoughts. Trauma in later life may have more impact on someone who has previously had PTSD (Solomon & Prager, 1992).

While Mr Jones is talking about his daughter, he becomes agitated and states that seeing his daughter reminded him of war-time images where emaciated prisoners looked like his daughter. He goes quiet and, when asked whether he thinks about his past experience, he remarks that images appear and that there is not much he can do about keeping them away.

PSYCHOLOGICAL THERAPY IN LATER LIFE

In our view, in all clinical psychological practice, whatever the age of the client, interventions need to be individually tailored, based on careful assessment and formulation. We acknowledge that there is a tension between this position and the drive towards therapies delivered in a standardized fashion, targeted at particular problems or groups of problems. Evaluations of such therapies, usually involving a randomized controlled trial design, form the core of the evidence base for the effectiveness of psychological therapies. Such studies are useful and helpful as a guide to the type of interventions that may be effective with a particular client, but in the clinical context, the question is not what is effective for a group of patients in a research trial, but rather what will make the desired difference for the specific patient (Woods, 2003).

Most psychological therapeutic work undertaken with older people is little different from that undertaken with younger people. A handful of intervention approaches are often described as being specific to older people, but essentially these are approaches to working with people with dementia, whatever the age of the person. The major group of approaches that might be said to be specifically geared to the developmental position of the older person are reminiscence and life review. These may readily be linked to the final phase of Erikson's life-span developmental model (Erikson, 1963; Erikson et al. 1986), where the task of late life is seen as involving a process of life review. The successful resolution of this stage involves a sense of integrity: accepting both what has been achieved and what will never now be possible; balancing disappointments and regrets with successes and positive experiences and memories. This position is contrasted with a sense of despair, of a life wasted, full of regret and disappointment, a sense of shame at the person one has become.

Although often used with people with dementia, typically in groups, primarily as a means of encouraging communication, enjoyment and well-being (Woods & McKiernan, 1995), life review and reminiscence therapy have also been widely used with older people experiencing symptoms of depression. Bohlmeijer et al. (2003) report a meta-analysis indicating strong empirical support for its use in this context. Life review is usually undertaken on a one-to-one basis, involving the person working through their life story chronologically, with the emphasis on evaluation of events and experiences, positive and negative, rather than simply the enjoyable recall of memories (Haight, 1992).

Some issues do arise more commonly in psychological therapy with older people, and may be considered as specific adaptations (Woods & Charlesworth, 2002); however, none are in fact age-specific:

Adversity

Older people referred for psychological therapy are often in the midst of difficult life circumstances – health problems, multiple bereavements, reduced social networks, enforced relocations. They may also face financial constraints and experience ageism. When the person reports negative thoughts these cannot always be conceptualized as cognitive distortions; they may well reflect the reality of the person's existence. A wise therapist does not rush in with bland reassurance or quick-fix solutions offering false hopes in such circumstances. Helping the person reflect on and reconsider the meanings underlying the negative thoughts is one approach used by therapists working in the field of life-threatening illness (e.g. Moorey, 1997) that is applicable in this context also. Helping the person develop pragmatic coping strategies is another approach – either problem-solving strategies to change an aspect of the difficult situation or emotion-focused, to assist in managing the person's emotional response to the situation.

Cognitive impairment

As well as those older people experiencing a dementia, a number of other potential clients for psychological therapy may have cognitive difficulties, e.g. those who have had a stroke, or have Parkinson's disease or who have mild cognitive impairment, as well as those whose depressed mood is associated with cognitive impairment. Such impairments do not rule out the use of therapies such as CBT – which have been shown to be feasible for treating depressed mood in people with dementia (Scholey & Woods, 2003). However, the therapist needs to adopt a flexible approach, using repetition and memory aids, summarizing clearly, working at the client's own pace, and where appropriate using behavioural methods, rather than focusing primarily on cognitions.

Physical health status

The person's health may place limitations on the progress of therapy, and may be a focus for the person's concerns. Sensory and mobility problems may require adaptations – in the use of written materials or in necessitating home visits. Depression and the person's physical condition can interact to reduce the person's function further, leading to excess disability, the reduction of which may be an important therapeutic goal. Working closely with medical colleagues who can advise on the effects of the person's health (and the associated medication) on function is essential.

Anti-therapy beliefs

Each succeeding generation of older people is more familiar with what is involved in psychological therapy – however, as with all cohorts, large individual differences remain in preparedness to engage in a 'talking therapy'. For some, where physical problems have already been diagnosed, seeing a psychologist implies that their problems are 'all in the mind' and appears to challenge the physical reality of their symptoms. Working with the person to move away from dichotomous thinking about 'body' and 'mind' is helpful here; recognizing that physical symptoms, including pain, can be worsened by stress and tension, and that the role of psychological therapy is to help manage these additional features, and to increase quality of life as far as possible.

Dependency on others

The dependency relationships of older people are often to the fore in psychological therapy. It is not possible to maintain the illusion sometimes fostered by the process of individual therapy with younger people that the person exists in isolation from a dynamic system of significant relationships. Relationships with spouse, adult children, care systems, medical practitioners: an understanding of each may be crucial to working with the older patient. Power imbalances loom large and problems may emerge when the person's attempts to maintain some control in the relationship are deemed inappropriate by those with more power. An interpersonal emphasis to therapy is often needed, with consideration given to joint sessions and the use of systemic therapy approaches and formulations (Pearce, 2002). The dependency of the person on the therapist may become an important issue; the therapist is viewed as a friend and the person feels bereft when treatment comes to an end. Issues of closure and consideration of the person's broader support system need careful reflection in supervision for experienced therapists as well as novices.

Chronicity of problems

Some older people referred for psychological therapy may have been experiencing difficulties over many years. They may have adapted to their problems in some ways, with them becoming literally part of their life; they may have had many previous experiences of treatments of various kinds. Being clear regarding the goals of treatment is important in such cases – improving quality of life and of the person's ability to cope may be acceptable goals; the person's efforts to cope with the problems over many years provide a store of experiences, which may be used to generate strategies for the present situation.

Although the evidence base for psychological therapies for mood disorders in older people is not large (older people are often excluded from treatment studies on the basis of their age), there is some evidence, from randomized controlled trials, that CBT in group and individual formats is effective in treating anxiety disorders in older people (e.g. Barrowclough et al., 2001). Cognitive therapy, behaviour therapy and brief psychodynamic psychotherapy appear to be equally effective treatment modalities for depression in older people (Thompson et al., 1987), with the effect size for cognitive therapy being comparable to that in younger people (Woods & Roth, 2005). A combined approach, using medication and monthly sessions of interpersonal psychotherapy, has been shown to be particularly helpful in preventing relapse for patients in this age group (Reynolds et al., 1999).

The initial formulation regarding Mr Jones's mood is that he is experiencing intrusive thoughts and images relating to both his daughter and his war-time experiences, and that his lack of opportunity to discuss these is hindering his ability to process and cope with these experiences. He is seen for a series of ten individual sessions where he is given the opportunity to talk about his life experiences and his losses and begin to integrate them as far as possible through structured life review using cognitive strategies, to help him reconsider his self-blame.

Mr Jones reports that he is beginning to be calmer about his daughter's death and now talks about her without crying. He is able to recall her as she was before the illness and recount stories about her when she was a younger girl. The flashbacks from the war have decreased in frequency and are generally less distressing. His improved mood is confirmed by his wife, and a fall in scores on the Hospital Anxiety & Depression Scale (HADS; Kenn et al., 1987) from the clinical to the normal range is also encouraging.

At a follow-up session four weeks later, to review the progress made during therapy, both Mr and Mrs Jones report maintained mood improvements, but the memory problems are still evident. It is decided to investigate these concerns further.

DEMENTIA ASSESSMENT

Cognitive assessment

In undertaking a cognitive assessment, the priority is again to establish a rapport with the client. The client will perform at their best if they feel supported and reassured; it is well worth investing time to try to allay any worries and anxieties they might have. Checking hearing aids are in place with a working battery and the availability of (reading) glasses is also helpful.

Establishing whether the client is literate is important, to avoid distress during assessments that assume basic reading and writing skills. The possibility of (undiagnosed) dyslexia needs to be kept in mind. Ascertaining the client's first language can help if the assessment is standardized on an English-speaking population. Some estimators of pre-morbid intelligence (NART; Nelson & Wilson, 1991; WTAR; Wechsler, 1999) may be unsuitable for this reason. The clinician must ensure that the assessment chosen has appropriate age norms and is validated for the cultural group one is working with.

It is advisable, where possible, to write down the complete answer given. This helps the examiner concentrate on the client and reduces the possibility of incorrect recording or scoring. The other advantage is that when interpreting the results, the quality of the answer and of any errors made can be illuminating. For example, if a task cannot be completed because of the client's difficulties in understanding the instructions, the interpretation may be different from where the client has difficulties concentrating.

To form a quick impression about the client's level of cognitive functioning, a range of short screening assessments are available. The Mini-Mental State Examination (Folstein et al., 1975) is a frequently used screening tool, comprising of twelve questions, which cover a variety of areas including memory and orientation. Recommended cut-off points and score ranges on such tests should be treated with caution, as they are influenced by education, mood and health, and the same score may be achieved by people showing quite different profiles of performance. Very brief screening tools such as the 6CIT (Brooke & Bullock, 1999) may be useful in some circumstances, but should be followed up with more detailed assessment. The Cambridge Cognitive Examination (revised) (CAMCOG-R; Roth et al., 1998), Middlesex Elderly Assessment of Mental State (MEAMS; Golding, 1989), Dementia Rating Scale (Mattis et al., 2002) and the Repeatable Battery for the Assessment of Neuropsychological Status (RBANS; Randolph, 1998) are more useful in providing a profile of the person's function across different areas of cognition. All need to be interpreted in the light of the best information regarding the person's pre-morbid intellectual and educational level, whether predicted from the National Adult Reading Test or from the person's occupation and education (Crawford et al., 1989). The same profile of scores would have a completely different interpretation for a retired headmaster as compared with a person whose predicted life-long intellectual level was in the below average range.

Often the results from one of the above measures will provide enough information, but if the findings are more ambiguous with more specific deficits, further assessment is usually indicated. A large and growing range of measures is available, examples of which for each key area of cognitive function are given in Table 23.1. Further assessment should be hypothesis-driven, with tests chosen to evaluate the emerging model of the person's strengths and weaknesses.

Based on his occupational history as a tax inspector, and supported by his performance on the NART, Mr Jones' pre-morbid IQ is estimated to be above the average (predicted IQ 118). His current IQ is just under average as estimated using the WASI (full-scale IQ 96). On a memory assessment, he shows difficulties in immediate and delayed recall of verbal information. His visual memory is somewhat better, although also impaired. It was also noted that Mr Jones was having perceptual problems, as confirmed by the Visual Object and Space Perception Battery (Warrington & James, 1991).

Table 23.1 Examples of measures available to assess different areas of cognitive function (most are available from Harcourt Assessment or NFER-Nelson)

Area to be assessed	*Examples of available measures*
Pre-morbid intellectual level	NART, WTAR
Screening of cognitive function	MMSE, 6-CIT
Profile of cognitive function	MEAMS, CAMCOG-R, RBANS
Current intellectual function	WASI, WAIS-III, Mill Hill Vocabulary/Raven's Matrices
Memory	Doors & People, Rivermead Behavioural Memory Test, Camden Memory Tests, Object Learning Test (Kendrick Assessment), Wechsler Memory Scale
Perceptual function	Visual Object & Space Perception Battery
Executive function	Behavioural Assessment of the Dysexecutive Syndrome, Hayling & Brixton, Verbal Fluency – FAS, Trail-making Test
Attention	Test of Everyday Attention
Language	Vocabulary from WASI; Graded Naming Test
Speed	Digit Copying Test (Kendrick Assessment)
Constructional abilities	Block Design from WASI

Collateral history

As a person with memory problems or limited insight might have difficulty recounting the onset and development of the symptoms, it is of great benefit to interview a person who knows the client well and can hopefully give a clearer account of the onset and nature of the changes that have taken place. Any particular concerns that this person might have, or risks he or she might perceive can be taken into account in the diagnostic process and will inform the nature of any possible intervention. This assessment can take the form of a structured instrument such as the IQ-CODE (Jorm et al., 1989). If the client still drives or has other responsibilities (e.g. care for a dependant, work) the views of the informant will be important again to inform whether other action might need to be taken.

Diagnostic process

Making the diagnosis of a dementia syndrome has become more important with the arrival of medication that may slow down cognitive decline, leading to many more people in the very early stages of dementia coming forward for assessment. Due to the complexity of the assessment and the range of variables that can have an impact on cognitive functioning, a multidisciplinary approach is essential. Findings should be viewed against one of the two major diagnostic frameworks for mental health problems, i.e. the *Diagnostic and statistical manual* (Fourth edition; DSM-IV: APA, 2000) or the *International classification of diseases* (ICD-10: WHO, 1992). Table 23.2 lists the major types of cognitive impairment seen in older people and their main features.

In general, the criteria for a dementia syndrome include the presence of the symptoms for more than six months, that these should not be explainable by any other physical cause and that the complaints should have an impact on day-to-day living. As well as memory problems, there should be difficulty in at least one of the following: problems in executive functioning (problem solving, logical and abstract thinking), apraxia (difficulty carrying out certain actions), aphasia (difficulty with expressive and or receptive communication) or agnosia (perceptual problems). Changes in personality can be noticed, either a complete change or an accentuation of previous characteristics.

Having diagnosed a dementia syndrome, the differential diagnosis of dementia subtype will be made on additional clinical features and a variety of classification systems are available for these (e.g. for Lewy body dementia or frontotemporal dementias). However, it is important to remember that post-mortem studies (where the neuropathology can be confirmed) of older people with dementia indicate that most patients have mixed pathologies, with Alzheimer's and vascular changes present (Xuereb et al., 2000). In addition, the evidence is now accumulating in support of Kitwood's (1990)

Table 23.2 Major types of cognitive impairment seen in older people and their main features

Name of disorder	*Clinical features*
Age-Associated Memory Impairment (AAMI), Mild Cognitive Impairment (MCI), etc.	A variety of terms have been used to describe states somewhere between 'normality' and 'dementia', e.g. minimal dementia; age-associated memory impairment (AAMI) (Dawe et al., 1992); age-associated cognitive decline (AACD) (Cullum et al., 2000); mild cognitive impairment (MCI) (Tuokko & Zarit, 2003). Typically, does not meet criteria for dementia, either does not affect day-to-day function, or only memory is impaired. Usually subjective complaint plus some deficits on objective testing. A proportion go on to fulfil diagnostic criteria for a dementia – but many do not
Alzheimer's disease	Most common form of dementia at all ages, characterized by loss of neurons, reflected in neuropathological changes – neurofibrillary tangles and amyloid plaques The progression is insidious and gradual. Severe episodic memory and mild problems with executive function, including verbal fluency, usually appear first. Other symptoms like aphasia, agnosia and apraxia may develop A number of medications, said to slow the progression of the disorder, are licensed
Lewy body dementia	Lewy bodies are neuropathological changes reported in Parkinson's disease in the basal ganglia. In Lewy body dementia they occur in cortical areas. Clinical features include hallucinations (visual or auditory), fluctuating cognition and parkinsonian symptoms. Neuroleptic medication (major tranquillizers) should be avoided, despite the presence of hallucinations, as they may lead to a rapid, irreversible deterioration
Vascular/multi-infarct dementia	Associated with mini-strokes or other vascular disease of the brain. The onset is usually more sudden and progression may be stepwise. Associated with other cardiovascular conditions (e.g. hypertension, angina) or diabetes. Cognitive problems tend to be more specific due to the more localized nature of this type of dementia, e.g. language problems or visuospatial difficulty. Infarcts may be seen on brain scan (CT or MRI), but not always evident. Treatment involves managing the risk factors for further vascular events About 20% of older people with dementia have vascular dementia, but there are also many mixed cases of Alzheimer's and vascular combined

Frontotemporal dementia	The main presentation in a frontotemporal dementia is a change in personality and social behaviour. The person may become more extrovert and impulsive, have difficulty maintaining social graces and obeying social etiquette; or may present as depressed, with lack of initiative and unwillingness to change routines. Quite often memory is relatively well preserved and will only deteriorate later in the illness. The management of the behavioural problems arising from this condition can be difficult in terms of risks and caregivers' stress
Pick's disease	A dementia affecting primarily the frontal lobes. The onset is usually between ages 50 and 60 and women are affected twice as often as men. A specific form of frontotemporal dementia, with the changes focusing on personality and behaviour rather than memory
Huntington's disease	Genetic condition – autosomal gene; rare. Genetic testing will confirm a differential diagnosis. The start of this condition is often in the late thirties, early forties. People might have presented as having (unresponsive) mental health conditions, such as depression and schizophrenia. The most salient clinical sign is the choreoform, jerky movements. There are associated changes in gait and dysarthria (slurred speech). Memory is less affected and insight is usually maintained which can lead to episodes of depression
Normal pressure hydrocephalus	A triad of symptoms alert to the need to consider this condition: progressive memory impairment and confusion, marked unsteadiness of gait (ataxia) and urinary incontinence. The problem is caused by an insufficient drainage of the cerebral fluid from the ventricles. Surgically can be ameliorated by the placement of a shunt (a valve). A CT scan can be used to ascertain a differential diagnosis
Semantic dementia	Sometimes described as a temporal lobe variant of frontotemporal dementia. Unusual initial presentation that seems to be typified by the presence of a specific difficulty in general knowledge, and an associated naming difficulty. Personality and behaviour remain intact
Creutzfeldt–Jakob disease	Includes the human variant of BSE (mad cow disease). Caused by a transmissible agent. The onset tends to be young, the deterioration rapid. The main presenting problems are neurological in nature, with ataxia, spasticity and extrapyramidal signs

Continued overleaf

Table 23.2 Continued

Name of disorder	*Clinical features*
Parkinson's disease	Some patients diagnosed as suffering from Parkinson's disease will develop memory problems and a general slowing of their information-processing skills. The organic changes are taking place in the subcortical structures of the brain, rather than the cortical structures (see also Lewy body dementia)
HIV/AIDS	Caused by the human immunodeficiency virus. Complaints of cognitive decline: poor memory, problem solving, reading and general slowing. Significant minority present with an affective disorder, psychosis or seizures. Range of physical and neurological symptoms: tremor, ataxia, hypertonia. Generally progresses quickly

proposition, that the manifestations of dementia are only attributable in part to neuropathological changes.

In older people, the link between clinical picture and pathology appears less clear than has conventionally been claimed. Snowdon (2003) commenting on the Nun Study, a longitudinal study of a population of older nuns, who have all agreed to regular examinations and to an eventual post-mortem, describes a sister who died at the age of eighty-five without apparent cognitive impairment on testing, but whose brain showed large amounts of Alzheimer-type pathology. He concludes:

> Given nearly the same location, type and amount of neuropathologic lesions, participants in our study show an incredible range of clinical manifestations, from no symptoms to severe symptoms.
>
> (Snowdon, 2003, p. 453)

Sharing the diagnosis

Based on the outcome of the pre-diagnostic counselling, the client and his or her representative can be invited for a meeting in which the findings of the assessment and the diagnosis are shared. It has to be acknowledged that this meeting might not be easy for the professionals involved and it is worth considering conducting a meeting like this with a colleague, ideally one who was involved in the assessment process and is known to the client.

Careful orientation as to the reason for the meeting should take place. Summarizing the assessments to date, without asking questions that can be experienced as another 'test', can help to bring a focus to the meeting. Introducing the possibilities for the outcome of the assessment should take place and it important to confirm that the client wishes to be informed about their diagnosis. Questions should be encouraged and a check should be made with the client that the conversation is being understood. Self-monitoring should take place to avoid jargon and complicated descriptions. Visual information can be useful for some clients to provide evidence, e.g. cognitive profile or brain scan. Throughout the session, verbal and non-verbal responses should be monitored to gauge the impact of the diagnosis. Checking whether a diagnosis has come as a surprise is useful. What were their expectations? Providing the space and time is important during this session, as this meeting should be considered the first step on the path of intervention. If these first steps can be carried out in a supportive manner, this will set the tone for future work.

Mr Jones is invited for a session to share the diagnosis. He decides that his wife can be present as well. The findings of all the investigations are explained and Mr Jones is given the opportunity to ask questions. He is told that the most likely diagnosis is one of vascular dementia. He has heard of Alzheimer's disease but is not familiar with this new term. The difference is explained and ways in which he can prevent further deterioration outlined, i.e. keeping his sugar levels and blood pressure under control, as well as maintaining a healthy lifestyle. He is already receiving aspirin, as a preventive measure against strokes. Mr Jones feels relieved that there is an explanation for some of his difficulties. He asks what might happen to him now. It is explained that although it is difficult to give an accurate prognosis, it is likely that his level of functioning would be stable for some time, before another deterioration might occur. He feels this provides a window of opportunity for him and his wife to do some things they have been wanting to do.

PSYCHOLOGICAL INTERVENTIONS IN DEMENTIA

Specific 'therapies' for people with dementia need to be implemented within a framework of values and principles that upholds the individuality of the person with dementia, offers choice, dignity and respect, and recognizes the human value and personhood of the person with dementia – all aspects that are too easily lost in caregiving systems (including the family), where the person with dementia may be devalued and depersonalized (Kitwood,

1997; Woods, 1999a). Within this framework, three major areas of focus for therapeutic endeavours may be identified (Woods, 2001):

Cognition-focused

Attempts to improve cognitive function in people with dementia have a long history, with reality orientation an early attempt to combat the therapeutic nihilism that prevailed in relation to dementia at the time (Holden & Woods, 1995). This approach has now been developed into a cognitive stimulation programme, delivered in a group context, with improvements noted in both cognition and quality of life (Spector et al., 2003). However, it is cognitive rehabilitation that offers the individually tailored, assessment and formulation driven approach that is the proper concern of psychological therapy (Clare, 2002). This approach identifies treatment goals relevant to the individual and aims to use the person's strengths – their relatively preserved abilities – to achieve these goals. The techniques might include the use of strategies to enhance learning (such as spaced retrieval and errorless learning), the use of external memory aids, to reduce reliance on memory and the use of anxiety reduction techniques where anxiety forms an obstacle to the person achieving his or her goals. Although much of the evidence base on this approach takes the form of single-cases (e.g. Clare et al., 2002), there is clearly a great deal of potential for assisting people in the early stages of dementia to maintain control and function in important and relevant areas of their lives.

> Mr Jones is keen to learn the names of the people he has met at the local club for people with dementia that he has begun to attend. Based on his cognitive profile as assessed, cognitive rehabilitation strategies are developed with him. He learns to associate faces with particular characteristics that he can then associate with the person's name. After three weeks of daily practice, he is able to recall three of the four people in the group.

Emotion-focused

The use of CBT for depression in dementia has been mentioned previously; caregivers have been also taught to use behavioural procedures (increasing involvement in enjoyed activities) to reduce depression in dementia (Teri et al., 1997). Progressive muscle relaxation has also been used successfully for anxiety symptoms in dementia (Suhr et al., 1999).

Psychotherapeutic interventions with individuals or in a group are developing (Cheston et al., 2003; Yale, 1995) where clients have an opportunity to explore the impact of the diagnosis and forgetting. The groups appear to be a great resource for people who might otherwise become more withdrawn as they do not know other people in a similar situation to themselves.

Reminiscence therapy has been used extensively with people with dementia, with benefits noted in well-being (Brooker & Duce, 2000) and interaction (Head et al., 1990).

Validation therapy (Feil, 1993) aims to help individuals with dementia communicate their feelings by providing a skilled listener, who is able to go beyond the actual words spoken to explore the underlying meanings, rather than jumping in to constantly correct the person. Resolution therapy has similar aims, emphasizing the importance of skilled listening (Stokes & Goudie, 1990).

Behaviour-focused

Behavioural approaches (specifically prompting, breaking tasks down into manageable chunks and social reinforcement) have been used to assist in improving and (just as important) maintaining function in people with dementia (Woods, 1999b). Self-care, dressing and toileting and orientation (McGilton et al., 2003) have been amongst the areas targeted.

Understanding and reducing challenging behaviour has also been a concern. Generally, approaches that have not been individually tailored have had limited success (Allen-Burge et al., 1999) and the need for careful assessment, functional analysis and individually tailored programmes demonstrated in several single-case series (Bird et al., 1995; Moniz-Cook et al., 2003; Moniz-Cook et al., 2001; Woods & Bird, 1999). Challenging behaviours targeted have included aggression, inappropriate urination, sexually disinhibited behaviour and entering other people's rooms.

Carers' interventions

Family caregiving has been the focus of extensive research (Zarit & Edwards, 1999). A distinction has been drawn between 'objective' and 'subjective' burden; two caregivers, looking after identical care recipients, would have potentially quite different outcomes, in terms of perceived strain, impact on their own health and depression. These differences are thought to be related to differences between caregivers in personality, coping skills and attributional styles, available resources, including social support and help from services and aspects of the relationship – past and present – between caregiver and recipient. Much of the literature focuses on strain and burden associated with care giving. Nolan et al. (1996) have been amongst those drawing attention to the satisfactions and rewards that may also be associated with caregiving, with many caregivers able to find meaning and purpose in their role, and feeling closer to the care recipient than previously, despite the many losses that are reported.

Four different strategies of psychological interventions may be considered (Woods & Roth, 2005):

- Using behavioural techniques to modify the behaviour of the person with dementia, and so reduce the stress experienced by the caregiver.
- Teaching stress reduction approaches such as relaxation, assertiveness, anger and anxiety management, to directly tackle the caregiver's feelings of stress.
- Providing an educational context, where carers' perceptions and attributions about the situation are challenged and problem-solving skills developed.
- Mobilizing family resources and enhancing social support and networks; identifying and making use of possible sources of help.

Often, these interventions are provided in group settings, with a mix of the above components included. The effectiveness research has been reviewed by Pusey and Richards (2001) and Brodaty et al. (2003). Although the evidence is mixed, some interventions (e.g. family counselling) have been successful in both reducing caregiver distress and delaying the point of entry of the person with dementia to institutional care (Mittelman et al., 1995). There is also optimism that depression and anxiety in caregivers will respond to psychological therapy in this group as in other older people.

Gallagher-Thompson and Steffen (1994) showed that CBT and brief psychotherapy were equally effective in reducing depression in family caregivers; however, psychotherapy was more effective with caregivers early in the process of adjustment, with CBT more effective with caregivers who had been providing care for 3.5 years or more. This suggests that support in the emotional adjustment required by the life-changing experience of becoming a caregiver may be an important intervention strategy also.

Other support can be provided through the provision of services, such as day care, home-helps and respite in the home or in a care-setting. Vernooij-Dassen et al. (1995) found that caregivers' sense of competence improved and admission into a care-setting could be delayed, by providing four hours per week of specially trained home-helps.

Mrs Jones appears to be hit harder by the diagnosis than her husband. She explains that she feels she has lost her anchor and is anxious about the responsibilities she now carries for things her husband always did previously. Mrs Jones is seen for eight sessions to help her come to terms with her changed role and the grieving process that has started. She finds some of her husband's behaviours particularly difficult to deal with and detailed discussion with her explores the underlying distress. Once she has been able to acknowledge her feelings, she begins to be able to try out some of the alternative approaches that were suggested. She begins to attend a carers' support group regularly.

Challenging behaviour

At a routine follow-up appointment, Mrs Jones is looking tired and reports she is suffering from high blood pressure, which is proving difficult to control. She explains that caring for her husband is getting harder as he is becoming more un-co-operative and on a few occasions has tried to hit her. Mrs Jones begins to cry and states that although she very much wishes to continue to look after her husband, she knows she has come to the limit of her ability. The possibility of respite care is discussed with her, where her husband will live in a care setting for set periods and live at home the rest of the time.

Mr Jones starts respite care, where it quickly becomes apparent that he is unco-operative while receiving help in his personal care. He is also observed trying to hit another resident.

Understanding a person's behaviour as a way of communicating a need, wish or feeling is a challenge for paid care-staff as well as for family caregivers. Many factors need to be considered in assessing challenging behaviour. Physical health (including pain); psychiatric phenomena, such as hallucinations or delusions; social aspects, such as the approach of others; psychological factors, such as personality and attachment style must all be taken into account (Stokes, 1996).

The staff are asked to make close observations in the first week and note when, where and with whom the behaviour is taking place. This shows that the incidents did not all occur during caregiving interventions and that other residents seemed to be at risk at irregular intervals.

More detailed functional analysis reveals a similar pattern. However, some staff seem to experience fewer difficulties with Mr Jones. Through team discussions they describe that they talk slowly and give Mr Jones one instruction at a time. This observation is consistent with the earlier findings in the cognitive assessment, where Mr Jones had problems with short-term memory and following a multi-stage command. It is also noted that Mr Jones was hard of hearing. The importance of clear communication is stressed, ensuring Mr Jones has understood before any intervention is started. Personal care has proved difficult and the possibility of a male carer or an older carer is explored. Mr Jones responds better to a male carer. Observations in the public areas show that Mr Jones becomes more restless around meal-times. His blood sugar levels are checked for ten days. It transpires that Mr Jones's sugar levels decrease; he is given some fruit about an hour before meal-times.

The staff report an improvement in Mr Jones's behaviour with the staff but there have been two more incidents where another resident was hit. It appears that another confused resident who wanders around had stood behind Mr Jones's chair on one occasion: Mr Jones had turned around and hit him. Mr Jones had looked anxious and scared. It is possible that his past war-time experience and PTSD could be related to the incidents. Due to Mr Jones's reducing cognitive abilities and perceptual problems, he is less able to evaluate a situation and his responses are more automatic. It is likely that the perceived threat is enough to trigger a self-defence response. Staff continue to monitor and try to ensure that the wandering resident does not get too close to Mr Jones unexpectedly.

The above scenario describes the complexity of an intervention with somebody who is challenging. A range of possibilities needs to be kept in mind from physiological to cognitive and emotional. As well as being able to have a hypothesis of the origins of the behaviour, it is important to have a working relationship with the person(s) who will be at the forefront in implementing any sort of intervention. This is often the most difficult part as either pre-existing relationship patterns get in the way or the care setting is such that well-being is not easily enhanced because of staffing difficulties or care philosophy.

IMPACT ON PROFESSIONALS

Working with clients like Mr Jones can be complex, where issues are multi-dimensional and require assessments and interventions that are ongoing. The, usually, younger, professional is first confronted with the age and generational difference that can lead to potential transference and counter-transference issues. Working with people who could be your parent or grandparent can raise dynamics in the relationship that need monitoring in supervision. The personal views that the younger professional holds about old age and ageing can influence what might be seen as normal and abnormal as well as colour the experience of the work. Being confronted with illness, deterioration and loss can be challenging and is likely to trigger some emotive responses. It is not always possible for the professional to improve the situation and make people 'better'. Lives have been lived and, as a therapist, one needs to work with certain facts that are a given.

At the same time, work with older people, because of its complexity, involves working at different levels, from individual work, to marital and family therapy, to systems and organizational work, including education and organizational consultancy. The individual work can entail (neuro-) psychological assessments, diagnostic uncertainty, diagnostic counselling, the full range of psychotherapeutic interventions as well as cognitive rehabilitation. The professional is required to have a range of skills and knowledge readily available as well as the passion to ensure that the approach towards the care of older adults is of the highest standard in accordance with the person-centred care philosophy, to enable the older person to achieve their full potential.

SUMMARY

Reviews of cognitive changes associated with ageing show remarkable stability in cognitive functioning across most of the lifespan. Longitudinal studies of ageing tend to show much less extensive cognitive decline than cross-sectional studies. Cohort effects are thought to account for a large proportion of age differences. 'Crystallized' abilities show change later than 'fluid' abilities. Speed of processing is possibly the fundamental cognitive change associated with ageing. Despite changes in neurophysiology, most older people maintain good cognitive functioning, by focusing resources on the areas of most importance or interest to them, by optimizing goal-relevant means, and by practising more or deploying compensatory strategies to address areas of declining functioning. Health problems and lifestyle choices may also affect cognitive functioning. To devise the most comprehensive intervention package, multi-disciplinary assessment is often needed. Pre-diagnostic counselling provides an opportunity to establish rapport with clients, understand their level of awareness of problems and concerns about assessment, and address issues of consent and confidentiality. Specific psychometric tests for assessing aspects of cognitive functioning are described. Other areas to cover at assessment are general and mental health, including mood and anxiety problems. Information from others close to the client, taken at interview or through questionnaires, is frequently useful. The DSM-IV-TR and ICD-10 provide diagnostic frameworks for dementia and the chapter also outlines the various subtypes of dementia. From the results of assessment, careful formulation and knowledge of the evidence base on interventions, an individualized treatment plan is made. Specific 'therapies' for people with dementia need to be implemented within a framework of values and principles that upholds the individuality of the person with dementia, offers choice, dignity and respect, and recognizes the human value and personhood of the person with dementia. Cognition, emotion and behaviour are the three major areas of focus for interventions. While there are a few specific interventions for dementia, such as reminiscence and life review work, most psychological therapeutic work with older people is little different from work with younger people. Issues that arise more commonly in treatment with older people include adversity, cognitive impairment, physical health status, anti-therapy beliefs, dependency on others and chronicity of problems. Carers' subjective experience of burden, in terms of perceived strain, impact on health and depression, relates to a variety of factors including the carer's personality, coping skills and attributional styles, and available resources, as well as to the relationship between carer and care recipient. In addition to burden, caring may also be associated with satisfaction and rewards. Interventions with carers may include using behavioural techniques to modify the behaviour of the care recipient, teach the carer techniques for managing stress and anxiety, provide education and problem-solving training to carers, mobilize family resources and enhance social support networks.

Psychological interventions are often undertaken with professional staff where clients exhibit challenging behaviour. The aim is to understand the behaviour as a communication of a need, wish or feeling, bearing in mind the client's physical and mental health, coping style, personality and attachment styles. Good supervision allows clinical psychologists to explore and recognize how personal views about age, ageing, illness and loss are impacting on them and their work.

EXERCISE 23.1

Using the case of Mr Jones from the chapter, assign roles of therapist, Mr and Mrs Jones and an observer. Role-play the following scenarios, changing roles after each:

1 Pre-diagnostic counselling session, at which you discuss Mr Jones's concerns and expectations about assessment, and address issues of consent and confidentiality.
2 Post-assessment session with Mr Jones, at which you outline the results of assessment, share the diagnosis, and discuss strategies for management.
3 A session with Mrs Jones at which you help her come to terms with her

changed role and the grieving process, as well as exploring alternatives she might try in coping with challenging behaviours.

FURTHER READING FOR FAMILIES AND CARERS

Alzheimer's Society (2002). *Caring for the person with dementia: A handbook for families and other carers*. London: Alzheimer's Society. Online. Available at: http://www.alzheimers.org.uk

Cayton, H., Graham, N. & Warner, J. (2002). *Dementia – Alzheimer's and other dementias*. London: Class Publishing.

Mace, N. & Rabins, P. (1999). *The 36-hour day: A family guide to caring for persons with Alzheimer's disease, related dementing illness and memory loss in later life* (Third Edition). Baltimore: Johns Hopkins University Press.

FURTHER READING FOR PRACTITIONERS

Jacoby, R. & Oppenheimer, C. (2002). *Psychiatry in the elderly* (Third Edition). Oxford: Oxford University Press.

Laidlaw, K., Thompson, L.W., Dick-Siskin, L. & Gallagher-Thompson, D. (2003). *Cognitive behaviour therapy with older people*. Chichester, UK: Wiley.

Woods, R. (1996). *Handbook of clinical psychology of ageing*. Chichester, UK: Wiley.

Woods, R. (1999). *Psychological problems of ageing: Assessment, treatment and care*. Chichester, UK: Wiley.

EVIDENCE SUMMARIES

Woods, R. & Roth, A. (2005). Effectiveness of psychological interventions with older people. In A. Roth and P. Fonagy (Eds.), *What works for whom? A critical review of psychotherapy research* (Second Edition, pp. 425–446). London: Guilford Press.

ASSESSMENT INSTRUMENTS

See also Table 23.1.

For instruments available from Harcourt Assessment and the Psychological Corporation, see http://www.harcourt-uk.com

Screening and profile of cognitive function

Brooke, P. & Bullock, R. (1999). Validation of a 6-item cognitive impairment test with a view to primary care usage. *International Journal of Geriatric Psychiatry*, 14(11), 936–940.

Folstein, M., Folstein, S. & McHugh, P. (1975). 'Mini-Mental State': A practical method for grading the cognitive state of patients for the clinician. *Journal of Psychiatric Research*, 12, 189–198. Available from Harcourt Assessment.

Golding, E. (1989). *Middlesex Elderly Assessment of Mental State*. London: Harcourt Assessment.

Mattis, S., Jurica, P. & Leitten, C. (2002). *Dementia Rating Scale – 2*. London: Harcourt Assessment.

Randolph, C. (1998). *The Repeatable Battery for the Assessment of Neuropsychological Status*. London: Harcourt Assessment.

Roth, M., Huppert, F.A., Mountjoy, C.Q. & Tym, E. (1998). *CAMDEX-R: The Cambridge Examination for Mental Disorders of the Elderly – revised.* Cambridge: Cambridge University Press.

Wechsler, D. (1999). *The Wechsler Abbreviated Scale of Intelligence*. London: Harcourt Assessment.

Pre-morbid ability

Nelson, H. & Willison, J. (1991). *The National Adult Reading Test – Manual*. Windsor, UK: NFER-Nelson.

Wechsler, D. (1999). *Wechsler Test of Adult Reading (WTAR)*. San Antonio, TX: Psychological Corporation.

Memory

Baddeley, A., Emslie, H. & Nimmo-Smith, I. (1994). *Doors and people: A test of visual and verbal recall and recognition*. London: Harcourt Assessment.

Benton, A. (1974). *The Revised Visual Retention test*. New York: Psychological Corporation.

Kendrick, D. & Watts, G. (1999). *Kendrick Assessment Scales for Cognitive Ageing*. Windsor, UK: NFER-Nelson.

Warrington, E. (1996). *The Camden Memory Tests*. Hove, UK: Psychology Press.

Wechsler, D. (1999). *The Wechsler Memory Scale – Third UK Edition*. London: Harcourt Assessment.

Wilson, B., Cockburn, J. & Baddley, A. (1985). *The Rivermead Behavioural Memory Test*. London: Harcourt Assessment.

Perceptual function

Warrington, E. & James, M. (1991). *Visual Object & Space Perception battery (VOSP)*. London: Harcourt Assessment.

Executive function

Burgess, P.W. & Shallice, T. (1997). *Hayling and Brixton Tests*. London: Harcourt Assessment.

Wilson, B., Alderman, N., Burgess, P.W., Emslie, H. & Evans, J.J. (1996). *Behavioural Assessment of the Dysexecutive syndrome*. London: Harcourt Assessment.

Attention

Robertson, I.H., Ward, T., Ridgeway, V. & Nimmo-Smith, I. (1994). *Test of Everyday Attention*. London: Harcourt Assessment.

Language

Benton, A.L. & Hamsher, K. (1976). *Multilingual Aphasia Examination*. Iowa City: University of Iowa Press. Includes the Verbal Fluency FAS test.

McKenna, P. & Warrington, E. K. (1983). *The Graded Naming Test*. Windsor, UK: NFER-Nelson.

Mood

Kenn, C., Wood, H., Kucyj, M., Wattis, J. P. & Cunane, J. (1987). Validation of the Hospital Anxiety and Depression Rating Scale (HADS) in an elderly psychiatric population. *International Journal of Geriatric Psychiatry*, 2, 189–193.

Yesavage, J., Brink, T. & Rose, T. (1983). Development and validation of a geriatric depression scale. A preliminary report. *Journal of Psychiatric Research*, 17, 37–49.

Behaviour problems

Brooker, D. (1998). *BASOLL – Behavioural Assessment Scale of Later Life*. Bicester, UK: Winslow.

Greene, J., Smith, R., Gardiner, M. & Timbury, G. (1982). Measuring behavioural disturbance of elderly demented patients in the community and its effects on relatives: A factor analytic study. *Age and Ageing*, 11, 121–126. Contains the behavioural and mood disturbance scale.

Moniz-Cook, E., Woods, R., Gardiner, E., Silver, M. & Agar, S. (2001). The Challenging Behaviour Scale (CBS): Development of a scale for staff caring for older people in residential and nursing homes. *British Journal of Clinical Psychology*, 40(3), 309–322.

Pattie, A. & Gilleard, C. (1979). *Manual for the Clifton Assessment Procedures for the Elderly (CAPE)*. Sevenoaks, UK: Hodder and Stoughton.

Overall staging of dementia

Hughes, C., Berg, L., Danzinger, W. et al. (1982). A new clinical scale for the staging of dementia. *British Journal of Psychiatry*, 140, 566–572. Contains the Clinical Dementia Rating (CDR) scale.

Reisberg, B., Ferris, S. H., DeLeon, M. J. & Crook, T. (1982). The Global Deterioration Scale for assessment of primary degenerative dementia. *American Journal of Psychiatry*, 139, 1136–1139.

Carer strain

Greene, J., Smith, R., Gardiner, M. & Timbury, G. (1982). Measuring behavioural disturbance of elderly demented patients in the community and its effects on relatives: A factor analytic study. *Age and Ageing*, 11, 121–126. Contains the Relative's Stress Scale.

Zarit, S., Reever, K. & Bach-Peterson, J. (1980). Relatives of the impaired elderly: Correlates of feelings of burden. *The Gerontologist*, 20, 649–655.

REFERENCES

Abas, M. A., Sahakian, B. J. & Levy, R. (1990). Neuropsychological deficits and CT scan changes in elderly depressives. *Psychological Medicine*, 20, 507–520.

Allen-Burge, R., Stevens, A. B. & Burgio, L. D. (1999). Effective behavioral interventions for decreasing dementia-related challenging behavior in nursing homes. *International Journal of Geriatric Psychiatry*, 14(3), 213–232.

American Psychiatric Association (APA) (2000). *Diagnostic and statistical manual of the mental disorders (Fourth Edition-Text Revision, DSM-IV-TR)*. Washington, DC: APA.

Baltes, P. B. & Baltes, M. M. (1990). Psychological perspectives on successful aging: The model of selective optimization with compensation. In P. B. Baltes & M. M. Baltes (Eds.), *Successful aging: Perspectives from the behavioral sciences* (pp. 1–34). Cambridge: Cambridge University Press.

Barrowclough, C., King, P., Colville, J., Russell, E., Burns, A. & Tarrier, N. (2001). A randomized trial of the effectiveness of cognitive-behavioral therapy and supportive counseling for anxiety symptoms in older adults. *Journal of Consulting and Clinical Psychology*, 69, 756–762.

Beats, B. C., Sahakian, B. J. & Levy, R. (1996). Cognitive performance in tests sensitive to frontal lobe dysfunction in the elderly depressed. *Psychological Medicine*, 26, 591–603.

Bird, M., Alexopoulos, P. & Adamowicz, J. (1995). Success and failure in five case studies: Use of cued recall to ameliorate behaviour problems in senile dementia. *International Journal of Geriatric Psychiatry*, 10, 305–311.

Bohlmeijer, E., Smit, F. & Cuijpers, P. (2003). Effects of reminiscence and life review on late-life depression: A meta-analysis. *International Journal of Geriatric Psychiatry*, 18, 1088–1094.

Bonwick, R. & Morris, P. (1996). Post-traumatic stress disorder in elderly war veterans. *International Journal of Geriatric Psychiatry*, 11, 1071–1076.

Breckenridge, J. N., Gallagher, D., Thompson, L. W. & Peterson, J. (1986). Characteristic depressive symptoms of bereaved elders. *Journal of Gerontology*, 41, 163–168.

Brodaty, H., Green, A. & Koschera, A. (2003). Meta-analysis of psychosocial interventions for caregivers of people with dementia. *Journal of American Geriatrics Society*, 51, 657–664.

Brooke, P. & Bullock, R. (1999). Validation of a 6-item cognitive impairment test with a view to primary care usage. *International Journal of Geriatric Psychiatry*, 14(11), 936–940.

Brooker, D. & Duce, L. (2000). Wellbeing and activity in dementia: A comparison of group reminiscence therapy, structured goal-directed group activity and unstructured time. *Aging and Mental Health*, 4(4), 354–358.

Cervilla, J. A. & Prince, M. J. (1997). Cognitive impairment and social distress as different pathways to depression in the elderly: A cross-sectional study. *International Journal of Geriatric Psychiatry*, 12, 995–1000.

Cheston, R., Jones, K. & Gilliard, J. (2003). Group psychotherapy and people with dementia. *Aging and Mental Health*, 7, 452–461.

Clare, L. (2002). Assessment and intervention in dementia of Alzheimer type. In A. Baddeley & M. D. Kopelman & B. A. Wilson (Eds.), *The handbook of memory disorders* (Second Edition, pp. 711–739). Chichester, UK: Wiley.

Clare, L., Wilson, B. A., Carter, G., Roth, I. & Hodges, J. R. (2002). Relearning face–name associations in early Alzheimer's disease. *Neuropsychology*, 16, 538–547.

Crawford, J. R., Stewart, L. E., Cochrane, R. H. B., Foulds, J. A., Besson, J. A. O. & Parker, D. M. (1989). Estimating premorbid IQ from demographic variables: Regression equations derived from a UK sample. *British Journal of Clinical Psychology*, 28, 275–278.

Cullum, S., Huppert, F., McGee, M., Dening, T., Ahmed, A., Paykel, E. S. & Brayne, C. (2000). Decline across different domains of cognitive function in normal ageing: Results of a longitudinal population-based study using CAMCOG. *International Journal of Geriatric Psychiatry*, 15, 853–862.

Davies, A. D. M. (1996). Life events, health, adaptation and social support in the clinical psychology of late life. In R. T. Woods (Ed.), *Handbook of the clinical psychology of ageing* (pp. 115–140). Chichester, UK: Wiley.

Dawe, B., Procter, A. & Philpot, M. (1992). Concepts of mild memory impairment in the elderly and their relationship to dementia – a review. *International Journal of Geriatric Psychiatry*, 7, 473–479.

Deary, I., Whalley, L. J., Lemmon, H., Crawford, J. R. & Starr, J. M. (2000). The stability of individual differences in mental ability from childhood to old age: Follow-up of the 1932 Scottish Mental Survey. *Intelligence*, 28, 49–55.

Dent, O. F., Waite, L. M., Bennett, H. P., Casey, B. J., Grayson, D. A., Cullen, J. S., Creasey, H. & Broe, G. A. (1999). A longitudinal study of chronic disease and depressive symptoms in a community sample of older people. *Aging and Mental Health*, 3(4), 351–357.

Elwood, P. C., Pickering, J., Bayer, A. & Gallacher, J. E. J. (2002). Vascular disease and cognitive function in older men in the Caerphilly cohort. *Age and Ageing*, 31, 43–48.

Erde, E. L., Nasal, E. C. & Scholl, T. O. (1988). On truth telling and the diagnosis of Alzheimer's disease. *Journal of Family Practice*, 326, 947–951.

Erikson, E. (1963). *Childhood and society* (Second Edition). New York: W. W. Norton.

Erikson, E. H., Erikson, J. M. & Kivnick, H. Q. (1986). *Vital involvement in old age*. New York: W.W. Norton.

Feil, N. (1993). *The validation breakthrough: Simple techniques for communicating with people with 'Alzheimer's type dementia'*. Baltimore: Health Professions Press.

Folstein, M. F., Folstein, S. E. & McHugh, P. R. (1975). 'Mini Mental State': A practical method for grading the cognitive state of patients for the clinician. *Journal of Psychiatric Research*, 12, 189–198.

Gallagher-Thompson, D. & Steffen, A. M. (1994). Comparative effects of cognitive-behavioral and brief psychodynamic psychotherapies for depressed family caregivers. *Journal of Consulting and Clinical Psychology*, 62, 543–549.

Golding, E. (1989). *Middlesex elderly assessment of mental state*. Titchfield, UK: Thames Valley Test Company.

Haight, B. (1992). The structured life-review process: A community approach to the ageing client. In G. M. M. Jones & B. M. L. Miesen (Eds.), *Care-giving in dementia* (pp. 272–292). London: Routledge.

Head, D., Portnoy, S. & Woods, R. T. (1990). The impact of reminiscence groups in two different settings. *International Journal of Geriatric Psychiatry*, 5, 295–302.

Henderson, A. S. (1994). Does ageing protect against depression? *Social Psychiatry and Psychiatric Epidemiology*, 29, 107–109.

Holden, U. P. & Woods, R. T. (1995). *Positive approaches to dementia care* (Third Edition). Edinburgh: Churchill Livingstone.

Holland, C. A. & Rabbitt, P. (1991). The course and causes of cognitive change with advancing age. *Reviews in Clinical Gerontology*, 1, 81–96.

Jorm, A. F., Scott, R. & Jacomb, P. (1989). Assessment of cognitive decline in dementia by informant questionnaire. *International Journal of Geriatric Psychiatry*, 4, 35–39.

Keady, J. & Nolan, M. (1994). Younger onset dementia: Developing a longitudinal model as the basis for a research agenda and a guide to interventions with sufferers and carers. *Journal of Advanced Nursing*, 19, 659–669.

Kenn, C., Wood, H., Kucyj, M., Wattis, J. P. & Cunane, J. (1987). Validation of the Hospital Anxiety and Depression Rating Scale (HADS) in an elderly psychiatric population. *International Journal of Geriatric Psychiatry*, 2, 189–193.

Kitwood, T. (1990). The dialectics of dementia: With particular reference to Alzheimer's disease. *Ageing and Society*, 10, 177–196.

Kitwood, T. (1997). *Dementia reconsidered: The person comes first*. Buckingham, UK: Open University Press.

Kraaij, V. & de Wilde, E. J. (2001). Negative life events and depressive symptoms in the elderly: A life span perspective. *Aging and Mental Health*, 5(1), 84–91.

Kuypers, J. A. & Bengtson, V. L. (1973). Social breakdown and competence. A model of normal aging, *Human Development*, 16, 181–201.

Laidlaw, K., Thompson, L. W., Dick-Siskin, L. & Gallagher-Thompson, D. (2003). *Cognitive behaviour therapy with older people*. Chichester, UK: Wiley.

Lam, D. H., Brewin, C. R., Woods, R. T. & Bebbington, P. E. (1987). Cognition and social adversity in the depressed elderly. *Journal of Abnormal Psychology*, 96, 23–26.

Lindesay, J., Briggs, K. & Murphy, E. (1989). The Guys/Age Concern survey: Prevalence rates of cognitive impairment, depression and anxiety in an urban elderly community. *British Journal of Psychiatry*, 155, 317–329.

Maguire, C. P., Kirby, M., Coen, R., Coakley, D., Lawlor, B. A. & O'Neill, D. (1996). Family members' attitudes toward telling the patient with Alzheimer's disease their diagnosis. *British Medical Journal*, 313, 529–530.

Mattis, S., Jurica, P. & Leitten, C. (2002). Dementia Rating Scale. (Second Edition; DRS-II). San Antonio, TX: Psychological Corporation.

McGilton, K. S., Rivera, T. M. & Dawson, P. (2003). Can we help persons with dementia find their way in a new environment? *Aging and Mental Health*, 7(5), 363–371.

McKiernan, F. M. (1996). Bereavement and attitudes to death. In R. T. Woods (Ed.), *Handbook of the clinical psychology of ageing* (pp. 159–182). Chichester, UK: Wiley.

Mittelman, M. S., Ferris, S. H., Shulman, E., Steinberg, G., Ambinder, A., Mackell, J. A. & Cohen, J. (1995). A comprehensive support program: Effect on depression in spouse-caregivers of AD patients. *Gerontologist*, 35, 792–802.

Moniz-Cook, E., Stokes, G. & Agar, S. (2003). Difficult behaviour and dementia in nursing homes: Five cases of psychosocial intervention. *Clinical Psychology and Psychotherapy*, 10(3), 197–208.

Moniz-Cook, E., Woods, R. T. & Richards, K. (2001). Functional analysis of challenging behaviour in dementia: The role of superstition. *International Journal of Geriatric Psychiatry*, 16(1), 45–56.

Moorey, S. (1997). When bad things happen to rational people: Cognitive therapy in adverse life circumstances. In P. Salkovskis (Ed.), *Frontiers of cognitive therapy* (pp. 450–469). New York: Guilford Press.

Murphy, E. (1982). Social origins of depression in old age. *British Journal of Psychiatry*, 141, 135–142.

Neal, L. A., Hill, N., Hughes, J., Middleton, A. & Busuttil, W. (1995). Convergent validity of measures of PTSD in an elderly population of former prisoners of war. *International Journal of Geriatric Psychiatry*, 10, 617–622.

Nelson, H. & Willison, J. (1991). *The National Adult Reading Test*. Windsor, UK: NFER-Nelson.

Nolan, M. R., Grant, G. & Keady, J. (1996). *Understanding family care*. Buckingham, UK: Open University Press.

Pearce, J. (2002). Systemic therapy. In Hepple, J., Pearce, J. & Wilkinson, P. (Eds.) *Psychological therapy with older people* (pp. 76–102). Hove, UK: Brunner-Routledge.

Pearlson, G. D., Rabins, P. V., Kim, W. S. & Speedie, L. J. (1989). Structural brain CT changes and cognitive deficits in elderly depressives with and without reversible dementia ('pseudodementia'). *Psychological Medicine*, 19, 573–584.

Poon, L. W. (1992). Towards an understanding of cognitive functioning in geriatric depression. *International Psychogeriatrics*, 4 (Suppl 2), 241–266.

Pusey, H., & Richards, D. (2001). A systematic review of the effectiveness of psychosocial interventions for carers of people with dementia. *Aging and Mental Health*, 5(2), 107–119.

Rabbitt, P. (1988). Social psychology, neurosciences and cognitive psychology need each other (and gerontology needs all three of them). *Psychologist*, 12, 500–506.

Randolph, C. (1998). *The Repeatable Battery for the Assessment of Neuropsychological Status*. Sidcup, UK: Psychological Corporation.

Reynolds, C. F., Frank, E., Perel, J. M., Imber, S. D., Cornes, C., Miller, M. D., Mazumdar, S., Houck, P. R., Dew, M. A., Stack, J. A., Pollock, B. G. & Kupfer, D. J. (1999). Nortriptyline and interpersonal psychotherapy as maintenance therapies for recurrent major depression: A randomized controlled trial in patients older than 59 years. *Journal of American Medical Association*, 281, 39–45.

Rimmer, T.W. (1993). Bad news – who should be informed first? *Journal of Cancer Care*, 2, 6–10.

Roth, M., Huppert, F.A., Mountjoy, C.Q. & Tym, E. (1998). CAMDEX-R: The Cambridge Examination for Mental Disorders of the Elderly – revised. Cambridge: Cambridge University Press.

Salthouse, T. A. (2000). Steps toward the explanation of adult age differences in cognition. In T. J. Perfect & E. A. Maylor (Eds.), *Models of cognitive ageing* (pp. 19–49). Oxford: Oxford University Press.

Schaie, K. W. (1990). Intellectual development in adulthood. In J. E. Birren & K. W. Schaie (Eds.), *Handbook of the psychology of aging* (Third Edition, pp. 291–309). San Diego, CA: Academic Press.

Schaie, K. W. (1996). *Intellectual development in adulthood: The Seattle Longitudinal Study*. Cambridge: Cambridge University Press.

Scholey, K. A. & Woods, B. T. (2003). A series of brief cognitive therapy interventions with people experiencing both dementia and depression: A description of techniques and common themes. *Clinical Psychology and Psychotherapy*, 10, 175–185.

Skilbeck, C. E. (1996). Psychological aspects of stroke. In R. T. Woods (Ed.), *Handbook of the clinical psychology of ageing* (pp. 283–301). Chichester, UK: Wiley.

Snowdon, D. A. (2003). Healthy aging and dementia: Findings from the Nun study. *Annals of Internal Medicine*, 139, 450–454.

Solomon, Z. & Prager, E. (1992). Elderly Israeli Holocaust survivors during the Persian Gulf War: A study of psychological distress. *American Journal of Psychiatry*, 149, 1707–1710.

Spector, A., Thorgrimsen, L., Woods, B., Royan, L., Davies, S., Butterworth, M. & Orrell, M. (2003). Efficacy of an evidence-based cognitive stimulation therapy programme for people with dementia: Randomised controlled trial. *British Journal of Psychiatry*, 183, 248–254.

Stokes, G. (1996). Challenging behaviour in dementia: A psychological approach. In R. T. Woods (Ed.), *Handbook of the clinical psychology of ageing* (pp. 601–628). Chichester, UK: Wiley.

Stokes, G. & Goudie, F. (1990). Counselling confused elderly people. In G. Stokes & F. Goudie (Eds.), *Working with dementia* (pp. 181–190). Bicester, UK: Winslow Press.

Stroebe, M. & Stroebe, W. (1991). Does 'grief-work' work? *Journal of Consulting and Clinical Psychology*, 59, 479–482.

Suhr, J., Anderson, S. & Tranel, D. (1999). Progressive muscle relaxation in the management of behavioural disturbance in Alzheimer's disease. *Neuropsychological Rehabilitation*, 9, 31–44.

Teri, L., Logsdon, R. G., Uomoto, J. & McCurry, S. M. (1997). Behavioral treatment of depression in dementia patients: A controlled clinical trial. *Journal of Gerontology*, 52B, P159–P166.

Thompson, L. W., Gallagher, D. & Breckenridge, J. S. (1987). Comparative effectiveness of psychotherapies for depressed elders. *Journal of Consulting and Clinical Psychology*, 55, 385–390.

Tuokko, L. W., Gallagher, D. & Breckenridge, J. S. (1987). Comparative effectiveness of psychotherapies for depressed elders. *Journal of Consulting and Clinical Psychology*, 55, 385–390.

Vernooij-Dassen, M., Huygen, F., Felling, A. & Persoon, J. (1995). Home care for dementia patients. *Journal of American Geriatrics Society*, 43, 456.

Warrington, E. & James, M. (1991). *Visual Object and Space Perception Battery (VOSP)*. Bury St Edmunds, UK: Thames Valley Test Company.

Wechsler, D. (1999). *Wechsler Test of Adult Reading (WTAR)*. San Antonio, TX: Psychological Corporation.

Windle, G. & Woods, R. T. (2004). Variations in subjective well-being: The mediating role of a psychological resource. *Ageing and Society*, 24, 583–602.

Woods, B. (2003). Evidence-based practice in psychosocial intervention in early dementia: How can it be achieved? *Aging and Mental Health*, 7, 5–6.

Woods, B. & Charlesworth, G. (2002). Psychological assessment and treatment. In R. Jacoby & C. Oppenheimer (Eds.), *Psychiatry in the elderly* (Third Edition, pp. 245–263). Oxford: Oxford University Press.

Woods, R. T. (1999a). Promoting well-being and independence for people with dementia. *International Journal of Geriatric Psychiatry*, 14, 97–109.

Woods, R. T. (1999b). Psychological 'therapies' in dementia. In R. T. Woods (Ed.), *Psychological problems of ageing* (pp. 311–344). Chichester, UK: Wiley.

Woods, R. T. (2001). Discovering the person with Alzheimer's disease: Cognitive, emotional and behavioural aspects. *Aging and Mental Health*, 5(Supp. 1), S7–S16.

Woods, R. T. & Bird, M. (1999). Non-pharmacological approaches to treatment. In G. Wilcock, K. Rockwood & R. Bucks (Eds.), *Diagnosis and management of dementia: A manual for memory disorders teams* (pp. 311–331). Oxford: Oxford University Press.

Woods, R. T. & McKiernan, F. (1995). Evaluating the impact of reminiscence on older people with dementia. In B. K. Haight & J. Webster (Eds.), *The art and science of reminiscing: Theory, research, methods and applications* (pp. 233–242). Washington, DC: Taylor & Francis.

Woods, R. T., Moniz-Cook, E., Iliffe, S., Campion, P., Vernooij-Dassen, M., Zanetti, O. & Franco, M. (2003). Dementia: Issues in early recognition and intervention in primary care. *Journal of the Royal Society of Medicine*, 96, 320–324.

Woods, R. T. & Roth, A. (2005). Effectiveness of psychological interventions with older people. In A. Roth & P. Fonagy (Eds.), *What works for whom? A critical review of psychotherapy research* (Second Edition, pp. 425–446). New York: Guilford Press.

World Health Organization (WHO) (1992). *The ICD-10 classification of mental and behavioural disorders. Clinical descriptions and diagnostic guidelines*. Geneva: WHO.

Xuereb, J. H., Brayne, C., Dufouil, C., Gertz, H., Wischik, C., Harrington, C., Mukaetova-Ladinska, E., McGee, M. A., O'Sullivan, A., O'Connor, D., Paykel, E. S. & Huppert, F. (2000). Neuropathological findings in the very old: Results from the first 101 brains of a population-based longitudinal study of dementing disorders. *Annals of the New York Academy of Sciences*, 903, 490–496.

Yale, R. (1995). *Developing support groups for individuals with early stage Alzheimer's disease: Planning, implementation and evaluation*. Baltimore: Health Profession Press.

Zarit, S. H. & Edwards, A. B. (1999). Family caregiving: Research and clinical intervention. In R. T. Woods (Ed.), *Psychological problems of ageing* (pp. 153–193). Chichester, UK: Wiley.

Chapter 24

Anger

Raymond W. Novaco and John L. Taylor

CASE EXAMPLE

Tim was a twenty-five-year old man with a history of serious sexual aggression against male and female children. At the age of fifteen he was convicted of the rape of a twelve-year-old girl, for which he spent two years in youth custody. Within a year of release, he carried out a series of indecent assaults on two twelve- and thirteen-year-old boys. Following conviction for these offences, Tim was admitted to an acute, low-secure hospital facility under sections 37/41 of the Mental Health Act (1983) on the grounds of 'mental impairment' as defined within the Act. Tim had a measured full-scale IQ of 77, which placed him in the 'borderline intelligence' range. He had attended mainstream school until the age of ten, when he was transferred to a local special needs school because of his learning difficulties.

Tim was the second youngest of six children, brought up by his parents in a seemingly stable home environment, although two of his siblings were also reported as having special educational needs. By the time he became a teenager it is reported that Tim's parents had little control over his unruly and aggressive behaviour, which was apparently activated with minimal provocation. He also began to abuse alcohol and drugs at that time. While in hospital, Tim continued to have regular and positive contact with his parents and siblings. Unfortunately, his father died four years after his admission to hospital and this affected him significantly.

About three years after hospital admission, Tim absconded with a fellow patient and stole a car, a crime for which they were both convicted. His progress in hospital was very patchy, with reports by ward nursing staff of frequent aggression and violence towards other patients, sexual aggression towards male and female patients, numerous absconsions from the hospital site, and generally un-co-operative, antisocial, and care-seeking attitudes and behaviour.

Prior to being considered for anger treatment, Tim had received two programmes of psychological intervention. Shortly after his admission he had responded positively to an individual behavioural intervention aimed at reducing levels of interpersonal conflict between him and other patients and direct care staff. He appeared to benefit from the structure and boundaries that this approach provided and was motivated by the sense of success he experienced, along with the positive attention from clinical staff that was associated with this improvement. Two years after his admission, Tim commenced, and ultimately completed, a sex-offender treatment programme that involved seventy sessions of group therapy over a period of three years. His responses to the specific elements of this treatment were mixed, but it emerged during this treatment that his sex-offending behaviour, along with his general aggression and violence towards others, was strongly associated with anger-control difficulties. Tim agreed that it might be beneficial for him to do some work on this particular problem area.

Tim completed several pre-treatment self-report measures (the Spielberger State Trait Anger Expression Inventory (STAXI; Spielberger, 1996) and the Novaco Anger Scale and Provocation Inventory (NAS and PI, Novaco, 1994, 2003)). His scores on both indicated high levels of anger compared to others in his patient population. His scores on these measures of anger disposition, reactivity, and expression were between 0.7 and 1.5 standard deviations above the means for his forensic inpatient reference group (cf. Novaco & Taylor, 2004). The anger psychometric measures are described later in the chapter. Using an informant rating scale, ward staff assessed Tim as demonstrating a range of behaviours associated with 'dissocial' and 'emotionally unstable – impulsive type' personality disorder characteristics.

Tim consented to take part in an eighteen-session, individualized cognitive-behavioural anger treatment specially designed for people with developmental disabilities and offending histories. The first six sessions constitute a 'preparatory' phase of treatment aimed at engaging and motivating clients, building the basic skills required for the treatment approach (e.g. self-monitoring), and providing opportunities for experiencing success. Perhaps unsurprisingly, given Tim's previous response to a structured and containing treatment approach, he responded well to this component of the treatment. In particular, as part of a 'decision matrix' exercise, he was able readily to identify the costs of remaining angry and aggressive and weigh these against the benefits of developing more appropriate ways of coping with and expressing his anger. At the end of this preparatory phase, Tim was motivated to continue with the next, more challenging phase of treatment.

The twelve-session 'treatment' phase follows a more customary CBT approach. It gives equal weight to modifying anger-maintaining cognitive distortions, the development of arousal reduction techniques and the rehearsal of pro-social anger coping skills within a sequential, but integrated, framework. The development of a shared formulation of the anger problems is pivotal in this approach. Tim was able to work with the therapist to identify priority areas for targeting during the treatment. These areas related to the particular types of situations likely to provoke anger arousal in him, the automatic thinking style that followed once his anger was activated, and his characteristic emotional and behavioural responses to such arousal. Together these make up Tim's 'anger signature' and treatment was aimed at helping him recognize and modify it.

During treatment, Tim progressively improved his tendency to ruminate about anger provocations, and he reduced the intensity of his anger arousal and the impulsiveness of his behavioural reactions. He perhaps showed greatest progress in modifying his thinking in response to situations in which he perceived that he had experienced injustice and disrespect at the hands of others.

Tim enthusiastically embraced the concepts of 'thought-catching' and thinking differently about situations by putting himself in others' shoes. His ability to implement this approach *in vivo*, in temporal conjunction with provocation events, was reflected in the 'thinking differently' sections of his daily anger log recordings.

His progress in treatment is reflected in clinically significant decreases in post-treatment anger assessment scores, which were maintained in one-month and eight-month follow-ups. These are presented in Table 24.1. With the empirical frame of reference being data on these psychometric measures obtained from 129 male patients in the same forensic hospital (cf. Novaco & Taylor, 2004), the change in Tim's scores from pre-treatment to post-treatment constitute reductions of 3.3 standard deviations on the NAS, 2.8 standard deviations on

Table 24.1 Tim's anger treatment evaluation scores

Anger measure	*Assessment point*			
	Pre-treatment	*Post-treatment*	*1-month follow-up*	*8-month follow-up*
Novaco Anger Scale				
Cognitive	40	26	25	27
Arousal	39	18	17	16
Behavioral	41	21	20	24
Total	120	65	62	66
Provocation Inventory	80	35	32	29
Spielberger STAXI				
Trait Anger	20	15	11	12
Anger Expression	39	16	14	19
Imaginal Provocation Test				
Anger Composite	36	17	–	–

Note: All assessments were administered by assistant psychologists independent of the therapist, using a structured interview format.

the PI, 2.1 standard deviations on STAXI Anger Expression, and .8 standard deviations on STAXI Trait Anger.

These self-reported changes in anger disposition, reactivity and expression were buttressed by the clinical impressions of ward staff. His key worker reported that following anger treatment '. . . there has been a marked improvement in the way Tim handles difficult situations. He tends to think rather than react, and afterwards discusses his feelings with staff'. Various aspects of clinical change that occurred with Tim will be given throughout this chapter to illustrate components of the treatment procedure.

INTRODUCTION

Interest in anger control has gained prominence in recent decades both in the general culture of Western societies and in clinical scientific literature (e.g. Beck, 1999). As emotion garnered broad attention in psychological research and theory, enthusiasm for the study of anger grew strongly, especially in conjunction with cardiovascular diseases (Chesney & Rosenman, 1985; Freidman, 1992; Siegman & Smith, 1994). Interest also mounted in broad-based efforts to find remedies for violent behaviour. In popular media, road rage metastasized into air rage, cinema rage, golf rage, rink rage, surf rage, trolley rage and royal rage. Anger management became a frequent prescription given by social gatekeepers, such as judicial officers, school administrators, mental health system directors, and prison and probation authorities. Thus, mental health professionals in many service delivery domains have now become familiar with client anger problems and have explored approaches to improving their clinical care capacity in this regard. Dissemination of programmes has occurred in schools, clinics, hospitals and prisons, especially of cognitive-behaviour therapy (CBT) interventions, with varying degrees of systematization in implementation. This chapter presents information on the epidemiology of anger problems, a summary of research on treatment of anger problems, information on the assessment and selection of clients for anger treatments, and an outline of a CBT approach to anger treatment. This treatment is based on a differentiated assessment of anger dyscontrol, incorporates an explicit treatment engagement component and delivers treatment as a way to foster self-regulation but also gives diligent attention to the psychosocial context of the person and the caregiving system.

Our attention to the provision of anger treatment concerns clinical populations with complex problems, such as the conjunction of impoverished family background, developmental disability, early conduct problems, substance use, serious offence history, institutionalization, re-offending, amalgamative emotional distress and recurrent challenging behaviour for mental healthcare staff. We have presented one such complex case in the case example. Tim has been a participant in a conjoined anger assessment and treatment project involving male forensic patients with developmental disabilities (Novaco & Taylor, 2004; Taylor et al., 2002, 2005). The successful treatment of persons with such multi-layered difficulties in regulating anger and aggressive behaviour bode well for downward extension to clients with less severe anger problems and less resource impairment.

CLINICAL FEATURES OF ANGER CONTROL PROBLEMS

As a normal human emotion, anger has considerable adaptive value, although there are sociocultural variations in the acceptability of its expression and the form that such expression takes. In the face of adversity, it can mobilize psychological resources, energize behaviours for corrective action and facilitate perseverance. Anger serves as a guardian to self-esteem, operates as a means of communicating negative sentiment, potentiates the ability to redress grievances, and boosts determination to overcome obstacles to our happiness and aspirations. Akin to aggressive behaviour, anger has functional value for survival.

For some clients, anger may be troublesome simply as a problem of psychosocial adjustment to stressful life circumstances. However, anger is a feature of a wide range of more problematic disorders encountered by clinical professionals in diverse settings. It is commonly observed in various personality, psychosomatic, and conduct disorders, in schizophrenia, in bipolar mood disorders, in organic brain disorders, in impulse control dysfunctions, and in a variety of conditions resulting from trauma. The central characteristic of anger in the context of such problem conditions is that it is 'dysregulated' – its activation, expression and experience occur without appropriate controls. This normal emotion, having no automatic status as a problem, becomes problematic by virtue of the adverse consequences to self and others that result from it and its reciprocal links to stressful life circumstances, psychopathology, and harm-doing behaviour.

Although the social distancing effect of anger is an obstacle to therapeutic change efforts, the designated recipients of real-life anger interventions have been highly diverse in problem condition, e.g. domestic violence perpetrators, traffic offenders, children with conduct problems, quarrelsome neighbours, explosive felons and persons with various psychiatric disorders being offered anger management as supplementary care. By contrast, a great many recipients of anger treatment in controlled studies have been college student volunteers, which unfortunately results in disproportionate attention to such studies with quasi-clinical clients in meta-analyses. Oddly, as six have now been published (Beck & Fernandez, 1998; Del Vecchio & O'Leary, 2004; DiGuiseppe & Tafrate, 2003; Edmondson & Conger, 1996; Sukhodolsky et al., 2004; Tafrate, 1995), there may be more meta-analyses of anger treatment than the number of high-quality clinical trials justify.

Providing services for people having recurrent anger problems is a challenging enterprise, as engaging them in the clinical process is often hard going. Seriously angry people appear to resist treatment, owing to the functional value of their anger routines. Howells and Day (2003), however, have turned the 'treatment resistance' notion on its head, asserting instead that the treatment engagement problem be understood as a matter of 'readiness'. They propose that readiness for anger management is affected by an array of impediments: the complexity of cases presenting with anger problems, institutional settings, client inferences about their problem, mandatory treatment, the client's personal goals, cultural differences and gender differences bearing on responsivity to provided programmes. This analysis by Howells and Day (2003) is insightful, particularly as it removes the onus of the problem from the dispositional status of the client. Our provision of the 'preparatory phase' component of the anger treatment to be described later seeks to address many of these core issues of readiness.

Behavioural-interpersonal features of anger problems

Because anger is a common precursor of aggressive behaviour, it can be unsettling for mental health professionals to engage as a treatment focus, regardless of its salience as a clinical need. Anger has been found to predict physical aggression by psychiatric hospital patients, prior to admission (McNeil et al. (2003), in the hospital (Novaco, 1994; Novaco & Renwick, in press; Novaco & Taylor, 2004; Wang & Diamond, 1999) and subsequently in the community after discharge (Monahan et al., 2001). Within a hospital, anger and aggression incur a great cost. High levels of direct-care staff injuries have been reported in studies done in secure hospitals in the US (Carmel & Hunter, 1989; Bensley et al. 1995), in the UK (National Audit Office, 2003) and in Australia (Cheung et al., 1996). Pertinent to the institutional context for our case study patient, violence faced by staff in a developmental disability service in the UK was found by Kiely and Pankhurst (1998) to entail nearly five times more incidents of patient-inflicted injury than that NHS Trust's sister psychiatric service, with 81% of staff reporting physical assault from service users during the previous twelve months. High turnover rates and burnout have indeed been found to be a consequence of staff exposure to the risk of violence in developmental disability services (Attwood & Joachim, 1994). Patient anger and aggression thus can be seen to carry heavy costs for a hospital system that is entrusted with providing security and rehabilitation.

Recurrent anger detracts from adaptive functioning in the contexts of work, family and social relationships. An angry person is not optimally alert, thoughtful, empathic, prudent or appreciative. Anger's embeddedness in other distressed emotions, such as shame and guilt (Tangney et al., 1992, 1996), as well as its involvement in clinical disorders such as depression (Bromberger & Matthews, 1996; Kopper & Epperson, 1996) paranoid delusional disorder (e.g. Kennedy et al., 1992), schizophrenia (e.g. Craig, 1982) and especially trauma (Andrews et al., 2000; Feeny et al., 2000; Novaco & Chemtob, 1998, 2002) further justify giving clinical attention to clients' anger regulatory difficulties.

In addition to being an activator of aggressive behaviour, anger can be problematic as an internal stressor, causing wear and tear on the body when recurrently activated, as reflected in its link to cardiovascular disease (cf. Chesney & Rosenman, 1985; Friedman, 1992; Siegman & Smith, 1994).

Designating anger as a problem condition is less than straightforward. Contrary to calls for a formal designation of 'anger disorders' (e.g. Eckhardt & Deffenbacher, 1995), it seems odd to pathologize an emotional state that has important energizing and potentiating functions and is a fundamental survival mechanism with extensions to freedom representational symbolic structures. Given that anger is a normal human emotion, ascertaining whether a person's anger experiences constitute a psychological problem condition hinges on the defining parameters. Frequency, intensity, duration and mode of expression comprise a set of such parameters, about which we will elaborate below.

EPIDEMIOLOGY OF ANGER

The judgement of whether someone has an 'anger problem' is dependent on the audience and its sociocultural context. Nevertheless, how often someone becomes angry, the degree of anger experienced, how long the arousal lasts and how one behaves when angry are dimensions by which a person's anger response patterns can be gauged to constitute a problem condition. Our case example, Tim, became angry frequently, at high intensity and with prolonged duration, connected with his rumination tendencies; he was also impulsively violent towards other patients. Clearly, the manifestations of his anger, and its association with substance abuse, sex offending and absconsions presented a multi-layered problem.

Anger frequency

How often people get angry surely varies culturally, but there is little data in this regard outside of North American samples. The study of normative patterns of anger began with G. Stanley Hall (1899) and was most extensively undertaken by Averill (1982). A variety of small sample studies have been conducted and, on the average in this research, people have reported becoming angry two or three times per week. Data reported by Kassinove et al. (1997) show general comparability between Russian (St Petersburg) and American (New York) participants, and no gender differences in anger frequency, which is a common finding. As Novaco and Jarvis (2002) showed in review and in examining US General Social Survey data, it is reasonable to infer that someone who reports becoming angry every day two or three times a day can be considered high in anger frequency.

Anger intensity

Unlike frequency, degree of anger intensity is more clearly indicative of dysfunction, because high arousal has cognitive interference effects and high intensity anger leads to impulsive behaviour, over-riding inhibitory controls. Although women and men seem to experience anger at comparable levels of intensity (e.g. Kopper & Epperson, 1996), even in response to trauma (e.g. Ehlers et al., 1998), men more often judge their anger intensity from their behaviour in an anger episode, while women are more inclined to weigh anger duration in judging their anger intensity (Frost & Averill, 1982). Persons with high anger dispositions are inclined to believe that their anger reactions are justified and readily defend their entitlement to anger on any occasion (i.e. frequency). In contrast, they can be more easily induced to consider that the anger reaction they did have was perhaps too strong.

Duration

The intensity of anger can be expected to influence anger duration, as greater elevation in physiological arousal is associated with longer time for recovery to baseline and because strong anger can escalate and extend as a product of angry behaviour. Another reason is that strongly bothersome events are likely to linger and not be resolved promptly, thus fostering rumination that prolongs anger and can re-vivify it.

The prolongation of anger arousal has several problematic consequences. First, blood pressure is significantly affected by prolonged anger and its non-expression, and this is a substantial factor in essential hypertension (Johnson, 1990). Second, when anger arousal does not return to baseline, there are likely to be 'excitation transfer' effects, whereby the undissipated arousal adds to arousal activation from new sources and raises the probability of aggressive behaviour (Zillmann & Bryant, 1974). Third, rumination about anger incidents interferes with optimal functioning and lessens positive inputs that are fortifying to the self.

Several of these ingredients to this dimension of anger duration are illustrated in an example incident from our case history. As recorded in his anger log, Tim had had some friction with a member of staff. When asked by the therapist to describe what had happened, the account was as follows:

Tim: Well, there was a mix-up about what time my drama session finished. I came back to the ward earlier than I should have 'cos the session finished early. The staff said I was lying.

Therapist: OK. And what were you thinking about when this happened? What thoughts were going through your mind?

Tim: I'm thinking to myself 'I did nothing wrong. Why me? It's always me that gets into bother – no-one else. They're always picking on me'.

Therapist: Right. And how were you feeling at this time?

Tim: Raging. I'm furious.

Therapist: Out of ten, how much would you say?

Tim: Ten out of ten!

Here an aversive experience readily maps onto an existing anger schema of being unfairly treated (also connected to a self-schema of diminished personal worth), the anger has strong intensity and, in Tim's sociophysical circumstances, he will be prone to ruminate about being 'picked-on', prolonging his anger experience. Both the rumination and duration dimensions are assessed by the NAS and can straightforwardly be obtained in clinical interview, giving added attention to the client's post-episode social functioning and conflict resolution strategies.

Mode of expression

A defining characteristic of anger is the engagement of antagonistic behaviour. Whether someone acts in an explicitly aggressive manner in any particular circumstance will vary with many factors, but is largely affected by inhibitory controls, internal and external. To be sure, the behavioural manifestation of anger is the clinical problem parameter having greatest societal import.

Anger impels both verbal and physical aggression. Verbal aggression pertains to threatening, abusive and derogatory statements, the common denominator of which is to produce distress in the target person. Physical aggression, which is overt behaviour intended to produce harm or damage, may be either directed at the provoking person or displaced to a substitute target. Anger can also motivate 'passive' aggression, which is harm-doing behaviour in a disguised form – pretended congeniality, deliberate interpersonal coldness or neglect – with the intention of producing distress in the target person. Alternatively, it may be expressed in constructively minded problem-solving behaviour or be given safe ventilation as a self-control tactic (e.g. removing oneself from a high-conflict situation and, in seclusion, shouting to an ethereal audience). When anger is suppressed by inhibitory mechanisms and there is no effective resolution of the instigating circumstances, the other three parameters (frequency, intensity and duration) will be affected.

SUMMARY OF RESEARCH ON RESPONSE TO ANGER TREATMENT

Research on anger treatment efficacy continues to lag far behind that for depression and anxiety. After CBT for anger was first implemented and evaluated by Novaco (1975, 1977), some controlled studies followed the stress inoculation approach (for a review of these, see Novaco, 1997; Novaco & Jarvis, 2002), and other more generic CBT approaches were adopted (e.g. Deffenbacher et al., 1987; Feindler & Ecton, 1986; Feindler et al., 1986; Hazaleus & Deffenbacher, 1986). Six meta-analyses of anger treatment studies have now been published (Beck & Fernandez, 1998; Del Vecchio & O'Leary, 2004; DiGuiseppe & Tafrate, 2003; Edmondson & Conger, 1996; Sukhodolsky et al., 2004; Tafrate, 1995); that by Sukhodolsky et al. is devoted to children and adolescents. These meta-analyses, except the latter, are overloaded with college student studies, and all fail to include case study reports and multiple baseline studies (see Novaco, 1997; Novaco & Jarvis, 2002), which have typically involved real clients with serious problems. Oddly, the controlled anger treatment trial by Chemtob et al. (1997), involving a seriously disordered population and published in a premier journal, was missed in both the Beck and Fernandez (1998) and the DiGuiseppe and Tafrate (2003) reviews.

Across the meta-analyses, anger treatments have produced medium to strong effect sizes. This indicates that approximately 75% of those receiving anger treatment improved compared to those in the control conditions. Most assuredly, more controlled treatment studies are needed with seriously disordered populations and with rigorous multi-model assessment designs. Little is known about the efficacy of anger treatment in reducing violent recidivism or other aggressive behaviour in the community.

Regarding forensic populations, it must be said that controlled treatment outcome evaluation studies have been thin, despite the common implementation of anger management in prison settings. A rather extensive outcome evaluation by Watt and Howells (1999) in two studies conducted in Western Australia with violent offenders in maximum- and minimum-security prisons produced discouraging results for a group anger management programme of ten two-hour sessions delivered over five weeks. Measures of anger knowledge, anger disposition, anger expression, observed aggressive behaviour and prison misconduct showed no treatment gains for the programme, compared to non-equivalent waiting-list controls. The non-randomness of the treatment group assignment may have been a factor in the non-significant effects, but the authors were inclined to attribute the absence of effects to 'low motivation for participants' and other programme administrative factors. We hope that the assessment and treatment provision contents of the present chapter will be useful in guiding future system-wide intervention studies.

For people like Tim, with developmental disabilities, anger treatment studies were reviewed by Taylor (2002); since that review, Lindsay and his colleagues with clients in the community (Lindsay et al., 2003, 2004) and Taylor et al. (2004, 2005) have reported successful anger treatment outcomes with hospitalized clients who had serious aggression problems. Very notably, the results of Lindsay and his colleagues have included lower re-offence and aggressive incident rates on follow-up for individuals who had received anger treatment.

The cognitive-behavioural treatment of anger has been shown to have applicability to a wide range of client populations. Anger dysregulation is associated with many clinical disorders and, in addition to it being indicative of subjective distress, self-report of anger is predictive of violent behaviour. Hospitalized patients with long-standing aggression histories, mental disorder and even intellectual disabilities can be engaged in CBT anger treatment and have been shown to benefit. While therapeutic mechanisms underlying treatment gains are not clear, nor their sustainability or generalizability, we are fortified in seeking further advances in providing remedies for this important clinical problem of anger dyscontrol.

ASSESSMENT OF ANGER PROBLEM PARAMETERS

Anger frequency

As outlined above with reference to the review by Novaco and Jarvis (2002), someone who reports becoming angry two or three times a day every day can be considered high in anger frequency.

Anger intensity

Ratings of anger intensity are a typical feature of anger psychometrics, such as Spielberger's (1996) State Trait Anger Expression Inventory (STAXI) and the Provocation Inventory (PI; Novaco, 2003). It is assumed that higher intensity ratings are indicative of greater disturbance, because the ratings are summed across items. Indeed, the intensity dimension functions as a qualitative discrimination, because we partly judge that we are angry, as opposed to being 'upset', 'bothered' or 'annoyed' by virtue of the affect intensity.

Anger intensity is a point of leverage for examining 'anger costs' to motivate treatment engagement and for making early inroads into anger control by means of arousal reduction techniques easily learned by clients, such as deep breathing and muscle relaxation. Anger intensity assessment can be done with various psychometric measures, such as the STAXI (Spielberger, 1996) or the NAS and PI (Novaco, 2003). The PI, in this regard, has an advantage, as it is an anger situational inventory and can facilitate an interview with the client about his or her anger experiences. This can be a very useful starting point with someone having difficulties disclosing or discussing anger control problems. On the PI, the person rates anger intensity on a 1–4 scale with regard to twenty-five common situations of provocation. Both high- and low-anger-rated items are informative. With the completed PI in hand, the clinician can first focus on the items endorsed as high-anger situations, asking the client to describe a recent experience in those situations and encouraging a full account of the episode. The incident account can provide useful information about cognitive structures affecting the perception of the event, the triggering elements, and the person's style of responding. Low-anger items are also useful, as they convey that the person does not get angry in all situations and giving some attention to these helps to overcome defensiveness. Low-anger items are also a basis for identifying coping skills and anger attenuating variables. The very act of talking about the hypothetical anger situations on the PI in a receptive and non-threatening atmosphere can help a person become comfortable with such discussions and to adopt an active role in the helping process.

Duration

Duration of anger, as well as rumination, are assessed by the NAS (Novaco, 2003). This measure can be obtained straightforwardly in clinical interview, giving added attention to the client's post-episode social functioning and conflict resolution strategies.

Someone who continues to dwell on anger experiences may also be imagining violent retaliation. A very useful assessment device in that regard is Grisso's Schedule for Imagined Violence (Grisso et al., 2000). This study, of over 1100 psychiatric patients, showed that the NAS Cognitive, Arousal and Behavioral subscales are very strongly related to imagined violence, especially NAS Cognitive.

Mode of expression

Regarding assessment of this mode of expression parameter, case record data are intrinsically useful, as the person's problematic behaviour is often duly noted and characterized for its stylistic features. There are several useful psychometric scales that differentiate mode of expression. The STAXI's Anger Expression subscales differentiate Anger In, Anger Out and Anger Control; the Aggression Questionnaire (AQ; Buss & Perry 1992) has subscales for Verbal Aggression and Physical Aggression, as well as for Anger and Hostility; the NAS Behavioral subscale has content category dimensions of impulsivity, verbal aggression, physical aggression and indirect expression, for which scores can be examined clinically (cf. Novaco, 2003). A recent review of measures of anger and hostility can be found in Eckhardt, Norlander and Deffenbacher (2004).

Returning to our case example, when the therapist inquired about how Tim responded to the staff challenging his explanation about getting back to the ward early:

Tim: Ha! I shouted and swore at 'em. Told them to 'eff off'. I argued with them and threatened to make a complaint.
Therapist: So, how well do you think you handled this situation?
Tim: Really bad. No good at all.

The high-intensity anger over-rode inhibitory control, resulting in impulsive verbal aggression that would have adverse consequences. Indicative here is that Tim recognizes that his angry behaviour is problematic and in need of change; however, when this episode occurred he had already begun to engage in treatment.

ANGER COSTS: PROMPTING MOTIVATION FOR TREATMENT

Treatment engagement follows from recognition that the costs of staying the same outweigh the costs of trying to be different. How sensitized a client is to the costs of recurrent anger reactions can be assessed from three lines of inquiry: (1) the degree to which he or she is aware of personal anger pattern features; (2) the degree of investment in anger habits; and (3) the degree to which the client is troubled by the experiential correlates and social products of his or her anger reactions.

Awareness of anger pattern features

At the core of anger dyscontrol problems is a deficiency in self-monitoring. Being aware of becoming angry, of the level of anger intensity, of the behavioural routines associated with their anger and of the instrumentality or gains produced by the routines is fundamental to self-regulation. Helping the client to see the reciprocity of anger in personal relationships and the detrimental effects that anger has on well-being are also important steps in shaping anger cost awareness.

Investment in anger habits

Reluctance to change follows from strong investment in anger routines. The degree of investment in anger can be detected from the person's inclination to externalize blame, quickness in justification for anger reactions, and belief in the efficacy of anger in responding to interpersonal conflict. The person's ability to consider constructive coping alternatives, as well as his or her inclination to use such alternatives, are also important to consider in assessing investment in anger habits and readiness to change.

Concern about anger experiential correlates

Most typically, clients' concern is prompted by the consequences that their angry behaviour has produced, such as loss of a relationship, judicial system sanctions or job difficulties. Sensitivity to social disapproval and valuation of negative feedback from significant others bears substantially on self-regulation. The person may be troubled by states of tension, agitation and irritability that demarcate anger or the ruminations and preoccupations that accompany anger.

Ascertaining recognition of the costs of anger can be done in a structured interview. For example, to learn about the client's awareness of anger patterns features, one might ask: 'What happens when you get angry?', 'Would anyone know that you are angry?', 'What are some signs that you are getting angry that others could see?' The client's responses to such questions can be followed with: 'How do other people react when you get angry?', 'What do you make of that?' The person's degree of investment in anger habits and concern about experiential correlates can be approached by questions such as: 'When you get really angry, what happens to you afterwards?', 'What thoughts do you have?', 'Do you ever wish that you had reacted differently?', 'How would your life be different, if you did not get angry so much?', 'What would you lose?', 'What would you gain?'

For many clients, readiness for therapeutic change must be enhanced through guided intervention that patiently induces motivation. Heightening recognition of anger costs is part of the anger treatment 'preparatory phase' that we have developed to facilitate treatment engagement (see also, Novaco, 1997; Renwick et al., 1997), although that initiative was pre-dated and more fully elaborated by the 'stages of change' model put forward by Prochaska and DiClemente (1983) and the motivational interviewing approach of Miller and Rollnick (1991). Here, to convey how we assist the client in identifying anger costs, some material from our case example is illustrative. This is taken from a 'decision matrix' exercise in Tim's preparatory phase work, occurring in session 5 of the six-session procedure. That session explored the costs and benefits of anger and aggression, both in the short and longer term, aiming to help the client to understand that the benefits of developing self-control over anger and aggression outweigh the believed benefits of these routines.

In the 'decision matrix' exercise, Tim referred to a situation he had recently recorded in his anger logs. This involved a friend (fellow patient) questioning his sexuality. This had made Tim angry and he shouted and swore at his friend; as a result, ward staff admonished him. Tim was asked to think about the immediate benefits of being aggressive in this situation. He explained that by reacting in this way 'I got the anger out of my system . . . stopped my mate from taking the mick out of me . . . and showed to the others [patients] that I'm not a soft touch'.

Despite the immediate benefits of the verbal aggression in release of the angry feelings, Tim was unable to identify any long-term advantages of behaving in this way. In the supportive context provided by the therapist, he was able to list many short- and long-term disadvantages of being angry and aggressive. Short-term consequences included getting into trouble with ward staff, losing points on the ward incentive scheme, falling out with his friend and the possibility that, if the situation had escalated, he and/or his friend might have been hurt. Moreover, Tim could identify longer-term problems associated with this style of responding, such as getting a bad reputation, letting people down (family, friends and staff), feeling ashamed and losing the trust and concern of carers. Using a worksheet depicting a set of scales, Tim readily weighed the costs of continuing to be aggressive against the costs of attempting to learn to respond to his anger in a calmer and more constructive manner.

Preparatory phase of anger treatment

An enlightened presentation of the many issues involved in readiness for anger therapy can be found in Howells and Day (2003), whose differentiation of impediments was noted earlier and who also discuss matters of therapeutic alliance, responsivity and prospective modification of therapeutic approach. In addition to what they denote, it can also be said that prospective participants in anger treatment often lack a number of pre-requisites for optimal involvement in a self-regulatory, coping skills intervention programme. Clients may have had some training in arousal control and thus may not have difficulty in identifying emotions or differentiating degrees of anger intensity. But they may be unaccustomed to making self-observations about their thoughts, feelings, and behaviour in rudimentary self-monitoring. Many may not recognize the degree to which thoughts, emotions and behaviour are interconnected. For others, however, such educational aspects of the preparatory phase are of less importance than the engagement issues.

The preparatory phase is thus constructed to 'prime' the client motivationally and to establish basic skills of emotion identification, self-monitoring, communication about anger experiences and arousal reduction. It serves to build trust in the therapist and the treatment programme, providing an atmosphere conducive to personal disclosure and to the collaboration required by this therapeutic approach. The latter includes building a common language about the model of anger that guides the treatment (Novaco, 1994). While designed to be relatively non-probing and non-challenging, for some institutionalized patients (cf. Novaco et al., 2000) it can elicit distress, as it raises vulnerability issues for them. Consequently, inter-session follow-up meetings with patients may be needed to support them in coping with the impact of the sessions. Because the preparatory phase can be pitched to the client as a 'trial period', its conclusion then leads to a more explicit and informed choice by the client about starting treatment proper. In effect, there is a bit of sleight-of-hand at play here in presenting the 'preparatory phase' to the client as something to 'try out', in the sense of it not being the 'real treatment', when indeed it is.

Formulation of anger problems

It commonly occurs that people are referred for anger treatment inappropriately, which typically happens in conjunction with concern about the person's violent behaviour. Not all violent offenders are candidates for anger treatment interventions. Howells (1989) cogently discussed the issue of suitability of clients for anger management interventions and provided case illustrations of congruities and incongruities. He states that anger treatment is not indicated for those whose violent behaviour is not emotionally mediated, whose violent behaviour fits their short-term or long-term goal structure or whose violence is anger mediated but not acknowledged. The latter condition is sought to be remedied by the 'preparatory phase' component but, at the outset, one must resolve the issue of whether the person's problematic behaviour, violent or otherwise, is an anger regulatory problem, implying that the acquisition or augmentation of anger control coping skills would reduce its probability.

At the time of segue to treatment, the therapist should have collated anger assessment data to construct a formulation of the client's anger regulatory problem and the treatment targets. That information should be derived from multiple sources and modes of assessment: (1) clinical interview with the client, significant others and clinical team or case workers; (2) self-report psychometric scales, such as the NAS-PI, STAXI or AQ, and also anger diary recordings, for which there are various formats (e.g. for adolescents in residential treatment; see Feindler & Ecton, 1986); (3) behavioural observation ratings, which can be provided by ward staff, such as the Staff Observation Aggression Scale, which has been revised as SOAS-R (Nijman et al., 1999) or the Ward Anger Rating Scale (Novaco, 1994; Novaco & Renwick, 2006); (4) coding of case files and incident reports (e.g. Novaco & Taylor, 2004); and possibly (5) structured provocation testing, which can be done via imaginal provocation procedures (cf. Novaco, 1975; Taylor et al., 2004).

As a general principle, it should be kept in mind that anger is an abstract construct that has many observable referents, none of which constitute a 'pure' index of anger. Proper assessment requires various modes of observation. For clinical purposes, multiple anger measures should be obtained and assessments should be made at different points in time. Attention should be given to minimizing contextual factors that are likely to impair validity, particularly as anger assessment is vulnerable to problems of *reactivity*, i.e. the person responding to inferences about the test situation, as opposed to responding to the explicit elements of the testing. Anger assessment, particularly in forensic settings, is prone to 'masking', referring to inclination to produce responses in anticipation of what those responses will mean to some audience.

Assessment of the anger regulatory problem is an ongoing process, as the therapist works progressively towards an individual anger problem formulation. During the first two or three sessions of the treatment phase, clients are encouraged to work on an *external events* × *internal processes* × *behavioural responses* analysis of their anger problems in order to reach a shared formulation of their difficulties. In the case of Tim, material from completed anger logs, from situations he described for his personal anger hierarchy, and from his profile of scores on the NAS and PI were used to reach a shared view of the key problems for him in controlling his anger and priorities for treatment. These were organized collaboratively within a simplified conceptual framework.

The situations about which Tim was most sensitive and strongly anger-reactive were those in which he was accused of doing things he had not done (unfairness/injustice). The types of thoughts that most characterized Tim's cognitive responses to such situations were 'I want to hit him . . . I should hit him . . . he deserves it' (justification). Moreover, he indicated that these thoughts 'go round and round in my head' (rumination). The feelings of anger that accompanied this type of situation were typically very strong (high intensity) and stayed with Tim for a prolonged period of time (long duration). His behavioural reactions in these circumstances were typically to swear and shout (verbal aggression) or to grab the other person and threaten him (impulsive confrontation). It was agreed with Tim that these would be the areas of focus in treatment, applying cognitive re-structuring, arousal reduction and behavioural skills training techniques for anger reduction. This shared formulation is of central importance. It is intrinsic to the collaborative emphasis given in CBT to promote self-control skills, especially the stress inoculation approach (Meichenbaum, 1985), and it is pivotal to enabling the client to extend treatment gains after completing therapy.

TREATMENT OF ANGER-CONTROL PROBLEMS

Levels of anger treatment intervention

Psychotherapeutic interventions for anger occur at several levels, which have different aims and degrees of sophistication. Intervention levels reflect the degree of systematization, complexity and depth of therapeutic approach. Increased depth is associated with greater individual tailoring to client needs. Correspondingly, greater specialization in techniques and in clinical supervision is required with more complex levels of intervention. These levels of intervention are full delineated in Novaco et al. (2000). To give a synopsis here, these levels are said to be:

General clinical care for anger

At this level, anger is identified as a relevant treatment issue and addressed as part of a wider mental healthcare programme involving counselling, psychodynamic therapies, cognitive and behavioural therapies, and/or psychopharmacology applied in an individual, couple, family or group format. General clinical care for anger, when its operational characteristics are explicitly designated, may indeed serve as a comparison condition for experimental anger treatment, as was done in the Chemtob et al. (1997) study with Vietnam veterans.

Anger management provision

This usually occurs as a structured, psychoeducational, group-based approach that imparts information about anger (its determinants, signs, manifestations and consequences) and about ways of controlling it, such as changing perceptions or beliefs, using relaxation and adopting alternative behaviours for dealing with provocation. Content and format varies but most existing forms of this intervention are guided by cognitive-behavioural principles. The term 'anger management' was coined in Novaco (1975) to describe an experimental cognitive-behavioural treatment, but it is now useful to distinguish this level of intervention from more specialized anger treatment. The group format does provide a forum for the sharing of anger experiences, peer support and peer modelling, as well as serving the through-put objectives of a clinical service system.

Compared to 'anger treatment', the provision of anger management is more time-limited, is generally homogenous in procedure and, while there is participant discussion, it is less interactive than treatment and more unidirectional in information flow. It involves less client disclosure and is thus less threatening; correspondingly, because of its structure, the personal investment for the client is lower. Importantly, it is not predicated on individual case formulation. Evaluative measures are often employed but explicit use of individual client assessment data tends not to occur.

Anger treatment provision

At this level of intervention, anger dyscontrol is approached in terms of the client's core needs. However, anger treatment is not a substitute for psychotherapy and should be understood as an adjunctive treatment. It focuses on the psychological deficits in self-regulation articulated in individual case formulation, and explicitly integrates assessment with treatment. It often involves clients who are high in threat-sensing, suspicion and avoidance and, therefore, hinges on the provision of a therapeutic relationship.

Anger treatment targets enduring change in cognitive, arousal and behavioural systems. It centrally involves substantial cognitive restructuring and the acquisition of arousal reduction and behavioural coping skills. It achieves cognitive and behaviour change in large measure through changing valuations of personal priorities and augmenting self-monitoring capacity. Because it addresses anger as grounded and embedded in aversive and often traumatic life experiences, it entails the evocation of distressed emotions, i.e. fear and sadness, as well as anger. In the stress inoculation CBT approach, therapist-guided exposure to provocation occurs in graduated hierarchy procedures. As high-anger clients, particularly those with comorbid mental/personality disorders, tend to push people away as part of their external blaming and avoidant styles, advanced therapeutic skill and supervision is essential in delivering anger intervention at this level.

CBT anger treatment: Stress inoculation for anger control

Model and rationale

This cognitive-behavioural approach to anger treatment involves the following key components: (1) client education about anger, stress and aggression; (2) self-monitoring of anger frequency, intensity and situational triggers; (3) construction of a personal anger provocation hierarchy, created from the self-monitoring data and used for the practice and testing of coping skills; (4) arousal reduction techniques of progressive muscle relaxation, breathing-focused relaxation, and guided imagery training; (5) cognitive restructuring by altering attentional focus, modifying appraisals and using self-instruction; (6) training behavioural coping in communication and respectful assertiveness as modelled and rehearsed with the therapist; and (7) practising the cognitive, arousal regulatory and behavioural coping skills while visualizing and role-playing progressively more intense anger-arousing scenes from the personal hierarchies.

Self-monitoring

Anger regulation cannot occur in the absence of self-monitoring. One must detect a signal that there is departure from equilibrium and that deviation must be assigned negative valuation. Persons with serious anger problems have great impairment in self-monitoring capacity and boosting that capacity is a central and fundamental therapeutic objective. This is accomplished by concerted notation and feedback on client-maintained anger incident logs, as well as the psychometric instruments and therapist-distributed handout material for client education about anger and aggression.

When people report anger experiences, they most typically give accounts of things that have 'happened to them'. For the most part, they describe events physically and temporally proximate to their anger arousal. As a rule, they provide accounts of provocations ascribed to events in the immediate situation of the anger experience, portrayed in the telling as being something about which anger is quite fitting. This can be viewed as a 'proximity bias' in the understanding of anger (Novaco, 1993).

The response to the question, 'What makes you angry?' hinges on self-monitoring proficiencies. People are commonly neither good nor objective observers when they are angry. Anger is very much a blaming reaction. Far less commonly do people disaggregate their anger experiences into source components, some of which may originate from distal sources and ambient circumstances (e.g. work overload, economic strain or family stress) rather than from acute, proximal occurrences. Concerted attention to the client's anger logs by the therapist provides for the identification of anger triggers, for understanding the contextual surround and for enabling clients to recognize how their cultivated world-view provides the landscape for their anger.

Cognitive restructuring

To illustrate cognitive change efforts, we return to our case example and to the incident when Tim was questioned by a member of staff about coming back to the ward early. The therapist first would have introduced the concept of 'thought-catching', i.e., monitoring of automatic thoughts occurring at the time of provocation. Clients are asked to record in their anger logs the thoughts they had at the time of an incident. These thoughts, and their role in experience and expression of anger, are discussed and explored in the sessions. Clients are encouraged to try to think differently about the situation by, for example, putting themselves in the shoes of the person with whom they were angry. The following excerpt from a session with Tim illustrates how this process is aimed at disconnecting the threat perception that drives hostile thinking and aggressive behaviour. Recall that Tim said that he was being picked-on, he had done nothing wrong, he was furious and then swore and shouted at the staff member. Here, the therapist works the cognitive restructuring:

Therapist: OK then Tim, let's think about how you might have handled this differently. Let's say you're in exactly the same situation. You come back to the ward early because a session has finished early. The staff are suspicious about why you have come back when you shouldn't have. They are asking you why you aren't at your session when you should be. Just the same as what happened to you here. OK?

Tim: Yes.

Therapist: Right. So straight away you start thinking these angry thoughts. Like 'I've done nothing wrong. They're picking on me. It's not fair'. That sort of thing.

Tim: Right.

Therapist: But instead of thinking those thoughts, which make you angry straight away, can you think of any other reasons why staff might have behaved like they did?

Tim: Umm.

Therapist: Well, try to put yourself in their shoes – see the situation from their point of view.

Tim: Er, OK.

Therapist: If you were a member of staff and a patient turns up on the ward when they should be in a session, what are you going to be thinking?

Tim: Yeah right – well for one thing I'd be saying to myself 'This guy's maybe trying it on – he shouldn't be leaving sessions early'.

Therapist: OK, well that sounds possible. Can you think of any other reasons why staff might be concerned?

Tim: Well it's their job to be worried about where patients are, isn't it? It's to do with security. You can't have patients just coming and going at all times.

Therapist: So if you are thinking like that, how are you feeling in this situation?

Tim: I'd be less angry – say five out of ten.

Therapist: And what about your body?

Tim: Oh, I think it wouldn't be as tensed up. Less shaky. Maybe two out of ten.

Therapist: Do you think you would have behaved in a different way?

Tim: I think so.

Therapist: How?

Tim: Maybe I wouldn't have flew off the handle. I'd have tried to explain to the staff what happened with the class finishing early. Calm like.

(*during this dialogue the therapist has been using a worksheet with graphics to record two lines: what actually happened (actual), and then what could have happened (possible)*)

Therapist: So if you look at what actually happened, and then look at what might have happened, you had exactly the same situation to begin with but very different endings. What do you think made the difference?

Tim: Well maybe thinking about it in a different way helped. Not thinking straight-off that they were trying to get me.

Once introduced, cognitive restructuring work is a component part of each session. Between sessions, clients record provocation incidents in their anger logs and are encouraged to try 'thinking differently' about these experiences, so as to move the cognitive re-framing temporally closer to actual incidents. A central goal of the cognitive change effort is to modify the entrenched anger schemas that produce anger reactions with considerable automaticity. For high-anger people, anger is often a default response to aversive events, intrinsically linked to threat-sensing. For example, seeing the person with whom one is enamoured conversing with a potential suitor, no matter how remote the prospect, can elicit a strong anger reaction in conjunction with a 'betrayal' appraisal. Having to wait for staff attention in some service sector (e.g. a social service agency, clinic or shop) can provoke anger that follows from appraisals of being 'ignored' or 'deemed worthless', which may be coupled with a entitlement schema. Cognitive restructuring seeks to alter the fixed frameworks that operate as the lens through which such social encounters are viewed and experienced. Because those appraisal systems have been shaped by self-protective motives, the therapist must provide a context of safety and support in order for alternative appraisal and expectation structures to be established.

Arousal reduction

There is no more central metaphor for anger than hot fluid in a container. Physiological activation is a defining feature of anger (Novaco, 1994). The cardiovascular, respiratory and skeletal systems are key components (Robins & Novaco, 2000; Siegman & Smith, 1994), and neural structures and transmitting mechanisms are progressively being identified for their activating and modulating functions (e.g. Anderson & Silver, 1998; Davidson et al., 2000; Harmon-Jones & Sigelman, 2001). Field and laboratory studies in abundance have provided ample evidence of the negative health consequences of 'hot' anger reactivity (cf. Williams & Williams, 1993), and suppressed anger has well-established links to elevated physiological arousal and sustained hypertension (cf. Robins & Novaco, 2000). Importantly, residual arousal from anger events can transfer to future conflicts and further intensify the anger reactivity to instigating events (Zillmann, 1988; Zillmann & Bryant, 1974). The somatic arousal component should perhaps be the primary treatment target in anger treatment for persons affected by trauma, as it has been found to be strongly linked to non-anger post-traumatic stress disorder (PTSD) symptoms and independent PTSD diagnosis (Novaco & Chemtob, 2002).

Arousal reduction procedures begin with helping the person to identify signs of arousal, including its intensity, duration and lability, as well as latency in reactivity. As discussed earlier, intensity is a gateway parameter, as modifying intensity can provide a foothold for treatment. Fundamental to arousal reduction is the regulation of breathing, which is the central rhythm of the body. Slow, deep breathing is therefore demonstrated and induced in each session, and clients are encouraged to practise on their own. Progressive muscle relaxation, akin to the classic Jacobsen (1939) procedures of systematically tensing and relaxing sequences of muscle groups is taught to clients as a core relaxation induction procedure. Other classic methods, such as autogenic procedures (Schultz & Lutne, 1959), emphasizing images of heaviness and warmth, are good supplements or substitutes for physically impaired patients (e.g. spinal-cord-injury patients) or for someone who is averse to muscle tensing, e.g. of the face. Guided relaxation imagery is also used, vividly portraying tranquil scenes to the client to induce a light somnambulistic state. Supplementary resources are marshalled when possible within institutions (e.g. music, art, horticulture) to bolster arousal reduction efforts, and clients in any context are encouraged to engage in personally chosen practices having arousal reduction aims, such as yoga, tai chi, meditation, aerobics or aesthetic appreciation.

Behavioural coping skills

Behavioural responses play an important role in shaping and defining anger. Implicit in the cognitive labelling of anger is an inclination to act in an antagonistic or confrontative manner. Such action impulses have a role in defining the emotional state as anger, as opposed to some other emotion. As anger is often the product of behavioural exchanges that escalate aversive events, the development of anger schemas and scripts for anger episodes are rooted in encodings of behavioural routines. Huesmann's (1998) social information-processing model is particularly valuable for understanding these constructs and the reciprocities between cognitive and behavioural systems.

Proficient self-monitoring can prompt negative feedback to counter the escalation of anger and aggression, breaking the self-fulfilling prophecy chain whereby angry, antagonistic outputs elicit antagonism in reply, which then confirms the belief that others are malevolent. Behavioural coping skills are essential for anger management and are part of all such CBT programmes. Goldstein and Keller (1987), for example, offered valuable procedures for training pro-social skills, communication, negotiation and contracting. Feindler and Ecton's (1986) work with adolescents is also rich with verbal and non-verbal coping skills.

For dealing with anger-evoking interpersonal situations, three main categories of behavioural skill should be inculcated: (1) *diplomacy*, whereby the person can effectively convey a conflict-neutralizing sentiment, offer a modicum of empathy, and seek a mutually satisfying solution; (2) *strategic withdrawal*, removal of oneself from a high-conflict situation when resolution is not currently feasible, followed by cool-down techniques and later constructive re-engagement; and (3) *respectful assertiveness*, maintaining poise and control with a repertoire of verbal skills and courteous firmness. Therapist-directed role-play is the principal mode in both individual and group treatment for teaching behavioural skills, but visual-motor imaginative rehearsal (as would be used with sports competitors) is always a useful technique. In the stress inoculation approach to CBT anger treatment (e.g., Chemtob et al. 1997; Novaco, 1977), provocation hierarchy work is a central platform by which behavioural skills rehearsed with the therapist are then applied and tested.

Provocation hierarchy work

Provocation is simulated in the therapeutic context by imaginal and role-play exposure to anger incidents anchored in the client's life experiences, as directed by the therapist. The provocation incidents are graduated in anger intensity and are arranged as a hierarchy, which is produced collaboratively. This graduated, hierarchical exposure, done in conjunction with the teaching of coping skills across sessions, is the basis for the 'inoculation' metaphor (cf. Meichenbaum, 1985). The therapist helps the client to arrange a gradation of personally provoking situations, constructing scenes providing sufficient detail to generate a good imaginal image. The scenarios are described in matter-of-fact terms but incorporate wording that captures the client's perceptual sensitivities on provoking elements, such as the antagonist's tone of voice or nuances of facial expression. Each scenario ends with provocative aspects of the situation, not denoting the client's reaction, so that it serves as a stimulus scene (see also Taylor et al., 2004, 2005). For example:

> You are sitting in the day room, watching your favourite television programme. You are really enjoying it. Another person comes in and, without asking, walks up to the TV, switches to another channel and then sits down to watch a different programme.

In constructing hierarchy items, the therapist should identify moderating variables that will exacerbate or buffer the magnitude of the anger reaction, should the scene need to be intensified or attenuated. Prior to the presentation of a scene, whether in imaginal or role-play mode, anger control coping is rehearsed and arousal reduction is induced through deep breathing and muscle relaxation. Imaginal presentation should occur before role-play is attempted. If the client experiences anger while imagining the scene (thirty-seconds exposure), he or she signals this by raising a finger. The therapist notes the latency and firmness of the finger-raising as information about the degree of anger experienced and scene appropriateness for its hierarchy position. Details about the procedure for individual treatment are given in a therapist manual (Novaco, 2001) and are elaborated further in Taylor and Novaco (2005). The latter book provides a comprehensive guide to anger treatment for clients with developmental disabilities, along with theoretical and empirical background.

SUMMARY

Anger is a normal human emotion that in many circumstances is adaptive and helpful. However, anger can also cause problems when it is dysregulated, that is, when it is activated too frequently or expressed too intensely without appropriate controls. In addition, the designation of anger as a 'problem' depends on the sociocultural context in which it is viewed. Problematic anger is a feature of many mental health problems, leading to adverse consequences for the client and others. While anger management has been offered to people presenting with a range of problems, most of the research to date has been conducted on college-student samples. Meta-analysis shows that anger treatments have medium to strong effect sizes, with about 75% of those in receipt of treatment improving compared to controls. Anger affects a client behaviourally, interpersonally and physiologically, all of which need to be understood at assessment and formulation, and addressed in treatment planning.

Comprehensive assessment of anger problems includes gathering information on the frequency of anger, the degree of anger, how long it lasts and the behaviours associated with anger. Very often, a preparatory phase or 'trial period' of therapy is offered to clients before embarking on anger treatment, to increase motivation for treatment and to establish basic skills of emotion identification, self-monitoring, communication about anger experiences, and arousal reduction. This trial period serves to build trust in the therapist and the treatment programme, and provides an atmosphere conducive to personal disclosure and the collaboration required by this therapeutic approach. In making a formulation, the therapist brings together information from the preparatory phase of treatment; clinical interview with the client, significant others and clinical team or case workers; self-report psychometric scales and anger diary recordings; behavioural observation ratings, review and coding of case files and incident reports; and structured provocation testing. Formulation occurs in collaboration with the client over a number of sessions, using an external events × internal processes × behavioural responses analysis of anger. Treatments for anger control problems include general clinical care for anger, where anger is addressed as an issue as part of a mental health treatment plan; anger management where information is provided, usually in a structured group format, about anger and ways of controlling it, usually within a cognitive-behavioural model; and anger treatment, which aims to produce enduring changes in cognitive, arousal, and behavioural systems. Anger treatment occurs within the context of an individualized formulation and a therapeutic relationship. Key components of anger treatment include: (1) client education about anger, stress and aggression; (2) self-monitoring of anger frequency, intensity and situational triggers; (3) construction of a personal anger provocation hierarchy, created from the self-monitoring data and used for the practice and testing of coping skills; (4) arousal reduction techniques of progressive muscle relaxation, breathing-focused relaxation and guided imagery training; (5) cognitive restructuring by altering attentional focus, modifying appraisals, and using self-instruction; (6) training behavioural coping in communication and respectful assertiveness as modelled and rehearsed with the therapist; and (7) practising the cognitive, arousal regulatory and behavioural coping skills while visualizing and role-playing progressively more intense anger-arousing scenes from the personal hierarchies. Finally, for some couples who have been involved in domestic violence, anger management training may be offered as part of a multi-modal programme, which also includes behavioural couples therapy.

EXERCISE 24.1

Using the case of Tim from the chapter, assign roles of therapist, Tim and an observer. Role-play the following scenarios, changing roles after each:

1 Part of a preparatory session with Tim in which you work with him on one of the following skills: emotion identification, self-monitoring, communication about anger experiences or arousal reduction.
2 Part of a session in which you collaboratively formulate with Tim about his anger control problems using the external events × internal processes × behavioural responses analysis of anger problems.
3 Part of a therapy session with Tim in which you either construct with him a personal anger provocation hierarchy from his self-monitoring data or work on teaching and practising arousal reduction techniques of progressive muscle relaxation, breathing-focused relaxation, or guided imagery training.
4 Part of a therapy session with Tim in which you work with him on cognitive restructuring, either by altering attentional focus, modifying appraisals, or using self-instruction.

EVIDENCE SUMMARY

Beck, R. & Fernandez, E. (1998). Cognitive-behavioural therapy in the treatment of anger. A meta-analysis. *Cognitive Therapy and Research*, 22, 63–74.

FURTHER READING FOR CLIENTS

Bilodeau, L. (1992). *The anger workbook*. Minneapolis, MN: Compcare.

Potter-Efron, R. & Potter-Efron, R. (1995). *The ten most common anger styles and what to do about them*. Oakland, CA: New Harbinger.

Tavris, C. (1989). *Anger: The misunderstood emotion* (revised and updated). New York. Touchstone.

FURTHER READING FOR PRACTITIONERS

Link, S. (1997). *Assessment and management of patients presenting risk to others*. Leicester: British Psychological Society, core miniguide series.

Novaco, R. (1975). *Anger control: The development and evaluation of an experimental treatment*. Lexington, MA: Heath.

Novaco, R. & Jarvis, K. (2002). Brief cognitive behavioural intervention for anger. In F. Bond & W. Dryden (Eds.), *Handbook of brief cognitive behaviour therapy* (pp. 77–100). Chichester, UK: Wiley.

Taylor, J. L. & Novaco, R. W. (2005). *Anger treatment for people with developmental disabilities: A theory, evidence and manual based approach*. Chichester, UK: Wiley.

ASSESSMENT INSTRUMENTS

Novaco, R. W. (2003). *The Novaco Anger Scale and Provocation Inventory (NAS-PI)*. Los Angeles: Western Psychological Services.

Speilberger, C. (1988). *Manual for the State Trait Anger Expression Inventory*. Tampa, FL: Psychological Assessment Resources.

REFERENCES

Anderson, K. & Silver, J. M. (1998). Modulation of anger and aggression. *Seminars in Clinical Neuropsychiatry*, 3, 232–241.

Andrews, B., Brewin, C. R., Rose, S. & Kirk, M. (2000). Predicting PTSD symptoms in victims of violent crime: The role of shame, anger, and childhood abuse. *Journal of Abnormal Psychology*, 109, 69–73.

Attwood, T. & Joachim, R. (1994). The prevention and management of seriously disruptive behavior in Australia. In N. Bouras (Ed.), *Mental health in mental retardation: Recent advances and practices* (pp. 365–374). Cambridge: Cambridge University Press.

Averill, J. R. (1982). *Anger and aggression: An essay on emotion*. New York: Springer-Verlag.

Beck, R. & Fernandez, E. (1998). Cognitive-behavioral therapy in the treatment of anger: A meta-analysis. *Cognitive Therapy and Research*, 22, 63–74.

Bensley, L., Nelson, N., Kaufman, J., Silverstein, B. et al. (1995). Patient and staff views of factors influencing assaults on psychiatric hospital employees. *Issues in Mental Health Nursing*, 16(5), 433–446.

Bromberger, J. T. & Matthews, K. A. (1996). A 'feminine' model of vulnerability to depressive symptoms: A longitudinal investigation of middle-aged women. *Journal of Personality and Social Psychology*, 70, 591–598.

Buss, A. H. & Perry, M. (1992). The Aggression Questionnaire. *Journal of Personality and Social Psychology*, 63, 452–459.

Carmel, H. & Hunter, M. (1989). Staff injuries from inpatient violence. *Hospital and Community Psychiatry*, 40(1), 41–46.

Chemtob, C. M., Novaco, R. W., Hamada, R. S. & Gross, D. M. (1997). Cognitive-behavioral treatment for severe anger in post-traumatic stress disorder. *Journal of Consulting and Clinical Psychology*, 65, 184–189.

Chesney, M. & Rosenman, R. (1985). *Anger and hostility in behavioral and cardiovascular disorders*. New York: Hemisphere.

Cheung, P., Schweitzer, I., Tuckwell, V. & Crowley, K. C. (1996). A prospective study of aggression among psychiatric patients in rehabilitation wards. *Australian and New Zealand Journal of Psychiatry*, 30, 257–262.

Craig, T. J. (1982). An epidemiological study of problems associated with violence among psychiatric inpatients. *American Journal of Psychiatry*, 139, 1262–1266.

Davidson, K., Putnam, K. M. & Larsen, C. L. (2000). Dysfunction in the neural circuitry of emotion regulation – a possible prelude to violence. *Science*, 289, 591–594.

Deffenbacher, J. L., Story, D. A., Stark, R. S., Hogg, J. A. & Brandon, A. D. (1987). Cognitive-relaxation and social skills interventions in the treatment of general anger. *Journal of Counseling Psychology*, 34(2), 171–176.

Del Vecchio, T. & K. D. O'Leary (2004). Effectiveness of anger treatments for specific anger problems: A meta-analytic review. *Clinical Psychology Review*, 24, 15–34.

DiGuiseppe, R. & Tafrate, R. C. (2003). Anger treatments for adults: A meta-analytic review. *Clinical Psychology: Science and Practice*, 10, 70–84.

Eckhardt, C. I. & Deffenbacher, J. L. (1995). Diagnosis of anger disorders. In H. Kassinove (Ed.), *Anger disorders: Definition, diagnosis, and treatment* (pp. 27–48). Washington, DC: Taylor & Francis.

Eckhardt, C., Norlander, B. & Deffenbacher, J. (2004). The assessment of anger and hostility: A critical review. *Aggression and Violent Behavior*, 9, 17–43.

Edmonson, C. B. & Conger, J. C. (1996). A review of treatment efficacy for individuals with anger problems: Conceptual, assessment, and methodological issues. *Clinical Psychology Review*, 16, 251–275.

Ehlers, A., Mayou, R. A. & Bryant, B. (1998). Psychological predictors of chronic posttraumatic stress disorder after motor vehicle accidents. *Journal of Abnormal Psychology*, 107, 508–519.

Feeny, N. C., Zoellner, L. A. & Foa, E. B. (2000). Anger dissociation, and post-traumatic stress disorder among female assault victims. *Journal of Traumatic Stress*, 13, 89–100.

Feindler, E. L. & Ecton, R. B. (1986). *Adolescent anger control: Cognitive therapy techniques*. New York: Pergamon Press.

Feindler, E. L., Ecton, R. B., Kingsley, R. B. & Dubey, D. R. (1986). Group anger-control training for institutionalized psychiatric male adolescents. *Behavior Therapy*, 17, 109–123.

Freidman, H. S. (1992). *Hostility, coping, and health*. Washington, DC: American Psychological Association.

Frost, W. D. & Averill, J. R. (1982). Differences between men and women in the everyday experience of anger. In J. Averill (Ed.), *Anger and aggression: An essay on emotion* (pp. 281–316). New York: Springer-Verlag.

Goldstein, A. P. & Keller, H. (1987). *Aggressive behavior: Assessment and intervention*. New York: Pergamon Press.

Grisso, T., Davis, J., Vesselinov, R., Appelbaum, P. S. & Monahan, J. (2000). Violent thoughts and violent behavior following hospitalization for mental disorder. *Journal of Consulting and Clinical Psychology*, 68, 388–398.

Hall, G. S. (1899). A study of anger. *American Journal of Psychology*, 10, 516–591.

Harmon-Jones, E. & Sigelman, J. (2001). State anger and prefrontal brain activity: Evidence that insult-related relative left-prefrontal activation is associated with experienced anger and aggression. *Journal of Personality and Social Psychology*, 80, 797–803.

Hazaleus, S. L. & Deffenbacher, J. L. (1986). Relaxation and cognitive treatments of anger. *Journal of Consulting and Clinical Psychology*, 54, 222–226.

Howells, K. (1989). Anger management methods in relation to the prevention of violent behaviour. In, J. Archer & K. Browne (Eds.), *Human aggression: Naturalistic accounts* (pp. 153–181). London: Routledge.

Howells, K. & Day, A. (2003). Readiness for anger management: Clinical and theoretical issues. *Clinical Psychology Review*, 23, 319–337.

Huesmann, L. R. (1998). The role of social information processing and cognitive schema in the acquisition and maintenance of habitual aggressive behavior. In R. G. Geen & E. Donnerstein (Eds.), *Human aggression: Theories, research, and implications for social policy* (pp. 73–109). San Diego, CA: Academic Press.

Jacobsen, E. (1939). *Progressive relaxation*. Chicago: University of Chicago Press.

Johnson, E. H. (1990). *The deadly emotions: The role of anger, hostility, and aggression in health and emotional well-being*. New York: Praeger.

Kassinove, H., Sukhodolsky, D. G., Tsytsarev, S. V. & Solovyova, S. (1997). Self-reported anger episodes in Russia and America. *Journal of Social Behavior and Personality*, 12, 301–324.

Kennedy, H. G., Kemp, L. I. & Dyer, D. E. (1992). Fear and anger in delusion (paranoid) disorder: The association with violence. *British Journal of Psychiatry*, 160, 488–492.

Kiely, J. & Pankhurst, H. (1998). Violence faced by staff in a learning disability service. *Disability and Rehabilitation*, 20, 81–89.

Kopper, B. A. & Epperson, D. I. (1996). The experience and expression of anger: Relationships with gender, gender role socialization, depression, and mental health functioning. *Journal of Counseling Psychology*, 43, 158–165.

Lindsay, W. R., Allan, R., Macleod, F., Smart, N. & Smith, A. H. W. (2003). Long-term treatment and management of violent tendencies of men with intellectual disabilities convicted of assault. *Mental Retardation*, 41, 47–56.

Lindsay, W. R., Allan, R., Parry, C., Macleod, F., Cottrell, J., Overend, H. & Smith, A. H. (2004). Anger and aggression in people with intellectual disabilities: Treatment and follow-up of consecutive referrals and a waiting list comparison. *Clinical Psychology and Psychotherapy*, 11(4), 255–264.

McNeil, D. E., Eisner, J. P. & Binder, R. L. (2003). The relationship between aggressive attributional style and violence by psychiatric patients. *Journal of Consulting and Clinical Psychology*, 71, 399–403.

Meichenbaum, D. (1985). *Stress inoculation training*. New York: Pergamon Press.

Miller, W. R., & Rollnick, S. (1991). *Motivational interviewing: Preparing people to change addictive behavior*. New York: Guilford Press.

Monahan, J., Steadman, H. J., Silver, E. et al. (2001). *Rethinking risk assessment: The MacArthur study of mental disorder and violence*. Oxford: Oxford University Press.

National Audit Office (2003). *A safer place to work: Protecting NHS hospital and ambulance staff from violence and aggression*. London: Report by the Comptroller and Auditor General (HC 527).

Nijman, H. L. I., Muris, P., Merckelbach, H. L. G. J., Palmstierna, T., Wistedt, B., Vos, A. M., van Rixtel, A. & Allertz, W. (1999). The Staff Observation Scale – Revised (SOAS-R). *Aggressive Behavior*, 25, 197–209.

Novaco, R. W. (1975). *Anger control: The development and evaluation of an experimental treatment*. Lexington, MA: D. C. Heath.

Novaco, R. W. (1977). Stress inoculation: A cognitive therapy for anger and its application to a case of depression. *Journal of Consulting and Clinical Psychology*, 45, 600–608.

Novaco, R. W. (1993). Clinicians ought to view anger contextually. *Behaviour Change*, 10, 208–218.

Novaco, R. W. (1994). Anger as a risk factor for violence among the mentally disordered. In J. Monahan & H. Steadman (Eds.), *Violence and mental disorder: Developments in risk assessment* (pp. 21–59). Chicago: University of Chicago Press.

Novaco, R. W. (1997). Remediating anger and aggression with violent offenders. *Legal and Criminological Psychology*, 2, 77–88.

Novaco, R. W. (2001). Stress inoculation treatment for anger control: Therapist procedures. Unpublished treatment manual (revised).

Novaco, R. W. (2003). *The Novaco Anger Scale and Provocation Inventory (NAS-PI)*. Los Angeles: Western Psychological Services.

Novaco, R. W. & Chemtob, C. M. (1998). Anger and trauma: Conceptualization, assessment, and treatment. In V. M. Follette, J. I. Ruzek & F. Abueg (Eds.), *Cognitive-behavioral therapies for trauma* (pp. 162–190). New York: Guilford Press.

Novaco, R. W. & Chemtob, C. M. (2002). Anger and combat-related posttraumatic stress disorder. *Journal of Traumatic Stress*, 15, 123–132.

Novaco, R. W. & Jarvis, K. L. (2002). Brief cognitive behavioral intervention for anger. In F. Bond & W. Dryden (Eds.), *Handbook of brief cognitive behavioural therapy* (pp. 77–100). London: John Wiley.

Novaco, R. W., Ramm, M. & Black, L. (2000). Anger treatment with offenders. In C. Hollin (Ed.), *Handbook of offender assessment and treatment* (pp. 281–296). London: John Wiley.

Novaco, R.W. & Renwick, S.J. (2006). Anger predictors and the validation of a ward behavior scale for anger and aggression. Manuscript submitted for publication.

Novaco, R. W. & Taylor, J. L. (2004). Assessment of anger and aggression in male offenders with developmental disabilities. *Psychological Assessment*, 16, 42–50.

Prochaska, J. O. & DiClemente, C. C. (1983). Stages and processes of self-change of smoking: Toward an integrative model of change. *Journal of Consulting and Clinical Psychology*, 51, 390–395.

Renwick, S., Black, L., Ramm, M. & Novaco, R. W. (1997). Anger treatment with forensic hospital patients. *Legal and Criminological Psychology*, 2, 103–116.

Robins, S. & Novaco, R. W. (2000). Anger control as a health promotion mechanism. In D. I. Mostofsky & D. H. Barlow (Eds.), *The management of anxiety in medical disorders* (pp. 361–377). Boston: Allyn & Bacon.

Schultz, J. & Lutne, W. (1959). *Autogenic training*. New York: Grune & Stratton.

Siegman, A. W. & Smith, T. W. (1994). *Anger, hostility, and the heart*. Hillsdale, NJ: Lawrence Erlbaum Associates.

Spielberger, C.D. (1996). *State–Trait Anger Expression Inventory Professional Manual*. Odessa, FL: Psychological Assessment Resources.

Sukhodolsky, D. G., Kassinove, H. & Gorman, B. S. (2004). Cognitive-behavior therapy for anger in children and adolescents: A meta-analysis. *Aggression and Violent Behavior*, 9(3), 247–269.

Tafrate, R. C. (1995). Evaluation of treatment strategies for adult anger disorders. In H. Kassinove (Ed.), *Anger disorders: Definition, diagnosis, and treatment* (pp. 109–129). Washington, DC: Taylor and Francis.

Tangney, J. P., Wagner, P. E., Fletcher, C. & Gramzow, R. (1992). Shamed into anger: The relation of shame and guilt to anger and self-reported aggression. *Journal of Personality and Social Psychology*, 62, 669–675.

Tangney, J. P., Wagner, P. E., Hill-Barlow, D., Marschall, D. E. & Gramzow, R. (1996). Relation of shame and guilt to constructive versus destructive responses to anger across the lifespan. *Journal of Personality and Social Psychology*, 70, 797–809.

Taylor, J.L. (2002). A review of assessment and treatment of anger and aggression in offenders with intellectual disability. *Journal of Intellectual Disability Research*, 46 (Suppl. 1), 57–73.

Taylor, J. L. & Novaco, R. W. (2005). *Anger treatment for people with developmental disabilities: A theory, evidence and manual based approach*. Chicester, UK: Wiley.

Taylor, J. L., Novaco, R. W., Gillmer, B. T., Robertson, A. & Thorne, I. (2005). Individual cognitive-behavioural anger treatment for people with mild-borderline intellectual disabilities and histories of aggression: A controlled trial. *British Journal of Clinical Psychology*, 44, 367–382.

Taylor, J. L., Novaco, R. W., Gillmer, B. & Thorne, I. (2002). Cognitive-behavioural treatment of anger intensity in offenders with intellectual disabilities. *Journal of Applied Research in Intellectual Disabilities*, 15, 151–165.

Taylor, J. L., Novaco, R. W., Guinan, C. & Street, N. (2004). Development of an imaginal provocation test to evaluate treatment for anger problems in people with intellectual disabilities. *Clinical Psychology and Psychotherapy*, 11(4), 233–246.

Wang, E. W. & Diamond, P. M. (1999). Empirically identifying factors related to violence risk in corrections. *Behavioral Sciences and the Law*, 17, 377–389.

Watt, B. D. & Howells, K. (1999). Skills training for aggression control: Evaluation of an anger management programme for violent offenders. *Legal and Criminological Psychology*, 4, 285–300.

Williams, R. & Williams, V. (1993). *Anger kills*. New York: Harper Perennial.

Zillmann, D. (1988). Cognition-excitation interdependencies in aggressive behavior. *Aggressive Behavior*, 14, 51–64.

Zillmann, D. & Bryant, J. (1974). Effect of residual excitation on the emotional response to provocation and delayed aggressive behavior. *Journal of Personality and Social Psychology*, 30, 782–791.

Chapter 25

Depersonalization disorder

Alberto Blanco-Campal

CASE EXAMPLE

Sean was a twenty-four-year old, single, second-year law student referred for psychological intervention by his GP who noted clinical features of panic disorder and low mood. At interview he appeared anxious and when asked about his chief complaint he started by saying 'You might think I am mad but . . . it is hard to explain . . . I feel as if I am not the real me. It's like I am permanently looking at my own thoughts . . . I know it's me thinking but it feels as though I am not in control of them. It feels as though the world around me has changed. It's as if I am in a film or looking through a goldfish bowl, everything looks strange'. It was evident that no metaphor was to Sean's full satisfaction. He offered to share some notes that he had gathered ahead of his consultation and proceeded to read a list of expressions describing his experiences. 'It's weird but I often look at my parents and they look strange almost unreal, they don't feel like my parents and the more I look at their faces the more unfamiliar they get', 'I often feel as if my arms don't belong to me and I have to move them to convince myself that it's me who is moving them', 'Sometimes my voice sounds weird not like mine, as though I have no control over it'. Sean explained that his biggest fear was that he was 'going mad'. He was terrified that the use of marijuana had permanently damaged his brain and that he was developing Alzheimer's dementia, which was causing him to forget about his own identity. This feeling was particularly acute in situations where he found himself 'as if suspended, as though my memories had no continuity, no past and no future, and I am afraid I may forget who I am'. Sean reported spending most of his day checking if he was still himself but it never felt right. He occasionally looked into the mirror to see if he had changed and he often tried to recall past personal events in order to reassure himself that he did not have Alzheimer's.

History of the problem

Sean's first episode of depersonalization (DP) occurred after smoking marijuana while away from home with friends. He remembered lying in bed feeling dizzy and all of a sudden he felt like he was losing his sense of self and control over his body. He immediately thought that he was going to lose consciousness or die. He described an 'eerie' feeling and felt disconnected from his body as if he was 'vanishing'. He panicked and ran to the bathroom to look in the mirror to check that he was still himself. He explained that he could not connect the image in the mirror with his own sense of self. In a state of terror he rang his parents. His mother answered the phone and he remembered feeling frightened by the fact that he felt as if she was 'distant, not herself'. He felt disconnected from his mother and without any feelings towards her, which increased his anxiety. His friends reassured him and brought him to the local hospital where a doctor told him that it was 'just a panic attack' and prescribed 'Xanax'. The following day he returned home.

These episodes of DP were initially short-lived (lasting from a few minutes to hours) but over time had become more prolonged and recurrent (lasting from a day to a few weeks). They were exacerbated by physiological states of fatigue or sleep deprivation, post-alcohol consumption, and situational factors including driving alone, socializing and fluorescent lighting. He was adamant that his symptoms were identical to those he experienced while intoxicated with cannabis. After four months of persisting symptoms, his parents sought a private psychiatric evaluation. Sean was diagnosed with first-episode schizophrenia and started on a course of neuroleptics. He reported little benefit from this medication. In fact, he noted some exacerbation of his symptoms and after two weeks discontinued this medication without medical advice.

With time, Sean developed a fear of venturing far from home and struggled to go to college. He avoided driving, unless he was accompanied, since driving increased his DP. Formerly gregarious and outgoing, with a great interest in sports, Sean was now finding it hard to socialize with friends. He gave up drinking socially, explaining that although he felt some relief while drinking, the day after he suffered a ten-fold increase in his symptoms, often ending in the local A&E department feeling 'panicky'.

Once a bright student and a high achiever, Sean's college attendance had become very poor and he was forced to repeat two academic years complaining of difficulties concentrating and learning new material. A year after the onset of symptoms, he attended a second psychiatrist who diagnosed him with panic disorder with agoraphobia and started Sean on a course of selective serotonin reuptake inhibitors (SSRIs) (fluoxetine). Although his anxiety reduced somewhat, his 'strange feelings' were still present, although they were slightly more tolerable. Nevertheless, he admitted to being hopeless about his future, thinking that he had no control over his situation. When seen for psychological assessment, seven years after the onset of the original symptoms, he was on a course of fluoxetine.

Sean was the younger of two siblings. His thirty-two-year-old brother had been hospitalized for a month with a major depressive episode. Family psychiatric history was otherwise unremarkable. Sean denied a personal history of psychiatric illness. Apart from sporadic drug use (i.e. cannabis) he denied a history of alcohol or drug abuse.

The above information was gathered from Sean over three assessment sessions during which he completed two self-report measures. The Dissociative Experience Scale, assessing dissociative symptoms in general, and the Cambridge Depersonalization Scale, a depersonalization-specific scale (DES; Bernstein-Carlson & Putnam, 1986; CDS, Sierra & Berrios, 2000). On the DES-total he scored 23, below the cut-off score of 30. However, he scored highly on the DES depersonalization/derealization taxon (DES DP/DR = 41). His score on both the Trait and State version of the CDS were well within the clinical range (139 and 181, respectively). In addition, two self-report measures of anxiety and depression were used. He scored 29 on the Beck Depression Inventory-II (Beck, 1996) and 27 on the Beck Anxiety Inventory (Beck, 1990); both scores were indicative of clinically significant anxiety and depression fulfilling diagnostic criteria for panic disorder and depression. Sean met diagnostic criteria for primary depersonalization disorder (DPD) (DSM-IV-TR; American Psychiatric Association (APA), 2000) due to him having severe and recurrent symptoms; his reality testing was intact and his symptoms caused him clinically significant distress and interfered with social and vocational functioning. He suffered DP episodically with episodes lasting from minutes to weeks.

From the clinical history it was clear that his predominant complaint was DP. Although his experiences of DP co-existed with panic disorder, they persisted after the resolution of episodes of panic. Depersonalization predated the onset of his depression, which represented a demoralized response to unremitting symptoms, and had led to social withdrawal.

Formulation

Guided by the general cognitive-behavioural model outlined in Figure 25.1 and based on initial assessment, an individualized case formulation (Figure 25.2) was developed with Sean. In his case, depresonalization (DP) had an acute onset, with cannabis intoxication being the main precipitant. Sean experienced this as very frightening, interpreting his transient symptoms of drug-induced DP as impending death or insanity.

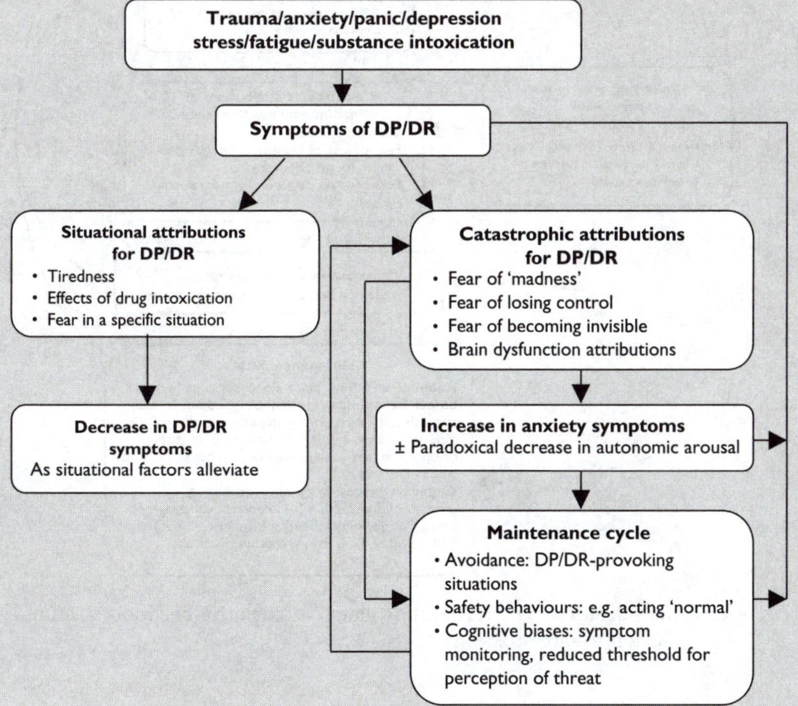

Figure 25.1 Cognitive-behavioural model of depersonalization disorder (Hunter et al., 2003).

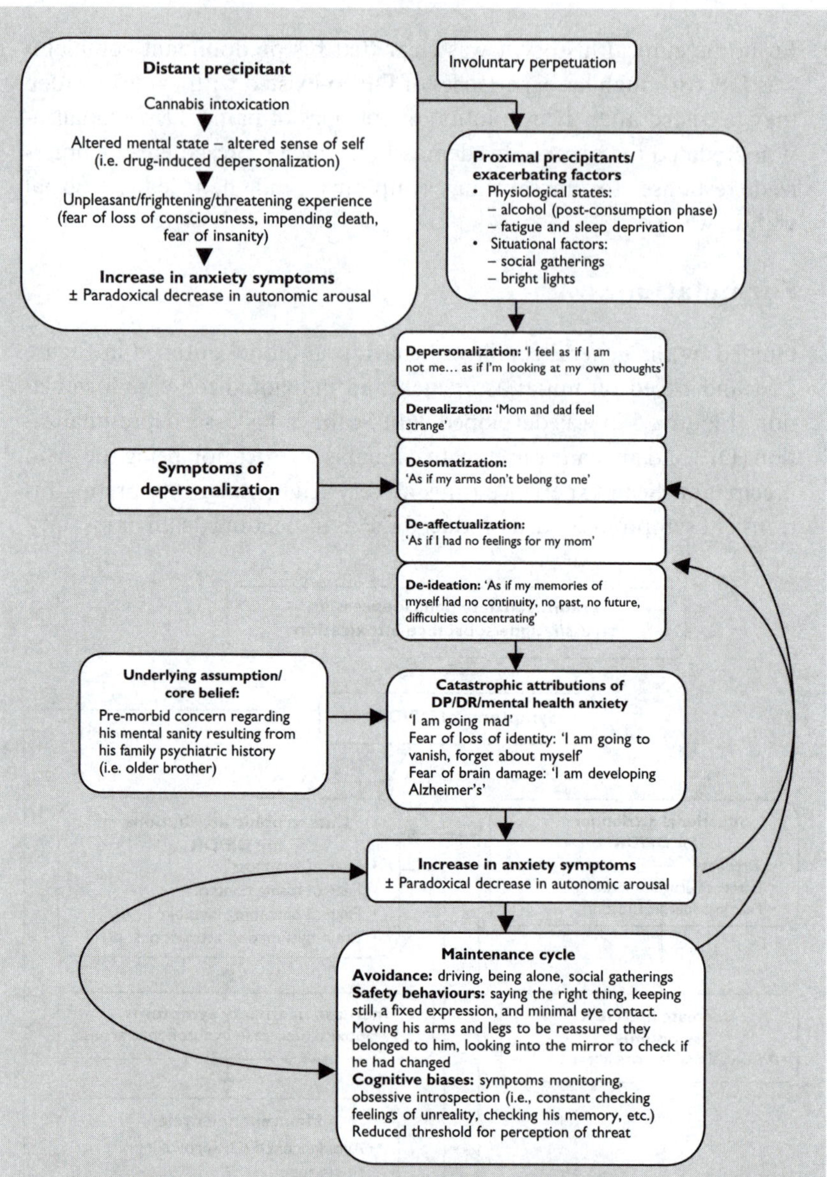

Figure 25.2 Individualized case formulation under a cognitive-behavioural framework presented to Sean.

This subjective life-threatening situation set in motion a hard-wired protective brain response characterized by emotional numbing and reduced autonomic response resulting from an abnormally increased regulation by prefrontal regions. This 'shut down' of emotional reactivity with associated loss of emotional tone in the experience of his 'self' and his surroundings (including his family and friends) generated the unpleasant and unfamiliar feelings that he described. This, in turn, generated an anxiety reaction, which served to exacerbate his symptoms of DP, thus creating a vicious circle. A predisposing factor in his case might have been the family history of depression, which might have led to pre-morbid concerns regarding his vulnerability to mental illness. Depersonalization was maintained by a pattern of catastrophic attributions of his symptoms, interpreting them as a sign of madness or confirmation of permanent brain damage signalling the beginning of Alzheimer's disease. Such beliefs set in place a 'vicious semi-autonomous cycle' of anxiety followed by DP. Thus, fear of impending episodes of DP led to an increase in self-focus on symptoms. This pattern resulted in a reduced threshold for the perception of 'unreality feelings' causing an increase in anxiety and consequent DP, which was set in motion by the same brain response. Unremitting DP had led to secondary panic disorder with non-pervasive agoraphobia and social withdrawal, causing Sean to feel demoralized and depressed.

Treatment

On the basis of this formulation, Sean was offered a contract for fifteen sessions of cognitive-behavioural therapy (CBT), spaced at weekly intervals, which he accepted. Therapy focused primarily on DP and secondarily on his comorbid anxiety and depression. The treatment programme developed by Hunter et al. (2004, 2005) was used in this case. The programme consisted of three phases.

Phase I

In the first five sessions the objective was to reduce Sean's overall level of distress and increase his level of activity, general motivation and mood. This was achieved by means of: (1) psychoeducation; (2) normalizing his experience; and (3) inviting him to monitor his DP symptoms.

The first two sessions were devoted to psychoeducation and normalization. During psychoeducation, information regarding DPD gathered from the literature was shared with Sean. This involved explaining that transient symptoms of DP are very common in the 'normal' population, particularly during states of extreme anxiety. Sean found it reassuring to learn that symptoms of DP are very rarely accompanied by psychotic symptoms (e.g. hallucination of voices) and that in most cases several years go on without an escalation to a psychotic illness.

To normalize Sean's experience of DP, it was reframed in terms of a 'normal' human reaction, a protective mechanism for dealing with overwhelming states of anxiety by distancing oneself. Sean experienced an enormous sense of relief when he was told that what he felt were incomprehensible symptoms signalling madness actually had a clinical name and could be explained as a normal human reaction.

Sessions three to five were dedicated to symptom monitoring. Sean was invited to keep a DP symptoms record. Sean focused initially on episodes where his DP was particularly distressing. This technique helped the clinician determine the idiosyncratic precipitants of DP and Sean's reactions to DP in terms of thoughts and behaviour. Sean was asked to describe the circumstances that increased or decreased his symptoms (i.e. alleviating and exacerbating factors) and he jotted down the specific fears (i.e. catastrophic attributions) they activated. To identify the presence of avoidance and safety behaviours, he wrote down what he thought helped to prevent his fears (e.g. going mad). Through this intervention Sean became aware of the link between his behaviour and thoughts and the level of his DP. He discovered that his symptoms increased in situations in which he anticipated an episode of uncontrolled DP (e.g. while driving, when socializing and in crowded public places, particularly where there was fluorescent lighting). He also noticed a decrease in symptoms when he managed to focus his attention 'outside' (e.g. when watching a film that he enjoyed). This helped Sean to appreciate that his symptoms were not uncontrollable. The DP record highlighted a general low level of activity, which was contributing to his low mood and motivation and set the scene for a pattern of symptom-focus. At this point a behavioural programme of scheduling of pleasant activities was initiated to improve Sean's overall mood.

Phase 2

In sessions six to thirteen the efforts centred on effecting change in factors thought to maintain his symptoms (i.e. avoidance, safety behaviours, catastrophic attributions and checking of symptoms). This phase involved specific interventions that were individually tailored.

First, a number of behavioural interventions (i.e. graded exposure, videotaping and role-play) were used to reduce avoidance of feared situations and the use of safety behaviours when dealing with them. Using the DP record Sean identified a number of situations in which he anticipated an episode of uncontrolled DP and therefore avoided. These included driving alone, socializing with friends and attending crowded places. The DP record revealed a series of safety behaviours that Sean used to prevent feared outcomes (i.e. developing Alzheimer's, going mad and people noticing his madness) in these situations. These included keeping a fixed expression, keeping very still, making minimal eye contact and going to look in the mirror to see if he had changed. In sessions 6 to 9, two behavioural strategies used in cognitive-behavioural interventions for social anxiety, videotaping of social interactions and role-play with and without safety behaviours, were used to reduce avoidance (see Chapter 15 for a detailed explanation of CBT for social anxiety). In the initial role-play Sean identified two safety behaviours that he would 'drop' during the exercise (i.e. saying the right thing and making little eye contact). This was operationalized in terms of looking into the clinician's eyes during conversation and asking for details regarding one of the clinician's arguments, thus avoiding saying 'the right thing'. To make the role-play more real, the clinician invited Sean to voluntarily induce an episode of DP. A list of situations that normally induce symptoms of DP – such as fatigue, fluorescent lighting, and staring at his face in a mirror – were presented. Sean chose to stare at his face in the mirror, which soon induced a tolerable exacerbation of his DP. Role-playing with and without safety behaviours was videotaped and helped to reassure him that his symptoms were undetectable to others. This then served to dispel his belief that his safety behaviours prevented him from going mad or developing Alzheimer's dementia. More importantly, role-playing helped Sean appreciate the role of safety behaviours in increasing his DP symptoms by way of simply 'going through the motions of the social interactions', creating a sense of emotional detachment from others (especially friends and family).

Sean initially found these exercises anxiety-provoking but over time he reported feeling more in control of his experiences.

Second, two cognitive strategies (task concentration training and cognitive restructuring) were used to facilitate the reduction of self-focused attention (SFA, constantly checking his memory and his feelings of unreality), and modification of catastrophic attributions:

Reductions of SFA

In sessions 10 to 13, Sean underwent a programme of task concentration training (TCT) and cognitive restructuring. In the first stage of training, the clinician drew Sean's attention to the fact that his pattern of attending to internal stimuli, checking whether his feeling of unreality were still present (e.g. Is this real? Am I losing my mind? Let's check if I can remember things from the past?), reduced his threshold for perception of threat serving to increase his level of anxiety. This in turn led to a sense of emotional detachment and an increase in DP, thus creating a vicious circle. Informed by the DP-record, Sean gained insight into the time he dedicated to: (1) internal stimuli (i.e. SFA) (e.g. Am I going mad? Is this real?); (2) external task-related stimuli (e.g. listening to a conversation in a social situation or a lecture in college); and (3) external task-irrelevant stimuli (e.g. the colour of the walls in the classroom). Once he understood the difference between these types of attention, a number of increasingly complex exercises were carried out in therapy (i.e. non-threatening situations). In the first exercise, Sean sat with his back to the clinician while the clinician told him a two-minute neutral story. Sean was encouraged to concentrate on the story and to summarize the same story afterwards. He was also asked to estimate the percentage of attention that he directed towards observing his unreality feelings, the task and towards the environment while listening.

In the second exercise, Sean listened to a similar story but this time he alternated attention between the task of listening and his feelings of unreality, thus gaining control over re-focusing attention towards external task-related stimuli. In the last exercise, it was Sean who spoke while concentrating on observing if the therapist was listening and understanding his message. TCT was subsequently practised in everyday non-threatening situations (e.g. at home talking to his family) and everyday life (e.g. while driving, in college, etc.). After four weeks of practice, Sean was surprised with the results, reporting that when he focused his attention outwards, he was able to feel a natural flow of emotions, feeling familiar warmth towards his friends and family.

Challenging catastrophic assumptions

Using the thought record it became clear that Sean's fears regarding DP symptoms revolved around three topics: (1) fear of going mad; (2) fear of forgetting about himself and others; and (3) fears of having permanent brain damage (e.g. Alzheimer's disease/tumour). Classic cognitive interventions were used to challenge his thoughts. For example, in relation to his fear of going mad, Sean was asked to describe in concrete terms what this would entail. Sean said that he would 'start hearing voices and start shouting in public'. Once his fear was operationalized, a number of techniques were used to challenge this thought. Sean generated evidence for and against his thought and came up with an alternative balanced belief. In addition, Sean agreed to carry out a behavioural experiment in therapy to test the validity of his hypothesis. Using the same technique of staring into the mirror in order to generate a state of heightened DP, Sean tested the validity of his feared prediction.

Regarding his fear of forgetting about himself, Sean believed that during an episode of DP he would not be able to remember anything about his past and would find it difficult to think about his future. While experiencing DP, Sean engaged in casual conversation with the clinician, giving him details about a past (more than 10 years ago) holiday and about his future plans while the clinician took notes about the level of his detail. Sean realized that despite experiencing intense DP, he was still able to recall past events with a great deal of specificity. Sean agreed that this would be atypical for cases of Alzheimer's disease.

Phase 3

The last three sessions involved modifying Sean's core beliefs regarding his vulnerability to mental illness. In addition, Sean summarized and consolidated what he had learned and, together with his therapist, worked on a plan for relapse prevention. Sean attended a follow-up booster session eight weeks after his episode of treatment, at which he reported overall good maintenance of gains, based on self-report and self-rating measures of DP (i.e. DES and the CDS).

DEFINITIONS

Depersonalization (DP) was first described by Maurice Krishaber (1872) and subsequently coined by the French psychiatrist, Ludovic Dugas in the late nineteenth century (Dugas, 1898). Within DSM-IV-TR, DP is defined as an alteration in the perception or experience of the self so that one feels 'detached from, and as if one is an outside observer of, one's mental processes or body (e.g. feeling like one is in a dream)' (APA, 2000, p. 532).

Depersonalization is often accompanied by the symptom of *derealization* defined as an alteration in the perception or experience of the external world so that it seems strange or unreal (e.g. people may seem unfamiliar or mechanical) (APA, 2000). Derealization was only described in the early twentieth century to describe an aspect of DP (Sierra & Berrios, 2001) and with some exceptions (e.g. Coons, 1996; Fleiss et al., 1975) has traditionally been viewed as a subset of DP (Jacobs & Bovasso, 1992). Both experiences are not delusional since reality testing remains intact; the sufferer recognizes that these are subjective phenomena rather than objective reality. In this chapter, depersonalization (DP) will be used as a broad term, encompassing symptoms of both depersonalization and derealization (DR).

Depersonalization occurs on a continuum in the general population from 'normal' (mild transient episodes without clinical significance occurring in non-clinical populations) to 'abnormal' (recurrent or persistent episodes associated with morbidity, i.e. depersonalization disorder) (DPD; Simeon & Hollander, 1993; Simeon et al., 1995). From here on, depersonalization will be used as a broad term, encompassing symptoms of both depersonalization and derealization.

In normal, healthy individuals, DP can occur under conditions such as fatigue (Mayer-Gross, 1935), states of meditation or relaxation (Castillo, 1990; Fewtrell, 1984; Kennedy, 1976), sleep deprivation (Bliss et al., 1959), sensory deprivation (Reed & Sedman, 1964), acute alcohol intoxication (Raimo et al., 1999; Wenzetl et al., 1996) and during or after illicit drug use including 'ecstasy' (Cohen & Cocores, 1997; McGuire et al., 1994), LSD (Waltzner, 1972) and, more commonly, cannabis (Mathew et al., 1993, 1999; Melges et al., 1970), with a small case-series reporting cannabis-induced chronic DPD (Keshaven & Lishman, 1986; Medford et al., 2003; Moran, 1986; Szymanski, 1981).

Depersonalization can present as a chronic, disabling and clinically significant phenomenon, either as a primary disorder or secondary (i.e. as a symptom/feature) to other psychiatric or organic condition (Medford et al., 2005).

The term 'secondary depersonalization' refers to cases in which symptoms of DP arise in the context of a primary psychiatric (e.g. anxiety, depression, etc.) or general medical condition (e.g. temporal lobe epilepsy). This is also occasionally referred to as symptomatic DP. Depersonalization, as a symptom, is extremely common and has been described as being the third most common psychiatric symptom after depression and anxiety (Cattell & Cattell, 1974).

Specific psychiatric conditions where symptoms of DP have been described include panic disorder during panic attacks (e.g. Cox et al., 1994), unipolar depression (Noyes et al., 1977; Sedman & Reed, 1963; Strickland et al., 2002), schizophrenia (Watts, 1985), PTSD (Bremmer et al., 1998; Davidson et al., 1990; Mayou et al., 2001), eating disorders (Meyer & Waller, 1998) and obsessive-compulsive disorder (OCD) (Lochner et al., 2004; Torch, 1978).

Symptoms of DP have been described in a number of medical conditions including: temporal lobe epilepsy (associated with the pre-ictal aura and some post-ictal states, e.g. Devinsky et al., 1989; Kenna & Sedman, 1965; Roth & Harper, 1962), cerebral tumours (Lilja & Salford, 1997), cerebrovascular disease (Morioka et al., 1997), temporal-lobe migraine (Ogunyemi, 1995) and traumatic brain injury (Blanco-Campal et al., 2003; Cantagallo et al., 1999; Grigsby & Kaye, 1993; Paulig et al., 1998). Lambert et al. (2002) provide an excellent review of cases of organic DP in which the authors proposed the introduction of an organic subtype of DP in the DSM analogous to 'mood disorder due to a general medical condition' to fulfil a clinical need and advance research in this area.

The symptoms in primary DPD are phenomenologically similar to those experienced in transient episodes of DP, the only difference being that in DPD they run a chronic course and result in functional impairment (Hunter et al., 2003). Moreover, despite the usefulness of the clinical distinction between primary and secondary DP, both conditions are often difficult to distinguish. In a recent study, Lambert et al. (2001a) found that two self-report measures of DP, the Dissociative Experience Scale (DES; Bernstein-Carlson & Putnam, 1986) and the Fewtrell Depersonalization Scale (FDS; Fewtrell, 2000) failed to distinguish primary and secondary DP. The authors concluded that, 'the validity of this distinction based on psychopathology ratings alone remains questionable' (Lambert et al., 2001a, p. 254).

This chapter examines DP as a primary disorder, although the assessment and psychotherapeutic treatment presented is also applicable to patients in whom DP has become chronic and pervasive in the context of another disorder.

Despite having been described more than a century ago (Dugas, 1898), DPD remains a relatively under-reported and under-researched phenomenon. A recent revival in the interest in this disorder has led to the establishment of the Depersonalization Research Unit at the Maudsley Hospital in London (website: http://www.iop.klc.uk/depersonalization; Phillips et al., 2001b; Senior et al., 2001), which devotes its efforts to the understanding of the disorder and the development of effective treatment strategies. Established in 1998, the unit takes referrals from within the local NHS Trust, throughout the UK and internationally. On the other side of the Atlantic, the Depersonalization and Dissociation Research Program at the Mount Sinai

School of Medicine in New York (website: http://www.mssm.edu/psychiatry/ddrp.shtml) is another clinic uniquely devoted to the study of dissociation in general and DP in particular.

CLINICAL PRESENTATION AND CLINICAL FEATURES

The experience of depersonalization (DP) is difficult for patients to describe and they often fear that these experiences signify impending psychosis (i.e. 'I am going mad'). Sufferers often feel that their experiences are 'unique' and fear being labelled 'insane'. Patients are often at pains to elaborate satisfactory similes or metaphors that could communicate their experience. They often start describing their experience by saying it's 'as if'. Despite enduring an often disabling, highly unpleasant and sometimes horrifying subjective experience, patients frequently fail to convey to the clinician the distress they experience. Clinicians should be aware that DP is rarely the presenting complaint and sufferers often present with other symptoms such as anxiety or depression. Patients may refer to their truly terrifying experiences as 'anxiety' or 'depression' in an effort to sound less bizarre.

Clinical features

Table 25.1 contains diagnostic criteria for DPD (i.e. primary DPD) from DSM-IV-TR (APA, 2000) and ICD-10 (WHO, 1992). Although both classifications describe the core clinical features, DP is clinically far more complex. Clinicians attempting to understand DP should be aware that the older literature is rich in phenomenological descriptions and remains an invaluable source of information (e.g. Ackner, 1954a, 1954b; Mayer-Gross, 1935; Shorvon et al., 1946). In an exceptional historical exploration of the phenomenology of DP, Sierra and Berrios (2001) confirmed that a core of symptoms, including emotional numbing, visual derealization and altered body experiences, have remained stable over the past century. Symptoms of DP can be divided into five major domains: depersonalization, derealization, desomatization, de-affectualization and de-ideation. Table 25.2 provides a glossary of symptoms of DP, their definition, and an example from patients' descriptions subsumed under these main domains. The clinician should be aware that along with these core symptoms DP may bring about impairment and distortion in the domains of affect, cognition and physiological/perceptual functioning (Hunter et al., 2003) (Table. 25.3).

Depersonalization

With regard to depersonalization, there is a disturbing sense of being 'separate from oneself', observing oneself as if from outside, feeling like a robot or

Table 25.1 Diagnostic criteria for depersonalization disorder

DSM-IV-TR	*ICD-10*
A. Persistent or recurrent experiences of feeling detached from, and as if one is an outside observer of, one's mental processes or body (e.g. feeling like one is in a dream) B. During the depersonalization experience, reality testing remains intact C. The depersonalization causes clinically significant distress or impairment in social, occupational, or other important areas of functioning D. The depersonalization experience does not occur exclusively during the course of another mental disorder, such as schizophrenia, panic disorder, acute stress disorder or another dissociative disorder, and is not due to the direct physiological effects of a substance (e.g. a drug of abuse, a medication) or a general medical condition (e.g. temporal lobe epilepsy)	For the diagnosis, there must be either or both of (a) and (b), plus (c) and (d): (a) Depersonalization symptoms, i.e. the individual feels that his or her own feelings and/or experiences are detached, distant, not his or her own, lost, etc. (b) Derealization symptoms, i.e. objects, people, and/or surroundings seem unreal, distant, artificial, colourless, lifeless, etc. (c) An acceptance that this is a subjective and spontaneous change, not imposed by outside forces or other people (i.e. insight) (d) A clear sensorium and absence of toxic confusional state or epilepsy

Note: Adapted from DSM-IV-TR (APA, 2000) and ICD-10 (WHO, 1992).

automaton. Some patients describe the experience of looking in the mirror and feeling detached from one's image. Some patients develop an obsessive need to observe the self constantly, finding themselves stuck in a chronic self-observation (e.g. 'I look in the mirror and I don't see me. I don't know who it is that I see and I don't know where the real me has gone . . . I spend all day checking myself and it's never me'). In fact, many sufferers report that the thought that they must be depersonalized often precedes their experience. The case example presented in this chapter illustrates this clinical aspect. Sufferers may report watching themselves from a distance and feeling 'as if' one part of them is acting while the other is observing. Individuals may fear that their identity is vanishing or disappearing. In extreme cases, individuals may report feeling 'as if' they were dead. Patients may attempt to describe their experience in the following terms: 'I am unreal and truly alone – like an outsider looking on'; 'I am here but not here'.

Derealization

With respect to derealization, there is a threatening sense of unfamiliarity or unreality in the environment, perceptual anomalies may be present, and other people may feel like actors in a play. Patients frequently describe the

Table 25.2 Clinical symptoms present in depersonalization disorder under the neurobiological mechanism thought to mediate the origin of each experiential feature (adapted from Sierra & Berrios, 1998, 2001)

Symptoms	*Definition*	*Example*
Inhibitory component: State of hypoemotionality and autonomic dampening		
Depersonalization		
Loss of feeling of agency	The feeling that one is not in charge of one's movements or mental activity	'It seemed rather pointless to reply to remarks made, but I heard my voice doing so' 'I was walking and talking, as though automatically, I couldn't feel any movement and yet I knew I was walking'
Derealization		
Changes in visual experience	Any complaint of 'unreality' concerning visual modality	'Everything seems just a painted picture, deathly quiet' 'Things looked dull, flat, and lifeless'
Changes in auditory experience	Complaints of unreality affecting the auditory modality	'Is there something wrong with my ears? I hear you clearly, yet your voice sounds far away, distant and unreal'. 'I could hear my voice and that of other people's very remotely although there was no lessening of sound'
Changes in tactile experience	Complaints of unreality affecting the haptic modality	'[The patient complained that] things that he touched lacked vividness and reality'
Changes in gustatory experience	Change in gustatory experience, so that the flavour of meals is no longer accompanied by feelings of pleasure or distaste	'I taste but it does not mean anything to me. I'll eat anything put before me. We had walnut cake which I normally adore – but it might have been dry bread'
Change in olfactory experience	Change in olfactory experience, so that smells are no longer accompanied by feelings of pleasure or dislike	'Perfume doesn't smell pleasant any longer. I'd have no preference for the smell of these roses over the smell of cabbage cooking'
Desomatization		
Changes in body experience	Subjective feeling of body change regarding size of parts of the body, the feeling of being weightless, or the feeling 'as if' parts of the body didn't belong to self	'My hands do not seem to be mine . . . The top part of my head often seems to disappear' 'Generally my head and lower jaw feel disproportionately large for my body and my arms and fingers pencil thin'

De-affectualization		
Emotional numbing	Absence of reduction in the experience of emotional feelings. In depersonalization the latter complaint occurs in the context of apparently normal motor emotional expression	'He had unexplained crying episodes but he said not to be able to feel sadness nor happiness'
Excitatory component: Increased alertness generating a state of vigilant alertness combined with emotional inhibition		
De-ideation		
Feelings of thought emptiness	The feeling of having the mind empty of thoughts or not being able to think	'Nothing comes into my head, there is an emptiness there. I don't seem to think unless anyone says anything to me'. 'I am not able to think, I don't have any thoughts, everything seems the same in my head, I try to think but I can't, my head is so weak, I can talk about anything, but nothing happens in my head'. 'I can't collect my thoughts sufficiently. My thinking isn't clear'
Distortions in the experiencing of time	Subjective changes in the perception of duration (i.e. time is experienced slower, faster or as at a standstill), and in time perspective, e.g. an inability to conceive past or future	'Time doesn't seem to go at all; the whole day seems exactly the same. If I look at the clock it doesn't mean anything to me at all. I couldn't give you the remotest idea now what the time is [asked, said it was twelve o'clock, actually 11:50]. It's difficult to think of the past at all . . . everything seems to have gone out of my head'
Changes in the subjective experiencing of memory	The subjective feeling of not being able to recall things (e.g. memory episodes) or having the feeling that the person was not part of the episode	'When he recalled events in his life, he felt as though he was "not in them"' 'He had doubts as to whether his memories were of real events or of just a vivid dream'
Heightened self-observation	State of increased self-awareness in which one has the feeling of being a disembodied observer contemplating one's actions and mental activity	'I seemed to be completely apart from myself. I felt that I was somewhere above looking down on the scene of which I was a part and yet not a part'. 'I was completely unable to tell whether I myself was still present or whether I was the part which had gone. In short there were two different beings, the one watching the other'

Continued overleaf

Table 25.2 Continued

Symptoms	*Definition*	*Example*
Subjective feeling of an inability to evoke images	The feeling of having the mind empty of thoughts or not being able to think	'I can't picture things vividly or recall them properly'. 'He would constantly try to imagine his wife or his home, but he wouldn't succeed'

Table 25.3 Clinical symptoms of depersonalization disorder (adapted from Hunter et al., 2003)

Affective
- Emotional numbing (for both positive and negative affect)
- Lack of empathy
- Sense of isolation
- Depression
- Anxiety
- Dream-like state
- Loss of motivation
- Loss of a sense of the consequences of one's behaviour

Cognitive
- Impaired concentration
- Mind 'emptiness' or 'racing thoughts'
- Memory impairments
- Impaired visual imagery
- Difficulty in processing new information

Physiological/perceptual
- Partial or total physiological numbing
- Feelings of weightlessness/hollowness
- Lack of a sense of physical boundaries
- Sensory impairments (e.g. taste, touch, microscopia and/or macroscopia)
- Sensory distortions (e.g. sound, loss of colour)
- Dizziness
- External world appears flat and two dimensional
- Objects do not appear solid
- Loss of sense of recognition to one's own reflection and voice
- Changed perception of time

experience of something between their eyes and the outside world (e.g. 'curtain', 'blind', 'glass wall', etc.; Shorvon et al., 1946). Derealization is often experienced in the visual modality (e.g. 'I see things as if they were two-dimensional, without depth') although it may also be experienced in other sensory modalities (e.g. objects feel strange to touch; sounds coming from the distance, muffled and distorted). Patients may attempt to describe their experience in the following terms: 'It's like living inside a bubble'; 'It is as if I am living in a film, it is all black and white and 2D'; 'It is like walking around with a goldfish bowl on your head' (examples taken from case descriptions in Baker et al., 2003).

Desomatization

With regard to desomatization, there is a diminution, loss or alteration of bodily sensations and a sense of disembodiment. Patients may refer to a sense of the physical body acting while the mind observes; of not being in full control of one's voice, movements or behaviour; or feeling detached from body parts or the whole body. Patients may attempt to describe their experience in the following terms: 'It is as if I were a phantom body', 'My hands seem not to belong to me'. There may also be a raised pain threshold.

De-affectualization

De-affectualization concerns a diminution or loss of emotional reactivity. Emotions may seem to lack spontaneity and subjective validity. Patients often experience a sense of emotional numbness or an inability to experience feelings. Patients may describe their experience in the following terms 'My emotions are gone, nothing affects me'; 'I am unable to have any emotions, everything is detached from me'. This experience may seriously affect intimate relationships.

De-ideation

Experiencing de-ideation, patients might report significant distortions and complaints regarding cognitive functioning. These may include: (1) inability to evoke images (e.g. 'When I close my eyes, I can't picture a blue sky or blue sea. I can think it but cannot see it with my mind'); (2) changes in the subjective experiencing of memory function; (3) distortion in the experiencing of time (e.g. 'If I do anything in the morning it seems like weeks ago'; Shorvon et al., 1946); (4) complaints of feeling that their mind is empty of thoughts or feeling unable to think (e.g. 'It is as if my mind is blank').

CLASSIFICATION

Both DSM-IV-TR (APA, 2000) and ICD-10 (WHO, 1992) classifications denote a degree of uncertainty regarding the nosological status of DP. DSM classifies DP as a dissociative disorder, i.e. 'a disruption in the usually integrated functions of consciousness, memory, identity, or perception of the environment' (APA, 2000), alongside dissociative amnesia, fugue states and dissociative identity disorder (DID). In contrast, the ICD-10 classifies depersonalization–derealization syndrome under the vague heading of 'other neurotic disorders' (F48.1).

The two sets of criteria are very similar, with both requiring that individuals affected must have intact reality testing and good insight into the psychological nature of their symptoms (i.e. the individual is aware that the symptoms of DP are a subjective experience and not real). The most notable differences between the two diagnostic systems are: (1) an explicit mention of impairment in functioning (criterion C, DSM-IV-TR) is not included in the ICD-10; (2) ICD-10 groups DR and DP symptoms together requiring the presence of 'either or both' for a definite diagnosis, whereas the DSM-IV-TR criteria separates these two clinical entities reserving the term 'derealization unaccompanied by depersonalization' (DSM-IV-TR, 300.15) for cases of pure derealization. The occurrence of DR in the absence of DP is relatively rare. A recent large-scale study of 204 cases of primary DPD found that 73% of the individuals reported symptoms of both DP and DR and only 6% reported symptoms of DR as a single phenomenon (Baker et al., 2003). Similarly, Lambert et al. (2001a) found only four cases of 'pure DR' among forty-two cases of both primary and secondary DP. These findings would appear to support the placing together of DP and DR as in the ICD-10 classification.

The classification of DPD as a dissociative disorder has been disputed and its conceptualization as an anxiety disorder has been advocated (Hunter et al., 2003; Tyrer, 1989), in light of the strong association between DPD and anxiety disorders in general and panic disorder in particular (e.g. Cassano et al., 1989). Hunter et al. (2003) listed several aspects in which DPD differs from dissociative disorders. First, individuals with DPD rarely experience significant periods of memory loss typically seen in dissociative amnesia, fugue states or dissociative identity disorder (e.g. Baker et al., 2003; Simeon et al., 1997). Second, whereas a lack of subjective awareness of change is the hallmark of true dissociation, in DPD sufferers are 'frighteningly aware' of their altered experience of themselves and/or their surroundings. Third, unlike other dissociative disorders, where the pattern is one of alternating between non-dissociative and dissociative states, in DPD the pattern is characterized by unremitting symptomatology. Fourth, there is a strong association between trauma (e.g. childhood physical or sexual abuse) and dissociative disorders (van Ijzendoorn & Schuengel, 1996). In contrast, despite the strong association between traumatic events (e.g. road traffic accidents) and transient symptoms of DP (Mayou et al., 2001; Noyes & Kletti, 1977) no such strong connection has been established between childhood trauma and chronic DPD, although Simeon et al. (2001b) found childhood emotional abuse to be a predictor of DPD. Further studies are needed to clarify the role of trauma in the development of the chronic condition of DPD. Finally, in DPD, comorbidity with other dissociative disorders is rare whereas anxiety disorders and depressive states often co-exist with DPD (e.g. Baker et al., 2003).

It is also true that DPD has dissociative features in that individuals experience a disruption in their previous integrated sense of self and a subjective detachment from themselves and/or the world, warranting its conceptualization as a dissociative disorder. Some authorities argue that DPD lies on a 'continuum of dissociation', representing a mild pathological form, which suggests that all dissociative phenomena are qualitatively similar (Braun, 1997). In contrast, Holmes et al. (2005) suggested the existence of two 'qualitatively' distinct dissociative phenomena, with possibly discrete underlying biological/physiological basis: (1) dissociative 'compartmentalization' (i.e. dissociative amnesia, dissociative fugue and dissociative identity disorder); and (2) dissociative 'detachment' (i.e. depersonalization/derealization). The authors concluded that using this dichotomy could lead to clearer case formulation and an improved choice of treatment strategy.

In summary, current classification systems betray a degree of uncertainty regarding the nosological status of DP. Its classification under 'other neurotic disorders' is extremely vague, whereas its classification as a dissociative disorder is arguable given the many *ways* in which DPD differs from other dissociative disorders. On the other hand, DP is strongly associated with the anxiety disorders, prompting its conceptualization within an anxiety disorder framework. Accepting depersonalization under a dissociative framework, a two-part taxonomy revealing two qualitatively distinct phenomena (i.e. dissociative detachment–depersonalization and derealization vs. dissociative compartmentalization–dissociative amnesia, dissociative fugue and dissociative identity disorder) can clarify the use of the terms dissociation and DP in theory, research and clinical practice.

PREVALENCE

Transient symptoms of depersonalization

Epidemiological surveys demonstrate that transient symptoms of DP/DR are very common (Hunter et al., 2004). For example, lifetime prevalence rates of transient symptoms of DP/DR range from 26% to 70% in college students (Sedman, 1966, 1970; Trueman, 1984), with one-year prevalence rates ranging from 46% to 74% (Dixon, 1963; Jacobs & Bovasso, 1992). A recent and more rigorous survey in a random rural US sample (1008 adults) found a one-year prevalence rate of symptoms of either DP/DR to be 23.4% (Aderibigbe et al., 2001). Peritraumatic symptoms of DP are also very common, with two studies reporting prevalence rates ranging from 31% in hospitalized accident victims to 66% in survivors of 'life-threatening danger' (Noyes et al., 1977; Noyes & Kletti, 1977). Taken together, these findings suggest that DP is part of a 'normal' human response to trauma.

Secondary depersonalization

Depersonalization (DP) is exceptionally common in a wide range of psychiatric conditions. One survey found lifetime experiences of DP/DR in 80% of psychiatric inpatients, of whom 12% described them as chronic and disabling (Brauer et al., 1970).

Prevalence of DP/DR in specific psychiatric disorders is higher in inpatient than outpatient samples. For instance, in schizophrenia prevalence rates range from 6.9% reporting current symptoms in a GP practice to 36% for the duration of the illness in inpatients (Watts, 1985; Noyer et al., 1977, respectively). In obsessive-compulsive disorder, a recent survey found that 6% of individuals met criteria for comorbid DPD (Lochner et al., 2004). In depression prevalence rates range from 4% in a sample of women attending GP services to 60% in inpatients (Strickland et al., 2002; Noyes et al., 1977, respectively). The highest prevalence rates are found in panic disorder (PD), ranging from 24.1% to 82.6% (Cox et al., 1994; Seguí et al., 2000). In fact DP/DR are among the symptoms most commonly present in a panic attack according to both DSM-IV-TR (APA, 2000) and ICD-10 (WHO, 1992) criteria (see Table 12.1, p. 460). Moreover, symptoms of DP in PD have been regarded as a marker of severity and a poor prognosis, arguing for a possible typification of PD with predominant DP symptoms (e.g. Cassano et al., 1989; Márquez et al., 2001; Seguí et al., 1998, 2000). For example, Cassano et al. (1989) divided 150 patients with PD into two groups based on the presence/absence of DP/DR. Symptoms of DP/DR were found in 34.7% of cases. Clinical comparisons found the DP subgroup to be a more severe form of PD, with an earlier age of onset (25.4 vs. 30.4), more avoidance behaviour and agoraphobia (86.6% vs. 65.3%), and a higher rate of co-morbidity with other psychiatric disorders such as obsessive-compulsive disorder (11.5% vs. 2%) and GAD (61.5% vs. 29.6%). More recently, the Spanish group of Seguí and co-workers (2000) confirmed and extended these results. In a sample of 274 PD patients, 24.1% exhibited DP/DR during the attacks. In line with Cassano and colleagues, this group was significantly younger (40.5 vs. 45.3) with an earlier age of onset (31.2 vs. 37.4). Overall, they displayed a more severe disorder with a higher number of attacks over the past month (15.4 vs. 10.3), higher indices of anxiety and depression, more anticipatory anxiety and agoraphobia and greater comorbidity with simple phobia and phobic avoidance behaviour. The authors concluded that, 'PD with DP during panic attacks may be distinguished as a distinct subcategory of PD' (Seguí et al., 2000, p. 176).

Primary depersonalization disorder

The prevalence of primary DPD in the general population is largely unknown. However, community surveys employing standardized diagnostic interviews to measure clinically significant symptoms of DP (i.e. primary DPD) reported rates of between, 1.2% and 1.7% for a one-month prevalence in two UK samples (Bebbington et al., 1981, 1997) and a 2.4% current prevalence rate in a Canadian urban sample. Thus, primary DPD is more infrequent than secondary DP, but equally prevalent as other thoroughly documented conditions such as obsessive-compulsive disorder (1–2%; Bebbington, 1998) and schizophrenia (0.5–1.5%; APA, 2000).

In addition, two recent large-scale studies with clinical samples of primary DPD with sample sizes ranging from 117 (73% recruited via media advertisement, 18% self-referred, and 9% referred by their doctor; Simeon et al., 2003a) to 204 (recruited from clinical referrals to a Depersonalization Research Unit (*n* = 130), the unit's website (*n* = 55) and media articles (*n* = 14); Baker et al., 2003) suggest that this condition is not as 'rare' as previously thought. These findings should assist in dispelling the common belief that primary DPD is a rare disorder (WHO, 1992, p. 172).

If DPD is not as rare as once thought, it remains *under-diagnosed* (Lambert et al., 2000). Simeon (2004) outlined several factors accounting for this situation: (1) limited familiarity on the part of many clinicians regarding the entity and its typical presentation; (2) reluctance on the part of many patients to disclose their symptoms because of an expectation that they will not be understood or will sound crazy; (3) patients' inability to articulate their DP experiences; and (4) a trend to diagnose DPD as just a variant of depression or anxiety, even when the diagnosis of a distinct condition is clearly warranted. Moreover, DPD is also often *misdiagnosed*. Of particular concern is the finding that patients with DPD have an average time of seven to ten years before being given a correct diagnosis (Steinberg et al., 1993). In terms of clinical presentation, it is not uncommon for many individuals to have received a previous psychiatric diagnosis. For example, Baker et al. (2003) found that 50% of their sample reported a previous psychiatric diagnosis, including depression (62%), anxiety disorder (41%) and even schizophrenia (7%). In addition, 42% reported a previous psychiatric admission, of which 57% reported more than one. This situation is illustrated in the case example presented in this chapter.

ONSET

Primary depersonalization

Age of onset for primary DPD is typically late adolescence or early adulthood. The mean age of onset was sixteen in a US study (*n* = 117) (Simeon et al., 2003a, 2003b) and 22.8 in a UK clinical survey ($n = 204$) (Baker et al., 2003). This study found that very early onset (five to sixteen years) represented a more severe disorder with higher DP symptomatology and greater levels of anxiety and depression (Baker et al., 2003; see also Brauer et al., 1970), although Simeon et al. (2003a) failed to replicate these results.

The gender distribution of DP has been controversial, with early studies showing a greater female incidence, ranging from 2 to 4:1 (Mayer-Gross, 1935; Roberts, 1960; Simeon et al., 1997). In contrast, recent large studies have confirmed a 1:1 gender ratio (Baker et al., 2003; Simeon et al., 2003a). No familial pattern of inheritance has been described (Maldonado et al., 2002), with only 5% of individuals reporting DP in a first-degree relative in a US sample (Simeon et al., 2003a, 2003b) and 10% in a UK sample (Baker et al., 2003). In contrast, a family history of other psychiatric illnesses is not uncommon. For instance, Baker et al. (2003) found that 30% of patients reported a family history of some psychiatric illness, with 28% reporting depression (see also Simeon et al., 2003a).

The onset of DP can be acute or insidious. With acute onset, some patients give a vivid account of their first episode, providing details of the exact moment, setting and circumstances (Simeon, 2004). Both types of onset are largely seen in equal proportion. For example, in the UK study of primary DP, 38% of patients reported a clear precipitant to their illness, while 16% reported a gradual onset and the majority (46%) were unclear (Baker et al., 2003). Simeon et al. (2003a) found relatively similar results, with 49% of patients identifying a clear precipitating factor of their illness while 51% were unable to identify an immediate precipitant.

Three main categories of precipitants can be identified from the UK (Baker et al., 2003) and the US studies (Simeon et al., 2003a, 1997): (1) substance misuse (mainly marijuana); (2) severe and/or prolonged stress (e.g. interpersonal, financial occupational, etc.) or a traumatic event (e.g. relative's death, etc.); and (3) a change in mental state (i.e. anxiety, depression). While childhood trauma is a well-documented precipitant of various dissociative disorders (van Ijzendoorn & Schuengel, 1996), its role in the pathogenesis of DPD remains a topic of debate. In a recent study, Simeon and colleagues (2001b) found a strong association between childhood interpersonal trauma, in particular emotional abuse, and DPD whereas Baker et al. (2003) found trauma (including physical/sexual abuse) a contributing factor in just 14% of their sample ($n = 204$).

When the onset is insidious, DP can be so remote that the individual fails to remember it, or it may begin with limited episodes of lesser severity and gradually become more pronounced (Simeon, 2004).

Clinical features and illness severity are similar whether the onset is acute or insidious (Baker et al., 2003; Simeon et al., 2003a), or whether the precipitating factor is substance misuse or a mental illness (Medford et al., 2003).

COURSE

Primary depersonalization

DP can be suffered episodically or continuously (i.e. DP is present at all time) but the disorder typically runs a chronic course. Most patients describe a continuous pattern with little or no fluctuation, and one third suffer it episodically (Baker et al., 2003; Simeon et al., 2003a). The duration of single episodes varies from individual to individual, ranging from minutes to years, generally resolving gradually. In a large proportion of cases, DP can first present episodically and subsequently become continuous (i.e. DP is always present or with a degree of fluctuation; Simeon, 2004).

Factors alleviating and exacerbating the symptoms differ from individual to individual. Three main factors can be identified:

1 *Environmental*: alleviating factors include task-focusing activities such as watching TV, social interaction; exacerbating factors include fluorescent lighting, over-stimulation or noise, travel to unfamiliar places and sensory deprivation.
2 *Physiological states*: alleviating factors include sleep, hygiene and rest, physical exercise and mental discipline; exacerbating factors include fatigue, sleep deprivation, viral illness. With alcohol, individuals often refer to a sense of temporary relief during alcohol consumption. However, they refer to a 'ten-fold' increase during the post-consumption phase, turning a mild experience into a 'absolute terror'.
3 *Psychological factors*: alleviating factors include emotional stimulation; exacerbating factors include negative affects such as anxiety, depression and symptom-focused attention.

Primary DPD is often accompanied by significant distress and marked reduction in well-being (Lambert et al., 2001a). In this regard, Baker et al. (2003) found that 79% of patients reported impaired social and/or vocational functioning. At an interpersonal level, individuals affected often feel distressed by their intense sense of emotional detachment from those close to them (Simeon, 2004).

COMORBIDITY

Primary depersonalization disorder

Axis I mood and anxiety disorders are frequently comorbid with primary DPD (Baker et al., 2003; Simeon et al., 1997, 2003a). These sometimes more obvious symptoms can often mask the primary chronic disturbance of DP. Simeon et al. (2003a, 2003b) found that 73% of their sample (n = 117) had a lifetime comorbid unipolar mood disorder and 64% a comorbid anxiety disorder. Current comorbidity was also high, with 28.2% presenting with social phobia, 16.2% with generalized anxiety disorder, and 12% with panic disorder. Largely in keeping with these findings, Baker et al. (2003) found that 62% of cases (n = 204) with primary DP reported a previous diagnosis of depression. In addition, 71% reported suffering 'panic attacks' and 59% stated that they were 'afraid to go out alone'.

Axis II personality disorders are also found comorbid with primary DPD, the most common cases being borderline ones, avoidant and obsessive-compulsive (Simeon et al., 2003a).

Comorbidity is often secondary to DP, such as depression and hopelessness arising as a demoralized response to the suffering and impairment imposed by unremitting DP. Likewise, DP may begin with a disturbing and frightening drug experience (i.e. a bad trip) that results in unpleasant and unfamiliar DP symptoms generating further anxiety, leading to increased DP, thus creating a vicious circle (e.g. Moran, 1986).

DIFFERENTIAL DIAGNOSIS

A DSM-IV-TR diagnosis of depersonalization disorder (i.e. primary DPD) cannot be made if the 'symptoms are due to the physiological consequences of a specific general medical condition' (e.g. temporal lobe epilepsy, traumatic brain injury, etc.) or occur only during the course of another Axis I mental disorder (e.g. panic disorder, social or specific phobia or post-traumatic or acute stress disorder). In these cases, symptoms of DP should be considered as a secondary phenomenon precluding a primary diagnosis.

In DSM-IV-TR, DP that is caused by the direct physiological effects of a substance is distinguished from DPD by the fact that a substance (e.g. illicit drug or medication) is thought to be aetiologically related to the DP. However, the clinician should be aware that although acute symptoms of DP arising either during or after intoxication could truly be drug induced (e.g. Mathew et al., 1993, 1999; Melges et al., 1970; Raimo et al., 1999), in which case their transient course precludes a diagnosis of DPD, in many cases individuals go on to experience a perpetuation of symptoms in the absence of drug use. In these cases a diagnosis of primary DPD (according to DSM-IV-TR) is warranted (e.g. Keshaven & Lishman, 1986; Medford et al., 2003; Moran, 1986; Szymanski, 1981). Interestingly, Medford et al. (2003) compared the clinical features of forty individuals with primary DPD who related the onset of symptoms to an episode of illicit drug use (mainly cannabis use only) with an age and sex matched sample of forty cases with non-drug-induced chronic primary DPD. The authors concluded that 'drug-induced DP does not appear to represent a distinct clinical syndrome. The neurocognitive mechanisms of the genesis and maintenance of DP are likely to be similar across clinical groups, regardless of precipitants' (Medford et al., 2003, p. 1731).

Depersonalization should not be diagnosed separately when the symptoms occur only during a panic attack that is part of panic disorder, social or specific phobia, or post-traumatic or acute stress disorder. To illustrate, an individual may suffer from distressing symptoms of DP and/or DR while having a panic attack but these symptoms abate when the panic episode ceases (e.g. Seguí et al., 2000) (see Chapter 12 for an illustration of a case in point).

In contrast to schizophrenia, intact reality testing is maintained in DPD. However, differentiating DPD from delusions of DP, which are sometimes seen in schizophrenia, may be difficult since the disturbance in the 'sense of self', regarded as the central phenomenon to schizophrenia, has a striking resemblance to DP (Sedman & Kenna, 1963). Clinicians must seek to distinguish DPD from its delusional or psychotic counterpart by its 'as if' quality. As Kuipers and colleagues note, 'people who suffer from delusions of depersonalization do not merely feel *as if* they are unreal, but that in some sense they *are* unreal' (see Chapter 21, p. 847), although, as they also note, 'detachment of the emotional component of perception' (see Chapter 21, p. 848) may be the process underlying both the neurotic and the psychotic psychopathological entities.

The feeling of numbness associated with DP may mimic depression. However, feelings of numbness in individuals with DPD are associated with other manifestations of DP (e.g. a sense of detachment from one's self) and occur even when the individual is not depressed. A remarkable feature of de-affectualization (i.e. diminution or loss of emotional reactivity) seen in DP is that it is not usually accompanied by an objectively blunted affect. Thus, 'clinical observation supports that, in the absence of feelings, the motor expression of some emotions seems normal in depersonalisation' (Sierra & Berrios, 1998 p. 900). This feature can help clinicians to draw a differential diagnosis (Medford et al., 2005).

AETIOLOGY

Historically, theories regarding the aetiology of DP can be divided into two main categories (see also Sierra & Berrios, 1997, for a comprehensive conceptual history of DP):

Theories regarding DP as a disturbance of an individual mental function

These include, 'sensory theories', 'affective theories' and 'memory theories'. A common denominator of these theories is their reductionist view, providing a partial explanation for a complex disorder. In essence, each theory is derived from over-emphasis of a particular feature or symptom isolated from the whole structure (Sedman, 1970).

SENSORY THEORIES

Historically, 'sensory theories' considered the disturbance of sensory perception as the central aetiological factor in DP. This theory emphasized the clinical feature of visual derealization. The theory was extrapolated from patients' complaints regarding their impression of flatness or lack of depth, and a lack of movement in what they perceived (e.g. 'I can see things, but I cannot exactly take it in', 'Everything is flat, still, artificial, altered'). This theory was later disputed based on the fact that many patients with clear sensory pathology did not report feelings of unreality and conversely, other patients with DP presented intact sensory functioning (Sierra & Berrios, 1997).

AFFECTIVE THEORIES

Historically, 'affective theories' regarded the inhibition of emotional feelings as the central aetiological factor responsible for DP. The theory was extrapolated from patients' complaints such as 'My emotions are gone, nothing affects me', 'I am unable to have any emotions, everything is detached from me'. A variation of this theory came from Loewy (in Mayer-Gross, 1935) who postulated a loss of the specific feelings accompanying action as responsible for DP (e.g. 'My movements feel automatic, like a machine'). A further variation came again from Mayer-Gross (1935), who noted a lack of feelings in patients' thinking rather than patients' activity (e.g. 'I have no thoughts at all . . . thoughts are so far away . . . I am like an automaton led about without will of his own. I have no active thoughts'). This variation attempted to explain the now-termed 'de-ideation' symptoms (e.g. 'mind emptiness').

MEMORY THEORIES

Historically, 'memory theories' regarded a disturbance of memory as the central aetiological factor of DP. In essence, 'feelings of unreality' were considered to result from the loss of 'feelings of familiarity', that is, a failure to recognize objects and persons as familiar due to an inability to create a strong association between the percept and earlier memories giving it a certain '*jamais vu*' quality. Janet (1903) proposed a variant of this theory, suggesting a 'hyperactivity of memory' as a central causal factor where individuals continually contrasted their depersonalized state with their former healthy state.

Theories regarding DP as a neurological/organic dysfunction

These vary, depending on their degree of localization of lesion responsible for the disorder.

BODY IMAGE THEORY

From a neurological perspective, the theory of 'body image' regarded the loss of the experiential body awareness that resulted from the image of our own body formed in our mind, as the central aetiological factor responsible for DP (e.g. L'Hermitte, 1939). The parietal and angular gyri of the brain are thought to be responsible for the experience of body image. The theory was extrapolated from patients' complaints of detachment from their physical self (e.g. 'I feel funny, I feel I have no body, I am only a head'), and attempted to explain symptoms now referred to as desomatization (i.e. loss of feelings of body ownership and loss of feelings of agency, that is, the feeling that one is not in charge of one's movements).

There is recent evidence supporting the role of body image in the development of specific features of DP (i.e. visual derealization and desomatization). For example, Sierra et al. (2002a) have recently drawn attention to the phenomenological similarities between asomatognosia, a neurological condition characterized by an alteration of body awareness associated with right parietal lesions, and the desomatization symptoms found in DPD. However, Simeon et al. (2000) distinguished between a neurological and a 'psychiatric version' of body schema distortion characterized by an 'as if' quality (more subtle, functionally based and less neurologically damaged) seen in DP disorder. In a PET scan study, the authors found evidence of metabolic abnormalities in brain networks responsible for an integrated body schema, including the angular gyrus, which is implicated in somatosensory–visual–auditory integration.

PREFORMED THEORY

Mayer-Gross (1935) considered DP as a 'non-specific' and non-localized preformed functional response of the brain, analogous to other preformed mechanisms such as delirium and seizures, which could be triggered by a number of factors.

The role of anxiety

The role of anxiety in the aetiology of DP has long been advocated. From a psychoanalytic standpoint, DP was thought to result from unconscious defences that become operative after signal anxiety has been experienced and serve to protect the individual from a breakthrough of aggressive or libidinal impulses (e.g. Levy & Wachtel, 1978).

In 1960, Roth described a phobic anxiety–depersonalization syndrome, proposing that DP was a 'specific' vestigial brain response, shaped by evolution and called into action when fear and anxiety threaten to overwhelm the individual. Roth and Harper (1962) proposed that DP represents an adaptive mechanism that combines opposing reaction tendencies, one serving to intensify alertness and the other to dampen potentially disorganizing emotion, called into action under catastrophic circumstances such as bereavement or a threat to life. This view finds support in a number of studies (e.g. Nuller, 1982; Trueman 1984), in particular those showing a high prevalence of transient DP in response to extreme danger or its associated anxiety (e.g. Noyes & Kletti, 1977; Noyes et al., 1977).

More recently, Hunter et al. (2003) have argued that there is substantial evidence supporting the conceptualization of DPD as an anxiety disorder. For example: (1) cognitive symptoms experienced in DPD are similar to those of increased arousal (e.g. racing thoughts, mind emptiness and subjective deficits in concentration); (2) clinical features of DPD are similar to those found in anxiety disorders such as acute stress disorder or PTSD (e.g. emotional anaesthesia, a sense of detachment or of being in a daze, and estrangement from others); (3) in keeping with panic disorder, individuals suffering from DPD report symptoms such as feeling dizzy or faint, or experiences of parasthesias, and the behavioural consequence of experiencing DPD often results in avoidance of situations that evoke greater levels of anxiety (e.g. social situations); (4) there is a high comorbidity of DP symptoms in anxiety disorders in general and PD in particular.

Two recent models of DP embrace the view that anxiety plays a significant role in its pathogenesis (Hunter et al., 2003; Sierra & Berrios, 1998).

A neurobiological model

In line with other authors (Mayer-Gross, 1935; Roth, 1960), Sierra and Berrios's (1998) neurobiological model, endorses the view that DP is a 'hard-wired vestigial response for dealing with extreme anxiety combining a state of increased alertness with a profound inhibition of the emotional response system' (p. 903). The model has the advantage of accounting for the syndromal complexity of the disorder, including affective dampening and cognitive complaints. A combination of two simultaneous neurocircuitries is postulated as responsible for the clinical features of DP (Figure 25.3):

1 An inhibitory component mediated by the left prefrontal cortex inhibiting neural regions important for emotion processing (i.e. amygdala and related limbic structures), causing a reduction in emotional response and a dampening of sympathetic outflow. This 'shut down' of emotional

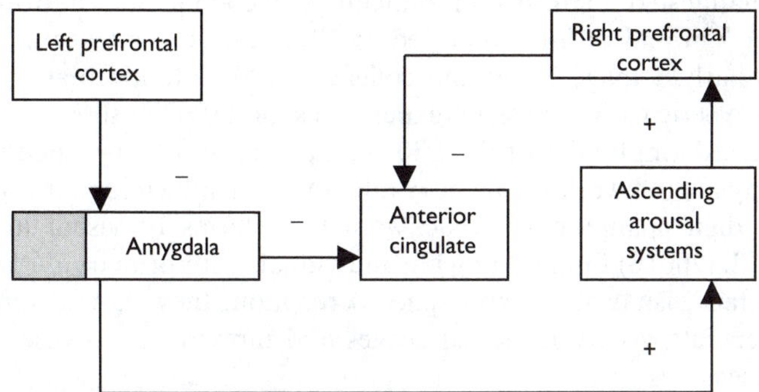

Figure 25.3 A neurobiological model of depersonalization (Sierra & Berrios, 1998). It is proposed here that depersonalization results from the combination of two mechanisms: an *inhibitory component* mediated by a left-sided prefrontal mechanism that inhibits the amygdala (and indirectly other structures such as the anterior cingulate), causing a reduction of emotional response and dampening of sympathetic outflow; and an *excitatory component* driven by uninhibited amygdala circuits (hatched area) controlling both cholinergic and amino-aminergic ascending arousal systems; this would lead to activation of the right prefrontal cortex and a reciprocal inhibition of the anterior cingulate and generate a state of vigilant attention. The simultaneous activity of these two opposing mechanisms explains many of the experiential features of depersonalization.

response leads to the central feature of de-affectualization with associated loss of emotional tone in the experience of oneself (depersonalization, desomatization) and one's surroundings (derealization).

2 An excitatory component driven by uninhibited amygdala circuits controlling both cholinergic and amino-aminergic ascending arousal systems, leading to activation of the right prefrontal cortex and a reciprocal inhibition of the anterior cingulate. This generates a state of vigilant attention responsible for the experiential feature of 'mind emptiness' and other related cognitive complaints (de-ideation). The anterior cingulate mediates the ability to focus attention on a specific stimulus (sustain attention) and inhibit distracting stimuli (selective attention) (Posner & Rothbart, 1992). Thus, it is not surprising that patients with DP complain of difficulties concentrating, and more importantly, that they experience symptom relief when managing to reduce self-focus attention and engage in externally focused attention (e.g. watching TV).

There is objective evidence supporting patients' subjective cognitive complaints in the domains of attention and visual imagery. Relative to attention, Guralnik and colleagues (2000) studying patients with primary DPD found specific cognitive alterations in patients' ability to effortfully control attention, leading to poor performance on auditory–verbal recall memory tasks.

This was manifested in terms of difficulties encoding new information, against a background of intact delayed recall and overall intellectual functioning. Similarly, Papageorgiou and colleagues (2002) found that 'normal' individuals experiencing transient experiences of DP/DR showed significantly decreased amplitudes of the P300 component of event-related potentials, indexing altered working memory and attention allocation on cognitive testing (i.e. digit span forwards/backwards). In terms of visual imagery, Lambert et al. (2001b) found that while individuals with primary DPD demonstrated intact visual object and space perception, they showed impaired ability to generate visual images of scenes and movements, assessed using self-report measures.

The pattern of neural response described by Sierra and Berrios's neurobiological model is considered as highly adaptive in situations of overwhelming threat, where the individual has no control over the environment and the source of danger is unknown or unlocalized (e.g. earthquake). It allows the inhibition of non-functional emotional responses (i.e. disorganized levels of fear) while maintaining a vigilant alertness, allowing for simultaneous multi-sensory scanning. In contrast, the emergence and persistence of this response in non-threatening situations, which patients with DPD are unable to 'switch off', results in de-affectualization with associated loss of emotional tone in the experience of the self and surroundings. These unpleasant and unfamiliar experiences are disturbing and frightening, generating further anxiety, and thus creating a vicious circle.

Neuroimaging (Phillips et al., 2000, 2001a) and psychophysiological (Kelly & Walter, 1968; Lader & Wing, 1966; Sierra et al., 2002b) studies lend empirical support to the neurobiological model proposed by Sierra and Berrios (1998).

Two studies investigated the processing of affective material in DPD. Using functional neuroimaging (fMRI), Phillips et al. (2000, 2001a) compared the emotional responses to emotionally salient stimuli (i.e. aversive or disgusted scenes) in patients with DPD, OCD, and healthy controls. The results showed that a pattern of reduced activation in limbic regions implicated in emotional processing (i.e. insula and cingulate gyrus) combined with an increased activation in prefrontal regions (i.e. right ventral prefrontal cortex) implicated in the inhibition of emotional response regions distinguished the DPD group.

In addition, two studies found objective evidence of autonomic under-arousal in response to emotional stimuli in DPD. As early as 1968, Kelly and Walter, using forearm blood flow as an index of sympathetic autonomic functioning, found that patients with DPD showed the lowest basal recordings of a range of psychiatric disorders and controls. In line with these findings, Sierra et al. (2002b) found a pattern of significantly reduced skin conductance response (SCR) to unpleasant pictures in fifteen patients with chronic DPD, indicative of a phasic inhibitory mechanism on emotional processing. Moreover, patients with DPD and those with anxiety disorders showed a shorter latency of SCR to unwarned stimulus (e.g. clapping), suggestive of a state of heightened state of alertness as predicted by the neurobiological model of DPD.

A cognitive-behavioural conceptualization of DPD

Based on the strong evidence linking DPD with the anxiety disorders, Hunter et al. (2003) proposed a speculative cognitive model of DPD in which anxiety plays a central role.

In line with other cognitive models of anxiety disorders, such as panic (Clark, 1986) and health anxiety (Warwick & Salkovskis, 2001), the model proposes that the chronic condition of DPD results from catastrophic misinterpretation of transient symptoms of DP, which are common in the 'normal' population. These may be precipitated by a range of factors, including physiological states (e.g. fatigue, substance intoxication), affective states (e.g. anxiety, panic, depression, etc.) and acute trauma or severe ongoing stress.

The model draws attention to the idiosyncratic or disorder-specific nature of the belief system present in DPD. In contrast to patients with panic disorder or health anxiety, where the focus is on catastrophic misinterpretations of the physical symptoms of anxiety (interpreting them as a sign of an imminent heart attack), patients with DPD are more troubled by the meaning of the cognitive symptoms of anxiety (interpreting them as a sign of madness or brain damage). Hunter et al. (in press) refer to this as a form of 'mental health anxiety'. Table 25.4 illustrates these symptom-specific cognitions in the case of panic disorder. In support of this claim the group of the Depersonalization Research Unit in London found that twelve out of fifteen patients with DPD (i.e. 80%) endorsed the statement 'something has gone wrong with my brain' (e.g. Creutzfeldt–Jakob disease) as being a likely cause of their symptoms. Other mediating attributions include 'fear of loss of identity' (Fewtrell, 1986).

Fundamental to the understanding of this cognitive-behavioural model is the mediating function played by a neurobiological reaction. This is characterized by decreased emotional response and decreased autonomic arousal in response to increasing levels of anxiety and mediated by catastrophic attributions of DP symptoms (Sierra & Berrios, 1998).

In line with other cognitive models of anxiety and mood disorders, Hunter et al. (2003) postulate that the automatic misattributions of symptoms stem from underlying assumptions or core beliefs about the self. Thus, whereas most people who experience transient DP/DR will attribute them to situational explanations (e.g. tiredness, stress, drug intoxication), and believe that once their circumstances change their symptoms will dissipate, those who go on to suffer the chronic condition of DPD may have premorbid concerns regarding their vulnerability to mental illness. This makes

Table 25.4 Examples of main sensations, misinterpretations and safety behaviours in patients with panic disorder (adapted from Wells, 1997)

Sensations	*Misinterpretation*	*Safety behaviour/avoidance*
Chest palpitations	Heart attack Dying	Relax Slow down heart rate Sit down, avoid exercise Avoid physical exertion
Unreality (dissociation)	Loss of control Madness	Keep control of mind Check memory Try to control thoughts Look for exits
Breathlessness	Suffocating	Take deep breaths Sit by open windows Go into open air Suck menthol sweets
Throat tightness	Choking	Carry bottle of water Try to clear throat
Dizziness	Fainting Collapsing	Control breathing Sit down Hold on to partner Avoid going out alone
Blurred vision	Blindness Stroke	Check vision Wear sunglasses Take aspirin Avoid stress
Jelly legs	Falling Collapsing	Leave situations Stiffen legs while standing Walk close to walls Wear flat shoes

transient DP/DR symptoms more threatening since they appear to confirm their fears.

In support of this claim, a recent survey of 204 cases with primary DPD found that 10% reported a family member with a history of DPD, and 30% reported a history of psychiatric disorder in a first-degree relative (Baker et al., 2003).

In keeping with other anxiety disorders, the model proposes that a range of behaviours and cognitive biases are responsible for the maintenance cycle. In the case of behaviours, these may include avoidance of situations likely to trigger the symptoms (e.g. social situations) and safety behaviours adopted to try to prevent the feared outcome (e.g. 'acting normal'). In support of this element of the model, Simeon et al. (1997) found a high degree of comorbidity (i.e. 47%) between DPD and social phobia. Cognitive or attentional biases may include an increase in symptoms monitoring leading to a reduced threshold in the perception of threat.

ASSESSMENT

Clinical interview

The initial assessment should ideally be carried out by a multi-disciplinary team that includes psychology and psychiatry. A full psychiatric and general medical history and a mental state examination should be part of a thorough clinical assessment. A detailed treatment history (i.e. pharmacological and psychotherapeutic) should also be included. A neurological examination may be sought when an underlying organic condition is suspected (e.g. epilepsy). Clinicians may find it helpful to divide their assessment into four symptom categories: depersonalization, derealization, desomatization and de-affectualization. In light of the difficulties of patients in communicating their experiences, a rating scale embracing the phenomenological complexity of DP should be added with the view to checking symptoms and tracking changes over time. The Cambridge Depersonalization Scale (Sierra & Berrios, 2000) is particularly useful since it offers 'trait' and 'state' versions. Given that Axis I mood and anxiety symptoms often co-exist with depersonalization, the clinician should search for the presence of these features, in particular anxiety, panic, depression, obsessions and compulsions. Self-report measures such as the Beck Depression and Anxiety Inventories and others can be used to this end (BDI-II; Beck, 1996; BAI; Beck, 1990). More importantly, the clinician should clarify the relationship between DP and co-existing psychological illness. The primary aim here is to clarify whether DP has always existed exclusively in the context of these illnesses, or whether DP predated, persisted after their resolution, or occurred independently of these. This should enable the distinction between primary and secondary DP. The assessment should link predisposing, precipitating and maintaining factors as well as factors alleviating and exacerbating the condition. From a cognitive-behavioural perspective it is critical to enquire about the patient's attribution and interpretation of the symptoms.

Standardized measures

Various procedures have been developed for the assessment and diagnosis of DP, ranging from self-report questionnaires (Dixon, 1963; Fewtrell, 2000; Jacobs & Bovasso, 1992) to clinician-rated scales (e.g. Simeon, 2001a) and structured interviews (e.g. Steinberg et al., 1990, 1993). Sierra and Berrios (2000) noted that many of the existing self-rating scales, such as the Dixon's

Scale (Dixon, 1963) or the Jacobs and Bovasso's DP scale (Jacobs & Bovasso, 1992), either lack construct validity or fail to embrace the phenomenological complexity of DP. On the other hand, commonly used structured interviews, such as the structured clinical interview for DSM-IV dissociative disorders (SCID-D; Steinberg et al., 1990, 1993), may take up to three hours, limiting their use in clinical practice or for frequently measuring change over time.

Other measures have been developed to assess DP as a symptom in situations of trauma (Marmar & Weiss, 1990) and as a feature in the context of an anxiety- and/or trauma-related phenomena (e.g. Cox & Swinson, 2002; Simeon et al., 2001a).

This section emphasizes two measures. First the Dissociative Experiences Scale (DES) is presented given that it is widely reported in studies of DP. The main emphasis here will be to illustrate its strengths and shortcomings when used in DP. Second, a DP-specific measure, the Cambridge Depersonalization Scale (CDS) is described since it can help clinicians detect, describe, quantify and measure change in DP over time.

The dissociative experiences scale (DES): A general dissociation scale

The DES (Bernstein-Carlson & Putnam 1986) is possibly the most widely used instrument for the screening and measuring of dissociation in a range of clinical and non-clinical populations (Bernstein-Carlson & Putnam, 1986). It is a twenty-eight-item self-report measure of dissociative experiences using a visual analogue scale (0–100%) to yield a quantitative index of dissociation. A second version has been developed that is easier to score in that the response scale has a numerical format from 0 to 100 (by 10s) (DES-II; Carlson & Putnam, 1993). The DES has been shown to have good reliability and validity (Carlson & Putnam, 1993). Factor analysis revealed three dissociative dimensions: (1) amnesia for dissociative experiences (DES-Amnesia); (2) depersonalization/derealization (DES-DP/DR); and (3) absorption and imaginative involvement (DES-Absorption). This factorial solution was replicated in DPD (Simeon et al., 1998).

The DES presents two shortcomings when used in DPD: (1) it records lifetime frequency of dissociative experiences (i.e. it's a trait measure), making it difficult to assess changes in the level of DP overtime; (2) the recommended cut-off would often miss cases of primary DPD. For example, two large-scale studies with primary DPD showed DES-mean scores ranging from to 23.8 (14.9) to 24.9 (14.7) (Baker et al., 2003; Simeon et al., 2003a). A markedly lower cut-off score of 12 has been found to yield a sensitivity of 80%, with a specificity of 95% for the detection of DPD (Simeon et al. 1998, 2003a, 2003b).

When using the DES, clinicians have the alternative of using the DES-taxon (Waller et al., 1996), which combines eight items (3, 5, 7, 8, 12, 13, 22, 27) and has been found useful as a screen for pathological dissociation. In this case, a cut-off score of 13 yielded 80% sensitivity with a specificity of 100% (Simeon et al. 1998).

The Cambridge depersonalization scale (CDS): A depersonalization-specific scale

Given the phenomenological complexity of depersonalization (DP), the initial clinical interview should be supported with a comprehensive self-report measure capturing all clinical aspects of DP in a comprehensive manner. The Cambridge Depersonalization Trait Scale (CDTS; Sierra & Berrios, 2000) is a comprehensive, twenty-nine-item self-rating questionnaire measuring the severity of trait DP/DR symptoms from the onset of the condition. An exhaustive review of the descriptive psychopathology of DP was a source of item selection (Sierra & Berrios, 1996, 1997, 1998). It captures the frequency and duration of DP symptoms over the 'last 6 months'. When tested on a sample of thirty-five patients with DSM-IV primary DPD, twenty-two with anxiety disorders, and twenty with temporal lobe epilepsy, the CDTS was able to differentiate the three clinical groups reflecting its high discriminative validity. This is of significance in light of the high prevalence of symptoms of DP (i.e. secondary DP) in neurological and Axis I anxiety disorder in general and PD in particular (see the case example in Chapter 12 for an illustration of a case in point). The CDTS showed high internal consistency and good reliability (Cronbach alpha = .89; split-half reliability = .92). The twenty-two-item Cambridge Depersonalization State Scale (CDSS), was derived from the CDTS and uses a visual analogue scale, from 0% to 100%, to ask respondents to rate the intensity of twenty-two symptoms, as they are currently experienced.

TREATMENT

Depersonalization has traditionally been considered refractory to psychotherapeutic treatment. To date, there are no randomized controlled studies of psychological interventions for DP. With the exception of three group studies (Ackner, 1954a, 1954b; Hunter et al., 2003, 2005), psychological treatments for DP are limited to single-case studies.

Psychotherapeutic approaches

Psychoeducation

Psychoeducation has been regarded as an invaluable tool in the treatment of DP (Fewtrell, 1986; Torch, 1978). Fewtrell (1986) noted that patients with chronic DPD can experience 'great relief' when encouraged 'to articulate the subjective sensations for the first time' and suggested that sharing examples from individuals suffering similar experiences quoted in the literature may be helpful (Fewtrell, 1986, p. 266). Moreover, Steinberg (2001) reported that when patients have an explanation for their symptoms, which they can share with their families affected by it, it serves to reduce their general anxiety and their overall stress level. In some cases, it may be beneficial to offer psychoeducation to families with the view to reducing the patient's fear of being thought insane.

Behaviour modification techniques

Record keeping and contingent positive reward

Dollinger (1983) reported on a single-case study of DPD in a fifteen-year-old girl treated with behavioural modification techniques within the context of family therapy. The patient was encouraged to keep a record of her episodes of DP and was subject to a reward contingency plan, where she was allowed to drive as a reward for symptoms reduction. After fifteen weeks of treatment, DP episodes decreased from between six and ten per day pre-treatment to none. At three-year follow-up the patient remained symptom free.

Flooding

Sookman and Solyom (1978) described flooding treatment both in fantasy and *in vivo* with two patients, a forty-eight-year-old woman and a forty-year-old man, reporting persistent symptoms of DP. The first patient was treated by 'flooding in fantasy', using grossly exaggerated taped narratives of DP episodes based on the patients' descriptions of their anxiety-provoking thoughts. The second patient was treated by 'flooding *in vivo*', involving exposure to precipitants of DP. Flooding in fantasy was found to be more effective than *in vivo*. The authors concluded that since DP is itself an experience of the imagination, it might be more effectively treated in imagination.

Paradoxical intention

Blue (1979) reported on the successful treatment of a fifty-year-old woman with DP disorder using a programme of seven-week directive therapy. The patient was invited to perform an undesirable task (i.e. house cleaning) whenever she depersonalized. At week four, she reported marked symptom reduction. At week five she was invited to induce the feelings of DP within herself to make her feel that she was in control of her symptoms. At three-month follow-up the patient remained symptom free.

This approach is similar to the 'controlled dissociation' strategy described by Gil (1988), where patients are invited to deliberately increase or decrease the intensity of their DP symptoms whenever an episode takes place in order to regain a sense of control.

Cognitive-behavioural therapy

Based on the cognitive-behavioural model of DPD outlined, Hunter et al. (2003) proposed a package of treatment with three phases:

Phase I

The initial phase employs a number of techniques that are non-specific to DPD. The main objective here is the reduction of distress, increasing the levels of activity, motivation and mood. This can be achieved by means of psychoeducation, normalizing the client's experiences, and symptom monitoring. In addition, standard CBT interventions can be used to treat comorbid anxiety and depression when present. Therapists should be aware that over-reliance on physiological interventions aimed to decrease arousal such as applied relaxation training or Jacobsen's progressive relaxation (Jacobsen, 1983; Ost, 1987) may in some cases result in a paradoxical outcome referred to as 'relaxation-induced anxiety' resulting in inducing under-arousal in patients where this represents a factor underlying feelings of unreality (e.g. Fetwtrell, 1984).

PSYCHOEDUCATION AND NORMALIZATION

In CBT, engaging patients by means of sharing an understanding of a clear rationale for their symptoms and treatment is crucial for its effectiveness. This is even more essential in patients with DP disorder since on average they suffer the disorder for between seven and ten years before being given a correct diagnosis; this figure was around twelve years in a UK sample (Baker et al., 2003; Steinberg et al., 1993). As Simeon (2004, p. 344) noted, 'patients can feel tremendous relief from contact with a clinician who is able to recognise their symptoms for what they are, is familiar with the basic presenting features of the disorder and is able to give this elusive condition a name'.

Psychoeducation involves sharing information regarding the almost universal experience of transient symptoms of DP/DR, particularly under situations of stress or life-threat. For those with comorbid panic states, the therapist can share information concerning the high prevalence of transient DP/DR during panic attacks. Normalization of the experience can be gained by describing the role of DP as a protective mechanism for dealing with overwhelming anxiety by distancing oneself from it.

DIARY KEEPING

This exercise serves two purposes: (1) it helps patients appreciate the causal relationship that may exist between their behaviour and thoughts and an increase in symptoms of DP/DR and so may facilitate their belief that their symptoms are controllable and not a sign of neurological damage or impending madness; (2) it provides information regarding the presence of low level of engagement in pleasurable activities that may be contributing to low mood and increased introspection and symptom monitoring, in which case the therapist may want to increase the levels of activity.

Phase 2

The emphasis in this phase is on effecting change in those factors thought to be maintaining the disorder. The treatment involves specific interventions, individually tailored to target specific symptoms of DPD. This entails: (1) reducing avoidance of DPD-provoking situations; (2) reducing the use of safety behaviours; (3) symptom monitoring and self-focused attention; and (4) challenging catastrophic misattributions related to DPD symptoms.

REDUCING AVOIDANCE

The goal here is to reduce: (1) the use of 'safety behaviours' (e.g. saying the right thing), and (2) avoidance of situations that the client has identified as anxiety provoking due to fear of an episode of uncontrolled DP (e.g. socializing, crowded public places, driving). In this phase, standard CBT strategies proven to be effective in the treatment of social anxiety will be helpful.

REDUCING SELF-FOCUSED ATTENTION

In DPD it is suggested that the concept of the 'self' and the world may become the subject of obsessive focus resulting in the experience of both the self and the external world appearing unreal or unfamiliar. Two types of cognitive techniques can be helpful in dealing with increased symptom-focus depending on the course of symptoms of DP. First, refocusing and grounding techniques can be useful strategies for individuals suffering DP intermittently, helping them to break the cycle of increasing self-focused attention and orienting them to their immediate environment. With refocusing, the individual concentrates on a specific aspect of the environment (e.g. the colour and texture of curtains, the feel of the arms of a chair). With grounding techniques, the individual employs a word (e.g. any word that is meaningful and grounds the person to the present), an object (e.g. stress ball, a herb bag, a rubber band), a mental image (e.g. a safe and soothing place) or a self-statement (e.g. I'm John, I'm real, my family is real and they are there for me no matter what!). There is evidence suggesting the benefit of these strategies in overcoming a range of dissociative symptoms (Kennerley, 1996).

Second, for individuals who experience DP persistently or with little fluctuation, these techniques are inadequate and the person could potentially develop them into maladaptive 'safety behaviours'. For these cases, interventions developed to reduce self-focused attention in social phobia (Clark & Wells, 1995), hypochondriasis (Salkovskis & Bass, 1997) and panic (Wells, 1990) are more appropriate. Two such interventions are attention training (Wells, 1990; Wells et al., 1997) and task concentration training (TCT; Bögels et al., 1997), which have been successfully applied in cases of panic disorder and social phobia.

In attention training, patients improve their ability to control their sustained attention, attention shifting and divided attention skills through a series of exercises.

TCT consists of three phases: In phase 1, patients are encouraged to gain insight into the differences between attention that focuses on: (1) internal stimuli; (2) external, irrelevant stimuli; and (3) external task-related stimuli, and the proportion of time patients dedicate to each one of them. In phase 2, patients receive specific training to increase the degree of externally focused task-related attention by way of increasingly more complex exercises in non-threatening situations (i.e. therapy and everyday life non-threatening situations). In phase 3, the training in phase 2 is extended to threatening situations. This therapeutic approach is illustrated in the case example.

CHALLENGING CATASTROPHIC THOUGHTS

Cognitive restructuring exercises in which negative cognitions can be reality tested and more balanced thoughts offered as replacements can be used to rectify catastrophic thoughts (e.g. fear of becoming invisible). This can be achieved by two means: (1) education (i.e. discussing the probabilities that symptoms of DP/DR may result in the patient becoming invisible using a Socratic-type dialogue); and (2) experimentation or interoceptive exposure (i.e. systematic exposure to the feared sensations of DP/DR, thereby allowing habituation while disconfirming the feared consequences).

A number of non-pharmacological and benign methods for inducing dissociation in the laboratory have been successfully employed in clinical and non-clinical populations. Miller, Brown, DiNardo and Barlow (1994) administered several focusing techniques (i.e. dot-staring, staring at one's own reflection in a mirror and silently repeating one's name) to ten patients with panic disorder with DP/DR, ten patients with panic disorder without DP/DR and ten non-anxious controls. Results showed that mirror and dot-staring tasks were the most successful tasks at eliciting DP/DR and that patients with panic disorder and DP/DR experienced the highest degree of DP/DR. These results have recently been replicated and extended with a larger non-clinical population of college students (n = 78) using dot-staring, pulsed photic and audio stimulation and stimulus deprivation techniques (Leonard et al., 1999). Results revealed that the multi-modal stimulus technique showed the highest dissociative powers.

Phase 3

This phase focuses on maintaining progress and focusing on precipitating factors to guarantee relapse prevention. Here, the patient and clinician review the triggers that worsen their DP symptoms and work on strategies to prevent these situations. Discussion on sleep hygiene, exercise and diet can be worthy of inclusion in this phase.

Hunter et al. (2005) have reported on an open study where twenty-one patients with primary DP, attending the Depersonalization Disorder clinic in London, were successfully treated with this CBT approach. The mean duration of the disorder was fourteen years, 81% of the sample had a comorbid anxiety and/or depression and most of them were being treated with a combination of SSRI and lamotrigine, although with little alleviation of symptoms. Following an average of thirteen sessions, the authors found significant reduction of symptoms of DP, anxiety and depression together with improvement in general functioning, with 29% of patients no longer meeting criteria for primary DP. More importantly, these improvements were maintained or increased at six-month follow-up.

Pharmacological approaches

Relatively little work has been devoted to the development of pharmacological treatments of DPD (Simeon, 2004). The field has been restricted to medications developed originally for other conditions, such as anxiety, depression and epilepsy. At present there is no recognized treatment for DPD and in the UK there is no licensed drug for the treatment of DP (Medford et al., 2005).

Selective serotonin reuptake inhibitors (SSRIs)

There is a collection of anecdotal reports of the beneficial effects of SSRIs in DP (Fichtner et al., 1992; Hollander et al., 1989; Ratliff & Kerski, 1995; Strohle et al., 2000). Retrospective treatment reviews in patients with primary DPD showed modest reduction in symptoms associated with SSRI therapy (Simeon et al., 1997, 2003a). In a relatively small sample-size study, Hollander et al. (1990) found a good response to fluoxetine or fluvoxamine in six patients with primary DPD and comorbid panic or obsessive-compulsive features. In addition, Simeon et al. (1998) found that clomipramine (a tricyclic with a mode of action similar to SSRIs) had beneficial effects in seven patients with primary DPD, although only two showed significant improvement. Four-year follow-up showed complete remission in one case. In contrast, a more recent placebo-controlled trial using fluoxetine (10–60 mg/day) in fifty-four individuals with primary DPD failed to show specific anti-depersonalization effects (Simeon et al., 2004).

Lamotrigine

There has been a recent surge of interest in the treatment of DPD with lamotrigine, an anticonvulsive medication used to treat epilepsy that acts at the presynaptic membrane to reduce the release of glutamate (Medford et al., 2005). A preliminary open-label trial with lamotrigine (dose range 50–250 mg a day), used as an add-on therapy to SSRIs in six patients with chronic (two to fifteen years) and continuous DPD showed promising results, with patients reporting substantial symptom reduction and no adverse side effects (Sierra et al. 2001). However, a recent cross-over, placebo-controlled trial failed to replicate these findings in nine patients with pure DPD, that is without psychiatric or neurological comorbidity (Sierra et al., 2003). Medford et al. (2005) suggested that lamotrigine might have a beneficial effect on DP but only when used in conjunction with an SSRI.

Neuroleptics

Neuroleptics have been used in non-controlled, non-blind studies, with some patients benefiting and others experiencing an exacerbation of their symptoms (Pauw, 2000). Nuller (1982) reported favourable response in nine out of fifteen patients reporting DP as their primary complaint, after a four-to-six-week trial with clozapine, an antipsychotic with a marked anxiolytic effect (doses between 150–600 mg/day orally or intramuscularly). However, the author noted that cases of chronic depersonalization were less responsive to the antipsychotic. In contrast, Ambrosino (1973) found antipsychotics ineffective in the treatment of DP. More recently, Medford et al. (2005) reported that a number of their patients with primary DPD, who had been previously misdiagnosed with schizophrenia and started on antipsychotic medications, had invariably resulted in worsening of symptoms. The opening case example in this chapter illustrates this situation.

Benzodiazepines

A number of isolated case reports (Hollander et al., 1989; Sachdev, 2002; Stein & Uhde, 1989) and a group study describe the efficacy of benzodiazepines in the alleviation of depersonalization (Nuller, 1982). Stein and Uhde (1989) reported on the beneficial effects of clonazepam in a patient with chronic DPD. More recently Sachdev (2002) reported the successful treatment of a twenty-four-year-old woman with a three-year history of primary DPD and mild symptoms of depression with the combination of citalopram–clonazepam. Sachdev noted that similar reports had been posted on an internet bulletin board by a number of patients (http://www.depersonalisation.hypermart.net/combo.net). In a group study, Nuller (1982) reported that phenazepam was successful in reducing episodes of DP in thirty-four of forty-three patients with severe DP.

Opiod agonists

In an open-label study, Bohus et al. (1999) found beneficial effects of naltrexone (25–100 mg/day) in treating dissociative symptoms in borderline personality disorder over a two-week period. More recently, Nuller et al. (2001) reported on the favourable effects of intravenous naloxone in ten of fourteen patients with chronic DP, with three individuals reporting complete remission and seven a marked improvement.

SUMMARY

Depersonalization (DP) is the subjective sense of detachment from various aspects of the self, such as one's body, cognitions, feelings or actions. This is often accompanied by derealization, a subjective sense of detachment from the external world, so that it seems strange or unreal, and other people may seem unfamiliar or mechanical. Depersonalization can occur as a primary disorder (i.e. primary depersonalization disorder; DPD), or as a secondary disorder, a feature or symptom of another psychiatric or organic condition (i.e. secondary DP). Current prevalence rates for primary DPD are about 2.4%. Yet, DP remains under-diagnosed and is often misdiagnosed. Age of onset is typically late adolescence or early adulthood (mean age of onset sixteen). Large studies have confirmed a 1:1 gender ratio; no familial pattern of inheritance has been found. Acute and insidious onsets are equally found. Most patients describe experiencing the symptoms continuously and one-third of cases suffer them episodically, with episodes lasting from minutes to years. The disorder typically runs a chronic course and is associated with marked distress, social and/or vocational impairment. Precipitating factors include substance misuse (mainly marijuana), prolonged stress, trauma and mental illness (particularly anxiety and depression). Depersonalization disorder is often comorbid with axis I anxiety and mood disorders. Comorbidity with axis II personality disorders has also been reported. There is ample evidence supporting the role of anxiety in the aetiology and maintenance of DP, prompting a conceptualization of DP as an anxiety disorder. The role of anxiety is central in recent neurobiological and cognitive-behavioural models of DP. Assessment should ideally be carried out by a multi-disciplinary team that includes a psychiatrist and psychologist. A full psychiatric and general medical history and a mental state examination should be part of a thorough clinical assessment. Clinical assessment should explore symptoms in the domains of depersonalization, derealization, desomatization and de-affectualization. A self-report measure should be added with the view to checking symptoms and tracking changes over time. Depersonalization has traditionally been considered refractory to treatment. To date there are no recognized psychopharmacological treatment guidelines for DPD and at present there is no licensed drug for its treatment in the UK, although a combination of a SSRI, and lamotrigine, have shown promising results. There are no evidence-based psychological therapies for DPD. However, preliminary results from a CBT open study with twenty-one patients have found promising results. Further studies with larger sample sizes and more rigorous research methodology are eagerly awaited.

EXERCISE 25.1

Divide into groups of three and assign roles of Sean, the psychologist and an observer. Role-play with Sean two parts of session (listed below), rotating roles after each role-play. The observer's role is to listen attentively and, after the role-play, to give feedback to the psychologist on three specific and behavioural aspects of what he or she did well and at most two suggestions of things to do differently. These should revolve around the psychologist's ability to: (1) confirm Sean's intact reality testing; (2) arrive at a differential diagnosis of schizophrenia, depression, and panic disorder; and (3) conclude that this was a case of primary depersonalization and not a case where symptoms of DP are secondary to anxiety and depression.

1 Part 1, where the psychologist offers Sean information regarding depersonalization to normalize his experience. Remember that the language must be simple but accurate.
2 Part 2, where the psychologist presents Sean with an individualized case formulation using a cognitive-behavioural framework.

After the role-plays, reflect on your experience of conveying your distressing experiences (in the case of Sean) and (in the case of the psychologist) trying to understand what Sean is struggling to convey.

FURTHER READINGS FOR PRACTITIONERS

Cattell, J.P. & Cattell, J.S. (1974). Depersonalisation: Psychological and social perspectives. In Arieti, S. (Ed.), *American handbook of psychiatry* (pp. 767–799). New York: Basic Books.

Coons, P.M. (1996). Depersonalisation and derealisation. In L.K. Michelson & W.J. Ray (Eds.), *Handbook of dissociation: Theoretical, empirical, and clinical perspectives* (pp. 291–305). New York: Basic Books.

Pauw, K.W. (2000). Depersonalisation disorder. In M. Gelder, J. López-Ibor & N. Andreasen (Eds.), *New Oxford textbook of psychiatry* (Volume 1, Section 4.9, pp. 831–833). Oxford: Oxford University Press.

Senior, C., Hunter, E., Lambert, M.V., Medford, N.C., Sierra, M., Phillips, M.L. & David, A.S. (2001). Depersonalisation. *The Psychologist*, 14, 128–132.

Steinberg, M. (2001). Depersonalisation. In G. Gabbard (Ed.), *Treatments of psychiatric disorders* (Third Edition, Volume 2, pp. 1695–1714). Washington, DC: American Psychiatric Press.

FURTHER READINGS FOR CLIENTS

Depersonalisation.info. http://www.depersonalisation.info This is an independent, non-profit discussion site providing information about depersonalization disorder and depersonalization as a symptom of other conditions.

Depersonalisation Research Unit: http://www.iop.klc.ac.uk/depersonalisation. This site contains information about depersonalization, a frequently-asked-questions (FAQs) section, and a list of links relevant to depersonalization. This group of researchers are currently designing a self-help booklet for sufferers of depersonalization disorder

Depersonalisation Self-help.com: http://www.dpselfhelp.com. This is a depersonalization support site providing information about depersonalization, including a forum/chatroom section.

EVIDENCE SUMMARIES

Hunter, E.C., Baker, D., Phillips, M.L., Sierra, M. & David, A.S. (2005). Cognitive-behaviour therapy for depersonalisation disorder: An open study. *Behaviour Research and Therapy*, 43, 1121–1130.

Maldonado, J.R., Butler. L.S. & Spiegel, D. (2002). Treatments for dissociative disorders. In P. Nathan & J. Gorman (Eds.), *A guide to treatments that work* (Second Edition, pp. 463–496). New York: Oxford University Press.

ASSESSMENT INSTRUMENTS

General dissociation scales

Bernstein-Carlson, E.M. & Putnam, F.W. (1986). Development, reliability, and validity of a dissociation scale. *Journal of Nervous and Mental Disease*, 174, 727–735. Contains the DES.

Bremner, J.D., Krystal, J.H., Putnam, F.W., Southwick, S., Marmar, C., Charney, D.S. & Mazure, C. (1998). Measurement of dissociative states with the Clinician-

Administered Dissociative Scale (CADSS). *Journal of Traumatic Stress*, 11, 135–136. This is a self-report scale (19 items) assessing state symptoms of dissociation, including eight clinical-rated items. It contains three subscales: amnesia (items 14 and 15), depersonalization (items 3–7) and derealization (items 1, 2, 8–13, 16–19). Available at: http://info.med.yale.edu/psych/org/ypi/trauma/cadds.txt

Carlson, E.B. & Putnam, F.W. (1993). An update on the Dissociative Experiences Scale. *Dissociation*, 6, 16–27. Contains the DES-II scale.

Depersonalization-specific scales

Dixon, J.C. (1963). Depersonalisation phenomena in a sample population of college students. *British Journal of Psychiatry*, 109, 371–375. Contains the Dixon's Depersonalisation Scale. This is a ten-item self-report scale.

Fewtrell, W.D. (2000). Fewtrell Depersonalisation Scale (FDS). Washington, DC: American Psychiatric Press.

Jacobs, J.R. & Bovasso, G.B. (1992). Toward the clarification of the construct of depersonalisation and its association with affective and cognitive dysfunctions. *Journal of Personality Assessment*, 59, 352–365. Contains a list of the items included in the Jacobs and Bovasso's Depersonalisation Scale.

Sierra, M. & Berrios, G.E. (2000). The Cambridge Depersonalisation Scale: A new instrument for the measurement of depersonalisation. *Psychiatry Research*, 93, 153–164. Contains the Cambridge Depersonalisation Scale-State (CDS-S).

Steinberg, M., Cicchetti, D., Buchanan, J., Hall, P. & Rounsaville, B. (1993). Clinical assessment of dissociative symptoms and disorders: The Structured Clinical Interview for DSM-IV Dissociative Disorders (SCID-D). *Dissociation*, 6, 3–15.

Steinberg, M., Rounsaville, B. & Cicchetti, D.V. (1990). The Structured Clinical Interview for DSM-III-R Dissociative Disorders: Preliminary report on a new diagnostic instrument. *American Journal of Psychiatry*, 147, 76–82.

Wing, J.K., Cooper, J.E. & Sartorius, N. (1974). *Present State Examination*. Cambridge: Cambridge University Press. The PSE includes items for depersonalization and derealization.

Depersonalization scales for use in anxiety and trauma-related phenomena

Cox, B.J. & Swinson, R.P. (2002). Instrument to assess depersonalisation-derealisation in panic disorder. *Depression and Anxiety*, 15, 172–175. Contains the Depersonalisation-Derealisation Inventory (DDI). This is a self-report measure (28 items) for use with clinically anxious patients.

Simeon, D., Guralnik, O. & Schmeidler, J. (2001). Development of a depersonalisation severity scale. *Journal of Traumatic Stress*, 14, 341–349. Contains the Depersonalisation Severity Scale (DSS). This is a short (six-item) clinician-rated scale developed for use in clinical trials of Depersonalization Disorder and trauma-related disorders in general.

Peri-traumatic depersonalization and derealization

Marmar, C.R. & Weiss, D. (1990). Peritraumatic Dissociative Experiences Questionnaire. San Francisco Medical School. The scale can be found on pp. 249–252 of J.D. Bremner & C.R. Marmar (Eds.) (1998). *Trauma, memory and dissociation*. Washington, DC: American Psychiatric Press.

REFERENCES

Ackner, B. (1954a). Depersonalisation I. Aetiology and phenomenology. *Journal of Mental Science*, 100, 838–853.

Ackner, B. (1954b). Depersonalisation II. Clinical syndromes. *Journal of Mental Science*, 100, 854–872.

Aderibigbe, Y.A., Bloch, R.M. & Walker, W.R. (2001). Prevalence of depersonalisation and derealisation experiences in a rural population. *Social Psychiatry and Psychiatric Epidemiology*, 36, 63–69.

Ambrosino, S.V. (1973). Phobic anxiety-depersonalisation syndrome. *New York State Journal of Medicine*, 73, 419–425.

American Psychiatric Association (APA) (2000). *Diagnostic and statistical manual of the mental disorders (Fourth Edition, Text Revision, DSM-IV-TR)*. Washington, DC: APA.

Baker, D., Hunter, E., Lawrence, E., Medford, N., Patel, M., Senior, C., Sierra, M., Lambert, M.V., Phillips, M.L. & David, A.S. (2003). Depersonalisation disorder: Clinical features of 204 cases. *British Journal of Psychiatry*, 182, 428–433.

Bebbington, P.E. (1998). Epidemiology of obsessive-compulsive disorder. *British Journal of Psychiatry*, 173, 2–6.

Bebbington, P.E., Hurry, J., Tennant, C., Sturt, E. & Wing, J.K. (1981). Epidemiology of mental disorders in Camberwell. *Psychological Medicine*, 11, 561–579.

Bebbington, P.E., Marsden, L. & Brewin, C.R. (1997). The need for psychiatric treatment in the general population: The Camberwell needs for care survey. *Psychological Medicine*, 27, 821–834.

Beck, A.T. (1990). *Beck Anxiety Inventory (BAI)*. San Antonio, TX: The Psychological Corporation.

Beck, A.T. (1996). *Beck Depression Inventory (BDI-II)*. San Antonio, TX: The Psychological Corporation.

Bernstein-Carlson, E.M. & Putnam, F.W. (1986). Development, reliability, and validity of a dissociation scale. *Journal of Nervous and Mental Disease*, 174, 727–735.

Blanco-Campal, A., Carton, S. & Delargy, M. (2003). Organic depersonalisation unaccompanied by depersonalisation after severe traumatic brain injury: A single case study. *Brain Injury*, 17, 152–153.

Bliss, E.L., Clark, L.D. & West, C.D. (1959). Studies of sleep deprivation – relationship to schizophrenia. *Archives of Neurological Psychiatry*, 81, 348–359.

Blue, F.R. (1979). Use of directive therapy in the treatment of depersonalisation neurosis. *Psychological Reports*, 45, 904–906.

Bögels, S.M., Mulkens, S. & De Jong, P.J. (1997). Task concentration training and fear of blushing. *Clinical Psychology and Psychotherapy*, 4, 251–258.

Bohus, M.J., Landwehrmeyer, G.B., Stiglmayr, C.E., Limberger, M.F., Böhme, R.

& Schmahl, C.G. (1999). Naltrexone in the treatment of dissociative symptoms in patients with borderline personality disorder: An open-label trial. *Journal of Clinical Psychiatry*, 60, 598–603.

Brauer, R., Horrow, M. & Tucker, G. (1970). Depersonalisation phenomena in psychiatric patients. *British Journal of Psychiatry*, 117, 509–515.

Braun, B.G. (1993). Multiple personality disorder and posttraumatic stress disorder: Similarities and differences. In J. Wilson & B. Raphael (Eds.), *International handbook of traumatic stress syndromes* (pp. 35–47). New York: Plenum Press.

Bremner, J.D., Krystal, J.H., Putnam, F.W., Southwick, S., Marmar, C., Charney, D.S. & Mazure, C. (1998). Measurement of dissociative states with the clinician-administered dissociative scale (CADSS). *Journal of Traumatic Stress*, 11, 135–136.

Cantagallo, A., Grassi, L. & Della Sala, S. (1999). Dissociative disorder after traumatic brain injury. *Brain Injury*, 13, 219–228.

Carlson, E.B. & Putnam, F.W. (1993). An update on the dissociative experiences scale. *Dissociation*, 6, 16–27.

Cassano, G.B., Petracca, A., Perugi, G., Toni, C., Tundo, A. & Roth, M. (1989). Derealisation in panic attacks: A clinical evaluation on 150 patients with panic disorder/agoraphobia. *Comprehensive Psychiatry*, 30, 5–12.

Castillo, R.J. (1990). Depersonalisation and meditation. *Psychiatry*, 53, 158–168.

Cattell, J.P. & Cattell, J.S. (1974). Depersonalisation: Psychological and social perspectives. In Arieti, S. (Ed.), *American handbook of psychiatry* (pp. 767–799). New York: Basic Books.

Clark, D.M. (1986). A cognitive approach to panic. *Behaviour Research and Therapy*, 24, 461–470.

Clark, D.M. & Wells, A. (1995). A cognitive model of social phobia. In R.G. Heimberg, D.H. Liebowitz & F. Schneier (Eds.), *Social phobia: Diagnosis, assessment and treatment* (pp. 9–93). New York: Guilford Press.

Cohen, R.S. & Cocores, J. (1997). Neuropsychiatric manifestations following the use of 3,4-methylenedioxymethampthetamine (MDMA; 'ecstasy'). *Progress in Neuro-Psychopharmacology and Biological Psychiatry*, 21, 727–734.

Coons, P.M. (1996). Depersonalisation and derealisation. In L.K. Michelson & W.J. Ray (Eds.), *Handbook of dissociation. Theoretical, empirical, and clinical perspectives* (pp. 291–305). New York: Plenum Press.

Cox, B.J. & Swinson, R.P. (2002). Instrument to assess depersonalisation–derealisation in panic disorder. *Depression and Anxiety*, 15, 172–175.

Cox, B.J., Swinson, R.P., Endler, N.S. & Norton, G.R. (1994). The symptoms structure of panic attacks. *Comprehensive Psychiatry*, 35, 349–353.

Davison, J.R., Kudler, H.S., Saunders, W.B. & Smith, R.D. (1990). Symptoms and comorbidity patterns in World War II and Vietnam veterans with posttraumatic stress disorder. *Comprehensive Psychiatry*, 31, 162–170.

Devinsky, O., Feldmann, O., Burrowes, K. & Bromfield, E. (1989). Autoscopy phenomena with seizures. *Archives of Neurology*, 46, 1080–1088.

Dixon, J.C. (1963). Depersonalisation phenomena in a sample population of college students. *British Journal of Psychiatry*, 109, 371–375.

Dollinger, S. (1983). A case report of dissociative neuosis (depersonalisation disorder) in an adolescent treated with family therapy and behaviour modification. *Journal of Consulting and Clinical Psychology*, 51, 479–484.

Dugas, L. (1898). Un cas de dépersonnalisation. Introduced and translated by Sierra, M. & Berrios, G.E. (1996). *History of Psychiatry*, 7, 451–461.

Fewtrell, W.D. (1984). Relaxation and depersonalisation. *British Journal of Psychiatry*, 145, 217 (letter).

Fewtrell, W.D. (1986). Depersonalisation: A description and suggested strategies. *British Journal of Guidance and Counselling*, 14, 263–268.

Fewtrell, W.D. (2000). Fewtrell Depersonalisation Scale (FDS). Washington, DC: American Psychiatric Press.

Fichtner, C.G., Horevitz, R.P. & Braun, B.G. (1992). Fluoxetine in depersonalisation disorder (letter). *American Journal of Psychiatry*, 149, 1750–1751.

Fleiss, J.L., Gurland, B.J. & Goldberg, K. (1975). Independence of depersonalisation–derealisation. *Journal of Consulting and Clinical Psychology*, 43, 110–111.

Gil, E. (1988). *Treatment of adult survivors of childhood abuse*. Walnut Creek, CA: Launch Press.

Grigsby, J. & Kaye, K. (1993). Incidence and correlates of depersonalisation following head trauma. *Brain Injury*, 7, 507–513.

Guralnik, O., Schmeidler, J. & Simeon, D. (2000). Feeling unreal: Cognitive processes in depersonalisation. *American Journal of Psychiatry*, 157, 103–109.

Hollander, E., Fairbanks, J., Decaria, C. & Liebowitz, M.R. (1989). Pharmacological dissection of panic and depersonalisation. *American Journal of Psychiatry*, 146, 402.

Hollander, E., Liebowitz, M.R., DeCaria, C.M., Fairbanks, J., Fallon, B. & Klein, D.F. (1990). Treatment of depersonalisation with serotonin reuptake blockers. *Journal of Clinical Psychopharmacology*, 10, 200–203.

Holmes, E.A., Brown,R.J., Mansell, W., Fearon, R.P., Hunter, E.C., Frasquilho, F. & Oakley, D.A. (2005). Are there two qualitatively distinct forms of dissociation? A review and some clinical implications. *Clinical Psychology Review*, 25, 1–23.

Hunter, E.C., Baker, D., Phillips, M.L., Sierra, M. & David, A.S. (2005). Cognitive-behaviour therapy for depersonalisation disorder: An open study. *Behaviour Therapy and Research*, 43, 1121–1130.

Hunter, E.C., Phillips, M.L., Chalder, T., Sierra, M. & David, A.S. (2003). Depersonalisation disorder: A cognitive-behavioural conceptualisation. *Behaviour Research and Therapy*, 41, 1451–1467.

Hunter, E.C., Sierra, M. & David, A.S. (2004). The epidemiology of depersonalisation and derealisation. *Society of Psychiatry and Psychiatric Epidemiology*, 39, 9–18.

Jacobs, J.R. & Bovasso, G.B. (1992). Toward the clarification of the construct of depersonalisation and its association with affective and cognitive dysfunctions. *Journal of Personality Assessment*, 59, 352–365.

Jacobsen, E. (1983). *Progressive relaxation*. Chicago: University Press.

Janet, P. (1903). *Les Obsessions et la Psychasthénie*. Paris: Alcan.

Kelly, D.H. & Walter, C.J. (1968). The relationship between clinical diagnosis and anxiety assessed by forearm blood flow and other measurements. *British Journal of Psychiatry*, 114, 611–626.

Kenna, J.C. & Sedman, G. (1965). Depersonalisation in temporal lobe epilepsy and the organic psychoses. *British Journal of Psychiatry*, 111, 293–299.

Kennedy, R.B. (1976). Self-induced Depersonalisation Syndrome. *American Journal of Psychiatry*, 133, 1326–1328.

Kennerley, H. (1996). Cognitive therapy of dissociative symptoms associated with trauma. *British Journal of Clinical Psychology*, 35, 325–340.

Keshaven, M.S. & Lishman, W.A. (1986). Prolonged depersonalisation following cannabis abuse. *British Journal of Addiction*, 81, 140–142.

Krishaber, (1872). De la névropathie cérébrocardiaque. *Gazette Sciéntifique Médicale*. Bordeaux.

Lader, M.H. & Wing, L. (1975). *Physiological measures, sedative drugs and morbid anxiety*. Maudsley Monographs no. 14. London: Oxford University Press.

Lambert, M.V., Senior, C., Fewtrell, D., Phillips, M.L. & David, A.S. (2001a). Primary and secondary depersonalisation disorder: A psychometric study. *Journal of Affective Disorders*, 63, 249–256.

Lambert, M.V., Senior, C., Phillips, M.L., Sierra, M., Hunter, E. & David, A.S. (2001b). Visual imagery and depersonalisation. *Psychopathology*, 34, 259–264.

Lambert, M.V., Sierra, M., Phillips, M.L. & David, A.S. (2000). Depersonalisation in cyberspace. *The Journal of Nervous and Mental Disease*, 188, 764–771.

Lambert, M.V., Sierra, M., Phillips, M.L. & David, A.S. (2002). The spectrum of organic depersonalisation: A review plus four new cases. *Journal of Neuropsychiatry and Clinical Neurosciences*, 1, 141–154.

Leonard, K.N., Telch, M.J. & Harrington, P.J. (1999). Dissociation in the laboratory: A comparison of strategies. *Behaviour Research and Therapy*, 37, 49–61.

Levy, J.S. & Watchtel, P.L. (1978). Depersonalisation: An effort at clarification. *American Journal of Psychoanalysis*, 38, 291–300.

L'Hermitte, J. (1939). *L'image de Notre Corps*. Paris: Nouvelle Review Critique.

Lilja, A. & Salford, L.G. (1997). Early mental changes in patients with astrocytomas with special reference to anxiety and epilepsy. *Psychopathology*, 30, 316–323.

Lochner, C., Seedat, S., Hemmings, S., Kinnear, C., Corfield, V., Niehaus, D., Moolman-Smook, J. & Stein, D. (2004). Dissociative experiences in obsessive-compulsive disorder and trichotillomania: Clinical and genetic findings. *Comprehensive Psychiatry*, 45, 384–391.

Maldonado, J.R., Butler, L.S. & Spiegel, D. (2002). Treatments for dissociative disorders. In P. Nathan & J. Gorman (Eds.), *A guide to treatments that work* (Second Edition, pp. 463–496). New York: Oxford University Press.

Marmar, C.R. & Weiss, D. (1990). Peritraumatic dissociative experiences questionnaire. In J.D. Bremner & C.R. Marmar (Eds.) (1998). *Trauma, memory and dissociation* (pp. 249–252). Washington, DC: American Psychiatric Press.

Márquez, M., Seguí, J., García, L., Canet, J. & Ortiz, M. (2001). Is panic disorder with psychosensorial symptoms (depersonalisation-derealisation) a more severe clinical subtype? *Journal of Nervous and Mental Disease*, 189, 332–335.

Mathew, R.J., Wilson, W., Chiu, N.Y., Turkington, T.G., Degrado, T.R. & Coleman, R.E. (1999). Regional cerebral blood flow and depersonalisation after tetrahydrocannabinol adminstration. *Acta Psychiatrica Scandinavica*, 100, 67–75.

Mathew, R.J., Wilson, W., Humphreys, D., Lowe, J.V. & Weithe, K.E. (1993). Depersonalisation after marijuana smoking. *Biological Psychiatry*, 33, 431–441.

Mayer-Gross, W. (1935). On depersonalisation. *British Journal of Medical Psychology*, 15, 103–126.

Mayou, R., Bryant, R. & Ehlers, A. (2001). Prediction of psychological outcomes one year after a motor vehicle accident. *American Journal of Psychiatry*, 165, 391–395.

McGuire, P.K., Cope, H. & Fahy, T.A. (1994). Diversity of psychopathology associated with use of 3,4-methylenedioxymethamphetamine ('ecstasy'). *British Journal of Psychiatry*, 165, 391–395.

Medford, N., Baker, D., Hunter, E., Sierra, M., Lawrence, E., Phillips, M.L. & David, A.S. (2003). Chronic depersonalisation following illicit drug use: A controlled analysis of 40 cases. *Addiction*, 98, 1731–1736.

Medford, N., Sierra, M., Baker, D. & David, A.S. (2005). Understanding and treating depersonalisation disorder. *Advances in Psychiatric Treatment*, 11, 92–100.

Melges, F.T., Tinklenberg, J.R., Hollister, L.E. & Gillepsie, H.K. (1970). Temporal disintegration and depersonalisation during marijuana intoxication. *Archives of General Psychiatry*, 23, 204–210.

Meyer, C. & Waller, G. (1998). Dissociation and eating psychopathology: Gender differences in a nonclinical population. *International Journal of Eating Disorders*, 23, 217–221.

Miller, P.P., Brown, T.A., DiNardo, P.A. & Barlow, D.H. (1994). The experimental induction of depersonalisation and derealisation in panic disorder and nonanxious subjects. *Behaviour Research and Therapy*, 32, 511–519.

Moran, C. (1986). Depersonalisation and agoraphobia associated with marijuana use. *British Journal of Medical Psychology*, 59, 187–196.

Morioka, H., Nagatomo, I., Horikiri, T., Kita, K., Ueyama, K. & Takigawa, M. (1997). A case of pontine infarction with depersonalisation. *International Medical Journal*, 4, 133–134.

Noyes, R., Hoenk, P.R., Kuperman, S. & Slymen, D.J. (1977). Depersonalisation in accident victims and psychiatric patients. *Journal of Nervous and Mental Disease*, 164, 401–407.

Noyes, R. & Kletti, R. (1977). Depersonalisation in response to life-threatening danger. *Comprehensive Psychiatry*, 8, 375–384.

Nuller, Y.L. (1982). Depersonalisation: Symptoms, meaning, and therapy. *Acta Psychiatrica Scandinavica*, 66, 451–458.

Ogunyemi, A.O. (1995). Migraine with prolonged aura: Correlation of clinical and EEG features. *Behavioural Neurology*, 8(2), 109–114.

Ost, L.G. (1987). Applied relaxation: Description of a coping technique and review of controlled studies. *Behaviour Research and Therapy*, 25, 397–410.

Papageorgiou, C., Ventouras, E., Uzunoglu, N., Rabavillas, A. & Stefanis, C. (2002). Changes of P300 elicited during a working memory test individuals with depersonalisation–derealisation experiences. *Neuropsychobiology*, 46, 70–75.

Paulig, M., Bottger, S. & Prosiegel, M. (1998). Depersonalisation syndrome after acquired brain damage: Overview based on 3 case reports and the literature and discussion of etiological models. *Nervanarzt*, 69, 1100–1106.

Pauw, K.W. (2000). Depersonalisation disorder. In M. Gelder, J. López-Ibor & N. Andreasen (Eds.), *New Oxford textbook of psychiatry* (Volume 1, Section 4.9, pp. 831–833). Oxford: Oxford University Press.

Phillips, M.L., Medford, N., Senior, C., Bullmore, E.T., Brammer, M.J., Andrew, C., Sierra, M., Williams, C.R. & David, A.S. (2000). Depersonalisation disorder: Thinking without feeling. *Biological Psychiatry*, 47 (Suppl. 1), S94–S95.

Phillips, M.L., Medford, N., Senior, C., Bullmore, E.T., Suckling, J., Brammer, M.L., Andrew, C., Sierra, M., Williams, C.R. & David, A.S. (2001a). Depersonalisation disorder: Thinking without feeling. *Psychiatry Research: Neuroimaging Section*, 108, 145–160.

Phillips, M.L., Sierra, M., Hunter, E., Lambert, M.V., Medford, N., Senior, C. &

David, A.S. (2001b). Service innovations: A depersonalisation research unit progress report. *Psychiatric Bulletin*, 25, 105–108.

Posner, M. & Rothbart, M.K. (1992). Attentional mechanisms and conscious experience. In A.D. Miller & M.D. Rugg (Eds.), *The neuropsychology of consciousness* (pp. 91–111). New York: Academic Press.

Raimo, E.B., Roemer, R.A., Moster, M. & Shan, Y. (1999). Alcohol-induced depersonalisation. *Biological Psychiatry*, 45, 1523–1526.

Ratliff, N.B. & Kerski, D. (1995). Depersonalisation treated with fluoxetine (letter). *American Journal of Psychiatry*, 152, 1689–1690.

Reed, G.F. and Sedman, G. (1964). Personality and depersonalization under sensory deprivation conditions. *Perceptual & Motor Skills*, 18: 659–660.

Roberts, W.W. (1960). Normal and abnormal depersonalisation. *Journal of Mental Sciences*, 106, 478–493.

Roth, M. (1960). The phobic-anxiety-depersonalisation syndrome and some general aetiological problems in psychiatry. *Journal of Neuropsychiatry*, 1, 293–306.

Roth, M. & Harper, M. (1962). Temporal lobe epilepsy and the phobic anxiety-depersonalisation syndrome II. *Comprehensive Psychiatry*, 3, 215–226.

Sachdev, P. (2002). Citalopram-clonazepan combination for primary depersonalisation disorder: A case report. *New Zealand Journal of Psychiatry*, 36, 424–425.

Salkovskis, P.M. & Bass, C. (1997). Hypochondriasis. In D.M. Clark & C.G. Fairburn (Eds.), *Science and practice of cognitive behaviour therapy* (pp. 313–339). Oxford: Oxford University Press.

Sedman, G. (1966). Depersonalisation in a group of normal subjects. *British Journal of Psychiatry*, 112, 907–912.

Sedman, G. (1970). Theories of depersonalisation: A reappraisal. *British Journal of Psychiatry*, 117, 1–14.

Sedman, G. & Kenna, J.C. (1963). Depersonalisation and mood changes in schizophrenia. *British Journal of Psychiatry*, 109, 669–673.

Sedman, G. & Reed, G.F. (1963). Depersonalisation phenomena in obsessional personalities and in depression. *British Journal of Psychiatry*, 109, 376–379.

Seguí, J., Márquez, M., García, L., Canet, J., Salvador-Carulla, L. & Ortiz, M. (2000). Depersonalisation in panic disorder: A clinical study. *Comprehensive Psychiatry*, 41, 172–178.

Seguí, J., Salvador-Carulla, L., Canet, J., Ortiz, M., & Farré, J.M. (1998). Semiology and subtyping of panic disorders. *Acta Psychiatrica Scandinavica*, 97, 272–277.

Senior, C., Hunter, E., Lambert, M.V., Medford, N.C., Sierra, M., Phillips, M.L. & David, A.S. (2001). Depersonalisation. *The Psychologist*, 14, 128–132.

Shorvon, H.J., Hill, J.D.N., Burkitt, E. & Halstead, H. (1946). The depersonalisation syndrome. *Proceedings of the Royal Society of Medicine*, 39, 779–792.

Sierra, M. & Berrios, G.E. (1996). A case of depersonalisation. *History of Psychiatry*, 7, 451–461.

Sierra, M. & Berrios, G.E. (1997). Depersonalisation: A conceptual history. *History of Psychiatry*, 8, 213–229.

Sierra, M. & Berrios, G.E. (1998). Depersonalisation: Neurobiological perspectives. *Biological Psychiatry*, 44, 898–908.

Sierra, M. & Berrios, G.E. (2000). The Cambridge Depersonalisation Scale: A new instrument for the measurement of depersonalisation. *Psychiatry Research*, 93, 153–164.

Sierra, M. & Berrios, G. (2001). The phenomenological stability of depersonalisation: Comparing the old with the new. *The Journal of Nervous and Mental Disease*, 189, 629–636.

Sierra, M., Lopera, F., Lambert, M.V., Phillips, M.L. & David, A.S. (2002a). Separating depersonalisation and derealisation: The relevance of the lesion method. *Journal of Neurology, Neurosurgery and Psychiatry*, 72, 530–532.

Sierra, M., Phillips, M.L., Ivin, G., Lambert, M.V., Krystal, J. & David, A.S. (2003). A placebo-controlled, cross-over trial of lamotrigine in depersonalisation disorder. *Journal of Psychopharmacology*, 17, 103–107.

Sierra, M., Phillips, M.L., Lambert, M.V., Senior, C., Krystal, J. & David, A.S. (2001). Lamotrigine in the treatment of depersonalisation disorder. *Journal of Clinical Psychiatry*, 62, 826–827.

Sierra, M., Senior, C., Dalton, J., McDonough, M., Bond, A., Phillips, M.L., O'Dwyer, A.M. & David, A.S. (2002b). Autonomic response in depersonalisation disorder. *Archives of General Psychiatry*, 59, 833–838.

Simeon, D. (2004). Depersonalisation disorder: A contemporary overview. *CNS Drugs*, 18, 343–354.

Simeon, D. & Hollander, E. (1993). Depersonalisation disorder. *Psychiatric Annals*, 23, 382–388.

Simeon, D., Gross, S., Guralnik, O., Stein, D.J., Schmeidler, J. & Hollander, E. (1997). Feeling unreal: 30 cases of DSM-III-R depersonalisation disorder. *American Journal of Psychiatry*, 154, 1107–1113.

Simeon, D., Guralnik, O., Hazlett, E.A., Spiegel-Cohen, J., Hollander, E. & Buchsnaum, M.S. (2000). Feeling unreal: A PET study of depersonalisation disorder. *American Journal of Psychiatry*, 157, 1782–1788.

Simeon, D., Guralnik, O. & Schmeidler, J. (2001a). Development of a depersonalisation severity scale. *Journal of Traumatic Stress*, 14, 341–349.

Simeon, D., Guralnik, O., Schmeidler, J. & Knutelska, M. (2004). Fluoxetine therapy in depersonalisation disorder: Randomised controlled trial. *British Journal of Psychiatry*, 185, 31–36.

Simeon, D., Guralnik, O., Schmeidler, J., Sirof, B. & Knutelska, M. (2001b). The role of childhood interpersonal trauma in depersonalisation disorder. *American Journal of Psychiatry*, 158, 1027–1033.

Simeon, D., Knutelska, M., Nelson, D. & Guralnik, O. (2003a). Feeling unreal: A depersonalisation disorder update of 117 cases. *Journal of Clinical Psychiatry*, 64, 990–997.

Simeon, D., Knutelska, M., Nelson, D., Guralnik, O. & Schmeidler, J. (2003b). Examination of the pathological dissociation taxon in depersonalisation disorder. *The Journal of Nervous and Mental Disease*, 11, 738–744.

Simeon, D., Stein, D.J. & Hollander, E. (1995). Depersonalisation disorder and self-injurious behaviour. *Journal of Clinical Psychiatry*, 56, 36–40.

Simeon, D., Stein, D.J. & Hollander, E. (1998). Treatment of depersonalisation disorder with clomipramine. *Biological Psychiatry*, 44, 302–303.

Sookman, D. & Solyom, L. (1978). Severe depersonalisation treated by behaviour therapy. *American Journal of Psychiatry*, 135, 12.

Stein, M.B. & Udde, T.W. (1989). Depersonalisation disorder: Effects of caffeine and response to pharmacotherapy. *Biological Psychiatry*, 26, 315–320.

Steinberg, M. (2001). Depersonalisation. In G. Gabbard (Ed.), *Treatments of psychiatric disorders* (Third Edition, Volume 2, pp. 1695–1714). Washington, DC: American Psychiatric Press.

Steinberg, M., Cicchetti, D., Buchanan, J., Hall, P. & Rounsaville, B. (1993). Clinical assessment of dissociative symptoms and disorders: The Structured Clinical Interview for DSM-IV Dissociative Disorders (SCID-D). *Dissociation*, 6, 3–15.

Steinberg, M., Rounsaville, B. & Cicchetti, D.V. (1990). The Structured Clinical Interview for DSM-III-R Dissociative Disorders: Preliminary report on a new diagnostic instrument. *American Journal of Psychiatry*, 147, 76–82.

Strickland, P.L., Deakin, J.F.W., Percival, C., Dixon, J., Gater, R.A. & Goldberg, D.P. (2002). Bio-social origins of depression in the community – interactions between social adversity, cortisol and serotonin neurotransmission. *British Journal of Psychiatry*, 180, 168–173.

Strohle, A., Kumpfel, T. & Sonntag, A. (2000). Paroxetine for depersonalisaiton associated with multiple sclerosis. *American Journal of Psychiatry*, 157, 150.

Szymanski, H.V. (1981). Prolonged depersonalisation after marijuana use. *American Journal of Psychiatry*, 138, 231–233.

Torch, E.M. (1978). Review of the relationship between obsession and depersonalisation. *Acta Psychiatrica Scandinavica*, 58, 191–198.

Trueman, D. (1984). Depersonalisation in a nonclinical population. *The Journal of Psychology*, 116, 107–112.

Tyrer, P. (1989). *Classification of neurosis*. New York: Wiley.

Van Ijzendoorn, M.H. & Schuengel, C. (1996). The measurement of dissociation in normal and clinical populations: Meta-analytic validation of the Dissociative Experiences Scale (DES). *Clinical Psychology Review*, 16, 365–383.

Waller, N.G., Putnam, F.W. & Carlson, E.B. (1996). Types of dissociation and dissociative types: A taxometric analysis of dissociative experiences. *Psychological Methods*, 1, 300–321.

Waltzner, H. (1972). Depersonalisation and the use of LSD: A psychodynamic study. *American Journal of Psychoanalysis*, 32, 45–52.

Warwick, H.M.C. & Salkovskis, P.M. (2001). Cognitive-behavioural treatment of hypochondriasis. In V. Starcevic & D.R. Lipsih (Eds.), *Hypochondriasis: Modern perspectives on an ancient malady* (pp. 314–328). Oxford: Oxford University Press.

Watts, C.A. (1985). A long-term follow-up of schizophrenia patients: 1946–1983. *Journal of Clinical Psychiatry*, 46, 210–216.

Wells, A. (1990). Panic disorder in association with relaxation induced anxiety: An attentional training approach to treatment. *Behaviour Therapy*, 21, 273–380.

Wells, A. (1997). *Cognitive therapy of anxiety disorders: A practice manual and conceptual guide*. Chichester, UK: Wiley.

Wells, A., White, J. & Carter, K. (1997). Attention training: Effects on anxiety and beliefs in panic and social phobia. *Clinical Psychology and Psychotherapy*, 4, 226–232.

Wenzel, K., Bernstein, D.P., Handelsman, L., Rinaldi, P., Rugiero, J. & Higgins, B. (1996). Levels of dissociation in detoxified substance abusers and their relationship to chronicity of alcohol and drug abuse. *Journal of Nervous and Mental Disease*, 184, 220–227.

World Health Organization (WHO) (1992). *The ICD-10 classification of mental and behavioural disorders*. Geneva: WHO.

Index